The Wordsworth
School Dictionary

–

Edited by Catherine Schwarz

Wordsworth Reference

First published in the UK as *Chambers New School Dictionary*
by W&R Chambers Ltd, Edinburgh, 1990.

This edition published 1996 by Wordsworth Editions Ltd.
8b East Street, Ware, Hertfordshire SG12 9HJ.

Copyright © W&R Chambers 1990.

· 4 6 8 10 9 7 5 3

ISBN 1-85326-359-1

Printed and bound in Great Britain by Mackays of Chatham plc.

PREFACE

This *New School Dictionary* is the latest in a renowned line of Chambers school dictionaries. Up-to-date and reliable, it covers the everyday vocabulary of children of upper primary age, as well as the vocabulary of their extraordinarily varied contemporary environment.

The range of entries is wide—from **bag lady** to **BSE, poll tax** to **pollutants, tagliatelle** to **triathlon**—and the entries themselves are clear, well-spaced and immediately readable. Many examples of words in context are given, to show how words are used as well as what they mean; pronunciations are given for unusual or particularly difficult words.

Chambers New School Dictionary is an attractive and accessible companion for young users of present-day English.

Notes on using the dictionary

The main entries (headwords) are listed alphabetically, from **a** to **zucchini**. In this list are included abbreviations (such as **BA, NATO** and **oz**) and cross-references to other main entries (such as **alliance** to **ally** and **despatch** to **dispatch**).

Within each main entry related words (subheads) with their meanings, are listed alphabetically, except when an undefined word follows the word from which it is formed. For example, **hastily** comes after **hasty** and **idealization** comes after **idealize**. Beside each headword and subhead its part of speech is given. Phrases are given in a separate list at the end of the entry.

Abbreviations, as well as the labels (*old, myth* and so on) that are found in brackets before some meanings, are explained on page v.

Many verbs in English can be spelt with either **-ize** or **-ise** as their ending; their related nouns are spelt with **-ization** or **-isation**. Both forms (*eg* **realize/realization** and **realise/realisation**) are acceptable. This dictionary uses the **-z-** form.

Pronunciation guide

Accented syllables

In most words of two or more syllables, one syllable is accented, or stressed, more strongly than the other or others. Where pronunciations are given in this dictionary, the accented syllable is shown by the mark , which is placed *after* the syllable.

Vowels

in accented syllables

Sound

ā	as in	bare	ö	as in	all
ä	as in	far	oo	as in	moon
a	as in	bat	oo	as in	foot
ē	as in	deer	ū	as in	pure
e	as in	pet	u	as in	bud
ī	as in	mine	û	as in	her
i	as in	bid	ow	as in	house
ō	as in	note	oi	as in	boy
o	as in	got			

in unaccented syllables

These are marked with a dot to show that they are not pronounced as distinctly as in accented syllables: ē·on (**aeon**), a·līn (**align**).

Consonants

b, d, f, h, j, k, l, m, n, p, r, s, t, v, w and z are pronounced as in standard English. The following other symbols are used:

ch	as in	cheap	th	as in	thin
g	as in	good	TH	as in	then
hw	as in	where	y	as in	yet
ng	as in	sing	zh	as in	azure
sh	as in	shine			

Additional sounds

ans and ons are French nasal vowels, as in **timbre** (tansbr) and **avant-garde** (a-vons-gärd).

Abbreviations used in the dictionary

Austr Australian
cap capital letter
coll colloquial
comput computing
E. East
eg for example
esp especially
etc and so on, and other things
Fr French
Ger German
gram grammar
hist historical
ie that is
It Italian
L Latin
maths mathematics

myth mythological
N. North
orig originally
® registered trade mark
RC Roman Catholic
S. South
Sp Spanish
TV television
UK United Kingdom
US(A) United States (of America)
USSR Union of Soviet Socialist
  Republics
usu usually
vulg vulgar
W. West

Labels used in the dictionary

label	denotes words or meanings that:
(coll)	are common and generally acceptable in spoken or informal English – *eg* **clout, doss**
(comput)	relate to computers – *eg* **memory, program**
(hist)	are used of something no longer in use or existence – *eg* **cubit, turnpike**
(myth)	refer to someone or something found only in stories and that never actually existed – *eg* **cockatrice, dryad**
(old)	are no longer commonly used in modern English – *eg* **damsel, twain**
(slang)	are less generally acceptable, even in informal English, than *(coll)* – *eg* **nick, quid**
(US)	are American – *eg* **closet, sidewalk**
(vulg)	are not generally acceptable, even in informal use

a or **an** *adjective* one: *A boy came into the garden*; any: *An ant has six legs*; in, to or for each: *four times a day*. The form *a* is used before words beginning with a consonant, *eg* boy; *an* is used before words beginning with a vowel, *eg* ant.

aback: taken aback surprised.

abacus *noun* (*plural* **abacuses**) a frame with beads on wires for counting.

abandon *verb* to leave, without meaning to return to; to give up (an idea *etc*). – *noun* **abandonment**.

abase *verb* to humble. – *noun* **abasement**.

abashed *adjective* embarrassed, confused.

abate *verb* to make or grow less. – *noun* **abatement**.

abattoir *a'bà t-wär*, *noun* a (public) slaughter-house.

abbess *noun* (*plural* **abbesses**) the female head of an abbey or a convent.

abbey *noun* (*plural* **abbeys**) a monastery or convent ruled by an abbot or an abbess; the church now or formerly attached to it.

abbot *noun* the male head of an abbey.

abbreviate *verb* to shorten (a word, phrase *etc*). – *noun* **abbreviation** a shortened form of a word *etc* used instead of the whole word (*eg maths* for *mathematics*).

abdicate *verb* to give up (a duty, position, *esp* that of king or queen). – *noun* **abdication**.

abdomen *noun* the part of the human body between the chest and the hips. – *adjective* **abdominal**.

abduct *verb* to take away by force or fraud. – *noun* **abduction**.

abet *verb* (*past tense* **abetted**) to help or encourage (*usu* to do wrong).

abeyance: in abeyance undecided, not to be dealt with for the time being.

abhor *verb* (*past tense* **abhorred**) to look on with horror, to hate. – *noun* **abhorrence**. – *adjective* **abhorrent** hateful.

abide *verb* to put up with, tolerate. – *adjective* **abiding** lasting. – **abide by** to keep, act according to.

ability *noun* (*plural* **abilities**) power or means to do a thing; talent.

abject *adjective* miserable, degraded.

ablaze *adjective* burning fiercely; gleaming like fire.

able *adjective* having power, means *etc* (to do a thing); clever. – *adverb* **ably**.

ablution *noun* (*usu plural*) washing of the body.

abnormal *adjective* not normal (in behaviour *etc*); unusual. – *noun* **abnormality** (*plural* **abnormalities**).

aboard *adverb, preposition* on (to) or in(to) (a means of transport).

abode *noun* a dwelling place.

abolish *verb* to do away with (*eg* a custom). – *noun* **abolition**. – *noun* **abolitionist** one who tries to do away with anything, *esp* slavery.

abominate *verb* to hate very much. – *adjective* **abominable** hateful. – *noun* **abomination** great hatred; anything hateful. – **the Abominable Snowman** (also **Yeti**) a large animal which may exist in the Himalayas.

aborigines *ab-ò r-ij'in-ēz*, *noun plural* the original or native inhabitants of a country (*esp* Australia). – *adjective* **aboriginal**.

abort *verb* (of a plan *etc*) to come to nothing; to stay undeveloped; to lose a baby before birth. – *noun* **abortion** the (deliberate) loss of an unborn child. – *adjective* **abortive** coming to nothing, useless: *an abortive attempt*.

abound *verb* to be very plentiful; (with **in**) to have many or much.

about *preposition* around: *Look about you*; near (in time, size *etc*): *It is about ten o'clock. It measures about two metres*; here and there in: *scattered about the room*. – *adverb* around: *They stood about waiting*; in motion or in action: *running about*; in the opposite direction: *He turned about and walked away*. – **about to** on the point of (doing something).

above *preposition* over, in a higher position than: *above his head*; greater than: *above average*; too good for: *He's above jealousy*. – *adverb* overhead, on high; earlier on (in a book *etc*). – *adjective, adverb* **above board** open(ly).

abrasion *noun* the act of rubbing off; a graze on the body. – *noun* **abrasive**

something used for rubbing or polishing. – *adjective* able to wear down; (of persons) able to hurt people's feelings.

abreast *adverb* side by side. – **abreast of** up to date with: *abreast of the times.*

abridge *verb* to shorten (a book, story *etc*). – *noun* **abridgement** or **abridgment**.

abroad *adverb* in another country; outside: *Witches go abroad after dark*; in all directions.

abrupt *adjective* sudden, without warning; (of speech *etc*) bad-tempered, short, blunt.

abscess *noun* (*plural* **abscesses**) a boil or similar collection of pus in the body.

abscond *verb* to run away secretly.

absent *adjective* away, not present. – *verb* (with **oneself**) to keep away. – *noun* **absence** the state of being away. – *noun* **absentee** a person who is absent. – *adjective* **absent-minded** forgetful.

absolute *adjective* complete, not limited by anything: *absolute power*. – *adverb* **absolutely** completely.

absolve *verb* to pardon. – *noun* **absolution** forgiveness, pardon.

absorb *verb* to soak up; to take up the whole attention of. – *adjective* **absorbed**. – *adjective* **absorbent** able to soak up (liquid). – *noun* **absorption** the act of absorbing; complete mental concentration.

abstain *verb* (with **from**) to hold oneself back. – *noun* **abstainer** a person who abstains from something, *esp* from alcoholic drink. – *noun* **abstention** a holding back, *esp* from voting.

abstemious *adjective* not greedy, sparing (in food, drink *etc*).

abstention *see* **abstain**.

abstinence *noun* holding back (from alcoholic drink *etc*).

abstract *adjective* existing only as an idea, not as a real thing. – *noun* a summary.

abstruse *adjective* difficult to understand.

absurd *adjective* clearly wrong, ridiculous. – *noun* **absurdity** (*plural* **absurdities**).

abundance *noun* a plentiful supply. – *adjective* **abundant** plentiful.

abuse *verb* to use wrongly; to insult, speak unkindly to, treat badly. – *noun* wrongful use; insulting language. – *adjective* **abusive**.

abyss *noun* (*plural* **abysses**) a bottomless depth. – *adjective* **abysmal** bottomless; (*coll*) very bad.

AC *abbreviation* alternating current.

a/c *abbreviation* account.

acacia *noun* a family of thorny shrubs and trees.

academy *noun* (*plural* **academies**) a college for special study or training; a society for encouraging science or art; in Scotland, a senior school. – *adjective* **academic** learned; not practical: *purely of academic interest*; of universities *etc*. – *noun* a university or college teacher.

ACAS *abbreviation* Advisory, Conciliation and Arbitration Service.

accede *verb* to agree (to).

accelerate *verb* to increase in speed. – *noun* **acceleration**. – *noun* **accelerator** a lever, pedal *etc* by which speed is increased.

accent *noun* (a mark used to show the) stress on a syllable or word; in French a mark used to show the quality of a vowel; emphasis: *The accent must be on hard work*; a special way of saying words in a particular region *etc*: *a Scottish accent*. – *verb* **accentuate** to make more obvious, emphasize.

accept *verb* to take something offered; to agree; to submit to. – *adjective* **acceptable** satisfactory; pleasing. – *noun* **acceptance** the act of accepting.

access *noun* right or means of approach or entry. – *adjective* **accessible** easily approached or reached. – *noun* **accessibility**. – *noun* **accession** a coming to: *the accession of a king to his throne*. – *noun* **accessory** (*plural* **accessories**) a (small) additional fitting (to a car *etc*) or article of dress (as a handbag *etc*); a helper (*esp* in crime).

accident *noun* an unexpected event (often unwanted or causing injury *etc*); a mishap. – *adjective* **accidental** happening by chance.

acclaim *verb* to welcome enthusiastically. – *noun* **acclamation** noisy sign of approval.

acclimatize *verb* to accustom (*esp* to another climate). – *noun* **acclimatization**.

accommodate *verb* to find room for; to make suitable; to oblige; to supply (with). – *adjective* **accommodating**

obliging. – *noun* **accommodation** space; lodgings.

accompany *verb* (*past tense* **accompanied**) to go or be with; to play an instrument (*eg* a piano) while a singer sings *etc*. – *noun* **accompaniment** that which goes along with (something); the music played while a singer sings *etc*. – *noun* **accompanist** a person who plays an accompaniment.

accomplice *noun* a person who helps another (*esp* in crime).

accomplish *verb* to complete; to bring about. – *adjective* **accomplished** completed; skilled (as in music *etc*). – *noun* **accomplishment** completion; something one is good at.

accord *verb* to agree (with); to give, grant. – *noun* agreement. – *noun* **accordance** agreement. – *adverb* **accordingly** therefore. – **according to** as told by; in relation to: *paid according to your work*; **of one's own accord** of one's own free will.

accordion *noun* a musical instrument with bellows, a keyboard and metal reeds.

accost *verb* to approach and speak to.

account *verb* to give a reason (for). – *noun* a bill; a reckoning up of money; a description (of events *etc*); an explanation. – *adjective* **accountable** answerable, responsible. – *noun* **accountant** a keeper or inspector of accounts. – **on account of** because of.

accoutrements *à-koo'tèr-mènts*, *noun plural* (*esp* military) dress and equipment.

accredited *adjective* given the official power to act.

accrue *verb* to be given or added to: *Interest accrues to savings deposited in a bank*. – *adjective* **accrued**.

accumulate *verb* to collect; to increase. – *noun* **accumulation** a collection; a mass or pile. – *noun* **accumulator** a type of battery (as in a car).

accurate *adjective* correct, exact. – *noun* **accuracy**.

accursed *adjective* under a curse; hateful.

accuse *verb* to bring a (criminal) charge against. – *noun* **accusation** a charge brought against anyone. – *noun* **accused** a person charged with wrongdoing. – *noun* **accuser**.

accustomed *adjective* used to: *accustomed to travel*; usual.

ace *noun* the one on playing-cards; a person who is expert in anything.

acetylene *noun* a kind of gas used for giving light and heat.

ache *noun* a continuous pain. – *verb* to be in continuous pain.

achieve *verb* to get (something) done, accomplish; to win. – *noun* **achievement**.

acid *adjective* (of taste) sharp; sarcastic. – *noun* a substance containing hydrogen which will dissolve metals. – *verb* **acidify** (*past tense* **acidified**) to make or become acid. – *noun* **acidity** the state of being acid. – *noun* **acid rain** rain containing sulphur and nitrogen compounds and other pollutants.

acknowledge *verb* to admit the truth of; to (write to) say one has received something. – *noun* **acknowledgement** or **acknowledgment**.

acme *noun* the highest point, perfection.

acne *noun* a common skin disease with pimples.

acorn *noun* the fruit of the oak tree.

acoustic *adjective* of hearing or sound. – *noun plural* **acoustics** the study of sound; the characteristics (of a hall *etc*) which affect the hearing of sound in it.

acquaint *verb* to make (someone) familiar (with). – *noun* **acquaintance** knowledge; a person whom one knows slightly.

acquiesce *ak-wi-es'*, *verb* (*usu* with **in**) to agree (to). – *noun* **acquiescence**.

acquire *verb* to get (as a possession), gain. – *adjective* **acquired** gained, not born with. – *noun* **acquisition** the act of getting; something got. – *adjective* **acquisitive** eager to get.

acquit *verb* (*past tense* **acquitted**) to declare (someone) innocent of a crime. – *noun* **acquittal** a legal judgement of 'not guilty'. – **acquit oneself well** or **badly** to do well or badly; to be successful or unsuccessful.

acre *noun* a land measure containing 4840 square yards or about 4000 square metres. – *noun* **acreage** the number of acres in a piece of land.

acrid *adjective* harsh, bitter.

acrimony *noun* bitterness of feeling or speech. – *adjective* **acrimonious**.

acrobat *noun* a person who performs feats of agility, rope-walking *etc*. – *adjective* **acrobatic.**

acronym *noun* a word formed from the initial letters of other words (*eg radar* for radio detecting and ranging).

across *adverb, preposition* to or at the other side (of): *They swam across the river. He saw her across the table.* – **across the board** involving all (things or persons).

acrostic *noun* a poem *etc* in which the first or last letters of each line, taken in order, spell a word or words.

acrylic *noun* a synthetically produced fibre. – Also *adjective.*

act *verb* to do something; to behave: *act foolishly*; to play a part (as in a play). – *noun* something done; a government law; a part of a play. – *noun* **action** a deed, an act; a law-case; what happens (in a film, play *etc*). – *adjective* **actionable** likely to cause a law-case: *an actionable statement.* – *verb* **activate** to start (something) working. – *adjective* **active** busy; lively; able to work *etc*; of the form of a verb in which the subject performs the action of the verb as in 'The dog *bit* the man'. – *noun* **activity** (*plural* **activities**). – *noun* **actor** (*masculine*), **actress** (*feminine*) (*plural* **actresses**) a person who acts a part in a play or film.

actual *adjective* real, existing in fact. – *noun* **actuality.** – *adverb* **actually** really.

actuary *noun* (*plural* **actuaries**) a person who works out the price of insurance. – *adjective* **actuarial.**

actuate *verb* to put into action; to drive or urge on.

acumen *noun* quickness of understanding.

acupuncture *noun* a method of treating illness by piercing the skin with needles.

acute *adjective* quick at understanding; (of a disease) severe, but not lasting very long; (of an angle) less than a right angle. – *noun* **acuteness.** – *noun* **acute accent** a stroke leaning forwards placed over letters in some languages to show their pronunciation.

AD *abbreviation* in the year of our Lord (*eg* AD 1900) (*anno Domini* [L]).

ad *noun* short for **advertisement.**

adage *noun* an old saying, a proverb.

adamant *adjective* unwilling to give way.

Adam's apple *noun* the natural lump which sticks out from the throat.

adapt *verb* to make suitable, to alter (so as to fit). – *adjective* **adaptable** easily altered to suit new conditions. – *noun* **adaptation.** – *noun* **adaptor** a device which enables an electrical plug to be used in a socket for which it was not designed, or several plugs to be used on the same socket.

add *verb* to make one thing join another to give a sum total or whole; to mix in: *add eggs to the flour*; to say further. – *noun* **addition** the act of adding; something added. – *adjective* **additional.** – *noun* **additive** a substance (often a chemical) added to another.

addendum *noun* (*plural* **addenda**) something added.

adder *noun* the common name of the viper, a poisonous snake.

addict *noun* a person who is dependent on something (often on a drug or alcohol), either physically or mentally. – **addicted to** dependent on.

addition, additive *see* **add.**

address *verb* to speak to; to write the address on (a letter *etc*). – *noun* (*plural* **addresses**) the name of the house, street, and town where a person lives *etc*; a speech.

adenoids *noun plural* a mass of tissue at the back of the nose which, when swollen, hinders breathing.

adept *adjective* very skilful.

adequate *adjective* sufficient, enough. – *noun* **adequacy.**

adhere *verb* to stick (to); to give support (to) or be loyal (to). – *noun* **adherence.** – *adjective* **adherent** sticking (to). – *noun* a follower, a person who supports a cause *etc*.

adhesion *noun* the act of sticking (to). – *adjective* **adhesive** sticky, gummed. – *noun* something which makes things stick to each other.

ad hoc *adjective* (of a committee *etc*) set up for a particular purpose only.

ad infinitum *adverb* for ever.

adjacent *adjective* (with **to**) lying next to.

adjective *noun* a word which tells something about a noun (as 'The *black* dog bites. The work is *hard'*.). – *adjective* **adjectival**.

adjoin *verb* to be joined to. – *adjective* **adjoining**.

adjourn *verb* to stop (a meeting *etc*) with the intention of continuing it at another time or place; to go to another place (*eg* another room). – *noun* **adjournment**.

adjudicate *verb* to give a judgement on (a dispute *etc*); to act as a judge at a (musical *etc*) competition. – *noun* **adjudication**. – *noun* **adjudicator** a person who adjudicates.

adjunct *noun* something joined or added.

adjust *verb* to rearrange or alter to suit the circumstances. – *adjective* **adjustable**. – *noun* **adjustment**.

adjutant *noun* a military officer who assists a commanding officer.

ad-lib *verb* (*past tense* **ad-libbed**) to speak without plan or preparation. – *adjective* without preparation.

administer *verb* to manage or govern; to carry out (the law *etc*); to give (help, medicine *etc*). – *verb* **administrate** to manage or govern. – *noun* **administration** management; (the body that carries on) the government of a country *etc*. – *adjective* **administrative**. – *noun* **administrator** a person involved in the administration of a country *etc*.

admiral *noun* the commander of a navy. – *noun* **admiralty** the government office which manages naval affairs.

admire *verb* to think very highly of; to look at with pleasure. – *adjective* **admirable** worthy of being admired. – *adverb* **admirably**. – *noun* **admiration**. – *noun* **admirer**.

admit *verb* (*past tense* **admitted**) to let in; to acknowledge the truth of, confess; (with **of**) to leave room for, allow: *This admits of no other explanation*. – *adjective* **admissible** allowable. – *noun* **admission** (the price of) being let in; anything admitted. – *noun* **admittance** the right or permission to enter.

admonish *verb* to warn; to rebuke, scold. – *noun* **admonition** a warning. – *adjective* **admonitory**.

ado *noun* trouble, fuss.

adolescent *noun*, *adjective* (a person) between childhood and the adult state. – *noun* **adolescence**.

adopt *verb* to take as one's own (*esp* a child of other parents). – *noun* **adoption**.

adore *verb* to love very much; to worship. – *adjective* **adorable** worthy of being loved. – *adverb* **adorably**. – *noun* **adoration** worship; great love.

adorn *verb* to decorate (with ornaments *etc*). – *noun* **adornment** ornament.

adrenaline *noun* a hormone produced in response to fear, anger, *etc*, prepositionaring the body for quick action.

adrift *adverb* drifting, floating.

adroit *adjective* skilful.

adulation *noun* great flattery. – *adjective* **adulatory**.

adult *adjective* grown up. – *noun* a grown-up person.

adulterate *verb* to make impure by adding something else. – *noun* **adulteration**.

adultery *noun* breaking of the marriage promise, unfaithfulness to one's wife or husband. – *noun* **adulterer** (*masculine*), **adulteress** (*feminine*).

advance *verb* to go forward; to put forward (a plan *etc*); to help the progress of; to pay before the usual or agreed time. – *noun* movement forward; improvement; a loan. – *adjective* **advanced** well forward in progress. – *noun* **advancement** progress. – **in advance** beforehand.

advantage *noun* a better position, superiority; gain or benefit. – *verb* to help, benefit. – *adjective* **advantageous** profitable; helpful. – **take advantage of** to make use of (a situation, person *etc*) in such a way as to benefit oneself.

advent *noun* coming, arrival: *the advent of television*. – *noun* **Advent** in the Christian church, the four weeks before Christmas.

adventitious *adjective* happening by chance.

adventure *noun* a bold or exciting undertaking or experience. – *noun* **adventurer** one who takes risks, *esp* in the hope of making a lot of money; a soldier who fights for any side who will pay him.

adverb *noun* a word which gives a more definite meaning to a verb, adjective, or other adverb (as 'He writes *neatly*. The sky is *beautifully* clear. He works *very* slowly'.). – *adjective* **adverbial** of or like an adverb.

adversary *noun* (*plural* **adversaries**) an enemy; an opponent.

adverse *adjective* unfavourable. – *noun* **adversity** (*plural* **adversities**) misfortune.

advert *noun* short for **advertisement**.

advertise *verb* to make known to the public; to stress the good points of (a product for sale). – *noun* **advertisement** anything (as a film, picture) which is intended to persuade the public to buy a particular product.

advice *noun* something said as a help to someone trying to make a decision *etc*; a formal notice. – *adjective* **advisable** wise, sensible. – *noun* **advisability**. – *verb* **advise** to give advice to; to recommend (an action *etc*). – *noun* **adviser**. – *adjective* **advisory** advice-giving.

advocate *noun* a person who pleads for another; (in Scotland) a court lawyer. – *verb* to plead or argue for; to recommend.

advt *abbreviation* advertisement.

adze or (*US*) **adz** *noun* a kind of axe used by a carpenter.

aegis *ē'jis, noun* protection; patronage.

aeon or **eon** *ē'ŏn, noun* a very long period of time, an age.

aerate *verb* to put air (or some other gas) into (a liquid).

aerial *adjective* of, in or from the air; placed high up or overhead (as an *aerial* railway). – *noun* a wire or rod (or a set of these) by means of which radio or television signals are received or sent.

aerobatics *noun plural* stunts performed by an aircraft.

aerobics *noun* a system of rhythmic physical exercise which aims to strengthen the heart and lungs by increasing the body's oxygen consumption.

aerodrome *noun* a landing and maintenance station for aircraft.

aeronautics *noun* the science or art of navigation in the air.

aeroplane *noun* a flying machine heavier than air, with wings.

aerosol *noun* a container of liquid and gas under pressure, from which the liquid is squirted as a mist.

aesthetic *adjective* of beauty or its appreciation; artistic, pleasing to the eye.

affable *adjective* pleasant, easy to speak to. – *noun* **affability**.

affair *noun* events *etc* which are connected with one person or thing: *the Belgrano affair*; (often in *plural*) business, concern; a love affair.

affect *verb* to act upon; to have an effect on; to move the feelings of; to pretend to feel *etc*. – *noun* **affectation** pretence. – *adjective* **affected** moved in one's feelings; not natural, sham. – *adjective* **affecting** moving the feelings.

affection *noun* a strong liking. – *adjective* **affectionate** loving. – *adverb* **affectionately**.

affidavit *noun* a written statement made on oath.

affiliated *adjective* (with **with** or **to**) connected, attached. – *noun* **affiliation**.

affinity *noun* (*plural* **affinities**) a close likeness or agreement.

affirm *verb* to state firmly. – *noun* **affirmation** a firm statement. – *adjective* **affirmative** saying 'yes'.

affix *verb* to attach to.

afflict *verb* to give continued pain or distress to. – *adjective* **afflicted** suffering. – *noun* **affliction** great suffering, misery.

affluent *adjective* wealthy. – *noun* a stream flowing into a river or lake. – *noun* **affluence** wealth.

afford *verb* to be able to pay for; to give, yield.

afforest *verb* to cover land with forest. – *noun* **afforestation**.

affray *noun* a fight, a brawl.

affront *verb* to insult openly. – *noun* an insult.

aflatoxin *noun* (possibly carcinogenic) toxin produced in foodstuffs by species of the mould Aspergillus.

afloat *adverb*, *adjective* floating.

afoot *adverb* happening or about to happen.

aforesaid *adjective* said or named before.

afraid *adjective* struck with fear; (*coll*) sorry to have to admit that.

aft *adverb* near or towards the stern of a vessel.

after *preposition* later in time than: *after dinner*; following: *They entered one after another. Day after day it rained*; in memory or honour of: *named after his* *father*; in pursuit of: *run after the bus*; about: *ask after someone's health*; despite: *After all his efforts, he still failed*; in the style of: *after (the manner of) Shakespeare*. – *adverb* later in time or place: *They arrived soon after*. – *conjunction* later than the time when: *After she arrived, things improved greatly*. – *adjective, prefix* **after(-)** later in time or place: *In after years it was forgotten. It had an aftertaste*. – **after all** all things considered: *After all, he's not very well*; despite everything said or done before: *He's coming after all*.

afterbirth *noun* the placenta and membranes expelled from the uterus after a birth.

aftermath *noun* the bad results of something, *eg* of war *etc*.

afternoon *noun* the time between noon and evening.

aftershave *noun* a lotion used on the face after shaving.

afterthought *noun* a later thought.

afterwards *adverb* later.

again *adverb* once more: *play the tune again*; in(to) the original state, place *etc*: *there and back again*; on the other hand: *Again, I might be wrong*; (*coll*) at another (later) time: *I'll see you again*.

against *preposition* in opposition to: *It is against the law to sell alcohol to children*. He fought *against his brother*; in the opposite direction to: *against the wind*; on a background of: *against the sky*; close to, touching: *lean against the wall*; as protection from: *immunized against diphtheria*.

agate *noun* a kind of precious stone.

age *noun* a long period of time; the time a person or thing has lived or existed. – *verb* to grow or make (obviously) older. – *adjective* **aged** old; of the age of: *aged five*. – *noun* **ageism** discrimination on grounds of age. – **of age** legally an adult.

agenda *noun* a list of things to be done, *esp* at a meeting.

agent *noun* a person or thing that acts; a person who acts for another; a spy. – *noun* **agency** (*plural* **agencies**) the office or business of an agent; action, means by which something is done.

aggrandize *verb* to make greater. – *noun* **aggrandizement**.

aggravate *verb* to make worse; (*coll*) to annoy. – *adjective* **aggravating**. – *noun* **aggravation**.

aggregate *noun* a total.

aggressive *adjective* ready to attack first; quarrelsome. – *noun* **aggression**. – *adverb* **aggressively**. – *noun* **aggressiveness**. – *noun* **aggressor**.

aggrieved *adjective* hurt, upset.

aghast *adjective* struck with horror.

agile *adjective* active, nimble. – *noun* **agility**.

agitate *verb* to stir up; to excite, disturb. – *noun* **agitation**. – *noun* **agitator** a person who stirs up (*usu* political) feeling.

agm *abbreviation* annual general meeting.

agnostic *noun* a person who believes that we cannot know whether God exists or not. – *noun* **agnosticism**.

ago *adverb* in the past: *Two years ago I went to Rome*.

agog *adjective* eager, excited.

agony *noun* (*plural* **agonies**) great pain. – *adjective* **agonized** showing great pain. – *adjective* **agonizing** causing great pain. – *noun* **agony aunt** a person, *usu* a woman, who gives advice in an agony column. – *noun* **agony column** the part of a newspaper or magazine in which readers submit and receive advice about personal problems; a column containing advertisements dealing with personal problems.

agoraphobia *noun* great fear of open spaces.

agrarian *adjective* of farmland or farming.

agree *verb* to be alike (*esp* in opinions, decisions *etc*); to say that one will do something, consent; (with **with**) to suit. – *adjective* **agreeable** pleasant; ready to agree. – *adverb* **agreeably**. – *noun* **agreement** likeness (*esp* of opinions); a written statement making a bargain.

agriculture *noun* the cultivation of the land, farming. – *adjective* **agricultural**.

aground *adjective, adverb* (of boats) stuck on the bottom of the sea or a river: *The ship ran aground*.

ague *ā'gū, noun* (*old*) a fever.

ahead *adverb* in front; in advance: *ahead of time*.

aid *verb* to help, assist. – *noun* help.

aide-de-camp *ā-dè-konᵍ, noun* (*plural* **aides-de-camp**) an officer who carries messages to and from a general on the field.

AIDS or **Aids** *noun* short for Acquired Immune Deficiency Syndrome, a viral disease.

ail *verb* to be ill; to trouble. – *noun* **ailment** a trouble, disease.

aileron *noun* a hinged flap on the back edge of an aeroplane's wing, used to control balance.

aim *verb* to point at (*esp* with a gun); to intend to do; to have as one's purpose. – *noun* the act of, or skill in, aiming; the point aimed at, goal, intention. – *adjective* **aimless** without aim or purpose.

air *noun* the mixture of gases (mainly oxygen and nitrogen) which we breathe, the atmosphere; a light breeze; fresh air; space overhead; a tune; the look or manner (of a person). – *verb* to expose to the air; to make known (an opinion *etc*). – *noun* **airbed** a mattress which can be inflated. – *adjective* **airborne** in the air, flying. – *adjective* **air-conditioned** of buildings *etc* in which the air is cleaned and kept to a certain temperature by a special system. – *noun plural* **aircraft** flying machine(s). – *noun* **air force** the branch of the armed forces using aircraft. – *noun* **air-gun** a gun worked by means of compressed air. – *noun* **air hostess** a woman whose duty is to serve and look after the passengers on aircraft. – *adverb* **airily** lightheartedly. – *noun* **airing** the act of exposing to the air. – *adjective* **airless**. – *noun* **airlock** a bubble in a pipe obstructing the flow of a liquid; a compartment with two doors for entering and leaving an airtight spaceship *etc*. – *noun* **airman** (*masculine*), **airwoman** (*feminine*) an aviator or aviatrix. – *noun* **air-miss** a near collision between aircraft. – *noun* **airport** a place where aircraft land and take off, with buildings for customs, waiting-rooms *etc*. – *noun* **air-pump** a pump for forcing air in or out of something. – *noun* **air-raid** an attack by aeroplanes. – *noun* **airship** a large balloon which can be steered and driven. – *noun* **airstream** a flow of air. – *adjective* **airtight** made so that air cannot pass in or out. – *adjective* **airy** of or like the air; well supplied with fresh air; light-hearted. – **on the air** broadcasting.

aisle *il*, *noun* the side part of a church; a passage between seats (*esp* in a church).

ajar *adverb* (of doors *etc*) partly open.

akimbo *adverb* with hand on hip and elbow bent outward.

akin *adjective* similar.

à la carte *adjective, adverb* according to the menu – each dish chosen and priced separately.

alacrity *noun* briskness, cheerful readiness.

alarm *noun* sudden fear; something which rouses to action or gives warning of danger. – *verb* to frighten. – *adjective* **alarming**. – *noun* **alarmist** a person who frightens others needlessly.

alas! *interjection* a cry showing grief.

albatross *noun* (*plural* **albatrosses**) a type of large sea-bird.

albino *noun* (*plural* **albinos**) a person or animal with no natural colour in their skin and hair (which are white) and eye pupils (which are pink).

album *noun* a book with blank pages for holding photographs, stamps *etc*; a long-playing record; recordings issued under one title.

albumen *noun* the white of eggs.

alchemy *noun* (*hist*) the early form of chemistry which aimed to change other metals into gold. – *noun* **alchemist** a person who practised alchemy.

alcohol *noun* the pure spirit in strong drinks. – *adjective* **alcoholic** of or containing alcohol. – *noun* a person suffering from alcoholism. – *noun* **alcoholism** dependence on alcoholic drinks.

alcove *noun* a recess in a room's wall.

alder *noun* a type of tree which grows beside ponds and rivers.

alderman *noun* formerly, a councillor next in rank to the mayor of a town *etc*; (*US*) a member of the governing body of a city.

ale *noun* a drink made from malt, hops *etc*.

alert *noun* signal to be ready for action. – *verb* to make alert, warn. – *adjective* watchful; quick-thinking. – **on the alert** on the watch (for).

alfalfa *noun* a kind of grass.

alfresco *adjective, adverb* in the open air.

algae *noun plural* a group of simple plants which includes seaweed.

algebra *noun* a method of counting, using letters and signs.

alias *adverb* (*plural* **aliases**) otherwise known as: *Smith alias Jones*. – *noun* a false name.

alibi *noun* the plea that a person charged with a crime was elsewhere when it was done; the state or fact of being elsewhere when a crime was committed.

alien *adjective* foreign. – *noun* a foreigner. – *verb* **alienate** to make (a person) strange or unfriendly. – **alien to** not in keeping with: *alien to his nature.*

alight *verb* to climb *etc* down; to settle, land. – *adjective, adverb* on fire, burning.

align *à-līn¹, verb* to set in line; to take sides in an argument *etc.* – *noun* **alignment** arrangement in a line.

alike *adjective* like one another, similar. – *adverb* in the same way, similarly.

alimentary *adjective* of food. – *noun* **alimentary canal** the passage through the body which begins at the mouth.

alimony *noun* an allowance paid by a husband to his wife, or a wife to her husband, to provide support, when they are legally separated.

alive *adjective* living; full of activity. – **alive to** aware of.

alkali *noun* a substance such as soda or potash (opposite of **acid**). – *adjective* **alkaline**.

all *adjective, pronoun* every one (of): *All men are equal. All must go;* the whole (of): *He ate all the cake.* – *adverb* wholly, completely: *dressed all in red.* – *noun* **all-rounder** one who shows ability in many kinds of work, sport *etc.* – **all in** with everything included; (*coll*) exhausted; **all-in wrestling** wrestling in which no holds are against the rules; **all over** over the whole of; everywhere; finished, ended.

Allah *noun* the name for God in the Islamic religion.

allay *verb* to make less, relieve; to calm.

allege *verb* to say without proof. – *noun* **allegation**.

allegiance *noun* loyalty.

allegory *noun* (*plural* **allegories**) a story or fable which deals with a subject in a way which is meant to suggest a deeper, more serious subject: *'Pilgrim's Progress' is an allegory of the Christian's life.* – *adjective* **allegorical**.

allergy *noun* (*plural* **allergies**) abnormal sensitiveness (of the body) to something. – *adjective* **allergic**.

alleviate *verb* to make lighter, to lessen. – *noun* **alleviation**.

alley *noun* (*plural* **alleys**) a narrow passage or lane; an enclosure for bowls or skittles.

alliance *see* **ally**.

alligator *noun* a kind of large reptile like a crocodile.

alliteration *noun* the repetition of the same sound at the beginning of two or more words close together (*eg* 'Sing a Song of Sixpence').

allocate *verb* to give to each a share. – *noun* **allocation**.

allot *verb* (*past tense* **allotted**) to give to each a share, distribute. – *noun* **allotment** the act of distributing; a small plot of ground for growing vegetables *etc.*

allow *verb* to let (someone do something); (with **for**) to take into consideration (in sums, plans *etc*); to admit, confess; to give, *esp* at regular intervals: *She allows him £5 a week.* – *adjective* **allowable**. – *noun* **allowance** a fixed sum or amount given regularly. – **make allowance(s) for** to treat differently because of taking into consideration special circumstances *etc.*

alloy *noun* a mixture of two or more metals.

allude *verb* (with **to**) to mention in passing. – *noun* **allusion**. – *adjective* **allusive**.

allure *verb* to tempt, draw on by promises *etc.* – *noun* **allurement**. – *adjective* **alluring**.

alluvium *noun* (*plural* **alluvia**) earth, sand *etc* brought down and left by rivers in flood. – *adjective* **alluvial**.

ally *verb* (*past tense* **allied**) to join oneself to (by treaty *etc*). – (*plural* **allies**) a friend, person *etc* in alliance with another. – *noun* **alliance** a joining together of two people, nations *etc* (*esp* against an enemy of both). – *adjective* **allied**.

almanac *noun* a calendar of days, weeks, and months of any year, *usu* with information (about the phases of the moon *etc*).

almighty *adjective* having much power. – **the Almighty** God.

almond *noun* the kernel of the fruit of the almond-tree.

almost *adverb* very nearly but not quite: *He is almost five years old. We are almost at our destination.*

alms *noun plural* gifts to the poor.

aloft *adverb* on high; upward.

alone *adjective* not accompanied by others, solitary: *He found he was alone again.* – *adverb* only, without anything or anyone else: *That alone is bad enough*; not accompanied by others: *He lived alone*.

along *preposition* over the length of: *He walked along the road.* – *adverb* onward: *Hurry along!* – *preposition* **alongside** beside. – *adverb* near a ship's side. – **along with** together with.

aloof *adjective, adverb* at a distance, apart; showing no interest in others. – *noun* **aloofness**.

aloud *adverb* so as to be heard.

alpha *noun* the first letter of the Greek alphabet.

alphabet *noun* letters of a language given in a fixed order. – *adjective* **alphabetic** or **alphabetical** in the order of the alphabet.

alphasort *verb* (*comput*) to sort into *esp* alphabetical order.

alpine *adjective* of the Alps or other high mountains.

already *adverb* before this or that time: *I've already done that*; now, before the expected time: *You haven't finished already, have you?*

alsatian *noun* a German shepherd dog.

also *adverb* in addition, besides, too: *He also must go.* – *noun* **also-ran** a person or thing who competed (as in a race) but was not among the winners.

altar *noun* a raised place for offerings to a god; in Christian churches, the communion table.

alter *verb* to change. – *noun* **alteration**.

altercation *noun* an argument or quarrel.

alternate *verb* (of two things *etc*) to do or happen in turn. – *adjective* happening *etc* in turns. – *adverb* **alternately**. – *noun* **alternation**. – *adjective* **alternative** offering a second possibility *etc*. – Also *noun*.

although *conjunction* though, in spite of the fact that.

altimeter *noun* an instrument for measuring height above sea level.

altitude *noun* height above sea level.

alto *noun* (*plural* **altos**) the male voice of the highest pitch; the female voice of lowest pitch (also **contralto**).

altogether *adverb* considering everything, in all: *Altogether there were 20 of them*; completely: *I am not altogether satisfied.*

altruism *noun* unselfish concern for the good of others. – *adjective* **altruistic**.

aluminium or (*US*) **aluminum** *noun* an element, a very light metal.

always *adverb* for ever: *I'll always remember this day*; every time: *He always says the same thing.*

am *abbreviation* before noon (*ante meridiem* [L]).

am *see* **be**.

amalgam *noun* a mixture (*esp* of metals). – *verb* **amalgamate** to join together, combine; to mix. – *noun* **amalgamation**.

amass *verb* to collect in large quantity.

amateur *noun* a person who takes part in a thing for the love of it, not for money (opposite of **professional**). – Also *adjective*. – *adjective* **amateurish** not done properly; not skilful.

amaze *verb* to surprise greatly. – *noun* **amazement**.

Amazon *noun* (*myth*) one of a nation of warrior women; a very strong or manlike woman.

ambassador (*masculine*), **ambassadress** (*feminine*) *noun* a government minister sent to look after the interests of one country in another country; a representative.

amber *noun* a hard yellowish fossil resin used in making jewellery. – *adjective* made of amber; of the colour of amber.

ambidextrous *adjective* able to use both hands with equal skill. – *noun* **ambidexterity**.

ambience *noun* environment, atmosphere.

ambiguous *adjective* having two possible meanings; not clear. – *noun* **ambiguity** (*plural* **ambiguities**).

ambition *noun* the desire for success, power, fame *etc*. – *adjective* **ambitious**.

amble *verb* to walk without hurrying. – Also *noun*.

ambrosia *noun* (*myth*) the food of the gods, which gave eternal youth and beauty.

ambulance *noun* a vehicle for carrying the sick or injured.

ambush *noun* (*plural* **ambushes**) the act of lying hidden in order to make a surprise attack; the people hidden in this way; their place of hiding. – *verb* to attack suddenly from a position of hiding.

amenable *adjective* open to advice or suggestion.

amend *verb* to correct, improve; to alter slightly. – *noun* **amendment** a change (*usu* in something written). – **make amends** to make up for having done wrong.

amenity *noun* (*plural* **amenities**) a pleasant or convenient feature of a place *etc*.

amethyst *noun* a type of precious stone of a bluish-violet colour.

amiable *adjective* likeable; friendly. – *noun* **amiability.**

amicable *adjective* friendly.

amid or **amidst** *preposition* in the middle of, among: *She seemed calm amidst all the confusion.*

amiss *adverb* wrong(ly); badly.

amity *noun* friendship.

ammonia *noun* a strong-smelling gas made of hydrogen and nitrogen.

ammunition *noun* gunpowder, shot, bullets, bombs *etc*.

amnesia *noun* loss of memory.

amnesty *noun* (*plural* **amnesties**) a general pardon of wrongdoers.

amoeba *noun* (*plural* **amoebas** or **amoebae**) a very simple form of animal life found in ponds *etc*.

amok or **amuck**: **run amok** to become furious or mad and do a lot of damage.

among or **amongst** *preposition* in the midst or in the middle of: *We live in a house among trees. We are among friends*; in shares, in parts: *Divide the chocolate amongst yourselves*; in the group of: *Among all his novels, this is the best.*

amoral *adjective* incapable of distinguishing between right and wrong.

amorous *adjective* loving; ready or inclined to love.

amount *verb* to add up (to). – *noun* total, sum (*usu* of money).

amp *noun* an ampère, the standard unit of electric current; short for amplifier.

amphetamine *noun* a type of drug used as a stimulant.

amphibian *noun* any animal that lives on land and in water; a vehicle for use on land and in water. – Also *adjective*. – *adjective* **amphibious.**

amphitheatre *noun* (*hist*) a theatre with seats surrounding a central arena.

ample *adjective* plenty of; large enough.

amplify *verb* (*past tense* **amplified**) to increase; to make louder. – *noun* **amplification.** – *noun* **amplifier** an electrical device for increasing loudness.

amplitude *noun* largeness; size.

ampoule *noun* a small *usu* glass container of medicine for injection.

amputate *verb* to cut off (*esp* a human limb). – *noun* **amputation.**

amuck *see* **amok.**

amuse *verb* to make to laugh; to give pleasure to. – *noun* **amusement.** – *adjective* **amusing** giving pleasure; funny.

an *see* **a.**

anabolic steroids *noun plural* steroids used to increase the build-up of body tissue, *esp* muscle.

anachronism *noun* the act of mentioning something which did not exist or was not yet invented at the time spoken about.

anaconda *noun* a type of large S. American water snake.

anaemia or (*US*) **anemia** *noun* a shortage of red cells in the blood. – *adjective* **anaemic** suffering from anaemia; pale or ill-looking.

anaesthetic or (*US*) **anesthetic** *noun* a substance which produces lack of feeling for a time in a part of the body, or which makes a person unconscious. – *noun* **anaesthetist** a doctor who gives anaesthetics.

anagram *noun* a word or sentence formed by rewriting (in a different order) the letters of another word or sentence (*veil* is an anagram of *evil*).

anal *see* **anus.**

analogy *noun* (*plural* **analogies**) a likeness, resemblance in certain ways. – *adjective* **analogous** similar, alike in some way.

analysis *noun* (*plural* **analyses**) a breaking up of a thing into its parts; a detailed examination (of something). – *verb* **analyse** or (*US*) **analyze.** – *noun* **analyst.**

anarchy *noun* lack or absence of government; disorder or confusion. – *noun* **anarchist**.

anathema *noun* a curse; a hated person or thing.

anatomy *noun* the study of the parts of the body; the body. – *noun* **anatomist**.

ANC *abbreviation* African National Congress.

ancestor *noun* one from whom a person is descended by birth, a forefather. – *adjective* **ancestral**. – *noun* **ancestry** line of ancestors.

anchor *noun* a heavy piece of iron, with hooked ends, for holding a ship fast to the bed of the sea *etc*. – *verb* to fix by anchor; to let down the anchor. – *noun* **anchorage** a place where a ship can anchor. – **cast anchor** to let down the anchor; **weigh anchor** to pull up the anchor.

anchovy *noun* (*plural* **anchovies**) a type of small fish of the herring family.

ancient *adjective* very old; of times long past.

ancillary *adjective* serving or supporting something more important.

and *conjunction* joining two statements, pieces of information *etc*: *I opened the door and went inside. The hat was blue and red*; in addition to: *2 and 2 make 4*.

anecdote *noun* a short, interesting or amusing story, *esp* a true one.

anemometer *noun* an instrument for measuring the speed of the wind.

anemone *noun* a type of woodland or garden flower.

aneroid barometer *noun* one in which the pressure of the air is measured without the use of mercury.

angel *noun* a messenger or attendant of God; a very good or beautiful person. – *adjective* **angelic**.

angelica *noun* a plant whose candied leaf-stalks are used as cake decoration.

anger *noun* a bitter feeling (against someone), annoyance, rage. – *verb* to make angry. – *adjective* **angry**. – *adverb* **angrily**.

angina *noun* a type of painful heart disease.

angle *noun* a corner; the V-shape made by two lines meeting at a point; a point of view. – *verb* to try to get by hints *etc*: *angling for a job*. – *noun* **angler** a person who fishes with rod and line. – *adjective* **angular** having angles; thin, bony.

Anglican *adjective* of the Church of England.

anglicize *verb* to turn into the English language; to make English in character.

Anglo-Saxon *adjective*, *noun* (of) the people of England before the Norman Conquest; (of) their language.

angora *noun* wool made from the hair of the Angora goat or rabbit. – *noun* **Angora cat** or **goat** or **rabbit** a type of cat, goat or rabbit with long silky hair.

angry *see* **anger**.

anguish *noun* very great pain or distress.

angular *see* **angle**.

animal *noun* a living being which can feel and move of its own accord; an animal other than man. – *adjective* of or like an animal.

animate *verb* to give life to; to make lively. – *adjective* living. – *adjective* **animated** lively; (of puppets, cartoon figures *etc*) made to move as if alive. – *noun* **animation**.

animosity *noun* bitter hatred, enmity.

aniseed *noun* a kind of seed with a flavour like that of liquorice.

ankle *noun* the joint connecting the foot and leg.

annals *noun plural* (yearly) historical accounts of events.

anneal *verb* to soften (or toughen) glass or metal by heating strongly and cooling slowly.

annex *verb* to take possession of; to add, attach. – *noun* (also **annexe**) a building added to another. – *noun* **annexation**.

annihilate *ă-nī'hil-āt, verb* to destroy completely. – *noun* **annihilation**.

anniversary *noun* (*plural* **anniversaries**) the day of each year when some event is remembered.

annotate *verb* to make notes upon; to add notes or explanation to. – *noun* **annotation**.

announce *verb* to make (publicly) known. – *noun* **announcement**. – *noun* **announcer** in radio *etc* a person who announces programmes or reads the news.

annoy *verb* to make rather angry, irritate. – *noun* **annoyance.**

annual *adjective* yearly. – *noun* a plant that lives only one year; a book published yearly. – *verb* **annualize** to convert to a yearly rate, amount *etc*. – *adverb* **annually.**

annuity *noun* (*plural* **annuities**) a yearly payment made for a certain time or for life.

annul *verb* (*past tense* **annulled**) to put an end to; declare no longer valid. – *noun* **annulment.**

anodyne *adjective* soothing, relieving pain. – *noun* something that soothes pain.

anoint *verb* to smear with ointment or oil (as part of a religious ceremony).

anomaly *noun* (*plural* **anomalies**) something unusual, not according to rule. – *adjective* **anomalous.**

anon short for **anonymous,** used when the author of a poem *etc* is not known.

anonymous *adjective* without the name (of the author, giver *etc*) being known or given.

anorak *noun* a hooded waterproof jacket.

anorexia *noun* lack of appetite; anorexia nervosa. – *noun* **anorexia nervosa** an emotional illness causing the sufferer to refuse food and become sometimes dangerously thin. – *adjective* **anorexic** relating to or suffering from anorexia. – Also *noun.*

another *adjective* a different (thing or person): *He moved to another job*; one more of the same kind: *Have another biscuit.* – Also *pronoun*.

answer *verb* to speak, write *etc* in return or reply; to find the result or solution (of a sum, problem *etc*); (with **for**) to be responsible; (with **for**) to suffer, be punished. – *noun* something said, written *etc* in return or reply; a solution. – *adjective* **answerable** able to be answered; responsible.

ant *noun* a type of small insect, thought to be hard-working.

antagonist *noun* an enemy; an opponent. – *noun* **antagonism** hostility, opposition, enmity. – *adjective* **antagonistic** opposed (to) unfriendly, hostile. – *verb* **antagonize** to make an enemy of, cause dislike.

Antarctic *adjective* of the South Pole or regions round it.

ante- *prefix* before.

antecedent *adjective* going before in time. – *noun* a person who lived at an earlier time, an ancestor; (*plural*) previous conduct, history *etc*.

antedate *verb* to date before the true time; to be earlier in date than.

antediluvian *adjective* very old or old-fashioned.

antelope *noun* a kind of graceful, swift-running, animal like a deer.

antenatal *adjective* before birth.

antenna *noun* (*plural* **antennas** or **antennae**) a feeler of an insect; an aerial.

anteroom *noun* a room leading into a large room.

anthem *noun* a piece of music for a church choir; any song of praise.

anthology *noun* (*plural* **anthologies**) a collection of specially chosen poems, stories *etc*.

anthracite *noun* a kind of coal that burns with a hot, smokeless flame.

anthrax *noun* an infectious disease of cattle, sheep *etc*, sometimes caught by man.

anthropoid *adjective* (*esp* of apes) man-like.

anthropology *noun* the study of mankind. – *noun* **anthropologist.**

anti- *prefix* against; opposite.

antibiotic *noun* a type of medicine taken to kill disease-causing bacteria.

antibody *noun* (*plural* **antibodies**) a substance produced in *eg* the human body to fight bacteria *etc*.

anticipate *verb* to look forward to, to expect; to see or know in advance; to act before (someone or something). – *noun* **anticipation** expectation; excitement.

anticlimax *noun* a dull or disappointing ending.

anticlockwise *adjective, adverb* in the opposite direction to the hands of a clock.

antics *noun plural* tricks, odd or amusing actions.

anticyclone *noun* a circling movement of air or wind round an area of high air pressure *usu* causing calm weather.

antidote noun something given to act against the effect of poison.

antifreeze noun a chemical with a low freezing-point, added to the water in a car's radiator to stop it freezing.

antihistamine noun a medicine used to treat an allergy.

antipathy noun dislike.

antipodes noun plural places on the earth's surface exactly opposite each other, (esp Australia and New Zealand, which are opposite to Europe). – adjective **antipodean.**

antique adjective old, from earlier times; old-fashioned. – noun an old, usu interesting or valuable object from earlier times. – adjective **antiquated** grown old, or out of fashion. – noun **antiquity** ancient times, esp those of the Greeks and Romans; great age; (plural **antiquities**) objects from earlier times.

antiseptic adjective germ-destroying. – noun something which destroys germs.

antisocial adjective not fitting in with, harmful to other people; disliking the company of other people.

antithesis noun (plural **antitheses**) the direct opposite.

antler noun the horn of a deer.

anus ān'ủs, noun the lower opening of the bowel through which faeces pass. – adjective **anal.**

anvil noun a metal block on which blacksmiths hammer metal into shape.

anxious adjective worried about what may happen. – noun **anxiety** (plural **anxieties**).

any adjective one: any book; some: any bread; every, no matter which: Any time you go, he's always there. – pronoun some: There aren't any left. – pronoun **anybody** any person. – adverb **anyhow** in any case: Anyhow I'll go and see him; carelessly: The papers were scattered anyhow over his desk. – pronoun **anyone** any person. – pronoun **anything** a thing of any kind. – adverb **anyway** at any rate. – adverb **anywhere** in any place. – **at any rate** in any case, whatever happens.

apart adverb aside; in or into pieces; in opposite directions. – **apart from** separate(ly) from; except for.

apartheid noun (the policy of) keeping people of different races apart.

apartment noun a room in a house; a set of rooms, a flat.

apathy noun lack of feeling or interest. – adjective **apathetic.**

ape noun any of a group of animals related to monkeys, but larger, tail-less and walking upright. – verb to imitate.

aperture noun an opening, a hole.

APEX abbreviation Association of Professional, Executive, Clerical and Computer Staff.

apex noun (plural **apexes** or **apices**) the highest point of anything.

aphid noun a type of small insect which feeds on plants.

aphrodisiac noun a drug etc that increases sexual desire. – Also adjective.

apiary noun (plural **apiaries**) a place where bees are kept. – noun **apiarist** a person who keeps an apiary or who studies bees.

apiece adverb to or for each one.

aplomb noun self-confidence.

apocryphal à-pok'rif-àl, adjective unlikely to be true.

apology noun (plural **apologies**) an expression of regret that one has done wrong. – adjective **apologetic** showing regret about having done wrong. – verb **apologize** to make an apology.

apoplexy noun sudden loss of ability to feel, move etc, a stroke. – adjective **apoplectic.**

apostle noun a person sent to preach the gospel, esp one of the twelve disciples of Christ; a leader of a movement or cause (such as for free speech etc).

apostrophe noun a mark (') to show possession: John's hat; or that a letter etc has been missed out: isn't (for is not).

apothecary noun (plural **apothecaries**) (old) a person who makes and supplies medicines etc, a chemist.

appal verb (past tense **appalled**) to horrify, shock. – adjective **appalling** shocking.

apparatus noun an instrument or machine; instruments, tools or material required for a piece of work.

apparel noun clothing.

apparent adjective easily seen, evident. – adverb **apparently.**

apparition noun something strange or remarkable which appears suddenly; a ghost.

appeal *verb* to ask earnestly (for help *etc*); (in law) to take a case that one has lost to a higher court; to be pleasing (to). – Also *noun*. – *adjective* **appealing** asking earnestly; arousing liking or sympathy.

appear *verb* to come into view; to arrive; to seem. – *noun* **appearance.**

appease *verb* to soothe or satisfy, *esp* by giving what was asked for.

appendix *noun* (*plural* **appendices** or **appendixes**) a part added at the end of a book; a small worm-shaped part of the bowels. – *noun* **appendicitis** a disease, an inflammation of this part of the body.

appertain *verb* to belong (to).

appetite *noun* desire (for food). – *adjective* **appetizing** tempting to the appetite.

applaud *verb* to praise (by clapping the hands). – *noun* **applause.**

apple *noun* a type of round firm fruit, *usu* red or green.

apply *verb* (*past tense* **applied**) to put on (an ointment *etc*); to use; to ask formally (for); to be suitable or relevant; (with **to**) to affect. – *noun* **appliance** a tool, instrument, machine *etc*; a fire engine. – *adjective* **applicable** able to be applied; suitable, relevant. – *noun* **applicant** a person who applies or asks. – *noun* **application** the act of applying; the thing applied (*eg* an ointment); hard work, close attention; a formal request (*usu* on paper). – **apply oneself** to work hard.

appoint *verb* to fix (a date *etc*); to place in a job: *He was appointed manager.* – *noun* **appointment** the act of appointing; a job, a post; an arrangement to meet someone.

apportion *verb* to divide in fair shares.

apposite *adjective* suitable, appropriate.

appraise *verb* to estimate the value or quality of. – *noun* **appraisal.** – *adjective* **appraising** (of a glance *etc*) quickly summing up.

appreciate *verb* to see or understand the good points, beauties *etc* of; to understand; to rise in value. – *adjective* **appreciable** noticeable, considerable. – *noun* **appreciation.**

apprehend *verb* to arrest; to understand. – *noun* **apprehension.** – *adjective* **apprehensive** afraid.

apprentice *noun* a person who is learning a trade. – *noun* **apprenticeship** the time during which one is an apprentice.

appro *noun* short for **approval.**

approach *verb* to come near; to be nearly equal to; to speak to in order to ask for something. – *noun* (*plural* **approaches**) a coming near to; a way leading to a place. – *adjective* **approachable** able to be reached; (of persons) easy to speak to, friendly.

approbation *noun* good opinion, approval.

appropriate *adjective* suitable, fitting. – *verb* to take possession of; to set (money *etc*) apart for a purpose. – *noun* **appropriation.**

approve *verb* to agree to, permit; (with **of**) to think well of. – *noun* **approval.** – **on approval** (of goods) on trial, for return (to shop *etc*) if not bought.

approx. *abbreviation* approximate(ly).

approximate *adjective* more or less accurate. – *verb* (with **to**) to be or come near (a number *etc*). – *noun* **approximation** a rough estimate.

APR *abbreviation* annual percentage rate.

apricot *noun* a type of orange-coloured fruit like a small peach.

April *noun* the fourth month of the year.

apron *noun* a garment worn to protect the front of the clothes; a hard surface for aircraft to stand on. – *noun* **apron stage** the part of the stage in front of the curtains in a theatre.

apropos: apropos of in connection with, concerning.

apse *noun* a rounded domed section, *esp* at the east end of a church.

apt *adjective* (with **to**) likely to; suitable, fitting. – *noun* **aptitude** talent, ability. – *noun* **aptness** suitability.

aqualung *noun* a breathing apparatus worn by divers.

aquamarine *noun* a type of bluish-green precious stone.

aquarium *noun* (*plural* **aquaria**) a tank or tanks for keeping fish or water animals.

aquatic *adjective* living, growing or taking place in water.

aqueduct *noun* a bridge for taking water, such as a canal, across a valley.

aquiline *adjective* like an eagle; (of a nose) curved or hooked.

arable *adjective* fit for ploughing; (of land *etc*) growing crops.

arbiter *noun* a judge, an umpire, someone chosen by opposing parties to decide between them; (with **of**) a person having control over. – *noun* **arbitrage** the practice of buying (currency, goods *etc*) in one market, and selling in another to make a profit from the differences in price. – *adjective* **arbitrary** fixed not by rules but by someone's decision or opinion. – *verb* **arbitrate** to act as a judge between people or their claims *etc*. – *noun* **arbitration** the act of judging between claims *etc*; the settlement of a dispute by an arbiter. – *noun* **arbitrator** an arbiter.

arboreal *adjective* of trees, living in trees.

arbour *noun* a seat in a garden shaded by tree-branches *etc*.

arc *noun* part of the circumference of a circle, a curve. – *noun* **arc-lamp** or **arc-light** a bright lamp lit by a special kind of electric current.

arcade *noun* a covered walk, *esp* one with shops on both sides.

arch *noun* (*plural* **arches**) the curved part above one's head in a gateway or the curved support for a bridge, roof *etc*. – *adjective* mischievous, roguish. – *verb* to raise or curve in the shape of an arch. – *noun* **archway** a passage or road beneath an arch.

arch- *prefix* chief (as in **arch-enemy**).

archaeology *noun* the study of the people of earlier times from the remains of their buildings *etc*. – *adjective* **archaeological**. – *noun* **archaeologist**.

archaic *adjective* (*esp* of words) no longer used, old-fashioned.

archangel *noun* a chief angel.

archbishop *noun* a chief bishop.

archdeacon *noun* a clergyman next in rank below a bishop.

archduke *noun* (*hist*) the title of the ruling princes of Austria.

archer *noun* a person who shoots arrows from a bow. – *noun* **archery** the art of shooting with a bow and arrows.

archipelago *noun* (*plural* **archipelagoes** or **archipelagos**) a group of small islands.

architect *noun* a person who plans and designs buildings. – *noun* **architecture** the style of a building; the study of building.

archives *noun plural* (a place for keeping) historical papers, written records *etc*.

Arctic *adjective* of the district round the North Pole. – *adjective* **arctic** very cold.

ardent *adjective* eager, passionate. – *noun* **ardour**.

arduous *adjective* difficult. – *noun* **arduousness**.

are *see* **be**.

area *noun* extent (of a surface) measured in square metres *etc*; a region, a piece of land or ground.

arena *noun* any place for a public contest, show *etc*; (*hist*) the centre of an amphitheatre *etc* where gladiators *etc* fought.

argosy *noun* (*plural* **argosies**) a large trading-ship with a valuable cargo.

argue *verb* to quarrel in words; to (try to) prove by giving reasons (that); to suggest or urge. – *adjective* **arguable** that can be argued as being true. – *noun* **argument** a heated discussion, quarrel; reasoning (for or against something). – *adjective* **argumentative** fond of arguing.

aria *noun* a song for solo voice in an opera *etc*.

arid *adjective* dry. – *noun* **aridity** or **aridness**.

arise *verb* (*past tense* **arose**, *past participle* **arisen**) to rise up; to come into being.

aristocracy *noun* those of the nobility and upper class. – *noun* **aristocrat** a member of the aristocracy. – *adjective* **aristocratic** of the aristocracy; having a distinguished appearance.

arithmetic *noun* a way of counting and calculating by using numbers. – *adjective* **arithmetical**.

ark *noun* the covered boat in which Noah lived during the Flood.

arm *noun* the part of the body between the shoulder and the hand; anything jutting out like this; (*plural*) weapons. – *verb* to equip with weapons. – *noun* **armchair** a chair with arms at each side. – *adjective* **armed** carrying a weapon, now *esp* a gun. – *noun* **arm-pit** the hollow under the arm at the shoulder.

armada *noun* a fleet of armed ships.

armadillo *noun* (*plural* **armadillos**) a type of small American animal whose body is protected by bony plates.

armaments noun plural equipment for war, esp the guns of a ship, tank etc.

armistice noun in war, a halt in the fighting, a truce.

armorial adjective of a coat-of-arms.

armour noun (hist) a protective suit of metal worn by knights. – adjective **armoured** (of a vehicle) protected by metal plates. – noun **armoury** (plural **armouries**) an arms store.

army noun (plural **armies**) a large number of men armed for war; a great number.

aroma noun a sweet smell. – adjective **aromatic**.

arose see **arise**.

around preposition in a circle about; on all sides of, surrounding: *Flowers grew around the tree*; all over, at several places in: *papers scattered around the room*; somewhere near in time, place, amount: *I left him around here. Come back around three o'clock.* - adverb on every side: *Children stood around and sang.* – **get around** (of a fact, rumour etc) to become known to all; (of a person) to be active.

arouse verb to awaken; to stir, move (a feeling or person).

arraign verb to accuse publicly.

arrange verb to put in some order; to plan, to settle. – noun **arrangement**.

arras noun a screen of tapestry.

array noun order, arrangement; clothing. – verb to put in order; to dress, to adorn.

arrears: in arrears not up to date, behindhand (with payments etc).

arrest verb to seize, capture esp by power of the law; to stop; to catch (the attention etc). – noun capture by the police; stopping.– adjective **arresting** striking, capturing one's attention.

arrive verb to reach a place. – noun **arrival** the act of arriving; person or thing that arrives. – **arrive at** to reach, come to (a decision etc).

arrogant adjective proud, haughty, self-important.– noun **arrogance**.

arrow noun a straight, pointed weapon made to be shot from a bow; an arrow-shape (on road signs etc) showing direction.

arse noun (vulg) the buttocks. – **arse around** to fool about, waste time.

arsenal noun a factory or store for weapons, ammunition etc.

arsenic noun an element that, combined with oxygen, makes a strong poison.

arson noun the crime of setting fire to a house etc on purpose.

art noun drawing, painting, sculpture etc; cleverness, skill; cunning; (plural) non-scientific school or university subjects. – adjective **artful** wily, cunning. – adjective **artless** simple, frank.

artefact or **artifact** noun an object made by man.

artery noun (plural **arteries**) a tube which carries blood from the heart to pass through the body. – adjective **arterial** of or like arteries. – noun **arterial road** a main traffic road.

artesian well noun one in which water rises to the surface by natural pressure.

artichoke noun a type of thistle-like plant, part of whose flower-head is eaten. – noun **Jerusalem artichoke** a type of plant whose roots are used as food.

article noun a thing, object; a section of a document; (plural) an agreement made up of clauses: *articles of apprenticeship*; a composition in a newspaper, journal etc; (in grammar) the name of the words *the, a, an*. – verb to bind (an apprentice etc) by articles.

articulate adjective expressing thoughts or words clearly. – noun **articulation**. – noun **articulated lorry** one with a cab which can turn at an angle to the main part of the lorry, making cornering easier.

artifact see **artefact**.

artificial adjective not natural; made by man. – noun **artificiality**. – noun **artificial insemination** the insertion of sperm into the uterus by means other than sexual intercourse.

artillery noun big guns; the part of the army that uses these.

artisan noun a skilled workman.

artist noun a person who paints pictures; a person skilled in anything; an artiste. – adjective **artistic** of artists; having or showing a talent for art. – noun **artistry** skill as an artist.

artiste är-tēst', noun a person who performs in a theatre, circus etc.

as adverb, conjunction in phrases expressing comparison or similarity: *He is as good as* *his brother. That cup is the same as this one.* – *conjunction* while, when: *He fell as I watched*; because, since: *As it's wet we can't go*; in the same way that: *He thinks as I do.* – *adverb* for instance. – **as for** concerning, regarding; **as if, as though** as it would be if; **as to** regarding; **as well (as)** too, in addition (to).

asbestos *noun* a thread-like mineral which can be woven and which will not burn. – *noun* **asbestosis** a lung disease caused by inhaling asbestos dust.

ascend *verb* to climb, go up; to rise or slope upwards. – *noun* **ascendancy** or **ascendency** control (over). – *adjective* **ascendant** or **ascendent** rising. – *noun* **ascent** a going up; a slope upwards. – **ascend the throne** to be crowned king or queen.

ascertain *verb* to find out; to make certain.

ascetic *noun* a person who keeps away from all kinds of pleasure. – Also *adjective*.

ascribe *verb* to think of as belonging to (a person or thing) or due to (a cause).

ash *noun* (*plural* **ashes**) a type of hard-wood tree with silvery bark; (often in *plural*) what is left after anything is burnt. – *adjective* **ashen** very pale.

ashamed *adjective* feeling shame.

ashore *adverb* on (to the) shore.

aside *adverb* on or to one side; apart. – *noun* words spoken (*esp* by an actor) which other persons nearby are supposed not to hear.

asinine *adjective* of an ass; stupid.

ask *verb* to request information about: *Ask where to go*; to invite.

askance: look askance at to look at with suspicion.

askew *adverb* off the straight, to one side.

asleep *adjective* sleeping; (of limbs) numbed.

ASLEF *abbreviation* Associated Society of Locomotive Engineers and Firemen.

asp *noun* a small poisonous snake.

asparagus *noun* a type of plant whose young shoots are eaten as a vegetable.

aspect *noun* look, appearance; view, point of view; side of a building *etc* or the direction it faces in.

aspen *noun* a kind of poplar tree.

asperity *noun* harshness, sharpness of temper; bitter coldness.

asphalt *noun* a tarry mixture used to make pavements, paths *etc*.

asphyxia *as-fiks'i-â, noun* suffocation (as by smoke or other fumes). – *verb* **asphyxiate** to suffocate. – *noun* **asphyxiation.**

aspidistra *noun* a kind of pot-plant with large leaves.

aspire *verb* (with **to** or **after**) to try to achieve or reach (something difficult, ambitious *etc*). – *noun* **aspiration.**

aspirin *noun* a pain-killing drug.

ass *noun* (*plural* **asses**) a horse-like animal with long ears, a donkey; a stupid person; (*US*) arse.

assail *verb* to attack. – *noun* **assailant** a person who attacks.

assassin *noun* a person who assassinates, a murderer. – *verb* **assassinate** to murder (*esp* a politically important person). – *noun* **assassination.**

assault *noun* an attack, *esp* a sudden one. – Also *verb*.

assemble *verb* to bring (people) together; to put together (a machine *etc*); to meet together. – *noun* **assemblage** a collection (of persons or things). – *noun* **assembly** (*plural* **assemblies**) a putting together; a gathering of people, *esp* for a special purpose. – *noun* **assembly line** series of machines and workers necessary for the manufacture of an article.

assent *verb* to agree. – *noun* agreement.

assert *verb* to state firmly; to insist on (a right *etc*). – *noun* **assertion.** – *adjective* **assertive** not shy, inclined to assert oneself. – **assert oneself** to make oneself noticed, heard *etc*.

assess *verb* to fix an amount (to be paid in tax *etc*); to estimate the value, power of *etc*. – *noun* **assessment.** – *noun* **assessor** a person who assesses.

asset *noun* an advantage, a help; (*plural*) the property of a person, company *etc*.

assiduous *adjective* persevering; hard-working.

assign *â-sīn', verb* to give to someone as a share or task; to fix (a time or place). – *noun* **assignation** *â-sig-nā'shôn,* an appointment to meet. – *noun*

assignment *à-sīn'mènt*, an act of assigning; a task given.

assimilate *verb* to take in. – *noun* **assimilation.**

assist *verb* to help. – *noun* **assistance.** – *noun* **assistant** a helper, *esp* someone who helps a senior worker; a person who serves in a shop *etc*.

assizes *noun plural* the name of certain law courts in England.

Assoc. *abbreviation* Association.

associate *verb* to keep company with; to join (with) in partnership or friendship; to connect in thought. – *adjective* joined or connected (with). – *noun* a friend, partner, companion. – *noun* **association** a club, society, union *etc*; a partnership, friendship; a connection made in the mind.

assorted *adjective* various, mixed. – *noun* **assortment** a variety, mixture.

assuage *verb* to soothe, ease (pain, hunger *etc*).

assume *verb* to take upon oneself; to take as true without further proof, take for granted; to put on (a disguise *etc*). – *adjective* **assumed** taken upon oneself; pretended. – *noun* **assumption** act of assuming; something taken for granted.

assure *verb* to make (someone) sure; to state positively (that). – *noun* **assurance** a feeling of certainty; confidence; a promise; insurance. – *adjective* **assured** certain; confident.

asterisk *noun* a star (*) used in printing for various purposes, *esp* to point out a note added.

astern *adverb* (in ships) at or towards the back part.

asthma *noun* an illness causing difficulty in breathing, and wheezing, coughing *etc*. – *noun, adj* **asthmatic** (a person) suffering from asthma.

astonish *verb* to surprise greatly. – *noun* **astonishment** amazement, wonder.

astound *verb* to surprise greatly, amaze. – *adjective* **astounding.**

astrakhan *noun* lamb-skin with a curled wool.

astral *adjective* of the stars.

astray *adverb* out of the right way, straying.

astride *adverb* with legs apart. – *preposition* with legs on each side of.

astringent *adjective, noun* (of) a type of lotion *etc* used for closing up the skin's pores. – *adjective* (of a manner *etc*) sharp, sarcastic.

astrology *noun* the study of the stars and their supposed power over the lives of humans. – *noun* **astrologer.**

astronaut *noun* a person who travels in space.

astronomy *noun* the study of the stars and their movements. – *noun* **astronomer.** – *adjective* **astronomical** of astronomy; (of numbers) very large.

astute *adjective* cunning, clever.

asunder *adverb* apart, into pieces.

asylum *noun* a place of refuge or safety; an old name for a home for the mentally ill.

at *preposition* showing position, time *etc*: *I will be at home. Come at 3 o'clock*; costing: *cakes at 25 pence each*. – **at all** in any way: *not worried at all.*

ate *see* **eat.**

atheism *ā'thē-izm, noun* belief that there is no God. – *noun* **atheist** a person who does not believe in a God.

athlete *noun* someone good at sport, *esp* running, gymnastics *etc*. – *adjective* **athletic** of athletics; good at sports, strong, powerful. – *noun plural* **athletics** running, jumping *etc* or competitions in these.

atlas *noun* (*plural* **atlases**) a book of maps.

atmosphere *noun* the air round the earth; any surrounding feeling; *a friendly atmosphere*. – *adjective* **atmospheric.** – *noun* **atmospheric pressure** the pressure exerted by the atmosphere at the surface of the earth, due to the weight of the air. – *noun plural* **atmospherics** in radio *etc*, air disturbances causing crackling noises.

atoll *noun* a coral island or reef.

atom *noun* the smallest part of an element; anything very small. – *noun* **atom(ic) bomb** a bomb in which the explosion is caused by nuclear energy. – *noun* **atomic energy** nuclear energy.

atone *verb* to make up for wrong-doing. – *noun* **atonement.**

atrocious *adjective* cruel or wicked; (*coll*) very bad. – *noun* **atrociousness.** – *noun* **atrocity** (*plural* **atrocities**) a terrible crime; (*coll*) something very ugly.

attach *verb* to fasten or join (to); to think of (something) as having: *attach importance to the event.* – *adjective* **attached** fastened; fond (of) – *noun* **attachment** something attached; a joining by love or friendship.

attaché-case *noun* a small case for papers *etc.*

attack *verb* to fall upon suddenly or violently; to speak or write against. – *noun* an act of attacking; a fit (of an illness *etc*).

attain *verb* to reach; to gain. – *adjective* **attainable** able to be attained. – *noun* **attainment** act of attaining; the thing attained, an achievement or accomplishment.

attempt *verb* to try. – *noun* a try or effort; an attack (on someone's life *etc*).

attend *verb* to be present at; to pay attention to; to wait on, look after; to accompany. – *noun* **attendance** act of waiting on or of being present; the number of persons present. – *adjective* **attendant** going along with. – *noun* a person who attends; a person employed to look after (something): *a cloakroom attendant.* – *noun* **attention** careful notice; concentration; care; in (army) drill, a stiffly straight standing position. – *adjective* **attentive** giving or showing attention; polite.

attic *noun* a room just under the roof of a house.

attire *verb* to dress. – *noun* clothing.

attitude *noun* way of thinking or feeling; position of the body.

attorney *noun* (*plural* **attorneys**) a person who has legal power to act for another.

attract *verb* to draw to or towards; to arouse liking or interest. – *noun* **attraction** act or power of attracting; that which attracts. – *adjective* **attractive** pleasing; good-looking, likeable.

attribute *verb* to think of as belonging to, or due to (a person or cause). – *adjective* **attributable**. – *noun* **attribute** something that is part of the nature of a person or thing, a quality.

aubergine *ō'bĕr-zhēn, noun* a plant with an oval dark purple fruit, eaten as a vegetable.

auburn *adjective* (*esp* of hair) reddish-brown in colour.

auction *noun* a public sale in which articles are sold to the person who offers the highest price. – *verb* to sell by auction. – *noun* **auctioneer** a person who sells by auction.

audacious *adjective* daring, bold. – *noun* **audacity**.

audible *adjective* able to be heard. – *noun* **audibility**. – *adverb* **audibly**.

audience *noun* a number of people gathered to watch or hear (a performance *etc*); a formal interview with someone important: *an audience with the Pope.*

audio *noun* the reproduction of recorded or radio sound. – *adjective* relating to such sound: *an audio tape.*

audio-typist *noun* a typist able to type from a recording on a tape-recorder *etc*.

audio-visual *adjective* concerned with hearing and seeing at the same time. – *noun plural* **audio-visual aids** films, recordings *etc* used in teaching.

audit *verb* to examine accounts officially. – Also *noun*. – *noun* **auditor** a person who audits accounts.

audition *noun* a hearing to test an actor, singer *etc*. – *noun* **auditorium** (*plural* **auditoria** or **auditoriums**) the part of a theatre *etc* where the audience sits. – *adjective* **auditory** *adjective* of hearing.

augment *verb* to increase in size, number or amount. – *noun* **augmentation**.

augur: augur well or **augur ill** to be a good or bad sign for the future.

August *noun* the eighth month of the year.

august *adjective* full of dignity, stately.

aunt *noun* a father's or a mother's sister or an uncle's wife.

au pair *ō pãr, noun* a foreign girl who does domestic duties in return for board, lodging and pocket money.

aural *adjective* pertaining to the ear. – *adverb* **aurally**. – *adjective* **auriform** ear-shaped.

auspices: under the auspices of under the control or supervision of.

auspicious *adjective* favourable; promising luck.

austere *adjective* severe; without luxury *etc*, simple. – *noun* **austerity**.

authentic *adjective* true, real, genuine. – *verb* **authenticate** to show to be true or real. – *noun* **authenticity**.

author (*masculine*), **authoress** (*feminine*) *noun* the writer of a book, poem, play *etc*.

authority *noun* (*plural* **authorities**) power or right; a person whose opinion is reliable, an expert; a person or body of people having control (over something); (*plural*) persons in power. – *adjective* **authoritative** said *etc* by an expert or someone in authority.

authorize *verb* to give (a person) the power or the right to do something; to give permission (for something to be done).

autism *noun* an abnormality of children affecting their ability to relate to and communicate with other people. – *adjective* **autistic**.

autobiography *noun* (*plural* **autobiographies**) the story of a person's life written by herself or himself. – *adjective* **autobiographical**.

autocrat *noun* a ruler who has complete power. – *noun* **autocracy** government by such a ruler. – *adjective* **autocratic** of an autocrat; expecting complete obedience.

autograph *noun* one's own signature; one's own handwriting. – *verb* to write one's own name (on).

automatic *adjective* (of a machine *etc*) self-working; (of an action) unconscious, without thinking. – *noun* something automatic (*eg* an automatic washing-machine); a kind of self-loading gun. – *adverb* **automatically**. – *noun* **automation** the use in factories *etc* of machines for controlling other machines. – *noun* **automaton** (*plural* **automatons** or **automata**) a (human-shaped) machine that can be operated to move by itself; a person who acts like a machine. – **automatic teller machine** an electronic panel set into the exterior wall of a bank *etc* from which one can obtain cash or information about one's bank account.

automobile *noun* (*US*) a motor car.

autonomy *noun* the power or right of a country *etc* to govern itself. – *adjective* **autonomous**.

autopsy *noun* (*plural* **autopsies**) an examination of the body after death.

autumn *noun* the season of the year when leaves change colour and fruits *etc* are ripe. – *adjective* **autumnal** of or like autumn.

auxiliary *adjective* helping; additional. – *noun* (*plural* **auxiliaries**) a helper.

AV *abbreviation* audio-visual; Authorized Version.

avail: avail oneself of to make use of; **to no avail** without any effect, of no use.

available *adjective* able or ready to be made use of. – *noun* **availability**.

avalanche *noun* a mass of snow and ice sliding down from a mountain; a great amount: *an avalanche of work*.

avant-garde *a-vons-gärd*, *adjective* (*esp* of literature, art, music) ahead of fashion, very modern: *an avante-garde writer*.

avarice *noun* greed, *esp* for riches. – *adjective* **avaricious**.

avenge *verb* to take revenge for (a wrong). – *noun* **avenger**.

avenue *noun* a (tree-bordered) street or approach to a house; means, way: *avenue of escape*.

average *noun* the result got by adding several amounts and dividing the total by the number of amounts (The *average* of 3, 7, 9, 13 is 8 (32÷4)). – *adjective* obtained by working out an average (of amounts *etc*): *The average price was £5. The average temperature was too low*; ordinary, usual; of medium size *etc*. – *verb* to form an average; to find the average of.

averse *adjective* not fond of, opposed (to). – *noun* **aversion** dislike; something that is hated.

avert *verb* to turn (one's eyes *etc*) away; to prevent.

aviary *noun* (*plural* **aviaries**) a place for keeping birds.

aviation *noun* (the science of) flying in aircraft. – *noun* **aviator** (*masculine*), **aviatrix** (*feminine*) a person who flies an aircraft.

avid *adjective* eager, greedy. – *noun* **avidity**.

avoid *verb* to escape, keep clear of. – *adjective* **avoidable**. – *noun* **avoidance**.

avoirdupois *adjective, noun* (of) the system of measuring weights in pounds and ounces.

avow *verb* to declare openly. – *noun* **avowal**. – *adjective* **avowed**.

await *verb* to wait for.

awake *verb* to rouse (from sleep); to stop sleeping. – *adjective* not asleep;

watchful. – verb **awaken** to awake; to arouse (interest etc). – noun **awakening** or **awaking.**

award verb to give, grant (a prize etc); to grant legally. – noun what is awarded (such as a payment, prize etc).

aware adjective having knowledge (of), conscious (of); alert. – noun **awareness.**

away adverb to or at a distance from the person or thing spoken about: *Throw it away. He is away;* in the opposite direction: *He turned away;* into nothing: *The sound died away;* constantly: *working away.* – **do away with** to abolish, get rid of; **get away with** to do (something) without being punished; **make away with** to destroy; to steal and escape with; **right away** immediately.

awe noun wonder mixed with fear; dread. – adjective **awesome** causing fear. – adjective **awestruck** full of fear and wonder.

awful adjective (coll) bad: *an awful headache;* (coll) very great: *an awful lot;* terrible. –

adverb **awfully** (coll) very much: *awfully grateful.* – noun **awfulness.**

awkward adjective clumsy, not graceful; difficult (to deal with). – noun **awkwardness.**

awl noun a pointed tool for boring small holes.

awning noun a covering (of canvas etc) to give shelter.

awry à-rī', adjective, adverb crooked; not according to plan, wrong.

axe noun (plural **axes**) a tool for chopping. – verb to cancel (a plan etc); to reduce greatly (costs, services etc).

axis noun (plural **axes**) the line, real or imaginary, on which a thing turns (as the axis of the earth, from North to South Pole, around which the earth turns); a fixed line taken as a reference, as in a graph.

axle noun the rod on which a wheel turns.

azure adjective sky-coloured, clear blue.

B

BA abbreviation British Airways; Bachelor of Arts.

babble verb to talk indistinctly or foolishly; (of a stream etc) to murmur. – Also noun.

babe noun a baby.

baboon noun a kind of large monkey with a dog-like snout.

baby noun (plural **babies**) a very young child, an infant. – noun **babyhood** the time when one is a baby. – noun **babysitter** someone who stays in the house with child(ren) while parents are out.

bachelor noun an unmarried man. – noun **Bachelor of Arts, Bachelor of Science** etc a person who has passed examinations at a certain level in subjects at a university etc.

bacillus bà-sil'ùs, noun (plural **bacilli**) a rod-shaped kind of germ.

back noun the part of the body in man from the neck to the base of the spine; the upper part of the body in animals;

the part of anything situated behind; a person who plays behind the forwards in football, hockey etc. – adjective of or at the back. – adverb to or in the place from which a person or thing came; to or in a former time or condition etc. – verb to move backwards; to bet on (a horse etc); (often with **up**) to help or support. – noun **backbone** the spine; the main support of anything; firmness. – noun **backer** a supporter. – verb **backfire** (of a motor car etc) to make an explosive noise in the exhaust pipe; (of a plan etc) to go wrong. – noun **background** the space behind the principal figures etc (of a picture); details etc that explain something; one's family and upbringing. – noun **backhand** (in tennis etc) a stroke played with the back of the hand facing the ball. – adjective **backhanded** (of a compliment etc) having a double or unflattering meaning. – noun **backing** support; material used on the back of something (esp a picture); (esp on a record) a musical accompaniment. – noun **backlash** a (violent) reaction (against something). – noun **backstroke** a stroke used in swimming on the back. – noun **back-wash** a backward current, such as that caused by a wave going out. – noun **backwater** a river pool not in the main stream; a place not affected by what is happening in the world outside. – **back down** to change one's opinion *etc*; **back out** to move out backwards; to excuse oneself from keeping to an agreement *etc*; **put one's back into** to work hard at; **put someone's back up** to irritate someone; **with one's back to the wall** in desperate difficulties.

backgammon noun a game rather like draughts, played with dice.

backward adjective moving towards the back; slow in learning or development. – adverb **backward(s)** towards the back; towards the past.

bacon noun pig's flesh salted and dried, used as food.

bacteria noun plural kinds of germs found in the air, water, earth, in living and dead bodies, and *usu* in things going rotten. – adjective **bacterial**. – noun **bacteriology** the study of bacteria. – noun **bacteriologist**.

bad adjective not good; wicked; (*usu* with **for**) hurtful: *Smoking is bad for you*; (of food) rotten; severe, serious: *a bad cut in his foot*; faulty; unwell. – noun **bad language** swearing *etc*. – adverb **badly** not well; seriously. – noun **badness**.

badge noun a mark or sign or brooch-like ornament giving some information about the wearer.

badger noun a burrowing animal of the weasel family which comes out at night. – verb to pester or annoy.

badminton noun a game rather like tennis, played with shuttlecocks.

baffle verb to prevent (*eg* a plan) from being carried out, to hinder; to be too difficult or too clever for, to puzzle.

bag noun a holder or container *usu* of a soft material; the quantity of fish or game caught. – adjective **baggy** (of clothes) large and loose. – noun **bag lady** a homeless woman who carries her belongings with her in shopping bags.

bagatelle noun a board game, in which balls are struck into numbered holes; something unimportant.

baggage noun luggage.

bagpipes noun plural musical instrument made up of a bag and several pipes.

bail verb (with **out**) to get an untried prisoner out of prison for the time being by giving money which will be returned only if he comes back for his trial; *see* also **bale**. – noun money given to bail out a prisoner; in cricket, one of the crosspieces on the top of the wickets.

bailie noun (in Scotland) formerly a burgh magistrate.

bailiff noun an officer who works for a sheriff; a landowner's agent.

bait noun food put on a hook to make fish bite, or in a trap *etc* to attract animals; anything tempting. – verb to put bait on a hook or trap; to worry, annoy.

baize noun a coarse woollen cloth.

bake verb to cook (in an oven); to dry or harden in the sun or in an oven. – noun **baker** a person who bakes or sells bread *etc*. – noun **bakery** or **bakehouse** a place used for baking in. – noun **baking powder** a powder added to flour to make cakes *etc* rise.

balalaika noun a type of Russian musical instrument, like a guitar.

balance noun a weighing machine; the money needed to make the two sides of an account equal; steadiness. – verb to be the same in weight; to make both sides of an account the same; to make or keep steady.

balcony noun (plural **balconies**) a platform built out from the wall of a building; an upper floor or gallery in theatres, cinemas *etc*.

bald adjective without hair; (of a statement *etc*) plain, bare.

balderdash noun nonsense.

bale noun a large tight bundle (of cotton, hay *etc*). – verb (with **out**) to escape by parachute from an aircraft in an emergency; to scoop water out of a boat (also **bail out**).

baleful adjective harmful; full of hate.

balk verb to hinder, to baffle; (with **at**) to refuse (to do something).

ball¹ noun anything round; the round object used in playing many games. – noun plural **ball-bearings** in machinery *etc*, small steel balls that sit loosely in grooves and ease the revolving of one part over another. – noun **ballpoint (pen)** a pen with a tiny ball as the writing point.

ball² *noun* a formal party at which dancing takes place. – *noun* **ballroom**.

ballad *noun* a simple poem telling a story *usu* in verses of four lines; a simple song.

ballast *noun* heavy material (such as sand, gravel *etc*) put into a ship *etc* to steady it.

ballerina *noun* a female ballet dancer.

ballet *noun* a kind of graceful dancing which tells a story by mime.

ballistic missile *noun* one which moves under power and is guided on its way, but simply falls on to its target.

balloon *noun* a bag filled with gas to make it float in the air; a toy made of thin rubber *etc* filled with air or gas and sealed to form a lightweight ball.

ballot *noun* a way of voting in secret by marking a paper and putting it into a special box.

balm *noun* anything that soothes; a sweet-smelling healing ointment. – *noun* **balminess**. – *adjective* **balmy** mild, soothing; sweet-smelling.

balsa *noun* a type of tropical American tree giving a very light wood (**balsa-wood**).

balsam *noun* a kind of flowering plant; an oily sweet-smelling substance obtained from certain trees.

balustrade *noun* a row of pillars (on a balcony *etc*) joined by a rail.

bamboo *noun* the hard, woody, jointed stem of a very tall Indian grass.

bamboozle *verb* to trick, puzzle.

ban *noun* an order forbidding something. – *verb* (*past tense* **banned**) to forbid officially (the publication of a book *etc*).

banal *adjective* lacking originality or wit, commonplace. – *noun* **banality**.

banana *noun* the long yellow fruit of a type of tropical tree.

band *noun* a group of people; a group of musicians playing together; a strip of some material to put round something; a stripe (of colour *etc*); (in radio) a group of wavelengths. – *verb* to join together.

bandage *noun* a strip of cloth *etc* or special dressing for a wound *etc*.

B and B *abbreviation* bed and breakfast.

bandeau *noun* (*plural* **bandeaux**) hair-band.

bandit *noun* an outlaw, robber, *esp* a member of a gang of robbers.

bandolier or **bandoleer** *noun* a belt across the body for carrying cartridges.

bandy *adjective* (of legs) bent outward at the knee. – **bandy words** to argue.

bane *noun* (a cause of) ruin or trouble.

bang *noun* a sudden, loud noise; a heavy blow. – *verb* to close with a bang, slam; to hit, strike: *He banged his head on the door*.

bangle *noun* a large ring worn on arms (or legs).

banish *verb* to order to leave (a country); to drive away (doubts, fear *etc*). – *noun* **banishment**.

banister *noun* the posts and handrail of a staircase.

banjo *noun* (*plural* **banjoes or banjos**) a type of musical stringed instrument like a guitar, having a long neck and a round body.

bank *noun* a mound or ridge of earth *etc*; the edge of a river *etc*; a place where money is put for safety, lent *etc*; a place where blood *etc* is stored till needed. – *noun* **banker** one who manages a bank. – *noun* **bank holiday** a day on which all banks (and most other shops *etc*) are closed. – *noun* **banknote** a piece of paper money issued by a bank. – *noun* **bankrupt** a person who has no money to pay their debts. – *adjective* unable to pay one's debts; utterly lacking (in ideas *etc*). – *noun* **bankruptcy** (*plural* **bankruptcies**). – **bank on** to depend on, count on.

banner *noun* a kind of flag carried in processions *etc*, *usu* hung between two poles; any flag.

banns *noun plural* a public announcement that a marriage is to take place.

banquet *noun* a feast or ceremonial dinner.

bantam *noun* a small kind of hen.

banter *verb* to tease in fun. – Also *noun*.

baptize *verb* to dip in, or sprinkle with, water as a sign of being taken into the Christian church; to christen, give a name to. – *noun* **baptism**. – *adjective* **baptismal**.

bar *noun* a rod of anything solid; a broad line or band; a cake (of soap, chocolate *etc*); something standing in the way, a hindrance; a bank of sand *etc*, lying at the mouth of a river; the counter across which drinks are served in a public house; the room where drinks are served in a public house, hotel *etc*; a public house; the rail at which prisoners stand for trial; the lawyers who plead in a court; a division in music. – *preposition* except: *All the runners, bar John, finished the race.* – *verb* (*past tense* **barred**) to fasten with a bar; to hinder or shut out. – *preposition* **barring** except for, but for: *They have all gone, barring you and me. Barring accidents he will be there.*

barb *noun* the backward-pointing spike on an arrow, fish-hook *etc*. – *adjective* **barbed** having a barb or barbs. – *noun* **barbed wire** wire with clusters of sharp points placed regularly along it, used for fencing *etc*.

barbarian *adjective, noun* (of) an uncivilized person. – *adjective* **barbaric** uncivilized; cruel. – *noun* **barbarity.**

barbecue *noun* a frame on which to grill meat *etc*, *esp* outdoors; a party at which a barbecue is used. – *verb* to cook (meat *etc*) on a barbecue.

barber *noun* a person who shaves beards and cuts hair, a men's hairdresser.

bard *noun* a poet.

bare *adjective* uncovered, naked; plain, simple; empty. – *verb* to uncover or expose. – *adjective* **barefaced** impudent. – *adverb* **barely** hardly, scarcely.

bargain *noun* an agreement (about buying or selling something); something bought cheaply. – *verb* to argue about a price *etc*. – **bargain for** to expect: *more than he bargained for*; **into the bargain** in addition, besides.

barge *noun* a flat-bottomed boat used on rivers and canals. – *verb* to move or rush clumsily; to push or bump (into); to push one's way into rudely.

baritone *noun* (a male singer with) a voice between high (tenor) and low (bass).

bark *noun* the sharp cry made by a dog *etc*; the rough outer covering of a tree's trunk and branches. – *verb* to utter a bark; to speak sharply or angrily; to injure by scraping the skin.

barley *noun* a type of grain used for food and for making malt liquors and spirits. – *noun* **barley sugar** sugar candied by melting and cooling to make a sweet. –

noun **barley water** a drink made from pearl barley.

barn *noun* a building in which grain, hay *etc* are stored.

barnacle *noun* a type of shellfish which sticks to rocks, ships' hulls *etc*.

barometer *noun* an instrument which measures the weight or pressure of the air and shows changes in the weather.

baron *noun* a nobleman, the lowest in the British peerage; (*hist*) a powerful nobleman; a powerful person *esp* a businessman: *drug baron*. – *noun* **baroness** (*plural* **baronesses**) a baron's wife or a female baron. – *adjective* **baronial.**

baronet *noun* the lowest title that can be passed on to an heir. – *noun* **baronetcy** the rank of baronet.

barracks *noun plural* a place for housing soldiers.

barrage *noun* something that hinders an enemy, *esp* heavy gunfire; an overwhelming number (of questions *etc*); a bar across a river to make the water deeper.

barrel *noun* a wooden cask or vessel with curved sides; the metal tube of a gun through which the shot is fired.

barren *adjective* not able to produce (fruit, crops, children *etc*), infertile. – *noun* **barrenness.**

barricade *noun* a barrier put up to block a street *etc*. – *verb* to block (a street *etc*) in this way; to make (doors *etc*) strong against attack; to shut behind a barrier.

barrier *noun* something (*eg* a strong fence *etc*) standing in the way; any obstacle.

barring see **bar.**

barrister *noun* a lawyer who pleads cases in English or in Irish courts.

barrow *noun* a small hand-cart; (*hist*) a mound raised over a grave.

Bart or **Bt** *abbreviation* baronet.

barter *verb* to give one thing in exchange for another. – *noun* trading by exchanging goods without using money.

basalt *noun* a hard, dark-coloured rock thrown up as lava from volcanoes.

base *noun* that on which a thing stands or rests; the lowest part; a place from which a military or other action is carried on. – *verb* to use as a foundation:

I base my opinion on what I have heard. – *adj* worthless, cowardly. – *noun* **baseball** an American ball game, rather like rounders. – *adjective* **baseless** without a foundation; untrue. – *noun* **basement** a storey below ground level in a building.

bash *verb* to hit hard. – *noun* a heavy blow. – **have a bash** (*coll*) to make an attempt at.

bashful *adjective* shy.

basic *adjective* of, forming a base; necessary, fundamental.

basil *noun* a herb used as flavouring.

basilisk *noun* (*myth*) a reptile whose look or breath killed; a type of American lizard.

basin *noun* a wide, open dish; a washhand basin; any large hollow holding water (*eg* a dock); the land drained by a river and its tributaries.

basis *noun* (*plural* **bases**) that on which a thing rests, the foundation:. *Mutual trust was the basis of their friendship;* the main ingredient.

bask *verb* to lie in warmth; to enjoy, feel great pleasure (in).

basket *noun* a container made of strips of wood, rushes *etc* woven together; anything resembling a basket in shape. – *noun* **basketball** a team game in which goals are scored by throwing a ball into a raised net.'

bass¹ *bās, noun* (*plural* **basses**) the low part in music; (a male singer with) a deep voice. – *adjective* low or deep in tone.

bass² *bas, noun* (*plural* **bass** or **basses**) a kind of fish of the perch family.

bassoon *noun* a kind of musical wind instrument with low notes.

bastard *noun* a child born to parents who are not married to each other; (*coll*, showing anger, dislike, sympathy *etc*) a person: *He's a cruel bastard.*

baste *verb* to spoon fat over (meat) while roasting to keep (it) from burning; to sew loosely together with big stitches, to tack.

bastion *noun* a defence; a kind of tower on a castle *etc*.

bat *noun* a shaped piece of wood *etc* for striking a ball in some games; a kind of mouse-like flying animal. – *verb* (*past tense* **batted**) to use the bat in cricket *etc*; to flutter (one's eyelids *etc*). – *noun* **batsman** a person who bats in cricket *etc*.

batch *noun* (*plural* **batches**) a quantity of things made *etc* at one time.

bated: with bated breath anxiously.

bath *noun* a vessel which holds water in which to wash the body; the water in which to wash; a washing or soaking of the body in water *etc*; (*plural*) an artificial pool or a building where one may bath or bathe: *Swimming lessons are available at the local baths.* – *verb* to wash (oneself or another) in a bath. – *noun* **bathchair** an old-fashioned wheelchair.

bathe *verb* to swim in water; to wash gently; to take a bath. – Also *noun*. – **bathed in** covered with.

bathyscaphe or **bathysphere** *noun* a deep-sea observation chamber.

batik *noun* a method of dyeing patterns on cloth by waxing certain areas so that they remain uncoloured.

batman *noun* an army officer's servant.

baton *noun* a small wooden stick; a light stick used by a conductor of music.

battalion *noun* a part of a regiment of foot soldiers.

batten *noun* a piece of sawn timber; in ships, a strip of wood used to fasten down the hatches when a storm is imminent. – Also *n*.

batter *verb* to hit repeatedly. – *noun* a beaten mixture *usu* of flour, milk and eggs, for cooking. – *adjective* **battered** beaten, ill-treated; worn out by use *etc*. – *noun* **battering-ram** (*hist*) in warfare, a machine with a heavy beam for breaking through walls *etc*.

battery *noun* (*plural* **batteries**) in an army, a number of large guns; a device for storing and transmitting electricity; a series of cages *etc* in which farm animals are reared or fattened, or birds are kept for egg-laying.

battle *noun* a fight, *esp* between armies. – Also *verb*. – *noun* **battleaxe** (*hist*) a kind of axe used in fighting; (*coll*) a fierce, domineering woman. – *noun* **battlefield**. – *noun* **battleship** a heavily armed and armoured warship.

battlement *noun* a wall on the top of a building, with openings or notches for firing guns *etc* from.

bauble *noun* a brightly-coloured ornament of little value.

bawl *verb* to shout or cry out loudly. – Also *noun*.

bay *noun* a wide inlet of the sea in a coastline; a space in a room *etc* set back, a recess; a compartment in an aircraft; the laurel tree. – *verb* (of dogs) to bark. – *noun* **bay window** a window that forms a recess. – **hold at bay** to fight off; **stand at bay** to stand and face attackers *etc*.

bayonet *noun* a steel stabbing blade that can be fixed to the muzzle of a rifle. – *verb* to stab with this.

bazaar *noun* a sale of goods for charity *etc*; an Eastern market-place; a shop.

BB *abbreviation* Boys' Brigade.

BBC *abbreviation* British Broadcasting Corporation.

BC *abbreviation* before Christ (*eg* 55 BC).

be *verb* to live, exist: *There may be a few sweets left*; to have a position, quality *etc*: *He wants to be a dentist. He will be angry.* – Also used to form tenses of other verbs. – *present tense* **am, are, is**, *past tense* **was, were**, *past participle* **been**. – *noun* **being** existence; any living person (or thing).

beach *noun* (*plural* **beaches**) the shore of the sea *etc*, *esp* when sandy or pebbly. – *verb* to drive or haul a boat up on the beach. – *noun* **beachcomber** a person who searches beaches for useful or saleable articles.

beacon *noun* a (flashing) light or other warning signal; (*hist*) a fire on a hill used as a signal of danger.

bead *noun* a small pierced ball of glass or other hard material (for threading along with others to form a necklace *etc*); a drop of liquid.

beadle *noun* an officer of a church or college.

beagle *noun* a small hound used in hunting hares.

beak *noun* the hard, horny part of a bird's mouth with which it gathers food; anything pointed or projecting.

beaker *noun* a tall cup or glass, *usu* without a handle.

beam *noun* a long straight piece of wood or metal; a shaft of light; a radio signal; the greatest breadth of a ship. – *verb* to shine; to smile broadly; to divert by radio wave.

bean *noun* a kind of pod-bearing plant; the seed of this used as food.

bear *noun* a heavy animal with shaggy fur and hooked claws. – *verb* (*past tense* **bore**, *past participle* **borne** (but *usu* **born** of children, ideas *etc*. *The baby was born last year.*) to carry; to endure, put up with; to produce (fruit, children *etc*). – *adjective* **bearable** able to be borne or endured. – *noun* **bearer** a carrier or messenger. – *noun* **bearing** behaviour; direction; connection; part of a machine supporting a moving part. – *noun* **bearskin** the high fur cap worn by the Guards in the British Army. – **bear in mind** to remember, to take into account; **bear out** to confirm: *What has happened bears out what you said yesterday*; **bear with** to be patient with; **bring to bear** to bring into use.

beard *noun* the hair that grows on a man's chin and cheeks. – *verb* to face up to, defy.

beast *noun* a four-footed animal; a brutal person. – *adjective* **beastly** like a beast in actions or behaviour; horrible; (*coll*) unpleasant. – *noun* **beastliness**.

beat *verb* (*past tense* **beat**, *past participle* **beaten**) to hit (repeatedly); to overcome or defeat; (of a heart or pulse) to move or throb in the normal way; to mark (time) in music *etc*; to stir (a mixture *etc*) with quick movements; to strike bushes *etc* to rouse birds. – *noun* a stroke; a round or course which one (*eg* a policeman) follows regularly. – *adjective* **beaten** (of metal) shaped; (of earth) worn smooth by treading; defeated. – **beat up** to injure by repeated hitting, kicking *etc*.

beatific *bē-à-tif'ik*, *adjective* of, or showing, great happiness.

beauty *noun* (*plural* **beauties**) (of a person or thing) very pleasing appearance; (of music, poetry, voices *etc*) pleasing sound; a very attractive woman *etc*. – *adjective* **beautiful** or, *esp* in poetry *etc* **beauteous**. – *verb* **beautify** (*past tense* **beautified**) to make beautiful.

beaver *noun* a type of gnawing animal that can dam streams; its fur; a member of the most junior branch of the Scout Association.

becalmed *adjective* (of a sailing ship) unable to move for lack of wind.

because for the reason that: *He didn't go because it was raining.* – *adverb* (with **of**) on account of: *Because of his interference, I shall not succeed.*

beck: **at one's beck and call** obeying all one's orders or requests.

beckon *verb* to make a sign (with the finger) to summon someone.

become *verb* to come to be: *He became angry*; to suit: *That dress becomes you.* – *adj* **becoming** (of clothes *etc*) suiting well; (of behaviour) suitable.

bed *noun* a place on which to rest or sleep; a plot (for flowers *etc*) in a garden; the bottom of a river *etc*. – *verb* (*past tense* **bedded**) to plant in soil *etc*; to provide a bed for; (*coll*) to have sexual intercourse with. – *noun plural* **bedclothes** bed-covers. – *noun* **bedding** mattress, bed-covers *etc*; straw *etc* for cattle to lie on. – *adjective* **bedridden** kept in bed by weakness, illness *etc*. – *noun* **bedrock** the solid rock under the soil. – *noun* **bedroom** a room for sleeping. – *noun* **bedspread** a top cover for a bed. – *noun* **bedstead** a frame for supporting a bed.

bedlam *noun* a place of uproar, confusion.

bedraggled *adjective* (wet and) untidy.

bee *noun* a type of winged insect that makes honey in wax cells; a gathering for combined work *etc*. – *noun* **beehive** a (dome-shaped) case or box in which bees are kept. – **make a beeline for** to go directly towards.

beech *noun* (*plural* **beeches**) a type of forest tree with grey smooth bark.

beef *noun* the flesh of an ox or cow, used as food. – *noun* **beefeater** a guardian of the Tower of London; a member (Yeoman) of the (Queen's or King's) Guard. – *adjective* **beefy** stout, muscular.

been *see* **be**.

beer *noun* an alcoholic drink flavoured with hops.

beet *noun* a kind of plant with a carrot-like root, one type (**sugar beet**) used as a source of sugar, the other with a root (**beetroot**) used as a vegetable.

beetle *noun* a kind of insect with four wings, the front pair forming hard covers for the back pair; a kind of hammer.

beetling *adjective* (of cliffs *etc*) over-hanging; (of eyebrows) heavy, frowning.

befall *verb* to happen (to): *A disaster befell him.*

befit *verb* to be suitable or right for.

before *preposition* in front of: *He stood before the entrance to the cave*; earlier than: *before three o'clock*; rather than, in preference to: *He would die before he would give in.* – *adverb* in front; earlier. – *conjunction* earlier than the time that. – *adverb* **beforehand** previously, before the time when something else is done.

befriend *verb* to act as a friend to, to help.

beg *verb* (*past tense* **begged**) to ask for money *etc*; to ask earnestly. – *noun* **beggar** a person who begs; a very poor person. – *verb* to make poor. – *adjective* **beggarly** poor; worthless. – **beggar description** to be greater than the speaker *etc* can find words to describe; **beg the question** to take as being proved the very point that needs to be proved.

began *see* **begin**.

beget *verb* (*present participle* **begetting**, *past tense* **begat**, *past participle* **begotten**) to be the father of; to cause.

begin *verb* (*present participle* **beginning**, *past tense* **began**, *past participle* **begun**) to make a start on. – *noun* **beginning**.

begone *interjection* be off, go away!

begrudge *verb* to grudge, envy: *He be-grudged Jane her success.*

beguile *verb* to cheat; to pass (time) pleasantly; to amuse, entertain.

begun *see* **begin**.

behalf: **on behalf of** as the representative of; in aid of: *collecting on behalf of the blind.*

behave *verb* to conduct oneself (well); to act (in a certain way). – *noun* **behaviour**. – *adjective* **well-behaved** or **badly-behaved** having good or bad manners.

behead *verb* to cut off the head of.

behest *noun* command.

behind *preposition* at or towards the back of: *behind the door*; after; in support of, encouraging: *His friends were behind him in his struggle.* – *adverb* at the back; not up to date: *behind with his work.*

behold *verb* to look (at), see.

beholden *adjective* grateful because of a good turn: *beholden to them.*

behove: **it behoves one to** it is right for one to.

belabour *verb* to beat, thrash. – **belabour the point** to discuss a subject at too great length.

belated *adjective* arriving late.

belay *verb* on ships, to fasten a rope round a peg.

belch *verb* to bring up wind (noisily) from the stomach through the mouth; (of a fire *etc*) to send up (smoke *etc*) violently.

beleaguer *bi-lēg'èr, verb* to besiege.

belfry *noun* (*plural* **belfries**) the part of a steeple or tower in which the bells are hung.

belie *verb* (*present participle* **belying**, *past tense* **belied**) to prove false.

believe *verb* to think of as true or as existing; to trust (in); to think or suppose. – *noun* **belief** what we think to be true; faith. – **make believe** to pretend.

belittle *verb* to make to seem small or unimportant.

bell *noun* a hollow object *usu* of metal which gives a ringing sound when struck by the tongue or clapper inside.

bellicose *adjective* inclined to fight, quarrelsome.

belligerent *adjective* carrying on war; quarrelsome, aggressive.

bellow *verb* to roar like a bull. – Also *noun*.

bellows *noun plural* an instrument for making a blast of air.

belly *noun* (*plural* **bellies**) the abdomen; the underpart of an animal's body; the bulging part of anything. – *verb* (*past tense* **bellied**) to swell or bulge out.

belong *verb* to be someone's property: *That book belongs to me*; to be a member of (a club *etc*); to be born in or live in: *I belong to Glasgow*; (of an object) to have its place in: *Those knives belong in the kitchen drawer*. – *noun plural* **belongings** what a person possesses.

beloved *adjective* much loved, very dear. – Also *noun*.

below *preposition* lower in position, rank *etc* than: *Her skirt reached below her knees. A captain ranks below a major*. – *adverb* in a lower position: *We looked down at the river below*.

belt *noun* a band or strip of leather, cloth *etc* worn around the waist; a continuous band of tough material used in machines or for conveying objects in a factory *etc*; a broad strip of anything (such as land). – *verb* to put a belt round; to thrash with a belt; (*coll*) to beat, hit. – *adjective* **belted** wearing or having a belt.

bemoan *verb* to weep about, mourn.

bench *noun* (*plural* **benches**) a long seat; a work-table; the judges of a court.

bend *verb* (*past tense* **bent**) to curve; (of persons) to stoop. – *noun* a turn (in a road *etc*).

beneath *preposition* under, in a lower position than. *A toad sat beneath the dripping tap*; covered by. *Beneath her coat she wore a black dress*; (felt to be) too low a task *etc* for. *Sweeping floors was beneath him*. – *adverb* below.

benediction *noun* a blessing.

benefactor *noun* a person who does good to others.

beneficial *adjective* bringing gain or advantage (to). – *noun* **beneficiary** (*plural* **beneficiaries**) a person who receives a gift, a legacy, an advantage *etc*.

benefit *noun* something good to receive or have done to one; money or services received from the government: *unemployment benefit*. – *verb* to do good to; to gain advantage.

benevolence *noun* wish to do good; a kind act. – *adjective* **benevolent** kindly.

benign *bè-nīn', adjective* gentle, kindly; (of disease) not causing death (opposite of **malignant**).

bent *noun* a natural liking. – *adjective* curved, crooked; (*coll*) dishonest; (*coll*) homosexual. – **be bent on** to be determined on. – *See* also **bend**.

bequeath *verb* to leave by will. – *noun* **bequest** money *etc* left by will.

berate *verb* to scold.

bereaved *adjective* deprived by death of a relative *etc*. – *noun* **bereavement**.

bereft *adjective* lacking, deprived (of).

beret *ber'ā, noun* a flat, round hat.

berry *noun* (*plural* **berries**) a (*usu* juicy) fruit enclosing seeds.

berserk *adverb* in a frenzy, mad.

berth *noun* a room or sleeping place in a ship *etc*; the place where a ship is tied up in a dock. – *verb* to moor (a ship). – **give a wide berth to** to keep well away from.

beryl *noun* a type of precious stone such as an emerald or aquamarine.

beseech *verb* to ask earnestly.

beset *verb (present participle* **besetting**, *past tense* and *past participle* **beset**) to attack from all sides; to surround.

beside *preposition* by the side of, near: *the house beside the river;* compared with: *Beside her sister she seems plain;* away from, wide of: *beside the point.* – **be beside oneself** to lose self-control; **beside the point** irrelevant.

besides *preposition* in addition to: *Besides me, there are plenty others;* other than, except: *nothing at all besides water.* – *adverb* also, moreover. *Besides, you can't go;* in addition: *plenty more besides.*

besiege *verb* to surround (a town *etc*) with an army; to crowd round.

besmirch *verb* to stain (a person's name *etc*).

besotted: besotted with foolishly fond of.

bespoke *adjective* (of clothes) ordered to be made.

best *adjective* good in the most excellent way. – *adverb* in the most excellent way. – *verb* to defeat. – *noun* **best man** a person who attends a man who is being married. – *noun* **best part** the largest or greatest part. – *noun* **bestseller** a book *etc* which sells exceedingly well. – **at best** under the most favourable circumstances; **do one's best** to try as hard as one can; **make the best of** do as well as possible with.

bestial *adjective* like a beast, beastly.

bestir *verb* to waken up, make lively.

bestow *verb* to give.

bet *noun* money put down to be lost or kept depending on the outcome of a race *etc*. – *verb (past tense* **bet** or **betted)** to place a bet.

betake: betake oneself to go.

bête noir *bet nwär, noun* a person or thing that a person particularly dislikes.

betray *verb* to give up (secrets, one's friends *etc*) to an enemy; to show signs of: *His face betrayed no emotion.* – *noun* **betrayal.**

betroth *verb* to promise in marriage. – *noun* **betrothal.** – **betrothed to** engaged to be married to.

better *adjective* good to a greater degree, of a more excellent kind; (of persons) healthier; completely recovered (from an illness). – *adjective* in a more excellent way. – *verb* to improve. – **better off** in a better position, wealthier; **get the better of** to defeat, to overcome; **had better** would be wise to; ought to; **think better of** to change one's mind about.

between *preposition* in or through the space dividing (two persons, places, times *etc*): *between 3 o'clock and 6 o'clock;* in parts, in shares to (two people): *Divide the chocolate between you;* from one (thing) to another: *the road between the cities;* one or the other of: *Choose between the boys.*

bevel *noun* a slanting edge. – *verb (past tense* **bevelled)** to give a slanting edge to. – *adjective* **bevelled.**

beverage *noun* a liquid for drinking.

bevy *noun (plural* **bevies)** a group of women or girls; a flock of birds (*eg* quails).

bewail *verb* to mourn loudly over.

beware *verb* to be watchful for (something dangerous).

bewilder *verb* to puzzle, confuse. – *noun* **bewilderment** confusion.

bewitch *verb* to put under a spell; to charm. – *adjective* **bewitching** charming; very beautiful.

beyond *preposition* on the far side of: *beyond the post office;* later than: *beyond three o'clock;* more than: *beyond what was required;* too far gone for: *beyond repair;* too difficult for: *The problem was beyond him.* – *adverb* on or to the far side, further away.

bi- *prefix* twice; having two; occurring *etc* twice (in a period of time) or once in every two (periods of time).

bias *noun* a favouring of one person, one side of an argument *etc* rather than another; a tendency to move *etc* in a particular direction; a weight on or in an object making it move in a particular direction. – *verb (past tense* **biassed** or **biased)** to give a bias to. – *noun* **bias binding** a piece of material cut on the slant and used for finishing hems *etc*.

bib *noun* a piece of cloth *etc* put under a child's chin to prevent his clothes being stained by food *etc*; the part (of an apron, overalls *etc*) covering the front, upper part of the body.

Bible *noun* the holy book of the Christian Church. – *adjective* **Biblical.**

bibliography *noun* (*plural* **bibliographies**) a list of books (about a subject). – *noun* **bibliographer** a person who puts together a bibliography.

bibliophile *noun* a lover of books.

bicentenary *noun* (*plural* **bicentenaries**) the two-hundredth year after an event *eg* someone's birth.

biceps *noun* the muscle in front of the upper part of the arm.

bicker *verb* to quarrel (*usu* over small matters).

bicycle *noun* a cycle with two wheels and driven by foot-pedals.

bid *verb* to offer a price (for); to tell, say: *I bid you farewell*; to command; to invite. – *noun* an offer of a price; a bold attempt: *a bid for freedom*.

bidet *bē'dā*, *noun* a low wash-basin for washing the genital area *etc*.

biennial *adjective* lasting two years; happening once every two years. – *noun* a plant that flowers only in its second year.

bier *bēr*, *noun* a carriage or frame for carrying a dead body.

big *adjective* (*comp* **bigger**, *superl* **biggest**) large, great in size, amount, extent *etc*; important; boastful.

bigamy *noun* the crime of or state of having two wives or two husbands at once. – *noun* **bigamist**. – *adjective* **bigamous**.

bight *noun* a small bay.

bigot *noun* one who too strongly believes or supports anything. – *noun* **bigotry**.

bike *noun* short for **bicycle**.

bikini *noun* (*plural* **bikinis**) a woman's brief two-piece bathing suit.

bilateral *adjective* having two sides; affecting two sides, parties *etc*: *a bilateral agreement*.

bilberry *noun* a type of plant with an edible dark-blue berry.

bile *noun* a fluid coming from the liver. – *adjective* **bilious** ill with too much bile; sick; greenish-yellow in colour. – *noun* **biliousness**.

bilge *noun* the broadest part of a ship's bottom; bilgewater; (*slang*) nonsense. – *noun* **bilgewater** water which lies in the ship's bottom.

bilingual *adjective* using or speaking two languages (well).

bill *noun* the beak of a bird; an account for money; an early version of a law before it has been passed by parliament; a printed sheet of information.

billet *noun* a lodging, *esp* for soldiers. – *verb* to lodge (soldiers) in private houses.

billiards *noun* a game played with a cue and balls on a table.

billion *noun* a million millions (1 000 000 000 000); (*US*, now often in Britain) a thousand millions (1 000 000 000).

billow *noun* a great wave. – *verb* to rise in billows. – *adjective* **billowy**.

billy (*pl* **billies**) or **billycan** *noun* a container for cooking, making tea *etc*, *esp* outdoors. – *noun* **billy-goat** a male goat.

bimbo *noun* (*plural* **bimbos**) a woman, *esp* an attractive but not very clever youngster.

bin *noun* a container for storing corn, wine *etc* or for holding dust and ashes.

binary *adjective* made up of two. – *noun* **binary system** a mathematical system in which numbers are expressed by two digits only, 1 and 0.

bind *verb* (*past tense* **bound**) to tie with a band; to fasten together; to make to promise. – *noun* **binding** anything that binds; the cover, stitching *etc* which holds a book together.

bingo *noun* a popular gambling game using numbers.

binoculars *noun* *plural* a small double telescope.

biodegradable *adjective* (of substances) able to be broken down into parts by bacteria.

biography *noun* (*plural* **biographies**) a written account of the life of a person. – *noun* **biographer** a person who writes a biography. – *adjective* **biographical**.

biology *noun* the study of living things. – *adjective* **biological**.

biped *noun* an animal with two feet (*eg* a bird).

birch *noun* (*plural* **birches**) a type of hardwood tree; a bundle of birch twigs, used for beating people. – *verb* to beat (as if) with a birch.

bird *noun* a feathered, egg-laying creature. – *noun* **birdwatching** the study of birds in their natural surroundings. –

bird of prey a bird (*eg* a hawk) which kills and eats animals (*esp* mammals) or birds; **bird's-eye view** a wide view, as would be seen from above.

Biro® *noun* a type of ballpoint pen.

birth *noun* the very beginning of a person's (or animal's) life in the world. – *noun* **birthday** the day on which a person is born; the day of the same date each year. – *noun* **birthmark** a mark on the body from birth. – *noun* **birthright** the right which one may claim because of one's parentage.

biscuit *noun* dough baked hard in small cakes.

bisect *verb* to cut in two equal parts.

bishop *noun* a clergyman of high rank (next to an archbishop) in the Roman Catholic Church and the Church of England. – *noun* **bishopric** the district ruled by a bishop.

bison *noun* (*plural* **bison**) a large wild ox of which there are two types, the American one, commonly called **buffalo,** and the European one, which is almost extinct.

bit¹ *noun* a small piece; a small tool for boring; the part of the bridle which the horse holds in its mouth; (*comput*) the smallest unit of information.

bit² *see* **bite.**

bitch *noun* (*plural* **bitches**) a female dog, wolf *etc*; (*coll*) an unpleasant, ill-tempered woman.

bite *verb* (*past tense* **bit,** *past participle* **bitten**) to grip, cut or tear with the teeth. – *noun* a grip with the teeth; the part bitten off; (in fishing) a nibble at the bait; a wound on the body caused by an animal's or insect's bite.

bitter *adjective* unpleasant to the taste; harsh: *bitter cold*; resentful, angry through disappointment.

bittern *noun* a type of bird like a heron.

bivouac *noun* a rest for the night in the open air without tents. – Also *verb* (*past tense* **bivouacked**).

bi-weekly *adjective* happening twice a week or once every two weeks.

bizarre *adjective* odd, strange.

blab *verb* (*past tense* **blabbed**) to talk much; to let out a secret.

black *adjective* dark and colourless. – *noun* black colour. – *adjective* **black-and-blue**

badly bruised. – *noun* **black belt** an award for skill in judo. – *noun* **blackberry** a type of black-coloured soft fruit growing on a prickly stem. – *noun* **blackbird** a type of black, thrush-like bird. – *noun* **blackboard** a dark-coloured board for writing on in chalk. – *noun* **blackcock** a kind of grouse. – *verb* **blacken** to make black or dark; to make to appear wicked. – *noun* **black eye** a bruised area round the eye *usu* as result of a blow. – *noun* **blackguard** a wicked person. – *noun* **blackleg** a person who works when other workers are on strike. – *noun* **blackmail** the crime of threatening to reveal a person's secrets unless money is paid. – *noun* **blackmailer.** – *noun* **blackmarket** illegal or dishonest buying and selling. – Also *adjective.* – *noun* **blackout** (a period of) total darkness caused by putting out or obscuring all lights; a faint, loss of consciousness. – *verb* **black out** to become unconscious. – *noun* **black sheep** a person who is less successful or less righteous than others in a group (*usu* the family). – *noun* **blacksmith** a person who makes or repairs articles of iron. – *noun* **black widow** a type of very poisonous American spider.

bladder *noun* a thin bag of skin *etc, esp* that in which urine collects in the body.

blade *noun* the cutting part of a knife, sword *etc*; a leaf of grass or corn.

blame *verb* to find fault with; to consider responsible for. – *noun* fault; responsibility (for something bad). – *adjective* **blameless.** – *adjective* **blameworthy** deserving blame.

blancmange *blâ-monzh*, *noun* a type of jelly-like pudding made with milk.

bland *adjective* polite, gentle; mild, not irritating; dull, not exciting.

blandishments *noun plural* acts or words meant to flatter.

blank *adjective* (of paper *etc*) without writing or marks; expressionless: *a blank look*. – *noun* an empty space; a cartridge without a bullet. – *noun* **blank verse** poetry without rhyme.

blanket *noun* a bedcovering of wool *etc*; a covering. – *adjective* covering a group of things: *a blanket agreement.* – *verb* to cover (with something thick).

blare *verb* to sound loudly. – Also *noun.*

blarney *noun* flattery or coaxing talk.

blaspheme *verb* to speak lightly or wickedly of God; to curse and swear. – *noun*

blasphemer. – *adjective* **blasphemous.** – *noun* **blasphemy** (*plural* **blasphemies**).

blast *noun* a blowing or gust of wind; a loud note (as on a trumpet); an explosion. – *verb* to break (stones, a bridge *etc*) by explosion; to wither, destroy; to produce a loud noise: *Music blasted from the radio.* – *noun* **blast furnace** a furnace (such as is used in iron-smelting) into which hot air is blown. – *noun* **blast-off** the moment of the launching of a rocket. – Also *verb.* – **at full blast** as quickly, strongly *etc* as possible.

blatant *adjective* very obvious; shameless. – *adverb* **blatantly.**

blaze *noun* a rush of light or flame. – *verb* to burn with a strong flame; to throw out a strong light. – *noun* **blazer** a kind of jacket worn by schoolchildren, sportsmen *etc*.

blazon *verb* to make known publicly; to display very obviously.

bleach *verb* to whiten, remove the colour from. – *noun* (*plural* **bleaches**) a substance which bleaches, used for cleaning, whitening clothes *etc*.

bleak *adjective* dull and cheerless; cold, unsheltered. – *noun* **bleakness.**

bleary *adjective* (of eyes) tired and inflamed.

bleat *verb* to cry like a sheep; to complain in an irritating or whining way. – Also *noun.*

bleed *verb* (*past tense* **bled**) to lose blood; to draw blood from. – *noun* **bleeding** a flow of blood.

bleep *verb* to give out a high-pitched intermittent sound. – Also *noun.*

blemish *noun* (*plural* **blemishes**) a stain; a fault or flaw. – *verb* to stain or spoil.

blend *verb* to mix together. – Also *noun.* – *noun* **blender** an electric machine which mixes thoroughly and liquidizes.

bless *verb* to wish happiness to; to make happy; to make holy. – *adjective* **blessed** or (in poetry *etc*) **blest** happy; fortunate; made holy, consecrated. – *noun* **blessing** a wish or prayer for happiness or success; any means or cause of happiness: *The children were a blessing to them.*

blight *noun* a disease in plants which withers them; anything that destroys. – *verb* to destroy.

blind *adjective* unable to see. – *noun* a window screen; something which deceives. – *verb* to make blind; to dazzle. – *noun* **blindness.** – *noun* **blind alley** a street open only at one end; anything which leads nowhere. – *adjective* **blindfold** having the eyes bandaged, so as not to see. – *noun* **blindman's buff** a game in which a blindfold person tries to catch others.

blink *verb* to close the eyes for a moment; to shine unsteadily. – Also *noun.* – *noun plural* **blinkers** pieces of leather over a horse's eyes to prevent it seeing in any direction except in front.

bliss *noun* very great happiness. – *adjective* **blissful.**

blister *noun* a thin bubble on the skin full of watery matter. – *verb* to rise up in a blister.

blithe *adjective* happy, merry.

blitz *noun* (*plural* **blitzes**) a sudden violent attack (*esp* from the air).

blizzard *noun* a fierce storm of wind and snow.

bloated *adjective* swollen, puffed out. – *noun* **bloater** a type of smoked herring.

blob *noun* a drop of liquid; a round spot. .

block *noun* a lump (of wood, stone *etc*); a connected group (of buildings *etc*); something which hinders or obstructs: *a road block*; an engraved piece of wood or metal for printing; (*hist*) the wood on which people were beheaded. – *verb* to hinder, prevent from going on. – *noun* **blockhead** a stupid person. – *noun plural* **block letters** capital letters written in imitation of printing type (*eg* NAME).

blockade *verb* to surround a fort or country so that food *etc* cannot reach it. – Also *noun.*

blonde *adjective, noun* (of) a woman of fair skin and light-coloured hair. – *adjective* **blond** light-coloured; fair-haired.

blood *noun* the red liquid which flows in the bodies of human beings and animals; one's descent or parentage: *royal blood.* – *noun* **blood donor** a person who gives blood which is stored and given to ill people. – *noun* **blood group** any one of the types into which human blood is divided. – *noun* **bloodhound** a breed of large dog with a good sense of smell. – *adjective* **bloodless.** – *noun* **bloodshed** the shedding of blood, slaughter. – *adjective* **bloodshot** (of eyes) inflamed with blood. – *adjective* **bloodthirsty** cruel, eager to kill. – *noun*

blood-vessel a vein or artery (of the body) in which the blood circulates. – *adjective* **bloody** covered or stained with blood; (*coll* showing anger *etc*): *What a bloody mess.*

bloom *verb* (of plants) to flower; to be in good health. – *noun* a blossom or flower; rosy colour; freshness, perfection; a powder on the skin of fresh fruits.

blossom *noun* a flower; the flowers on a fruit tree. – *verb* to put forth flowers; to open out, develop, flourish.

blot *noun* a spot or stain (of ink *etc*). – *verb* (*past tense* **blotted**) to spot or stain; to dry writing with **blotting paper**. – **blot out** to remove or conceal from sight or memory.

blotch *noun* (*plural* **blotches**) a spot or patch of colour *etc*. – *verb* to mark with blotches. – *adjective* **blotched**. – *adjective* **blotchy**.

blouse *noun* a loose piece of clothing for the upper body.

blow *noun* a hard stroke or knock (*eg* with the fist); (*coll*) a sudden piece of bad luck. – *verb* (*past tense* **blew**, *past participle* **blown**) (of air or wind) to move; to drive air upon or into; to sound (a wind instrument); to breathe hard or with difficulty. – *noun* **blowfly** a fly which lays its eggs in dead flesh *etc*, a bluebottle. – *noun* **blowlamp** or **blowtorch** a lamp for aiming a very hot flame at a particular spot. – *adjective* **blowy** windy. – **blow over** to pass and be forgotten; **blow up** to destroy by explosion.

blubber *noun* the fat of whales and other sea animals.

bludgeon *noun* a short stick with a heavy end.

blue *adjective, noun* (of) the colour of a clear sky; (*coll*) unhappy, depressed. – *noun plural* **blues** or **the blues** a slow, sad, *orig* American Negro, song. – *noun* **bluebell** the wild hyacinth; (in Scotland) the harebell. – *noun* **bluebottle** a large fly with a blue abdomen. – *noun* **Blue Peter** a blue flag with white centre, raised when a ship is about to sail. – *noun* **blueprint** a sketch-plan of work to be done. – *noun* **bluestocking** a learned lady. – **out of the blue** unexpectedly.

bluff *adjective* rough and jolly in manners, outspoken. – *verb* to (try to) deceive (by a display of self-confidence). – *noun* a high steep bank overlooking the sea or a river; deception, trickery.

blunder *verb* to make a bad mistake. – Also *noun*.

blunderbuss *noun* (*plural* **blunderbusses**) a short hand gun with a wide mouth.

blunt *adjective* having an edge or point that is not sharp; rough in manner. – *verb* to make less sharp or less painful. – *adverb* **bluntly** frankly, straightforwardly.

blur *noun* a spot, thing *etc* that cannot be seen clearly; a smudge, a smear. – Also *verb* (*pt* **blurred**). – *adjective* **blurred**.

blurt *verb* (*usu* with **out**) to speak suddenly and without thinking.

blush *noun* (*plural* **blushes**) a red glow on the face caused by shame *etc*; a reddish glow. – *verb* to go red in the face.

bluster *verb* to blow strongly; to boast noisily (but without good reason). – *noun* a blast or roaring as of the wind; words of noisy, empty boasting.

BMA *abbreviation* British Medical Association.

boa *noun* a long scarf of fur or feathers. – *noun* **boa (constrictor)** a type of large snake which kills its prey by winding itself round it and crushing it.

boar *noun* the male pig; a wild pig.

board *noun* a sheet of wood; a group of people who run a business *etc*: *board of directors*; stiff card used in the binding of books; food: *bed and board*. – *verb* to cover with boards; to supply with food at fixed terms; to enter (a ship *etc*). – *noun* **boarder** a person who receives food and lodging. – *noun* **boarding-house** a house where paying guests receive meals at a fixed price. – *noun* **boarding-school** a school in which food and lodging is given.

boast *verb* to brag, to speak proudly and exaggeratedly, *esp* about oneself and one's actions. – *noun* something said in a bragging or boasting manner. – *adjective* **boastful** fond of boasting.

boat *noun* a vessel for sailing or rowing; a ship; a boat-shaped dish: *a sauceboat.* – *verb* to sail about in a boat. – *noun* **boater** a straw hat with a brim.

boatswain or **bosun** both *bō'sn*, *noun* an officer who looks after a ship's boats, rigging *etc*.

bob verb (past tense **bobbed**) to move up and down; to cut (hair) to about neck level.

bobbin noun a reel or spool on which thread is wound.

bobsleigh noun a long sledge or two short sledges joined together with one long seat.

bode: bode well or **bode ill** to be a good or bad sign.

bodice noun the (close-fitting) part of a woman's or a child's dress above the waist.

bodkin noun a large blunt needle.

body noun (plural **bodies**) the whole or main part of a human being or animal; a corpse; the main part of anything; a mass (esp of persons). – adverb all in one piece, as one whole. – noun **bodyguard** a person or group of people whose job is to protect another person from harm or attack. – adjective **bodily** of the body. – noun **body language** communication by means of conscious or unconscious gestures, attitudes, facial expressions etc. – noun **body-popping** a form of dancing with robot-like movements. – noun **body-warmer** a padded sleeveless jacket.

boffin noun (coll) a (research) scientist.

bog noun a marsh. – adjective **boggy**. – **bog down** to hinder, prevent from making progress.

bogey noun something greatly feared.

boggle verb to be astonished at, refuse to believe.

bogus adjective false.

boil verb (of a liquid) to reach the temperature at which it turns to vapour; to bubble up owing to heat; (coll) to be hot; (coll) to be angry. – noun a kind of inflamed swelling. – noun **boiler** a container in which water is heated or steam is produced. – noun **boiling-point** the temperature at which a liquid turns to vapour (of water, 100°C).

boisterous adjective wild, noisy; (of weather) stormy.

bold adjective daring, full of courage; cheeky; striking, well-marked: *a picture in bold colours*; (of printing type) thick and clear.

bollard noun on ships or quays, a post for fastening ropes to; in a street, a short post used in controlling traffic.

bollocks noun plural (vulg) the testicles; (slang) rubbish.

bolster noun a long pillow or cushion. – verb (with **up**) to support.

bolt noun a (small) metal sliding bar used to fasten a door etc; a large screw or pin; a roll of cloth. – verb to fasten with a bolt; to swallow (food) hurriedly; to rush away, escape. – **bolt upright** (sitting) with a very straight back.

bomb noun a case containing explosive or other harmful material thrown, dropped, timed to go off automatically etc; (with **the**) the nuclear bomb. – verb to drop bombs on. – noun **bomber** an aeroplane built for bombing; a person who throws, plants etc bombs. – noun **bombshell** formerly, a bomb; a startling piece of news.

bombard verb to attack with artillery; to batter or pelt. – noun **bombardment.**

bombast noun pompous language. – adjective **bombastic.**

bona fide *bō'na fī'dā,* adjective real, genuine: *a bona fide excuse.*

bond noun (often pl) that which binds (eg chains, ropes etc); that which brings people together: *Their interest in ballet was a bond between them*; a (written) promise to pay or do something. – noun **bondage** slavery. – noun **bonded store** or **bonded warehouse** one where goods are kept until taxes have been paid on them. – **in bond** in a bonded warehouse.

bone noun a hard material forming the skeleton of animals; one of the connected pieces of a skeleton: *the hip bone.* – verb to take the bones out of (meat etc). – adjective **bony** (of food) full of bones; not fleshy, thin; made of bone or bone-like substance.

bonfire noun a large fire in the open air.

bonk noun (the sound of) a blow; (coll) an act of sexual intercourse.

bonnet noun a type of hat for women, usu fastened by ribbons etc; the covering over a motor-car engine.

bonny adjective good-looking; healthy-looking.

bonus noun (plural **bonuses**) an extra payment in addition to wages etc; something extra.

boo verb make a sound of disapproval. – Also noun.

boob noun (coll) a mistake; (coll) a woman's breast.

booby noun (pl **boobies**) a silly or stupid person. – noun **booby prize** a prize for the person who is last in a competition. – noun **booby trap** an explosive or other harmful device hidden or disguised as something harmless, intended to injure the first person to come near it.

book noun (printed) pages bound together; a written work which has appeared, or is intended to appear, in the form of a book: *I read your book and enjoyed it.* – verb to order (places etc) beforehand. – noun **book-keeping** the keeping of accounts. – noun **booklet** a small (paper-covered) book. – noun **book-maker** (also (coll) **bookie**) a person who takes bets and pays winnings. – noun **bookworm** a person who is very fond of reading; a grub that eats holes in books.

boom verb to make a hollow sound or roar; to increase in prosperity, success etc. – noun a loud, hollow sound; a rush or increase of trade, prosperity etc: *the oil boom*; a pole by which a sail is stretched.

boomerang noun a curved piece of wood which when thrown returns to the thrower, used as a hunting weapon by Australian aborigines.

boon noun a blessing or favour to be grateful for. – noun **boon companion** a close friend whose company one enjoys.

boor noun a rough or rude person. – adjective **boorish.**

boost verb to push up, raise, increase: *A good advertisement will boost the sales of shampoo. Another injection will boost his resistance to polio.* – Also noun. – noun **booster** that which boosts; a device for increasing the power of a machine etc; the first of several stages of a rocket.

boot noun a covering (of leather etc) for the foot and lower part of the leg; a place for stowing luggage in a car. – verb to kick. – noun **bootee** a (knitted) boot for a baby. – **to boot** in addition, as well.

booth noun a covered stall (at a fair or market); a small (enclosed) compartment (for telephoning, voting etc).

bootlegger noun a person who deals illegally in alcoholic drink.

booty noun plunder or gains usu taken in war etc.

border noun the edge or side of anything; the boundary of a country; a flowerbed in a garden. – verb (usu with **on** or **upon**) to be near to: *His behaviour borders on madness.* – adjective **bordered** edged.

bore[1] verb to make a hole by piercing; to weary, seem tiresome or dull to. – noun a hole made by boring; the size across the tube of a gun; a tiresome person or thing; a flood or wave that rushes up some river mouths at high tide. – noun **boredom** lack of interest, weariness.

bore[2] see **bear.**

born adjective by birth, natural: *a born athlete.* – verb see **bear.** – **be born** (of a baby) to come out of the mother's womb; to come into existence.

borne see **bear.**

borough noun (hist) a town with special privileges granted by royal charter; a town that elects Members of Parliament; see also **burgh.**

borrow verb to get (from another) on loan.

borzoi noun a breed of long-haired dog.

bosh noun nonsense.

bosom noun the breast; midst, centre: *the bosom of his family.* – adjective (of friends etc) close.

boss noun (plural **bosses**) a leader or master. – verb to manage, order about in a highhanded way. – adjective **bossy** tending to boss others too much, domineering.

bosun see **boatswain.**

botany noun the study of plants. – adjective **botanic** or **botanical.** – noun **botanist** a person who studies or is an expert in botany. – noun **botanic garden** a large public garden where plants and trees of different countries are grown.

botch verb to mend clumsily; to do badly. – noun a badly done piece of work.

both adjective, pronoun the two, the one and the other: *We both went. Both of us went. Both (the) men are dead. The men are both dead. Both are dead.* – adverb equally, together: *He is both dishonest and cunning.*

bother verb to be a nuisance to; to trouble (oneself or others). – noun trouble, inconvenience.

bothy noun (plural **bothies**) (in Scotland) a hut to give shelter to climbers etc; a simply furnished hut for farm labourers.

bottle *noun* a hollow narrow-necked vessel for holding liquids. – *verb* to put in a bottle. – *noun* **bottleneck** a narrow part of a road likely to become crowded with traffic; any stage in a process where progress is held up. – **bottle up** to keep in, hold in (one's feelings).

bottom *noun* the lowest part or underside of anything; the sitting part of the body, the buttocks. – *adjective* **bottomless** extremely deep.

botulism *noun* food-poisoning caused by bacteria in infected tinned food *etc*.

boudoir *bood'wär*, *noun* a lady's private room.

bough *noun* a branch of a tree.

bought *see* **buy**.

boulder *noun* a large stone.

bounce *verb* to (cause to) jump or spring up after striking the ground *etc*; to move about noisily. – Also *noun*. – *noun* **bouncer** a person whose job it is to force troublemakers (at a club *etc*) to leave. – *adjective* **bouncing** (large and) lively.

bound *noun* a leap; a jump; (*usu plural*) borders, limits. – *verb* to jump, leap; to limit; to surround; *see* also **bind**. – *noun* **boundary** (*plural* **boundaries**) (line *etc* marking) the edge or limit. – *adjective* **boundless** having no limit, vast. – **bound for** ready to go to, on the way to; **bound to** certain to: *He is bound to notice it*; **out of bounds** beyond the permitted limits.

bounty *noun* (*plural* **bounties**) a gift; generosity; money given as a help. – *adjective* **bounteous** or **bountiful** generous; plentiful.

bouquet *book'ā*, *noun* a bunch of flowers; a scent (of wine).

bourgeois *boor'zhwä*, *noun*, *adjective* (a person) of the middle class.

bout *noun* a (round in a) fight or contest; a period, spell, fit (of illness *etc*).

boutique *noun* a small shop *usu* selling goods (*esp* clothes) of the latest fashion.

bovine *adjective* of or like cattle; stupid.

bow¹ *verb* to bend; to nod the head or bend the body in greeting; to give in; to weigh down, crush. – *noun* a bending of the head or body; (*usu plural*) the front part of a ship.

bow² *noun* anything in the shape of a curve or arch; a weapon for shooting arrows, made of a stick of springy wood bent by a string; a looped knot; a wooden rod with horsehair stretched along it, by which the strings of a violin *etc* are played. – *adjective* **bow-legged** having legs curving outwards. – *noun* **bowman** a soldier *etc* who uses a bow. – *noun* **bow window** a window built in a curve.

bowels *noun plural* in the body, the large and small intestines; the inner-most parts of anything: *in the bowels of the earth*.

bower *noun* a shady spot in a garden.

bowl *noun* a basin for holding liquids *etc*; a basin-shaped hollow in anything; a heavy wooden ball for rolling along the ground, as in the game skittles; (*plural*) a game played on a green with specially weighted bowls. – *verb* to play at bowls; to move speedily like a bowl; (in cricket) to send the ball at the wicket; to put out a batsman by knocking his wicket with the ball. – *noun* **bowler** a person who bowls in cricket; a (black) hat with a rounded top. – **bowl over** to knock down; to surprise greatly.

box *noun* (*plural* **boxes**) a case for holding anything; a hardwood tree; an evergreen shrub; (in a theatre) private closed-in seats. – *verb* to enclose, confine in a box or any small space; to strike with the hand or fist; to fight with the fists, wearing padded gloves, as a sport. – *noun* **boxer** a person who boxes as a sport; a breed of large smooth-haired dog with a head like a bulldog's. – *noun* **boxing** the name of this sport. – *noun* **Boxing Day** December 26, the day (now often the first weekday) after Christmas Day. – *noun* **box office** an office where theatre tickets *etc* may be bought.

boy *noun* a male child; a male servant. – *adjective* **boyish**. – *noun* **boyhood** the time of being a boy. – *noun* **Boy Scout** *see* **Scout**.

boycott *verb* to refuse to do business or trade with. – Also *noun*.

BR *abbreviation* British Rail.

bra *noun* short for **brassière**.

brace *noun* anything that draws together and holds tightly; a piece of wire fitted over teeth to straighten them; a pair or couple (*esp* of pheasant, grouse *etc* when shot); a carpenter's tool used in boring; (*plural*) shoulder-straps for holding up trousers. – *verb* to tighten or strengthen, give firmness to. – *adjective* **bracing** giving strength.

bracelet *noun* an ornament for the wrist; (*coll*) a handcuff.

bracken *noun* a coarse kind of fern.

bracket *noun* a support for something fastened to a wall; in printing *etc* a mark (*eg* (), []) used to group together several words *etc*. – *verb* to enclose in brackets; to group together.

brackish *adjective* (of water) rather salty.

bradawl *noun* a tool to pierce holes.

brag *verb* (*past tense* **bragged**) to boast. – Also *noun*.

braid *verb* to plait (the hair). – *noun* decorative ribbon used as trimming; a plait of hair.

braille *noun* a system of raised marks on paper which blind people can read by feeling.

brain *noun* the part of the body inside the skull, the centre of feeling and thinking. – *verb* to knock out the brains of; to hit on the head. – *noun* **brainwashing** forcing (a person) to change their views. – *noun* **brainwave** a good idea. – *adjective* **brainy** (*coll*) clever.

braise *verb* to stew (meat) in little liquid.

brake *noun* a part of a vehicle, used for stopping or slowing down. – *verb* to slow down by using the brake(s).

bramble *noun* the blackberry bush; (in Scotland) its fruit.

bran *noun* the inner husks of wheat *etc*, *usu* separated from flour after grinding.

branch *noun* (*plural* **branches**) a shoot or arm-like limb of a tree; a small shop, bank, library *etc* belonging to a bigger one. – *verb* to spread out like branches.

brand *noun* a make of goods (having a special trademark); a burning piece of wood; a permanent mark *esp* one made by a red-hot iron. – *verb* to mark with a brand; to put a permanent mark on, impress deeply; to mark with disgrace: *branded as a thief*. – *adjective* **brand-new** absolutely new.

brandish *verb* to wave (a weapon *etc*) about.

brandy *noun* (*plural* **brandies**) a strong drink, a spirit made from wine.

brass *noun* (*plural* **brasses**) metal made by mixing copper and zinc; (in music) brass wind instruments: *a brass band*. – *adjective* of, made of brass; playing brass musical instruments: *a brass band*. – *noun* **brass plate** a nameplate on a door *etc*. – *adjective* **brassy** like brass; showily dressed or harsh-voiced.

brassière *noun* an article of women's underwear for supporting the breasts.

brat *noun* a disapproving name for a child.

bravado *noun* a show of bravery, bold pretence.

brave *adjective* ready to meet danger, pain *etc* without showing fear, courageous; noble. – *verb* to face or meet boldly and without fear. – *noun* a Red Indian warrior. – *noun* **bravery**.

bravo *interjection* well done!

brawl *noun* a noisy quarrel; a fight. – Also *verb*.

brawn *noun* muscle power. – *adjective* **brawny** big and strong.

bray *noun* a cry (like that) of an ass. – Also *verb*.

brazen *adjective* of or like brass; impudent, shameless: *a brazen hussy*. – **brazen (it) out** to face (a difficult situation) with bold impudence.

brazier *noun* a kind of iron basket for holding burning coals.

brazil-nut *noun* the three-sided nut from a type of tree found in Brazil.

breach *noun* (*plural* **breaches**) break or gap; a breaking of a law, of a promise *etc*; a quarrel. – *verb* to make a breach or opening in. – **breach of the peace** a breaking of the law by noisy, offensive behaviour.

bread *noun* food made of flour or meal and baked; necessary food, means of living. – *noun* **breadwinner** one who earns a living for a family.

breadth *noun* distance from side to side, width; extent.

break *verb* (*past tense* **broke,** *past participle* **broken**) to (cause to) fall to pieces or apart; to act against (a law, promise *etc*); to interrupt (a silence *etc*); to tell (news); to check, soften the effect of (a fall); to cure (a habit); (of a teenage boy's voice) to drop to a deep male tone; (often with **in**) to tame or train (a horse). – *noun* an opening; a pause; (*coll*) a lucky chance. – *adjective* **breakable**. – *noun* **breakage** the act of breaking; the thing broken. – *noun*

breakdance or **breakdancing** a form of dance to rock or disco music using some gymnastic routines. – noun **breakdown** see **break down** below. – noun **breaker** a large wave. – noun **break-in** illegal entry (by force) of a house etc with intent to steal. – noun **breakthrough** a sudden success after effort. – noun **breakwater** a barrier to break the force of waves. – **break down** to divide into parts; (of engines etc) to fail; to be overcome with weeping or (nervous) exhaustion (noun **breakdown**); **break into** to get into by force; **break out** to appear suddenly; to escape; (with **in**) to become covered (with a rash etc); **break up** to (cause to) fall to pieces or apart; to separate, depart: *The meeting broke up.*

breakfast noun the first meal of the day. – Also verb.

bream noun a type of small fish.

breast noun the front part of a human or animal body between neck and belly; either of the milk-producing parts of the body of a woman. – noun **breastplate** a piece of armour for the breast.

breath noun the air drawn into and then sent out from the lungs; one act of breathing; a very slight breeze. – noun **breathalyser** a device into which a person breathes to indicate the amount of alcohol in the blood. – adjective **breathless** breathing very fast, panting; excited.

breathe verb (present participle **breathing**) to draw in and send out air from the lungs; to whisper. – noun **breather** a rest or pause.

bred see **breed**.

breech noun the back part, esp of a gun; (plural) **breeches** trousers (esp those coming just below the knee).

breed verb (past tense **bred**) to produce (children, a family); to mate and rear (animals); to cause: *Dirt breeds disease.* – noun a group (of animals or people) alike in looks etc, being descended from the same ancestor, race, type; kind, sort: *a new breed of salesmen.* – noun **breeding** act of producing or rearing; good manners; education and training.

breeze noun a gentle wind. – adjective **breezy** windy; bright, lively.

brethren noun old plural of **brother**.

brevity noun shortness.

brew verb to make beer; to make (tea etc); (of a storm, trouble etc) to be gathering or forming; to plot, plan: *brewing mischief.* – noun **brewery** (plural **breweries**) a place where beer is made.

briar or **brier** noun the wild rose; a type of heather plant whose wood is used for making tobacco pipes.

bribe noun a gift (usu money) given to persuade a person to do something usu dishonest. – verb to win over with a bribe. – noun **bribery**.

bric-à-brac noun small odds and ends.

brick noun an (oblong) block of baked clay for building; a toy building-block of wood etc.

bride noun a woman about to be married, or newly married. – adjective **bridal** of a bride or a wedding. – noun **bridegroom** a man about to be married, or newly married. – noun **bridesmaid** an unmarried woman who attends the bride at a wedding.

bridge noun something built to carry a track or road across a river etc; the captain's platform on a ship; a card game; the bony part of the nose; a thin piece of wood holding up the strings of a violin etc. – verb to be or build a bridge over; to get over (a difficulty).

bridle noun the harness on a horse's head to which the reins are attached. – verb to put on a bridle; to toss the head indignantly. – noun **bridle-path** a path for horseriders.

brief adjective short; taking a short time. – noun (a set of notes giving) information or instructions, esp to a lawyer about a law case; (plural) close-fitting legless pants or underpants. – verb to instruct or inform. – **in brief** in a few words.

brier see **briar**.

brig noun a sailing vessel with two masts and square-cut sails.

brigade noun a body (usu two battalions) of soldiers. – noun **brigadier** a senior army officer.

brigand noun a robber, bandit.

bright adjective shining; full of light; clever; cheerful. – verb **brighten** to make or grow bright.

brilliant adjective very clever; sparkling; splendid – noun **brilliance**.

brim noun the edge (of a cup etc); the outer edge of a hat which sticks out. – verb (past tense **brimmed**) to be full. – adjective **brimful** full to the brim.

brimstone *noun* sulphur.

brine *noun* salt water. – *adjective* **briny**.

bring *verb* (*past tense* **brought**) to fetch, lead or carry (to a place); to cause to come: *The medicine brings him relief*. – **bring about** to cause; **bring home to** to make (someone) realize (something); **bring off** to do (something) successfully; **bring to** to revive; **bring up** to rear, to feed and educate; to mention: *He brought up that point in his speech*.

brink *noun* the edge (of a cliff, *etc*). – **on the brink of** almost at the point of, on the verge of: *on the brink of war*.

brisk *adjective* moving quickly; lively and efficient: *a brisk manner*. – *noun* **briskness**.

bristle *noun* a short, stiff hair (as of a pig). – *verb* (of hair *etc*) to stand on end; to show anger and indignation. – *adjective* **bristly** having bristles; rough.

brittle *adjective* hard but easily broken.

broach *verb* to begin to talk about (a subject *etc*); to open, begin using (*eg* a cask of wine).

broad *adjective* wide, extensive; (of an accent *etc*) strong, obvious. – *noun* **broadness**. – *verb* **broadcast** to send out by radio, television *etc*. – Also *noun*. – *verb* **broaden** to make or grow broader. – *noun* **broadside** a shot by all the guns on one side of a ship; a strong attack (in an argument *etc*).

brocade *noun* a silk cloth on which fine patterns are sewn.

broccoli *noun* a hardy variety of cauliflower with small green or purple flower-heads.

brochure brōˈshoor, *noun* a booklet: *a holiday brochure*.

brogue brōg, *n* a strong shoe; a broad accent (*esp* Irish) in speaking.

broil *verb* to grill; to make or be very hot.

broke *adjective* (*coll*) without money. – *verb* see **break**.

broken see **break**.

broker *noun* one who buys and sells (stocks and shares *etc*) for others.

bronchitis *noun* an illness (affecting the windpipe) in which breathing is difficult. – *adjective* **bronchial** having to do with the windpipe.

bronco *noun* (*plural* **broncos**) (*US*) a half-tamed horse.

brontosaurus *noun* a type of large extinct dinosaur.

bronze *noun* a golden-brown mixture of copper and tin. – Also *adjective*. – *adjective* **bronzed** sunburnt (to a colour like that of bronze).

brooch *noun* (*plural* **brooches**) an ornament pinned to the clothing.

brood *verb* (of a hen *etc*) to sit on eggs; to think (anxiously) for some time. – *noun* a number of young birds hatched at one time; young animals or children of the same family.

brook *noun* a small stream. – *verb* to put up with, endure.

broom *noun* a type of shrub with yellow flowers; a brush for sweeping. – *noun* **broomstick** the handle of a broom.

Bros *abbreviation* Brothers.

broth *noun* soup, *esp* one made with vegetables.

brother *noun* a male born of the same parents as oneself; a companion, a fellow-worker *etc*. – *noun* **brotherhood** an association of men. – *noun* **brother-in-law** the brother of one's husband or of one's wife; the husband of one's sister or of one's sister-in-law. – *adjective* **brotherly** of or like a brother; affectionate.

brought see **bring**.

brow *noun* the forehead; an eyebrow; the edge of a hill. – *verb* **browbeat** to bully.

brown *adjective* of a dark colour made by mixing red, yellow, black *etc*; suntanned. – Also *noun*.

brownie *noun* (*myth*) a helpful fairy or goblin; a Brownie Guide. – *noun* **Brownie Guide** a junior Girl Guide.

browse *verb* to feed (on the shoots or leaves of plants); to glance through (books), reading here and there.

bruise *noun* a mark, a discoloured area (*eg* on the body) where it has been struck *etc*. – *verb* to cause bruises (to).

brunette *noun* a woman with dark hair.

brunt: bear or **take the brunt** to take the chief strain.

brush *noun* (*plural* **brushes**) an instrument with tufts of bristles, hair, wire *etc* for smoothing the hair, cleaning, painting *etc*; a disagreement, a brief quarrel or fight; the tail of a fox; undergrowth. – *verb* to pass a brush over; to remove by sweeping; to touch lightly in passing. – noun **brushwood** broken branches, twigs *etc*; undergrowth.

brusque *broosk, adjective* sharp and short in manner, rude. – noun **brusqueness**.

Brussels sprouts *noun plural* a type of vegetable with sprouts like small cabbages on the stem.

brute *noun* an animal; a cruel person. – *adjective* **brutal** like a brute, cruel. – *noun* **brutality**. – *noun* **brute strength** pure physical strength. – *adjective* **brutish** like a brute, savage, coarse.

BSc *abbreviation* Bachelor of Science.

BSE *abbreviation* bovine spongiform encephalopathy, a *usu* fatal disease of cattle that affects the nervous system.

BST *abbreviation* British Summer Time.

Bt *abbreviation see* **Bart.**

bubble *noun* a thin ball of liquid blown out with air. – *verb* to rise in bubbles. – *adjective* **bubbly.**

buccaneer *noun* (*hist*) pirate. – *adjective* **buccaneering** like a pirate.

buck *noun* the male of the deer, goat, hare and rabbit; (*US coll*) a dollar. – *verb* (of a horse *etc*) to attempt to throw a rider by rapid jumps into the air.

bucket *noun* a container for water *etc*.

buckle *noun* a clip (of metal *etc*) for fastening straps or belts. – *verb* to fasten with a buckle. – *noun* **buckler** a small shield.

buckshot *noun* large lead shot fired from a shotgun.

bud *noun* the first shoot of a tree or plant. – *verb* to produce buds. – *adjective* **budding** showing signs of becoming: *a budding author.*

Buddhism *noun* a religion whose followers worship Buddha. – *noun, adj* **Buddhist.**

budge *verb* to move slightly, stir.

budgerigar *noun* a kind of small parrot often kept as a pet.

budget *noun* the plan for a government's spending made each year by parliament; anyone's plan of their future spending. – *verb* to allow for in a budget.

budgie *noun* short for **budgerigar**.

buff *noun* a light yellowish brown colour. – *verb* to polish.

buffalo *noun* (*plural* **buffaloes**) a large kind of ox, *esp* one used in Asia to draw loads; (*US*) the American bison.

buffer *noun* something which lessens the force of a blow or collision.

buffet[1] *buf'it, noun* a slap or a blow. – *verb* to strike, knock about.

buffet[2] *boof'ā, noun* a counter or café where food and drink may be bought; a (cold) meal set out on tables for people to serve themselves.

buffoon *noun* a clown, fool. – *noun* **buffoonery.**

bug *noun* a name for any small insect, *esp* one which is disliked; a disease germ: *a tummy bug*; a tiny device which may be concealed in a room to record conversations. – *verb* (*past tense* **bugged**) to put such a device in (a room *etc*). – *noun* **bugbear** a thing that frightens or annoys.

buggy *noun* (*plural* **buggies**) a child's push-chair.

bugle *noun* a type of small trumpet. – *noun* **bugler** a person who plays the bugle.

build *verb* (*past tense* **built**) to put together the parts of anything. – *noun* (of persons) physical type: *a man of heavy build*. – *noun* **builder.** – *noun* **building** the act or trade of building (houses *etc*); a house or other built dwelling *etc*. – *noun* **building society** an institution like a bank which accepts investments and whose main business is to lend people money to buy a house. – *adjective* **built-up** (of an area *etc*) containing houses and other buildings.

bulb *noun* the rounded part of the stem of certain plants (*eg* hyacinth, onion) which store their food; a glass globe surrounding the element of an electric light. – *adjective* **bulbous** bulb-shaped.

bulge *noun* a swelling; a (temporary) noticeable increase. – *verb* to swell out.

bulk *noun* (large) size; the greater part. – *noun* **bulkhead** a wall in the inside of a ship, meant to keep out water in a collision. – *adjective* **bulky** taking up much room.

bull *noun* the male of animals of the ox family, also of the whale, elephant *etc*. – *noun* **bulldog** a breed of strong, fierce-looking dog. – *verb* **bulldoze** to use a bulldozer on; to force. – *noun* **bulldozer** a machine for levelling land and clearing away obstacles. – *noun*

bullfight (in Spain *etc*) a public entertainment in which a bull is angered and *usu* finally killed. – *noun* **bullfinch** a small pink-breasted bird. – *noun* **bullfrog** a type of large frog. – *noun* **bullring** the arena in which bullfights take place. – *noun* **bull's-eye** the mark in the middle of a target; a striped sweet.

bullet *noun* the piece of metal fired from a gun. – *adjective* **bullet-proof** not able to be pierced by bullets.

bulletin *noun* a report (as of a person's health, of news *etc*).

bullion *noun* gold or silver in the form of bars *etc*.

bullock *noun* a young bull.

bully *noun* (*plural* **bullies**) one who unfairly uses his size and strength to hurt or frighten weaker persons. – *verb* to act like a bully. – *verb* **bully-off** (formerly in hockey *etc*) to put the ball in play (*see* **pass-back**).

bulrush *noun* (*plural* **bulrushes**) a type of large strong reed which grows on wet land or in water.

bulwark *bool'wàrk, noun* anything strong for defence (such as a wall).

bumble-bee *noun* a type of large bee.

bump *verb* to strike heavily; to knock by accident. – *noun* the sound of a heavy blow; the act of striking (by accident); a raised lump. – *noun* **bumper** a bar round the front and back of a car's body to protect it from damage. – *adjective* large: *a bumper crop*.

bumpkin *noun* a clumsy, awkward, country person.

bumptious *adjective* self-important.

bun *noun* a kind of cake; hair wound into a rounded mass.

bunch *noun* (*plural* **bunches**) a number of things tied together or growing together. – *verb* to crowd together.

bundle *noun* a number of things loosely bound together. – *verb* to tie in a bundle; to push roughly: *He bundled the children into the car.*

bung *noun* the stopper of the hole in a barrel, bottle *etc*. – *verb* to stop up with a bung. – *noun* **bung-hole**.

bungalow *noun* a house of one storey, *usu* standing by itself.

bungle *verb* to do a thing badly or clumsily. – Also *noun*.

bunion *noun* a lump or swelling on the joint of the big toe.

bunk *noun* a narrow bed *esp* in a ship's cabin. – *noun* **bunkbed** one of a pair of narrow beds one above the other. – *noun* **bunker** a large box for keeping coal; a sandpit on a golf course; an underground shelter.

bunkum *noun* nonsense.

bunny *noun* (*plural* **bunnies**) a child's name for a rabbit.

bunting *noun* a thin cloth used for making flags; flags; a type of bird of the finch family.

buoy *boy, noun* a floating mark which acts as a guide or as a warning for ships; something which acts as a float (*eg* a lifebuoy). – *noun* **buoyancy** ability to float, lightness; ability to recover quickly. – *adjective* **buoyant** light cheerful.

bur(r) *noun* the prickly seedcase or head of certain plants.

burden *noun* a load; something difficult to bear (*eg* poverty, sorrow); (*old*) the chorus of a song. – *adjective* **burdensome**.

bureau *noun* (*plural* **bureaux** or **bureaus**) a writing table; an office.

bureaucracy *bū-rok'ra-si, noun* government by officials. – *noun* **bureaucrat** an administrative official. – *adjective* **bureaucratic**.

burgh *noun* (in Scotland) a borough.

burglar *noun* a person who breaks into a house to steal. – *noun* **burglary** (*plural* **burglaries**).

burial *see* **bury**.

burlesque *noun* a piece of writing, acting *etc*, making fun of somebody.

burly *adjective* broad and strong.

burn *verb* (*past tense* **burnt** or **burned**) to set fire to; to be on fire, or scorching; to injure by burning. – *noun* a hurt or mark caused by fire; (in Scotland) a small stream. – *noun* **burner** the part of a lamp or gas-jet from which the flame rises.

burnish *verb* to polish. – Also *noun*.

burnt *see* **burn**.

burrow *noun* a hole or passage in the ground dug by certain animals for shelter. – *verb* to make a passage beneath the ground.

burst *verb* to break suddenly (after increased pressure); to move, speak *etc* suddenly or violently. – Also *noun*.

bury *verb* (*past tense* **buried**) to put beneath the earth (*esp* a dead body); to cover, hide. – *noun* **burial.**

bus *noun* (*plural* **buses**) a large (public) road vehicle for carrying many passengers. – *noun* **bus stop** an official stopping place for buses.

busby *noun* (*plural* **busbies**) a tall, fur hat worn by certain soldiers.

bush *noun* (*plural* **bushes**) a growing thing between a plant and a tree in size; wild, unfarmed country (*esp* in Africa *etc*). – *noun* **bush-baby** a type of small lemur. – *noun* **bush-ranger** in Australia, an outlaw living in the wilds. – *noun* **bush telegraph** the quick passing-on of news from person to person. – *adjective* **bushy** full of bushes; like a bush; (of hair *etc*) thick.

business *noun* (*plural* **businesses**) one's work or job; trade; commerce: *Business is good just now;* something that concerns a person: *Her behaviour is none of my business.* – *adjective* **businesslike** practical, methodical, alert and prompt. – *noun* **businessman** (*masculine*), **businesswoman** (*feminine*) a person who works in commerce.

busk *verb* to play or sing in the street *etc* for money. – *noun* **busker.**

bust *noun* a work of art (*usu* a sculpture) showing only the head and shoulders of the person; a woman's breasts.

bustard *noun* a kind of large, swift-running bird similar to a turkey.

bustle *verb* to busy oneself noisily. – *noun* noisy activity, fuss; a stuffed pad once worn by ladies under the skirt of their dress.

busy *adjective* (*comparative* busier, *superlative* **busiest**) having a lot to do. – *adverb* **busily.** – *noun* **busybody** a person too concerned with others' affairs. – **busy oneself with** to occupy oneself with.

but *conjunction* showing a contrast between two ideas *etc*: *John was there but Peter was not. Her eyes are not brown but blue;* except that, without that: *It never rains but it pours.* – *preposition* except, with the exception of: *No one but John had any money. The next road but one is where we turn left (ie the second road).* – *adverb* only: *We can but hope.* – **but for** were it not for: *But for your help we would have been late.*

butch *adjective* (of a woman) looking, and often acting aggressively like a man.

butcher *noun* a person whose work is to (kill animals for food and) sell meat. – *verb* to kill cruelly. – *noun* **butchery** great or cruel slaughter.

butler *noun* the chief manservant in a household who looks after the wines *etc*, and who serves them.

butt *noun* a large cask, a barrel; a person of whom others make fun; the thick heavy end of a rifle *etc*; the end of a finished cigarette or cigar; a push with the head. – *verb* to strike with the head. – **butt in** to interrupt or interfere.

butter *noun* a fatty food made by churning cream. – *verb* to spread over with butter. – *noun* **buttercup** a plant with a cup-like yellow flower. – *noun* **buttermilk** the milk that is left after butter has been made. – *noun* **butterscotch** a kind of hard toffee made with butter.

butterfly *noun* (*plural* **butterflies**) a kind of insect with large (*usu* coloured) wings.

buttocks *noun plural* the two fleshy parts of the body on which one sits, the rump.

button *noun* a knob or disc of metal, plastic *etc* used to fasten clothing; a knob pressed to work an electrical device (*eg* a doorbell). – *verb* to fasten by means of buttons. – *noun* **buttonhole** a hole through which a button is passed. – *verb* to catch the attention of (someone) and force (them) to listen.

buttress *noun* (*plural* **buttresses**) a support (as on the outside of a wall). – *verb* to support, as by a buttress.

buxom *adjective* plump and pretty.

buy *verb* (*past tense* **bought**) to get by giving money for. – *noun* **buyer.**

buzz *verb* to make a humming noise like bees; (of aircraft) to fly close to. – Also *noun*. – *noun* **buzzer** a device which makes a buzzing noise as a signal. – *noun* **buzz word** a word well-established in a particular jargon, its use suggesting up-to-date specialized knowledge.

buzzard *noun* a type of large bird of prey.

by *adverb* near: *A crowd stood by, watching;* past: *A dog trotted by;* aside: *money put by for an emergency.* – *preposition* next to, near: *standing by the door;* past: *going by the house;* through, along, across: *We came by the main road;* showing person *etc* who does something: *written by him;*

(of time) not after: *Do it by four o'clock*; during the (time of): *by day*; by means of: *by train*; to the extent of: *taller by a head*; used to express measurements, compass directions *etc*: *We built on a room 6 metres by 4 metres. Sail North by East*; in the quantity of: *We sell potatoes by the pound. They're paid by the week*. – noun **by-election** an election for parliament during a parliamentary session. – *adjective* **bygone** past. – *noun plural* **bygones** old grievances or events that are or should be forgotten. – *noun* **by-law** or **bye-law** a local (not a national) law. – noun **bypass** a road built round a town *etc* so that traffic need not pass through it. – *noun* **bypath** or **byroad** or **byway** a side road. – *noun* **by-product** something useful obtained during the manufacture of something else. – *noun* **bystander** a person who stands watching something. – *noun* **byword** a common saying; someone or something well-known for some special quality.

bye *noun* in cricket, a ball bowled past the wicket; a run made from this.

C

°C *abbreviation* degree(s) Celsius or centigrade.

c or **ca** *abbreviation* about (*circa* [L])

cab *noun* a taxi; (*hist*) a hired carriage.

cabaret *kab'ä r-ä, noun* a restaurant with variety acts; an entertainment given in such a restaurant.

cabbage *noun* a type of vegetable, the leaves of which are eaten.

cabin *noun* a hut; a small room, *esp* in a ship.

cabinet *noun* a cupboard which has shelves and doors; a similar container for storage *etc*; a wooden case with drawers; a selected number of government ministers who decide on policy. – *noun* **cabinet-maker** a maker of fine furniture.

cable *noun* a strong rope or thick metal line; a line of covered telegraph wires laid under the sea or underground; a telegram sent by such a line; an underground wire. – *verb* to telegraph by cable. – *noun* **cable television** the transmission of television programmes to individual subscribers by cable.

cacao *noun* a tree from whose seeds cocoa and chocolate are made.

cache *kash, noun* a store or hiding place of treasure, arms *etc*; things hidden.

cackle *noun* the sound made by a hen or goose; a laugh which sounds like this.

cacophony *noun* (*plural* **cacophonies**) an unpleasant noise. – *adjective* **cacophonous.**

cactus *noun* (*plural* **cactuses** or **cacti**) a type of prickly plant.

CAD *abbreviation* computer-aided design.

cad *noun* a mean, despicable person.

cadaverous *adjective* corpse-like, very pale and thin.

caddie *noun* a golfer's assistant (and adviser) who carries his clubs.

caddy *noun* (*plural* **caddies**) a box in which tea is kept.

cadence *noun* the fall of the voice (as at the end of a sentence); a group of chords which ends a piece of music.

cadet *noun* a youth training to be an officer in the armed forces or to be a police officer; a schoolboy who takes military training.

cadge *verb* to get by begging; to beg. – *noun* **cadger.**

café *noun* a small restaurant where coffee, tea, snacks *etc* are served.

cafeteria *noun* a self-service restaurant.

caffeine *noun* a drug found in coffee and tea *etc*.

caftan *noun* a kind of long-sleeved garment reaching to the ankles.

cage *noun* a box made of metal *etc* rods in which birds or animals are enclosed; in a mine, a lift used by the miners. – *verb* to close up in a cage.

cagey or **cagy** *adjective* unwilling to speak freely, wary. – *noun* **caginess.**

cagoule *noun* a lightweight anorak.

cairn *noun* a heap of stones, *esp* one set up over a grave, or as a mark on a mountain-top; a breed of small terrier. – *noun* **cairngorm** a brown or yellow variety of quartz, used for brooches *etc*.

cajole *verb* to coax by flattery. – *noun* **cajolery.**

cake *noun* a baked piece of dough *etc*, *usu* sweetened; anything pressed into a lump: *a cake of soap*. – *verb* to form into a mass, harden. – **have one's cake and eat it** to enjoy both of two alternative things.

calamine *noun* a pink powder containing a zinc salt, used in lotion or ointment to soothe skin.

calamity *noun* (*plural* **calamities**) a great disaster, a misfortune. – *adjective* **calamitous.**

calcium *noun* an element, a metal which forms the chief part of lime.

calculate *verb* to count, work out by mathematics; to think out in an exact way. – *adjective* **calculable** able to be counted or measured. – *adjective* **calculating** thinking selfishly. – *noun* **calculation** a mathematical reckoning, a sum. – *noun* **calculator** a machine which makes mathematical calculations. – *noun* **calculus** a mathematical system of calculation.

calendar *noun* a table or list showing the year divided into months, weeks and days.

calf *noun* (*plural* **calves**) the young of cattle *etc*; its skin cured as leather; the back of the lower part of a person's leg.

calibrate *verb* to mark the scale on (a measuring instrument); to check or adjust the scale of (a measuring instrument).

calibre or (*US*) **caliber** *noun* measurement across the opening of tube or gun; (of a person) quality of character, ability.

calico *noun* a kind of cotton cloth. – Also *adjective*.

call *verb* to cry aloud; to name; to summon; to make a short visit; to telephone. – Also *noun*. – *noun* **calling** someone's trade or job.

calligraphy *noun* (beautiful) handwriting. – *noun* **calligrapher.** – *adjective* **calligraphic.**

callipers or **calipers** *noun plural* an instrument like compasses, used for measuring thicknesses of tubes *etc*; (*singular*) a splint to support the leg, made of two metal rods.

callous *adjective* cruel, hardhearted. – *noun* **callousness.**

callow *adjective* not mature, inexperienced.

callus *noun* (*plural* **calluses**) a hard thickening of the skin.

calm *adjective* still or quiet; not anxious or flustered. – *noun* absence of wind; quietness, peacefulness. – *verb* to make peaceful. – *noun* **calmness.**

calorie *noun* a measure of heat; a measure of the energy-giving value of food. – *noun* **calorimeter** an instrument for measuring heat.

calumny (*plural* **calumnies**) *noun* a false accusation or lie about a person.

calve *verb* to give birth to a calf.

calypso *noun* (*plural* **calypsos**) a West Indian folksong made up as the singer goes along.

calyx *kā'liks*, *noun* (*plural* **calyces** or **calyxes**) the outer covering or cup of a flower.

CAM *abbreviation* computer-aided manufacturing.

camber *noun* a slight curve or bulge on a road *etc* making the middle higher than the sides.

camcorder *noun* a video camera and video recorder combined in one hand-held unit.

came *see* **come.**

camel *noun* a type of animal of Asia and Africa with a humped back, used for both carrying and riding.

cameo *noun* (*plural* **cameos**) a gem or other stone on which a carved figure or design stands out.

camera *noun* an instrument for taking photographs. – **in camera** in private.

camomile *noun* a type of plant, or its dried flowers, used in medicine.

camouflage *kam'oo-fläzh*, *noun* the disguising of the appearance of (something) so that it is not easily seen against its background; such an appearance occurring naturally (in animals *etc*), protective colouring. – Also *verb*.

camp *noun* a group of tents, huts *etc* in which people (holidaymakers, explorers *etc*) live for a short time; fixed military quarters or settlement. – *verb* to pitch tents; to set up a temporary home. – *noun* **camp bed** a small portable folding bed. – *noun* **campsite** (official) place for pitching tents.

campaign *noun* organized action in support of a cause or movement; a war or part of a war. – *verb* to organize support; to serve in a military campaign.

campanology *noun* the study or art of bell-ringing.

campus *noun* (*plural* **campuses**) the grounds (often including the buildings) of a university, college *etc*.

can¹ *verb* (*past tense* **could**) *usu* used with another verb to express the ability to do something: *He can play the guitar*; used to express permission given: *You can go swimming tomorrow*. – **can but** can only: *We can but wait*.

can² *noun* a tin container for liquids, preserved food *etc*. – *verb* to put (food) into a closed tin to keep it from going bad. – *noun* **canned music** previously recorded music: *Many supermarkets play canned music*. – *noun* **cannery** (*plural* **canneries**) a place where food is canned.

canal *noun* a waterway for boats, made by man.

canary *noun* (*plural* **canaries**) a type of yellow-feathered songbird kept as a pet.

canasta *noun* a kind of card-game.

cancan *noun* a high-kicking dance.

cancel *verb* (*past tense* **cancelled**) to put off permanently, call off: *cancel one's holiday plans*; to cross out by crossing with lines. – **cancel out** to make ineffective by balancing each other: *His sins and good deeds cancel one another out*.

cancer *noun* a malignant growth. – *adjective* **cancerous**.

candid *adjective* saying just what one thinks, frank. – *noun* **candour**.

candidate *noun* a person who enters for an examination or competition for a job, prize *etc*. – *noun* **candidacy**. – *noun* **candidature**.

candied *see* **candy**.

candle *noun* a stick of wax, containing a wick, used for giving light. – *noun*

candle-power the amount of light given by one candle. – *noun* **candlestick** a holder for a candle. – *noun* **candle-wick** a cotton tufted material, used for bedspreads *etc*.

candour *see* **candid**.

candy *noun* sugar crystallized by boiling; (*US*) (*plural* **candies**) a sweet. – *verb* to preserve in sugar, to coat with sugar. – *adjective* **candied**.

cane *noun* the stem of certain kinds of plant (such as bamboo and sugar cane); a walking stick. – *verb* to beat with a cane. – *noun* **cane sugar** sugar got from the sugar cane. – *noun* **caning** a thrashing with a cane.

canine *adjective* of dogs. – *noun* **canine (tooth)** any of the four sharp-pointed teeth, one on each side of the upper and lower jaw.

canister *noun* a box or case, *usu* of tin, for holding tea *etc*.

canker *noun* a spreading sore; a disease in trees, plants *etc*.

cannabis *noun* a narcotic drug got from the hemp plant.

cannibal *noun* a person who eats human flesh; an animal that eats its own kind. – *noun* **cannibalism**.

cannon *noun* a large, *usu* mounted gun. – *noun* **cannonball** a solid metal ball to be shot from a cannon – **cannon into** to run into, collide with.

cannot *verb* *usu* used with another verb to express the inability to do something: *I cannot understand this*; used to refuse permission: *I've told him he cannot go today*.

canny *adjective* wise, shrewd, cautious. – *noun* **canniness**.

canoe *noun* a light narrow boat driven by paddles.

canon *noun* a law or rule; a standard to judge by; a clergyman connected with a cathedral; a list of saints. – *verb* **canonize** to put someone on the list of saints.

cañon *see* **canyon**.

canopy *noun* (*plural* **canopies**) a covering over a throne, bed, pulpit *etc*.

cant *noun* words understood by people in a particular occupation *etc* only: *thieves' cant*; talk which is not sincere; a slope; a tilted position. – *verb* to tilt something from a level position.

can't *verb* short for **cannot**.

cantankerous *adjective* crotchety, bad-tempered, quarrelsome.

cantata *noun* a short piece of music for a choir of singers.

canteen *noun* a place where drink and food may be bought and eaten (*usu* in some place of work); a water-flask; a case containing cutlery.

canter *verb* to move at an easy gallop. – Also *noun*.

cantilever *noun* a large projecting bracket used in building for holding up heavy parts like balconies and stairs. – *noun* **cantilever bridge** a bridge made of a row of upright piers with cantilevers extending to meet one another.

canton *noun* one of the Swiss federal states.

canvas *noun* (*plural* **canvases**) a coarse, strong cloth used for sails, tents *etc* and for painting on.

canvass *verb* to go round asking for votes, money *etc*.

canyon or **cañon** *noun* a deep, steep-sided valley containing a river or stream.

cap *noun* a soft hat *usu* with a peak; a cover or top (as of a bottle, pen *etc*); a contraceptive diaphragm. – *verb* (*past tense* **capped**) to put a cap on; to give a university degree to; to choose (a player) for a national sports team (*esp* football or cricket); to do better than, improve on: *He capped my story with a funnier one.*

capable *adjective* able to cope with difficulties without help; (often with **of**) able or likely (to): *capable of doing great things*. – *noun* **capability** (*plural* **capabilities**).

capacious *adjective* roomy, wide.

capacitor *noun* an apparatus for collecting and storing electricity.

capacity *noun* (*plural* **capacities**) power of understanding; ability to do a thing; the amount that something can hold; position: *in his capacity as leader*. – **to capacity** to the greatest extent possible: *The tank is filled to capacity. We are working to capacity.*

cape *noun* a covering for the shoulders; a point of land running into the sea.

caper *verb* to leap, dance about. – *noun* a leap; (*coll*) a prank or adventure; the

flower-bud of a shrub which, when pickled, is used in sauces.

capercaillie or **capercailzie** *noun* a kind of large grouse.

capillary *adjective* very fine, like a hair. – *noun* (*plural* **capillaries**) a very fine tube; a tiny blood vessel.

capital *adjective* chief, most important; involving death; excellent. – *noun* the chief city (of a country); a large letter (as that which begins a sentence); money for carrying on a business; money invested, accumulated wealth. – *noun* **capitalism** a system in which the country's wealth is owned by individuals, not by the State. – *noun* **capitalist** a person who supports or practises capitalism. – *verb* **capitalize** to write in capitals; to turn to one's advantage. – *noun* **capital punishment** punishment by death. – **make capital out of** to turn to one's advantage.

capitulate *verb* to give in (*eg* to an enemy). – *noun* **capitulation**.

capon *noun* a young castrated fattened cock bred for food.

caprice *kà-prēs',* *noun* a sudden, impulsive change of mind or mood. – *adjective* **capricious** full of caprice, apt to change one's mind often.

capsize *verb* to upset, to overturn.

capstan *noun* on a ship or quay, a machine turned by spokes or by a steam engine, used for winding or hauling.

capsule *noun* the case containing the seeds of a plant; a small gelatine case for powdered medicine; a space capsule.

Capt. *abbreviation* captain.

captain *noun* the commander of a company of soldiers, a ship or an aircraft; the leader of a team, club *etc*. – *verb* to lead. – *noun* **captaincy** (*plural* **captaincies**) the rank of a captain.

caption *noun* a heading (for a newspaper article, photograph *etc*).

captious *adjective* ready to find fault.

captivate *verb* to charm, fascinate.

captive *noun* a prisoner. – *adjective* taken or kept as a prisoner; not able to get away: *a captive audience*. – *noun* **captivity** the state of being a prisoner. – *noun* **captor** a person who takes a prisoner. – *verb* **capture** to take by force; to get hold of, seize: *capture the imagination.* – *noun* the act of capturing; the thing captured.

car *noun* a motor-car; (*esp US*) a carriage of a train. – *noun* **car park** a place where motor-cars *etc* may be left for a time.

carafe *noun* a bottle for serving wine, water *etc*.

caramel *noun* sugar melted and browned; a kind of sweet, made of sugar and butter.

carat *noun* a measure of the purity of gold; a measure of the weight of gems.

caravan *noun* a house on wheels drawn originally by horse, now *usu* by car; a number of travellers *etc* crossing the desert together. – *noun* **caravanserai** an inn where desert caravans stop.

caraway *noun* a type of plant whose spicy seeds are used to flavour cakes *etc*.

carbine *noun* a short light musket.

carbohydrate *noun* a compound of carbon, hydrogen and oxygen, such as sugar, starch *etc*.

carbon *noun* an element of which charcoal is one form. – *noun* **carbon copy** a copy of a piece of typing *etc* made by using carbon paper; an exact copy. – *noun* **carbon dioxide** a gas present in the air and breathed out by humans and animals. – *adjective* **carbonic** (made) of carbon. – *adjective* **carboniferous** producing or containing coal or carbon. – *noun* **carbon monoxide** a poisonous gas with no smell. – *noun* **carbon paper** a paper coated with black ink for making copies in typing *etc*.

carbuncle *noun* a type of fiery-red precious stone; an inflamed swelling under the skin.

carburettor or **carburetter** or (*US*) **carburetor** *noun* the part of a motor-car engine which changes the petrol into vapour.

carcass or **carcase** *noun* the dead body (of an animal).

carcinogen *kär sin'ō-jen, noun* a substance that encourages the growth of cancer. – *adjective* **carcinogenic** causing cancer.

carcinoma *kär-sin-ō'mà, noun* (*plural* **carcinomas** or **carcinomata**) a cancer.

card *noun* (a piece of) pasteboard or very thick paper; a tool for combing wool *etc*; (*plural*) any of the many types of games played with a pack of special cards. – *verb* to comb wool *etc*. – *noun* **cardboard** stiff pasteboard.

cardiac *adjective* of the heart: *cardiac failure*.

cardigan *noun* a knitted woollen jacket.

cardinal *adjective* principal, important. – *noun* a person of high rank in the Roman Catholic Church. – *noun plural* **cardinal numbers** numbers telling how many (1, 2, 3 *etc*).

care *noun* close attention; worry, anxiety; protection, keeping: *in my care.* – *verb* to be concerned or worried; (with **for**) to look after; to feel affection or liking (for). – *adjective* **carefree** having no worries. – *adjective* **careful** attentive, taking care. – *adjective* **careless** paying little attention, not taking care. – *noun* **carelessness**. – *noun* **caretaker** a person who looks after a building. – *adjective* in temporary charge: *a caretaker government.* – *adjective* **careworn** looking very worried, worn out by anxiety. – **care of** or **c/o** at the house of.

career *noun* one's life work, trade, profession; course, progress through life, headlong rush. – *verb* to move or run rapidly and wildly.

caress *verb* to touch gently and lovingly. – Also *noun* (*plural* **caresses**).

cargo *noun* (*plural* **cargoes**) a ship's load.

caribou *noun* the N. American reindeer.

caricature *noun* a picture of someone which exaggerates certain of their features. – *verb* to draw a caricature of. – *noun* **caricaturist**.

caries *noun* decay, *esp* of the teeth. – *adjective* **carious**.

carillon *kà-ril'yòn, noun* a set of bells on which tunes can be played; the tune played on these.

carmine *adjective, noun* (of) a bright red colour.

carnage *noun* slaughter, killing.

carnation *noun* a type of garden flower, often pink, red or white.

carnival *noun* a celebration with merriment, feasting *etc*.

carnivore *noun* a flesh-eating animal. – *adjective* **carnivorous**.

carol *noun* a song of joy or praise (*esp* one sung at Christmas).

carouse *verb* to take part in a drinking bout.

carousel noun (US) a merry-go-round; a rotating or moving conveyor, eg for luggage at an airport.

carp noun a freshwater fish found in ponds. – verb to find fault with small errors, complain about nothing.

carpenter noun a worker in wood, esp as used in buildings etc. – noun **carpentry** the trade of a carpenter.

carpet noun the woven covering of floors, stairs etc. – verb to cover with a carpet.

carriage noun the act or cost of carrying; a vehicle for carrying people; way of walking: *She has a dignified carriage.*

carrion noun rotting animal flesh.

carrot noun a type of vegetable whose long orange-coloured root is eaten.

carry verb (past tense **carried**) to pick up and take to another place; to contain and take to a destination: *cables carrying electricity*; to bear, have as a mark: *carry a scar*; (of a voice etc) to be able to be heard at a distance; to win, succeed: *carry the day*; to keep for sale: *carry cigarettes*. – noun **carrier** a person who carries goods; a machine or container for carrying; a person who passes on a disease. – noun **carrier pigeon** a pigeon which carries letters. – **carried away** overcome by one's feelings; **carry on** to continue (doing); **carry out** to bring to a successful finish.

cart noun a two-wheeled vehicle (drawn by a horse) used on farms for carrying loads; a small wheeled vehicle pushed by hand. – verb to carry (in a cart); to drag (off). – noun **carter** a person who drives a cart. – noun **cart-horse** a large, heavy horse, used for working. – noun **cartwheel** the wheel of a cart; a sideways somersault with hands touching the ground. – noun **cartwright** a maker of carts.

cartilage noun gristle, a strong elastic material in the bodies of humans and animals.

cartography noun the science of map-making.

carton noun a container made of cardboard, plastic etc.

cartoon noun a comic drawing with a comic caption; a (usu amusing) film made of a series of drawings of animals etc which gives an impression of their movement; a large drawing on paper, later to be copied in its final form. – noun **cartoonist**.

cartridge noun a case holding the powder and bullet fired by a gun; a spool of film or tape enclosed in a case; a tube of ink for loading a pen; the part of a record-player which holds the stylus.

carve verb to make or shape by cutting; to cut up (meat) into slices.

cascade noun a waterfall. – verb to fall like or in a waterfall.

case noun a container or outer covering; that which happens, an occurrence; statement of facts, argument; state of affairs, what is true; a trial in a law-court: *a murder case.*

casement noun a window-frame; a window that swings on hinges.

cash noun money in the form of coins and notes. – verb to turn into, or change for, money. – noun **cash card** a card issued by a bank etc that allows the holder to use a cash dispenser. – noun **cash dispenser** an automatic teller machine. – noun **cashier** a person who looks after the receiving and paying of money. – verb to dismiss (esp from the army or navy) in disgrace. – noun **cash register** a machine for holding money that records the amount put in. – **cash in on** to profit from (in terms of money or advantage).

cashew noun a type of kidney-shaped nut, or the large tropical tree that bears it.

cashmere noun fine soft goats' wool.

casino noun (plural **casinos**) a building in which gambling takes place.

cask noun a barrel (usu containing wine etc).

casket noun a small box (for holding jewels etc); (US) a coffin.

cassava noun a kind of tropical plant from whose roots tapioca is obtained.

casserole noun a covered dish in which food can be cooked and served; the food cooked in it.

cassette noun a holder for film, magnetic tape for recording sound etc; the magnetic tape itself.

cassock noun a long robe worn by priests.

cassowary noun (plural **cassowaries**) a type of large, flightless bird of Australia and New Guinea.

cast verb (past tense **cast**) to throw or fling (objects, light etc); to throw off, drop, shed; to shape (*esp* metal) in a mould; to choose (actors *etc*) for a play or film; to give a part to (an actor *etc*). – *noun* something shaped in a mould; the actors in a play; a small heap of earth thrown up by a worm; a type: *cast of mind*; a squint (in the eye). – *noun* **castaway** a deserted or shipwrecked person. – *noun* **cast iron** unpurified iron melted and moulded into shape. – *adjective* **cast down** depressed. – *adjective* **cast off** used by someone else, second-hand.

castanets *noun plural* hollow shells of ivory or hard wood, which are clicked together to accompany a dance.

caste *noun* a class or rank of people (*esp* in India).

castellated *adjective* having walls, towers *etc* like those of a castle.

caster *see* **castor.**

castigate *verb* to scold; to punish. – *noun* **castigation.**

castle *noun* a fortified house or fortress.

castor *noun* a small wheel (as on the legs of furniture). – Also **caster.** – *noun* **castor-oil** an oil made from a kind of palm, used as a medicine. – *noun* **castor sugar** or **caster sugar** very fine granulated sugar.

castrate *verb* to remove the testicles (of a male animal) and deprive of the ability to reproduce.

casual *adjective* happening by chance; not regular, temporary: *casual labour*; (of clothes) informal: *She wears casual clothes at the weekend*; not careful, unconcerned: *a casual attitude to work*. – *noun* **casualty** (*plural* **casualties**) a person who is killed or wounded; a casualty department. – *noun* **casualty department** a hospital department for treating accidental injuries *etc*.

cat *noun* a sharp-clawed furry animal kept as a pet; one of the cat family which includes lions, tigers *etc*. – *noun* **cat-burglar** a burglar who breaks into houses by climbing walls *etc*. – *noun* **cat flap** a small door set in a larger door to allow a cat entry and exit. – *noun* **catgut** cord made from the stomachs of sheep, used as strings for violins *etc*. – *noun* **cat litter** a granular absorbent material used to line a tray on which a cat may urinate and defecate. – *noun* **cat-o'-nine-tails** a whip with nine tails or lashes. – *noun* **cat's cradle** a children's

game with string. – *noun* **cat's-eye®** a small mirror fixed in the surface of a road to reflect light and so guide drivers at night.

cataclysm *noun* a great flood of water; a violent change.

catacomb *noun* an underground burial place.

catalogue *noun* a list of names, books, objects for sale *etc* set out in some order. – *verb* to list in order.

catalyst *noun* any substance which helps or prevents a chemical reaction without itself changing; anything that brings about a change.

catamaran *noun* a boat with two parallel hulls.

catapult *noun* a small forked stick with a length of elastic fixed to the two prongs, used for firing small stones *etc*; (*hist*) a weapon for throwing heavy stones in warfare.

cataract *noun* a waterfall; a disease of the outer eye.

catarrh *noun* inflammation of the lining of the nose and throat causing a discharge; the discharge caused.

catastrophe *kà t-as'trò-fi*, *noun* a sudden disaster. – *adjective* **catastrophic.**

catch *verb* (*past tense* **caught**) to take hold of, capture; to take (a disease): *catch a cold*; to be in time for: *catch the train*; to surprise (in an act): *catch him stealing*. – *noun* a haul (of fish); something one is lucky to have got or won; a hidden flaw or disadvantage; something which fastens: *a window-catch*. – *adjective* **catching** infectious, liable to be caught. – *noun* **catchment area** an area from which a river or a reservoir draws its water supply; an area from which the pupils in a school are drawn. – *noun* **catch-phrase** or **catchword** phrase or word which is popular for a while. – *adjective* **catchy** (of a tune) not easily forgotten. – **catch on** to become popular; **catch up on** to draw level with, overtake, to get up-to-date with (work *etc*).

catechize *verb* to ask many questions. – *noun* **catechism** a book (*esp* a religious one) which teaches by asking questions and giving the answers; a series of searching questions.

category *noun* (*plural* **categories**) a class or division of things (or people) of the same kind. – adjective **categorical** allowing of no doubt or argument. – adverb **categorically.**

cater verb to provide food; to supply what is required: *They cater for all tastes.* – noun **caterer.** – noun **catering.**

caterpillar noun the larva of an insect that feeds upon the leaves of plants. – adjective moving on endless metal belts: *a caterpillar tractor*.

caterwaul verb to howl or yell like a cat. – noun **caterwauling.**

catgut see **cat.**

cathedral noun the church of a bishop; the chief church in the district ruled by a bishop.

catherine-wheel noun a firework which turns like a wheel when burning.

cathode ray tube noun a device in which a narrow beam of electrons strikes against a screen, as a television set.

catholic adjective wide, comprehensive: *catholic taste in books.* – adjective **Catholic** (short for **Roman Catholic**) of the Roman Catholic Church.

catkin noun a tuft or spike of small flowers on certain trees, *esp* the willow and hazel.

cattle noun plural animals that eat grass, *esp* oxen, bulls and cows.

caught see **catch.**

cauldron noun a large pan.

cauliflower noun a kind of cabbage, of which one eats the white flower-head.

cause noun that which makes something happen; a reason (for action): *cause for complaint*; an aim for which a group or person works: *the cause of peace.* – verb to make happen.

causeway noun a raised road over wet ground or shallow water.

caustic adjective burning, corroding; bitter, severe: *caustic wit.*

cauterize verb to burn away flesh with a caustic substance or a hot iron in order to make a sore heal cleanly.

caution noun a warning; carefulness (owing to presence of some danger). – verb to warn. – adjective **cautionary** giving a warning. – adjective **cautious** careful, showing caution.

cavalcade noun a procession on horseback, in cars *etc*.

cavalier noun (hist) a supporter of the king in the Civil War of the 17th century. – adjective offhand: *in a cavalier fashion*.

cavalry noun horse soldiers.

cave noun a hollow place in the earth or in rock. – noun **caveman** prehistoric man who lived in caves. – **cave in** (to cause) to fall or collapse inwards.

cavern noun a deep hollow place in the earth. – adjective **cavernous** huge and hollow; full of caverns.

caviare or **caviar** noun the pickled eggs of the sturgeon.

cavil verb (past tense **cavilled**) to make objections over small, unimportant details.

cavity noun (plural **cavities**) hollow place, a hole.

cavort verb to dance or leap around.

caw verb to call like a crow. – Also noun.

cayenne noun a type of very hot red pepper.

cayman noun (plural **caymans**) any of various kinds of alligator, *esp* those of S. America.

CB abbreviation Companion of the Order of the Bath.

CBE abbreviation Companion of the Order of the British Empire.

CBI abbreviation Confederation of British Industry.

cc abbreviation cubic centimetre(s).

CD abbreviation compact disc.

cease verb to come or bring to an end. – adjective **ceaseless** without stopping.

cedar noun a type of large evergreen tree with a hard sweet-smelling wood.

cede verb to yield or give up (to another).

ceiling noun the inner roof of a room; the upper limit.

celandine noun a type of small yellow wild flower.

celebrate verb to feast and make merry in honour of a marriage, birthday or other happy event. – adjective **celebrated** famous. – noun **celebration.** – noun **celebrity** (plural **celebrities**) a famous person; fame.

celery noun a type of vegetable the stalks of which are eaten.

celestial adjective of the sky: *Stars are celestial bodies*; heavenly.

celibacy *noun* the state of not being married. – *adjective* **celibate** abstaining from sexual intercourse.

cell *noun* a small room in a prison, monastery *etc*; the smallest, fundamental part of living things; the part of an electric battery containing electrodes. – *noun* **cellphone** a pocket telephone for use in a cellular radio system based on a network of transmitters. – *adjective* **cellular** made of or having cells or small hollow spaces.

cellar *noun* an underground room, *esp* one for storing coal, wine *etc*.

cello *noun* (short for **violoncello**) a type of large musical, stringed instrument similar in shape to a violin. – *noun* **cellist** a person who plays the cello.

cellophane® *noun* a kind of transparent wrapping material.

cellular *see* **cell**.

celluloid *noun* a very hard elastic substance used for making film *etc*.

cellulose *noun* a substance found in plants and wood used to make paper, textiles *etc*.

Celsius *sel'si-ŭs, adjective* of a temperature scale of a hundred degrees, on which water freezes at 0° and boils at 100°; as measured on this scale: *10° Celsius*.

cement *noun* the mixture of clay and lime used to stick bricks together in buildings; anything that makes two things stick together. – *verb* to put together with cement; to join firmly.

cemetery *noun* (*plural* **cemeteries**) a place where the dead are buried.

cenotaph *noun* a monument to a person or persons buried elsewhere.

censor *noun* a person whose job is to examine books, films *etc* with power to delete any of the contents. – *adjective* **censorious** fault-finding.

censure *noun* blame, expression of disapproval. – *verb* to blame, criticize.

census *noun* (*plural* **censuses**) a counting of the people in a country.

cent *noun* a coin which is the hundredth part of a larger coin (*eg* of a dollar).

centaur *noun* (*myth*) a monster, half man and half horse.

centenary *noun* (*plural* **centenaries**) a hundredth birthday; the hundredth year since an event took place. – *noun*

centenarian a person a hundred or more years old. – *adjective* **centennial** having lasted a hundred years; happening every hundred years.

centigrade *adjective* of a temperature scale, having a hundred degrees; as measured on this scale: *5° centigrade*; Celsius.

centigramme *noun* a hundredth part of a gramme.

centilitre *noun* a hundredth part of a litre.

centimetre *noun* a hundredth part of a metre.

centipede *noun* a small crawling creature with many legs.

centre or (*US*) **center** *noun* the middle point or part; a place built or used for some special activity or service: *sports centre*. – *adjective* **central** belonging to the centre; chief. – *noun* **central heating** heating of a building by water, steam or air from a central point. – *verb* **centralize** to group in a single place: to bring (government authority) under one central control. – *noun* **central locking** in a vehicle, the automatic locking of all the doors by the locking of the driver's door.

centrifugal *adjective* moving away from the centre.

centripetal *adjective* moving towards the centre.

centurion *noun* (*hist*) a commander of 100 Roman soldiers.

century *noun* (*plural* **centuries**) a hundred years; a hundred in number (such as runs in cricket).

ceramic *adjective* of (the making of) pottery. – *noun* something made of pottery; (*plural*) the art of pottery.

cereal *noun* grain used as food; a (breakfast) food prepared from grain.

cerebral *adjective* of the brain.

ceremony *noun* (*plural* **ceremonies**) the formal acts and solemn show or display that go with an important event. *the marriage ceremony*. – *adjective* **ceremonial** with or of ceremony. – *adjective* **ceremonious** full of ceremony.

cerise *sĕr-ēz', adjective, noun* (of) the colour of cherries, red.

certain *adjective* sure; not to be doubted; fixed, settled; some or one, not definitely named: *The tour bus will stop at* *certain places. I know of a certain shop that stocks what you need.* – adverb **certainly**. – noun **certainty**.

certificate noun a written or printed statement that something has happened or been done: *birth certificate*. – verb **certify** (past tense **certified**) to put down in writing as an official promise, statement etc.

cervix noun the neck of the womb. – noun **cervical smear** the collection of a sample of cells from the cervix, and the examination of these cells under a microscope as a test for early cancer.

cessation noun a ceasing or stopping, ending.

cesspool noun a pool or tank in which liquid waste or sewage is collected.

cf abbreviation compare.

CFC abbreviation chlorofluorocarbon.

chafe verb to make hot or sore by rubbing; to wear away by rubbing; to become annoyed.

chaff noun the husks of corn after threshing; anything of no great value; good-natured teasing. – verb to tease jokingly.

chaffinch noun (plural **chaffinches**) a type of small bird.

chagrin sha'grin, noun annoyance.

chain noun a number of links or rings (esp of metal) passing through one another; (plural) these used to tie prisoners' limbs, fetters; a number of connected things: *a mountain chain*; a group of things owned by one person or firm: *a chain of shops*; a number of atoms of an element joined together. – verb to fasten or imprison with a chain. – noun **chain letter** a letter, usu containing promises or threats, requesting the recipient to send a similar letter to a (sometimes specified) number of other people. – noun **chain mail** armour made of iron links. – noun **chain reaction** a (chemical) process in which each reaction in turn causes a similar reaction. – noun **chain saw** a power-driven saw, with teeth on an endless chain. – verb **chain-smoke** to smoke (eg cigarettes) continuously. – noun **chain-smoker**. – noun **chain-store** one of several shops under the same ownership.

chair noun a seat for one person with a back to it; an official position (as of the person in charge of a meeting or of a university professor). – noun **chairlift** a row of chairs on an endless cable for carrying people up mountains etc. – noun **chairman** or **chairwoman** or **chairperson** someone who presides at or is in charge of a meeting.

chalet noun a small wooden house often used by holidaymakers; a summer hut used by Swiss herdsmen in the Alps.

chalice noun a cup for wine, esp that used in church services.

chalk noun a type of limestone; a similar substance used for writing, drawing. – verb to mark with chalk. – adjective **chalky** of chalk; white, pale.

challenge verb to question another's right to do a thing etc; to ask (someone) to take part in a contest of some kind eg to settle a quarrel. – noun a call to a contest of any kind, esp to a duel. – noun **challenger**. – adjective **challenging** (of a problem etc) interesting but difficult.

chamber noun a room; the place where an assembly (such as parliament) meets, or where legal cases are heard by a judge; an enclosed space or cavity; the part of a gun that holds the cartridges. – noun **chamber music** music for a small group of players, suitable for performance in a room rather than in a large hall. – noun **chamberpot** or **chamber** a receptacle for urine etc, used (esp formerly) in the bedroom.

chamberlain noun a person appointed by a king or local authority to carry out certain duties.

chameleon kà-mēl'yòn, noun a type of small lizard able to change its colour to match its surroundings.

chamois sham'wà, noun a type of goat-like deer living in mountainous country; (also **shammy**) a soft kind of leather made from its skin.

champ verb to chew noisily. – **champing at the bit** impatient to act.

champagne sham-pān', noun a type of white sparkling wine.

champion noun a person, animal etc who has beaten all others in a competition; one who strongly supports a cause (such as freedom of speech etc). – verb to support the cause of (a person, freedom etc). – noun **championship** the act of championing; a contest to find a champion; the title of champion.

chance noun a risk, possibility; something unexpected, not planned; an opportunity. – verb to risk; to happen by accident. – *adjective* happening by accident. – *adjective* **chancy** risky. – **by chance** not arranged, unexpectedly; **chance upon** to meet or find unexpectedly.

chancel *noun* the part of a church near the altar.

chancellor *noun* a high government minister (*eg Chancellor of the Exchequer* who is in charge of government spending, *Lord Chancellor* the head of the English legal system); the head of a university.

chancery *noun* (in England) the Lord Chancellor's court.

chandelier *noun* a fixture hanging from the ceiling with branches for holding lights.

change *verb* to make or become different; to give up or leave one thing for another (*eg* one's job, house); to put on different clothes; to give or get (money of one kind) in exchange for (money of another kind). – *noun* the act of making or becoming something different; another set of clothing; money in the form of coins; money given back by a shopkeeper when a buyer gives more than the price of an article. – *adjective* **changeable** likely to change; often changing. – *noun* **changeling** a child secretly taken or left in place of another. – **change of life** the menopause.

channel *noun* the bed of a stream; a passage for ships; a narrow sea; a groove; a gutter; a band of frequencies for radio or television signals. – *verb* (*past tense* **channelled**) to direct into a particular course.

chant *verb* to sing; to recite in a singing manner. – Also *noun*.

chanty *see* **shanty**.

chaos *kā'os*, *noun* disorder, confusion. – *adjective* **chaotic**.

chap *noun* (*coll*) a man. – *adjective* **chapped** (of skin) cracked by cold or wet weather.

chapel *noun* a small part of a larger church; a small church for (private) worship.

chaperone *noun* an older lady who attends a younger one when she goes out in public. – *verb* to act as a chaperone to.

chaplain *noun* a clergyman with the army, navy, or air force or on a ship *etc*.

chapter *noun* a division of a book; (a meeting of) the clergy of a cathedral. – **chapter of accidents** a series of accidents.

char *verb* (*past tense* **charred**) to burn until black; to do odd jobs of housework, cleaning *etc*. – *noun* **charwoman** a woman hired to do housework for other people.

charabanc *noun* a long motor-coach with rows of seats.

character *noun* the nature and qualities of a person *etc*; the good points and bad points which make up a person's nature; self-control, firmness; a person noted for odd or strange ways; reputation; a person in a play, story, film *etc*. – *noun* **characteristic** a point or feature which is typical of a person *etc* and easily noticed. – *adjective* typical. – *verb* **characterize** to be typical of; to describe (as).

charade *noun* a word-guessing game, in which the syllables of a word and then the whole word are acted.

charcoal *noun* wood burnt black.

charge *verb* to accuse: *He was charged with murder*; to ask (a price); to attack; to load (a gun *etc*); to fill (with); to lay a task upon a person. – *noun* blame, accusation (for a crime); price, fee; an attack; the gunpowder in a shell or bullet; care: *The money was given into my charge*; someone looked after by another person. – *noun* **charger** a horse used in battle. – **in charge** in command or control; **take charge of** to take command of.

chariot *noun* (*hist*) (two-wheeled) carriage used in battle. – *noun* **charioteer** chariot-driver.

charisma *ka-riz'mà*, *noun* a personal quality that impresses others. – *adjective* **charismatic**.

charity *noun* (*plural* **charities**) giving of money to the poor *etc*; an organization which collects money and gives it to those in need; love for all people; kindness. – *adjective* **charitable** giving to the poor; kindly; of a charity.

charlatan *noun* someone who claims greater powers, abilities *etc* than they really have.

charm *noun* something thought to have magical powers; a spell; power to attract (by appearance, manner *etc*). – *verb* to please greatly, delight; to put under a spell.

chart 55 cherish

chart *noun* a table or diagram giving some form of information (*eg* a temperature chart); a map, *esp* one of seas or lakes, showing rocks, islands, currents, depth *etc*; a rough map. – *verb* to make a chart of; to plan.

charter *noun* a written paper showing the granting of rights, favours, lands *etc*, *esp* by a king or a government. – *verb* to hire (a boat, aeroplane *etc*). – *adjective* **chartered** having a charter; (of an aeroplane *etc*) hired for a special purpose.

charwoman *see* **char.**

chary *adjective* cautious, careful (of).

chase *verb* to run after, pursue; to hunt. – *noun* a pursuit; a hunt.

chasm *kazm*, *noun* a deep hole or drop between high rocks *etc*; a wide difference.

chassis *shas'ē*, *noun* (*plural* **chassis**) the frame, wheels, and machinery of a motor-car; an aeroplane's landing carriage.

chaste *adjective* pure, virtuous. – *noun* **chastity.**

chasten *verb* to make humble; to punish, *usu* by scolding. – *adjective* **chastened.**

chastise *verb* to punish, *usu* by whipping or beating. – *noun* **chastisement.**

chat *verb* (*past tense* **chatted**) to talk in an easy, friendly way (about unimportant things). – Also *noun*. – *noun* **chat-show** a radio or TV programme in which personalities talk informally with their host. – *adjective* **chatty** willing to talk, talkative.

chateau *shä'tō*, *noun* (*plural* **chateaux**) a French castle or country house.

chattels *noun plural* movable possessions. – **goods and chattels** personal possessions.

chatter *verb* to talk idly, rapidly or indiscreetly; (of teeth) to rattle together through cold *etc*. – Also *noun*. – *noun* **chatterbox** a person who chatters a great deal.

chauffeur *shōf'ėr*, *noun* a person employed to drive a motor-car.

cheap *adjective* low in price, inexpensive; of little value, worthless. – *verb* **cheapen** to make cheap.

cheat *verb* to deceive; to act dishonestly to gain an advantage. – *noun* a person who cheats; a dishonest trick.

check *verb* to bring to a stop; to hinder or hold back; to see if something (*eg* a sum) is correct or accurate; to see if something (*eg* a machine) is in good condition or working properly. – *noun* a sudden stop; something that hinders; a test of the correctness or accuracy of; a square (*eg* on a draughtboard); (a fabric with) a pattern of squares. – *adjective* **checked.** – *noun* **checkmate** in chess, a position from which the king cannot escape. – *noun* **checkout** a place where payment is made in a supermarket. – **check in** or **check out** to record one's arrival at or departure from (*eg* work, an airport *etc*).

checkers *see* **chequers.**

cheek *noun* the side of the face below the eye; insolence, disrespectful speech or behaviour. – *noun* **cheekiness.** – *adjective* **cheeky** impudent, insolent.

cheep *verb* to make a faint sound like a small bird. – Also *noun*.

cheer *noun* a shout of approval or welcome. – *verb* to shout approval; to encourage, urge on; to comfort, gladden. – *adjective* **cheerful** happy, in good spirits. – *adjective* **cheerless** sad, gloomy. – *adjective* **cheery** lively and merry. – **cheer up** to make or become less gloomy.

cheerio *interjection* goodbye!

cheese *noun* a solid food made from milk. – *adjective* **cheeseparing** mean.

cheetah *noun* a type of swift-running animal like the leopard.

chef *noun* a male head cook.

chemistry *noun* the study of the elements and the ways they combine or react with each other. – *adjective* **chemical** of chemistry or reactions between elements *etc* – *noun* a substance which is formed by or used in a chemical process. – *noun* **chemist** a person who studies chemistry; a person who makes up and sells medicines, a pharmacist.

cheque or (*US*) **check** *noun* a written order to a banker telling him to pay money from one's bank account to another person. – *noun* **cheque book** a book containing cheques.

chequers or **checkers** *noun* a pattern of squares, as on a chessboard; the game of draughts. – *adjective* **chequered** or **checkered** marked like a chessboard; partly good, partly bad: *a chequered life.*

cherish *verb* to protect and treat with fondness or kindness; to keep in one's mind or heart: *cherish a hope.*

cheroot *noun* a small cigar.

cherry *noun* (*plural* **cherries**) a type of small bright-red fruit with a stone, or the tree that bears it.

cherub *noun* (*plural* **cherubs** or **cherubim**) an angel having wings and the plump face and body of a child; a beautiful child.

chess *noun* a game for two persons, played with pieces (**chessmen**) which are moved on a board marked off into alternate black and white squares (**chessboard**).

chest *noun* a large strong box, the part of the body between the neck and the stomach. – **chest of drawers** a piece of furniture fitted with a set of drawers.

chesterfield *noun* a kind of sofa.

chestnut *noun* a type of reddish-brown nut, or the tree that bears it; a reddish-brown horse; an old joke.

cheviot *noun* a kind of sheep.

chevron *noun* a V-shape (*esp* on a badge, road-sign *etc*).

chew *verb* to break up (food) with the teeth before swallowing.

chic *shĕk*, *adjective* smart and fashionable. – *noun* style, fashionable elegance.

chicanery *noun* dishonest cleverness.

chick or **chicken** *noun* the young of (domestic) fowls, *esp* of the hen. – *adjective* **chicken-hearted** cowardly. – *noun* **chickenpox** an infectious disease which causes red, itchy spots.

chicory *noun* a type of plant whose root is ground to mix with coffee and whose leaves are used as a vegetable.

chide *verb* to scold by words.

chief *adjective* head; main, most important; largest. – *noun* a leader or ruler; the head (of a department, organization *etc*). – *adverb* **chiefly** mainly, for the most part. – *noun* **chieftain** the head of a clan or tribe.

chiffon *noun* a thin flimsy material.

chilblain *noun* a painful swelling which occurs in cold weather on hands and feet.

child *noun* (*plural* **children**) a young human being; a son or daughter (of any age). – *noun* **childhood** the time of being a child. – *adjective* **childish** of or like a child; silly. – *adjective* **childlike** innocent.

chill *noun* coldness; an illness that causes shivering, a feverish cold; (of manner *etc*) lack of warmth or enthusiasm. – *adjective* cold. – *verb* to make cold (without freezing). – *adjective* **chilly** cold.

chilli or **chili** *noun* the dried, hot-tasting pod of a kind of pepper; a sauce made with this.

chime *noun* the sound of bells ringing; (*plural*) a set of bells (as in a clock). – *verb* to ring; (of clocks) to strike.

chimney *noun* (*plural* **chimneys**) a passage for the escape of smoke or heated air from a fire. – *noun* **chimneypot** a pipe of earthenware, iron *etc* placed at the top of a chimney. – *noun* **chimneystack** a tall, *esp* factory, chimney; a number of chimneys built up together. – *noun* **chimneysweep** a person who sweeps or cleans chimneys.

chimpanzee *noun* a type of African ape.

chin *noun* the part of the face below the mouth.

china *noun* fine kind of earthenware, porcelain; articles made of this.

chinchilla *noun* a type of small S. American animal, valued for its soft grey fur.

chink *noun* a narrow opening; a sound like that of coins striking together.

chintz *noun* (*plural* **chintzes**) a cotton cloth with brightly coloured patterns.

chip *verb* (*past tense* **chipped**) to break or cut small pieces (from or off) *noun* a small piece chipped off; a part damaged by chipping; a long thin piece of potato fried; (*US*) a (potato) crisp.

chipmunk *noun* a kind of N. American squirrel.

chipolata *noun* a type of small sausage.

chiropodist *noun* a person who treats minor disorders and diseases of the feet (*eg* corns). – *noun* **chiropody** the treatment of these.

chirp or **chirrup** *noun* the sharp, shrill sound (of birds *etc*). – Also *verb*. – *adjective* **chirpy** merry, cheerful.

chisel *noun* an iron or steel tool to cut or hollow out wood, stone *etc*. – *verb* (*past tense* **chiselled**) to cut with a chisel.

chit *noun* a short note; a child, a young woman: *chit of a girl*. – *noun* **chit-chat** gossip, talk.

chivalry *shiv'ăl-ri*, *noun* kindness, *esp* towards women or the weak; (*hist*) the standard of behaviour expected of knights in medieval times. – *adjective* **chivalrous.**

chive *noun* a herb like the leek and onion, used as flavouring.

chlorine *noun* an element, a yellowish-green gas with a sharp, distinctive smell, used as a bleach and disinfectant. – *verb* **chlorinate** to add chlorine or a substance containing it to (*eg* water).

chloroform *noun* a liquid, the vapour of which when breathed in, causes unconsciousness.

chock-a-block or **chockfull** *adjective* completely full.

chocolate *noun* paste got from the seeds of the cacao tree, used in sweet-making; a sweet made from this paste when hardened; a drink made from it. – *adjective* dark brown in colour, like chocolate.

choice *noun* the act or power of choosing; something chosen. – *adjective* of a high quality: *choice vegetables.*

choir *noun* a group or society of singers; the part of a church where the choir sits. – *adjective* **choral** of or for a choir.

choke *verb* to stop or partly stop the breathing of; to block or clog (a pipe *etc*); to have one's breathing stopped or interrupted (*eg* by smoke or chemicals). – *noun* a valve in a petrol engine which controls the flowing-in of air.

cholera *kol'ėr-à*, *noun* a deadly disease, commonest in hot countries.

choose *verb* (*past tense* **chose**, *past participle* **chosen**) to pick out and take (one) from two or several things, to select; to decide, prefer to: *We chose to go.*

chop *verb* (*past tense* **chopped**) to cut into small pieces; to cut with a sudden blow. – *noun* a chopping blow; a slice of mutton, pork *etc*, containing a bone. – *noun* **chopper** a knife or axe for chopping; (*coll*) a helicopter. – *adjective* **choppy** (of the sea) not calm, having small waves. – **chop and change** to keep changing.

chopsticks *noun plural* two small sticks of wood, ivory *etc* used by the Chinese *etc* instead of a knife and fork.

choral *see* **choir.**

chord *noun* a musical sound made by the playing of several notes together; a straight line joining any two points on a curve.

chore *noun* dull, boring job; (*plural*) housework.

choreography *noun* the arrangement of dancing and dance steps (in a ballet *etc*). – *noun* **choreographer.**

chorister *noun* a member of a choir.

chortle *verb* to laugh, chuckle.

chorus *noun* (*plural* **choruses**) a band of singers and dancers; a choir or choral group; the repeated part of a song.

chose, chosen *see* **choose.**

chow *noun* a breed of dog, *orig* from China, with a bushy coat and a blue-black tongue.

christen *verb* to baptize and give a name to. – *noun* **christening.**

Christian *noun* a follower of Christ. – Also *adjective.* – *noun* **Christianity** the religion having Christ as its centre. – *noun* **Christian name(s)** (a) first or personal name (or names): *John William* Smith.

Christmas *noun* a yearly holiday or festival, in memory of the birth of Christ, held on December 25. – *noun* **Christmas Eve** December 24. – *noun* **Christmas tree** an evergreen tree hung with lights, decorations and gifts at Christmas.

chromatic *adjective* of colours; coloured. – *noun* **chromatic scale** a series of musical notes, each separated from the next by a semitone.

chromium *noun* an element, a metal which does not rust.

chronic *adjective* (*esp* of a disease) lasting a long time; (*coll*) very bad.

chronicle *noun* a record of events in order of time. – *verb* to write down events in order. – *noun* **chronicler.**

chronological *adjective* arranged in the order of the time of happening.

chronometer *noun* an instrument for measuring time.

chrysalis *noun* an insect (*esp* a butterfly or moth) at an early part of its life when it is without wings and shut up in a soft covering or cocoon.

chrysanthemum *noun* a type of garden flower with a large, bushy head.

chubby *adjective* (*comparative* **chubbier**, *superlative* **chubbiest**) plump. – *noun* **chubbiness.**

chuck verb to throw, toss; to pat gently (under the chin). – **chuck out** (coll) to expel (a person); (coll) to throw away, get rid of.

chuckle noun a quiet laugh. – verb to laugh quietly.

chum noun (coll) a close friend.

chunk noun a thick piece.

church noun (plural **churches**) a building used for public, esp Christian, worship; any group of people of the same beliefs who meet together for worship. – noun **churchyard** the burial ground round a church.

churlish adjective bad-mannered, rude.

churn noun a machine used for making butter. – verb to make (butter) in a churn; to shake or stir about violently.

chute shōōt, noun a sloping trough for sending things (eg water, logs, parcels) down to a lower level; a similar structure with steps in a playground, for children to slide down.

chutney noun (plural **chutneys**) any of various sauces made from vegetables, fruits, vinegar.

CIA abbreviation (US) Central Intelligence Agency.

CID abbreviation Criminal Investigation Department.

cider noun an alcoholic drink made from the juice of apples.

cigar noun a roll of tobacco leaves for smoking. – noun **cigarette** a tube of fine tobacco enclosed in thin paper.

C-in-C abbreviation Commander-in-Chief.

cinder noun a burnt-out piece of coal.

cinema noun a place where films are shown; (with **the**) films generally, or films regarded as a form of art.

cinnamon noun a yellowish-brown spice got from the bark of a tree.

cipher noun a secret writing, code; nought, 0; a person of no importance.

circa preposition about (esp a date): circa 1100 BC.

circle noun a figure formed from an endless curved line, ○; something in the form of a circle, a ring; any society or group of people; a balcony or tier of seats in a theatre etc. – verb to enclose in a circle; to move round (something). – noun **circlet** a little circle, esp one used as an ornamental headband.

circuit noun a movement in a circle; a connected group of places, sporting events etc: the American tennis circuit; the path of an electric current. – adjective **circuitous** (of a route etc) not direct, roundabout.

circular adjective round, like a circle. – noun a letter sent round to a number of persons. – verb **circularize** to send a circular to.

circulate verb to move round (as the blood moves in the body); to send round. – noun **circulation** the act of circulating; the movement of the blood; the total sales of a newspaper, magazine etc.

circumference noun (the length of) the outside line of a circle.

circumlocution noun a roundabout way of saying something.

circumnavigate verb to sail round (eg the world). – noun **circumnavigator**.

circumscribe verb to draw a line round; to lay down limits (eg for a person's actions), restrict. – noun **circumscription**.

circumspect adjective wary, looking carefully at circumstances, cautious. – noun **circumspection** caution.

circumstance noun a condition (of time, place, manner etc) which affects a person, an action or an event; (plural) the state of a person's (financial) affairs. – verb **circumstantiate** to prove by giving details. – noun **circumstantial evidence** evidence which points to a conclusion but does not give proof of it.

circumvent verb to get round (a difficulty); to outwit. – noun **circumvention**.

circus noun (plural **circuses**) a travelling company of performing animals, acrobats, clowns etc; a large arena for sports events.

cirrhosis noun a disease of the liver.

cirrus noun a fleecy kind of cloud.

cistern noun a tank for holding or storing water.

citadel noun fortress, esp one in a city.

cite verb to quote as an example or as proof; to summon a person to appear in court. – noun **citation** something quoted; a summons to appear in court; official recognition of an achievement, a brave act etc.

citizen noun a person who lives in a city, town or state. – noun **citizenship** the rights of or state of being a citizen.

citric acid *noun* a type of sharp-tasting acid found in citrus fruits.

citron *noun* a type of fruit similar to a lemon.

citrus fruit *noun* any one of certain fruits including the orange, lemon and lime.

city *noun* (*plural* **cities**) a large town; a town with a cathedral. – **the City** that part of London regarded as the centre of business.

civic *adjective* having to do with a city or a citizen. – *noun plural* **civics** the study of one's duties as a citizen.

civil *adjective* of the ordinary people of a country, not its armed forces; polite. – *noun* **civil engineer** an engineer who plans bridges, roads *etc*. – *noun* **civilian** one who is not in the armed forces. – *noun* **civility** politeness, good manners. – *noun* **civil law** law concerned with the rights of a citizen, not concerned with criminal acts. – *noun* **civil list** the expenses of the king's or queen's household. – *noun* **civil marriage** a marriage which does not take place in church. – *noun plural* **civil rights** the rights of a citizen. – *noun* **civil service** the paid administrative officials of the country who are not in the armed forces. – *noun* **civil war** war between citizens of a country.

civilize *verb* to bring (a people) under a regular system of laws, education *etc* from a primitive state. – *noun* **civilization** making or becoming civilized; life under a civilized system; the civilized nations as a whole. – *adjective* **civilized** living under such a system; not savage.

clad *adjective* clothed (in).

claim *verb* to demand as a right; to state as a truth, assert (that). – Also *noun*. – *noun* **claimant** a person who makes a claim.

clairvoyance *noun* the supposed power to see into the future or into the world of spirits. – *noun*, *adjective* **clairvoyant**.

clam *noun* a type of large shellfish with two shells hinged together.

clamber *verb* to climb awkwardly or with difficulty.

clammy *adjective* moist and sticky.

clamour *noun* a loud, continuous noise or outcry. – *verb* to cry aloud; to make a loud demand (for). – *adjective* **clamorous** noisy.

clamp *noun* a piece of timber, iron *etc* used to fasten things together. – *verb* to bind with a clamp. – **clamp down on** to stop (something, *eg* vandalism) by forceful action.

clan *noun* (in Scotland) a tribe, or a number of families, under a chieftain *usu* having the same surname. – *adjective* **clannish** loyal to one another, like the members of a clan, and showing little interest in other people. – *noun* **clansman** a member of a clan.

clandestine *adjective* hidden, secret, underhand.

clang *verb* to make a loud, deep, ringing sound. – Also *noun*.

clank *noun* a sound like that made by metal hitting metal. – Also *verb*.

clap *noun* the noise made by the sudden striking together of two things (*esp* the hands); a burst of sound, *esp* thunder. – *verb* (*past tense* **clapped**) to strike noisily together (*esp* the hands to show pleasure); (*coll*) to put or place suddenly: *Clap him in jail*. – *noun* **clapper** the tongue of a bell. – *noun* **claptrap** meaningless words, nonsense.

claret *noun* a type of red wine.

clarify *verb* (*past tense* **clarified**) to make clear and understandable; to make (*eg* a liquid) clear and pure.

clarinet *noun* a type of musical wind instrument, *usu* of wood. – *noun* **clarinettist** a person who plays the clarinet.

clarion *noun* (*old*) a kind of trumpet; a shrill, rousing noise. – *noun* **clarion call** a loud, clear call to action.

clarity *noun* clearness.

clash *noun* (*plural* **clashes**) a loud noise, as of the striking together of weapons; a disagreement or fight. – *verb* to bang noisily together; to disagree; (of events) to take place at the same time; (*usu* with **with**) not to look well together: *The two shades of red clashed with each other*.

clasp *noun* a hook *etc* for fastening; a fastening for the hair; a handshake; an embrace. – *verb* to hold closely; to grasp; to fasten.

class *noun* (*plural* **classes**) a rank or order of persons or things; a number of schoolchildren or students who are taught together; (of animals, plants *etc*) a group of different kinds, all of which have something in common. – *verb* to place in a class; to arrange in some order. – *verb* **classify** (*past tense*

classified) to arrange in classes; to put into a class or category. – *noun* **classification**.

classic *noun* any great writer, book or other work of art; (*plural*) (the study of) ancient Greek and Latin writers' works. – *adjective* excellent; standard: *the classic example*; simple and elegant in style. – *adjective* **classical** of a classic or the classics; (of music) serious, not light.

clatter *noun* noise as of plates *etc* banged together.

clause *noun* a part of a sentence containing a finite verb; a part of a will, act of parliament *etc*.

claustrophobia *noun* an abnormal fear of enclosed spaces. – *adjective* **claustrophobic**.

claw *noun* one of the hooked nails of an animal or bird; the foot of an animal or bird with hooked nails. – *verb* to scratch or tear.

clay *noun* soft, sticky earth, different kinds of which are used in making pottery, bricks *etc*. – *adjective* **clayey**.

claymore *noun* (*hist*) a kind of large sword once used by the Scottish Highlanders.

clean *adjective* free from dirt; pure; neat; complete: *a clean break*. – *adverb* completely: *He got clean away*. – *verb* to make clean, or free from dirt. – *noun* **cleaner** a person whose job is to clean; something which cleans. – *noun* **cleanliness**. – *adverb* **cleanly**. – *noun* **cleanness**.

cleanse *verb* to make clean.

clear *adjective* bright, undimmed; free from mist or cloud; transparent; free from difficulty or hindrance; easy to see or hear or understand; after deductions and charges have been made: *clear profit*; without a stain; without touching, without being caught by: *Steer clear of the rocks. We got clear of the enemy*. – *verb* to make clear; to empty: *clear the streets of snow*; to free from blame; to leap over (without touching); (of the sky, weather) to become bright. – *noun* **clearance** act of clearing. – *adjective* **clear-cut** distinct, obvious. – *noun* **clearing** land free of trees. – *noun* **clearness**. – **clear out** or **clear off** to go away.

cleave *verb* (*past tense* **clove** or **cleft**, *past participle* **cloven** or **cleft**) to divide, split; to crack; to stick (to). – *noun* **cleavage** the act of splitting; the way in which

two things are split or divided; the hollow between the breasts. – *noun* **cleaver** that which cleaves, a chopper.

clef *noun* a musical sign fixing the pitch of the notes.

cleft *noun* an opening made by splitting; a crack. – *verb see* **cleave**. – *noun* **cleft palate** a congenital defect causing a fissure in the roof of the mouth.

cleg *noun* a type of horsefly.

clematis *noun* a flowering, climbing shrub.

clement *adjective* mild; merciful. – *noun* **clemency** readiness to forgive; mercy.

clench *verb* to press firmly together: *He clenched his teeth*.

clergy *noun* the ministers of the Christian religion. – *noun* **clergyman** one of the clergy; a minister.

cleric *noun* a clergyman.

clerk *noun* a person who works in an office, writing letters, keeping accounts *etc*. – *verb* to act as clerk. – *adjective* **clerical** of office work; of the clergy.

clever *adjective* quick in learning and understanding; skilful. – *noun* **cleverness**.

cliché *klē'shā, noun* something (*esp* an idea, phrase *etc*) that has been used too much and has little meaning.

click *noun* a short sharp sound like a clock's tick. – Also *verb*.

client *noun* a customer of a shopkeeper *etc*; a person who goes to a lawyer *etc* for advice. – *noun* **clientele** the customers of a lawyer, shopkeeper *etc*.

cliff *noun* a very steep, rocky slope, *esp* one by the sea.

climate *noun* the weather conditions (heat, cold, rain, wind *etc*) of a place or country; the conditions (*eg* economic) in a country *etc*. – *adjective* **climatic**.

climax *noun* (*plural* **climaxes**) (of events *etc*) the point of greatest interest, feeling or importance.

climb *verb* to go to the top of; to go up using the hands or feet or both; to slope upward. – *noun* an act of climbing; a place for climbing. – *noun* **climber** a person who climbs; a plant which climbs up other plants, walls *etc*.

clinch *verb* to grasp tightly; to settle (an argument, bargain *etc*). – *noun* (*plural*

clinches) (in boxing) a position in which the boxers hold each other with their arms; a passionate embrace.

cling *verb* (*past tense* **clung**) to stick or hang on (to). – *noun* **clingfilm** thin transparent plastic material used to wrap food.

clinic *noun* a place or part of a hospital where a particular kind of medical advice or treatment is given. – *adjective* **clinical** of a clinic; based on observation: *clinical medicine*; objective, cool and unemotional: *a clinical view of the situation*.

clink *noun* a ringing sound. – Also *verb*.

clinker *noun* the waste stuff when iron is smelted or coal burnt.

clip *verb* to cut (off); to fasten with a clip. – *noun* the thing clipped off; a small fastener (*eg* for paper); (*coll*) a smart blow. – *noun* **clipper** a fast-sailing vessel; (*plural*) tool for clipping.

clique *klēk*, *noun* a small group of people who help each other but keep others at a distance.

cloak *noun* a loose outer garment; something which hides: *cloak of darkness*. – *verb* to cover as with a cloak; to hide. – *noun* **cloakroom** a place where coats, hats *etc* may be left for a time.

cloche *noun* (*plural* **cloches**) a transparent frame for protecting plants.

clock *noun* a machine for measuring time. – *adjective* **clockwise** turning or moving in the same direction as the hands of a clock. – *adjective*, *noun* **clockwork** (worked by) machinery such as that of a clock. – **clock in** or **clock out** (or **clock on** or **clock off**) to record one's time of arrival or departure (*usu* at one's place of work). – **like clockwork** smoothly, without difficulties.

clod *noun* a thick lump, *esp* of turf; a stupid man. – *noun* **clodhopper** a stupid clumsy person. – *adjective* **clodhopping**.

clog *noun* a shoe with a wooden sole. – *verb* (*past tense* **clogged**) to block (pipes *etc*).

cloister *noun* a covered-in walk in a monastery or convent; a monastery or convent. – *adjective* **cloistered** shut up in a monastery *etc*; sheltered.

close¹ *adjective* near in time, place *etc*; shut up, with no opening; without fresh air, stuffy; narrow, confined;

mean; secretive; beloved, very dear: *a close friend*; decided, won by a small amount: *a close contest*. – *noun* a narrow passage off a street; the gardens, walks *etc* near a cathedral. – *noun* **closeness**. – *noun* **close-up** a film or photograph taken very near the subject.

close² *verb* to shut; to finish; to come closer to and fight (with). – *noun* the end. – *noun* **closed-circuit television** a system of television cameras and receivers for private use (as in shops *etc*). – *noun* **closed shop** a place of work where only members of a (particular) trade union are employed. – *noun* **closure** the act of closing.

closet *noun* (*US*) a cupboard. – *verb* to take into a room *etc* for a private conference. – **closeted with** in private conference with.

closure *see* **close²**.

clot *noun* a lump or thickening that forms in some liquids (*eg* blood, cream); (*coll*) a stupid person. – *verb* (*past tense* **clotted**) to form into clots.

cloth *noun* woven material of cotton, wool, linen, silk *etc*; a piece of this; a table-cover.

clothes *noun plural* things worn to cover the body and limbs (as shirt, trousers, skirt *etc*); bedclothes. – *verb* **clothe** to put clothes on; to provide with clothes: *He has barely enough money to clothe the children*; to cover. – *noun* **clothing** clothes.

cloud *noun* a mass of tiny drops of water or ice floatng in the sky; a great number or quantity of anything small in the air (*eg* locusts, dust). – *verb* to blot out, hide or become dark, as with a cloud. – *noun* **cloudburst** a sudden heavy fall of rain. – *adjective* **clouded**. – *adjective* **cloudless**. – *adjective* **cloudy** darkened with clouds; not clear or transparent.

clout *noun* (*coll*) a blow; (*coll*) influence. – *verb* (*coll*) to hit.

clove *noun* a flower bud of the clove tree, used as a spice; a small section of a bulb of garlic *etc*. – *verb see* **cleave.**

cloven-hoofed *adjective* having the hoof divided, as the ox, sheep *etc*.

clover *noun* a type of field plant with leaves *usu* in three parts, common in pastures. – **in clover** in luxury.

clown *noun* a comedian with a painted face and comical clothes in a circus; a fool. – *noun* **clowning** silly or comical behaviour. – *adjective* **clownish** like a clown; awkward.

cloy *verb* (of *eg* something sweet) to become unpleasant when too much is taken. – *adjective* **cloying**.

club *noun* a heavy stick; a bat or stick used in certain games, *esp* golf; a group of people who meet for study, games, entertainment *etc*; the place where these people meet sometimes provided with refreshments, entertainment *etc*; (*plural*) one of the four suits in playing-cards. – *verb* (*past tense* **clubbed**) to beat with a club. – **club together** (of a group of people) to put money into a joint fund for some purpose.

cluck *noun* a sound like that made by a hen. – Also *verb*.

clue *noun* any sign or piece of evidence that helps to solve a mystery, problem *etc*.

clump *noun* a cluster of trees or shrubs. – *verb* to walk heavily.

clumsy *adjective* (*comparative* **clumsier**, *superlative* **clumsiest**) awkward in movement or actions; tactless, not skilfully carried out: *a clumsy apology*. – *noun* **clumsiness**.

clung *see* **cling**.

cluster *noun* a bunch; a crowd. – *verb* to group together in clusters.

clutch *verb* to hold firmly; to seize or grasp. – *noun* (*plural* **clutches**) a grasp; part of a motor-car engine used in changing the gears.

clutter *noun* a collection (of objects) in a crowded or confused state; disorder, confusion, untidiness. – *verb* to crowd together untidily; (with **up**) to fill or cover in an untidy, disordered way.

cm *abbreviation* centimetre.

CND *abbreviation* Campaign for Nuclear Disarmament.

CO *abbreviation* carbon monoxide; Commanding Officer.

Co *abbreviation* Company; County.

c/o *abbreviation* care of.

co- *prefix* joint, working *etc* with, as in **co-author, co-driver**.

coach *noun* (*plural* **coaches**) a bus for long-distance travel; a large, closed, four-wheeled horse carriage; a railway carriage; a private teacher, *esp* one who trains sportsmen. – *verb* to prepare (someone) for an examination, sports contest *etc*.

coagulate *verb* to (cause to) become a thickened mass (as when milk goes sour or blood clots).

coal *noun* a black substance (the wood of prehistoric trees *etc*) dug out of the earth and used for burning, making gas *etc*. – *noun* **coalfield** a district where there is coal to be mined. – *noun* **coal gas** the mixture of gases, obtained from coal, used for lighting and heating. – *noun* **coalmine** a mine from which coal is dug.

coalesce *kō-ȧl-es*', *verb* to come together and unite.

coalition *noun* a joining together of different parts of parties.

coarse *adjective* not fine in texture *etc*, rough; harsh; vulgar. – *verb* **coarsen** to make coarse. – *noun* **coarseness**.

coast *noun* the side or border of land next to the sea. – *verb* to sail along or near a coast; to move without the use of any power (as downhill on a bike, car *etc*). – *adjective* **coastal**. – *noun* **coastguard** a person who acts as a guard along the coast to prevent smuggling and help those in danger in boats *etc*.

coat *noun* an outer garment with sleeves; hair or wool (of an animal); a covering (*eg* paint). – *verb* to cover with a coat or layer. – *noun* **coating** a covering. – **coat of arms** the badge or crest of a family.

coax *verb* to get (someone) to do what is wanted without using force.

cob *noun* a head of corn, wheat *etc*; a male swan.

cobalt *noun* an element, a silvery metal; a blue colouring got from it.

cobble *noun* a rounded stone used in paving roads. – Also **cobblestone**. – *verb* to mend (shoes); to repair, patch roughly or hurriedly. – *noun* **cobbler** a person who mends shoes.

cobra *noun* a type of poisonous snake, found in India and Africa.

cobweb *noun* a spider's web.

cocaine *noun* a narcotic drug.

cochineal *noun* a scarlet dye, used to colour food, made from the dried bodies of certain insects.

cock *noun* the male of most kinds of bird, *esp* the male of the farmyard hen; a tap or valve for controlling the flow of a liquid *etc*; a hammer-like part of a gun which, when the trigger is pulled, fires the shot; a small heap (of hay). – *verb* to draw back the cock of a gun; to set upright (ears *etc*); to tilt to one side (*eg* one's head). – *noun* **cockerel** a young cock. – *noun* **cocker spaniel** a breed of small spaniel. – *noun* **cockpit** the space for the pilot or driver in an aeroplane, small boat or racing car; a pit or enclosed space where game cocks fight. – *noun* **cockroach** (*plural* **cockroaches**) a type of crawling insect. – *noun* **cockscomb** the comb or crest of a cock's head. – *adjective* **cocksure** quite sure, often without cause. – *noun* **cocktail** a mixed alcoholic drink. – *adjective* **cocky** conceited, self-confident.

cockade *noun* a knot of ribbons or something similar worn on the hat.

cockatoo *noun* a kind of parrot.

cockatrice *noun* (*myth*) a monster like a cock with a dragon's tail.

cockerel *see* **cock**.

cockle *noun* a type of shellfish. – *noun* **cockleshell** the shell of a cockle.

cockney *noun* (*plural* **cockneys**) a person born in the East End of London, *esp* one born within the sound of Bow Bells; the way of speaking in this area. – Also *adjective*.

cocoa *noun* a drink made from the ground seeds of the cacao tree.

coconut *noun* the large, hard-shelled nut of a type of palm tree.

cocoon *noun* a covering or case of silk spun by the larva (grub) of certain insects to protect it while it turns into a butterfly, moth *etc*.

cod *noun* a fish much used as food, found in the nothern seas.

c.o.d. *abbreviation* cash on delivery.

coddle *verb* to treat as an invalid, pamper, over-protect.

code *noun* a way of signalling or sending secret messages, using words, letters *etc* agreed on beforehand; a book or collection of laws, rules *etc*. – *verb* **codify** (*past tense* **codified**) to arrange in an orderly way, classify.

codicil *noun* a note added to a will or treaty.

coeducation *noun* the education of boys and girls together. – *adjective* **coeducational** or (*coll*) **co-ed**.

coerce *verb* to make (to do), to compel. – *noun* **coercion**. – *adjective* **coercive** using force.

coeval *adjective* of the same age or time.

coexist *verb* to exist at the same time. – *noun* **coexistence**. – *adjective* **coexistent**.

C of E *abbreviation* Church of England.

coffee *noun* a drink made from the ground beans or seeds of the coffee shrub; a pale brown colour.

coffer *noun* a chest for holding money, gold *etc*. – *noun* **coffer-dam** a watertight dam placed in a river inside which the foundations of a bridge are built.

coffin *noun* the box in which a dead body is buried or cremated.

cog *noun* a tooth on a wheel. – *noun* **cogwheel** a toothed wheel.

cogent *adjective* (of speaking or writing) convincing, having the power to make people believe what is said. – *noun* **cogency**.

cogitate *verb* to think carefully. – *noun* **cogitation**.

cognac *noun* a kind of French brandy.

cognizance *noun* awareness, notice. – **take cognizance of** to take notice of, take into consideration.

cohere *verb* to stick together. – *noun* **coherence** connection (between thoughts, ideas *etc*). – *adjective* **coherent** sticking together; clear and logical in thought or speech. – *noun* **cohesion** the act of sticking together. – *adjective* **cohesive**.

cohort *noun* (*hist*) a tenth part of a Roman legion.

coiffure *noun* a style of hairdressing.

coil *verb* to wind in rings, to twist. – *noun* a coiled arrangement (of hair, rope *etc*); a contraceptive device fitted in the uterus.

coin *noun* a piece of stamped metal used as money. – *verb* to make metal into money; to make up (a new word *etc*). – *noun* **coinage** the act of coining; coins; the system of coins used in a country; a newly-made word.

coincide *verb* (sometimes with **with**) to be like or the same as: *Their interests coincide. His story coincides with hers*; (sometimes with **with**) to happen at the same time as: *Her arrival coincided with* *his departure.* – *noun* **coincidence** the happening of one thing at the same time as another, by chance or without planning. – *adjective* **coincidental.**

coir *noun* outside fibre of the coconut.

coke *noun* a type of fuel made by heating coal till the gas is driven out.

Col. *abbreviation* Colonel.

colander *noun* a kind of bowl with small holes in it for straining vegetables *etc*.

cold *adjective* low in temperature; lower in temperature than is comfortable; causing shivering; unfriendly. – *noun* the state of being cold or of feeling the coldness of one's surroundings; a disease, due to germs, causing shivering, running nose *etc*. – *noun* **coldness.** – *adjective* **cold-blooded** (of fishes *etc*) having cold blood; cruel; lacking in feelings. – *noun* **cold feet** lack of courage. – *noun* **cold war** a struggle between nations for power without the use of open warfare.

coleslaw *noun* a salad made from raw cabbage.

colic *noun* a severe stomach pain.

collaborate *verb* to work together (with); to work with (an enemy) to betray one's country *etc*. – *noun* **collaboration.** – *noun* **collaborator.**

collage *kol-äzh'*, *noun* a design made of scraps of paper and other odds and ends pasted on paper *etc*.

collapse *verb* to fall or break down; to cave or fall in; to become unable to continue. – Also *noun*. – *adjective* **collapsible** (of a chair *etc*) able to be folded up.

collar *noun* a band, strip *etc* worn round the neck by humans or animals; the part of an article of clothing at the neck. – *verb* (*coll*) to seize. – *noun* **collarbone** either of two bones joining the breast bone and shoulderblade.

collate *verb* to examine and compare; to gather together and arrange in order: *Please photocopy and then collate the report.* – *noun* **collation** a light (often cold) meal; a comparison.

collateral *noun* an additional security for repayment of a debt.

colleague *noun* a person who does the same kind of work as another or who works in the same firm *etc* as another.

collect *verb* to bring together; to gather together. – *adjective* **collected** gathered

together; (of persons) calm. – *noun* **collection** the act of collecting; a number of objects or people; money gathered at a meeting, *esp* a church service. – *adjective* **collective** acting together; of several things or persons, not of one. – *noun* a business *etc* owned and managed by the workers. – *noun* **collector** a person who collects (tickets, money, stamps *etc*).

college *noun* (a building used by) a group of people gathered together to learn and study; a building which is part of a university *etc*. – *adjective* **collegiate.**

collide *verb* (of moving things *etc*) to come together with great force. – *noun* **collision** a violent meeting of two moving things, *esp* vehicles; a disagreement, clash (of interests *etc*).

collie *noun* a breed of long-haired dog with a pointed nose, a sheepdog.

collier *noun* a person who works in a coalmine; a coal ship. – *noun* **colliery** (*plural* **collieries**) a coalmine.

colloquial *adjective* used in everyday talk but not in very correct writing or speaking. – *noun* **colloquialism** an example of colloquial speech.

collusion *noun* a secret agreement (*usu* for some dishonest purpose).

colon *noun* in punctuation, the mark (:), used to show a break in a sentence; a part of the bowel.

colonel *kûr'nèl*, *noun* a senior army officer fulfilling a staff appointment.

colonnade *noun* a row of columns or pillars.

colony *noun* (*plural* **colonies**) a group of settlers or the settlement they make in another country; any group of people, animals *etc* of the same type living together. – *adjective* **colonial** of colonies abroad. – *noun* **colonist** a settler. – *verb* **colonize** to set up a colony in.

colossal *adjective* huge, enormous. – *noun* **colossus** anything enormous (*eg* a huge statue).

colour or (*US*) **color** *noun* a quality that an object shows in the light, as redness, blueness *etc*; any shade or tint, vividness, brightness; (*plural*) a flag or standard. – *verb* to put colour on; to blush; to influence: *Unemployment coloured his attitude to life.* – *adjective* **colour-blind** unable to distinguish certain colours (*eg* red and green). – *adjective* **coloured**

having colour; not white-skinned. – *adjective* **colourful** brightly coloured; vivid, interesting. – *noun* **colouring** the putting on of colours; the effect of combining colours; complexion. – *adjective* **colourless** without colour; dull. – **off colour** unwell.

colt *noun* a young horse.

column *noun* a stone (or wooden) pillar standing upright; anything of a long or tall, narrow shape; a line of print, figures *etc* stretching from top to bottom of a page; an arrangement (of troops, ships *etc*) one behind the other.

coma *noun* unconsciousness lasting a long time. – *adjective* **comatose** in or of a coma; drowsy, sluggish.

comb *noun* a toothed instrument for separating, smoothing or cleaning hair, wool, flax *etc*; the crest of certain birds; a collection of cells for honey. – *verb* to arrange, smooth or clean with a comb; to search (a place) thoroughly.

combat *verb* to fight or struggle against. – *noun* a fight or struggle. – *noun, adjective* **combatant** (a person who is) fighting. – *adjective* **combative** quarrelsome; involving fighting.

combine *verb* to join together. – *noun* a number of traders *etc* who join together. – *noun* **combination** a joining together of things or people; a set of things or people combined; the series of letters or figures dialled to open a safe; (*plural*) an article of underwear for the body and legs. – *noun* **combine harvester** a machine that both cuts and threshes crops.

combustible *adjective* liable to catch fire and burn. – *noun* anything that will catch fire. – *noun* **combustion** burning.

come *verb* (*past tense* **came**, *past participle* **come**) to move towards this place (opposite of **go**): *Come here!*; to draw near: *Christmas is coming*; to arrive: *We'll have tea when you come*; to happen, occur: *The index comes at the end of the book*. – **come about** to happen; **come across** or **come upon** to meet, find accidentally; **come by** to obtain; **come into** to get (by inheriting); **come of age** to reach the age at which one becomes an adult for legal purposes; **come round** or **come to** to recover (from a faint *etc*); **come upon** *see* **come across**; **to come** in the future.

comedy *noun* (*plural* **comedies**) a play of light-hearted or amusing kind (opposite of **tragedy**). – *noun* **comedian** a

performer who tells jokes, acts in comedy *etc*.

comely *adjective* good-looking, pleasing. – *noun* **comeliness**.

comet *noun* a kind of star which has a tail of light.

comfort *verb* to help, soothe (someone in pain or distress). – *noun* ease, quiet enjoyment; state of being comfortable; anything that makes one happier or more at ease. – *adjective* **comfortable** at ease, free from trouble, pain, hardship *etc*; giving comfort.

comic *adjective* of comedy; funny. – *noun* someone amusing, *esp* a professional comedian; a (comic) picture paper. – *adjective* **comical** funny, amusing. – *noun* **comic strip** a strip of small pictures showing stages in an adventure.

comma *noun* in punctuation, the mark (,).

command *verb* to give an order; to be in charge of; to look over or down upon (a view *etc*). – *noun* an order; control. – *noun* **commandant** an officer who has command of a place or of troops. – *noun* **commander** a person who commands; in the navy, an officer next in rank below captain. – *adjective* **commanding** powerful; having a wide view. – *noun* **commandment** an order or command.

commandeer *verb* to seize (something) *esp* for the use of an army.

commando *noun* (*plural* **commandoes**) (a soldier serving in) a unit of the army trained for hard or dangerous tasks.

commemorate *verb* to bring to memory by some solemn act; to serve as a memorial of. – *noun* **commemoration**.

commence *verb* to begin. – *noun* **commencement**.

commend *verb* to praise; to give into the care of. – *adjective* **commendable** praiseworthy. – *noun* **commendation** praise. – *adjective* **commendatory** praising.

commensurate *adjective* (with **with**) equal in size, importance *etc*, in proportion to.

comment *noun* a remark or series of remarks; a criticism. – Also *verb*. – *noun* **commentary** (*plural* **commentaries**) a description of an event *etc* (by one who is watching it) (also **running commentary**); a set of explanatory notes for a book *etc*. – *noun* **commentator** a person who gives or writes a commentary.

commerce *noun* the buying and selling of goods between people or nations; trade, dealings. – *adjective* **commercial** of commerce; (of radio, TV *etc*) paid for by advertisements. – *noun* an advertisement on radio, TV *etc*.

commiserate *verb* to sympathize (with). – *noun* **commiseration** pity.

commissar *noun* (in USSR) the head of a government department.

commissariat *noun* that part of an army or other organization that looks after the food supply.

commission *noun* the act of committing; a warrant or document giving authority to an officer in the armed forces; an order *esp* for a work of art; a fee for doing business *etc* on another's behalf; a body of persons appointed to investigate something. – *verb* to give a commission or power to. – *noun* **commissionaire** a uniformed doorkeeper. – *noun* **commissioner** a person who represents high authority in a district *etc*; a member of a commission. – **in (out of) commission** in (not in) use.

commit *verb* (*past tense* **committed**) to give or hand over, to entrust; (with **oneself** *etc*) to promise; to do (something *usu* wrong): *commit a crime*. – *noun* **commitment** a promise; a task that must be done. – *noun* **committal** the act of committing. – *adjective* **committed** pledged to support (something): *a committed communist*. – *noun* **committee** a number of people chosen from a larger body to attend to some special business.

commodious *adjective* roomy, spacious.

commodity *noun* (*plural* **commodities**) an article to be bought or sold; (*plural*) goods, produce.

commodore *noun* an officer next above a captain in the navy.

common *adjective* shared by all or by many, seen or happening often, ordinary; without special rank. – *noun* land belonging to the people of a town, parish *etc*. – *noun* **commoner** someone who is not a noble. – *noun* **common law** unwritten law based on custom. – *noun* **Common Market** an association of certain European countries to establish free trade (without duty, tariffs *etc*) among them. – *noun* **common noun** a

name for any one of a class of things (opposite of **proper noun**). – *adjective* **commonplace** ordinary. – *noun* **common-room** in a school *etc*, a sitting-room for the use of a group. – *noun* **Commons (House of Commons)** the lower House of Parliament. – *noun* **common sense** practical good sense. – *noun* **commonwealth** an association of self-governing states.

commotion *noun* a disturbance *esp* among people.

commune *noun* a group of people living together, sharing work *etc*. – *verb* to talk together. – *adjective* **communal** common, shared.

communicate *verb* to make known, tell; to pass on; to get in touch (with); to have a connecting door. – *adjective* **communicable** able to be passed on to others: *a communicable disease*. – *noun* **communication** an act or means of conveying information; a message; a way of passing from place to place. – *adjective* **communicative** willing to give information, talkative.

communiqué *kom-ū'ni-kā*. *noun* an official announcement.

Communion *noun* in the Christian Church, the celebration of the Lord's supper. – *noun* **communion** the act of sharing (thoughts, feelings *etc*), fellowship.

communism *noun* (often with *cap*) the kind of socialism developed in Russia or China where industry is controlled by the state. – *adjective* **communist** of communism. – *noun* (often with *cap*) a person who believes in communism.

community *noun* (*plural* **communities**) a group of people living in one place; the public in general. – *n* **community charge** a tax related to property, charged according to the number of residents, to pay for local public services.

commute *verb* to travel regularly between two places *esp* to work (in a city *etc*) from one's home; to change (a punishment) for one less severe. – *noun* **commuter** a person who travels regularly to work from home in a different place.

compact *adjective* fitted or packed closely, neatly together. – *noun* a bargain or agreement. – *noun* **compact disc** a small audio disc on which digitally recorded sound is registered as a series of pits that are readable by a laser beam.

companion noun someone or something that accompanies; a friend. – adjective **companionable** friendly. – noun **companionship** friendship; the act of accompanying. – noun **companionway** on a ship, a staircase from deck to cabin.

company noun (plural **companies**) a gathering of persons; a number of persons who have joined together for trade etc, a business firm; part of a regiment; a ship's crew; companionship.

compare verb to set things together to see how far they are or are not alike; to liken. – adjective **comparable**. – adjective **comparative** judged by comparing with something else: a comparative improvement; (gram) the degree of adjective or adverb between positive and superlative (eg blacker, better, more courageous). – noun **comparison** the act of comparing. – **beyond compare** much better than all rivals.

compartment noun a separate part or division (eg of a railway carriage).

compass noun (plural **compasses**) an instrument with a magnetized needle for showing direction; (usu plural) an instrument (made up of a fixed leg and a movable leg) for drawing circles.

compassion noun pity for another's suffering; mercy. – adjective **compassionate** pitying, merciful.

compatible adjective able to live with, agree with etc. – noun **compatibility**.

compatriot noun a fellow-countryman.

compel verb (past tense **compelled**) to force (someone to do something).

compensate verb to make up for wrong or damage done, esp by giving money. – noun **compensation** something (usu money) given to make up for wrong or damage.

compère (masculine), **commère** (feminine) noun a person who introduces different acts of an entertainment. – Also verb.

compete verb to try to beat others (in a race etc). – noun **competition**. – adjective **competitive** (of sport etc) based on competitions; (of a person) fond of competing. – noun **competitor** a person who competes; a rival.

competent adjective capable, efficient; skilled; properly trained or qualified. – noun **competence**.

competition, competitive see **compete**.

compile verb to make (a book etc) from information that one has collected. – noun **compilation**. – noun **compiler**.

complacent adjective satisfied (with oneself). – noun **complacence**. – noun **complacency**.

complain verb to express dissatisfaction (about something); to grumble. – noun **complaint** a statement of one's dissatisfaction, sorrow etc; an illness: The common cold is not a serious complaint.

complement noun that which completes or fills up; the full number or quantity needed to fill (something); the angle that must be added to a given angle to make up a right angle. – adjective **complementary** completing; together making up a whole; (of an angle) making up a right angle.

complete adjective having nothing missing; finished; whole. – verb to finish; to make perfect. – noun **completeness**. – noun **completion** the act of completing.

complex adjective made up of many parts; complicated, difficult. – noun (plural **complexes**) a set of repressed emotions and ideas which affect a person's behaviour; an exaggerated reaction (to something), an obsession: a complex about her weight; a group of related buildings etc: a shopping complex. – noun **complexity** (plural **complexities**).

complexion noun the colour or look of the skin of the face; appearance.

compliance see **comply**.

complicate verb to make difficult. – adjective **complicated** difficult to understand; detailed. – noun **complication** a (new) difficulty; a development (in an illness etc) which makes things worse.

complicity noun (plural **complicities**) a share in a crime or other misdeed.

compliment noun an expression of praise or flattery; (plural) good wishes. – verb to praise, to congratulate (on). – adjective **complimentary** flattering, praising; given free: a complimentary ticket.

comply verb (past tense **complied**) (to agree) to do something that someone else orders or wishes. – noun **compliance**. – adjective **compliant** yielding, giving agreement.

component adjective forming one of the parts of a whole. – noun a part (of a machine etc).

compose *verb* to put together or in order, to arrange, form; to create (a piece of music, a poem *etc*). – *adjective* **composed** quiet, calm. – *noun* **composer** a person who writes music. – *adjective* **composite** made up of parts. – *noun* **composition** the act of composing; the thing composed, *esp* a piece of writing or music; a mixture of substances. – *noun* **compositor** a person who puts together the types for printing. – *noun* **composure** calmness.

compost *noun* a gardener's mixture of natural manures.

compound *adjective* made up of a number of different parts; not simple. – *noun* (in chemistry) a substance formed from two or more elements; an enclosure (round a building).

comprehend *verb* to understand; to include. – *adjective* **comprehensible** able to be understood. – *noun* **comprehension** the act or power of understanding. – *adjective* **comprehensive** taking in or including much or all. – *noun* **comprehensive school** a school providing all types of secondary education.

compress *verb* to press together; to force into a narrower or smaller space. – *noun* a folded cloth or pad used to create pressure on a part of the body or to reduce inflammation. – *noun* **compression**.

comprise *verb* to include, contain; to consist of.

compromise *noun* a settlement, an agreement reached by both sides giving up something. – *verb* to make a compromise; to put in a difficult or embarrassing position.

compulsion *noun* a force driving a person to do a thing. – *adjective* **compulsory** requiring to be done; forced upon one.

compunction *noun* regret.

compute *verb* to count, calculate. – *noun* **computation**. – *noun* **computer** an electronic machine that carries out many stages of calculations and stores and sorts information of various kinds.

comrade *noun* a companion, a friend.

con *verb* (*past tense* **conned**) to trick, play a confidence trick on. – *noun* **con-man** one who (regularly) cons people. – *noun* **con-trick** a confidence trick.

concave *adjective* hollow or curved inwards (opposite of **convex**). – *noun* **concavity** (*plural* **concavities**) a hollow.

conceal *verb* to hide, keep secret. – *noun* **concealment** the act of hiding; a hiding-place.

concede *verb* to give (up), yield; to admit (the truth of something): *I concede that you may be right*.

conceit *noun* a too high opinion of oneself or of one's abilities. – *adjective* **conceited** having a very good opinion of oneself, vain. – *noun* **conceitedness**.

conceive *verb* to form in the mind, to imagine; to become pregnant. – *adjective* **conceivable** able to be imagined.

concentrate *verb* to direct all one's attention or effort towards (something); to bring together to one place. – *adjective* **concentrated** (of an acid *etc*) made stronger or less dilute. – *noun* **concentration**.

concentric *adjective* (*esp* of circles placed one inside the other) having the same point for centre.

concept *noun* a general idea about something. – *noun* **conception** the act of conceiving; an idea.

concern *verb* to have to do with; to make uneasy; to interest, to affect; (with **oneself** *etc*) to be interested or anxious. – *noun* that which concerns; anxiety; a business. – *preposition* **concerning** about: *concerning your inquiry*.

concert *noun* a musical entertainment, performance or show. – *adjective* **concerted** planned or practised together. – **in concert** together.

concertina *noun* a type of musical wind instrument, with bellows and keys.

concerto *noun* (*plural* **concertos**) a long piece of music for solo instrument with an accompaniment from an orchestra.

concession *noun* a granting or allowing of something: *a concession for oil exploration*; that which is granted, allowed; *plural* (referring to ticket prices *etc*) certain groups of people, *usu* children, unemployed and old age pensioners, granted a reduction in price.

conch *noun* (*plural* **conches**) a kind of sea-shell.

conciliate *verb* to win over (someone previously unfriendly or angry). – *noun* **conciliation**. – *adjective* **conciliatory**.

concise *adjective* brief, in a few words. – *noun* **conciseness**.

conclude *verb* to end; to reach a decision or a judgement; to settle. – *adjective*

concluding last, final. – *noun* **conclusion** end; decision, judgement. – *adjective* **conclusive** settling, deciding: *They offered conclusive proof.*

concoct *verb* to mix (a food or drink); to make up, invent: *concoct a story.* – *noun* **concoction.**

concord *noun* agreement.

concourse *noun* a crowd; a crowding together; a large open space in a building *etc.*

concrete *adjective* solid, real; made of concrete. – *noun* a mixture of gravel, cement *etc* used in building.

concur *verb* (*past tense* **concurred**) to agree. – *noun* **concurrence.** – *adjective* **concurrent** happening *etc* together; agreeing.

concussion *noun* temporary harm done to the brain when one receives a knock on the head.

condemn *verb* to blame; to give judgement against or to sentence to a certain punishment; to declare (houses *etc*) unfit for use. – *noun* **condemnation.** – *noun* **condemned cell** a cell for a prisoner condemned to death.

condense *verb* to make to go into a smaller space; (of steam, vapour) to turn to liquid. – *noun* **condensation** the act of condensing; drops of liquid formed from vapour.

condescend *verb* to act towards someone as if one is better than he is; to make oneself humble. – *adjective* **condescending.** – *noun* **condescension.**

condiment *noun* something that seasons or flavours food, *esp* salt or pepper.

condition *noun* the state in which anything is; something that must happen or be done before some other thing happens or is done; a term of or a point in a bargain, treaty *etc.* – *adjective* **conditional** depending on certain things happening.

condole *verb* to share another's sorrow, to sympathize. – *noun* **condolence.**

condom *noun* a contraceptive rubber sheath worn by a man.

condone *verb* to forgive, allow (an offence) to pass unchecked.

conducive *adjective* helping, favourable (to): *conducive to peace.*

conduct *verb* to lead, guide; to control, be in charge of, organize; to direct (an orchestra *etc*); to pass on, transmit (electricity *etc*); (with **oneself**) to behave. – *noun* act or method of controlling or organizing; behaviour. – *noun* **conduction** a passing on, transmission of heat, electricity *etc.* – *noun* **conductor** one who directs an orchestra *etc;* (**conductor** (*masculine*), **conductress** (*feminine*)) a person in charge of a bus *etc;* something that transmits (heat, electricity *etc*).

conduit *kon'dit, noun* a channel or pipe to carry water, electric wires *etc.*

cone *noun* a shape or figure, round at the bottom and coming to a point; anything cone-shaped (*eg* a fir-cone). – *adjective* **conical** cone-shaped.

coney *see* **cony.**

confectioner *noun* a person who makes or sells sweets, cakes *etc.* – *noun* **confectionery** sweets, cakes *etc;* the shop or business of a confectioner.

confederate *adjective* joined together by treaty. – *noun* a person who has agreed to act with others (often for an evil purpose). – *noun* **confederacy** (*plural* **confederacies**) a league, alliance. – *noun* **confederation** a union, a league (of states *etc*).

confer *verb* (*past tense* **conferred**) to talk together; to give, grant. – *noun* **conference** a meeting for discussion.

confess *verb* to own up, to admit (*eg* that one has done wrong). – *adjective* **confessed** admitted, not secret. – *noun* **confession** owning up to (a crime or fault).

confetti *noun* small pieces of coloured paper thrown at weddings or other celebrations.

confide *verb* (with **in**) to tell (secrets *etc*) to; to hand over to someone's care. – *noun* **confidant** (*masculine*), **confidante** (*feminine*) a person trusted with a secret. – *noun* **confidence** trust or belief; self-reliance; boldness; something told privately. – *noun* **confidence trick** a trick to get money *etc* from someone by first gaining his trust. – *adjective* **confident** very sure; bold. – *adjective* **confidential** to be kept as a secret: *confidential information;* having to keep secrets: *confidential secretary.* – *adjective* **confiding** trusting.

confine *verb* to shut up, imprison; to keep within limits. – *noun* **confinement** the state of being confined; imprisonment;

(the time of) giving birth to a child. – noun plural **confines** limits.

confirm verb to make firm, strengthen; to make sure; to show to be true; to take into the Church. – noun **confirmation** a making sure; proof; the cer-emony in which a person is made a full member of the Church. – adjective **confirmed** settled in a habit etc: a confirmed bachelor.

confiscate verb to take away, as a punishment. – noun **confiscation**.

conflagration noun a big fire.

conflict noun a struggle or contest; a battle. – verb (of statements etc) to contradict each other. – adjective **conflicting**.

confluence noun a place where rivers join.

conform verb to follow the example of most other people (in behaviour, dress, religion etc). – noun **conformation** form, shape or structure. – noun **conformity** (plural **conformities**) likeness; the act of conforming.

confound verb to puzzle, confuse.

confront verb to face, meet (eg an enemy, a difficulty); to bring face to face (with): He was confronted with the evidence. – noun **confrontation**.

confuse verb to mix up, to put in disorder; to mix up in the mind; to puzzle; to embarrass. – noun **confusion**.

congeal verb to become solid esp by cooling; to freeze.

congenial adjective agreeable, pleasant.

congenital adjective (of a disease etc) present in a person from birth.

conger noun a kind of large sea-eel.

congested adjective overcrowded; clogged; (of a part of the body) too full of blood. – noun **congestion** (of traffic etc) overcrowded condition; a gathering of too much blood in one part of the body.

conglomeration noun a heap or collection.

congratulate verb to express one's joy (to a person) at their success. – noun **congratulation** (often in plural). – adjective **congratulatory**.

congregate verb to come together in a crowd. – noun **congregation** a gathering esp of people in a church.

congress noun (plural **congresses**) a large meeting of persons from different places for discussion. – noun **Congress** the name given to the parliament of the United States.

congruent adjective (of triangles etc) exactly matching.

congruous adjective suitable, appropriate. – noun **congruity**.

conical see **cone**.

conifer noun a cone-bearing tree. – adjective **coniferous**.

conjecture noun a guess. – verb to guess. – adjective **conjectural**.

conjugal adjective of marriage.

conjugate verb to give the different parts of a verb. – noun **conjugation**.

conjunction noun a word that joins sentences, phrases etc (eg and, but); a union, combination with. – **in conjunction with** together with, acting with.

conjunctivitis noun a kind of inflammation of the inside of the eyelid and surface of the eye.

conjure verb to perform tricks that seem magical. – noun **conjuror** or **conjurer** a person who performs conjuring tricks.

conker noun a horse-chestnut, esp one used in a game (**conkers**) in which one tries to hit and destroy one's opponent's chestnut.

connect verb to join or fasten together. – noun **connection** something that connects; a state of being connected; a train, aeroplane etc which takes one on the next part of one's journey; a friend, relation, business acquaintance etc. – **in connection with** concerning.

conning-tower noun the place on a warship or submarine from which orders for steering are given.

connive verb (with **at**) to take no notice of, disregard (a misdeed etc). – noun **connivance**.

connoisseur kon-ès-ur', noun a person who has an expert knowledge (of pictures, music, wines etc).

connotation noun a meaning; what is suggested by a word in addition to its simple meaning.

connubial adjective of marriage.

conquer verb to gain by force; to overcome. – noun **conqueror** a person who conquers. – noun **conquest** something won by force or effort; an act of conquering.

conscience *noun* one's inward sense of what is right and wrong. – *adjective* **conscientious** careful and earnest in one's work *etc*. – *noun* **conscientiousness**.

conscious *adjective* aware of oneself and one's surroundings, awake (after being unconscious); aware, knowing; deliberate, intentional. – *noun* **consciousness**.

conscript *noun* a person who is obliged by law to serve in the armed forces. – *verb* to compel to serve (in the armed forces). – *noun* **conscription**.

consecrate *verb* to set apart for a holy use. – *noun* **consecration**.

consecutive *adjective* coming in order, one after the other.

consensus *noun* an agreement (of opinion).

consent *verb* to agree (to). – *noun* agreement; permission.

consequence *noun* that which comes after, result; importance. – *adjective* **consequent** following as a result. – *adjective* **consequential** following as a result; important.

conserve *verb* to keep from being wasted, spoilt or lost. – *noun* **conservation** the act of conserving (old buildings, countryside, wild animals and flowers *etc*). – *noun* **conservationist** one who encourages and practises conservation. – *adjective* **conservative** not liking changes; (of a guess or estimate) moderate, not exaggerated. – *noun, adjective* **Conservative** (a supporter) of the Conservative Party. – *noun* **Conservative Party** one of the main political parties of the UK. – *noun* **conservatory** (*plural* **conservatories**) a glass-house for plants.

consider *verb* to think; to think about (carefully); to think of as, regard as; to pay attention to the wishes *etc* of (someone). – *adjective* **considerable** (fairly) large; important. – *adjective* **considerate** thoughtful about others' wishes *etc*, kind. – *noun* **consideration** serious thinking; thoughtfulness for others; a small payment. – *preposition* **considering** taking into account: *considering his age*.

consign *kö n-sīn'*, *verb* to give into the care of. – *noun* **consignment** a load (*eg* of goods).

consist *verb* to be made up (of). – *noun* **consistency** (*plural* **consistencies**) thickness or firmness; the quality of (always) being the same. – *adjective* **consistent** not changing, regular; (of statements *etc*) not contradicting each other.

console *verb* to comfort, cheer up. – *noun* **consolation** something that makes trouble *etc* more easy to bear.

consolidate *verb* to make or become solid or strong; to unite. – *noun* **consolidation**.

consonant *noun* a letter of the alphabet that is not a vowel (*eg* b, c).

consort *noun* a husband or wife; a companion. – *verb* to keep company (with).

conspicuous *adjective* clearly seen, noticeable.

conspire *verb* to plan or plot together. – *noun* **conspiracy** (*plural* **conspiracies**) a plot by a group of people. – *noun* **conspirator** a person who takes part in a conspiracy.

constable *noun* a policeman; (*hist*) a high officer of state or the keeper of a castle. – *noun* **constabulary** the police force.

constant *adjective* never stopping; never changing; faithful. – *noun* **constancy**. – *adverb* **constantly** always; often.

constellation *noun* a group of stars.

consternation *noun* dismay, astonishment.

constipation *noun* too slow working of the bowels. – *verb* **constipate** to cause constipation.

constitute *verb* to step up, establish; to form or make up. – *noun* **constituency** (*plural* **constituencies**) (the voters in) a district which has a member of parliament. – *adjective* **constituent** making or forming. – *noun* a necessary part; a voter in a constituency. – *noun* **constitution** the way in which a thing is made up; the natural condition of a body with regard to strength, health *etc*; a set of rules, laws *etc* by which a country or body of people is governed. – *adjective* **constitutional** of a constitution. – *noun* a short walk for the sake of one's health.

constrain *verb* to force (a person) to act in a certain way. – *noun* **constraint** compulsion, force; embarrassment.

constrict *verb* to press together tightly, to cramp; to surround and squeeze.

construct *verb* to build, make. – *noun* **construction** the act of constructing;

anything built; the arrangement of words in a sentence; meaning. – *adjective* **constructive** of construction; helping to improve: *constructive criticism*.

consul *noun* a person who looks after their country's affairs in a foreign country; in ancient Rome, a chief ruler. – *adjective* **consular**. – *noun* **consulate** the official residence of a consul; the duties and authority of a consul.

consult *verb* to seek advice or information from. – *noun* **consultant** one (*esp* a doctor) who gives professional or expert advice; the senior grade of hospital doctor. – Also *adjective*. – *noun* **consultation** the act of consulting (for expert advice). – *noun* **consulting room** a room where a doctor *etc* sees patients.

consume *verb* to eat up; to use (up); to destroy. – *noun* **consumer** one who buys, eats or uses (goods *etc*).

consummate *verb* to complete; to make (marriage) legally complete by sexual intercourse. – *adjective* complete, perfect.

consumption *noun* the act of consuming; the amount consumed; (*old*) tuberculosis.

cont. or **contd** *abbrev* continued.

contact *noun* touch; meeting; communication; an acquaintance, *esp* one who can be of help; a person who has been with someone suffering from an infectious disease. – *verb* to get into contact with. – *noun* **contact lens** a, *usu* plastic, lens worn in contact with the eyeball instead of spectacles.

contagious *adjective* (of disease *etc*) spreading from person to person (*esp* by touch).

contain *verb* to hold or have inside; to hold back: *contain her anger*. – *n* **container** a box, tin, jar *etc* for holding anything.

contaminate *verb* to make impure or dirty. – *noun* **contamination**.

contd *see* **cont**.

contemplate *verb* to look at or think about attentively; to intend. – *noun* **contemplation**.

contemporary *adjective, noun* (of) a person living at or belonging to the same time.

contempt *noun* complete lack of respect, scorn. – *adjective* **contemptible** deserving scorn, worthless. – *adjective* **contemptuous** scornful. – **contempt of** court deliberate disobedience to and disrespect for the law and those who carry it out.

contend *verb* to struggle against; to hold firmly to a belief, maintain (that). – *noun* **contention** an opinion strongly held; a quarrel, dispute. – *adjective* **contentious** quarrelsome.

content *adjective* happy, satisfied. – *noun* happiness, satisfaction. – *verb* to make happy or to satisfy. – *noun* (often *plural*) that which is contained in anything. – *adjective* **contented** happy, content. – *noun* **contentment** happiness, content.

contention, contentious *see* **contend**.

contest *verb* to fight for, argue against. – *noun* a fight, a competition. – *noun* **contestant** a person who contests.

context *noun* the place in a book, speech *etc* to which a certain part belongs; the setting, background of an event *etc*.

contiguous *adjective* touching, close. – *noun* **contiguity**.

continent *noun* one of the five great divisions of the earth's land surface (Europe, Asia, Africa, Australia, America). – *adjective* **continental** of or like a continent; European. – **the Continent** the mainland of Europe.

contingent *adjective* depending (on something else). – *noun* a batch, a group (*esp* of soldiers). – *noun* **contingency** (*plural* **contingencies**) a chance happening.

continue *verb* to keep on, go on (doing something). – *adjective* **continual** going on without stop. – *noun* **continuance** the state of going on without interruption. – *noun* **continuation** the act of carrying something farther or continuing; a part that continues, an extension. – *noun* **continuity** the state of having no gaps or breaks. – *adjective* **continuous** coming one after the other (without a gap or break).

contort *verb* to twist or turn violently. – *noun* **contortion** a violent twisting. – *noun* **contortionist** a person who can twist their body violently.

contour *noun* (often *plural*) outline, shape. – *noun* **contour line** a line drawn on a map through points all at the same height above sea-level.

contraband *noun* goods, legally forbidden to be brought into a country; smuggled goods. – Also *adjective*.

contraception *noun* the prevention of conceiving children. – *adjective, noun*

contraceptive (of) a drug or device which prevents the conceiving of children.

contract *verb* to become or make smaller; to bargain for; to promise in writing. – *noun* a (written) agreement. – *noun* **contraction** a shortening; a shortened form (*esp* of a word). – *noun* **contractor** a person who promises to do work, or supply goods, at an arranged price.

contradict *verb* to say the opposite of; to deny. – *noun* **contradiction**. – *adjective* **contradictory**.

contralto *noun* (*plural* **contraltos**) the deepest or lowest singing voice in women.

contraption *noun* a machine, a device.

contrapuntal *see* **counterpoint**.

contrary¹ *adjective* opposite. – *noun* the opposite. – **on the contrary** just the opposite.

contrary² *adjective* always doing or saying the opposite, perverse. – *noun* **contrariness**.

contrast *verb* to compare so as to show differences; to show a marked difference from. – *noun* a difference between (two) things.

contravene *verb* to break (a law *etc*). – *noun* **contravention**.

contretemps *kon̄ʂˈtrè-tonʂ*, *noun* a mishap at an awkward moment.

contribute *verb* to give (money, help *etc*) along with others; to supply, give (written articles to a magazine *etc*); to help to cause (something). – *noun* **contribution**. – *noun* **contributor**.

contrite *adjective* very sorry for having done wrong. – *noun* **contrition**.

contrive *verb* to plan; to bring about (with difficulty), manage. – *noun* **contrivance** an act of contriving; an invention.

control *noun* power or authority to guide, rule, manage, restrain *etc*; (often *plural*) means by which a driver keeps a machine powered or guided. – *verb* to exercise control over; to have power over. – *adjective* **controlled**. – *noun* **controller**. – *noun* **control tower** an airport building from which landing and take-off instructions are given.

controversy *noun* (*plural* **controversies**) an argument, a disagreement. – *adjective* **controversial** likely to cause argument.

conundrum *noun* a riddle, a question.

conurbation *noun* a group of towns forming a single built-up area.

convalesce *verb* to recover health gradually after being ill. – *noun* **convalescence** a gradual return to health and strength. – *adjective*, *noun* **convalescent** (of) a person convalescing.

convection *noun* the spreading of heat by movement of heated air or water. – *noun* **convector** a heater which works by convection.

convene *verb* to call or come together. – *noun* **convener** a person who calls a meeting; the chairman or chairwoman of a committee.

convenient *adjective* suitable; easy to reach or use, handy. – *noun* **convenience** suitableness, handiness; any means of giving ease or comfort; (*coll*) a (public) lavatory. – **at your convenience** when it suits you best.

convent *noun* a dwelling for nuns (or monks).

conventicle *noun* (*hist*) a secret meeting (for worship).

convention *noun* a way of behaving that has become usual, a custom; a large meeting or assembly; a treaty or agreement. – *adjective* **conventional** done by habit or custom.

converge *verb* to come together, meet at a point – *noun* **convergence**. – *adjective* **convergent**.

converse *verb* to talk. – *noun* talk; the opposite. – *adjective* opposite. – *noun* **conversation** talk, exchange of ideas, news *etc*. – *adjective* **conversational** of or used in conversation; talkative.

convert *verb* to change (from one thing into another); to turn from one religion to another, or from an evil to a religious life. – *noun* a person who has been converted. – *noun* **conversion** the act of converting; something converted to another use. – *adjective* **convertible** able to be changed (from one thing to another). – *noun* a car with a folding roof.

convex *adjective* curved on the outside (opposite of **concave**). – *noun* **convexity** (*plural* **convexities**).

convey *verb* to carry, transport; to send; (in law) to hand over: *convey property*. – *noun* **conveyance** the act of conveying; a vehicle of any kind. – *noun* **conveyor**

or **conveyor belt** an endless moving mechanism for conveying articles, *esp* in a factory.

convict *verb* to declare or to prove that a person is guilty. – *noun* a person found guilty of a crime (and sent to prison). – *noun* **conviction** (in a law court) the passing of a sentence upon a guilty person; a strong belief.

convince *verb* to make (someone) believe that something is true; to persuade (someone) by showing.

convivial *adjective* jolly, festive. – *noun* **conviviality**.

convocation *noun* a meeting *esp* of bishops, or of heads of a university.

convolvulus *noun* a kind of twining plant with trumpet-shaped flowers.

convoy *verb* to go along with and protect. – *noun* merchant ships protected by warships; a line of army lorries with armed guard.

convulse *verb* to cause to shake violently: *convulsed with laughter*. – *noun* **convulsion** a sudden stiffening or jerking of the muscles; a violent disturbance. – *adjective* **convulsive**.

cony or **coney** *noun* a rabbit or its fur.

coo *verb* to make a sound like that of a dove. – Also *noun*.

cook *verb* to prepare (food) by heating; (*coll*) to alter (accounts *etc*) dishonestly. – *noun* a person who cooks and prepares food ready for table. – *noun* **cooker** a stove for cooking; an apple *etc* used in cooking, not for eating raw. – *noun* **cookery** the art of cooking.

cool *adjective* slightly cold; calm, not excited; rather cheeky. – *verb* to make or grow cool; to calm. – *adjective* **coolly**. – *noun* **coolness**.

coop *noun* a box or cage for hens *etc*. – *verb* to shut (up) as in a coop. – *noun* **cooper** a person who makes barrels.

co-operate *verb* to work or act together. – *noun* **co-operation** a working together; willingness to act together. – *noun* **co-operative** a business or farm *etc* owned by the workers. – *noun* **co-operative society** or **co-op** a trading organization in which the profits are shared among members.

co-opt *verb* to choose (someone) to join a committee or other body.

co-ordinate *verb* to make things fit in or work smoothly together. – *noun* **co-ordination**.

coot *noun* a type of water-bird with a white spot on the forehead.

cope *verb* to struggle or deal successfully (with), manage.

coping *noun* the top layer of stone in a wall. – *noun* **coping-stone** the top stone of a wall.

copious *adjective* plentiful.

copper *noun* an element, a hard reddish-brown metal; a coin made from (metal containing) copper; a large vessel made of copper, *usu* to boil water in. – *noun* **copperplate** very fine and regular handwriting.

copra *noun* the dried kernel of the coconut, yielding coconut oil.

copse or **coppice** *noun* a wood of low-growing trees.

copy *noun* (*plural* **copies**) an imitation; a print or reproduction (of a picture *etc*); an individual example of a certain book *etc*. – *verb* to make a copy of; to imitate. – *noun* **copyright** the right of one person or body to publish a book, perform a play, print music *etc*. – *adjective* of or protected by the law of copyright.

coquette *noun* a woman who flirts.

coral *noun* a hard surface made up of the skeletons of a kind of tiny animal, gradually building up from the sea-bottom to form a rock-like mass (**coral reef**).

cord *noun* thin rope or strong string; anything of cord-like appearance.

cordial *adjective* cheery, friendly. – *noun* a refreshing drink. – *noun* **cordiality**.

cordite *noun* a kind of explosive.

cordon *noun* a line of guards, police *etc* to keep people back. – *adjective, noun* **cordon bleu** (of) a first class cook.

corduroy *noun* a ribbed cloth (*usu* cotton) looking like velvet.

core *noun* the inner part of anything, *esp* fruit. – *verb* to take out the core of fruit.

co-respondent *noun* a man or woman charged with adultery, and proceeded against along with the wife or husband who is the **respondent**.

corgi *noun* a breed of short-legged dog.

cork *noun* the outer bark of the cork-tree (an oak found in southern Europe *etc*); a stopper for a bottle *etc* made of cork. – *adjective* made of cork. – *verb* to plug, to stop up (with a cork). – noun **corkscrew** a tool with a screw-like spike for taking out corks. – adjective shaped like a cork-screw.

corm noun the bulb-like underground stem of certain plants.

cormorant noun a type of big sea-bird.

corn noun (a grain or seed of) wheat, oats or maize; a little lump of hard skin usu on a toe. – noun **corncrake** a kind of bird with a harsh croaking cry. – noun **corned beef** salted (tinned) beef. – noun **cornflour** finely ground (maize) flour. – noun **cornflower** a type of plant, with a blue flower.

cornea noun the transparent covering of the eyeball.

corner noun the point where two lines, walls, roads etc meet; a small (quiet) place; (coll) a difficult situation. – verb to drive into a place from which there is no escape. – noun **cornerstone** the stone at the corner of (the foundation of) a building; something upon which much depends.

cornet noun a type of musical instrument like a trumpet; an ice-cream in a cone-shaped wafer.

cornice noun an ornamental border round a ceiling.

corolla noun the petals of a flower.

corollary noun (plural **corollaries**) something which may be taken for granted when something else has been proved; a natural result.

coronary noun (plural **coronaries**) (short for **coronary thrombosis**) a heart disease caused by blockage of one of the arteries supplying the heart.

coronation noun the crowning of a king or queen.

coroner noun a government officer who holds inquiries into the causes of sudden or accidental deaths.

coronet noun a small crown; a crown-like head-dress.

corporal noun in the British Army, the rank next below sergeant. – adjective of the body. – noun **corporal punishment** beating, caning etc.

corporate adjective of or forming a whole, united. – noun **corporation** a body of people acting as one, eg for administrative or business purposes.

corps kör, noun (plural **corps**) a division of an army; an organized group.

corpse noun a dead body.

corpulence noun fatness of body. – adjective **corpulent.**

corpuscle noun a very small particle or cell in a fluid (esp blood).

corral noun (US) a fenced space for (captured) animals; (US) a circle of wagons formed for defence.

correct verb to remove faults and errors from; to set right; to punish. – adjective having no errors; true. – noun **correction** the putting right of a mistake; punishment. – adjective **corrective.**

correspond verb to write letters to; to be similar (to), to match. – noun **correspondence** letters; likeness to. – noun **correspondent** a person who writes letters; a person who contributes reports to a newspaper etc.

corridor noun a passageway.

corrigendum noun (plural **corrigenda**) a correction to a book etc.

corroborate verb to give evidence which strengthens evidence already given. – noun **corroboration.** – adjective **corroborative.**

corrode verb to rust; to eat away, as acid eats into metal. – noun **corrosion.** – adjective **corrosive.**

corrugated adjective folded or shaped into ridges: corrugated iron.

corrupt verb to make evil or rotten; to bribe. – adjective dishonest, taking bribes; bad, rotten. – adjective **corruptible** able to be corrupted or bribed. – noun **corruption** evil, sin; bribery.

corsair noun a pirate; a pirate-ship.

corset noun a tight-fitting under-garment to support the body.

cortège noun a (funeral) procession.

corvette noun a type of small swift warship, used against submarines.

cosh noun (plural **coshes**) a short heavy stick. – verb to hit with a cosh.

cosmetic noun something designed to improve the appearance, esp of the face. – adjective improving the appearance of.

cosmic adjective of the universe or outer space.

cosmonaut noun an astronaut esp of the USSR.

cosmopolitan adjective belonging to all parts of the world; made up of people of many races; used to, feeling at home in, many different parts of the world.

cosset *verb* to treat with too much kindness, pamper.

cost *verb* (*past tense, past participle* **cost**) to be priced at; to cause loss (of something) as though in payment: *War costs lives.* – *noun* what must be spent or suffered in order to get something. – *adjective* **costly** high-priced, valuable. – *noun* **costliness**.

costume *noun* (a set of) clothes; clothes to wear in a play; fancy dress; a swimming costume. – *noun* **costume jewellery** inexpensive, imitation jewellery.

cosy *adjective* warm and comfortable. – *noun* (*plural* **cosies**) a covering used for a teapot *etc* to keep it warm.

cot *noun* a small bed with high sides for children; (*US*) a small bed which can be folded away, a camp bed; (in poetry *etc*) a cottage. – *noun* **cot death** the sudden unexplained death in sleep of an apparently healthy baby.

coterie *noun* a number of persons interested in the same things who tend to exclude other people.

cottage *noun* a small house, *usu* in the countryside or a village. – *noun* **cottage cheese** a soft, white cheese made from skim-milk. – *noun* **cottager** a person who lives in a cottage.

cotton *noun* a soft fluffy substance got from the seeds of the cotton plant; cloth made of cotton. – Also *adjective*. – *noun* **cottonwool** cotton in a fluffy state, used for wiping, absorbing.

couch *noun* (*plural* **couches**) a sofa. – *verb* to express (in words): *The letter was couched in old-fashioned English.* – *noun* **couch grass** a kind of grass, a troublesome weed.

couchette *koo-shet'*, *noun* a sleeping berth on a continental train *etc*, convertible into an ordinary seat.

cougar *noun* (*esp US*) the puma.

cough *noun* a noisy effort of the lungs to throw out air and harmful matter from the throat. – *verb* to make this effort.

could *verb* the form of the verb **can** used to express a condition: *He could do it if he tried. I could understand a small mistake, but this is ridiculous; see* also **can¹**.

coulomb *noun* a unit of electric charge.

council *noun* a group of (elected) persons who meet to discuss or give advice

about policy, government *etc*. – *noun* **councillor** a member of a council.

counsel *noun* advice; a person who advises in matters of law, a lawyer. – *verb* (*past tense* **counselled**) to give advice to. – *noun* **counsellor** a person who gives advice.

count *verb* to find the total number of, add up; to say numbers in order (1, 2, 3, *etc*); to think, consider: *Count yourself lucky!* – *noun* the act of counting; the number counted; a charge, accusation; a point being considered; a nobleman in certain countries (*feminine* **countess**). – *noun* **counter** a person who or a thing which counts; a token used in counting; a small plastic disc used in ludo *etc*; a table on which money is counted or goods are laid for show. – *adjective* **countless** too many to be counted, very many. – **count on** to rely on, depend on.

countenance *noun* the face; the look on a person's face. – *verb* to allow, encourage.

counter *verb* to answer or oppose (a move, act *etc*) by another. – *adverb* in the opposite direction. – *adjective* opposed; opposite. – *noun see* **count.**

counter- *prefix* against, opposing; opposite.

counteract *verb* to block or defeat (an action) by doing the opposite.

counterattack *noun* an attack made by the defenders upon an attacking enemy. – Also *verb.*

counterattraction *noun* something which draws away the attention from something else.

countercharge *verb* to bring a charge against someone who has accused one. – Also *noun.*

counterfeit *adjective* not genuine, not real; made in imitation *esp* with a dishonest purpose: *counterfeit money.* – Also *noun.* – *verb* to make a copy of for dishonest purposes.

counterfoil *noun* a part of a cheque, postal order *etc* kept by the payer or sender.

countermand *verb* to give an order which goes against one already given.

counterpane *noun* a top cover for a bed.

counterpart *noun* something which is just like or which corresponds to something or someone.

counterpoint *noun* the combining of two or more melodies to make a piece of music. – *adjective* **contrapuntal.**

counterpoise *noun* a weight which balances another weight.

countersign *verb* to sign one's name after another has done so to show that a document is genuine.

countess *see* **count** and **earl.**

country *noun* (*plural* **countries**) a nation; a land under one government; the land in which one lives; a district which is not in a town or city; an area or stretch of land. – *adjective* belonging to the country. – *noun* **countryside** the parts of the country other than towns and cities.

county *noun* (*plural* **counties**) a division of a country.

coup *kōō, noun* any sudden outstandingly successful move or act; a sudden and violent change in government: *The president was killed during the coup.* – *noun* **coup d'état** *kōō dā-tü¹,* a sudden and violent change in government.

couple *noun* a pair, two of a kind together; husband and wife. – *verb* to join together. – *noun* **couplet** two lines of rhyming verse. – *noun* **coupling** a kind of link for joining parts of machinery, railway carriages *etc.*

coupon *noun* a part of a ticket *etc* that can be torn off *esp* a piece cut from an advertisement *etc* which may be exchanged for goods or money; (**football coupon**) a form in which one tries to forecast the result of football matches in the hope of winning money.

courage *noun* bravery, lack of fear. – *adjective* **courageous.**

courgette *noun* a type of vegetable, a small marrow.

courier *noun* a person who acts as guide for tourists; a messenger.

course *noun* a path in which anything moves; the act of moving from point to point; the road or ground on which one runs, travels, plays games *etc*; the direction to be followed: *The ship held its course;* line of action (what one should do); a part of a meal; a number of things following each other: *a course of twelve lectures;* one of the rows of bricks in a wall. – *verb* to move quickly; to hunt. – *noun* **courser** a swift horse. – *noun*

coursing the hunting of hares with greyhounds. – **in due course** after a while, when it is the proper time; **in the course of** during.

court *noun* a shut-in space (*eg* one surrounded by houses, or one used for certain sports such as tennis); the persons who attend a king, queen *etc*; any place where a king, queen *etc* lives; the place where legal cases are heard or tried. – *verb* to try to persuade (a woman) to marry one, to woo; to try to gain (*eg* admiration) or seem to be trying to gain (danger *etc*). – *adjective* **courteous** polite; obliging. – *noun* **courtier** a member of a royal court. – *adjective* **courtly** having fine manners. – *noun* **court-martial** (*plural* **courts-martial**) a court held by navy or army officers to try those who break navy or army laws. – *noun* **courtship** the act or time of courting or wooing. – *noun* **courtyard** a court or enclosed space beside a house.

courtesy *kûr¹ti-si, noun* politeness.

courtier *see* **court.**

cousin *noun* the son or daughter of an uncle or aunt.

cove *noun* a small inlet on the sea coast; a bay.

coven *noun* a gathering of witches.

covenant *noun* an important agreement or promise between people to do or not to do something.

cover *verb* to put or spread something on, over or about; to hide; to stretch over (an area or a length of time): *Trees covered the land. His diary covered three years;* to include; to be enough for: *Five pounds should cover the cost;* to travel over: *He covers 3 kilometres a day;* to point a weapon at: *He had the gangster covered.* – *noun* something that covers, hides or protects. – *noun* **coverage** the area covered; the amount or extent of news covered by a newspaper *etc*; the amount of protection given by an insurance policy; something which covers. – *noun* **coverlet** a bed cover. – **cover up** to cover completely; to conceal deliberately (a wrong, an illegal or dishonest deed *etc*) (*noun* **cover-up**).

covert *adjective* secret, not done openly. – *noun* a hiding place (trees, bushes *etc*) for animals or birds when hunted.

covet *verb* to desire eagerly, *esp* something belonging to another person. –

adjective **covetous.** – *noun* **covetousness.**

covey *noun* (*pl* **coveys**) a flock of birds, *esp* partridges.

cow *noun* the female animal of the ox kind used for giving milk; the female of certain other animals (*eg* elephant, whale). – *verb* to frighten, subdue. – *adjective* **cowed.** – *noun* **cowboy** a man who has the charge of cattle on a ranch in America. – *noun* **cowherd** one who looks after cows.

coward *noun* a person who has no courage and shows fear easily. – *noun* **cowardice** lack of courage. – *adjective* **cowardly.**

cowed *see* **cow.**

cower *verb* to crouch down or shrink back, through fear.

cowl *noun* a cap or hood, *esp* that of a monk; a cover for a chimney.

cowslip *noun* a type of yellow wild flower.

cox *noun* short for **coxswain.**

coxcomb *noun* (*hist*) a strip of red cloth notched like a cock's comb, which court jesters used to wear; a person who is conceited *esp* about dress.

coxswain *noun* a person who steers a boat; an officer in charge of a boat and crew.

coy *adjective* too modest or shy.

coyote *koi-ōt'i*, *noun* (*plural* **coyote** or **coyotes**) a type of small wolf of N. America.

coypu *noun* a type of large, beaverlike animal living in rivers and marshes.

crab *noun* a kind of sea animal with a shell and five pairs of legs, the first pair of which have large claws. – *noun* **crab apple** a type of small, bitter apple. – *adjective* **crabbed** *krab'id*, bad-tempered. – *adjective, adverb* **crabwise** (moving) sideways like a crab.

crack *verb* to (cause to) make a sharp sudden sound; to break partly without falling to pieces; to break into (a safe); to solve, decipher (a code); to break open (a nut); to make (a joke). – *noun* a sharp sound; a split or break; a narrow opening; (*coll*) a sharp, witty remark; (*coll*) a pure form of cocaine. – *adjective* excellent: *a crack tennis player.* – *adjective* **cracked** split, damaged, crazy. – *noun* **cracker** a hollow tube of paper, often containing a small gift, which breaks with a bang when the ends are pulled; a thin, crisp biscuit. – **crack up** to fail suddenly, go to pieces, collapse.

crackle *verb* to make a continuous cracking noise. – *noun* **crackling** a cracking sound; the rind or outer skin of roast pork.

cradle *noun* a baby's bed *esp* one in which it can be rocked; anything shaped like a cradle in which something is laid (*eg* a frame under a ship that is being built).

craft *noun* a trade or skill; a boat or small ship; slyness. – *noun* **craftsman** or **craftswoman** a person who works at a trade. – *adjective* **crafty** cunning, sly.

crag *noun* a rough steep rock. – *adjective* **craggy** rocky; (*usu* of faces) with strong or rough features.

cram *verb* (*past tense* **crammed**) to fill full, stuff; to learn up in a short time facts for an examination.

cramp *noun* a painful stiffening of the muscles. – *verb* to put into too narrow or small a space; to hinder, restrict. – *adjective* **cramped** without enough room; (of handwriting) small and closely-written.

crampon *noun* a metal plate with spikes, fixed to the boots when climbing on ice *etc*.

cranberry *noun* a type of red, sour berry.

crane *noun* a kind of large wading bird with long legs, neck and bill; a machine for lifting heavy weights. – *verb* to stretch out the neck (to see round or over something).

cranium *noun* (*plural* **crania** or **craniums**) the skull.

crank *noun* a handle with which something (*eg* an axle) can be made to turn; a lever or arm which turns movement to and fro into movement round and round; a person with unusual or odd ideas. – *verb* to start (an engine) with a crank. – *adjective* **cranky** odd, with unusual ideas *etc*; cross, irritable.

cranny *noun* (*plural* **crannies**) a small opening or crack.

crape *see* **crêpe.**

crash *noun* (*plural* **crashes**) a noise of heavy things breaking or banging together; a collision, a violent meeting together of a vehicle (*eg* car, train, aeroplane) with another vehicle or another object (*eg* a tree, the ground) *usu* resulting in damage; the failure of a business. – *adjective* short but intensive: *a crash course in French.* – *verb* (of a car *etc*) to be involved in a crash; (of a business) to fail; (of a computer system or program) to have a complete breakdown; to force one's way noisily through; (*coll*) to attend (a party) uninvited (also **gatecrash**). – *noun* **crash-helmet** a covering for the head worn for protection by motor-cyclists *etc*. – *verb* **crash-land** to land (an aircraft), *usu* in an emergency, in a way which damages it. – *noun* **crash-landing**.

crass *adjective* stupid.

crate *noun* an openwork container, *usu* made of wooden slats, for carrying goods, sometimes with compartments for bottles. – Also *v*.

crater *noun* the bowl-shaped mouth of a volcano; a hole in the earth made by an explosion.

cravat *noun* a scarf worn in place of a tie.

craven *adjective* cowardly.

crawfish *see* **crayfish**.

crawl *verb* to move on hands and knees; to move slowly; to be covered (with): *crawling with wasps*; to behave in too humble a manner. – *noun* the act of crawling; a kind of swimming stroke.

crayfish or **crawfish** *noun* a kind of shellfish, something like a small lobster.

crayon *noun* a coloured pencil or stick used for drawing.

craze *noun* a temporary fashion or enthusiasm. – *adjective* **crazy** mad, unreasonable. – *noun* **crazy paving** paving made with stones of irregular shape.

creak *verb* to make a sharp, grating sound like the sound of a hinge in need of oiling.

cream *noun* the fatty substance which forms on milk and gives butter when churned; anything like cream: *Use cleansing cream instead of soap. Eat your ice cream*; the best part of anything: *cream of society*. – *verb* to take off the cream; to take away the best part of anything: *The school creamed off the best pupils and put them in one class.* – *adjective* **creamy** full of or like cream.

crease *noun* a mark made by folding or doubling anything; (in cricket) a line showing the position of a batsman and

bowler. – *verb* to make creases in; to become creased.

create *verb* to bring into being; to make; (*coll*) to make a fuss. – *noun* **creation** the act of creating; that which is created. – *adjective* **creative** having the ability to create, artistic. – *noun* **creator** a person who creates. – **the Creator** God.

creature *noun* an animal or person.

crèche *noun* a (public) nursery for children.

credentials *noun plural* evidence, *esp* letters which a person carries to show people that they may trust him.

credible *adjective* able to be believed. – *noun* **credibility**.

credit *noun* recognition of good qualities, achievements *etc*: *Give him credit for some common sense*; good qualities, honour; source of honour: *a credit to the school*; trustworthiness regarding ability to pay for goods *etc*; time allowed for payment of goods *etc*; the sale of goods to be paid for at a later time; the side of an account on which payments received are entered; a sum of money which one has in an account at a bank; belief, trust; (*plural*) (the giving of) the names of people who have helped in a film *etc*. – *verb* to believe; to enter on the credit side of an account; (with **with**) to give credit for; to think (someone) has: *I credited him with more sense.* – *adjective* **creditable** bringing honour or good reputation to. – *noun* **credit card** a card allowing the holder to pay for purchased articles at a later date. – *noun* **creditor** a person to whom money is due.

credulous *adjective* believing too easily. – *noun* **credulity**.

creed *noun* what is believed, *esp* in one's religion.

creek *noun* a small inlet or bay on the sea coast; a short river.

creep *verb* (*past tense* **crept**) to move slowly or secretly and silently; to move on hands and knees or with the body close to the ground; to shiver with fear or disgust: *It makes your flesh creep*; (of a plant *etc*) to grow along the ground or a wall *etc*. – *noun* a moving in a creeping way; (*coll*) a person one dislikes; (*plural*) great fear or disgust: *Spiders give me the creeps.* – *noun* **creeper** a plant growing along the ground, or up a wall. – **creep up on** to approach (*usu* from behind) unseen.

cremate verb to burn (a dead body). – noun **cremation**. – noun **crematorium** a place where dead bodies are burnt.

crenellated adjective having battlements.

creosote noun an oily liquid made from wood tar, used to keep wood from rotting.

crêpe or **crape** noun a type of fine, crinkly material. – noun **crêpe paper** paper with a crinkled appearance.

crept see **creep**.

crescent adjective curve-shaped, like the new or old moon, not the full moon. – noun anything shaped in a curve; a name for a curved road or street.

cress noun a type of plant with leaves of a slightly bitter taste, used in salads.

crest noun the tuft on the head of a cock or other bird; the top of a hill, wave etc; feathers on the top of a helmet; a badge. – adjective **crestfallen** downhearted, discouraged.

crevasse krè-vas¹, noun a deep crack or split in snow or ice.

crevice noun a crack or narrow opening.

crew noun the people who man a ship, aircraft, bus etc; a gang or mob. – verb to act as a member of a crew; see **crow**. – noun **crewcut** a hairstyle in which the hair is very, very short.

crib noun a manger; a child's bed; a ready-made translation etc used by schoolchildren to avoid preparing their own. – verb (past tense **cribbed**) to copy the work of another.

cribbage noun a type of card game.

crick noun a sharp pain (in the neck). – verb to produce a crick in.

cricket noun a game played with bats, ball and wickets, between two sides of 11 each; a kind of insect similar to a grasshopper. – noun **cricketer** a person who plays cricket. – noun **cricket match** a game of cricket.

cried see **cry**.

crier noun short for **town-crier**.

crime noun an act or deed which is against the law. – adjective **criminal** forbidden by law; very wrong. – noun a person guilty of a crime.

crimson adjective, noun (of) a deep red colour.

cringe verb to crouch or shrink back in fear etc; to behave in too humble a way.

crinkle verb to wrinkle, crease; to make a crackling sound. – adjective **crinkly** having a wrinkled appearance.

crinoline noun a petticoat or skirt made to stick out all round by means of hoops.

cripple noun a lame or disabled person. – verb to make lame; to make less strong, less efficient etc, throw out of action: *The strike crippled the country*. – adjective **crippled**.

crisis noun (plural **crises**) a deciding moment or turning point; a time of great danger or suspense.

crisp adjective stiff and so dry as to be crumbled easily, brittle; cool and fresh: *crisp air*; firm and fresh: *a crisp lettuce*; sharp. – noun a thin crisp piece of fried potato eaten cold. – noun **crispness**. – adjective **crispy**.

criss-cross adjective, noun (having) a pattern of crossing lines. – Also adverb.

criterion noun (plural **criteria**) a means or rule by which something can be judged, a test, a standard.

critic noun a person who judges the good points or faults in a thing (such as a picture, play, book etc); a person who finds faults in a thing or person. – adjective **critical** fault-finding; of criticism; of or at a crisis; very ill; serious; very important. – noun **criticism** a judgement or opinion on (something) esp one showing up faults; the act of criticizing. – verb **criticize** to find fault with; to give an opinion or judgement on.

croak verb to make a low, hoarse sound. – Also noun. – adjective **croaky**.

crochet krō¹shā, noun a kind of knitting done with one hooked needle (a **crochet hook**).

crock noun an earthenware pot or jar; a worthless, old and decrepit person or thing. – noun **crockery** china or earthenware dishes.

crocodile noun a type of large reptile found in rivers in Asia, Africa etc; a procession (usu of children) walking two by two. – noun plural **crocodile tears** pretended tears.

crocus noun (plural **crocuses**) a type of yellow, purple or white flower which grows from bulb.

croft noun a small farm with a cottage esp in the Scottish Highlands. – noun **crofter**.

crone *noun* an ugly old woman.

crony *noun* (*plural* **cronies**) (*coll*) a close friend.

crook *noun* anything bent (such as a shepherd's or bishop's stick bent at the end); a criminal; a cheat. – *verb* to bend or form into a hook. – *adjective* **crooked** bent like a crook; not straight; not honest. – *noun* **crookedness.**

croon *verb* to sing or hum in a low voice. – *noun* **crooner.** – *noun* **crooning.**

crop *noun* that which is gathered for food from fields, trees or bushes; a part of a bird's stomach; a kind of riding whip; the hair on the head; a short haircut. – *verb* (*past tense* **cropped**) to cut short; to gather a crop (of wheat *etc*). – **come a cropper** to fail badly; to have a fall; **crop up** to happen unexpectedly.

croquet *krō'kā*, *noun* a game in which the players, using long-handled wooden hammers (mallets), try to drive wooden balls through hoops in the ground.

cross *noun* anything shaped like this: + or × ; a frame consisting of two bars of wood *etc* placed across each other, of the type on which Christ and criminals were nailed; a monument in a street, often but not always cross-shaped, where proclamations used to be made and markets held; the result of breeding an animal or plant with one of another kind: *a cross between a horse and a donkey*; a trouble or grief that one must bear. – *verb* to mark with a cross; to go to the other side of (a room, road *etc*); to lie or pass across; to meet and pass; to go against the wishes of, annoy; to draw two lines across (cheques); to breed (one kind) with (another). – *adjective* ill-tempered, angry. – *noun* **crossbow** a bow fixed crosswise to a wooden stand with a device for pulling back the bowstring. – *noun, adjective* **cross-country** (a race) across fields *etc*, not on roads. – *verb* **cross-examine,** *verb* **cross-question** to test the truth of someone's words (in a court) by close questioning. – *adjective* **cross-eyed** having a squint. – *noun* **crossing** a place where a street, river *etc* may be crossed; a journey over the sea. – *noun* **crossness** bad temper, sulkiness. – *noun* **cross-reference** in a book such as a dictionary, a statement that what is looked for will be found in another place. – *noun* **crossroads** a place where roads cross each other. –

noun **cross-section** a section made by cutting across (something); a sample, a part or quantity taken as being representative of the whole: *a cross-section of voters*. – *noun* **crossword** a form of word puzzle.

crotchet *noun* a note of a certain length in music. – *adjective* **crotchety** bad-tempered.

crouch *verb* to stand with the knees well bent; (of an animal) to lie close to the ground.

croup *kroop*, *noun* a disease of children causing difficulty in breathing and a harsh cough; the hindquarters of a horse.

croupier *noun* a person who collects the money and pays the winners at gambling.

crow *noun* a type of large bird, generally black; the cry of a cock; the happy sounds made by a baby. – *verb* (*past tense* **crew** or **crowed**) to cry like a cock; (*past tense* **crowed**) to boast; (*past tense* **crowed**) (of a baby *etc*) to make happy noises. – *noun* **crowbar** a large iron bar used as a lever. – *noun* **crow's foot** one of the wrinkles near the eye, produced by ageing. – *noun* **crow's-nest** a sheltered and enclosed platform near the mast-head of a ship from which a lookout is kept. – **as the crow flies** in a straight line.

crowd *noun* a number of persons or things together (without order or arrangement). – *verb* to gather into a crowd; to fill (a room *etc*) too full; to give too little space to, to hinder by being too close.

crown *noun* the jewelled head-dress worn by kings or queens on great occasions; the best or most magnificent part of anything; the highest part or top of anything (*eg* of the road, the head); an old coin which was worth five shillings. – *verb* to set a crown on; to make king; (*coll*) to hit on the head; to reward, finish happily: *Her efforts were crowned with success.*

crucial *adjective* testing, involving making a decision: *the crucial moment*; of great and far-reaching importance: *The crucial question is whether he will succeed.*

crucible *noun* a small container for melting metals *etc*.

crucify *verb* (*past tense* **crucified**) to put to death by fixing the hands and feet to a cross. – *noun* **crucifix** (*plural* **crucifixes**) a figure or picture of Christ fixed to the cross. – noun **crucifixion** the act of crucifying; death on the cross, *esp* that of Christ.

crude *adjective* raw, not purified or refined: *crude oil*; roughly made or done; rude, blunt, tactless. – noun **crudeness**. – noun **crudity**.

cruel *adjective* causing pain or distress; having no pity for others' sufferings. – noun **cruelty** (*plural* **cruelties**).

cruet *noun* a small jar for salt, pepper, sauces *etc*; two or more such jars on a stand.

cruise *verb* to travel (by car, ship *etc*) at a steady speed. – noun a journey by ship made for pleasure and relaxation. – noun **cruiser** a middle-sized warship.

crumb *noun* a small bit of anything, *esp* bread. – verb **crumble** to break into crumbs or small pieces; to fall to pieces. – adjective **crumbly**.

crumpet *noun* a kind of soft cake, baked on a griddle and eaten with butter.

crumple *verb* to crush into creases or wrinkles; to become creased; to collapse.

crunch *verb* to chew anything hard, and so make a noise; to crush. – noun a noise as of crunching; (*coll*) a testing moment or turning-point.

crusade *noun* any movement undertaken for some good cause; (*hist*) an expedition of Christians to win back the Holy Land from the Turks. – noun **crusader** one who goes on a crusade.

crush *verb* to squeeze together; to beat down or overcome; to crease or crumple (a dress *etc*). – noun a violent squeezing; a vast crowd of persons or things; a drink made by squeezing fruit. – adjective **crushed** squeezed, squashed; completely defeated or miserable.

crust *noun* the hard outside coating of anything (such as bread, a pie, the earth *etc*). – adjective **crusty** having a crust; (of people) cross.

crustacean *krus-tā'shèn, noun* any of a large group of animals, often having a hard shell, including crabs, lobsters, shrimps *etc*.

crutch *noun* (*plural* **crutches**) a stick with a bar across the top for lame people; any support.

crux *noun* the difficult or most important part of a problem.

cry *verb* (*past tense* **cried**) to make a loud sound, as in pain or sorrow; to weep; to call loudly. – Also *noun* (*plural* **cries**). – adjective **crying** weeping; calling loudly; calling for, requiring notice or attention: *a crying need*. – **cry off** cancel: *cry off a match*; **cry over spilt milk** to be worried about a misfortune that is past and cannot be helped.

crypt *noun* an underground cell or chapel, *esp* one used for burial. – adjective **cryptic** full of mystery, secret; difficult to understand: *a cryptic remark*.

crystal *noun* a special kind of very clear glass often used for cut-glass ornaments *etc*; the regular shape taken by each small part of certain substances (*eg* salt, sugar). – adjective **crystalline** made up of (or like) crystals. – verb **crystallize** to form into the shape of a crystal; to take a form or shape, become clear. – noun **crystallization**.

cub *noun* the young of certain animals (such as foxes); a Cub Scout. – noun **Cub Scout** a junior Scout.

cube *noun* a solid body having six equal square sides; the answer to a sum in which a number is multiplied by itself twice (8 is the cube of 2). – adjective **cubic** of cubes; having the shape of a cube.

cubicle *noun* a small room closed off in some way from a larger one.

cubit *noun* (*hist*) the distance from élbow to middle-finger tip, once used as a means of measurement.

cuckoo *noun* a type of bird, named after its call, which visits Britain in summer and lays its eggs in the nests of other birds.

cucumber *noun* a creeping plant with a long green fruit used in salads.

cud *noun* food brought back from the stomach and chewed a second time by certain animals (*eg* the sheep, cow).

cuddle *verb* to put one's arms round, hug. – Also *noun*.

cudgel *noun* a heavy stick, a club. – verb (*past tense* **cudgelled**) to beat with a cudgel.

cue *noun* a hint or sign (telling a person when to speak, or what to say next); the stick used in billiards and snooker.

cuff *noun* the end of a sleeve (of a shirt, coat *etc*) near the wrist; the turned back hem of a trouser leg; a blow with the open hand. – *verb* to hit with the hand. – *noun plural* **cufflinks** two ornamental buttons *etc* joined by a small bar, chain *etc* used to fasten a shirt cuff. – **off the cuff** without planning or rehearsal.

cuisine *kwi-zēn'*, *noun* (the art of) cookery.

cul-de-sac *noun* a street closed at one end.

culinary *adjective* of kitchen or cookery.

cull *verb* to gather; to choose from a group; to pick out (seals, deer *etc*) from a herd and kill for the good of the herd. – *noun* such a killing.

culminate *verb* to reach the highest point; to reach the most important or greatest point, to end (in). – *noun* **culmination**.

culpable *adjective* guilty, blameworthy.

culprit *noun* a person who is to blame for something; (in English and US law) a prisoner accused but not yet tried.

cult *noun* worship or religious belief; a strong devotion to or enthusiasm for a person, thing or idea: *the cult of physical fitness*.

cultivate *verb* to grow (vegetables *etc*); to plough, sow *etc* (land); to try to develop and improve: *He cultivated their friendship.* – *adjective* **cultivated** having been cultivated; educated, informed. – *noun* **cultivation** ploughing *etc*; developing and refining.

culture *noun* a form or type of civilization of a certain race or nation and the customs associated with it: *Jewish culture*; improvement or development of the mind *etc* by education, training *etc*; educated tastes in art, music, literature; cultivation (of plants *etc*). – *adjective* **cultured** well-developed *esp* in literature, art *etc*.

culvert *noun* an arched drain for carrying water under a road, railway *etc*.

cumbersome *adjective* heavy, difficult to manage, handle *etc*.

cummerbund *noun* a sash worn around the waist.

cumulative *adjective* increasing as parts *etc* are added on.

cumulus *noun* a kind of cloud common in summer, made up of rounded heaps.

cunning *adjective* sly, clever in a deceitful way; skilful, clever. – *noun* slyness; skill, knowledge.

cup *noun* a hollow container to hold liquid for drinking; an ornamental vessel *usu*

of metal, given as a prize in sports events *etc*. – *verb* (*past tense* **cupped**) to make or put in the shape of a cup: *She cupped her hands.* – *noun* **cupful** (*plural* **cupfuls**) as much as fills a cup. – *noun* **cup-tie** (in football *etc*) one of a series of games *eg* in a competition for which the prize is a cup.

cupboard *noun* a recess in a room with a door and shelves or a box with doors, often hung on walls, used for storing things.

cupidity *noun* greed.

cupola *kū'pò-là*, *noun* a curved ceiling or dome on the top of a building.

cur *noun* a dog of mixed breed; a cowardly person.

curare *noun* a kind of poison used by some S. American Indians on the tips of their arrows.

curate *noun* a Church of England clergyman assisting a rector or a vicar.

curator *noun* a person who has charge of a museum, art gallery *etc*.

curb *verb* to hold back, try to prevent from going on. – Also *noun*.

curd *noun* milk thickened by acid; the cheese part of milk, as opposed to the **whey**. – *verb* **curdle** to turn into curd. – **curdle someone's blood** to shock or terrify someone.

cure *noun* the act of freeing from disease, healing; that which heals. – *verb* to heal; to get rid of (a bad habit *etc*); to preserve, *eg* by drying, salting *etc*. – *adjective* **curable**. – *adjective* **curative** likely to cure.

curfew *noun* an order forbidding people to be in the streets after a certain hour; (*hist*) the ringing of an evening bell, as a signal to put out all fires and lights.

curio *noun* (*plural* **curios**) an article valued for its oddness or rareness.

curious *adjective* anxious to find out; unusual, odd. – *noun* **curiosity** (*plural* **curiosities**) strong desire to find out; anything unusual.

curl *verb* to twist (hair) into small coils or rolls; (of hair) to grow naturally in small coils; (of smoke *etc*) to move in a spiral; to twist out of shape, form a curved shape; to play at the game of curling. – *noun* a small coil or roll as of hair. – *noun* **curling** a game played by throwing round, flat stones along a sheet of ice. – *adjective* **curly** having curls.

curlew *noun* a type of wading bird with very long slender bill and legs.

currant *noun* a kind of small black raisin; any of various kinds of small, soft, round fruit: *redcurrant.*

current *adjective* belonging to the present time: *the current year*; passing from person to person, generally accepted: *That story is current.* – *noun* a stream of water, air or electrical power moving in a certain direction. – *noun* **currency** (*plural* **currencies**) the money (notes and coins) of a country; state or time of being current or well-known: *The story gained currency.* – *noun* **current account** a bank account from which money may be withdrawn by cheque.

curriculum *noun* the course of study at a university, school *etc.* – *noun* **curriculum vitae** a brief account of the main events of a person's life.

curry *noun* (*plural* **curries**) a kind of food (meat, vegetables *etc*) containing a mixture of spices which gives a strong, peppery flavour. – *verb* (*past tense* **curried**) to cook (meat *etc*) using the spices necessary for a curry; to rub down (a horse). – *noun* **curry powder** a selection of spices ground together used in making a curry. – **curry favour** to try hard to be someone's favourite.

curse *verb* to use swear words; to wish evil on (someone). – *noun* a wish for evil or a magic spell: *The witch put a curse on him*; an evil or a great misfortune or the cause of this. – *adjective* **cursed** under a curse; hateful.

cursor *noun* a flashing device that appears on a VDU screen to show position *eg* of the end of the last entry.

cursory *adjective* hurried.

curt *adjective* impolitely short, abrupt. – *noun* **curtness.**

curtail *verb* to make less, reduce. – *noun* **curtailment.**

curtain *noun* a piece of material hung to cover a window, stage *etc.*

curtsy or **curtsey** *noun* (*plural* **curtsies**) a bow made by women by bending the knees.

curve *noun* a rounded line, like part of the edge of a circle: anything shaped like this: *a curve in the road.* – *noun* **curvature** a curving or bending; a curved piece (of something); an abnormal curving, as of the spine.

cushion *noun* a casing of some soft material filled with stuffing (feathers, foam rubber *etc*) for resting on; any soft pad.

cushy *adjective* (*coll*) easy and comfortable: *a cushy job.*

custard *noun* a dish consisting of milk, eggs *etc* flavoured, and cooked together.

custody *noun* care, guardianship; imprisonment. – *noun* **custodian** a keeper; a caretaker (*eg* of a museum).

custom *noun* something done by habit or because it is usual; the regular or frequent doing of something; habit; the regular buying of goods at the same shop *etc*; (*plural*) taxes on goods coming into a country; (*plural*) the department of the government that collects these or the place where they are collected. – *adjective* **customary** usual. – *adjective* **custom-built** built to suit a particular demand or purpose. – *noun* **customer** someone who buys (regularly) from a shop; (*coll*) a person: *an awkward customer.*

cut *verb* (*present participle* **cutting**, *past tense* **cut**) to make a slit or opening in, or divide, with something sharp (*eg* scissors, a knife): *He cut a hole in it. I cut a slice of bread for toasting*; to wound; to remove with something sharp (*eg* scissors, lawnmower): *Get your hair cut. Cut the grass*; to reduce in amount; to shorten (a play, book *etc*) by removing parts (of it); to ignore (a person one knows); to divide in two (a pack of cards); to stop filming; (*coll*) to stay away from: *cut school for the day.* – *noun* a slit or opening made by cutting; a wound made with something sharp; a stroke or blow; a thrust with a sword; the way a thing is cut; the shape and style (of clothes); a piece (of meat). – *adjective* **cut-and-dried** (of plans *etc*) arranged carefully and exactly. – *noun* **cut glass** glass with ornamental patterns cut on the surface, used for vases, drinking-glasses *etc.* – *adjective* **cut-price** sold at a price lower than usual. – *noun* **cut-throat** a wicked dangerous person. – *noun* **cutting** a piece cut from a newspaper; a trench or passage, cut in the earth or rock for a railway or road; a twig or shoot of a tree or plant. – *adjective* **cut-up** distressed. – **cut down** to take down by cutting; to reduce (supply, amount taken *etc*); **cut in** to interrupt; **cut off** to separate: *They were cut off from the mainland by the tide*; to stop: *cut off supplies*; **cut out** to shape (a dress *etc*) by cutting; *(coll)* to stop; of an engine, to fail.

cute *adjective* smart, clever; pretty and pleasing.

cuticle *noun* the skin at the bottom and edges of finger and toe nails.

cutlass *noun* (*plural* **cutlasses**) a short broad sword.

cutlery *noun* knives, forks, spoons *etc*.

cutlet *noun* a slice of meat *usu* with the bone attached.

cuttlefish *noun* a type of sea creature like a squid.

cv *abbreviation* curriculum vitae.

cwt *abbreviation* hundredweight.

cyanide *noun* a kind of poison.

cycle *noun* short for **bicycle**; a number or round of events coming one after the other, over and over again: *the cycle of the seasons*; a period of time in which events happen in this way; a number of poems, songs, stories, written about one main person or event. – *verb* to ride

a bicycle. – *noun* **cyclist** a person who rides a bicycle.

cyclone *noun* a whirling windstorm; a system of winds blowing in a spiral. – *adjective* **cyclonic**.

cygnet *noun* a young swan.

cylinder *noun* a solid or hollow tube-shaped object; in machines, motor-car engines *etc*, the hollow tube in which a piston works. – *adjective* **cylindrical** shaped like a cylinder.

cymbals *noun plural* brass, plate-like musical instruments, beaten together in pairs.

cynic *noun* a person who believes the worst about people. – *noun* **cynicism**. – *adjective* **cynical** sneering; believing the worst of people.

cynosure *noun* centre of attraction.

cypress *noun* a type of evergreen tree.

cyst *noun* a kind of liquid-filled blister on an internal part of the body or just under the skin.

cystitis *noun* inflammation of the bladder.

czar *see* **tsar**.

D

dab *verb* (*past tense* **dabbed**) to touch gently with a pad, cloth *etc*, *eg* to soak up moisture. – *noun* the act of dabbing; a small lump of anything soft or moist; a gentle blow, pat; a small kind of flounder. – *noun* **dab-hand** (*coll*) an expert.

dabble *verb* to play in water with hands or feet; to do (something) in a half-serious way or as a hobby: *He dabbles in witchcraft*. – *noun* **dabbler**.

dace *noun* a type of small river fish.

dachshund *daks'hoond*, *noun* a breed of dog with short legs and a long body.

dad or **daddy** *noun* (*coll*, or child's names for) **father**.

dado *noun* (*plural* **dadoes**) the lower part of an inside wall when decorated in a different way from the rest.

daffodil *noun* a type of yellow flower which grows from a bulb.

daft *adjective* silly.

dagger *noun* a short sword for stabbing.

dahlia *noun* a type of garden plant with large flowers.

daily *adjective, adverb* every day. – *noun* (*plural* **dailies**) a paper published every day; a person who is paid to clean a house regularly (also **daily help**).

dainty *adjective* small and neat; pleasant-tasting. – *noun* (*plural* **dainties**) anything pleasant (*esp* tasty food). – *noun* **daintiness**.

dairy *noun* (*plural* **dairies**) the place where milk is kept, and butter and cheese are made; a shop which sells milk *etc*. – *noun* **dairy cattle** cows kept for their milk, not their meat. – *noun* **dairy farm** a farm mainly concerned with the production of milk, butter *etc*. – *noun* **dairymaid** or **dairyman** woman or man working in a dairy.

dais *noun* (*plural* **daises**) a raised floor at the upper end of a hall *etc*.

daisy *noun* (*plural* **daisies**) a type of small common flower with white petals.

dale *noun* low ground between hills.

dally *verb* (*past tense* **dallied**) to waste time by idleness or play; to play (with). – *noun* **dalliance**.

Dalmatian *noun* a breed of large spotted dog.

dam *noun* a bank or wall of earth, concrete *etc* to keep back water; the water kept in like this; a mother, *esp* of animals. – *verb* (*past tense* **dammed**) to keep back by a dam; to hold back, to control (tears *etc*).

damage *noun* hurt or injury *esp* to a thing; (*plural*) money paid, by order of a law court, by one person to another to make up for injury, insults *etc*. – *verb* to spoil, make less effective or unusable.

damask *noun* silk, linen or cotton cloth, with figures and designs in the weave.

dame *noun* a comic woman in a pantomime, *usu* played by a man dressed up as a woman. – *noun* **Dame** the title of a woman of the same rank as a knight.

damn *verb* to sentence to unending punishment (in hell); to condemn as wrong, bad *etc*. – *interjection* expression of annoyance. – *adjective* **damnable** deserving to be condemned; hateful. – *noun* **damnation** unending punishment; condemnation. – *adjective* **damning** leading to conviction or ruin: *damning evidence*.

damp *noun* moist air; wetness. – *verb* to wet slightly; to make less fierce or intense (*eg* a fire). – *adjective* moist, slightly wet. – *noun* **dampness**. – *verb* **dampen** to make or become damp or moist; to lessen (enthusiasm *etc*). – *noun* **damper** that which damps or dampens.

damsel *noun* (*old*) an unmarried girl.

damson *noun* a type of small dark-red plum.

dance *verb* to move in time to music. – Also *noun*. – *noun* **dancer**.

dandelion *noun* a type of common plant with a yellow flower.

dandruff *noun* dead skin which collects under the hair and falls off in small pieces.

dandy *noun* (*plural* **dandies**) a man who pays great attention to his dress and looks.

danger *noun* something which may harm: *The canal is a danger to children*; a state in which one may be harmed: *He is in danger*. – *adjective* **dangerous** unsafe, likely to cause harm; full of risks.

dangle *verb* to hang loosely.

dank *adjective* moist, wet.

dapper *adjective* small and neat.

dappled *adjective* marked with spots or splashes of colour.

dare *verb* to be brave or bold enough (to); to lay oneself open to, to risk: *dare his anger*; to challenge: *He dared him to cross the railway line*. – *noun* **dare-devil** a rash person fond of taking risks. – Also *adjective*. – *adjective* **daring** bold, fearless. – *noun* boldness. – **I dare say** I suppose: *I dare say you're right*.

dark *adjective* without light; black or of a colour near to black; gloomy; evil: *dark deeds*. – *noun* **dark** or **darkness**. – *verb* **darken** to make or grow dark or darker. – *adjective* **dark-haired** having dark-brown or black hair. – **a dark horse** a person about whom little is known; **in the dark** knowing nothing (about something); **keep dark** to keep (something) secret.

darling *noun* a word showing affection; one dearly loved; a favourite.

darn *verb* to mend (clothes) with crossing rows of stitches. – *noun* the place so mended.

dart *noun* a pointed, arrow-like weapon for throwing or shooting; something which pierces; (*plural*) a game in which small darts are aimed at a board (**dartboard**) marked off in circles and numbered sections. – *verb* to move quickly and suddenly.

dash *verb* to throw, knock *etc* violently, *esp* so as to break; to ruin (*esp* hopes); to depress, sadden (spirits *etc*); to rush with speed or violence. – *noun* (*plural* **dashes**) a rush; a short race; a small amount (as of soda water *etc*); liveliness; in writing, a short line (–) to show a break in a sentence *etc*. – *adjective* **dashing** hasty; spirited, smart.

dastardly *adjective* cowardly.

DAT or **Dat** or **dat** *abbreviation* digital audio tape.

data *noun plural* (*singular* **datum**) available facts (from which conclusions may be drawn); facts stored in a computer. – *noun* **databank** (*comput*) a library of files, possibly including databases. – *noun* **database** (*comput*) a collection of systematically stored files that are often connected with each other.

date¹ *noun* a statement of time expressed in terms of the day, month and year (*eg* 23 December 1995); the time at which an event occurs or occurred; the period of time to which something belongs; an appointment: *I have a date with her next Wednesday*. – *verb* to give a date to; to belong to a certain time: *This castle dates from the 12th century*; to become old-fashioned: *That dress will date quickly*. – **out of date** old-fashioned; no longer used; no longer valid; **up to date** in fashion, modern; including, or knowledgeable about, the latest information; at the point (in work *etc*) that one should be.

date² *noun* a type of palm tree, or its fruit.

datum *see* **data**.

daub *verb* to smear; to paint roughly or without skill.

daughter *noun* a female child (when spoken of in relation to her parents). – *noun* **daughter-in-law** a son's wife.

daunt *verb* to frighten; to be discouraging. – *adjective* **dauntless** unable to be frightened.

Davy-lamp *noun* an early kind of safety lamp for coalminers.

dawdle *verb* to move slowly. – *noun* **dawdler**.

dawn *noun* beginning (*esp* of a day). – *verb* to become day; to begin to appear. – *noun* **dawning** dawn. – **dawn on** to become suddenly clear to (someone).

day *noun* the time of light, from sunrise to sunset; twenty-four hours, from one midnight to the next; the time or hours *usu* spent at work; (sometimes *plural*) a particular time or period: *in the days of steam*. – *noun* **daydream** a dreaming or imagining of pleasant events while awake. – Also *verb*. – *noun* **daylight** the light of day, of the sun. – *noun* **day-release** time off from work for education. – **day in, day out** on and on, continuously; **the other day** recently.

daze *verb* to make to feel confused *eg* by a blow, to stun; to bewilder.

dazzle *verb* (of a strong light) to prevent one from seeing clearly; to shine brilliantly; to fascinate, impress deeply.

dB *abbreviation* decibel(s).

DC *abbreviation* District of Columbia; direct current.

DDR *abbreviation* German Democratic Republic (East Germany) (*Deutsche Demokratische Republik* [*Ger*]).

deacon (*masculine*), **deaconess** (*feminine*) *noun* the lowest rank of clergy in the Church of England; a church official in other churches.

dead *adjective* without life; cold and cheerless; numb; (of an engine *etc*) not working; no longer in use; complete: *dead silence*; exact: *dead centre*; certain: *a dead shot*. – *adverb* completely: *dead certain*; suddenly and completely: *stop dead*. – *noun* those who have died: *Speak well of the dead*; the time of greatest stillness, coldness, darkness *etc*: *the dead of night*. – *adjective* **dead-and-alive** dull, having little life. – *adjective* **deadbeat** having no strength left. – *verb* **deaden** to lessen pain *etc*. – *noun* **dead end** a road *etc* closed at one end; a job *etc* not leading to promotion. – Also *adjective*. – *noun* **dead heat** a race in which two or more runners are equal. – *noun* **deadline** a date by which something must be done. – *noun* **deadlock** a standstill resulting from a complete failure to agree. – *adjective* **deadly** likely to cause death, fatal; intense, very great. – *adverb* intensely, extremely. – *noun* **deadliness**. – *adjective* **deadpan** without expression on the face. – *noun* **dead ringer** (*coll*) a person or thing looking exactly like someone or something else.

deaf *adjective* unable to hear; refusing to listen. – *verb* **deafen** to make deaf; to have an unpleasant effect on the hearing; to make (walls *etc*) soundproof. – *noun, adjective* **deafening** (of) something that deafens. – *noun* **deaf-mute** a person who is both deaf and dumb. – *noun* **deafness**.

deal *noun* a (business) agreement or arrangement; an amount or quantity: *a good deal of paper*; the dividing out of playing-cards in a game; a kind of softwood. – *verb* to divide, give out; to trade (in); to do business (with); (with **with**) to take action concerning, cope with: *He deals with all the problems*. – *noun* **dealer** a person who deals; a trader.

dean *noun* the chief clergyman in a cathedral church; an important official of a university.

dear *adjective* high in price; highly valued; much loved. – *noun* a person who is loved; a person who is lovable or charming. – *adverb* at a high price. – *adverb* **dearly**. – *noun* **dearness**.

dearth *noun* a scarcity, shortage.

death *noun* the state of being dead, the end of life; the end (of something): *the death of music halls*. – *noun* **death-blow** a blow that causes death; an event *etc* that causes the end of something. – *adjective, adverb* **deathly** like death; very pale or ill-looking. – *noun* **death-mask** a plastercast taken of a dead person's face. – *noun* **death rattle** a rattling in the throat which is sometimes heard before a person's death. – *noun* **death roll** a list of the dead. – *noun* **deathwatch beetle** a kind of insect that makes a ticking noise and whose larva destroys wood.

debar *verb* (*past tense* **debarred**) to keep from, prevent.

debase *verb* to lessen in value; to make bad, wicked *etc*. – *adjective* **debased**. – *noun* **debasement**.

debate *noun* a discussion, *esp* a formal one before an audience; an argument. – Also *verb*. – *adjective* **debatable** able to be argued about, doubtful: *a debatable point*.

debauchery *noun* excessive indulgence in drunkenness and other (immoral) pleasures. – *adjective* **debauched** given to, inclined to debauchery.

debilitate *verb* to make weak. – *noun* **debility** weakness of the body.

debit *noun* a debt. – *verb* to mark something down as a debt.

debonair *adjective* of pleasant and cheerful appearance and manners.

debouch *verb* to come out from a narrow or confined place.

debrief *verb* to gather information (from an astronaut, spy *etc*) after a mission.

debris *deb'rē*, *noun* the remains of something broken, destroyed *etc*; rubbish.

debt *det*, *noun* what one person owes to another. – *noun* **debtor** a person who owes a debt. – **in debt** owing money; **in someone's debt** under an obligation to someone, owing someone a favour *etc*.

début *dā-bū*, *noun* the first public appearance (*eg* of an actor). – *noun* **debutante** a young woman making her first appearance in upper-class society.

decade *noun* a period of ten years; a set or series of ten.

decadence *noun* a falling (from high) to low standards in morals, the arts *etc*. – *adjective* **decadent**.

decamp *verb* to run away.

decant *verb* to pour (wine) from a bottle into a decanter. – *noun* **decanter** a bottle (*usu* ornamental) with a glass stopper for wine, whisky *etc*.

decapitate *verb* to cut the head from. – *noun* **decapitation**.

decathlon *noun* a contest consisting of ten events in the Olympic Games *etc*.

decay *verb* to become bad, worse or rotten. – Also *noun*. – *adjective* **decayed**.

decease *noun* death. – *adjective* **deceased** dead. – *noun* (with **the**) a dead person.

deceit *noun* the act of deceiving. – *adjective* **deceitful**.

deceive *verb* to tell untruths so as to mislead; to cheat. – *noun* **deceiver**.

decelerate *verb* to slow down.

December *noun* the twelfth month of the year.

decent *adjective* respectable; good enough, adequate: *a decent salary*; kind: *It's decent of you to help*. – *noun* **decency**.

deception *noun* the act of deceiving, cheating; something that deceives or is intended to deceive. – *adjective* **deceptive** different from what it seems or looks, misleading: *Appearances may be deceptive*. – *adverb* **deceptively**.

decibel *noun* a unit of loudness of sound.

decide *verb* to make up one's mind (to do something); to settle (an argument *etc*). – *adjective* **decided** clear: *a decided difference*; with one's mind made up. – *adverb* **decidedly** definitely.

deciduous *adjective* (of trees) having leaves that fall in autumn.

decimal *adjective* numbered by tens; of ten parts or the number 10. – *noun* a decimal fraction. – *noun* **decimal currency** a system of money in which each coin or note is either a tenth of another or ten times another in value. – *noun* **decimal fraction** a fraction expressed as so many tenths, hundredths, thousandths *etc* and written using a **decimal point** like this: $0 \cdot 1 = \frac{1}{10}$, $2 \cdot 33 = 2\frac{33}{100}$. – *verb* **decimalize** to convert (figures or a country's currency) to decimal form. – *noun* **decimalization**.

decimate *verb* to make much smaller in numbers, *esp* by destruction.

decipher *verb* to translate (writing in code) into ordinary, understandable language; to make out the meaning of (something difficult to read).

decision *noun* the act of deciding; the ability to decide; judgement; firmness: *He acted with decision.* – *adjective* **decisive** final, putting an end to a contest *etc*: *a decisive defeat*; showing decision and firmness: *a decisive manner*.

deck *verb* to put ornaments *etc* on, adorn. – *noun* a platform extending from one side of a ship *etc* to the other and forming the floor; a floor on a bus *etc*; a pack (of playing-cards); the turntable of a record-player; the part of a tape-recorder or computer on or in which the tapes are placed to be played. – *noun* **deck-chair** a collapsible chair of wood and canvas *etc*.

declaim *verb* to make a speech in impressive dramatic language; to speak violently (against someone). – *noun* **declamation.** – *adjective* **declamatory.**

declare *verb* to make known (*eg* goods on which duty is payable, income on which tax is payable); to announce *esp* formally or publicly: *declare war*; to say firmly; (in cricket) to end an innings before ten wickets have fallen. – *noun* **declaration.**

decline *verb* to say 'no' (to an invitation, offer *etc*), refuse; to become less strong, less good *etc*; to slope down. – *noun* a downward slope; a gradual worsening (of health *etc*).

declivity *noun* (*plural* **declivities**) a downward slope.

decode *verb* to translate (a coded message) into ordinary, understandable language.

decompose *verb* to rot, decay; to separate in parts or elements. – *noun* **decomposition.**

décor *dā-kör, noun* the decoration of a room *etc* and the arrangement of objects in it.

decorate *verb* to add some form of ornament to (someone or something); to make more beautiful, impressive *etc*; to paint, paper the walls of (a room *etc*); to pin a badge or medal on (someone) as a mark of honour. – *noun* **decoration.** – *adjective* **decorative** ornamental; pretty. – *noun* **decorator** a person who decorates houses, rooms *etc*.

decorous *adjective* behaving in an acceptable or dignified way. – *noun* **decorum** good behaviour.

decoy *verb* to lead into a trap or into evil. – *noun* something or someone intended to lead another into a trap.

decrease *verb* to make or become less in number. – *noun* a growing less.

decree *noun* an order or law; a judge's decision. – *verb* (*past tense* **decreed**) to give an order.

decrepit *adjective* weak and infirm because of old age; in ruins or disrepair. – *noun* **decrepitude.**

decry *verb* (*past tense* **decried**) to make (something) seem worthless, belittle; to express disapproval of.

dedicate *verb* to give up wholly to, devote to: *She is dedicated to teaching. He was dedicated to football*; to set apart *esp* for a holy or sacred purpose; to name, in the front pages of a book *etc*, the person for whom, or in honour of whom, it is written: *I dedicate this book to my father.* – *noun* **dedication.**

deduce *verb* to find out something by putting together all that is known. – *noun* **deduction.**

deduct *verb* to subtract, take away (from). – *noun* **deduction** a subtraction; an amount subtracted.

deed *noun* something done, an act; (in law) a signed statement or bargain.

deep *adjective* being or going far down; hard to understand; cunning; occupied or involved to a great extent: *deep in debt*; intense, strong: *of a deep red colour*; heartfelt: *deep love*; low in pitch. – *noun* (with **the**) the sea. – *verb* **deepen** to make deep. – *noun* **deep freeze** a type of low temperature refrigerator that can freeze food and preserve it frozen for a long time. – Also *verb*. – *adjective* **deep-seated** firmly fixed, not easily removed. – **in deep water** in difficulties or trouble.

deer *noun* (*plural* **deer**) a kind of animal with antlers (*usu* in the male only), such as the reindeer.

deface *verb* to spoil the appearance of, disfigure. – *noun* **defacement.**

defame *verb* to (try to) harm the reputation of. – *noun* **defamation.** – *adjective* **defamatory.**

default *verb* to fail to do something one ought to do, *eg* to pay a debt. – Also *noun.* – *noun* **defaulter.**

defeat *verb* to beat, win a victory over (in a fight, competition *etc*). – Also *noun.*

defecate *verb* to empty the bowels of waste matter.

defect *noun* a lack of something necessary for completeness or perfection, a flaw. – *verb* to desert a country, political party *etc* to join or go to another: *defect to the West*. – *noun* **defection** failure in duty; desertion. – *adjective* **defective** faulty; incomplete; (of a person) not having normal mental or physical ability.

defence or (*US*) **defense** *noun* the act or action of defending against attack; a means or method of protection; in a law-court, the defending lawyer(s); the argument put forward by such lawyer(s). – *adjective* **defenceless** without defence.

defend *verb* to guard or protect against attack; to conduct the defence of in a law-court. – *noun* **defendant** one who resists attack; the accused person in a law case. – *adjective* **defensible** able to be defended. – *adjective* **defensive** defending or protecting. – **on the defensive** prepared to defend oneself against attack or criticism.

defer *verb* (*past tense* **deferred**) to put off to another time; to give way (to the wishes *etc* of another). – *noun* **deference** respect, willingness to consider the wishes *etc* of others; the act of giving way to another. – *adjective* **deferential** showing deference or respect.

defiance *noun* open disobedience or opposition. – *adjective* **defiant**.

deficient *adjective* lacking in what is needed. – *noun* **deficiency** (*plural* **deficiencies**) lack, want; the amount lacking.

deficit *noun* amount by which something (*eg* a sum of money) is too little.

defile *verb* to make dirty, to soil; to corrupt, make bad or evil. – *noun* **defilement**.

define *verb* to fix the bounds or limits of; to outline or show clearly; to state the exact meaning of. – *adjective* **definite** having clear limits, fixed; exact; certain; clear. – *noun* **definiteness**. – *noun* **definite article** the name given to the adjective *the*. – *noun* **definition** an explanation of the exact meaning of a word or phrase; sharpness or clearness of outline. – *adjective* **definitive** quite fixed, final, settling once and for all.

deflate *verb* to let the air or gas out of (a tyre *etc*); to reduce (a person's) self-importance or self-confidence. – *noun* **deflation**.

deflect *verb* to turn aside (from a fixed course or direction). – *noun* **deflection**.

deform *verb* to spoil the shape of; to make ugly. – *adjective* **deformed** badly or abnormally formed. – *noun* **deformity** (*plural* **deformities**) a part abnormal in shape; state of being badly shaped.

defraud *verb* to cheat; (with **of**) to take by cheating or fraud.

defray *verb* to pay for (the expenses of anything).

defrost *verb* to remove frost or ice (from a refrigerator), thaw.

deft *adjective* clever (*esp* with the fingers). – *noun* **deftness**.

defunct *adjective* no longer active or in use.

defy *verb* (*past tense* **defied**) to dare someone (to do something), to challenge; to resist boldly or openly; to make impossible: *Her beauty defies description*.

degenerate *adjective* having become immoral or very bad. – *verb* to become or grow bad or worse. – *noun* **degeneration**.

degrade *verb* to lower in grade, rank *etc*; to disgrace. – *adjective* **degrading**. – *noun* **degradation**.

degree *noun* a step or stage in a process *etc*; rank or grade; amount, extent: *a degree of certainty*; a unit of temperature; a unit by which angles are measured, one 360th part of the circumference of a circle; a title or certificate given by a university (gained by examination or as an honour).

dehydrate *verb* to remove water from (*esp* food), dry out. – *adjective* **dehydrated** (of people) deprived of fluid. – *noun* **dehydration**.

deify *verb* (*past tense* **deified**) to worship as a god.

deign *verb* to do as a favour, or act as if one is doing a favour: *She deigned to answer us*.

deity *noun* (*plural* **deities**) a god or goddess.

déjà vu *dā-zhä vū*, *noun* the feeling of having experienced something before that is in fact being experienced for the first time.

dejected *adjective* gloomy, dispirited. – *noun* **dejection**.

delay verb to put off to a later time; to keep back, hinder. – Also noun.

delectable adjective delightful, pleasing.

delegate verb to give (a task) to someone else to do. – noun someone acting on behalf of another or others, a representative. – noun **delegation** a group of delegates.

delete verb to rub or strike out (eg a piece of writing). – noun **deletion**.

deleterious adjective harmful.

deliberate verb to think carefully or seriously (about). – adjective intentional, not by accident; slow in deciding; not hurried. – adverb **deliberately**. – noun **deliberation** careful thought; calmness, coolness; (plural) formal discussions.

delicate adjective not strong, frail; easily damaged; of fine texture; dainty, done by fine work; pleasing to the senses, esp the taste; tactful; requiring careful handling. – noun **delicacy** (plural **delicacies**) the state of being delicate; tact; something delicious to eat.

delicatessen noun a shop selling food (esp imported cheeses, meats etc) cooked or prepared ready for serving.

delicious adjective pleasant to the taste; giving pleasure. – noun **deliciousness**.

delight verb to please highly; to take great pleasure (in). – Also noun. – adjective **delighted**. – adjective **delightful**.

delinquent adjective guilty of an offence or misdeed; not carrying out one's duties. – noun a person who is guilty of an offence; a person who fails in his duty. – noun **delinquency** wrongdoing, misdeeds; failure in duty.

delirious adjective raving, wandering in the mind (usu as a result of fever); wildly excited. – noun **delirium** state of being delirious; wild excitement. – noun **delirium tremens** a delirious disorder of the brain produced by over-absorption of alcohol.

deliver verb to hand over; to give out (eg a speech, blow); to set free; to rescue; to assist at the birth of (a child). – noun **deliverance** a freeing. – noun **delivery** (plural **deliveries**) a handing over (as of letters, parcels etc); the birth of a child; way of speaking.

delphinium noun a kind of branching garden plant, usu with blue flowers.

delta noun the triangular stretch of land at the mouth of a river which reaches the sea in two or more branches.

delude verb to deceive. – noun **delusion** the act of deluding; a false belief, esp as a symptom of mental illness.

deluge noun a great flow of anything, esp water (also work to be done, letters to be answered etc). – verb to flood (with water, work etc).

delve verb to dig; to search deeply and carefully.

demand verb to ask, or ask for, firmly or sharply; to insist; to require, call for: This demands instant attention. – noun a request which seems like a command; urgent claim: demands on my time; a wish or willingness to buy or a need for (certain goods etc).

demean verb to lower, degrade (esp oneself).

demeanour noun behaviour, conduct.

demented adjective out of one's mind, insane.

demise noun death.

demob verb, noun short for **demobilize** or **demobilization**.

demobilize verb to break up an army after a war is over; to free (a soldier) from army service. – noun **demobilization**.

democracy noun government of the people by the people through their elected parliament – noun **democrat** a person who believes in this kind of government. – noun (US) **Democrat** a member of the American Democratic Party. – adjective **democratic**. – adjective, noun (US) **Democratic** (of, belonging to) one of the two chief political parties in the USA.

demography noun the study of population size and movement. – noun **demographer**. – adjective **demographic**.

demolish verb to lay in ruins, pull or tear down (a building etc). – noun **demolition**.

demon noun an evil spirit, a devil.

demonstrate verb to show clearly; to prove; to show (a machine etc) in action; to express a (usu political) opinion by marching, showing placards etc in public. – adjective **demonstrable** able to be shown clearly. – noun **demonstration** a show; a display; proof; a public expression of opinion by processions, mass-meetings etc. – adjective **demonstrative**

pointing out; proving; (in the habit of) showing one's feelings openly. – *noun* **demonstrator** a person who shows (*eg* the working of a machine); a person who takes part in a public demonstration.

demoralize *verb* to take away the confidence of.

demote *verb* to reduce to a lower rank or grade. – *noun* **demotion.**

demur *verb* (*past tense* **demurred**) to object, say 'no'.

demure *adjective* shy and modest. – *noun* **demureness.**

den *noun* the lair or cave of a wild animal; a small private room for working *etc.*

denier *noun* a unit of weight of nylon, silk, rayon yarn.

denigrate *verb* to attack the reputation of, defame.

denim *noun* a type of cotton cloth used for jeans, overalls *etc.*

denizen *noun* a dweller, an inhabitant.

denomination *noun* name or title; a value (as of a coin, stamp *etc*); a group of people of the same religious beliefs. – *adjective* **denominational.** – *noun* **denominator** the lower number in a vulgar fraction by which the upper number is divided (as the 3 in ⅔).

denote *verb* to mean, be a sign of.

dénouement *noun* the most important part of a story (*eg* where a mystery is solved).

denounce *verb* to accuse (of a crime *etc*) publicly; to inform against: *He denounced him to the enemy.* – *noun* **denunciation.**

dense *adjective* closely packed together; thick; very stupid. – *noun* **denseness.** – *noun* **density** (*plural* **densities**) the state of being dense; the weight of a standard volume of something (*eg* water).

dent *noun* a hollow made by a blow or pressure. – *verb* to make a dent in.

dental *adjective* of a tooth or teeth.

dentist *noun* a person who cures tooth troubles (by filling, taking teeth out *etc*). – *noun* **dentistry** the work of a dentist. – *noun* **denture** (often *plural*) a set of false teeth.

denude *verb* to make bare, strip (something) of a covering of any kind: *The wind denuded the trees of leaves.* – *noun* **denudation.**

denunciation *see* **denounce.**

deny *verb* (*past tense* **denied**) to declare to be untrue: *I deny that I did it;* to refuse, forbid: *I deny you the right to leave.* – *noun* **denial.** – **deny oneself** to do without (things that one desires or needs).

deodorant *noun* something that removes or hides unpleasant smells.

depart *verb* to go away; to turn aside from: *depart from one's plans.* – *noun* **departure.** – **a new departure** a new course of action of some kind.

department *noun* a separate part or branch (of a shop, university, government *etc*).

depend *verb* (with **on** or **upon**) to rely on; (with **on**) to receive necessary support (*esp* financial) from; (with **on** or **upon**) to be controlled or decided by: *It all depends on the weather.* – *adjective* **dependable** to be trusted. – *noun* **dependant** a person who is kept or supported by another. – *noun* **dependence** the state of being dependent. – *adjective* **dependent** depending; relying on another for (*esp* financial) support.

depict *verb* to draw, paint *etc*; to describe.

depilatory *adjective* taking hair off. – Also *noun.*

deplete *verb* to make smaller in amount, number *etc.* – *noun* **depletion.**

deplore *verb* to feel or express disapproval or regret about (something). – *adjective* **deplorable** regrettable; very bad.

deploy *verb* to place in position ready for action.

depopulate *verb* to reduce greatly the number of people in (an area *etc*). – *adjective* **depopulated** empty of people; reduced in population.

deport *verb* to send (a person) out of a country. – *noun* **deportation.** – *noun* **deportment** way of carrying or holding oneself; behaviour.

depose *verb* to remove from a high position (*esp* a king from his throne). – *noun* **deposition** the act of deposing; *see* also **deposit.**

deposit *verb* to place; to put or set down; to put in for safe keeping (*eg* money in a bank). – *noun* money paid in part payment of something which one means to buy; money put in a bank; a solid that has settled at the bottom of a liquid; a layer (of coal, iron *etc*) occurring naturally in rock *etc*. – *noun* **deposit account** a bank account from which money must be withdrawn in person, not by cheque. – *noun* **deposition** a written piece of evidence. – *noun* **depository** (*plural* **depositories**) a place where anything is deposited.

depot *dep'ō, noun* a storehouse; a military station where stores are kept; the place where railway engines, buses *etc* are kept and repaired.

deprave *verb* to make wicked. – *adjective* **depraved** wicked. – *noun* **depravity**.

deprecate *verb* to show disapproval of, condemn as bad. – *noun* **deprecation**.

depreciate *verb* to lessen the value of; to fall in value. – *noun* **depreciation**.

depredation *noun* (often *plural*) plundering.

depress *verb* to make gloomy, unhappy or of low spirits; to press down; to lower in value, amount *etc*. – *noun* **depression** low spirits, gloominess; a hollow; a lowering in value *etc*; a period in which the economic situation of a country is bad with unemployment, lack of trade *etc*; a region of low atmospheric pressure.

deprive *verb* to take away: *They deprived the king of his power*. – *noun* **deprivation** the act of depriving; the state of being deprived. – *adjective* **deprived** suffering from hardship *etc*, disadvantaged.

Dept *abbreviation* department.

depth *noun* deepness; a deep place; the deepest part; the middle: *depth of winter*; intensity, strength. – **in depth** thorough(ly), careful(ly); **out of one's depth** in water deeper than one can stand up in; concerned in problems too difficult to understand.

deputation *noun* persons chosen (and sent) to speak or act for others. – *verb* **deputize** to take another's place for a time, act as substitute. – *noun* **deputy** (*plural* **deputies**) a person acting in place of another; a delegate, representative.

derail *verb* to cause to leave the rails. – *noun* **derailment**.

derange *verb* to put out of place or out of working order. – *adjective* **deranged** out of one's mind, insane; out of order. – *noun* **derangement**.

derelict *adjective* broken-down, abandoned (*esp* buildings, ships *etc*). – *noun* **dereliction** the neglecting of what should be attended to: *dereliction of duty*.

deride *verb* to laugh at, mock. – *noun* **derision** act of deriding; mockery. – *adjective* **derisive**.

derive *verb* to be descended or formed (from); to trace (a word) back to the beginning of its existence; to receive, obtain: *derive satisfaction*. – *noun* **derivation**. – *noun*, *adjective* **derivative** (something) derived from something else, not original; a word made from another word (*eg fabulous* from *fable*).

dermatitis *noun* inflammation of the skin.

dermatology *noun* the study and treatment of skin diseases. – *noun* **dermatologist**.

derogatory *adjective* harmful to one's reputation, dignity *etc*; scornful, belittling, disparaging.

derrick *noun* a kind of crane for lifting weights; a framework over an oil well that holds the drilling machinery.

descant *noun* (in music) a tune played or sung above the main tune.

descend *verb* to go or climb down; to slope downwards; (with *from*) to have as one's ancestor: *I'm descended from Napoleon*; to go from a greater to a lesser or worse state. – *noun* **descendant** a person descended from another. – *noun* **descent** the act or state of descending; a downward slope; the way down.

describe *verb* to give an account of in words; to draw the outline of, trace. – *noun* **description** the act of describing; an account in words; sort, kind: *people of all descriptions*. – *adjective* **descriptive**.

descry *verb* (*past tense* **descried**) to notice, see.

desecrate *verb* to spoil (something sacred); to treat without respect. – *noun* **desecration**.

desert¹ *verb* to run away (from) (*eg* the army); to leave, abandon: *He deserted his family. His courage deserted him*. – *noun* **deserter** a person who deserts *esp* from the army *etc*. – *noun* **desertion** the act of deserting (*esp* from the army *etc*).

desert² *noun* a stretch of barren country, *usu* hot, dry and sandy with very little water. – noun **desert island** an uninhabited island in a tropical area.

deserve verb to have earned as a right by one's actions etc, be worthy of. – adjective **deserving**. – adverb **deservedly** justly.

desiccate verb to dry up; to preserve by drying: desiccated coconut.

design verb to make a plan or a sketch of something (eg a building) before it is made; to intend. – noun a plan or sketch; a painted picture, pattern etc; an intention or plan. – adjective **designing** crafty, cunning. – **have designs on** to plan to get (someone or something) for oneself.

designate verb to point out, indicate; to name; to appoint, select (for a duty etc). – adjective appointed to a post but not yet occupying it: director designate. – noun **designation** a name, title.

desire verb to wish for (greatly). – noun a longing for; a wish. – adjective **desirable** pleasing; worth having. – noun **desirability**. – **desirous of** wishing for, wanting something.

desist verb to stop (doing something).

desk noun a table for writing, reading etc.

desolate adjective lonely; sorrowful, unhappy; empty of people, deserted; barren. – adjective **desolated** overcome by grief; made desolate. – noun **desolation** the state of being desolated; loneliness; deep sorrow; barren land; ruin.

despair verb to give up hope. – noun lack of hope; that which causes despair: He was the despair of his parents. – adjective **despairing** having no hope.

despatch see dispatch.

desperado noun (plural **desperadoes** or **desperados**) a bold or violent criminal, a gangster.

desperate adjective having lost all hope, despairing; very bad; reckless; violent. – noun **desperation**.

despicable adjective contemptible, worthless and hateful.

despise verb to look upon with contempt, regard as worthless or hateful.

despite preposition in spite of: Despite the rain they went to the seaside.

despoil verb to rob, plunder. – noun **despoliation**.

despondent adjective downhearted, dejected. – noun **despondency**.

despot noun someone (usu king or ruler of a country) with unlimited power, a tyrant. – adjective **despotic**. – noun **despotism**.

dessert noun fruits, sweets etc served at the end of a meal; pudding, the sweet course in a meal.

destine verb to set apart for a certain use etc. – noun **destination** the place to which someone or something is going. – adjective **destined** bound (for a place); intended (as if by fate): destined to succeed. – noun **destiny** (plural **destinies**) what is destined to happen; fate.

destitute adjective in need of food, shelter etc; (with **of**) completely lacking in: destitute of kindness. – noun **destitution**.

destroy verb to pull down, knock to pieces; to ruin; to kill. – noun **destroyer** a person who destroys; a type of fast warship.

destruction noun the act of destroying or being destroyed; ruin; death. – adjective **destructible** able to be destroyed. – adjective **destructive** causing destruction; doing great damage; (of criticism etc) pointing out faults without suggesting improvements.

desultory adjective moving from one thing to another without a fixed plan; (of conversation etc) changing from subject to subject, rambling.

detach verb to unfasten, remove (from). – adjective **detachable** able to be taken off: a detachable lining. – adjective **detached** standing apart, by itself: a detached house; separated; not personally involved, showing no emotion or prejudice. – noun **detachment** state of being detached; the act of detaching; a body or group (eg of troops on special service).

detail noun a small part, fact, item etc. – verb to describe fully, give particulars of; to set (a person) to do a special job or task: The pilot was detailed for night-flying. – adjective **detailed** with nothing left out. – **in detail** giving attention to details, item by item.

detain verb to hold back; to keep late; to keep under guard. – noun **detention** imprisonment; a forced stay (as a punishment at school at the end of the day).

detect verb to discover; to notice. – noun **detection**. – noun **detective** a person who tries to find criminals or watches suspected persons.

détente *dā-tonᵍt, noun* a lessening of hostility between nations.

detention *see* **detain.**

deter *verb* (*past tense* **deterred**) to discourage or prevent from (by frightening). – *adjective, noun* **deterrent** (of) something (*esp* a weapon) which deters.

detergent *noun* a (soapless) substance used with water for washing dishes *etc.*

deteriorate *verb* to grow worse: *His health is deteriorating rapidly.* – *noun* **deterioration.**

determine *verb* to decide; to fix or settle: *He determined his course of action.* – *noun* **determination** the state of being determined; the act of determining; stubbornness, firmness of character and purpose. – *adjective* **determined** having one's mind made up, decided: *determined to succeed*; stubborn; fixed; settled.

deterrent *see* **deter.**

detest *verb* to hate greatly. – *adjective* **detestable** very hateful. – *noun* **detestation** great hatred.

dethrone *verb* to remove from a throne. – *noun* **dethronement.**

detonate *verb* to (cause to) explode. – *noun* **detonation** an explosion. – *noun* **detonator** something which sets off an explosive.

detour *noun* a circuitous route.

detract *verb* to take away (from), lessen (an achievement, value *etc*). – *noun* **detraction.**

detriment *noun* harm, damage, disadvantage. – *adjective* **detrimental** disadvantageous, causing harm or damage.

de trop *di trō, adjective* (of a person) in the way, unwelcome.

deuce *noun* a playing-card with two pips; (in tennis scoring) having forty points each.

devastate *verb* to lay waste, leave in ruins; to overcome (a person) with grief *etc.* – *noun* **devastation.**

develop *verb* to (make to) grow bigger or to a more advanced state; to acquire gradually (an interest *etc*); to become active, visible *etc*: *Spots developed on her face*; to unfold gradually; to use chemicals (called **developer**) to make a photograph appear. – *noun* **development.**

deviate *verb* to turn aside, *esp* from the right, normal or standard course. – *noun* **deviation.**

device *noun* something made for a purpose *eg* a tool or an instrument; a plan; a picture or design on a coat of arms.

devil *noun* the spirit of evil, Satan; any evil spirit or person. – *adjective* **devilish** of or like a devil; very wicked. – *adjective* **devil-may-care** not caring what happens. – *noun* **devilment** or **devilry** mischief.

devious *adjective* not direct, roundabout; not straightforward.

devise *verb* to make up, put (quickly) together; to plan or plot.

devoid *adjective* (with **of**) empty of, free from: *devoid of generosity.*

devolve *verb* to fall as a duty (upon someone).

devote *verb* to give up wholly (to). – *adjective* **devoted** loving and loyal; given up (to): *devoted to his work.* – *noun* **devotee** a keen follower. – *noun* **devotion** great love.

devour *verb* to eat up greedily; to destroy.

devout *adjective* earnest, sincere; religious. – *noun* **devoutness.**

dew *noun* tiny drops of water coming from the air as it cools at night. – *adjective* **dewy.**

dexterity *noun* skill, quickness. – *adjective* **dexterous** or **dextrous.**

DHSS *see* **DSS.**

diabetes *noun* a disease in which there is too much sugar in the blood – *adjective, noun* **diabetic.**

diabolic or **diabolical** *adjective* devilish, very wicked.

diadem *noun* a kind of crown.

diagnose *verb* to say what is wrong (with a sick person) after making an examination. – *noun* **diagnosis** (*plural* **diagnoses**). – *adjective* **diagnostic.**

diagonal *noun, adjective* (a line) going from one corner to the opposite corner.

diagram *noun* a drawing to explain something.

dial *noun* the face of a clock or watch; the turning disc over the numbers on a telephone; any disc *etc* containing numbers and a pointer. – *verb* (*past tense* **dialled**) to turn a telephone dial or use a keypad to get a number.

dialect *noun* a way of speaking found only in a certain district or among a certain class or group of people.

dialogue *noun* a talk between two (or more) people.

diameter *noun* the line (drawn) across a circle, passing through its centre.

diamond *noun* a very hard, precious stone; a kind of four-cornered shape: ◇; a playing-card bearing red marks of this shape.

diaper *noun* (*US*) a baby's nappy.

diaphragm *dī'à-fram*, *noun* a layer of muscle separating the lower part of the body from the chest; any thin dividing layer; a contraceptive device a woman fits over her cervix.

diarrhoea *dī-à-rē'à*, *noun* too frequent emptying of the bowels, with too much liquid in the faeces.

diary *noun* (*plural* **diaries**) a (small book containing a) record of daily happenings.

diatribe *noun* an angry attack in words or writing.

dice *noun* (*singular* also **die**) (*plural* **dice**) a small cube *usu* with numbered sides or faces, used in certain games. – *verb* to cut (food) into small cubes.

Dictaphone® *noun* a type of machine which records what is spoken into it, used in offices for dictation.

dictate *verb* to read out (something) so that another may write (it) down; to give firm commands. – *noun* an order, command. – *noun* **dictation.** – *noun* **dictator** an all-powerful ruler. – *adjective* **dictatorial** of or like a dictator; domineering, in the habit of giving orders.

diction *noun* manner of speaking; choice of words.

dictionary *noun* (*plural* **dictionaries**) a book having the words of a language in (alphabetical) order, together with their meanings; a book containing other information alphabetically arranged.

did *see* **do.**

die *verb* (*present participle* **dying,** *past tense* **died**) to lose life; to wither. – *noun* a

stamp or punch for making raised designs on money *etc*; *see* also **dice.**

diesel engine *noun* an internal combustion engine in which heavy oil is ignited by heat generated by compression.

diet *noun* food; a course of recommended foods *eg* for the purpose of losing weight; a meeting of a court *etc*. – *verb* to eat certain kinds of food only, *esp* to lose weight. – *adjective* **dietetic** of a diet or diets.

differ *verb* (*past tense* **differed**) (with **from**) to be unlike; to disagree. – *noun* **difference** a point in which things are unlike; the amount by which one number is greater than another; a disagreement. – *adjective* **different** unlike. – *verb* **differentiate** to make a difference or distinction between.

difficult *adjective* not easy, hard to do, understand or deal with; hard to please. – *noun* **difficulty** (*plural* **difficulties**) lack of easiness, hardness; anything difficult; anything which makes something difficult, an obstacle, hindrance *etc*; (*plural*) troubles.

diffident *adjective* shy, not confident. – *noun* **diffidence.**

diffuse *verb* to spread in all directions. – *adjective* widely spread.

dig *verb* (*present participle* **digging,** *past tense* **dug**) to turn up (earth) with a spade *etc*; to make (a hole) by this means; to poke or push (something) into. – *noun* a poke or thrust; a digging up (or the place dug) to find archaeological remains. – *noun* **digger** a machine for digging.

digest *verb* to break up food (in the stomach) and turn it into a form in which the body can make use of it; to think over. – *noun* a summing-up; a collection of written material. – *adjective* **digestible** able to be digested. – *noun* **digestion** the act or power of digesting. – *adjective* **digestive** making digestion easy.

digit *noun* a finger or toe; any of the numbers 0–9. – *adjective* **digital** (of an electronic calculator, clock *etc*) using the numbers 0–9. – *noun* **digital audio tape** a magnetic audio tape on which sound has been recorded digitally. – *noun* **digital recording** a very accurate process of recording sound by storing electrical pulses representing the audio signal on compact disc, digital audio tape *etc*; such a recording.

digitalis *noun* a family of plants, including the foxglove, from which a medicine used in heart disease is obtained.

dignified *adjective* stately, serious. – *noun* **dignitary** (*plural* **dignitaries**) a person of high rank or office. – *noun* **dignity** a stately or serious manner; manner showing a sense of one's own worth or the seriousness of the occasion; high rank.

digress *verb* to wander from the point in speaking or writing. – *noun* **digression**.

dike, dyke *noun* a wall; an embankment; a ditch; (*coll*) a lesbian.

dilapidated *adjective* falling to pieces, needing repair.

dilate *verb* to make or grow larger, swell out. – *noun* **dilatation** or **dilation**.

dilatory *adjective* slow (in doing things), inclined to delay.

dilemma *noun* a position or situation giving a choice of two things, neither of which is pleasant.

dilettante *noun* a person who has a slight but not serious interest in several subjects.

diligent *adjective* hard-working, industrious. – *noun* **diligence**.

dilly-dally *verb* (*past tense* **dilly-dallied**) to loiter, waste time.

dilute *verb* to lessen the strength of a liquid *etc*, *esp* by adding water. – Also *adjective*. – *adjective* **diluted**. – *noun* **dilution**.

dim *adjective* not bright or clear; not seeing or understanding clearly. – *verb* (*past tense* **dimmed**) to make or become dim. – *noun* **dimness**.

dime *noun* the tenth part of a N. American dollar, ten cents.

dimension *noun* a measurement (of length, width or thickness); (*plural*) size, measurements.

diminish *verb* to make or grow less. – *noun* **diminution** a lessening. – *adjective* **diminutive** very small.

dimple *noun* a small hollow, *esp* on the cheek or chin.

din *noun* a loud, lasting noise. – *verb* (*past tense* **dinned**) (with **into**) to put (information *etc*) into someone's mind by constant repetition.

dine *verb* to take dinner.

dinghy *noun* (*plural* **dinghies**) a small rowing boat, *esp* one carried on board a bigger boat.

dingy *adjective* dull, faded, or dirty-looking. – *noun* **dinginess**.

dinner *noun* the main meal of the day.

dinosaur *noun* any of various types of extinct (giant) reptile.

dint *noun* a hollow made by a blow, a dent. – **by dint of** by means of.

diocese *noun* a bishop's district.

Dip. *abbreviation* diploma.

dip *verb* (*past tense* **dipped**) to plunge into any liquid for a moment; to lower (*eg* a flag) and raise again; to slope down; to look briefly into (a book *etc*). – *noun* a liquid substance in which anything is dipped; a creamy sauce into which biscuits *etc* are dipped: *a cheese dip*; a downward slope; a hollow; a short bathe.

DipEd *abbreviation* Diploma in Education.

diphtheria *noun* an infectious throat disease.

diphthong *noun* two vowel-sounds pronounced as one syllable (as in *out*).

diploma *noun* a written statement giving an honour, or saying that one has passed a certain examination.

diplomacy *noun* the business of making agreements, treaties *etc* between countries; cleverness in making people agree, tact. – *noun* **diplomat** a person engaged in diplomacy. – *adjective* **diplomatic** of diplomacy; tactful.

dire *adjective* dreadful: *in dire need*.

direct *adjective* straight, not roundabout; (of a person's manner) straightforward, outspoken. – *verb* to point or aim at; to show the way; to order, instruct; to control, organize; to put a name and address on (a letter). – *noun* **direction** the act of directing; the place or point to which one moves, looks *etc*; an order; guidance; (*plural*) instructions. – *noun* **directness**. – *noun* **director** a person who directs, *esp* one who guides or manages (a business *etc*). – *noun* **directory** (*plural* **directories**) a book of names and addresses *etc*. – *noun* **direct speech** speech reported in the speaker's exact words. – *noun* **direct tax** a tax on income or property.

dirge *noun* a lament; a funeral hymn.

dirk *noun* a kind of dagger.

dirt *noun* any unclean substance, such as mud, dust, dung *etc.* – *noun* **dirt track** an earth track for motor-cycle racing. – *adjective* **dirty** not clean, soiled; bad, obscene, evil. – *verb* (*past tense* **dirtied**) to soil with dirt. – *adverb* **dirtily.** – *noun* **dirtiness.**

disable *verb* to take away (wholly or partly) the power or strength from, cripple. – *noun* **disability** (*pl* **disabilities**) something which disables. – *noun* **disablement** the act of disabling; state of being disabled.

disabuse *verb* to set right (someone) about a wrong belief or opinion: *You must disabuse him of that idea.*

disadvantage *noun* an unfavourable circumstance, a drawback. – Also *v.* – *adjective* **disadvantaged** having a disadvantage of some kind *esp* poverty, homelessness. – *adjective* **disadvantageous** not advantageous.

disaffected *adjective* discontented, rebellious. – *noun* **disaffection.**

disagree *verb* (sometimes with **with**) to hold different opinions *etc* (from another); to quarrel; (of food) to be unsuitable (to someone) and cause illness. – *adjective* **disagreeable** unpleasant. – *noun* **disagreement.**

disallow *verb* not to allow.

disappear *verb* to go out of sight, vanish. – *noun* **disappearance.**

disappoint *verb* to fail to come up to the hopes or expectations (of); to fail to fulfil. – *adjective* **disappointed.** – *noun* **disappointment.**

disapprove *verb* to have an unfavourable opinion (of). – *noun* **disapproval.**

disarm *verb* to take weapons away from; to get rid of war weapons; to make less angry *etc*, to charm. – *noun* **disarmament** the act of doing away with war weapons. – *adjective* **disarming** gaining friendliness, charming: *a disarming smile.*

disarrange *verb* to throw out of order, make untidy. – *noun* **disarrangement.**

disarray *noun* disorder.

disaster *noun* an extremely unfortunate happening, *esp* one that causes great damage, loss *etc*. – *adjective* **disastrous.**

disband *verb* to (cause to) break up: *The gang disbanded.* – *noun* **disbandment.**

disbelieve *verb* not to believe. – *noun* **disbelief.** – *noun* **disbeliever.**

disburse *verb* to pay out. – *noun* **disbursement.**

disc or **disk** *noun* a flat, round shape; a pad of cartilage between vertebrae; a gramophone record; (*comput*) a flat round shape coated with magnetic material on which data are stored. – *noun plural* **disc brakes** car *etc* brakes using pads that are hydraulically forced against discs on the wheels. – *noun* **disc drive** (*comput*) part of a computer system that records data on to and retrieves data from discs. – *noun* **disc jockey** one who introduces and plays recorded music (for radio programmes *etc*).

discard *verb* to throw away as useless.

discern *verb* to see, realize. – *adjective* **discernible** able to be seen (or understood. – *adjective* **discerning** quick or clever at noticing or understanding. – *noun* **discernment** the state of quality of being discerning.

discharge *verb* to unload (cargo); to set free; to dismiss; to fire (a gun); to perform (duties); to pay (a debt); to give off (*eg* smoke), let out (*eg* pus). – *noun* unloading; setting free; firing (of a gun); dismissal; something discharged (*eg* pus); the performance (of duties); payment.

disciple *noun* someone who believes in another's teaching, *esp* one of the followers of Christ.

discipline *noun* training in an orderly way of life; order kept by means of control. – *verb* to bring to order; to punish. – *noun* **disciplinarian** a person who insists on strict discipline. – *adjective* **disciplinary** of or enforcing discipline (by punishment).

disclaim *verb* to refuse to have anything to do with, deny. – *noun* **disclaimer** a denial.

disclose *verb* to uncover, reveal, make known. – *noun* **disclosure** the act of disclosing; something disclosed.

disco (also **discotheque**) *noun* (*plural* **discos**) a club, hall or event at which recorded music is played for dancing; the equipment and records used to provide such music.

discolour or (*US*) **discolor** *verb* to change or spoil the colour of; to stain. – *noun* **discoloration.**

discomfiture *noun* embarrassment; defeat.

discomfort *noun* want of comfort, uneasiness.

disconcert *verb* to upset, embarrass.

disconnect *verb* to separate, break the connection between. – *adjective* **disconnected** separated, no longer connected; (of speech *etc*) not well joined together, rambling.

disconsolate *adjective* sad, disappointed.

discontent *noun* dissatisfaction. – *adjective* **discontented** dissatisfied, cross. – *noun* **discontentment**.

discontinue *verb* to stop, cease to continue.

discord *noun* disagreement, quarrelling; (in music) a jarring of notes. – *adjective* **discordant**.

discotheque *see* disco.

discount *noun* a small sum taken off the price of something: *He received a 10% discount on his order.* – *verb* to leave out, not to consider; to allow for exaggeration in (*eg* a story).

discourage *verb* to take away the confidence, hope *etc* of: *His low marks discouraged him*; to try to prevent (by showing disapproval of): *She discouraged his attempts.* – *noun* **discouragement.** – *adjective* **discouraging** giving little hope or encouragement.

discourse *noun* a speech, sermon, lecture; an essay; a conversation. – *verb* to talk.

discourteous *adjective* not polite, rude. – *noun* **discourtesy.**

discover *verb* to find out; to find by chance, *esp* for the first time. – *noun* **discoverer.** – *noun* **discovery** (*plural* **discoveries**) the act of finding or finding out; the thing discovered.

discredit *noun* loss of good reputation, disgrace; disbelief. – *verb* to refuse to believe; to cause disbelief in; to disgrace. – *adjective* **discreditable** disgraceful.

discreet *adjective* wise, cautious, tactful. – *noun* **discretion.**

discrepancy *noun* (*plural* **discrepancies**) a difference, disagreement (between two stories, amounts of money *etc*).

discretion *see* discreet.

discriminate *verb* to make differences (between), to distinguish; to treat (people) differently. – *adjective* **discriminating** showing good sense in judging things *etc*. – *noun* **discrimination** the act of or ability in discriminating.

discus *noun* a heavy disc thrown in a kind of athletic competition.

discuss *verb* to talk about. – *noun* **discussion.**

disdain *verb* to look down on, scorn (something); to be too proud (to do something). – *noun* scorn. – *adjective* **disdainful.**

disease *noun* illness. – *adjective* **diseased.**

disembark *verb* to put or go ashore. – *noun* **disembarkation.**

disembodied *adjective* (of a spirit, soul *etc*) separated from the body.

disengage *verb* to separate, free. – *adjective* **disengaged** separated, freed; not busy; vacant, not engaged.

disentangle *verb* to free from entanglement, to unravel.

disfavour *noun* the state of being out of favour; dislike.

disfigure *verb* to spoil the beauty or appearance of. – *noun* **disfigurement.**

disfranchise *verb* to take away the right to vote.

disgorge *verb* to vomit; to throw out; to give up (what has been taken).

disgrace *noun* the state of being out of favour; shame. – *verb* to bring shame upon. – *adjective* **disgraceful** shameful; very bad.

disgruntled *adjective* sulky, discontented.

disguise *verb* to change the appearance of, by a change of dress *etc*; to hide (feelings *etc*). – *noun* a disguised state; that which disguises.

disgust *noun* strong dislike, loathing; indignation. – *verb* to arouse dislike, loathing or indignation. – *adjective* **disgusting** sickening; causing disgust.

dish *noun* (*plural* **dishes**) a plate, bowl *etc* for food; food prepared for table. – *verb* to put into a dish, serve out. – *noun* (also **dish aerial**) a large aerial, shaped like a dish, used *eg* in satellite television.

dishearten *verb* to take away courage or hope from. – *adjective* **disheartened.** – *adj* **disheartening.**

dishevelled *adjective* untidy, with hair *etc* disordered.

dishonest adjective not honest, deceitful. – noun **dishonesty.**

dishonour noun disgrace, shame. – verb to cause shame to. – adjective **dishonourable** having no sense of honour; disgraceful.

disillusion verb to take away a false belief from. – Also noun. – adjective **disillusioned.** – noun **disillusionment.**

disinclined adjective unwilling.

disinfect verb to destroy disease-causing germs in. – noun **disinfectant** a substance that kills germs.

disinherit verb to take away the rights of an heir.

disintegrate verb to fall into pieces; to break up into parts. – noun **disintegration.**

disinterested adjective unselfish, not influenced by private feelings or interests.

disjointed adjective (esp of speech etc) not well connected together.

disk see **disc.**

dislike verb not to like, to disapprove of. – Also noun.

dislocate verb to put (a bone) out of joint; to upset, to put out of order. – noun **dislocation.**

dislodge verb to drive from a place of rest, hiding or defence; to knock out of place accidentally.

disloyal adjective not loyal, unfaithful. – noun **disloyalty.**

dismal adjective gloomy; sorrowful, sad.

dismantle verb to strip off or take down fittings, furniture etc; to take to pieces.

dismay verb to surprise and upset. – Also noun.

dismember verb to tear to pieces; to cut the limbs from.

dismiss verb to send or to put away; to send (a person) from a job, sack; to stop, close (a law-case) etc. – noun **dismissal.**

dismount verb to come down off a horse, bicycle etc.

disobey verb to fail or refuse to do what is commanded. – noun **disobedience.** – adjective **disobedient** refusing or failing to obey.

disobliging adjective not willing to carry out the wishes of others.

disorder noun lack of order, confusion; disturbance; disease. – verb to throw out of order. – adjective **disorderly** out of order; behaving in a lawless (noisy) manner. – noun **disorderliness.**

disown verb to refuse or cease to recognize as one's own.

disparage verb to speak of as being of little worth or importance, belittle. – noun **disparagement.** – adjective **disparaging.**

disparity noun (plural **disparities**) great difference, inequality.

dispassionate adjective favouring no one, unbiassed; judging calmly, cool.

dispatch or **despatch** verb to send off (a letter etc); to kill, finish off; to do or deal with quickly. – noun (plural **dispatches** or **despatches**) the act of sending off; a report (eg to a newspaper); speed in doing something; killing; (plural) **dispatches** official papers (esp military or diplomatic). – noun **dispatch rider** a carrier of military dispatches by motorcycle.

dispel verb (past tense **dispelled**) to drive away, make to disappear.

dispense verb to give or deal out; to prepare (medicines, prescriptions) for giving out. – adjective **dispensable** able to be done without. – noun **dispensary** (pl **dispensaries**) a place where medicines are given out. – noun **dispensation** special leave to break a rule etc. – noun **dispenser** a person who dispenses; a machine which dispenses. – **dispense with** to do without.

disperse verb to scatter; to spread; to (cause to) vanish. – noun **dispersal** or **dispersion** a scattering.

dispirited adjective sad, discouraged.

displace verb to put out of place; to disarrange; to put (a person) out of office. – noun **displaced person** a person forced to leave his or her own country because of war, political opinions etc. – noun **displacement** a movement out of place; the quantity of water moved out of place by a ship etc when floating.

display verb to set out for show. – noun a show, exhibition.

displease verb not to please; to offend, annoy. – noun **displeasure** annoyance, disapproval.

dispose verb to arrange, settle; to get rid (of); to make inclined. – adjective

disposable intended to be thrown away. – *noun* **disposal** the act of disposing. – *adjective* **disposed** inclined, willing. – **at one's disposal** available for one's use.

disposition *noun* arrangement; nature, personality; (in law) a giving over of (property *etc*) to another.

dispossess *verb* to take away from, deprive of ownership (of).

disproportionate *adjective* too big or too little, not in proportion.

disprove *verb* to prove to be false.

dispute *verb* to argue (about). – *noun* an argument, quarrel. – *adjective* **disputable** not certain, able to be argued about. – *noun* **disputation** an argument.

disqualify *verb* (*past tense* **disqualified**) to put out of a competition *etc* for breaking rules; to take away a qualification or right. – *noun* **disqualification**.

disquiet *noun* uneasiness, anxiety. – Also *verb*.

disregard *verb* to pay no attention to, ignore. – *noun* want of attention, neglect.

disrepair *noun* the state of being out of repair.

disrepute *noun* bad reputation. – *adjective* **disreputable** having a bad reputation, not respectable.

disrespect *noun* rudeness, lack of politeness. – *adjective* **disrespectful**.

disrupt *verb* to break up; to throw (a meeting *etc*) into disorder. – *noun* **disruption**. – *adjective* **disruptive** breaking up or causing disorder.

dissatisfy *verb* (*past tense* **dissatisfied**) not to satisfy, to displease. – *noun* **dissatisfaction**. – *adjective* **dissatisfied**.

dissect *verb* to cut into parts in order to examine; to study and criticize. – *noun* **dissection**.

dissemble *verb* to hide, disguise (one's true intentions *etc*).

disseminate *verb* to scatter, spread. – *noun* **dissemination**.

dissent *verb* to have a different opinion; to refuse to agree. – *noun* disagreement. – *noun* **dissension** disagreement, quarrelling. – *noun* **dissenter** a member of a church that has broken away from the officially established church.

dissertation *noun* a long piece of writing or talk on a particular (often scholarly) subject.

disservice *noun* harm, an ill turn.

dissident *noun* a person who disagrees, *esp* politically.

dissimilar *adjective* not the same. – *noun* **dissimilarity** (*plural* **dissimilarities**).

dissipate *verb* to (cause to) disappear; to waste. – *adjective* **dissipated** having wasted one's energies *etc* on too many pleasures. – *noun* **dissipation**.

dissociate *verb* to separate. – **dissociate oneself from** to refuse to be associated with.

dissolve *verb* to melt; to break up; to put an end to. – *noun* **dissolution**.

dissolute *adjective* having bad habits, wicked.

dissonance *noun* discord, *esp* when deliberately used in music; disagreement. – *adjective* **dissonant**.

dissuade *verb* to stop (from doing something) by advice or persuasion. – *noun* **dissuasion**.

distaff *noun* the stick which holds the bunch of flax or wool in spinning. – *adjective* of women, female: *on the distaff side*.

distance *noun* the space between things *etc*; a far-off place or point: *in the distance*; coldness of manner. – *adjective* **distant** far off or far apart in place or time; not close: *a distant cousin*; cold in manner.

distaste *noun* dislike. – *adjective* **distasteful** disagreeable, unpleasant.

distemper *noun* a kind of paint used chiefly for walls; a disease of dogs. – *verb* to paint with distemper.

distend *verb* to swell; to stretch outwards. – *noun* **distension**.

distil *verb* (*past tense* **distilled**) to get (a liquid) in a pure state by heating to a steam or vapour and cooling; to extract the spirit or essence from something by this method; to (cause to) fall in drops. – *noun* **distillation** the act of distilling. – *noun* **distillery** (*plural* **distilleries**) a place where distilling (of whisky, brandy *etc*) is done.

distinct *adjective* clear; easily seen or made out; different. – *noun* **distinction** a difference; outstanding worth or merit; a mark of honour. – *adjective* **distinctive** different, special. – *noun* **distinctiveness.**

distinguish *verb* to recognize a difference (between); to mark off as different; to make out, recognize; to give distinction to. – *adjective* **distinguished** outstanding, famous.

distort *verb* to twist out of shape; to turn or twist (a statement *etc*) from the true meaning; to cause (a sound) to be unclear and harsh. – *noun* **distortion.**

distract *verb* to draw aside (the attention); to trouble, confuse; to make mad. – *adjective* **distracted** mad (with pain, grief *etc*). – *noun* **distraction** something which draws away attention; anxiety, confusion; amusement; madness.

distraught *adjective* extremely agitated or anxious.

distress *noun* pain, trouble, sorrow; a cause of suffering. – *verb* to cause pain or sorrow to. – *adjective* **distressed.** – *adjective* **distressing.**

distribute *verb* to divide among several, deal out; to spread out widely. – *noun* **distribution.**

district *noun* a region of a country or town.

distrust *noun* lack of trust or faith; suspicion. – *verb* to have no trust in. – *adjective* **distrustful.**

disturb *verb* to throw into confusion; to worry, make anxious; to interrupt. – *noun* **disturbance** an act of disturbing; a noisy or disorderly happening; an interruption.

disuse *noun* the state of being no longer used. – *adjective* **disused** no longer used.

ditch *noun* (*plural* **ditches**) a long narrow hollow trench dug in the ground, *esp* one for water.

dither *verb* to hesitate, be undecided; to act in a nervous, uncertain manner. – *noun* a state of indecision or nervousness.

ditto often written **do.,** the same as already written or said.

ditty *noun* (*plural* **ditties**) a simple, little song.

divan *noun* a long, low couch without a back; a kind of bed without a headboard.

dive *verb* to plunge headfirst into water; to swoop through the air; to go down steeply and quickly. – Also *noun*. – *noun* **diver** a person who dives; a person who works under water using special breathing equipment *etc*; any of several types of diving bird.

diverge *verb* to separate and go in different directions; to differ. – *noun* **divergence.** – *adjective* **divergent.**

diverse *adjective* different, various. – *verb* **diversify** (*past tense* **diversified**) to make or become different or varied.

diversion *noun* turning aside; an alteration to a traffic route; (an) amusement.

diversity *noun* difference; variety.

divert *verb* to turn aside, change the direction of; to amuse. – *adjective* **diverting** amusing.

divest *verb* to strip or deprive of: *They divested him of his authority.*

divide *verb* to separate into parts; to share (among); to (cause to) go into separate groups; in arithmetic, to find out how many times one number contains another. – *noun* *plural* **dividers** measuring compasses used in geometry.

dividend *noun* that which is to be divided (see **divisor**); a share of profit (of a business *etc*).

divine *adjective* of God; holy. – *verb* to guess; to foretell, predict. – *noun* **divination** (the art of) foretelling. – *noun* **diviner** a person who claims a special ability in finding hidden water or metals. – *noun* **divining rod** a (hazel) stick, used by water diviners. – *noun* **divinity** (*plural* **divinities**) a god; the nature of a god; religious studies. – **the Divinity** God.

division *noun* the act of dividing; a barrier, something which divides or separates; a part or section (of an army *etc*); separation; disagreement. – *adjective* **divisible** able to be divided. – *noun* **divisibility.** – *adjective* **divisional** of a division. – *noun* **divisor** the number by which another number (the **dividend**) is divided.

divorce *noun* the legal ending of a marriage; a complete separation. – *verb* to end one's marriage with; to separate (from).

divulge *verb* to let out, make known (a secret *etc*).

DIY *abbreviation* do-it-yourself.

dizzy *adjective* giddy, confused; causing giddiness: *dizzy heights.* – *noun* **dizziness.**

DJ *abbreviation* disc jockey.

do *verb* (*present tense* **do, does**, *past tense* **did**, *past participle* **done**) to carry out, perform (a job *etc*); to carry out some action on, *eg* to wash or clean (dishes *etc*), to cook or make (a meal *etc*), to comb *etc* (hair); (*slang*) to swindle; to act: *Do as you please*; to get on: *He is doing well*; to be enough: *A penny will do*; used to avoid repeating a verb: *I seldom see her, but when I do, she runs away*; used with a more important verb (1) in questions: *Do you see?* (2) in sentences with **not**: *I do not know*; (3) to emphasize: *I do hope.* – *noun* (*plural* **dos**) (*coll*) an affair; a festivity, party. – *noun* **doer.** – *noun plural* **doings** actions. – *adjective* **done** finished. – **do away with** to put an end to, destroy.

do. *see* **ditto.**

docile *adjective* (of a person or animal) easy to manage. – *noun* **docility.**

dock *noun* (often *plural*) a deepened part of a harbour *etc* where ships go for loading, unloading, repair *etc*; the box in a law court where the accused person stands; a kind of weed with large leaves. – *verb* to put in or enter a dock; to clip or cut short; to (make spaceships) join together in space. – *noun* **docker** a person who works in the docks. – *noun* **dockyard** a naval harbour with docks, stores *etc*.

docket *noun* a label or note giving the contents of something.

doctor *noun* a person who is trained to treat ill people; a person who has the highest university degree in any subject. – *verb* to treat, as a doctor does a patient; to tamper with, add something harmful to.

doctrine *noun* a belief that is taught.

document *noun* a written statement, giving proof, evidence, information *etc*. – *adjective* **documentary** of or found in documents; of a documentary. – *noun* (*plural* **documentaries**) a film, programme *etc* giving information about a certain subject.

dodder *verb* to shake, tremble, *esp* as a result of old age.

dodge *verb* to avoid (by a sudden or clever movement). – *noun* a trick.

dodo *noun* (*plural* **dodoes** or **dodos**) a type of large extinct bird.

doe *noun* the female of certain animals (as deer, rabbit, hare).

doer, does *see* **do.**

doff *noun* to take off (one's hat *etc*).

dog *noun* a type of animal often kept as a pet; one of the dog family which includes wolves, foxes *etc*; the male of this animal. – *adjective* (of animal) male. – *verb* (*past tense* **dogged**) to follow and watch constantly. – *noun* **dog-collar** a collar for dogs; a clergyman's collar. – *adjective* **dog-eared** (of the pages of a book) turned down at the corner. – *noun* **dogfish** a kind of small shark. – *noun* **dog-rose** the wild rose. – *noun* **dogsbody** (*coll*) a person who is given odd jobs, *esp* unpleasant ones. – *noun* **dog's life** a life of misery. – *adjective* **dog-tired** completely worn out. – *noun* **dogwatch** on a ship, the period of lookout from 4 to 6 p.m. or 6 to 8 p.m.

dogged *adjective* refusing to give in, determined. – *noun* **doggedness.**

doggerel *noun* bad poetry.

dogma *noun* an opinion accepted or fixed by an authority (such as the Church); opinion that is not to be contradicted. – *adjective* **dogmatic** of dogma; forcing one's opinions on others.

doily or **doyley** *noun* (*plural* **doilies** or **doyleys**) a fancy napkin (as on plates in a cakestand).

doldrums *noun plural* those parts of the ocean about the equator where calms and variable winds are common; low spirits.

dole *verb* to deal (out) in small pieces. – *noun* money given by a government to unemployed people. – *adjective* **doleful** sad, unhappy. – *noun* **dolefulness.**

doll *noun* a toy in the shape of a small human being.

dollar *noun* the main unit of money in some countries, *esp* that of N. America.

dolmen *noun* an ancient tomb in the shape of a stone table.

dolphin *noun* a type of sea animal like a porpoise.

dolt *noun* a stupid person. – *adjective* **doltish.**

domain *noun* a kingdom; land in the country, an estate; an area of interest or knowledge.

dome *noun* anything shaped like a half-ball (*esp* a roof). – *adjective* **domed.**

domestic *adjective* of the home or household; (of animals) tame, sharing man's life or used by man; not foreign, of one's own country: *domestic products.* – *noun* a servant in a house. – *adjective* **domesticated** (of an animal) accustomed to live near man; (of a person) fond of doing jobs associated with running a house. – *noun* **domestic help** (a person paid to give) assistance with housework. – *noun* **domesticity** home life. – *noun* **domestic science** the study of subjects associated with running a house (*eg* cookery, sewing).

domicile *noun* the country, place *etc* in which a person lives permanently.

dominant *adjective* ruling; most powerful, most important. – *noun* **dominance**.

dominate *verb* to have command or influence over; to be most strong, or most noticeable *etc*; to tower above, overlook. – *noun* **domination**.

domineering *adjective* overbearing, like a tyrant.

dominion *noun* lordship, rule; an area with one ruler, owner, or government.

domino *noun* (*plural* **dominoes**) a hooded cloak with a mask for the face; one of the 28 wooden or ivory pieces marked with dots used in the game of **dominoes**.

don *noun* a college or university lecturer *etc.* – *verb* (*past tense* **donned**) to put on (a coat *etc*).

donation *noun* a gift of money or goods. – *verb* **donate** to present a gift.

done *see* **do**.

donkey *noun* (*plural* **donkeys**) an ass, a type of animal with long ears, related to the horse.

donor *noun* a giver of a gift or of a part of the body to replace a diseased *etc* part of someone else's body.

don't *verb* short for **do not**.

doom *noun* judgement; fate; ruin. – *adjective* **doomed** condemned; destined, certain (to fail, be destroyed *etc*).

door *noun* the hinged barrier, *usu* of wood, which closes the entrance to a room, house *etc*; the entrance itself. – *noun* **doorstep** the step in front of the door of a house. – *noun* **doorway** the space *usu* filled by a door, entrance.

dope *verb* to drug. – *noun* (*coll*) any drug or drugs; an idiot.

dormant *adjective* sleeping; not active: *a dormant volcano.*

dormer *noun* (also **dormer window**) a small window jutting out from a sloping roof.

dormitory *noun* (*plural* **dormitories**) a room with beds for several people.

dormouse *noun* (*plural* **dormice**) a type of small animal which hibernates.

dorsal *adjective* of the back: *dorsal fin.*

dose *noun* the quantity of medicine to be taken at one time; any unpleasant thing (*eg* an illness, punishment) that must be endured. – *verb* to give medicine to.

doss *verb* (*coll*) to lie down to sleep in a makeshift or temporary place. – *noun* **doss-house** (*coll*) a cheap lodging-house.

dossier *dos'i-ā, noun* a set of papers containing information about a person or subject.

dot *noun* a small, round mark. – *verb* (*past tense* **dotted**) to mark with a dot; to scatter.

dotage *noun* the foolishness and childishness of old age.

dote: dote on to be foolishly fond of.

double *verb* to multiply by two; to fold. – *noun* twice as much: *He ate double the amount*; a person so like another as to be mistaken for them. – *adjective* containing *etc* twice as much: *a double dose*; made up of two of the same sort together; folded over; deceitful: *a double game.* – *adverb* **doubly**. – *noun* **double agent** a spy paid by each of two countries hostile to each other, but who is loyal to only one of them. – *noun* **double bass** a type of large stringed musical instrument. – *adjective* **double-breasted** (of a suit or coat) having one half of the front overlapping the other and a double row of buttons but a single row of buttonholes. – *verb* **doublecross** to cheat. – Also *noun*. – *noun* **double-dealer** a deceitful, cheating person. – *noun* **double-dealing**. – *noun* **double-decker** a vehicle (*usu* a bus) with two floors. – *noun* **double glazing** two sheets of glass in a window to keep in the heat or keep out noise. – **at the double** very quickly; **double back** to turn sharply and go back the way one has come.

doublet *noun* (*hist*) a close-fitting jacket, once worn by men.

doubloon *noun* (*hist*) an old Spanish gold coin.

doubt *verb* to be unsure or undecided about; not to trust. – *noun* a feeling of not being sure; suspicion, a thing doubted. – *adjective* **doubtful**. – *adverb* **doubtless**.

dough *noun* a mass of flour, moistened and kneaded; (*coll*) money. – *noun* **doughnut** a ring-shaped cake fried in fat.

doughty *adjective* strong; brave.

dove *noun* a pigeon. – *noun* **dovecote** a pigeon house. – *verb* **dovetail** to fit one thing exactly into another.

dowdy *adjective* not smart, badly dressed.

down *adverb* towards or in a lower place or position; to a smaller size *etc*: *to grind down*; from an earlier to a later time: *handed down from father to son*; on the spot, in cash: £2 *down*. – *preposition* towards or in the lower part of; along: *down the road*. – *adjective* descending, going, *etc* downwards: *the down escalator*. – *noun* light, soft feathers; (*plural*) low, grassy hills. – *adjective* **down-at-heel** (of shoes) worn down at the heel; shabby. – *adjective* **downcast** sad. – *noun* **downfall** (of a person) ruin, defeat. – *adjective* **downhearted** discouraged. – *noun* **Downie**® a duvet. – *noun* **downpour** a heavy fall of rain. – *adjective, adverb* **downstairs** on or to a lower floor (of a house *etc*). – *adverb* **downstream** further down a river or stream (in the direction of its flow). – *adjective* **downtrodden** kept in a humble, inferior position. – *adverb* **downwards** moving, leading *etc* down. – *adjective* **downy** soft like feathers. – **go** or **be down with** to become or be ill with: *He has gone down with flu*.

dowry *noun* (*plural* **dowries**) money and property brought by a woman to her husband on their marriage.

doyley *see* **doily**.

doz. *abbreviation* dozen.

doze *verb* to sleep lightly. – Also *noun*.

dozen *adjective, noun* twelve.

DPU *abbreviation* data processing unit.

Dr *abbreviation* doctor.

drab *adjective* of dull colour.

draft *noun* a rough sketch or outline of something; a group (*eg* of soldiers) picked out for a special purpose; (*US*) conscription into the army *etc*; an order for payment of money. – *verb* to make a rough plan; to pick out (*esp* soldiers) for some special purpose; (*US*) to conscript into the army *etc*. – *noun* **draftsman** (also **draughtsman**) a person who draws plans.

drag *verb* to pull *esp* roughly or by force; to move slowly and heavily; (to cause) to trail along the ground *etc*; to search (the bed of a lake *etc*) by means of a net or hook. – *noun* (*coll*) a boring, dreary job, event or person; women's clothing worn by men, or sometimes vice versa.

dragon *noun* (*myth*) a winged, fire-breathing serpent; a fierce or rather frightening person. – *noun* **dragonfly** a kind of winged insect with a long body and double wings.

dragoon *noun* a heavily-armed horse soldier. – *verb* to force or bully (a person into doing something).

drain *verb* to clear (land) of water by trenches or pipes; to drink everything in (a cup *etc*); to use up completely (money, strength *etc*). – *noun* anything (such as a ditch, waterpipe, trench) in which liquids may flow away. – *noun* **drainage** the drawing-off of water by rivers, pipes *etc*. – *adjective* **drained** emptied of liquid; with no strength left.

drake *noun* the male of the duck.

drama *noun* a play for acting on the stage; an exciting or tense happening. – *adjective* **dramatic** having to do with plays; exciting, thrilling; unexpected, sudden. – *noun* **dramatist** a writer of plays. – *verb* **dramatize** to turn (a story) into a play for acting; to make real events seem like scenes from a play; to make vivid, striking or sensational. – *noun* **dramatization**.

drank *see* **drink**.

draper *noun* a dealer in cloth and cloth goods. – *verb* **drape** to arrange (cloth coverings) to hang gracefully. – *noun* **drapery** cloth goods; a draper's shop. – *noun plural* **drapes** (*US*) curtains.

drastic *adjective* severe; thorough.

draught *noun* the act of drawing or pulling; something drawn out; an amount of liquid drunk at once, without stopping; a current or rush of air; *see also* **draft**; (*plural*) a game for two, played by moving pieces on a squared board. – *noun* **draughtsman** same as **draftsman**. – *adjective* **draughty** full of air currents, cold.

draw *verb* (*past tense* **drew**, *past participle* **drawn**) to make a picture (*esp* with pencil, crayons *etc*); to pull after or along; to attract (a crowd, attention *etc*); to obtain money from a fund *etc*: *to draw a pension*; to require depth for floating: *This ship draws 20 feet*; to move or come (near *etc*): *Night draws near*; to score equal points in a game: *Their team might draw with ours.* – *noun* **drawback** a disadvantage. – *noun* **drawbridge** a bridge (at the entrance to a castle) which can be drawn up or let down. – *noun* **drawer** a person who draws; a sliding box for clothes *etc* which fits into a chest, cabinet, table *etc*. – *noun* **drawing** a picture made by pencil, crayon *etc*. – *noun* **drawing-pin** a pin with a large flat head for fastening paper on a board *etc*. – *noun* **drawing-room** a sitting-room. – **draw a conclusion** to form an opinion from evidence heard; **drawn and quartered** (*hist*) having the body cut in pieces after being hanged; **draw up** (of a car *etc*) to stop; to move closer; to plan, write out (a contract *etc*).

drawl *verb* to speak in a slow, lazy manner. – Also *noun*.

drawn *see* **draw**.

dread *noun* great fear. – *adjective* terrifying. – *verb* to be greatly afraid of. – *adjective* **dreadful** terrible; (*coll*) very bad. – *noun* **dreadnought** (*hist*) a kind of battleship.

dream *noun* thoughts, pictures in the mind that come mostly during sleep; something imagined, not real; something very beautiful; a hope or ambition. – *verb* (*past tense, past participle* **dreamed** or **dreamt**) to see visions and pictures in the mind while asleep. – *adjective* **dreamy** looking as if not quite awake; vague, dim; beautiful. – **dream up** to invent.

dreary *adjective* gloomy, cheerless.

dredge *verb* to drag a net, bucket *etc* along the bed of a river or sea in order to bring up fish, mud *etc*; to sprinkle with (*eg* sugar). – *noun* an instrument for dredging a river *etc*. – *noun* **dredger** a ship which deepens a channel *etc* by lifting mud from the bottom; a box or jar with a sprinkler top (*eg* a sugar dredger).

dregs *noun plural* sediment, the solid part that falls to the bottom of a liquid: *dregs of wine*; the least useful part of anything; the last remaining part.

drench *verb* to soak.

dress *verb* to put on clothes or a covering; to prepare (food *etc*) for use *etc*; to arrange (hair); to treat and bandage (wounds). – *noun* (*plural* **dresses**) covering for the body; a lady's gown, frock *etc*; style of clothing. – *adjective* (of clothes *etc*) for wearing on formal occasions. – *noun* **dress-coat** a black tailcoat. – *noun* **dresser** a kitchen sideboard for dishes *etc*. – *noun* **dressing** something put on as a covering; a seasoned sauce added to salads *etc*; a bandage *etc* to cover a wound. – *noun* **dressing-gown** a loose, light coat worn indoors over pyjamas *etc*. – *noun* **dress rehearsal** the final rehearsal of a play, in which the actors wear their costumes. – *adjective* **dressy** fond of stylish clothes; stylish, smart.

drew *see* **draw**.

drey *noun* (*plural* **dreys**) a squirrel's nest.

dribble *verb* to (cause to) fall in small drops; to let saliva run down the chin; (in football) to kick the ball on, little by little. – Also *noun*.

dried *see* **dry**.

drift *noun* something driven by wind (such as ice, snow, sand); the direction in which a thing is driven; (of words spoken or written) the general meaning. – *verb* to go with the tide or current; (of snow *etc*) to be driven into heaps by the wind; to wander or live aimlessly. – *noun* **drifter** a person who drifts; a fishing boat that uses nets (**drift-nets**) which remain near the surface of the water. – *noun* **driftwood** wood driven on to the seashore by winds or tides.

drill *verb* to make a hole in; to make with a drill; to exercise soldiers *etc*; to sow (seeds) in rows. – *noun* a tool for making holes in wood *etc*; exercise, practice *esp* of soldiers; a row of seeds or plants.

drink *verb* (*past tense* **drank**, *past participle* **drunk**) to swallow (a liquid); to take alcoholic drink, *esp* to too great an extent. – *noun* something to be drunk; alcoholic liquids. – **drink in** to take eagerly into the mind, listen eagerly; **drink to** to wish (someone) well while drinking, to toast; **drink up** to drink (a liquid) to the last drop.

drip *verb* (*past tense* **dripped**) to fall in drops; to let (water *etc*) fall in drops. – *noun* a drop; a continual dropping (*eg* of water); liquid that drips; a device for adding liquid slowly to a vein *etc*. – *verb*

drip-dry to dry (a garment) by hanging it up to dry without squeezing moisture out of it in any way; (of a garment) to dry in this way. – *adjective* able to be dried in this way. – *noun* **dripping** fat from meat in roasting *etc*.

drive *verb* (*past tense* **drove**, *past participle* **driven**) to control or guide (a car *etc*); to go in a vehicle; to force or urge along; to hurry on; to hit hard (a ball, nail *etc*); to bring about: *drive a bargain*. – *noun* a journey in a car; a private road to a house; an avenue or road; energy, enthusiasm; a campaign: *a drive to put an end to racialism*; a hard stroke with a club or bat (in golf, cricket, tennis *etc*). – *noun* **driver** a person who drives; a wooden-headed golf club. – *noun* **drive-in** (*US*) a cinema, restaurant where people are catered for while remaining in their cars. – **what are you driving at?** what are you suggesting or implying?

drivel *noun* (*coll*) nonsense. – *verb* (*past tense* **drivelled**) (*coll*) to talk nonsense.

driven *see* **drive**.

drizzle *noun* rain in small drops. – Also *verb*. – *adjective* **drizzly**.

droll *adjective* funny, amusing; odd.

dromedary *noun* (*plural* **dromedaries**) a type of Arabian camel with one hump.

drone *verb* to make a low humming sound; to speak in a dull boring voice. – *noun* a low humming sound; a dull boring voice; the low-sounding pipe of a bagpipe; the male of the bee; a lazy, idle person.

drool *verb* to let saliva flow in anticipation of food; to anticipate (something) in a very obvious way.

droop *verb* to hang down: *The hem of her dress is drooping*; to grow weak, faint or discouraged.

drop *noun* a small round or pear-shaped particle of liquid, *usu* falling: *raindrop*; a small quantity (of liquid); a fall or descent from a height: *a drop of six feet*; a small sweet: *acid drop*. – *verb* (*past tense* **dropped**) to fall suddenly; to let fall; to fall in drops; to set down from a car *etc*; to give up, abandon (a friend, habit *etc*). – *noun* **droplet** a tiny drop. – *noun plural* **droppings** dung (of animals or birds). – **drop off** to fall asleep; **drop out** to withdraw (*eg* from a university course).

dross *noun* the scum which metals throw off when melting; small or waste coal; waste matter, impurities; anything worthless.

drought *noun* a period of time when no rain falls, *esp* when this causes hardship.

drove *noun* a number of moving cattle or other animals; a crowd (of people). – *verb see* **drive**. – *noun* **drover** a person who drives cattle.

drown *verb* to sink in water and so die; to kill (a person or animal) in this way; to flood or soak completely; to cause (a sound) not to be heard by making a louder sound.

drowsy *adjective* sleepy.

drub *verb* (*past tense* **drubbed**) to beat or thrash. – *noun* **drubbing** a thrashing.

drudge *verb* to do very humble or boring work. – *noun* a person who does such work. – *noun* **drudgery** hard, uninteresting work.

drug *noun* a substance used in medicine (*eg* to kill pain); a substance taken habitually by people to achieve a certain effect *eg* great happiness or excitement. – *verb* (*past tense* **drugged**) to give a drug or drugs to; to make to lose consciousness by a drug. – *noun* **druggist** a person who deals in drugs; a chemist. – *noun* **drugstore** (*US*) a shop which sells various articles (*eg* cosmetics, newspapers, soft drinks) as well as medicines.

drum *noun* a musical instrument of skin *etc* stretched on a round frame of wood or metal, and beaten with sticks; anything shaped like a drum (*eg* a container for oil). – *verb* (*past tense* **drummed**) to beat a drum; to tap continuously (with the fingers). – *noun* **drummer**. – *noun* **drumstick** a stick for beating a drum; the lower part of the leg of a cooked chicken *etc*.

drunk *adjective* suffering from or showing the effects (giddiness, unsteadiness *etc*) of taking too much alcoholic drink. – *noun* a person who is drunk; a person who is often drunk. – *verb see* **drink**. – *noun* **drunkard** a person who is in the habit of drinking too much alcohol. – *adjective* **drunken** drunk; in the habit of being drunk; resulting from too much drink: *a drunken stupor*; involving too much drink: *a drunken orgy*. – *noun* **drunkenness**.

dry *adjective* not moist or wet; thirsty; uninteresting; (of manner) reserved, matter-of-fact; (of wine) not sweet. – verb (past tense **dried**) to make or become dry. – adverb **dryly** or **drily**. – verb **dry-clean** to clean (clothes etc) with chemicals, not with water. – noun **dry-rot** a disease of wood, in which it becomes dry and crumbly. – adjective **dry-stone** (of walls) built of stone without cement or mortar.

dryad noun (myth) a nymph of the woods.

DSO abbreviation Distinguished Service Order.

DSS abbreviation Department of Social Services (previously **DHSS** Department of Health and Social Security).

dual adjective double; made up of two. – noun **dual carriageway** a road divided by a central barrier or boundary, with each side used by traffic moving in one direction. – adjective **dual-purpose** able to be used for more than one purpose.

dub verb (past tense **dubbed**) to declare (someone) a knight by touching each shoulder with a sword; to name or nickname; to add sound-effects to a film etc; to provide (a film) with a new sound-track (eg in a different language).

dubbin or **dubbing** noun a grease for softening leather or making it waterproof.

dubious adjective doubtful, uncertain; probably not honest: dubious dealings. – noun **dubiety**.

ducal adjective of a duke.

ducat noun (hist) an old European gold coin.

duchess noun (plural **duchesses**) the wife, or widow, of a duke; a woman of the same rank as a duke in her own right.

duchy noun (plural **duchies**) the land owned, or ruled over, by a duke.

duck noun a kind of web-footed bird, with a broad flat beak; (in cricket) a score of no runs. – verb to push (someone's head) under water; to lower the head quickly as if to avoid a blow. – noun **duckling** a baby duck.

duck-billed platypus see **platypus**.

duct noun a tube or pipe for carrying liquids (eg in the human body), electric cables etc.

dudgeon: in high dudgeon very angry, indignant.

due adjective owed, that ought to be paid etc; expected to be ready, to arrive etc;

proper: due care. – adverb directly: due south. – noun that which is owed; what one has a right to; (plural) the amount of money charged for some service or for belonging to a club etc. – **due to** brought about by, caused by: His success was due to hard work.

duel noun (hist) a fight (with pistols or swords) between two people. – Also verb. – noun **duellist** a person who fights in a duel.

duet noun musical piece for two singers etc.

duffel-coat or **duffle-coat** noun a coat of coarse woollen cloth, usu with toggles instead of buttons.

dug see **dig**.

dugout noun a boat made by hollowing out the trunk of a tree; a rough shelter dug out of a slope or bank or in a trench; at a football match etc, the bench where managers, trainers, and players who are not on the field sit.

duke noun a nobleman next in rank below a prince. – noun **dukedom** the title, rank, or lands of a duke.

dulcet adjective sweet to the ear; melodious.

dulcimer noun a type of musical instrument with stretched wires which are struck with small hammers.

dull adjective not lively; (of persons) slow to understand or learn; not exciting or interesting; (of weather) cloudy, not bright or clear; not bright in colour; (of sounds) not clear or ringing; blunt, not sharp. – Also verb. – adverb **dully**. – noun **dullness** the state of being dull.

dulse noun a type of eatable seaweed.

duly adverb at the proper or expected time; as expected: He duly handed it over.

dumb adjective without the power of speech; silent; (coll) stupid. – noun **dumbness**. – adverb **dumbly** in silence. – verb **dumbfound** to astonish. – noun **dumb show** acting without words.

dummy noun (plural **dummies**) a person who is dumb; something which seems real but is not (eg an empty package for shop-window display); a model of a human used for displaying clothes etc; an artificial teat put in a baby's mouth to comfort it. – noun **dummy run** a try-out, a practice.

dump verb to throw down heavily; to unload and leave (rubbish etc); to sell at a low price. – *noun* a place for leaving rubbish; (*plural*) depression, low spirits: *He's in the dumps today.*

dumpling *noun* a ball of cooked dough.

dumpy *adjective* short and thick or fat.

dun *adjective* greyish-brown, mouse-coloured. – *verb* (*past tense* **dunned**) to demand payment.

dunce *noun* one slow at learning; a stupid person.

dune *noun* a low hill of sand.

dung *noun* the waste matter passed out of an animal's body, manure. – *noun* **dunghill** a heap of dung in a farmyard.

dungarees *noun plural* trousers made of coarse, hard-wearing material with a bib.

dungeon *noun* a dark underground prison.

dupe *noun* one easily cheated. – *verb* to deceive; to trick.

duplicate *adjective* exactly the same. – *noun* another of exactly the same kind; an exact copy. – *verb* to make a copy or copies of. – *noun* **duplication**.

duplicity *noun* deceit, double-dealing.

durable *adjective* lasting, able to last; wearing well.

duration *noun* the time a thing lasts.

duress *noun* illegal force used to make someone do something. – **under duress** under the influence of force, threats *etc*.

during *preposition* throughout all or part of: *We lived here during the war*; at a particular point within (a period of time): *He died during the night.*

dusk *noun* twilight, partial dark. – *adjective* **dusky** dark-coloured. – *noun* **duskiness**.

dust *noun* fine grains or specks of earth, sand *etc*; anything in the form of fine powder. – *verb* to free from dust: *She dusted the table*; to sprinkle lightly with powder. – *noun* **dustbin** a container for household rubbish. – *noun* **dust-bowl** an area with little rain in which the wind raises storms of dust. – *noun* **duster** a cloth for removing dust. – *noun* **dust jacket** a paper cover on a book. – *noun* **dustman** a person whose job it is to collect household rubbish. – *adjective* **dusty** covered with dust.

duty *noun* (*plural* **duties**) something one ought to do; an action or task required to be done; a tax; (*plural*) the various tasks involved in a job. – *adjective* **dutiable** (of goods) on which tax is to be paid. – *adjective* **dutiful** obedient; careful to do what one should. – *adjective* **duty-free** not taxed.

duvet *doo'vā, noun* a kind of quilt stuffed with feathers, down *etc*, used instead of blankets.

dux *noun* (*plural* **duxes**) (in Scotland) the top boy or girl in a school or class.

DV *abbreviation* if God is willing (*deo volente* [*L*]).

dwarf *noun* (*plural* **dwarfs** or **dwarves**) an under-sized person, animal or plant. – *verb* to make to appear small: *A seven-foot man dwarfs one of ordinary height.* – *adjective* not growing to full or usual height.

dwell *verb* to live or stay (somewhere); (with **on**) to think or speak for a long time (about something): *Don't dwell on the past.*

dwindle *verb* to grow less, waste away.

dye *verb* to give a colour to clothes, cloth *etc*. – *noun* a powder or liquid for colouring. – *noun* **dyeing** the putting of colour into cloth.

dying *see* **die**.

dyke *see* **dike**.

dynamic *adjective* of force; (of a person) forceful, energetic. – *noun* **dynamics** the scientific study of movement and force.

dynamite *noun* a type of powerful explosive.

dynamo *noun* (*plural* **dynamos**) a machine for turning the energy produced by movement into electricity.

dynasty *noun* (*plural* **dynasties**) a succession of kings *etc* of the same family. – *adjective* **dynastic**.

dysentery *noun* an infectious disease causing fever, pain and diarrhoea.

dyslexia *noun* great difficulty in learning to read and in spelling. – *adjective* **dyslexic**.

dyspepsia *noun* indigestion. – *noun, adjective* **dyspeptic** (a person) suffering from indigestion.

E

E *abbreviation* east; eastern.

each *adjective* (of two or more things *etc*) every one taken individually: *A tree stood on each side of the fence. They arrived late on each occasion.* – *pronoun* every one individually: *Each of them received a prize.* – **each other** used when an action takes place between two (loosely, between more than two) people: *We don't see each other often.*

eager *adjective* keen, anxious to do or get (something). – *noun* **eagerness.**

eagle *noun* a kind of large bird of prey. – *noun* **eaglet** a young eagle.

ear *noun* the part of the body through which one hears sounds; the ability to tell one sound from another: *a good ear (for music)*; a spike or head (of corn *etc*). – *noun* **eardrum** the membrane in the middle of the ear. – *verb* **earmark** to mark or set aside for a special purpose. – *n* **earphone** a device held in or over the ear for listening to the radio *etc*. – *adjective* **ear-piercing** very loud or shrill. – *noun* **earshot** the distance at which a sound can be heard. – *noun* **earwig** a type of insect with pincers at its tail. – **lend an ear** to listen.

earl (*masculine*), **countess** (*feminine*) *noun* a member of the British aristocracy ranking between a marquis and a viscount. – *noun* **earldom** the lands or title of an earl.

early *adjective* (*comparative* **earlier**, *superlative* **earliest**) in good time; at or near the beginning (of a period of time, an event, a book *etc*); sooner than expected; soon. – Also *adverb*. – *noun* **earliness.** – *noun* **early bird** an early riser; a person who gains an advantage by acting more quickly than rivals.

earn *verb* to get (money) by work; to deserve. – *noun plural* **earnings** pay for work done.

earnest *adjective* serious, serious-minded. – *noun* seriousness; something (*usu* money) given to make sure that a bargain will be kept. – *noun* **earnestness.** – **in earnest** meaning what one says or does.

earth *noun* the planet on which we live; its surface; soil; the hole of a fox, badger *etc*; an electrical connection (*usu* a wire) with the ground. – *verb* to connect electrically with the ground. – *adjective* **earthen** made of earth or clay. – *noun* **earthenware** pottery, dishes made of clay. – *adjective* **earthly** of the earth as opposed to heaven. – *noun* **earthquake** a shaking of the earth's crust. – *adjective* **earthshattering** of great importance. – *noun* **earth-tremor** a slight earthquake. – *noun* **earthwork** a man-made fortification (*usu* a bank) of earth. – *noun* **earthworm** the common worm – *adj* **earthy** like soil; covered in soil; (of persons *etc*) coarse, not refined.

ease *noun* freedom from difficulty; freedom from pain, worry or embarrassment; rest from work. – *verb* to make or become less painful, strong, difficult *etc*; to put carefully and gradually (into or out of a position). – *adjective* **easy** (*comparative* **easier**, *superlative* **easiest**) not hard to do; free from pain, worry or discomfort. – *adverb* **easily.** – *noun* **easiness.** – **stand at ease** to stand with the legs apart and arms behind one's back.

easel *noun* a stand for an artist's picture, a blackboard *etc*.

east *noun* one of the four chief directions, that in which the sun rises. – Also *adjective*. – *adjective* **easterly** coming from or facing the east. – *adjective* **eastern** of the east. – *adjective* **eastward(s)** towards the east. – Also *adverbs*.

Easter *noun* the time when Christ's rising from the dead is celebrated.

easy see **ease.**

eat *verb* (*past tense* **ate**, *past participle* **eaten**) to chew and swallow (food); to destroy gradually, waste away. – *adjective* **eatable** fit to eat, edible.

eaves *noun plural* the edge of a roof overhanging the walls. – *verb* **eavesdrop** to listen secretly to a private conversation. – *noun* **eavesdropper.**

ebb *noun* the flowing away of the tide after high tide; a lessening, a worsening. – *verb* to flow away; to grow less or worse.

ebony *noun* a type of black, hard wood. – *adjective* made of ebony; black as ebony.

ebullient *adjective* lively and enthusiastic. – *noun* **ebullience.**

EC *abbrev* European Community.

eccentric *adjective* odd, acting strangely; (of circles) not having the same centre. – *noun* **eccentricity** (*plural* **eccentricities**) oddness of manner or conduct.

ecclesiastic or **ecclesiastical** *adjective* of the church or clergy.

ECG *abbreviation* electrocardiogram (or -graph).

echo *noun* (*plural* **echoes**) the repeating of a sound caused by its striking a surface and coming back. – *verb* to send back sound; to repeat (a thing said); to imitate.

eclipse *noun* the disappearance of the whole or part of a heavenly body, as of the sun when the moon comes between it and the earth; loss of glory or brilliance. – *verb* to throw into the shade; to blot out (a person's success *etc*) by doing better.

ecology *noun* the study of plants, animals *etc* in relation to their natural surroundings. – *adjective* **ecological**. – *noun* **ecologist.**

economy *noun* (*plural* **economies**) the management of the money affairs of a country *etc*; the careful use of something *esp* money. – *adjective* **economic** concerning economy or economies; making a profit. – *adjective* **economical** careful in spending or using *esp* money, not wasteful. – *noun* **economics** the study of how men and nations make and spend money. – *noun* **economist** a person who studies or is an expert on economics. – *verb* **economize** to be careful in spending or using.

ecstasy *noun* (*plural* **ecstasies**) very great joy or pleasure. – *adjective* **ecstatic.**

ecumenical *adjective* of or concerned with the unity of the whole Christian church.

eczema *noun* a type of skin disease.

eddy *noun* (*plural* **eddies**) a current of water, air *etc* running against the main stream, causing a circular movement. – Also *verb.*

edelweiss *ā\del-vīs*, *noun* a kind of Alpine plant with white flowers.

edge *noun* the border of anything, the part farthest from the middle; the cutting side of a knife, weapon *etc*; sharpness, as of appetite, mind *etc*; advantage. – *verb* to put an edge or border on; to move little by little: *edge forward.* – *adverb* **edgeways** sideways. – *noun* **edging** a border or fringe. – *adjective* **edgy** on edge, unable to relax, irritable.

edible *adjective* fit to be eaten.

edict *noun* an order, command.

edifice *noun* a large building.

edify *verb* (*past tense* **edified**) to improve the mind. – *adjective* **edifying**. – *noun* **edification** progress in knowledge.

edit *verb* to prepare matter for printing, broadcasting *etc*. – *noun* **edition** the form in which a book *etc* is published after being edited; the number of copies of a book, newspaper *etc* printed at one time; an issue of a newspaper altered in some way for a particular area (*eg* with local news added). – *noun* **editor** a person who edits a book *etc*. – *adjective* **editorial** of an editor. – *noun* the part of a newspaper *etc* written by its editor.

educate *verb* to teach (persons), *esp* in a school, college *etc*. – *noun* **education**. – *adjective* **educational** of education.

EEC *abbreviation* European Economic Community.

EEG *abbreviation* electroencephalogram (or -graph).

eel *noun* a kind of long ribbon-shaped fish.

eerie *adjective* causing fear of the unknown.

efface *verb* to rub out; (with **oneself**) to keep from being noticed.

effect *noun* the result of an action; strength, power (of a drug *etc*); an impression produced: *the effect of the lighting*; general meaning; use, operation: *That law is not yet in effect*; (*plural*) goods, property. – *verb* to bring about. – *adjective* **effective** producing the desired effect; actual. – *adjective* **effectual** able to do what is required.

effeminate *adjective* unmanly, womanish.

effervesce *verb* to froth up; to be very lively, excited *etc*. – *noun* **effervescence**. – *adjective* **effervescent.**

efficacious *adjective* effective. – *noun* **efficacy.**

efficient *adjective* able to do things well, fit, capable. – *noun* **efficiency.**

effigy *noun* (*plural* **effigies**) a likeness of a person, *esp* made of stone, wood *etc*.

effluent *noun* a stream flowing from another stream or lake; liquid industrial waste; sewage.

effort *noun* a try, *esp* one using all one's strength, ability *etc*; hard work.

effrontery *noun* impudence.

effusive *adjective* pouring forth words.

eg *abbreviation* for example (*exempli gratia* [*L*]).

egg *noun* an almost round object, laid by birds, insects *etc* from which their young are produced. – *noun* **egg plant** the aubergine. – **egg on** to urge.

egoism *noun* the habit of considering only one's own interests, selfishness; egotism. – *noun* **egoist**. – *adjective* **egoistic**. – *noun* **egotism** the habit of speaking much of oneself, boastfulness. – *noun* **egotist**.

eider or **eider-duck** *noun* a northern sea duck. – *noun* **eiderdown** soft feathers from the eider; a quilt.

eight *noun* the number 8. – *adjective* 8 in number. – *adjective* **eighth** the last of eight. – *noun* one of eight equal parts.

eighteen *noun* the number 18. – *adjective* 18 in number. – *adjective* **eighteenth** the last of eighteen (things *etc*). – *noun* one of eighteen equal parts.

eighty *noun* the number 80. – *adjective* 80 in number. – *adjective* **eightieth** the last of eighty. – *noun* one of eighty equal parts.

either *adjective, pronoun* one or other of two: *Either bus will take you there. Either of the boys can play*; each of two, both: *Trees grow on either side of the river.* – *conjunction* used with **or** to show alternatives: *Either you go or he does.* – *adverb* any more than another: *I cannot go either. That doesn't work either.*

ejaculate *verb* to emit semen; to shout out, exclaim. – *noun* **ejaculation**.

eject *verb* to throw out; to make (someone) leave a house, job *etc*. – *noun* **ejection**.

eke: eke out to make enough (by adding to in some way): *She eked out the stew by adding vegetables.*

elaborate *verb* to work out in detail: *You must elaborate your escape plan*; (often with **on**) to explain (too) fully. – *adjective* done with fullness and exactness, often too much so; having much ornament or decoration. – *noun* **elaboration**.

élan *noun* enthusiasm, dash.

eland *noun* a type of African deer.

elapse *verb* (of time) to pass.

elastic *adjective* able to stretch and spring back again, springy. – *noun* a piece of cotton *etc* made springy by having rubber woven into it. – *noun* **elasticity**.

elated *adjective* in high spirits, very pleased. – *noun* **elation**.

elbow *noun* the joint where the arm bends. – *verb* to push with the elbow, jostle. – *noun* **elbow grease** hard rubbing. – *noun* **elbow-room** plenty of room to move.

elder *adjective* older; having lived a longer time. – *noun* a person who is older; an office-bearer in certain churches; a type of tree with purple-black berries (**elderberries**). – *adjective* **elderly** nearing old age. – *adjective* **eldest** oldest.

elect *verb* to choose (someone) by voting; to choose (to). – *adjective* chosen; chosen for a post but not yet in it: *president elect*. – *noun* **election** the choosing, *usu* by voting (of people to sit in parliament *etc*). – *verb* **electioneer** to try to get votes in an election. – *noun* **electorate** all those who have the right to vote.

electricity *noun* a form of energy used to give light, heat and power. – *adjective* **electric** or **electrical** of, produced by, worked by *etc* electricity. – *noun* **electric charge** a quantity of electricity *eg* that stored in a battery. – *noun* **electrician** a person skilled in working with electricity. – *verb* **electrify** (*past tense* **electrified**) to supply with electricity; to excite or surprise greatly. – *verb* **electrocute** to kill by an electric current.

electrode *noun* a conductor through which an electric current enters or leaves a battery *etc*.

electron *noun* a very light particle within an atom, having the smallest possible charge of electricity. – *adjective* **electronic** of or using electrons or electronics. – *noun* **electronics** a branch of physics dealing with the movement and effects of electrons, and with their application to machines *etc*.

elegant *adjective* graceful, well-dressed, fashionable; (of clothes *etc*) well-made and tasteful. – *noun* **elegance**.

elegy *noun* (*plural* **elegies**) a poem about sad things, such as the death of a friend.

element *noun* a part of anything; a substance that cannot be split into simpler substances by chemical means, as oxygen, iron *etc*; surroundings necessary for life or those which suit one best; the heating wire carrying the current in an electric heater *etc*; (*plural*) first steps in learning; (*plural*) the powers of nature, the weather. – *adjective* **elemental** of the elements. – *adjective* **elementary** at the first stage; simple.

elephant *noun* a type of very large animal, with a thick skin, a trunk and two ivory tusks. – *adjective* **elephantine** big and clumsy.

elevate *verb* to raise to a higher position; to make cheerful; to improve (the mind). – *noun* **elevation** the act of raising up; rising ground; height; a drawing of a building as seen from the side; an angle measuring height: *the sun's elevation.* – *noun* **elevator** (*US*) a lift in a building.

eleven *noun* the number 11. – *adjective* 11 in number. – *noun* a team (for cricket *etc*) of eleven people. – *noun* **elevenses** coffee, biscuits *etc* taken around eleven o'clock in the morning. – *adjective* **eleventh** the last of eleven (things *etc*). – *noun* one of eleven equal parts.

elf *noun* (*plural* **elves**) (*myth*) a mischief-working fairy. – *adjective* **elfin** or **elfish** or **elvish**.

elicit *verb* to draw out (information *etc*).

eligible *adjective* fit or worthy to be chosen. – *noun* **eligibility**.

eliminate *verb* to get rid of; to exclude, omit: *He was eliminated at the first interview.* – *noun* **elimination**.

élite or **elite** *ā-lēt′, n* those thought to be the best people, as the richest, best educated *etc*.

elixir *noun* a liquid which people once thought would make them live for ever or would turn iron *etc* into gold.

elk *noun* a very large kind of deer.

ell *noun* an old measure of length.

ellipse *noun* (*plural* **ellipses**) an oval shape. – *adjective* **elliptic** or **elliptical** oval; having part of the words or meaning left out.

elm *noun* a type of tree with a rough bark and leaves with saw-like edges.

elocution *noun* the art of what is thought to be correct speech; style of speaking.

elongate *verb* to stretch out lengthwise, make longer. – *noun* **elongation**.

elope *verb* to run away from home to get married. – *noun* **elopement**.

eloquent *adjective* good at putting one's thoughts *etc* into spoken words (to influence others). – *noun* **eloquence**.

else *adverb* otherwise: *Eat or else you will starve*; apart from the person or thing mentioned: *Someone else has taken her place.* – *adverb* **elsewhere** in or to another place.

elucidate *verb* to make (something) easy to understand.

elude *verb* to escape (by a trick); to be too difficult to remember or understand. – *adjective* **elusive** hard to catch.

elver *noun* a young eel.

elves, elvish *see* **elf**.

emaciated *adjective* very thin, like a skeleton.

emanate *verb* to flow, come out from. – *noun* **emanation** something given out by a substance, as gas, rays *etc*.

emancipate *verb* to set free, as from slavery or strict or unfair social conditions. – *noun* **emancipation**.

embalm *verb* to preserve (a dead body) from decay by treating it with spices or drugs.

embankment *noun* a bank of earth or stone to keep water back, to carry a railway *etc* over low-lying places *etc*.

embargo *noun* (*plural* **embargoes**) an official order forbidding something, *esp* trade with another country.

embark *verb* to put or go on board ship; (with **on**) to start (a new career *etc*). – *noun* **embarkation**.

embarrass *verb* to make to feel uncomfortable and self-conscious; to put difficulties (sometimes lack of money) in the way of. – *noun* **embarrassment**.

embassy *noun* (*plural* **embassies**) the offices *etc* of an ambassador in a foreign country.

embellish *verb* to make beautiful, to decorate; to add details to (a story *etc*). – *noun* **embellishment**.

ember *noun* a piece of wood or coal glowing in a fire.

embezzle *verb* to use for oneself money given to one to look after. – *noun* **embezzlement**.

emblazon *verb* to set out in bright colours or in some very noticeable way.

emblem *noun* an object, picture *etc* which represents something: *The dove is the emblem of peace. The leek is the emblem of Wales;* a badge.

embody *verb* (*past tense* **embodied**) to include; to give form or expression (to an idea *etc*): *His first novel embodies the hopes of youth.* – *noun* **embodiment.**

emboss *verb* to make a pattern which stands out from a flat surface (of leather, metal *etc*). – *adjective* **embossed.**

embrace *verb* to throw the arms round in affection; to include; to accept, adopt eagerly (a political party *etc*). – Also *noun.*

embrocation *noun* an ointment for rubbing on the body (for stiffness *etc*).

embroider *verb* to ornament with designs in needlework; to add (untrue) details to (a story *etc*). – *noun* **embroidery.**

embroil *verb* to get (a person) into a quarrel, or into a difficult situation *etc*; to throw into confusion.

embryo *noun* (*plural* **embryos**) the young of an animal or plant in its earliest stages in the womb, egg or seed; the beginning of anything. – *adjective* **embryonic** in an early stage of development.

emend *verb* to remove faults or errors from. – *noun* **emendation.**

emerald *noun* a type of gem of a bright green colour.

emerge *verb* to come out; to become known or clear. – *noun* **emergence.** – *noun* **emergency** (*plural* **emergencies**) an unexpected happening, *usu* dangerous or worrying, requiring very quick action. – *noun* **emergency exit** a way out of a building for use in an emergency. – *adjective* **emergent** arising; newly formed or newly independent: *emergent nation.*

emery *noun* a very hard mineral, for smoothing and polishing, used in **emery paper, emery board** *etc.*

emetic *adjective* causing vomiting. – Also *noun.*

emigrate *verb* to leave one's country to settle in another. – *noun* **emigration.** – *noun* **emigrant** a person who emigrates.

eminent *adjective* famous, notable. – *noun* **eminence** distinction, fame; a title of honour; a rising ground, hill. – *adverb* **eminently** very, obviously: *eminently suitable.*

emissary *noun* (*plural* **emissaries**) a person sent on private (often secret) business.

emit *verb* (*past tense* **emitted**) to send, give out (light, sound *etc*). – *noun* **emission** the act of emitting.

emollient *adjective, noun* softening and smoothing (substance).

emolument *noun* wages, salary.

emotion *noun* any feeling that disturbs or excites the mind (fear, love, hatred *etc*). – *adjective* **emotional** moving the feelings; (of persons) having feelings easily excited. – *adjective* **emotive** causing emotion (rather than thought).

empathy *noun* the ability to share another person's feelings *etc*. – *verb* **empathize.**

emperor (*masculine*), **empress** (*feminine*) *noun* the ruler of an empire.

emphasis *noun* greater force of voice used on some words or parts of words to make them more noticeable; greater attention or importance: *The emphasis is on freedom.* – *verb* **emphasize** to put emphasis on; to call attention to. – *adjective* **emphatic** spoken strongly.

empire *noun* a large and powerful nation or group of nations (*usu* ruled by an emperor); area of power or control.

empirical *adjective* based on experiment and experience, not on theory alone. – *noun* **empiricism.**

employ *verb* to give work to; to use; to occupy the time of. – *noun* **employ** employment. – *noun* **employee** a person who works for an **employer**. – *noun* **employment** work, trade, occupation.

emporium *noun* (*plural* **emporia** or **emporiums**) a market; a shop, *esp* a big shop.

empress *see* **emperor.**

empty *adjective* having nothing (or no one) in it; unlikely to result in anything: *empty threats.* – *verb* (*past tense* **emptied**) to make or become empty. – *noun* (*plural* **empties**) an empty bottle *etc*. – *noun* **emptiness.**

EMS *abbreviation* European Monetary System.

emu *noun* a type of Australian bird which cannot fly.

emulate *verb* to try to do as well as, or better than. – *noun* **emulation.**

emulsion *noun* a milky liquid, *esp* that made by mixing oil and water.

enable *verb* to make it possible for, allow: *The money enabled him to retire.*

enact *verb* to act, perform; to make a law.

enamel *noun* any thin, hard, glossy coating, as paint on metal; the smooth white coating of the teeth *etc*. – *verb* (*past tense* **enamelled**) to coat or paint with enamel. – *noun* **enamelling.**

enamoured: enamoured of fond of.

encampment *noun* a camp for troops *etc*.

enchant *verb* to delight, please greatly; to put a spell or charm on. – *noun* **enchanter** (*masculine*), **enchantress** (*feminine*). – *noun* **enchantment** state of being enchanted; act of enchanting.

enclose *verb* to put inside an envelope *etc* with a letter *etc*; to put (*eg* a wall) around. – *noun* **enclosure** the act of enclosing; something enclosed.

encompass *verb* to surround; to include.

encore *ong-kör[1]*, *noun* an extra performance of a song *etc* given in reply to a call from an audience; this call.

encounter *verb* to meet, *esp* unexpectedly; to come up against (a difficulty, enemy *etc*). – *noun* a meeting, a fight.

encourage *verb* to give hope or confidence to; to urge (to do). – *noun* **encouragement.**

encroach *verb* to go beyond one's rights or land and interfere with another's. – *noun* **encroachment.**

encumbrance *noun* something which hinders or weighs heavily on (someone).

encyclopaedia or **encylopedia** *noun* a book or books containing much information, either on all subjects or on one particular subject. – *adjective* **encyclopaedic** or **encyclopedic** giving complete information.

end *noun* the last point or part; death; the farthest point of the length of something, as of a table *etc*; purpose or object aimed at, the result; a small piece left over. – *verb* to bring or come to an end. – *noun* **ending** the last part. – **on end** standing *etc* on one end; in a row or series, without a stop: *He fasted for days on end.*

endanger *verb* to put in danger or at risk.

endear *verb* to make dear or more dear. – *noun* **endearment** a word of love.

endeavour *verb* to try hard (to). – *noun* a determined attempt.

endemic *adjective* of a disease *etc* found regularly in a certain area.

endive *noun* a type of plant whose curly leaves are eaten as a salad.

endorse *verb* to give one's support to something said or written; to write on the back of a cheque to show that money has been received for it; to indicate on a motor licence that the owner has broken a driving law. – *noun* **endorsement.**

endow *verb* to give money for the buying and upkeep of: *He endowed a bed in the hospital;* to give a talent, quality *etc* to: *Nature endowed her with a good brain.* – *noun* **endowment.**

endure *verb* to bear without giving way; to last. – *adjective* **endurable** bearable. – *noun* **endurance** the power of enduring.

enemy *noun* (*plural* **enemies**) a person who wishes to harm one; a person, army *etc* armed to fight against one; a person who is against (something): *an enemy of communism.* – *noun* **enmity** (*plural* **enmities**).

energy *noun* (*plural* **energies**) strength to work; vigour; ability to work, play *etc* very actively; power (such as electricity, heat *etc*). – *adjective* **energetic** active, lively.

enervate *verb* to take strength out of.

enforce *verb* to cause (a law *etc*) to be carried out.

engage *verb* to begin to employ (workmen *etc*); to book in advance; to take or keep hold of (a person's attention *etc*); to be busy with, occupied in; (of machine parts) to fit together; to begin fighting. – *adjective* **engaged** bound by a promise *esp* of marriage; busy (on something); in use. – *noun* **engagement** a promise of marriage; an appointment (to meet someone); a fight: *naval engagement.* – *adjective* **engaging** pleasant, charming.

engine *noun* a machine in which heat or other energy is used to produce motion; the part of a train which pulls the coaches *etc*. – *noun* **engineer** a person who makes or works with any kind of engine or machine; a person who designs machines, engines *etc*; a person who designs or makes bridges, roads, canals *etc*. – *verb* to bring about by clever or cunning planning. – *noun* **engineering** the science of machines, roadmaking *etc*.

engrave *verb* to write or draw with a special tool on wood, steel *etc*; to make a deep impression on: *The event was engraved on his memory.* – *noun* **engraving** (a print made from) a cut-out drawing *etc* in metal or wood.

engross *verb* to take up the whole interest or attention.

engulf *verb* to swallow up wholly.

enhance *verb* to make to appear greater or better: *Candlelight enhances her beauty.*

enigma *noun* anything or anyone difficult to understand, a mystery. – *adjective* **enigmatic**.

enjoy *verb* to find or take pleasure in; to be in the habit of having, *esp* something of advantage: *He enjoys good health.* – *adjective* **enjoyable**. – *noun* **enjoyment**. – **enjoy oneself** to have a pleasant time.

enlarge *verb* to make larger; (with **on**) to say much or more about something. – *noun* **enlargement** an increase in the size of anything; a larger photograph made from a smaller one.

enlighten *verb* to give more knowledge or information to. – *noun* **enlightenment**.

enlist *verb* to join an army *etc*; to obtain the support and help of.

enliven *verb* to make more active or cheerful.

en masse *ong mas, adverb* all together, in a body.

enmity *see* **enemy**.

enormous *adjective* very large. – *noun* **enormity** hugeness; great wickedness; ability to shock: *The enormity of his remarks silenced all.*

enough *adjective, pronoun* (in) the number or amount wanted or needed: *I have enough coins. Do you have enough money? He has quite enough now.* – *adverb* as much as is wanted or necessary: *She's been there often enough to know her way.*

enquire *see* **inquire**.

enrage *verb* to make angry.

enrol or **enroll** *verb* (*past tense* **enrolled**) to enter (a name) in a register or list. – *noun* **enrolment**.

en route *ong root, adverb* on the way.

ensconce: ensconce oneself to settle comfortably.

ensemble *noun* all the parts of a thing taken together; an outfit of clothes; (a performance given by) a group of musicians *etc*.

ensign *noun* the flag of a nation, regiment *etc*: *the White Ensign of the Royal Navy*; (*hist*) a young officer who carried the flag.

ensue *verb* to follow, come after; to result (from).

ensure *verb* to make sure.

entail *verb* to leave land so that the heir cannot sell any part of it; to bring as a result, involve: *The exam entailed extra work.*

entangle *verb* to make tangled or complicated; to involve (in difficulties).

enter *verb* to go or come in or into; to put (a name *etc*) into a list; to take part (in); to begin (on, upon).

enterprise *noun* anything new (*esp* if risky or difficult) undertaken; a spirit of boldness in trying new things; a business concern. – *adjective* **enterprising** showing boldness *esp* in attempting new things.

entertain *verb* to amuse; to receive as a guest; to give a party; to consider (*eg* a suggestion); to hold in the mind: *He entertained the belief that he was Napoleon.* – *noun* **entertainer** a person who entertains, *esp* one paid to amuse people. – *adjective* **entertaining** amusing. – *noun* **entertainment** something that entertains, as a theatrical show, a party *etc*.

enthral *verb* (*past tense* **enthralled**) to give great delight to.

enthusiasm *noun* great interest and keenness. – *verb* **enthuse** to be enthusiastic (over). – *noun* **enthusiast**. – *adjective* **enthusiastic** acting with all one's powers; greatly interested, keen. – *adverb* **enthusiastically**.

entice *verb* to draw on by promises, rewards *etc*. – *noun* **enticement** a bribe, promise or reward. – *adjective* **enticing**.

entire *adjective* whole, complete. – *noun* **entirety**.

entitle *verb* to give a name to a book *etc*; to give (a person) a right to.

entity *noun* (*plural* **entities**) something which exists.

entomology *noun* the study of insects. – *noun* **entomologist.**

entrails *noun plural* the inner parts of an animal's body, the bowels.

entrance¹ *noun* a place for entering (*eg* a door); the act of coming in; the right to enter. – *noun* **entrant** a person who comes in; a person who goes in for a race, competition *etc.*

entrance² *verb* to fill with great delight; to bewitch. – *adjective* **entrancing** charming.

entreat *verb* (*plural* **entreaties**) to ask earnestly. – *noun* **entreaty.**

entrenched *adjective* firmly established, difficult to move or change.

entrust or **intrust** *verb* to trust (something) to the care of (someone else).

entry *noun* (*plural* **entries**) the act of entering; a place for entering; something written in a book, as a name *etc.*

E number *noun* an identification code for food additives *eg* E102 for tartrazine.

enumerate *verb* to count; to mention individually. – *noun* **enumeration.**

enunciate *verb* to pronounce distinctly; to state formally. – *noun* **enunciation.**

envelop *verb* to cover by wrapping; to surround entirely: *enveloped in mist.* – *noun* **envelope** a wrapping or cover, *esp* for a letter.

environment *noun* surroundings, circumstances in which a person or animal lives.

envisage *verb* to picture in one's mind and consider.

envoy *noun* a messenger, *esp* one sent to deal with a foreign government.

envy *verb* (*past tense* **envied**) to look greedily at someone and wish to have what they have. – Also *noun* (*plural* **envies**). – *adjective* **enviable** worth envying, worth having. – *adjective* **envious** feeling envy.

enzyme *noun* a substance produced in a living body which affects the speed of chemical changes without itself changing.

eon *see* **aeon.**

epaulet or **epaulette** *noun* a shoulder ornament on a uniform.

ephemeral *adjective* lasting a very short time.

epic *noun* a long poem, story, film *etc* about great deeds. – *adjective* of or like an epic; heroic; greater than usual.

epicure *noun* a person who is fond of eating and drinking good things. – *adjective* **epicurean.**

epidemic *noun* an outbreak (*eg* of disease or crime) which affects many people.

epidermis *noun* the top covering of the skin.

epidural *noun* (also **epidural anaesthetic**) the injection of anaesthetic into the lowest portion of the spine to ease pain in the lower half of the body.

epiglottis *noun* a piece of skin at the back of the tongue which closes the windpipe during swallowing.

epigram *noun* any short, neat, witty saying in prose or verse. – *adjective* **epigrammatic.**

epilepsy *noun* an illness causing attacks of unconsciousness and (*usu*) fits. – *adjective* **epileptic** suffering from epilepsy; of epilepsy: *an epileptic fit.* – *noun* a person suffering from epilepsy.

epilogue or (*US*) **epilog** *noun* the very end part of a book, programme *etc*; a speech at the end of a play *etc.*

episcopal *adjective* of or ruled by bishops. – *adjective* **episcopalian** believing in **episcopacy**, the ruling of the Church by bishops.

episode *noun* one of several parts of a story *etc*; an interesting event or happening. – *adjective* **episodic** of episodes; happening at irregular intervals.

epistle *noun* a (formal) letter *esp* one from an apostle of Christ in the Bible.

epitaph *noun* words about a dead person put on a gravestone.

epithet *noun* a describing word, an adjective.

epitome *e-pit'o-mi*, *noun* something or someone that represents something on a small scale: *He is the epitome of politeness*; a summary (of a book, story). – *verb* **epitomize** to make or be the epitome (of something).

epoch *noun* an event or time marking the beginning of a new period in history, development *etc*; an extended period of time, *usu* marked by an important series of events. – *adjective* **epoch-making** marking an important point in history.

equable *adjective* of calm temper; (of climate) neither very hot nor very cold.

equal *adjective* of the same size, value, quantity *etc*; evenly balanced; (with **to**) able, fit for: *equal to the job.* – *noun* a person of the same rank, cleverness *etc* (as another). – *verb* (*past tense* **equalled**) to be or make equal to; to be the same as. – *noun* **equality** the state of being equal. – *verb* **equalize** to make equal.

equanimity *noun* evenness of temper, calmness.

equate *verb* to regard or treat as being in some way the same; to state the equality of. – *noun* **equation** a statement, *esp* in mathematics, that two things are equal.

equator *noun* an imaginary line around the earth, halfway between the North Pole and the South Pole. – *adjective* **equatorial** of, situated on or near, the equator.

equerry *noun* (*plural* **equerries**) an official who attends a king or prince *etc*.

equestrian *adjective* of horse-riding; on horseback. – *noun* a horseman or horsewoman.

equi- *prefix* equal. – *adjective* **equidistant** equally distant. – *adjective* **equilateral** having all sides equal.

equilibrium *noun* a state of equal balance between weights, forces *etc*; a balanced state of mind or feelings.

equine *adjective* of or like a horse or horses.

equinox *noun* either of the times (about 21st March and 23rd September) when the sun crosses the equator, making night and day equal in length. – *adjective* **equinoctial**.

equip *verb* (*past tense* **equipped**) to supply with everything needed (for a task). – *noun* **equipage** carriages, attendants *etc* for a rich or important person. – *noun* **equipment** a set of articles needed to equip (a person or thing).

equity *noun* fairness, just dealing. – *noun* **Equity** British actors' and actresses' trade union. – *adjective* **equitable** fair, just.

equivalent *adjective* equal in value, power, meaning *etc*. – Also *noun*.

equivocal *adjective* having more than one meaning; uncertain, doubtful. – *verb* **equivocate** to use words with more than one meaning in order to mislead, to tell lies cleverly.

era *noun* a number of years counting from an important point in history: *the Elizabethan era*; a period of time marked by an important event or events: *the era of steam*.

eradicate *verb* to get rid of completely. – *noun* **eradication**.

erase *verb* to rub out; to remove. – *noun* **eraser** something which erases, a rubber. – *noun* **erasure** the act of erasing; something erased.

ere *preposition, conjunction* before: *ere long*.

erect *verb* to build; to set upright. – *adjective* standing straight up. – *noun* **erection** the act of erecting; anything erected; (achieving) an erect penis.

ermine *noun* a stoat; its white fur.

ERNIE *abbreviation* (*comput*) electronic random number indicator equipment.

erode *verb* to wear away, destroy gradually. – *noun* **erosion**.

erotic *adjective* of or arousing sexual desire.

err *verb* to make a mistake; to sin. – *adjective* **erratic** irregular, wandering, not following a fixed course; not steady or reliable in behaviour. – *noun* **erratum** (*plural* **errata**) an error in a book.

errand *noun* a (*usu* short) journey on which a person is sent to say or do something for someone else; the purpose of this journey.

errant *adjective* doing wrong; straying; wandering in search of adventure: *a knight errant*.

erratic, erratum *see* **err**.

error *noun* a mistake; wrongdoing. – *adjective* **erroneous** wrong.

erudite *adjective* clever, having learned much from books. – *noun* **erudition**.

erupt *verb* to break out or through. – *noun* **eruption** a breaking or bursting forth, as a volcano, a rash on the body *etc*.

escalate *verb* to increase in amount, intensity *etc*. – *noun* **escalation**. – *noun* **escalator** a moving stairway.

escape *verb* to get away safe or free; (of gas *etc*) to leak; to slip from (the memory *etc*). – *noun* the act of escaping. – *noun* **escapade** a mischievous adventure. – *noun* **escapement** something which controls the movement of a watch *etc*. – *noun* **escapism** the (habit of) trying to escape from reality into daydreaming *etc*.

escarpment *noun* the steep, cliff-like side of a hill *etc*.

escort *noun* person(s), ship(s) *etc* accompanying others for protection, courtesy *etc*. – *verb* to act as escort to.

escutcheon *noun* a shield on which a coat of arms is shown.

Eskimo *noun* (*plural* **Eskimos**) one of a people inhabiting the Arctic regions; Inuit.

esoteric *adjective* of or understood by a small number of people.

ESP *abbreviation* extrasensory perception.

esparto *noun* a type of strong grass grown in Spain and N. Africa, used for making paper, ropes *etc*.

especial *adjective* more than ordinary; particular. – *adverb* **especially**.

espionage *noun* spying; the use of spies, *esp* by one country to find out the secrets of another.

esplanade *noun* a level roadway, *esp* one along a seafront.

Esq *see* **Esquire**.

Esquire *noun* (*usu* written **Esq**) a title of politeness after a man's name: *John Brown, Esq*.

essay *noun* a written composition; an attempt. – *verb* to try. – *noun* **essayist** a writer of essays.

essence *noun* the most important part or quality; substance got from a plant *etc* in concentrated form: *vanilla essence*.

essential *adjective* absolutely necessary. – Also *noun*. – *adverb* **essentially** basically; necessarily.

establish *verb* to settle in position; to found, set up; to show to be true, prove (that). – *adjective* **established** firmly set up; accepted, recognized; (of a church) officially recognized as national. – *noun* **establishment** anything established, *esp* a place of business, residence *etc*. – **The Establishment** the people holding important, influential positions in a community.

estate *noun* a large piece of land owned by a person or group of people; a person's total possessions; land developed for houses, factories *etc*. – *noun* **estate agent** a person whose job it is to sell houses. – *noun* **estate car** a car with a large inside luggage compartment and an additional door at the back.

esteem *verb* to think highly of, to value. –Also *noun*. – *adjective* **esteemed**.

estimate *verb* to judge the size, amount, value of something *esp* roughly, without measuring. – Also *noun*. – *noun* **estimation** opinion, judgement.

estranged *adjective* no longer friendly.

estuary *noun* (*plural* **estuaries**) the wide lower part of a river, up which the tide travels.

et al *abbreviation* and others (*et alii* or *aliae* or *alia* [L]).

etc *see* **et cetera**.

et cetera (written **etc**) and other things of the same sort (*et ceteri* or *cetera* [L]).

etch *verb* to make drawings on metal, glass *etc* by eating out the lines with acid. – *noun* **etching** the picture from the etched plate.

eternal *adjective* lasting for ever; seemingly endless. – *noun* **eternity** time without end; the time or state after death.

ether *noun* a colourless liquid used to dissolve fats, to deaden feeling *etc*. – *adjective* **ethereal** delicate, fairy-like.

ethical *adjective* having to do with right behaviour, justice, duty; right, just, honourable. – *adverb* **ethically**. – *noun* **ethics** the study of right and wrong; (belief in) standards leading to right, ethical behaviour.

ethnic *adjective* of race; of the customs, dress, food of a particular race or group.

ethnology *noun* the study of the different races of mankind.

etiquette *noun* (rules setting out) polite or correct behaviour.

etymology *noun* (*plural* **etymologies**) the study of the history of words; a (short) description of the history of a word. – *adjective* **etymological**. – *noun* **etymologist**.

eucalyptus *noun* (*plural* **eucalyptuses** or **eucalypti**) a type of large Australian evergreen tree giving timber, oils, gum.

eulogize *verb* to praise greatly. – *noun* **eulogy** (*plural* **eulogies**) great praise, written or spoken.

euphemism *noun* a pleasant name for something unpleasant (*eg* 'passed on' for 'died'). – *adjective* **euphemistic.**

euphonious *adjective* pleasant in sound. – *noun* **euphonium** a brass musical instrument with a low tone. – *noun* **euphony.**

euphoria *noun* a feeling of great happiness, joy. – *adjective* **euphoric.**

eurhythmics *noun* the art of graceful movement of the body, *esp* to music.

euthanasia *noun* the killing of someone painlessly, *esp* to end suffering.

evacuate *verb* to (cause to) leave *esp* because of danger; to make empty. – *noun* **evacuation.** – *noun* **evacuee** a person who has been evacuated (from danger).

evade *verb* to avoid or escape *esp* by cleverness or trickery. – *noun* **evasion.** – *adjective* **evasive** with the purpose of evading; not straightforward: *an evasive answer.*

evaluate *verb* to find or state the value of.

evanescent *adjective* passing away quickly.

evangelical *adjective* spreading Christ's teaching. – *noun* **evangelist.**

evaporate *verb* to (cause to) change into vapour: *Heat evaporates water;* to vanish. – *noun* **evaporation.**

evasion *see* **evade.**

eve *noun* the evening or day before a festival: *Christmas Eve;* the time just before an event: *on the eve of the battle.*

even *adjective* level, smooth; (of numbers) able to be divided by 2 without a remainder; calm. – *adverb* used to emphasize a word or words: *The job was even harder than before. Even young children could understand that;* exactly, just. – *verb* to make even or smooth. – *noun* **evenness.** – **get even with** to harm (someone) who has harmed one.

evening *noun* the last part of the day and early part of the night.

event *noun* something (*esp* something important) that happens; an item in a sports programme *etc.* – *adjective* **eventful** exciting. – *adjective* **eventual** final; happening as a result. – *noun* **eventuality** (*plural* **eventualities**) a possible happening. – *adverb* **eventually** at last, finally.

ever *adverb* always; at any time. – *noun* **evergreen** a kind of tree *etc* with green leaves all the year round. – *adverb* **evermore** for ever.

every *adjective* each (of several things *etc*) without exception. – *pronoun* **everybody** or **everyone** every person. – *adjective* **everyday** daily; common, usual. – *pronoun* **everything** all things. – *adverb* **everywhere** in every place. – **every other** one out of every two, alternate.

evict *verb* to put (someone) out of house and home *esp* by force of law. – *noun* **eviction.**

evident *adjective* easily seen or understood. – *adverb* **evidently.** – *noun* **evidence** a clear sign; proof; information given in a law case.

evil *adjective* wicked; harmful; unpleasant. – *noun* wickedness.

evince *verb* to show: *The men evinced surprise at these words.*

evoke to draw out, produce: *The house evoked memories of their childhood.* – *adjective* **evocative** evoking, *eg* memories, a certain atmosphere.

evolve *verb* (to cause) to develop; to work out (a plan *etc*). – *noun* **evolution** gradual development; the teaching or belief that the higher forms of life have gradually developed out of the lower. – *adjective* **evolutionary.**

ewe *noun* a female sheep.

ewer *noun* a large jug with a wide spout.

ex- *prefix* no longer, former: *the ex-president;* outside, not in: *an ex-directory (telephone) number.*

exact *adjective* accurate; punctual; careful. – *verb* to compel to pay, give *etc.* – *adjective* **exacting** asking too much; tiring. – *noun* **exactness** accuracy, correctness.

exaggerate *verb* to make (something) seem larger, greater *etc* than it is. – *noun* **exaggeration.**

exalt *verb* to raise in rank; to praise; to make joyful. – *noun* **exaltation.**

examine *verb* to put questions to (pupils *etc*) to test knowledge; to question (a witness); to look at closely, inquire into; (of a doctor) to look at (a person's body) to check for illness or disease. – *noun* **examination** a test of knowledge (also **exam**); a close inspection or inquiry; formal questioning. – *noun* **examiner.**

example 121 **exemplify**

example noun one case given to show what other things of the same kind are like; a warning: Let this be an example to you.

exasperate verb to make very angry. – noun **exasperation**.

excavate verb to dig, scoop out; to uncover by digging. – noun **excavation** the act of digging out; a hollow made by digging. – noun **excavator** a machine used for excavating.

exceed verb to go beyond, be greater than. – adverb **exceedingly** very.

excel verb (past tense **excelled**) to do very well; to be better than. – noun **excellence** the state of being excellent, very high quality. – noun **Excellency** (plural **Excellencies**) a title of ambassadors etc. – adjective **excellent** unusually or extremely good.

except preposition leaving out, not counting. – conjunction with the exception (that). – verb to leave out, not to count. – preposition **excepting** except. – noun **exception** something left out; something that is unlike the rest: an exception to the rule. – adjective **exceptional** standing out from the rest. – adverb **exceptionally** very. – **except for** with the exception of; **take exception to** to object to, be offended by.

excerpt noun a part chosen from a whole work: an excerpt from a play.

excess noun a going beyond what is usual or proper; the amount by which one thing is greater than another; (plural) **excesses** very bad behaviour. – adjective beyond the amount allowed. – adjective **excessive** too much, too great etc. – adverb **excessively**.

exchange verb to give one thing and get another in return. – noun the act of exchanging; exchanging money of one country for that of another; the difference between the value of money in different places; a central office or building (eg where telephone lines are connected); a place where business shares are bought and sold.

exchequer noun the part of government that has to do with the money affairs of a country. – **Chancellor of the Exchequer** see chancellor.

excise[1] verb to cut off or out. – noun **excision**.

excise[2] noun tax on goods etc made and sold within a country and on certain licences etc.

excite verb to rouse the feelings of; to move to action. – adjective **excitable** easily excited. – noun **excitement**. – adjective **exciting**.

exclaim verb to cry or shout out. – noun **exclamation** a sudden shout. – noun **exclamation mark** in punctuation, a mark (!) to show that an exclamation has been made. – adjective **exclamatory**.

exclude verb to shut out; to prevent from sharing; to leave out (of consideration). – noun **exclusion**. – adjective **exclusive** shutting out unwanted persons, select: an exclusive club; not obtainable elsewhere: an exclusive offer. – **exclusive of** not including.

excommunicate verb to expel from membership of a church, to forbid to take part in church sacraments. – noun **excommunication**.

excrescence noun something unwanted which grows outwards (such as a wart).

excrete verb to cast out, discharge waste matter from the body. – noun **excrement** the waste matter cast out by humans or animals.

excruciating adjective (of pain etc) very severe.

excursion noun an outing, usu for pleasure (such as a picnic).

excuse verb to forgive, pardon; to set free from a duty or task. – noun a person's reason or explanation for having done something wrong. – adjective **excusable** pardonable.

execrable adjective very bad.

execute verb to perform: execute a dance step; to carry out: execute commands; to put to death legally. – noun **execution** a doing or performing; killing by order of the law. – noun **executioner** a person whose duty it is to put to death condemned persons. – adjective **executive** having power to act, carry out laws. – noun the part of a government (or society) having such power; a person in a business organization who has the power to act on important decisions. – noun **executor** a person who sees to the carrying out of what is stated in a will.

exemplary adjective worth following as an example: exemplary conduct; acting as a warning: exemplary punishment.

exemplify verb (past tense **exemplified**) to be an example of; to show by giving example.

exempt *verb* to grant freedom from some duty, task, payment, *etc*. – *adjective* free (from), not liable (to do something that others have to do). – *noun* **exemption**.

exercise *noun* a task for practice; training for body, mind *etc*. – *verb* to give exercise to; to use: *Exercise great care!*

exert *verb* to bring into action, use: *He exerts great influence on her.* – *noun* **exertion** effort; hard work. – **exert oneself** to make a great effort.

exhale *verb* to breathe out. – *noun* **exhalation**.

exhaust *verb* to tire out; to use up completely: *exhaust our supplies*; to say all that can be said about (a subject *etc*). – *noun* the way out for the waste products of fuel-using engines (steam, fumes *etc*). – *adjective* **exhausted** tired out; emptied; used up. – *noun* **exhaustion** great tiredness, weariness; the act of exhausting. – *adjective* **exhaustive** saying all that can be said.

exhibit *verb* to show (in public). – *noun* anything shown (*eg* a picture in a picture gallery). – *noun* **exhibition** a public show, an open display. – *noun* **exhibitionism** a tendency to try to attract people's attention. – *noun* **exhibitionist**. – *noun* **exhibitor**.

exhilarate *verb* to make joyful or lively, refresh. – *adjective* **exhilarating**.

exhort *verb* to urge (to do). – *noun* **exhortation**.

exhume *verb* to dig out (*esp* a body from a grave). – *noun* **exhumation**.

exigent *adjective* demanding immediate attention, urgent. – *noun* **exigency** (*plural* **exigencies**) an urgent need or demand: *He was forced by the exigencies of the situation to sell his house.*

exile *noun* a person who lives outside their own country, either by choice or unwillingly; a (*usu* long) stay in a foreign land. – *verb* to drive (a person) away from their own country, to banish.

exist *verb* to be, have life; to live; to live in poor circumstances. – *noun* **existence**. – *adjective* **existent**.

exit *noun* a way out; the act of going out.

exodus *noun* a going away of many people (*esp* those leaving a country for ever).

exonerate *verb* to free from blame. – *noun* **exoneration**.

exorbitant *adjective* going beyond what is usual or reasonable: *an exorbitant price*. – *noun* **exorbitance**.

exorcize *verb* to drive out (an evil spirit or spell); to free (someone or something) from an evil spirit dwelling in them. – *noun* **exorcism** the act of driving away evil spirits or spells. – *noun* **exorcist**.

exotic *adjective* coming from a foreign country; unusual, colourful.

expand *verb* to grow wider or bigger; to open out. – *noun* **expanse** a wide stretch (as of land *etc*). – *noun* **expansion** a growing, stretching or spreading – *adjective* **expansive** spreading out; (of persons) talkative, telling much.

expatiate *verb* to talk a great deal (about something).

expatriate *adjective* living outside one's native country. – Also *noun*.

expect *verb* to think of as likely to happen, come *etc* soon; to think, assume: *I expect he's too busy.* – *noun* **expectancy** state of expecting; hope. – *adjective* **expectant** hopeful, expecting; expecting to become (*esp* a mother). – *noun* **expectation** state of expecting; what is expected. – *adjective* **expecting** (*coll*) pregnant.

expedient *adjective* suited to the time and to the occasion but sometimes not just or fair. – *noun* something done to get round a difficulty. – *noun* **expedience** or **expediency**.

expedite *verb* to hasten, hurry on. – *adjective* **expeditious** swift, speedy.

expedition *noun* a journey with a purpose (often exploration); people making such a journey.

expel *verb* (*past tense* **expelled**) to drive or force out; to send away in disgrace (*esp* from a school). – *noun* **expulsion**.

expend *verb* to spend, use up. – *noun* **expenditure** amount spent or used up, *esp* money.

expense *noun* cost; cause of spending: *The house was a continual expense*; (*plural*) money spent in carrying out a job *etc*. – *adjective* **expensive** costing much money.

experience *noun* any event in which one is involved: *a horrible experience*; wisdom, knowledge gained from events, practice *etc*. – *verb* to go through, undergo. – *adjective* **experienced** skilled, knowledgeable.

experiment noun a trial, test (of an idea, machine etc). – verb to carry out experiments. – adjective **experimental**.

expert adjective highly skilful or knowledgeable (in a particular subject). – noun a person who is highly skilled or knowledgeable. – noun **expertise** skill.

expiate verb to make up for (a crime etc). – noun **expiation**.

expire verb to die; to come to an end. – noun **expiry** the end or finish.

explain verb to make clear; to give reasons for. – noun **explanation** a statement which makes clear something difficult or puzzling; a reason (eg for one's behaviour). – adjective **explanatory** meant to make clear.

expletive noun an exclamation, esp a swear word.

explicable adjective able to be explained.

explicit adjective plainly stated; outspoken.

explode verb to blow up like a bomb with loud noise; to prove (a theory etc) to be wrong. – noun **explosion** a sudden burst or blow-up, with a loud noise. – adjective **explosive** liable to explode; hot-tempered. – noun anything (such as gunpowder) that will explode.

exploit noun a daring deed; a feat. – verb to make use of selfishly; to make good use of (resources etc). – noun **exploitation**.

explore verb to make a journey of discovery. – noun **exploration**. – noun **explorer**.

explosion see **explode**.

exponent noun a person who shows skill in a particular art or craft: an exponent of karate. – adjective **exponential**.

export verb to sell goods etc in a foreign country. – noun an act of exporting; something exported. – noun **exportation**.

expose verb to place (something) where all can see it; to show up (a hidden evil, crime etc); to lay open to sun, wind, cold etc; to allow light to reach and act on (a film). – noun **exposition** a public show; a statement which makes clear a writer's meaning. – noun **exposure**.

expostulate verb to protest. – noun **expostulation**.

expound verb to explain fully.

express verb to show by action; to put into words; to press or squeeze out. – adjective clearly stated: express instructions; sent in haste: express messenger. – noun a fast train. – noun **expression** the look on someone's face; showing meaning, feeling by means of language, art etc; a show of feeling in a performance of music etc; a word or phrase: a slang expression; pressing or squeezing out. – adjective **expressive** expressing; expressing meaning or feeling clearly.

expropriate verb to take (property etc) away from its owner.

expulsion see **expel**.

expunge verb to rub out, remove.

exquisite adjective of great beauty; excellent; (of pleasure etc) very great; keen, sharp.

extant adjective still existing.

extempore iks-tem'pò-ri, adverb, adj at a moment's notice, without preparation. – verb **extemporize** to make up (music, a speech etc) as one plays, speaks etc.

extend verb to stretch, make longer; to hold out: he extended his hand; to last: This holiday extends into next week. – noun **extension** a part added (to a building, a holiday etc); a telephone connected with a main one. – adjective **extensive** wide; covering a large space; happening or being in many places. – noun **extent** the space something covers; degree: to a great extent.

extenuate verb to lessen; to make to seem less bad. – noun **extenuation**.

exterior adjective lying etc on the outside, outer: an exterior wall. – noun the outside (of something).

exterminate verb to destroy completely, kill off (a race, a type of animal etc). – noun **extermination**.

external adjective outside; on the outside.

extinct adjective no longer active: an extinct volcano; of a kind no longer found alive: The dodo is extinct. – noun **extinction** making or becoming extinct.

extinguish verb to put out (fire etc); to put an end to. – noun **extinguisher** a spray containing chemicals for putting out fires.

extol verb (past tense **extolled**) to praise greatly.

extort verb to take by force or threats. – noun **extortion**. – adjective **extortionate** (of a price) much too high.

extra *adjective* more than is usual or necessary; additional. – *adverb* unusually. – *noun* anything extra; a person employed to be one of a crowd in a film.

extra- *prefix* outside, beyond, as in **extraterrestrial** outside, or from outside the earth.

extract *verb* to draw or pull out *esp* by force; to choose and take out parts of a book *etc*; to take out (a substance forming part of something else) by pressure *etc* or by chemical means. – *noun* a part chosen (from a book *etc*); a substance obtained by extraction. – *noun* **extraction** act of extracting; a person's descent: *He was of English extraction.*

extradite *verb* to hand over to the police of another country (someone wanted by them). – *noun* **extradition**.

extraneous *adjective* having nothing to do with the subject: *extraneous information*.

extraordinary *adjective* not usual, exceptional; very surprising; specially employed: *ambassador extraordinary*.

extrasensory *adjective* beyond the range of the ordinary senses.

extravagant *adjective* spending too freely; wasteful; too great: *extravagant praise*. – *noun* **extravagance**.

extravert or **extrovert** *noun* an outgoing, sociable person.

extreme *adjective* far from the centre; far from the ordinary or usual; very great. – *noun* an extreme point. – *noun*

extremist a person who carries ideas foolishly far. – *noun* **extremity** (*plural* **extremities**) the farthest-off part or place; great distress or pain; farthest-off parts of the body, as hands, feet.

extricate *verb* to set free (from difficulties *etc*).

extrovert *see* **extravert**.

exuberant *adjective* in very high spirits. – *noun* **exuberance**.

exude *verb* to give off (in great amounts): *He exudes sweat after playing squash. The bride exuded happiness.*

exult *verb* to be very glad, rejoice greatly: *They exulted in their victory.* – *adjective* **exultant**. – *noun* **exultation**.

eye *noun* the part of the body with which one sees; the ability to notice: *an eye for detail*; sight; anything like an eye (*eg* the hole in a needle *etc*). – *verb* to look at. – *noun* **eyeball** the round part of the eye; the eye itself (the part between the eyelids). – *noun* **eyebrow** the hairy ridge above the eye. – *noun* **eyeglass** a lens to correct faulty eyesight. – *noun* **eyelash** one of the hairs on the edge of the eyelid. – *noun* **eyelet** a small hole for a lace *etc*. – *noun* **eyelid** the skin cover of the eye. – *noun* **eye-opener** that which shows up something unexpected. – *noun* **eyesore** anything that is ugly (*esp* a building). – *noun* **eyewitness** a person who sees a thing done (*eg* a crime committed).

eyrie or **eyry** *īr'i*, *noun* the nesting place of eagles or other birds of prey.

F

°F *abbreviation* degree(s) Fahrenheit.

FA *abbreviation* Football Association.

fable *noun* a story (about animals *etc*) that has a lesson or moral. – *adjective* **fabulous** existing (only) in fable: *The griffin is a fabulous creature*; (*coll*) very good.

fabric *noun* cloth; the outside parts (walls *etc*) of a building.

fabricate *verb* to make up (lies). – *noun* **fabrication**.

façade *fä-säd*, *noun* the front of a building; a deceptive appearance.

face *noun* the front part of the head; the front of anything; appearance. – *verb* to turn, stand *etc* in the direction of; to stand opposite to; to put an additional surface (**facing**) on. – *noun* **face pack** a creamy cosmetic mixture put on to the face for a certain time. – *noun* **facepowder** powder put on the face as a cosmetic. – **face up to** to meet or accept boldly: *He faced up to his responsibilities.*

facet *noun* a side of a many-sided object, *esp* a cut gem; an aspect.

facetious *adjective* funny, joking. – *noun* **facetiousness.**

facial *adjective* of the face.

facile *adjective* not deep or thorough, superficial; easily persuaded; (too) fluent. – *verb* **facilitate** to make easy. – *noun* **facility** ease; skill in doing a thing; *(plural)* **facilities** the means for doing a thing (easily).

facsimile *noun* an exact copy.

fact *noun* something known or held to be true; reality; (in law) a deed. – **in fact** actually, really.

faction *noun* a group of people (part of a larger group) acting together: *The rival factions hated each other.* – *adjective* **factious** trouble-making, riotous.

factor *noun* something which affects the course of events; a person who does business for another; a number which exactly divides into another (*eg* 3 is a factor of 6). – *verb* **factorize** to find factors of.

factory *noun* (*plural* **factories**) a workshop where goods are made in large quantities.

factotum *noun* a person employed to do all kinds of work.

faculty *noun* (*plural* **faculties**) power of the mind, *eg* reason *etc*; a natural power of the body, as hearing *etc*; ability, aptitude; a department of study in a university *etc*: *Faculty of Science.*

fad *noun* an odd like or dislike. – *adjective* **faddy.**

fade *verb* to (make to) lose colour, strength *etc*; to go from sight, hearing *etc*, disappear (gradually).

faeces *fē'sēz, n* solid excrement.

fag *verb* (*past tense* **fagged**) to work hard; to weary; (*coll*) to work as a school fag. – *noun* any tiresome bit of work; (*coll*) a young schoolboy forced to do jobs for an older one; (*US*) (*slang*) a male homosexual; (*slang*) a cigarette.

faggot or **fagot** *noun* a bundle of sticks; (*US*) (*slang*) a male homosexual.

Fahrenheit *adjective* of a temperature scale on which water freezes at 32° and boils at 212°; as measured on this scale: *70° Fahrenheit.*

fail *verb* to (declare to) be unsuccessful; to break down, stop; to lose strength; to be lacking, not to be enough; to disappoint. – *noun* **failing** a fault ; a weakness. – *adjective* **fail-safe** made so that if a fault occurs it will be automatically corrected or made safe. – *noun* **failure** the act of failing; someone or something which fails. – **without fail** certainly: *Do it without fail by tomorrow.*

fain *adverb* (in poetry *etc*) willingly.

faint *adjective* lacking in strength, brightness *etc*; about to lose consciousness. – *verb* to become faint; to fall down unconscious. – *noun* a loss of consciousness. – *adverb* **faintly** dimly, not clearly. – *noun* **faintness.**

fair[1] *adjective* of a light colour *esp* of hair; free from rain; not favouring one side, just; good enough but not excellent; beautiful. – *noun* **fairness.** – *adjective* **fair-haired** having light-coloured hair, blond. – *noun* **fairway** the deep-water part of a channel, river *etc*; the mown part on a golf course, between the tee and the green.

fair[2] *noun* a large market held at fixed times; an exhibition of goods from different countries, firms *etc*; a sale of goods for charities; a collection of entertainments (merry-go-rounds *etc*) which moves from place to place.

fairy *noun* (*plural* **fairies**) (*myth*) a (small) being like a man or woman with magical powers. – *noun* **fairy light** a small coloured light for decoration (of Christmas trees *etc*). – *noun* **fairy story** or **fairy tale** an old story of fairies, giants *etc*; (*coll*) a lie.

fait accompli *fet à-kom'pli, noun* something already done, an accomplished fact.

faith *noun* trust, belief (*eg* in God); loyalty to a promise: *He kept faith with them.* – *adjective* **faithful** loyal; keeping one's promises; true, accurate: *a faithful account of events*; believing (in God). – *adjective* **faithless.**

fake *verb* to make an imitation of (*esp* in order to deceive). – *adjective* not genuine, forged. – *noun* someone who is not what they pretend to be; a forgery.

falcon *noun* a kind of bird of prey. – *noun* **falconry** the training of falcons for hunting.

fall *verb* (*past tense* **fell**, *past participle* **fallen**) to drop down; to become less; (of a fortress *etc*) to be captured; to die in battle; to happen, occur: *Christmas falls on Tuesday this year.* – *noun* a dropping down; something that falls: *a fall of snow*; lowering (in value *etc*); (*US*) autumn; an accident in which one falls (as from a horse, when running *etc*); ruin, downfall, surrender; (*plural*) a waterfall. – *noun* **fallout** radioactive dust resulting from the explosion of an atomic bomb *etc*. – **fall flat** to fail to have the intended effect; **fall in love** to begin to be in love; **fall out with** to quarrel with; **fall through** (of plans *etc*) to fail, come to nothing.

fallacy *noun* (*plural* **fallacies**) a wrong idea or belief; something which is thought to be true but is really false; unsound argument or reasoning. – *adjective* **fallacious** misleading, false; not showing sound reasoning.

fallible *adjective* liable to make a mistake or to be wrong. – *noun* **fallibility**.

fallow *adjective* (of land) left unsown for a time after being ploughed; of a yellowish-brown colour. – *noun* **fallow deer** a type of yellowish-brown deer.

false *adjective* untrue; not real, fake; not natural: *false teeth*. – *noun* **falsehood** a lie, an untruth. – *noun* **falseness** or **falsity** quality of being false. – *verb* **falsify** (*past tense* **falsified**) to make false, alter for a dishonest purpose: *He falsified the firm's accounts.*

falter *verb* to stumble or hesitate.

fame *noun* the quality of being well-known or much talked about, renown. – *adjective* **famed** or **famous** well-known, having fame. – *adverb* **famously** (*coll*) very well.

familiar *adjective* well-known; seen, known *etc* before; well-acquainted (with); too friendly, cheeky. – *noun* **familiarity**. – *verb* **familiarize** to make quite accustomed or acquainted (with).

family *noun* (*plural* **families**) a man, his wife and their children; the children alone; a group of people related to one another; a group (such as plants, animals, languages) having some likeness.

famine *noun* great shortage *esp* of food or water.

famished *adjective* very hungry.

famous *see* **fame**.

fan *noun* a device or appliance for making a rush of air; a small hand-held device,

usu shaped like part of a circle, for cooling the face; an admirer (of an actor, singer *etc*). – *verb* (*past tense* **fanned**) to cause a rush of air with a fan; to increase the strength of: *fan his anger.* – *noun* **fanlight** a window above a door, *esp* one shaped like a half circle. – **fan out** to spread out in the shape of a fan.

fanatic *noun* a person who is over-enthusiastic or eager about something (*esp* religion). – *adjective* **fanatic** or **fanatical** wildly or excessively enthusiastic.

fancy *noun* (*plural* **fancies**) a sudden liking or desire; the power of the mind to imagine things *esp* things unlike reality; something imagined. – *adjective* not plain; ornamented. – *verb* (*past tense* **fancied**) to picture, imagine; to have a sudden wish for; to think without being sure. – *noun* **fancier** one whose hobby is to keep prize animals, birds *etc*. – *adjective* **fanciful** inclined to have fancies; imaginary, not real. – *noun* **fancy dress** dress chosen for fun, *esp* for a party, and usually representing a famous type or character.

fanfare *noun* a great blowing of trumpets or bugles.

fang *noun* a tooth of a wild animal (*esp* a fierce one); the poison-tooth of a snake.

fantasy *noun* (*plural* **fantasies**) an imaginary (*esp* unreal) scene, story *etc*; an idea not based on reality. – *adjective* **fantastic** very unusual, strange; (*coll*) very great; (*coll*) excellent.

far *adverb* at or to a long way: *far off*; very much: *far better*. – *adjective* (*comparative* **farther**, *superlative* **farthest**) a long way off, distant: *a far country*; more distant: *the far side*. – *adjective* **far-fetched** very unlikely: *a far-fetched story*. – *adjective* **far-flung** extending over a great distance. – *adjective* **far-sighted** foreseeing what is likely to happen and preparing for it. – *See* also **further**.

farce *noun* a play with unlikely and ridiculous characters and plot; anything silly and useless. – *adjective* **farcical** absurd, ridiculous.

fare *verb* to get on (well, badly): *He fared well in the competition.* – *noun* the price of a journey; a person who pays to be carried on a journey; food. – *interjection*, *noun* **farewell** goodbye.

farm *noun* an area of land used for growing crops, breeding and feeding cows, sheep *etc*; a place where certain animals, fish *etc* are reared: *an oyster farm.* – *verb* to work the lands *etc* of a farm. – *noun* **farmer** the owner or tenant of a farm who works the land *etc.* – *noun* **farmhouse** the house where a farmer lives. – *noun* **farmstead** a farm and farmhouse. – *noun* **farmyard** the yard surrounded by farm buildings. – **farm out** to give (work) to others to do for payment.

farrow *noun* a litter of baby pigs. – *verb* to give birth to a litter of pigs.

farther, farthest *see* **far.**

farthing *noun* an old coin, worth ¼ of an old penny.

fascinate *verb* to charm, attract or interest irresistibly; to make (a victim) still and powerless: *The snake fascinated the rabbit.* – *adjective* **fascinating.** – *noun* **fascination.**

fashion *noun* the make or cut of a thing (*esp* clothes); a way of behaving, dressing *etc* which is popular for a time; a way of doing a thing: *acting in a strange fashion.* – *verb* to shape (according to a pattern). – *adjective* **fashionable** agreeing with the latest style of dress, way of living *etc.* – **in fashion** fashionable.

fast *adjective* quick-moving; (of a clock *etc*) showing a time in advance of the correct time; of colour (in clothes *etc*) fixed, not likely to be removed by washing. – *adverb* quickly; firmly: *stand fast.* – *verb* to go without food (of one's own free will). – *noun* abstinence from food. – *noun* **fastness** (of colour, dye *etc*) permanence; a stronghold, fortress, castle.

fasten *verb* to fix; to make firm (by tying, nailing *etc*).

fastidious *adjective* difficult to please.

fat *noun* an oily substance made by the bodies of animals and by plants. – *adjective* having much fat; plump; thick, wide. – *verb* **fatten** to make or become fat.

fatal *adjective* causing death or disaster. – *noun* **fatality** (*plural* **fatalities**) (an accident causing) death.

fate *noun* what the future holds for someone, fortune, luck; end or death: *He met his fate bravely.* – *adjective* **fated** controlled by fate; doomed. – *adjective* **fateful** having important results.

father *noun* a male parent; a priest; a person who first makes, invents *etc*

something: *Jules Verne is the father of science fiction.* – *verb* to become the father of. – *noun* **father-in-law** the father of one's husband or wife. – *noun* **fatherland** one's native land.

fathom *noun* a measure of depth of water (6 feet, 1·83 metres). – *verb* to understand, get to the bottom of (a mystery *etc*).

fatigue *fa-tēg'*, *noun* great tiredness; weakness or strain (of metals *etc*) caused by use. – *verb* to tire out.

fatuous *adjective* very foolish.

faucet *noun* (*US*) a tap.

fault *noun* a mistake; a flaw, something bad or wrong (*eg* with a machine). – *adjective* **faultless.** – *adjective* **faulty** having a fault or faults.

faun *noun* (*myth*) an imaginary creature, half man, half animal.

fauna *noun* the animals of a district or country as a whole.

faux pas *fō pä*, *noun* a mistake.

favour *noun* a kind action; goodwill, kindness, approval; gift, token, badge *etc.* – *verb* to show preference for; to be an advantage to: *The darkness favoured his escape.* – *adjective* **favourable** friendly; showing approval; advantageous, helpful (to). – *noun* **favourite** a liked or best-loved person or thing; one, *esp* a horse, likely to win. – *adjective* best liked. – *noun* **favouritism** showing favour towards one person *etc* more than another. – **in favour of** in support of; for the benefit of.

fawn *noun* a young deer; its colour, a light yellowish-brown. – *adjective* of this colour. – *verb* to show affection as a dog does; (with **upon**) to flatter in too humble a way.

fax *noun* a copy produced by a **fax machine**, a machine that scans a document *etc* electronically and transfers the information by a telephone line to a receiving machine that produces a copy. – Also *verb.*

FBI *abbreviation* (*US*) Federal Bureau of Investigation.

FDR *abbreviation* Free Democratic Republic (West Germany) (*Freie Demokratische Republik* [*Ger*]).

fear *noun* an unpleasant feeling caused by danger, evil *etc.* – *adjective* **fearful** timid; afraid; terrible; (*coll*) very bad: *a fearful* *headache.* – *adjective* **fearless** brave, daring.

feasible *adjective* able to be done, likely. – *noun* **feasibility**.

feast *noun* a rich and plentiful meal; a festival day on which some event is remembered. – *verb* to hold or eat a feast.

feat *noun* a deed difficult to do.

feather *noun* one of the growths which form the outer covering of a bird. – *adjective* **feathery** having or covered in feathers; soft; light.

feature *noun* a mark by which anything is known, a characteristic; an important or special article in a newspaper *etc*; the main film *etc* in a programme; a special attraction; (*plural*) the various parts of a person's face (eyes, nose *etc*). – *verb* to show or exhibit as a feature; to take part (in); be prominent in.

February *noun* the second month of the year.

fecund *adjective* fertile. – *noun* **fecundity**.

fed *see* **feed**.

federal *adjective* joined by treaty or bargain. – *adjective* **federated** joined after an agreement is made. – *noun* **federation** those joined together for a common purpose, a league.

fee *noun* a price paid for work done, or for some special service or right.

feeble *adjective* weak. – *noun* **feebleness**. – *adverb* **feebly**.

feed *verb* (*past tense* **fed**) to give food to; to eat food; to supply with necessary materials. – *noun* food for animals: *cattle feed*. – **fed up** tired, bored and disgusted.

feel *verb* (*past tense* **felt**) to explore by touch; to experience, be aware of (pain, pleasure *etc*); to believe, consider; to think (oneself) to be: *I feel ill*; to be sorry (for): *I feel for you in your sorrow.* – *noun* **feeler** one of two thread-like parts of an insect's body (on the head) by which it senses danger *etc*. – *noun* **feeling** sense of touch; emotion: *He spoke with great feeling*; affection; an impression, belief; (*pl*) what a person feels inside such as love, anger. – **feel like** to want, have an inclination to or for: *He feels like going out. He feels like an apple.*

feet *see* **foot**.

feign *fān, verb* to pretend to feel or be: *He feigned illness.*

feint *noun* a pretence; a move to put an enemy off guard. – Also *verb*.

felicity *noun* happiness. – *noun plural* **felicitations** good wishes, congratulations. – *adjective* **felicitous** lucky; well-chosen, suiting well.

feline *adjective* cat-like; of the cat family.

fell *noun* a barren hill. – *verb* to bring to the ground; to cut down; *see* also **fall**. – *adjective* cruel, fierce.

fellow *noun* an equal; one of a pair; a member of a learned society, college *etc*; a man, boy. – *noun* **fellowship** state of being on equal terms; friendship; an award to a university graduate.

felon *noun* a person who has committed a serious crime. – *noun* **felony** (*plural* **felonies**) serious crime.

felt *noun* a type of rough cloth made of rolled and pressed wool. – *verb see* **feel**.

female *noun, adjective* (one) of the sex which produces young.

feminine *adjective* womanly; having to do with women. – *noun* **femininity**. – *noun* **feminism** the movement which aims to win rights for women equal to those of men. – *noun* **feminist** a supporter of this movement.

femur *noun* the thigh bone.

fen *noun* low marshy land, often covered with water.

fence *noun* a railing, hedge *etc* for closing in animals or land; (*slang*) a receiver of stolen goods. – *verb* to close in with a fence; to fight with swords; to give answers that tell nothing. – *noun* **fencing** fences; material for fences; the sport of fighting with swords, using blunted weapons.

fend: fend for oneself to look after, provide for oneself.

fender *noun* a low guard round a fireplace to keep in coals *etc*; something (a piece of matting *etc*) lowered over a ship's side to act as a buffer against the quay; (*US*) the bumper of a car *etc*.

fermentation *noun* the change which takes place when certain substances are brought together (as when yeast is added to the dough in the making of bread); a state of great excitement. – *verb* **ferment** (of a mixture) to change by fermentation; to stir up trouble *etc*. – Also *noun*.

fern *noun* a kind of plant with no flowers and feather-like leaves.

ferocious *adjective* fierce, savage. – *noun* **ferocity.**

ferret *noun* a type of small weasel-like animal used to chase rabbits out of their warrens. – *verb* to search busily and persistently.

ferrule *noun* a metal ring or cap on the tip of a walking stick or umbrella.

ferry *verb* (*past tense* **ferried**) to carry (people, cars *etc*) over water by boat or overland by aeroplane *etc*. – *noun* (*plural* **ferries**) a crossing place for boats; the boat which crosses.

fertile *adjective* fruitful, producing much; full of ideas. – *noun* **fertility** fruitfulness, ability of land to produce crops *etc*, ability of a woman or female animal to produce offspring. – *verb* **fertilize** to make (soil *etc*) fertile or more fertile. – *n* **fertilization.** – *noun* **fertilizer** a substance (*eg* manure, chemicals) for making fields (more) fertile.

fervent *adjective* very eager; intense. – *noun* **fervour.**

fester *verb* (of a cut, sore) to have pus in it because of infection.

festive *adjective* of a feast; in a happy, celebrating mood, joyful. – *noun* **festival** a celebration; a feast; a season of musical, theatrical or other performances. – *noun* **festivity** (*plural* **festivities**) joyfulness, merrymaking.

festoon *verb* to decorate with chains of ribbons, flowers *etc*.

fetch *verb* to go and get; to bring in (a price): *The vase fetched £100 at the auction.*

fete or **fête** *noun* an occasion with stalls, competitions, displays *etc* to raise money (often for charity). – *verb* to entertain lavishly, make much of (a person).

fetid *adjective* having a rotten smell, stinking.

fetish *noun* (*plural* **fetishes**) something of which a person is excessively (and unnaturally) fond.

fetlock *noun* the part of a horse's leg just above the foot.

fetters *noun plural* chains, bonds (for imprisonment).

fettle: in fine fettle in good health or condition.

feud *noun* a private, drawn-out war *esp* between families, clans, tribes *etc*.

feudal *adjective* (*hist*) of the system by which, in earlier times, certain services were given to the overlord by the tenants, as a return for their lands. – *noun* **feudalism.**

fever *noun* (any illness causing) high body temperature and quickened pulse. – *adjective* **fevered** having a fever; very excited. – *adjective* **feverish** having a slight fever; excited; too eager.

few *adjective, noun* not many: *A few (pounds) were left. He took the few (pounds) which were left.* – **a good few** or **quite a few** several, a considerable number.

fez *noun* (*plural* **fezzes**) a close-fitting red hat (shaped like a flowerpot) with a tassel and formerly the national headdress of the Turks.

fiancé (*masculine*), **fiancée** (*feminine*) *fēon͡s'sä*, *noun* a person to whom one is engaged to be married.

fiasco *noun* (*plural* **fiascos**) a complete failure.

fib *verb* (*past tense* **fibbed**) to lie about something unimportant. – Also *noun*.

fibre *noun* any fine thread or threadlike stuff. – *adjective* **fibrous.** – *noun* **fibreglass** a material made of very fine threadlike pieces of glass used for many purposes *eg* building boats.

fickle *adjective* changeable, not constant or loyal.

fiction *noun* stories *etc* which tell of imagined characters and events; an untruth, a lie. – *adjective* **fictional** (of novels, stories *etc*) about imagined characters and events. – *adjective* **fictitious** not real, imaginary; untrue.

fiddle *noun* a violin. – *verb* to play the violin; to make restless, aimless movements (with); to interfere, tamper (with); (*coll*) to falsify (accounts *etc*) with the intention of cheating.

fidelity *noun* faithfulness; truth; accuracy.

fidget *verb* to move (the hands, feet *etc*) restlessly.

field *noun* a piece of ground enclosed for pasture, crops, sports *etc*; an area of land which contains a natural resource (*eg* coal, gold); an area or branch of interest, knowledge *etc*; those taking part in a race, competition *etc*. – *verb* (in cricket *etc*) to catch the ball and return it. – *noun* **field-day** a day of unusual activity or success. – *noun plural* **fieldglasses** a small double telescope.

– *noun* **field-gun** a light, mobile cannon.
– *noun* **field-marshal** an officer of the highest rank in the army.

fiend *noun* an evil spirit; a wicked person.
– *adjective* **fiendish**.

fierce *adjective* very angry-looking, hostile, likely to attack; intense, strong; *fierce competition*. – *noun* **fierceness**.

fiery *adjective* like fire; easily made angry; high-spirited.

fife *noun* a type of small flute.

fifteen *noun* the number 15. – *adjective* 15 in number. – *adjective* **fifteenth** the last of fifteen (things *etc*). – *noun* one of fifteen equal parts.

fifth *see* **five.**

fifty *noun* the number 50. – *adjective* 50 in number. – *adjective* **fiftieth** the last of fifty (things *etc*). – *noun* one of fifty equal parts.

fig *noun* a soft, pear-shaped fruit containing many seeds and often eaten dried; the tree which bears it.

fight *verb* (*past tense* **fought**) to struggle (with) with fists, weapons *etc*; to quarrel; to go to war with. – *noun* a struggle; a battle. – *noun* **fighter** a person who fights; a fast military aircraft armed with guns.

figment *noun* a made-up story or an idea which has no real existence.

figure *noun* outward form or shape; a number; a geometrical shape; a person: *A mysterious figure approached*; (in a book *etc*) a diagram or drawing; a set of movements (as in skating *etc*). – *verb* to appear: *He figures in the story*; (*usu* with **out**) to work out, understand. – *adjective* **figurative** (of words) used not in the ordinary meaning but to show likenesses (*eg* in 'He was a lion in battle' for 'He was as brave as or like a lion in battle.'). – *adjective* **figured** marked with a design: *figured silk*. – *noun* **figurehead** a person who does little but who serves as a leader.

filament *noun* a slender threadlike object (*eg* the thin wire in an electric-light bulb).

filch *verb* to steal.

file *noun* a folder, loose-leaf book *etc* to hold papers; a line of soldiers *etc* walking one behind another; a steel tool with a roughened surface for smoothing or wearing away wood, metal *etc*. – *verb* to put (papers *etc*) in a file; to rub with a file; to walk in a file.

filial *adjective* of or natural to a son or daughter.

filibuster *noun* a very long speech made to delay the passing of a law. – Also *verb*.

filigree *noun* very fine gold or silver thread lace-work.

fill *verb* to put (something) into (until there is no room for more): *He fills the bucket with water*; to become full: *Her eyes filled with tears*; to satisfy, fulfil (a requirement *etc*); to occupy: *fill a post*; to appoint a person to (a job *etc*): *Have you filled the vacancy?*; to put something in a hole (in a tooth *etc*) to stop it up. – *noun* as much as is needed to fill: *He ate his fill*. – *noun* **filler** a funnel for pouring liquids through; a substance added to a material to increase its bulk, improve its quality *etc*; a material used to fill up holes in wood, plaster *etc*. – *noun* **filling** anything used to fill a hole or gap. – *adjective* (of food) satisfying. – *noun* **filling-station** a garage where petrol is sold. – **fill in** to fill (*esp* a hole); to complete (a form *etc*); to do another person's job while they are absent: *I'm filling in for George*; **fill up** to fill completely.

fillet *noun* a piece of meat or fish without bones. – *verb* to remove the bones from.

fillip *noun* an encouragement.

filly *noun* (*plural* **fillies**) a young female horse.

film *noun* a thin skin or coating; a thin celluloid strip with a chemical coating on which photographs are taken; a story, play *etc* photographed on film and shown in a cinema, on television *etc*. – *verb* to photograph on a film. – *noun* **filmstar** a famous actor or actress in films.

Filofax® *noun* a personal organizer.

filter *noun* a strainer or other device for removing solid material from liquids; a green arrow on a traffic light which allows one lane of traffic to move while the main stream is held up. – *verb* to purify by a filter; to come in drops or gradually; (of cars *etc*) to join gradually a stream of traffic; (of a lane of traffic) to move in the direction shown by the filter.

filth *noun* dirt. – *adjective* **filthy** very dirty.

fin *noun* a part of a fish's body with which it balances itself and swims.

final *adjective* last; allowing of no argument: *The judge's decision is final.* – *n* the last contest in a competition. – *noun* **finality** the quality of being final and decisive. – *verb* **finalize** to get or put (*eg* plans) in a final or finished form.

finale *fi-nä'li, n* the last part of anything (*eg* a concert).

finance *noun* money affairs; the study or management of these; (*plural*) the money one has to spend. – *verb* to supply with sums of money. – *adjective* **financial**. – *noun* **financier** a person who manages (public) money.

finch *noun* (*plural* **finches**) a kind of small bird.

find *verb* (*past tense* **found**) to come upon or meet with either accidentally (*I found this ring in the street*) or after searching (*After looking everywhere I found my book under the bed*); to discover; to judge to be: *I find it difficult.* – *noun* something found, *esp* something of interest or value. – **find out** to discover; to detect.

fine *noun* money to be paid as a punishment. – Also *verb.* – *adjective* made up of very small pieces, drops *etc*; not coarse: *fine linen*; thin, delicate; slight: *a fine distinction*; beautiful, handsome; of good quality; pure; bright, not rainy; well, healthy. – *noun plural* **fine arts** painting, sculpture, music. – *noun* **finery** splendid clothes *etc*.

finesse *noun* cleverness and subtlety (in handling situations *etc*).

finger *noun* one of the five branching parts of the hand. – *verb* to touch with the fingers. – *noun* **fingering** (in music) the positioning of the fingers in playing an instrument; the showing of this by numbers. – *noun* **fingerprint** the mark made by the tip of a finger, used by the police as a means of identification.

finish *verb* to end or complete the making *etc* of; to stop: *finish work for the day.* – *noun* the end (*eg* of a race); the last touch (of paint, polish *etc*) that makes a perfect job. – *adjective* **finished** ended; complete; perfect; (of a person) ruined, not likely to achieve further success *etc*.

finite *adjective* having an end or limit.

fiord or **fjord** *noun* a long narrow inlet between steep hills (*esp* in Norway).

fir *noun* a kind of cone-bearing tree. – *noun* **fir-cone**.

fire *noun* the heat and light given off by something burning; a mass of burning material, objects *etc*; a heating device: *electric fire*; eagerness, keenness. – *verb* to set on fire; to make eager: *fired by his enthusiasm*; to make (a gun) explode; to shoot. – *noun* **fire alarm** a device (*eg* a system of bells) to give warning of a fire. – *noun* **firearm** a gun *eg* a pistol. – *noun* **fire brigade** a company of firemen. – *noun* **fire-damp** a dangerous gas found in coal mines. – *noun* **fire engine** a vehicle carrying firemen and their equipment. – *noun* **fire escape** a means of escape (*esp* an outside metal staircase) from a building in case of fire. – *noun* **firefly** a type of insect which glows in the dark. – *noun* **fire-guard** a framework of iron placed in front of a fireplace for safety. – *noun* **fireman** one whose job it is to put out fires. – *noun* **fireplace** a recess in a room below a chimney for a fire. – *noun* **firewood** wood for burning on a fire. – *noun plural* **fireworks** squibs, rockets *etc* sent up at night for show; (*coll*) angry behaviour.

firkin *noun* a small barrel.

firm *adjective* not easily moved, bent or shaken; with mind made up. – *noun* a business company.

firmament *noun* the heavens, sky.

first *adjective, adverb* before all others in place, time or rank. – *adjective* before doing anything else. – *noun* **first-aid** treatment of a wounded or sick person before the doctor's arrival. – *noun* **first-born** the eldest child. – *adjective* **first-class** of the highest standard, best kind *etc*. – *adjective* **first-hand** direct. – *noun* **first name** a person's name that is not their surname. – *adjective* **first-rate** first class.

firth *noun* a narrow arm of the sea, *esp* at a river mouth.

fiscal *adjective* of the public revenue; of financial matters.

fish *noun* (*plural* **fish** or **fishes**) a kind of animal that lives in water, and breathes through gills. – *verb* to (try to) catch fish with rod, nets *etc*; to search (for): *She fished for a handkerchief in her bag*; to try cunningly to obtain: *fish for compliments.* – *noun* **fisherman** a man who fishes (*esp* for a living). – *noun* **fishmonger** a person who sells fish for food. – *adjective* **fishy** like a fish; doubtful, arousing suspicion.

fission *noun* splitting.

fissure *noun* a crack.

fist *noun* a tightly-shut hand. – *noun plural* **fisticuffs** a fight with the fists.

fit *adjective* suited to a purpose; proper; in good training or health. – *noun* a sudden attack or spasm of laughter, illness *etc*. – *verb* (*past tense* **fitted**) to be of the right size or shape; to be suitable. – *adjective* **fitful** coming or doing in bursts or spasms. – *noun* **fitness**. – *adjective* **fitting** suitable. – *noun* something fixed or fitted *esp* in a room, house *etc*.

five *noun* the number 5. – *adjective* 5 in number. – *adjective* **fifth** the last of five (things *etc*). – *noun* one of five equal parts.

fives *noun plural* a handball game played in a walled court.

fix *verb* to make firm; to fasten; to mend, repair. – *adjective* **fixed** settled; set in position. – *adverb* **fixedly** steadily, intently: *He stared fixedly at me*. – *noun* **fixture** anything fixed (such as a shelf); a match or race that has been arranged.

fizz *verb* to make a hissing sound. – *noun* a hissing sound. – *adjective* **fizzy** of a drink in which tiny bubbles form on the surface.

fizzle: fizzle out to fail, coming to nothing.

fjord *see* **fiord**.

flabbergasted *adjective* very surprised.

flabby *adjective* not firm, soft, limp; weak, feeble. – *noun* **flabbiness**.

flaccid *flas'id, adjective* hanging in loose folds, not firm, limp.

flag *noun* a banner, standard, or ensign; a flat paving-stone; a type of waterplant, *esp* an iris. – *verb* (*past tense* **flagged**) to become tired or weak.

flagellation *noun* whipping.

flagon *noun* a large container for liquid.

flagrant *adjective* conspicuous; openly wicked. – *noun* **flagrancy**.

flail *verb* to wave or swing in the air. – *noun* (*old*) a tool for threshing corn.

flair *noun* talent, skill: *a flair for organizing*.

flak *noun* anti-aircraft fire; strong criticism.

flake *noun* a thin slice or chip of anything; a very small piece (as of snow *etc*). – *verb* to form into flakes. – **flake off** to break off in flakes.

flamboyant *adjective* splendidly coloured; too showy, intended to attract notice.

flame *noun* the bright leaping light of a fire. – *verb* to burn brightly. – *adjective* **flaming** burning; red; violent: *a flaming temper*.

flamingo *noun* (*plural* **flamingoes**) a type of long-legged bird of pink or bright-red colour.

flammable *adjective* easily set on fire.

flan *noun* a flat, open tart.

flange *noun* a raised edge on the rim of a wheel.

flank *noun* the side of anything (as of a person's or animal's body, of an army *etc*). – *verb* to go by the side of; to be situated at the side of.

flannel *noun* loosely woven woollen cloth; a small piece of material used *esp* for washing the face; (*plural*) trousers of this or similar material. – *noun* **flannelette** cotton cloth made in imitation of flannel.

flap *noun* anything broad and loose-hanging: *the flap of a tent*; the sound made when such a thing moves; a time of feverish activity; a panic. – *verb* (*past tense* **flapped**) to hang down loosely; to (cause to) move with a flapping noise; to get into a panic.

flare *verb* to blaze up. – *noun* a bright light, *esp* one used at night as a signal, to show the position of a boat in distress *etc*.

flash *noun* (*plural* **flashes**) a quick burst of light; a moment, instant; a distinctive mark on a uniform. – *verb* to shine out suddenly; to pass quickly. – *noun* **flashlight** a burst of light in which a photograph is taken; an electric torch. – *adjective* **flashy** dazzling for a moment; showy, gaudy; cheaply smart. – **in a flash** suddenly.

flask *noun* a narrow-necked bottle; a small flat bottle; an insulated bottle or vacuum flask.

flat *adjective* level: *a flat surface*; (of drinks) no longer fizzy; leaving no doubt, downright: *a flat denial*; below the right musical pitch; (of a tyre) punctured; dull, uninteresting. – *adverb* stretched out: *lying flat on her back*. – *noun* an apartment which lies on one storey of a building; a sign (*b*) in music which lowers a note; a punctured tyre. – *noun* **flatness**. – *noun* **flatfish** a sea fish with a flat body (*eg* a sole). – *noun* **flat race** a race over level ground without hurdles. – *noun* **flat rate** a rate which is the same in all cases. – verb **flatten** to make or become flat. – **flat out** as fast as possible, with as much effort as possible.

flatter verb to praise insincerely; to make out (a person or thing) to be better than they really are. – noun **flattery.**

flatulence noun wind in the stomach. – adjective **flatulent.**

flaunt verb to display in an obvious way.

flautist noun a flute-player.

flavour noun taste: *the flavour of lemons*; quality or atmosphere: *The celebrations had an Eastern flavour.* – verb to give a taste to. – noun **flavouring** anything used to give a special taste.

flaw noun a fault, an imperfection, a defect. – adjective **flawless** without fault or blemish.

flax noun a type of plant whose fibres are woven into linen cloth. – adjective **flaxen** made of or looking like flax; (of hair) fair.

flay verb to strip the skin off.

flea noun a type of small, wingless, blood-sucking insect having great jumping power.

fleck noun a spot, a speck. – adjective **flecked** marked with spots or patches.

fled see **flee.**

fledgling noun a young bird with fully-grown feathers.

flee verb (past tense **fled**) to run away (from danger etc).

fleece noun a sheep's coat of wool. – verb to clip wool from; (coll) to rob by cheating. – adjective **fleecy** soft and fluffy like wool.

fleet noun a number of ships; a number of vehicles (taxis etc). – adjective swift; nimble, quick in movement. – adjective **fleeting** passing quickly. – noun **fleetness** swiftness.

flesh noun the soft substance (muscle etc) which covers the bones of animals; meat; the body; the soft eatable part of fruit. – adjective **fleshy** fat, plump. – **flesh and blood** relations, family; human nature.

flew see **fly.**

flex verb to bend. – noun a length of covered wire attached to electrical devices. – noun **flexibility** ease in bending; willingness etc to adapt. – adjective

flexible easily bent; (of persons) willing or able to adapt to new or different conditions. – noun **flexitime** a system in which an agreed number of hours' work is done at times partly chosen by the worker.

flick verb to strike lightly with a quick, sharp movement; to remove (dust etc) with a movement of this kind. – noun a quick, sharp movement: *a flick of the wrist.*

flicker verb to flutter; to burn unsteadily. – Also noun.

flight noun the act of flying; a journey by plane; the act of fleeing or escaping; a flock (of birds); a number (of steps). – adjective **flighty** changeable, impulsive.

flimsy adjective thin; easily torn or broken etc; weak: *a flimsy excuse.*

flinch verb to move or shrink back in fear, pain etc.

fling verb (past tense **flung**) to throw. – noun a throw; a casual attempt; a period of time devoted to pleasure.

flint noun a kind of hard stone. – adjective made of flint. – noun **flintlock** a gun fired by sparks from a flint.

flip verb (past tense **flipped**) to toss lightly. – noun a light toss or stroke. – noun **flipper** a limb of a seal, walrus etc.

flippant adjective joking, not serious. – noun **flippancy.**

flirt verb to play at courtship without any serious intentions. – noun a person who flirts. – noun **flirtation.** – adjective **flirtatious** fond of flirting.

flit verb (past tense **flitted**) to move quickly and lightly from place to place.

float verb to keep on the surface of a liquid; to set going: *float a fund.* – noun a cork etc on a fishing line; a raft; a van (for milk etc); a large lorry for transporting cattle etc; a platform on wheels, used in processions etc; a sum of money set aside for giving change etc.

flock noun a number of animals or birds together; a large number of people; the congregation of a church; a shred or tuft of wool; wool or cotton waste. – verb (usu with **together**) to gather in a crowd; to go in a crowd.

floe noun a sheet of floating ice.

flog verb (past tense **flogged**) to beat, lash. – noun **flogging.**

flood noun a great flow (esp of water); the rise or flow of the tide; a great quantity:

a flood of letters. – *verb* to (cause to) overflow; to cover or fill with water. – *verb* **floodlight** (*past tense* and *past participle* **floodlit**) to illuminate with floodlighting. – *noun* a light used to floodlight. – *noun* **floodlighting** strong artificial lighting to illuminate an exterior or stage.

floor *noun* the part of a room on which one walks; a storey of a building. – *verb* to make a floor; (*coll*) to knock flat; (*coll*) to puzzle.

flop *verb* (*past tense* **flopped**) to sway or swing about loosely; to fall or sit down suddenly and heavily; to move about in a heavy, clumsy way; to fail badly. – Also *noun*. – *adjective* **floppy** flopping, soft and flexible. – *noun* **floppy disc** (*comput*) a thin bendable disc used to store information.

flora *noun* the plants of a district or country as a whole. – *adjective* **floral** (made) of flowers. – *noun* **florist** a seller or grower of flowers.

florid *adjective* (of persons) high-coloured, flushed; too ornate.

floss *noun* fine silk thread.

flotilla *noun* a fleet of small ships.

flotsam *noun* floating objects washed from a ship or wreck.

flounce *verb* to walk (away) suddenly and impatiently (*eg* in anger). – *noun* a gathered decorative strip sewn onto the hem of a dress.

flounder *verb* to struggle to move one's legs and arms (in water, mud *etc*); to have difficulty in speaking or thinking clearly or in acting efficiently. – *noun* a small flatfish.

flour *noun* finely-ground wheat; anything crushed to powder. – *adjective* **floury**.

flourish *verb* to be successful, *esp* financially; (of flowers *etc*) to grow well, thrive; to be healthy; to wave (something) as a show or threat. – *noun* (*plural* **flourishes**) fancy strokes in writing; a sweeping movement (with the hand, sword *etc*); showy splendour; an ornamental passage in music.

flout *verb* to treat with contempt, defy openly.

flow *verb* to run, as water; to move smoothly; (of the tide) to rise. – Also *noun*.

flower *noun* the part of a plant or tree from which fruit or seed grow; the best of

anything. – *verb* (of plants *etc*) to produce a flower; to be at one's best, flourish. – *adjective* **flowery** full of, decorated with flowers; of a piece of writing, using fine-sounding, fancy language.

flown *see* **fly**.

fl. oz. *abbreviation* fluid ounce(s).

flu *noun* short for **influenza**.

fluctuate *verb* to vary (in number, price *etc*); to be always changing. – *noun* **fluctuation**.

flue *noun* a passage for air and smoke in a stove or chimney.

fluent *adjective* finding words easily in speaking or writing without any awkward pauses. – *noun* **fluency**.

fluff *noun* any soft, downy stuff. – *adjective* **fluffy**.

fluid *noun* a substance whose particles can move about freely. – a liquid or gas; a liquid. – *adjective* flowing; not settled.

fluke *noun* a type of small worm which harms sheep; the part of an anchor which holds fast in sand; a success due to chance.

flung *see* **fling**.

fluoride *noun* a substance containing the element **fluorine** which prevents tooth decay. – *verb* **fluoridize** or **fluoridate** to add fluoride to drinking water. – *noun* **fluoridation**.

flurry *noun* (*plural* **flurries**) a sudden rush (of wind *etc*). – *verb* (*past tense* **flurried**) to excite.

flush *noun* (*plural* **flushes**) a reddening of the face; freshness, glow. – *verb* to become red in the face; to clean by a rush of water. – *adjective* (with **with**) having the surface level (with the surface around); (*coll*) well supplied with money.

fluster *noun* excitement caused by hurry. – Also *verb*.

flute *noun* a type of high-pitched musical wind instrument. – *adjective* **fluted** decorated with grooves.

flutter *verb* to move (*esp* wings) quickly. – *noun* a quick beating (of pulse *etc*); nervous excitement.

flux *noun* an ever-changing flow: *Events are in a state of flux.*

fly *noun* (*plural* **flies**) a type of small winged insect; a fish-hook made to look like a fly; a flap of material with buttons or a zip *esp* at the front of trousers. – *verb* (*past tense* **flew,** *past participle* **flown**) to move through the air on wings or in an aeroplane; to run away. – *noun* **flying squad** a body of police organized for fast action or movement or available for duty where needed. – *noun* **flyover** a road *etc* built on pillars to cross over another. – *noun* **flysheet** the outer covering of a tent. – *noun* **flywheel** a heavy wheel which enables a machine to run at a steady speed.

FM *abbreviation* frequency modulation.

foal *noun* a young horse. – *verb* to give birth to a foal.

foam *noun* a mass of small bubbles on liquids. – *verb* to produce foam. – *noun* **foam rubber** sponge-like form of rubber for stuffing chairs, mattresses *etc*.

fob *noun* a small watch pocket; a fancy chain hanging from the watch pocket. – *verb* (*past tense* **fobbed**) to make (someone) accept (something worthless *etc*): *I was fobbed off with a silly excuse.*

fo'c'sle *see* **forecastle.**

focus *noun* (*plural* **focuses** or **foci** *fō'sī*) meeting point for rays of light; point to which light, a look, attention, is directed. – *verb* to get the right length of ray of light for a clear picture; to direct (one's attention *etc*) to one point. – *adjective* **focal** of or at a focus.

fodder *noun* dried food (hay, oats *etc*) for farm animals.

foe *noun* an enemy.

foetus *noun* a young human being or animal in the womb or in the egg.

fog *noun* thick mist. – *verb* to cover in fog; to bewilder, confuse. – *adjective* **foggy.** – *noun* **foghorn** a horn used as a warning to or by ships in fog.

foil *verb* to defeat, disappoint. – *noun* metal in the form of paper-thin sheets; a dull person or thing against which someone or something else seems brighter; a blunt sword with a button at the end, used in fencing practice.

foist *verb* to pass off as genuine; to palm off (something undesirable on someone).

fold *noun* a part laid on top of another; an enclosure for sheep *etc*. – *verb* to lay one part on top of another. – *noun* **folder** a cover to hold papers.

foliage *noun* leaves.

folio *noun* (*plural* **folios**) a leaf (two pages) of a book; a page number; a sheet of paper folded once.

folk *noun* people; a nation, race; (*plural*) one's family or relations. – *noun* **folklore** the study of the customs, beliefs, fairy tales *etc* of a people. – *noun* **folksong** a song passed on from person to person over a period of time.

follow *verb* to go or come after; to happen as a result; to act according to; to understand; to work at (a trade). – *noun* **follower** someone who follows; a supporter, disciple. – *noun* **following** supporters. – *preposition* after, as a result of: *Following the fire, the house collapsed.*

folly *noun* (*plural* **follies**) foolishness.

foment *verb* to stir up, encourage growth of (a rebellion *etc*).

fond *adjective* loving; tender. – *noun* **fondness.** – **fond of** having a liking for.

fondle *verb* to caress.

font *noun* the basin holding water for baptism.

food *noun* that which living beings eat. – *noun* **food processor** electrical appliance for chopping, blending *etc* food. – *noun* **foodstuff** something used for food.

fool *noun* a silly person; (*hist*) a court jester; a pudding made of fruit, sugar and cream. – *verb* to deceive; to play the fool. – *adjective* **foolhardy** rash, taking foolish risks. – *adjective* **foolish.** – *noun* **foolishness** or **foolery** foolish behaviour. – *adjective* **foolproof** (of engines, plans *etc*) unable to go wrong. – **fool about** to behave in a playful or silly manner.

foolscap *noun* paper for writing or printing, 17×13½ in. (43×34 cm.).

foot *noun* (*plural* **feet**) the part of the leg below the ankle; the lower part of anything; twelve inches, 30 cm. – *verb* to pay (a bill *etc*). – *noun* **football** (a game played by kicking) a large ball. – *noun* **foothill** a smaller hill at the foot of a mountain. – *noun* **foothold** a place to put the foot in climbing; a firm position from which one can begin to do something. – *noun* **footing** balance; degree of friendship, seniority *etc*. – *noun* **footlight** a light at the front of a stage, which shines on the actors. – *noun* **footnote** a note at the bottom of a page. – noun **footpad** (*hist*) a highway robber. – noun **footplate** a driver's platform on a railway engine. – noun **footprint** a mark of a foot. – noun **footstep** the sound of a person's foot when walking. – noun **footwear** shoes *etc*.

fop noun a man who is vain about his dress. – adjective **foppish.**

for preposition sent to or to be given to: *a letter for you*; towards: *They headed for home*; during (a period): *They waited for three hours*; on behalf of: *Do it for me*; because of: *for good reason*; as the price of: *£1 for a saucepan*; (in order) to have: *He did it for the money*.

forage noun food for horses and cattle. – verb to search for food, fuel *etc*.

foray noun a sudden raid for plunder.

forbade see **forbid.**

forbearance noun control of temper. – adjective **forbearing** patient.

forbid verb (*past tense* **forbade**) to order not to. – adjective **forbidden.** – adjective **forbidding** rather frightening.

force noun strength; violence; the police; a group of workers, soldiers *etc*; (*plural*) soldiers, sailors, airmen. – verb to make, compel: *They forced him to go*; to get by violence: *force an entry*; to break open; to hurry on; to make vegetables *etc* grow more quickly. – adjective **forced** done unwillingly, with effort: *a forced laugh*. – adjective **forceful** acting with power. – adjective **forcible** done by force.

forceps noun a (surgical) tool with two arms for holding or lifting.

ford noun a shallow crossing place in a river. – verb to cross (water) on foot.

fore- prefix before; beforehand; in front.

forearm[1] noun the part of the arm between elbow and wrist.

forearm[2] verb to prepare beforehand.

foreboding noun a feeling of coming evil.

forecast verb to tell (about) beforehand, to predict. – Also noun.

forecastle, fo'c'sle both *fŏk'sl*, noun a raised deck at the front of a ship; the part of ship under the deck where the crew live.

forefather noun an ancestor.

forefinger noun the finger next to the thumb.

forefront noun the very front.

foregone: a foregone conclusion a result that can be guessed rightly in advance. *See also* **forgo.**

foreground noun the part of a view (or picture of one) nearest the front or nearest the person looking at it.

forehead noun the part of the face above the eyebrows.

foreign adjective belonging to another country; not belonging naturally in a place *etc*: *a foreign body in an eye*; not familiar. – noun **foreigner** a person from another country; somebody unfamiliar.

foreleg noun a front leg (of an animal).

forelock noun the lock of hair next to the forehead.

foreman noun (*plural* **foremen**) an overseer or leader of a group (such as workmen, jury).

foremast noun ship's mast nearest the bow.

foremost adjective the most famous or important.

forensic adjective having to do with courts of law or the investigation of crime.

forerunner noun a person or thing which is a sign of what is to follow.

foresee verb (*past tense* **foresaw,** *past participle* **foreseen**) to see or know beforehand. – noun **foresight** ability to see what will happen later; a fitting on the front of the barrel of a rifle to make correct aiming possible.

foreshore noun the part of the shore between high and low tidemarks.

foresight see **foresee.**

forest noun a large piece of land covered with trees; a stretch of country kept for game (such as deer). – noun **forester** a worker in a forest. – noun **forestry** (the science of) forest-growing.

forestall verb to upset someone's plan by acting earlier than they are expecting: *He forestalled his brother*.

foretaste noun sample of what is to come.

foretell verb (*past tense* **foretold**) to tell before, to prophesy.

forethought noun thought or care for the future.

foretold see **foretell.**

forewarn verb to warn beforehand. – noun **forewarning.**

forewent *see* **forgo.**

forewoman *noun* a woman overseer; a head woman in a shop or factory.

foreword *noun* a piece of writing at the beginning of a book.

forfeit *verb* to lose (a right) as a result of doing something. – *noun* that which must be given up for some (criminal) action; a fine. – *noun* **forfeiture** the loss of something as a punishment.

forge *noun* a blacksmith's workshop; a furnace in which metal is heated. – *verb* to hammer (metal) into shape; to imitate for criminal purposes; to move steadily on: *He forged ahead with his plans.* – *noun* **forgery** (*plural* **forgeries**) something imitated for criminal purposes; the act of criminal forging.

forget *verb* (*past tense* **forgot,** *past participle* **forgotten**) to lose or put away from the memory. – *adjective* **forgetful** likely to forget. – *noun* **forgetfulness.**

forgive *verb* (*past tense* **forgave,** *past participle* **forgiven**) to be no longer angry with (someone); to overlook (a fault, debt *etc*). – *noun* **forgiveness** pardon; readiness to pardon. – *adjective* **forgiving.**

forgo *verb* (*past tense* **forewent** or **forwent,** *past participle* **foregone** or **forgone**) to give up, do without.

forgot, forgotten *see* **forget.**

fork *noun* a pronged tool for piercing and lifting things; anything divided like a fork (*eg* a road, tree branch). – *verb* to divide into two branches *etc*. – *noun* **fork-lift truck** a power-driven truck with steel prongs that can lift, carry and stack heavy packages.

forlorn *adjective* pitiful, unhappy. – *noun* **forlorn hope** a wish which seems to have no chance of being granted.

form *noun* shape or appearance; kind, type; a paper with printed questions and space for the answers; a long seat; a school class; the nest of a hare. – *verb* to give shape to; to make. – *adjective* **formal** (of a person's manner) cold, business-like; done according to established rule, custom or convention. – *noun* **formal dress** the kind of clothes required to be worn on certain social (ceremonial) occasions *eg* balls, banquets *etc*. – *noun* **formality** (*plural* **formalities**) something which must be done but has little meaning: *The chairman's speech was only a formality*; cold

correctness of manner. – *noun* **formation** the act of forming; arrangement (as of aeroplanes when flying).

format *noun* (of books) the size, shape, kind of print *etc*; the design or arrangement of an event *etc* (such as a television programme); (*comput*) the description of the way data is, or is to be, arranged on a disc *etc*. – *verb* to arrange a book *etc* into a specific format; (*comput*) to arrange data for use on a disc *etc*; (*comput*) to prepare a disc *etc* for use by dividing it into sectors.

former *adjective* of an earlier time; of the first-mentioned of two (opposite of **latter**). – Also *noun*. – *adverb* **formerly** in earlier times.

formidable *adjective* causing fear; difficult to overcome.

formula *noun* (*plural* **formulae** or **formulas**) a set of rules to be followed; an arrangement of signs or letters used in chemistry, arithmetic *etc* to express an idea briefly (such as H_2O = water). – *verb* **formulate** to set down clearly; to make into a formula.

forsake *verb* (*past tense* **forsook**) to desert. – *adjective* **forsaken** left alone; miserable.

forswear *verb* to give up (something).

fort *noun* a place of defence against an enemy.

forte *för'tā, noun* that at which one is very good.

forth *adverb* forward; onward. – *adjective* **forthcoming** happening or appearing soon; (of a person) willing to tell what they know; friendly and open. – *adjective* **forthright** outspoken, straightforward. – *adverb* **forthwith** immediately.

fortify *verb* (*past tense* **fortified**) to strengthen (against attack). – *noun plural* **fortifications** walls *etc* built to strengthen a position.

fortitude *noun* courage in meeting danger or bearing pain.

fortnight *noun* two weeks. – *adjective* or *adverb* **fortnightly** once a fortnight.

fortress *noun* (*plural* **fortresses**) a fortified place.

fortuitous *adjective* happening by chance.

fortune *noun* luck (good or bad); large sum of money. – *adjective* **fortunate** lucky.

forty *noun* the number 40. – *adjective* 40 in number. – *adjective* **fortieth** the last of forty (things *etc*). – *noun* one of forty equal parts.

forum *noun* (*list*) market-place in ancient Rome; any public place where speeches are made; a meeting to talk about a particular subject.

forward *adjective* advancing: *a forward movement*; near or at the front; (of fruit *etc*) ripe earlier than usual; too ready in word or action, pert. – *verb* to help (towards success): *forward one's plans*; to send on (*eg* letters). – *adverb* **forward** or **forwards** onward; towards the front.

forwent *see* **forgo.**

fossil *noun* the hardened remains of the shape of a plant or animal found in rock. – *verb* **fossilize** to change into a fossil.

foster *verb* to bring up or nurse (*esp* a child not one's own); to help on, encourage (something). – *noun* **foster-child** (also **-brother** or **-sister**) a boy or girl fostered by a family. – *noun* **foster-mother** or **foster-father** a mother or father who brings up a fostered child.

fought *see* **fight.**

foul *adjective* very dirty; smelling or tasting bad; (of weather, temper) stormy. – *verb* to become entangled with; to dirty; to play unfairly. – *noun* a breaking of the rules of a game. – *noun* **foul play** a criminal act.

found *verb* to establish, set up; to shape by pouring melted metal into a mould; *see also* **find.** – *noun* **foundation** that on which anything rests; a sum of money left or set aside for a special purpose *eg* to support an organization *etc*; an organization *etc* supported in this way. – *noun* **founder** a person who founds. – *noun* **foundry** (*plural* **foundries**) workshop where metal founding is done.

founder *verb* (of a ship) to sink; (of a horse) to stumble or go lame. – *noun see* **found.**

foundling *noun* a child abandoned by its parents.

fountain *noun* a jet of water rising up; the pipe or structure from which it comes; the beginning of anything.

four *noun* the number 4. – *adjective* 4 in number. – *adjective* **fourth** the last of four (things *etc*). – *noun* one of four equal parts.

fourteen *noun* the number 14. – *adjective* 14 in number. – *adjective* **fourteenth** the last of fourteen (things *etc*). – *noun* one of fourteen equal parts.

fowl *noun* a bird, *esp* of the farmyard or poultry kind.

fox *noun* (*plural* **foxes**) a type of dog-like reddish-brown animal of great cunning. – *verb* to trick by cleverness or cunning; to puzzle, baffle. – *noun* **fox-glove** a tall wild flower. – *noun* **fox-hound** a breed of dog trained to chase foxes. – *noun* **fox terrier** a breed of dog trained to drive foxes from their earths. – *noun* **foxtrot** a dance made up of walking steps and turns. – *adjective* **foxy** cunning.

foyer *fwä'yā*, *noun* an entrance hall to a theatre, hotel *etc*.

FP *abbreviation* Former Pupil.

fracas *frak'ä*, *noun* uproar; a noisy quarrel.

fraction *noun* a part, not a whole number (such as ½, ¾, ⅞ *etc*); a small part.

fractious *adjective* cross, quarrelsome.

fracture *noun* a break in something hard, *esp* in a bone of the body.

fragile *adjective* easily broken.

fragment *noun* a part broken off; something not complete. – *verb* to break into pieces. – *adjective* **fragmentary** broken.

fragrant *adjective* sweet-smelling. – *noun* **fragrance** sweet scent.

frail *adjective* weak; easily tempted to do wrong. – *noun* **frailty** (*plural* **frailties**) weakness.

frame *verb* to put a frame round; to put together, to construct; (*slang*) to make (someone) appear to be guilty of a crime. – *noun* a case or border round anything; build of human body; state (of mind). – *noun* **framework** the outline, shape, or skeleton of anything.

franc *noun* the standard unit of French, Belgian and Swiss money.

franchise *noun* the right to vote (*esp* in a general election).

frank *adjective* open, speaking one's mind. – *verb* to mark a letter by machine to show that postage has been paid.

frankfurter *noun* a kind of smoked sausage.

frankincense *noun* a sweet-smelling resin used as incense.

frantic *adjective* wildly excited or anxious.

fraternal *adjective* brotherly; of a brother. – *noun* **fraternity** (*plural* **fraternities**) a company of persons who regard each other as equals. – *verb* **fraternize** to make friends with.

fratricide *noun* the murder or murderer of a brother.

fraud *noun* deceit, dishonest dealing; a pretender, impostor; a fake. – *adjective* **fraudulent.**

fraught *adjective* anxious, tense; (with **with**) filled.

fray *noun* a fight, a brawl. – *verb* to wear away.

freak *noun* an unusual event; an odd or unconventional person or thing.

freckle *noun* a brown spot on the skin.

free *adjective* not bound or shut in; generous; frank (in manner); costing nothing. – *verb* to make or set free; (with **from** or **of**) to get rid. – *noun* **freedom** liberty. – *adjective* **freehand** (of drawing) done without the help of rulers, tracing *etc.* – *adjective* **freehold** (of an estate) belonging to the holder or his heirs for all time. – *noun* **freelance** a person working independently (such as a writer who is not employed by any one newspaper). – *noun* **Freemason** a member of a certain men's society, sworn to secrecy. – *adjective* **free-range** (of poultry) allowed to move about freely and feed out of doors; (of eggs) laid by poultry of this kind. – *noun* **free speech** the right to express opinions of any kind. – *adjective* **freestyle** (of swimming race *etc.*) in which any style may be used.

freeze *verb* (*past tense* **froze,** *past participle* **frozen**) to turn into ice; to make (food) very cold in order to preserve; to go stiff (as with cold, fear); to fix (prices, wages *etc.*) at a certain level. – *noun* **freezer** a type of cabinet in which food is made, or kept, frozen. – *noun* **freezing-point** the point at which liquid becomes a solid (of water, $0°$ C).

freight *noun* load, cargo; charge for carrying a load. – *verb* to load with goods. – *noun* **freighter** a ship or aircraft that carries cargo. – *noun* **freight train** a goods train.

French: *noun* **French polish** a kind of varnish for furniture. – *noun* **French window** a long window also used as a door. – **take French leave** to go or remain absent without permission.

frenetic *adjective* frantic.

frenzy *noun* a fit of madness; wild excitement. – *adjective* **frenzied** mad.

frequent *adjective* happening often. – *verb* to visit often. – *noun* **frequency** (*plural* **frequencies**) the rate at which something happens; the number per second of vibrations, waves *etc.*

fresco *noun* (*plural* **frescoes** or **frescos**) a picture painted on a wall while the plaster is still damp.

fresh *adjective* new, unused; (of food) newly made, gathered *etc.*, not preserved; (of weather) cool, refreshing; (of persons) not tired; cheeky. – *adjective* newly: *fresh-laid eggs.* – *verb* **freshen** to make fresh; to grow strong. – *noun* **freshman** or **fresher** a first-year university student. – *adjective* **freshwater** of inland rivers, lakes *etc.*, not of the sea.

fret *verb* (*past tense* **fretted**) to worry or show discontent. – *noun* one of the ridges on the fingerboard of a guitar. – *adjective* **fretful.**

fretwork *noun* decorated cut-out work in wood. – *noun* **fretsaw** a narrow-bladed, fine-toothed saw for fretwork.

friar *noun* a member of one of the brotherhoods of the Church, *esp* one who has vowed to live in poverty. – *noun* **friary** (*plural* **friaries**) the friars' house.

friction *noun* rubbing of two things together; the wear caused by rubbing; quarrelling, bad feeling.

Friday *noun* sixth day of the week.

fridge *noun* (*coll*) refrigerator.

fried *see* **fry.**

friend *noun* a person who likes and knows well another person: *He is my friend. We are good friends;* sympathizer, helper. – *adjective* **friendly** kind; (with **with**) on good terms. – *noun* **friendliness.** – *noun* **friendship.**

frieze *noun* a part of a wall below the ceiling, often ornamented with designs; a picture on a long strip of paper *etc.*, often displayed on a wall.

frigate *noun* a small warship.

fright *noun* sudden fear: *It gave me a fright. He took fright and ran away.* – *verb* **frighten** to make afraid. – *adjective* **frightful** causing terror; (*coll*) very bad.

frigid *adjective* frozen, cold; cold in manner. – *noun* **frigidity** coldness.

frill *noun* an ornamental edging (of linen, lace *etc*); something unnecessary added on (to a thing, action *etc*).

fringe *noun* a border of loose threads; hair cut to hang over the forehead; a border (*esp* of soft material, paper *etc*). – *verb* to edge round.

Frisbee ® *noun* a plastic plate-like object skimmed through the air as a game.

frisk *verb* to skip about playfully; (*coll*) to search (a person) for weapons *etc*. – *adjective* **frisky**.

fritter *noun* a piece of fried batter containing fruit *etc*. – *verb* (with **away**) to waste time *etc*.

frivolous *adjective* playful, not serious. – *noun* **frivolity** (*plural* **frivolities**).

frizzy *adjective* (of hair) massed in small curls.

fro: to and fro forwards and backwards.

frock *noun* a woman's or girl's dress; a monk's wide-sleeved garment. – *noun* **frock-coat** a man's long coat.

frog *noun* a small greenish jumping animal living on land and in water. – *noun* **frogman** an underwater swimmer wearing flippers and breathing apparatus.

frolic *noun* merrymaking or an outburst of gaiety. – *verb* (*past tense* **frolicked**) to play gaily. – *adjective* **frolicsome**.

from *preposition* used before the place, thing, person *etc* that is the starting point of an action, period of time *etc*: *We sail from England to France. The office is closed from Friday to Monday. The castle is open from the first of March (onwards). Jam is made from fruit and sugar*; used to show separation: *Warn them to keep away from there. Take it from him.*

frond *noun* a leaf-like growth *esp* a branch of a fern or palm.

front *noun* the part of anything nearest the person who sees it; the part which faces the direction in which the thing moves; (in war) the fighting line. – Also *adjective*. –*noun* **frontage** front part of a building. – **in front of** at the head of, before.

frontier *noun* a boundary between countries. – Also *adjective*.

frontispiece *noun* a picture at the very beginning of a book.

frost *noun* frozen dew; the coldness of weather needed to form ice. – *verb* to cover with frost or anything sparkling like it. – *adjective* **frosted**. – *adjective* **frosty**.

froth *noun* foam on liquids. – *verb* to throw up foam. – *adjective* **frothy**.

frown *verb* to wrinkle the brows (in deep thought, disapproval *etc*). – Also *noun*. **frown on** to look upon with disapproval.

frowzy *adjective* rough and tangled.

froze, frozen *see* **freeze**.

frugal *adjective* careful in spending, thrifty; costing little, small: *a frugal meal*. – *noun* **frugality**.

fruit *noun* the part of a plant containing the seed; result: *Their hard work bore fruit*. – *noun* **fruiterer** a person who sells fruit. – *adjective* **fruitful** producing (much) fruit; producing good results. – *noun* **fruition** ripeness; a good result. – *adjective* **fruitless** useless, done in vain. – *noun* **fruit machine** a gambling machine into which coins are put.

frump *noun* a plain, badly or unfashionably dressed woman. – *adjective* **frumpish**.

frustrate *verb* to make (someone feel) powerless; to bring to nothing: *They frustrated his wishes*. – *noun* **frustration**.

fry *verb* (*past tense* **fried**) to cook in hot fat. – *noun* anything fried; young fishes. – **small fry** people or things of little importance.

ft *abbreviation* foot, feet.

fuchsia *fū'shi-à*, *n* a type of shrub with long hanging flowers.

fuddle *verb* to make stupid (with drink).

fudge *noun* a soft, sugary sweet.

fuel *noun* any substance (*eg* coal, oil, petrol, gas) by which a fire, engine *etc* is kept going.

fugitive *adjective* running away (from police *etc*). – *noun* a person who is running away (from someone or something): *a fugitive from justice*.

fugue *fūg*, *noun* a piece of music with several interwoven tunes.

fulcrum *noun* (*plural* **fulcrums** or **fulcra**) the point on which a lever turns, or a balanced object rests.

fulfil *verb* (*past tense* **fulfilled**) to carry out (a task, promise *etc*). – *noun* **fulfilment**.

full *adjective* holding as much as can be held; (with **of**) having plenty; plump: *full face.* – *adverb* (used with *adjectives*) fully: *full-grown.* – *noun* **fullness.** – *adverb* **fully.** – *noun* **full moon** the moon when it appears at its largest. – *noun* **full stop** point (.) placed at the end of a sentence.

fulmar *noun* a type of white seabird.

fulminate *verb* to flash like lightning; (with **against**) to speak fiercely. – *noun* **fulmination.**

fulsome *adjective* overdone: *fulsome praise.*

fumble *verb* to use the hands awkwardly; to drop (something thrown, as a ball).

fume *noun* (*usu plural*) smoke or vapour. – *verb* to give off smoke or vapour; to be (quietly) in a rage.

fumigate *verb* to kill germs by means of strong fumes. – *noun* **fumigation.**

fun *noun* enjoyment, a good time: *to have fun.* – *noun* **funfair** amusement park. – *adjective* **funny** amusing; odd. – *adverb* **funnily.** – *noun* **funny bone** part of the elbow. – **make fun of** to tease, make others laugh at.

function *noun* a special job, use or duty (of a machine, person, part of the body *etc*); (large) arranged gathering of people. – *verb* (of a machine *etc*) to work, operate; to carry out usual duties. – *noun* **functionary** (*plural* **functionaries**) a person holding an office, an official.

fund *noun* a sum of money for a special purpose; a store or supply.

fundamental *adjective* of great or far-reaching importance; going to the very bottom of the matter. – *noun* a necessary part; (*plural*) the groundwork or first stages.

funeral *noun* the ceremony of burial or cremation. – *adjective* **funereal** mournful.

fungus *noun* (*plural* **fungi**) a soft, spongy plant growth (*eg* toadstool, mushroom); disease-growth on animals and plants.

funicular railway *noun* a kind of railway in which carriages are pulled uphill by a cable.

funnel *noun* a vessel, *usu* a cone ending in a tube for pouring liquids into bottles; a tube or passage for escape of smoke, air *etc*.

fur *noun* the short fine hair of certain animals; their skins covered with fur (used for clothing); a coating on the tongue, on the inside of kettles, boilers *etc*. – *verb* (*past tense* **furred**) to line or cover with fur. – *noun* **furrier** a person who buys, sells, or works with furs. – *adjective* **furry.**

furbish *verb* to rub up until bright.

furious *see* **fury.**

furlong *noun* one-eighth of a mile (220 yards, 201·17 metres).

furnace *noun* a very hot oven or closed-in fireplace for melting iron ore, making steam for heating *etc*.

furnish *verb* to fit up (a room or house) completely; to supply: *He was furnished with enough food for a week.* – *noun plural* **furnishings** fittings of any kind. – *noun* **furniture** moveable articles in a house *etc* (as tables, chairs).

furore *fū-rōr'ā*, *noun* uproar; excitement.

furrow *noun* the groove made by a plough; any groove; a deep wrinkle. – *verb* to cut deep grooves in; to wrinkle.

furry *see* **fur.**

further *adverb, adjective* to a greater distance or degree; in addition. – *verb* to help on or forward. – *adverb* **furthermore** in addition to what has been said. – *adverb* **furthest** to the greatest distance or degree.

furtive *adjective* stealthy, sly; done in a sly manner.

fury *noun* violent anger. – *adjective* **furious.**

furze another name for **gorse.**

fuse *verb* to melt; to join together; to put a fuse in (a plug *etc*); (of a circuit *etc*) to stop working because of the melting of a fuse. – *noun* easily-melted wire put in an electric circuit for safety; any device for causing an explosion to take place automatically. – *noun* **fusion** a melting; close union of things, as if melting into one another.

fuselage *noun* the body of an aeroplane.

fuss *noun* unnecessary activity, excitement or attention, often about something unimportant; strong complaint. – *verb* to be unnecessarily concerned about details; to worry overmuch. – *adjective* **fussy.**

fusty *adjective* mouldy; stale-smelling.

futile *adjective* useless; having no effect. – *noun* **futility** uselessness.

future *adjective* happening *etc* later in time. – *noun* (with **the**) the time to come; (in grammar) the future tense.

fuzz *noun* fine, light hair, feathers *etc*; (*slang*) the police. – *adjective* **fuzzy** covered with fuzz, fluffy; curly.

G

g *abbreviation* gramme or gram.

gabble *verb* to talk fast, chatter. – Also *noun*.

gaberdine *noun* a kind of cloth; a kind of coat.

gable *noun* the triangular area of wall at the end of a building with a ridged roof.

gadabout *noun* a person who loves travelling about.

gadfly *noun* a fly which bites cattle.

gadget *noun* a (small) simple machine or tool.

Gaelic *noun* the language of the Scottish Highlanders and the Irish.

gaff *noun* a large hook used for landing fish, such as salmon; a spar made from a mast, for raising the top of a sail. – **blow the gaff** (*coll*) to let out a secret.

gag *verb* (*past tense* **gagged**) to silence by stopping the mouth. – *noun* something put in a person's mouth to silence him; (*coll*) a joke or funny story.

gaggle *noun* a flock (of geese).

gaiety, gaily *see* **gay**.

gain *verb* to win; to earn; to reach; to get closer, *esp* in a race; (of clocks, watches) to go ahead (of correct time); to take on (*eg* weight). – *noun* something gained; profit.

gait *noun* way or manner of walking.

gaiter *noun* a cloth ankle-covering, fitting over the shoe, sometimes reaching to the knee.

gala *noun* a time of rejoicing and merrymaking; a sports meeting: *swimming gala*.

galaxy *noun* (*plural* **galaxies**) a system of stars; a splendid gathering (*eg* of women, famous people). – *noun* **Galaxy** or **the Galaxy** the Milky Way.

gale *noun* a strong wind.

gall *noun* bile (a bitter fluid coming from the liver and stored in the **gallbladder**); bitterness of feeling; a growth (caused by insects) on oaks and other trees and plants. – *verb* to annoy. – *adjective* **galling**.

gallant *adjective* brave; noble; paying great attention to ladies. – *noun* a man who is a favourite with ladies because of his fine manners. – *noun* **gallantry** bravery; politeness to ladies.

galleon *noun* (*hist*) a large Spanish sailing ship.

gallery *noun* (*plural* **galleries**) a long passage; the top floor of seats in a theatre; a room for showing paintings *etc* (also **art gallery**).

galley *noun* (*plural* **galleys**) (*hist*) a long, low-built ship driven by oars; a place where cooking is done on board ship. – *noun* **galley-slave** (*hist*) a prisoner condemned to work at the oars of a galley.

gallon *noun* a measure for liquids (8 pints, 3·636 litres).

gallop *verb* to move by leaps; to (cause to) move very fast. – *noun* a fast pace.

gallows *noun* a wooden framework on which criminals were hanged.

galore *adverb* in great plenty: *whisky galore*.

galosh or **golosh** *noun* (*plural* **galoshes** or **goloshes**) a rubber shoe worn over ordinary shoes in wet weather.

galvanism *noun* electricity got by action of chemicals (*usu* acids) on metal. – *adjective* **galvanic**. – *verb* **galvanize** to stir into activity; to stimulate by electricity; to coat (iron *etc*) with zinc. – *noun* **galvanometer** an instrument for measuring electric currents.

gambit *noun* a first move (as in chess) in which something is lost in order to make one's position stronger; an opening move in a transaction or an opening remark in a conversation.

gamble *verb* to play games for money; to risk money on the result of a game, race *etc*; to take a wild chance. – Also *noun*.

gambol *verb* (*past tense* **gambolled**) to leap playfully. – Also *noun*.

game *noun* a contest played according to rules; (*plural*) athletic competition: *Olympic Games*; wild animals and birds hunted for sport. – *adjective* plucky; (of limbs *etc*) lame. – *noun* **gamekeeper** one who looks after game birds, animals, fish *etc*. – *noun, adjective* **gaming** gambling. – **big game** large hunted animals (*eg* lions).

gammon *noun* leg of a pig, salted and smoked.

gamut *noun* the whole range of notes which a voice or instrument can produce; any whole extent.

gander *noun* a male goose.

gang *noun* any group of people who meet regularly; a team of criminals; a number of labourers. – *noun* **ganger** foreman of a company of workmen (*eg* labourers). – *noun* **gangster** one of a gang of criminals.

gangrene *noun* the rotting of some part of the body. – *adjective* **gangrenous.**

gangster *see* **gang.**

gangway *noun* a passage between rows of seats; a moveable bridge leading from a quay to a ship.

gannet *noun* a type of large white sea bird.

gantry *noun* (*plural* **gantries**) a platform or structure for supporting (a travelling crane *etc*).

gaol, gaoler *see* **jail, jailer.**

gap *noun* an opening or space between things.

gape *verb* to open the mouth wide (as in surprise); to be wide open.

garage *noun* a building for storing a car (or cars); a shop where car repairs are done, and petrol, oil *etc* sold.

garb (*old*) *noun* dress. – *verb* to clothe.

garbage *noun* rubbish.

garble *verb* to mix up, muddle: *a garbled account of what happened.*

garden *noun* a piece of ground on which flowers or vegetables are grown. – *verb* to work in a garden; to take care of a garden. – *noun* **gardener.** – *noun* **garden party** a large tea party, held out of doors.

gargantuan *adjective* extremely large, huge.

gargle *verb* to wash the throat with (but without swallowing) a soothing or germ-killing liquid.

gargoyle *noun* a jutting-out roof-spout, carved in the shape of a human or animal head.

garish *adjective* over-bright.

garland *noun* flowers or leaves tied or woven into a circle.

garlic *noun* an onion-like plant with a strong smell and taste, used in cooking.

garment *noun* any article of clothing.

garnet *noun* a semi-precious stone *usu* red in colour.

garnish *verb* to decorate (a dish of food). – Also *noun* (*plural* **garnishes**). – *noun* **garnishing.**

garret *noun* a room next to the roof of a house.

garrison *noun* a body of troops for guarding a fortress.

garrotte *verb* to strangle (by tightening a noose of rope *etc* round someone's neck, *orig* by tightening an iron collar).

garrulous *adjective* fond of talking. – *noun* **garrulity** or **garrulousness.**

garter *noun* a broad elastic band to keep a stocking up.

gas *noun* (*plural* **gases**) a substance like air (though some gases may be smelled); natural or manufactured form of this which will burn and is used as a fuel; (*US*) petrol. – *verb* (*past tense* **gassed**) to poison with gas. – *adjective* **gaseous.** – *noun* **gas mask** a covering for the face to prevent breathing in of poisonous gas. – *noun* **gasoline** or **gasolene** (*US*) petrol. – *noun* **gasometer** a tank for storing gas. – *noun* **gasworks** place where gas is made.

gash *noun* (*plural* **gashes**) a deep, open wound. – Also *verb*.

gasp *noun* sound made by a sudden intake of the breath. – *verb* to breathe with difficulty; to say breathlessly; (*coll*) to want badly: *gasping for a drink.*

gastric *adjective* of the stomach.

gate *noun* (that which closes) the opening in a wall, fence *etc*; the number of people at a (football) match; the total sum they pay to get in. – noun **gate-crasher** a person who comes to a party uninvited. – verb **gatecrash**. – noun **gateway** an opening containing a gate; an entrance.

gateau *gat'ō*, noun (*plural* **gateaus** or **gateaux**) a rich cake, *usu* layered and with cream.

gather verb to bring together, or to meet, in one place; to pick (flowers *etc*); to increase in: *The car gathered speed*; to learn, come to the conclusion (that): *I gather that you have finished.* – noun **gathering** a crowd.

gauche *gōsh*, adjective awkward and clumsy in people's company.

gaucho noun (*plural* **gauchos**) a cowboy of the S. American plains, noted for horse-riding.

gaudy adjective showy; vulgarly bright in colour. – noun **gaudiness**.

gauge verb to measure; to make a guess. – noun a measuring device. – noun **broad-gauge** or **narrow-gauge** railways having the distance between rails greater or less than the *standard gauge* (4 ft 8½ in, 1·435 metre).

gaunt adjective thin, haggard.

gauntlet noun a long glove (often of leather) with a guard for the wrist used by motor-cyclists *etc*; (*hist*) the iron glove of armour.

gauze noun thin cloth that can be seen through.

gavotte noun (music for) a type of lively dance.

gawky adjective awkward.

gay adjective lively; merry, full of fun; brightly coloured; (*coll*) homosexual. – noun (*coll*) a homosexual. – noun **gaiety**. – adverb **gaily**.

gaze verb to look steadily. – noun a fixed look.

gazelle noun a type of small deer.

gazette noun a newspaper, *esp* one having lists of government notices. – noun **gazetteer** a geographical dictionary.

GB abbreviation Great Britain.

GC abbreviation George Cross.

GCSE abbreviation General Certificate of Secondary Education.

GDR abbreviation German Democratic Republic (East Germany).

gear noun anything needed for a particular job, sport (*eg* harness, tools, clothes); (in cars *etc*) a connection by means of a set of toothed wheels between the engine or source of power and the wheels. – verb (with **to**) to adapt to, design for what is needed.

geese see **goose**.

geisha *gā'shä*, noun a Japanese girl trained to entertain.

gelatine noun a jelly-like substance made from hooves, animal bones *etc*, and used in food. – adjective **gelatinous** jelly-like.

gelding noun a castrated horse.

gem noun any precious stone, *esp* when cut to shape; anything greatly valued.

gender noun (in grammar, *esp* in languages other than English) any of three types of noun – masculine, feminine or neuter.

gene noun the basic unit of heredity responsible for passing on specific characteristics from parents to off-spring. – adjective **genetic**.

genealogy noun (*plural* **genealogies**) history of families from generation to generation; the ancestors of a person or family shown as a plan. – adjective **genealogical**. – noun **genealogist** a person who studies or makes genealogies.

general adjective not detailed, broad: *a general idea of the person's interests*; involving everyone: *a general election*; to do with several different things: *general knowledge*; of most people: *the general opinion*. – noun a high-ranking army officer. – noun **generalization** a (too) general view, statement *etc*. – verb **generalize** to make a broad general statement (meant to cover all individual cases). – adverb **generally** usually, in most cases; by most people. – noun **general practitioner** a doctor who treats most ordinary illnesses. – **in general** generally.

generate verb to produce, bring into being: *generate electricity*: *generate hatred*. – noun **generation** act of creating or making; a step in family descent; people born at about the same time. – noun **generator** a machine for making electricity *etc*.

generic see **genus**.

generous adjective giving plentifully; kind. – noun **generosity**.

genesis *noun* beginning.

genetic *see* **gene**.

genial *adjective* good-natured.

genie *noun* (*plural* **genii**) a guardian spirit.

genitals *noun plural* the organs of sexual reproduction.

genius *noun* (*plural* **geniuses**) unusual cleverness; a person who is unusually clever.

genteel *adjective* good-mannered (*esp* excessively).

gentile *noun* (in the Bible) anyone not a Jew.

gentility *noun* noble birth, aristocracy; good manners, refinement often to too great an extent.

gentle *adjective* (of persons) soft in manner, not brutal; (of things) mild, not extreme: *gentle breeze*. – *noun* **gentleness**.

gentleman *noun* a man (opposite of **lady**), *esp* one of noble birth; a well-mannered man. – *adjective* **gentlemanly** behaving in a polite manner.

gentry *noun* a wealthy, land-owning class of people.

genuine *adjective* real, not fake; (of persons) honest and straightforward. – *noun* **genuineness**.

genus *noun* (*plural* **genera**) a group (*usu* of living things) made up of a number of kinds. – *adjective* **generic** general, applicable to any member of a group or class.

geography *noun* the study of the surface of the earth and its inhabitants. – *noun* **geographer** a person who studies geography. – *adjective* **geographic** or **geographical**.

geology *noun* the study of the earth's history as shown in its rocks and soils. – *adjective* **geological**. – *noun* **geologist**.

geometry *noun* the branch of mathematics which deals with the study of lines, angles, and figures. – *adjective* **geometric** or **geometrical** having regular shape; (of patterns *etc*) made up of angles and straight lines.

geranium *noun* a kind of plant, often with bright red flowers.

gerbil *noun* a type of small, rat-like desert animal, often kept as a pet.

germ *noun* a very small living thing which may cause a disease; the smallest form of what will become a living thing (as a fertilized egg, a flower bud); that from which anything grows: *germ of an idea*. – *noun* **germicide** a germ-killer.

germane *adjective* closely related.

German shepherd dog *noun* a breed of large wolf-like dog, an alsatian.

germinate *verb* to begin to grow, to sprout. – *noun* **germination**.

gesticulate *verb* to wave hands and arms about in excitement *etc*. – *noun* **gesticulation**.

gesture *noun* a movement of the hands, head *etc*; an action made to show one's feelings: *a gesture of friendship*.

get *verb* (*past tense, past participle* **got,** (*US*) *past participle* **gotten**) to obtain, to go or move; to cause to be done: *get your hair cut*; to receive: *get a letter*; to cause to be in some condition: *get the car going*; to arrive: *get home*; to catch, or have (a disease); to become: *get old*. – **get at** to reach; to hint at; to criticize continually; (*slang*) to try to influence by bribes or threats; **get away with** to do and escape punishment for; **get on with** to be on friendly terms with; **get over** to recover from; **get up** to stand up; to get out of bed.

geyser *gē'zėr, noun* a hot spring which spouts water into the air; a gas or electric water heater.

ghastly *adjective* very pale, death-like; ill; *feeling ghastly*; horrible, ugly; (*coll*) very bad. – *noun* **ghastliness**.

gherkin *noun* a small pickled cucumber.

ghetto *noun* (*plural* **ghettos**) a (poor) part of a city *etc* in which a certain group (*esp* of immigrants) lives.

ghost *noun* a spirit, *usu* of a dead person. – *adjective* **ghostly** like a ghost. – *noun* **ghostliness**.

ghoul *gool, noun* an evil spirit which plunders dead bodies; a person unnaturally interested in death and disaster. – *adjective* **ghoulish**.

GHQ *abbreviation* general headquarters.

giant (*masculine*), **giantess** (*feminine*) *noun* (in old stories) a huge being like a human being in shape; a person of great height or size. – *adjective* huge.

gibber *verb* to speak nonsense; to make meaningless noises. – *noun* **gibberish** words without meaning.

gibbet *noun* (*hist*) a gallows on which criminals used to be executed or hung up after execution.

gibbon *noun* a large, tail-less ape.

gibe *see* **jibe**.

giblets *noun plural* eatable parts from the inside of a fowl *etc*.

giddy *adjective* unsteady, dizzy; causing dizziness: *from a giddy height*. – *noun* **giddiness**.

gift *noun* something freely given (*eg* a present); a natural talent: *a gift for music*; (*coll*) something easily done *etc*: *The examination paper was a gift*. – *adjective* **gifted** having special natural power or ability. – **look a gift horse in the mouth** to find fault with a gift.

gigantic *adjective* huge, of giant size.

giggle *verb* to laugh in a nervous or silly manner. – Also *noun*.

gild *verb* to cover with gold; to make bright. – *noun* **gilt** the gold covering used in gilding. – *adjective* covered with thin gold; coloured like gold. – *adjective* **gilt-edged** not risky, safe to invest in: *gilt-edged stocks*. – **gild the lily** to try to improve something already beautiful enough.

gill¹ *jil, noun* a measure (¼ pint, 11·36 cubic centimetres) for liquids.

gill² *gil, noun* one of the openings on the side of a fish's head through which it breathes.

gillie *noun* a man who helps and guides a sportsman while fishing or shooting (*esp* in Scotland).

gilt *see* **gild**.

gimcrack *adjective* cheap and badly-made.

gimlet *noun* a small tool for boring holes by hand.

gimmick *noun* something meant to attract attention.

gin *noun* an alcoholic drink made from grain, and flavoured with juniper berries; a trap or snare.

ginger *noun* a hot-tasting root, used as a seasoning in food. – *adjective* flavoured with ginger; reddish-brown in colour (*esp* hair). – *noun* **gingerbread** cake flavoured with ginger. – *adverb* **gingerly** very carefully.

gingham *noun* a striped or checked cotton cloth.

gipsy *see* **gypsy**.

giraffe *noun* a type of African animal with very long legs and neck.

gird *verb* to bind round. – *noun* **girder** a beam of iron, steel, or wood used in building. – *noun* **girdle** belt, cord *etc* which goes round something (*usu* the waist).

girl *noun* a female child or young woman. – *noun* **girlhood** the state or time of being a girl. – *adjective* **girlish** like a girl. – *noun* **Girl Guide** *see* **Guide**.

giro *noun* a system by which payment may be made through banks, post offices *etc*; (also **girocheque**) a form like a cheque by which such payment is made; (*coll*) a system of social security payment (by giro-cheque).

girth *noun* measurement round the middle; a strap that keeps a saddle on a horse *etc*.

gist *noun* the main points or ideas (of a story, argument *etc*).

give *verb* (*past tense* **gave**, *past participle* **given**) to hand over freely or in exchange; to utter (a shout, cry); to break or crack: *The bridge gave under the weight of the train*; to produce: *This lamp gives a good light*. – *noun* **giver**. – **give away** to hand over (something) to someone without payment; to betray; **give in** to yield; **give over** (*coll*) to stop (doing something); **give rise to** to cause; **give up** to hand over; to yield; to stop, abandon (a habit *etc*); **give way** to yield; to collapse; to let traffic crossing one's path go before one.

glacé *adjective* iced or sugared.

glacier *noun* a slowly-moving river of ice in valleys between high mountains. – *adjective* **glacial** of ice or glaciers.

glad *adjective* pleased; giving pleasure: *the glad news*. – *verb* **gladden** to make glad. – *noun* **gladness**.

glade *noun* an open space in a wood.

gladiator *noun* (*hist*) in ancient Rome, a man trained to fight with other men or with animals for the amusement of spectators.

glamour *noun* fascination, charm, beauty, *esp* artificial. – *adjective* **glamorous**.

glance *noun* a quick look. – *verb* to take a quick look at; (with **off**) to hit and fly off sideways.

gland *noun* a part of the body which takes substances from the blood and stores them either for use or so that the body may get rid of them. – *adjective* **glandular**.

glare *noun* an unpleasantly bright light; an angry or fierce look. – *verb* to shine with an unpleasantly bright light; to look angrily. – *adjective* **glaring** dazzling; very clear, obvious: *a glaring mistake*.

glasnost *noun* the Soviet policy of openness and forthrightness.

glass *noun* (*plural* **glasses**) a hard transparent substance made from certain metal oxides and other oxides; anything made of glass *esp* a glass drinking vessel or a mirror; a pair of lenses set in a frame used to correct bad eyesight, spectacles. – *adjective* made of glass. – *noun* **glasshouse** a greenhouse. – *adjective* **glassy** (of eyes) without expression.

glaze *verb* to cover with a thin coating of glass or other shiny stuff; to make shiny; to put panes of glass in a window; of eyes, to become glassy. – *noun* a shiny surface; a sugar-coating. – *noun* **glazier** a person who sets glass in window-frames.

gleam *verb* to glow; to flash. – *noun* a beam of light; brightness.

glean *verb* to collect (*esp* things overlooked before); (*old*) to gather corn in handfuls after the reapers.

glee *noun* joy; a song in parts. – *adjective* **gleeful** merry.

glen *noun* in Scotland, a long narrow valley.

glib *adjective* speaking smoothly and fluently (often insincerely and superficially); (of a reply *etc*) quick and ready, but showing little thought. – *noun* **glibness**.

glide *verb* to move smoothly and easily; to travel by glider. – *noun* the act of gliding. – *noun* **glider** an aeroplane without an engine.

glimmer *verb* to burn or shine faintly. – *noun* a faint light; a faint appearance (of): *a glimmer of hope*.

glimpse *noun* a brief view. – *verb* to get a brief look at.

glint *verb* to sparkle, gleam. – Also *noun*.

glisten *verb* to sparkle.

glitter *verb* to sparkle. – Also *noun*.

gloaming *noun* twilight, dusk.

gloat *verb* to look at or think about with wicked joy: *She gloated over his defeat*.

globe *noun* a ball; the earth; a ball with a map of the world drawn on it; a glass covering for a lamp. – *adjective* **global** of, or affecting, the whole world; applying generally: *global increase in earnings*. – *adjective* **globular** ball-shaped. – *noun* **globule** a drop; a small ball-shaped piece.

gloom *noun* dullness, darkness; sadness. – *adjective* **gloomy** dimly lighted; sad, depressed.

glory *noun* (*plural* **glories**) fame, honour; great show, splendour. – *verb* to rejoice, take great pleasure (in). – *verb* **glorify** (*past tense* **glorified**) to make glorious; to praise highly. – *adjective* **glorious** spendid; deserving great praise; delightful.

gloss *noun* brightness on the surface. – *verb* to make bright; to explain; (with **over**) to try to hide (a fault *etc*) by treating (it) rapidly or superficially or by giving (it) a false appearance. – *adjective* **glossy** shiny, highly polished.

glossary *noun* (*plural* **glossaries**) a list of words with their meanings.

glove *noun* a covering for the hand with a separate covering for each finger; a boxing glove.

glow *verb* to burn without flame; to give out a steady light; to be flushed (from heat, cold *etc*); to tingle (with an emotion): *She glowed with pride*. – *noun* a glowing state; great heat; bright light. – *adjective* **glowing** giving out a steady light; tingling; flushed; full of praise: *I hear glowing accounts of his bravery*. – *noun* **glow-worm** a kind of beetle which glows in the dark.

glower *verb* to stare (at) with a frown. – *adjective* **glowering** scowling; threatening.

glucose *noun* a kind of sugar found in the juice of fruits.

glue *noun* a substance for sticking things together. – *verb* to join with glue. – *adjective* **gluey** sticky.

glum *adjective* sad, gloomy.

glut *verb* (*past tense* **glutted**) to take one's fill greedily; to supply too much to (a market). – *noun* an over-supply (of something): *a glut of fish on the market*.

glutton *noun* a person who eats too much; someone who is eager (for anything): *a glutton for punishment*. – *adjective* **gluttonous** fond of overeating; eating greedily. – *noun* **gluttony** greediness in eating.

glycerine *noun* a colourless, sticky, sweet-tasting liquid.

GMT *abbreviation* Greenwich Mean Time.

GMWU *abbreviation* General and Municipal Workers Union.

gnarled *närld, adjective* knotty, twisted.

gnash *nash, verb* to grind (the teeth).

gnat *nat, noun* a small (blood-sucking) fly, a midge.

gnaw *nö, verb* to bite at with a scraping action.

gnome *nōm, noun* (*myth*) a goblin who lives underground, often guarding treasure.

GNP *abbreviation* gross national product.

gnu *noo, noun* a type of African antelope.

go *verb* (*past tense* **went**, *past participle* **gone**) to move: *Please go home. You go to London*; to leave: *time to go*; to lead: *The road goes north*; to become: *go mad*; to work: *The machine is going at last*; to intend (to do): *I'm going to eat an apple*; to be removed, taken away *etc*: *The food's all gone*; to be given, awarded *etc*: *The prize has gone to John*. – *noun* the act or process of going; energy, spirit; (*coll*) attempt, try; (*coll*) fashion, style. – *adjective* **go-ahead** eager to succeed. – *noun* permission to act. – *noun* **go-between** a person who helps two people to communicate with each other. – *noun* **go-kart** a small low-powered racing car. – **from the word go** from the start; **go about** to try, set about; **go ahead** to proceed, to begin on an action *etc*; **go along with** to agree with; **go back on** to fail to keep (a promise *etc*); **go for** to aim to get; to attack; **go off** to explode; to become rotten; to come to dislike (a person *etc*); **go on** to continue; to talk too much; **go round** to be enough for everyone: *Will the food go round?*; **go steady (with)** to court (a person); **go the whole hog** to do (something) thoroughly; **go under** to be ruined; **on the go** very active.

goad *noun* a sharp-pointed stick for driving oxen *etc*; anything that urges on. – *verb* to urge on by annoying.

goal *noun* the upright posts between which the ball is to be driven in football and other games; a score in football and other games; anything aimed at or wished for.

goat *noun* a type of animal of the sheep family with horns and a long-haired coat.

gobble *verb* to swallow quickly; to make a noise like a turkey.

goblet *noun* (*hist*) a large cup without handles; a drinking glass with a stem.

goblin *noun* (*myth*) a mischievous and ugly spirit.

god (*masculine*), **goddess** (*feminine*) *noun* a being who is worshipped, an idol. – *noun* **God** the creator and ruler of the world in the Christian, Jewish *etc* religions. – *noun* **godfather** (*masculine*), **godmother** (*feminine*) a person who says that he or she will see that a child is brought up according to the beliefs of the Christian Church. – *adjective* **godly** holy, good living. – *noun* **godsend** a very welcome piece of unexpected good fortune. – *noun* **godspeed** a wish for success or for a safe journey.

goggle-eyed *adjective* with staring eyes.

goggles *noun plural* spectacles for protecting the eyes from dust *etc*.

goitre *noun* a swelling in the neck.

gold *noun* an element, a precious yellow metal; riches. – *adjective* of, or like, gold. – *noun* **gold-digger** a woman who views men merely as a source of wealth. – *adjective* **golden** of, or like, gold; very fine. – *noun* **golden wedding** *etc* a 50th anniversary of a wedding *etc*. – *noun* **goldfield** a place where gold is found. – *noun* **goldfinch** a type of small many-coloured bird. – *noun* **goldfish** a kind of golden-yellow Chinese carp, often kept as a pet. – *noun* **gold-leaf** gold beaten to a thin sheet. – *noun* **goldsmith** a maker of gold articles.

golf *noun* a game in which a ball is struck with various clubs. – *noun* **golfer** a person who plays golf. – *noun* **golf club** a club used in golf; a society of players of golf; the place where they meet.

gollywog *noun* a doll with a black face and bristling hair.

golosh *see* **galosh.**

gondola *noun* a boat used on Venice canals; the car suspended from an airship, cable railway *etc*; a unit with shelves for displaying goods in a supermarket *etc*. – *noun* **gondolier** a boatman who rows a gondola.

gone *see* **go.**

gong *noun* a metal plate which, when struck, gives a booming sound, used *eg* to call people to meals.

good *adjective* having the qualities which the speaker wants in the thing or person spoken of: *A good fire will warm us. A good butcher will bone it for you*; virtuous: *a good person*; kind: *She was good to me*; pleasant, enjoyable: *a good time*; large: *a good income.* – *adjective* **good-for-nothing** useless, lazy. – *noun* **good morning, good-day, good afternoon, good evening, good night** or **good-bye** words used as greeting when meeting or leaving someone. – *noun* **good name** (good) reputation. – *adjective* **good-natured** kind, cheerful. – *noun* **goodness** the quality of being good. – *noun plural* **goods** one's belongings; things to be bought and sold. – *noun* **good taste** a feeling for what is right or socially acceptable. – *noun* **goodwill** kind wishes; a good reputation in business.

goose *noun* (*plural* **geese**) a web-footed bird larger than a duck. – *noun plural* **goosepimples** small bumps on the skin caused by cold or fear.

gooseberry *noun* an eatable *usu* green berry.

gore *noun* (a thick mass of) blood; a triangular-shaped piece of cloth in a garment *etc.* – *verb* to pierce with horns, tusks *etc.* – *adjective* **gory** covered with blood; of blood or bloodshed.

gorge *noun* the throat; a narrow valley between hills. – *verb* to swallow greedily till one is full.

gorgeous *adjective* showy, splendid; beautiful, very attractive; (*coll*) excellent, enjoyable, very fine *etc.*

gorgon *noun* (*myth*) a monster whose glance turned people to stone; any very stern-looking person.

gorgonzola *noun* a kind of strong cheese.

gorilla *noun* the largest kind of ape.

gorse *noun* a kind of prickly bush with yellow flowers.

gory *see* **gore**.

gosling *noun* a young goose.

gospel *noun* the teaching of Christ; (*coll*) the absolute truth.

gossamer *noun* fine spider-threads floating in the air or lying on bushes; any very thin material.

gossip *noun* (a person who listens to and passes on) talk, not necessarily true, about someone's personal affairs *etc.* – *verb* to pass on gossip; to chatter.

got *see* **get**.

gouache *goo'ash*, *noun* a kind of paint containing water, gum and honey; a painting done with this paint.

gouge *gowj*, *noun* a chisel with a hollow blade for cutting grooves. – *verb* to scoop (out).

goulash *noun* (*plural* **goulashes**) a stew of meat and vegetables, highly seasoned.

gourd *noun* a large fleshy fruit; the skin of a gourd used as a bottle, cup *etc.*

gourmand *noun* a glutton.

gourmet *goor'mā*, *noun* one with a taste for good wines or food.

gout *noun* a painful swelling of the smaller joints, *esp* of the big toe. – *adjective* **gouty**.

govern *verb* to rule, control; to put into action the laws *etc* of a country. – *noun* **governess** a woman who teaches young children at their home. – *noun* **government** rule; control; the persons who rule and administer the laws of a country. – *noun* **governor** a person who rules.

gown *noun* a woman's dress; a loose robe worn by clergymen, lawyers, teachers *etc.*

GP *abbreviation* general practitioner.

GPO *abbreviation* General Post Office.

grab *verb* (*past tense* **grabbed**) to seize or grasp suddenly; to lay hands on, *esp* by rough or unjust means. – *noun* a sudden grasp or catch.

grace *noun* beauty of form or movement; a short prayer at a meal; the title of a duke or archbishop; favour or mercy: *God's grace.* – *adjective* **graceful** beautiful in appearance; done in a neat way. – *adjective* **gracious** kind, polite. – **with good** (or **bad**) **grace** willingly (or unwillingly).

grade *noun* a step or placing according to quality or rank; class. – *verb* to arrange in order (*eg* from easy to difficult). – *noun* **gradation** arrangement in order (of rank, difficulty *etc*). – *noun* **gradient** a slope (on a road, railway *etc*). – *adjective* **gradual** step by step; going slowly but steadily. – *adverb* **gradually**. – **make the grade** to do as well as is necessary (in a job, examination *etc*).

graduate *verb* to divide into regular spaces; to pass university examinations and receive a degree. – *noun* a person who has done so. – *noun* **graduation** the act of getting a degree from a university.

graffiti *noun plural* words or drawings scratched or painted on a wall *etc*.

graft *verb* to fix a shoot or twig of one plant upon another, so that it may grow there; to fix (skin) from one part of the body upon another part; to transfer (a part of the body) from one person to another; to get illegal profit by graft. – *noun* living tissue (*eg* skin) which is grafted; a shoot *etc* grafted; hard work; profit gained by illegal or unfair means.

Grail *noun* the plate said to be used by Christ at the Last Supper.

grain *noun* a seed (*eg* of wheat, oats); corn in general; a very small quantity; a very small measure of weight; the run of the lines of fibre in wood, leather *etc*. – **against the grain** against (a person's) natural feelings.

gram *see* **gramme**.

grammar *noun* (the study of) the correct use of words in speaking or writing: *His grammar is bad*. – *noun* **grammarian** an expert on grammar. – *noun* **grammar school** a kind of secondary school. – *adjective* **grammatical** correct according to rules of grammar.

gramme or **gram** *noun* the basic unit of weight in the metric system.

gramophone *noun* an older name for a record-player.

granary *noun* (*plural* **granaries**) a storehouse for grain.

grand *adjective* great; noble; fine. – *noun* **grandchild, grand-daughter** or **grandson** one's son's or daughter's child. – *noun* **grand duke** in some countries a duke of specially high rank. – *noun* **grandfather** one's father's or mother's father. – *noun* **grand master** a chess-player of the greatest ability. – *noun* **grandmother** one's father's or mother's mother. – *noun* **grand opera** opera without spoken dialogue. – *noun* **grand piano** a piano with a large flat top. – *noun* **grandstand** rows of raised seats at a sports ground giving a good view.

grandee *noun* a man of high rank.

grandeur *noun* greatness.

grandiloquent *adjective* speaking in a high-sounding language.

grandiose *adjective* planned on a large scale.

granite *noun* a hard rock of greyish or reddish colour.

granny *noun* (*plural* **grannies**) (*coll*) a grandmother.

grant *verb* to give; to allow (something asked for); to admit as true. – *noun* something given (normally money) for a special purpose. – *conjunction* **granted** or **granting** (often with **that**) (even) if, assuming: *granted that you are right*. – **take for granted** to assume (that something will happen) without checking; to treat (a person) casually, without respect or kindness.

granule *noun* a tiny grain or part. – *adjective* **granular** made up of grains. – *adjective* **granulated** broken into grains.

grape *noun* the green or black smooth-skinned berry from which wine is made. – *noun* **grapefruit** a fruit like a large yellow orange. – *noun* **grapeshot** shot which scatters when fired.

graph *noun* line (or lines) drawn on squared paper to show changes in quantity (*eg* in temperature, money spent). – *adjective* **graphic** to do with writing, drawing or painting; vivid, well told. – *noun* a painting, print, illustration or diagram.

graphite *noun* a form of carbon used in making pencils.

grapple *verb* to struggle (with); to try to deal (with a problem *etc*).

grasp *verb* to clasp and grip with the fingers or arms; to understand. – *noun* a grip with one's hand *etc*; one's power of understanding. – *adjective* **grasping** greedy, mean.

grass *noun* (*plural* **grasses**) the plant covering fields of pasture; a kind of plant with long narrow leaves (*eg* wheat, reeds, bamboo). – *noun* **grasshopper** a type of jumping insect. – *noun* **grass-snake** a type of green harmless snake. – *noun* **grass-widow** a woman whose husband is temporarily away. – *adjective* **grassy** covered with grass.

grate *noun* a framework of iron bars for holding a fire. – *verb* to rub down into small pieces; to make a harsh, grinding sound; to irritate. – *noun* **grater** an instrument with a rough surface for rubbing cheese *etc* into small pieces. – *n* **grating** a frame of iron bars.

grateful *adjective* feeling thankful; showing or giving thanks. – *noun* **gratification** pleasure; satisfaction. – *verb*

gratify (*past tense* **gratified**) to please; to satisfy. – *noun* **gratitude** thankfulness; desire to repay kindness shown.

gratis *adverb* for nothing, without payment.

gratuity *noun* (*plural* **gratuities**) a money gift in return for something done, a tip. – *adjective* **gratuitous** uncalled-for, done without good reason or excuse: *a gratuitous insult*.

grave *noun* a pit in which a dead person is buried. – *adjective* serious, important: *grave problems*; not cheerful, dignified, solemn. – *adverb* **gravely**. – *noun* **graveness** or **gravity**. – *noun* **gravestone** a stone placed to mark a grave. – *noun* **graveyard** a place where the dead are buried, a cemetery.

gravel *noun* small stones or pebbles.

graven *adjective* (*old*) carved: *graven images*.

gravity *noun* seriousness, importance: *the gravity of the situation*; seriousness, lack of gaiety, solemnity; weight; the force which attracts things towards earth and causes them to fall to the ground. – *verb* **gravitate** to move towards as if strongly attracted (to). – *noun* **gravitation**.

gravy *noun* (*plural* **gravies**) the juices from meat that is cooking; a sauce made from these.

gray *see* **grey**.

graze *verb* to feed on (growing grass); to scrape the skin of; to touch lightly in passing. – *noun* a scraping of the skin; a light touch. – *noun* **grazing** grass land for animals to graze in.

grease *noun* thick animal fat; oily substance of any kind. – *verb* to smear with grease, apply grease to. – *adjective* **greasy**. – *noun* **greasepaint** a kind of make-up used by actors *etc*.

great *adjective* very large; powerful; very important, distinguished; very talented: *a great singer*; of high rank, noble. – *noun* **greatness**. – *noun* **great-grandchild** the son or daughter of a grandson or granddaughter. – *noun* **great-grandparents** the father and mother of a grandfather or grandmother.

grebe *noun* a fresh-water diving bird.

greed *noun* great and selfish desire (for food, money *etc*). – *adjective* **greedy**. – *noun* **greediness**.

green *adjective* of the colour of growing grass *etc*; without experience; easily fooled; concerned with care of the environment. – *noun* the colour of growing grass; a piece of ground covered with grass; a member of the Green Party, an environmentalist; (*plural*) green vegetables for food. – *noun* **green belt** open land surrounding a city *etc*. – *noun* **greenery** green plants. – *noun* **greenfly** the aphid. – *noun* **greengage** a kind of plum, green but sweet. – *noun* **greengrocer** a person who sells fresh vegetables. – *noun* **greenhouse** a building, *usu* of glass, in which plants are grown. – *noun* **Green Party** a political party concerned with conserving natural resources and decentralizing political and economic power. – **greenhouse effect** the warming-up of the earth's surface due to too much carbon dioxide in the atmosphere; **have green fingers** to be a skilful gardener; **the green light** permission to begin (anything).

greet *verb* to meet a person with kind words; to say 'Hullo,' 'Good-day,' *etc*; to react to, respond to: *They greeted his speech with approval*; to become evident to. – *noun* **greeting** words of welcome or kindness; reaction, response.

gregarious *adjective* living in flocks and herds; liking the company of others.

grenade *noun* a small bomb thrown by hand.

grew *see* **grow**.

grey or **gray** *adjective, noun* (of) a colour between black and white; grey-haired, old. – *noun* grey colour; a grey horse. – *noun* **greyhound** a breed of fast-running dog. – *noun* **grey matter** (*coll*) brains.

grid *noun* a grating of bars; a network of lines, *eg* for helping to find a place on a map; a network of wires carrying electricity through the country. – *noun* **grid-iron** a frame of iron bars for cooking food over a fire.

grief *noun* deep sorrow. – **come to grief** to meet with misfortune.

grieve *verb* to feel sorrow; to make sorrowful. – *noun* **grievance** a cause for complaining. – *adjective* **grievous** painful; serious; causing grief.

griffin or **griffon** *noun* (*myth*) an animal with the body and legs of a lion and the beak and wings of an eagle.

grill *verb* to cook directly under heat (provided by an electric or gas cooker);

to cook on a gridiron over a fire; to question (someone) closely. – *noun* a frame of bars for grilling food on; grilled food; the part of a cooker used for grilling; a restaurant serving grilled food.

grille *noun* a metal grating over a door, window *etc*.

grim *adjective* stern, fierce-looking; terrible; very unpleasant: *a grim sight*; unyielding, stubborn: *grim determination*. – *noun* **grimness**.

grimace *noun* a twisting of the face in fun or pain. – Also *verb*.

grime *noun* dirt. – *adjective* **grimy**.

grin *verb* (*past tense* **grinned**) to smile broadly. – Also *noun*. – **grin and bear it** to suffer something without complaining.

grind *verb* (*past tense* **ground**) to crush to powder; to sharpen by rubbing; to rub together (*eg* the teeth). – *noun* hard or unpleasant work. – *noun* **grinder** a person or thing that grinds. – *noun* **grindstone** a revolving stone for grinding or sharpening tools. – **back to the grindstone** back to work; **keep one's nose to the grindstone** to work, or make someone work, without stopping.

grip *noun* a firm hold, grasp; a way of holding or grasping; control; the handle or part by which anything is held; a travelling bag, a holdall. – *verb* (*past tense* **gripped**) to take a firm hold of.

gripe *noun* a sharp pain in the stomach; a complaint. – *verb* to complain.

grisly *adjective* frightful, hideous.

grist *noun* corn for grinding. – **grist to the mill** something which brings profit or advantage.

gristle *noun* a tough elastic substance in meat. – *adjective* **gristly**.

grit *noun* tiny pieces of stone; courage. – *verb* (*past tense* **gritted**) to apply grit to (*eg* icy roads); to clench (one's teeth). – *adjective* **gritty**.

grizzled *adjective* grey, or mixed with grey. – *adjective* **grizzly** of a grey colour. – *noun* (*plural* **grizzlies**) or **grizzly bear** a type of large bear of N. America.

groan *verb* to utter a moaning sound (in pain, disapproval *etc*); to be loaded: *a table groaning with food*.

groats *noun plural* oat grains without the husks.

grocer *noun* a dealer in certain kinds of food and household supplies. – *noun plural* **groceries** food (sold by grocers).

groggy *adjective* weak and staggering (from blows or illness).

groin *noun* the part of the body where the inner part of the thigh joins the rest of the body.

groom *noun* a person who has charge of horses; a man who is being married (*usu* **bridegroom**). – *verb* to look after (*esp* a horse); to make smart and tidy.

groove *noun* a furrow, a long hollow. – *verb* to cut a groove.

grope *verb* to search (for) by feeling as if blind.

gross *adjective* coarse; very fat; great, obvious: *gross error*; (of sums of money) total, before any deductions (*eg* income tax) are made: *gross profit*. – *noun* the whole taken together; twelve dozen. – *noun* **grossness** coarseness.

grotesque *adjective* very odd or strange-looking.

grotto *noun* (*plural* **grottoes** or **grottos**) a cave.

ground *noun* the surface of the earth; a good reason: *ground(s) for complaint*; (*plural*) lands surrounding a castle, large house *etc*; (*plural*) dregs: *coffee grounds*. – *verb* (of ships) to strike the sea-bed *etc* and remain stuck; to prevent (aeroplanes) from flying; *see* also **grind**. – *adjective* **grounded** (of aeroplanes) unable to fly. – *noun* **ground floor** the storey of a building at street level. – *noun* **groundhog** same as **marmot**. – *noun* **grounding** the first steps in learning something. – *adjective* **groundless** without reason. – *noun* **ground-swell** broad ocean waves. – *noun* **groundwork** the first stages of a task.

groundsel *noun* a type of common wild plant with small yellow flowers.

group *noun* a number of persons or things together. – *verb* to form or gather into a group; to classify.

grouse *noun* (*plural* **grouse**) a kind of game bird hunted on moors and hills); (*plural* **grouses**) a grumble, complaint. – *verb* to grumble, complain.

grove *noun* a small group of trees.

grovel *verb* (*past tense* **grovelled**) to crawl or lie on the ground; to make oneself too humble.

grow *verb* (*past tense* **grew**, *past participle* **grown**) to become bigger or stronger; to become: *grow old*; to rear, cause to grow (plants, trees *etc*). – *noun* **growth** growing; increase; something that grows; something abnormal that grows on the body.

growl *verb* to utter a deep sound like a dog. – Also *noun*.

grown *see* **grow**.

grub *noun* the form of an insect after being hatched from the egg (*eg* a caterpillar); (*coll*) food. – *verb* (*past tense* **grubbed**) to dig. – *adjective* **grubby** dirty. – *noun* **grubbiness**.

grudge *verb* to be unwilling to give, grant, allow *etc*: *I grudge him his success*; to give *etc* unwillingly, with reluctance. – *noun* feeling of resentment: *I bear a grudge against him*.

gruel *noun* a thin mixture of oatmeal boiled in water. – *adjective* **gruelling** very tiring.

gruesome *adjective* horrible.

gruff *adjective* rough in manner; (of voice *etc*) deep and harsh.

grumble *verb* to complain in a bad-tempered, discontented way. – Also *noun*.

grumpy *adjective* cross, badtempered.

grunt *verb* to make a sound like that of a pig. – Also *noun*.

guarantee *noun* a (written) promise (to do something); a statement by the maker that something will work well; money put down which will be given up if a promise is broken. – *verb* to give a guarantee. – *noun* **guarantor** a person who promises to pay if another person fails to keep an agreement to pay.

guard *verb* to keep safe from danger or attack. – *noun* a person or a group of people whose duty it is to protect; something (*eg* a fireguard) which protects from danger; a person in charge of a railway train or coach; a position of defence (in boxing, cricket, fencing *etc*). – *adjective* **guarded** careful. – *noun* **guardian** a person who has the legal right to take care of an orphan; a person who protects or guards.

guava *noun* a type of yellow pear-shaped fruit, or the tree that bears it.

gudgeon *noun* a type of small freshwater fish.

guerrilla *noun* a member of a small band which makes sudden attacks on a larger army but does not fight openly. – *adjective* of a method of fighting in which many small bands acting independently make sudden raids on an enemy.

guess *verb* to say without sure knowledge; to say what is likely to be the case. – Also *noun* (*plural* **guesses**). – *noun* **guesswork** guessing.

guest *noun* a visitor received and entertained in another's house or in a hotel *etc*.

guffaw *verb* to laugh loudly. – Also *noun*.

guide *verb* to show the way to, lead, direct; to influence. – *noun* a person who shows the way (to travellers *etc*); a person who points out interesting things about a place; a book (**guide-book**) telling about a place. – *noun* **Guide** a girl belonging to the Girl Guides organization. – *noun* **guidance** help or advice towards doing something *etc*. – *noun* **guided missile** an explosive rocket which after being fired can be guided to its target by radio waves.

guild *noun* a company or association of persons working in the same trade or profession or sharing the same interests; a name used by some societies or clubs.

guile *noun* cunning, deceit.

guillemot *noun* a type of diving sea-bird.

guillotine *gil'ò-tēn*, *noun* an instrument for beheading (formerly used in France); a machine for cutting paper; the limiting of discussion time in parliament by prearranging voting times. – *verb* to behead with the guillotine; to cut (paper) with a guillotine; to use a parliamentary guillotine on.

guilt *noun* a sense of shame; blame for wrongdoing (*eg* breaking the law). – *adjective* **guilty**.

guinea *noun* (*hist*) a British gold coin; now a word for £1·05, sometimes used in expressing prices, fees *etc*. – *noun* **guinea-fowl** a bird, something like a pheasant, having white-spotted feathers. – *noun* **guinea-pig** a gnawing animal about the size of a rabbit; a person used as the subject of an experiment.

guise *noun* appearance, dress *esp* a disguised or false appearance: *in the guise of a priest*.

guitar *noun* a type of stringed musical instrument.

gulch noun (plural **gulches**) a narrow rocky valley.

gulf noun a large inlet of the sea.

gull see **seagull**.

gullet noun a passage by which food goes down into the stomach.

gullible adjective easily tricked.

gully noun (plural **gullies**) a channel worn by water.

gulp verb to swallow eagerly or in large mouthfuls. – Also noun.

gum noun the firm flesh in which the teeth grow; sticky juice got from some trees and plants; a kind of sweet. – verb (past tense **gummed**) to stick with gum. – adjective **gummy** sticky.

gumption noun good sense.

gun noun any weapon firing bullets or shells. – noun **gunboat** a small warship with heavy guns. – noun **gun-carriage** a wheeled support for a field-gun. – noun **gun dog** a dog trained to fetch birds etc after they have been shot. – noun **gunfire** the firing of guns. – noun **gun-metal** a mixture of copper and tin. – noun **gunpowder** an explosive in powder form. – noun **gun-running** bringing guns into a country illegally. – **stick to one's guns** to keep determinedly to one's opinion.

gunwale or **gunnel**, both gun'l, noun the upper edge of a boat's side.

gurgle verb to flow making a bubbling sound; to make such a sound. – Also noun.

gush verb to flow out in a strong stream; to talk at great length, exaggerating one's emotions, enthusiasms etc: She would gush about her daughter's wedding for hours. – noun (plural **gushes**) a strong or sudden flow.

gusset noun a cornered piece of cloth put into a garment to strengthen part of it.

gust noun a sudden blast (such as wind). – adjective **gusty** windy.

gusto noun enthusiasm.

gut noun a narrow passage in the lower part of the body; animal intestines made for use as violin-strings etc. – verb (past tense **gutted**) to take out the inner parts of: gut a fish; to destroy completely (often by fire): a gutted building.

gutter noun a water channel (on the roof, at the edge of a roadside etc). – noun **gutter press** that part of the press that specializes in sensational journalism. – noun **guttersnipe** a poor child who spends most of his time in the streets.

guttural adjective harsh in sound, as if formed in the throat.

guy noun a steadying rope for a tent etc; an image of Guy Fawkes made of old clothes etc, burned in Britain on 5th November; (coll) a man.

guzzle verb to eat or drink greedily.

gym noun short for **gymnasium** or **gymnastics**.

gymkhana noun a meeting for competitions (often between horse-riders).

gymnasium noun (plural **gymnasiums** or **gymnasia**) a building or room fitted out for physical exercises. – noun **gymnast** one who does gymnastics. – adjective **gymnastic**. – noun plural **gymnastics** exercises to strengthen the body.

gypsum noun a softish chalk-like mineral.

gypsy or **gipsy** noun (plural **gypsies** or **gipsies**) a member of a wandering people; a Romany.

gyrate verb to whirl round. – noun **gyration**. – adjective **gyratory**.

H

haberdashery noun materials for sewing, mending etc. – noun **haberdasher** a person who sells haberdashery.

habit noun something one is used to doing; a person's ordinary behaviour; dress: a monk's habit. – adjective **habitual** usual, formed by habit. – verb **habituate** to make accustomed.

habitable adjective that may be lived in. – noun **habitat** the natural home of an animal or plant. – *noun* **habitation** a dwelling place.

hack *verb* to cut or chop up roughly; to ride on horseback *esp* along ordinary roads. – *noun* a rough cut, gash; a person who does hard work for low pay, *esp* a writer; an ordinary riding horse (kept for hire). – *noun* **hacksaw** a saw for cutting metal.

hackles *noun plural* the feathers on the neck of a farmyard cock; the hair on a dog's neck. – **make someone's hackles rise** to make someone angry.

hackneyed *adjective* (*esp* of sayings *etc*) too much used, not fresh or original. – *noun* **hackney carriage** or **hackney cab** a carriage or taxi let out for hire.

haddock *noun* (*plural* **haddock** or **haddocks**) a small eatable sea-fish.

Hades *noun* (*myth*) the dwelling place of the dead, hell.

hadj *noun* a Muslim pilgrimage to Mecca.

haemoglobin or (*US*) **hemoglobin,** both *hē-mō-glō'bin*, *noun* the oxygen-carrying substance in the red blood cells.

haemorrhage or (*US*) **hemorrhage,** both *hem'òr-ij*, *noun* bleeding, *esp* in great quantity.

haft *noun* a handle (of a knife *etc*).

hag *noun* an ugly old woman; a witch.

haggard *adjective* thin-faced, hollow-eyed *etc*, with tiredness.

haggis *noun* (*plural* **haggises**) a Scottish food made from the chopped-up heart, lungs and liver of a sheep and cooked in a sheep's stomach.

haggle *verb* to argue in a determined way (*esp* over a price).

ha-ha *noun* a sunken fence.

hail *verb* to greet, welcome; to call to. – *noun* a call from a distance; greeting; welcome; frozen raindrops; a shower (*eg* of bullets, things thrown *etc*). – *verb* to shower with hail: *It's hailing*; to pour down: *Arrows hailed down.* – *noun* **hailstone** a piece of hail. – **hail from** to come from, belong to (a place).

hair *noun* a thread-like growth on the skin of an animal; the whole mass of these (as on the head). – *noun* **hair-breadth** or **hair's-breadth** a very small distance. – *noun* **hair-dresser** a person who cuts, washes and sets hair. – *adjective* **hair-raising** causing great fear. – *noun* **hair-spring** a very fine spring in a watch *etc*.

– *adjective* **hairy** covered with hair. – **split hairs** to be very particular over unimportant details.

hake *noun* a kind of eatable sea-fish something like a cod.

halberd *noun* (*hist*) a battleaxe fixed on a long pole. – *noun* **halberdier** a soldier armed with a halberd.

halcyon *hal'si-òn*: **halcyon days** a time of peace and happiness.

hale: **hale and hearty** healthy.

half *noun* (*plural* **halves**) one of two equal parts. – *adjective* being one of two equal parts; not full or complete: *She bought a half bottle of wine. He gave a half smile.* – *adverb* partly, to some extent. – *noun* **half-breed** or **half-caste** a person having father and mother of different races, *esp* white and black. – *noun plural* **half-brothers** or **half-sisters** brothers or sisters sharing only one parent. – *noun* **half-crown** (*hist*) a coin in old British money of the value of two shillings and sixpence (12½ pence). – *adjective* **half-hearted** not eager. – *noun* **half-life** the time in which the radioactivity of a substance falls to half its original value. – *adverb* **half-mast** (of flags) hoisted half-way up the mast to show that some well-known person has died. – *noun* **halfpenny** *hā'pni*, (*hist*) a coin worth half of a penny. – *noun* **half-time** in sport, a short rest half-way through a game. – *adverb, adjective* **half-way** at or of a point equally far from the beginning and the end (of a distance, journey, period of time, task *etc*). – *adjective* **half-witted** weak in the mind.

halibut *noun* a kind of large eatable flatfish.

halitosis *noun* bad breath.

hall *noun* a passage or large room at the entrance to a house; a large public room; a large country house, the home of a squire or landowner. – *noun* **hallmark** a mark put on gold and silver articles to show the quality of the gold or silver; any mark which shows that a thing is good.

hallo *see* **hello.**

hallow *verb* to make holy; to set apart for holy use. – *noun* **Hallowe'en** the evening of October 31st, when witches and spirits are supposed to be around.

hallucination *noun* the seeing of something that is not really there: *He had hallucinations after he took the drugs.* –

adjective **hallucinatory** causing hallucinations.

halo *noun* (*plural* **haloes** or **halos**) a circle of light round the sun or moon or around a person's head (as in the pictures of a saint).

halt *verb* to come or bring to a stop; to be lame, limp; to hesitate, be uncertain. – *adjective* lame. – *noun* a stop, standstill; stopping place. – *adverb* **haltingly** hesitantly.

halter *noun* a head-rope for holding and leading a horse.

halve *verb* to cut, divide in two.

halyard *noun* a rope for raising or lowering a sail or flag.

ham *noun* the thigh of a pig salted and dried; the back of the thigh; (*coll*) an amateur radio operator. – *noun* **hamburger** a round cake of minced beef, usually fried. – *adjective* **ham-fisted** clumsy.

hamlet *noun* a small village.

hammer *noun* a tool for beating or breaking hard substances or driving nails; a striking piece in a clock, piano, pistol *etc*. – *verb* to drive or shape with a hammer; to defeat overwhelmingly. – **hammer and tongs** violently.

hammock *noun* a length of netting, canvas *etc* hung up by the corners, and used as a bed.

hamper *verb* to hinder. – *noun* a large basket with a lid.

hamster *noun* a kind of animal, similar to a rat, with large cheek pouches.

hamstring *noun* a tendon at the back of the knee. – *verb* to lame by cutting this; to make ineffective or powerless.

hand *noun* the part of the human body at the end of the arm; a pointer (*eg* of a clock); help: *lend a hand*; a measure (four inches, 10·16 centimetres) used for measuring the height of horses; a workman; one's style of handwriting; side or direction: *left-hand side*; a set of playing-cards dealt to a person; clapping, applause: *a big hand*. – *verb* to pass (something) with the hand; (with **over**) to give. – *noun* **handbag** a small bag carried by women for personal belongings. – *noun* **handbill** a small printed notice. – *noun* **handbook** a small book giving information or directions (a guidebook). – *noun plural* **handcuffs** steel bands, joined by a

short chain, put round the wrists of prisoners. – *noun* **handful** as much as can be held in one hand; a small amount. – *noun* **handhold** something which the hand can grip (*eg* in climbing). – *adjective* **hand-picked** chosen carefully. – *adjective* **hands-on** operated by hand; involving practical experience, knowledge or method of working. – *adjective* **hand-to-mouth** (of an existence *etc*) with barely enough to live on and nothing to spare. – *noun* **handwriting** writing with pen or pencil. – **at hand** near by; **hand-to-hand fighting** fighting in which those involved are in close contact with each other; **in hand** in one's possession: *cash in hand*; in preparation; under control; **out of hand** out of control; at once.

handicap *noun* something that makes doing something more difficult; (in a race, competition *etc*) a disadvantage (*eg* having to run a greater distance in a race) given to the best competitors so that others have a better chance of winning; the race, competition *etc*; a physical or mental disability. – Also *verb*. – *adjective* **handicapped** having or given a handicap; physically or mentally disabled.

handicraft *noun* skilled work done by hand, not machine.

handiwork *noun* thing(s) made by hand; work done by, or a result of the action of a particular person *etc*: *This is the handiwork of a vandal*.

handkerchief *noun* a cloth for wiping the nose *etc*.

handle *verb* to touch, hold or use with the hand; to manage, cope with. – *noun* that part of anything meant to be held in the hand. – *noun plural* **handlebars** (on a bicycle) a bar at the front with a handle at each end, used for steering.

handsome *adjective* good-looking; generous: *a handsome gift*.

handy *adjective* useful or convenient to use; easily reached, near; clever with the hands. – *noun* **handiness**. – *noun* **handyman** a man who does odd jobs.

hang *verb* (*past tense* **hung**) to fix or be fixed to some point off the ground *esp* with string *etc*; to remain more or less still in the air (*eg* of a hawk, a cloud); (with **down**) to droop, fall or incline downwards; to depend (on); to attach wall-paper to a wall; (*past tense* **hanged**) to put a criminal to death by putting a rope round his neck and letting him fall. – *adjective* **hangdog** guilty-looking. – *noun* **hanger** that on which a coat *etc* is hung. – *noun* **hanger-on** (*plural* **hangers-on**) one who stays near someone in the hope of gaining some advantage. – *noun* **hang-gliding** a sport in which one hangs in a harness under a large kite. – *noun* **hanging** the killing of a criminal by hanging. – *noun* **hangman** the man who hangs criminals. – *noun* **hangover** uncomfortable after-effects of being drunk; something remaining (from). – **get the hang of** to understand, learn how to use; **hang about** or **around** to remain near, loiter; **hang back** to hesitate; **hang fire** to delay.

hangar *noun* a shed for aeroplanes.

hank *noun* a coil or loop of string, rope, wool *etc*.

hanker *verb* to long for.

hankie or **hanky** *noun* (*plural* **hankies**) short for **handkerchief**.

hansom-cab *noun* a light two-wheeled cab with the driver's seat raised behind.

haphazard *adjective* depending on chance, without planning or system. – Also *adverb*.

hapless *adjective* unlucky.

happen *verb* to take place; to occur by chance; to chance to do: *I happened to find him.* – *noun* **happening** an event.

happy *adjective* (*comparative* **happier**, *superlative* **happiest**) joyful; contented; lucky: *a happy chance*; willing: *happy to help.* – *adverb* **happily**. – *noun* **happiness**. – *adjective* **happy-go-lucky** easy-going, taking things as they come.

hara-kiri *noun* suicide as practised in Japan in earlier times.

harangue *noun* an intense, rousing speech (to a crowd). – Also *verb*.

harass *verb* to annoy (often); to make sudden attacks on. – *noun* **harassment**.

harbinger *noun* a sign of something to come: *harbinger of spring*.

harbour *noun* a place of shelter for ships; any place of shelter or safety. – *verb* to give shelter or refuge; to store (*eg* unkind thoughts) in the mind.

hard *adjective* solid, firm; not easily broken or put out of shape; not easy to do, understand *etc*; not easy to please;

not easy to bear; having no kind or gentle feelings; (of water) containing many minerals and so not lathering well when soap is added; (of drugs) habit-forming. – *adverb* strongly, violently. – *verb* **harden** to make hard. – *adjective* **hard-headed** clever, shrewd. – *adjective* **hard-hearted** having no kind feelings. – *adjective* **hard hit** hurt, badly affected (as by a loss of money). – *noun* **hard labour** tiring work given to prisoners as part of their punishment. – *adverb* **hardly** scarcely; only just; with difficulty. – *noun* **hardness** the state of being hard. – *noun* **hardship** something not easy to bear (*eg* cold, lack of money). – *noun* **hard shoulder** the surfaced strip on the outer edges of a motorway, used when stopping in an emergency. – *adjective* **hard up** short of money. – *noun* **hardware** goods such as pots and pans; equipment (machinery, weapons *etc*); part or parts of a computer (*see* **software**). – *noun* **hardwood** the wood of certain trees (as oak, ash, elm *etc*). – **hard and fast** (*esp* of rules) strict; **hard of hearing** rather deaf.

hardy *adjective* daring, brave; strong, tough. – *noun* **hardiness**.

hare *noun* a type of fast-running animal, like a large rabbit. – *noun* **harebell** a plant with blue, bell-shaped flowers. – *adjective* **hare-brained** careless about what one does; mad, foolish. – *noun* **hare-lip** a split in the upper lip at birth, like that of a hare.

harem *hār'èm*, *noun* the women's rooms in an Islamic house; the women who occupy these.

haricot *har'i-kō*, *noun* a type of bean.

hark! *interjection* listen! – **hark back** to refer back to what was being spoken of earlier.

harlequin *noun* a comic character in a dress of several colours, in a pantomime or comedy.

harm *noun* hurt; damage. – *verb* to cause damage; to do a wrong to. – *adjective* **harmful**. – *adjective* **harmless**.

harmony *noun* (*plural* **harmonies**) agreement of one part, colour or sound with another; agreement between people: *living in harmony*. – *adjective* **harmonic** having to do with harmony. – *noun* **harmonica** a mouth organ. – *adjective* **harmonious** pleasant-sounding; peaceful, without disagreement. – *noun* **harmonium** a type of musical wind instrument like a small organ. – verb **harmonize** to be in, or bring into, harmony; to agree, go well (with); (in music) to add the different parts to a melody.

harness noun the leather and other fittings for a horse at work; an arrangement of straps etc for attaching a piece of equipment to the body: a parachute harness. – verb to put harness on a horse; to use (a source of power etc) for a special purpose. – **in harness** working, not on holiday or retired.

harp noun a musical instrument played by plucking the strings with the fingers. – noun **harpist**. – **harp on** to talk too much about.

harpoon noun a spear tied to rope, used for killing whales. – verb to strike with a harpoon.

harpsichord noun a kind of musical instrument something like a piano.

harpy noun (plural **harpies**) (myth) a monster with the body of a woman, and the wings, feet and claws of a bird of prey; a cruel woman.

harrier noun a breed of small dog for hunting hares; a kind of bird of prey; a cross-country runner.

harrow noun a frame with iron spikes for breaking up lumps of earth in ploughed land. – verb to drag a harrow over; to distress greatly. – adjective **harrowing** very distressing.

harry verb (past tense **harried**) to plunder, lay waste (an area, country etc); to harass, worry (a person).

harsh adjective rough, bitter; cruel. – noun **harshness**.

hart noun the stag or male deer, esp from the age of six years.

hartebeest or **hartbeest** noun a type of S. African antelope.

harvest noun the time of the year when the ripened crops are gathered in; the crops gathered at this time. – verb to gather in (a crop). – noun **harvester** a person or machine that harvests; a kind of creature like a spider. – noun **harvest home** the feast held when the harvest is gathered in.

hash noun a dish of chopped meat etc. – **make a hash of** to spoil completely.

hashish noun the strongest form of the drug made from hemp.

hasp noun a clasp (of a padlock etc).

hassle verb to cause problems for. – noun difficulty, trouble.

hassock noun a thick cushion used as a footstool or for kneeling on.

haste noun speed, hurry. – verb **hasten** to hurry (on); to drive forward. – adjective **hasty** hurried; done without thinking. – adverb **hastily**. – **make haste** to hurry.

hat noun a kind of covering for the head. – noun **hatter** a person who makes or sells hats. – noun **hat-trick** (in cricket) the putting out of three batsmen by three balls in a row; (in football etc) three goals scored by the same player; any action performed three times in a row. – **keep (something) under one's hat** to keep secret.

hatch noun (plural **hatches**) (the door or cover of) an opening in a floor, wall etc. – verb to produce young from eggs; to form and set working a plan (usu evil); to shade (part of a picture etc) with fine lines. – noun **hatchback** a car with a sloping rear door which opens upwards. – noun **hatchery** (plural **hatcheries**) a place for hatching eggs (esp of fish). – noun **hatchway** an opening in a floor or ship's deck.

hatchet noun a small axe. – adjective **hatchet-faced** thin-faced, with sharp features. – **bury the hatchet** to put an end to a quarrel.

hate verb to dislike very much. – noun great dislike. – adjective **hateful** causing hatred. – noun **hatred** extreme dislike.

haughty adjective proud, looking on others with scorn. – noun **haughtiness**.

haul verb to drag, pull with force. – noun a strong pull; (coll) a difficult or tiring job: a long haul; that which is caught at one pull: a haul of fish; a rich find, booty. – noun **haulage** (money charged for) the carrying of goods.

haunch noun (plural **haunches**) the fleshy part of the hip; a leg and loin of meat (esp venison).

haunt verb to visit often; (of a ghost) to stay about a place: A ghost haunts this house. – noun a place often visited. – adjective **haunted** inhabited by ghosts.

have verb (past tense **had**) used with another verb to show that an action is in the past and completed: I have bought a shirt; to own or possess: I have a fur coat; to hold, contain: This house has *three bedrooms*; to give birth to: *to have a baby*; to suffer from: *to have a cold*; to cause (to be done): *have your hair cut*; to put up with: *I won't have her being so rude*. – **have done with** to finish; **have it out** to settle (as an argument).

haven *noun* a safe harbour; a place of safety.

haversack *noun* a bag made of canvas *etc* with shoulder-strap, for carrying food *etc*.

havoc *noun* great destruction.

haw *see* **hawthorn**.

hawk *noun* a bird of prey of the falcon kind. – *verb* to hunt birds with trained hawks; to carry goods about for sale. – *noun* **hawker** a door-to-door salesman.

hawthorn *noun* a type of prickly tree, with white flowers and small red berries (**haws**).

hay *noun* grass, cut and dried, used as cattle food. – *noun* **hay-cock** a pile of hay in a field. – *noun* **hay-fever** an illness like a bad cold caused by pollen *etc*. – *noun* **hay-fork** a long-handled fork used in turning and lifting hay. – *noun* **hayrick** or **haystack** hay built up into a house-like block. – *adjective* **haywire** tangled, in a state of disorder.

hazard *noun* chance; risk of harm or danger. – *verb* to risk; to put forward (a guess *etc*) at the risk of being wrong. – *adjective* **hazardous** dangerous, risky.

haze *noun* a thin mist. – *adjective* **hazy** misty; not clear, vague. – *noun* **haziness**.

hazel *noun* a type of light-brown nut, or the tree that bears it.

he *pronoun* some male person or animal already spoken about (used only as the subject of a verb): *He ate a banana*.

head *noun* the uppermost part of the body, containing the brain, jaw *etc*; the chief part, place or person. – *verb* to lead; to go in front of; to go in the direction of: *They headed for home*; to hit (a ball) with the head; (with **off**) to turn aside: *head off an attack*. – *noun* **headache** a pain in the head; a worrying problem. – *noun* **headband** a band worn round the head. – *noun* **headboard** a board across the top end of a bed. – *noun* **headdress** a covering for the head. – *noun* **header** a dive, head first. – *adverb* **headfirst** with the head first; rashly, without thinking. – *noun*

heading that which stands at the head (such as the title of a book or chapter). – *noun* **headland** a point of land running out into the sea, a cape. – *noun* **headlight** a strong light on the front of a motor car *etc*. – *noun* **headline** a line in large letters at the top of a page in a newspaper *etc*. – *adjective, adverb* **headlong** with the head first; without stopping; without thought. – *noun* **headmaster** (*masculine*) or **headmistress** (*feminine*) or **head-teacher** the principal teacher of a school. – *adjective, adverb* **head-on** with the head or front first. – *noun plural* **headphones** a listening device that fits over the ears. – *noun* **headquarters** place from which the chief officers of an army *etc* control their operations; the chief office (of a business *etc*). – *noun* **headstone** a gravestone. – *adjective* **headstrong** determined to do as one likes. – *noun* **headway** forward movement. – *noun* **headwind** a wind blowing straight in one's face. – *adjective* **heady** exciting. – **head over heels** in a somersault; completely, thoroughly.

heal *verb* to make or become healthy or sound, cure. – *noun* **health** the state of one's body *etc*; soundness of body *etc*; a wish (said while drinking) that someone may have good health. – *adjective* **healthy** in good health or condition; encouraging good health.

heap *noun* a pile of things thrown one on top of another; a great many (of). – *verb* to throw in a pile.

hear *verb* (*past tense* **heard**) to receive (sounds, news, music) by the ear; to listen to. – *noun* **hearing** the act or power of listening; a court case. – *noun* **hearsay** what one hears people say, rumour. – **Hear! Hear!** a cry to show agreement with a speaker; **will not hear of** will not allow: *He would not hear of her going home alone*.

hearse *noun* a car for carrying a dead body to the grave.

heart *noun* the part of the body which acts as a blood pump; the inner or chief part of anything; courage; eagerness; one of the signs on playing-cards. – *noun* **heartache** sorrow. – *adjective* **heartbroken** very upset, very sad. – *noun* **heartburn** a burning feeling in the chest after eating, indigestion. – *verb* **hearten** to cheer on, encourage. – *noun* **heart-failure** (death caused by) the sudden stopping of the heart's beating. – *adjective* **heartfelt** felt deeply, sincere.

– *adjective* **heartless** cruel. – *adjective* **hearty** strong, healthy; (of a meal) large; done eagerly; over-cheerful. – *adverb* **heartily.**

hearth *noun* (the floor of) the fireplace.

heat *noun* (high) temperature; anger; a division or round in a competition, race *etc*. – *verb* to make or become hot. – *noun* **heat wave** a period of hot weather. – **in heat** (of female animals) ready for mating in the breeding season.

heath *noun* barren, open country; heather.

heathen *noun* a person who does not believe in God, *esp* one who worships idols. – Also *adjective.*

heather *noun* a plant with small purple or white flowers growing on moorland. – *adjective* of the colour of purple heather.

heave *verb* to lift by force; to throw; to rise and fall; to produce, let out (*esp* a sigh). – Also *noun.*

heaven *noun* the sky (often in *plural*); the dwelling place of (the Christian) God; the place of reward of the good after death; any place of great happiness. – *adjective* **heavenly** dwelling in heaven; (*coll*) delightful. – **heavenly bodies** the sun, moon and stars.

heavy *adjective* of great weight; great in amount, force *etc*: *heavy rainfall*; not easy to bear; slow; sleepy. – *adverb* **heavily.** – *noun* **heaviness.** – *noun* **heavy metal** a very loud repetitive form of rock music. – Also *adjective.*

heckle *verb* (in an election) to ask awkward questions of a public speaker. – *noun* **heckler** a person who heckles.

hectare *noun* 10 000 square metres.

hectic *adjective* rushed; feverish.

hector *verb* to bully.

hedge *noun* a fence of bushes, shrubs *etc*. – *verb* to make a hedge; to shut in with a hedge; to avoid giving a straight answer. – *noun* **hedgehog** a small prickly-backed animal. – *noun* **hedgerow** a row of bushes forming a hedge.

heed *verb* to give attention to, listen to. – *adjective* **heedless** careless. – **pay heed to** to take notice of.

heel *noun* the back part of the foot. – *verb* to hit (*esp* a ball) with the heel; to put a heel on (a shoe); (of ships) to lean over. – **take to one's heels** or **show a clean pair of heels** to run away.

hefty *adjective* (of persons) powerful, muscular; heavy.

Hegira *noun* the Muslim era, dating from AD 622.

heifer *hef'èr, noun* a young cow.

height *noun* the state of being high; distance from bottom to top; the highest point; (often *plural*) a high place. – *verb* **heighten** to make higher.

heinous *hā'nŭs, adjective* very wicked: *a heinous crime.*

heir (*masculine*), **heiress** (*feminine*) *noun* a person who by law receives a title or property on the death of the owner. – *noun* **heir-apparent** a person who is expected to receive a title or property when the present holder dies. – *noun* **heirloom** something that has been handed down in the family from generation to generation.

held *see* **hold.**

helicopter *noun* a flying machine kept in the air by propellers rotating on a vertical axis.

heliograph *noun* a means of signalling, using the sun's rays.

heliotrope *noun* a plant with small, sweet-smelling, lilac-blue flowers; a light purple colour.

helium *noun* an element, a very light gas.

hell *noun* in some religions, the place of punishment of the wicked after death; the dwelling place of the Devil; any place of great misery or pain. – *adjective* **hellish.** – **hellbent on** determined to.

hello or **hallo** or **hullo** *noun* (*plural* **hellos** or **helloes** *etc*) a greeting used between people: *I said hello to him. Hello! How are you?*

helm *noun* the wheel or handle by which a ship is steered. – *noun* **helmsman** the person who steers.

helmet *noun* an armoured or protective covering for the head.

help *verb* to aid, do something necessary or useful for; to give the means for doing something to; to stop oneself from (doing): *I cannot help liking him.* – *noun* aid, assistance; a person who assists. – *adjective* **helpful** useful, able to help. – *noun* **helping** a share (of food). – *adjective* **helpless** useless; powerless. – *noun* **helpmate** a partner. – **help oneself** serve oneself (with food).

helter-skelter *adverb* in a great hurry, in confusion. – *noun* a spiral slide in a fairground *etc.*

hem *noun* the border of a garment doubled down and stitched. – *verb* (*past tense* **hemmed**) to put or form a hem on; (with **in**) to surround.

hemisphere *noun* a half of the earth or a map of it: *western* or *eastern, northern* or *southern hemisphere*. – *adjective* **hemispherical** like half a ball in shape.

hemlock *noun* a type of poisonous plant.

hemoglobin *see* **haemoglobin**.

hemorrhage *see* **haemorrhage**.

hemp *noun* a type of plant used for making ropes, bags, sails *etc* and the drug cannabis.

hen *noun* a female bird; a female domestic fowl. – *verb* **henpeck** (of a wife) to worry (a husband) into always giving way.

hence *adverb* from this place or time: *ten years hence*; for this reason: *Hence, I shall have to stay.* – *adverb* **henceforth** or **henceforward** from now on.

henchman *noun* a follower; a servant.

henna *noun* a reddish dye taken from a plant for colouring the hair *etc*.

heptagon *noun* a seven-sided figure. – *adjective* **heptagonal**.

her *pronoun* a female person already spoken about (used only as the object in a sentence): *He helps her.* – *adjective* belonging to such a person: *her house.* – *pronoun* **hers**: *This house is hers.* – *pronoun* **herself** used reflexively: *She washed herself*; used for emphasis: *She herself won't be there but her brother will.*

herald *noun* something that is a sign of future things; (*hist*) a person who carries and reads important notices. – *verb* to announce loudly; to be a sign of. – *adjective* **heraldic** of heraldry. – *noun* **heraldry** the study of coats of arms, badges, crests *etc*.

herb *noun* a plant used in the making of medicines or in cooking. – *adjective* **herbaceous** (of a plant) with a stem which dies every year; (of a flower-bed) (to be) filled with such plants. – *adjective* **herbal** of or using herbs: *herbal remedy*. – *noun* **herbalist** a person who sells herbs used in cooking or medicine. – *adjective* **herbivorous** eating or living on grass *etc*.

Herculean *adjective* needing or showing great strength *etc*; very strong.

herd *noun* a group of animals of one kind; (with **the**) most people. – *verb* to treat or group together like a herd of animals.

here *adverb* at, in or to this place: *He's here already. Come here!* – *adverb* **hereabouts** approximately in this place. – *adverb* **hereafter** after this. – *adverb* **hereby** by this means. – **the hereafter** life after death.

heredity *noun* the passing on of qualities (appearance, intelligence *etc*) from parents to children. – *adjective* **hereditary** passed on in this way.

heresy *her'i-si, noun* (*plural* **heresies**) an opinion which goes against the official (*esp* religious) view. – *noun* **heretic** a person who holds or teaches such an opinion. – *adjective* **heretical**.

heritage *noun* something passed on by or inherited from an earlier generation, a parent *etc*.

hermaphrodite *hèr-maf'rō-dīt, noun* an animal which has the qualities of both male and female sexes.

hermetically: hermetically sealed closed completely and airtight.

hermit *noun* a person who lives alone (*esp* for religious reasons). – *noun* **hermitage** the dwelling of a hermit. – *noun* **hermit crab** a kind of crab which lives in the abandoned shell of a shellfish.

hernia *noun* the bursting out of (part of) a bodily organ through an opening or weak spot in the surrounding tissue.

hero (*masculine*) (*plural* **heroes**), **heroine** (*feminine*) *noun* a person admired (by many) for brave deeds; the chief person in a story *etc*. – *adjective* **heroic** brave as a hero; of heroes. – *noun* **heroism** bravery.

heroin *noun* a drug derived from morphine.

heron *noun* a type of large water bird, with long legs and neck.

herpes *noun* a name for various types of a skin disease.

herring *noun* (*plural* **herring** or **herrings**) an eatable sea fish.

hers, herself *see* **her**.

hertz *noun* a unit of frequency, used of radio waves *etc*.

hesitate *verb* to pause because of uncertainty; to be unwilling (to do something). – *noun* **hesitancy**. – *adjective* **hesitant**. – *noun* **hesitation**.

hessian noun a type of coarse cloth.

het: het up (coll) excited.

hew verb (past tense **hewed**, past participle **hewed** or **hewn**) to cut with blows; to shape with blows.

hexagon noun a six-sided figure. – adjective **hexagonal**.

heyday noun the time of greatest strength, the prime.

HGV abbreviation heavy goods vehicle.

hibernate verb to pass the winter in rest, as some animals do. – noun **hibernation**. – noun **hibernator**.

hiccup or **hiccough** noun a sharp gasp, caused by laughing, eating, drinking; (plural) a fit of such gasping. – Also verb.

hickory noun (plural **hickories**) a N. American tree.

hide verb (past tense **hid**, past participle **hidden**) to put or keep out of sight. – noun a place of hiding from which birds etc are watched; the skin of an animal. – adjective **hidden** out of sight; unknown. – adjective **hidebound** (of persons etc) not open to new ideas. – noun **hiding** a thrashing.

hideous adjective frightful; very ugly.

hierarchy hī'èr-är-ki, n a number of things or persons arranged in order of rank.

hieroglyphics hī-èr-ō-glif'iks, noun plural ancient Egyptian writing, in which pictures are used as letters; writing difficult to read.

hi-fi adjective short for **high fidelity**. – noun (coll) (high quality) equipment for reproducing recorded sound.

higgledy-piggledy adverb, adjective in great disorder.

high adjective raised far above; of (great) extent upward, tall; well up on any scale of measurement, judgement, rank etc; great, large: We have high hopes for her. Those high prices are due to shortages; (of sound) shrill, acute in pitch; (of food, esp meat) beginning to go bad. – adverb far above in the air; well up on any scale; to a high degree. – noun **highball** (US) liquor and an effervescent drink (e.g. whisky and soda) with ice in a tall glass. – adjective **high-born** of noble birth. – noun **highbrow** a person of intellectual tastes. – Also adjective. – noun **High Court** a supreme court. – adjective **high-explosive** (of shells, bombs) causing great damage. – adjective **high fidelity** reproducing sound very clearly. – adjective **high-flown** (of language, style) using words that sound too grand or pompous. – adjective **high-handed** (of actions) done without thought for others. – noun **Highlander** one who comes from the Highlands. – noun **highlight** a bright spot or area in a picture; a colour (in hair etc) made obvious by bright light; (most) memorable event or experience. – adverb **highly** very: highly delighted; in a high position or degree. – adjective **highly-strung** nervous, easily excited. – noun **highness** height. – noun **Highness** a title of a king etc. – noun **highroad** a main road. – adjective **high-spirited** bold, lively. – noun **high tea** a cooked meal in the late afternoon. – noun **high tide** or **high water** the time when the tide is farthest up the shore. – noun **high treason** the crime of acting against the safety of one's own country. – noun **highway** the public road. – noun **highwayman** (hist) a robber who attacks people on the public road. – **Highway Code** a set of official rules for road users in Britain; **the Highlands** a mountainous region, esp the north of Scotland; **the high seas** the open seas.

hijack verb to steal (a car, aeroplane etc) while it is moving; to force the driver or pilot (of a vehicle) to head for a place chosen by the **hijacker**. – Also noun.

hike verb to travel on foot. – Also noun. – noun **hiker**.

hilarious adjective very funny; very merry. – noun **hilarity**.

hill noun a mound of high land, less high than a mountain. – adjective **hilly**.

hillock noun a small hill.

hilt noun the handle, esp of a sword. – **up to the hilt** thoroughly, completely.

him pronoun a male person already spoken about (used only as the object in a sentence): Help him. What did you say to him? – pronoun **himself** used reflexively: He has cut himself; used for emphasis: He himself could not do the job but his friend could.

hind noun a female deer. – adjective placed behind. – adjective **hindmost** farthest behind. – noun **hindsight** wisdom or knowledge got only after something has happened.

hinder verb to keep back, delay, prevent. – noun **hindrance** something that hinders.

hinge *noun* a joint on which a door, lid *etc* turns. – *verb* to move on a hinge; to depend (on): *Everything hinges on the weather*.

hint *noun* a mention which suggests one meaning without stating it clearly; a slight impression, or one not clearly stated: *a hint of fear in his words*. – Also *verb*: *He hinted that he might go*.

hinterland *noun* the district lying inland from the coast.

hip *noun* the part of the side of the body just below the waist; the fruit of the (wild) rose.

hippopotamus *noun* (*plural* **hippopotami** or **hippopotamuses**) a large African animal living in and near rivers.

hire *noun* money paid for work done, or for the use of something belonging to another person. – *verb* to give or get the use of something by paying money. – *noun* **hire-purchase** a way of buying an article by paying for it in weekly or monthly parts or instalments.

hirsute *hûr'sūt, adjective* hairy, shaggy.

his *adjective* belonging to him: *his book*. – *pronoun* : *This book is his*.

hiss *verb* to make a sound like a snake. – *noun* (*plural* **hisses**) such a sound, made to show anger or displeasure.

history *noun* (*plural* **histories**) the study of the past; a description in speech or (*esp*) writing of past events, ways of living *etc*. – *noun* **historian** a person who writes history. – *adjective* **historic** important, likely to be remembered. – *adjective* **historical** of history; true of something in the past.

histrionic *adjective* having to do with stage-acting or actors. – *noun plural* **histrionics** a dramatically exaggerated display of strong feeling.

hit *verb* (*present participle* **hitting**, *past tense* **hit**) to strike with a blow *etc*; (with **upon**) to come upon, discover. – *noun* a blow; a stroke; a shot which hits a target; a success (*esp* a successful song, recording, play *etc*). – *noun* **hit parade** (*old*) (weekly) list of best-selling records (see **top ten**).

hitch *verb* to fasten (by a hook *etc*); to lift with a jerk; to hitch-hike. – *noun* (*plural* **hitches**) a jerk; an unexpected stop or delay; one of several kinds of knot. – *verb* **hitch-hike** to travel by relying on lifts in other people's vehicles. – *noun* **hitch-hiker**.

hither *adverb* to this place. – *adverb* **hitherto** up till now. – **hither and thither** back and forwards.

HIV *abbreviation* human immuno-deficiency virus.

hive *noun* place where bees live; a busy place: *hive of industry*.

HM *abbreviation* Her or His Majesty.

HMS *abbreviation* Her or His Majesty's Ship or Service.

HMSO *abbreviation* Her or His Majesty's Stationery Office.

hoard *noun* a (hidden) store (of treasure, food *etc*). – *verb* to store up (in secret).

hoarding *noun* a fence of boards.

hoarse *adjective* having a harsh voice, as from a cold or cough.

hoary *adjective* white with age; of great age. – *noun* **hoar-frost** white frost.

hoax *noun* (*plural* **hoaxes**) a trick played to deceive people. – *verb* to play a hoax on.

hob *noun* the top of an electric *etc* stove; an appliance heated by electricity *etc*, on which cooking pots are placed for heating; a small shelf next to a fireplace on which pans *etc* may be kept hot.

hobble *verb* to walk with difficulty with short steps. – Also *noun*.

hobby *noun* (*plural* **hobbies**) a favourite way of passing one's spare time. – *noun* **hobby-horse** a wooden horse on rockers or in a merry-go-round; a favourite subject, which one continually talks about.

hobgoblin *noun* (*myth*) a mischievous fairy.

hobnail *noun* a big-headed nail used for horseshoes and in the soles of heavy boots.

hobnob *verb* (*past tense* **hobnobbed**) to be on very friendly terms (with).

hobo *noun* (*plural* **hoboes**) a tramp.

hock *noun* a kind of white wine; a joint on the hind leg of an animal, below the knee.

hockey *noun* an eleven-a-side ball game played with clubs curved at one end.

hocus-pocus *noun* a juggler's trick; deception, trickery.

hod *noun* a wooden trough on a pole, for carrying bricks and mortar; a container for coal.

hoe *noun* a tool used for weeding, loosening earth *etc.* – *verb* to use a hoe.

hog *noun* a pig. – *verb* (*past tense* **hogged**) (*coll*) to take or use selfishly.

Hogmanay *noun* (in Scotland) the last day of the year (December 31) when many parties are held and people visit each other.

hoist *verb* to lift, to raise. – *noun* a lift, an elevator for goods.

hold *verb* (*past tense* **held**) to keep in one's hand or power; to have; to contain; to think, believe; to cause to take place: *hold a meeting*; to apply (still): *That rule doesn't hold any longer*; celebrate: *not to hold Christmas*. – *noun* grip, grasp; influence: *He has a hold over the others*; (in ships) a large space where cargo is carried. – *noun* **holdall** a (large) bag with a zip. – *noun* **holder** something made to hold something else; a person who holds. – *noun* **holding** the amount held (*eg* land, shares in a company).– *noun* **hold-up** an attack with intent to rob. – **hold forth** to speak at length; **hold good** to be true; **hold out** to continue to fight; **hold over** to keep till later; **hold up** to support; to hinder; to attack and demand money from.

hole *noun* an opening in something solid; a pit or burrow; a miserable place; (*coll*) a difficulty.

holiday *noun* a day (or longer time) of rest and amusement.

hollow *adjective* having empty space inside, not solid; fake, unreal: *a hollow victory*. – *noun* a sunken place; a dip in the land. – *verb* to scoop (out).

holly *noun* (*plural* **hollies**) a type of evergreen shrub with scarlet berries and prickly leaves.

hollyhock *noun* a type of tall garden plant.

holocaust *noun* a great destruction (by fire).

holster *noun* the (leather) case for a pistol.

holt *noun* an otter's den.

holy *adjective* of or like God; religious; set apart for use in worshipping God. – *noun* **holiness** the state of being holy. – *noun* **Holy Writ** the Bible.

homage *noun* a sign of respect: *to pay homage to the king*.

home *noun* the place where one *usu* lives or where one's family lives; the place from which anything comes originally: *America is the home of jazz*; a place where children or elderly or sick people live and are looked after. – *adjective* of one's dwelling place or one's country. – *adverb* to one's home; to the full length: *He drove the nail home*. – *noun plural* **home economics** the study of how to run a home. – *adjective* **homely** plain but pleasant; (*US*) plain, not attractive. – *adjective* **home-made** made at home. – *noun* **Home Secretary** (in Britain) the government minister who looks after matters relating to law and order, immigration *etc.* – *adjective* **homesick** longing for home. – *noun* **homestead** farmhouse. – *noun* **home truth** a plain statement of something true but unpleasant made to a person's face. – *adverb* **homewards** towards home. – *noun* **homework** work (*usu* for school) done at home. – *adjective* **homing** (*esp* of pigeons) having the habit of making for home. – **bring home** to make (someone) realize (something).

homeopathy or **homoeopathy** *noun* the system of treating illness by small quantities of substances that produce symptoms similar to those of the illness.

homicide *noun* the killing of a human being; a person who kills a human being. – *adjective* **homicidal**.

homogenize *verb* to treat (milk) so that the cream does not separate itself and rise to the surface. – *noun* **homogenization**.

homonyms *noun plural* words having the same sound but a different meaning (*eg* there, their).

homosexual *adjective* sexually attracted to one's own sex. – Also *noun*. – *noun* **homosexuality**.

Hon. *abbreviation* Honourable; Honorary.

hone *verb* to sharpen (a knife *etc*).

honest *adjective* truthful; not inclined to steal, cheat *etc.* – *noun* **honesty**.

honey *noun* a sweet, thick fluid made by bees from the nectar of flowers. – *noun* **honeycomb** a network of wax cells in which bees store honey. – *adjective* **honeycombed** having holes like the cells in an empty honeycomb. – *noun* **honeymoon** a holiday spent immediately after marriage. – *noun* **honeysuckle** a climbing shrub with sweet-smelling flowers.

honk *noun* a noise like the cry of the wild goose or the sound of a motor horn. – Also *verb*.

honorary *adjective* done to give honour; acting without payment. – *noun* **honorarium** a gift or fee for services not paid for by wages.

honour or *(US)* **honor** *noun* respect for truth, honesty *etc*; fame, glory; reputation, good name; a title which shows respect: *Your Honour*; a privilege; (often *plural*) recognition given for exceptional achievements *etc*. – *verb* to give respect to (what is good); to give high rank to; to pay money when due: *honour a debt.* – *adjective* **honourable** worthy of honour.

hood *noun* a covering for the head; anything which covers or protects like a hood; a folding cover over seats in a carriage, car *etc*; *(US)* the bonnet of a car.

hoodwink *verb* to deceive.

hoof *noun* (*plural* **hoofs** or **hooves**) the horny part on the feet of certain animals (*eg* horses).

hook *noun* a bent piece of metal *etc* for hanging things on (*eg* coats) or for catching things (*eg* fish). – *verb* to catch, hold or drag with (anything like) a hook. – *adjective* **hooked** curved like a hook; caught (by a hook); (*slang*) addicted to, fascinated by. – **by hook or by crook** by one means or another, whatever the cost.

hookah or **hooka** *noun* a tobacco pipe through which smoke is drawn through water, used by Turks and Arabs.

hooligan *noun* a wild, unruly person. – *noun* **hooliganism** unruly behaviour.

hoop *noun* a thin ring of wood or metal.

hoopoe *noun* a kind of bird with a large crest.

hooray *see* **hurrah.**

hoot *verb* to sound a motor horn *etc*; (of an owl) to call, cry; (of persons) to make a similar sound, *esp* in laughter. – *noun* the sound made by a motor horn, siren or owl; a shout of scorn *etc*. – *noun* **hooter** a device which makes a hooting sound (*eg* a motor horn).

Hoover® *noun* a kind of vacuum cleaner. – *verb* **hoover** to use a vacuum cleaner on (a floor *etc*).

hop *verb* (*past tense* **hopped**) to leap on one leg. – *noun* a short jump on one leg; a climbing plant, the bitter fruits of which are used in brewing beer. – *noun*

hopper a box or funnel for shaking down corn *etc* to the grinding (or other) machinery. – *noun* **hopscotch** a hopping game over lines drawn on the ground (scotches).

hope *noun* a state of mind in which one expects or wishes good to come; something desired. – *verb* to expect or wish good to happen. – *adjective* **hopeful.** – *adjective* **hopeless** without hope; very bad.

horde *noun* a large crowd or group.

horizon *noun* the line which seems to be formed by the meeting of the earth and sky; the limit of what a person can see or understand. – *adjective* **horizontal** lying level or flat.

hormone *noun* any of a number of substances produced by certain glands of the body, each of which makes some organ of the body active. – *adjective* **hormonal.**

horn *noun* a hard growth on the heads of certain animals (*eg* oxen, sheep, deer); something made of horn or curved or sticking out like an animal's horn; part of a motor car which gives a warning sound; a kind of wind instrument, once made of horn, now of brass. – *adjective* **horned** having horns or something like horns. – *adjective* **horny** hard like horn.

hornet *noun* a kind of large wasp.

hornpipe *noun* a lively sailor's dance.

horoscope *noun* the telling of a person's fortune by studying the position of the stars at his birth.

horror *noun* great fear, terror; something which causes fear; someone who causes great dislike (*esp* a child). – *adjective* **horrible** causing horror; very unpleasant or bad. – *adjective* **horrid** hateful; very unpleasant. – *verb* **horrify** (*past tense* **horrified**) to frighten greatly; to shock: *I was horrified by the child's behaviour.*

horse *noun* a type of four-footed animal with hooves and a mane; a wooden frame for hanging clothes to dry; an apparatus for vaulting *etc* in a gymnasium. – *noun* **horse-chestnut** a type of tree or its brown, shiny nut. – *noun* **horsefly** a large fly which bites. – *noun* **horse laugh** a loud, harsh laugh. – *noun* **horseplay** rough play, fooling around. – *noun* **horsepower** a unit of mechanical power used in giving power of cars *etc* (*usu* shortened to **hp**). – *noun* **horse-radish** a type of plant, the root of which has a sharp taste, used in sauces. – *noun* **horseshoe** a shoe for horses, made of a curved piece of iron; a horseshoe-shaped thing.

horticulture *noun* the study and art of gardening. – *adjective* **horticultural** having to do with gardening. – *noun* **horticulturist** a person skilled in gardening.

hosanna *noun* an exclamation of praise to God.

hose *noun* (*plural* **hose**) a covering for the legs or feet, stockings *etc*: *hose to wear with the kilt*; (*plural* **hoses**) a tubing of rubber *etc* for carrying water. – *noun* **hosiery** knitted goods (such as tights).

hospice *noun* a home which provides special nursing care for incurable invalids.

hospitable *adjective* showing kindness to guests or strangers. – *noun* **hospitality** a friendly welcome often including food, drink *etc* for guests or strangers.

hospital *noun* a building for the treatment of the ill and injured.

host *noun* (*feminine* **hostess**) a person who welcomes and entertains guests; (*feminine* **hostess**) an innkeeper or hotel-keeper; a very large number.

hostage *noun* a person held prisoner by an enemy or opponent to make sure that an agreement will be kept to or a condition fulfilled.

hostel *noun* a building providing rooms for students *etc*. – *noun* **hostelry** (*plural* **hostelries**) an inn. – *noun* **hostler** or **ostler** (*hist*) the servant who looks after the horses at an inn.

hostile *adjective* of an enemy; not friendly; showing dislike or opposition (to). – *noun* **hostility** unfriendliness; opposition; the state of being an enemy; (*plural*) **hostilities** acts of warfare.

hot *adjective* (*comparative* **hotter**, *superlative* **hottest**) very warm; (of food) having much spice; passionate; radioactive; (*slang*) stolen; (*slang*) not safe. – *noun* **hotbed** a place where there is much disease, wickedness *etc*: *a hotbed of rebellion*. – *adjective* **hot-blooded** passionate, easily roused to anger *etc*. – *noun* **hot-dog** a hot sausage in a roll. – *adverb* **hot-foot** in great haste. – *adjective* **hot-headed** inclined to act rashly without thinking. – *noun* **hothouse** a heated glasshouse for plants. – *noun* **hot line** a direct telephone line between heads of government. – **in(to) hot water** in(to) trouble.

hotchpotch *noun* (*plural* **hotchpotches**) a confused mixture.

hotel *noun* a building where travellers *etc* may stay for payment.

hound *noun* a dog used in hunting. – *verb* to hunt, pursue.

hour *noun* sixty minutes, the 24th part of a day; a time or occasion: *the hour of reckoning*. – *noun* **hour-glass** an instrument for measuring the hours by the running of sand from one glass into another. – *adjective* **hourly** happening or done every hour. – Also *adverb*.

house *noun* a building in which people (often a single family) live; a family household; a business firm; a building where school boarders stay. – *verb* to provide a house for; to shelter. – *noun* **houseboat** a river barge with a cabin for living in. – *noun* **housebreaker** a person who breaks into a house to steal. – *noun* **household** the people who live together in a house; a family. – *noun* **householder** a person who owns or pays the rent of a house; the chief person in a family. – *noun* **housekeeper** a person paid to look after the running of a house. – *noun* **housewarming** a party held when someone moves into a new house. – *noun* **housewife** a woman who looks after a house and her husband and family. – *noun* **housing** accommodation *eg* houses, flats *etc*; a casing or covering for machines *etc*. – **a household word** something which everyone is talking about.

hovel *noun* a small dirty dwelling.

hover *verb* (of birds *etc*) to remain in the air in the same spot; to stay near, linger (about); to be undecided or uncertain. – *noun* **hovercraft** a craft able to travel over land or sea supported on a cushion of air.

how *adverb* in what manner: *How is she dressed?*; to what extent: *How old are you?*; to a great extent: *How beautifully she sings*; by what means: *How do you do it?*; in what state of health, condition *etc*: *How are you?* – *adverb* **however** no matter how; in spite of that.

howdah *noun* a seat fixed on an elephant's back.

howitzer *noun* a short cannon used to attack a besieged town or trench.

howl *verb* to make a long, loud sound like that of a dog or wolf; to yell (as in pain, anger, joy). – Also *noun*. – *noun* **howler** (*coll*) a very silly mistake.

HP *abbreviation* hire-purchase; (also **hp**) horsepower.

HQ *abbreviation* headquarters.

HRH *abbreviation* Her or His Royal Highness.

hub *noun* the centre part of a wheel through which the axle passes; the centre of much traffic, business *etc*.

hubbub *noun* a confused sound of many voices.

huddle *verb* to crowd together. – *noun* a close group.

hue *noun* colour. – **hue and cry** an alarm and general chase.

huff *noun* a fit of bad temper and sulking. – *adjective* **huffy**.

hug *verb* (*past tense* **hugged**) to hold tightly with the arms; to keep close to: *The ships hug the shore.*

huge *adjective* of great size. – *noun* **hugeness**.

hula-hoop *noun* a light hoop for spinning round the waist.

hulk *noun* an old ship unfit for use; anything big and clumsy. – *adjective* **hulking** big and clumsy.

hull *noun* the body or framework of a ship.

hullabaloo *noun* a noisy disturbance.

hullo *see* **hello**.

hum *verb* (*past tense* **hummed**) to make a buzzing sound like that of bees; to sing with the lips shut; (of a place *etc*) to be noisily busy. – *noun* (also **humming**) the noise of bees; any buzzing, droning sound. – *noun* **humming-bird** a type of small brightly-coloured bird whose rapidly moving wings make a humming noise.

human *adjective* having to do with mankind as opposed to God or animals; (of persons) having the qualities, feelings *etc* natural to mankind. – *noun* a man, woman or child. – *adjective* **humane** kind, showing mercy, gentle. – *noun* **humanism** a set of ideas about or interest in ethics and mankind, not including religious belief. – *noun* **humanist**. – *adjective* **humanitarian** kind to one's fellow-men. – *noun* **humanity** men and women in general; kindness, gentleness.

humble *adjective* modest, meek; not of high rank, unimportant. – *verb* to make to feel low and unimportant. – **eat humble pie** to acknowledge openly that one has made a mistake.

humbug *noun* a fraud; nonsense; a kind of hard sweet.

humdrum *adjective* dull, not exciting.

humid *adjective* (of air, climate) moist, damp. – *noun* **humidity** moisture; amount of wetness.

humiliate *verb* to make to feel humble or ashamed, hurt someone's pride. – *adjective* **humiliating**. – *noun* **humiliation** something which humiliates; shame.

humility *noun* humble state of mind, meekness.

humour or (*US*) **humor** *noun* the ability to see things as amusing or ridiculous (also **sense of humour**); funniness; the amusing side of anything; one's state of mind, temper, mood. – *verb* to do as another wishes. – *noun* **humorist** a person who can bring out the amusing side of things. – *adjective* **humorous** funny, causing laughter.

hump *noun* a lump (*eg* on the back). – *noun* **humpback** a back with a hump; a person with a hump on his back. – *adjective* **humpbacked** having a hump on the back; (of a bridge *etc*) rising and falling so as to form a hump shape.

humus *hūm'ŭs*, *noun* soil made of rotted leaves *etc*.

hunch *noun* (*plural* **hunches**) a hump; a suspicion that something is untrue or is going to happen *etc*. – *noun* **hunchback** humpback. – *adjective* **hunchbacked** humpbacked.

hundred *noun* the number 100. – *adjective* 100 in number. – *adjective* **hundredth** the last of a hundred (things *etc*). – *noun* one of a hundred equal parts.

hundredweight *noun* 112 lb, 50·8 kilogrammes (*usu* written **cwt**).

hunger *noun* a desire for food; a strong desire for anything. – *verb* to go without food; to long (for). – *noun* **hunger-strike** a refusal to eat (*eg* by prisoners) as a protest. – *adjective* **hungry** wanting or needing food.

hunt *verb* to chase animals or birds for food or for sport; to search (for). – *noun* chasing wild animals; a search. – *noun* **hunter** (*masculine*), **huntress** (*feminine*) a person who hunts.

hurdle noun a frame to be jumped over in a race; any difficulty which must be overcome.

hurdygurdy noun a musical instrument played by turning a handle, a hand-organ, a barrel organ.

hurl verb to throw with force.

hurlyburly noun a great stir, uproar.

hurrah or **hurray** or **hooray** interjection a shout of joy, approval etc.

hurricane noun a violent storm of wind blowing at a speed of over 75 miles (120 kilometres) per hour. – noun **hurricane lamp** a lamp specially made to keep alight in strong wind.

hurry verb (past tense **hurried**) to act or move quickly; to make (someone) act etc quickly. – noun eagerness to act or move quickly, haste. – adjective **hurried** done in a hurry.

hurt verb to cause pain or distress; to wound; to damage. – noun a wound; damage. – adjective **hurtful** causing pain, distress or damage.

hurtle verb to (cause to) move at great speed.

husband noun a married man (the partner of a **wife**). – verb to spend or use (eg one's money, strength) carefully. – noun **husbandry** farming; management; care with one's money, thrift.

hush inter be quiet! – noun (coll) silence. – verb to make quiet. – adjective **hush-hush** (coll) top secret. – **hush up** to stop (a scandal etc) becoming public.

husk noun the dry thin covering of certain fruits and seeds.

husky adjective (of the voice) hoarse, rough in sound; big and strong. – noun (plural **huskies**) a Canadian sledge dog.

hussar noun a light-armed horse soldier.

hussy noun (plural **hussies**) a forward, cheeky girl.

hustings noun plural speeches, campaigning etc which take place just before an election.

hustle verb to push rudely; to hurry. – Also noun.

hut noun a small wooden building; a simple dwelling place.

hutch noun (plural **hutches**) a box in which pet rabbits are housed.

hyacinth noun a type of sweet-smelling flower which grows from a bulb.

hyaena see **hyena**.

hybrid noun something (usu an animal or plant) made or bred from two different kinds (eg a mule, which is a hybrid from a horse and an ass); a word which is formed of parts from different languages. – Also adjective.

hydra noun (myth) a many-headed water serpent that grew two heads for each one cut off; a water creature that can divide and re-divide itself.

hydrant noun a connection to which a hose can be attached to draw water off the main water supply.

hydraulic adjective carrying water; worked by water or other fluid.

hydro- prefix water. – noun **hydro** (short for **hydropathic**) (plural **hydros**) a type of hotel (originally with special swimming baths etc for health improvements). – noun **hydroelectricity** electricity got from water-power. – adjective **hydroelectric**.

hydrogen noun an element, the lightest gas, which with oxygen makes up water. – noun **hydrogen bomb** an exceedingly powerful bomb using hydrogen.

hydrophobia noun a fear of water, a symptom of rabies; rabies.

hyena, hyaena noun a dog-like wild animal with a howl sounding like laughter.

hygiene hī'jēn, noun (the study of) cleanliness as a means to health. – adjective **hygienic**.

hymen noun the thin membrane that partially closes the vagina of a virgin.

hymn noun a song of praise, esp one sung to God. – noun **hymnal** or **hymnary** (plural **hymnaries**) a book of hymns.

hype noun (coll) extravagant advertisement or publicity; (coll) a hypodermic syringe. – verb (coll) to promote extravagantly; to inject oneself with a drug. – **hype up** (coll) to hype.

hyper- prefix to a greater extent than usual, excessive as in **hyperactive**.

hyperbole hī-pûr'bŏl-i, noun exaggeration. – adjective **hyperbolical**.

hypermarket noun a very large self-service store which stocks a wide range of goods.

hyphen noun a short stroke (-) used to link or separate parts of a word or phrase; sweet-and-sour: re-create.

hypnotize *verb* to put a person into a sleep-like state in which suggestions are obeyed. – *noun* **hypnosis** a hypnotized state; hypnotism. – *adjective* **hypnotic** of hypnosis or hypnotism; causing hypnosis or a sleep-like state. – *noun* **hypnotism** the production of a hypnotized state; hypnosis. – *noun* **hypnotist**.

hypo- *prefix* below, under.

hypoallergenic *adjective* specially formulated in order to reduce the risk of allergy.

hypochondria *noun* over-anxiety about one's own health. – *noun, adjective* **hypochondriac**.

hypocrite *hip'o-krit, noun* a person who pretends to be good but is not. – *noun* **hypocrisy** false pretence of goodness. – *adjective* **hypocritical**.

hypodermic *noun* a hypodermic syringe. – *noun* **hypodermic syringe** an instrument with a fine, hollow needle (**hypodermic needle**) for giving an injection of a drug just below the skin.

hypotenuse *noun* the longest side of a right-angled triangle.

hypothesis *noun* (*plural* **hypotheses**) something taken as true (for the sake of argument). – *adjective* **hypothetical** supposed.

hysterectomy *noun* (*plural* **hysterectomies**) surgical removal of the womb.

hysteria *noun* a nervous excitement causing uncontrollable laughter, crying *etc*; a nervous illness. – *adjective* **hysterical**. – *noun plural* **hysterics** a fit of hysteria.

Hz *abbreviation* hertz.

I

I *pronoun* the word used by a speaker or writer in mentioning himself (as the subject of a verb): *He and I went together*.

IBA *abbreviation* Independent Broadcasting Authority.

ibex *noun* (*plural* **ibexes**) a wild mountain goat.

ice *noun* frozen water; ice cream. – *verb* to cover with icing; to freeze. – *noun* **ice age** an age when the earth was mostly covered with ice. – *noun* **iceberg** a huge mass of floating ice. – *noun* **icebox** (*US*) refrigerator. – *noun* **ice-cap** a permanent covering of ice, as at the north and south poles. – *noun* **ice cream** a sweet creamy mixture, flavoured and frozen. – *noun* **ice floe** a piece of floating ice. – *noun* **ice hockey** hockey played with a rubber disc (**puck**) on an ice rink. – *noun* **ice-skate** a skate for moving on ice. – Also *verb*. – *noun* **ice-skater**. – *noun* **ice-skating**. – *noun* **icing** powdered sugar, mixed with water or white of egg, flavoured and allowed to set. – *adjective* **icy** covered with ice; very cold. – *adverb* **icily**. – **dry ice** solid carbon dioxide.

ichthyology *noun* the study of fishes.

icicle *noun* a hanging, pointed piece of ice formed by the freezing of dropping water.

icon or **ikon** *noun* a painted or mosaic image (*eg* of Christ or of a saint).

iconoclasm *noun* the act of breaking images; the attacking of long-established beliefs.

ID *abbreviation* identification. – *noun* (*US*) a means of identification (*eg* a card or bracelet).

I'd short for **I would** or **I should** or **I had**: *I'd sooner go than stay*.

idea *noun* a thought, notion, mental picture; plan.

ideal *adjective* perfect; existing in imagination only (opposite of **real**). – *noun* that which is highest and best; a standard of perfection. – *noun* **idealism**. – *noun* **idealist** a person who thinks that perfection can be reached. – *verb* **idealize** to think of as perfect. – *noun* **idealization**. – *adverb* **ideally** in ideal circumstances: *Ideally all children under five should attend a play group*.

identical *adjective* the same in all details.

identify verb (past tense **identified**) to (claim to) recognize, prove to be the same: He identified the man as his attacker; to think of as the same: He identifies money with happiness. – noun **identification**. – **identify (oneself) with** to feel close to or involved with.

identikit picture noun a rough picture of a wanted person which police put together from descriptions.

identity noun (plural **identities**) who or what a person or thing is; the state of being the same.

ideology noun (plural **ideologies**) a set of (usually political) ideas. – adjective **ideological**.

idiocy see idiot.

idiom noun a common form of expression whose meaning cannot be guessed from the actual words. 'The boy turned up unexpectedly one day'. – adjective **idiomatic**.

idiosyncrasy noun (plural **idiosyncrasies**) a personal oddness of behaviour. – adjective **idiosyncratic**.

idiot noun a feeble-minded person; a fool. – noun **idiocy** feeble-mindedness, foolishness. – adjective **idiotic**.

idle adjective without work to do; lazy; meaningless: idle chatter. – verb to spend (time) in doing nothing; (of an engine) to run without doing any work. – noun **idleness**. – noun **idler**. – adverb **idly**.

idol noun an image worshipped as a god; a person or thing loved or honoured (too much). – verb **idolize** to love (too) greatly.

idyllic adjective very happy in a simple way.

ie abbreviation that is, that means (id est [L]).

if conjunction on condition that, supposing that: If you go, he will go; whether: I don't know if he's going.

iffy adjective (coll) dubious; uncertain.

igloo noun an Eskimo's snow hut.

igneous adjective having to do with fire; (of rock) formed by the action of great heat within the earth.

ignite verb to set on fire; to catch fire. – noun **ignition** the act of setting on fire or catching fire; the sparking part of a motor engine.

ignoble adjective dishonourable; of low birth.

ignominy ig'nò-min-i, noun (public) disgrace. – adjective **ignominious** dishonourable, disgraceful.

ignoramus ig-nò-rā'mùs, noun an ignorant person.

ignore verb to take no notice of. – adjective **ignorant** knowing very little; (with **of**) not knowing, not aware. – noun **ignorance**.

iguana noun a type of tree lizard.

ikon see **icon**.

I'll short for **I shall** or **I will**.

ill adjective unwell; evil, bad; unlucky. – adverb badly. – noun evil; (plural) misfortunes. – adjective **ill-at-ease** uncomfortable. – adjective **ill-gotten** (of profits etc) obtained in a wrongful way. – adjective **ill-humoured** or **ill-natured** bad-tempered. – noun **illness** disease, sickness. – adjective **ill-starred** unlucky. – verb **ill-treat** or **ill-use** to treat badly. – noun **ill-will** or **ill-feeling** dislike, resentment.

illegal adjective against the law. – noun **illegality** (plural **illegalities**).

illegible adjective (almost) impossible to read, indistinct.

illegitimate adjective born of parents not married to each other.

illicit adjective unlawful, forbidden.

illiterate adjective not able to read or write. – noun **illiteracy**.

illogical adjective not logical, not showing sound reasoning.

illuminate verb to light up; to make (more) clear. – adjective **illuminated** (of a document etc) decorated with (coloured) lettering etc. – noun **illumination** the act of illuminating; (plural) a decorative display of lights.

illusion noun something which deceives the mind or eye; a mistaken belief. – adjective **illusive**. – adjective **illusory**.

illustrate verb to draw pictures for (a book etc); to explain, show (through examples, diagrams, slides etc). – noun **illustration** a picture in a book etc; an example which illustrates. – adjective **illustrative**. – noun **illustrator** a person who illustrates.

illustrious adjective famous, distinguished.

I'm short for **I am**: I'm older now.

image noun a likeness made of someone or something; a striking likeness; a picture in the mind; public reputation. – noun **imagery** pictures suggested by words that help to make a piece of writing more vivid.

imagine verb to form a picture in the mind often of something that is not present or does not exist; to think, suppose. – adjective **imaginary** existing only in the imagination, not real. – noun **imagination** the power of forming pictures in the mind (of things not present); the creative ability of an artist etc. – adjective **imaginative** having a lively imagination; done with imagination: an imaginative piece of writing.

imago see **pupa**.

imam noun the officiating priest who leads the prayers in a mosque. – noun **Imam** a Muslim leader.

imbecile noun a feeble-minded person; a fool. – noun **imbecility** feeble-mindedness, stupidity.

imbibe verb to drink (in).

imbue verb to fill the mind (with): The general's actions imbued his troops with feelings of patriotism.

IMF abbreviation International Monetary Fund.

imitate verb to try to be the same as, to copy. – noun **imitation** a copy. – adjective made to look like: imitation leather. – noun **imitator**.

immaculate adjective spotless; very clean and neat.

immaterial adjective of little importance.

immature adjective not mature.

immediate adjective happening straight away: immediate reaction; close: immediate family; direct: his immediate successor. – noun **immediacy**. – adverb **immediately** without delay.

immemorial adjective going further back in time than can be remembered.

immense adjective very large. – noun **immensity**.

immerse verb to plunge into liquid. – noun **immersion**. – noun **immersion heater** an electric water-heating instrument (inside the hot water tank). – **immerse oneself in** to give one's whole attention to.

immigrate verb to come into a country and settle there. – adjective, noun **immigrant** (of) a person who immigrates. – noun **immigration**.

imminent adjective about to happen: imminent danger.

immobile adjective without moving; not easily moved. – noun **immobility**. – verb **immobilize** put out of action.

immoderate adjective going beyond reasonable limits.

immoral adjective wrong, evil; indecent: immoral suggestions. – noun **immorality**.

immortal adjective living for ever; famous for ever. – noun **immortality** unending life or fame. – verb **immortalize** to make immortal or famous for ever.

immovable adjective not able to be moved or changed.

immune adjective not likely to catch (a disease) or be affected by: She should be immune to measles after the inoculation. I am immune to his charm. – noun **immune system** the natural defensive system of an organism that identifies and neutralizes harmful matter within itself. – noun **immunity**. – verb **immunize** to make a person immune from (a disease) (esp by an injection of something to fight the disease).

imp noun mischievous child or fairy. – adjective **impish**.

impact noun the blow of one thing striking another; a collision; strong effect: Her appearance made an impact on the audience. – verb to press firmly together.

impair verb to damage, weaken. – noun **impairment**.

impala noun a large African antelope.

impale verb to pierce through (with a spear etc).

impart verb to tell to others (what one knows).

impartial adjective not favouring one side more than another; just. – noun **impartiality**.

impassable adjective (of roads etc) not able to be passed.

impasse am'päs, noun a situation from which there seems to be no way out.

impassioned adjective moved by strong feeling.

impassive adjective not easily moved either by pleasure or pain.

impatient adjective restlessly eager; irritable, short-tempered. – noun **impatience**.

impeach verb to accuse publicly (esp a high official) of misconduct. – noun **impeachment**.

impeccable adjective having no fault. – adverb **impeccably**: impeccably dressed.

impecunious adjective having little or no money.

impede verb to hinder, keep back. – noun **impediment** a hindrance; a defect in a person's speech eg a stutter or stammer.

impel verb (past tense **impelled**) to urge; to drive on.

impending adjective about to happen: an impending storm.

imperative adjective necessary, urgent; (gram) expressing command.

imperceptible adjective so small as not to be noticed.

imperfect adjective having a fault or flaw, not perfect. – noun **imperfection** a fault or a flaw.

imperial adjective of an emperor or empire. – noun **imperialism** the policy of gaining the territory of, and ruling other people. – noun **imperialist**.

imperil verb (past tense **imperilled**) to put in danger.

imperious adjective having an air of authority, haughty.

impermeable adjective not able to be passed through: Clay is impermeable by water.

impersonal adjective not showing or influenced by personal feelings; not connected with any person.

impersonate verb to dress up as, or act the part of, someone. – noun **impersonation**. – noun **impersonator**.

impertinent adjective cheeky, bad-mannered; not pertinent. – noun **impertinence**.

imperturbable adjective not easily worried, calm.

impervious adjective (with **to**) able to remain unaffected by: He is impervious to hints.

impetigo im-pi-tī'gō, noun a kind of skin disease.

impetuous adjective rushing into action, rash. – noun **impetuosity**.

impetus noun moving force: The impetus of the blow sent him flying; impulse.

impiety noun lack of respect for holy things. – adjective **impious** wicked.

impinge verb (with **on** or **upon**) to come in contact with; to trespass (on) (eg another person's rights or privacy).

implacable adjective not able to be soothed or calmed.

implant verb to fix in, plant firmly. – Also noun.

implement noun a tool (eg a spade, a painter's brush). – verb to carry out, to fulfil (eg a promise).

implicate verb to bring in, involve (a person): The statements of other gang members implicate you in the crime. – noun **implication** the act of implicating; something meant though not actually said.

implicit adjective understood, meant though not actually said; unquestioning: implicit obedience.

imply verb (past tense **implied**) to suggest: His silence implied disapproval.

impolite adjective not polite, rude.

import verb to bring in (goods) from abroad (for sale). – noun act of importing; something imported; meaning; importance. – noun **importation** act of importing.

important adjective worth taking notice of; special. – noun **importance**.

importune verb to keep asking for something. – adjective **importunate** repeatedly asking. – noun **importunity**.

impose verb to place something (as a tax burden etc) on (someone or something); (with **on**) to take advantage (of a person), to deceive. – adjective **imposing** impressive, making much show. – noun **imposition** a burden; an exercise given as a punishment.

impossible adjective not able to be done or to happen; (of a person etc) not able to be dealt with, intolerable. – noun **impossibility**.

impostor noun a person who pretends to be someone else in order to deceive. – noun **imposture** (the act of) deceiving in this way.

impotent adjective without power, strength or effectiveness; (of males) without sexual power. – noun **impotence**.

impound verb to take possession of (something) by law (eg furniture in payment of the rent).

impoverish *verb* to make (a person *etc*) poor; to make poor in quality. – *noun* **impoverishment.**

impracticable *adjective* not able to be done. – *noun* **impracticability.**

impractical *adjective* lacking common sense. – *noun* **impracticality.**

impregnable *adjective* too strong to be taken by, or overthrown by, attack.

impresario *noun* (*plural* **impresarios**) the organizer of a (musical) entertainment.

impress *verb* to arouse (someone's) interest or admiration; to mark by pressing upon; to fix deeply in the mind. – *noun* **impression** what a person thinks or feels about something: *The play left a lasting impression on me. My impression is that it's likely to rain;* a mark made by impressing; a quantity of copies of a book printed at one time. – *adjective* **impressionable** easily influenced or affected. – *noun* **impressionism** the attempt, in painting, writing, *etc* to reproduce the actual effect of something. – *noun* **impressionist** an entertainer who impersonates people. – *adjective* **impressive** having a great effect on the mind.

imprint *verb* to print; to mark; to set a permanent mark on (the mind *etc*). – *noun* that which is imprinted; the printer's name on a book.

imprison *verb* to shut up as in a prison. – *noun* **imprisonment.**

improbable *adjective* not likely to happen. – *noun* **improbability.**

impromptu *adjective, adverb* without preparation or rehearsal.

improper *adjective* not suitable; wrong; indecent. – *noun* **improper fraction** a fraction greater than 1 (as $5/4$, $2\frac{1}{8}$). – *noun* **impropriety** (*plural* **improprieties**) something improper.

improve *verb* to make or become better. – *noun* **improvement.**

improvident *adjective* taking no thought for future needs. – *noun* **improvidence.**

improvise *verb* to put together, produce from available materials or on the spur of the moment: *We improvised a stretcher. The pianist improvised a tune.* – *noun* **improvisation.**

impudent *adjective* cheeky, insolent. – *noun* **impudence.**

impulse *noun* a sudden force such as a push; a sudden urge resulting in sudden action. – *adjective* **impulsive** acting on impulse, without time to consider. – *noun* **impulsiveness.**

impunity *noun* freedom from punishment, injury or loss.

impure *adjective* mixed with other substances; not clean. – *noun* **impurity** (*plural* **impurities**).

impute *verb* to think of (something blameworthy) as being caused, done *etc* (by someone). – *noun* **imputation** suggestion of fault, blame.

in *preposition* showing position in space or time: *She was sitting in the garden. He was born in the year 1921;* showing state, condition, manner *etc*: *in part: in a high voice.* – *adverb* (towards the) inside, not out; in power; (*coll*) in fashion. – *adjective* that is in, inside or coming in; (*coll*) fashionable. – *abbreviation* inch(es). – **be in for** to be trying to get; to be about to receive (something unpleasant).

in- *prefix* into, on, towards, as in **inshore**; not, as in **inaccurate.**

inability *noun* (*plural* **inabilities**) lack of power, means *etc* (to do something).

inaccessible *adjective* not able to be (easily) reached, approached or obtained.

inaccurate *adjective* not correct; not exact. – *noun* **inaccuracy** (*plural* **inaccuracies**).

inactive *adjective* not active; not working, doing nothing. – *noun* **inaction** lack of action. – *noun* **inactivity** idleness; rest.

inadequate *adjective* not enough; unable to cope (in an emergency *etc*).

inadmissible *adjective* not allowable.

inadvertent *adjective* unintentional. – *adverb* **inadvertently.**

inane *adjective* silly, foolish. – *noun* **inanity** (*plural* **inanities**).

inanimate *adjective* without life.

inapplicable *adjective* not applicable.

inappropriate *adjective* not suitable.

inapt *adjective* not apt; unfit or unqualified. – *noun* **inaptitude** or **inaptness** unfitness, awkwardness. – *adverb* **inaptly.**

inarticulate *adjective* unable to express oneself (clearly); uttered indistinctly.

inasmuch as *conjunction* because, since.

inattentive *adjective* not paying attention. – *noun* **inattention.**

inaudible *adjective* not loud enough to be heard.

inaugurate *verb* to make a start on, *usu* with show or ceremony. – *adjective* **inaugural**. – *noun* **inauguration**.

inauspicious *adjective* unlucky, unlikely to end in success.

inbred *adjective* natural; resulting from **inbreeding** repeated mating within the family.

inc. *abbreviation* incorporated; inclusive; including.

incalculable *adjective* not able to be counted or estimated.

incandescent *adjective* white-hot.

incantation *noun* (words sung or said as) a spell.

incapable *adjective* unable (to do what is expected); helpless (through drink *etc*).

incapacitate *verb* to take away power, strength or rights; to disable. – *noun* **incapacity** inability; disability.

incarcerate *verb* to imprison.

incarnate *adjective* having human form. – *noun* **incarnation** appearance in the form of a human body.

incendiary *adjective* meant for setting (buildings *etc*) on fire: *an incendiary bomb*.

incense *verb* to make angry. – *noun* spices *etc* burned (*esp* in religious ceremonies) to give off a pleasant smell.

incentive *noun* that which encourages one to do something.

inception *noun* beginning.

incessant *adjective* going on without pause.

incest *noun* illegal sexual intercourse between close relatives.

inch *noun* (*plural* **inches**) one twelfth of a foot (about 2·5 centimetres). – *verb* to move very gradually.

incident *noun* a happening. – *noun* **incidence** how often or in what quantity a thing occurs; a falling (of a ray of light *etc*). – *adjective* **incidental** happening in connection with something: *an incidental expense*; casual. – *adverb* **incidentally** by the way.

incinerate *verb* to burn to ashes. – *noun* **incineration**. – *noun* **incinerator** an apparatus for burning rubbish *etc*.

incipient *adjective* beginning to exist: *an incipient dislike*.

incision *noun* the act of cutting into something; a cut, a gash. – *adjective* **incisive** (of words, manner *etc*) sharp, clear, firm. – *noun* **incisiveness**. – *noun* **incisor** a front tooth.

incite *verb* to move to action; to urge on. – *noun* **incitement**.

incivility *noun* (*plural* **incivilities**) impoliteness.

inclement *adjective* (of weather) stormy. – *noun* **inclemency**.

incline *verb* to lean or slope (towards); to bend, bow; to (cause to) have a liking, tendency, (slight) desire for. – *noun* a slope. – *noun* **inclination** liking, tendency; slope; bending. – *adjective* **inclined**.

include *verb* to count in, along with others. – *noun* **inclusion**. – *adjective* **inclusive** including everything mentioned *etc*: *From Tuesday to Thursday inclusive is 3 days*.

incognito *in-kòg-nē'tō, adjective, adverb* with one's identity concealed (by use of a disguise, false name *etc*). – *noun* (*plural* **incognitos**) a disguise.

incoherent *adjective* (of a speech *etc*) not coherent, unconnected, rambling; (of a person) speaking in this way. – *noun* **incoherence**.

incombustible *adjective* not able to be burned by fire.

income *noun* a person's earnings; gain or profit.

incoming *adjective* approaching; new, next.

incommode *verb* to cause bother or trouble to.

incommunicado *adjective, adverb* without means of communicating with others.

incomparable *adjective* without equal. – *adverb* **incomparably**.

incompatible *adjective* (of statements *etc*) contradicting each other; (of persons) bound to disagree. – *noun* **incompatibility**.

incompetent *adjective* not good enough at doing a job. – *noun* **incompetence**.

incomplete *adjective* not finished.

incomprehensible *adjective* not able to be understood, puzzling. – *noun* **incomprehension**.

inconceivable *adjective* not able to be imagined or believed.

inconclusive *adjective* not leading to a definite decision or conclusion.

incongruous *adjective* not matching well; out of place, unsuitable. – *noun* **incongruity** (*plural* **incongruities**).

inconsequential *adjective* unimportant.

inconsiderable *adjective* slight, unimportant.

inconsiderate *adjective* not thinking of others.

inconsistent *adjective* not consistent, contradicting.

inconsolable *adjective* not able to be comforted.

inconspicuous *adjective* not noticeable.

inconstant *adjective* often changing. – *noun* **inconstancy**.

incontinent *adjective* unable to control one's bladder and bowels; uncontrolled.

incontrovertible *adjective* not to be doubted.

inconvenient *adjective* causing awkwardness or difficulty. – *noun* **inconvenience**. – *verb* to cause inconvenience, trouble to.

incorporate *verb* to contain as part of a whole: *The new sports complex will incorporate a gymnasium, swimming pool etc;* to include within a group *etc.* – *adjective* **incorporated** (shortened to **inc.**) formed into a company or society.

incorrect *adjective* wrong.

incorrigible *adjective* too bad to be put right or reformed.

incorruptible *adjective* not able to be bribed; that can never decay.

increase *verb* to grow, to make greater or more numerous. – *noun* growth; the amount added by growth. – *adverb* **increasingly** more and more.

incredible *adjective* impossible to believe. – *adverb* **incredibly**. – *noun* **incredibility**.

incredulous *adjective* not believing (what is said). – *noun* **incredulity**.

increment *noun* an increase, *esp* one added annually to a salary.

incriminate *verb* to show that a person has taken part in a crime or misdeed.

incubator *noun* a large heated box for hatching eggs or one for rearing premature babies. – *verb* **incubate**. – *noun* **incubation period** the time (between being infected and the appearance of the symptoms) that it takes for a disease to develop.

inculcate *verb* to impress something on (a person's mind) by much repeating.

incumbent *adjective* resting on (someone) as a duty: *It is incumbent upon me to warn you.* – *noun* a person who holds an office, *esp* in the church.

incur *verb* (*past tense* **incurred**) to bring something (as blame, debt *etc*) upon oneself.

incurable *adjective* unable to be cured.

incursion *noun* an invasion, raid.

indebted *adjective* having cause to be grateful (to someone for something received). – *noun* **indebtedness**.

indecent *adjective* offending (often in a sexual sense) against normal or usual standards of behaviour. – *noun* **indecency**. – *noun* **indecent assault** an assault involving indecency but not rape.

indecision *noun* slowness in making up one's mind, hesitation. – *adjective* **indecisive** not coming to a definite result; unable to make up one's mind.

indeed *adverb* in fact; (used for emphasis) really. – *interjection* expressing surprise *etc*.

indefatigable *adjective* untiring.

indefensible *adjective* unable to be defended; (of behaviour *etc*) inexcusable.

indefinable *adjective* not able to be stated or described clearly.

indefinite *adjective* not fixed, uncertain; without definite limits. – *noun* **indefinite article** the name given to the adjectives *a, an*. – *adverb* **indefinitely** for an indefinite period of time.

indelible *adjective* unable to be rubbed out or removed.

indelicate *adjective* impolite, rude. – *noun* **indelicacy**.

indemnity *noun* money paid to make up for (possible) damage or loss.

indent *verb* to begin a new paragraph by going in from the margin; (with **for**) to apply for (stores, equipment *etc*). – *noun* **indentation** a hollow, dent; a notch or inward curve in an outline, coastline *etc.* – *noun* **indenture** a written agreement.

independent *adjective* free to think or act for oneself; not relying on someone (or something) else for support, guidance *etc.* – *noun* **independence.**

indescribable *adjective* not able to be described.

indestructible *adjective* not able to be destroyed.

indeterminate *adjective* not fixed, indefinite.

index *noun (plural* **indexes)** an alphabetical list giving the page number of subjects dealt with in a book; an indication; *(plural* **indices)** (in mathematics) an upper number which shows how many times a number is multiplied by itself *(eg* 4^3 means $4 \times 4 \times 4$); a numerical scale showing changes in the cost of living, wages *etc.* – *adjective* **index-linked** (of *eg* pensions) directly related to the cost-of-living index.

Indian: *noun* **Indian corn** maize. – *noun* **Indian ink** a very black ink used by artists. – *noun* **Indian summer** a period of summer warmth in autumn.

indiarubber *noun* rubber, *esp* a piece that is used for rubbing out pencil *etc.*

indicate *verb* to point out, show. – *noun* **indication** a sign. – *adjective* **indicative** pointing out, being a sign of: *indicative of his attitude.* – *noun* **indicator** that which indicates; a pointer; a name given to many instruments *etc* that give information *(esp* by means of a pointer, or as the left and right flashing lights on a vehicle).

indict *in-dīt¹*, *verb* to accuse of a crime *esp* formally or in writing. – *noun* **indictment.**

indifferent *adjective* neither very good nor very bad; (with **to**) showing no interest in. – *noun* **indifference.**

indigenous *adjective* native to a country or area.

indigent *adjective* living in want, poor. – *noun* **indigence.**

indigestion *noun* discomfort or pain experienced in digesting food. – *adjective* **indigestible** difficult to digest.

indignant *adjective* angry (*usu* because of wrong done to oneself or others). – *noun* **indignation.** – *noun* **indignity** *(plural* **indignities)** loss of dignity; insult.

indigo *adjective, noun* (of) a purplish-blue colour.

indirect *adjective* not straight or direct; not affecting or affected directly. – *noun* **indirect speech** speech reported not in the speaker's actual words. – *noun* **indirect tax** a tax on particular goods, paid by the customer in the form of a higher price.

indiscreet *adjective* rash, not cautious; giving away too much information. – *noun* **indiscretion** a rash or unwise saying or act.

indiscriminate *adjective* making no (careful) distinction between one thing (or person) and another: *The riot resulted in indiscriminate killing. Panic about shortages resulted in indiscriminate buying.*

indispensable *adjective* not able to be done without, necessary.

indisposed *adjective* unwell. – *noun* **indisposition.**

indisputable *adjective* not able to be denied.

indistinct *adjective* not clear.

indistinguishable *adjective* difficult to make out; too alike to tell apart.

individual *adjective* of a person or thing (out of a group) taken singly; distinctive; unusual. – *noun* a single person, animal or thing. – *noun* **individualist** a person who believes in independent actions *etc.* – *noun* **individuality** separate existence; quality of standing out from others.

indivisible *adjective* not able to be divided.

indoctrinate *verb* to fill with a certain teaching or set of ideas.

indolent *adjective* lazy. – *noun* **indolence.**

indomitable *adjective* unconquerable, unyielding.

indoor *adjective* done *etc* inside a building. – *adverb* **indoors** in or into a building *etc.*

indubitable *adjective* not to be doubted. – *adverb* **indubitably.**

induce *verb* to persuade; to bring on, cause. – *noun* **inducement** something which encourages or persuades: *Money is an inducement to work.*

induction *noun* the formal installing (of someone, *esp* a clergyman) in a new post; the production of electricity in something by placing it near something else containing electricity; the process of drawing a conclusion from particular cases. – *adjective* **inductive**.

indulge *verb* to be in the habit of giving in to the wishes of (someone): *She indulges that child too much*; to give way to, not to restrain: *He indulged in grief in private*. – *noun* **indulgence** the act of indulging; a pardon for a sin. – *adjective* **indulgent** not strict, kind.

industry *noun* (*plural* **industries**) (any branch of) trade or manufacture: *The clothing industry employs many people*; steady attention to work. – *adjective* **industrial**. – *noun* **industrialist** someone involved in organizing an industry. – *adjective* **industrious** hardworking.

inebriated *adjective* drunk.

inedible *adjective* not eatable.

ineffable *adjective* not able to be described.

ineffective *adjective* useless, having no effect. – *noun* **ineffectiveness**.

ineffectual *adjective* achieving nothing.

inefficient *adjective* not efficient, not capable; wasting time, energy *etc*. – *noun* **inefficiency** (*plural* **inefficiencies**).

inelegant *adjective* not graceful. – *noun* **inelegance**.

ineligible *adjective* not qualified, not suitable (to be chosen).

inept *adjective* clumsy; foolish. – *noun* **ineptitude**.

inequality *noun* (*plural* **inequalities**) lack of equality, unfairness; unevenness.

inert *adjective* without the power of moving; disinclined to move or act; not lively; chemically inactive. – *noun* **inertness**. – *noun* **inertia**. – *adjective* **inertia-reel** (of a car seat belt) running from a reel and designed to tighten on sudden braking.

inescapable *adjective* unable to be avoided.

inestimable *adjective* too good *etc* to be estimated.

inevitable *adjective* not able to be avoided. – *noun* **inevitability**. – *adverb* **inevitably**.

inexcusable *adjective* not to be excused.

inexhaustible *adjective* very plentiful; not likely to become used up.

inexorable *adjective* not able to be persuaded or moved by pleading, relentless.

inexpensive *adjective* cheap in price.

inexperience *noun* lack of (skilled) knowledge or experience. – *adjective* **inexperienced**.

inexplicable *adjective* not able to be explained.

inexpressible *adjective* not able to be told or described in words.

inextricable *adjective* not able to be disentangled. – *adverb* **inextricably**.

infallible *adjective* never making an error; certain to produce the desired result expected: *an infallible remedy*. – *noun* **infallibility**.

infamous *adjective* having a very bad reputation; disgraceful. – *noun* **infamy** (public) disgrace.

infant *noun* a baby. – *noun* **infancy** the state or time of being an infant; the beginning of anything: *Civilization was still in its infancy*. – *noun* **infanticide** the murder of a child; a person who murders a child. – *adjective* **infantile** of babies; childish.

infantry *noun* foot-soldiers.

infatuated *adjective* filled with foolish love. – *noun* **infatuation**.

infect *verb* to fill with disease-causing germs; to pass on disease to; to pass on, spread (*eg* enthusiasm). – *noun* **infection** the means (*usu* germs) by which disease is spread; a disease; anything that spreads widely and affects many people. – *adjective* **infectious** likely to spread from person to person.

infer *verb* (*past tense* **inferred**) to reach a conclusion (from facts or reasoning); to hint. – *noun* **inference**.

inferior *adjective* lower in any way; not of best quality. – *noun* a person lower in rank *etc*. – *noun* **inferiority**. – *noun* **inferiority complex** a constant feeling that one is less good in some way than others.

infernal *adjective* of hell; (*coll*) annoying. – *noun* **inferno** hell; (*plural* **infernos**) any place of horror or fire.

infertile *adjective* (of soil *etc*) not producing much; (of persons or animals) not able to bear young. – *noun* **infertility**.

infest *verb* to swarm over: *The dog is infested with lice*.

infidel *adjective* one who does not believe in religion (*esp* Christianity). – *noun* **infidelity** unfaithfulness, disloyalty.

in-fighting noun rivalry or quarrelling between members of the same group.

infiltrate verb to pass into secretly: *Enemy soldiers infiltrated our lines.* – noun **infiltration**.

infinite adjective without end or limit. – adjective **infinitesimal** very small. – noun **infinitive** part of the verb that expresses the action but has no subject (*eg* I hate *to lose*). – noun **infinity** space or time stretching so far as to be beyond our power of thinking.

infirm adjective feeble, weak. – noun **infirmary** (plural **infirmaries**) a name given to some hospitals. – noun **infirmity** (plural **infirmities**) a weakness of the body or of the character.

inflame verb to make hot or red; to cause violent feelings *esp* anger. – adjective **inflamed**. – adjective **inflammable** easily set on fire; easily excited. – noun **inflammation** heat in a part of the body, with pain, redness and swelling. – adjective **inflammatory** rousing to anger or excitement.

inflate verb to blow up (a balloon, tyre *etc*); to puff up (with pride), exaggerate: *She has an inflated sense of her own importance*; to increase to a great extent. – noun **inflation** the act of inflating; the state of a country's economy in which prices and wages keep forcing each other to increase.

inflection see **inflexion**.

inflexible adjective not yielding, unbending.

inflexion or **inflection** noun a change of tone in the voice.

inflict verb to bring down (something unpleasant *eg* blows, punishment) on. – noun **infliction**.

influence noun the power to affect other persons or things. – verb to have power over. – adjective **influential**.

influenza noun an infectious illness with fever, headache, a cold *etc*.

influx noun a flowing in; (of people *etc*) a coming in in large numbers.

inform verb to give knowledge to; (with **on**) to tell (something) against (someone), betray. – noun **informant** a person who informs. – noun **information** knowledge, news. – adjective **informative** giving information. – noun **informer** a person who gives information (to the police, authorities *etc*).

informal adjective not formal; relaxed, friendly. – noun **informality**.

infra- prefix below, beneath.

infra-red adjective of rays of heat with wavelengths longer than visible light.

infringe verb to break (a rule or law). – noun **infringement**.

infuriate verb to drive into a rage.

infuse verb to pour upon or over; to fill the mind (with a desire *etc*). – noun **infusion** the act of infusing; liquid (such as tea) formed by pouring water on something.

ingenious adjective skilful in inventing; cleverly thought out. – noun **ingenuity** cleverness; quickness of ideas.

ingenuous adjective frank; without cunning. – noun **ingenuousness**.

inglenook noun a fireside corner.

ingot noun a lump (*usu* cast in oblong shape) of unworked metal, *esp* of gold or silver.

ingrained adjective deeply fixed: *ingrained laziness*.

ingratiate verb to get oneself into the favour of someone. – adjective **ingratiating**.

ingratitude noun lack of gratitude or thankfulness.

ingredient noun one of the things of which a mixture is made.

inhabit verb to live in. – noun **inhabitant** someone who lives permanently in a place.

inhale verb to breathe in. – noun **inhalant** a medicine which is inhaled. – noun **inhalation** the act of inhaling; a medicine which is inhaled. – noun **inhaler** a device that enables a person to breathe in medicine, steam *etc*.

inherent adjective inborn, belonging naturally.

inherit verb to receive property *etc* as an heir; to possess the qualities of one's parents *etc*: *She inherits her quick temper from her mother*. – noun **inheritance** that which one gets (by will) when a relative dies. – noun **inheritor** an heir.

inhibit verb to hold back, prevent. – adjective **inhibited** unable to let oneself go. – noun **inhibition** a holding back (of natural impulses *etc*), restraint.

inhospitable adjective unwelcoming, unfriendly.

inhuman *adjective* not human; brutal. – *noun* **inhumanity**.

inhumane *adjective* cruel.

inimical *adjective* unfriendly, hostile.

inimitable *adjective* impossible to imitate.

iniquity *noun* (*plural* **iniquities**) wickedness; a sin. – *adjective* **iniquitous** unjust; wicked.

initial *adjective* of or at a beginning: *There were initial problems in running the new school.* – *noun* the letter beginning a word *esp* a name. – *verb* (*past tense* **initialled**) to put the initials of one's name to.

initiate *verb* to begin, start: *It was he who initiated the reforms*; to give first lessons to; to admit (*esp* with secret ceremonies) to a society *etc*. – *noun* **initiation**. – *noun* **initiative** (the right to take) the first step; readiness to take a lead.

inject *verb* to force (a fluid *etc*) into the veins or muscles by means of a needle and syringe; to put (*eg* enthusiasm) into. – *noun* **injection**.

injudicious *adjective* unwise.

injunction *noun* an order or command.

injure *verb* to harm, damage; to wrong. – *adjective* **injured** hurt; offended. – *noun* **injury** (*plural* **injuries**) hurt, damage, harm; a wrong.

injustice *noun* unfairness; a wrong.

ink *noun* a coloured (often dark blue or black) liquid used in writing, printing *etc*. – *verb* to mark with ink. – *adjective* **inky** of or covered in ink; very dark.

inkling *noun* a hint or slight sign.

inlaid *see* **inlay**.

inland *adjective* not beside the sea; carried on *etc* inside a country (as **inland revenue** taxes *etc* collected within the country). – *adverb* towards the inner part of a country.

inlay *noun* a kind of decoration done by fitting pieces of different shapes and colours into a background. – *verb* to do this kind of work. – *adjective* **inlaid**.

inlet *noun* a small bay.

inmate *noun* a resident or occupant (*esp* of an institution): *the inmates of the prison.*

inmost *adjective* the most inward, the farthest in.

inn *noun* a house for the lodging of travellers, a small country hotel. – *noun* **innkeeper** a person who keeps an inn.

innate *adjective* inborn, natural.

inner *adjective* farther in; (of feelings *etc*) hidden. – *adjective* **innermost** farthest in; most secret.

innings *noun* a team's turn for batting in cricket; a turn or a go (at something).

innocent *adjective* not guilty, blameless; harmless; (with **of**) lacking, without: *innocent of make-up.* – *noun* **innocence**.

innocuous *adjective* not harmful.

innovation *noun* something new.

innuendo *noun* (*plural* **innuendoes**) (a remark containing) a disagreeable hint.

innumerable *adjective* too many to be counted.

innumerate *adjective* having no understanding of arithmetic or mathematics. – *noun* **innumeracy**.

inoculate *verb* to give (a person *etc*) a mild form of a disease (by injecting germs in his blood) so that he may not easily catch it. – *noun* **inoculation**.

inoffensive *adjective* harmless, giving no offence.

inopportune *adjective* at a bad or inconvenient time.

inordinate *adjective* going beyond the limit, unreasonably great.

inorganic *adjective* not having the characteristics of living bodies.

in-patient *noun* a patient who lives in, as well as being treated in a hospital.

input *noun* an amount (of energy, labour *etc*) that is put into something; information fed into a computer.

inquest *noun* a legal inquiry into a case of sudden death.

inquire or **enquire** *verb* to ask. – *noun* **inquirer** or **enquirer**. – *adjective* **inquiring** or **enquiring** questioning; eager to find out. – *noun* **inquiry** or **enquiry** (*plural* **inquiries** or **enquiries**) a question; a search for information; an investigation.

inquisition *noun* a careful questioning or investigation. – *noun* **inquisitor** an official investigator.

inquisitive *adjective* eager to find out; fond of prying into the affairs of others.

inroad *noun* a raid, an advance (into). – **make inroads into** to use up large amounts of: *While unemployed he made inroads into his savings.*

insane *adjective* mad, not sane. – *noun* **insanity**.

insanitary *adjective* not sanitary, likely to help the spread of disease.

insatiable *adjective* not able to be satisfied.

inscribe *verb* to write or engrave on (*eg* a name on the first page of a book, or on a monument). – *noun* **inscription** the writing on a book, monument *etc*.

inscrutable *adjective* not able to be searched into and understood, mysterious.

insect *noun* any small six-legged creature with wings and a body divided into sections. – *noun* **insecticide** powder or liquid for killing insects. – *adjective* **insectivorous** (of plants and animals) feeding on insects.

insecure *adjective* not safe; not firm; not feeling secure or settled. – *noun* **insecurity**.

insensible *adjective* unconscious, unaware (of); not having feeling.

insensitive *adjective* (with **to**) not feeling: *insensitive to cold*; unsympathetic (to): *insensitive to her grief*; unappreciative of (*eg* beauty).

inseparable *adjective* not able to be separated or kept apart.

insert *verb* to put in or among. – *noun* something put in. – *noun* **insertion** the act of putting in; an insert.

inset *noun* something set in (*eg* a small picture, map *etc* in a corner of a larger one).

inshore *adjective* (of fishing *etc*) carried on near the shore. – *adverb* to or near the shore.

inside *noun* the side, space or part within; indoors. – *adjective* being on or in the inside; indoor; coming from or done by someone within an organization *etc*: *inside information*. – *adverb* to, in or on the inside. – *preposition* to the inside of; within.

insidious *adjective* likely to trap those who are not careful, treacherous; (of a disease *etc*) coming on gradually and unnoticed.

insight *noun* power of looking into a matter and understanding clearly.

insignia *noun plural* signs or badges showing that one holds an office, award *etc*.

insignificant *adjective* of little importance. – *noun* **insignificance**.

insincere *adjective* not sincere. – *noun* **insincerity**.

insinuate *verb* to hint (at a fault); to put in (something) gradually (and secretly); to work oneself into (favour). – *noun* **insinuation** a sly hint.

insipid *adjective* dull, without liveliness; tasteless.

insist *verb* to urge something strongly: *insist on punctuality*; to refuse to give way, to hold firmly to one's intentions *etc*: *He insists on walking there*; to go on saying (that): *He insists that he saw a ghost*. – *adjective* **insistent** holding fast to what one claims; compelling attention. – *noun* **insistence**.

insolent *adjective* rude, impertinent, insulting. – *noun* **insolence**.

insoluble *adjective* not able to be dissolved; (of a problem *etc*) not able to be solved.

insolvent *adjective* not able to pay one's debts. – *noun* **insolvency**.

insomnia *noun* sleeplessness. – *adjective, noun* **insomniac** (of) a person who suffers from insomnia.

inspect *verb* to look carefully into, to examine; to look over (troops *etc*) ceremonially. – *noun* **inspection** careful examination. – *noun* **inspector** an official who inspects; a police officer below a superintendent and above a sergeant in rank.

inspire *verb* to encourage, rouse; to be the source of (poetic) ideas; to breathe in. – *noun* **inspiration** something or someone that influences or encourages; a very good idea; breathing in. – *adjective* **inspired** seeming to be aided by higher powers; brilliantly good.

inst. *abbreviation* this month: *10th inst*.

instability *noun* lack of steadiness or stability (*esp* in the personality).

install or **instal** *verb* (*past tense* **installed**) to place in position, or put in ready for use (as electricity into a house); to introduce formally to a new job *etc*. – *noun* **installation** the act of installing; something installed.

instalment *noun* a part of a sum of money paid at fixed times until the whole amount is paid; one part of a serial story.

instance *noun* an example, a particular case. – *verb* to mention as an example. – **at the instance of** at the request of.

instant *adjective* immediate, urgent; able to be prepared *etc* almost immediately: *instant coffee.* – *noun* a very short time, a moment; point or moment of time. – *adjective* **instantaneous** done, happening very quickly. – *adverb* **instantly** immediately.

instead *adverb* in place of someone or something: *He will go instead.* – **instead of** in place of: *Walk instead of running.*

instep *noun* the arching, upper part of the foot.

instigate *verb* to stir up, encourage. – *noun* **instigation.**

instil *verb* (*past tense* **instilled**) to put in little by little (*esp* ideas into the mind).

instinct *noun* a natural feeling or knowledge, which living things seem to have without thinking and without being taught. – *adjective* **instinctive** due to instinct.

institute *verb* to set up, establish, start. – *noun* a society, organization *etc* or the building it uses. – *noun* **institution** a society, organization, building *etc* established for a particular purpose (*esp* care or education); an established custom. – *adjective* **institutional.**

instruct *verb* to teach; to direct or command. – *noun* **instruction** teaching; a command; (*plural*) rules showing how something is to be used. – *adjective* **instructive** containing or giving information or knowledge. – *noun* **instructor.**

instrument *noun* a thing used in doing something, a tool; something for producing musical sounds (such as a piano, trumpet). – *adjective* **instrumental** helpful in bringing (something) about; belonging to or produced by musical instruments. – *noun* **instrumentalist** a person who plays on a musical instrument.

insubordinate *adjective* rebellious, disobedient. – *noun* **insubordination.**

insufferable *adjective* not able to be endured.

insufficient *adjective* not enough. – *noun* **insufficiency.**

insular *adjective* of an island or islands; (of opinions) narrow, prejudiced.

insulate *verb* to cover (something) with a material that will not let through electrical currents, or heat, or sound; to cut off, isolate. – *noun* **insulation.**

insulin *noun* a substance used in the treatment of diabetes.

insult *verb* to treat with scorn or rudeness. – Also *noun.* – *adjective* **insulting** scornful, rude.

insuperable *adjective* that cannot be overcome.

insure *verb* to arrange for payment of a sum of money on (something) if it should be lost, damaged, stolen *etc.* – *noun* **insurance.**

insurgent *adjective* rising up in rebellion. – *noun* a rebel.

insurmountable *adjective* not able to be got over.

insurrection *noun* a rising up in rebellion.

intact *adjective* whole, unbroken.

intake *noun* a thing or quantity taken in.

intangible *adjective* not able to be felt by touch; difficult to define or describe, not clear.

integer *noun* a whole number, not a fraction. – *adjective* **integral** of or essential to a whole: *an integral part of the machine;* made up of parts forming a whole. – *verb* **integrate** to fit parts together to form a whole; to enable (racial) groups to mix freely with each other and live on equal terms. – *noun* **integration.** – *noun* **integrity** honesty; state of being whole.

intellect *noun* the thinking power of the mind. – *adjective* **intellectual** showing or requiring intellect. – *noun* a person of natural ability or with academic interests.

intelligent *adjective* clever, quick at understanding. – *noun* **intelligence** mental ability; information sent, news. – *adjective* **intelligible** able to be understood.

intemperate *adjective* going beyond reasonable limits, uncontrolled; having the habit of drinking too much. – *noun* **intemperance.**

intend *verb* to mean or plan to (do something). – *noun* **intent** purpose. – *adjective* with all one's mind (on), attentive; determined (on). – *noun* **intention** what one means to do; meaning. – *adjective* **intentional** done on purpose. – *adverb* **intentionally.**

intense *adjective* very great; (of a person) over-serious, inclined to feel strongly. – *verb* **intensify** (*past tense* **intensified**) to increase. – *noun* **intensity** (*plural* **intensities**) strength (of feeling, colour *etc*). – *adjective* **intensive** very thorough, concentrated. – *noun* **intensive care** a unit in a hospital where a patient's condition is carefully monitored.

inter- *prefix* between, among, together as in **intertwine.**

inter *verb* (*past tense* **interred**) to bury. – *noun* **interment.**

interact *verb* to act on one another.

intercede *verb* to act as peacemaker between two persons, nations *etc*. – *noun* **intercession.** – *noun* **intercessor.**

intercept *verb* to stop or seize on the way; to cut off, interrupt (a view, the light *etc*).

interchange *verb* to put each in the place of the other; to (cause to) alternate. – *noun* the act of interchanging; a junction of two or more major roads on separate levels to allow cars *etc* to transfer from one to another without lines of traffic crossing each other. – *adjective* **interchangeable** able to be used one for the other.

intercom *noun* a telephone system within a building, aeroplane *etc*.

intercourse *noun* communication; dealings between people *etc*; sexual intercourse.

interdict *noun* an order forbidding something.

interest *noun* special attention, curiosity; a thing with which one concerns oneself; advantage, benefit; a sum paid for the loan of money. – *verb* to catch or hold the attention of. – *adjective* **interested** having or taking an interest. – *adjective* **interesting** holding the attention.

interfere *verb* (with **in**) to take part in what is not one's business, meddle; (with **with**) to get in the way of, hinder; *interfere with the progress of the plan.* – *noun* **interference** the act of interfering; the spoiling of radio or television reception by another station or local disturbance (lightning, traffic *etc*).

interim *noun* time between; the meantime. – *adjective* temporary.

interior *adjective* inner; inside a building; inland. – *noun* the inside of anything; the inland part of a country.

interject *verb* to throw a remark in (to a conversation); to exclaim. – *noun* **interjection** word or words of exclamation (*eg* Ah! Oh dear!).

interlock *verb* to lock or clasp together; to fit into each other.

interloper *noun* a person who goes in without having the right to go in, an intruder.

interlude *noun* an interval, or what happens in it; a short piece of music played between the parts of a play, film *etc*.

intermarry *verb* (of a race or group) to marry with members of another race *etc*; to marry with members of the same group, race *etc*.

intermediary *noun* (*plural* **intermediaries**) someone who acts between two persons (*eg* in trying to settle a quarrel).

intermediate *adjective* in the middle; coming between.

interment *see* **inter.**

interminable *adjective* never-ending, boringly long.

intermission *noun* an interval, a pause.

intermittent *adjective* ceasing every now and then and starting again.

intern *verb* to keep someone from the enemy side prisoner in a country while a war is going on. – *noun* **internee** someone who is confined in this way. – *noun* **internment.**

internal *adjective* of the inner part *esp* of the body; inside, within (a country, organization *etc*).

international *adjective* happening between nations; concerning or involving more than one nation; world-wide. – *noun* a match between teams of two countries.

internecine *adjective* (of feuds *etc* within a group) causing deaths on both sides.

interplanetary *adjective* between the planets.

interplay *noun* the action of one thing on another.

interpose *verb* to place or come between, to put in (a remark *etc*) by way of interruption.

interpret *verb* to explain the meaning of something; to translate; to bring out the meaning of something (as music, a part in a play *etc*) in one's performance;

to take the meaning of something to be. – *noun* **interpretation**. – *noun* **interpreter** a person who translates (on the spot) the words of a speaker into the language of his hearers.

interregnum *noun* the time between the end of one reign and the beginning of the next.

interrogate *verb* to examine by asking questions, to question. – *noun* **interrogation**. – *noun* **interrogative** a word used in asking a question (*eg* Why? Who?). – *adjective* questioning. – *noun* **interrogator**.

interrupt *verb* to stop (a person) while they are saying or doing something; to stop (something that one is doing); to get in the way of, cut off (a view *etc*). – *noun* **interruption**.

intersect *verb* (of lines *etc*) to meet and cross. – *noun* **intersection** the point where two lines cross; a crossroads.

intersperse *verb* to scatter here and there in. – *noun* **interspersion**.

interstice *in-tûr'stis*, *noun* a small space between things placed close together, a chink.

intertwine *verb* to twine or twist together.

interval *noun* a time or space between; a short pause in a programme *etc*.

intervene *verb* to come or be between, or in the way; to join in (in order to stop) a fight or quarrel between other persons or nations. – *noun* **intervention**.

interview *noun* a formal meeting of one person with one or more others for purposes of business (*eg* an appointment to a job) or of publishing or broadcasting information. – Also *verb*.

intestate *adjective* without having made a will: *He died intestate.*

intestines *noun plural* the inside parts of the body, *usu* the bowels and passages leading to them. – *adjective* **intestinal**.

intimate *adjective* knowing much about, familiar (with); (of friends) close; private, personal; having a sexual relationship (with). – *noun* a close friend. – *verb* to hint; to announce. – *noun* **intimacy** (*plural* **intimacies**) close friendship; familiarity; sexual intercourse. – *noun* **intimation** a hint; an announcement.

intimidate *verb* to frighten (*esp* by threatening violence). – *adjective* **intimidating**. – *noun* **intimidation**.

into *preposition* to the inside: *into the room*; to a different state: *A tadpole changes into a frog*; (*maths*) expressing the idea of division: *2 into 4 goes twice*.

intolerable *adjective* not able to be endured. – *adjective* **intolerant** not willing to put up with (people of different ideas, race, religion *etc*). – *noun* **intolerance**.

intone *verb* to speak in a singing manner, to chant. – *noun* **intonation** the rise and fall of the voice.

intoxicate *verb* to make drunk; to excite. – *noun* **intoxicant** a strong drink. – *noun* **intoxication** drunkenness.

intra- *prefix* within.

intractable *adjective* difficult, stubborn.

intransigent *adjective* refusing to come to an agreement. – *noun* **intransigence**.

intransitive *adjective* (of verbs) not of the kind that can take an object (as *to go*, *to fall*).

intrepid *adjective* without fear, brave. – *noun* **intrepidity**.

intricate *adjective* complicated, having many twists and turns. – *noun* **intricacy** (*plural* **intricacies**) the state of being intricate; something intricate.

intrigue *noun* a secret plot or scheming; a secret love affair. – *verb* to plot; to rouse the curiosity of, fascinate. – *adjective* **intriguing**.

intrinsic *adjective* belonging to a thing as part of its nature.

introduce *verb* to bring in or put in; to make (a person) known (to another). – *noun* **introduction** the introducing of a person or thing; something written (or said) at the beginning of a book (or speech *etc*) briefly explaining its contents *etc*. – *adjective* **introductory** coming at the beginning.

introspective *adjective* inward-looking, fond of examining one's thoughts, feelings *etc*. – *noun* **introspection**.

intrude *verb* to thrust (oneself) in uninvited or unwanted. – *noun* **intruder** someone who breaks in or intrudes. – *noun* **intrusion**. – *adjective* **intrusive**.

intuition *noun* the power of grasping a fact or idea without thinking it out; an idea so grasped.

Inuit *noun* (one of) the Eskimo people; their language.

inundate *verb* to flood; to overwhelm: *I'm inundated with work.* – *noun* **inundation.**

inure *verb* to make accustomed (to pain *etc*).

invade *verb* to enter (a country *etc*) as an enemy intending to take possession; to interfere with (someone's rights, privacy *etc*). – *noun* **invader.** – *noun* **invasion.**

invalid[1] *adjective* (of a passport *etc*) not valid, not legally effective. – *verb* **invalidate** to make invalid. – *noun* **invalidity.**

invalid[2] *noun* a person who is ill or disabled. – Also *adjective*. – *verb* to cause to be an invalid; (with **out**) to discharge as an invalid (*esp* out of the army).

invaluable *adjective* too precious to have its value estimated, priceless.

invariable *adjective* unchanging. – *adverb* **invariably** always.

invasion *see* **invade.**

invective *noun* words of scorn or hate, violent abuse.

inveigle *verb* to coax, entice. – *noun* **inveiglement.**

invent *verb* to make or think up (a machine, scheme *etc*) for the first time; to make up (a story, an excuse). – *noun* **invention** something invented. – *adjective* **inventive** good at inventing, resourceful. – *noun* **inventor.**

inventory *noun* (*plural* **inventories**) a detailed list of articles (as the contents of a house *etc*).

invert *verb* to turn upside down; to reverse the order of. – *adjective* **inverse** opposite, reverse. – *noun* the opposite. – *adverb* **inversely.** – *noun* **inversion** a turning upside-down; a reversal. – *noun plural* **inverted commas** commas upside down ("—", '—') or similar marks used in writing to show where direct speech begins and ends.

invertebrate *adjective* (of animals) having no backbone (*eg* worms, insects). – Also *noun.*

invest *verb* to put money in a firm *etc* (*usu* in the form of shares) to make a profit; to clothe, surround something with a quality; to surround, lay siege to (a stronghold *etc*). – *noun* **investiture** a ceremony of giving (the robes *etc* of) high office to someone. – *noun* **investment** something (*esp* money) invested;

something in which money is invested; a siege. – *noun* **investor** a person who invests.

investigate *verb* to search into with care. – *noun* **investigation** a careful search. – *noun* **investigator.**

inveterate *adjective* firmly fixed in a habit by long practice: *an inveterate gambler*; (of a quality, habit *etc*) deep-rooted. – *noun* **inveteracy.**

invidious *adjective* likely to cause ill-will or envy.

invigilate *verb* to supervise (an examination *etc*). – *noun* **invigilator.**

invigorate *verb* to strengthen, refresh. – *adjective* **invigorating.**

invincible *adjective* not able to be defeated or surmounted. – *noun* **invincibility.**

inviolable *adjective* (of an oath, a right, a person) to be treated as sacred, not to be broken or disregarded or harmed. – *noun* **inviolability.** – *adjective* **inviolate** not violated, free from harm *etc*.

invisible *adjective* not able to be seen. – *noun* **invisibility.**

invite *verb* to ask a person politely to do something, *esp* to come (to one's house, to a meal *etc*); to ask for or to seem by one's behaviour to be asking for: *His behaviour invites punishment.* – *noun* **invitation** a (written) request (to come). – *adjective* **inviting** tempting, attractive.

in vitro *adjective* (*esp* of the fertilization of a human ovum) in a test tube, in a laboratory.

invocation *see* **invoke.**

invoice *noun* a letter sent with goods with details of price and quantity. – *verb* to make such a list.

invoke *verb* to call upon (in prayer); to ask for (*eg* help); to call forth (a spirit). – *noun* **invocation.**

involuntary *adjective* not done willingly or intentionally. – *adverb* **involuntarily.**

involve *verb* to have as a consequence, to require; to (cause a person to) take part (in) or be concerned (in): *She is involved in social work. His son was involved in the disgrace.* – *adjective* **involved** complicated. – *noun* **involvement.**

inward *adjective* placed within; situated in the mind or soul. – *adverb* (also **inwards**) towards the inside. – *adverb*

inwardly within; in the heart, privately.

iodine *noun* an element, used in liquid form to kill germs.

ion *noun* an electrically-charged atom or group of atoms.

iota *noun* a little bit.

IOU *noun* short for *I owe you*, a note given as a receipt for money borrowed.

IQ *abbreviation* Intelligence Quotient.

IRA *abbreviation* Irish Republican Army.

irascible *adjective* easily made angry. – *noun* **irascibility**.

ire *noun* anger. – *adjective* **irate** angry.

iridescent *adjective* coloured like a rainbow; shimmering with changing colours. – *noun* **iridescence**.

iris *noun* (*plural* **irises**) the coloured part of the eye round the pupil; a type of lily-like flower which grows from a bulb.

irk *verb* to weary, annoy. – *adjective* **irksome** tiresome.

iron *noun* an element, the most common metal, widely used to make tools *etc*; an iron instrument: *a branding iron*; a golf club *orig.* but now not necessarily, having an iron head; an appliance for smoothing clothes; (*plural*) a prisoner's chains. – *adjective* made of iron; like iron; stern; (of a rule *etc*) not to be broken. – *verb* to smooth with an iron; (with **out**) to smooth out (difficulties). – *noun* **ironmonger** a dealer in articles made of iron (**ironmongery**).

irony *noun* (*plural* **ironies**) a form of deliberate mockery in which someone says the opposite of what is obviously true; apparent mockery in a situation, words *etc: The irony of it was that she would have given him the money if he hadn't stolen it.* – *adjective* **ironic**. – *adjective* **ironical**.

irrational *adjective* against (the rules of) common-sense.

irregular *adjective* not regular; uneven, variable; against the rules. – *noun* **irregularity** (*plural* **irregularities**).

irrelevant *adjective* not having to do with what is being spoken about. – *noun* **irrelevancy** (*plural* **irrelevancies**).

irreparable *adjective* not able to be repaired.

irreplaceable *adjective* too good, precious, rare *etc* to be replaced.

irrepressible *adjective* (of high spirits *etc*) not able to be kept in check.

irreproachable *adjective* not able to be found fault with.

irresistible *adjective* too strong or too charming to be resisted.

irresolute *adjective* not able to make up one's mind or keep to one's decision.

irrespective *adjective* taking no account of: *He went every day irrespective of the weather.*

irresponsible *adjective* having no sense of responsibility, thoughtless.

irreverent *adjective* having no respect (*eg* for holy things). – *noun* **irreverence**.

irrevocable *adjective* not to be changed.

irrigate *verb* to supply (land) with water (by canals *etc*). – *noun* **irrigation**.

irritate *verb* to annoy; to cause discomfort, inflammation (to the skin, eyes *etc*). – *adjective* **irritable** cross, easily annoyed. – *noun* **irritation** annoyance; discomfort *etc* of the skin *etc*.

Islam *noun* the Muslim religion, founded by the prophet Mohammed; the Muslim world. – *adjective* **Islamic**.

island *noun* land surrounded with water; anything resembling this, as a **traffic island**, built in the middle of a street for pedestrians to stand on. – *noun* **islander** an inhabitant of an island.

isle *noun* an island.

isobar *noun* a line on the map connecting places where atmospheric pressure is the same.

isolate *verb* to place or keep someone or something separate from others; to consider a thing by itself. – *noun* **isolation**.

isosceles *adjective* (of a triangle) having two sides equal.

isotherm *noun* a line on the map connecting places which have the same temperature.

issue *verb* to go, flow, or come out; to give out (orders *etc*); to publish. – *noun* a flow; children: *He died without issue*; publication; the copies of a book published at one time; one number in the series (of a magazine *etc*); result, consequence; the actual question which is being argued about or discussed. – **to take issue** to disagree (with).

isthmus *noun* (*plural* **isthmuses**) a narrow neck of land connecting two larger portions.

it *pronoun* the thing spoken of: *My hat disappeared but I found it again*; used in sentences that have no real subject: *It snowed today. It is too late*; used in phrases as a kind of object: *Go it alone. Brave it out.* – *adjective* **its** belonging to it. – *pronoun* **itself** used reflexively: *The cat licked itself*; used for emphasis: *After we've seen the garden we'll see the house itself.*

italics *noun plural* a kind of type which *slopes to the right.* – *verb* **italicize** to print in italics.

itch *noun* an irritating feeling in the skin which is made better by scratching; a strong desire. – *verb* to have an itch; to long (to). – *adjective* **itchy.**

item *noun* a separate article or detail (in a list). – *verb* **itemize** to list item by item or in detail.

itinerant *adjective* making journeys from place to place (on business *etc*), travelling. – *noun* a person who travels around, *esp* a tramp, gypsy, pedlar *etc*.

itinerary *noun* (*plural* **itineraries**) a route or plan of a journey.

its, itself *see* **it.**

it's short for **it is.**

ITV *abbreviation* Independent Television.

IUCD or **IUD** *abbreviation* intra-uterine (contraceptive) device.

IVF *abbreviation* in vitro fertilization.

ivory *noun* (*plural* **ivories**) the hard white substance which forms the tusks of the elephant, walrus *etc*; a carving *etc* in ivory.

ivy *noun* (*plural* **ivies**) a creeping evergreen plant.

J

jab *verb* (*past tense* **jabbed**) to poke, stab. – *noun* a poke; a punch; (*coll*) an injection.

jabber *verb* to talk rapidly (and indistinctly). – Also *noun.*

jack *noun* an instrument for raising heavy weights such as motor cars; the playing-card between ten and queen, the knave. – *verb* (*usu* with **up**) to raise with a jack. – *noun plural* **jackboots** large boots reaching above the knee. – *noun* **jack-in-the-box** a figure that is fixed to a spring inside a box and leaps out when the lid is opened. – *noun* **jack-knife** a large folding knife; a dive resembling a jack-knife's action. – *verb* (of a vehicle and its trailer) to swing together to form a sharp angle.

jackal *noun* a dog-like wild animal.

jackass *noun* a male ass; (*coll*) a stupid person. – *noun* **laughing jackass** the Australian giant kingfisher or kookaburra.

jackdaw *noun* a type of small crow.

jacket *noun* a short coat; a covering, *esp* a loose paper cover for a book.

jackpot *noun* a fund of prize money which has mounted up because of being so far unwon.

Jacuzzi® *noun* a bath fitted with a mechanism that agitates the water.

jade *noun* hard green mineral substance used for ornaments. – *adjective* **jaded** tired.

jagged *adjective* rough-edged, uneven.

jaguar *noun* a type of South American animal like a leopard.

jail or **gaol** *noun* a prison. – *noun* **jailbird** or **gaolbird** a person who has been in jail. – *noun* **jailer** or **gaoler** a person who has charge of a jail or of prisoners.

jam *noun* fruit boiled with sugar till it is set; a crush; a stopping or blockage caused by crowding together; (*coll*) a difficult situation. – *verb* (*past tense* **jammed**) to press or squeeze tight; to crowd full; to stick and so be unable to move: *This wheel has jammed*; to cause interference with another radio station's broadcast.

jamb *noun* the side post of a door.

jamboree *noun* a large, lively gathering; a rally of Boy Scouts.

jangle *verb* to sound harshly with a ringing noise; to irritate.

janitor *noun* a caretaker; a doorkeeper.

January *noun* the first month of the year.

jar *noun* a glass or earthenware bottle with a wide mouth. – *verb* (*past tense* **jarred**) to have a harsh, startling effect; to hurt by a sudden (violent) movement. – *adjective* **jarring** harsh, startling.

jargon *noun* special words used within a particular trade, profession *etc*.

jasmine *noun* a shrub with white or yellow sweet-smelling flowers.

jaundice *noun* a disease which causes yellowness of the skin *etc*. – *adjective* **jaundiced** having jaundice; discontented, bitter.

jaunt *noun* a journey, *esp* one for pleasure. – *adjective* **jaunty** cheerful, gay.

javelin *noun* a long spear for throwing.

jaw *noun* the mouth, chin *etc*, the lower part of the face; (*plural*) the mouth (*esp* of an animal).

jay *noun* a brightly-coloured bird of the crow kind. – *noun* **jaywalker** a person who walks carelessly among traffic.

jazz *noun* popular music of American Negro origin.

JCB® *jā-sē-bĕ*, *noun* a type of mobile excavator.

jealous *adjective* wanting to have what someone else has, envious; carefully looking after what one thinks much of. – *noun* **jealousy**.

jeans *noun plural* denim trousers.

jeep *noun* a small army motor vehicle.

jeer *verb* to make fun of, scoff. – Also *noun*.

jelly *noun* (*plural* **jellies**) the juice of fruit boiled with sugar till it becomes firm; a transparent wobbly food *usu* fruit-flavoured; anything in a jelly-like state. – *noun* **jellyfish** a sea animal with a jelly-like body.

jemmy *noun* (*plural* **jemmies**) a burglar's iron tool.

jeopardy *noun* danger. – *verb* **jeopardize** to put in danger or at risk.

jerboa *noun* a small rat-like desert animal with very long hindlegs.

jerk *verb* to give a sudden sharp movement. – Also *noun*. – *adjective* **jerky** moving or coming in jerks.

jerkin *noun* a type of short coat.

jersey *noun* (*plural* **jerseys**) a sweater, pullover.

jest *noun* a joke. – *verb* to joke. – *noun* **jester** (*hist*) a court fool, once employed by kings, nobles *etc* to amuse them.

jet *noun* a hard black mineral substance, used for ornaments *etc*; a spout of flame, air or liquid; a jet plane. – *adjective* **jet-black** very black. – *noun* **jet lag** tiredness, lack of concentration *etc* caused by the body's inability to cope with the time changes resulting from rapid air travel. – *noun* **jet plane** one driven by jet propulsion. – *noun* **jet propulsion** high speed forward motion produced by sucking in air, liquid *etc* and forcing it out from behind. – *noun* **jet set** rich people who enjoy frequent jet travel and expensive holidays.

jetsam *noun* goods thrown overboard and washed ashore.

jettison *verb* to throw overboard; to abandon.

jetty *noun* (*plural* **jetties**) a small pier.

Jew *noun* one who is of the race or religion of the Israelites. – *adjective* **Jewish** of the Jews. – *noun* **Jew's harp** a small harp-shaped musical instrument played between the teeth.

jewel *noun* a precious stone; anything or anyone highly valued. – *adjective* **jewelled** or (*usu US*) **jeweled** set with jewels. – *noun* **jeweller** or (*usu US*) **jeweler** one who makes or deals in articles made of precious jewels and metals. – *noun* **jewellery** or (*usu US*) **jewelry** articles made or sold by a jeweller.

jib *noun* a three-cornered sail in front of a ship's foremast; the jutting-out arm of a crane. – *verb* (*past tense* **jibbed**) (with **at**) to refuse to (do something), object to.

jibe or **gibe** *verb* to jeer, scoff. – Also *noun*.

jig *noun* a lively dance. – *verb* (*past tense* **jigged**) to jump about.

jigsaw (puzzle) *noun* a puzzle consisting of many different shaped pieces that fit together to form a picture.

jilt *verb* to cast aside (a lover) after previously encouraging them.

jingle *noun* a clinking sound (as of coins); a simple rhyme. – Also *verb*.

job *noun* a person's daily work; any piece of work. – *adjective* **jobbing** doing odd jobs of work for payment; *jobbing gardener*. – *noun* **job centre** a government office where information about available jobs is shown. – *noun* **job-lot** a collection of odds and ends.

jockey *noun* (*plural* **jockeys**) a person who rides a horse in a race. – *verb* to push one's way (into a good position).

jocular *adjective* joking, merry.

jodhpurs *noun plural* riding breeches, fitting tightly from knee to ankle.

jog *verb* (*past tense* **jogged**) to nudge, push slightly; to travel slowly; to run at a gentle pace. – *noun* **jogger** a person who runs gently. – *noun* **jogging**.

joggle *verb* to shake slightly. – Also *noun*.

join *verb* to put or come together; to connect, fasten; to become a member of; to come and meet. – *noun* the place where two or more things join. – *noun* **joiner** a person who joins; a worker in wood. – *noun* **joint** the place where two or more things join; the place where two bones are joined (*eg* elbow or knee); meat containing a (joint) bone. – *adjective* united; shared among more than one. – *adverb* **jointly** together. – **join battle** to begin fighting in battle.

joist *noun* the beam to which the boards of a floor or the laths of a ceiling are nailed.

joke *noun* anything said or done to cause laughter. – Also *verb*. – *noun* **joker** a person who jokes; an extra playing-card in a pack.

jolly *adjective* merry. – *noun* **jollification** noisy (feasting and) merriment. – *noun* **jolliness** or **jollity** merriment.

jollyboat *noun* a small boat belonging to a ship.

jolt *verb* to shake suddenly; to go forward with sudden jerks. – *noun* a sudden jerk.

joss-stick *noun* a stick of gum which gives off a sweet smell when burned.

jostle *verb* to push or knock against.

jot *noun* a very small part. – *verb* (*past tense* **jotted**) to write down hurriedly or briefly. – *noun* **jotter** a book for note-taking.

joule *noun* a unit of energy.

journal *noun* an account kept of each day's doings, a diary; a newspaper, a magazine. – *noun* **journalism** the business of recording daily events for the media, *esp* papers and magazines. – *noun* **journalist**.

journey *noun* (*plural* **journeys**) a distance travelled. – *verb* to travel. – *noun* **journeyman** a person whose apprenticeship is finished.

joust *noun* (*hist*) the armed contest between two knights on horseback at a tournament. – *verb* to fight on horseback at a tournament.

jovial *adjective* cheerful, good-humoured. – *noun* **joviality**.

jowl *noun* the lower part of the jaw or cheek.

joy *noun* gladness. – *adjective* **joyful** or **joyous** full of joy. – *adjective* **joyless** dismal. – *noun* **joy-ride** a trip for amusement, *esp* reckless and in a stolen car.

JP *abbreviation* Justice of the Peace.

Jr *abbreviation* Junior: *John Brown Jr*.

jubilant *adjective* full of rejoicing, triumphant. – *noun* **jubilation**.

jubilee *noun* celebrations arranged in memory of some event (such as a wedding, coronation *etc*).

judge *verb* to hear the evidence *etc* in a question of law and make a decision on it; to form an opinion; to decide which is best in a competition *etc*. – *noun* (in the courts of law) one who hears cases and decides on them according to the country's laws; one skilled in finding out good and bad points (*esp* of those in a competition). – *noun* **judgement** or **judgment** a decision (in a court of law *etc*); an opinion; good sense in forming opinions.

judicial *adjective* of a judge or court of justice.

judiciary *noun* the judges of a country taken as a whole.

judicious *adjective* wise.

judo *noun* a form of wrestling for self-defence, *orig* practised in Japan.

jug *noun* a dish for liquids *usu* with a handle and a shaped lip for pouring.

juggernaut *noun* a large (articulated) lorry.

juggle *verb* to toss a number of things (balls, clubs *etc*) into the air and catch them; to handle or present in a deceitful way. – *noun* **juggler.**

jugular vein *noun* the large vein at the side of the neck.

juice *noun* the liquid in vegetables, fruits *etc*. – *adjective* **juicy.**

ju-jitsu *noun* an earlier form of **judo.**

jukebox *noun* a coin-operated machine which plays selected records automatically.

July *noun* the seventh month of the year.

Juma *noun* the Islamic Sabbath, Friday.

jumble *verb* to throw together without order, muddle. – *noun* a confused mixture. – *noun* **jumble sale** a sale of odds and ends, cast-off clothing *etc*.

jumbo *noun* (*plural* **jumbos**) a child's name for an elephant – *adjective* very large. – *noun* **jumbo jet** a large jet aircraft.

jump *verb* to leap; to make a sudden (startled) movement (upwards). – Also *noun*. – *adjective* **jumpy** easily startled.

jumper *noun* a sweater or jersey.

junction *noun* a place or point of joining (*eg* of roads or railway lines).

juncture *noun* point: *At this juncture in his lecture he collapsed.*

June *noun* the sixth month of the year.

jungle *noun* a dense growth of trees and plants in tropical areas.

junior *adjective* younger; in a lower class or rank. – Also *noun*.

juniper *noun* a type of evergreen shrub with berries and prickly leaves.

junk *noun* a Chinese flat-bottomed sailing ship, high in the bow and stern; worthless articles, rubbish. – *noun* **junk bond** a bond offering a high yield but with low security. – *noun* **junk food** food of little nutritional value,

unhealthy food. – *noun* **junkie** or **junky** (*plural* **junkies**) a (drug) addict. – *noun* **junk mail** unsolicited mail *eg* advertising material.

junket *noun* a dish made of curdled milk sweetened and flavoured. – *noun* **junketing** feasting, merriment.

junta *noun* a government formed following a successful coup d'état.

jurisdiction *noun* a legal authority or power; the district over which a judge, court *etc* has power.

jurisprudence *noun* the study or knowledge of law.

jury *noun* (*plural* **juries**) a group of men or women selected to reach a decision on whether an accused prisoner is guilty or not; a group of judges for a competition *etc*. – *noun* **juror, juryman** or **jurywoman** a person who serves on a jury.

just *adjective* not favouring one more than another, fair; in keeping with one's rights; correct. – *adverb* exactly; not long since; merely, only; really: *She's just lovely.*

justice *noun* fairness in making judgements; what is right or rightly deserved; a judge. – **Justice of the Peace** (shortened to **JP**) a citizen who acts as a judge for certain matters.

justify *verb* (*past tense* **justified**) to prove or show to be just, right or desirable. – *adjective* **justifiable** able to be justified or defended. – *noun* **justification** good reason.

jut *verb* (*past tense* **jutted**) to stand or stick out.

jute *noun* the fibre from certain plants for making sacking, canvas *etc*.

juvenile *adjective* young, of young people; childish. – *noun* a young person.

juxtapose *verb* to place side by side. – *noun* **juxtaposition.**

K

k *abbreviation* kilo-, one thousand.

kale *noun* a cabbage with open curled leaves.

kaleidoscope *noun* a tube-shaped toy in which loose, coloured shapes reflected in two mirrors can be seen changing patterns. – *adjective* **kaleidoscopic** with changing colours; changing quickly.

kangaroo *noun* a large Australian animal with long hindlegs and great power of leaping. The female carries its young in a pouch on the front of its body.

kapok *noun* light waterproof fibre fluff got from the seeds of a tropical tree, used for stuffing pillows *etc*.

karate *noun* a Japanese form of unarmed fighting using blows and kicks.

karma *noun* in Buddhism, (the force of one's actions determining) one's destiny.

kayak *noun* a canoe *esp* an Eskimo canoe made of sealskins stretched on a frame.

KB *abbreviation* Knight of the Bath.

KBE *abbreviation* Knight Commander of the British Empire.

KC *abbreviation* King's Counsel; Kennel Club.

kebab *noun* small pieces of meat *etc usu* cooked on a skewer.

kedgeree *noun* a dish made with rice, fish and other ingredients.

keel *noun* the long supporting piece of a ship's frame that lies lengthways along the bottom. – *verb* (with **over**) to overturn; to fall (over). – *verb* **keelhaul** (*hist*) to punish by hauling under the keel of a ship by ropes.

keen *adjective* eager, enthusiastic; very sharp; biting cold. – *noun* **keenness**.

keep *verb* (*past tense* **kept**) to hold on to, not to give or throw away; to look after; to feed and clothe; to have or use; to fulfil (one's promise); to stay, (cause to) remain in any position or state; (sometimes with **on**) to continue (doing something); (of food) to remain in good condition; to celebrate: *keep Christmas*. – *noun* food and other necessities; a castle stronghold. – *noun* **keeper** a person who looks after something. – *noun* **keeping** care; charge. – *noun* **keepsake** a gift in memory of the giver or an occasion *etc*. – **in keeping with** suited to; **keep out** to exclude; to stay outside; **keep up** to go on with, to continue (something); **keep up with** to go as fast *etc* as.

keg *noun* a small cask or barrel.

kelp *noun* a type of large brown seaweed.

kelvin *noun* a measure of temperature.

ken *noun* the amount or extent of one's knowledge or understanding: *beyond the ken of the average person*.

kennel *noun* a hut for a dog; (*plural*) a place where dogs can be looked after.

kept *see* **keep**.

kerb *noun* the edge of something, *esp* a pavement.

kerchief *noun* a square of cloth used in dress to cover the head *etc*.

kernel *noun* the softer substance in the shell of a nut or inside the stone of a pulpy fruit; the important part of anything.

kerosene *noun* paraffin oil.

kestrel *noun* a type of small falcon which hovers.

ketch *noun* (*plural* **ketches**) a two-masted sailing vessel.

ketchup *noun* a flavouring sauce made from tomatoes *etc*.

kettle *noun* a pot *usu* with a spout for heating liquids. – *noun* **kettledrum** a drum made of a metal bowl covered with stretched skin *etc*.

key *noun* that by which something (*eg* a door lock, a nut) is turned or screwed; in musical instruments, one of the small parts for sounding the notes; in a typewriter or computer, one of the parts which one presses to type letters or give commands; the chief note of a piece of music; that which explains a mystery, code *etc*; a book containing answers to exercises *etc*. – *verb* to type on a typewriter or computer. – *adjective* important, essential. – *noun* **keyboard** the keys in a piano or organ arranged along a flat board; the keys of a typewriter or computer; an electronic musical instrument with keys arranged as on a piano *etc*. – *noun* **keyhole** the hole in which a key of a door *etc* is placed. – noun **keynote** the chief note of a piece of music; the chief point about anything. – noun **keypad** a device with buttons that can be pushed to operate something, eg a television, a telephone. – noun **keystone** the stone at the highest point of an arch holding the rest in position. – adjective **keyed-up** excited.

kg abbreviation kilogramme(s).

KGB abbreviation Committee of State Security (*Komitet Gosudartsvennoi Bezopasnosti* [*Russ*]).

khaki adjective, noun (of) greenish-brown. – noun cloth of this colour used for soldiers' uniforms.

kibbutz noun (plural **kibbutzim**) a (farming) settlement in Israel in which all share the work.

kick verb to hit or strike out with the foot; (of a gun) to spring back violently when fired. – noun a blow with the foot; the springing-back of a gun when fired. – noun **kick-off** the start (of a football game). – **for kicks** for fun.

kid noun a young goat; goatskin; (coll) a child. – adjective made of kid leather.

kidnap verb (past tense **kidnapped**) to carry off (a person or child) by force, often demanding money in exchange for them. – noun **kidnapper**.

kidney noun (plural **kidneys**) one of a pair of urine-controlling organs placed in the lower part of the back, one on each side. Some animals' kidneys are used as meat.

kill verb to put to death; to put an end to. – noun the act of killing; the animals killed by a hunter. – noun **killer**. – **be in at the kill** to be there at the most exciting moment.

kiln noun a large oven or furnace for baking pottery, bricks etc or for drying grain, hops etc.

kilogramme noun a measure of weight – 1000 grammes (about 2½ lb).

kilometre noun a measure of length – 1000 metres (about ⅝ of a mile).

kilowatt noun a measure of electrical power.

kilt noun (in Scotland) a pleated tartan skirt reaching to the knee.

kimono noun (plural **kimonos**) a loose Japanese robe, fastened with a sash.

kin noun persons of the same family, relations. – **kith and kin** see kith; **next of kin** one's nearest relative.

kind noun a sort, type; goods, not money: *paid in kind*. – adjective having good feelings towards others; generous; gentle. – adjective **kindhearted** kind. – noun **kindliness**. – adverb **kindly**. – adjective kind: *a kindly old man*. – noun **kindness**.

kindergarten noun a school for very young children.

kindle verb to light a fire; to catch fire; to stir up (feelings). – noun **kindling** material for starting a fire.

kindred noun one's relatives. – adjective of the same sort; related.

kinetic adjective of or expressing motion: *kinetic sculpture*.

king noun the male ruler of a nation, inheriting his position by right of birth; the playing-card with a picture of a king; the most important chess piece. – noun **kingcup** marsh marigold. – noun **kingdom** the area ruled by a king; any of the three great divisions of natural objects – animal, vegetable or mineral. – noun **kingfisher** a type of fish-eating bird with brightly coloured feathers. – adjective **kingly** like a king; royal. – noun **kingpin** the most important person in an organization.

kink noun a bend or curl in a rope, hair etc; a peculiarity of the mind. – adjective **kinky** (coll) having sexual perversions.

kinsman (masculine), **kinswoman** (feminine) noun a person of the same family as oneself. – noun plural **kinsfolk** one's own people, relations.

kiosk noun a small stall for the sale of papers, sweets etc; a telephone box.

kipper noun a smoked and dried herring.

kirk noun (in Scotland) a church.

kiss verb to touch lovingly with one's lips; to touch gently. – Also noun (plural **kisses**). – **kiss of life** a mouth-to-mouth method of restoring breathing.

kit noun an outfit of clothes, tools etc (necessary for a particular job etc).

kitchen noun a room where food is cooked. – noun **kitchenette** a small kitchen. – noun **kitchen-garden** a vegetable garden.

kite noun a light frame, covered with paper or other material, for flying in the air; a kind of hawk.

kith: kith and kin friends and relatives.

kitten *noun* a young cat.

kittiwake *noun* a type of gull.

kitty *noun* (*plural* **kitties**) a sum of money set aside for a purpose.

kiwi *noun* a swift-running almost wingless bird of New Zealand.

kleptomania *noun* an uncontrollable desire to steal. – *noun, adjective* **kleptomaniac.**

km *abbreviation* kilometre(s).

knack *nak, noun* a special clever ability.

knacker *nak'èr, noun* a buyer of old horses for slaughter.

knapsack *nap·sak, noun* a bag for food, clothes *etc* slung on the back.

knave *nāv, noun* a cheating rogue; (in playing-cards) the jack. – *noun* **knavery** dishonesty. – *adjective* **knavish** cheating, wicked.

knead *nēd, verb* to work (dough *etc*) by pressing with the fingers; to massage.

knee *nē, noun* the joint at the bend of the leg. – *noun* **kneecap** the flat round bone on the front of the knee joint. – *verb* to cause to suffer **kneecapping,** a form of torture or punishment in which the victim is shot or otherwise injured in the kneecap.

kneel *nēl, verb* (*past tense* **knelt**) to go down on one or both knees.

knell *nel, noun* the tolling of a bell for a death or funeral; a warning of a sad end or failure.

knickerbockers *nik·èr-bok-èrz, noun plural* loose breeches tucked in at the knee.

knickers *nik·èrz, noun plural* women's and girls' underwear for the lower part of the body.

knick-knack *nik·nak. noun* a small, ornamental article.

knife *nīf, noun* (*plural* **knives**) a tool for cutting. – *verb* to stab. – **at knife point** under threat of injury.

knight *nīt, noun* (*hist*) one of noble birth, trained to use arms; a rank, with the title *Sir,* which does not go down from father to son; a piece used in chess. – *verb* to raise to the rank of knight. – *noun* **knight-errant** (*hist*) a knight who travelled in search of adventures. – *noun* **knighthood** the rank of a knight. – *adjective* **knightly** of knights; gallant, courageous.

knit *nit, verb* (*past tense* **knitted**) to form a garment or fabric from yarn or thread (by means of knitting needles); to join closely. – *noun* **knitting** work done by knitting. – *noun plural* **knitting needles** (a pair of) thin pointed rods used in knitting.

knob *nob, noun* a hard rounded part standing out from the main part; a (door-)handle.

knock *nok, verb* to strike, hit; to drive or be driven against; to tap on a door to have it opened. – *noun* a sudden stroke; a tap (on a door). – *noun* **knocker** a hinged weight on a door for knocking with. – *adjective* **knock-kneed** having knees that touch in walking. – **knock out** to hit (someone) hard enough to make him unconscious.

knoll *nōl, noun* a small rounded hill.

knot *not, noun* a hard lump, *esp* one made by tying string *etc,* or one in wood at the join between trunk and branch; a tangle; a small gathering, cluster (*eg* of people); a measure of speed for ships (about 1·85 kilometre per hour). – *verb* (*past tense* **knotted**) to tie in a knot. – *adjective* **knotted** full of knots. – *adjective* **knotty** having knots; difficult. – **get knotted!** (*coll*) interjection expressing anger, defiance *etc.*

know *nō, verb* (*past tense* **knew**) to be aware or sure of; to recognize. – *adjective* **knowing** clever; cunning. – *adverb* **knowingly** intentionally. – *noun* **knowledge** that which is known; information; ability, skill. – *adjective* **knowledgeable** showing or having knowledge.

knuckle *nuk l, noun* a joint of the fingers. – *verb* (with **under**) to give in, yield.

koala bear *noun* an Australian tree-climbing animal that looks like a small bear.

kookaburra *see* **jackass.**

Koran *noun* the holy book of the Muslims.

kosher *adjective* pure and clean according to Jewish law.

kowtow *verb* (with **to**) to treat with too much respect.

kraal *noun* a South African village.

Kt *abbreviation* Knight.

kudos *noun* fame, glory.

kung-fu *noun* a form of self-defence, developed in China.

kw *abbreviation* kilowatt.

L

l *abbreviation* litre.

lab *noun* short for **laboratory.**

label *noun* a small written note fixed on to something (to tell its contents, owner *etc*). – *verb* (*past tense* **labelled**) to fix a label to; to call something by a certain name.

labial *adjective* of the lips.

laboratory *noun* (*plural* **laboratories**) a scientist's workroom.

labour or (*US*) **labor** *noun* (hard) work; workmen on a job; (in a pregnant female) the process of childbirth. – *verb* to work hard; to move slowly or with difficulty; to emphasize (a point) too greatly. – *adjective* **laborious** requiring hard work; wearisome. – *adjective* **laboured** showing signs of effort. – *noun* **labourer** a person who does heavy unskilled work. – *noun* **Labour Party** one of the chief political parties of Great Britain.

laburnum *noun* a kind of tree with large hanging clusters of yellow flowers and poisonous seeds.

labyrinth *noun* a place full of puzzling windings, a maze.

lace *noun* a string or cord, for fastening shoes *etc*; decorative openwork fabric made with fine thread. – *verb* to fasten with a lace; to add alcohol to (a drink).

lacerate *verb* to tear, wound. – *noun* **laceration.**

lack *verb* to be in want; to be without. – *noun* want, need.

lackadaisical *adjective* bored, half-hearted.

lackey *noun* (*plural* **lackeys**) a manservant; a person who acts like a slave.

laconic *adjective* using few words to express one's meaning. – *adverb* **laconically.**

lacquer *noun* a varnish. – Also *verb*.

lacrosse *noun* a twelve-a-side ball game played with sticks having a shallow net at the end.

lactic *adjective* of milk.

lad *noun* a boy, a youth.

ladder *noun* a set of rungs or steps between two supports, for climbing up or down; a run from a broken stitch, in a stocking *etc*.

lade *noun* a channel for leading water to a millwheel.

laden *adjective* loaded, burdened. – *noun* **lading** that which is loaded; cargo.

ladle *noun* a large spoon for lifting out liquid. – *verb* to lift with a ladle.

lady *noun* (*plural* **ladies**) a woman (of good manners); a title of the wives of knights, lords and baronets, and of the daughters of noblemen; (*plural*) a (public) lavatory for women. – *noun* **ladybird** a small beetle, usually red with black spots. – **Her Ladyship** the title of a lady of high rank.

lag *verb* (*past tense* **lagged**) to move slowly and fall behind; to cover (a boiler or pipes) with a warm covering. – *noun* a delay. – *noun* **lagging** material for covering pipes *etc*.

lager *noun* a light beer. – *noun* **lager lout** a drunken pugnacious youth.

lagoon *noun* a shallow stretch of water separated from the sea by low sand-banks, rocks *etc*.

laid *see* **lay**[1].

lain *see* **lie.**

lair *noun* the den of a wild beast.

laird *noun* (in Scotland) a land-owner, squire.

laissez-faire *lā-sā-fār* , *noun* a general principle of not interfering.

laity *see* **lay**[2].

lake *noun* a large stretch of water surrounded by land.

lama *noun* a Buddhist priest of Tibet.

lamb *noun* a young sheep; the meat of this animal; a gentle person.

lame *adjective* unable to walk, crippled; not good enough: *a lame excuse*. – *verb* to make lame. – *noun* **lame duck** an inefficient or weak person or organization. – *noun* **lameness.**

lament *verb* to mourn, feel or express grief for; to regret. – *noun* a show of grief (also **lamentation**); a mournful poem or piece of music. – *adjective* **lamentable** pitiful; very bad.

laminated *adjective* made by putting layers together: *laminated glass.*

lamp *noun* a (glass-covered) light.

lampoon *noun* a violent criticism (in writing) of a person.

lamprey *noun* (*plural* **lampreys**) a type of fish like an eel.

lance *noun* a long shaft of wood, with a spearhead. – *verb* to cut open (a boil *etc*) with a knife. – *noun* **lance-corporal** a soldier with rank just below a corporal. – *noun* **lancer** a light cavalry soldier.

lancet *noun* a sharp surgical instrument.

land *noun* the solid portion of the earth's surface; ground; soil; a (part of a) country. – *verb* to set or come on land or on shore. – *adjective* **landed** consisting of or owning lands and estates: *Balmoral is a landed property. The landed gentry often enjoy field sports.* – *noun* **landfall** an approach to land after a voyage; the land approached. – *noun* **landing** a coming ashore or to ground; a place for getting on shore; the level part of a staircase between the flights of steps. – *adjective* **landlocked** almost shut in by land. – *noun* **landlord** (*masculine*), **landlady** (*feminine*) the owner of land or houses; the person who owns or manages an inn *etc* – *noun* **landlubber** a person who lives, works *etc* on land and knows little about the sea. – *noun* **landmark** any object on land that serves as a guide; an important event. – *noun* **land-mine** a type of bomb laid on or near the surface of the ground which explodes when something or someone passes over it. – *noun* **landscape** a (picture of a) view of inland scenery. – *noun* **landscape gardening** gardening for picturesque effect. – *noun* **landslide** a mass of land that slips down from the side of a hill. – *noun* **landslide victory** (in elections *etc*) one in which a great mass of votes goes to one side.

landau *noun* (*old*) a horse-drawn carriage with a removable top.

lane *noun* a narrow road, street or passage; a course or part of the road, sea *etc* to which cars, ships, aircraft *etc* must keep.

language *noun* human speech; the speech of a particular people or nation.

languid *adjective* lacking liveliness and spirit. – *verb* **languish** to grow weak, to droop; to long (for). – *adjective* **languishing**. – *noun* **languor** state of being languid.

laniard *see* **lanyard**.

lank *adjective* tall and thin; (of hair) straight and limp. – *adjective* **lanky** tall and thin.

lantern *noun* a case for holding or carrying a light. – *adjective* **lantern-jawed** hollow-cheeked, long-jawed.

lanyard or **laniard** *noun* (on a ship) a short rope used for fastening; a cord for hanging a whistle *etc* round the neck.

lap *verb* (*past tense* **lapped**) to lick up with the tongue; to wash or flow against; (with **up**) to accept (praise *etc*) greedily; to wrap round, surround; to make (something) lie partly (over); in a race, to get a lap ahead of other competitors. – *noun* the front part (from waist to knees) of a person seated; the clothes covering that part; a fold; one round of a racetrack or other competition course. – *noun* **lapdog** a small pet dog.

lapel *noun* the part of a coat joined to the collar and folded back on the chest.

lapidary *noun* (*plural* **lapidaries**) a person who cuts, polishes and shapes (precious) stones. – *adjective* engraved on stone.

lapse *verb* to fall (into evil ways or careless habits); to cease. – *noun* a mistake, a failure; a passing away (of time).

lapwing *noun* a type of bird of the plover family (also **peewit**).

larceny *noun* stealing, theft.

larch *noun* (*plural* **larches**) a kind of cone-bearing deciduous tree.

lard *noun* the melted fat of the pig. – *verb* to put strips of bacon *etc* in meat before cooking; to smear, lay on thickly.

larder *noun* a room or place where food is kept; stock of food.

large *adjective* great in size, amount *etc*. – *adverb* **largely** mainly, to a great extent. – *noun* **largeness**. – **at large** at liberty, free; in general: *the public at large.*

largesse *noun* a generous giving away of money *etc*.

lariat *noun* a rope for fastening horses while they are grazing; a lasso.

lark *noun* a general name for several kinds of singing bird; a piece of fun or mischief. – *verb* to fool about, behave mischievously.

larkspur *noun* a tall plant with blue, white or pink spurred flowers, a kind of delphinium.

larva noun (plural **larvae**) an insect in its first stage after coming out of the egg, a grub.

larynx noun (plural **larynxes** or **larynges**) the upper part of the windpipe containing the cords that produce the voice. – noun **laryngitis** a disease of the larynx.

lasagne noun plural flat sheets of pasta. – noun singular (also **lasagna**) a baked dish made with this.

lascivious adjective full of indecent desires, lustful.

laser noun (an instrument that concentrates light into) a very narrow powerful beam.

lash noun (plural **lashes**) a thong or cord of a whip; a stroke with a whip; an eyelash. – verb to strike with a whip; to fasten with a rope etc; to attack with bitter words.

lass noun (plural **lasses**) a girl.

lassitude noun lack of energy, weariness.

lasso noun (plural **lassoes** or **lassos**) a long rope with a loop that tightens when the rope is pulled, used for catching wild horses etc. – verb (past tense **lassoed**) to catch with a lasso.

last adjective coming after all the others: *He was the last person to arrive. The audience left before the last act;* most recent, next before the present: *His last job was boring.* – Also adverb. – verb to continue, go on; to remain in good condition. – noun a foot-like shape on which shoes are made or repaired. – adverb **lastly** finally. – noun plural **last rites** religious ceremonies performed for the dying. – **at last** in the end; **on one's last legs** completely worn out, about to collapse; **to the last** to the end.

latch noun (plural **latches**) a catch of wood or metal used to fasten a door; a light door-lock. – verb to fasten with a latch. – noun **latchkey** a door-key (to raise the latch of a door). – noun **latchkey child** a child who regularly returns home to an empty house.

late adjective coming after the expected time: *The train was late;* far on (in time): *It's getting late;* recent: *our late disagreement;* recently dead: *the late king;* recently, but no longer, holding an office or position: *the late chairman.* – Also adverb. – adverb **lately** recently. – noun **lateness**. – **of late** recently.

latent adjective hidden, undeveloped but capable of becoming developed or active: *This test will show up any latent ability. The police were aware of latent hostility in the area.*

lateral adjective of, at, to, or from the side. – noun **lateral thinking** thinking which seeks new ways of looking at a problem and does not merely proceed by logical steps from the starting point of what is known or believed.

latex noun the milky juice of plants esp of the rubber tree.

lath noun a thin narrow strip of wood.

lathe noun a machine for turning and shaping articles of wood, metal etc.

lather noun a foam or froth (eg from soap and water); (coll) a state of agitation. – verb to cover with lather.

Latin noun the language of ancient Rome.

latitude noun the distance, measured in degrees on the map, of a place north or south from the equator; freedom of action or choice: *His new job allows him far more latitude than his previous one.*

latter adjective the last of two mentioned; recent. – adjective **latter-day** of recent times. – adverb **latterly** recently.

lattice noun a network of crossed wooden etc strips (also **lattice-work**); a window having this.

laudable adjective worthy of being praised. – adjective **laudatory** expressing praise.

laugh verb to make sounds with the voice in showing amusement, happiness, scorn etc. – noun the sound of laughing. – adjective **laughable** comical, ridiculous. – noun **laughing stock** an object of scornful laughter. – noun **laughter** the act or noise of laughing.

launch verb to cause a boat, ship, to slide into the water; to cause a rocket etc to take off; to start (someone or something) off on a course; to put (a product) on the market with suitable publicity; to throw or hurl. – noun (plural **launches**) the act of launching; a large motor boat.

launder verb to wash and iron clothes etc. – noun **launderette** a shop where customers may wash clothes etc in washing machines. – noun **laundry** (plural **laundries**) a place where clothes are washed; clothes to be washed.

laurel *noun* the bay tree, from which wreaths were made for crowning victors *etc*; (*plural*) honours or victories gained.

lava *noun* molten rock *etc* thrown out by a volcano, becoming solid as it cools.

lavatory *noun* (*plural* **lavatories**) a toilet.

lavender *noun* a plant with small pale purple, sweet-smelling flowers; a pale-purple colour.

lavish *verb* to spend or give very freely. – *adjective* too free in giving or spending, very generous.

law *noun* the collection of rules according to which a country is governed; any one of such rules; (in science) a rule that says that in certain conditions certain things always happen. – *adjective* **law-abiding** obeying the law. – *noun* **law court** a place where people accused of crimes are tried. – *adjective* **lawful** allowed by law. – *adjective* **lawless** paying no attention to, and not observing the laws. – *noun* **lawsuit** a quarrel or dispute to be settled by a court of law. – *noun* **lawyer** a person whose work it is to give advice in matters of law.

lawn *noun* an area of smooth grass *eg* as part of a garden; a kind of fine linen. – *noun* **lawnmower** a machine for cutting grass. – *noun* **lawn tennis** tennis played on a hard or grass court.

lax *adjective* not strict; careless, negligent. – *noun* **laxative** a medicine which loosens the bowels. – *noun* **laxity.** – *noun* **laxness.**

lay¹ *verb* (*past tense* **laid**) to place or set down; to put (*eg* a burden, duty) on (someone); to beat down; to cause to disappear or subside: *lay a ghost*; to set in order, arrange; (of hens) to produce eggs; to bet, wager. – *adjective* **laid-back** (*coll*) relaxed, easy-going. – *adjective* **laid-up** ill in bed. – *noun* **layabout** a lazy idle person. – *noun* **layby** a parking area at the side of a road. – **lay about someone** to deal blows on all sides; **lay down** to assert; to store (*eg* wine); **lay off** to dismiss (workers) temporarily; (*coll*) to stop: *lay off arguing*; to talk at great length; **lay up** to store for future use; **lay waste** to ruin, destroy.

lay² *adjective* not of the clergy; without special training in or special knowledge of a particular subject. – *noun* **laity** ordinary people, not clergymen. – *noun* **layman** one of the laity; someone without special training in a subject.

lay³ *noun* (*old*) a short poem; a song.

layer *noun* a thickness, covering or level – *adjective* **layered** having a number of distinct layers: *a layered cake*.

layette *noun* a baby's complete outfit.

lazy *adjective* (*comparative* **lazier,** *superlative* **laziest**) not caring for work; idle. – *verb* **laze** to be lazy. – *noun* **laziness.**

lb *abbreviation* pound(s) (the weight).

lbw *abbreviation* leg before wicket.

LCD *abbreviation* liquid crystal display.

lea *noun* (*old*) a meadow.

lead¹ *verb* (*past tense* **led**) to show the way by going first; to direct; to guide; to persuade; to live (a busy *etc* life); (of a road) to form a way (to), go (to). – *noun* the first or front place; guidance, direction; a leash for a dog *etc*. – *noun* **leader** a person who or one which leads or goes first; a chief; a column in a newspaper expressing the editor's opinions. – *noun* **leadership** the state of being a leader; the ability to lead. – *noun* **leading question** a question asked in such a way as to suggest the desired answer.

lead² *noun* an element, a soft bluish-grey metal; the part of a pencil that writes, really made of graphite; a weight used for sounding depths at sea *etc*. – *adjective* **leaden** made of lead; lead-coloured; dull, heavy. – *adjective* **lead-free** (of petrol) unleaded.

leaf *noun* (*plural* **leaves**) a part of a plant growing from the side of a stem, *usu* green, flat and thin but of various shapes according to the plant; anything thin like a leaf; a page of a book; a hinged flap or movable extra part of a table *etc*. – *noun* **leaflet** a small printed sheet. – *adjective* **leafy.** – **turn over a new leaf** to begin again and do better.

league *noun* a union of persons, nations *etc* for the benefit of each other; an association of clubs for games; an old measure of distance, *usu* 3 miles (about 4·8 kilometres). – **in league with** allied with.

leak *noun* a hole through which liquid passes; an escape of gas *etc* or of secret information. – Also *verb*. – *noun* **leakage** that which enters or escapes by leaking.

lean *verb* (*past tense* **leant**) to slope over to one side, not to be upright; to rest (against); to rely (on). – *adjective* thin;

poor, scanty; (of meat) not fat. – noun **leaning** a liking (for something). – noun **lean-to** a shed etc built against another building or wall.

leap verb (past tense **leapt**) to move with jumps; to jump (over). – noun a jump. – noun **leapfrog** a game in which one player leaps over another's bent back. – noun **leap year** a year which has 366 days (February having 29), occurring every fourth year.

learn verb (past tense, past participle **learned** or **learnt**) to get to know (something); to gain skill. – adjective **learned** having or showing great knowledge. – noun **learner.** – noun **learning** knowledge.

lease noun (the period of) an agreement giving the use of a house etc on payment of rent. – verb to let or rent. – noun **leasehold** property, or land, held by lease.

leash noun (plural **leashes**) a lead by which a dog etc is held. – verb to put (a dog etc) on a leash.

least adjective, noun (something) which is the smallest (amount etc): She spent the least money. He has least. – adverb (often with **the**) the smallest or lowest degree: I like her least, anyway; **not in the least** not at all. – **at least** at any rate, anyway; **not in the least** not at all.

leather noun the skin of an animal, prepared (by tanning) for use. – verb to beat. – noun **leathering** a thrashing. – adjective **leathery** like leather; tough.

leave noun permission to do something (eg to be absent); (esp of soldiers, sailors) a holiday. – verb (past tense **left**) to allow to remain; to abandon, forsake; to depart (from); to make a gift to a person by one's will; to give to a person's charge, care etc: Leave the decision to him. – noun plural **leavings** things left over. – **take one's leave (of)** to part from; to say goodbye to.

lecherous adjective lustful in a sexual way. – noun **lechery.**

lectern noun a stand for a book to be read from.

lecture noun something written or read to an audience, on a certain subject; a scolding. – verb to deliver a lecture; to scold. – noun **lecturer** a person who lectures, esp to students.

led see **lead¹**.

ledge noun a shelf or an object that sticks out like a shelf: a window-ledge; an underwater ridge.

ledger noun the book of accounts of an office or shop.

lee noun the side away from the wind, the sheltered side. – adjective, adverb **leeward** in the direction towards which the wind blows. – noun **leeway** a drift (of a ship) off course; lost time, lost ground etc: He has a lot of leeway to make up since he has been off ill.

leech noun (plural **leeches**) a kind of blood-sucking worm.

leek noun a long green and white vegetable of the onion family.

leer noun a sly, sidelong or lustful look. – Also verb.

lees noun plural dregs that settle at the bottom of liquid esp wine.

left¹ adjective on, for, or belonging to the side of the body that in most people has the less skilful hand (opposite to **right**). – Also adverb. – noun the left side; a group with left-wing ideas etc. – adjective **left-handed** using the left hand rather than the right; awkward. – adjective **left-wing** extremely socialist or radical in political views, ideas etc.

left² see **leave.**

leg noun one of the limbs by which animals (including man) walk; a long slender support of anything (as of a table); one stage in a journey, contest etc. – noun plural **leggings** outer coverings for the lower legs. – adjective **leggy** having long legs.

legacy noun (plural **legacies**) something which is left by will; something left behind by someone who had one's job, house etc previously. – noun **legatee** a person to whom a legacy is left.

legal adjective allowed by law, lawful; of law. – noun **legality** (plural **legalities**) the state of being legal. – verb **legalize** to make lawful.

legation noun (the headquarters of) an official body of people acting on behalf of the government of their own country etc in another country, an embassy.

legend noun a story handed down from long ago, a myth; the words accompanying a picture, a caption. – adjective **legendary** of legend; famous; not to be believed.

legerdemain lej ėr-dė-mān, noun conjuring by quickness of the hand.

legible adjective (of writing) that can be read (easily). – noun **legibility.**

legion *noun* (*hist*) a body of Roman soldiers of from three to six thousand; a great many, a very large number. – *noun* **legionary** (*plural* **legionaries**) a soldier of a legion.

legislate *verb* to make laws. – *noun* **legislation**. – *adjective* **legislative** law-making. – *noun* **legislator** a person who makes laws. – *noun* **legislature** the part of the government which has the powers of making laws.

legitimate *adjective* lawful; (of a child) born of parents married to each other; correct, reasonable. – *noun* **legitimacy**.

leisure *noun* time free from work, spare time. – *adjective* **leisured** not occupied with business. – *adjective*, *adverb* **leisurely** taking plenty of time.

lemming *noun* a kind of small rat-like animal of the arctic regions.

lemon *noun* an oval fruit with pale yellow rind and very sour juice, or the tree that bears it. – *noun* **lemonade** a (fizzy) drink flavoured with lemons.

lemur *noun* a kind of animal related to the monkey but with a pointed nose.

lend *verb* (*past tense* **lent**) to give use of (something) for a time; to give, add (a quality) to someone or something: *His presence lent an air of respectability to the occasion.* – **lend itself to** to be suitable for, adapt easily to.

length *noun* the extent from end to end in space or time; the quality of being long; a great extent; a piece (of cloth *etc*). – *verb* **lengthen** to make or grow longer. – *adverb* **lengthways** or **lengthwise** in the direction of the length. – *adjective* **lengthy** long; tiresomely long. – **at length** in detail; at last.

lenient *adjective* merciful, punishing only lightly. – *noun* **lenience**. – *noun* **leniency**.

lens *noun* (*plural* **lenses**) a piece of glass *etc* curved on one or both sides, used in spectacles, contact lenses, cameras *etc*; a part of the eye.

Lent *noun* (in the Christian church) a period of fasting before Easter lasting forty days.

lent *see* **lend**.

lentil *noun* the seed of a pod-bearing plant, used in soups *etc*.

leonine *adjective* like a lion.

leopard *noun* a type of animal of the cat family with a spotted skin.

leotard *noun* a kind of tight-fitting garment worn for dancing, gymnastics *etc*.

leper *noun* a person with leprosy; an outcast. – *noun* **leprosy** a contagious skin disease.

leprechaun *noun* (*myth*) a kind of Irish fairy.

lesbian *noun* a female homosexual. – Also *adjective*.

less *adjective* not as much: *less time*; smaller: *Think of a number less than 40*. – *adverb* not as much, to a smaller extent: *He goes less (often) than he should*. – *noun* a smaller portion, amount: *He has less than I have*. – *preposition* minus: *5 less 2 equals 3*. – *verb* **lessen** to make smaller. – *adjective* **lesser** smaller.

lesson *noun* that which is learned or taught; a part of the Bible read in church; a period of teaching.

lest *conjunction* for fear that, in case.

let *verb* (*present participle* **letting**, *past tense*, *past participle* **let**) to allow; to grant use of (*eg* a house, shop, farm) in return for payment. – **let down** to fail to help *etc*, disappoint; **let off** to excuse, not to punish *etc*; **let up** to become less.

lethal *adjective* causing death.

lethargy *noun* a lack of energy or interest; sleepiness. – *adjective* **lethargic**.

letter *noun* a mark expressing a sound; a written message; (*plural*) learning: *a man of letters*. – *noun* **lettering** the way in which letters are formed; the letters formed. – **(to) the letter** (according to) the exact meaning of the words: *He followed his father's instructions to the letter*.

lettuce *noun* a kind of green plant whose leaves are used in a salad.

leukaemia *noun* a cancerous disease of the white blood cells in the body.

levee *noun* a reception, meeting *etc* held by a king or queen.

level *noun* a flat, smooth surface; a height, position, strength *etc* in comparison with some standard: *water level*; a kind of instrument for showing whether a surface is level: *spirit level*; suitable or appropriate position or rank. – *adjective* flat, even, smooth or horizontal. – *verb* (*past tense* **levelled**) to make flat, smooth or horizontal; to make equal; to aim (a gun *etc*); to pull down (a building *etc*). – *noun* **level crossing** a place where a road crosses a railway track. – *adjective* **level-headed** having good sense.

lever *noun* a bar of metal, wood *etc* used to raise up or shift something heavy; a bar or handle for operating a machine *etc*; any method of gaining advantage: *He used the information as a lever to get a better job.*

leveret *noun* a young hare.

leviathan *noun* a kind of huge (sea) monster; anything huge or powerful.

levitation *noun* (the illusion of) raising a heavy body in the air without support. – *verb* **levitate** to (cause to) float in the air.

levity *noun* lack of seriousness, frivolity.

levy *verb* (*past tense* **levied**) to collect by order (*eg* a tax, men for an army). – *noun* (*plural* **levies**) money, troops *etc* collected by order.

lewd *adjective* taking delight in indecent thoughts or acts. – *noun* **lewdness.**

lexicographer *noun* a maker of a dictionary.

liable *adjective* legally responsible (for) or bound to do something; likely or apt (to do something or happen); (with **to**) likely to have, get suffer from: *liable to colds.* – *noun* **liability** (*plural* **liabilities**) (legal) responsibility; a debt; a disadvantage.

liaison *li-ăz'ŏn, noun* contact, communication.

liar *see* **lie.**

libel *noun* anything written with the purpose of hurting a person's reputation. – Also *verb* (*past tense* **libelled**). – *adjective* **libellous.**

liberal *adjective* generous; broad-minded, tolerant. – *noun* **Liberal** a member of the former Liberal Party. – *noun* **liberality.** – *noun* **Liberal Party** formerly, one of the chief political parties of Great Britain.

liberate *noun* to set free. – *noun* **liberation.**

libertine *noun* a person who lives a wicked, immoral life.

liberty *noun* (*plural* **liberties**) freedom; too great freedom of speech or action; (*plural*) rights, privileges. – **take liberties** to behave rudely or impertinently.

library *noun* (*plural* **libraries**) (a building or room containing) a collection of books or some other collection (*eg* gramophone records). – *noun* **librarian** the keeper of a library.

libretto *noun* (*plural* **libretti** or **librettos**) (a book of) the words of an opera, musical show *etc*.

lice *see* **louse.**

licence *noun* a (printed) form giving permission to do something (*eg* to keep a dog, television set *etc*, to drive a car *etc*); too great freedom of action *etc*. – *verb* **license** to permit. – *noun* **licensee** a person to whom a licence (*esp* one to keep a hotel or public house) is given. – *adjective* **licentious** given to behaving immorally or improperly. – *noun* **licentiousness.**

lichen *lī'kĕn, noun* a large group of moss-like plants that grow on rocks *etc*.

lick *verb* to pass the tongue over; (of flames) to reach up, to touch. – *noun* the act of licking; a tiny amount. – **lick into shape** to make vigorous improvements on.

lid *noun* a cover for a box, pot *etc*; the cover of the eye.

lie *noun* a false statement meant to deceive. – *verb* (*present participle* **lying.** *past tense* **lied**) to tell a lie; (*past tense* **lay,** *past participle* **lain**) to rest in a flat position; (*past tense* **lay,** *past participle* **lain**) to be or to remain in a state or position. – *noun* the position or situation in which something lies. – *noun* **liar** a person who tells lies. – *adjective, noun* **lying.** – **lie in wait (for)** to keep hidden in order to surprise someone (with an attack); **lie low** to keep quiet or hidden; **the lie of the land** the state of affairs.

liege *lēj, noun* a loyal subject; a lord or superior. – *noun* **liege-lord** (*hist*) an overlord.

lieu: in lieu (of) instead of.

Lieut. *abbreviation* Lieutenant.

lieutenant *noun* an army officer next below captain; in the navy, an officer below a lieutenant-commander; a rank below a higher officer, as **lieutenant-colonel.**

life *noun* (*plural* **lives**) the period between birth and death; the state of being alive; liveliness; manner of living; the story of a person's life; living things: *animal life.* – *noun* **lifebelt** a ring or belt made of cork or filled with air for keeping a person afloat. – *noun* **lifeboat** a boat for rescuing people in difficulties at sea. – *noun* **life cycle** the various stages through which a living thing passes. –

adjective **lifeless** dead; not lively. – *adjective* **life-like** like a living person. – *adjective* **lifelong** lasting the length of a life. – *adjective* **life-size** (of a portrait *etc*) full size. – *noun* **life-support machine** or **system** a device or series of devices for keeping a human being alive in adverse circumstances, *eg* illness, space travel.

lift *verb* to bring to a higher position, raise; to take up; (*coll*) to steal; (of fog *etc*) to disappear. – *noun* a platform *etc* that moves up and down (between floors) carrying goods or people; a ride in someone's car *etc*; a raising (of spirits *etc*), a boost. – *noun* **lift-off** the take-off of a rocket *etc*.

ligament *noun* a tough substance that connects the bones of the body.

ligature *noun* something which binds.

light¹ *noun* the brightness given by the sun, moon, lamps *etc* that makes things able to be seen; a source of light (*eg* a lamp); a flame (of a match *etc*); knowledge. – *adjective* bright; (of a colour) pale; having light; not dark. – *verb* (*past tense* **lit** or **lighted**) to give light to; to set fire to. – *verb* **lighten** to make or become brighter; (of lightning) to flash. – *noun* **lightening** a making or becoming lighter or brighter. – *noun* **lighter** something used for lighting (a cigarette *etc*). – *noun* **lighthouse** a tower-like building with a flashing light to warn or guide ships. – *noun* **lighting** a means of providing light. – *noun* **lightship** a ship anchored in a fixed position to serve as a lighthouse. – *noun* **light-year** the distance light travels in a year (6 billion miles). – **bring to light** to reveal, cause to be noticed; **come to light** to be revealed or discovered; **in the light of** taking into consideration (information acquired *etc*).

light² *adjective* not heavy; easy to bear or to do; easy to digest; nimble; lively; not grave, cheerful; not serious: *light music*; (of rain *etc*) little in quantity. – *verb* **lighten** to make less heavy. – *noun* **lighter** a large open boat used in unloading and loading ships. – *adjective* **light-fingered** apt to steal. – *adjective* **light-headed** dizzy. – *adjective* **light-hearted** cheerful. – *adverb* **lightly**.

light³ *verb* (*past tense* **lighted** or **lit**) (with **on, upon**) to land, settle on; to come upon by chance.

lightning *noun* an electric flash in the clouds. – *noun* **lightning conductor** a metal rod that protects buildings *etc* from the electricity of lightning by conducting it down to earth.

lignite *noun* brown, woody coal.

like¹ *adjective* the same as or similar to. – *adverb* in the same way as: *He runs like a hare.* – *noun* something or someone that is the equal of or similar to another: *You won't see his like again.* – *noun* **likelihood** probability. – *adjective* **likely** probable; promising; liable (to do something). – *adverb* probably. – *verb* **liken** to think of as similar, to compare. – *noun* **likeness** a similarity, a resemblance; a portrait, photograph *etc* of someone. – *adverb* **likewise** in the same way; also.

like² *verb* to be pleased with; to be fond of. – *adjective* **likeable** or **likable** attractive, lovable. – *noun* **liking** a fondness; satisfaction: *to my liking.*

lilac *noun* a small tree with hanging clusters of pale purple or white flowers. – *adjective* of pale purple colour.

lilt *noun* (a tune *etc* with) a striking rhythm or swing. – Also *verb*.

lily *noun* (*plural* **lilies**) a tall plant grown from a bulb with large white or coloured flowers. – *noun* **lily-of-the-valley** a plant with small white bell-shaped flowers.

limb *noun* a leg or arm; a branch.

limber *adjective* easily bent, supple. – **limber up** to exercise so as to become supple.

limbo: in limbo forgotten, neglected.

lime *noun* the white substance, quicklime, left after heating limestone, used in making cement; a type of tree related to the lemon or its greenish-yellow fruit; another name for the **linden** tree. – **in the limelight** attracting publicity or attention.

limit *noun* the farthest point or place; a boundary; largest (or smallest) extent, degree *etc*; restriction. – *verb* to set or keep to a limit. – *noun* **limitation** that which limits; the act of limiting; a weak point about a person or thing.

limousine *noun* a kind of large motor car, *esp* one with a separate compartment for the driver.

limp *adjective* lacking stiffness; weak. – *verb* to walk lamely; (of a damaged ship *etc*) to move with difficulty. – *noun* the act of limping; a limping walk.

limpet *noun* a small cone-shaped shell-fish that clings to rocks; a person who is difficult to get rid of.

limpid *adjective* clear, transparent.

linchpin *noun* a pin-shaped rod used to keep a wheel on an axle.

linden *noun* (also called **lime**) a tree with small flowers and heart-shaped leaves.

line *noun* a cord, rope *etc*; a long thin stroke or mark; a wrinkle; a row (of printed words, ships, soldiers *etc*); a service of ships or aircraft; a railway; a telephone wire *etc*, or any connected system; a short letter; a family from generation to generation; course, direction; a kind or sort (of thing, activity *etc*); (*plural*) army trenches; (*plural*) a written school punishment exercise. – *verb* to mark out with lines; (*esp* with **up**) to place in a row or alongside of; to form lines along (a street); to cover on the inside: *line a dress*. – *noun* **lineage** one's descent, traced back to one's ancestors. – *adjective* **lineal** directly descended through the father, grandfather *etc*. – *noun* **lineament** a feature, *esp* of the face. – *adjective* **linear** made of lines; (of measurement) in one dimension (length, breadth or height) only. – *noun* **liner** a ship or aeroplane working on a regular service. – *noun* **linesman** (in sport) an umpire at a boundary line. – *noun* **lining** a covering on the inside. – **(ship** or **regiment) of the line** (a ship or regiment) belonging to the regular fighting forces.

linen *noun* cloth made of flax; articles made of linen (*eg* tablelinen, bedlinen).

ling *noun* a type of long slender fish like the cod; heather.

linger *verb* to remain for a long time or for longer than the expected time; to loiter, delay.

lingerie *noun* women's underwear.

lingua franca *noun* any (often simplified) language used amongst people from different nations *etc* so that they can talk together.

linguist *noun* a person skilled in languages; a person who studies language. – *adjective* **linguistic**. – *noun* **linguistics** the scientific study of languages and of language in general.

liniment *noun* an oil or ointment rubbed into the skin to cure stiffness in the muscles, joints *etc*.

link *noun* a ring of a chain; a single part of a series; anything connecting two things. – *verb* to connect as by a link; to join closely; to be connected.

links *noun plural* a stretch of flat or slightly hilly ground near the seashore; a golf course.

linnet *noun* a type of small songbird of the finch family.

lino *noun* short for **linoleum**. – *noun* **lino-cut** a design for printing cut into a block of linoleum.

linoleum *noun* a type of smooth, hard-wearing covering for floors.

linseed *noun* flax seed. – *noun* **linseed oil** oil from flax seed.

lint *noun* linen scraped into a soft woolly material for putting over wounds; fine pieces of fluff.

lintel *noun* a timber or stone over a doorway or window.

lion (*masculine*), **lioness** (*feminine*) *noun* a type of powerful animal of the cat family, the male of which has a shaggy mane. – *verb* **lionize** to treat (someone) as a celebrity. – **the lion's share** the largest share.

lip *noun* the fleshy rim of the mouth; the edge of an opening, container *etc*. – *noun* **lip-reading** reading what a person says from the movement of the lips. – *noun* **lip-service** saying one thing but believing another: *He pays lip-service to the rules*. – *noun* **lipstick** a stick of red, pink *etc* colouring for the lips.

liquefy *verb* (*past tense* **liquefied**) to make or become liquid. – *noun* **liquefaction**.

liqueur *noun* a strong alcoholic drink, strongly flavoured and sweet.

liquid *noun* a flowing, water-like substance. – *adjective* flowing; looking like water; soft and clear. – *verb* **liquidate** to close down, wind up the affairs of (a bankrupt business company); to get rid of by violence. – *noun* **liquidation**. – *noun* **liquidator**. – *verb* **liquidize** to make liquid; to make into a purée. – *noun* **liquidizer** a machine for liquidizing.

liquor *noun* any alcoholic drink, *esp* a strong kind (*eg* whisky).

liquorice or **licorice** *noun* a plant with a sweet root; a black, sticky sweet made from this root.

lira *noun* the standard unit of Italian money.

lisp *verb* to say *th* for *s* or *z* because of being unable to pronounce these letters correctly; to speak imperfectly, like a child. – Also *noun*.

lissome *adjective* nimble, bending easily.

list¹ *noun* a series *eg* of names, numbers, prices *etc* written down one after the other; *see* also **lists**. – *verb* to write (something) down in this way. – *noun* **listed building** one protected from being knocked down because it is of architectural or historical interest.

list² *verb* (of a ship) to lean over to one side. – *noun* a slope to one side.

listen *verb* to give attention to so as to hear or to pay attention to the advice of. – *noun* **listener**.

listerosis *noun* a disease affecting the brain caused by eating food contaminated with **listeria** bacteria.

listless *adjective* weary, without energy or interest. – *noun* **listlessness**.

lists *noun plural* (*hist*) the ground enclosed for a battle between knights on horseback.

lit *see* **light¹** and **light³**.

litany *noun* (*plural* **litanies**) a set form of prayer.

literal *adjective* following the exact or most obvious meaning, word for word with no exaggeration and nothing added by the imagination. – *adverb* **literally** exactly as stated: *He was literally blinded by the flash* means he actually lost the power of sight.

literary *adjective* of writing, books, authors *etc*; knowledgeable about books. – *noun* **literacy** ability to read and write. – *adjective* **literate** able to read and write.

literature *noun* the books *etc* that are written in any language, *esp* novels, poetry *etc*; anything in written form on a subject.

lithe *adjective* (of a person or body) bending easily, supple, flexible.

lithograph *noun* a picture made from a drawing done on stone or metal. – *noun* **lithographer**. – *noun* **lithography** printing done by this method.

litigation *noun* a law case. – *adjective* **litigious** fond of taking one's troubles to court.

litre *noun* a metric measure of liquids (1·76 pint).

litter *noun* an untidy mess of paper, rubbish *etc*; a heap of straw as bedding for animals *etc*; a number of animals born at one birth; (*hist*) a kind of bed for carrying the sick and injured. – *verb* to scatter carelessly about, *esp* rubbish *etc*; to produce a litter of young.

little *adjective* small in quantity or size. – *adverb* in a small quantity or degree; not much; not at all: *Little does he know.* – *pronoun* a small quantity, amount, distance *etc*: *Have a little more. Move a little to the right.*

liturgy *noun* (*plural* **liturgies**) the form of service of a church. – *adjective* **liturgical**.

live¹ *verb* to have life; to dwell; to pass one's life; to continue to be alive; to survive; (with **on**) to keep oneself alive; (with **on**) to be supported by; to be lifelike or vivid. – *noun* **livelihood** one's means of living (as one's daily work). – **live and let live** to allow others to live as they please; **live down** (*eg* one's past) to live until one's past acts are forgotten; **live up to** to be as good as expected.

live² *adjective* having life, not dead; full of energy; (of a television broadcast *etc*) seen as the event takes place, not recorded; apt to burn, explode, or give an electric shock. – *adjective* **lively** full of life, high spirits. – *noun* **liveliness**. – *verb* **liven** to make lively. – *noun* **livestock** farm animals. – *noun* **livewire** a very lively, energetic person.

livelong *adjective* whole: *the livelong day.*

liver *noun* a large gland in the body that carries out several important functions including purifying the blood. The liver of some animals is used as meat.

livery *noun* (*plural* **liveries**) the uniform of a manservant *etc*. – *noun* **livery stable** a stable where horses are kept for hire.

livid *adjective* of a bluish lead-like colour; (of a person) very angry.

living *adjective* having life; active, lively; (of a likeness) exact. – *noun* means of living. – *noun* **living-room** an informal sitting-room. – *noun* **living wage** a wage on which it is possible to live comfortably.

lizard *noun* a kind of four-footed reptile.

llama *noun* a type of S. American animal of the camel family without a hump.

lo! *interjection* look!

loach *noun* (*plural* **loaches**) a type of small river fish.

load verb to put on what is to be carried; to put the ammunition in (a gun); to put a film in (a camera); to weight for some purpose: *loaded dice*. – noun as much as can be carried at once; cargo; a heavy weight or task; the power carried by an electric circuit. – noun **loaded question** one meant to trap a person into making an admission which is harmful to him. – noun **loadline** a line along a ship's side to mark the waterline when fully loaded.

loaf noun (plural **loaves**) a shaped mass of bread. – verb to pass time idly or lazily. – noun **loafer**.

loam noun a rich soil. – adjective **loamy**.

loan noun anything lent *esp* money. – verb to lend.

loath or **loth** adjective unwilling (to).

loathe verb to dislike greatly. – noun **loathing** great hate or disgust. – adjective **loathsome** causing loathing or disgust, horrible.

loaves *see* **loaf**.

lob noun (in cricket) a slow, high ball bowled underhand; (in tennis) a ball high overhead dropping near the back of the court. – verb (past tense **lobbed**) to send such a ball; (*coll*) to throw.

lobby noun (plural **lobbies**) a small entrance hall; a passage off which rooms open; a group of people who try to influence the government or other authority in a particular way. – verb (past tense **lobbied**) to try to influence (public officials); to conduct a campaign to influence public officials.

lobe noun the hanging-down part of an ear; a division of the brain, lungs *etc*.

lobster noun a kind of shellfish with large claws, used for food. – noun **lobster pot** a basket in which lobsters are caught.

lobworm noun a kind of sea worm.

local adjective of or confined to a certain place. – noun (*coll*) one's nearest public house; (*usu plural*) the people living in a particular place or area. – noun **local colour** details in a story which make it more interesting and realistic. – noun **locale** the scene (of an) event. – noun **local government** administration of the local affairs of a district *etc* by elected inhabitants. – noun **locality** a particular place and the area round about. – verb **localize** to keep (something) to one area, keep from spreading. – verb **locate** to find; to set in a

particular place: *a house located in north London*. – noun **location** the act of locating; situation. – **on location** (of filming) in natural surroundings, not in a studio.

loch noun (in Scotland) a lake; an arm of the sea.

lock noun a fastening for doors *etc* (needing a key to open it); a part of a canal for raising or lowering boats; the part of a gun by which it is fired; a tight hold; a section of hair; (*plural*) hair. – verb to fasten with a lock; to become fastened; (with **up**) to shut in (with a lock). – noun **locker** a small cupboard. – noun **locket** a little ornamental case hung round the neck. – noun **lockjaw** a form of the disease tetanus which stiffens the jaw muscles. – noun **lockout** the act of locking out (*esp* of factory workers *etc* by their employer during wage disputes). – noun **locksmith** a smith who makes locks. – **lock, stock and barrel** completely.

locomotive noun a railway engine. – adjective of or capable of locomotion. – noun **locomotion** movement from place to place.

locum noun (plural **locums**) a person taking another's place (*esp* a doctor, dentist *etc*) for a time.

locust noun a type of large insect of the grasshopper family which destroys growing plants.

lodge noun a small house (*esp* one at the entrance to a larger building); a beaver's dwelling; a house occupied during the shooting or hunting season; (the meeting place of) a branch of some societies. – verb to live in rented rooms; to become fixed (in); to put in a safe place; to make (a complaint, appeal *etc*) officially. – noun **lodger** a person who stays in rented rooms. – noun **lodging** a place to stay, sleep *etc*; (*plural*) a room or rooms rented in another's house.

loft noun a room or space just under a roof; a gallery in a hall, church *etc*. – adjective **lofty** high up; noble, proud. – noun **loftiness**.

log noun a thick, rough piece of wood, part of a felled tree; a device for measuring a ship's speed; a logbook. – verb (past tense **logged**) to write down (events) in a logbook. – noun **logbook** an official record of (a ship's or aeroplane's) progress; a record (of progress, attendance *etc*); the registration documents of a motor vehicle.

loganberry *noun* a kind of fruit like a large raspberry.

loggerhead: at loggerheads quarrelling.

logic *noun* the study of reasoning correctly; correctness of reasoning. – *adjective* **logical** according to the rules of logic or sound reasoning. – *adverb* **logically.**

logo *noun* (*plural* **logos**) a badge or symbol (of a business firm *etc*) consisting of a simple picture or design and/or letters.

loin *noun* the back of an animal cut for food; (*plural*) the lower part of the back. – *noun* **loincloth** a piece of cloth worn round the hips, *esp* in India and south-east Asia.

loiter *verb* to proceed, move slowly; to linger; to stand around.

loll *verb* to lie lazily about; (of the tongue) to hang down or out.

lone *adjective* alone; standing by itself. – *adjective* **lonely** lone; lacking or wanting companionship; (of a place) having few people. – *noun* **loneliness.** – *adjective* **lonesome** lone; feeling lonely.

long *adjective* not short, measuring much from end to end; measuring a certain amount in distance or time: *Cut a strip 2 cm long. Her speech was only 2 minutes long;* far-reaching; slow to do something. – *adverb* for a great time; through the whole time: *all day long.* – *verb* to wish (for) very much. – *noun* **longbow** a large bow bent by the hand in shooting. – *noun* **longhand** ordinary writing, not shorthand. – *noun* **longing** an eager desire. – *adjective* **long-playing** (of a record) playing for a long time (approximately 45 minutes). – *adjective* **long-range** able to reach a great distance; (of a forecast) looking a long way into the future. – *adjective* **long-sighted** able to see things at a distance but not those close at hand. – *adjective* **long-suffering** putting up with troubles without complaining. – *adjective* **long-term** extending over a long time; taking the future, not just the present, into account. – *adjective* **long-winded** using too many words. – **before long** soon; **in the long run** in the end.

longevity *noun* great length of life.

longitude *noun* the distance, measured in degrees on the map, of a place east or west of the Greenwich meridian.

loo *noun* (*coll*) a toilet.

look *verb* to turn the eyes towards so as to see; to seem; to face: *This room looks south.* – *noun* the act of looking; the expression on one's face; appearance; (*plural*) personal appearance. – *noun* **looking-glass** a mirror. – *noun* **lookout** (a person who keeps) a careful watch; a high place for watching from; concern, responsibility. – **look down on** to despise, think of as being inferior; **look for** to search for; **look into** to investigate; **look on** to stand by and watch; to think of (as): *He looks on you as his mother;* **look out!** be careful! **look over** to examine briefly.

loom *noun* a machine for weaving cloth. – *verb* to appear indistinctly, often threateningly.

loop *noun* a doubled-over part in a piece of rope, string *etc*; a U-shaped bend (as in a river). – *noun* **loophole** a narrow slit in a wall; means of escaping or avoiding. – **loop the loop** to fly (an aircraft) upwards, back and down as if going round a circle.

loose *adjective* not tight, slack; not tied; free; not closely packed; vague, not exact; careless. – *adverb* **loosely.** – *verb* (also **loosen**) to make loose, to slacken; to untie. – *adjective* **loose-leaf** having a cover that allows pages to be inserted or removed. – **break loose** to escape; **on the loose** free.

loot *noun* goods stolen or plundered. – *verb* to plunder, ransack.

lop *verb* (*past tense* **lopped**) to cut off the top or ends of (*esp* a tree). – *adjective* **lop-eared** having ears hanging down. – *adjective* **lop-sided** leaning to one side, not having the sides the same.

lope *verb* to run with a long stride.

loquacious *adjective* talkative. – *noun* **loquaciousness** or **loquacity.**

lord *noun* the owner of an estate; a title given to noblemen, bishops and judges and used in other titles (as **Lord Mayor**); (mainly *hist*) a master, a ruler; **Lord** (with **the**) God. – *adjective* **lordly** like or belonging to a lord; noble, proud. – *noun* **Lord's day** Sunday. – *noun* **lordship** power, rule; used to or of a lord: *his lordship.* – (**House of**) **Lords** the upper (non-elected) house of the British parliament; **lord it over (someone)** to act like a lord, domineer.

lore *noun* knowledge, beliefs *etc* handed down.

lorgnette *noun* eyeglasses with a handle.

lorry *noun* (*plural* **lorries**) a motor vehicle for carrying heavy loads.

lose verb (past tense **lost**) to cease to have, have no longer; to have (something) taken away from; to put (something) where it cannot be found; to waste (time); to miss (the train, a chance etc); not to win (a game etc). – noun **loser** a person who loses. – noun **loss** (plural **losses**) the act of losing; that which is lost; waste, harm, destruction. – adjective **lost** not able to be found; no longer possessed; not won; thrown away; ruined; (with **in**) with attention totally taken up (by): *lost in thought*. – **at a loss** uncertain what to do, say etc.

loss, lost see **lose**.

lot noun a large number or quantity; one's fortune or fate; a separate portion. – **cast** (or **draw**) **lots** to decide who is to do something by drawing names out of a box etc.

loth see **loath**.

lotion noun a liquid for treating or cleaning the skin or hair.

lottery noun (plural **lotteries**) the sharing-out of money or of prizes won by chance, through drawing lots.

lotus noun (plural **lotuses**) kind of water-lily; (myth) a tree whose fruit was said to cause forgetfulness.

loud adjective making a great sound; noisy; showy, over-bright. – adverb **loud** or **loudly**. – noun **loudhailer** a megaphone with microphone and amplifier. – noun **loudspeaker** a device for converting electrical signals into sound.

lounge verb to lie back at one's ease; to move about lazily. – noun a sitting room. – noun **lounger** a lazy person. – noun **lounge suit** a man's suit for ordinary everyday (but not casual) wear.

lour see **lower²**.

louse noun (plural **lice**) a small blood-sucking insect sometimes found on the bodies of animals and people.

lout noun a clumsy, awkward fellow.

louvre or **louver** noun a slat that is set at an angle. – noun **louvre door** a door made up of sloping slats through which air and some light can pass. – noun **louvre window** a window covered with sloping slats; a window formed of narrow panes that can be set open at a narrow angle to admit air.

love noun a great fondness, liking, affection; a loved person; (in tennis etc) no score, nothing. – verb to be very fond of, to like very much. – adjective **lovable** worthy of love. – noun **love affair** a (temporary) relationship between people in love but not married. – adjective **lovely** beautiful; delightful. – noun **lover** a person who loves (someone); an admirer (of something); a person who is having a love affair with someone. – adjective **loving** full of love. – **in love (with)** feeling love and desire (for); having a great liking (for).

low adjective not high, not lying or reaching far up; (of a voice) not loud; cheap; feeling sad; humble; mean, unworthy. – verb to make the noise of cattle, to bellow or moo. – adverb in or to a low position; not loudly; cheaply. – adjective **lower** less high. – verb to make less high; to let or come down. – noun **lowing** bellowing, mooing. – noun **lowland** low or level country, without hills. – adjective **lowly** low in rank, humble. – noun **lowliness**. – noun **lowness**.

lower¹ see **low**.

lower² or **lour** verb (of the sky) to become dark and cloudy; to frown. – adjective **lowering**.

loyal adjective faithful, true. – noun **loyalist** one who is true to his king and country. – noun **loyalty** (plural **loyalties**).

lozenge noun a diamond-shaped figure; a small sweet for sucking.

LP noun a long-playing record.

LSD abbreviation lysergic acid diethyl-amide; pounds, shillings and pence (British coinage before decimalization).

Lt abbreviation Lieutenant.

Ltd abbreviation limited liability.

lubricate verb to oil (a machine etc) to make it move more easily and smoothly. – noun **lubricant** something which lubricates, oil. – noun **lubrication**.

lucerne noun a type of plant used for feeding cattle, alfalfa.

lucid adjective easily understood; (of a mind) clear, not confused. – noun **lucidity**.

luck noun fortune, whether good or bad; chance; good fortune. – adjective **luckless** unfortunate, unhappy. – adjective **lucky** (comparative **luckier**, superlative **luckiest**) fortunate, having good luck; bringing good luck.

lucrative adjective giving gain or profit.

lucre noun gain; money.

ludicrous adjective ridiculous.

ludo noun a game played with counters on a board.

lug verb (past tense **lugged**) to pull or drag with effort. – noun **lugger** a type of small sailing vessel.

luggage noun suitcases and other baggage of a traveller.

lugubrious adjective mournful, dismal.

lugworm noun a kind of large worm found on the seashore, used for bait by fishermen.

lukewarm adjective neither hot nor cold; not very eager, not enthusiastic.

lull verb to soothe or calm. – noun a period of calm. – noun **lullaby** (plural **lullabies**) a song to lull children to sleep.

lumbago noun a pain in the lower part of the back.

lumbar adjective of or in the lower part of the back.

lumber noun useless old furniture etc; timber sawn up. – verb to move about clumsily, heavily. – noun **lumberjack** a person who fells, saws and shifts trees.

luminous adjective giving light; shining; clear. – noun **luminosity**.

lump noun a small, solid mass of no particular shape; a swelling; the whole taken together: considered in a lump; a heavy, dull person. – verb to form into lumps; to treat as being alike, class (together). – adjective **lumpish** heavy; dull. – noun **lump sum** an amount of money given all at once, not in instalments. – adjective **lumpy** full of lumps.

lunacy see **lunatic**.

lunar adjective of the moon.

lunatic noun, adjective (a person who is) insane or crazy. – noun **lunacy**.

lunch noun (plural **lunches**) a midday meal. – verb to eat lunch. – noun **luncheon** lunch.

lung noun one of two bag-like parts of the body which fill and empty with air in the course of breathing.

lunge noun a sudden thrust or push. – Also verb.

lupin noun a type of plant with flowers on long spikes.

lurch verb to roll or pitch suddenly to one side, stagger. – Also noun. – **leave in the lurch** to leave in a difficult position without help.

lure noun that which attracts or leads on, bait. – verb to attract, entice away.

lurid adjective (of colour etc) glaring; horrifying, sensational; pale, like a ghost.

lurk verb to keep out of sight; to be hidden; to move or act secretly and slyly. – adjective **lurking** (of a feeling) vague, hidden.

luscious adjective sweet, delicious, juicy.

lush adjective (of grass etc) green, thick and plentiful.

lust noun a greedy desire (for power, riches etc); a strong sexual desire. – Also verb. – adjective **lustful**.

lustre noun brightness, splendour; gloss. – adjective **lustrous** bright, shining.

lusty adjective lively, strong.

lute noun an old type of stringed musical instrument.

luxury noun (plural **luxuries**) something pleasant (and expensive) but not necessary; the use or enjoyment of things of this sort. – adjective **luxuriant** having very great growth of leaves, branches etc; richly ornamented. – verb **luxuriate** to be luxuriant; to enjoy, take delight (in). – adjective **luxurious** supplied with luxuries; very comfortable.

lychgate noun a churchyard gate with a porch.

lying see **lie**.

lymph noun a colourless fluid in the body. – noun **lymph gland** one of the glands carrying lymph.

lynch verb to condemn and put to death without legal trial.

lynx noun (plural **lynxes**) a kind of wild animal of the cat family, noted for its keen sight.

lyre noun an old kind of musical instrument like the harp. – noun **lyrebird** a type of Australian bird with a lyre-shaped tail.

lyric noun a short poem (expressing the poet's feelings); (plural) the words of a song. – adjective of a lyric; full of (joyful) feeling. – adjective **lyrical** lyric; song-like; full of enthusiastic praise.

M

M *abbreviation a thousand (mille* [L]).

m *abbreviation* metre(s); miles; married; male; masculine.

MA *abbreviation* Master of Arts.

macabre *adjective* gruesome, horrible.

macadamize *verb* to surface (a road) with small broken stones.

macaroni *noun* a type of pasta made into (long) tubes and cooked.

macaroon *noun* a sweet cake or biscuit made mainly of almonds and sugar.

macaw *noun* a kind of long-tailed brightly-coloured parrot.

mace *noun* a heavy staff with an ornamental head (carried as a sign of office); (*hist*) a heavy stick; a spice made from the covering of a nutmeg.

machete *mà-shet'i, n* a kind of heavy knife used as a weapon *etc.*

machination *noun* (often *plural*) a crafty scheme, plot.

machine *noun* a working arrangement of wheels, levers, or other parts; a (motor) bicycle; a political party organization. – *verb* to sew (or do other jobs) with a machine. – *noun* **machine code** a system of symbols that can be understood by a computer. – *noun* **machine-gun** a gun which fires bullets very quickly one after the other. – *noun* **machinery** machines in general; the working parts of a machine; organization: *machinery of local government*. – *noun* **machine-tool** a power-driven machine for shaping metal, plastic or wood, *eg* a drill, a lathe. – *noun* **machinist** one who makes or works machinery.

Mach number *noun* the ratio of the speed of an aircraft to the velocity of sound (*eg* Mach 5 means 5 times the speed of sound).

mackerel *noun* a type of eatable seafish with wavy markings.

mackintosh *noun* (*plural* **mackintoshes**) a kind of waterproof overcoat.

mad *adjective* out of one's mind, insane; wildly foolish; furious with anger. – *noun* **madcap** a rash, hot-headed person. – *verb* **madden** to make angry or mad. – *noun* **madhouse** any place of confusion and noise; (*hist*) a house for mad people. — *noun* **madman** a person who is mad. – *noun* **madness**. – **like mad** very quickly, very energetically *etc*; **mad cow disease** (*coll*) BSE.

madam *noun* a polite form of address used to a woman.

made *see* **make**.

madeira *noun* a kind of wine; a kind of sponge cake.

Madonna *noun* the mother of Jesus, *esp* as shown in statues, pictures *etc*.

madrigal *noun* a part-song for several voices.

maelstrom *māl'stròm, noun* a whirlpool; any place of great confusion.

maestro *mī'strō, noun* (*plural* **maestros**) someone highly skilled in some art, *esp* a conductor or composer of music.

magazine *noun* a paper published weekly, monthly *etc*, containing articles, stories, pictures *etc*; a storage place for military equipment, gunpowder *etc*; in a rifle, a place for extra cartridges.

magenta *adjective, noun* (of) a reddish-purple colour.

maggot *noun* a small worm-like creature, the grub of a bluebottle *etc*. – *adjective* **maggoty** full of maggots.

magic *noun* any influence which produces results which cannot be explained or which are remarkable; conjuring tricks. – *adjective* using magic; used in magic; magical. – *adjective* **magical** of, produced by magic; very mysterious and beautiful; very wonderful or mysterious. – *noun* **magician** a person skilled in magic. – **black magic** magic which is done for an evil purpose, witchcraft.

magistrate *noun* a person who has the power of putting the law into force in a police court, or as a Justice of the Peace. – *adjective* **magisterial** of magistrates; having an air of authority.

magnanimity *noun* generosity. – *adjective* **magnanimous** very generous.

magnate *noun* a person of great power or wealth.

magnesium *noun* an element, a white metal which burns with a dazzling white light. – *noun* **magnesia** a white powder formed from magnesium.

magnet *noun* a piece of iron, steel *etc* which has the power to attract other pieces of iron *etc*; a person or thing that attracts strongly. – *adjective* **magnetic** having the powers of a magnet; (of a person) strongly attractive. – *noun* **magnetic north** the direction in which the magnetized needle of a compass points. – *noun* **magnetic tape** tape on which sound, pictures, computer material *etc* can be recorded. – *noun* **magnetism** the power of a magnet; the science which deals with magnets; attraction, great charm. – *verb* **magnetize** to make magnetic; to attract, influence.

magneto *noun* (*plural* **magnetos**) a device producing electric sparks, *esp* one for lighting the fuel in a motor-car engine.

magnification *see* **magnify**.

magnificent *adjective* splendid in appearance; great or noble in deeds; excellent, very fine. – *noun* **magnificence.**

magnify *verb* (*past tense* **magnified**) to make something appear larger (by using a magnifying glass); to exaggerate. – *noun* **magnification.**

magnitude *noun* greatness; size.

magnolia *noun* a type of tree with large white or purplish sweet-scented flowers.

magpie *noun* a black-and-white chattering bird of the crow family, known for its habit of collecting objects.

magus *noun* (*plural* **magi** *mā'jī*) an ancient Persian astrologer and magician. – **the Magi** the three magi who brought gifts to the infant Jesus.

Maharajah *noun* the title given to a great Indian prince. – *noun* **Maharani** or **Maharanee** a Maharajah's wife.

mahogany *noun* a type of tropical American tree or its hard reddish-brown wood, much used for furniture.

maid *noun* a female servant; an unmarried woman, a younger girl. – *noun* **maiden** an unmarried girl. – *adjective* of a maiden, unmarried; first: *He made a brief maiden speech. The Titanic sank on her maiden voyage.* – *noun* **maiden name** the surname of a married woman before her marriage. – *noun* **maiden over** (in cricket) an over in which no runs are made.

mail *noun* letters, parcels *etc* carried by post; body armour of steel rings or plates; armour. – *verb* to post. – *noun* **mail order** an order for goods to be sent by post. – *adjective* **mail-order.** – *noun* **mail shot** unsolicited advertising material sent by post.

maim *verb* to cripple, disable.

main *adjective* chief, most important. – *noun* the ocean; (often *plural*) a chief pipe, wire *etc* supplying gas, water or electricity. – *noun* **mainframe** the central processing unit and storage unit of a computer. – *adjective* (of a computer) of the large, powerful type rather than the small-scale kind. – *noun* **mainland** a large piece of land off whose coast smaller islands lie. – *adverb* **mainly** chiefly, mostly. – *noun* **mainsail** the principal sail of a ship or boat. – *noun* **mainspring** the chief spring, *esp* one which causes the wheels to move, in a watch or clock; the chief cause of action. – *noun* **mainstay** the chief support. – **in the main** for the most part.

maintain *verb* to keep (something) as it is; to continue to keep in good working order; to support (a family *etc*); to state (an opinion) firmly. – *noun* **maintenance** the act of maintaining; upkeep, repair; means of support, *esp* money for food, clothing *etc*.

maize *noun* a type of cereal crop grown widely in America.

Maj. *abbreviation* Major.

majesty *noun* (*plural* **majesties**) greatness of rank or manner; a title used to or of a king or queen (*eg* **Your Majesty**). – *adjective* **majestic** stately.

major *adjective* greater or great in size, importance *etc*; opposite of **minor**. – *noun* a senior army officer. – *noun* **majority** (*plural* **majorities**) the greater number or quantity; the difference in amount between the greater and the lesser number; the age when one becomes legally an adult, in UK 18.

make *verb* (*past tense* **made**) to form, construct; to cause to be: *you make me angry*; to bring about: *make trouble*; to amount to: *2 and 2 make 4*; to earn: *He makes £5 a day*; to force: *I made him do it*; to perform (a journey, an attempt *etc*); to prepare (*eg* a meal). – *noun* kind; shape, form; brand. – *noun* **maker.** – *noun, adjective* **makeshift** (a thing) used for a time for want of something better.

– *noun* **make-up** cosmetics for a woman, or for an actor or actress. – **make believe** to pretend (*noun* **make-believe**); **make good** to do well; to carry out (a promise); to make up for (a loss); **make light of** to treat as unimportant; **make much of** to fuss over, treat as important; **make nothing of** not to be able to understand, do *etc*; make light of; **make off** to run away; **make out** to see (in the distance or indistinctly); to declare, prove; to write out (a bill *etc*) formally; **make up** to form a whole: *Eleven players make up the side*; to put together, invent (a false story); to put make-up on the face; to be friendly again after a quarrel; **make up for** to give or do something in return for damage *etc* that one has done; **on the make** (*coll*) looking for personal gain; (*coll*) looking for a sexual partner.

maladjusted *adjective* unable to fit in happily in one's work, way of life *etc*.

maladministration *noun* bad management, *esp* of public affairs.

malady *noun* (*plural* **maladies**) illness, disease.

malaise *noun* a feeling of discomfort.

malapropism *noun* the use of a wrong word which sounds something like the one intended, *eg* contemptuous for contemporary.

malaria *noun* a fever caused by the bite of a certain type of mosquito.

male *adjective* of the sex that is able to father children or young, masculine. – Also *noun*.

malefactor *noun* an evildoer.

malevolent *adjective* wishing ill to others, spiteful. – *noun* **malevolence**.

malformation *noun* faulty or wrong shape.

malfunction *verb* to fail to work or operate properly. – Also *noun*.

malice *noun* ill will, spite. – *adjective* **malicious**.

malign *mà-līn*, *verb* to speak evil of, *esp* falsely.

malignant *adjective* wishing to do great harm, spiteful; (of a disease *etc*) likely to cause death.

malinger *verb* to pretend to be ill (to avoid work *etc*). – *noun* **malingerer**.

mallard *noun* the (male of the) common wild duck.

malleable *adjective* (of metal *etc*) able to be beaten out by hammering; (of people) easy to influence.

mallet *noun* a kind of wooden hammer.

malnutrition *noun* underfeeding or poor feeding.

malodorous *adjective* having a bad smell.

malpractice *noun* wrongdoing; failure to practise one's profession in a correct or proper way.

malt *noun* barley or other grain prepared for making beer or whisky.

maltreat *verb* to treat roughly or unkindly. – *noun* **maltreatment**.

mama or **mamma** *noun* a name sometimes used for **mother**.

mammal *noun* any of the kinds of animals of which the female parent feeds the young with her own milk.

mammoth *noun* a type of very large elephant, now extinct. – *adjective* huge.

man *noun* (*plural* **men**) a human being; the human race; a grown-up human male; a husband; a piece in chess or draughts. – *verb* (*past tense* **manned**) to supply with men: *man the boats*. – *adjective* **manful** courageous. – *adverb* **manfully**. – *verb* **manhandle** to handle roughly. – *noun* **manhole** a hole (into a drain, sewer *etc*) large enough to let a man through. – *noun* **manhood** the state of being a man; manly quality. – *noun* **mankind** the human race. – *adjective* **manly** brave, strong. – *adjective* **mannish** (of a woman) behaving, looking like a man. – *noun* **man-of-war** a warship. – *noun* **manpower** the number of people available for work. – *noun* **manslaughter** unintentional but blameworthy homicide. – **the man in the street** the ordinary person; **to a man** every single one.

manacle *noun* a handcuff. – Also *verb*.

manage *verb* to have control or have charge of; to deal with; to cope; to succeed. – *adjective* **manageable** easily managed or controlled. – *noun* **management** the people in charge of organizing a business *etc*; the art of managing a business *etc*. – *noun* **manager** (*masculine*), **manageress** (*feminine*) a person who looks after a business *etc*.

mandarin *noun* a type of fruit like a small orange; (*hist*) a senior Chinese official.

mandate *noun* a command; power given to a person or nation to act in the name of another. – *adjective* **mandatory** compulsory.

mandible *noun* the jaw or lower jawbone.

mandolin(e) *noun* a kind of round-backed stringed instrument like a guitar.

mane *noun* long hair on the head and neck *eg* on the horse and the male of the lion.

maneuver *see* **manoeuvre**.

manganese *noun* an element, a hard easily-broken metal of a greyish-white colour.

mange *noun* a skin disease of dogs, cats *etc.* – *adjective* **mangy** affected with mange; shabby; squalid.

mangel-wurzel *noun* a kind of beetroot, grown as food for cattle.

manger *noun* a box or trough holding dry food for horses and cattle.

mangetout *mon^szh-too,* *noun* a type of pea, of which the pod is also eaten.

mangle *noun* a machine for squeezing water out of clothes or for smoothing them. – *verb* to squeeze (clothes) through a mangle; to crush, tear, damage badly.

mango *noun* (*plural* **mangoes**) a type of tropical tree in India or its reddish, juicy fruit.

mangrove *noun* a type of tree which grows in swamps in hot countries.

mania *noun* a form of mental illness in which the sufferer is over-active, over-excited and unreasonably happy; (too) great fondness or enthusiasm (for something): *a mania for collecting records.* – *noun* **maniac** a madman; a very rash or over-enthusiastic person. – *adjective* **manic** suffering from mania; very energetic, very active, very excited.

manicure *noun* the care of hands and nails; professional treatment for the hands and nails. – Also *verb.* – *noun* **manicurist** a person who cares for and treats hands and nails.

manifest *adjective* easily seen or understood. – *verb* to show plainly. – *noun* **manifestation**. – *noun* **manifesto** (*plural* **manifestoes** or **manifestos**) a public announcement of intentions (*esp* by a political party).

manifold *adjective* many and various.

manipulate *verb* to handle or manage skilfully, cunningly or dishonestly.

mankind, manly *see* **man**.

manna *noun* in the Bible, the food provided miraculously for the Israelites in the wilderness; any unexpected or delicious treat.

mannequin *noun* a person, *usu* a woman, who wears clothes to show intending buyers how they look; a dummy figure.

manner *noun* the way (in which anything is done); the way in which a person behaves; (*plural*) (polite) behaviour *usu* towards others. – *noun* **mannerism** an odd and obvious habit in someone's behaviour *etc.* – *adjective* **mannerly** polite. – **all manner of** all kinds of.

manoeuvre, (*US*) **maneuver** *noun* a planned movement of troops, ships or aircraft; a trick, a cunning plan. – *verb* to perform a manoeuvre; to move or manage cunningly.

manor *noun* (*hist*) the land belonging to a lord or squire; a large house *usu* attached to a country estate. – *adjective* **manorial**.

manse *noun* the house of a minister of certain religious denominations *eg* the Church of Scotland.

mansion *noun* a large house.

mantelpiece *noun* a shelf over a fireplace.

mantilla *noun* a kind of veil covering the head and shoulders sometimes worn by Spanish women.

mantle *noun* a cloak or loose outer garment; a covering: *a mantle of snow;* a piece of thin, transparent, material round the light in gas or some paraffin lamps.

mantra *noun* a word or phrase, chanted or repeated inwardly in meditation.

manual *adjective* of the hand or hands; worked by hand; working with the hands: *manual worker.* – *noun* a handbook used *eg* to give instructions as to how to use something: *a car manual;* the keyboard of an organ *etc.*

manufacture *verb* to make (articles, materials *etc*), formerly by hand, now *usu* by machinery, and in large quantities. – *noun* the process of manufacturing; anything manufactured. – *noun* **manufacturer**.

manure *noun* a substance, *esp* animal dung, used to make soil more fertile. – *verb* to treat (soil, plants) with manure.

manuscript *noun* the prepared material for a book *etc* before it is printed; a book or paper written by hand.

Manx cat *noun* a type of cat that has no tail.

many *adjective* a large number of: *Many people were present.* – *pronoun* a large number: *Many survived.* – **many a** (followed by a *singular* noun) a large number of: *Many a man had to die before the war ended.*

map *noun* a flat drawing of (part of) the earth's surface, showing various details *eg* rivers, mountains *etc.* – *verb* (*past tense* **mapped**) to make a map of; (with **out**) to plan.

maple *noun* any of several kinds of tree of the same type as the sycamore, one of which produces sugar; its hard light-coloured wood used for furniture *etc.*

mar *verb* (*past tense* **marred**) to spoil: *The scar marred her beauty. Coughing marred his enjoyment of the concert.*

maraud *verb* to plunder, raid. – *noun* **marauder** a plundering robber. – *adjective* **marauding.**

marble *noun* any kind of limestone that takes a high polish, used for sculpture, decorating buildings *etc*; a little ball, now *usu* of glass, used in a children's game.

marcasite *noun* crystals formed from iron and used in jewellery.

March *noun* the third month of the year.

march *verb* (to cause) to walk in time with regular step; to go on steadily. – *noun* (*plural* **marches**) a marching movement; a piece of music for marching to; the distance covered by marching; a steady going forward (of events *etc*): *the march of time*; a boundary.

marchioness *see* **marquess.**

mare *noun* the female of the horse.

margarine *noun* a substance like butter, made mainly of vegetable fats.

margin *noun* an edge, border; the blank edge on the page of a book; something extra (*eg* time, money *etc*) beyond what seems to be needed. – *adjective* **marginal** placed in the margin; of or in a margin; borderline, close to a limit; (of a political constituency *etc*) without a clear majority for any one candidate or party; of little effect or importance: *a marginal improvement.*

marguerite *noun* a kind of large daisy.

marigold *noun* a kind of plant with a yellow flower.

marijuana *noun* a drug made from the plant hemp.

marina *noun* a place with moorings for yachts, sailing dinghies *etc.*

marinate or **marinade** *verb* to steep in wine, herbs or spices *etc.* – Also *noun.*

marine *adjective* of the sea. – *noun* a soldier serving on board a ship; shipping in general. – *noun* **mariner** a sailor.

marionette *noun* a puppet moved by strings.

marital *adjective* of marriage.

maritime *adjective* of the sea or ships; lying near the sea.

marjoram *noun* a type of sweet-smelling herb used as a flavouring.

mark *noun* a sign that can be seen; a stain, spot *etc*; a target, a thing aimed at; trace; a point or unit used in establishing how good a piece of work is (*esp* in schools); the starting-line in a race: *On your marks!*; the standard unit of German money. – *verb* to make a mark on; to observe, watch; to stay close to (an opponent in football *etc*); to award marks to (a piece of schoolwork *etc*); (with **off**) to separate, distinguish. – *adjective* **marked** easily noticed: *a marked improvement.* – *adverb* **markedly** noticeably. – *noun* **marker** a person who marks the score at games; any object (as a counter *etc*) used to mark the score. – *noun* **marksman** a person who shoots well. – **mark time** to move the feet up and down, as if marching, but without going forward; to keep things going without progressing; **up to the mark** coming up to the required standard.

market *noun* a public place for buying and selling; (a country, place *etc* where there is) a need or demand (for certain types of goods). – *verb* to put on sale. – *noun* **market forces** commerce not restricted by government intervention. – *noun* **market-garden** a garden in which fruit and vegetables are grown to be sold. – *noun* **marketing** the act or practice of (advertising and) selling. – *noun* **market leader** a company that sells more goods of a certain type than any other company; a brand of goods selling more than any other of its type. – **on the market** for sale: *His house is on the market.*

marlinspike *noun* a spike for separating the strands of a rope *etc*.

marmalade *noun* a jam made from oranges, grapefruit or lemons.

marmoset *noun* a type of small monkey found in America.

marmot *noun* a kind of burrowing animal of the squirrel family (also **woodchuck** or **groundhog**).

maroon *adjective, noun* (of) a brownish-red colour. – *noun* a firework used as a distress signal *etc*. – *verb* to leave on an island or in another lonely place without means of escape; to leave in a helpless or uncomfortable position.

marquee *noun* a large tent used for large gatherings (*eg* a wedding reception) or public entertainment (*eg* a circus).

marquess or **marquis** (*masculine*), **marchioness** (*feminine*) *noun* (*plural* **marquesses** or **marquises** (*masculine*), **marchionesses** (*feminine*)) a nobleman below a duke in rank.

marriage *see* **marry**.

marrow *noun* the soft substance in the hollow part of bones; a type of long thick-skinned vegetable.

marry *verb* (*past tense* **married**) to join (or be joined) together as husband and wife. – *noun* **marriage** the ceremony by which a man and a woman become husband and wife; a joining together. – *adjective* **marriageable** suitable or old enough for marriage.

marsh *noun* (*plural* **marshes**) a piece of low-lying wet ground. – *noun* **marshmallow** a type of marsh plant with pink flowers; a foam-like sweet sticky substance. – *noun* **marsh marigold** a type of marsh plant with yellow flowers (also **kingcup**). – *adjective* **marshy**.

marshal *noun* a high-ranking officer in the army or air force; a person who directs processions *etc*; (*US*) a kind of law-court official; (*US*) a head of a police force. – *verb* (*past tense* **marshalled**) to arrange (troops, facts, arguments *etc*) in order; to show the way, conduct, lead. – *noun* **marshalling yard** a place where railway wagons are shunted about to make up trains.

marsupial *noun* any animal which carries its young in a pouch (*eg* the kangaroo or opossum).

martello tower *noun* a round coastal fort.

marten *noun* a kind of animal related to the weasel, with valuable fur.

martial *adjective* warlike; of, or suitable for war. – *noun* **martial art** a type of combative sport or method of self-defence. – *noun* **martial law** the government of a country by army rules and rulers.

martin *noun* a kind of bird of the swallow family.

martinet *noun* a person who keeps strict order.

martini *noun* (*plural* **martinis**) a cocktail made with gin and vermouth. – *noun* **Martini**® a type of vermouth.

martyr *noun* a person who suffers death or hardship for what they believe. – *verb* to put a person to death or make them suffer for their beliefs. – *noun* **martyrdom** the death or suffering of a martyr.

marvel *noun* anything astonishing or wonderful – *verb* (*past tense* **marvelled**) to feel amazement (at). – *adjective* **marvellous** astonishing, extraordinary; (*coll*) excellent, very good.

marzipan *noun* a mixture of ground almonds, sugar *etc*, used in the making of sweets and cakes.

mascot *noun* a person, animal or thing that is supposed to bring good luck: *The football team's mascot was a teddy bear*.

masculine *adjective* of the male sex; manly. – *noun* **masculinity**.

mash *verb* to beat or crush into a pulp-like mixture. – *noun* mashed potato; a mixture, *esp* one of bran, meal *etc*, used as food for animals.

mask *noun* a cover for the face (for disguise or protection); something pretended, disguise. – *verb* to cover the face with a mask; to hide.

masochism *noun* an unnatural pleasure taken in being dominated or cruelly treated. – *noun* **masochist** a person who takes such pleasure.

mason *noun* a worker in stone; a Freemason. – *adjective* **masonic**. – *noun* **masonry** stonework.

masque *noun* an old type of theatre show in which the actors wore masks.

masquerade *noun* a dance at which masks are worn; pretence. – *verb* to pretend to be someone else: *He masqueraded as a butler.*

mass *noun* (*plural* **masses**) a lump or quantity gathered together; a large quantity; the main part or body; a measure of quantity of matter in an object. – *noun* **Mass** (in some Christian Churches) the celebration of Christ's last supper with his disciples; music for this celebration. – *adjective* of a mass; of or consisting of large numbers or quantities. – *verb* to form into a mass. – *adjective* **massive** bulky, heavy, huge. – *noun* **mass media** means of communicating information to a large number of people *eg* television. – *noun* **mass production** production in large quantities of articles all exactly the same. – **the masses** ordinary people.

massacre *noun* the cruel killing of great numbers of people. – *verb* to kill (large numbers) in a cruel way.

massage *noun* the rubbing of parts of the body (muscles, knees *etc*) *esp* to remove pain or stiffness. – Also *verb*. – *noun* **masseur** (*masculine*), **masseuse** (*feminine*) a person who massages.

mast *noun* a long upright pole, *esp* one holding up the sails *etc* in a ship or one holding an aerial, flag *etc*.

master *noun* a person who controls or commands; an owner (of a dog *etc*); an employer; a male teacher; the commander of a merchant ship: a person who is very skilled in something, an expert; a degree awarded by universities, as **Master of Arts, Science** *etc*. – *adjective* chief; controlling: *master switch*. – *verb* to overcome, defeat; to become able to do (a thing) thoroughly. – *adjective* **masterful** strong-willed. – *noun* **masterkey** a key which is so made that it opens a number of different locks. – *adjective* **masterly** showing the skill of an expert or master, clever. – *verb* **mastermind** to plan, work out the details of (a scheme *etc*). – Also *noun*. – *noun* **masterpiece** the best example of someone's work, *esp* a very fine picture, book, piece of music *etc*. – *noun* **masterstroke** a clever act or move. – *noun* **mastery** victory (over); control (of); great skill (in). – **master of ceremonies** the person who directs the form and order of events of a public occasion; a compère.

masticate *verb* to chew. – *noun* **mastication.**

mastiff *noun* a breed of large, powerful dog.

masturbate *verb* to stimulate (one's own) sexual organs to a state of orgasm. – *noun* **masturbation.**

mat *noun* a piece of material (coarse plaited plant fibre, carpet *etc*) for wiping shoes on, covering the floor *etc*; a piece of material, wood *etc* put below dishes at table. – *adjective see* **matt.** – *adjective* **matted** thickly tangled. – *noun* **matting** material from which mats are made.

matador *noun* the man who kills the bull in bullfights.

match *noun* (*plural* **matches**) a small stick of wood or other material (**matchstick**) tipped with a substance which easily catches fire when rubbed against something hard; a person or thing similar to or the same as another; a person or thing agreeing with or suiting another; an equal; a (person suitable for) marriage; a contest or game. – *verb* to be of the same make, size, colour *etc*; to set (two things, teams *etc*) against each other; to hold one's own with, be equal to. – *noun* **matchbox** a box for holding matches. – *adjective* **matchless** having no equal. – *noun* **matchwood** wood broken into small pieces.

mate *noun* a companion or fellow-worker; an assistant: *plumber's mate*; a husband or wife; either the male or female of a pair of animals, birds *etc*; a merchant ship's officer, next in rank to the captain; (*coll*) term of address by one man to another. – *verb* to marry; (of animals or birds) to bring or come together to breed.

material *adjective* made of matter, able to be seen and felt; not spiritual, concerned with physical comfort, money *etc*: *a material outlook on life*; important, essential: *a material difference*. – *noun* something out of which anything is, or may be, made; cloth. – *noun* **materialism** a tendency to attach too much importance to material things (*eg* physical comfort, money); the belief that only things we can see or feel really exist or are important. – *noun* **materialist.** – *adjective* **materialistic.** – *verb* **materialize** to appear in bodily form; to happen, come about. – *adverb* **materially** to a large extent, greatly.

maternal *adjective* of a mother; like a mother, motherly; related through one's mother: *maternal grandmother*. – *noun* **maternity** the state of being a mother, motherhood. – *adjective* of or for a woman having or about to have a baby: *maternity clothes*.

mathematics *noun* (often shortened to **maths**) the study of measurements, numbers and quantities. – *adjective* **mathematical** of or done by mathematics; very exact. – *noun* **mathematician** a person who is good at mathematics; a person whose job is concerned with mathematics.

matinée *noun* an afternoon performance in a theatre *etc*. – *noun* **matinée coat** a baby's short jacket.

matins *noun plural* the morning service in certain churches.

matricide *noun* the killing of one's own mother; a person who kills their own mother.

matriculate *verb* to admit, or be admitted to a university.

matrimony *noun* marriage. – *adjective* **matrimonial**.

matrix *noun* (*plural* **matrices**) a mould in which metals *etc* are shaped; a mass of rock in which gems *etc* are found.

matron *noun* a married woman; a senior nurse in charge of a hospital; formerly a woman in charge of housekeeping or nursing in a school, hostel *etc*. – *adjective* **matronly** (of a woman) dignified, staid; rather plump.

matt or **mat** *adjective* having a dull surface, not shiny or glossy.

matter *noun* anything that takes up space, can be seen, felt *etc*; material, substance; a subject written or spoken about; (sometimes *plural*) affair, business; trouble, difficulty: *What is the matter?*; importance: *It is of no great matter*; pus. – *verb* to be of importance: *It does not matter*; to give out pus. – *adjective* **matter-of-fact** keeping to the actual facts, not imaginative; uninteresting. – **a matter of course** something that is to be expected: *His promotion came as a matter of course*; **a matter of opinion** a subject on which different opinions are held; **as a matter of fact** in fact.

mattock *noun* a kind of tool like a pickaxe.

mattress *noun* (*plural* **mattresses**) a thick firm layer of foam rubber, padding covered in cloth *etc*, for lying on, *usu* as part of a bed.

mature *adjective* fully grown or developed; ripe, ready for use. – *verb* to (cause to) become mature; of an insurance policy *etc* to be due to be paid out. – *noun* **maturity** ripeness.

maudlin *adjective* silly, sentimental.

maul *verb* to hurt badly by rough or savage treatment.

mausoleum *noun* a very fine tomb.

mauve *adjective, noun* (of) a purple colour.

mawkish *adjective* weak and sentimental.

maxim *noun* a general truth or rule showing how one should behave *etc*.

maximum *adjective* greatest, most. – *noun* (*plural* **maxima**) the greatest number or quantity; the highest point or degree

May *noun* the fifth month of the year. – *noun* **Mayday** the first day of May. – *noun* **mayday** an international distress signal. – *noun* **maypole** a decorated pole for dancing round on Mayday.

may *verb* (*past tense* **might**) *usu* used with another verb to express permission, possibility *etc*: *Yes, you may watch the film. I thought I might find him there*; used to express a wish: *May you always be happy!*

maybe *adverb* perhaps.

mayonnaise *noun* a sauce made of eggs, oil, vinegar or lemon juice *etc*.

mayor *noun* (*masculine* and *feminine*) the chief elected public official of a city or town. – *noun* **mayoress** a mayor's wife.

maze *noun* a series of winding paths in a park *etc* deliberately laid out in such a way that it is difficult to find the way out; something complicated and confusing: *a maze of regulations*.

mazurka *noun* (the music for) a kind of lively Polish dance.

MBE *abbreviation* Member of the Order of the British Empire.

MC *abbreviation* Master of Ceremonies; Military Cross.

MCC *abbreviation* Marylebone Cricket Club.

MD *abbreviation* Doctor of Medicine (*Medicinae Doctor* [L]); Managing Director.

ME *abbreviation* myalgic encephalomyelitis (chronic fatigue and muscle pain following a viral infection).

me *pronoun* the word used by a speaker or writer in mentioning himself or herself (as the object in a sentence): *He hit me. Give it to me*.

mead *noun* an alcoholic drink made with honey.

meadow *noun* a field of grass. – *noun* **meadowsweet** a type of wild flower with sweet-smelling cream-coloured flowers.

meagre or (*US*) **meager** *adjective* thin; poor in quality; scanty, not enough. – *noun* **meagreness.**

meal *noun* the food taken at one time (*eg* breakfast, dinner, supper); grain ground to a coarse powder. – *adjective* **mealy-mouthed** not frank and straightforward in speech.

mean¹ *adjective* not generous with money *etc*; unkind, selfish; lowly, humble. – *noun* **meanness.**

mean² *adjective* middle, coming midway between two other things, points, quantities *etc*; average. – *noun* something lying midway between two other things *etc*; (*plural*) a method, instrument, action *etc* by which anything is brought about; money, property *etc*: *a man of means*. – **by all means** certainly, of course; in any or every way possibly; **by no means** certainly not; not at all; **(in the) meantime, meanwhile** in the time between two happenings.

mean³ *verb* (*past tense, past participle* **meant**) (to intend) to express, indicate: *'Halt' means 'stop'. By 'several' I mean three or more*; to Intend. – *noun* **meaning** what is (intended to be) expressed or conveyed; purpose, intention. – *adjective* (of a look, glance *etc*) full of expression indicating a certain feeling. – *adjective* **meaningful.** – *adjective* **meaningless.** – **mean well** (or **ill**) to have good (or bad) intentions.

meander *verb* (of a river) to flow in a winding course; to wander about slowly and aimlessly.

measles *noun singular* a kind of infectious disease, with red spots. – *adjective* **measly** (*coll*) ungenerous, mean.

measure *noun* size or amount (found by measuring); an instrument, container *etc* for measuring; musical time; (often *plural*) a plan of action: *They took measures to prevent their house from being burgled*; a law brought before parliament to be considered. – *verb* to find out the size, quantity *etc* by using some form of measure; to be of a certain length, amount *etc*; to indicate the measurement of (something): *A thermometer measures temperature*; to mark

(off), weigh (out) *etc* in portions. – *adjective* **measured** steady, unhurried. – *noun* **measurement** the act of measuring; the size, amount *etc* found by measuring. – **for good measure** as a bonus.

meat *noun* flesh of animals used as food. – *adjective* **meaty** full of meat; tasting of meat; (of a book *etc*) full of information.

mechanic *noun* a skilled worker with tools or machines. – *adjective* **mechanical** of machinery: *mechanical engineering*; worked by machinery; done without thinking. – *adverb* **mechanically.** – *noun* **mechanics** the study of forces and motion; the study and art of constructing machinery; the actual details of how something works: *The mechanics of his plan are beyond me*. – *noun* **mechanism** a piece of machinery; the way a piece of machinery works; an action by which a result is produced. – *verb* **mechanize** to equip (a factory *etc*) with machinery; to supply (troops) with armoured vehicles. – *noun* **mechanization.**

medal *noun* a piece of metal *etc* in the form of a coin or a coin-like object, with a design, inscription *etc* stamped on it, made in memory of an event or given as a reward for merit. – *noun* **medallion** a large medal or piece of jewellery like one. – *noun* **medallist** a person who has gained a medal.

meddle *verb* to concern oneself with things that are not one's business, to interfere or tamper (with). – *noun* **meddler.** – *adjective* **meddlesome** fond of meddling.

media *see* **medium.**

mediaeval *see* **medieval.**

mediate *verb* to act as a peacemaker (between). – *noun* **mediation.** – *noun* **mediator** a person who tries to make peace between people who are quarrelling.

medicine *noun* something given to a sick person in order to make them better; the science of the treatment of illnesses. – *adjective* **medical** of doctors or their work. – *noun* an examination to check one's physical health. – *noun* **medicament** a medicine. – *adjective* **medicated** mixed with a healing or disinfecting substance. – *noun* **medication** medical treatment; a medicine. – *adjective* **medicinal** used in medicine; used as a medicine; having the power to cure. – noun **medicine man** a witch doctor.

medieval or **mediaeval** adjective of the Middle Ages.

mediocre adjective not very good, ordinary. – noun **mediocrity.**

meditate verb to think deeply and in quietness; to contemplate religious or spiritual matters; to consider, think about. – noun **meditation** deep, quiet thought; contemplation on a religious or spiritual theme. – adjective **meditative** thoughtful.

medium noun (plural **media** or **mediums**) something (a means, a substance, a material etc) through which an effect is produced; (plural **media**) a means (esp television, radio or newspapers) by which news etc is made public; (plural **mediums**) a person through whom spirits (of dead people) are said to speak. – adjective middle or average in size, quality etc.

medley noun (plural **medleys**) a mixture; a piece of music put together from a number of other pieces.

meek adjective gentle, uncomplaining. – noun **meekness.**

meerschaum noun a fine white clay used to make tobacco pipes; a pipe made of this.

meet verb (past tense **met**) to come face to face (with); to come together, join; to make the acquaintance of; to pay (bills etc) fully; to be suitable for, satisfy (requirements, a demand etc). – noun a meeting of huntsmen or other sportsmen. – adjective proper, suitable. – noun **meeting** a coming together, esp of people; an assembly, gathering.

mega- prefix great, huge.

megalith noun a huge stone set up in prehistoric times.

megalomania noun an exaggerated idea of one's own importance or abilities.

megaphone noun a portable cone-shaped device with microphone and amplifier for making the sound of the voice louder.

megaton adjective of a bomb with an explosive force equalling a million tons of TNT.

melancholy noun lowness of spirits, sadness. – adjective sad, depressed.

melanin noun the dark pigment in skin, hair etc of humans.

mêlée noun a confused fight between two groups of people.

mellifluous adjective sweet-sounding.

mellow adjective (of fruit) ripe, juicy, sweet; having become pleasant or agreeable with age; (of light, colour etc) soft, not harsh. – verb to make or become mellow. – noun **mellowness.**

melodrama noun a type of play, intended to arouse great sympathy, horror etc. – adjective **melodramatic** of or like a melodrama, exaggerated, sensational, over-dramatic.

melody noun (plural **melodies**) a tune; sweet music. – adjective **melodic** of melody. – adjective **melodious** pleasing to the ear; tuneful.

melon noun a type of large juicy fruit or the plant that bears it.

melt verb to make or become liquid, esp by heat; to soften; to disappear: The crowd melted away; to become tender in feeling: His heart melted at the sight of the orphan. – noun **meltdown** the process in which the radioactive fuel in a nuclear reactor overheats and melts through the insulation into the environment.

member noun a person who belongs to any group, society etc; a limb or organ of the body. – noun **Member of Parliament** (shortened to **MP**) a person elected to the House of Commons. – noun **membership** the membership of a club etc; the state of being a member.

membrane noun a thin skin which covers or lines parts of a human or animal body, plants etc.

memento noun (plural **mementos**) something by which an event is remembered.

memo noun (plural **memos**) short form of **memorandum.**

memoir noun a written statement of what has happened; (plural) a person's account of their own life, an autobiography.

memorandum noun (plural **memoranda**) a note which helps one to remember; a written statement of a matter being discussed; a brief note sent round colleagues in an office etc.

memory noun (plural **memories**) the power to remember; the mind's store of remembered things; something remembered; (comput) a store of information; what is remembered about a person, their reputation. – *adjective* **memorable** worthy of being remembered, famous. – *noun* **memorial** something (*eg* a monument) which helps us to remember persons or events of the past. – *adjective* **commemorating**, honouring the memory of a person *etc*. – *verb* **memorize** to learn by heart. – **in memory of** in remembrance of or as a memorial of.

menace *noun* harm or danger that may happen; a threat. – *verb* to be a danger to; to threaten. – *adjective* **menacing** evil-looking; threatening.

ménage *mā-näzh'*, *noun* a household.

menagerie *noun* (a place for keeping) a collection of wild animals.

mend *verb* to put right something broken, torn *etc*, to repair; to make or grow better. – *noun* a part which has been mended. – **on the mend** getting better.

mendacious *adjective* untruthful. – *noun* **mendacity.**

mendicant *noun* a beggar. – Also *adjective*.

menial *adjective* (of work) humble, uninteresting, not requiring skill.

meningitis *noun* an illness caused by inflammation of the covering of the brain.

menopause *noun* the ending of menstruation in middle age.

menstruation *noun* (in women) the monthly discharge of blood from the womb. – *adjective* **menstrual** of menstruation. – *verb* **menstruate.**

mensuration *noun* the act or art of measuring length, height *etc*.

mental *adjective* of the mind; done, made, happening *etc* in the mind; (of illness) affecting the mind. – *noun* **mental hospital** a hospital for people suffering from mental illness. – *noun* **mentality** (*plural* **mentalities**) mental power; personality.

menthol *noun* a sharp-smelling substance got from peppermint oil.

mention *verb* to speak of briefly; to remark (that). – *noun* (act of) mentioning or remarking.

mentor *noun* a (wise) giver of advice.

menu *noun* (*plural* **menus**) (a card with) a list of dishes to be served at a meal; (*comput*) a list of options.

MEP *abbreviation* Member of the European Parliament.

mercantile *adjective* of buying and selling, trading.

mercenary *adjective* working for money; influenced by the desire for money. – *noun* (*plural* **mercenaries**) a soldier who is paid by a foreign country to fight in its army.

merchandise *noun* goods to be bought and sold.

merchant *noun* a person who carries on a business in the buying and selling of goods, a trader. – *adjective* of trade. – *noun* **merchant bank** a bank providing *esp* commercial banking services. – *noun* **merchantman** a trading ship. – *noun* **merchant navy** ships and crews employed in trading.

mercury *noun* an element, a heavy, silvery liquid metal (also **quicksilver**). – *adjective* **mercurial** lively, often changing.

mercy *noun* (*plural* **mercies**) kindness, forgiveness towards an enemy, wrongdoer *etc*; pity; (*coll*) a bit of good luck. – *adjective* **merciful** willing to forgive or to punish only lightly. – *adjective* **merciless** cruel. – **at one's mercy** in one's power.

mere *noun* a pool or a lake. – *adjective* nothing more than, no more than: *mere nonsense*. – *adverb* **merely** only, simply.

merge *verb* to (cause to) combine or join together; to blend, come together gradually. – *noun* **merger** a joining together *esp* of business firms *etc*.

meridian *noun* a (semi-)circle drawn round the globe passing through the north and south poles; the highest point of the sun's course; the highest point of success *etc*.

meringue *mě-rang'*, *noun* a cake made of sugar and white of egg.

merino *noun* (*plural* **merinos**) a kind of sheep which has very fine wool; soft cloth made from its wool.

merit *noun* that which deserves praise or reward; worth, value; (*plural*) the rights and wrongs (of a case, affair *etc*). – *verb* to deserve. – *adjective* **meritorious** deserving honour or reward.

mermaid (*feminine*), **merman** (*masculine*) *noun* an imaginary sea creature with a human's body down to the waist, and a fish's tail.

merry *adjective* full of fun, cheerful and lively; slightly drunk. – *noun* **merriment** fun; laughter. – *noun* **merry-go-round** a kind of roundabout with wooden horses, seats *etc* for riding on. – *noun* **merrymaking** cheerful celebrating, festivity.

mesh *noun* (*plural* **meshes**) the opening between the threads of a net; network.

mesmerize *verb* to hypnotize; to hold the attention of completely, fascinate. – *noun* **mesmerism**.

mess *noun* (*plural* **messes**) an untidy or disgusting sight; disorder, confusion; (in the army, navy *etc*) a number of persons who take their meals together; the place where they eat. – *verb* (*usu* with **up**) to make untidy, dirty, muddled. – *noun plural* **messmates** those who eat together.

message *noun* a piece of news or information sent from one person to another; a lesson, moral. – *noun* **messenger** a person who carries a message.

Messrs *noun plural* Sirs, Gentlemen; used as *plural* of Mr (*Messieurs* [F]).

metabolism *noun* the chemical changes in the cells of a living organism that provide energy for living processes and activity; the conversion of nourishment into energy.

metal *noun* any of a group of substances (*eg* gold, silver, iron *etc*) *usu* shiny and able to conduct heat and electricity. – *adjective* **metallic** made of metal; like metal. – *noun* **metallurgy** the study of metals. – *adjective* **metallurgic(al)**.

metamorphosis *noun* (*plural* **metamorphoses**) a change in appearance, form, character *etc*, a transformation; a change that takes place in some creature during growth (*eg* a tadpole into a frog).

metaphor *noun* a way of describing something by suggesting that it is, or has the qualities of, something else: *The camel is the ship of the desert*. – *adjective* **metaphorical**.

mete *verb* (with **out**) to deal out (punishment *etc*).

meteor *noun* a small mass, body *etc*, moving rapidly through space, becoming bright as it enters the earth's atmosphere, a shooting star. – *adjective* **meteoric** of, like a meteor; rapid; rapidly and brilliantly successful. – *noun* **meteorite** a metor which falls to the earth in the form of a piece of rock. – *noun* **meteorologist** a person who studies or makes forecasts about the weather. – *noun* **meteorology** the

study of weather and climate. – *adjective* **meteorological**.

meter *noun* an instrument for measuring the amount of gas, electricity, water *etc* used; *see also* **metre**.

method *noun* a (planned or orderly) way of doing something; orderly arrangement. – *adjective* **methodical** orderly, done or acting according to some plan.

methylated spirit(s) or (*coll*) **meth(s)** *noun* or *noun plural* a type of alcohol used as fuel in lamps, stoves *etc*.

meticulous *adjective* (too) careful and accurate about small details.

metre or (*US*) **meter** *noun* the chief unit of length in the metric system (about 1·1 yard); (in poetry, music) the arrangement of syllables or notes in a regular rhythm. – *adjective* **metric** of the metric system; metrical. – *adjective* **metrical** (in poetry) of, in metre; arranged in the form of verse. – *noun* **metrication** the change-over of a country's units of measurements to the metric system. – *noun* **metric system** the system of weights and measures based on tens (1 metre = 10 decimetres = 100 centimetres *etc*).

metronome *noun* an instrument that keeps a regular beat, used for music practice.

metropolis *noun* (*plural* **metropolises**) the capital city of a country; a chief centre. – *adjective* **metropolitan**.

mettle *noun* courage, pluck. – **on one's mettle** out to do one's best.

mew *noun* the cry of a cat; *see* **sea-mew**; (*plural*) stables (now often used as flats) built round a yard or in a lane. – *verb* to make the cry of a cat.

mezzo-soprano *noun* (*plural* **mezzo-sopranos**) (a person with) a singing voice between alto and soprano.

MI5 *noun* (*coll*) British government counter-espionage agency.

MI6 *noun* (*coll*) British espionage and intelligence agency.

miaow *noun* the sound made by a cat. – Also *verb*.

mic. *abbreviation* microphone.

mica *noun* a type of mineral which glitters and divides easily into thin transparent layers.

mice *see* **mouse**.

Michaelmas daisy *noun* a kind of large daisy, a kind of aster.

micro *noun* (*plural* **micros**) short for **microcomputer** or **microwave oven**.

micro- *prefix* very small.

microbe *noun* a kind of very tiny living thing; a germ.

microchip *noun* a tiny piece of silicon *etc* designed to act as a complex electronic circuit.

microcomputer *noun* a very small computer containing a microprocessor.

microcosm *noun* a version on a small scale: *The misery in the household was a microcosm of the misery to be found throughout the whole country.*

microfilm *noun* a very narrow photographic film on which whole books, documents *etc* can be reproduced on a tiny scale.

micrometer *noun* an instrument used for measuring tiny distances or angles.

microphone *noun* an instrument for picking up sound waves to be broadcast, recorded or amplified.

microprocessor *noun* a microcomputer (or part of one) consisting of one or more microchips.

microscope *noun* an instrument (containing magnifying glass) which makes small objects easily seen. – *adjective* **microscopic** tiny.

microwave *noun* a very short radio wave; short for microwave oven. – *noun* **microwave oven** an oven in which food is cooked by the heat produced by the passage of microwaves.

mid- *adjective, prefix* placed or coming in the middle. – *noun* **midday** noon. – *adjective* **midland** in the middle of a country, away from the coast. – *noun* **midnight** twelve o'clock at night. – *noun* **midshipman** formerly a junior naval officer, below sub-lieutenant. – *noun* **midsummer** the time about June 21 which is the longest day of the year. – *adjective, adverb* **midway** half-way. – *noun* **midwinter** the time about December 21 which is the shortest day of the year.

midden *noun* a rubbish or dung heap.

middle *adjective* equally distant from the ends or edges; coming between. – *noun* the middle point or part, centre; the course (of an action, job *etc*). – *adjective* **middle-aged** between youth and old age. – *noun* **Middle Ages** the time

roughly between the years AD 500 and AD 1500. – *noun* **middle-class** the class of people between the working and upper classes. – *adjective* **middling** of middle size, quality *etc*; not very good or bad.

midge *noun* any of several kinds of small fly.

midget *noun* a person who has not grown up to the normal size. – *adjective* very small.

midriff *noun* the middle of the body, just below the ribs.

midst *noun* the middle (*eg* of a job). – **in our midst** among us.

midwife *noun* (*plural* **midwives**) a woman who helps at the birth of babies. – *noun* **midwifery** the art of assisting at the birth of babies.

mien *mēn, noun* a look or appearance.

might *noun* power, strength. – *verb see* **may**. – *noun* **mightiness** greatness. – *adjective* **mighty** (*comp* **mightier**, *superl* **mightiest**) having great power; very great. – *adverb* (*coll*) very. – **with might and main** with all possible effort.

migraine *noun* a very severe type of headache.

migrate *verb* to change one's home to another region or country; to pass regularly from one region to another, as certain birds *etc* do. – *noun* **migration**. – *adjective, noun* **migrant** (of) a person, bird *etc* that migrates. – *adjective* **migratory** migrating; wandering.

mike *noun* short for **microphone**.

mild *adjective* gentle; (of a taste) not sharp or bitter; not harsh or severe; (of weather) not cold. – *noun* **mildness**.

mildew *noun* a mark on plants, cloth, leather *etc* caused by tiny fungi.

mile *noun* a measure of length (1·61 kilometre or 1760 yards). – *noun* **mileage** distance in miles; travel expenses (counted by the mile). – *noun* **milestone** a stone beside the road showing the number of miles to a certain place; something which marks an important event.

milieu *mēl-yû , noun* surroundings.

military *adjective* of, for soldiers or warfare. – *noun* the army. – *adjective* **militant** fighting, warlike; aggressive, favouring or taking part in forceful action. – *noun* a person who is militant.

– *verb* **militate** to fight, work (against); to work (against), act to one's disadvantage. – *noun* **militia** a body of men (not regular soldiers) trained to fight in emergencies.

milk *noun* a white liquid produced by female animals as food for their young; this liquid, *esp* from cows, used as a food or drink generally. – *verb* to draw milk from; to force, take (money *etc*) from. – *noun* **milk-float** a kind of vehicle that carries milk-bottles *etc* and makes deliveries of milk to homes *etc*. – *noun* **milkmaid** (*old*) a woman who milks cows. – *noun* **milkman** a man who sells or delivers milk. – *noun* **milk-tooth** a tooth from the first set of teeth in humans and mammals. – *adjective* **milky** of, like milk. – *noun* **Milky Way** bright band of stars stretching across the sky.

mill *noun* a machine for grinding or crushing grain, coffee *etc*; a building where grain is ground; a factory where things are made. – *verb* to grind; to put grooves round the edge of (a coin); to move round and round in a crowd. – *noun* **miller** a person who grinds grain. – *noun* **millrace** the stream of water which turns a millwheel and so drives the machinery of a mill. – *noun* **millstone** one of two heavy stones between which grain was ground; a great trouble or difficulty which keeps one from making progress. – *noun* **millwheel** a wheel, *esp* a water-wheel, used for driving a mill.

millennium *noun* (*plural* **millennia**) a period of a thousand years; a period of great happiness hoped for on earth.

millet *noun* a type of grain used for food.

milli- *prefix* thousand; a thousandth part of.

milligramme *noun* a thousandth of a gramme.

millilitre *noun* a thousandth of a litre.

millimetre *noun* a thousandth of a metre.

milliner *noun* a person who makes and sells women's hats. – *noun* **millinery** the goods sold by a milliner.

million *noun* a thousand thousands (1 000 000). – *noun* **millionaire** a person who has a million pounds (or dollars) or more.

millipede *noun* a type of small crawling creature with a long body and very many legs.

mime *noun* the use of, or the art of, using actions, movements of the arms *etc* in place of speech; a play performed through mime; an action in such a play. – *verb* to act using actions and movements but no words. – *verb* **mimic** (*past tense* **mimicked**) to imitate *esp* in a mocking way. – *noun* a person who mimics. – *noun* **mimicry** the act of mimicking; (in an animal) a likeness to its surroundings or to another animal.

mimosa *noun* a type of tree with bunches of yellow, scented flowers.

min. *abbreviation* minimum; minute (of time).

minaret *noun* a slender tower on an Islamic mosque.

mince *verb* to cut or chop into small pieces; to walk in a prim way with short steps. – *noun* meat chopped finely. – *noun* **mincemeat** a chopped-up mixture of dried fruit, suet *etc*. – *noun* **mince-pie** a pie filled with mincemeat. – *noun* **mincer** a machine for mincing. – **not to mince matters** not to try to soften an unpleasant statement by using tactful words.

mind *noun* the power by which we think *etc*; intelligence, understanding; intention: *I have a (good) mind to tell him so*. – *verb* to see to, look after: *Mind the baby*; to watch out for, be careful of: *Mind the step*; to object to: *I don't mind your saying so*. – *adjective* **mindful** paying attention (to). – *adjective* **mindless** foolish; without reason or thought. – **change one's mind** to change one's opinion or intention; **in two minds** undecided; **make up one's mind** to decide; **out of one's mind** mad; **presence of mind** ability to act calmly and sensibly; **speak one's mind** to speak frankly.

mine *pronoun* a thing or things belonging to me: *That book is mine*. – *noun* a place (*usu* a pit or system of underground tunnels) from which metals, coal *etc* are dug; a heavy charge of explosive material for blowing up (a vehicle, ship *etc*). – *verb* to dig or work a mine; to lay explosive mines in. – *noun* **minefield** an area covered with explosive mines. – *noun* **miner** a person who works in a (coal) mine. – *noun* **minesweeper** or **minelayer** a ship which places mines in, or removes them from, the sea.

mineral *adjective, noun* (of) any of the substances (coal, metals, gems *etc*) that are found in the earth and mined. – *noun* **mineralogy** the study of minerals.

– noun mineralogist. – noun mineral water water containing small amounts of minerals; a fizzy type of soft drink.

mingle *verb* to mix.

mini- *prefix* small (as in **minibus** *etc*). – *noun* **Mini**® a type of small car.

miniature *noun* a painting (or something else) made on a small scale. – *adjective* on a small scale.

minibus *noun* (*plural* **minibuses**) a type of small bus.

minim *noun* (in music) a note equal to two crotchets in length.

minimize *verb* to make to seem small or unimportant: *He minimized the help he received*; to make as little as possible. – *noun* **minimum** (*plural* **minima**) the smallest possible quantity. – *adjective* the least possible.

minion *noun* a slave-like follower.

minister *noun* the head of one of the divisions or departments of the government; a clergyman; a representative of a government in a foreign country. – *verb* (with **to**) to help, supply the needs of. – *adjective* **ministerial** of a minister. – *noun* **ministry** (*plural* **ministries**) a department of government or its headquarters; the work of a clergyman.

mink *noun* a small weasel-like kind of animal or its fur.

minnow *noun* a type of very small river or pond fish.

minor *adjective* of less importance, size *etc*; small, unimportant; opposite of **major**. – *noun* a person who has not come of age legally, in the UK a person under 18 years old. – *noun* **minority** (*plural* **minorities**) the smaller number or part; the state of being a minor.

minster *noun* a large church or cathedral.

minstrel *noun* (*hist*) a (travelling) musician; a singer, entertainer. – *noun* **minstrelsy** a collection of songs.

mint *noun* a type of plant with strong-smelling leaves, used as flavouring; a place where coins are made; (*coll*) a large sum (of money). – *verb* to make coins. – **in mint condition** in perfect condition, as good as new.

minuet *noun* (the music for) a kind of slow, graceful dance.

minus *preposition* used to show subtraction and represented by the sign (−): *Five minus two equals three*, or 5−2=3; (*coll*) without: *I'm minus my car today*. – *adjective, noun* (of) a quantity less than zero.

minute[1] *noun* the sixtieth part of an hour; in measuring an angle, the sixtieth part of a degree; a very short time; (*plural*) the notes taken of what is said at a meeting.

minute[2] *adjective* very small; very exact.

minx *noun* (*plural* **minxes**) a cheeky young girl.

miracle *noun* a wonderful act beyond the power of man; a fortunate happening that has no natural cause or explanation. – *adjective* **miraculous**.

mirage *noun* something not really there that one imagines one sees, *esp* an expanse of water imagined by travellers in the desert.

mire *noun* deep mud. – *adjective* **miry**.

mirror *noun* a surface that reflects light, *esp* a piece of glass which shows the image of the person looking into it. – *verb* to reflect as a mirror does.

mirth *noun* merriment, laughter. – *adjective* **mirthful**. – *adjective* **mirthless**.

mis- *prefix* wrong(ly), bad(ly).

misadventure *noun* an unlucky happening.

misanthropist *noun* a person who hates mankind. – *adjective* **misanthropic**. – *noun* **misanthropy**.

misappropriate *verb* to put to a wrong use *esp* to use (someone else's money) for oneself.

misbehave *verb* to behave badly. – *noun* **misbehaviour**.

misc. *abbreviation* miscellaneous.

miscarry *verb* (*past tense* **miscarried**) to go wrong or astray; to be unsuccessful; in pregnancy, to have a miscarriage. – *noun* **miscarriage** a going wrong, failure; in pregnancy, the loss of the baby from the womb before it is able to survive.

miscellaneous *adjective* assorted, made up of several kinds. – *noun* **miscellany** (*plural* **miscellanies**) a mixture or collection of things (*esp* writings) of different kinds.

mischance *noun* an unlucky accident.

mischief *noun* naughtiness; evil, harm, damage. – *adjective* **mischievous** naughty; teasing; causing trouble.

misconception *noun* a wrong idea, a misunderstanding.

misconduct *noun* bad or immoral behaviour.

misconstrue *verb* to take a wrong meaning from, misunderstand.

miscreant *noun* a wicked person.

misdeed *noun* a bad deed; a crime.

misdemeanour *noun* a misdeed or minor offence (*esp* against the law).

miser *noun* a person who hoards money and spends very little on anything or anybody; a mean person. – *adjective* **miserly** very mean.

misery *noun* (*plural* **miseries**) a great unhappiness, pain, poverty *etc*. – *adjective* **miserable** very unhappy; very poor, worthless or wretched.

misfire *verb* (of guns *etc*) to fail to go off; (of a plan *etc*) to go wrong.

misfit *noun* a person who cannot fit in happily at home, work *etc*; a thing that fits badly.

misfortune *noun* bad luck; an unlucky accident.

misgiving *noun* a feeling of fear or doubt (*eg* about the result of an action).

misguided *adjective* led astray, mistaken.

mishandle *verb* to treat badly or roughly.

mishap *noun* an unlucky accident.

mislay *verb* (*past tense* **mislaid**) to put (a thing) aside and forget where it is, to lose.

mislead *verb* (*past tense* **misled**) to give a false idea (to), to deceive. – *adjective* **misleading**.

misnomer *noun* a wrong or unsuitable name.

misogynist *mis-oj'in-ist*, *noun* one who hates women.

misprint *noun* a mistake in printing.

misquote *verb* to make a mistake in repeating what someone has written or said.

misrepresent *verb* to give a wrong idea (of someone's words, actions *etc*).

miss *noun* (*plural* **misses**) a form of address used before the name of an unmarried woman; a young woman or girl; the act of missing; a failure to hit the target; a loss. – *verb* to fail to hit, reach, catch, find, see, hear, take (an opportunity), understand; to discover the loss or absence of; to feel the lack of: *He misses his old friends*; (with **out**) to leave out; to be left out of (*esp* something worthwhile or advantageous). – *adjective* **missing** lost.

missal *noun* the Mass book of the Roman Catholic Church.

misshapen *adjective* badly, abnormally shaped.

missile *noun* a weapon or other object that is thrown or fired.

mission *noun* a task, duty *etc* that a person or group is sent to do; a group of representatives sent (to another country) for negotiations *etc*, or one sent to spread a religion; the headquarters of such groups; one's chosen task or purpose: *His mission in life is to make people happy*. – *noun* **missionary** (*plural* **missionaries**) a person who is sent to spread a religion.

missive *noun* something sent, *esp* a letter.

misspell *verb* to spell wrongly. – *noun* **misspelling**.

misspent *adjective* spent in the wrong way, wasted: *misspent youth*.

mist *noun* a cloud of moisture seen in the air, thin fog or drizzle; anything that blurs one's sight, judgement *etc*. – *verb* (with **up** or **over**) to cover or become covered with mist. – *adjective* **misty**.

mistake *verb* (*past tense* **mistook**, *past participle* **mistaken**) to misunderstand, be wrong or make an error about; to take (one thing or person) for another. – *noun* a wrong action, statement *etc*, an error. – *adjective* **mistaken** making an error, unwise: *mistaken belief*.

mister *see* **Mr**.

mistletoe *noun* a type of plant with white berries, used as a Christmas decoration.

mistress *noun* (*plural* **mistresses**) a female employer; a female teacher; a female owner (of a dog); a woman skilled in an art *etc*: *a mistress of sculpture*; a woman who is the lover though not the legal wife of a man; *see* **Mrs**.

mistrust *noun* a lack of trust or confidence in. – *verb* not to trust, not to have confidence in.

misunderstand *verb* to take a wrong meaning from what is said or done. –

noun **misunderstanding** a mistake about a meaning; a slight disagreement.

misuse *noun* bad or wrong use. – *verb* to use wrongly; to treat badly.

mite *noun* anything very small (*eg* a little child); a kind of very tiny spider; (*hist*) a very small coin.

mitigate *verb* to make (trouble, punishment, anger *etc*) less great or severe. – *noun* **mitigation**.

mitre *noun* the pointed head-dress worn by archbishops and bishops; a slanting joint between two pieces of wood.

mitt or **mitten** *noun* a kind of glove without separate divisions for the four fingers.

mix *verb* to unite or blend two or more things together to form one mass; (often with **up**) to confuse, muddle; to go into the company of others, associate (with): *He does not mix with his neighbours.* – Also *noun*. – *adjective* **mixed** jumbled together; confused, muddled; made up of, including different kinds (or sexes). – *noun* **mixer** a machine (or person) that mixes. – *noun* **mixture** the act of mixing; the state of being mixed; a number of things mixed together; a medicine. – **mixed up** confused; bewildered.

mizzen-mast *noun* the mast nearest the stern of the ship.

ml *abbreviation* millilitre(s).

MLR *abbreviation* minimum lending rate.

mm *abbreviation* millimetre(s).

mnemonic *ni-mon'ik*, *noun* something (*eg* a rhyme *etc*) which helps one to remember (something).

MO *abbreviation* medical officer.

moan *verb* to make a low sound of grief or pain. – Also *noun*.

moat *noun* a deep trench round a castle *etc*, *usu* filled with water.

mob *noun* a noisy crowd. – *verb* (*past tense* **mobbed**) to crowd round, or attack, in a disorderly way.

mobile *adjective* able to move; moving or moved easily; changing quickly. – *noun* a decorative object hung so that it moves slightly in the air. – *noun* **mobility**.

mobilize *verb* to gather (troops *etc*) together ready for active service. – *noun* **mobilization**.

moccasin *noun* a soft leather shoe of the type worn by the N. American Indians.

mocha *noun* a fine coffee; coffee or coffee and chocolate flavour; a deep brown colour.

mock *verb* to laugh at, make fun of. – *adjective* false, pretended, imitation: *a mock battle.* – *noun* **mockery** the act of mocking; a ridiculous imitation.

MOD *abbreviation* Ministry of Defence.

mode *noun* manner (of doing or acting); kind, sort; fashion. – *adjective* **modish** fashionable, smart.

model *noun* a design, pattern *etc* to be copied; a copy of something made in a small size: *model railway*; a living person who poses for an artist; someone who is employed to wear and show off new clothes. – *adjective* acting as a model; fit to be copied, perfect: *model behaviour.* – *verb* (*past tense* **modelled**) to make a model of; to shape; to form according to a particular pattern; to wear and show off (clothes).

moderate *verb* to make or become less great or severe. – *adjective* keeping within reasonable limits, not going to extremes; of medium or average quality, ability *etc*. – *adverb* **moderately**. – *noun* **moderation** a lessening or calming down; the practice of not going to extremes. – *noun* **moderator** the chairman at a meeting (*esp* of clergymen).

modern *adjective* belonging to the present or to a time not long past, not old. – *noun* **modernity**. – *verb* **modernize** to bring up to date.

modest *adjective* not exaggerating one's achievements *etc*, not boastful; not very large: *a modest salary*; behaving in a decent way, not shocking. – *noun* **modesty**.

modicum *noun* (*plural* **modicums**) a small quantity or amount: *a modicum of kindness.*

modify *verb* (*past tense* **modified**) to make a change in: *He modified the design*; to make less extreme: *He modified his demands.* – *noun* **modification**.

modish see **mode**.

modulate *verb* to vary or soften the tone or pitch of (the voice *etc*); to change key (in music). – *noun* **modulation**.

module *noun* (in architecture) a standard unit of size; a separate, self-contained section of a spacecraft; a set course forming a unit in an educational scheme.

mohair *noun* (fabric made from) the long silky hair of an Angora goat.

Mohammed *noun* a prophet, the founder of Islam.

moist *adjective* damp, very slightly wet. – *verb* **moisten** to make slightly wet or damp. – *noun* **moisture** slight wetness; water or other liquid in tiny drops in the atmosphere or on a surface. – *verb* **moisturize** to add moisture to. – *noun* **moisturizer** a cosmetic cream or liquid that restores moisture to the skin.

molar *noun* a back tooth which grinds one's food.

molasses *noun singular* a type of thick syrup left when sugar is made, treacle.

mole *noun* a kind of small burrowing animal, with very small eyes and soft fur; a spy who successfully infiltrates a rival organization; a small (often dark brown) spot on the skin; a stone jetty or pier. – *noun* **molehill** little heap of earth cast up by a burrowing mole.

molecule *noun* the smallest part of a substance that has the same qualities as the substance itself.

molest *verb* to annoy or torment; to injure, attack (*usu* a child or woman) sexually. – *noun* **molester.**

mollify *verb* – (*past tense* **mollified**) to calm down, soothe, or lessen the anger of.

mollusc *noun* the name of a group of boneless animals *usu* with hard shells (*eg* shellfish, snails).

mollycoddle *verb* to pamper, over-protect.

molten *adjective* (of metal, lava *etc*) melted.

moment *noun* a very short space of time, an instant; importance. – *adjective* **momentary** lasting for a moment. – *adjective* **momentous** of great importance. – *noun* **momentum** (*plural* **momenta**) the force of a moving body.

monarch *noun* a king, queen, emperor or empress. – *noun* **monarchy** (*plural* **monarchies**) government by a monarch; an area governed by a monarch.

monastery *noun* (*plural* **monasteries**) a house where a group of monks live. – *adjective* **monastic** of or like monasteries or monks. – *noun* **monasticism** the way of life in a monastery.

Monday *noun* the second day of the week.

monetary *adjective* of money or coinage.

money *noun* (*plural* **moneys** or **monies**) the coins and banknotes which are used for payment; wealth. – *adjective* **moneyed** or **monied** wealthy.

mongoose *noun* (*plural* **mongooses**) a type of small weasel-like animal which kills snakes.

mongrel *adjective, noun* (of) an animal, *esp* a dog, of mixed breed.

monitor *noun* any of several kinds of instruments used for checking if some system, apparatus *etc* is working correctly; a pupil who helps in the running of a school; a screen in a television studio showing the picture being transmitted; a screen as part of a computer; a kind of large lizard. – *verb* to use, or to be, a monitor; to check, keep a check on something; to listen to and report on foreign broadcasts *etc*.

monk *noun* one of a male religious group that lives apart from the world in a monastery.

monkey *noun* (*plural* **monkeys**) the type of animal most like man, *usu* the small long-tailed kind walking on four legs (unlike the apes); a mischievous child. – *verb* to meddle, tamper with something. – *noun* **monkey-nut** a peanut, groundnut. – *noun* **monkey-puzzle** a kind of pine tree with prickly spines along its branches.

mono- *prefix* one, single.

monochrome *adjective* in one colour; black and white.

monocle *noun* a single eyeglass.

monogamy *noun* a marriage to one wife or husband only at a time. – *adjective* **monogamous.**

monogram *noun* two or more letters (often a person's initials) made into a single design: *He wore his monogram on his shirt.*

monologue *noun* a long speech by one person.

monoplane *noun* an aeroplane having one pair of wings.

monopoly *noun* (*plural* **monopolies**) the right, not shared by others, of doing, making or selling something; complete unshared possession, control *etc*. – *verb* **monopolize** to have the full, unshared rights in anything; to take up the whole of (eg someone's attention, a conversation etc).

monorail noun a railway on which the trains run along a single rail.

monosyllable noun a word of one syllable. – adjective **monosyllabic.**

monotone noun a single, unchanging tone; dull. – noun **monotony** lack of variety.

monsoon noun a wind that blows in the Indian Ocean; the rainy season caused by the south-west monsoon in summer.

monster noun anything of unusual size or appearance; a huge creature, causing fear; a very wicked person. – adjective huge. – noun **monstrosity** (plural **monstrosities**) something not natural; something very ugly. – adjective **monstrous** huge, horrible.

montage mon'tāzh, noun a composite picture; a film made up of parts of other films.

month noun a twelfth part of a year, about four weeks. – adjective, adverb **monthly** happening once a month. – noun (plural **monthlies**) a paper published once a month.

monument noun a building, pillar, tomb etc built in memory of a person or an event. – adjective **monumental** of or acting as a monument; very great in size, quantity etc. – **ancient monument** any structure (such as a dwelling-place, grave etc) remaining from ancient times.

moo noun the sound made by a cow. – Also verb.

mood noun the state of a person's feelings or temper. – adjective **moody** often changing one's mood; ill-tempered, cross.

moon noun the heavenly body which travels round the earth once each month and reflects light from the sun. – verb to wander (about); to gaze dreamily (at). – noun **moonbeam** a beam of light from the moon. – noun **moonlight** the light of the moon. – noun **moonshine** the shining of the moon; rubbish, foolish ideas or talk. – noun **moonstone** a precious stone with a pearly shine.

moor noun a large stretch of open ground, often covered with heather. – verb to tie up or anchor (a ship etc). – noun **moorhen** a kind of water bird, a female coot.

– noun plural **moorings** the place where a ship is moored; the anchor, rope etc holding it. – noun **moorland** a stretch of moor.

moose noun (plural **moose**) a large kind of deer-like animal, found in N. America.

moot point noun a debatable point, a question that has no obvious solution.

mop noun a pad of sponge or a bunch of short pieces of coarse yarn etc on a handle for washing or cleaning; a thick head of hair. – verb (past tense **mopped**) to clean with a mop; to clean or wipe: He mopped his brow. – **mop up** to clean or wipe up.

mope verb to be unhappy and gloomy.

moped noun a pedal bicycle with a motor.

moraine noun a line of rocks and gravel left by a glacier.

moral adjective having to do with right and wrong behaviour and character; having to do with right behaviour or character. – noun the lesson of a fable or story; (plural) principles and standards of (esp sexual) behaviour. – noun **morality** (the right) moral standards. – verb **moralize** to draw a lesson from a story or happening. – noun **moral support** encouragement without active help. – noun **moral victory** a failure that can really be seen as a success.

morale noun spirit and confidence.

morass noun (plural **morasses**) a marsh or bog; something that bewilders (someone) or is difficult to cope with: involved in a morass of government regulations.

morbid adjective (of a person, thoughts etc) too concerned with gloomy, unpleasant things; diseased, unhealthy.

more adjective a greater number, amount of: The boys ate more cakes than the girls. We need more money every year. – adverb to a greater extent: more beautiful. I love you more than I can say. – noun a great proportion, amount; a further or additional number, amount: There's more where this came from. – adverb **moreover** besides.

morgue noun a place where dead bodies are laid, awaiting identification etc.

moribund adjective in a dying state.

morn noun (in poetry etc) morning.

morning noun the part of the day before noon. – adjective taking place in the

morning. – noun **morning star** Venus or another planet, when it rises before the sun.

morocco noun a fine goat-skin leather first brought from Morocco.

moron noun a person of low mental ability, an idiot. – adjective **moronic.**

morose adjective bad-tempered, gloomy.

morphia noun a kind of drug which causes sleep or deadens pain (also **morphine**).

morris-dance noun a kind of English country dance in which male dancers wear traditional clothes, decorated with bells.

morrow noun (in poetry etc) the next day, the day after.

morse noun a code of signals (made up of dots and dashes) used (esp formerly) in signalling and telegraphy.

morsel noun a small piece, esp of food.

mortal adjective liable to die; causing death, deadly. – noun a human being. – noun **mortality** (plural **mortalities**) the state of being mortal; the number of deaths; deaths in proportion to the population, death-rate. – adverb **mortally** fatally: mortally wounded.

mortar noun a kind of bowl in which substances are crushed and ground usu by a **pestle**; a short gun for throwing shells; a mixture of lime, sand and water, used for fixing stones in a building etc. – noun **mortarboard** a university or college cap with a square flat top.

mortgage noun a sum of money lent through a legal agreement for buying buildings, land etc (which the borrower must give up if he fails to repay the loan). – verb to offer buildings etc as security for money borrowed.

mortice see **mortise.**

mortify verb (past tense **mortified**) to make to feel ashamed or humble; (of a part of the flesh) to die. – noun **mortification.**

mortise or **mortice** noun a hole made in a piece of wood to receive the shaped end (**tenon**) of another piece. – noun **mortise-lock** or **mortice-lock** a lock whose mechanism is covered by being sunk into the edge of a door etc.

mortuary noun (plural **mortuaries**) a place where dead bodies are kept before burial or cremation.

mosaic noun a picture or design made up of many small pieces of coloured glass, stone etc.

Moslem see **Muslim.**

mosque noun an Islamic place of worship.

mosquito noun (plural **mosquitoes or mosquitos**) any of several types of biting or blood-sucking insects, some carrying disease.

moss noun (plural **mosses**) any of several kinds of very small flowerless plant, found in moist places; a bog. – adjective **mossy.**

most adjective the greatest number of, amount of: Most children attend school regularly. Most food can be frozen. – adverb very, extremely: I'm most grateful; (often with **the**) to the greatest extent: He was the most ill of the family. – noun the greatest number, amount: He got most. – adverb **mostly** mainly, chiefly. – **at most** not more than; **for the most part** mostly.

MOT certificate (coll) the former official name for the vehicle test certificate awarded following a successful **MOT** (Ministry of Transport) **test**, a compulsory regular examination of cars over a certain age to check that they are roadworthy.

motel noun a hotel built to accommodate motorists and their vehicles.

moth noun the name of a family of insects like butterflies, seen mostly at night; the cloth-eating grub of the **clothes-moth**. – noun **mothball** a small ball of a chemical used to protect clothes from moths. – verb to put aside for later use etc. – adjective **moth-eaten** (of cloth) full of holes made by moths; old, shabby.

mother noun a female parent; the female head of a convent. – verb to give birth to, be the mother of; to care for as a mother does. – noun **mother-country** or **mother-land** the country of one's birth. – noun **motherhood** the state of being a mother. – noun **mother-in-law** the mother of one's husband or wife. – adjective **motherly** of, like a mother. – noun **mother-of-pearl** the shining, hard, smooth substance which forms inside certain shells. – noun **mother-tongue** a person's native language.

motif noun (plural **motifs**) a distinctive feature or idea in a piece of music, a play, a design etc.

motion *noun* the act, state or power of moving; a single movement; a suggestion put before a meeting for discussion. – *verb* to make a signal or sign by a movement or gesture; to direct (a person) in this way: *The policeman motioned him forward.* – *adjective* **motionless** without movement.

motive *noun* that which causes a person to act or to do something, a reason. – *verb* **motivate** to cause (someone) to act in a certain way.

motley *adjective* made up of different colours or kinds.

motocross *noun* the sport of motor-cycle racing across rough terrain.

motor *noun* a machine (*usu* an engine worked by petrol) which brings about motion or does work; a motor-car. – Also *adjective.* – *verb* to go by motor vehicle. – *noun* **motor-bicycle (or -bike, -cycle, -boat, -bus, -car)** a bicycle (or boat *etc*) driven by an engine worked by petrol. – *noun* **motorist** a person who drives a motor-car. – *verb* **motorize** to supply with an engine: *He motorized his bicycle.* – *noun* **motorway** a special kind of dual carriageway on which traffic is allowed to drive faster than on other roads.

mottled *adjective* marked with spots of many colours or shades.

motto *noun* (*plural* **mottoes**) a short sentence or phrase, which acts as a guiding principle or rule of behaviour: *'Death before defeat' was the family motto.*

mould *noun* a shape into which a substance in liquid form is poured so that it may take on that shape when it cools or sets: *a jelly mould*; soil (containing rotted leaves *etc*); a fluffy growth found on stale food *etc.* – *verb* to form in a mould; to shape. – *verb* **moulder** to crumble away to dust. – *noun* **moulding** a decorated border (*usu* of moulded plaster) round a ceiling, picture frame *etc.* – *adjective* **mouldy** (*esp* of stale food *etc*) affected by mould.

moult *verb* (of birds) to shed the feathers.

mound *noun* a bank of earth or stones; a hill; a heap.

mount *verb* to go up; to get up, or place, on a horse, bicycle *etc*; to fix (a jewel *etc*) in a holder, or (a picture *etc*) on to a backing, for display; to fix anything on to a support; to prepare, organize (an exhibition). – *noun* a mountain; a support or backing on which something is displayed; a horse, bicycle *etc* to ride on. – **The Mounties** the Canadian mounted police.

mountain *noun* a large hill; a large heap or quantity. – *noun* **mountaineer** a climber of mountains. – *adjective* **mountainous** having many mountains; huge. – *noun* **mountain-ash** the rowan tree.

mountebank *noun* a person who makes untrue claims about themselves, their abilities *etc.*

mourn *verb* to grieve for (a person, loss *etc*); to be sorrowful. – *noun* **mourner.** – *adjective* **mournful** sad. – *noun* **mourning** the showing of grief; the dark-coloured clothes traditionally worn by mourners; a period of time during which signs of grief (*eg* dark-coloured clothes) are shown.

mouse *noun* (*plural* **mice**) a type of little gnawing animal (often greyish-brown) found in houses and in the fields; a shy, timid, uninteresting person; (*comput*) a device which when moved by hand causes the cursor to move on a screen. – *adjective* **mousy** of a light-brown colour; (of a person) shy, timid, uninteresting.

mousse *noun* a mixture, often containing cream, that has been whipped up and set.

moustache *noun* the hair upon the upper lip of men.

mouth *noun* the opening in the head by which an animal or person eats and utters sounds; that part of a river where it flows into the sea; an opening or entrance (of a bottle, a cave *etc*). – *verb* to speak; to shape words in an exaggerated way. – *noun* **mouthful** (*plural* **mouthfuls**) as much as fills the mouth. – *noun* **mouth-organ** a kind of small musical instrument played by the mouth. – *noun* **mouthpiece** the part of a musical instrument, tobacco-pipe *etc* held in the mouth; a person who speaks for others.

move *verb* to (cause to) change place or position; to change one's house; to rouse or affect the feelings of: *He was moved by the beautiful music*; to rouse into action; to propose, suggest. – *noun* an act of moving; a step or action; a shifting of pieces in a game (of chess *etc*). – *adjective* **movable** able to be moved, lifted, changed *etc.* – *noun* **movement** the act or manner of moving; a change of position; a division of a piece of music; a group of people united to achieve some aim; *the Communist movement*; an organized attempt to achieve an aim: *He took part in the movement to reform the divorce laws.* – *noun* **movie** a cinema film. – *adjective* **moving** in motion; causing emotion (*eg* pity).

mow *verb* to cut grass, hay *etc* with a scythe or machine; (with **down**) to destroy in great numbers. – *noun* **mower** machine for mowing.

MP *abbreviation* Member of Parliament; Military Police.

mpg *abbreviation* miles per gallon.

mph *abbreviation* miles per hour.

Mr (short for **mister**) the form of address used before the surname of men.

Mrs (short for **mistress**) the form of address used before the surname of married women.

MS *abbreviation* multiple sclerosis.

Ms a form of address sometimes used before the surnames of married or unmarried women; *abbreviation* manuscript.

MSc *abbreviation* Master of Science.

MSG *abbreviation* monosodium glutamate.

much *adjective* a great amount of. – *adverb* to, by a great extent: *much loved*: *much faster*. – *pronoun* a great amount; something important: *He made much of it.* – **much the same** nearly the same.

muck *noun* dung, dirt, filth.

mucus *noun* the slimy fluid from the nose *etc*. – *adjective* **mucous** like or covered by mucus.

mud *noun* a wet, soft earth. – *noun* **mudguard** a shield or guard over wheels to catch mudsplashes. – *adjective* **muddy** covered with or containing mud.

muddle *verb* to confuse, bewilder; to mix up; to make a mess of. – *noun* a mess; a (state of) confusion.

muesli *noun* a mixture of grains, nuts and fruit often eaten at breakfast with milk, yoghurt *etc*.

muezzin *noun* an Islamic priest who calls out the hour of prayer from a mosque.

muff *noun* a tube-shaped (often furry) cover to keep the hands warm. – *verb* to fail in trying to do something (*eg* catch a ball *etc*).

muffin *noun* a round, flat spongy cake to be toasted and eaten hot with butter;

(*US*) a small, round cake made of flour, bran *etc* eaten with butter.

muffle *verb* to wrap up for warmth *etc*; to deaden (a sound). – *noun* **muffler** a scarf; (*US*) a silencer for a car *etc*.

mufti *noun* clothes worn when off duty by someone normally in uniform.

mug *noun* a straight-sided cup; (*coll*) a stupid person. – *verb* (*past tense* **mugged**) to attack and rob (someone) in the street. – *noun* **mugger**.

muggy *adjective* (of the weather) close and damp.

mulatto *noun* (*plural* **mulattoes**) a person one of whose parents was coloured, the other white.

mulberry *noun* a kind of tree on whose leaves silkworms are fed; its purple berry.

mulch *noun* loose straw *etc* laid down to protect the roots of plants. – *verb* to cover with mulch.

mule *noun* an animal whose parents are a horse and an ass; a backless kind of slipper. – *adjective* **mulish** stubborn.

mull *verb* to think or ponder (over). – *adjective* **mulled** (of wine *etc*) sweetened, spiced and warmed.

mullet *noun* a type of eatable small sea fish.

mullion *noun* an upright (often stone) division in a window.

multi- *prefix* many.

multi-coloured *adjective* many-coloured.

multifarious *adjective* of many kinds.

multimillionaire *noun* a person who has property worth several million pounds.

multinational *adjective, noun* (of) a company which has branches in several different countries.

multiple *adjective* having or affecting many parts: *multiple injuries*; involving many things of the same sort, as vehicles in a *multiple crash*. – *noun* a number or quantity which contains another an exact number of times.

multiply *verb* (*past tense* **multiplied**) to increase; to increase a number by adding it to itself a certain number of times, as 2 multiplied by 3 (or 2×3)=$2+2+2=6$. – *noun* **multiplication** the act of multiplying. – *noun*

multiplicity a great number; the state of being many or varied. – noun **multiplier** the number by which another is to be multiplied.

multitude noun a great number; a crowd. – adjective **multitudinous** very many.

mum noun coll for **mother**. – adjective silent.

mumble verb to speak indistinctly.

mummy noun (plural **mummies**) coll or child's name for **mother**; a dead body kept whole for a very long time by wrapping in bandages and treating with wax, spices etc. – verb **mummify** (plural **mummified**) to make into a mummy.

mumps noun singular an infectious disease affecting certain glands at the side of the neck, causing swelling.

munch verb to chew (with the mouth shut).

mundane adjective dull, ordinary.

municipal adjective of, belonging to, owned by a city or town.

munificent adjective very generous. – noun **munificence**.

munitions noun plural weapons, ammunition etc used in war.

mural adjective of or on a wall. – noun a painting, design etc made on a wall.

murder verb to kill a person unlawfully and on purpose. – noun the act of murdering. – noun **murderer** (masculine), **murderess** (feminine). – adjective **murderous** capable of, guilty of murder; wicked.

murky adjective dark, gloomy.

murmur noun a low, indistinct, continuous sound; a low muttering or grumbling; hushed speech or tone. – verb to make a murmur; to complain, grumble.

muscle noun fleshy, bundle-like parts of the body which, by drawing together or stretching out, cause the movements of the body. – adjective **muscular** of muscles; strong.

muse verb to think (over) in a quiet, leisurely way. – noun (myth) one of the nine goddesses of poetry, music, dancing etc.

museum noun (plural **museums**) a building in which objects of artistic, scientific or historic interest are kept and displayed.

mush noun anything soft and pulpy; anything (eg a film, song) over-sentimental. – adjective **mushy.**

mushroom noun a kind of (eatable) fungus, usu umbrella-shaped. – adjective growing or springing up very quickly. – verb to grow very quickly: New buildings mushroomed all over the town.

music noun the art of arranging, combining etc certain sounds able to be produced by the voice, or by instruments; an arrangement of such sounds or its written form; any sweet or pleasant sound. – adjective **musical** of music; sounding sweet, pleasant; having a talent for music. – noun **music centre** apparatus consisting of a record-player, tape-recorder, and radio, with loudspeakers. – noun **musician** someone skilled in music; someone who plays a musical instrument.

musk noun a strong perfume, obtained from the male **musk-deer** (a small hornless deer found in Central Asia). – noun **musk-rat** same as **musquash.**

musket noun (hist) a kind of gun once used by soldiers. – noun (hist) **musketeer** a soldier armed with a musket.

Muslim noun a person who follows the Islamic religion.

muslin noun a kind of fine, soft, cotton cloth.

musquash noun (plural **musquashes**) a type of large N. American water-rat or its fur (also **musk-rat**).

mussel noun a kind of shellfish, used as food and having two separate halves to its shell.

must verb usu used with another verb to express necessity: You must learn to cross the road safely; to express compulsion: You must do as you're told; to express certainty or probability: This sum must be right. – noun something that must be done, a necessity.

mustang noun a kind of wild horse found in America.

mustard noun a type of plant with a sharp taste; a hot, dark yellow-coloured seasoning (for meat etc) made from its seeds.

muster verb to gather up or together (eg troops, courage). – **pass muster** to be accepted as satisfactory.

musty *adjective* smelling old and stale.

mute *adjective* dumb; silent; (of a letter in a word) not sounded. – *noun* a dumb person. – *adjective* **muted** (of sounds) made quieter, hushed; (of colours) not bright.

mutilate *verb* to cut off (a limb *etc*) from; to damage greatly. – *noun* **mutilation**.

mutiny *verb* (*past tense* **mutinied**) to rise against those in power; to refuse to obey the commands of officers in the army, navy or air force. – *noun* (*plural* **mutinies**) refusal to obey commands, *esp* in the armed forces. – *noun* **mutineer** a person who takes part in a mutiny. – *adjective* **mutinous** rebellious; refusing to obey orders.

mutter *verb* to speak words in a low voice; to grumble.

mutton *noun* the flesh of the sheep used as food.

mutual *adjective* given by each to the other(s): *mutual trust: mutual help*; common to two or more, shared by two or more: *a mutual friend*.

muzzle *noun* the nose and mouth of an animal; a fastening placed over the mouth of an animal to prevent biting; the open end of a gun. – *verb* to put a muzzle on (a dog *etc*); to prevent from speaking (freely): *The president muzzled the press.*

muzzy *adjective* cloudy, confused.

my *adjective* belonging to me. *This is my book.* – *pronoun* **myself** used reflexively: *I hurt myself*; used for emphasis: *I myself can't go, but my brother can.*

myopia *noun* short-sightedness. – *noun, adjective* **myopic**.

myriad *noun* a very great number. – *adjective* very many, countless.

myrrh *noun* a kind of resin with a bitter taste, used in medicines, perfumes *etc*.

myrtle *noun* a type of evergreen shrub.

myself *see* **my**.

mystery *noun* (*plural* **mysteries**) something that cannot be or has not been explained, something puzzling; a deep secret. – *adjective* **mysterious** puzzling, difficult to understand; secret, hidden. – *adjective* **mystic(al)** having a secret or sacred meaning beyond ordinary human understanding. – *noun* **mystic** a person who tries to commune with God or obtain knowledge of sacred or mystical things *esp* by going into a state of spiritual ecstasy. – *verb* **mystify** (*past tense* **mystified**) to puzzle greatly; to confuse, bewilder. – *noun* **mystique** an atmosphere of mystery about someone or something.

myth *noun* a story about gods, heroes *etc* of ancient times; a fable; something imagined or untrue. – *adjective* **mythical** of a myth; invented, imagined, never having existed. – *adjective* **mythological** of myth or mythology; mythical. – *noun* **mythology** a collection of myths; the study of myths. – *noun* **mythologist**.

myxomatosis *noun* a contagious disease of rabbits.

N

N *abbreviation* north; northern

nabob *noun* the title given to certain Indian princes.

nadir *noun* the point of the heavens opposite the **zenith**; the lowest point of anything.

nag *verb* (*past tense* **nagged**) to find fault with constantly. – *noun* a (small) horse.

naiad *noun* (*myth*) a goddess of rivers.

nail *noun* a horny covering, protecting the tips of the fingers and toes; a thin pointed piece of metal for fastening wood *etc*. – *verb* to fasten with nails; to fasten (something up) in this way (*eg* in a box); (*coll*) to catch, trap.

naive *nï-ēv'*, *adjective* simple in thought, manner or speech; inexperienced and lacking knowledge of the world. – *noun* **naiveté**.

NALGO *abbreviation* National and Local Government Officers Association.

naked *adjective* without clothes; having no covering. – *noun* **nakedness.**

namby-pamby *adjective* childish, insipid, lacking liveliness.

name *noun* a word by which a person, place or thing is known or called; fame, reputation: *He has made a name for himself*; authority: *I arrest you in the name of the king.* – *verb* to give a name to; to speak of by name, mention; to appoint. – *adjective* **nameless** without a name, not named. – *adverb* **namely** that is to say. – *noun* **nameplate** a piece of metal or other material, having on it the name of a person, house *etc.* – *noun* **namesake** a person having the same name as another.

nanny *noun* (*plural* **nannies**) a children's nurse.

nanny-goat *noun* a female goat.

nap *noun* a short sleep; a woolly or fluffy surface on cloth; a kind of card game. – *verb* (*past tense* **napped**) to take a short sleep. – **caught napping** taken unawares.

napalm *noun* petrol in a jelly-like form, used in bombs.

nape *noun* the back of the neck.

naphtha *noun* a kind of clear liquid which readily catches fire, obtained from coal and other substances.

napkin *noun* a small piece of cloth or paper for wiping the lips at meals; a nappy.

nappy *noun* (*plural* **nappies**) a piece of cloth folded and put between a baby's legs to absorb urine *etc*; a thick pad of absorbent paper for the same purpose.

narcissus *noun* (*plural* **narcissi** or **narcissuses**) a type of plant like a daffodil with a white, star-shaped flower.

narcotic *noun* a type of drug that brings on sleep or stops pain.

narrate *verb* to tell a story. – *noun* **narration** the telling of a story. – *noun* **narrative** a story. – *adjective* telling a story. – *noun* **narrator.**

narrow *adjective* of small extent from side to side, not wide: *a narrow road*; with little to spare: *a narrow escape*; lacking wide interests or experience: *narrow views.* – *verb* to make or become narrow. – *adverb* **narrowly** closely; barely. – *adjective* **narrow-minded** unwilling to

accept ideas different from one's own. – *noun plural* **narrows** a narrow sea passage, a strait.

narwal or **narwhal** *noun* a kind of whale with a large tusk.

NASA *abbreviation* (*US*) National Aeronautics and Space Administration.

nasal *adjective* of the nose; sounded through the nose.

nasturtium *noun* a climbing plant with brightly-coloured flowers.

nasty *adjective* dirty; very disagreeable or unpleasant; (of a problem *etc*) difficult to deal with. – *noun* **nastiness.**

NAS/UWT *abbreviation* National Association of Schoolmasters/Union of Women Teachers.

natal *adjective* of birth.

nation *noun* the people living in the same country, or under the same government; a race of people: *the Jewish nation.* – *adjective* **national** of or belonging to a nation or race. – *noun* a person belonging to a nation: *a British national.* – *noun* **national anthem** any nation's official song or hymn. – *noun* **national call** a long-distance, but not international, telephone call. – *noun* **nationalism** the desire to bring the people of a nation together under their own government. – *noun* **nationalist.** – *noun* **nationality** state of being a member of a particular nation. – *verb* **nationalize** to take (something *esp* industries) into the control of the government. – *noun* **nationalization.**

native *adjective* born in a person: *native intelligence*; of one's birth: *my native land.* – *noun* a person born in a certain place: *a native of Scotland*; one of those inhabiting a country from earliest times before its discovery by settlers *etc*. – **the Nativity** the birth of Christ.

NATO *abbreviation* North Atlantic Treaty Organization.

natty *adjective* trim, tidy, smart.

nature *noun* the world around us (animals, trees, grass, streams, mountains *etc*); the qualities which make a thing, person, animal what it or they are: *She has a kindly nature.* – *adjective* **natural** of nature; produced by nature, not artificial; (of a quality, ability *etc*) in one at birth, not learned afterwards; (of manner, personality) unaffected, simple; (of a result *etc*) expected, normal. – *noun* an idiot; a person having a natural ability; (in music) a note which is neither a sharp nor a flat (shown by the sign). – *noun* **natural gas** gas suitable for burning found in the earth or under the sea; *noun* **natural history** the study of animals and plants. – *adverb* **naturally** by nature; simply; of course. – *noun* **naturalist** one who studies animal and plant life. – *verb* **naturalize** to give the rights of a citizen to (one born in another country). – *noun* **natural resources** the natural wealth of a country (as forests, minerals, water *etc*). – **-natured** (used with another word) having a certain temper or personality: *good-natured*: *ill-natured etc*.

naught *noun* nothing; *see also* **nought.**

naughty *adjective* bad, misbehaving. – *noun* **naughtiness.**

nausea *noun* a feeling of sickness. – *verb* **nauseate** to make sick, to fill with disgust. – *adjective* **nauseous** sickening; disgusting.

nautical *adjective* of ships or sailors. –*noun* **nautical mile** 1·85 kilometre (6080 ft).

nautilus *noun (plural* **nautiluses** or **nautili)** a small type of sea creature related to the octopus.

naval *see* **navy.**

nave *noun* the middle or main part of a church.

navel *noun* the small hollow in the centre of the front of the belly.

navigate *verb* to direct, steer or pilot a ship, aircraft *etc* on its course; to sail on, over or through. – *adjective* **navigable** able to be used by ships. – *noun* **navigation** the art of navigating. – *noun* **navigator** one who steers or sails a ship *etc*.

navvy *noun (plural* **navvies)** a labourer working on roads *etc*.

navy *noun (plural* **navies)** a nation's fighting ships; the men serving on these. – *adjective* **naval** of the navy. – *adjective* **navy-blue** dark blue.

nay *adverb (old)* no.

NB or **nb** *abbreviation* note well *(nota bene* [L]).

NCO *abbreviation* non-commissioned officer.

neap *adjective* (of the tide) having the smallest extent between its low and high level.

near *adjective* not far away in place or time; close in relationship, friendship *etc*; nearside; barely avoiding or almost reaching (something): *a near disaster*. – *adverb* to, at a little distance (also **nearby**): *He lives quite near(by)*. – *preposition* close to. – *verb* to approach. – *adverb* **nearly** almost: *nearly four o'clock*; closely: *nearly related*. – *noun* **nearness.** – *adjective* **nearside** (of the side of a vehicle *etc*) furthest from the centre of the road. – *adjective* **near-sighted** short-sighted.

neat *adjective* trim, tidy; skilfully done; (of liquor *esp* alcoholic) not diluted with water *etc*.

nebula *noun (plural* **nebulae)** a shining cloud-like appearance in the night sky, produced by very distant stars or by a mass of gas and dust. – *adjective* **nebulous** hazy, vague.

necessary *adjective* not able to be done without. – *noun (plural* **necessaries)** something that cannot be done without, as food, clothing *etc*. – *verb* **necessitate** to make necessary; to force. – *noun* **necessity** *(plural* **necessities)** something necessary; great need; want, poverty.

neck *noun* the part between the head and body; anything like the neck: *the neck of a bottle: a neck of land*. – *noun* **necklace** a string of beads or precious stones *etc* worn round the neck. – *noun* **necktie** (US) a man's tie. – **neck and neck** (in a race *etc*) running side by side, staying exactly equal.

necromancer *noun* a person who deals in magic. – *noun* **necromancy.**

necropolis *noun (plural* **necropolises)** a cemetery.

nectar *noun* the sweet liquid collected from flowers by bees to make honey; *(myth)* the drink of the ancient Greek gods; a delicious drink.

nectarine *noun* a kind of peach.

née *adjective* born, used in stating a woman's surname before her marriage: *Mrs Janet Brown, née Black*.

need *verb* to be without, to be in want of; to require. – *noun* state of needing; necessity; difficulty, want, poverty. – *adjective* **needful** necessary. – *adjective* **needless** unnecessary. – *adjective* **needy** poor.

needle *noun* a small, sharp piece of steel, with a small hole (**eye**) at the top for thread, used in sewing; a similar, longer object with no eye, used for various purposes, *eg* in knitting, or hollowed out for hypodermic syringes *etc*; (in a compass) the moving pointer; the long, sharp-pointed leaf of a pine, fir *etc*; a stylus.

ne'er *adjective* (in poetry *etc*) never. – *adjective, noun* **ne'er-do-well** (of) a lazy, worthless person who makes no effort.

nefarious *adjective* very wicked.

negative meaning or saying 'no', as an answer; (of a person, attitude *etc*) timid, lacking spirit or ideas. – *noun* a word or statement by which something is denied; the photographic film, from which prints are made, in which light objects appear dark and dark objects appear light. – *verb* to prove the opposite; to refuse to accept, to reject (a proposal made at a meeting *etc*).

neglect *verb* to treat carelessly; to fail to give proper attention to; to fail to do. – *noun* lack of care and attention. – *adjective* **neglectful**.

negligée *noun* a type of loose dressing gown *usu* made of thin material, worn by women.

negligence *noun* lack of proper care. – *adjective* **negligent** careless. – *adjective* **negligible** not worth thinking about, very small: *a negligible amount*.

negotiate *verb* to bargain, discuss a subject (with), in order to reach agreement; to arrange (a treaty, a payment *etc*); to get past (an obstacle or difficulty). – *adjective* **negotiable** able to be negotiated. – *noun* **negotiation**. – *noun* **negotiator**.

Negro (*masculine*), **Negress** (*feminine*) (*plural* **Negroes** (*masculine*), **Negresses** (*feminine*)) a member of a dark-skinned African race. – *adjective* **negroid** of or like a Negro.

neigh *verb* to cry like a horse. – Also *noun*.

neighbour or (*US*) **neighbor** *noun* a person who lives near another. – *noun* **neighbourhood** (surrounding) district or area: *in the neighbourhood of Paris: a poor neighbourhood*. – *adjective* **neighbouring** near or next in position. – *adjective* **neighbourly** friendly. – **in the neighbourhood of** approximately, nearly.

neither *adjective, pronoun* not either: *Neither bus goes that way. Neither of us feels well*. – *conjunction* used (often with

nor) to show alternatives in the negative: *Neither John nor David is tall. He neither talks nor laughs*.

nem con *abbreviation* unanimously (*nemine contradicente* [L]).

nemesis *noun* fate, punishment that is bound to follow wrongdoing.

neo- *prefix* new, as in **neonatal** of new-born babies.

neologism *noun* a new word or expression.

neon lighting *noun* a form of lighting in which an electric current is passed through a small quantity of gas.

nephew *noun* the son of a brother or sister, or of a brother-in-law or sister-in-law.

nerve *noun* one of the fibres which carry feeling from all parts of the body to the brain; courage, coolness; (*coll*) impudence. – *verb* to strengthen the nerve or will of. – *adjective* **nervous** of the nerves; easily excited or frightened; timid. – *adjective* **nervy** excitable, jumpy. – *noun* **nervous system** the brain, spinal cord and nerves of an animal or human being.

nest *noun* a structure or place in which birds (and some animals and insects) live and rear their young; a shelter or den. – *verb* to build a nest and live in it. – *verb* **nestle** to lie close together as in a nest; to settle comfortably. – *noun* **nestling** a young newly hatched bird.

net *noun* cord, string or finer material knotted so as to form a loose arrangement of crossing lines and spaces, used for catching fish *etc* or for wearing over the hair *etc*; fine material made like a net, with meshes. – *adjective* (also **nett**) (of a profit *etc*) remaining after expenses *etc* have been paid; (of the weight of something) not including packaging. – *verb* (*past tense* **netted**) to catch or cover with a net; to put (a ball) into a net; to make by way of profit. – *noun* **netball** a type of team game in which a ball is thrown into a high net. – *noun* **netting** fabric of netted string, wire *etc*. – *noun* **network** an arrangement of lines crossing one another; a widespread organization; a system of linked radio stations *etc*.

nether *adjective* lower. – *adjective* **nethermost** lowest.

nett *see* **net**.

nettle *noun* a type of plant covered with hairs which sting sharply. – *verb* to make angry, provoke. – noun **nettle-rash** a skin rash, like that caused by a sting from a nettle.

neur(o)- *prefix* of the nerves.

neuralgia *noun* a pain in the nerves, *esp* in those of the head and face.

neurosis *noun* a type of mental illness in which the patient suffers from extreme anxiety. – *adjective* **neurotic** suffering from neurosis; in a bad nervous state. – Also *noun*.

neuter *adjective* (in grammar) neither masculine nor feminine; (of animals) neither male nor female; unable to bear or father young. – *verb* to make (a cat *etc*) unable to bear or father young.

neutral *adjective* taking no side (in a quarrel or war); (of a colour) not strong or definite. – *noun* a person or nation that takes no side in a war *etc*; the gear position *usu* used when a vehicle is remaining still. – *noun* **neutrality**. – *verb* **neutralize** to make neutral; to make useless or harmless.

neutron *noun* one of the particles (without electrical charge) which with protons make up the nucleus of an atom. – *noun* **neutron bomb** a type of nuclear bomb that kills people by intense radiation but leaves buildings intact.

never *adverb* not ever; at no time; under no circumstances. – *adverb* **nevertheless** in spite of that: *I feel ill. Nevertheless I shall come with you.*

new *adjective* recent; not before seen or known; different; not used or worn; fresh. – *noun* **newness**. – *noun* **newcomer** a person lately arrived. – *adjective* **newfangled** (of things, ideas *etc*) new and not thought very good. – *adverb* **newly**.

news *noun singular* report of a recent event; new information. – *noun* **newsagent** a shopkeeper who sells newspapers. – *noun* **newspaper** a paper printed daily or weekly containing news.

newt *noun* a small lizard-like kind of animal, living on land and in water.

next *adjective* nearest, closest in place, time *etc*: *the next page*. – *adverb* in the nearest place or at the nearest time: *She led and I came next. Do that sum next.*

NHS *abbreviation* National Health Service.

nib *noun* a pen point.

nibble *verb* to take little bites (of). – *noun* a little bite.

nice *adjective* agreeable, pleasant; careful, precise, exact. – *adverb* **nicely** pleasantly; very well. – *noun* **nicety** (*plural* **niceties**) a small fine detail. – **to a nicety** with great exactness.

niche *nēsh* or *nich*, *noun* a hollow in a wall for a statue, vase *etc*; a suitable place in life.

nick *noun* a little cut, notch; (*slang*) prison, jail. – *verb* to cut notches in; (*slang*) to steal.

nickel *noun* an element, a greyish-white metal used *esp* for mixing with other metals and for plating: *nickel-plating*; (in *US*) a 5-cent coin.

nickname *noun* a name used instead of a person or thing's real name, *usu* in fun or scorn.

nicotine *noun* a poisonous substance contained in tobacco.

niece *noun* the daughter of a brother or sister, or of a brother-in-law or sister-in-law.

niggardly *adjective* mean, ungenerous.

niggling *adjective* unimportant, trivial, fussy; (of a worry, fear *etc*) small but always present.

nigh *adjective* (*old*) near.

night *noun* the period of darkness between sunset and sunrise; darkness. – *adjective* of or for night; happening, active *etc* at night: *nightshift: a night worker.* – *noun* **nightdress** or **nightgown** a kind of garment worn in bed. – *noun* **nightfall** the beginning of night. – *noun* **nightjar** a kind of bird like a swallow which is active at night. – *adjective, adverb* **nightly** by night; every night. – *noun* **nightmare** a frightening dream. – *noun* **nightshade** a family of plants some of which have poisonous berries, *eg* deadly nightshade. – *noun* **night-watchman** a person who looks after a building during the night.

nightingale *noun* a type of small bird, the male of which sings beautifully by night and day.

nil *noun* nothing.

nimble *adjective* quick and neat (in action or thought). – *noun* **nimbleness**.

nimbus *noun* a rain cloud.

nincompoop *noun* a weak, foolish person.

nine *noun* the number 9. – *adjective* 9 in number. – *adjective* **ninth** the last of nine (things *etc*). – *noun* one of nine equal parts.

ninepins *noun* a game in which nine bottle-shaped objects, *usu* wooden, are set up and knocked down by a ball.

nineteen *noun* the number 19. – *adjective* 19 in number. – *adjective* **nineteenth** the last of nineteen (things *etc*). – *noun* one of nineteen equal parts.

ninety *noun* the number 90. – *adjective* 90 in number. – *adjective* **ninetieth** the last of ninety (things *etc*). – *noun* one of ninety equal parts.

ninny *noun* (*plural* **ninnies**) a fool.

nip *verb* (*past tense* **nipped**) to pinch, squeeze tightly (*eg* the skin); to be stingingly painful; to bite, cut (off); to check the growth of, to damage (plants *etc*); (*coll*) to go nimbly or quickly. – *noun* a pinch; a sharp coldness in the weather; a small quantity: *a nip of whisky*.

nipple *noun* the pointed part of the breast from which a baby sucks milk.

Nirvana *noun* the state to which a Buddhist or Hindu aspires as the best attainable. – *noun* **nirvana** a blissful state.

nit *noun* the egg of a louse or other small insect; (*coll*) a nitwit.

nitrate *noun* any of several substances formed from nitric acid, often used as soil fertilizers.

nitric acid *noun* a kind of strong acid containing nitrogen.

nitrogen *noun* an element, a type of gas forming nearly four-fifths of the air we breathe. – *noun* **nitro-glycerine** a powerful kind of explosive.

nitwit *noun* a very stupid person.

No or **no** *abbreviation* number.

no *adjective* not any: *We have no food*; not a: *She is no beauty*. – *adverb* not at all: *The patient is no better*. – *interjection* expressing a negative: *Are you feeling better today? No*. – *noun* (*plural* **noes**) a refusal; a vote against. – *pronoun* **nobody** not any person. – *noun* a person of no importance: *He is a nobody in politics*. – *pronoun* **no one** not any person, nobody.

noble *adjective* great and good, fine; brave; of high birth or rank. – *noun* a person of high rank or birth (also **nobleman**). – *adverb* **nobly**. – *noun*

nobility the nobles of a country; goodness, greatness of mind or character.

nobody *see* **no**.

nocturnal *adjective* happening or active (as certain kinds of animals) at night. – *noun* **nocturne** a piece of music intended to give a feeling of night-time.

nod *verb* (*past tense* **nodded**) to bend the head forward quickly (often as a sign of agreement); to let the head drop in weariness. – *noun* an action of nodding. – **nod off** to fall asleep.

node *noun* the swollen part of a branch or twig where leaf-stalks join it; a swelling. – *noun* **nodule** a small rounded lump.

Noël, Nowell *noun* Christmas.

noise *noun* a sound, often one which is loud or harsh. – *verb* to spread (a rumour *etc*). – *adjective* **noiseless**. – *adjective* **noisy** (*comparative* **noisier**, *superlative* **noisiest**) making a loud sound.

nomad *noun* one of a group of people without a fixed home who wander about with flocks of sheep *etc* in search of pasture; someone who wanders from place to place. – *adjective* **nomadic**.

no-man's-land *noun* land owned by no one, *esp* that lying between two opposing armies.

nom de plume *noun* (*plural* **noms de plume**) a name used by an author instead of his own name, a pen-name.

nomenclature *noun* (system of) naming; names.

nominal *adjective* in name only; very small: *a nominal fee*.

nominate *verb* to propose (someone) for a post or for election; to appoint. – *noun* **nomination**. – *noun* **nominee** a person whose name is put forward for a post.

non- *prefix* not – used with a great many words to change their meaning to the opposite.

nonagenarian *noun* a person from ninety to ninety-nine years old.

nonchalant *adjective* not easily roused or upset, cool. – *noun* **nonchalance**.

non-commissioned *adjective* belonging to the lower ranks of army officers, below second-lieutenant.

non-committal *adjective* unwilling to express, or not expressing, an opinion.

nonconformist *noun* a person who does not agree with those in authority, *esp* in church matters. – Also *adjective*.

nondescript *adjective* not easily described, lacking anything noticeable or interesting.

none *adverb* not at all: *none the worse*. – *pronoun* not one, not any.

nonentity *noun* (*plural* **nonentities**) a person of no importance.

non-existent *adjective* not existing, not real.

nonplussed *adjective* taken aback, confused.

nonsense *noun* words that have no sense or meaning; foolishness. – *adjective* **nonsensical**.

non sequitur *noun* a remark *etc* unconnected with what has gone before.

non-stop *adjective* going on without a stop.

noodle *noun* (*usu plural*) a long thin strip of pasta, eaten in soup *etc* or served with a sauce.

nook *noun* a corner; a small recess.

noon *noun* twelve o'clock midday.

no one *see* **no**.

noose *noun* a kind of loop in a rope *etc* that tightens when pulled.

nor *conjunction* used (often with **neither**) to show alternatives in the negative: *Neither Mary nor Susan has been here*.

norm *noun* a pattern or standard to judge other things from. – *adjective* **normal** ordinary, usual according to a standard.

north *noun* one of the four chief directions, that to the left of someone facing the rising sun (opposite to **south**). – Also *adjective, adverb* . – *adjective* **northerly** of, from or towards the north. – *adjective* **northern** of the north. – *adjective, adverb* **northward(s)** towards the north. – *noun* **north-east** (or **north-west)** the point of the compass midway between north and east (or west). – *noun* **north pole** *see* **pole**.

nose *noun* the part of the face by which people and animals smell and breathe; a jutting-out part of anything (*eg* the front of an aeroplane). – *verb* to track by smelling; (*coll*) to interfere in others' affairs, to pry (into); to push a way through: *The ship nosed through the ice*; to move forward cautiously. – *noun* **nosedive** a headfirst dive (by an aeroplane). – Also *verb*. – *noun* **nosegay** a bunch of flowers. – *adjective* **nos(e)y** inquisitive, fond of prying.

nostalgia *noun* a longing for past times; a longing for home. – *adjective* **nostalgic**.

nostril *noun* one of the openings of the nose.

not *adverb* expressing negative, refusal or denial: *I am not going. Give it to me, not to him. I did not break the window*.

notable *adjective* worth taking notice of; important, remarkable. – *noun* an important person. – *noun* **notability** (*plural* **notabilities**) a well-known person. – *adverb* **notably** in a notable or noticeable way; particularly.

notary (public) *noun* (*plural* **notaries (public)**) an official whose job is to see that written documents or statements are drawn up in a way required by law.

notation *noun* the showing of numbers, musical sounds *etc* by signs: *sol-fa notation*; a set of such signs.

notch *noun* (*plural* **notches**) a small V-shaped cut. – *verb* to make a notch. – *adjective* **notched**.

note *noun* a sign or piece of writing to draw someone's attention; (*plural*) ideas, details (for a speech, from a talk *etc*) set down in a short form; a short explanation; a short letter; a piece of paper used as money (*eg* a £5 note); a single sound or the sign standing for it in music; a key on the piano *etc*. – *verb* to make a note of; to notice. – *noun* **notebook** a small book in which to make notes. – *adjective* **noted** well-known. – *noun* **notepaper** writing paper. – *adjective* **noteworthy** notable, remarkable. – **of note** well-known, distinguished; **take note (of)** to notice particularly.

nothing *noun* no thing, not anything; (in arithmetic) nought; something of no importance. – *adverb* not at all: *He's nothing like his father*. – *noun* **nothingness** state of being nothing or of not existing; space, emptiness.

notice *noun* an announcement, made or shown publicly; attention: *The bright colour attracted my notice*; a warning given *eg* before leaving or before dismissing someone from a job, house *etc*. – *verb* to see, observe, take note of. – *adjective* **noticeable** (likely to be) easily noticed.

notify *verb* (*past tense* **notified**) to inform; to give notice of. – *adjective* **notifiable** that must be reported: *a notifiable disease*. – *noun* **notification**.

notion *noun* an idea; a vague belief or opinion.

notorious *adjective* well known because of badness: *He is a notorious thief*. – *noun* **notoriety**.

notwithstanding *preposition* in spite of: *Notwithstanding his poverty, he refused all help*.

nougat *noo'gä*, *noun* a sticky kind of sweet (containing nuts *etc*).

nought *noun* nothing; naught; the figure 0.

noun *noun* (in grammar) the word used as the name of any person or thing (as *John* and *box* in the sentence *John opened the box*).

nourish *verb* to feed; to encourage the growth of. – *adjective* **nourishing** giving the body what is necessary for health and growth. – *noun* **nourishment** food; an act of nourishing.

nouveau riche *noo-vō rēsh*, *noun* a person who has recently acquired wealth but *usu* not good taste.

novel *adjective* new and strange. – *noun* a book telling a long story. – *noun* **novelist** a writer of novels. – *noun* **novelty** (*plural* **novelties**) something new and strange; newness; a small, *usu* cheap, manufactured article, *orig* of unusual design, sold as a souvenir or toy: *These crackers have novelties inside them*.

November *noun* the eleventh month of the year.

novice *noun* a beginner.

now *adverb* at the present time: *I can see him now*; immediately before the present time: *I thought of her just now*; in the present circumstances: *I can't go now because my mother is ill*. – *conjunction* (*usu* **now that**) because, since: *I can go out now that it's fine*. – *adverb* **nowadays** in present times. – **now and then** or **now and again** sometimes, from time to time: *I see him now and again*.

nowhere *adverb* not in, or to, any place.

noxious *adjective* harmful: *noxious fumes*.

nozzle *noun* a spout fitted to the end of a pipe, tube *etc*.

NSPCC *abbreviation* National Society for the Prevention of Cruelty to Children.

nuance *noun* a slight difference in meaning or colour *etc*.

nucleus *noun* (*plural* **nuclei**) the central part of an atom; the central part round which something collects or from which something grows: *the nucleus of his collection of books*; the part of a plant or animal cell that controls its development. – *adjective* **nuclear** of a nucleus, *esp* that of an atom; produced by the splitting of the nuclei of atoms. – *noun* **nuclear energy** energy released or absorbed during reactions taking place in atomic nuclei. – *noun* **nuclear family** the family unit made up of the father and mother with their children. – *noun* **nuclear fission** the splitting of atomic nuclei. – *noun* **nuclear fusion** the creation of a new nucleus by merging two lighter ones, with release of energy. – *noun* **nuclear missile** a missile whose warhead is an atomic bomb. – **nuclear reactor** apparatus for producing nuclear energy.

nude *adjective* without clothes, naked. – *noun* an unclothed human figure; a painting or statue of such a figure. – *noun* **nudism**. – *noun* **nudist** a person who approves of going without clothes. – *noun* **nudity** the state of being nude. – **in the nude** naked.

nudge *noun* a gentle push, *usu* with the elbow. – Also *verb*.

nugget *noun* a lump, *esp* of gold.

nuisance *noun* a person or thing that is annoying or troublesome.

NUJ *abbreviation* National Union of Journalists.

null: null and void having no legal force.

nullify *verb* (*past tense* **nullified**) to make useless or of no effect; to declare to be null and void.

NUM *abbreviation* National Union of Mineworkers.

numb *adjective* having lost the power to feel or move. – *verb* to make numb.

number *verb* a word or figure showing how many, or showing a position in a series (as house numbers in a street); a collection of things or persons; one issue of a newspaper or a magazine; a popular song or piece of music. – *verb* to count; to give numbers to; to amount to in number. – *adjective* **numberless** more than can be counted.

numeral *noun* a figure (*eg* 1, 2 *etc*) used to express a number. – *noun* **numerator**

(in vulgar fractions) the number above the line (as 2 in ⅔). – *adjective* **numerical** of, in, using or consisting of numbers. – *adjective* **numerous** many.

numerate *adjective* having some understanding of mathematics and science.

numismatist *noun* a person who collects and studies coins. – *noun* **numismatics** the study of coins.

numskull *noun* a stupid person.

nun *noun* a member of a female religious group living in a convent. – *noun* **nunnery** (*plural* **nunneries**) a house where a group of nuns live.

NUPE *abbreviation* National Union of Public Employees.

nuptial *adjective* of marriage. – *noun plural* **nuptials** a wedding ceremony.

NUR National Union of Railway-men.

nurse *noun* a person who looks after sick or injured people, or small children. – *verb* to look after sick people *etc*, *esp* in hospital; to give (a baby) milk from the breast; to hold or look after with care: *He nurses his tomato plants*; to encourage (feelings, as anger, hope *etc*) in oneself: *He nurses a grudge against her*. – *noun* **nursery** (*plural* **nurseries**) a room for young children; a place where young plants are reared; a nursery school. – *noun* **nursery school** a school for very young children. – *noun* **nursing home** a small private hospital.

nurture *verb* to bring up, rear; to nourish: *nurture tenderness*. – *noun* care, upbringing; food, nourishment.

NUT *abbreviation* National Union of Teachers.

nut *noun* a fruit having a hard shell and, in it, a kernel; a small block *usu* of metal with a hole in it for screwing on the end of a bolt. – *noun plural* **nutcracker(s)** any of several types of instruments for cracking nuts open. – *noun* **nuthatch** (*plural* **nuthatches**) a small kind of bird living on nuts and insects. – *adjective* **nutty** containing, or having the flavour of nuts; (*coll*) mad. – **in a nutshell** expressed very briefly.

nutmeg *noun* a hard kind of seed used as a spice in cooking.

nutrient *adjective*, *noun* (of) a substance giving nourishment. – *noun* **nutriment** nourishment, food. – *noun* **nutrition** act or process of nourishing; food. – *adjective* **nutritious** or **nutritive** valuable as food, nourishing.

nuzzle *verb* to press, rub or caress with the nose; to lie close to, snuggle, nestle.

nylon *noun* a type of material made from chemicals; (*plural*) stockings made of nylon.

nymph *noun* (*myth*) a goddess of the rivers, trees *etc*; a beautiful girl; an insect not yet fully developed.

nymphomania *noun* strong, *esp* excessive, sexual desire in women.

O

O! or **Oh!** *interjection* expressing surprise, admiration, pain *etc*.

oaf *noun* (*plural* **oafs**) a stupid or clumsy person.

oak *noun* a type of tree having acorns as fruit; its hard wood. – *adjective* **oak** or **oaken** made of oak. – *noun* **oak apple** a kind of growth on the leaves and twigs of oaks, caused by insects.

OAP *abbreviation* Old Age Pension or Pensioner.

oar *noun* a pole for rowing, with a flat, blade-like end. – *verb* to row. – *noun*

oarsman or **oarswoman** a person who rows. – **put one's oar in** to interfere in.

oasis *noun* (*plural* **oases**) in a desert, a place where water is found and trees *etc* grow.

oast *noun* a large oven to dry hops. – *noun* **oast-house** a building containing this.

oath *noun* (*plural* **oaths**) a solemn promise to speak the truth, to keep one's word, to be loyal *etc*; a swear word.

oats *noun plural* a type of grassy plant or its grain, used as food. – *noun* **oatcake** a thin flat cake made of oatmeal. – *noun*

oatmeal meal made by grinding down oat grains.

obdurate *adjective* stubborn, firm, unyielding.

OBE *abbreviation* Officer of the Order of the British Empire.

obedience, obedient *see* **obey.**

obeisance *noun* a bow or curtsy showing respect.

obelisk *noun* a tall four-sided pillar with a pointed top.

obese *adjective* very fat. – *noun* **obesity.**

obey *verb* to do what one is told to do: *She did not obey the instructions. The dog will obey an order.* – *noun* **obedience** the act of obeying; willingness to obey. – *adjective* **obedient.**

obituary *noun* (*plural* **obituaries**) a notice (*usu* in a newspaper) of a person's death.

object *noun* anything that can be seen or felt; an aim or purpose: *His main object was to make money;* (in grammar) the word in a sentence which stands for the person or thing on which the action of the verb is done (as *me* in the sentences *He hit me. He likes me.*). – *verb* (often with **to**) to feel or show disapproval of. – *noun* **objection** the act of objecting; a reason for objecting. – *adjective* **objectionable** nasty, disagreeable. – *adjective* **objective** not influenced by personal interests, fair. – *noun* aim, purpose, goal.

oblige *verb* to force or compel: *I was obliged to go home;* to do a favour or service to: *Oblige me by shutting the door.* – *noun* **obligation** a promise or duty by which one is bound: *I am under an obligation to help him;* a debt of gratitude for a favour received. – *adjective* **obligatory** compulsory; required as a duty. – *adjective* **obliged** owing or feeling gratitude. – *adjective* **obliging** ready to help others.

oblique *adjective* slanting; not straight or direct; not straightforward: *an oblique reference.*

obliterate *verb* to blot out; to destroy completely. – *noun* **obliteration.**

oblivion *noun* forgetfulness; state of being forgotten. – *adjective* **oblivious** (with **of** or **to**) unaware, not paying attention; forgetful.

oblong *noun* a figure of this shape: ☐. – Also *adjective.*

obnoxious *adjective* offensive, causing dislike.

oboe *noun* (*plural* **oboes**) a type of high-pitched woodwind instrument – *noun* **oboist** a person who plays the oboe.

obscene *adjective* (sexually) indecent; disgusting. – *noun* **obscenity** (*plural* **obscenities**).

obscure *adjective* dark; not clear or easily understood; unknown, humble: *an obscure painter.* – *verb* to darken; to make less clear. – *noun* **obscurity.**

obsequious *adjective* trying to win favour by being too humble or too ready to agree, flatter *etc.*

observe *verb* to notice; to watch with attention; to remark; to obey (a law *etc*); to keep, preserve: *observe a tradition.* – *noun* **observance** the act of keeping (a law, a tradition *etc*). – *adjective* **observant** good at noticing. – *noun* **observation** the act or habit of seeing and noting; attention; a remark. – *noun* **observatory** (*plural* **observatories**) a place for making observations of the stars, weather *etc.* – *noun* **observer** a person who sees or observes; a person who is sent to listen to, but not take part in, a discussion *etc.*

obsess *verb* to fill the mind completely. – *noun* **obsession** a feeling or idea from which the mind cannot get away; the state of being obsessed. – *adjective* **obsessive** of obsession; having or liable to have an obsession.

obsolete *adjective* gone out of use. – *adjective* **obsolescent** going out-of-date. – *noun* **obsolescence.**

obstacle *noun* something which stands in the way and hinders. – *noun* **obstacle race** a race in which obstacles have to be passed, climbed, gone through, *etc.*

obstetrics *noun plural* the study and act of helping women before, during and after the birth of babies. – *adjective* **obstetric** or **obstetrical** of obstetrics. – *noun* **obstetrician** a doctor trained in this.

obstinate *adjective* stubborn; not yielding – *noun* **obstinacy** stubbornness.

obstreperous *adjective* noisy, unruly.

obstruct *verb* to block up, keep from passing; to hold back. – *noun* **obstruction** something which hinders; something which blocks up.

obtain *verb* to get, gain; to be in use: *This rule still obtains.* – *adjective* **obtainable** able to be got.

obtrude verb to thrust (something unwanted on someone); to thrust (oneself) forward when not wanted. – noun **obtrusion**. – adjective **obtrusive** too noticeable; pushing, impudent.

obtuse adjective (of an angle) greater than a right angle; blunt, not pointed; stupid, not quick to understand.

obverse noun the side of a coin showing the head or main design.

obviate verb to remove, prevent or get round (a difficulty etc).

obvious adjective easily seen or understood, plain, evident.

OC abbreviation Officer Commanding.

occasion noun a particular time: on that occasion; a special event: a great occasion; a cause or reason; opportunity. – verb to cause. – adjective **occasional** happening (or used) now and then. – adverb **occasionally**.

Occident noun the West. – adjective **occidental**.

occult adjective secret, mysterious; supernatural. – Also noun.

occupy verb (past tense **occupied**) to dwell in; to keep busy; to take up, fill (space, time, a place etc); to seize, capture (a town, fort etc). – noun **occupancy** (plural **occupancies**) the act, fact or period of occupying. – noun **occupant**. – noun **occupation** state of being occupied; that which occupies one; one's trade or job; possession (of a house etc). – noun **occupier** a person who has possession (of a house etc).

occur verb (past tense **occurred**) to happen; to appear or to be found; (with **to**) to come into the mind of: That never occurred to me. – noun **occurrence** a happening or event; the act or fact of occurring.

ocean noun the stretch of salt water surrounding the land of the earth; one of its five great divisions (Atlantic, Pacific, Indian, Arctic, Antarctic).

oche ok'i, noun the line, groove etc behind which a darts player must stand to throw.

ochre noun a type of fine pale-yellow or red clay, used for colouring.

octa- or **octo-** or **oct-** prefix eight.

octagon noun an eight-sided figure. – adjective **octagonal**.

octave noun (in music) a series or stretch of eight notes (as from one C to the C next above it).

octet noun a group of eight (lines of poetry, singers etc).

October noun the tenth month of the year.

octogenarian noun a person from eighty to eighty-nine years old.

octopus noun (plural **octopuses**) a type of sea creature with eight arms.

ocular adjective of the eye.

oculist noun a person who specializes in diseases and defects of the eye.

OD abbreviation overdose.

odd adjective (of a number) not even, leaving a remainder of one when divided by two (eg the numbers 3, 17, 315); unusual, strange; not one of a matching pair, set or group etc, something left out or left over: an odd glove: odd screw: odd minute; (plural) chances or probability: The odds are that he will win; (plural) difference: It makes no odds. – noun **oddity** (plural **oddities**) queerness, strangeness; a queer person or thing. – noun plural **oddments** scraps. – **at odds** quarrelling; **odd jobs** jobs of different kinds, not part of regular employment; **odds and ends** objects, scraps etc of different kinds.

ode noun a type of poem, usu written to a person or thing.

odious adjective hateful. – noun **odium** dislike, hatred.

odour noun smell (pleasant or unpleasant). – adjective **odourless** without smell.

oedema ē-dēm'à, noun the accumulation of fluid in body tissue resulting in swelling.

oesophagus noun the gullet.

of preposition belonging to: the house of my parents; from (a place, person etc): within two miles of his home; from among: one of my pupils; made from, made up of: a house of bricks; indicating an amount, measurement etc: a gallon of petrol; about, concerning: talk of old friends; with, containing: I teach a class of twenty children. Bring me a cup of water; as a result of: die of hunger; indicating removal or taking away: He robbed her of her jewels; indicating a connection between an action and its object: the joining of the pieces; indicating character, qualities etc: He is a man of judgement. It was good of you to come; (US) (in telling the time) before, to: ten (minutes) of eight.

off adverb away from a place, from a particular state, standard, position etc): *He walked off rudely. Your work has gone off. The light was switched off*; entirely, completely: *Finish off your work.* – adjective cancelled: *The expedition is off*; not up to the required or normal standard or condition: *The meat is off*; not working, not on: *The control is in the off position*; not quite pure in colour: *off-white.* – preposition not on, away from: *It fell off the table*; taken away: *10% off the usual price*; below the normal standard: *off his game.* – **badly off** or **well off** poor or rich; **off and on** occasionally.

offal noun the parts of an animal unfit for use as food; certain internal organs of an animal (heart, liver etc) that are eaten.

off-chance noun a slight chance.

off-colour adjective not feeling well.

offend verb to make angry or hurt the feelings of; to displease; to do wrong. – noun **offence** (any cause of) anger, displeasure, hurt feelings; a crime, a sin. – noun **offender**. – noun **offensive** the position of one who attacks; an attack. – adjective annoying; insulting; disgusting; used in attacking or assaulting: *an offensive weapon.* – **take offence at** to be angry or feel hurt at.

offer verb to put forward (a gift, payment etc) for acceptance or refusal; to lay (a choice, chance etc) before; to say that one is willing to do something. – noun an act of offering; a bid of money; something proposed. – noun **offering** a gift; collection of money in church.

offhand adjective said or done without thinking or preparation; lacking politeness. – adverb without previous preparation.

office noun a place where business is carried on; the people working in such a place; a duty, a job; a position of authority, esp in the government; (plural) services, helpful acts. – noun **officer** a person who carries out a public duty; a person holding a commission in the army, navy or air force. – adjective **official** done, given out by those in power: *The ministry made an official announcement. The police took no official action*; forming part of one's task when holding a job or office: *official duties*; having full and proper authority. – noun a person who holds an office in the service of the government etc. –

adverb **officially** as an official, formally; as announced or said in public (though not necessarily truthfully). – verb **officiate** to perform a duty or service, esp as a clergyman at a wedding etc. – adjective **officious** fond of interfering esp in a pompous way.

offing: in the offing at a place or time not far off.

off-licence noun a shop selling alcohol which must not be drunk on the premises.

off-putting adjective causing aversion.

offset verb to weigh against, to make up for: *The high cost of the project was partly offset by a government grant.*

offshoot noun a shoot growing out of the main stem; anything (of lesser importance) growing out of or starting from something else: *That firm is an offshoot of an international firm.*

offshore adjective, adverb in or on the sea close to the coast; at a distance from the shore; from the shore: *offshore winds.*

offside adjective, adverb (in sport) illegally ahead of the ball eg (in football) in a position between the ball and the opponent's goal; (of the side of a vehicle etc) nearest to the centre of the road.

offspring noun one's child or children; the young (of animals etc).

oft adverb (in poetry etc) often.

often adverb many times.

ogle verb to eye (someone) impudently in order to show admiration.

ogre noun (myth) a (man-eating) giant; someone or something that frightens or threatens.

Oh! see **O!**

OHMS abbreviation On Her (or His) Majesty's Service.

oil noun a greasy liquid, got from plants (eg olive oil), from animals (eg whale oil), and from minerals (eg petroleum); (plural) oil colours for painting. – verb to smear with oil, put oil on or in. – noun **oil colour** paint made by mixing a colouring substance with oil. – noun **oilfield** an area where mineral oil is found. – noun **oil painting** a picture painted in oil colours. – noun **oilrig** a structure set up for drilling an oil-well. – noun **oilskin** cloth made waterproof by means of oil; a garment of this. –

noun **oil-well** a hole drilled into the earth's surface or into the sea bed to obtain petroleum. – adjective **oily** of or like oil; (of person, manner etc) trying to be too friendly or flattering.

ointment noun any of many greasy substances rubbed on the skin to soothe, heal etc.

OK or **okay** interjection, adjective, adverb all right. – verb **okay** (past tense **okayed**) to mark or pass as being all right.

old adjective advanced in age, aged; having a certain age: ten years old; not new, having existed a long time; belonging to far-off times; worn, worn-out; out-of-date, old-fashioned. – noun **old age** the later part of life. – adjective **old-fashioned** in a style common in the past, out-of-date. – **of old** long ago.

olfactory adjective of or used in smelling: olfactory glands.

olive noun a type of fruit which gives an oil used for cooking; the tree that bears it. – adjective of a yellowish-green colour. – noun **olive branch** a sign of a wish for peace.

Ombudsman noun an official appointed to look into complaints against the government.

omega noun the last letter of the Greek alphabet.

omelette or **omelet** noun beaten eggs fried (and usu folded over) in a pan.

omen noun a sign of future events. – adjective **ominous** suggesting future trouble.

omit verb (past tense **omitted**) to leave out; to fail to do. – noun **omission** something omitted; the act of omitting.

omnibus noun (plural **omnibuses**) an old word for **bus**. – adjective widely comprehensive; of miscellaneous contents. – noun **omnibus book** a book containing several works, either by one writer or on one topic. – noun **omnibus edition** a radio or TV programme made up of material from preceding editions of the series.

omnipotent adjective having absolute, unlimited, power: the omnipotent ruler. – noun **omnipotence**.

omniscient adjective knowing everything – noun **omniscience**.

omnivorous adjective feeding on all kinds of food.

on preposition touching, fixed etc to the outer or upper side etc of a thing or person: on the table; supported by: standing on one foot; receiving, taking etc: He has been suspended on half-pay. She is on drugs; occurring in the course of a specified time etc: on the following day; about: a book on churches; with: He had his wallet on him; next to, near: a city on the Thames; indicating membership of: He is on the committee; in the condition, process or state of: He put his house on sale. The designs are on show; by means of: He played the tune on the piano; followed by: disaster on disaster. – adverb so as to be touching, or fixed to the outer or upper side etc of a thing: Put your coat on; onwards, further: They carried on towards London. From now on we shall pay you more; at a further point: later on. – adjective working, performing: The television is on; arranged, planned: Do you have anything on this afternoon?

once adverb at an earlier time in the past: Men once lived in caves; for one time only: I've been to London once in the last ten years. – noun one time only. Do it just this once. – conjunction when: Once you've finished, go! – **all at once** suddenly: All at once he appeared from nowhere; see also **at once**; **at once** without delay: Come here at once!; (sometimes with **all**) at the same time, together: She did several things (all) at once; **once (and) for all** for the last time; **once upon a time** at some time in the past, often used at the beginning of stories.

oncology noun the study of tumours. – noun **oncogen** something that causes cancerous tumours; – noun **oncogene** a type of gene involved in the onset and development of cancer. – adjective **oncogenic**.

oncoming adjective approaching from the front: oncoming traffic.

one noun the number 1; a particular member of a group: She's the one I hate most. – pronoun a single particular person or thing: one of my cats; in formal or pompous English used instead of **you**, meaning anyone: One must beware of thieves. – adjective 1 in number; a single: Only one man survived; identical, the same: We're all of one mind; some (unnamed time): one day soon. – pronoun **oneself** used reflexively: wash oneself; used for emphasis: One always has to go oneself, because nobody else will. – adjective **one-sided** (of a contest etc) with one person, side *etc* having a great advantage over the other. – *adjective* **one-way** (of a road, street) meant for traffic moving in one direction only. – **one another** used when an action takes place between more than two (loosely, between two) people: *They hit one another*.

onerous *adjective* heavy, hard to bear or do: *an onerous task*.

ongoing *adjective* continuing: *an ongoing task*.

onion *noun* a type of vegetable with a strong taste and smell.

onlooker *noun* a person who watches (an event).

only *adverb* not more than: *only two matches left*; alone, solely: *Only you went*; not longer ago than: *I saw him only yesterday*; indicating the unavoidable result (of an action): *He'll only be offended if you ask*; (with **too**) extremely: *I'll be only too pleased to come*. – *adjective* single, solitary: *an only child*. – *conjunction* (*coll*) but, except that: *I'd like to go, only I have to work*.

ono *abbreviation* or nearest offer.

onrush *noun* a rush forward.

onset *noun* beginning; a fierce attack.

onslaught *noun* a fierce attack.

onus *noun* burden; responsibility.

onward *adjective* going forward in place or time. – *adverb* **onward** or **onwards**.

onyx *noun* a type of precious stone with layers of different colours.

ooze *verb* to flow gently or slowly. – *noun* soft mud; a gentle flow.

opacity *see* **opaque**.

opal *noun* a type of bluish-white precious stone, with flecks of various colours.

opaque *adjective* not able to be seen through. – *noun* **opacity**.

OPEC *abbreviation* Organization of Petroleum-Exporting Countries.

open *adjective* not shut, allowing entry or exit; not enclosed or fenced; showing the inside or inner part; uncovered; not blocked; free for all to enter; honest, frank; (of land) without many trees. – *verb* to make open; to unlock; to begin. – *noun* **open air** any place not indoors or underground *etc*. – *adjective* **open-air**. – *noun* **opener** something that opens

(something): *a tin opener*. – *noun* **opening** a hole or gap; an opportunity; a vacant job. – *adverb* **openly** without trying to hide or conceal anything. – *adjective* **open-minded** ready to take up new ideas. – *noun* **open verdict** a verdict of death, with no cause stated, given by a coroner's jury. – **in the open** out-of-doors, in the open air; **open to** likely or willing to receive *etc*: *That position is open to attack*: *This writer is open to criticism*.

opera *noun* a play in which music by voices and orchestra is of the greatest importance; *see* also **opus**. – *adjective* **operatic**.

operate *verb* to act, work; to bring about an effect; to perform an operation. – *adjective* **operating** of or for an operation on a person's body. – *noun* **operation** action; method or way of working; the cutting of a part of the human body in order to cure disease; (*plural*) movements of armies, troops. – *adjective* **operative** working, in action; (of a rule *etc*) in force, having effect. – *noun* a workman in a factory *etc*. – *noun* **operator** a person who works a machine; a person who connects telephone calls.

operetta *noun* a play with music and singing.

ophthalmic *adjective* relating to the eye: *an ophthalmic surgeon*. – *noun* **ophthalmologist** a doctor who specializes in diseases of and injuries to the eye.

opiate *noun* a drug containing opium used to make a person sleep; anything that calms or dulls the mind or feelings.

opinion *noun* what one thinks or believes; (professional) judgement, point of view: *He wanted another opinion on his son's case*; what one thinks of the worth or value of someone or something: *I have a low opinion of her*. – *adjective* **opinionated** having strong opinions which one is confident are right.

opium *noun* a drug made from the dried juice of a type of poppy.

opossum *noun* a type of small American animal that carries its young in a pouch.

opponent *see* **oppose**.

opportune *adjective* coming at the right or convenient time. – *noun* **opportunism** the state of being an opportunist. – *noun* **opportunist** a person who takes advantage of any opportunity or circumstance which will be to their advantage. – noun **opportunity** (plural **opportunities**) a chance (to do something).

oppose verb to struggle against, resist; to stand against, compete against. – noun **opponent** a person who opposes; an enemy; a rival. – adjective **opposite** facing, across from; lying on the other side (of); as different as possible. – preposition facing, across from: He lives opposite the post office; acting a rôle (in a play, opera etc) corresponding in importance to: She played Ophelia opposite his Hamlet. – noun something as different as possible (from something else): Black is the opposite of white. – noun **opposition** resistance; those who resist; (in parliament) the party which is against the governing party.

oppress verb to govern harshly like a tyrant; to treat cruelly; to distress or worry greatly. – noun **oppression**. – adjective **oppressive** oppressing; cruel, harsh; (of weather) close, tiring.

opprobrium noun a great or public disgrace; something that brings great disgrace. – adjective **opprobrious** disgraceful; scornful.

opt verb (with **for**) to choose; to decide (to do). – **opt out** to decide not to (do something).

optic or **optical** adjective having to do with the eye or sight. – noun **optical illusion** an impression that something seen is different from what it is. – noun **optician** a person who makes and sells spectacles. – noun **optics** the science of light.

optimism noun the habit of taking a bright, hopeful view of things (opposite of **pessimism**). – noun **optimist** a person who is in the habit of taking such a view. – adjective **optimistic**.

optimum adjective best, most favourable: optimum conditions.

option noun choice; the right or power to choose; the thing chosen. – adjective **optional** left to one's choice.

opulent adjective wealthy; luxurious. – noun **opulence** riches.

opus noun (plural **opera**) a work, esp a musical composition.

or conjunction used (often with **either**) to show alternatives: You can either go out or stay in. Do you prefer tea or coffee?; because if not: You'd better go or you'll miss your bus.

oracle noun a person thought to be very wise or knowledgeable; (hist) a holy place where a god was thought to give answers to difficult questions; an answer of this kind; a person through whom such answers were made known.

oral adjective spoken, not written; having to do with the mouth. – noun an oral examination or test. – adverb **orally** by mouth.

orange noun a type of juicy citrus fruit, with a thick reddish-yellow skin.

orang-utan noun a type of large, man-like ape.

oration noun a public speech esp one in fine formal language. – noun **orator** a public speaker, esp a very eloquent one. – noun **oratory** the art of speaking well in public.

oratorio noun (plural **oratorios**) a sacred story set to music, performed by soloists, choir and usu orchestra.

orb noun anything in the shape of a ball, a sphere.

orbit noun the path of a planet etc round another heavenly body, of a space capsule round the earth etc; range or area of influence: within his orbit. – verb to go round the earth etc in space: The spacecraft orbited the earth.

orchard noun a large garden of fruit trees.

orchestra noun a group of musicians playing together under a conductor. – verb **orchestrate** to arrange (a piece of music) for an orchestra; to organize in such a way as to produce the best effect.

orchid noun a kind of plant usu with brightly coloured or unusually shaped flowers.

ordain verb to declare something to be law; to receive (a clergyman) into the Church. – noun **ordinance** a command; a law. – noun **ordination** the receiving of a clergyman into the church.

ordeal noun a hard trial or test; suffering, painful experience.

order noun an instruction to act (made from a position of authority): The captain gave his orders to his lieutenants; a request, list of requests: He left his order with the grocer; an arrangement according to a system; an accepted way of doing things; a tidy or efficient state; peaceful conditions: law and order;

rank, position, class; a society or brotherhood (*eg* of monks). – *verb* to tell (to do something) from a position of authority; to give an order for; to arrange. – *adjective* **orderly** in proper order; well-behaved, quiet. – *noun* (*plural* **orderlies**) a soldier who carries the orders and messages of an officer; a hospital attendant who does routine jobs. – **in order** correct according to what is regularly done; in a tidy arrangement; **in order to** for the purpose of: *In order to live you must eat*; **out of order** not working; not the correct way of doing things; not in a tidy arrangement.

ordinal numbers *noun plural* those showing order (as first, second, third *etc*).

ordinance *see* **ordain**.

ordinary *adjective* common, usual; normal; not unusually good *etc*. – **out of the ordinary** unusual.

ordination *see* **ordain**.

Ordnance Survey *noun* a government office which produces official detailed maps.

ore *noun* a mineral from which a metal is obtained (*eg* iron ore).

organ *noun* a part of the body (*eg* the liver); a large musical wind instrument with a keyboard; a means of spreading information, *eg* a newspaper: *an organ of communism*. – *adjective* **organic** of or produced by the bodily organs; of living things; made up of parts all having their own work to do; (of food) grown without the use of artificial fertilizers *etc*. – *noun* **organism** any living thing. – *noun* **organist** a person who plays the organ.

organdie *noun* a fine thin stiff muslin.

organize *verb* to arrange, set up (an event *etc*); to form into a whole. – *noun* **organization** the act of organizing; a body of people working together for a purpose.

orgasm *noun* the climax of sexual pleasure.

orgy *noun* (*plural* **orgies**) a drunken or other unrestrained celebration.

Orient *noun* the East. – *adjective* **oriental**.

orientate *verb* to find one's position and sense of direction; to set or put facing a particular direction. – *noun* **orientation**. – *noun* **orienteering** the sport of finding one's way across country with the help of map and compass.

orifice *noun* an opening.

origami *noun* Japanese art of folding paper.

origin *noun* the starting point; the place from which a person or thing comes; cause. – *adjective* **original** first in time; not copied; able to think or do something new. – *noun* the earliest version; a model from which other things are made. – *verb* **originate** to bring or come into being; to produce.

ornament *noun* anything that adds, or is supposed to add, beauty. – *verb* to adorn, decorate. – *adjective* **ornamental** used for ornament; beautiful. – *noun* **ornamentation**.

ornate *adjective* richly decorated.

ornithologist *noun* a person who studies or is an expert on birds. – *noun* **ornithology**.

orphan *noun* a child who has lost one or both parents (*usu* both). – *noun* **orphanage** a home for orphans.

orthodox *adjective* holding (*esp* religious) views that are held generally in one's country, religion *etc*. – *noun* **orthodoxy**.

orthography *noun* a correct or usual spelling.

orthopaedics or (*US*) **orthopedics** *noun* the branch of medicine which deals with bone diseases and injuries. – *adjective* **orthopaedic**.

oscillate *verb* to swing to and fro like the pendulum of a clock; to keep changing one's mind. – *noun* **oscillation**.

osier *noun* a type of willow tree, the twigs of which are used in making baskets *etc*; one of the twigs.

osprey *noun* (*plural* **ospreys**) a type of eagle which eats fish.

ostensible *adjective* (of reasons *etc*) outwardly shown, apparent, but not always real or true.

ostentatious *adjective* showy, meant to catch the eye. – *noun* **ostentation**.

osteopath *noun* a person who treats injuries to bones, muscles *etc* by manipulating the patient's body, not by drugs or surgery.

ostler *see* **hostler**.

ostracize *verb* to banish (someone) from the company of a group of people. – *noun* **ostracism**.

ostrich *noun* (*plural* **ostriches**) a type of large bird which cannot fly.

other *adjective* second of two: *the other shoe*; remaining, not previously mentioned: *the other men*; different, additional: *some other reason*; (with **every**) second: *every other day*; recently past: *the other day*. – *pronoun* the second of two; those remaining, those not previously mentioned: *The others went home later*; the previous one: *one after the other*. – **other than** except: *no hope other than to retreat*; **someone** or **something or other** a person or thing not named or specified: *There's always someone or other here*.

otter *noun* a type of river animal living on fish.

ottoman *noun* a kind of low, cushioned seat without a back.

ought *verb* used with other verbs to indicate duty or need: *He ought to set an example. You ought to keep yourself tidy*; or to indicate what can be reasonably expected: *The weather ought to be fine*.

ounce *noun* a unit of weight, one-sixteenth of a pound, 28·35 grammes.

our *adjective* belonging to us: *our house*. – *pronoun* **ours**: *The green car is ours*. – *pronoun* **ourselves** used reflexively: *We exhausted ourselves playing football*; used for emphasis: *We ourselves don't like it, but other people may*.

oust *verb* to drive out (from position or possessions); to take the place of: *She ousted him as leader of the party*.

out *adverb* into, towards the open air: *Go out for a walk*; from within: *Take out a pencil*; not inside: *He's out of prison now*; far from here: *out at sea*; not at home, not in the office *etc*: *He's out at the moment*; aloud: *shouted out*; to or at an end: *Hear me out*; inaccurate: *The calculation was two miles out*; (*coll*) on strike; published: *The book isn't out yet*; no longer hidden or secret; dismissed from a game (of cricket, baseball *etc*); finished, having won (at cards *etc*); no longer in power or office; determined: *out to win*. – *adjective* **outer** nearer the edge, surface *etc*; further away. – *adjective* **outermost** nearest the edge *etc*; furthest. – *noun* **outing** a trip, excursion. – *adjective* **out-and-out** complete, total, thorough: *an out-and-out villain*.

outback *noun* (in Australia) wild inland areas.

outbid *verb* (*present participle* **outbidding**, *past tense* **outbid**) to offer a higher price than (somebody else).

outboard *adjective* on the outside of a ship or boat: *an outboard motor*.

outbreak *noun* beginning (of a war, of disease *etc*).

outbuilding *noun* a shed or building that is separate from the main buildings.

outburst *noun* a bursting out, *esp* of angry feelings.

outcast *noun* a person driven away from friends and home.

outcome *noun* result.

outcrop *noun* the part of a rock formation that can be seen at the surface of the ground.

outcry *noun* (*plural* **outcries**) a show of anger, disapproval *etc* (*esp* by the general public).

outdo *verb* (*past tense* **outdid**, *past participle* **outdone**) to do better than.

outdoor *adjective* of or in the open air. – *adverb* **outdoors**.

outfit *noun* a set of clothes worn together (sometimes for a special occasion *etc*): *her wedding outfit*. – *noun* **outfitter** a seller of outfits, *esp* men's clothes.

outgoings *noun plural* money spent or being spent.

outgrow *verb* (*past tense* **outgrew**, *past participle* **outgrown**) to get too big or old for (clothes, toys *etc*).

out-house *noun* a shed.

outlandish *adjective* looking or sounding very strange.

outlaw *noun* someone put outside the protection of the law; a robber or bandit. – *verb* to place someone beyond the protection of the law; to ban, forbid.

outlay *noun* money paid out.

outlet *noun* a passage outwards *eg* for a water-pipe; a means of letting something out (*esp* a feeling, energy *etc*): *Football was an outlet for his high spirits*; a market for goods.

outline *noun* the outer line (as of a figure in a drawing); a sketch showing only the main lines; a rough sketch; a brief description. – *verb* to draw or describe an outline of.

outlive *verb* to live longer than.

outlook *noun* a view (from a window *etc*); what is thought likely to happen: *the weather outlook*.

outlying *adjective* far from the centre, distant.

outnumber *verb* to be greater in number than: *Their team outnumbered ours.*

out-of-date *adjective* obsolete, no longer valid: *This is an out-of-date voucher.* – **out of date**: *This voucher is out of date.*

out-patient *noun* a patient who does not live in a hospital while receiving treatment.

outpost *noun* a military station in front of or far from the main army; an outlying settlement.

output *noun* the goods produced by a machine, factory *etc*; the amount of work done by a person.

outrage *noun* a wicked act of great violence; an act which hurts the feelings or that causes offence. – *verb* to injure, hurt by violence; to insult, shock. – *adjective* **outrageous** violent, very wrong; not moderate.

outright *adverb* completely. – *adjective* complete, thorough.

outset *noun* start, beginning.

outside *noun* the outer surface or place: *the outside of the box.* – *adjective* in, on, or of the outer surface or place: *the outside seat*; connected with leisure *etc* rather than one's full-time job: *outside interests*; slight: *an outside chance of winning*. – *adverb* beyond the limits (of): *The prisoners never go outside the walls: The building is locked outside working hours*; out-of-doors, in(to) the open air. – *preposition* beyond the borders *etc* of, not within. – *noun* **outsider** a stranger; a person who is not included in a particular social group *etc*; a runner *etc* whom no one expects to win. – **at the outside** at the most: *ten miles at the outside.*

outsize *adjective* of a very large size. – Also *noun*.

outskirts *noun plural* the outer borders of a city *etc*.

outspoken *adjective* bold and frank in speech.

outstanding *adjective* well-known; very good; (of accounts, debts) unpaid.

outstretched *adjective* (*esp* of one's hand) reaching out.

outvote *verb* to defeat (*eg* in an election *etc*) by a greater number of votes.

outward *adjective* towards or on the outside; (of a journey) away from home, not towards it. – *adverb* **outwardly** or **outwards**.

outweigh *verb* to be more important than: *The advantages outweigh the disadvantages.*

outwit *verb* (*past tense* **outwitted**) to defeat by cunning.

ova *see* **ovum**.

oval *adjective* having the shape of an egg. – Also *noun*.

ovary *noun* (*plural* **ovaries**) the part of the female body in which eggs are formed.

ovation *noun* an outburst of cheering, hand-clapping *etc*.

oven *noun* a covered place for baking; a small furnace.

over *preposition* higher than, above in position, number, rank *etc*: *The number is over the door. He won over £10. She has ruled over the people for 30 years*; across: *going over the bridge*; on the other side of: *the house over the road*; on top of: *He threw his coat over the body*; here and there on: *paper scattered over the carpet*; about: *They quarrelled over their money*; by means of: *over the telephone*; during, throughout: *over the years*; while doing, having *etc*: *He fell asleep over his dinner*. – *adverb* above, higher in position or movement: *Two birds flew over*; across (a distance): *He walked over and spoke*; downwards: *I fell over*; above in number *etc*: *anyone aged four and over*; as a remainder: *three left over*; through: *read the passage over*. – *adjective* finished: *The war is over*. – *noun* (in cricket) a fixed number of balls bowled from one end of the wicket. – **over again** once more.

over- *prefix* often meaning too much, to too great an extent: *Do not overcook the vegetables. The over-excited children were tearful*.

overall *noun* a garment worn over ordinary clothes to protect them against dirt; trousers with a bib made of hard-wearing material worn by workmen *etc*. – *adjective* from one end to the other: *overall length*; including everything: *overall cost*. – **over all** altogether.

overawe *verb* to make silent by fear or astonishment.

overbalance *verb* to (make to) lose one's balance and fall.

overbearing *adjective* too sure that one is right, domineering.

overboard *adverb* out of a ship into the water: *Man overboard*.

overcast *adjective* (of the sky) cloudy.

overcharge *verb* to charge too great a price; to fill or load too heavily.

overcoat *noun* an outdoor coat worn over all other clothes.

overcome *verb* to get the better of, conquer. – *adjective* helpless (from exhaustion, emotion *etc*).

overdo *verb* to do too much; to exaggerate: *They rather overdid the sympathy*; to cook (food) too long.

overdose *noun* too great an amount (of medicine, a drug *etc*). – Also *verb*.

overdraw *verb* to draw more money from the bank than one has in one's account. – *noun* **overdraft** the amount of money overdrawn from a bank, sometimes by official arrangement.

overdue *adjective* later than the stated time: *The train is overdue*; (of a bill *etc*) still unpaid although the time for payment has passed.

overflow *verb* to flow over the edge or limits of: *The river overflowed its banks. The crowd overflowed into the next room*; to be so full as to flow over. – *noun* a running-over of liquid; a pipe or channel for getting rid of extra or waste water *etc*.

overgrown *adjective* covered (with wild growth of plants); grown too large.

overhang *verb* to jut out over.

overhaul *verb* to examine carefully and carry out repairs. – Also *noun*.

overhead *adverb* above, over one's head. – Also *adjective*. – *noun plural* the general expenses of a business *etc*.

overhear *verb* to hear what one was not meant to hear.

overjoyed *adjective* filled with great joy.

overland *adverb*, *adjective* on or by land, not sea.

overlap *verb* to extend over and cover a part of: *The two pieces of cloth overlapped*; (of work *etc*) to cover a part of the same area or subject (as another), partly to coincide. – *noun* the amount by which something overlaps.

overload *verb* to load or fill too much.

overlook *verb* to look down upon from a higher point, to have or give a view of: *The hill overlooked the town*; to fail to see, to miss; to pardon, not to punish.

overlord *noun* (*hist*) a lord, *esp* one who may command other lords.

overmuch *adverb* too much.

overnight *adverb* during the night: *He stayed overnight with a friend*; in a very short time: *He changed completely overnight*. – *adjective* for the night: *an overnight bag*; got or made in a very short time: *an overnight success*.

overpass *noun* a road going over above another road, railway, canal *etc*.

overpower *verb* to defeat by a greater strength; to overwhelm, make helpless. – *adjective* **overpowering** unable to be resisted; overwhelming, very strong *etc*: *an overpowering smell*.

overrate *verb* to value more highly than one ought.

overreach: overreach oneself to try to do or get more than one can and so fail.

override *verb* to ignore, set aside: *He overrode the teacher's authority*.

overrule *verb* to go against or cancel an earlier judgement or request.

overrun *verb* to grow or spread over: *The garden is overrun with weeds and the house with mice*; to take possession of (a country).

overseas *adjective*, *adverb* abroad; beyond the sea.

oversee *verb* to watch over, supervise. – *noun* **overseer.**

overshadow *verb* to lessen the importance of by doing better than.

oversight *noun* a mistake (*eg* when something has been left out); failure to notice.

overstep *verb* to go further than (a set limit, rules *etc*).

overt *adjective* not hidden or secret; openly done.

overtake *verb* to catch up with and pass.

overthrow *verb* to defeat.

overtime *noun* time spent in working beyond one's set hours; payment, *usu* at a special rate, for this.

overture *noun* a proposal or offer often intended to open discussions: *overtures of peace*; a piece of music played as an introduction to an opera *etc*.

overwhelm *verb* to defeat completely; to load, cover *etc* with too great an

amount: *overwhelmed with work*; (of emotion *etc*) to overcome, make helpless: *overwhelmed with grief*. – *adjective* **overwhelming.**

overwork *verb* to work more than is good for one. – *adjective* **overworked.**

overwrought *adjective* excessively nervous or excited, agitated.

ovum *noun* (*plural* **ova**) the egg from which the young of animals and people develop.

owe *verb* to be in debt to: *He owes John ten pence*; to have (a person or thing) to thank for: *I owe my success to my family*. – **owing to** because of.

owl *noun* a kind of bird of prey which comes out at night. – *noun* **owlet** a young owl.

own *verb* to have as a possession; to admit, confess to be true. – *adjective* belonging to the person mentioned: *Is that your own penknife?* – *noun* **owner** a person who possesses. – *noun* **ownership** possession. – **on one's own** by one's own efforts; alone.

ox *noun* (*plural* **oxen** used for male and female cattle) the male of the cow (*usu castrated*) used for drawing loads *etc*.

oxygen *noun* an element, a gas without taste, colour or smell, forming part of the air and of water.

oyster *noun* a type of eatable shellfish.

oz abbreviation for **ounce(s).**

ozone *noun* a form of oxygen. – *noun* **ozone layer** a layer of the upper atmosphere which protects the earth from the sun's ultraviolet rays.

P

p *abbreviation* page; pence.

PA *abbreviation* public address (system); personal assistant.

pa *abbreviation* per annum.

pace *noun* a step; rate (of walking *etc*). – *verb* to measure by steps; to walk backwards and forwards. – *noun* **pacemaker** a person who sets the pace (as in a race); a device used to correct weak or irregular heart rhythms.

pachyderm *noun* a thick-skinned animal such as an elephant.

pacify *verb* (*present participle* **pacifying**, *past tense* **pacified**) to make peaceful; to calm, soothe. – *noun* **pacifist** a person who is against war and works for peace.

pack *noun* a bundle, *esp* one carried on one's back; a set of playing-cards; a number of animals (*esp* dogs, wolves *etc*). – *verb* to place (clothes *etc*) in a case or trunk for a journey; to press or crowd together closely. – *noun* **package** a bundle or parcel. – *verb* to put into a container; to wrap. – *noun* **package holiday** or **package tour** a holiday or tour arranged by an organizer before it is advertised. – *noun* **packet** a small parcel; a container made of paper,

cardboard *etc*. – *noun* **pack-ice** a mass of large pieces of floating ice driven together by wind, currents *etc*. – *noun* **packing** the act of putting things in cases, parcels *etc*; material for wrapping goods to pack; something used to fill an empty space. – *noun* **packing case** a wooden box in which goods are transported. – **send packing** to send (a person) away roughly.

pact *noun* an agreement; a bargain or contract.

pad *noun* a soft cushion-like object to prevent jarring or rubbing *etc*; sheets of paper fixed together; the paw of certain animals; a rocket-launching platform. – *verb* (*past tense* **padded**) to stuff or protect with anything soft; (often with **out**) to fill up (*eg* a book) with unnecessary material; to walk making a dull, soft, noise. – *noun* **padding** stuffing material; (in writing or speech) words, sentences put in just to fill space or time.

paddle *verb* to move forward by the use of paddles; to row; to wade in shallow water. – *noun* a short, broad spoon-shaped oar. – *noun* **paddle-steamer** a steamer driven by two large wheels made up of paddles.

paddock *noun* a small closed-in field *usu* near a house or stable, used for pasture.

paddy-field *noun* a muddy field in which rice is grown.

padlock *noun* a removable lock with hinged hook.

paediatrics or (*US*) **pediatrics** *noun* the treatment of children's diseases. – *noun* **paediatrician**.

paedophile or (*US*) **pedophile** *noun* a person who has sexual desire for children.

pagan *noun* a person who does not believe in any religion; a heathen. – Also *adjective*. – *noun* **paganism**.

page *noun* one side of a blank, written or printed sheet of paper; a boy servant; a boy who carries the train of the bride's dress in a marriage service.

pageant *noun* a show or procession made up of scenes from history; any fine show. – *noun* **pageantry** splendid show or display.

pagoda *noun* an Eastern temple, *esp* in China and India.

paid *see* **pay**.

pail *noun* an open vessel of tin, zinc, plastic *etc* for carrying liquids, a bucket.

pain *noun* feeling caused by hurt to mind or body; threat of punishment: *under pain of death*; (*plural*) care: *He takes great pains with his work.* – *verb* to cause suffering to, distress. – *adjective* **pained** showing pain or distress. – *adjective* **painful**. – *adjective* **painless**. – *adjective* **painstaking** very careful.

paint *verb* to put colour on in the form of liquid or paste; to describe in words. – *noun* something in liquid form used for colouring and put on with a brush, a spray *etc*. – *noun* **painter** a person whose trade is painting; an artist; a rope used to fasten a boat. – *noun* **painting** the act or art of covering with colour of making a picture; a painted picture.

pair *noun* two of the same kind; a set of two. – *verb* to join to form a pair; to go two and two; to mate.

pal *noun* (*coll*) a friend.

palace *noun* the house of a king, queen, archbishop or nobleman.

palaeolithic or **paleolithic** *adjective* of the early Stone Age when man used stone tools.

palate *noun* the roof of the mouth; taste. – *adjective* **palatable** pleasant to the taste; acceptable, pleasing: *The truth is often not palatable.*

palatial *adjective* like a palace, magnificent.

palaver *noun* an (unnecessary) fuss.

pale[1] *noun* a piece of wood, a stake, used in making a fence to enclose ground. – *noun* **paling** a row of stakes of wood *etc* in the form of a fence; a pale.

pale[2] *adjective* light or whitish in colour; not bright. – *verb* to make or turn pale.

palette *noun* an oval board on which an artist mixes paints.

palfrey *noun* (*old*) a horse for riding (not a horse used in battle).

palindrome *noun* a word *etc* that reads the same backwards as forwards (*eg* level).

paling *see* **pale**.

palisade *noun* a fence of pointed (wooden) stakes.

pall *noun* the cloth over a coffin at a funeral; a dark covering or cloud: *a pall of smoke.* – *verb* to become dull or uninteresting. – *noun* **pallbearer** one of those carrying or walking beside the coffin at a funeral.

pallet *noun* a straw bed or mattress; a platform or tray (that can be lifted by a fork-lift truck) for holding or stacking goods.

palliative *adjective* making less severe or harsh. – *noun* something which lessens pain, *eg* a drug.

pallid *adjective* pale. – *noun* **pallor** paleness.

palm *noun* a kind of tall tree, with broad, spreading fan-shaped leaves, which grows in hot countries; the inner surface of the hand between the wrist and the start of the fingers. – *noun* **palmist** someone who claims to tell fortunes by the lines and markings of the hand. – *noun* **palmistry** the telling of fortunes in this way. – **palm off** to give with the intention of cheating: *That shopkeeper palmed off a foreign coin on me.*

palpable *adjective* able to be touched or felt; easily noticed, obvious.

palpate *verb* (*esp* of a doctor *etc*) to examine by touch. – *noun* **palpation**.

palpitate *verb* (of the heart) to beat rapidly, to throb. – *noun* (often in *plural*)

palpitation uncomfortable rapid beating of the heart.

palsy *noun* a loss of power and feeling in the muscles. – *adjective* **palsied.**

paltry *adjective* of little value.

pampas *noun plural* the vast treeless plains of S. America.

pamper *verb* to spoil (a child *etc*) by giving too much attention to.

pamphlet *noun* a small book, stitched or stapled, often with a light paper cover.

pan *noun* a broad shallow pot used in cooking, a saucepan; a shallow dent in the ground; the bowl of a toilet. – *verb* (*past tense* **panned**) to move a television or film camera so as to follow an object or give a wide view. – *noun* **pancake** a thin cake of flour, eggs, sugar and milk, fried in a pan. – **pan out** to turn out (well or badly); to come to an end.

pan- *prefix* all, whole, as in **Pan American** including all America or Americans, North and South.

panacea *pan-à-sē'à, noun* a cure for all things.

panache *noun* a sense of style, swagger. *He always does things with great panache.*

pancake *see* **pan.**

panda *noun* a large black-and-white bear-like animal found in Tibet *etc*; a raccoon-like animal found in the Himalayas. – *noun* **panda car** (*coll*) a police patrol car.

pandemic *adjective* (of a disease *etc*) occurring over a wide area and affecting a large number of people.

pandemonium *noun* a state of confusion and uproar.

pander *verb* (with **to**) to be over-anxious to give way (to other people or their wishes).

p and p or **p & p** *abbreviation* postage and packing.

pane *noun* a sheet of glass.

panegyric *pan-i-jir'ik, noun* a speech praising highly (a person, achievement *etc*).

panel *noun* a flat rectangular piece of wood such as is set into a door or wall; a group of people chosen for a particular purpose *eg* to judge a contest, take part in a television quiz *etc*. – *adjective* **panelled.**

pang *noun* a sudden sharp pain.

panic *noun* a sudden and great fright; fear that spreads from person to person. – *verb* (*past tense* **panicked**) to throw into panic; to act wildly through fear.

pannier *noun* a basket, *esp* one slung on a horse's back.

panoply *noun* (*plural* **panoplies**) all the splendid and magnificent dress, equipment *etc* associated with a particular event *etc*: *the panoply of a military funeral;* (*hist*) a full suit of armour.

panorama *noun* a wide view of a landscape, scene *etc*.

pansy *noun* (*plural* **pansies**) a kind of flower like the violet but larger.

pant *verb* to gasp for breath; to say breathlessly; to wish eagerly (for). – *noun plural* **panties** women's or children's knickers with short legs. – *noun plural* **pants** underpants; women's short-legged knickers; trousers.

pantechnicon *noun* a large van for transporting furniture.

panther *noun* a large leopard; (*US*) a puma.

pantihose *noun plural* tights.

pantomime *noun* a Christmas play, with songs, jokes and dancing, based on a popular fairy tale *eg* Cinderella.

pantry *noun* (*plural* **pantries**) a room for storing food.

papa *noun* a name sometimes used for father.

papacy *noun* the position or the power of the Pope. – *adjective* **papal.**

paper *noun* a material made from rags, grass, wood *etc* used for writing, wrapping *etc*; a single sheet of this; a newspaper; an essay on a learned subject; a set of examination questions; (*plural*) documents proving one's identity, nationality *etc*. – *verb* to cover up (*esp* walls) with paper. – *noun* **paperback** a book bound in a flexible paper cover. – *noun* **paper-chase** a game in which one runner leaves a trail of paper so that others may track him. – *noun* **paperweight** a heavy glass, metal *etc* object used to keep a pile of papers in place.

papier-mâché *pap'yä-mä'shä, noun* a substance consisting of paper pulp and some sticky liquid or glue, shaped (by moulding) into models, bowls, boxes *etc*.

papoose *noun* a N. American Indian baby.

paprika *noun* a type of red pepper powder.

papyrus *noun (plural* **papyri** or **papyruses)** a type of reed from which people used to make paper.

par *noun* an accepted standard, value, level *etc*; (in golf) the number of strokes allowed for each hole if the play is perfect. – **below par** not up to standard; not feeling very well; **on a par with** equal to or comparable with.

parable *noun* a story (*esp* in the Bible) which teaches a moral lesson.

parachute *noun* an umbrella-shaped arrangement made of a light material and rope with which a person may drop slowly and safely to the ground from an aeroplane. – *verb* to drop by parachute. – *noun* **parachutist** a person dropped by parachute from an aeroplane.

parade *noun* an orderly arrangement of troops for inspection or exercise; a procession of people, vehicles *etc* often in celebration of some event. – *verb* to arrange (troops) in order; to march in a procession; to display in an obvious way.

paradigm *par'à-dīm, noun* an example showing a certain pattern.

paradise *noun* any place or state of great happiness. – *noun* **Paradise** heaven.

paradox *noun (plural* **paradoxes)** a saying which seems to contradict itself but which may be true. – *adjective* **paradoxical.** – *adverb* **paradoxically.**

paraffin *noun* an oil which burns and is used as a fuel (for heaters, lamps *etc*).

paragliding *noun* the sport of gliding, supported by a modified type of parachute.

paragon *noun* a model of perfection or excellence: *This boy is a paragon of good manners.*

paragraph *noun* a division of a piece of writing shown by beginning the first sentence on a new line, *usu* leaving a short space at the beginning of the line; a short item in a newspaper.

parakeet *noun* a type of small parrot.

parallel *adjective* (of lines) going in the same direction and never meeting, always remaining the same distance apart; similar or alike in some way: *The judge treats all parallel cases in the same way.* – *noun* a parallel line; something comparable in some way with something else; a line drawn east and west across a map or round a globe at a set distance from the equator to mark latitude. – *noun* **parallelogram** a foursided figure, the opposite sides of which are parallel and equal in length.

paralyse or (*US*) **paralyze** *verb* to affect with paralysis; to make helpless or ineffective; to bring to a halt: *The strike paralysed production at the factory.* – *noun* **paralysis** loss of the power to move and feel in one or more parts of the body. – *adjective* **paralytic** suffering from paralysis; (*coll*) helplessly drunk. – *noun* a paralysed person.

paramedic *noun* a person helping doctors and nurses *eg* an ambulanceman. – Also *adjective*. – *adjective* **paramedical.**

parameter *noun* a boundary or limit.

paramilitary *adjective* on military lines and intended to supplement the military; organized (illegally) as a military force. – Also *noun*.

paramount *adjective* above all others in rank or power; the very greatest: *of paramount importance.*

paramour *noun* (*old*) a lover *esp*. of a married person.

paranoia *noun* a form of mental disorder characterized by delusions of *eg* grandeur, persecution; intense (*esp* irrational) fear or suspicion.

parapet *noun* a low wall on a bridge or balcony to prevent persons from falling off.

paraphernalia *noun plural* one's belongings, equipment *etc*.

paraphrase *verb* to express (a piece of writing) in other words. – Also *noun*.

paraplegia *noun* paralysis of the lower part of the body and legs. – *adjective, noun* **paraplegic** (of) a person who suffers from this.

parasite *noun* an animal, plant or person living on another without being any use in return. – *adjective* **parasitic.**

parasol *noun* a light umbrella used as a sunshade.

paratroops *noun plural* soldiers carried by air to be dropped by parachute into enemy country. – *noun* **paratrooper.**

parboil *verb* to boil (food) slightly.

parcel *noun* thing(s) wrapped and tied, *usu* to be sent by post. – *verb (past tense* **parcelled**) (*usu* with **out**) to divide into portions. – **part and parcel** an absolutely necessary part.

parch *verb* to make hot and very dry; to make thirsty. – *adjective* **parched.**

parchment *noun* the dried skin of a goat or sheep used for writing on; paper resembling this.

pardon *noun* to forgive; to free from punishment; to allow to go unpunished. – *noun* forgiveness; the act of pardoning. – *adjective* **pardon- able** able to be forgiven.

pare *verb* to peel or cut off the edge, outer surface or skin of; to make smaller little by little. – *noun plural* **parings** small pieces cut away or peeled off.

parent *noun* a father or mother. – *noun* **parentage** descent from parents or ancestors: *of noble parentage.* – *adjective* **parental** of parents; with the manner or attitude of a parent.

parenthesis *noun (plural* **parentheses**) a word or group of words inserted in a sentence as an explanation, comment *etc*, *usu* separated from the rest of the sentence by brackets, dashes *etc*: *His father (so he said) was dead;* (*plural*) brackets. – *adjective* **parenthetical.**

pariah *noun* a person driven out from a community or group, an outcast.

parish *noun (plural* **parishes**) a district having its own church and minister or priest. – *noun* **parishioner** a member of a parish.

parity *noun* the state of being equal.

park *noun* a public place for walking, with grass and trees; an enclosed piece of land surrounding a country house. – *verb* to stop and leave (a car *etc*) in a place for a time.

parka *noun* a type of thick jacket with a hood.

parley *verb (past tense* **parleyed**) to hold a conference, *esp* with an enemy. – *noun* (*plural* **parleys**) a meeting between enemies to settle terms of peace *etc*.

parliament *noun* the chief law-making council of a nation – in Britain, the House of Commons and the House of Lords. – *adjective* **parliamentary.**

parlour *noun* a sitting room in a house. – *noun* **parlourmaid** a woman or girl whose job is to wait at table.

parochial *adjective* having to do with a parish; interested only in local affairs; narrow-minded.

parody *noun (plural* **parodies**) an amusing imitation of a serious author's subject and style. – *verb (past tense* **parodied**) to make a parody of.

parole *noun* the release of a prisoner before the end of his sentence on condition that he will have to return if he breaks the law.

paroxysm *noun* a fit of pain, rage, laughter *etc*.

parquet *noun* a type of flooring of wooden blocks arranged in a pattern.

parr *noun* a young salmon before it leaves a river for the sea.

parricide *noun* the murder of a parent or a close relative; a person who commits such a crime.

parrot *noun* a kind of bird found in warm countries with a hooked bill and *usu* brightly coloured feathers, a good imitator of human speech.

parry *verb (past tense* **parried**) to keep off, turn aside (a blow, question *etc*).

parse *verb* to name the parts of speech of (words in a sentence) and say how the words are connected with each other.

parsimony *noun* great care in spending one's money, meanness.

parsley *noun* a type of bright green leafy herb, used in cookery.

parsnip *noun* a type of plant with an eatable yellowish root shaped like a carrot.

parson *noun* a clergyman, *esp* one in charge of a parish. – *noun* **parsonage** a parson's house.

part *noun* a portion or share; a piece, something which, together with other things, makes up a whole: *the various parts of a car engine;* character taken by an actor in a play; a rôle in an action, campaign *etc: the part he played in the war;* (in music) the notes to be played or sung by a particular instrument or voice; (*plural*) talents: *a man of many parts.* – *verb* to divide; to separate, to send or go in different ways; to put or keep apart. – *noun* **parting** the act of separating or dividing; a place of separation; a going away (from each other), a leave-taking; a line dividing hair on the head brushed in opposite directions. – *adverb* **partly** not wholly or completely. – *noun* **part-song** a song in which singers sing different parts in harmony. – **in good part** without being hurt or taking offence; **part of speech** one of the grammatical groups into which words are divided, *eg* noun, verb, adjective, preposition; **part with** to let go, be separated from: *He refused to part with his stick*; **take someone's part** to support someone in an argument *etc*.

partake *verb* (*past tense* **partook**, *past participle* **partaken**) (*usu with* **of**) to eat or drink some of something; to take a part (in).

partial *adjective* in part only, not total or complete: *partial payment*; having a liking for (a person or thing): *partial to cheese*. – *noun* **partiality** the favouring of one side *etc* more than another, bias; a particular liking for.

participate *verb* to take part (in); to have a share in. – *noun* **participant** or **participator** a person who takes part in. – *noun* **participation** the act of taking part.

participle *noun* a form of a verb which can be used with other verbs to form tenses: 'He was *eating*. He had *turned*'; used as an adjective: '*stolen* jewels'; used as a noun: '*Running* makes me tired'.

particle *noun* a very small piece: *a particle of sand*.

particular *adjective* of, relating to *etc* a single definite person, thing *etc* considered separately from others: *This particular waiter ignored us. Answer this particular question*; special: *I have one particular friend. Take particular care of the china*; very exact, difficult to please: *particular about his food*. – *noun plural* the facts or details about any thing or person.

partisan *adjective* giving strong and enthusiastic support or loyalty to a particular cause, theory *etc*, *esp* without considering other points of view. – Also *noun*.

partition *noun* a division; something which divides, as a wall between rooms. – *verb* to divide into parts; to divide by making a wall *etc*.

partner *noun* a person who shares the ownership of a business *etc* with another or others; one of a pair *esp* in games, dancing *etc*; a husband or wife.

– *verb* to act as someone's partner. – *noun* **partnership** state of being partners: *business partnership*: *dancing partnership*; a joining of people as partners.

partridge *noun* a type of bird which is shot as game.

party *noun* (*plural* **parties**) a gathering of guests: *a birthday party*; a group of people travelling *etc* together: *a party of tourists*; a number of people having the same plans or ideas: *a political party*; a person taking part in, knowing of, or approving an action. – *noun* **party line** a shared telephone line; policy laid down by the leaders of a political party.

pass *verb* (*past tense* **passed**) to go, move, travel *etc*: *He passed out of sight over the hill*; to cause to go or move (to another person or place): *pass the salt*; to go by: *I saw the bus pass our house*; to overtake: *He passed me because I slowed down*; (of parliament *etc*) to put (a law) into force; to be (declared) successful in an examination *etc*; to be declared healthy or in good condition (in an inspection); to come to an end: *The feeling of sickness soon passed*; to hand on, give: *He passed the story on to his son*; to spend (time): *He passed a pleasant hour by the river*; to make, utter (*eg* a remark). – *noun* a narrow passage, *esp* over or through a range of mountains; a ticket or card allowing one to go somewhere; success in an examination. – *adjective* **passable** fairly good; (of a river, ford *etc*) able to be crossed. – *noun* **pass-back** a move in hockey, putting the ball (back) into play. – *noun* **passer-by** (*plural* **passers-by**) a person who happens to pass by when something happens. – *adjective* **passing** going by: *a passing car*; not lasting long: *a passing interest*; casual: *a passing remark*. – *noun* the act of someone or something which passes; a going away, coming to an end; death. – *noun* **passport** a card or booklet which gives the name and description of a person, and which is needed to travel in another country. – *noun* **password** a secret word which allows those who know it to pass.

passage *noun* the act of passing: *passage of time*; a journey (*esp* in a ship); a long narrow way, a corridor; a way through; a part of what is written in a book. – *noun* **passageway** a passage, a way through.

passenger *noun* a traveller, not a member of the crew, in a train, ship, aeroplane *etc*.

passion noun strong feeling, esp anger or love. – noun **Passion** the sufferings (esp the death) of Christ. – adjective **passionate** easily moved to passion; full of passion.

passive adjective making no resistance; acted upon, not acting – noun **passiveness** or **passivity**. – noun **passive smoking** the involuntary inhaling of smoke from tobacco smoked by others.

past noun (with **the**) the time gone by; a person's previous life or career; (in grammar) the past tense. – adjective of an earlier time: He thanked me for past kindnesses; just over, recently ended: the past year; gone, finished: The time for argument is past. – preposition after: It's past midday; up to and beyond, further than: Go past the church. – adverb by: He marches past, looking at no one.

pasta noun a dough used in making spaghetti, macaroni etc; the prepared shapes, eg spaghetti.

paste noun a mixture of flour, water etc used for pies, pastry etc; a sticky liquid for sticking paper etc together; any soft mixture: almond paste; a kind of fine glass used in making imitation gems. – noun **pasteboard** cardboard.

pastel adjective (of colours) soft, pale. – noun a chalk-like crayon used in drawing; a drawing made with this.

pasteurize verb to heat food (esp milk) in order to kill harmful germs in it.

pastille noun a small sweet, sometimes sucked as a medicine etc.

pastime noun a hobby, a spare-time interest.

pastor noun a clergyman. – adjective **pastoral** having to do with country life; of a clergyman or his work.

pastry noun (plural **pastries**) a flour paste used in the making of pies, tarts etc; a small cake.

pasture noun ground covered with grass on which cattle graze. – noun **pasturage** grazing land.

pasty[1] adjective like paste; pale.

pasty[2] noun a pie containing meat and vegetables in a covering of pastry.

pat noun a light, quick blow or tap, usu with the hand; a small lump (esp of butter). – verb (past tense **patted**) to strike gently. – **off pat** memorized thoroughly, ready to be said when necessary.

patch verb to mend (clothes) by putting in a new piece of material to cover a hole; (with **up**) to mend, esp hastily or clumsily; patch up the roof; (with **up**) to settle (a quarrel). – noun (plural **patches**) a piece of material sewn on to mend a hole; a small piece of ground. – noun **patchwork** a piece of material formed of small patches or pieces of material sewn together. – adjective **patchy** uneven, mixed in quality: Her work is very patchy.

pate noun the head: a bald pate.

pâté noun a paste made of finely minced meat, fish or vegetable, flavoured with herbs, spices etc.

patent noun an official written statement which gives to one person or business for a stated number of years the sole right to make or sell something that they have invented. – adjective protected from copying by a patent; open, easily seen. – verb to obtain a patent for. – **patent (leather)** leather with a very glossy surface. – adverb **patently** openly, clearly: patently obvious.

paternal adjective of a father; like a father, fatherly; on one's father's side of the family: my paternal grandfather. – noun **paternity** the state or fact of being a father.

path noun a way made by people or animals walking on it, a track: a hill-path; the route to be taken (by a person or vehicle): in the lorry's path; a course of action, way of life. – noun **pathway** a path.

pathetic see pathos.

pathology noun the study of diseases. – noun **pathologist** a doctor who studies the causes and effects of disease; a doctor who makes post-mortem examinations.

pathos noun the quality (of something) that causes one to feel pity: The pathos of the situation made me weep. – adjective **pathetic** causing pity; causing contempt; totally useless or inadequate: a pathetic attempt.

patient adjective suffering delay, pain, discomfort etc without complaint or anger. – noun a person under the care of a doctor etc. – noun **patience** the ability or willingness to be patient; a card game played usu by one person.

patio noun (plural **patios**) a paved open yard attached to a house.

patois *pat'wä, noun* a dialect of language spoken by the ordinary people of a certain area.

patriarch *noun* the male head of a family or tribe; the head of the Greek Orthodox Church *etc*. – *adjective* **patriarchal**.

patrician *adjective* aristocratic.

patricide *noun* the murder of one's own father; one who commits such a murder.

patrimony *noun* property handed down from one's father or ancestors.

patriot *noun* a person who loves (and serves) his country. – *adjective* **patriotic**. – *noun* **patriotism** love of and loyalty to one's country.

patrol *verb* (*past tense* **patrolled**) to keep guard or watch by moving (on foot or in a vehicle) to and fro. – *noun* the act of keeping guard in this way; the people *etc* keeping watch; a small group of Scouts or Girl Guides. – Also *adjective*: *the patrol van*.

patron *noun* someone who protects or supports (a person, an artist, a form of art *etc*); a customer of a shop *etc*. – *noun* **patronage** the support given by a patron. – *verb* **patronize** to act as a patron toward: *He patronizes his local shop*; to treat a person as if one is superior to him: *He patronizes his brother-in-law*. – *noun* **patron saint** a saint chosen as a protector: *St Patrick is the patron saint of Ireland*.

patter *verb* (of falling rain, footsteps *etc*) to make a quick tapping sound. – *noun* the sound of falling rain, of footsteps *etc*; chatter, rapid talk, *esp* that used by salesmen to encourage people to buy their goods.

pattern *noun* an example suitable to be copied; a model or guide for making something; a decorative design; a sample: *a book of tweed patterns*. – *adjective* **patterned** having a design, not self-coloured.

patty *noun* (*plural* **patties**) a small flat cake of chopped meat *etc*.

paucity *noun* smallness of number or quantity: *There's a paucity of good builders*.

paunch *noun* (*plural* **paunches**) a fat stomach.

pauper *noun* a very poor person.

pause *noun* a short stop, an interval; a break or hesitation in speaking or writing; (in music) (a mark showing) the holding of a note or rest. – *verb* to stop for a short time.

pave *verb* to lay (a street or pathway) with stone or concrete pieces to form a level surface for walking on. – *noun* **pavement** a paved surface *esp* a paved footway at the side of a road for pedestrians. – **pave the way for** to prepare or make the way easy for.

pavilion *noun* a building in a sports ground in which sportsmen change their clothes; a large ornamental building; a large tent.

paw *noun* the foot of an animal. – *verb* of an animal, to scrape with one of the front feet; to handle or touch roughly, clumsily or rudely; to strike out wildly with the hand: *paw the air*.

pawn *verb* to put (an article of some value) in someone's keeping in exchange for a sum of money which, when repaid, buys back the article. – *noun* (in chess) a small piece of the lowest rank; a person who lets themselves be used by another for some purpose: the state of having been pawned: *My watch is in pawn*. – *noun* **pawnbroker** a person who lends money in exchange for pawned articles. – *noun* **pawnshop** a pawnbroker's place of business.

pay *verb* (*past tense* **paid**) to give (money) in exchange for (goods *etc*): *He paid £10 for it*; to suffer the punishment (for); to be advantageous or profitable: *It pays to be careful*; to give (*eg* attention). – *noun* money given or received for work *etc*, wages. – *adjective* **payable** requiring to be paid. – *adjective* **pay-as-you-earn** of a system of collecting income tax by deducting it from the pay or salary before this is given to the worker. – *noun* **payee** a person to whom money is paid. – *noun* **payment** the act of paying; money paid (or its value in goods *etc*). – *noun* **pay-roll** a list of persons entitled to receive pay, with the amounts due to each. – *noun* **payroll** the money for paying wages. – **pay off** to pay in full and discharge (workers) owing to lack of work *etc*; to have good results: *His hard work paid off*; **pay out** to spend; to give out (a length of rope *etc*).

PAYE *abbreviation* pay as you earn.

PC *abbreviation* police constable; privy councillor.

pc *abbreviation* postcard.

PE *abbreviation* physical education.

pea *noun* a kind of climbing plant, having round green seeds in pods; the seed itself, eaten as a vegetable.

peace *noun* quietness; freedom from war or disturbance; a treaty bringing this about. – *adjective* **peaceable** of a quiet nature, fond of peace. – *adjective* **peaceful** quiet; calm. – *noun* **peace-offering** something offered to bring about peace.

peach *noun* (*plural* **peaches**) a type of juicy, velvet-skinned fruit; the tree that bears it; an orangey-pink colour.

peacock (*masculine*), **peahen** (*feminine*) *noun* a type of large bird, the male noted for its splendid feathers, *esp* in its tail.

peak *noun* the pointed top of a mountain or hill; the highest point; the jutting-out part of the brim of a cap. – *verb* to rise to a peak; to reach the highest point: *Prices peaked in July and then fell steadily.* – *adjective* **peaked** pointed; (of a hat, cap) having a peak. – *adjective* **peaky** looking pale and unhealthy.

peal *noun* a set of bells tuned to each other; the changes rung on such bells; a loud sound or succession of loud sounds: *peals of laughter.* – *verb* to sound loudly.

peanut *noun* a type of nut similar to a pea in shape (also **groundnut, monkey-nut**). – *noun* **peanut butter** a paste of ground roasted peanuts, spread on bread *etc.*

pear *noun* a type of fruit narrowing towards the stem and bulging at the end; the tree that bears it. – *adjective* **pear-shaped**: *a pear-shaped woman.*

pearl *noun* a gem formed in the shell of the oyster and several other shellfish; something resembling a pearl in shape, size, colour or value: *pearls of wisdom.*

peasant *noun* a person who works and lives on the land, *esp* in a primitive or underdeveloped area.

peat *noun* a kind of turf, cut out of boggy places, dried and used as fuel.

pebble *noun* a small, roundish stone. – *noun* **pebble dash** a kind of coating for outside walls. – *adjective* **pebbly** full of pebbles.

pecan *noun* a kind of oblong, thin-shelled nut, common in N. America; the tree bearing it.

peccadillo *noun* (*plural* **peccadilloes** or **peccadillos**) a wrong or sin felt to be unimportant.

peck *verb* to strike with the beak; to pick up with the beak; to eat little, nibble (at); to kiss quickly and briefly. – *noun* a sharp blow with the beak; a brief kiss. – *adjective* **peckish** slightly hungry.

pectoral *adjective* of or on the breast or chest: *pectoral muscles.*

peculiar *adjective* belonging to one person or thing in particular and to no other: *a custom peculiar to France*; strange, odd: *He is a very peculiar person.* – *noun* **peculiarity** (*plural* **peculiarities**) that which marks a person or thing off from others in some way; something odd. – *adverb* **peculiarly.**

pecuniary *adjective* of money.

pedagogue *noun* a teacher. – *adjective* **pedagogic** *ped-à-goj'ik*, of a teacher or of education.

pedal *noun* a lever worked by the foot, as on a bicycle, piano *etc*; (on an organ) a key worked by the foot. – *verb* (*past tense* **pedalled**) to work the pedals of; to ride on a bicycle.

pedant *noun* a person who makes a great show of their knowledge; a person who considers minor details to be of great importance. – *adjective* **pedantic.** – *noun* **pedantry** too great a concern with unimportant details; a display of knowledge.

peddle *verb* to travel from door to door selling small objects. – *noun* **pedlar** a person who peddles, a hawker.

pedestal *noun* the foot or support of a pillar, statue *etc.*

pedestrian *adjective* going on foot; for those on foot; unexciting, dull: *a pedestrian account of his adventures.* – *noun* a person who goes or travels on foot. – *noun* **pedestrian crossing** a place where pedestrians may cross the road when the traffic stops.

pedigree *noun* a list of the ancestors from whom a person or animal is descended; (distinguished) descent or ancestry. – *adjective* of an animal, pure-bred, from a long line of ancestors of the same breed.

pedlar *see* **peddle.**

pedometer *noun* an instrument for measuring the distance covered by a walker.

pee verb (past tense **peed**) (coll) to urinate. – noun (coll) act of urinating; (coll) urine.

peek verb to peep, glance esp secretively. – Also noun.

peel verb to strip off the outer covering or skin of: peel an apple; (of skin, paint, bark etc) to come off in small pieces; to lose skin in small flakes (as a result of sunburn etc). – noun skin, rind.

peep verb to look through a narrow opening, round a corner etc; to look slyly or quickly (at); to begin to appear: The sun peeped out; to make a high, small sound. – noun a quick look, a glimpse (usu from a hidden position); a high, small sound.

peer verb to look at with half-closed eyes, (as if) with difficulty. – noun one's equal in rank, merit or age; a nobleman of the rank of baron upwards; a member of the House of Lords. – noun **peerage** a peer's title; the peers as a group. – adjective **peerless** without any equal, better than all others.

peevish adjective ill-natured, cross, fretful.

peewit noun the lapwing.

peg noun a pin or stake of wood, metal etc; a hook fixed to a wall for hanging clothes etc. – verb (past tense **pegged**) to fasten with a peg; to fix (prices etc) at a certain level.

pejorative adjective showing disapproval, dislike, scorn etc: a pejorative remark.

Pekinese or **Pekingese** noun a breed of small dog with long coat and flat face.

pelican noun a type of large waterbird with a pouched bill for storing fish. – noun **pelican crossing** a street-crossing where the lights are operated by pedestrians.

pellet noun a little ball (of shot etc); a small pill.

pell-mell adverb in great confusion; headlong.

pelmet noun a strip or band (of wood etc) hiding a curtain rail.

pelt noun the (untreated) skin of an animal. – verb to throw (things) at; to run fast; (of rain, sometimes with **down**) to fall heavily. – **at full pelt** at top speed.

pelvis noun the frame of bone which circles the body below the waist.

pemmican noun dried meat, pressed hard into cakes.

pen noun an instrument for writing in ink: a small enclosure, for sheep, cattle etc; a female swan. – verb (past tense **penned**) to shut up, enclose in a pen; to write (eg a letter). – noun **pen-friend** a person one has never seen (usu living abroad) with whom one exchanges letters. – noun **penknife** a pocket knife with folding blades. – noun **pen-name** a name adopted by a writer instead of his or her own name.

penal adjective of, or as, punishment. – verb **penalize** to punish; to put under a disadvantage. – noun **penalty** (plural **penalties**) punishment; a disadvantage put on a player or team which breaks a rule of a game. – noun **penal servitude** imprisonment with hard labour as an added punishment.

penance noun punishment willingly suffered by a person to make up for a wrong.

pence see penny.

pencil noun an instrument containing a length of graphite or other substance for writing, drawing etc. – verb (past tense **pencilled**) to draw, mark etc with a pencil.

pendant noun an ornament hung from a necklace etc; a necklace with such an ornament.

pendent adjective hanging.

pending adjective awaiting a decision or attention: This matter is pending. – preposition awaiting, until the coming of: pending confirmation.

pendulum noun a swinging weight which drives the mechanism of a clock.

penetrate verb to pierce or pass into or through; to enter (usu by force). – adjective **penetrating** (of a sound) piercing; keen, probing: a penetrating look. – noun **penetration** the act of breaking through or into; cleverness in understanding.

penguin noun a kind of large sea bird of Antarctic regions, which cannot fly.

penicillin noun a medicine got from mould, which kills many bacteria.

peninsula noun a piece of land almost surrounded by water. – adjective **peninsular**.

penis noun the part of the body of a male human or animal used in sexual intercourse and for urinating.

penitent *adjective* sorry for one's sins. – *noun* a penitent person. – *noun* **penitentiary** (*US*) a prison.

pennant *noun* a long flag coming to a point at the end.

penny *noun* a coin worth ¹⁄₁₀₀ of £1; *plural* **pence** used to show an amount in pennies: *A ticket costs ten pence; plural* **pennies** used for a number of coins: *I need five pennies for the coffee machine.* – *adjective* **penniless** having no money.

pension *noun* a sum of money paid regularly to a retired person, a widow, a person wounded in a war *etc.* – *adjective* **pensionable** having or giving the right to a pension: *She has reached pensionable age. She applied for a pensionable post.* – *noun* **pensioner** a person who receives a pension. – **pension off** to dismiss or allow to retire with a pension.

pensive *adjective* thoughtful.

pent or **pent-up** *adjective* shut up, not allowed to go free; (of emotions *etc*) not freely expressed.

pentagon *noun* a five-sided figure. – *adjective* **pentagonal**.

pentathlon *noun* a five-event contest in the Olympic Games *etc.*

penthouse *noun* a (luxurious) flat at the top of a building.

penultimate *adjective* last but one.

penury *noun* poverty, want.

peony *noun* (*plural* **peonies**) a type of garden plant with large red, white or pink flowers.

people *noun* the men, women and children of a country or nation; persons generally. – *verb* to fill with living beings, *esp* people; to inhabit, make up the population of.

pepper *noun* a type of plant whose berries are dried, powdered and used as seasoning; the powder so used; any of several hollow fruits containing many seeds, used as a food either raw, cooked or pickled. – *verb* to sprinkle with pepper; (with **with**) to throw at or hit: *He peppered him with bullets.* – *adjective* **pepper-and-salt** mixed black and white: *pepper-and-salt hair.* – *noun* **peppercorn** the dried berry of the pepper plant. – *noun* **pepper mill** a small device for grinding peppercorns for flavouring food. – *noun* **peppermint** a type of plant with a powerful taste

and smell; a flavouring taken from this and used in sweets *etc.* – *adjective* **peppery** containing much pepper; inclined to be hot-tempered.

pep-talk *noun* a talk meant to encourage or arouse enthusiasm.

per *preposition* in, out of: *five per cent* (often written as 5%) *ie* five out of every hundred; for each: *£1 per dozen*; in each: *six times per week.* – **per annum** [*L*] in each year; **per head** for each person.

peradventure *adverb* (*old*) by chance.

perambulator *see* **pram.**

perceive *verb* to become aware of through the senses; to see; to understand. – *adjective* **perceptible** able to be seen *etc* or understood. – *noun* **perception** the art of perceiving; the ability to perceive; understanding. – *adjective* **perceptive** able or quick to perceive or understand.

percentage *noun* the rate per hundred.

perch *noun* (*plural* **perches**) a type of freshwater fish; a rod on which birds roost; any high seat or position. – *verb* to roost.

perchance *adverb* (*old*) by chance; perhaps.

percolate *verb* (of a liquid) to drip or drain through small holes; to cause (a liquid) to do this; (of news *etc*) to pass slowly down or through. – *noun* **percolator** a device for percolating: *a coffee percolator*.

percussion *noun* a striking of one object against another; musical instruments played by striking, *eg* drums, cymbals *etc.*

perdition *noun* utter loss or ruin; everlasting punishment.

peregrine *noun* a type of falcon used in hawking.

peremptory *adjective* urgent; (of a command *etc*) to be obeyed at once; (of a manner) commanding in an arrogant way, dictatorial.

perennial *adjective* lasting through the year; everlasting, perpetual; (of plants) growing from year to year without replanting or sowing. – *noun* a perennial plant.

perestroika *noun* in Russia, reconstruction, restructuring (of the state *etc*).

perfect *adjective* complete; finished; faultless; exact. – *verb* to make perfect;

to finish. – noun **perfection** the state of being perfect; complete freedom from flaws; the highest state or degree. – noun **perfectionist** a person who is satisfied only by perfection.

perfidious adjective treacherous, unfaithful. – noun **perfidiousness**. – noun **perfidy**.

perforate verb to make a hole or holes through. – adjective **perforated** pierced with holes.

perforce adverb (old) of necessity, unavoidably.

perform verb to do or act; to act (a part), as on the stage; to provide any kind of entertainment for an audience; to play (a piece of music). – noun **performance** an entertainment (in a theatre etc); the act of doing something; the level of success of a machine, a car etc. – noun **performer** a person who acts or performs.

perfume noun sweet smell, fragrance; a liquid which gives off a sweet smell when put on the skin, scent. – verb to put scent on or in; to give a sweet smell to. – noun **perfumery** the shop or factory where perfume is sold or made.

perfunctory adjective done carelessly or half-heartedly: a perfunctory inspection. – adverb **perfunctorily**.

perhaps adverb it may be (that), possibly: Perhaps I'll forget to do it.

peri- prefix around.

peril noun a great danger. – adjective **perilous** very dangerous. – **at one's peril** at one's own risk.

perimeter noun the outside line enclosing a figure or shape: perimeter of a circle; the outer edge of any area: He went outside the perimeters of the city.

period noun any stretch of time; the time during which something (eg a revolution of the earth round the sun) takes place; a stage in the earth's development or in history; a full stop, as after a sentence; a sentence; an occurrence of menstruation. – adjective **periodic** of a period; happening at regular intervals (eg every month, year); happening every now and then; a periodic clearing out of rubbish. – adjective **periodical** issued, done etc, at regular intervals; periodic. – noun a magazine which appears at regular intervals.

peripatetic adjective moving from place to place: a peripatetic salesman.

periphery noun (plural **peripheries**) the line surrounding something; the outer boundary or edge (of something). – adjective **peripheral** of or on a periphery; away from the centre; not essential, of little importance.

periscope noun a tube with mirrors by which an observer in a trench or submarine is able to see objects on the surface.

perish verb to be destroyed or pass away completely; to die; to decay, rot. – adjective **perishable** liable to go bad quickly.

periwig noun (hist) a wig.

periwinkle noun a type of small shellfish, shaped like a small snail, eaten as food when boiled; a type of creeping evergreen plant, with a small blue flower.

perjure verb (with **oneself** etc) to tell a lie when one has sworn to tell the truth, esp in a court of law. – noun **perjurer**. – noun **perjury**.

perk noun short for **perquisite**. – adjective **perky** jaunty, in good spirits. – **perk up** to recover one's energy or spirits.

perm noun short for **permanent wave**. – verb to give a permanent wave to (hair).

permafrost noun permanently frozen subsoil.

permanent adjective lasting, not temporary. – noun **permanence**. – noun **permanency** (plural **permanencies**) the state of being permanent; a person or thing that is permanent. – noun **permanent wave** a wave or curl put into the hair by a special process and usu lasting for some months.

permeate verb to pass into through small holes, to soak into; to fill every part of. – adjective **permeable**.

permit verb (plural **permitted**) to agree to another's action, to allow; to make possible. – noun a written order, allowing a person to do something: a fishing permit. – adjective **permissible** allowable. – noun **permission** freedom given to do something. – adjective **permissive** allowing something to be done; (too) tolerant.

permutation noun the arrangement of things, numbers, letters etc in a certain order; the act of changing the order of things.

pernicious adjective destructive.

pernickety adjective fussy about small details.

peroration *noun* the closing part of a speech; a speech.

peroxide *noun* a chemical (hydrogen peroxide) used for bleaching hair *etc*. – *noun* **peroxide blonde** (*coll*) a woman whose hair has been bleached.

perpendicular *adjective* standing upright, vertical; at right angles (to). – *noun* a line at right angles to another.

perpetrate *verb* to do or commit (a sin, error *etc*). – *noun* **perpetration**. – *noun* **perpetrator**.

perpetual *adjective* everlasting, unending. – *adverb* **perpetually**. – *verb* **perpetuate** to cause to last for ever or for a long time. – *noun* **perpetuity**. – **in perpetuity** for ever; for the length of one's life.

perplex *verb* to puzzle, bewilder; to make more complicated. – *noun* **perplexity** a puzzled state of mind; something which puzzles.

perquisite *noun* something of value one is allowed in addition to one's pay.

persecute *verb* to harass, worry, *usu* over a period of time; to kill, make to suffer, *esp* because of religious beliefs. – *noun* **persecution**. – *noun* **persecutor**.

persevere *verb* to keep trying to do a thing (in spite of difficulties). – *noun* **perseverance** the act of persevering.

persist *verb* to hold fast to something (*eg* an idea); to continue to do something in spite of difficulties; to survive, last: *The idea that snakes are slimy still persists.* – *adjective* **persistent** (of persons) obstinate, refusing to be discouraged; lasting, not dying out. – *noun* **persistence**.

person *noun* a human being; one's body: *He had jewels hidden on his person*; form, shape: *Trouble arrived in the person of Jeremy.* – *adjective* **personable** good-looking. – *noun* **personage** a (well-known) person. – *adjective* **personal** one's own; private; (of remarks) insulting, offensive to the person they are aimed at. – *noun* **personal column** a newspaper column containing personal messages, advertisements *etc*. – *noun* **personality** (*plural* **personalities**) all of a person's characteristics (of feeling, mind, body *etc*) as seen by others; a well-known person. – *adverb* **personally** speaking from one's own point of view; by one's own act, not using an agent or representative: *He thanked me personally.* – *noun* **personal**

organizer a small loose-leaf filing system containing a diary and a selection of information, *eg* addresses, maps, indexes. – *noun* **personal stereo** a small portable cassette player (and radio) with earphones. – *verb* **personify** (*past tense* **personified**) to talk about things, ideas *etc* as if they were living persons (as in 'Time marches on.'); to be typical or a perfect example of. – *noun* **personification**. – **in person** personally, not represented by someone else.

personnel *noun* the people employed in a firm *etc*.

perspective *noun* a point of view; in painting *etc*, (the art of giving) a sense of depth, distance *etc* like that in real life. – **in perspective** (of an object *etc* in a photograph *etc*) having the size *etc* in relation to other things that it would have in real life; (of an event *etc*) in its true degree of importance *etc* when considered in relation to other events *etc*: *You must learn to see things in perspective.*

Perspex® *noun* a transparent plastic which looks like glass.

perspicacious *adjective* of clear or sharp understanding. – *noun* **perspicacity** keenness of understanding.

perspicuity *noun* clearness in expressing one's thoughts.

perspire *verb* to sweat. – *noun* **perspiration** sweat.

persuade *verb* to bring a person to do or think something, by arguing with them or advising them. – *noun* **persuasion** act of persuading; a firm belief *esp* a religious belief. – *adjective* **persuasive** having the power to convince. – *noun* **persuasiveness**.

pert *adjective* saucy, cheeky.

pertain (with **to**) to belong, have to do with: *duties pertaining to the job.*

pertinacious *adjective* holding strongly to an idea, obstinate. – *noun* **pertinacity**.

pertinent *adjective* connected with the subject spoken about, to the point.

perturb *verb* to disturb greatly; to make anxious or uneasy. – *noun* **perturbation** great worry, anxiety.

peruse *verb* to read (with care). – *noun* **perusal**.

pervade *verb* to spread through: *Silence pervaded the room.*

perverse *adjective* obstinate in holding to the wrong point of view; unreasonable. – *noun* **perverseness** or **perversity** stubbornness; wickedness.

pervert *verb* to turn away from what is normal or right: *pervert the course of justice*; to turn (a person) to crime or evil. – *noun* a person who commits unnatural or perverted acts. – *noun* **perversion** the act of perverting; an unnatural or perverted act.

peseta *noun* the standard unit of Spanish currency.

pessimism *noun* the habit of thinking that things will always turn out badly (opposite of **optimism**). – *noun* **pessimist** a person who tends to think in this way. – *adjective* **pessimistic**.

pest *noun* a troublesome person or thing; a creature that is harmful or destructive, *eg* a mosquito. – *noun* **pesticide** any substance which kills animal pests. – *noun* **pestilence** a deadly, spreading disease. – *adjective* **pestilent** very unhealthy; troublesome.

pester *verb* to annoy continually.

pestle *noun* a tool for pounding things to powder.

pet *noun* a tame animal *usu* kept in the home (such as a cat *etc*); a favourite (child); a fit of sulks. – *adjective* kept as a pet; favourite; chief: *my pet hate*. – *verb* (*past tense* **petted**) to fondle. – *adjective* **pettish** sulky. – *noun* **pet name** one used to express affection or love.

petal *noun* one of the leaf-like parts of a flower.

peter: peter out to fade or dwindle away to nothing.

petite *adjective* small and neat in appearance.

petition *noun* a request, *esp* one signed by many people and sent to a government or authority. – Also *verb*. – *noun* **petitioner**.

petrel *noun* a kind of small, long-winged sea-bird.

petrify *verb* (*past tense* **petrified**) to turn into stone; to turn (someone) stiff, *esp* with fear. – *noun* **petrifaction**.

petroleum *noun* oil in its raw, unrefined form, extracted from natural wells below the earth's surface. – *noun* **petrol** petroleum when refined as fuel for use in motor-cars *etc*.

petticoat *noun* an underskirt worn by women.

petty *adjective* of little importance, trivial. – *noun* **pettiness**. – *noun* **petty cash** money paid or received in small sums. – *noun* **petty officer** a rank of officer in the navy (equal to a non-commissioned officer in the army).

petulant *adjective* cross, irritable; unreasonably impatient. – *noun* **petulance**.

pew *noun* a seat or bench in a church.

pewter *noun* a mixture of tin and lead.

PG *abbreviation* parental guidance (certificate awarded to a film denoting possible unsuitability for young children).

phalanx (*plural* **phalanxes**) *n* a company of foot soldiers, drawn up for battle in an oblong-shaped body; a group of supporters.

phallus *noun* (symbol of) the penis. – *adjective* **phallic**.

phantasy *see* **fantasy**.

phantom *noun* a ghost.

Pharaoh *noun* (*hist*) a ruler of Egypt in ancient times.

pharmaceutical *adjective* having to do with the making up of medicines and drugs. – *noun* **pharmacist** a person who prepares and sells medicines. – *noun* **pharmacy** (*plural* **pharmacies**) the art of preparing medicines; a chemist's shop.

pharmacology *noun* the scientific study of drugs and their effects. – *noun* **pharmacologist**.

pharynx *noun* the back part of the throat behind the tonsils. – *noun* **pharyngitis** an illness in which the pharynx becomes inflamed.

phase *noun* one in a series of changes in the shape, appearance *etc* of something (*eg* the moon); a period, stage in the development of something (*eg* a war, a scheme *etc*).

PhD *abbreviation* Doctor of Philosophy.

pheasant *noun* a type of bird with brightly-coloured feathers which is shot as game.

phenomenon *noun* (*plural* **phenomena**) any happening or fact (*esp* in nature) that is observed by the senses: *the phenomenon of lightning*; anything remarkable or very unusual, a wonder. – *adjective* **phenomenal** very unusual, remarkable.

phial *noun* a small glass bottle.

philander *verb* to make love, to flirt. – *noun* **philanderer.**

philanthropy *noun* the love of mankind, *usu* as shown by money given or work done for the benefit of others. – *adjective* **philanthropic** doing good to one's fellow men. – *noun* **philanthropist** a person who does good to others.

philately *noun* the study and collecting of stamps. – *noun* **philatelist.**

philharmonic *adjective* (*usu* in names of orchestras *etc*) music-loving.

philology *noun* the study of words and their history. – *noun* **philologist.**

philosopher *noun* a person who studies philosophy. – *adjective* **philosophic** or **philosophical** of philosophy; calm, not easily upset. – *noun* **philosophy** (*pl* **philosophies**) the study of the nature of the universe, or of man and his behaviour; a person's view of life.

phlegm *flem, noun* the thick slimy matter brought up from the throat by coughing; coolness of temper, calmness. – *adjective* **phlegmatic** not easily aroused.

phlox *noun* a type of garden plant with flat white or purplish flowers.

phobia *noun* an intense (*usu* irrational) fear, dislike or hatred.

phoenix *fē'niks, noun* (*myth*) a bird which was said to burn itself and to rise again from its ashes.

phone *noun* short for **telephone.** – *noun* **phonecard** a card that can be used instead of cash to operate certain public telephones.

phonetic *adjective* of the sounds of language; spelt according to sound (as *flem* for **phlegm**). – *noun* **phonetics** the study of the sounds of language; a system of writing according to sound.

phoney or **phony** *adjective* (*coll*) fake, not genuine.

phosphorus *noun* an element, a wax-like, poisonous substance that gives out light in the dark. – *noun* **phosphate** a kind of soil fertilizer containing phosphorus. – *noun* **phosphorescence** faint glow of light in the dark. – *adjective* **phosphorescent.**

photocopy *noun* a copy of a document *etc* made by a device which photographs and develops images of the document. – Also *verb.*

photogenic *adjective* being a good or striking subject for a photograph.

photography *noun* the art of taking pictures by means of a camera, making use of the action of light on special films or plates. – *noun* **photograph** (*coll* **photo** (*plural* **photos**)) a picture so made. – *verb* to take a picture with a camera. – *noun* **photographer.** – *noun* **Photo-fit®** or **photophit** a method of making identification pictures by combining photographs of individual features. – *noun* **Photostat®** a type of special camera for making photographic copies of documents, pages of books *etc*; a photographic copy so made.

phrase *noun* a small group of words expressing a single idea, *eg* 'after dinner', 'on the water'; a short saying or expression; (in music) a short group of bars forming a distinct unit. – *verb* to express in words: *You could have phrased your excuse more tactfully.* – *noun* **phraseology** one's choice of words and phrases used in expressing oneself.

physical *adjective* of the body: *He has great physical strength: She practises physical exercises;* of things that can be seen or felt. – *adverb* **physically.** – *noun* **physician** a doctor (specializing in medical rather than surgical treatment). – *noun* **physicist** a person who specializes in physics. – *noun* **physics** the science which includes the study of heat, light, sound, electricity, magnetism *etc*.

physiognomy *noun* (the features or expression of) the face.

physiology *noun* the study of the way in which living bodies work (including blood circulation, food digestion, breathing *etc*). – *noun* **physiologist.**

physiotherapy *noun* the treatment of disease by bodily exercise, massage *etc* rather than by drugs. – *noun* **physiotherapist.**

physique *noun* the build of one's body; bodily strength.

piano *noun* (*plural* **pianos**) a type of large musical instrument played by striking keys. – *noun* **pianist** a person who plays the piano.

piazza *noun* a market-place, square in a town *etc* surrounded by buildings.

pibroch *noun* a kind of bagpipe music.

picador *noun* a bullfighter armed with a lance and mounted on a horse.

piccolo *noun* (*plural* **piccolos**) a kind of small, high-pitched flute.

pick *verb* to choose; to pluck, gather (flowers, fruit *etc*); to peck, bite, nibble (at); to poke, probe (teeth *etc*); to open (a lock) with a tool other than a key. – *noun* choice; the best or best part; a kind of heavy tool for breaking ground *etc* pointed at one end or both ends; any instrument for picking (*eg* a toothpick). – *noun* **pickaxe** a pick. – *noun* **pickpocket** a person who robs people's pockets. – **pick a quarrel** to start a quarrel deliberately; **pick on** to single out *usu* for something unpleasant; to nag at; **pick up** to lift up; to learn (a language, habit *etc*); to take into a vehicle, give someone a lift; to find or get by chance; to improve, gain strength.

picket *noun* a pointed stake; a small sentry-post or guard; a number of men on strike who prevent others from working or from going into work. – *verb* to fasten (a horse *etc*) to a stake; to place a guard of soldiers or a group of strikers at (a place).

pickle *noun* a liquid in which food is preserved; vegetables preserved in vinegar; (*coll*) an awkward, unpleasant situation. – *verb* to preserve with salt, vinegar *etc*.

picnic *noun* a meal eaten out-of-doors, *usu* during an outing *etc*. – Also *verb* (*past tense* **picnicked**).

pictorial *see* **picture**.

picture *noun* a painting or drawing; a portrait; a photograph; a film; (*plural*) the cinema; a vivid description; representation. – *verb* to make a picture of; to form a likeness of in the mind, to imagine. – *adjective* **pictorial** having pictures; consisting of pictures; calling up pictures in the mind. – *adjective* **picturesque** such as would make a good or striking picture, pretty, colourful.

pie *noun* meat, fruit or other food baked in a casing or covering of pastry. – *adjective* **pie-eyed** (*coll*) drunk.

piebald *adjective* (*esp* of horses) white and black in patches; spotted.

piece *noun* a part or portion of anything; a single article or example: *a piece of paper*; a composition in music, writing, painting or other form of art: *a piece of popular music*; a coin; a man in chess, draughts *etc*. – *verb* to put (together). – *adverb*

piecemeal by pieces, little by little. – *noun* **piecework** work paid for according to how much work is done, not according to the time spent on it.

pièce de résistance *pyes dè rä-zēs-tonⁿs*, *noun* the best item.

pied *adjective* with two or more colours in patches.

pied à terre *pyä da ter*, *noun* a (small) second home (in a city).

pier *noun* a platform of stone, wood *etc* stretching from the shore into the sea *etc* as a landing place for ships; a pillar (supporting an arch, bridge *etc*).

pierce *verb* to make a hole through; to force a way into; to move (the feelings) deeply. – *adjective* **piercing** shrill, loud; sharp.

pierrot *pē'èr-ō*, *noun* a comic entertainer with a white face and loose white clothes.

piety *see* **pious**.

piffle *noun* nonsense.

pig *noun* a type of farm animal, from whose flesh ham and bacon are made; an oblong moulded piece of metal (*eg* pig-iron). – *noun* **piggery** (*plural* **piggeries**) or **pigsty** a place where pigs are kept. – *adjective* **pig-headed** stubborn. – *noun* **pigskin** a kind of leather made from a pig's skin. – *noun* **pigtail** the hair of the head formed into a plait.

pigeon *noun* a kind of bird of the dove family. – *noun* **pigeon-hole** a small division in a case or desk for papers *etc*. – *verb* lay aside; to classify, put into a category.

pigment *noun* paint or other substance used for colouring; a substance in animals and plants that gives colour to the skin *etc*. – *noun* **pigmentation** colouring (of skin *etc*).

pigmy *see* **pygmy**.

pike *noun* a type of freshwater fish; a weapon like a spear, with a long shaft and a sharp head.

pilchard *noun* a small type of herring-like sea fish used as food.

pile *noun* a number of things lying one on top of another, a heap; a great quantity; a large building; a large stake or pillar driven into the earth as a foundation for a building, bridge *etc*; the thick, soft surface on carpets *etc* and on certain kinds of cloth, *eg* velvet. – *verb* (often with **up**) to make or form a pile or heap.

pilfer *verb* to steal small things. – *noun* **pilfering**.

pilgrim *noun* a traveller to a holy place. – *noun* **pilgrimage** a journey to a holy place.

pill *noun* a little tablet, ball *etc* of medicine; (sometimes with **the**) a contraceptive in the form of a small tablet taken by mouth.

pillage *verb* to seize goods, money *etc esp* as loot in war. – *noun* the act of plundering in this way.

pillar *noun* an upright support for roofs, arches *etc*; an upright post or column as a monument *etc*; anything or anyone that supports: *He is a pillar of the church.* – *noun* **pillarbox** a *usu* pillar-shaped box with a slot through which letters *etc* are posted.

pillion *noun* a seat for a passenger on a motor-cycle; (*old*) a light saddle for a passenger on horseback, behind the main saddle.

pillory *noun* (*plural* **pillories**) (*hist*) a wooden frame (with holes for the head and hands) in which wrongdoers were placed in a standing position. – *verb* (*present participle* **pillorying,** *past tense* **pilloried**) to mock in public.

pillow *noun* a kind of cushion for the head. – *verb* to rest or support on, or as if on, a pillow. – *noun* **pillowcase** or **pillowslip** a cover for a pillow.

pilot *noun* the person who steers a ship in or out of a harbour; the person flying an aeroplane; a guide, leader. – *verb* to steer or guide. – *noun* **pilot-light** a small gas-light from which larger jets are lit; an electric light showing that a current is switched on. – *noun* **pilot scheme** a scheme introduced on a small scale to act as a guide to a full-scale one.

pimp *noun* a man who manages prostitutes and takes money from them; one who is paid to seek customers for prostitutes.

pimpernel *noun* a kind of plant of the primrose family, with small pink or scarlet flowers.

pimple *noun* a small round infected swelling on the skin. – *adjective* **pimpled** or **pimply** having pimples.

pin *noun* a short pointed piece of metal with a small round head, used for fastening, *esp* in dressmaking; a wooden or metal peg or nail; a skittle. –

verb (*present participle* **pinning,** *past tense* **pinned**) to fasten with a pin; to hold fast, pressed against something: *The fallen branch pinned him to the ground.*

pinafore *noun* a covering to protect the front of a dress, a kind of apron; (also **pinafore dress**) a sleeveless dress worn over a jersey, blouse *etc*.

pince-nez *panss¹-nā,* *noun* a pair of eye-glasses with a spring for gripping the nose.

pincers *noun plural* a kind of tool like pliers, but with sharp points for gripping, pulling out nails *etc*; the claw of a crab or lobster.

pinch *verb* to squeeze (*esp* flesh) between the thumb and forefinger, to nip; to grip tightly, hurt by tightness; (*coll*) to steal. – *noun* (*plural* **pinches**) a squeeze, a nip; a small amount (*eg* of salt *etc*). – *adjective* **pinched** (of a face) looking cold, pale or thin. – **at a pinch** if really necessary or urgent; **feel the pinch** to suffer from the lack of something (*usu* money).

pine *noun* any of several kinds of ever-green, cone-bearing trees with needle-like leaves; the soft wood of such a tree used for furniture *etc*. – *verb* to waste away, lose strength (with pain, grief *etc*); to long (for something). – *noun* **pineapple** a type of large fruit shaped like a pine-cone.

ping *noun* a whistling sound such as that of a bullet. – Also *verb*. – *noun* **ping-pong®** table-tennis.

pinion *noun* a bird's wing; a small toothed wheel. – *verb* to hold (someone) fast by binding or holding their arms; to cut or fasten the wings (of a bird).

pink *noun* a pale red colour; a type of sweet-scented garden flower like a carnation; good state: *in the pink of health.* – *verb* (*esp* of an engine) to make a faint clinking noise; to cut (cloth *etc*) leaving a zig-zag edge with **pinking scissors** or **pinking shears.**

pinnacle *noun* a slender spire or turret; a high pointed rock or mountain; the highest point.

pint *noun* a liquid measure equal to just over ½ litre.

pioneer *noun* a person who goes before to clear the way for others; an explorer; someone who is the first to do, study, use *etc* something. – *verb* to act as a pioneer (in).

pious *adjective* respectful in religious matters. – *noun* **piety**.

pip *noun* a seed (of fruit); a spot or symbol on dice, cards *etc*; a star on an army officer's tunic; a short high-pitched note given on the radio or telephone as a time signal *etc*.

pipe *noun* any tube, *esp* one of earthenware, metal *etc* for carrying water, gas *etc*; a kind of tube with a bowl at the end, for tobacco smoking; a kind of musical instrument in which the sound is made by blowing in a tube; (*plural*) a type of musical instrument made of several small pipes joined together; (*plural*) bagpipes. – *verb* to play (notes, a tune) on a pipe or pipes; to whistle, chirp; to speak in a shrill high voice; to convey (*eg* water) by pipe. – *noun* **pipe clay** a kind of fine white clay used to whiten leather *etc* and in making clay pipes. – *noun* **piped music** continuous background music played throughout a building or in public places. – *noun* **pipeline** a long line of pipes such as carry oil from an oil-field. – *noun* **piper** a person who plays a pipe, *esp* the bagpipes. – *adjective* **piping** high-pitched, shrill; piping hot. – *noun* a length of tubing; a system of pipes; a narrow kind of cord for trimming clothes *etc*; a strip of decorative icing round a cake. – **in the pipeline** in preparation, soon to become available; **pipe down** to become silent, stop talking; **piping hot** very hot.

pipette *noun* a kind of small glass tube used *esp* in laboratories.

pippin *noun* a kind of apple.

piquant *pē'kànt, adjective* sharp; appetizing; arousing interest.

pique *pēk, noun* anger caused by wounded pride, spite, resentment. – *verb* to wound the pride of; to arouse (curiosity).

pirate *noun* someone who robs ships at sea; their ship; someone who, without permission, prints or broadcasts what another has written *etc*. – *noun* **piracy**. – *adjective* **piratical**.

pirouette *noun* a rapid whirling on the toes in dancing. – Also *verb*.

pistachio *noun* (*plural* **pistachios**) a kind of greenish seed or nut, used as a flavouring.

piste *pēst, noun* a ski trail.

pistil *noun* the seed-bearing part of a flower.

pistol *noun* a small gun held in the hand.

piston *noun* a round piece of metal that moves up and down inside a cylinder (in engines, pumps *etc*). – *noun* **piston-rod** the rod to which the piston is fitted.

pit *noun* a hole in the ground; a place from which minerals (*eg* coal) are dug; the ground floor of a theatre behind the stalls; (often *plural*) a place beside the racecourse for repairing and refuelling racing cars *etc*. – *verb* (*past tense* **pitted**) to set one thing or person against another: *I had to pit my wits against his*. – *adjective* **pitted** marked with small holes.

pitch *verb* to fix a tent *etc* in the ground; to throw; to fall heavily: *He suddenly pitched forward*; (of a ship) to lurch; to set the level or key of a tune. – *noun* (*plural* **pitches**) a thick dark substance obtained by boiling down tar; a throw; the height or depth of a note; a peak, an extreme point, intensity: *His anger reached such a pitch that he hit her*; the field, ground for certain games; (in cricket) the ground between wickets; the slope (of a roof *etc*); the part of a street *etc* where a street seller or street-entertainer is stationed. – *adjective* **pitch-dark** very dark. – *noun* **pitched battle** a battle on chosen ground between sides that have been arranged in position beforehand. – *noun* **pitchfork** a fork for lifting and throwing hay. – *verb* to throw (someone) suddenly into (a position or state).

pitcher *noun* a kind of large jug.

piteous *see* **pity**.

pitfall *noun* a trap, a possible danger.

pith *noun* the soft substance in the centre of the stems of plants; the white substance under the rind of an orange *etc*; the important part of anything. – *adjective* **pithy** full of pith; very full of meaning, to the point: *a pithy saying*.

pittance *noun* a very small wage or allowance.

pity *noun* a feeling for the sufferings of others, sympathy; a cause of grief; a regrettable fact. – *verb* (*past tense* **pitied**) to feel sorry for. – *adjective* **piteous** or **pitiable** deserving pity; wretched. – *adjective* **pitiful** sad; poor, wretched.

pivot *noun* the pin or centre on which anything turns; that on which something or someone depends to a great extent: *He is the pivot of the firm*. – *verb* to turn on a pivot; to depend (on). – *adjective* **pivotal**.

pixy or **pixie** *noun* (*plural* **pixies**) (*myth*) a kind of fairy.

pizza *noun* a flat piece of dough spread with tomato, cheese *etc* and baked.

placard *noun* a printed notice (as an advertisement *etc*) placed on a wall *etc*.

placate *verb* to calm, soothe, make less angry *etc*.

place *noun* a city, town, village; a dwelling or home; a building, room, area *etc*; a particular spot; an open space in a town: *a market place*; a seat in a theatre, train, at table *etc*; a position (as in football *etc*); job or position (often one won by competing against others); rank. – *verb* (*present participle* **placing**) to put in a particular place; to find a place for; to give (an order for goods *etc*); to remember who a person is. *I can't place him*. – *adjective* **placed** having a place; among the first three in a race *etc*. – **in place** in the proper position; suitable; **in place of** instead of; **out of place** not in the proper position; unsuitable.

placenta *noun* the structure within the womb that unites the unborn mammal to its mother, shed at birth.

placid *adjective* calm, not easily disturbed.

plagiarize *verb* to steal or borrow from the writings or ideas of another. – *noun* **plagiarism**. – *noun* **plagiarist**.

plague *noun* a fatal infectious disease *esp* a fever caused by rat fleas; a great and troublesome quantity: *a plague of flies*. – *verb* to pester or annoy continually or frequently.

plaice *noun* a type of eatable flatfish.

plaid *noun* a long piece of (tartan) cloth worn over the shoulder.

plain *adjective* flat, level; simple, ordinary; without ornament or decoration; without luxury; clear, easy to see or understand; not good-looking, not attractive. – *noun* a level stretch of land. – *adjective* **plain-clothes** (of a police detective *etc*) wearing ordinary clothes, not uniform. – *adjective* **plain-spoken** speaking one's thoughts frankly.

plaintiff *noun* a person who takes action against another in the law courts.

plaintive *adjective* sad, sorrowful.

plait *noun* a length of hair arranged by intertwining three (or more) separate pieces; any material so intertwined. – *verb* to form into a plait.

plan *noun* a diagram of a building, town *etc* as if seen from above; a scheme or arrangement to do something. – *verb* (*past tense* **planned**) to make a sketch or plan of; to decide or arrange to do, or how to do (something).

plane *noun* short for **aeroplane**; any level surface; a kind of carpentry tool for smoothing wood; a level or standard (of achievement *etc*); a type of tree with broad leaves. – *adjective* flat, level. – *verb* to smooth with a plane; to glide (over water *etc*).

planet *noun* any of the bodies (such as the earth) which move round the sun or round another fixed star. – *adjective* **planetary**.

plank *noun* a long, flat piece of timber.

plankton *noun* very tiny living creatures floating in seas, lakes *etc*.

plant *noun* anything growing from the ground, having stem, root and leaves; a factory or machinery. – *verb* to put (something) into the ground so that it will grow; to put (an idea *etc*) into the mind; to put in position: *plant a bomb*; to set down firmly; (*coll*) to place (something) as false evidence. – *noun* **plantation** a place planted *esp* with trees; a colony; an estate for growing cotton, sugar, rubber, tobacco *etc*. – *noun* **planter** the owner of a plantation.

plantain *noun* a type of plant with broad leaves spreading out flat over the ground; a kind of banana.

plaque *noun* a plate of metal, china *etc* (for fixing to a wall) as a decoration or as a memorial; a film or deposit of saliva and bacteria which forms on the teeth.

plasma *noun* the liquid part of blood and of certain other fluids.

plaster *noun* a mixture of lime, water and sand which sets hard, for covering walls *etc*; a finer mixture (**plaster of Paris**) containing gypsum used for making moulds, supporting broken limbs *etc*; a piece of sticky tape to hold a dressing on a wound *etc*; a small dressing which can be stuck over a wound. – *adjective* made of plaster. – *verb* to apply plaster to; to cover too thickly (with). – *noun* **plaster cast** a mould made of plaster of Paris; a mould made of plaster of Paris and gauze put round an injured limb *etc*. –

noun **plasterer** a person who plasters (walls).

plastic *adjective* easily moulded or shaped; made of plastic. – *noun* any of many chemically manufactured substances that can be moulded when soft, formed into fibres *etc*. – *noun* **plastic bullet** a cylinder of PVC fired from a gun. – *noun* **plastic explosive** mouldable explosive material. – *noun* **plasticity** the state or quality of being plastic or easily moulded. – *noun* **plastic surgery** operation(s) to repair or replace damaged areas of skin or to improve the appearance of a facial feature *eg* a nose.

Plasticine® *noun* a soft clay-like substance used for modelling.

plate *noun* a shallow dish for holding food; a flat piece of metal, glass, china *etc*; gold and silver articles; a sheet of metal used in printing; a book illustration *usu* on glossy paper; the part of false teeth that fits to the mouth. – *verb* to cover with a coating of metal. – *noun* **plate-glass** a kind of glass, in thick sheets, used for shop windows, mirrors *etc*. – *noun* **plating** a thin covering of metal.

plateau *noun* (*plural* **plateaus** or **plateaux**) a broad level stretch of high land; a steady, unchanging state or condition: *Prices have now reached a plateau.*

platform *noun* a raised level surface, such as that for passengers at a railway station; a raised floor, *esp* one for speakers, entertainers *etc*.

platinum *noun* an element, a kind of heavy and very valuable steel-grey metal.

platitude *noun* a dull, ordinary remark made as if it were important.

platonic *adjective* (of a relationship *etc*) not involving sexual love.

platoon *noun* (in the army) a section of a company of soldiers.

platter *noun* a kind of large, flat plate.

platypus *noun* (*plural* **platypuses**) a small type of water animal of Australia that has webbed feet and lays eggs (also **duck-billed platypus**).

plaudit *noun* (*usu plural*) applause, praise.

plausible *adjective* seeming (often misleadingly) to be truthful or honest; seeming probable or reasonable. – *noun* **plausibility**.

play *verb* to amuse oneself; to take part in a game; to gamble; to act (on a stage *etc*); to perform (on a musical instrument); to carry out (a trick); to trifle or fiddle (with): *The child is playing with his food*; to (cause to) flicker over: *The firelight played on his face*; to (cause to) splash over: *The firemen played their hoses over the house*. – *noun* amusement, recreation; gambling; a story for acting, a drama; a way of acting or behaving: *foul play*; (of machinery *etc*) freedom of movement. – *noun* **playboy** an irresponsible rich (young) man only interested in pleasure. – *noun* **player** an actor; one who plays a game, musical instrument *etc*. *noun* **playfellow** or **playmate** a friend with whom one plays. – *adjective* **playful** wanting to play: *a playful kitten*; fond of joking *etc*, not serious. – *noun* **playground** a place for playing in at school, in a park *etc*. – *noun* **playgroup** a group of children (*usu* aged less than five) who play together supervised by adults. – *noun* **playing-card** one of a pack of cards used in playing card games. – *noun* **play-off** a game to decide a tie; a game between the winners of other competitions. – *noun* **playschool** a nursery school or playgroup. – *noun* **plaything** a toy. – *noun* **playwright** a writer of plays. – **a play on words** a pun *etc*; **play at** to treat or act towards in a light-hearted, not serious way: *He only plays at being a business man*; **play off** to set off (one person) against another to gain some advantage for oneself; **play on** to make use of (someone's feelings *etc*) to turn to one's own advantage; **play the game** to act fairly and honestly.

PLC *abbreviation* public limited company.

plea *noun* an excuse; a prisoner's answer to a charge in a law-court; an urgent request.

plead *verb* to state one's case, *esp* in a law-court; (with **with**) to beg earnestly; to give as an excuse. – **plead guilty** or **not guilty** (in a law-court) to admit or deny one's guilt.

please *verb* to give pleasure or delight (to); to satisfy; to choose, like (to do): *Do as you please*. – *interjection* if you are willing (added for politeness to a command or request): *Pass me the sugar, please. Please keep off the grass*. – *adjective* **pleasant** giving pleasure; agreeable. – *noun* **pleasantness**. – *noun* **pleasantry** (*plural* **pleasantries**) a good-humoured joke or joking. – *adjective* **pleasurable**

delightful, pleasant. – noun **pleasure** enjoyment, joy, delight; what one wishes: *What is your pleasure?* – **at pleasure** when or if one pleases; **if you please** please.

pleat noun a fold in cloth, which has been pressed or stitched down. – verb to put pleats in. – adjective **pleated**.

plebeian adjective of the ordinary or common people. – Also noun (hist). – noun **plebiscite** a system of deciding a matter by asking everybody to give their vote, for or against.

plectrum noun a small piece of horn, metal etc used for plucking the strings of a guitar etc.

pledge noun something handed over by a person who borrows money etc which will not be given back if the loan is not repaid etc; a solemn promise. – verb to give as security, to pawn; to promise solemnly to do something: *He pledged himself to carry out the plan*; to drink to the health of, to toast.

plenary adjective full, complete.

plenty noun a full supply, as much as is needed; a large number or quantity (of). – adjective **plenteous** or **plentiful** not scarce; abundant.

plethora noun too large a quantity of anything: *a plethora of politicians.*

pleurisy noun an illness in which the covering of the lungs becomes inflamed.

pliable adjective easily bent or folded; easily persuaded. – adjective **pliant** pliable.

pliers noun plural a kind of tool used for gripping tightly, bending and cutting (wire) etc.

plight noun situation, state (usu bad). – verb to promise solemnly.

plimsoll noun a light rubber-soled canvas shoe, used for sports etc. – noun **Plimsoll line** or **mark** loadline.

plinth noun the square slab at the foot of a column; the base or pedestal of a statue, vase etc.

PLO abbreviation Palestine Liberation Organization.

plod verb (past tense **plodded**) to travel slowly and steadily; to work on steadily. – noun **plodder** a dull or slow but hard-working person.

plop noun the sound like that of a small object falling into water. – Also verb (past tense **plopped**).

plot noun a small piece of ground; a plan, esp for doing evil; the story of a play, novel etc. – verb (past tense **plotted**) to plan secretly; to make a chart, plan, graph etc of; to mark points on one of these. – noun **plotter**.

plough noun a type of farm tool for turning up the soil. – verb to turn up the ground in furrows; to work one's way through slowly: *He is ploughing through his homework.* – noun **ploughshare** the blade of the plough. – **the Plough** a group of seven stars forming a shape like an old plough.

plover noun any of several kinds of birds that nest on the ground in open country.

pluck verb to pull, pull out or off; to pick (flowers, fruit etc); to strip off the feathers of (a bird which is to be cooked). – noun courage, spirit. – adjective **plucky** brave, determined. – **pluck up courage** to prepare oneself (to face a danger, difficulty etc).

plug noun an object which can be fitted into a hole to stop it up; a fitting put into a socket to connect an appliance to an electric current. – verb (past tense **plugged**) to stop up with a plug; (coll) to advertise, publicize etc by mentioning repeatedly.

plum noun a kind of fruit, usu dark red or purple with a stone in the centre; the tree that bears it. – adjective very good, very profitable etc: *a plum job.* – noun **plum cake** or **pudding** a rich cake or pudding containing raisins, currants etc.

plumage see plume.

plumb noun a lead weight hung on a string (**plumbline**), used eg to test if a wall has been built straight up. – adjective, adverb standing straight up, vertical. – verb to test the depth of (the sea etc).

plumber noun a person who fits and mends water, gas and sewage pipes. – noun **plumbing** the work of a plumber; the drainage and water systems of a building etc.

plume noun a feather, esp a large showy one, or one worn as an ornament on a hat etc; something looking like a feather: *a plume of smoke*; a crest. – noun **plumage** the feathers of a bird.

plummet noun a weight of lead hung on a line, for taking depths at sea. – verb to plunge.

plump *adjective* fat, rounded, well filled out. – *verb* to (cause to) grow fat, swell; to beat or shake cushions *etc* back into shape; to sit or sink down heavily; (with **for**) to choose, give one's vote for.

plunder *verb* to carry off (another's) goods by force, to loot, rob. – *noun* goods seized by force.

plunge *verb* to throw oneself (into water *etc*), to dive; to rush or lurch forward; to put or thrust suddenly into water or other material *etc*: *He plunged the knife into its neck.* – *noun* an act of plunging; a dive.

plural *adjective* more than one. – *noun* (in grammar) the form which shows more than one (*eg mice* is the plural of *mouse*).

plus *preposition* used to show addition and represented by the sign (+): *Five plus two equals seven,* or 5 + 2 = 7. – *adjective, noun* (of) a quantity more than zero. – *adverb* (*coll*) and a bit extra: *He earns £9000 plus.*

plush *noun* a type of cloth with a soft velvety surface on one side. – *adjective* luxurious.

plutocrat *noun* a wealthy person or one who is powerful because of being wealthy. – *adjective* **plutocratic.**

ply *verb* (*past tense* **plied**) to work at steadily; to make regular journeys: *This ferry plies between Dover and Calais;* to use (energetically), *eg* a tool *etc*; to keep supplying someone with something (*eg* food, questions to answer *etc*). – *noun* **plier** a person who plies; (*see also* **pliers**). – *noun* **plywood** a board made up of thin sheets of wood glued together. – *adjective* **two-** (or **three-** *etc*) **ply** having two (or three *etc*) layers, strands *etc*.

PM *abbreviation* prime minister.

pm *abbreviation* after noon (*post meridiem* [*L*]).

PMS *abbreviation* premenstrual syndrome.

PMT *abbreviation* premenstrual tension.

pneumatic *nū-mat'ik, adjective* filled with air; worked by air: *pneumatic drill.*

pneumonia *nū-mō'ni-ā, noun* a type of disease in which the lungs become inflamed.

PO *abbreviation* post office; postal order.

poach *verb* to cook something (as eggs without their shells) in boiling water, or other liquid; (to trespass in order) to catch fish or hunt game illegally. – *noun* **poacher** a person who steals game.

pocket *noun* a small pouch or bag (as in a garment, suit, billiard table); one's supply of money; a small isolated area or group: *a pocket of unemployment.* – *verb* to put in the pocket; to steal. – *noun* **pocket-book** a wallet for holding papers or money carried in the pocket. – *noun* **pocket money** (an allowance of) money for personal spending. – **in,** or **out of, pocket** having gained, or having lost, money on a deal *etc*.

pockmark *noun* a scar or small hole in the skin left by smallpox *etc*.

pod *noun* a long seed-case of the pea, bean *etc*. – *verb* (*past tense* **podded**) to remove from the pod; to form pods.

podgy *adjective* (short and) fat.

poem *noun* a piece of writing (of a striking or imaginative kind) set out in lines which *usu* have a regular rhythm and often rhyme. – *noun* **poet** a person who writes poetry. – *adjective* **poetic** of or like poetry. – *noun* **poetry** the art of writing poems; poems.

pogrom *noun* an organized killing or massacre of certain people (*esp* the Jews).

poignant *adjective* sharp, keen; very painful, sad or moving; pathetic. – *noun* **poignancy.**

point *noun* a sharp end of anything; a headland; a dot: *a decimal point;* (in punctuation) a full stop; an exact place or spot; an exact moment of time; the chief matter or a detail of an argument; the meaning of a joke *etc*; a mark (*eg* in a competition); a purpose, advantage: *There is no point in going;* a movable rail to direct a railway engine from one line to another; an electrical wall socket into which plugs are inserted; a mark of character: *He has many good points.* – *verb* to make pointed: *Point your toes;* to direct, aim; to call attention to: *He pointed to the building;* to fill the joints (of a wall) with mortar. – *adjective* **point-blank** (of a shot) fired from very close range; (of a question *etc*) direct. – *adjective* **pointed** having a (sharp) point; sharp; (of a remark *etc*) obviously aimed at someone. – *noun* **pointer** a rod for pointing; a type of dog that can show a huntsman *etc* where game is. – *adjective* **pointless** having no meaning or purpose.

poise *verb* to balance, keep (something) in a steady position; to hover in the air. – *noun* state of balance; dignity, self-confidence. – *adjective* **poised** balanced; having poise; (with **for**) prepared or ready for action.

poison *noun* any substance which, when taken into the body, kills or harms; anything harmful. – *verb* to kill or harm with poison; to make harmful by adding poison to; to make bitter or bad (*eg* someone's mind). – *adjective* **poisonous** harmful because of having poison in it; causing evil. – *noun* **poison pill** (*coll*) an action (*eg* a merger) taken by a company to prevent a threatened takeover bid.

poke *verb* to push (something *eg* a finger, stick into something), prod, thrust at; to search about, *esp* inquisitively. – *noun* a nudge or a prod; a prying search. – *noun* **poker** a kind of rod for stirring up a fire; a kind of card game. – *adjective* **poky** small, cramped, shabby.

polar *see* **pole**.

Polaroid® *noun* a kind of plastic through which light is seen less brightly; (*plural*) sunglasses; a camera that develops each individual picture in a few seconds.

polder *noun* land below the level of the sea reclaimed for use.

pole *noun* a long rounded rod or post; formerly, a measure of length (about 5 metres) or area (about 27·6 square metres; the north or south end of the earth's axis (**the north** or **south pole**); (*plural*) the points in the heavens opposite to the north and south poles; (*plural*) the opposite points of a magnet or electric battery. – *adjective* **polar** of the regions round the north or south poles. – *noun* **pole-star** the star nearest to the north pole of the heavens.

polecat *noun* a large kind of weasel; (*US*) a skunk.

police *noun* the body of men and women whose work it is to keep order, see that the laws are obeyed *etc*. – *verb* to keep law and order (in a place) by use of police. – *noun* **policeman** (*masculine*), **policewoman** (*feminine*). – *noun* **police station** the headquarters of the police in a district.

policy *noun* (*plural* **policies**) a (planned or agreed) course of action; a written agreement with an insurance company.

polio *noun* short for **poliomyelitis**.

poliomyelitis *noun* a kind of disease of the spinal cord, causing weakness or paralysis of the muscles.

polish *verb* to make smooth and shiny by rubbing; to improve (a piece of writing *etc*); to make polite or refined (a person's manner *etc*). – *noun* a gloss on a surface; a substance used for polishing; fine manners, style *etc*.

polite *adjective* having good manners, courteous. – *noun* **politeness**.

politic *adjective* wise, cautious. – *adjective* **political** of government, politicians, or politics. – *noun* **politician** someone (*eg* a member of parliament) whose business is politics. – *noun* **politics** the art or study of government.

polka *noun* a kind of lively dance or the music for it.

poll *noun* a counting of voters at an election; total number of votes; the testing of public opinion by means of questioning (also **opinion poll**). – *verb* to cut or clip off (hair, horns, branches *etc*); to receive a certain number of votes: *He polled 5000 votes*. – *noun* **polling station** a place where voting is done. – *noun* **poll tax** community charge.

pollard *noun* a tree having the whole top cut off, so that new branches grow from the top of the stem. – *verb* to cut the top off (a tree).

pollen *noun* the fertilizing powder of flowers. – *verb* **pollinate** to fertilize with pollen. – *noun* **pollination**.

pollute *verb* to make dirty or impure; to make (any feature of the environment) harmful to life. – *noun* **pollutant** something that pollutes. – *noun* **pollution** the act of polluting; dirt.

polo *noun* a kind of game like hockey played on horseback. – *noun* **polo neck** on a garment, a close fitting neck with a part turned over at the top; a garment with a neck like this.

poltergeist *noun* a kind of ghost said to move furniture and throw objects around a room.

poly- *prefix* many, much.

polygamy *noun* the custom or state of having more than one wife (or husband) at the same time. – *noun* **polygamist**. – *adjective* **polygamous**.

polyglot *adjective* speaking (or written in) many languages. – Also *noun*.

polygon *noun* a figure of many angles and sides. – *adjective* **polygonal.**

polysyllable *noun* a word of three or more syllables. – *adjective* **polysyllabic.**

polytechnic *noun* a kind of college in which technical subjects such as engineering, building *etc* are taught.

polythene *noun* the name of several types of plastic that can be moulded when hot.

pomegranate *noun* a type of fruit with a thick skin and many seeds.

pommel *noun* the knob on the hilt of a sword; the high part of a saddle.

pomp *noun* solemn and splendid ceremony, magnificence. – *adjective* **pompous** self-important in manner or speech, excessively dignified.

poncho *noun* (*plural* **ponchos**) a type of S. American cloak made of, or made like, a blanket with a hole for the head.

pond *noun* a small lake or pool.

ponder *verb* to think over, consider. – *adjective* **ponderous** weighty; clumsy; sounding very important.

poniard *noun* a kind of small dagger.

pontiff *noun* (in the Roman Catholic Church) a bishop, *esp* the pope. – *adjective* **pontifical** of, belonging to a pontiff; pompous in speech. – *verb* **pontificate** to speak in a pompous manner.

pontoon *noun* a kind of flat-bottomed boat used with others to support a temporary bridge or roadway (a **pontoon bridge**); a kind of card-game.

pony *noun* (*plural* **ponies**) a small horse. – *noun* **pony-trekking** riding cross-country in small parties.

poodle *noun* a breed of dog, with curly hair often clipped in a fancy way.

pool *noun* a small area of still water; a deep part of a stream or river; a (joint) fund, stock or supply (*eg* of money, typists *etc*); the money played for in certain games, gambles *etc*. – *verb* to put money *etc* into a joint fund. – *noun plural* (**football**) **pools** organized betting on football match results.

poop *noun* the back part (or stern) of a ship; a high deck in the stern.

poor *adjective* having little money or property; not good: *Your work is poor*; lacking (in): *poor in sports facilities*; deserving pity: *Poor Tom has broken his leg*. – *noun* (with **the**) those with little money. – *adjective* **poorly** in bad health, ill.

pop *noun* a sharp quick kind of noise, like that made by a cork as it comes out of a bottle; a kind of fizzy drink; popular music. – *verb* (*past tense* **popped**) to (cause to) make a pop; to move quickly: *pop in*. – *adjective* (of music *etc*) short for **popular.** – *noun* **popcorn** a kind of maize that bursts open when heated.

pope *noun* (also with *cap*) the bishop of Rome, head of the Roman Catholic Church.

popinjay *noun* a person who is conceited, *esp* about his dress.

poplar *noun* a type of tall, narrow quick-growing tree.

poplin *noun* strong (cotton) cloth.

poppy *noun* (*plural* **poppies**) a type of plant with large *usu* red flowers.

populace *noun* the common people.

popular *adjective* of the people: *popular vote*; liked by most people; widely held or believed: *popular belief*. – *noun* **popularity** the state of being generally liked. – *verb* **popularize** to make popular or widely known.

population *noun* the (number of) people living in a place. – *verb* **populate** to fill (an area *etc*) with people. – *adjective* **populous** full of people.

porcelain *noun* a kind of fine china.

porch *noun* (*plural* **porches**) a covered entrance to a building.

porcupine *noun* one of the largest kinds of gnawing animals, covered with sharp quills.

pore *noun* a tiny hole *esp* that of a sweat gland in the skin. – *verb* (with **over**) to study closely or eagerly. – *adjective* **porous** having pores; (of a material *etc*) allowing fluid to pass through.

pork *noun* the flesh of the pig.

pornography *noun* literature or art that is indecent in a sexual way. – *adjective* **pornographic.**

porous *see* **pore.**

porpoise *noun* a type of blunt-nosed sea animal of the dolphin family, about 1½ metres (5 feet) long.

porridge *noun* a food made from oatmeal boiled in water (or milk).

port *noun* a harbour, or a town with a harbour; the left side of a ship as one faces the front; a strong, dark-red kind of sweet wine. – *noun* **porter** a person who carries luggage, pushes hospital trolleys *etc*; a doorkeeper; a kind of dark brown beer.

portable *adjective* able to be lifted and carried.

portal *noun* an entrance or doorway, *usu* of a grand kind.

portcullis *noun* (*plural* **portcullises**) a grating of crossed woodwork or ironwork which can be let down quickly to close a gateway (as in old castles).

portend *verb* to give warning of, foretell. – *noun* **portent** a warning sign. – *adjective* **portentous** like a warning; strange or wonderful; important, solemn.

porter *see* **port**.

portfolio *noun* (*plural* **portfolios**) a case for carrying papers, drawings *etc*; the post or job of a government minister.

port-hole *noun* a small (*usu* round) window in a ship's side.

portico *noun* (*plural* **porticoes** or **porticos**) a row of columns in front of a building forming a porch or covered walk.

portion *noun* a part; a share, a helping (of food *etc*). – *verb* to divide into parts.

portly *adjective* stout (and dignified).

portmanteau *noun* a kind of large leather travelling bag.

portrait *noun* a drawing, painting, or photograph of a person; a description (of a person, place *etc*). – *verb* **portray** (*past tense* **portrayed**) to paint or draw (someone or something); to describe in words; to act the part of. – *noun* **portrayal** an act of portraying; a description or portrait.

pose *noun* a position or attitude of the body: *a relaxed pose*; a manner or some kind of behaviour put on to impress others, a pretence. – *verb* to place or position oneself (for a photograph, for a good effect *etc*); (with **as**) to pretend or claim to be what one is not: *He posed as a doctor*; to put forward or set (a problem, question *etc*). – *noun* **poser** a person who poses; a difficult question. – *noun* **poseur** a person who puts on poses.

posh *adjective* (*coll*) high-class; smart.

position *noun* place, situation: *the position of the house*; manner of standing, sitting *etc*, posture: *in a crouching position*; a rank or job: *a high position in a bank*. – *verb* to place.

positive *adjective* meaning or saying 'yes': *a positive answer*; not able to be doubted: *positive proof*; certain, convinced: *I am positive that she did it*; definite: *a positive improvement*; (of a quantity) greater than zero; (in grammar) of the first degree of comparison of adjectives or adverbs *eg* *big* in 'He is big but she is bigger'.

posse *noun* a force or body (of police *etc*).

possess *verb* to own or to have; to take hold of one's mind: *Anger possesses me*. – *adjective* **possessed** in the power of a driving (and evil) force or spirit; self-possessed, calm. – *noun* **possession** the state of possessing; the state of being possessed; something owned. – *adjective* **possessive** showing possession *esp* in grammar, as the adjectives *my*, *your*, *his etc*; regarding or treating (a person *eg* one's child) as a possession. – *noun* **possessor** the owner.

possible *adjective* able to happen or to be done; able to be true, not unlikely (as a reason, explanation *etc*). – *noun* **possibility** (*plural* **possibilities**) the state of being possible; something that may happen or that may be done. – *adverb* **possibly** perhaps.

post *noun* a pole or stake (of wood, iron *etc*) *usu* fixed upright in the ground; (the system of carrying) letters and other mail; a job: *a teaching post*; a place of duty: *The soldier remained at his post*; a settlement, camp *etc* often in a remote area: *a military post: trading post*. – *verb* to put (a letter) in a postbox for collection; to send or to station somewhere: *His army unit was posted abroad*; to put up, stick up (a notice *etc*). – *noun* **postage** money paid for sending a letter *etc* by post. – *noun* **postage stamp** a small printed label to show that postage has been paid. – *adjective* **postal** of or by post. – *noun* **postal order** a paper form bought at a post office which can be exchanged for the amount of money printed on it. – *noun* **postbox** a box with an opening in which to post letters *etc*. – *noun* **postcard** a card on which a message may be sent by post, often sent by people on holiday. – *noun* **post code** a short series of letters and numbers (*eg* EH7 4AZ) that identify a very small area, used for sorting mail by machine. – *noun* **poster** a large notice or placard; a large printed picture. – *adverb* **post-free** without charge for postage. – *adverb* **post-haste** with great speed. – *noun* **postman** a person who delivers letters. – *noun* **postmark** a mark showing the date, put on a letter at a post office. – *noun* **postmaster** an official in charge of a post office. – *noun* **post office** an office for receiving and sending off letters by post *etc*.

post- *prefix* after.

posterior *adjective* situated behind, coming after. – *noun* the buttocks.

posterity *noun* all future generations; a person's descendants.

postern *noun* a back door or gate (to a castle *etc*).

postgraduate *adjective* (of studies, degree *etc*) following on from a first university degree. – *noun* a person continuing to study after gaining a first degree.

posthumous *adjective* (of a book) published after the author's death; (of a child) born after the father's death.

postil(l)ion *noun* (*old*) a person who guides the horses of a carriage, and rides on one of them.

postmortem *noun* an examination of a dead body (to find out the cause of death).

postpone *verb* to put off to a future time, to delay. – *noun* **postponement.**

postscript *noun* a part added as an afterthought at the end of a letter, after the sender's name.

postulate *verb* to assume or take for granted (that).

posture *noun* the manner in which one holds oneself in standing, walking *etc*; a position or pose.

postwar *adjective* of, belonging to the time after a war.

posy *noun* (*plural* **posies**) a small bunch of flowers.

pot *noun* any one of many kinds of deep vessels, containers, jars *etc* used in cooking, for holding foods, liquids *etc*, or for growing plants; (*slang*) marijuana; (*plural*) (*coll*) a great deal of: *pots of money*. – *verb* (*past tense* **potted**) to plant in a pot; to make articles of baked clay. – *noun* **pothole** a hole made in a rock by swirling water, a deep cave (sometimes explored by **potholers**); a hole worn in a road surface. – *adjective*

potted (of meat *etc*) pressed down and preserved in a pot or jar; (of a book *etc*) made shorter and easier to understand. – **take pot-luck** to have a meal with someone as a guest without any special preparations being made.

potash *noun* potassium carbonate, a substance obtained from the ashes of wood.

potassium *noun* an element, a type of silvery-white metal.

potato *noun* (*plural* **potatoes**) a type of plant with round underground stems (**tubers**) which are used as a vegetable; the vegetable itself.

potent *adjective* powerful, strong. – *noun* **potency.** – *noun* **potentate** someone with power, a prince, a ruler. – *adjective* **potential** that may develop, possible. – *noun* the possibility or promise of further development. – *noun* **potentiality** (*plural* **potentialities**) a possibility; something that may develop.

potion *noun* a drink (often one containing medicine or poison).

pot-pourri *noun* a scented mixture of dried petals *etc*; a mixture or medley.

potter *noun* a person who makes articles of baked clay. – *verb* to. do small odd jobs; to dawdle. – *noun* **pottery** articles made of baked clay; (*plural* **potteries**) a place where such things are made; the art of making them.

pouch *noun* (*plural* **pouches**) a kind of pocket or small bag; a bag-like formation, *esp* that on the front of a kangaroo, for carrying its young.

pouffe *noun* a kind of low, stuffed seat.

poultice *noun* a (hot) wet and sticky type of dressing spread on a bandage and put on inflamed areas of skin. – *verb* to put a poultice on.

poultry *noun* farmyard fowls, *eg* hens, ducks, geese, turkeys. – *noun* **poulterer** a person who sells poultry and game for food.

pounce *verb* (with **on**) to fall upon, swoop down on, and seize or attack. – *noun* a sudden swoop; the claw of a bird.

pound *noun* the standard unit of money in Britain, shown by the sign (£), 100 new pence; a measure of weight, written lb (about ½ kilogramme, 16 ounces); a pen or enclosure (*esp* one for animals). – *verb* to beat into small pieces or powder; to beat or bruise; to walk or run with heavy steps.

pour *verb* to (cause to) flow in a stream: *The blood poured out. She poured the tea;* to rain heavily: *It is pouring.*

pout *verb* to push out the lips sulkily to show displeasure. – Also *noun*.

poverty *noun* the state of being poor; want or need: *poverty of ideas.*

POW *abbreviation* prisoner of war.

powder *noun* any substance made up of very fine particles, fine dust; gunpowder; face powder. – *verb* to sprinkle with powder, put powder on; to grind down to powder. – *adjective* **powdered** in the form of a fine dust; covered with powder. – *adjective* **powdery** covered with powder; like powder: *powdery snow.*

power *noun* strength; force; ability to do things; authority or legal right; a strong nation; a person or persons in authority; rule; the force used for driving machines: *electric power: steam power;* (in physics *etc*) the rate of doing work; (in mathematics) the product obtained by multiplying a number by itself a given number of times (*eg* $2 \times 2 \times 2$ or 2^3 is the third power of 2). – *adjective* **power-driven** worked by electricity *etc*, not by hand. – *adjective* **powered** supplied with mechanical power. – *adjective* **powerful**. – *adjective* **powerless** without power or ability. – *noun* **power station** a building where electricity is produced.

pow-wow *noun* (*hist*) a discussion with, or held by, N. American Indians; (*coll*) any conference.

pp *abbreviation* pages.

PR *abbreviation* proportional representation; public relations.

practicable *adjective* able to be used or done.

practical *adjective* liking action (rather than thought *etc*); efficient; learned by practice, rather than from books: *He has practical knowledge of carpentry.* – *noun* **practical joke** a joke consisting of action, not words, *usu* causing annoyance to the person it is played on. – *adverb* **practically** in a practical way; in effect or reality; (*coll*) almost: *practically empty.*

practice *noun* habit: *It is my practice to get up early;* the actual doing (of something): *I always intend to get up early but in practice I stay in bed late;* exercise by means of repeated performance to gain skill (in playing a musical instrument, in preparation for a race, match *etc*); the business of a doctor, lawyer, dentist *etc.*

practise or (*US*) **practice** *verb* to do exercises in, train in, take lessons in so as to get and keep a skill: *He practises judo nightly;* to put into action or practice, make a habit of: *to practise self-control;* to follow (one's profession): *He used to practise as a surgeon.* – *noun* **practitioner** a person engaged in a profession: *a medical practitioner.*

pragmatic or **pragmatical** *adjective* concerned with matters of fact, rather than ideas and theories, practical.

prairie *noun* (in N. America) a stretch of level land, without trees and covered with grass.

praise *verb* to speak highly of (a person or thing); to glorify (God) by singing hymns *etc*. – *noun* an expression of approval or honour. – *adjective* **praiseworthy** deserving to be praised.

pram *noun* a kind of small four-wheeled carriage for pushing a baby in (short for **perambulator**).

prance *verb* to strut or swagger about; to dance or jump about; (of a horse) to spring from the hind legs.

prank *noun* a trick played for mischief.

prate *verb* to talk foolishly.

prattle *verb* to talk or chatter meaninglessly or in a childish way. – Also *noun*.

prawn *noun* a type of shellfish like the shrimp.

pray *verb* to ask earnestly, beg; to speak to God in prayer. – *noun* **prayer** an act of praying, an earnest request for something; (often *plural*) that part of worship in which requests are made, and thanks given to God.

pre- *prefix* before.

preach *verb* to give a sermon; to teach, speak in favour of: *He preaches caution.* – *noun* **preacher**.

preamble *noun* something said as an introduction.

prearrange *verb* to arrange beforehand.

precarious *adjective* uncertain, risky, dangerous.

precaution *noun* care taken beforehand (to avoid an accident, a disease *etc*). – *adjective* **precautionary**.

precede *verb* to go before in time, rank or importance. – *noun* **precedence** the act or right of going before. – *noun* **precedent** a past action which may serve as an example or rule in the future. – *adjective* **preceding** going before; previous.

precept *noun* a rule to guide one's action; a commandment.

precinct *noun* the ground enclosed by the boundary walls of a building *esp* a cathedral; (*plural*) the area closely surrounding any place; (*esp US*) an administrative district. – **shopping precinct** a shopping centre *esp* when closed to cars *etc*.

precious *adjective* of great price or worth; highly valued.

precipice *noun* a steep cliff. – *adjective* **precipitous** very steep.

precipitate *verb* to throw head foremost; to force into (hasty action *etc*); to bring on suddenly, to hasten (death, illness *etc*). – *adjective* headlong; hasty, rash. – *noun* the substance which settles at the bottom of a liquid. – *noun* **precipitation** an act of precipitating; great hurry; rash haste; (the amount of) rainfall.

precipitous *see* **precipice**.

précis *prā-sē, noun* (*plural* **précis**) a summary of a piece of writing.

precise *adjective* definite; exact, accurate. – *noun* **precision** preciseness; exactness, accuracy.

preclude *verb* to prevent; to make impossible.

precocious *adjective* (often of children, their speech or knowledge) unexpectedly advanced or well-developed. – *noun* **precocity**.

preconceive *verb* to form (ideas *etc*) before having actual knowledge or experience. – *noun* **preconception** an act of preconceiving; an idea formed without actual knowledge.

precursor *noun* a person or thing which goes before, *esp* as a sign of something to come: *the precursor of jazz*.

predator *noun* a bird or animal that attacks and kills others for food; a creature that plunders (crops *etc*). – *adjective* **predatory** of a predator; (of a person) in the habit of using others for one's own gain, *esp* financial.

predecease *verb* to die before (someone).

predecessor *noun* a person who has held an office or position before another.

predetermine *verb* to settle beforehand.

predicament *noun* an unfortunate or difficult situation.

predicate *noun* (in grammar) what is said about the subject of a sentence (as *is sad* in the sentence *Jack is sad*).

predict *verb* to foretell, forecast. – *adjective* **predictable** able to be foretold, forecast. – *noun* **prediction** an act of predicting; something predicted.

predilection *noun* a preference, a liking for something.

predispose *verb* to turn a person in favour of (something) beforehand: *We were predisposed to believe her*; to make liable or subject (to): *His weak chest predisposes him to colds*. – *noun* **predisposition**.

predominate *verb* to be the stronger or the greater in number; to have control (over). – *noun* **predominance**. – *adjective* **predominant** ruling; most or more noticeable or outstanding.

pre-eminent *adjective* outstanding, excelling all others. – *noun* **pre-eminence**.

preen *verb* to arrange feathers, as birds do; to smarten one's appearance *esp* in a conceited way. – **preen oneself** to take or show obvious pride in one's achievements *etc*.

prefabricated *adjective* (of a building *etc*) made of parts manufactured beforehand, ready to be fitted together.

preface *noun* an introduction (to a book *etc*). – *verb* to start or introduce with a preface: *He prefaced his rebuke with a smile*.

prefect *noun* someone set in authority over others; (in schools) a senior pupil having certain powers.

prefer *verb* (*past tense* **preferred**) to like better, choose one thing rather than another: *I prefer tea to coffee. I prefer to walk rather than go by bus*; to put forward (a claim or request). – *adjective* **preferable** more desirable. – *noun* **preference** greater liking, the choice of one thing rather than another; the thing that is preferred. – *adjective* **preferential** showing, giving preference. – *noun* **preferment** promotion.

prefix *noun* (*plural* **prefixes**) a syllable or word put at the beginning of a word to alter its meaning (as *dis-*, *un-*, *re-*, in *dislike*, *unhappy*, *regain*).

pregnant *adjective* carrying an unborn baby (or young) in the womb; (of

words, a pause *etc*) full of meaning. –
noun **pregnancy** (*plural* **pregnancies**)
the state of being pregnant.

prehensile *adjective* able to grasp or hold
on to something: *a prehensile tail*.

prehistoric *adjective* belonging to the time
before history was written down. –
noun **prehistory**.

prejudge *verb* to judge or decide (something) before hearing the facts of a case.

prejudice *noun* an unreasonable or unfair
feeling (for or against anything); an
opinion formed without careful
thought; harm, injury: *to the prejudice of
your chances*. – *verb* to fill with prejudice;
to do harm to, damage: *His late arrival
prejudiced his chances of success in the
examination*. – *adjective* **prejudiced**
having, showing prejudice. – *adjective*
prejudicial damaging, harmful.

prelate *noun* a bishop, archbishop or
other clergyman of high rank. – *noun*
prelacy (*plural* **prelacies**) the office of a
prelate.

preliminary *adjective* going before, preparing the way: *a preliminary investigation*. – *noun* (*plural* **preliminaries**) something that goes before.

prelude *noun* a piece of music played as an
introduction to the main piece; an
event *etc* that goes before and acts as an
introduction: *That first success was a
prelude to a brilliant career*.

premarital *adjective* before marriage.

premature *adjective* coming, born *etc*
before the right, proper or expected
time.

premeditate *verb* to think out
beforehand, plan, intend: *premeditated
murder*. – *noun* **premeditation**.

premenstrual *adjective* before menstruation.

premier *adjective* first, leading, foremost.
– *noun* a prime minister. – *noun*
première a first performance (of a play
etc).

premise or **premiss** *noun* (*plural* **premises**
or **premisses**) something assumed
from which a conclusion is drawn.

premises *noun plural* a building (or part of a
building) and its grounds: *These
premises are used by the local football team*.

premium *noun* (*plural* **premiums**) a
reward; (yearly) payment on an insurance policy. – **at a premium** much

valued or desired and so difficult to
obtain: *Tickets for the cup final were at a
premium*.

premonition *noun* feeling that something
is going to happen; a warning.

preoccupy *verb* to take up completely the
attention of (someone). – *noun* **pre-
occupation** the act of preoccupying;
the state of being preoccupied; that
which preoccupies. – *adjective* **preoccupied** deep in thought.

prepaid *see* **prepay.**

prepare *verb* to make or get ready; to train
or equip. – *noun* **preparation** an act of
preparing; (shortened to **prep**) study
for a lesson in class; something prepared, made ready (*eg* a medicine,
face-cream *etc*). – *adjective* **preparatory**
acting as an introduction or first step. –
adjective **prepared** ready; willing. – *noun*
preparatory school a private school
educating children in preparation for a
public or other senior school. – **preparatory to** before, in preparation for.

prepay *verb* (*past tense* **prepaid**) to pay
beforehand. – *noun* **prepayment.**

preponderance *noun* greater weight,
power, or number: *There was a preponderance of young people in the audience*.

preposition *noun* (in grammar) a word
placed before a noun or pronoun to
show how it is related to another word,
as '*through* the door', '*in* the town',
'written *by* me'.

prepossessing *adjective* pleasant, attractive, making a good impression.

preposterous *adjective* very foolish,
absurd.

prerequisite *noun* something necessary
before a thing can be done or can
happen.

prerogative *noun* a privilege or right
enjoyed by a person because of rank or
position.

presage *verb* to foretell, warn of.

Presbyterian *adjective* (of a church)
having business and other affairs managed by **presbyters** (ministers and
elders). – *noun* **presbytery** (*plural* **pres-
byteries**) a body of presbyters; (in the
Roman Catholic Church) a priest's
house.

prescribe *verb* to lay down as a rule; to
order the use of (a medicine). – *noun*
prescription a doctor's (*usu* written)

instructions for the preparing of a medicine; something prescribed; the act of prescribing. – adjective **prescriptive** laying down rules; (of rights etc) based on custom or habit.

presence noun the state of being present (opposite of **absence**); one's personal appearance, manner etc. – adjective **present** being here or in the place spoken of, thought of etc; belonging to the time in which we are: The present rates of pay are adequate. We need courage in the present situation. – noun the time we are now at; a gift; (in grammar) the present tense. – verb to hand over (a gift) esp formally; to offer; to set forth, put forward; to introduce (a person) to another. – adjective **presentable** fit to be seen (or given). – noun **presentation** the act of handing over a present; the present itself; a setting forth (of a statement, ideas etc); a showing (of a play etc); – adverb **presently** soon. – **in one's presence** while one is present; **presence of mind** calmness, ability to act sensibly in an emergency, difficulty etc; **present oneself** to introduce oneself; to arrive.

presentiment noun a feeling that something unpleasant is about to happen, a foreboding.

preserve verb to keep safe from harm; to keep in existence, to maintain; to treat (food) in such a way that it will not go bad or rotten. – noun private ground; a place where game animals, birds etc are protected; jam. – noun **preservation** the act of preserving; the state of being preserved. – noun **preservative** something that preserves, esp something that helps to prevent food from going bad.

preside verb to be chairman or to be in charge at a meeting etc. – noun **presidency** (plural **presidencies**) the office or rank of a president. – noun **president** the leading member of a club, institution etc; the head of a republic.

press verb to push on, against or down; to squeeze; to urge, force; to smooth out, iron (clothes etc). – noun an act of pressing; a crowd; a printing machine; newspapers and magazines as a whole; those involved in writing and producing newspapers etc. – adjective **pressing** requiring action at once, insistent. – noun **pressure** the act of pressing; the state of being pressed; force on or against a surface; strong persuasion, compulsion; stress, strain; urgency. –

noun **pressure cooker** a type of pan in which food is cooked quickly by steam under great pressure. – noun **pressure group** a group of people who try to persuade the authorities etc to take a particular course of action. – verb **pressurize** to fit (an aeroplane etc) with a device that maintains normal air pressure; to force (someone to do something).

pressgang noun (hist) a body of men once employed to carry off men by force into the army or navy. – verb (hist) to carry off men by force for the army or navy; to force (someone to do something): We pressganged him on to the committee.

prestige noun reputation, influence due to rank, success etc.

presume verb to take for granted; to act impertinently, take the liberty of (doing something); (with **on**) to take advantage of (someone's kindness etc). – adverb **presumably** probably. – noun **presumption** something supposed; a strong likelihood; impertinent behaviour. – adjective **presumptuous** unsuitably bold.

presuppose verb to take for granted.

pretend verb to make believe: Pretend you are a witch; to put on a false show or make a false claim: He pretended to be ill. – noun **pretence** the act of pretending; make-believe; a (false) claim. – noun **pretender** a person who lays claim to something (esp to the title of king). – noun **pretension** a claim (whether true or not); self-importance. – adjective **pretentious** claiming more than is deserved or justified; self-important; showy, ostentatious.

preternatural adjective beyond what is natural, abnormal.

pretext noun an excuse.

pretty adjective pleasing or attractive to see, listen to etc. – adverb fairly, quite: pretty good. – noun **prettiness.**

prevail verb (with **against** or **over**) to gain control or victory over; to win, succeed; (with **on**, **upon**) to persuade: He prevailed upon me to stay; to be (most) usual or common. – adjective **prevailing** controlling; most common. – adjective **prevalent** common, widespread. – noun **prevalence.**

prevaricate verb to avoid telling the truth. – noun **prevarication.**

prevent *verb* to hinder; to prevent from happening. – *noun* the act of preventing. – *noun, adjective* **preventive** (something) that helps to prevent (illness *etc*).

preview *noun* a viewing of a performance, exhibition *etc* before it is open to the public.

previous *adjective* going before in time; former. – *adverb* **previously.**

prey *noun* animals (that may be) killed by others for food; a victim. – *verb* (with **on** or **upon**) to seize and eat: *The hawk preys upon smaller birds*; to (hunt and) harass: *The attacker preyed on women out walking alone*.

price *noun* the money for which a thing is bought or sold, the cost; something that one must give up or suffer in order to gain something: *The price of victory was the lives of many*. – *adjective* **priceless** of very great value; (*coll*) very funny.

prick *verb* to pierce slightly; to give a sharp pain to; to stick up (the ears). – *noun* an act of piercing; a feeling of being pierced with a small sharp point. – *noun* **prickle** a sharp point growing on a plant or animal. – *verb* to be prickly; to feel prickly. – *adjective* **prickly** full of prickles; stinging, pricking.

pride *noun* the state of feeling proud; too great an opinion of oneself; a feeling of pleasure in having done something well; dignity; a group of lions. – **pride oneself on** to allow oneself to feel or show pride (about some achievement): *I pride myself on my writing*.

priest *noun* a clergyman in some Christian religions; **priest** (*masculine*), **priestess** (*feminine*) an official in a non-Christian religion. – *noun* **priesthood** the office, position of a priest; those who are priests.

prig *noun* a smug, self-righteous person. – *adjective* **priggish.**

prim *adjective* (of a person, manner *etc*) unnecessarily formal and correct.

prima ballerina *noun* the leading female dancer of a ballet company. – *noun* **prima donna** a leading female opera singer; a woman who is over-sensitive and temperamental.

primary *adjective* first; chief. – *noun* **primary colours** those from which all others can be made *eg* red, blue and yellow. – *noun* **primary school** a school for the early stages of education.

primate *noun* a member of the highest order of mammals (man, monkeys, apes, lemurs); an archbishop.

prime *adjective* first in time, rank or importance; of highest quality, excellent. – *noun* the time of greatest health and strength: *the prime of life*. – *verb* to prepare by putting something in or on: *He primed the wood before painting it. He primed the pump*; to supply with detailed information: *She was well primed before the meeting*. – *noun* **prime minister** the head of a government. – *noun* **primer** a simple introductory book on any subject; something that primes (a surface to be painted *etc*).

primeval *adjective* of, belonging to the first ages of the world.

primitive *adjective* belonging to very early times; old-fashioned; not skilfully made, rough, clumsy.

primrose *noun* a kind of pale-yellow spring flower common in woods and hedges.

prince (*masculine*), **princess** (*feminine*) (*plural* **princesses**) *noun* a member of a royal family, *esp* the child of a king or queen; a title given to the ruler of some states or countries. – *adjective* **princely** fit for a prince; splendid.

principal *adjective* highest in rank or importance; chief. – *noun* the head of a school, college or university; someone who takes a leading part (in a show *etc*); money in a bank *etc* on which interest is paid. – *noun* **principality** (*plural* **principalities**) a country ruled by a prince. – *adverb* **principally** chiefly, mostly.

principle *noun* a general truth, rule or law; the theory on which the working of a machine *etc* is based: *the principle of the combustion engine*; (*plural*) one's own rules of behaviour, sense of right and wrong.

print *verb* to mark letters on paper with type (*eg* by using a printing press); to write in capital letters or unjoined small letters; to publish (a book *etc*) in printed form; to stamp patterns on (cloth *etc*); to make a finished photograph. – *noun* a mark made by pressure: *footprint*; printed lettering; a photograph made from a negative; a printed state: *The book is in print*; a printed reproduction of a painting or drawing; cloth printed with a design. – *noun* **printer** a person who prints books, newspapers *etc*; a machine that prints *eg* attached to a computer system. – *noun* **print-out** the printed information produced by a computer *etc*.

prior¹ *adjective* earlier; previous (to). – *noun* **priority** (*plural* **priorities**) the state of being first in time or position; the right to be first: *An ambulance must have priority in traffic*; something that must be considered or done first: *Our priority is to get him into hospital.*

prior² (*masculine*), **prioress** (*feminine*) *noun* the head of a priory. – *noun* **priory** (*plural* **priories**) a building where a community of monks or nuns live.

prise *verb* to force open or off with a kind of lever: *He prised open the safe. He prised off the lid.*

prism *noun* a solid body with parallel sides whose two ends are the same shape and size; a glass prism (often with triangular ends).

prison *noun* a building for holding criminals, a jail; any place where someone is shut up against his will. – *noun* **prisoner** someone under arrest or locked up in jail; a captured enemy soldier or anyone held in captivity. – **prisoner of war** a person captured during the war, especially a member of the armed forces.

pristine *adjective* in the original or unspoilt state.

privacy *noun* the state of being away from company or from observation; secrecy.

private *adjective* of, belonging to a person (or a group of people), not to the general public; hidden from view; secret, not made generally known; personal. – *noun* the lowest rank of ordinary soldier (not an officer). – *noun plural* **private parts** the external sexual organs.

privateer *noun* an armed private vessel with orders from a government to seize and plunder enemy ships.

privation *noun* want, poverty, hardship; the act of taking away, loss.

privet *noun* a type of shrub used for hedges.

privilege *noun* a favour or right granted to or available to one person or to only a few people. – *adjective* **privileged** having privileges.

privy: privy council *noun* a body of statesmen appointed as advisers to a king or queen. – **privy to** knowing about (something secret).

prize *noun* reward for good work *etc*; something won in a competition; something captured, *esp* an enemy ship; something highly valued. – *adjective* very fine, worthy of a prize. – *verb*

to value highly. – *noun* **prize fight** a boxing match fought for money.

pro *noun* short for **professional**.

pro- *prefix* before, forward, front; in favour of: *pro-British*. – **pros and cons** the arguments for and against (a plan *etc*).

probable *adjective* likely; that may happen; that is likely to be true. – *noun* **probability** (*plural* **probabilities**) likelihood; something that is probable. – *adverb* **probably** very likely.

probation *noun* the testing of a person's conduct, powers, or character; a system of letting law-breakers go without punishment on condition that they commit no more offences and report to social workers (**probation officers**) regularly. – *noun* **probationer** a person who is training to be a member of a profession.

probe *noun* a long, thin instrument *eg* used by doctors to examine a wound; a thorough investigation; a spacecraft for exploring space. – *verb* to examine very carefully; to investigate thoroughly to try to find out information.

probity *noun* honesty, goodness of character.

problem *noun* a question to be solved; a matter which is difficult to deal with. – *adjective* **problematic** or **problematical** doubtful, uncertain.

proboscis *noun* (*plural* **proboscises**) the nose of an animal or mouth of an insect; the trunk of an elephant.

proceed *verb* to go on; to begin (to do something); to go on with, continue; to take legal action (against). – *noun* **procedure** the order or method of doing business; a course of action, or a particular action. – *noun* **proceeding** a step, a going forward; an action; (*plural*) a record of matters dealt with at the meetings of a society *etc*; (*plural*) a law action. – *noun plural* **proceeds** money, profit made from a sale *etc*.

process *noun* (*plural* **processes**) a method or series of operations used in manufacturing goods; a series of events, actions *etc* producing change or development; course; a law-court case. – **in the process of** in the course of: *He lost his watch in the process of moving house.*

procession *noun* a line of persons or vehicles moving forward in order.

proclaim *verb* to announce publicly, declare openly. – *noun* **proclamation**

an official announcement made to the public.

procrastinate *verb* to put off, delay doing something till a later time. – *noun* **procrastination**.

procure *verb* to obtain; to bring about. – *noun* **procurator-fiscal** (in Scotland) the law officer of a district.

prod *verb* (*past tense* **prodded**) to poke; to urge on.

prodigal *adjective* spending one's money *etc* without care or thought, wasteful. – *noun* **prodigality**.

prodigy *noun* (*plural* **prodigies**) something astonishing or strange; a person of amazing cleverness: *a child prodigy*. – *adjective* **prodigious** strange, astonishing; enormous.

produce *verb* to bring forth, bring out; to bring into being, to yield; to bring about, cause; to prepare (a programme, play *etc*) for the stage, television *etc*; to make, manufacture. – *noun* something that is produced, *esp* on a farm or in a garden, as crops, eggs, milk *etc*; *noun* **producer** a person who produces anything, *esp* a play, film *etc*. – *noun* **product** a thing produced; a result; (*plural*) the goods which a country produces; (in mathematics) the number that results from the multiplication of two or more numbers. – *noun* **production** the act or process of producing; that which is produced. – *adjective* **productive** fruitful, producing much; bringing results. – *noun* **productivity** the rate or efficiency of work done *esp* in industrial production.

Prof. *abbreviation* Professor.

profane *adjective* not sacred; treating holy things without respect. – *noun* **profanity** (*plural* **profanities**) swearing; lack of respect for sacred things.

profess *verb* to declare (a belief *etc*) openly; to pretend or to claim: *He professed to be an expert on Shakespeare.* – *adjective* **professed** declared; pretended. – *noun* **profession** an occupation (of a non-mechanical kind) requiring special knowledge (as the work of a doctor, lawyer *etc*); an open declaration. – *adjective* **professional** of a profession; earning (one's living) from a game or an art (opposite of **amateur**): *He became a professional footballer. She is a professional singer*; showing the skill *etc* of one who is trained. – Also *noun*. – *noun* **professor** a teacher of the highest rank in a university; (*US*) a university teacher.

proffer *verb* to offer.

proficiency *noun* skill. – *adjective* **proficient** skilled, expert.

profile *noun* an outline; a side view of a face, head *etc*; a short description of someone's life, achievements *etc*.

profit *noun* gain, benefit; the money got by selling an article for a higher price than was paid for it. – *verb* to gain or receive benefit (from); to bring gain or benefit to. – *adjective* **profitable** bringing profit or gain. – *noun* **profiteer** a person who makes large profits unfairly. – Also *verb*.

profligate *adjective* living an immoral life; very extravagant. – Also *noun*. – *noun* **profligacy**.

pro forma or **pro-forma** *adjective* (of an invoice) made out to show the market price of specified goods, with goods being paid for before dispatch. – Also *noun*.

profound *adjective* very deep; (of a feeling) deeply felt; showing great knowledge or understanding: *a profound comment*. – *noun* **profundity** depth; the state or quality of being profound.

profuse *adjective* abundant, lavish, extravagant: *He was profuse in his thanks.* – *noun* **profusion** great abundance.

progenitor *noun* an ancestor. – *noun* **progeny** children.

prognosticate *verb* to foretell. – *noun* **prognostication**.

programme or (*US*) **program** *noun* (a booklet or sheet giving details of) the items in an entertainment, ceremony *etc*; a scheme or plan. – **program** a set of instructions given to a computer to carry out certain actions. – *verb* (*past tense* **programmed**) to prepare the series of operations to be carried out (by a machine, *esp* a computer).

progress *noun* advance, forward movement; improvement. – *verb* to go forward; to improve. – *noun* **progression** advance; onward movement. – *adjective* **progressive** going forward; advancing by stages; favouring reforms.

prohibit *verb* to forbid; to prevent. – *noun* **prohibition** an act of forbidding; the forbidding by law of making and selling alcoholic drinks. – *adjective* **prohibitive** prohibiting; (of prices) so high as to make buying almost impossible.

project *noun* a plan, scheme; a task; a piece of study or research. – *verb* to throw out, forward or up; to jut out; to cast (an image, a light *etc*) on to a surface *etc*; to plan or propose. – *noun* **projectile** a missile. – *noun* **projection** an act of projecting; something projected; something which juts out. – *noun* **projector** a machine for projecting pictures on a screen.

proletariat *noun* the ordinary working people.

proliferate *verb* to grow or increase rapidly. – *adjective* **prolific** producing much, fruitful; abundant.

prolix *adjective* using too many words, tiresomely long. – *noun* **prolixity**.

prologue *noun* a preface or introduction (*esp* to a play *etc*).

prolong *verb* to make longer.

promenade *noun* a level roadway or walk for the public (*esp* alongside the sea); a walk or a stroll. – *verb* to walk for pleasure. – *noun* **promenade concert** a concert at which a large part of the audience stands instead of being seated (also **prom**).

prominent *adjective* standing out; easily seen; famous, distinguished. – *noun* **prominence**.

promiscuous *adjective* having many sexual relationships; mixed in kind; not making distinctions between one thing or person and another. – *noun* **promiscuity**.

promise *verb* to say, give one's word (that one will do or will not do something); to say that one will give (a gift, help *etc*); to show signs for the future: *The weather promises to improve.* – *noun* (a statement of) something promised; a sign (of something to come); a sign of future success: *His essay showed great promise.* – *adjective* **promising** showing signs of turning out well or being successful.

promontory *noun* (*plural* **promontories**) a headland jutting out into the sea.

promote *verb* to raise to a higher rank or position; to help onwards, encourage (a scheme, a charity *etc*); to advertise, encourage the buying of (goods). – *noun* **promotion**.

prompt *adjective* acting without delay, quick, immediate; punctual. – *verb* to

move to action: *She prompted him to demand higher wages;* to supply words to a speaker (*esp* an actor) who has forgotten what to say. – *noun* **prompter**. – *noun* **promptness** quickness, readiness; punctuality.

promulgate *verb* to make widely known. – *noun* **promulgation**.

prone *adjective* lying face downward; inclined (to); *prone to laziness.*

prong *noun* the spike of a fork. – *adjective* **pronged** having prongs.

pronoun *noun* a word used instead of a noun (*eg* I, you, who).

pronounce *verb* to speak (words, sounds); to announce (one's opinion), declare. – *adjective* **pronounced** noticeable, marked. – *noun* **pronouncement** a statement, announcement. – *noun* **pronunciation** the way a word is said; the act of saying something.

proof *noun* evidence that makes something clear beyond doubt; the standard of strength of whisky *etc*; a copy of a printed sheet for correction before the final printing and publication. – *adjective* able to keep out or withstand: *proof against attack;* (also used as part of a word: *waterproof, bulletproof*).

prop *noun* something that holds up, a support; short for **propeller**: *turbo-prop aeroplane;* (*plural*) short for stage **properties**. – *verb* (*past tense* **propped**) to hold up by placing something under or against.

propaganda *noun* the spreading of ideas *etc* to influence opinions; the material used *eg* film, posters, leaflets. – *noun* **propagandist** a person who sees to the spreading of such ideas.

propagate *verb* to spread; to (cause plants or animals to) produce seedlings or young *etc*. – *noun* **propagator**.

propel *verb* (*past tense* **propelled**) to drive forward. – *noun* **propellant** an explosive for firing a rocket; the gas in an aerosol spray. – *noun* **propeller** a shaft with blades which revolves to drive forward ships, aircraft *etc*. – *noun* **propulsion** an act of driving forward.

propensity *noun* (*plural* **propensities**) a natural inclination: *He has a propensity to criticize. She has a propensity for bumping into things.*

proper *adjective* right, correct: *the proper way to fire a gun;* full, thorough: *a proper* *search*; prim, well-behaved: *a very proper young lady*. – *adverb* **properly** in the right way; (*coll*) thoroughly. – *noun* **proper noun** or **name** (in grammar) a noun or name, naming a particular person, thing, place: *John, New York*.

property *noun* (*plural* **properties**) that which one owns; land or buildings; a quality: *Hardness is a property of the diamond*; (*plural*) the furniture *etc* required by actors in a play.

prophesy *verb* (*past tense* **prophesied**) to (try to) tell what will happen in the future, predict. – *noun* **prophecy** (*plural* **prophecies**) foretelling the future; something prophesied. – *noun* **prophet** someone who claims to be able to foretell events *etc* to come; someone who tells what they believe to be the will of God.

propinquity *noun* nearness.

propitiate *verb* to calm the anger of. – *adjective* **propitious** favourable: *propitious circumstances*.

proportion *noun* a part of a total amount: *A large proportion of income is taxed*; the relation in size, number, amount, degree of a thing or part as compared with other things or parts: *The proportion of girls to boys is small*. – *adjective* **proportional** or **proportionate** in proportion. – *noun* **proportional representation** a voting system intended to give parties a representation as close as possible to the proportion of their voting strength. – **in** (**out of**) **proportion** suitable or appropriate (unsuitable or not appropriate) in size, quantity or degree when compared with other parts or things: *An elephant's tail seems out of proportion to the rest of its body*.

propose *verb* to put forward (a plan, someone's name for a job *etc*) for consideration, to suggest: *He proposed his cousin for president*; to intend; to make an offer *esp* of marriage. – *noun* **proposal** an act of proposing; anything proposed; an offer of marriage. – *noun* **proposition** a proposal, suggestion; a statement; a situation, thing *etc* that must be dealt with: *a tough proposition*.

propound *verb* to state, put forward for consideration.

proprietor (*masculine*), **proprietress** or **proprietrix** (*feminine*) *noun* an owner: *the proprietor of the hotel*.

propriety *noun* (*plural* **proprieties**) rightness, fitness, suitability; right behaviour, decency. *She always behaves with propriety*.

propulsion *see* **propel**.

pro rata [*L*] in proportion.

prosaic *adjective* dull, not interesting.

proscribe *verb* to outlaw; to prohibit.

prose *noun* writing which is not in verse; ordinary written or spoken language.

prosecute *verb* to bring a law-court action against; to carry on (one's studies, an investigation *etc*). – *noun* **prosecution** an act of prosecuting; those bringing the case in a law court.

prospect *noun* a view, a scene; what one may expect to happen, one's outlook for the future: *The prospect of starvation frightens the refugees. He has a job with good prospects*. – *verb* to make a search (*esp* for gold or other minerals). – *adjective* **prospective** likely to be or to happen: *the prospective headmaster*. – *noun* **prospector** a person who prospects, *esp* for minerals. – *noun* **prospectus** (*plural* **prospectuses**) a booklet giving information about a school, organization *etc*.

prosper *verb* to get on well or succeed. – *noun* **prosperity** success, good fortune, wealth. – *adjective* **prosperous**.

prosthesis *noun* (*plural* **prostheses**) an artificial replacement part for the body.

prostitute *noun* a person (*usu a woman*) who offers sexual intercourse for payment.

prostrate *adjective* lying flat, *esp* face downwards; worn out, exhausted, in a state of collapse. – *verb* to throw forwards to the ground: *They prostrated themselves before the king*; to exhaust, tire out completely. – *adjective* **prostrated** worn out (by grief, tiredness *etc*). – *noun* **prostration**.

protagonist *noun* a chief character (in a play *etc*).

protect *verb* to shield or defend from danger, keep safe. – *noun* **protection** the act of protecting; safety, shelter. – *adjective* **protective** giving protection; intended to protect. – *noun* **protector** a guardian, defender. – *noun* **protectorate** a country which is partly governed and defended by another country.

protégé (*masculine*), **protégée** (*feminine*) *noun* a person who is guided and helped in their career by someone important or powerful.

protein noun any of a large number of substances (present in milk, eggs, meat etc) necessary as part of the food of human beings and animals.

protest verb to express a strong objection (against); to declare solemnly: to protest one's innocence. – noun a strong statement or demonstration of disapproval or objection. – noun **protestation** a solemn declaration; a protest.

Protestant noun a member of one of the Christian churches that broke away from the Roman Catholic Church at the time of the Reformation.

protocol noun correct (diplomatic) procedure.

proton noun a particle with a positive electrical charge, forming part of the nucleus of an atom or the whole of the nucleus of a hydrogen atom.

protoplasm noun the half-liquid substance which is the chief material found in all living cells.

prototype noun the first or original model from which anything is copied.

protract verb to draw out or lengthen in time. – noun **protractor** an instrument for drawing and measuring angles on paper.

protrude verb to stick out, or thrust forward: His front teeth protrude. – noun **protrusion** the act of sticking or thrusting out; something that sticks out.

protuberance noun a swelling, a bulge. – adjective **protuberant.**

proud adjective thinking too highly of oneself, haughty; having a feeling of pleasure, satisfaction at an achievement etc; showing a spirit of independence: He was too proud to accept the offer of help.

prove verb to show to be true or correct; to try out, test; to turn out (to be): His remarks proved correct.

provender noun food, esp for horses and cattle.

proverb noun a well-known wise saying (eg 'Nothing venture, nothing gain'). – adjective **proverbial** like a proverb; widely known, spoken about by everybody: His kindness is proverbial.

provide verb to supply. – conjunction **provided (that)** or **providing** on condition (that).

providence noun foresight; thrift; the care of God for all creatures. – noun **Providence** God. – adjective **provident** showing thought for and making plans for the future; thrifty. – adjective **providential** fortunate, coming as if by divine help.

province noun a division of a country; the extent or scope of one's duties or knowledge: Mending fuses is not my province; (plural) all parts of a country outside the capital. – adjective **provincial** of a province; of the provinces; rough in manners, narrow in one's views, interests etc.

provision noun an act of providing; an agreed arrangement; a rule or condition; a supply or store; (plural) (a supply of) food. – adjective **provisional** arranged for the time being; temporary.

proviso noun (plural **provisos**) a condition laid down beforehand.

provoke verb to cause, result in (laughter, trouble etc); to rouse to anger or action: Don't let him provoke you. – noun **provocation** an act of provoking; an act which arouses anger. – adjective **provocative** tending to cause anger; intended to or likely to arouse interest etc: a provocative neckline. – adjective **provoking** annoying.

prow noun the front part of a ship.

prowess noun skill, ability.

prowl verb to go about stealthily in search of prey or plunder.

proximity noun nearness.

proxy noun (plural **proxies**) a person who acts or votes on behalf of another; a document giving someone the authority to act on behalf of another; such authority.

prude noun an over-modest, priggish person. – noun **prudery** the attitude of such a person. – adjective **prudish.**

prudent adjective wise and cautious. – noun **prudence.**

prune noun a dried plum. – verb to trim (a tree etc) by cutting off unneeded twigs etc; to shorten, reduce (eg a story, expenditure etc).

pry verb (past tense **pried**) to look or inquire closely into things that are not one's business. – adjective **prying.**

PS *abbreviation* postscript.

psalm *säm*, *noun* a sacred song, *esp* one in the Book of Psalms. – *noun* **psalmist** a writer of psalms.

psalter *söl'tèr*, *noun* a book of psalms.

pseud(o)- *sūd(ō)*, *prefix* false.

pseudo or **pseud** *sūd'ō* or *sūd*, *(coll)* *adjective* false, fake, pretended: *His Spanish accent is pseudo.* – *noun* **pseud** *(coll)* a fraud.

pseudonym *sū'dò-nim*, *noun* a false name used by an author.

psych(o)- *sīk'(ō)*, *prefix* mind.

psychiatry *sī-kī'à-tri*, *noun* the treatment of mental diseases. – *adjective* **psychiatric** of, or needing, such treatment. – *noun* **psychiatrist** a person who treats diseases of the mind.

psychic *sīk'ik* or **psychical** *sīk'ikl*, *adjective* of the mind or soul; of mysterious forces and influences on the mind and senses; sensitive to feeling such forces: *She thinks she is psychic because she guessed his thoughts.*

psychoanalysis *sī-kō-à-nal'i-sis*, *noun* a method of treating a mental illness by discussing with the patient its possible causes in the patient's past.

psychology *sī-köl'i-ji*, *noun* the science which studies the human mind. – *adjective* **psychological** of psychology or the mind. – *noun* **psychologist**.

PT *abbreviation* physical training.

pt *abbreviation* part; pint.

PTA *abbreviation* parent teacher association.

ptarmigan *tär'mi-gàn*, *noun* a type of mountain-dwelling bird of the grouse family, which turns white in winter.

Pte *abbreviation* Private (military).

pterodactyl *te-rò-dak'til*, *noun* a kind of extinct flying reptile.

PTO *abbreviation* please turn over.

pub *noun* short for **public house**.

puberty *noun* the time during youth when the body becomes sexually mature.

pubic *adjective* of the lowest part of the abdomen.

public *adjective* of, concerning, open to, shared by the people (of a community or nation) in general: *Politicians should be aware of public opinion. She made a* public announcement. *I borrowed a book from the public library;* generally or widely known: *a public figure.* – *noun* people in general. – *noun* **publican** the keeper of an inn or public house. – *noun* **publication** the act of making (news *etc*) public; the act of publishing (a book, newspaper *etc*); something published (*eg* a book, magazine *etc*). – *noun* **public house** a building where alcoholic drinks are sold to the public and consumed. – *noun* **publicist** an advertising agent. – *noun* **publicity** the act of bringing something to the notice of the public, often through advertising; public notice or attention. – *noun* **public relations** the relations between a person *etc* and the public; the business of setting up and maintaining favourable relations; a department of a firm, organization *etc* dealing with this. – **in public** in front of, among other people; **public address system** a system of devices (*eg* microphones, amplifiers, loudspeakers) used to enable (large) groups of people to hear voices, music *etc*.

publish *verb* to make generally known; to prepare, and put out a book *etc* for sale. – *noun* **publisher** a person who publishes books.

puce *adjective* of a brownish-purple colour.

pucker *verb* to wrinkle. – *noun* a wrinkle or fold.

pudding *noun* the sweet course of a meal; any of several types of soft foods made with eggs, flour, milk *etc*; any of several types of sausages.

puddle *noun* a small (muddy) pool.

puerile *adjective* childish, silly.

puff *verb* to blow out in small gusts; to breathe heavily (as after running); to blow up, inflate; to swell (up, out). – *noun* a short, sudden gust of wind, breath *etc*; a powder puff; a piece of advertising. – *adjective* **puffy** swollen, flabby; breathing heavily. – *noun* **puff pastry** a light, flaky kind of pastry.

puffin *noun* a type of sea bird, with a short, thick beak.

pug *noun* a breed of small dog with a snub nose.

pugilist *noun* a boxer. – *noun* **pugilism** boxing.

pugnacious *adjective* quarrelsome, fond of fighting. – *noun* **pugnacity**.

pull *verb* to move or try to move (something) towards oneself *esp* by using force; to drag, tug; to stretch or strain: *to pull a muscle*; to tear: *to pull to pieces*. – *noun* the act of pulling; a pulling force (*eg* of a magnet *etc*); a handle for pulling; (*coll*) advantage, influence. – **pull oneself together** to regain one's self-control or self-possession; **pull through** to get safely to the end of a difficult or dangerous experience; **pull up** to stop, halt.

pullet *noun* a young hen.

pulley *noun* (*plural* **pulleys**) a grooved wheel fitted with a cord and set in a block, used for lifting weights *etc*.

pullover *noun* a knitted garment for the top half of the body, a jersey.

pulmonary *adjective* of, affecting, the lungs.

pulp *noun* the soft fleshy part of a fruit; a soft mass (made of wood *etc*) which is made into paper; any soft mass. – *verb* to reduce to pulp.

pulpit *noun* an enclosed platform in a church, for the preacher.

pulsar *noun* a distant source of regular radio signals in space, possibly a star.

pulse *noun* the beating or throbbing of the heart and blood vessels of the body as blood flows through them; beans, peas, lentils and other similar edible seeds. – *verb* to beat or throb (also **pulsate**).

pulverize *verb* to make or crush into powder.

puma *noun* a type of American wild animal like a large cat.

pumice or **pumice stone** *noun* (a piece of) a light kind of solidified lava used for smoothing skin *etc* and for rubbing away stains.

pummel *verb* (*past tense* **pummelled**) to beat with the fists.

pump *noun* a machine used for making water *etc* rise to the surface; a machine for drawing out or forcing in air, gas *etc*: *a bicycle pump*; any of several kinds of thin- or soft-soled shoes for dancing, gymnastics *etc*. – *verb* to raise or force with a pump; (*coll*) to draw out information from (a person) by cunning questions.

pumpkin *noun* a kind of large roundish, thick-skinned, yellow fruit, used for food.

pun *noun* a play upon words alike in sound but different in meaning, as 'They went and told the sexton, and the sexton tolled the bell'. – *verb* (*past tense* **punned**) to make a pun.

punch *verb* to beat with the fist; to make a hole in with a tool or machine: *The conductor punched the ticket*. – *noun* (*plural* **punches**) a blow with the fist; a tool used for punching holes; a kind of drink made of spirits or wine, water, sugar *etc*. – *noun* **punch-bowl** a bowl for mixing punch. – *adjective* **punchdrunk** (of a boxer) dizzy from blows. – *noun* **punch line** the sentence or phrase that gives the main meaning or point to a story (*esp* a joke).

punctilious *adjective* paying great care to small points, *esp* in one's behaviour.

punctual *adjective* up to time, not late; strict in keeping time of appointments. – *noun* **punctuality**.

punctuate *verb* to divide up sentences by commas, full stops *etc*; to interrupt at intervals: *The silence was punctuated by occasional coughing*. – *noun* **punctuation** the act of punctuating; the use of punctuation marks. – *noun plural* **punctuation marks** the symbols used in punctuating sentences, as full stop, comma, colon, question mark *etc*.

puncture *noun* an act of pricking or piercing; a small hole made with a sharp point; a hole in a tyre.

pundit *noun* a learned man, an expert: *The pundits disagree about the state of the economy*.

pungent *adjective* sharp-tasting or sharp-smelling; (of remarks *etc*) strongly sarcastic.

punish *verb* to cause (a person) to suffer for a fault or crime; to inflict suffering on; to treat roughly or harshly. – *adjective* **punishable** (of crimes *etc*) likely or liable to be punished. – *noun* **punishment** pain or unpleasantness inflicted (for a fault or crime) – *adjective* **punitive** inflicting punishment or suffering.

punnet *noun* a small basket made of strips of wood *etc* for holding fruit.

punt *noun* a type of flat-bottomed boat with square ends. – *verb* to move (a punt) by pushing a pole against the bottom of a river *etc*.

puny *adjective* little and weak.

pup *noun* a young dog (also **puppy**); one of the young of certain other animals, *eg* the seal *etc*.

pupa *noun* (*plural* **pupae**) the stage (often passed inside a cocoon) in the growth of an insect in which it changes from a larva (*eg* a caterpillar) to its perfect form or **imago** (*eg* a butterfly).

pupil *noun* a person who is being taught by a teacher; the round opening in the middle of the eye through which the light passes.

puppet *noun* a doll which is moved by strings or wires; a kind of doll that fits over the hand and is moved by the fingers; a person who acts just as told by another.

puppy *see* **pup.**

purchase *verb* to buy. – *noun* the act of buying; that which is bought; the power to lift or shift got by using a lever *etc*; firm grip or hold. – *noun* **purchaser** a person who buys.

pure *adjective* clean, spotless; free from dust, dirt, infection *etc*; not mixed with other (polluting or adulterating) substances; free from faults or sin, innocent: *a pure young girl*; utter, absolute, nothing but: *pure nonsense.* – *adverb* **purely** in a pure way; wholly, entirely: *purely on merit*; merely, only: *purely for the sake of appearance.* – *verb* **purify** (*past tense* **purified**) to make pure. – *noun* **purification.** – *noun* **purist** a person who insists on correctness. – *noun* **purity** the state of being pure.

purée *noun* food made into a pulp by being put through a sieve or liquidizing machine.

purge *verb* to make clean, purify; to clear (something) of anything unwanted: *He purged his party of those who disagreed with him.* – *noun* **purgative** a medicine which clears waste matter out of the body. – *noun* **purgatory** in the Roman Catholic Church, a place where it is believed that a soul is made pure before entering heaven; any state of suffering for a time.

purification, purify *see* **pure.**

puritan *noun* a strict, *usu* narrow-minded person. – *noun* **Puritan** (*hist*) one of a group believing in strict simplicity in worship and daily life. – *adjective* **puritanical.**

purity *see* **pure.**

purl *verb* to knit in stitches made with the wool *etc* in front of the work.

purloin *verb* to steal.

purple *noun* a dark colour formed by the mixture of blue and red.

purport *noun* meaning. – *verb* to mean; to seem or appear (to be, to do): *He purports to be an expert on the theatre.*

purpose *noun* the aim towards which an effort or action is directed; intention; use, function (of a tool *etc*). – *verb* to intend. – *adverb* **purposely** intentionally. – **on purpose** intentionally; **to the purpose** to the point.

purr *noun* the low, murmuring sound made by a cat when pleased. – Also *verb.*

purse *noun* a small bag for carrying money; (*US*) a handbag. – *verb* to close (the lips) tightly. – *noun* **purser** the officer who looks after a ship's money.

pursue *verb* to follow after (in order to overtake or capture), chase; to be engaged in, carry on (studies, an enquiry *etc*); to follow (a route, path *etc*). – *noun* **pursuer** a person who pursues. – *noun* **pursuit** the act of pursuing; an occupation or hobby.

purvey *verb* to provide, supply (food *etc*) *usu* as a business. – *noun* **purveyor.**

pus *noun* a thick yellowish liquid produced from infected wounds *etc*.

push *verb* to press hard against; to move or thrust (something) away with force, to shove; to urge on; to make a thrust or an effort. – *noun* a thrust; effort; (*coll*) energy and determination. – *noun* **push-chair** a folding chair on wheels for a young child. – *adjective* **pushing** determined to get what one wants, aggressive.

pusillanimous *adjective* cowardly.

pustule *noun* a small pimple containing pus.

put *verb* (*present participle* **putting**, *past tense* **put**) to place; to lay or set: *Put the book on the table*; to bring to a certain position or state: *Put the light on. He put it out of his mind*; to express: *You did not put your question very politely.* – **put about** to change course at sea; to spread (news); **put by** to set aside, save up; **put down** to defeat; **put in for** to make a claim for, apply for; **put off** to delay or end (an arrangement *etc*); to turn (a person) away from an intention or purpose; **put out** to extinguish (a fire *etc*); to annoy or embarrass; **put up** to build; to propose, suggest (a plan, candidate *etc*); to let someone stay in one's house *etc*; to stay as a guest in someone's house; **put-up job** (*coll*) a dishonest scheme; **put up with** to bear patiently, tolerate.

putative *adjective* supposed, commonly accepted.

putrefy *verb* (*past tense* **putrefied**) to go bad, to rot. – *noun* **putrefaction**. – *adjective* **putrid** rotten; stinking.

putt *verb* (in golf) to send a ball gently forward. – *noun* **putter** a golf club used for this.

putty *noun* a type of cement made from ground chalk, used in putting glass in windows *etc*.

puzzle *verb* to present with a problem which is difficult to solve or with a situation *etc* which is difficult to understand; to be difficult (for someone) to understand: *Her attitude puzzled him*; (with **out**) to think long and carefully (about) and *usu* solve a problem. – *noun* a difficulty which causes much thought; a problem, a kind of toy or riddle to test one's thinking, knowledge or skill: *a crossword puzzle: a jigsaw puzzle*.

PVC *abbreviation* polyvinyl chloride.

pygmy or **pigmy** (*plural* **pygmies** or **pigmies**) *noun* one of a race of very small human beings.

pyjamas *noun plural* a sleeping suit consisting of trousers and a jacket.

pylon *noun* a high, tower-like steel construction for supporting electric power cables; a guiding mark at an airfield.

pyramid *noun* a solid shape having flat sides which come to a point at the top; something built in this shape, *esp* one of these used as tombs in ancient Egypt.

pyre *noun* a pile of wood on which a dead body is burned.

Pyrex® *noun* a type of glassware for cooking that will withstand heat.

pyrotechnics *noun* (a display of) fireworks.

Pyrrhic: Pyrrhic victory *noun* a victory gained at so great a cost that it is equal to a defeat.

python *noun* a type of large, non-poisonous snake which crushes its victims.

Q

QC *abbreviation* Queen's Counsel.

qt *abbreviation* quart; quiet.

quack *noun* the cry of a duck; a person who claims to have skill and knowledge (*esp* in medicine) that he does not possess. – *verb* to make the noise of a duck.

quad *noun* short for **quadruplet**; short for **quadrangle**.

quadr(i)- *prefix* four.

quadrangle *noun* (in mathematics) a figure having four equal sides and angles; a four-sided courtyard surrounded by buildings, *esp* in a school, college *etc*. – *adjective* **quadrangular**.

quadrant *noun* one quarter of the circumference or area of a circle; an instrument used in astronomy, navigation *etc* for measuring heights.

quadrennial *adjective* happening *etc* every four years.

quadrilateral *noun* a four-sided figure or area.

quadrille *noun* a dance for four couples arranged to form a square.

quadruped *noun* any four-footed animal.

quadruple *adjective* four times as much or many; made up of four parts. – *verb* to make or become four times greater: *He quadrupled the price*. – *noun* **quadruplet** one of four children born of one mother at one birth.

quaff *verb* to drink up eagerly.

quagmire *noun* wet, boggy ground.

quail *verb* to shrink back in fear. – *noun* a type of small bird like a partridge.

quaint *adjective* pleasantly odd, unusual, *esp* because of being old-fashioned.

quake *verb* (*present participle* **quaking**) to shake, tremble, *esp* with fear.

qualify *verb* to (cause to) become fit or suitable to follow a profession or trade *etc*, or to hold a position; to prove oneself fit for this, *esp* by passing a test; to reach a certain standard of knowledge or ability; to lessen the force of a statement by adding something that makes it less strong: *That's good – no, I'd better qualify that – quite good.* – *noun* **qualification** the act of qualifying; something which qualifies (*eg* a statement); a skill or achievement that makes a person suitable or fit for a job *etc*. – *adjective* **qualified** having the necessary qualification for a job *etc*.

quality *noun* (*plural* **qualities**) an outstanding feature of a person or thing: *Kindness is a quality admired by all*; degree of worth: *cloth of poor quality*. – *adjective* **qualitative** having to do with quality rather than quantity.

qualm *noun* doubt about whether one is doing right.

quandary *noun* (*plural* **quandaries**) a state of uncertainty; a situation in which it is difficult to decide what to do.

quango *noun* (*plural* **quangos**) an official body, funded and appointed by government, that supervises some part of national activity or culture *etc*.

quantity *noun* (*plural* **quantities**) amount: *a large quantity of paper*; a symbol which represents an amount: *x is the unknown quantity*. – *adjective* **quantitative** having to do with quantity, not quality.

quarantine *noun* the (period of) keeping apart of people or animals who might be carrying an infectious disease: *My dog was in quarantine for six months*; the state of being kept apart for this reason. – *verb* to put in quarantine.

quarrel *noun* an angry disagreement or argument. – *verb* (*past tense* **quarrelled**) to disagree violently or argue angrily (with); to find fault (with a person or action). – *adjective* **quarrelsome** fond of quarrelling, inclined to quarrel.

quarry *noun* (*plural* **quarries**) a pit or other place from which stone is taken for building *etc*; a hunted animal; an intended victim; anything eagerly looked for, chased *etc*. – *verb* (*past tense* **quarried**) to dig (stone *etc*) from a quarry.

quart *noun* a measure of liquids, 1·136 litre (2 pints).

quarter *noun* any one of four equal parts (of a thing); a fourth part of a year (three months); direction: *No help came from any quarter*; a district: *in a poor quarter of the city*; mercy shown to an enemy: *No quarter was given by either side*; (*plural*) lodgings (*esp* for soldiers). – *verb* to divide into four equal parts; to place (*esp* soldiers) in lodgings. – *noun* **quarter-deck** the part of the upper deck of a ship between the stern and the mast nearest it. – *noun* **quarter-final** a match in a competition immediately before a semi-final. – Also *adjective*. – *adjective, adverb* **quarterly** (happening *etc*) every three months. – *noun* (*plural* **quarterlies**) a magazine *etc* published every three months. – *noun* **quartermaster** an officer who looks after the lodging of soldiers and their supplies.

quartet *noun* a group of four players or singers; a piece of music written for such a group.

quartz *noun* a kind of hard substance often in crystal form, found in rocks.

quasar *noun* a star-like object (not really a star) which gives out light and radar waves.

quash *noun* to crush, put down (*eg* a rebellion); to wipe out, annul (*eg* a judge's decision).

quasi- *prefix* apparently or to some extent, but not completely: *quasi-historical*.

quaver *verb* to shake, tremble; to speak or sing in a shaking voice. – *noun* a trembling of the voice; (in music) a note equal to half a crotchet in length.

quay *kē, n* a solid landing place, built for the loading and unloading of boats.

queasy *adjective* as if about to vomit, sick; easily shocked or disgusted. – *noun* **queasiness.**

queen *noun* a female ruler; the wife of a king; the most powerful piece in chess; a high value of playing-card with a picture of a queen; the egg-laying female of certain kinds of insect (*esp* bees, ants and wasps). – *adjective* **queenly** of or like a queen – *noun* **queen mother** the mother of the reigning king or queen who was once herself queen.

queer *adjective* odd, strange. – *noun, adjective* (*coll*) used offensively, (a) homosexual.

quell *verb* to crush (a rebellion *etc*); to remove (fears, suspicions *etc*).

quench *verb* to drink and so satisfy (one's thirst); to put out (*eg* a fire).

querulous *adjective* complaining.

query *noun* (*plural* **queries**) a question mark(?). – *verb* (*past tense* **queried**) to question (*eg* a statement).

quest *noun* a search.

question *noun* something requiring an answer (*eg* 'Where are you going?'); a subject, matter *etc*: *the energy question: a question of ability*; a matter for dispute or doubt: *There's no question of him leaving.* – *verb* to ask questions of (a person); to express doubt about. – *adjective* **questionable** doubtful. – *noun* **question mark** in writing, a mark (?) put after a question. – *noun* **questionnaire** a written list of questions to be answered by a series of people to provide information for a (statistical) report or survey. – **out of the question** not even to be considered, unthinkable.

queue *noun* a line of people waiting (*eg* for a bus). – *verb* to stand in, or form, a queue.

quibble *verb* to avoid an important part of an argument *eg* by quarrelling over details. – Also *noun*.

quiche *kēsh*, *noun* an open pastry case filled with beaten eggs, cheese *etc* and baked.

quick *adjective* done or happening in a short time; acting without delay, fast-moving: *a quick brain.* – *noun* a very tender part of the body, *esp* under the nails; (*old*) (with **the**) the living. – *verb* **quicken** to speed up, become or make faster. – *noun* **quicklime** lime which has not been mixed with water. – *adverb* **quickly** (*coll* **quick**) without delay, rapidly. – *noun* **quicksand** sand that sucks in anyone who stands on it. – *noun* **quicksilver** mercury. – *adjective* **quick-tempered** easily made angry.

quid *noun* (*slang*) a pound (£1).

quiescent *adjective* not active.

quiet *adjective* making little or no noise; calm: *a quiet life.* – *noun* the state of being quiet; lack of noise, peace. – *verb* to make or become quiet. – *verb* **quieten** to make or become quiet. – *noun* **quietness**.

quill *noun* a large feather, *esp* the feather of a goose or other bird made into a pen; one of the sharp spines of certain animals (*eg* the porcupine).

quilt *noun* a bedcover filled with down, feathers *etc*. – *adjective* **quilted** (of clothes) made of two layers of material with padding or stuffing between them.

quin short for **quintuplet**.

quince *noun* a type of pear-like fruit with a sharp taste, used in jams *etc*.

quinine *noun* a bitter drug taken from the bark of a type of tree, used as a medicine, *esp* for malaria.

quinquennial *adjective* happening once every five years; lasting five years.

quintessence *noun* the most important part of anything; the purest part or form of something. – *adjective* **quintessential**.

quintet *noun* a group of five players or singers; a piece of music written for such a group.

quintuplet *noun* one of five children born to a mother at the same time.

quip *noun* a witty remark or reply. – Also *verb* (*past tense* **quipped**).

quire *noun* a set of 24 sheets of paper.

quirk *noun* an odd feature of (a person's) behaviour; a trick or sudden turn (*esp* of fate). – *adjective* **quirky**.

quit *verb* (*past tense* **quitted** or **quit**) to give up, stop: *I'm going to quit smoking*; (*coll*) to leave, resign from (a job). – **be quits** to be even with each other.

quite *adverb* completely, entirely: *quite empty*; fairly, moderately: *quite warm*.

quiver *noun* a case for arrows; a tremble, shake. – *verb* to tremble, shake.

quixotic *adjective* having noble but foolish and unrealistic aims which cannot be carried out.

quiz *verb* (*past tense* **quizzed**) to question. – *noun* (*plural* **quizzes**) a competition to test knowledge. – *adjective* **quizzical** (of a look *etc*) as if asking a question, *esp* humorously or mockingly.

quoits *noun* a game in which heavy flat rings (**quoits**) are thrown on to small rods.

quorum *noun* the least number of people who must be present at a meeting before any business can be done.

quota *noun* a part or share to be given or received by each member of a group.

quote *verb* to repeat the words of (anyone) exactly as they were said or written; to state (a price for something). – *noun* **quotation** the act of repeating something said or written; the words repeated; a price stated. – *noun plural* **quotation marks** marks used in writing to show that someone's words are being repeated exactly (*eg* He said 'I'm going out.').

quoth *verb* (*old*) said: *'The stagecoach awaits,' quoth he.*

quotient *noun* the result obtained by dividing one number by another: *4 is the quotient when 12 is divided by 3.*

qv *abbreviation* which see (*quod vide* [L]).

qwerty *noun* (*plural* **qwertys**) a standard arrangement of keys on a typewriter keyboard; a keyboard with keys set out in the standard arrangement. – Also *adjective*.

R

R *abbreviation* King or Queen (*rex* or *regina* [L]).
® registered trade mark.

RA *abbreviation* Royal Academy.

rabbi *noun* (*plural* **rabbis**) a Jewish priest or teacher of the law.

rabbit *noun* a type of small, burrowing, long-eared animal.

rabble *noun* a disorderly, noisy crowd.

rabid *adjective* (of dogs) suffering from **rabies**, a disease which causes madness; violently enthusiastic or extreme: *a rabid nationalist.*

raccoon or **racoon** *noun* a type of small furry animal of N. America.

race[1] *noun* a group of living beings with the same ancestors and physical characteristics; the state of belonging to a particular one of these groups; descent: *of noble race.* – *adjective* **racial** of or according to race. – *noun* **racialism** the belief that some races of men are better than others; prejudice on the grounds of race. – *noun* **racialist** a person who believes in, or practises, racialism. – Also *adjective.* – *noun* **racism** racialism; the (political) belief that ability *etc* is determined by one's race. – *noun* **racist** a person who believes in or practises racism. – Also *adjective.*

race[2] *noun* a competition to find the fastest (person, animal, vehicle *etc*). – *verb* to run fast; to take part in a race. – *noun* **racecourse** or **racetrack** a course over which races are run. – *noun* **racehorse** a horse bred and used for racing. – *adjective* **racy** (of stories) full of action (often involving sexual exploits).

dividing one number by another: *4 is the quotient when 12 is divided by 3.*

rack *noun* a framework for holding objects (*eg* letters, plates, hats *etc*); (*hist*) an instrument for torturing victims by stretching the joints; a bar with teeth which fits into and moves a toothed wheel *etc*. – **rack and ruin** a state of neglect and decay; **rack one's brains** to think hard (about something).

racket[1] or **racquet** *noun* a kind of bat made up of a strong frame strung with nylon *etc* for playing tennis, badminton *etc*; (*plural*) a form of tennis played against a wall.

racket[2] *noun* great noise; a dishonest way of making a profit. – *noun* **racketeer** a person who makes money dishonestly.

raconteur *noun* a person who tells stories (*esp* in an entertaining way).

racoon *see* **raccoon.**

racquet *see* **racket.**

RADA *abbreviation* Royal Academy of Dramatic Art.

radar *noun* a method of detecting solid objects using radio waves which bounce back off the object and form a picture of it on a screen.

radiant *adjective* sending out rays of light, heat *etc*; showing joy and happiness: *a radiant smile.* – *noun* **radiance** brightness; splendour.

radiate *verb* to send out rays of light, heat *etc*; to spread out or send out from a centre. – *noun* **radiation** the act of radiating; the giving off of rays of light, heat *etc* or of those from radioactive substances; radioactivity. – *noun* **radiator** any of various devices (*esp* a series of connected hot-water pipes) which send out heat; the part of a motor car which cools the engine.

radical *adjective* thorough: *a radical change*; basic, deep-seated: *radical differences*; (in politics) wishing for, involving *etc* great changes in the method of government. – *noun* a person who has radical political views.

radio *noun* (*plural* **radios**) (an apparatus for) the sending and receiving of signals by means of electromagnetic waves. – *verb* (*past tense* **radioed**) to send a message to (a person) in this way. – *adjective* **radioactive** (of some metals *etc*) giving off rays which are often dangerous but which can be used in medicine. – *noun* **radioactivity**. – *noun* **radiography** photography of the interior of the body *etc* by X-rays *etc*. – *noun* **radiology** the science of radioactive substances and radiation; (the branch of medicine involving) the use of these (*eg* X-rays and radium). – *noun* **radiotherapy** the treatment of certain diseases by X-rays or radioactive substances.

radish *noun* (*plural* **radishes**) a type of plant with a sharp-tasting root, eaten raw in salads.

radium *noun* an element, a radioactive metal used in radiotherapy.

radius *noun* (*plural* **radii**) a straight line from the centre to the circumference of a circle; an area within a certain distance from a central point.

RAF *abbreviation* Royal Air Force.

raffia *noun* strips of fibre from the leaves of a type of palm tree, used in weaving mats *etc*.

raffle *noun* a way of raising money by selling numbered tickets, one or more of which wins a prize. – *verb* to give as a prize in a raffle.

raft *noun* a number of logs *etc* fastened together and used as a boat.

rafter *noun* one of the sloping beams supporting a roof.

rag *noun* a torn or worn piece of cloth; (*plural*) worn-out, shabby clothes. – *adjective* made of rags: *a rag doll*. – *verb* (*past tense* **ragged**) to tease or play tricks on (someone). – *adjective* **ragged** in torn, shabby clothes; torn and tattered.

ragamuffin *noun* a ragged, dirty, *usu* young, person.

rage *noun* great anger, fury. – *verb* to be violently angry; to be violent (*eg* of a storm, an argument, a battle). – **all the rage** very fashionable or popular.

ragwort *noun* a large coarse weed with a yellow flower.

raid *noun* a short, sudden, *usu* unexpected attack; an unexpected visit by the police (to catch a criminal, recover stolen goods *etc*). – Also *verb*. – *noun* **raider**.

rail *noun* a bar of metal used in fences *etc*; (*plural*) strips of steel which form the track on which trains run; the railway: *I came here by rail*. – *verb* (with **against, at**) to speak angrily or bitterly. – *noun* **railing** a fence or barrier of rails. – *noun* **railway** or (*US*) **railroad** a track laid with steel rails on which trains run.

raiment *noun* (*old*) clothing.

rain *noun* water falling from the clouds in drops; a great number (of things) falling. – *verb* to pour or fall in drops: *It's raining today.* – *noun* **rainbow** the brilliant coloured bow or arch sometimes to be seen in the sky opposite the sun when rain is falling; a member of the most junior branch of the Girl Guides. – *noun* **raincoat** a waterproof coat to keep out the rain. – *noun* **rainfall** the amount of rain that falls in a certain time. – *noun* **rain-forest** tropical forest with very heavy rainfall. – *adjective* **rainy** full of rain: *rainy skies*; showery, wet: *a rainy day*.

raise *verb* to lift up: *raise the flag*; to cause to rise, make higher: *raise the price*; to bring up (a subject) for consideration; to bring up (a child, family *etc*); to breed or grow (*eg* pigs, crops); to collect, get together (a sum of money).

raisin *noun* a dried grape.

rajah *noun* an Indian prince.

rake *noun* a tool, like a large comb with a long handle, for smoothing earth, gathering hay *etc*; (*usu old*) a person who lives an immoral life. – *verb* to draw a rake over; to scrape (together); to aim gunfire at (*eg* a ship) from one end to the other. – *adjective* **rakish** at a slanting, jaunty angle.

rally *verb* (*past tense* **rallied**) to gather again: *The general rallied his troops after the defeat*; to come together for a joint action or effort: *The club's supporters rallied to save it*; to recover from an illness. – *noun* (*plural* **rallies**) the act of rallying; a gathering; a (political) mass meeting; an improvement in health after an illness; (in tennis *etc*) a long series of shots before the point is won or lost; a competition to test driving skills and vehicles over an unknown route. – *noun* **rallying** long-distance motor-racing over public roads.

RAM *abbreviation (comput)* random access memory.

ram *noun* a male sheep; something heavy, *esp* as part of a machine, for ramming. – *verb (past tense* **rammed)** to press or push down hard; (of ships, cars *etc*) to run into and cause damage to: *The destroyer rammed the submarine.*

Ramadan *noun* the ninth month of the Muslim calendar, the month of fasting by day; the fast itself.

ramble *verb* to walk about for pleasure, *esp* in the countryside; to speak in an aimless or confused way. – *noun* a walk (*esp* in the countryside) for pleasure. – *noun* **rambler** a person who rambles; a climbing rose or other plant.

ramekin *noun* a baked mixture of cheese and eggs; a baking dish for one person.

ramification *noun* a branch or part of a subject, plot (of a play, book) *etc*; a consequence (*esp* indirect and one of several).

ramp *noun* a sloping surface (*eg* of a road).

rampage *verb* to rush about angrily or violently. – **on the rampage** rampaging.

rampant *adjective* widespread and uncontrolled: *Vandalism is rampant in the city*; (in heraldry) standing on the left hind leg: *lion rampant.*

rampart *noun* a mound or wall built as a defence.

ramshackle *adjective* badly made, falling to pieces.

ran *see* **run.**

ranch *noun (plural* **ranches)** (*esp* in America) a farm for rearing cattle or horses.

rancid *adjective* (*esp* of butter) smelling or tasting stale.

rancour *noun* ill-will, hatred. – *adjective* **rancorous.**

rand *noun* the standard unit of S. African money.

R and B *abbreviation* rhythm and blues.

R and D *abbreviation* research and development.

random *adjective* done *etc* without any aim or plan in mind, chance: *a random sample.* – **at random** without any plan or purpose; **random access memory** a computer memory in which data can be directly located.

randy *adjective* lustful.

range *noun* a line or row: *a range of mountains*; extent, number: *a wide range of goods*; a piece of ground with targets where shooting, archery *etc* is practised; the distance which an object can be thrown, sound can be heard *etc*; the distance between the top and bottom notes of a voice *etc*; a large kitchen stove with a flat top. – *verb* to set in a row or in order; to wander (over); to stretch, extend: *His kingdom ranged from the Trent to the Humber.* – *noun* **ranger** a keeper who looks after a forest or park. – *noun* **Ranger Guide** an older member of the Girl Guide movement.

rank *noun* a row or line (*esp* of soldiers); class or order: *the upper ranks of society*: *the rank of captain*; (*plural*) private soldiers (not officers). – *verb* to place in order (of importance, merit *etc*); to have a place in an order: *Apes rank above dogs in intelligence.* – *adjective* (of plants *etc*) growing too plentifully; having a strong, unpleasant taste or smell; absolute: *rank nonsense.* – **rank and file** soldiers of the rank of private; ordinary people, the majority.

rankle *verb* to cause lasting annoyance, bitterness *etc*.

ransack *verb* to search thoroughly; to plunder.

ransom *noun* the price paid for the freeing of a captive. – *verb* to pay money to free (a captive).

rant *verb* to talk foolishly and angrily for a long time. – *noun* **ranting.**

rap *noun* a sharp blow or knock. – *verb (past tense* **rapped)** (often with **on**) to strike with a quick, sharp blow; (with **out**) to speak hastily.

rapacious *adjective* greedy, eager to seize as much as possible.

rape *verb* to have sexual intercourse with (someone) against their will (*usu* by force). – *noun* the act of raping; the act of seizing and carrying off by force; a type of plant like the turnip whose seeds give oil.

rapid *adjective* quick, fast: *a rapid rise to fame.* – *noun plural* a part in a river where the current flows swiftly. – noun **rapidity** swiftness.

rapier noun a type of light sword with a narrow blade.

rapt adjective having the mind etc fully occupied: rapt attention.

rapture noun great delight. – adjective **rapturous**.

rare adjective seldom found, uncommon; (of meat) lightly cooked. – verb **rarefy** or **rarify** (past tense **rarefied** or **rarified**) to make thin, less dense. – noun **rarity** (plural **rarities**) something uncommon; uncommonness.

raring: raring to go very keen to go, start etc.

rascal noun a naughty or wicked person.

rash adjective acting, or done, without thought. – noun redness or outbreak of spots on the skin. – noun **rashness** the state of being rash.

rasher noun a thin slice (of bacon or ham).

rasp noun a coarse file; a rough, grating sound. – verb to rub with a file; to make a rough, grating noise; to say in a rough voice. – adjective **rasping** (of a sound, voice) rough and unpleasant.

raspberry noun a type of red berry similar to a blackberry, or the bush which bears it.

rat noun a kind of gnawing animal, larger than a mouse. – verb (past tense **ratted**) to hunt or kill rats. – noun **rat-race** a fierce, unending competition for success, wealth etc. – adjective **ratty** irritable. – **rat on** to inform against; to desert.

ratchet noun (a wheel with a toothed edge and) a catch allowing winding in one direction only (eg in a watch); a toothed wheel (also **ratchet-wheel**).

rate noun the frequency with which something happens or is done: a high rate of road accidents; speed: speak at a tremendous rate; level of cost, price etc: paid at a higher rate; (usu plural) the sum of money to be paid by the owner of a house (before this charge was replaced by the community charge), shop etc to pay for local public services. – verb to work out the value of (for taxation etc); to value: I don't rate his work very highly. – noun **rat(e)able value** a value of a shop etc used to work out the rates to be paid on it. – **rate cap** to set an upper limit on the rates that can be levied by a local authority. – noun **rate-capping**.

rather adverb somewhat, fairly: It's rather cold today; more willingly: I'd rather talk about it now than later; more correctly speaking: He agreed, or rather he didn't say no.

ratify verb (past tense **ratified**) to approve officially and formally: Parliament ratified the treaty. – noun **ratification**.

rating noun in the navy, a sailor below the rank of an officer.

ratio noun (past tense **ratios**) the proportion of one thing to another: a ratio of two girls to one boy in the class.

ration noun a measured amount of food given out at intervals to a person or animal; an allowance. – verb to deal out (eg food) in measured amounts; to allow only a certain amount to (a person etc).

rational adjective able to reason; sensible; based on reason: rational arguments. – verb **rationalize** verb to think up a good reason for (an action or feeling) so as not to feel guilty about it. – noun **rationalization**.

rattle verb to (make to) give out short, sharp, repeated sounds: The coins rattled in the tin when he shook it; (usu with **off**) to speak quickly. – noun a sharp noise, quickly repeated; a toy or instrument which makes such a sound. – noun **rattlesnake** or **rattler** a type of poisonous snake having bony rings on its tail which rattle when shaken.

ratty see **rat**.

raucous adjective hoarse, harsh: a raucous voice.

ravage verb to cause destruction or damage in, plunder. – noun plural damaging effects: The ravages of time had affected her beauty.

rave verb to talk wildly, as if mad; (coll) to talk very enthusiastically (about). – noun, adjective **raving**.

raven noun a type of large black bird of the crow family. – adjective (of hair) black and glossy.

ravenous adjective very hungry.

ravine noun a deep, narrow valley between hills.

ravioli noun little pasta cases with savoury fillings.

ravish verb to plunder; to rape; to fill with delight. – adjective **ravishing** filling with delight.

raw *adjective* not cooked: *raw onions*; not prepared, not refined *etc*, in its natural state: *raw cotton*; (of weather) cold; sore. – **a raw deal** unjust treatment.

ray *noun* a line of light, heat *etc*; a small degree or amount: *a ray of hope*; one of several lines going outwards from a centre; a kind of flat-bodied fish.

rayon *noun* a type of artificial silk.

raze *verb* to destroy, knock flat (a town, house *etc*).

razor *noun* a sharp-edged instrument for shaving. – *noun* **razorbill** a type of seabird of the auk family. – *noun* **razor-fish** a type of long narrow shellfish.

RC *abbreviation* Roman Catholic.

re *preposition* concerning, about.

re- *prefix* again, once more, as in **recreate**; back, as in **reclaim**.

reach *verb* to arrive at: *We reached the summit of the hill. Your message never reached me*; to stretch out (the hand) so as to touch *etc*: *I couldn't reach the top shelf*; to extend: *His influence reached as far as the next town*. – *noun* a distance that can be travelled easily: *within reach of home*; the distance one can stretch one's arm; a straight part of a stream or river between bends.

react *verb* to act or behave in response to something done or said; to undergo a chemical change: *Metals react with sulphuric acid*. – *noun* **reaction** behaviour as a result of action; a chemical change; a (movement for a) return to things as they were: *a reaction against Victorian morality*. – *adjective* **reactionary** favouring a return to old ways, laws *etc*. – Also *noun* (*plural* **reactionaries**).

read *verb* (*past tense* **read**) to look at and understand, or say aloud (written or printed words); to study a subject (*esp* in a university or college or for a profession): *He is reading law*. – *adjective* **readable** quite interesting. – *noun* **reader** a person who reads (books *etc*); a person who reads manuscripts of books *etc* for a publisher; a senior university lecturer; a reading book (*esp* for children). – *noun* **read-out** (the retrieval of) data from a computer *etc*; data from a radio transmitter. – **read only memory** (*comput*) a memory device that can only be read, not written to.

ready *adjective* prepared: *packed and ready to go*; willing: *always ready to help*; quick: too ready to find fault; available (for use *etc*): *Your coat is ready for collection*. – *noun* **readiness**. – *adverb* **readily** easily; willingly. – *adjective* **readymade** (*esp* of clothes) made for sale to anyone whom they will fit or suit, not made specially for one person.

real *adjective* actually existing, not imagined; not imitation, genuine: *real leather*; sincere: *a real love of art*. – *noun* **realism** the showing or viewing of things as they really are. – *noun* **realist** a person who claims to see life as it really is. – *adjective* **realistic** life-like; viewing things as they really are. – *noun* **reality** (*plural* **realities**) that which is real and not imaginary; truth. – *adverb* **really** in fact; very: *really dark hair*.

realize *verb* to come to understand, know: *I never realized you were here*; to make real, accomplish, fulfil: *The soldier realized his ambition when he became a general*; get (money) for: *He realized £16 000 on the sale of his house*. – *noun* **realization**.

realm *noun* a kingdom, a country; an area of activity, interest *etc*: *the realm of sport*.

ream *noun* a measure for paper, 20 quires; (*plural*) a large quantity (*esp* of paper): *She wrote reams in her English exam*.

reap *verb* to cut and gather (corn *etc*); to gain: *He reaped the benefit of his hard work*. – *noun* **reaper** a person who reaps; a machine for reaping.

rear *noun* the back part (of anything); the last part of an army or fleet. – *verb* to bring up (children); to breed (animals); (of animals) to stand on the hindlegs. – *noun* **rear-admiral** an officer who commands the rear division of the fleet. – *noun* **rearguard** troops which protect the rear of an army. – **bring up the rear** to come or be last (*eg* in a line of walkers).

reason *noun* cause, excuse: *What is the reason for this noise?*; purpose: *What is your reason for going to London?*; the power of the mind to form opinions, judge right and truth *etc*; common sense. – *verb* to think out (opinions *etc*); (with **with**) to try to persuade (a person) by arguing. – *adjective* **reasonable** sensible; fair.

reassure *verb* to take away (a person's) doubts or fears. – *noun* **reassurance**.

rebate *noun* a part of a payment or tax which is given back to the payer.

rebel *noun* a person who opposes or fights against those in power. – *verb* (*past tense*

rebelled) to take up arms against or oppose those in power. – *noun* **rebellion** an open or armed fight against those in power; a refusal to obey. – *adjective* **rebellious**.

rebound *verb* to bounce back: *The ball rebounded off the wall.* – *noun* the act of rebounding; a reaction following an emotional situation or crisis.

rebuff *noun* a blunt refusal or rejection. – Also *verb*.

rebuke *verb* to scold, blame. – *noun* a scolding.

rebut *verb* (*past tense* **rebutted**) to deny (what has been said). – *noun* **rebuttal**.

recalcitrant *adjective* stubborn; disobedient. – *noun* **recalcitrance**.

recall *verb* to call back: *The soldier was recalled to headquarters;* to remember. – *noun* a signal or message to return; the act of recalling or remembering.

recant *verb* to take back what one has said; to reject publicly one's beliefs. – *noun* **recantation**.

recap *noun* or *verb* (*past tense* **recapped**) short for **recapitulation** or **recapitulate**.

recapitulate *verb* to go over again quickly the chief points of anything (*eg* a discussion). – *noun* **recapitulation**.

recapture *verb* to capture (what has escaped or been lost).

recast *verb* (*past tense* **recast**) to fashion or shape in a new form.

recede *verb* to go back; to become more distant; to slope backwards. – *adjective* **receding** going or sloping backwards; becoming more distant.

receipt *noun* the act of receiving (*esp* money or goods); a written note saying that money has been received.

receive *verb* to have something given or brought to one: *receive a gift: receive a letter;* to meet and welcome; to take goods, knowing them to be stolen. – *noun* **receiver** a person who receives stolen goods; the part of a telephone through which words are heard and into which they are spoken; an apparatus through which television or radio broadcasts are received.

recent *adjective* happening, done or made only a short time ago. – *adverb* **recently**.

receptacle *noun* an object to receive or hold things, a container.

reception *noun* a welcome: *The new boy had a good reception;* a large meeting to welcome guests; the quality of radio or television signals. – *noun* **receptionist** a person employed (*eg* in an office, hotel) to receive callers, answer the telephone *etc*. – *adjective* **receptive** quick to take in or accept ideas *etc*.

recess *noun* (*plural* **recesses**) part of a room set back from the rest, an alcove; the time during which parliament or the law-courts do not work; remote parts: *in the recesses of my memory*.

recession *noun* the act of moving back; a temporary fall in (a country's or world) business activities: *a trade recession*.

recipe *noun* instructions on how to prepare or cook a certain kind of food.

recipient *noun* someone who receives.

reciprocal *adjective* both given and received: *their reciprocal affection.* – *verb* **reciprocate** to feel or do the same in return: *I reciprocate his dislike of me.*

recite *verb* to repeat aloud from memory. – *noun* **recital** the act of reciting; a musical performance; the facts of a story told one after the other. – *noun* **recitation** a poem *etc* recited.

reckless *adjective* rash, careless. – *noun* **recklessness**.

reckon *verb* to count; to consider; to believe. – *noun* **reckoning** the settling of debts, grievances *etc*; payment for one's sins; a bill; a sum, calculation.

reclaim *verb* to claim back; to win back (land from the sea) by draining, building banks *etc*; to make waste land fit for use. – *noun* **reclamation**.

recline *verb* to lean or lie on one's back or side. – *adjective* **reclining**.

recluse *noun* a person who lives alone and avoids other people.

recognize *verb* to know from a previous meeting *etc*; to admit, acknowledge: *Everyone recognized his skill;* to show appreciation of: *They recognized his courage by giving him a medal.* – *adjective* **recognizable**. – *noun* **recognition** act of recognizing.

recoil *verb* to shrink back (in horror or fear); (of guns) to jump back after a shot is fired. – Also *noun*.

recollect *verb* to remember. – *noun* **recollection** the act or power of remembering; a memory, something remembered.

recommend *verb* to urge, adverbise: *I recommend that you take a long holiday*; to speak highly of. – *noun* **recommendation** the act of recommending; a point in favour of a person or thing.

recompense *verb* to pay money to or reward (a person) to make up for loss, inconvenience *etc*. – Also *noun*.

reconcile *verb* to bring together in friendship, after a quarrel; to show that two statements, facts *etc* do not contradict each other; (with **to**) to make to accept patiently: *I became reconciled to her absence*. – *noun* **reconciliation**.

recondite *adjective* secret, little-known.

reconnaissance *noun* a survey to obtain information (*esp* before a battle).

reconnoitre *verb* to make a reconnaissance of.

reconstitute *verb* to put back into its original form: *The dried milk must be reconstituted before use*; to make up, form in a different way.

record *verb* to write something down for future reference; to put (the sound of music, speech *etc*) on tape or disc so that it can be listened to later; to show, *esp* in writing (*eg* one's vote); (of an instrument) to show, register: *The thermometer recorded 30°C yesterday*. – *noun* a written report of any fact or facts; a round, flat piece of plastic on which sounds are recorded for playing on a record-player; (in races, games *etc*) the best known performance: *John holds the school record for the mile*. – *noun* **recorder** one who or that which records; a type of simple musical wind instrument; a judge in certain courts. – *noun* **recording** the act of recording; recorded music, speech *etc*. – *noun* **record-player** a machine for playing records. – **break** or **beat the record** to do better than any previous performance (in a sporting event); **off the record** (of a comment, remark *etc*) not to be made public.

recount *verb* to count again; to tell (the story of). – *noun* a second count (*eg* of votes).

recoup *verb* to make good, recover (expenses, losses *etc*).

recourse: have recourse to to make use of in an emergency.

recover *verb* to get possession of again; to become well again after an illness. – *adjective* **recoverable** able to be recovered. – *noun* **recovery** (*plural* **recoveries**) a return to health; the act of getting back (something lost *etc*).

re-cover *verb* to cover again.

re-create *verb* to describe or create again (something past). – *noun* **re-creation**.

recreation *noun* a pleasurable or refreshing activity (*eg* a sport, hobby) done in one's spare time.

recriminate *verb* to accuse one's accuser in return. – *noun* **recrimination** (often *pl*) accusation made by one who is himself accused. – *adjective* **recriminatory**.

recruit *noun* a newly-enlisted soldier, member *etc*. – *verb* to enlist (someone in an army, political party *etc*). – *noun* **recruitment**.

rectangle *noun* a four-sided figure with all its angles right angles and its opposite sides equal in length, an oblong. – *adjective* **rectangular**.

rectify *verb* (*past tense* **rectified**) to put right. – *adjective* **rectifiable**.

rectitude *noun* honesty; correctness of behaviour.

rector *noun* in the Church of England, a clergyman in charge of a parish; (in Scotland) the headmaster of some secondary schools; (in Scotland) a university official elected by the students. – *noun* **rectory** (*plural* **rectories**) the house of a Church of England rector.

rectum *noun* the lower part of the alimentary canal.

recumbent *adjective* lying down.

recuperate *verb* to recover strength or health. – *noun* **recuperation**.

recur *verb* (*past tense* **recurred**) to happen again. – *noun* **recurrence** the act of happening again: *a recurrence of his illness*. – *adjective* **recurrent** happening every so often.

recycle *verb* to remake into something different; to treat (material) by some process and use (it) again.

red *adjective, noun* (of) the colour of blood. – *noun* **redness**. – *noun* **redbreast** the robin. – *noun* **red deer** a type of reddish-brown deer. – *verb* **redden** to make or grow red. – *adverb* **red-handed** in the act of doing wrong: *The police caught the thief red-handed*. – *noun* **red herring** something mentioned to lead a discussion away from the main subject;

a false clue. – noun **Red Indian** a member of the N. American red-skinned race. – adjective **red-letter** (of a particular day) especially important or happy for some reason. – noun **red light** a danger signal; a signal to stop. – noun **redskin** a Red Indian. – noun **red tape** unnecessary and troublesome rules about how things are to be done. – noun **redwood** a type of American tree which grows to a great height. – **see red** to become very angry.

redeem verb to buy back (eg articles from a pawnbroker); to save from sin or condemnation; to make amends for. – noun **Redeemer** Jesus Christ. – adjective **redeeming** making up for other faults: Good spelling was the redeeming feature of his composition. – noun **redemption** the act of redeeming; the state of being redeemed.

redeploy verb to move (eg soldiers, workers) to a different place where they will be more useful.

redolent adjective sweet-smelling; smelling (of); suggestive, making one think (of): a house redolent of earlier times.

redouble verb to make twice as great: redouble your efforts.

redoubtable adjective brave, bold.

redress verb to set right, to make up for (a wrong etc). – noun something done or given to make up for a loss or wrong, compensation.

reduce verb to make smaller; to lessen; to bring to the point of by force of circumstances: He was reduced to begging in the streets; to bring (to a lower rank or state); to change into other terms: reduce pounds to pence. – adjective **reducible**. – noun **reduction**.

redundant adjective more than what is needed; (of a worker) no longer needed because of the lack of a suitable job – noun **redundance**. – noun **redundancy** (plural **redundancies**).

reed noun a kind of tall stiff grass growing in moist or marshy places; a part, originally made of reed, in certain wind instruments (eg the oboe) which vibrates when the instrument is played. – adjective **reedy** full of reeds; like a reed; sounding like a reed instrument: a reedy voice.

reef noun a chain of rocks lying at or near the surface of the sea. – noun **reef knot** a square, very secure knot.

reefer noun a short coat, as worn by sailors; (slang) a marijuana cigarette.

reek noun a strong (usu unpleasant) smell; smoke. – verb to send out smoke; to smell strongly.

reel noun a cylinder of plastic, metal or wood on which thread, cable, film, fishing lines etc may be wound; a length of cinema film; a lively Scottish or Irish dance. – verb to wind on a reel; (with **in**) to draw, pull in (a fish on a line); to stagger. – **reel off** to repeat or recite quickly, without pausing.

ref abbreviation referee; reference.

refectory noun (plural **refectories**) a dining hall, for monks, students etc.

refer verb (past tense **referred**) (with **to**) to mention; to turn (to) for information; to relate, apply (to); to direct (to) for information, consideration etc: I refer you to the managing director. – noun **referee** a person to whom a matter is taken for settlement; (in games) a judge; a person willing to provide a note about one's character etc. – n **reference** the act of referring; a mention; a note about a person's character, work etc. – noun **reference book** a book to be consulted for information, eg an encyclopaedia. – noun **reference library** a library of books to be looked at for information but not taken away.

referendum noun (plural **referenda** or **referendums**) a vote given by the people of a country about some important matter.

refine verb to purify; to improve, make more exact, elegant etc. – adjective **refined** purified; polite in one's manners, free of vulgarity. – noun **refinement** good manners, taste, learning; an improvement. – noun **refinery** (plural **refineries**) a place where sugar, oil etc are refined.

refit verb (past tense **refitted**) to repair damages (esp to a ship).

reflect verb to throw back (light or heat): The white sand reflected the sun's heat; to give an image of: reflected in the mirror; (with **on**) to throw blame: Her behaviour reflects on her mother; (with **on**) to think over something carefully. – noun **reflection** the act of throwing back (eg a ray of light, an image of a person etc in a mirror); the image of a person etc reflected in a mirror; blame, unfavourable criticism. – adjective **reflective** thoughtful. – noun **reflector** something (*eg* a piece of shiny metal or a piece of glass) which throws back light.

reflex *noun* (*plural* **reflexes**) an action which is automatic, not intended (*eg* jerking the leg when the kneecap is struck). – Also *adjective*.

reflexive *adjective* in grammar, showing that the object (**reflexive pronoun**) of the verb (**reflexive verb**) is the same as its subject (*eg* in 'He cut himself', *himself* is a *reflexive pronoun* and *cut* a *reflexive verb*).

reform *verb* to improve, remove faults from (a person, one's conduct, an organization *etc*); to give up bad habits, evil *etc*. – *noun* an improvement. – *noun* **reformation** a change for the better. – *n* **Reformation** the religious movement in the Christian Church in the 16th century from which the Protestant Church arose. – *noun* **reformer** a person who wishes to bring about improvements.

re-form *verb* to form again (*eg* a society).

refract *verb* to change the direction of (a ray of light). – *noun* **refraction.**

refractory *adjective* (of persons) unruly, not easily controlled.

refrain *noun* a chorus coming at the end of each verse of a song. – *verb* to keep oneself back (from doing something): *Please refrain from smoking.*

refresh *verb* to give new strength, power, or life to. – *adjective* **refreshing** bringing back strength; cooling. – *noun* **refreshment** that which refreshes (*eg* food and drink). – *noun* **refresher course** a course of study intended to keep up or increase skill or knowledge that one already has. – **refresh one's memory** to go over facts again so that they are clear in one's mind.

refrigerator *noun* a storage machine which keeps food cold and so prevents it from going bad. – *verb* **refrigerate.** – *noun* **refrigeration.**

refuel *verb* (*past tense* **refuelled**) to supply with, or take in, fresh fuel.

refuge *noun* a place of safety (from attack, danger *etc*). – *noun* **refugee** a person who seeks shelter (from persecution *etc*) in another country.

refund *verb* to pay back. – Also *noun.*

refuse¹ *verb* to say that one will not (do something): *He refused to leave the room*; to withhold, not to give (*eg* permission). – *noun* **refusal.**

refuse² *noun* that which is thrown aside as worthless, rubbish.

refute *verb* to prove wrong (something that has been said or written). – *noun* **refutation.**

regain *verb* to win back again; to get back to. *He jumped from the boat and regained the shore in ten minutes.*

regal *adjective* kingly, royal. – *noun plural* **regalia** certain marks or signs of royalty (*eg* crown and sceptre).

regale *verb* to entertain in a splendid way.

regard *verb* to look upon, consider: *I regard you as a nuisance*; to look at carefully; to pay attention to. – *noun* concern; affection; respect; (*plural*) good wishes. – *preposition* **regarding** concerning, to do with: *He received a reply regarding his application for a job.* – **regardless of** paying no care or attention to; **with** (or **in**) **regard to** concerning.

regatta *noun* a meeting for yacht or boat races.

regency *see* **regent.**

regenerate *verb* to make new and good again. – *noun* **regeneration.**

regent *noun* someone who governs in place of a king or queen. – *noun* **regency** (*plural* **regencies**) (a time of) rule by a regent.

reggae *noun* strongly rhythmic type of rock music, originally introduced from the West Indies.

regicide *noun* the killing of a king; one who kills a king.

régime or **regime** *noun* method or system of government or administration.

regimen *noun* diet and habits to be followed.

regiment *noun* a body of soldiers, commanded by a colonel. – *verb* to organize or control too strictly. – *adjective* **regimental** of a regiment. – *noun* **regimentation** too strict control *etc*.

region *noun* a stretch of land; an area or district. – *adjective* **regional.** – **in the region of** somewhere near (in position or amount): *in the region of the stomach.*

register *noun* a written list (*eg* of attendances at school, of people who have votes *etc*); the distance between the highest and lowest notes of a voice or instrument. – *verb* to write down, or have one's name put, in a register; to record, make (one's vote *etc*); to show, record: *A thermometer registers temperature.* – *noun* **registered letter** one insured against loss by the post office. – *noun* **registrar** a person whose duty it is to keep a register of births, deaths, marriages. – *noun* **registry** (*plural* **registries**) an office where a register is kept. – *noun* **registry office** one where records of births, marriages and deaths are kept and where marriages may be performed.

regret *verb* (*past tense* **regretted**) to be sorry about: *I regret any inconvenience you have suffered. I regret that I missed him*; to be sorry (to have to say something). – *noun* sorrow for anything. – *adjective* **regretful**. – *adjective* **regrettable** to be regretted, unwelcome.

regular *adjective* done according to rule or habit; usual; arranged in order; even: *regular teeth*; happening at certain fixed times. – *noun* a soldier of the regular army. – *noun* **regularity**. – *verb* **regulate** to control by rules; to adjust to a certain order or rate. – *noun* **regulation** a rule or order. – *noun* **regular army** the part of the army which is kept always in training, even in peacetime. – *n* **regulator** a person or thing that regulates.

regurgitate *verb* to bring back into the mouth after swallowing. – *noun* **regurgitation**.

rehabilitate *verb* to give back rights, powers or health to; to train or accustom (a disabled person *etc*) to live a normal life. – *noun* **rehabilitation**.

rehearsal *noun* a private practice of a play, concert *etc* before performance in public; any practice for a future event or action. – *verb* **rehearse** to practise beforehand; to tell (facts, events *etc*) in order.

reign *noun* rule; the time during which a king or queen rules. – *verb* to rule; to prevail: *Silence reigned at last.*

reimburse *verb* to pay (a person an amount) to cover expenses. – *noun* **reimbursement**.

rein *noun* one of two straps attached to a bridle for guiding a horse; (*plural*) a simple device for controlling a child when walking. – *verb* to control (with reins).

reincarnation *noun* the rebirth of the soul in another body after death.

reindeer *noun* (*plural* **reindeer**) a type of deer found in the far North.

reinforce *verb* to strengthen (*eg* an army with men, concrete with iron). – *noun* **reinforcement** the act of reinforcing; anything which strengthens.

reinstate *verb* to put back in a former position. – *noun* **reinstatement**.

reiterate *verb* to repeat, *esp* several times. – *noun* **reiteration**.

reject *verb* to throw away, cast aside; to refuse to take: *She rejected his offer of help*; to turn down (*eg* an application, request). – Also *noun*. – *noun* **rejection**.

rejoice *verb* to feel or show joy. – *noun* **rejoicing**.

rejoinder *noun* an answer to a reply.

rejuvenate *verb* to make young again. – *noun* **rejuvenation**.

relapse *verb* to fall back (*eg* into ill health, bad habits). – Also *noun*.

relate *verb* to show a connection between (two or more things); to tell (a story). – *adjective* **related** (often with **to**) of the same family (as): *I'm related to him*; connected. – *noun* **relation** a person who is of the same family, either by birth or marriage; a connection between two or more things. – *noun* **relationship** connection. – *noun* **relative** one who is of the same family *etc*. – *adjective* comparative: *the relative speeds of a car and a train.*

relax *verb* to become or make less tense; to slacken (*eg* one's grip or control); to make (laws, rules) less severe. – *noun* **relaxation** a slackening; rest from work: *He played tennis for relaxation.*

relay *verb* (*past tense* **relayed**) to receive and pass on (*eg* news, a message, a television programme). – *noun* the sending out of a radio or television broadcast received from another station; a fresh set of people *etc* to replace others at some job, task *etc*. – *noun* **relay race** a race in which members of each team take over from each other, each member running *etc* an arranged distance. – **in relays** in groups which take over from one another in doing something.

release *verb* to set free; to let go; to allow (news *etc*) to be made public. – Also *noun*.

relegate *verb* to put down (to a lower position, group *etc*); to leave (a task *etc* to someone else). – *noun* **relegation**.

relent *verb* to become less severe (with a person). – *adjective* **relentless** without pity; refusing to be turned from one's purpose.

relevant *adjective* having to do with what is being spoken about. – *noun* **relevance.**

reliable, reliance *see* **rely.**

relic *noun* something left over from a past time.

relief *noun* a lessening of pain or anxiety; release from a post or duty; person(s) taking over one's duty *etc*; help given to those in need: *famine relief*; the act of freeing (a town *etc*) from a siege; a way of carving or moulding in which the design stands out from its background. – *verb* **relieve** to lessen (pain or anxiety); to take over a duty from (someone else); to come to the help of (a town *etc* under attack).

religion *noun* belief in, or worship of, a god. – *adjective* **religious.**

relinquish *verb* to give up, abandon: *relinquish control.*

relish *verb* to enjoy; to like the taste of. – *noun* (*plural* **relishes**) enjoyment; flavour; something which gives flavour.

reluctant *adjective* unwilling. – *noun* **reluctance.**

rely *verb* (*past tense* **relied**) to have full trust in, depend (on). – *noun* **reliability** or **reliance** trust. – *adjective* **reliable** able to be trusted or counted on. – *adjective* **reliant.**

remain *verb* to stay, not to leave; to be left: *Only two tins of soup remained*; to be still (the same): *The problem remains unsolved.* – *noun* **remainder** that which is left behind after removal of the rest; (in arithmetic) the number left after subtraction or division. – *noun plural* **remains** that which is left; a dead body.

remand *verb* to put a person back in prison until more evidence is found. – **on remand** having been remanded.

remark *verb* to say; to comment (on); to notice. – *noun* something said. – *adjective* **remarkable** deserving notice, unusual.

remedy *noun* (*plural* **remedies**) a cure for an illness, evil *etc*. – *verb* to cure; to put right.

remember *verb* to keep in mind; to recall to the mind after having forgotten; to send one's best wishes (to): *Remember me to your mother*; to reward, give a present to: *He remembered her in his will.* – *noun* **remembrance** the act of remembering; memory; something given *etc* to remind someone of a person or an event, a keepsake, a souvenir; (*plural*) a friendly greeting.

remind *verb* to bring (something) back to a person's mind: *Remind me to post that letter*; to cause (someone) to think about (a person or thing) by resembling (the person or thing) in some way: *She reminds me of her sister. Her nose reminds me of a pig's snout.* – *noun* **reminder** one who or that which reminds.

reminiscence *noun* something (*eg* an event) remembered from the past; (*plural*) memories (*esp* when told or written). – *adjective* **reminiscent** reminding one of: *reminiscent of Paris*; in a mood to remember and think about past events *etc*. – *verb* **reminisce** to think and talk about things remembered from the past.

remiss *adjective* careless: *It was remiss of me to forget your birthday.*

remission *noun* the act of remitting; a shortening (of a person's prison sentence); (of a disease *etc*) a lessening in force or effect.

remit *verb* (*past tense* **remitted**) to pardon, excuse (a crime *etc*); to wipe out, cancel (a debt *etc*); to lessen, (cause to) become less intense; to send (money); to hand over (*eg* a prisoner to a higher court). – *noun* **remittance** the sending of money *etc esp* to a distance; the money sent.

remnant *noun* a small piece or small number of things left over from a larger piece or number.

remonstrate *verb* to make a protest: *He remonstrated with me about my extravagance.* – *noun* **remonstrance.**

remorse *noun* regret about something bad or wrong which one has done. – *adjective* **remorseful.** – *adjective* **remorseless** having no remorse; cruel.

remote *adjective* far away in time or place; far from any (other) village, town *etc*; slight: *a remote chance.*

remove *verb* to take (something) from its place; to dismiss (a person from a post); to take off (clothes *etc*); to get rid of: *I can't remove this stain from my skirt.* – *noun* a stage or degree away (from): *one remove from tyranny.* – *noun* **removal** the act of removing, *esp* of furniture *etc* to a new home. – *adjective* **removed** separated or distant (from); (of cousins) separated by a generation: *first cousin once removed* (*eg* a cousin's child).

remunerate *verb* to pay (someone) for something done. – *noun* **remuneration** pay, salary. – *adjective* **remunerative** profitable.

renal *adjective* of the kidneys.

rend *verb* (*past tense* **rent**) to tear (apart), divide.

render *verb* to give back (*eg* property); to give (*eg* thanks): to translate into another language; to perform (music *etc*); to cause to be: *His words rendered me speechless*. – *noun* **rendering** a translation; a performance.

rendezvous *ron'di-voo, noun* (*plural* **rendezvous**) a meeting place fixed beforehand; the meeting itself.

renegade *adjective, noun* (of) a person who deserts their own side, religion or beliefs.

renew *verb* to make as if new again; to begin again: *renew one's efforts*; to make usable for a further period of time (*eg* a driving licence); to replace: *renew the water in the tank*. – *noun* **renewal.**

rennet *noun* a substance used in curdling milk for making cheeses *etc*.

renounce *verb* to give up, *esp* publicly or formally: *He renounced his claim to the title*. – *noun* **renunciation.**

renovate *verb* to make (something) like new again, to mend. – *noun* **renovation.**

renown *noun* fame. – *adjective* **renowned** famous.

rent *noun* a tear, a split; a payment made for the use of a house, shop, land *etc*. – *verb see* **rend**; to pay or receive rent for a house *etc*. – *noun* **rental** money paid as rent. – *noun* **rent-boy** a young male homosexual prostitute. – **rent out** to give for use in return for money.

renunciation *see* **renounce.**

reorganize *verb* to put in a different order. – *noun* **reorganization.**

rep *noun* short for **representative** (salesman) or **repertory.**

repair *verb* to mend; to make up for (a wrong); (*old*) to go: *He repaired once more to his house*. – *noun* the condition in which a thing is: *The house is in bad repair*; the act or process of mending: *in need of repair*; a mended place. – *noun* **reparation** something which makes up for a wrong.

repartee *noun* a quick witty reply; an exchange of witty remarks between people; skill in witty conversation.

repast *noun* (*old*) a meal.

repatriate *verb* to send (someone) back to their own country. – *noun* **repatriation.**

repay *verb* (*past tense* **repaid**) to pay back; to give or do something in return: *He repaid her kindness with a gift*. – *noun* **repayment** the act of repaying; that which is paid back.

repeal *verb* to do away with, cancel (*esp* a law). – Also *noun*.

repeat *verb* to say or do over again; to say from memory; to tell, pass on (someone's words), sometimes when one ought not to. – *noun* something repeated (*eg* a television programme, a passage of music). – *adverb* **repeatedly** again and again. – *noun* **repeater** a gun which fires several shots. – *noun* **repetition** the act of repeating; something repeated. – *adjective* **repetitive** repeating (something) too often.

repel *verb* (*past tense* **repelled**) to drive back or away; to disgust. – *adjective* **repellent** disgusting. – *noun* something that drives away (something): *an insect repellent*.

repent *verb* to be sorry (for what one has done); (with **of**) to regret. – *noun* **repentance**. – *adjective* **repentant** repenting.

repercussion *noun* an indirect or resultant effect of something which has happened: *The event, though itself minor, had wide repercussions.*

repertoire *rep'èr-twär, noun* the range of works that a performer, singer, theatre company *etc* is able or ready to perform.

repertory *noun* (*plural* **repertories**) repertoire. – *noun* **repertory theatre** a theatre with a more or less permanent company which performs a series of plays.

repetition *see* **repeat.**

repetitive *see* **repeat.**

replace *verb* to put (something) back where it was; to put (something or someone) in place of another: *He replaced the cup he had broken with the new one.*

replenish *verb* to fill up one's supply (of something) again.

replete *adjective* full.

replica *noun* an exact copy (of a picture, a piece of furniture *etc*).

reply *verb* (*past tense* **replied**) to speak or act in answer to something. – *noun* (*plural* **replies**) an answer.

report *verb* to pass on news; to give a description (of an event *etc*); to tell about; to write down and take notes of (a speech, meeting *etc*) *esp* for a newspaper; to make a complaint against (*esp* to the police or the authorities). – *noun* a statement of facts; an account, description, *esp* in a newspaper or on radio or television; a rumour; a written description of a pupil's work; a loud noise, *esp* the sound made by the firing of a gun. – *noun* **reporter** a person who reports, *esp* one who writes articles for a newspaper *etc*.

repose *noun* sleep, rest. – *verb* to rest; to place (*eg* trust in a person). – *noun* **repository** (*plural* **repositories**) a place where things are stored *esp* for safe keeping.

reprehensible *adjective* deserving blame.

represent *verb* to speak or act on behalf of a person or a group of people: *He represents the tenants' association*; to stand for, to be a sign or symbol of: *Each letter represents a sound*; to claim to be: *He represents himself as an expert*; to explain, point out. – *noun* **representation** the act of representing or being represented; an image, picture; (often *pl*) a strong claim or appeal. – *adjective* **representative** typical, having the characteristics of all its kind: *a representative specimen*; standing or acting for another or others. – *noun* a person who acts or speaks on behalf of a group of people (*eg* in parliament, at a conference); a travelling salesman for a firm.

repress *verb* to keep down by force; to keep under control. – *noun* **repression**.

reprieve *verb* to pardon (a criminal); to give a period of freedom (from trouble, difficulty) to. – Also *noun*.

reprimand *verb* to scold severely. – Also *noun*.

reprint *verb* to print again; to print more copies of (a book *etc*). – *noun* another printing of a book.

reprisal *noun* the act of paying back wrong for wrong: *The attack was a reprisal for an earlier one by the other side*.

reproach *verb* to express disappointment or displeasure; to scold; to blame. – *noun* the act of reproaching; blame, discredit; something that brings blame or discredit: *This pile of rubbish is a reproach to the council*. – *adjective* **reproachful** showing that one blames: *a reproachful glance*.

reprobate *noun* a person of evil or immoral habits. – Also *adjective*.

reproduce *verb* to produce a copy of; (of humans, animals and plants) to produce (young, seeds *etc*). – *noun* **reproduction** the act or process of reproducing; something reproduced, a copy.

reproof *noun* a scolding, criticism for a fault or wrong. – *verb* **reprove** to scold, blame. – *adjective* **reproving**.

reptile *noun* any of the group of creeping, cold-blooded animals which includes snakes, lizards *etc*. – *adjective* **reptilian**.

republic *noun* a form of government in which power is in the hands of the people's elected representatives with a president instead of a king *etc*. – *adjective* **republican**. – *adjective*, *noun* **Republican** (*US*) (of, belonging to) one of the two chief political parties in the United States.

repudiate *verb* to refuse to acknowledge as one's own; to refuse to recognize or accept: *He repudiated the committee's suggestion*. – *noun* **repudiation**.

repugnant *adjective* hateful, distasteful. – *noun* **repugnance**.

repulse *verb* to drive back (an enemy *etc*); to reject, snub (a person). – Also *noun*. – *noun* **repulsion** disgust. – *adjective* **repulsive** causing disgust, loathsome.

reputation *noun* the opinion held by people in general of a particular person; good name. – *adjective* **reputable** having a good reputation, well thought of. – *noun* **repute** reputation. – *adjective* **reputed** considered, thought (to be something): *reputed to be dangerous*; supposed: *the reputed author of the book*. – *adverb* **reputedly** in the opinion of most people.

request *verb* to ask for. – *noun* the act of asking for (something); something asked for.

requiem *noun* a hymn or mass sung for the dead; the music for this.

require *verb* to need; to demand, order. – *noun* **requirement** something needed; a demand.

requisite *adjective* required; necessary. – *noun* something needed or necessary. – *noun* **requisition** a (formal) demand or request for supplies (*eg* for a school or an army). – Also *verb*.

requite *verb* to repay, give back in return; to repay or avenge (one action) by another. – *noun* **requital** payment in return.

rescind *ri-sind¹*, *verb* to do away with, cancel (an order or law).

rescue *verb* to save from a dangerous situation; to free from capture. – *noun* an act which saves (someone or something) from danger or capture.

research *noun* (*plural* **researches**) a close and careful (scientific) study or investigation to try to find out new facts (about something): *cancer research*. – *verb* to study carefully; (with **into**) to take part in such a study or investigation. – *noun* **researcher** a person who researches.

resemble *verb* to look like or be like: *He doesn't resemble his sister.* – *noun* **resemblance** likeness.

resent *verb* to feel injured, annoyed or insulted by. – *adjective* **resentful**. – *noun* **resentment** ill will, bitterness, annoyance.

reserve *verb* to set aside (for future or special use); to book, have kept for one (*eg* a seat, a table, a library book). – *noun* something reserved; (*esp plural*) troops or forces outside the regular army kept ready to help those already fighting; a piece of land set apart for some reason: *nature reserve*; the habit of not speaking or acting in an open friendly manner, shyness. – *noun* **reservation** the act of reserving, booking; an exception or condition: *He agreed to the plan, but with certain reservations*; doubt, objection: *I had reservations about his appointment*. – *adjective* **reserved** unwilling to speak one's thoughts openly or to behave in a friendly way; kept back for a particular person or purpose.

reservoir *noun* a place (*usu* a man-made lake) where water is kept in store.

reside *verb* to live, have one's home (in); (of power, authority *etc*) to be present in, be placed (in). – *noun* **residence** a house or other place (*esp* an impressive or large building) where one lives; the act of living in a place; the period of time one lives in a place. – *noun* **resident** a person whose home is in a particular place or area: *a resident of Blackpool*. – *adjective* living in (a place); living in, or having to live in, the place where one works: *resident caretaker*. – *adjective* **residential** (of an area) containing houses rather than shops, factories *etc*; providing living accommodation: *The university runs a residential course*.

residue *noun* what is left over. – *adjective* **residual**.

resign *verb* to give up (one's job, position *etc*). – *noun* **resignation** the act of resigning; a letter to say one is resigning; patient, calm acceptance of a situation. – *adjective* **resigned** patient, not actively complaining. – *adverb* **resignedly**. – **resign oneself to** to accept (a situation *etc*) with patience and calmness.

resilient *adjective* (of a person) readily recovering from misfortune, hurt *etc*; (of an object) readily recovering its original shape after being bent, twisted *etc*. – *noun* **resilience**.

resin *noun* a sticky substance produced by certain plants (*eg* firs, pines). – *adjective* **resinous**.

resist *verb* to struggle against, oppose (*esp* successfully); to stop oneself from (doing something). – *noun* **resistance** the act of resisting; any organized opposition to something (*esp* a force occupying a country); the ability of a substance to turn an electric current passing through it into heat.

resolute *adjective* determined, with mind made up. – *noun* **resolution** firmness or determination of mind or purpose; a firm decision (to do something); a proposal put before a meeting; an opinion or decision formally expressed by a group of people *eg* a public meeting.

resolve *verb* to decide firmly (to do something); to solve (a difficulty); to break up into parts. – *noun* a firm purpose.

resonate *verb* to echo. – *noun* **resonance** a deep, echoing tone. – *adjective* **resonant** echoing, resounding.

resort *verb* to begin to use *etc*, turn (to) *esp* in a difficulty: *Finally he had to resort to violence.* – *noun* a frequently visited place (*esp* for holidays). – **in the last resort** when all else fails.

resound *verb* to sound loudly; to echo. – *adjective* **resounding** echoing; thorough: *a resounding victory*.

resource *noun* (*usu plural*) a source or means of supplying what is required; (*usu plural*) a natural source of wealth in a country *etc*; (*plural*) money or other property; an ability to handle situations skilfully and cleverly. – *adjective* **resourceful** good at finding ways out of difficulties.

respect *verb* to show or feel a high regard or admiration for; to treat with care or consideration: *respect his wishes.* – *noun* high regard, esteem, admiration; consideration; a detail, way: *alike in some respects*; (*plural*) good wishes. – *noun* **respectability** the state of being respectable. – *adjective* **respectable** worthy of respect; having a good reputation; considerable, large, fairly good: *a respectable score.* – *adjective* **respectful** showing respect. – *adjective* **respective** belonging to each (person or thing mentioned) separately: *Peter and George went to their respective homes* (*eg* each went to his own home). – *adverb* **respectively** in the order given: *Peter, James and John were first, second and third respectively.* – **in respect of** concerning, as regards; **with respect to** with reference to.

respire *verb* to breathe. – *noun* **respiration** breathing. – *noun* **respirator** a mask worn over the mouth and nose to purify the air breathed in *eg* in the presence of gas; a device used to help very ill or injured people breathe, when they are unable to do so naturally.

respite *noun* a pause, rest: *no respite from work.*

resplendent *adjective* very bright or splendid in appearance.

respond *verb* to answer; to act or react in response to (something or an action): *The baby responded to her new toy with a smile. I smiled but she did not respond*; to show a reaction to *esp* as a sign of improvement: *He responded to treatment.* – *noun* **response** a reply; an action, feeling *etc* in return for or in answer to another action *etc*; the answer made to the priest during church services. – *adjective* **responsible** (sometimes with **for**) being the cause of: *responsible for this mess*; liable to be called to account for or blamed for (actions, standard of work *etc*) to (someone in authority): *He is responsible to the manager for the conduct of his staff*; involving the making of important decisions *etc*: *a responsible post*;

trustworthy. – *noun* **responsibility** (*plural* **responsibilities**). – *adjective* **responsive** quick to react *eg* to show interest, sympathy *etc*.

rest *noun* a pause or break in work; a sleep; a support or prop for something: *a book rest*; (with **the**) what is left, the remainder: *the rest of the meat*; all the other people not mentioned: *Jack went home but the rest went to the cinema.* – *verb* to stop working *etc* for a time; to be still; to sleep; to depend (on), be based on: *The case rests on your evidence*, to stop, develop no further: *I can't let the matter rest there*; to lean, lie or place on a support. – *adjective* **restful** relaxing; relaxed. – *adjective* **restive** restless, impatient; not easily managed or controlled. – *adjective* **restless** unable to keep or lie still; getting no rest; agitated. – **rest with** to be the duty, right or responsibility of: *The choice rests with you.*

restaurant *noun* a place where meals may be bought and eaten. – *noun* **restaurateur** the owner or manager of a restaurant.

restitution *noun* the act of giving back what has been lost or taken away; compensation for harm or injury done.

restive *see* **rest**.

restore *verb* to put or give back; to repair (a building, a painting *etc*) so that it looks as it used to; to cure (a person). – *noun* **restoration**.

restrain *verb* to hold back (from); to keep under control. – *noun* **restraint** the act of restraining; the state of being restrained; self-control.

restrict *verb* to limit, keep within the bounds of space, time, quantity *etc*: *There is only a restricted space available for parking cars*; (of an area *etc*) to make open only to certain people: *Only residents were able to enter the restricted area. The restricted zone is guarded by soldiers.* – *noun* **restriction** the act of restricting; something (*esp* a rule, law *etc*) which restricts. – *adjective* **restrictive** having the effect or aim of restricting.

result *noun* anything which is due to something already done, said *etc*; a consequence; the answer to a sum; (in games) the score. – *verb* (with **from**) to be the result or effect (of something done, said *etc*); (with **in**) to have as a result: *The match resulted in a draw.* – *adjective* **resultant**.

resume verb to begin again after a pause or interruption: resume a discussion; to take again: He resumed his seat by the fire. - noun **resumption.**

résumé rā'zü-mā, noun a summary; (US) a curriculum vitae.

resurgent adjective rising again. - noun **resurgence** a rising again into activity or prominence.

resurrection noun a rising from the dead, esp (**Resurrection**) of Christ; the act of bringing back into use. - verb **resurrect** to bring back to life or into use.

resuscitate verb to bring back to consciousness, revive. - noun **resuscitation.**

retail verb to sell goods to the person who is going to use them (not to someone who is going to sell them to someone else); to tell (eg a story) fully and in detail. - noun the sale of goods to the actual user not to another seller. - noun **retailer** a person who retails (goods); a shopkeeper.

retain verb to keep possession of, continue to have; to keep (something) in mind; to reserve (a person's services) by paying a fee beforehand; to hold back, keep in place. - noun **retainer** a fee for services paid beforehand; (old) a servant (to a family).

retake verb to take or capture again. - noun the filming of part of a film again.

retaliate verb to return like for like, to hit back: If you insult him he will retaliate. - noun **retaliation.**

retard verb to keep back, hinder; to make slow or late. - noun **retardation.** - adjective **retarded** slow in mental or physical growth.

retch verb to make the muscular actions and sound of vomiting, usu without actually vomiting.

retd abbreviation retired.

retention noun the act of holding in; the act of keeping possession of; the act of retaining the services of (eg a lawyer). - adjective **retentive** able to hold or retain: a retentive memory.

reticent adjective unwilling to speak, or not in the habit of speaking, openly and freely, reserved. - noun **reticence.**

retina noun (plural **retinas** or **retinae**) the part of the back of the eye that receives the image of what is seen.

retinue noun the attendants who follow a person of rank or importance.

retire verb to give up work permanently usu because of age; to go to bed; to draw back, retreat. - noun **retiral** retirement. - adjective **retired** having given up work; (of a place) out-of-the-way, quiet. - noun **retirement** the act of retiring from work; one's life after one has given up work. - adjective **retiring** shy, liking to avoid being noticed.

retort verb to make a quick and sharp or witty reply. - noun a ready and sharp reply; a bottle of thin glass, (esp one with its neck pointing downwards and used for distilling liquids).

retrace verb to go over again: He retraced his steps to the place he started from.

retract verb to take back (what one has said or given); to draw back: The cat retracted its claws. - adjective **retractable** able to be retracted. - noun **retraction.**

retreat verb to draw back, withdraw; to go away. - noun the act of moving backwards before the advance of an enemy or opponent, or from danger etc; a withdrawal; a quiet, peaceful place.

retribution noun punishment.

retrieve verb to get back, recover (eg something lost); to search for and fetch: The dog retrieved the pheasant. - noun **retriever** a breed of dog trained to find and fetch birds which have been shot.

retrograde adjective going backward; going from a better to a worse stage.

retrospect: in restrospect in considering or looking back on the past. - adjective **retrospective** looking back on past events; (of a law etc) applying to the past as well as the present and the future: The new tax laws were made retrospective.

return verb to go or come back; to give, send, pay etc back; to elect (a person to parliament etc).- noun the act of returning; a profit: a return on your investment; a statement of income etc (for calculating one's income tax). - adjective **returnable** able to be returned; that must be returned. - noun **return match** a second match played between the same team or players. - noun **return ticket** a ticket which covers a journey both to and from a place. - **by return** (of a letter etc) sent by the first post back.

reunion noun a meeting of people who have been apart for some time. - verb

reunite to join after having been separated.

Rev or **Revd** *abbreviation* Reverend.

reveal *verb* to make known; to show. – *noun* **revelation** the act of revealing; that which is made known, *esp* something unexpected.

reveille *ri-val'i*, *noun* a bugle call at daybreak to waken soldiers.

revel *verb* (*past tense* **revelled**) to take great delight (in); to make merry. – *noun* (*usu plural*) merrymaking. – *noun* **reveller**. – *noun* **revelry** noisy merrymaking.

revelation *see* **reveal**.

revenge *noun* harm done to another person in return for harm which he has done; the desire to do such harm. – *verb* to inflict punishment, injury *etc* in return for harm or injury done: *He revenged his father's murder*; (with **oneself**) to take revenge: *He revenged himself on his enemies*.

revenue *noun* money received as payment, income (*esp* that of a country) from all sources.

reverberate *verb* to echo and re-echo, resound. – *noun* **reverberation**.

revere *verb* to look upon with great respect. – *noun* **reverence** great respect; expression of this. – *adjective* **reverend** worthy of respect. *adjective* **Reverend** (*usu* written **Rev**) a title given to a clergyman. – *adjective* **reverent** or **reverential** showing respect.

reverie *noun* a daydream.

reverse *verb* to turn upside down or the other way round; to (cause to) move backwards; to undo (a decision, policy *etc*). – *noun* the opposite (of); the other side (of a coin *etc*); a defeat. – *noun* **reversal** the act of reversing or being reversed. – *adjective* **reversible** (of clothes *etc*) able to be worn with either side out.

revert *verb* to come or go back to an earlier subject; (of an object, title *etc*) to return or be returned to its previous owner or members of his family. – *noun* **reversion**.

review *verb* to give a written opinion or criticism of (*eg* a new book); to look at or consider again; to inspect (*eg* troops). – *noun* a written critical opinion and account (of a book, play *etc*); a magazine consisting of such accounts; a second look at or consideration of; an inspection of troops *etc*. – *noun* **reviewer** a person who reviews, a critic.

revile *verb* to say harsh things about.

revise *verb* (to examine in order) to correct faults and make improvements; to study one's previous work, one's notes *etc* as preparation for an examination; to change (*eg* one's opinion). – *noun* **revision** the act of revising; a revised form (of something *esp* a book).

revive *verb* to bring or come back to life, use, strength, or fame. – *noun* **revival** a return to life, use *etc*; (a time of) a fresh show of interest: *a religious revival*. – *noun* **revivalist** a person who helps to create a religious revival.

revoke *verb* to do away with, cancel (a decision *etc*); (in card games) to fail to follow suit.

revolt *verb* to rise up (against), to rebel; to feel disgust (at); to disgust. – *noun* a rising against those in power, a rebellion. – *adjective* **revolting** causing disgust.

revolution *noun* a full turn round a centre, as that made by a record on a record-player; the act of turning round a centre; a rising of a people or party against those in power; a complete change (as in ideas, way of doing things). – *adjective* **revolutionary** (aimed at) bringing about great changes (as in government, ideas); tending to do this; turning. – *noun* (*plural* **revolutionaries**) a person who is involved in or who is in favour of revolution. – *verb* **revolutionize** to bring about a complete change in.

revolve *verb* to roll or turn round. – *noun* **revolver** a kind of pistol.

revue *noun* a light theatre show, *usu* with short plays or sketches, often based on recent events.

revulsion *noun* disgust; a sudden change of feeling (*esp* from love to hate).

reward *noun* something given in return for service or work done or for good behaviour *etc*; a sum of money offered for finding or helping to find a criminal, lost property *etc*. – *verb* to give a reward to (a person); to give a reward for (a service). – *adjective* **rewarding** giving pleasure, satisfaction, profit *etc*.

RGN *abbreviation* Registered General Nurse.

rhapsody *noun* music, poetry, or speech which shows strong feeling or excitement: – *verb* **rhapsodize** to talk or write wildly and enthusiastically (about). – **go into rhapsodies over** to show wild enthusiasm for.

rhetoric *noun* the art of good speaking or writing; language which is too showy, consisting of unnecessarily long or difficult words *etc*. – *adjective* **rhetorical**. – *noun* **rhetorical question** one which the asker answers, or which does not need an answer.

rheumatism *noun* a disease which causes stiffness and pain in one's joints. – *adjective* **rheumatic**.

rhino (*plural* **rhinos**) short for **rhinoceros**.

rhinoceros *noun* (*plural* **rhinoceros** or **rhinoceroses**) a type of large, thick-skinned animal, with one horn (or two) on the nose.

rhododendron *noun* a type of flowering shrub with thick evergreen leaves and large flowers.

rhubarb *noun* a plant, the stalks of which are used in cooking.

rhyme *noun* in poetry, a likeness between the sounds of words or of their endings (such as *humble* and *crumble* or *convention* and *prevention*); a word which is like another word in this way; a short poem. – *verb* (sometimes with **with**) to sound like, to be rhymes. ('Star' rhymes with 'car'.)

rhythm *noun* a regular repeated pattern of sounds, beats or stresses in music, speech (*esp* poetry) *etc*; a regularly repeated pattern of movements. – *adjective* **rhythmic** or **rhythmical**. – **rhythm and blues** a type of music combining the styles of rock-and-roll and the blues.

rib *noun* any one of the bones which curve round and forward from the backbone, enclosing the heart and lungs; one of the spars of wood which form the framework of a boat, curving up from the keel. – *adjective* **ribbed** arranged in ridges and furrows.

ribald *adjective* (of jokes, songs *etc*) coarse, vulgar.

ribbon *noun* a narrow strip or band of silk or other material, used in decorating clothes, tying hair *etc*.

rice *noun* the seeds of a plant, grown in well-watered ground in tropical countries, used as a food.

rich *adjective* possessing much money or much of value, wealthy; valuable: *a rich reward*; (with **in**) having much of: *a country rich in natural resources*; (of food) containing much fat, eggs, sugar *etc*; (of material, clothes *etc*) splendid; (of a colour) deep in tone. – *noun plural* **riches** wealth. – *adverb* **richly**. – *noun* **richness**.

rickets *noun* a disease of children, causing softening and bending of the bones: *Rickets is caused by lack of calcium*. – *adjective* **rickety** suffering from rickets; unsteady: *a rickety table*.

rickshaw *noun* a two-wheeled carriage pulled by a man, used in Japan etc.

ricochet *rik'ò-shā*, *verb* (*past tense* **ricocheted** *rik-ò-shād* or **ricochetted** *rik-ò-shet'id*) (of a bullet *etc*) to rebound at an angle from a surface. – Also *noun*.

rid *verb* (*past tense, past participle* **rid**) to free from, clear of: *to rid the city of rats*. – **get rid of** to free oneself of; **good riddance to** I am happy to have got rid of.

riddle *noun* a puzzle in the form of a question *etc* which describes an object or person in a misleading or mysterious way; anything difficult to understand, a mystery; a tray with holes for separating large objects from smaller ones, or solid objects from something in a powder-like form (*eg* stones from soil).

ride *verb* (*past tense* **rode**, *past participle* **ridden**) to travel, be carried on a horse, bicycle *etc*, or in car, train *etc*; to travel on and control (a horse); (of a ship) to float at anchor. – *noun* a journey on horseback, bicycle *etc*; a path *esp* through a wood, for riding horses. – *noun* **rider** a person who rides; something added to what has already been said. – **ride up** to work itself up out of position: *Her skirt is riding up*.

ridge *noun* a raised part between furrows or anything resembling this; a long crest on high ground.

ridicule *verb* to laugh at, mock. – Also *noun*. – *adjective* **ridiculous** deserving to be laughed at, very silly.

rife *adjective* very common: *Disease was rife in the country*.

riff-raff *noun* used insultingly, worthless people.

rifle *noun* a gun fired from the shoulder. – *verb* to search through and rob; to steal.

rift *noun* a crack; a disagreement between friends. – *noun* **rift valley** a long valley formed by the fall of part of the earth's crust between faults in the rock.

rig *verb* (*past tense* **rigged**) (with **out**) to clothe, to dress; (with **up**) to fit (a ship) with sails and ropes; to manage or control (a ballot, an election result) illegally or dishonestly. – *noun* an oilrig. – *noun* **rigging** ship's spars, ropes *etc*. – **rig up** to make or build (*esp* hastily).

right *adjective* on, for, or belonging to the side of the body which in most people has the more skilful hand (opposite to **left**); correct, true; just, good; straight. – *adverb* to or on the right side; correctly; straight; all the way: *right along the pier and back*. – *noun* that which is correct or good, and which ought to be done; something one is entitled to: *a right to a fair trial*; the right-hand side, direction, part *etc*; a group holding the more traditional conservative beliefs. – *verb* to mend, set in order, to put back in the proper position. – *noun* **right angle** an angle like one of those in a square, an angle of 90°. – *adjective* **righteous** living a good life; just. – *noun* **righteousness**. – *adjective* **rightful** by right, proper: *the rightful king*. – *adjective* **right-handed** using the right hand more easily than the left. – *adjective* **Right Honourable** used before the names of cabinet ministers in the British government. – *noun* **right-of-way** a road or path over private land along which people may go as a right. – *adjective* **right-wing** in politics, of Conservative political beliefs. – **by right** because one has the right; **in one's own right** not because of anyone else, independently: *a peeress in her own right*.

rigid *adjective* not easily bent; stiff; strict.

rigmarole *noun* a long, rambling speech.

rigour *noun* strictness; harshness. – *adjective* **rigorous** very strict.

rill *noun* a small stream.

rim *noun* an edge or border, *esp* the outer ring of a wheel or the top edge of a cup *etc*.

rime *noun* thick white frost; old form of **rhyme**.

rind *noun* a thick firm covering, *esp* the peel of fruit, the skin of bacon, the outer covering of cheese.

ring *noun* a small round hoop, *esp* of metal, worn on the finger, in or on the ear *etc*; a hollow circle; anything in the shape of a ring; an enclosed space, as for boxing, circus performances *etc*; the sound of a bell or a similar sound; a small group of people *esp* one formed for business or criminal purposes: *a drug ring*. – *verb* (*past tense* **ringed**) to encircle, go round; to mark (a bird *etc*) by putting on a ring; (*past tense* **rang**, *past participle* **rung**) to make the sound of a bell, or a strong clear sound; to cause (a bell *etc*) to sound; to telephone. – *noun* **ringleader** one who takes the lead in mischief *etc*. – *noun* **ringlet** a long curl of hair. – *noun* **ringmaster** a person who is in charge of the performance in a circus ring. – *noun* **ring road** a road that circles a town *etc* avoiding the centre. – *noun* **ringworm** a skin disease causing circular red patches.

rink *noun* a sheet of ice, often artificially made, for skating or curling.

rinse *verb* to wash lightly to remove soap *etc*; to clean (a cup, one's mouth *etc*) by putting in and emptying out water. – *noun* the act of rinsing; a liquid for rinsing, *esp* one for tinting the hair.

riot *noun* a noisy disturbance, disorder among a group of people; a striking display (of colour). – *verb* to take part in a riot. – *adjective* **riotous** noisy, uncontrolled.

RIP *abbreviation* may he or she rest in peace.

rip *verb* (*past tense* **ripped**) to tear apart or off; to come apart. – *noun* a tear.

ripe *adjective* (of fruit, grain *etc*) ready to be gathered in or eaten; fully developed, mature. – *verb* **ripen** to make or become ripe or riper. – *noun* **ripeness**.

ripple *noun* a little wave or movement on the surface of water; a soft sound *etc* that rises and falls quickly and gently: *a ripple of laughter*.

rise *verb* (*past tense* **rose**, *past participle* **risen**) to get up from bed; to stand up; to move upwards, go up, become higher; (of a river *etc*) to have its source (in), to start (in): *The Rhone rises in the Alps*; to rebel: *The people rose against the tyrant*. – *noun* a slope upwards; an increase in wages, prices *etc*. – *noun* **rising** an act of rising; rebellion. – **give rise to** to cause.

risk *noun* a chance of loss or injury; a danger. – *verb* to take the chance of: *to risk death*; to take the chance of losing: *to risk one's life, health etc*. – *adjective* **risky** possibly resulting in loss or injury.

risotto *noun* a dish made with rice.

rissole *noun* a fried cake or ball of minced meat, fish *etc.*

rite *noun* a solemn ceremony, *esp* a religious one. – *noun* **ritual** a traditional or set way of carrying out religious worship *etc.* – *adjective* of or forming a rite or ceremony.

rival *noun* a person who tries to equal or beat (another). – *verb* (*past tense* **rivalled**) to (try to) equal. – *noun* **rivalry** (*plural* **rivalries**).

riven *adjective* (*old*) split.

river *noun* a large stream of water flowing across land.

rivet *noun* a bolt for fastening plates of metal together. – *verb* to fasten with a rivet; to fix firmly (someone's attention *etc*): *riveted by the play: riveted to the spot.*

rivulet *noun* a small stream.

RN *abbreviation* Royal Navy.

RNIB *abbreviation* Royal National Institute for the Blind.

RNLI *abbreviation* Royal National Lifeboat Institution.

roach *noun* (*plural* **roaches**) a type of freshwater fish.

road *noun* a way (*usu* with a hard, level surface) for vehicles and people; a way of getting to (somewhere), a route; (*plural*) a place where ships may lie at anchor (also **roadstead**). – *noun* **roadie** a member of the crew who transport, set up and dismantle equipment for (rock, jazz *etc*) musicians. – *noun* **roadway** the part of a road used by cars *etc*. – *adjective* **roadworthy** (of a vehicle) fit to be used on the road.

roam *verb* to wander about.

roan *noun* a horse with a dark-brown coat spotted with grey or white.

roar *verb* to give a loud, deep sound; to laugh loudly; to say (something) loudly. – Also *noun.*

roast *verb* to cook or be cooked in an oven or over or in front of a fire. – *adjective* roasted: *roast beef.* – *noun* meat roasted; meat for roasting.

rob *verb* (*past tense* **robbed**) to steal from (a person or place). – *noun* **robber**. – *noun* **robbery** (*plural* **robberies**) the act of stealing.

robe *noun* a long loose garment; (*US*) a dressing gown; (*plural*) the dress (as of a judge *etc*) showing rank or position. – *verb* to dress.

robin *noun* a type of small bird, known by its red breast.

robot *noun* a mechanical man or woman; a machine that can do the work of a person. – *adjective* **robotic.**

robust *adjective* strong, healthy.

rock *noun* a large lump or mass of stone; a hard sweet made in sticks; music or songs with a heavy beat and *usu* with a simple melody (also **rock music**). – *verb* to sway backwards and forwards or from side to side. – *noun* **rock-and-roll** a simpler, earlier form of rock music (also **rock'n'roll**). – *noun* **rocker** a curved support on which anything (*eg* a cradle *etc*) rocks. – *noun* **rockery** (*plural* **rockeries**) a collection of stones amongst which small plants are grown. – *noun* **rocking-chair** or **-horse** a chair or a toy horse which rocks backwards and forwards on rockers. – *adjective* **rocky** full of rocks; inclined to rock, unsteady.

rocket *noun* a tube containing materials which, when set on fire, give off a jet of gas driving the tube forward, used for launching a spacecraft, for signalling, and as a firework; a spacecraft so launched. – *verb* to move, *esp* upwards, very rapidly. *House prices are rocketing.*

rod *noun* a long thin stick or bar; a fishing rod; an old measure of distance, about 5 metres.

rode *see* **ride.**

rodent *noun* any gnawing animal (as the rat, beaver *etc*).

rodeo *noun* (*plural* **rodeos**) a roundup of cattle for marking; a show of riding by cowboys.

roe *noun* the eggs of fishes; (also **roe deer**) a small kind of deer; a female red deer. – *noun* **roebuck** the male roe deer.

rogue *noun* a dishonest person; a mischievous person, a rascal. – *noun* **roguery** dishonesty; mischief. – *adjective* **roguish** mischievous; wicked.

rôle *noun* a part played, *esp* by an actor.

roll *verb* to move along by turning over like a wheel or ball; (of a ship *etc*) to rock or move from side to side; (of thunder, drums *etc*) to rumble; to wrap round and round: *to roll up a carpet*; to flatten with roller(s): *to roll the lawn*. – *noun* anything *eg* a sheet of paper, length of cloth *etc* rolled or formed into the shape of a tube or cylinder; a very small loaf of bread; a rocking or turning over movement; a list of names; a long, rumbling sound. – *noun* **rollcall** the calling of names from a list; – *noun* **roller** something cylinder-shaped, often for flattening; a tube-shaped object on which something (*eg* hair) is rolled up; a small solid wheel; a long heavy wave on the sea. – *noun* **rollerskate** a skate with wheels instead of a blade. – *noun* **rolling pin** a roller of wood *etc* for flattening dough. – *noun* **rolling stock** the stock of engines, carriages, wagons *etc* that run on a railway.

rollicking *adjective* noisy and full of fun.

ROM *abbreviation* (*comput*) read-only memory.

Romans *adjective* (of a number, numerals) written in letters, as I, II, III, IV *etc* for 1, 2, 3, 4 *etc*. – **Roman Catholic Church** the Church whose head is the Pope, the Bishop of Rome.

romance *noun* a tale about heroic, adventurous *etc* events not likely to happen in real life nowadays; a love story; a love affair. – *verb* to write or tell tales rich in imagination. – *adjective* **romantic** of romance; full of feeling and imagination; dealing with love.

romp *verb* to play in a lively way; to move quickly and easily. – *noun* a lively game. – *noun plural* **rompers** a short suit for a baby.

rood *noun* (*old*) a measure of area (a quarter of an acre); a cross carrying an image of Christ.

roof *noun* (*plural* **roofs**) the top covering of a building, car *etc*; the upper part of the mouth. – *verb* to cover with a roof.

rook *noun* a kind of crow; (in chess) the castle. – *noun* **rookie** (*coll*) a new recruit. – *noun* **rookery** (*plural* **rookeries**) a nesting place of rooks in a group of trees; a breeding place of penguins or seals.

room *noun* an inside division or compartment in a house; space: *room for everybody*; (*plural*) lodgings. – *adverb* **roomy** having plenty of space.

roost *noun* a perch on which a bird rests at night. – *verb* to sit or sleep on a roost. – *noun* **rooster** a farmyard cock.

root *noun* the underground part of a plant; the base of anything, as a tooth *etc*; a cause, a source; a word from which other words have developed. – *verb* to form roots and begin to grow; to be fixed; (of an animal) to turn up ground *etc* in a search for food; to search (about). – *adjective, adverb* **root-and-branch** thorough(ly), complete(ly). – *adjective* **rooted** firmly planted. – **root out** or **root up** to tear up by the roots; to get rid of completely; **take root** to form roots and grow firmly; to become firmly fixed.

rope *noun* a thick cord, made by twisting strands of hemp, nylon *etc*; anything resembling a thick cord. – *verb* to fasten or catch with a rope; to enclose, mark off with a rope. – *adjective* **ropy** like ropes, stringy; (*coll*) bad, not well.

rosary *noun* (*plural* **rosaries**) a set of prayers; a string of beads used in saying prayers; a rose garden.

rose *verb see* **rise**. – *noun* a type of flower, often scented, growing on a *usu* prickly bush; a deep pink colour. – *adjective* **rosy** red, pink; (of the future *etc*) bright, hopeful.

rosemary *noun* a kind of evergreen sweet-smelling shrub, used as a flavouring herb in cooking.

rosette *noun* a kind of badge shaped like a rose, made of ribbons.

roster *noun* a list showing a repeated order of duties *etc*.

rostrum *noun* (*plural* **rostrums** or **rostra**) a platform for public speaking.

rot *verb* (*past tense* **rotted**) to go bad or cause to go bad, to decay. – *noun* decay; (*coll*) nonsense. – *adjective* **rotten** (of meat, fruit *etc*) having gone bad, decayed; worthless, disgraceful. – *noun* **rotter** (*coll*) a very bad, worthless person.

rota *noun* a list of duties *etc* to be repeated in a set order.

rotary *adjective* turning round like a wheel.

rotate *verb* to turn round like a wheel; to (cause to) go through a repeating series of changes. – *noun* **rotation**.

rote: by rote off by heart, automatically.

rotor *noun* a turning part of a motor, dynamo *etc*.

rotten, rotter *see* **rot**.

rotund *adjective* round; plump.

rouble or **ruble** *noun* a standard unit of Russian coinage.

rouge *noun* a powder or cream used to give colour to the cheeks.

rough *adjective* not smooth; uneven; coarse, harsh; boisterous, wild; not exact: *a rough guess*; stormy. – *noun* a hooligan or bully; rough ground. – *noun* **roughage** bran or fibre in food. – *noun* **roughcast** plaster mixed with fine gravel, used to coat outside walls. – *verb* **roughen** to make rough. – **rough and ready** not fine or carefully made, but effective; **rough out** to sketch or shape roughly.

roulette *noun* a game of chance, played with a ball which is placed on a wheel.

round *adjective* shaped like a ring or circle; plump; even, exact: *a round dozen*. – *adverb, preposition* on all sides (of), around: *look round the room*; in a circle (about): *The earth moves round the sun*; from one (person, thing, place *etc*) to another: *The news went round*. – *noun* a circle or something round in shape; a single bullet or shell; a burst of firing, cheering *etc*; a song in which the singers take up the tune in turn; a usual route: *a postman's round*; a series of calls or deliveries: *The milkman was late starting his round*; set of tasks *etc*: *a round of duties*; each stage of a boxing match or other contest *etc*. – *verb* to make or become round; (of a ship) to go round (*eg* a headland). – *noun* **roundabout** a revolving machine for riding on, a merry-go-round; a meeting place of roads, where traffic must move in a circle. – *adjective* not straight or direct. – *noun* **rounders** a type of ball game played with a bat. – *adverb* **roundly** boldly, plainly. – *noun* **round trip** a journey to a place and back. – **round on** to make a sudden attack on; **round up** to gather or drive together.

rouse *verb* to awaken; to stir up, excite. – *adjective* **rousing** stirring, exciting.

rout *noun* a disorderly flight (of an army *etc*); a complete defeat. – *verb* to defeat utterly.

route *noun* the course to be followed, a way of getting to somewhere. – *verb* to fix the route of.

routine *noun* a fixed, unchanging order of doing things. – *adjective* regular, ordinary, usual: *routine enquiries*.

rove *verb* to wander or roam. – *noun* **rover** a wanderer; an unsettled person; (*hist*) a pirate. – *noun* **Rover Scout** an older member of the Scout Association.

row[1] *noun* a line of persons or things; an act of rowing; a trip in a rowing boat. – *verb* to drive (a boat) by oars. – *noun* **rower** a person who rows. – *noun* **rowing boat** a boat rowed by oars.

row[2] *noun* a noisy quarrel; a noise; (*coll*) a scolding.

rowan *noun* a type of tree with clusters of bright red berries, the mountain ash.

rowdy *adjective* noisy, disorderly. – *noun* **rowdyism**.

rowlock *noun* a place to rest an oar on the side of a rowing boat.

royal *adjective* of, or given by, a king or queen; splendid, magnificent: *royal feast*. – *noun* **royal blue** a deep, bright blue. – *noun* **royalist** a person who supports a king or queen. – *noun* **royalty** (*plural* **royalties**) the state of being royal; a royal person, or royal persons as a whole; a sum paid to the author of a book *etc* for each copy sold.

rpm *abbreviation* revolutions per minute.

rps *abbreviation* revolutions per second.

RSPB *abbreviation* Royal Society for the Protection of Birds.

RSPCA *abbreviation* Royal Society for the Prevention of Cruelty to Animals.

RSSPCC *abbreviation* Royal Scottish Society for Prevention of Cruelty to Children.

RSVP *abbreviation* reply if you please. (*répondez, s'il vous plaît* [Fr]).

Rt Hon *abbreviation* Right Honourable.

Rt Rev *abbreviation* Right Reverend.

rub *verb* (*past tense* **rubbed**) to move one thing against the surface of another; to wipe, clean, polish (something); (with **out, away**) to remove (a mark). – *noun* the act of rubbing; a wipe. – **rub in** to work into (a surface) by rubbing; to keep reminding (someone of something unpleasant).

rubber *noun* a tough elastic substance made from the juice of certain plants (or an artificial substitute for this), used in tyres *etc*; (also **indiarubber**) a piece of rubber used for rubbing out pencil *etc* marks; an odd number (three or five) of games in cards, cricket *etc*. – *noun* **rubber stamp** an instrument with rubber figures or letters for stamping names, dates *etc* on books or papers. – *verb* **rubber-stamp** to authorize, approve.

rubbish *noun* waste material, litter; nonsense.

rubble *noun* small rough stones, bricks *etc* used in building, or remaining from a ruined building.

rubicund *adjective* red or rosy-faced.

ruble *see* **rouble**.

ruby *noun* (*plural* **rubies**) a type of red, precious stone.

ruck *noun* a wrinkle or crease.

rucksack *noun* a type of bag carried on the back by walkers, climbers *etc*.

rudder *noun* the flat piece of wood or metal fixed by a hinge to the stern of a boat for steering; a similar object fixed to the tail of an aeroplane.

ruddy *adjective* red; (of the face, complexion *etc*) rosy, as in good health.

rude *adjective* showing bad manners, not polite; roughly made: *a rude shelter*; rough, not refined; startling and sudden: *a rude awakening*; coarse, vulgar, indecent.

rudiments *noun plural* the first simple rules or facts of anything. – *adjective* **rudimentary** in an early stage of development.

rue *noun* a type of shrub with bitter leaves. – *verb* to be sorry for (having done something), regret. – *adjective* **rueful** sorrowful, regretful.

ruff *noun* (*hist*) a pleated frill worn round the neck; a frill-like band of feathers or hair on a bird or animal's neck.

ruffian *noun* a rough, brutal person. – *adjective* **ruffianly**.

ruffle *verb* to disturb the smoothness of anything (*eg* hair, a bird's feathers *etc*); to annoy, offend.

rug *noun* a mat for the floor; a thick covering or blanket (also **travelling rug**).

Rugby or **rugby** *noun* a form of football using an oval ball.

rugged *adjective* of rough, uneven surface or appearance; strong; stern, harsh.

ruin *noun* complete loss of money *etc*; (a cause of) downfall; a wrecked or decayed state; (*plural*) broken-down remains of buildings *etc*. – *verb* to destroy; cause to decay; to spoil completely: *ruin his chances*; to make very poor. – *noun* **ruination** the act of ruining; the state of being ruined; something which ruins. – *adjective* **ruined** in ruins; destroyed, in ruins. – *adjective* **ruinous** ruined; likely to bring ruin.

rule *noun* government: *a country under military rule*; an order or regulation: *school rules*; what usually happens, is done *etc*; a general idea guiding one's actions: *My rule is never to lend books*; a marked strip of wood, metal *etc* for measuring length. – *verb* to govern (as king *etc*), be in power; to decide (that); to draw (a line); to mark with lines. – *noun* **ruler** a person who rules; an instrument for drawing straight lines. – *adjective* **ruling** governing; most important. – *noun* a decision or rule. – **as a rule** usually; **rule out** to leave out, not to consider.

rum *noun* a type of alcoholic drink, a spirit made from sugar-cane.

rumble *verb* to make a low rolling noise like that of thunder *etc*. – Also *noun*.

ruminant *adjective, noun* (of) an animal, such as a cow, that chews the cud. – *verb* **ruminate** to chew the cud; to be deep in thought. – *noun* **rumination** deep thought.

rummage *verb* to turn things over in search. – Also *noun*.

rummy *noun* a kind of card game.

rumour *noun* general talk; a story *etc* passed from person to person which may not be true. – *verb* to spread a rumour of; to tell widely.

rump *noun* the hind part of an animal; the meat from this part.

rumple *verb* to make untidy; to crease.

rumpus *noun* uproar, a noisy disturbance.

run *verb* (*present participle* **running**, *past tense* **ran**, *past participle* **run**) to move swiftly, hurry; to race; (of trains) to travel; (of water) to flow; (of machines) to work; to spread (rapidly): *This colour runs*; to go on, continue, extend: *The programme runs for two hours*; to cause (vehicles, machinery *etc*) to run or work; to organize, conduct (a business *etc*). – *noun* an act of running; a trip; a distance run; a time or spell of running; a period, continuous stretch: *a run of good luck*; a ladder (in a stocking *etc*); free use of: *the run of the house*; a single score in cricket; an enclosure for hens *etc*. – *noun* **runner** one who runs; a messenger; a rooting stem of a plant; a blade of a skate or sledge. – noun **running** the act of moving fast, flowing etc; management, control. – adjective for use in running: *running shoes*; giving out fluid: *a running sore*; carried on continuously: *a running commentary*. – adverb one after another: *three days running*. – noun **runaway** a person, animal or vehicle etc that runs away. – Also adjective. – adjective **run-down** in poor health or condition. – noun **runner-up** (plural **runners-up**) one who comes second in a race or competition. – adjective **run-of-the-mill** ordinary. – noun **runway** a path for aircraft to take off from or land on. – **in (out of) the running** having (or not having) a chance of success; **run a risk** to take a chance of harm, loss, failure etc; **run down** (of a vehicle or driver) to knock (someone) down; to speak ill of; **run into** to bump into, collide with; to meet (someone) accidentally; **run out of** to become short of; **run over** to knock down or pass over with a car etc.

rune noun one of the letters of an early kind of alphabet used in some ancient writings. – adjective **runic.**

rung noun a step of a ladder. – verb see **ring.**

runnel noun a little stream or river.

runner see **run.**

rupee noun the standard coin of India, Pakistan, Sri Lanka.

rupture noun a breaking (eg of friendship, peace etc); a tear or burst (often in a part of the body). – verb to break or burst.

rural adjective of the country.

ruse noun a trick or cunning plan.

rush verb to move quickly, hurry; to make (someone) hurry; to take (a fort etc) by a quick, sudden attack. – noun (plural **rushes**) a quick, forward movement; a hurry; a kind of tall grasslike plant growing near water.

rusk noun a kind of hard biscuit like toast.

russet adjective reddish-brown. – noun a type of apple of russet colour.

rust noun the reddish-brown coating (caused by air and moisture) which forms on iron and steel. – verb to form rust. – adjective **rustless** or **rustproof** not rusting. – adjective **rusty** covered with rust; (coll) showing lack of practice: *My French is rusty.*

rustic adjective of the country; roughly made; simple, unsophisticated. – noun a countryman; a peasant.

rustle verb (of silk, straw etc) to make a soft, whispering sound; to steal (cattle); (coll) (with **up**) to get, prepare quickly: *rustle up a meal.* – Also noun. – noun **rustler** a person who steals (cattle).

rut noun a deep track made by a wheel etc. – adjective **rutted** full of ruts. – **in a rut** having a fixed, rather dull, routine or way of life.

ruthless adjective without pity, cruel.

rye noun a kind of grain. – noun **rye-bread** a bread made with flour from this grain. – noun **rye-grass** a kind of grass grown for cattle-feeding.

S

s abbreviation second(s).

Sabbath noun the day of the week regularly set aside for religious services and rest (among Muslims, Friday, Jews, Saturday, and Christians, Sunday).

sable noun a small type of animal like the weasel, or its dark brown or blackish fur. – adjective black, dark.

sabot *sab ò*, noun a kind of wooden shoe.

sabotage noun deliberate destruction of machinery etc by enemies, dissatisfied workers etc. – verb to destroy, damage or cause to fail.

sabre noun (hist) a curved sword used by the cavalry. – noun **sabre-rattling** an obvious display of force or military power to frighten the enemy.

sac noun (in plants and in animals' bodies) a bag often containing a liquid.

saccharine *noun* a very sweet substance used as a substitute for sugar.

sachet *noun* a small bag (to hold handkerchiefs *etc*); a (small) sealed packet containing something in a liquid or powder form, *eg* shampoo.

sack *noun* a large bag of coarse cloth for holding grain, flour *etc*; dismissal from one's job; a plundering (of a captured town). – *verb* to dismiss (someone) from a job; to plunder (a captured town). – *noun* **sackcloth** coarse cloth for making sacks; a garment made of this worn as a sign of repentance. – *noun* **sacking** a coarse cloth or canvas used for sacks *etc*. – **get the sack** (*coll*) to be dismissed from one's job.

sacrament *noun* a religious ceremony such as baptism.

sacred *adjective* holy; devoted to or dedicated to some purpose or person: *sacred to her memory*; connected with religion: *The choir sang sacred music. The galley holds a collection of sacred art.*

sacrifice *noun* the act of offering something (as an animal that has been specially killed) to a god; the thing offered; something given up in order to benefit another person or to gain something more important: *He became successful because of the sacrifices his mother made*; the giving up of something for this purpose. – *verb* to offer (an animal *etc*) as a sacrifice to God in worship; to give up something for someone or something else. – *adjective* **sacrificial** of sacrifice.

sacrilege *noun* the using of a holy thing or place in a wicked way. – *adjective* **sacrilegious.**

sacrosanct *adjective* very sacred; not to be harmed.

sad *adjective* sorrowful, unhappy; showing sorrow; causing sorrow. – *verb* **sadden** to make or become sad.

saddle *noun* a seat for a rider used on the back of a horse or on a bicycle *etc*; a certain cut or joint of meat (from the back of an animal). – *verb* to put a saddle on; (with **with**) to put a load or burden on (a person): *His son saddled him with debts*. – *noun* **saddler** a maker of saddles and harness.

sadism *sād'izm, noun* taking pleasure in, or enjoyment of, cruelty to others. – *noun* **sadist.** – *adjective* **sadistic.**

sae *abbreviation* stamped addressed envelope.

safari *noun* an expedition, *esp* for observing or hunting wild animals. – *noun* **safari park** an enclosed area where wild animals are kept in the open, on view to visitors.

safe *adjective* unharmed; free or secure from harm or danger; reliable, trustworthy. – *noun* a heavy metal chest or box in which money and jewels may be locked away; a kind of cupboard for meat *etc*. – *noun* **safeguard** anything that gives protection or security. – *verb* to protect. – *noun* **safety** freedom from harm or danger. – *adjective* giving protection or safety: *safety belt*. – *noun* **safety belt** a seat-belt. – *noun* **safety-pin** a curved pin in the shape of a clasp, with a guard covering its point. – **safe and sound** unharmed.

saffron *noun* a type of crocus from which is obtained a yellow food dye and flavouring agent.

sag *verb* (*past tense* **sagged**) to droop or sink *esp* in the middle.

saga *noun* an ancient story about the deeds of heroes *etc*; a novel or series of novels about several generations of a family; a long detailed story.

sagacious *adjective* very wise, quick at understanding. – *noun* **sagacity.**

sage *noun* a type of herb with grey-green leaves which are used for flavouring; a wise man. – *adjective* wise.

sago *noun* a white starchy substance (got from certain Eastern palms) often used in puddings.

sahib *noun* a term of respect given in India to persons of rank *etc*.

said *adjective* mentioned before: *the said shopkeeper*. – *verb* see **say.**

sail *noun* a sheet of canvas *etc* spread out to catch the wind by which a ship or boat may be driven forward; a journey in a ship or boat; an arm of a windmill. – *verb* to go by water in a ship or boat (with or without sails); to navigate or steer a ship or boat; to begin a (sea) voyage; to glide along easily. – **sailboard** *noun* a surfboard fitted with a mast and sail. – Also *verb*. – *noun* **sailor** a person who sails; a member of a ship's crew, a seaman. – **set sail** to set out on a (sea) voyage.

saint *noun* a very good or holy person; a title given by the Roman Catholic Church or other church after death to very holy persons (often shortened to

St *esp* if used in names of places *etc*: *St John's Road*). – *adjective* **sainted** or **saintly** very holy or very good.

Saint Bernard or **St Bernard** *noun* a breed of large dog.

sake *noun* cause, purpose: *He did it for the sake of making money*; benefit, advantage: *for my sake*.

salaam *noun* an Eastern greeting; a deep bow. – Also *verb*.

salad *noun* a dish of vegetables, *eg* lettuce, cucumber *etc* cut up and served raw. – *noun* **salad cream** or **salad dressing** a kind of sauce for putting on salad.

salamander *noun* a kind of small lizard-like animal.

salami *noun* a type of highly seasoned sausage.

salary *noun* (plural **salaries**) fixed wages regularly paid for work (*esp* to someone in a profession).

sale *noun* the exchange of anything for money; a selling of goods at reduced prices; an auction. – *noun* **saleroom** an auction room. – *noun* **salesman** (*masculine*), **saleswoman** (*feminine*) a person who sells or shows goods to customers.

salient *adjective* (of an angle *etc*) pointing outwards; standing out, chief: *the salient points of a speech*.

saline *adjective* containing salt, salty: *saline solution*.

saliva *noun* the liquid that forms in the mouth to help digestion, spittle. – *adjective* **salivary** of saliva. – *verb* **salivate** to form saliva.

sallow *adjective* (of a face, complexion) pale, yellowish. – *noun* a type of willow tree.

sally *noun* (plural **sallies**) a sudden rushing forth; a trip, an excursion; a witty remark, a joke. – *verb* (past tense **sallied**) to rush out suddenly; (with **forth**) to go out *eg* for a walk.

salmon *noun* a large type of fish with yellowish-pink flesh.

salmonella *noun* a bacterium which causes food poisoning.

salon *noun* a place, shop, in which hairdressing *etc* is done; a large room for receiving or entertaining notable people; a gathering of such people.

saloon *noun* a passengers' dining-room or sitting-room in a ship; a covered-in motor car; a public-house, bar.

salt *noun* a substance used for seasoning, either mined from the earth or obtained from sea water; any other substance formed (as salt is) from a metal and an acid; (*coll*) a sailor. – *adjective* containing salt; tasting of salt; preserved in salt. – *verb* to sprinkle with salt; to preserve with salt. – *noun* **salt cellar** a small table dish or container for salt. – *noun* **saltpan** a dried-up hollow near the sea where salt can be found. – *adjective* **salty**.

salubrious *adjective* (of a place, climate *etc*) healthy.

salutary *adjective* giving health or safety; having a good effect: *a salutary lesson*.

salute *verb* to greet (a person) with words, a kiss or other gesture; (in the armed forces *etc*) to raise the hand to the forehead to show respect (to); to honour a person by a firing of guns *etc*. – *noun* an act or way of saluting. – *noun* **salutation** an act of greeting.

salvage *noun* goods saved from destruction or waste; the act of saving a ship or cargo, or of saving goods from a fire *etc*; payment made for this act. – *verb* to save from loss or ruin.

salvation *noun* the act, means, or cause of saving: *The arrival of the police was his salvation*; the saving of man from sin.

salve *noun* an ointment for healing or soothing. – *verb* to soothe (pride, conscience *etc*).

salver *noun* a small tray often of silver *etc*.

salvo *noun* (plural **salvos**) a great burst of gunfire, of bombs, or of clapping.

same *adjective* exactly alike, identical: *They both had the same feeling*; not different; unchanged: *He still looks the same*; mentioned before: *The same person came again*. – *pronoun* the thing just mentioned. – *noun* **sameness** lack of change or variety. – **all the same** or **just the same** in spite of that; **at the same time** still, nevertheless.

sampan *noun* a kind of small boat used in Far Eastern countries.

sample *noun* a small part taken from something to show what the whole is like. – *verb* to test a sample of: *sample a cake*. – *noun* **sampler** a person who samples; a piece of embroidery *etc* to show one's skill.

sanatorium *noun* a hospital, *esp* for people suffering from a disease of the lungs; a place set aside for those who are ill, in a school, college etc.

sanctimonious adjective trying to appear full of holiness and goodness, priggish.

sanction noun permission, approval; a penalty for not keeping a law, rule of conduct etc; (often in plural) a measure applied, eg to a nation, to force it to stop a course of action: The country enforced sanctions against the neighbouring republic.

sanctity noun holiness; sacredness. – verb (past tense **sanctified**) to make holy, sacred or free of sin. – noun **sanctification**.

sanctuary noun (plural **sanctuaries**) a sacred place; (the most sacred part of) a temple or church; a place where one can be safe from arrest or violence; an area within which birds, animals etc are protected, a nature reserve.

sand noun a mass of tiny particles of crushed or worn rocks etc; (plural) stretch of sand (on the seashore). – verb to sprinkle with sand; to add sand to; to smooth or polish (with sandpaper). – noun **sandbag** a bag filled with sand, used as a protective barrier or covering. – noun **sand dune** a ridge of sand blown up by the wind. – noun **sand martin** a type of small bird which nests in sandy banks. – noun **sandpaper** paper with a layer of sand glued to it for smoothing and polishing. – noun **sandpiper** a type of wading bird. – noun **sandshoe** a light shoe, usu with a rubber sole. – noun **sandstone** a kind of soft rock make of layers of sand pressed together. – adjective **sandy** having much sand; like sand; (of hair) yellowish-red in colour.

sandal noun a shoe in which the sole is held on to the foot by straps.

sandwich noun (plural **sandwiches**) two slices of bread with any kind of food between. – verb to place, fit something between two other objects.

sane adjective of sound mind, not mad; sensible. – noun **saneness**. – noun **sanity** soundness of mind; mental health; good sense or judgement.

sanguine adjective hopeful, cheerful; (of a complexion) red. – adjective **sanguinary** bloodthirsty, bloody.

sanitary adjective of conditions or arrangements that encourage good health, eg good drainage; free from dirt, infection etc. – noun **sanitation** arrangements for protecting health, esp drainage, sewage disposal etc. – noun **sanitary towel** a pad of absorbent material worn to soak up menstrual blood.

sanity see **sane**.

sank see **sink**.

sap noun the juice in plants, trees etc. – verb (past tense **sapped**) to weaken (a person's strength etc). – noun **sapling** a young tree.

sapphire noun a kind of precious stone of a deep blue colour.

sarcasm noun a hurtful remark made in scorn; the use of such remarks. – adjective **sarcastic** containing sarcasm; often using sarcasm, scornful.

sarcophagus noun a stone coffin.

sardine noun a type of small fish of the herring kind often tinned in oil.

sardonic adjective bitter, mocking, scornful.

sari noun a long piece of cloth worn by Indian women, wrapped round the waist and hanging loose over the shoulder.

sarong noun kind of skirt worn by Malay men and women.

sartorial adjective having to do with dress, or with tailor-made clothes: sartorial elegance.

SAS abbreviation Special Air Service.

sash noun (plural **sashes**) a band, ribbon or scarf worn round the waist or over the shoulder; a frame (usu one that slides up and down) for panes of glass: window sash.

sat see **sit**.

Satan noun the Devil. – adjective **Satanic** of Satan, devilish.

satchel noun a small bag for carrying schoolbooks etc.

sate verb (old) to satisfy fully or give more than enough to. – adjective **sated**.

satellite noun a smaller body moving round a larger – as the moon round the earth; a man-made object fired into space to travel round a planet (**artificial satellite**); a state etc controlled by a more powerful neighbouring one. – noun **satellite television** the broadcasting of television programmes via artificial satellite.

satiate *verb* to satisfy fully; to give more than enough to. – *noun* **satiety** state of being satiated.

satin *noun* a closely woven silk with a glossy surface. – *noun* **satinwood** a smooth kind of wood.

satire *noun* a piece of writing *etc* which makes fun of certain people or their ways; ridicule, scorn. – *adjective* **satirical**. – *noun* **satirist** a writer of satire.

satisfy *verb* (*past tense* **satisfied**) to give enough (of something) to (a person); to please, make content; to give enough to quieten or get rid of (hunger, curiosity *etc*); to convince: *I was satisfied that he was innocent*; to fulfil (conditions, requirements for a job *etc*). – *noun* **satisfaction** the act of satisfying or state of being satisfied; a feeling of pleasure or comfort; something that satisfies; a making up for (damage *etc*), compensation. – *adjective* **satisfactory** satisfying; fulfilling the necessary requirements.

saturate *verb* to soak or fill completely (with water *etc*); to cover (an area) completely *eg* with bombs. – *noun* **saturation**.

Saturday *noun* the seventh day of the week.

saturnine *adjective* gloomy, sullen.

satyr *noun* (*myth*) a god of the woods who was half man, half goat.

sauce *noun* a liquid seasoning added to food to improve flavour; (*coll*) cheek, impudence. – *noun* **saucepan** a rather deep pan, often with a long handle, for boiling, stewing food *etc*. – *adjective* **saucy** cheeky.

saucer *noun* a small, shallow dish for placing under a cup.

sauerkraut *noun* a dish of cabbage cut up fine and pickled in salt *etc*.

saunter *verb* to stroll about without hurry. – Also *noun*.

sausage *noun* minced meat seasoned and stuffed into a tube of animal gut *etc*.

savage *adjective* wild; fierce and cruel; uncivilized; very angry. – *noun* a human being in an uncivilized state; a fierce or cruel person. – *verb* to attack very fiercely. – *noun* **savagery** cruelty.

savanna or **savannah** *noun* a grassy, treeless plain.

save *verb* to bring out of danger, rescue; to protect from harm, damage, loss; to keep from spending or using (money, time, energy *etc*); to put money aside for the future. – *preposition* except (for): *All were broken save one*. – *noun* **savings** money put aside for the future. – *noun* **saviour** a person who saves from harm or evil. – *noun* **Saviour** Jesus Christ. – *noun* **saving grace** a good quality that makes up for faults. – **save up** to put money aside for future use.

savour *noun* characteristic taste or flavour; an interesting quality. – *verb* to taste or smell of; to taste (with enjoyment); to have a trace or suggestion (of): *Her reaction savours of jealousy*; to experience. – *adjective* **savoury** having a pleasant taste or smell; salt or sharp in flavour, not sweet. – *noun* (*plural* **savouries**) a savoury dish; a small savoury item of food.

savoy *noun* a type of winter cabbage.

saw *noun* a tool with a toothed edge for cutting wood *etc*; (*old*) a wise saying. – *verb* (*past tense* **sawed**, *past participle* **sawn** or **sawed**) to cut with a saw; *see* also **see**. – *noun* **sawdust** a dust of fine fragments of wood, made in sawing. – *noun* **sawmill** a mill where wood is sawn up.

sax *noun* short for **saxophone**.

saxifrage *noun* a type of rock plant.

saxophone *noun* a kind of wind instrument, with a curved metal tube and keys for the fingers.

say *verb* (*past tense* **said**) to speak, utter a (word *etc*): *to say 'Yes'*; to express in words, to state or tell: *They say they are going*. – *noun* the right to speak: *I have no say in the matter*; the opportunity to speak: *I have had my say*. – *noun* **saying** something often said, *esp* a proverb. – **I say!** an exclamation expressing surprise or protest or trying to attract someone's attention; **that is to say** in other words.

scab *noun* a crust formed over a sore; any of several diseases of animals or plants; a blackleg. – *adjective* **scabby**.

scabbard *noun* the sheath in which the blade of a sword is kept.

scabies *noun* an itchy skin disease.

scaffold *noun* a platform on which people are put to death. – *noun* **scaffolding** the poles and wooden platforms used by men at work on a building.

scald *verb* to burn with hot liquid or steam; to cook or heat (milk *etc*) just short of boiling point. – *noun* a burn caused by hot liquid or steam.

scale *noun* a set of regularly spaced marks made on something (*eg* a thermometer *etc*) for use as a measure; a series or system of increasing values: *salary scale*; (in music) a group of notes going up or down in order; the measurements of a map, model, plan *etc* compared with the actual size of country, object, area *etc* that is shown by them: *a map drawn to the scale 1:50000*; the size of an activity, business *etc*: *manufacture on a small (or large) scale*; a small thin flake or layer on the skin of a fish, snake *etc*, or on a leaf bud; (*plural*) a weighing machine. – *verb* to climb up; to clear of scales; to remove in thin layers. – *adjective* **scaly** having flakes or scales.

scallop *noun* a type of shellfish with a pair of hinged fan-shaped shells. – *adjective* **scalloped** (of a hem or edge of a garment *etc*) cut into curves or notches, wavy.

scallywag *noun* a rogue.

scalp *noun* the outer covering of the skull; the skin and hair of the top of the head. – *verb* to cut the scalp from.

scalpel *noun* a doctor's small, thin-bladed knife.

scamp *noun* a rascal.

scamper *verb* to run about playfully; to run off in haste.

scampi *noun* *plural* Norway lobsters (which are large prawns) cooked and used as food.

scan *verb* (*past tense* **scanned**) to count the beats in a line of verse; (of verse) to have the correct number of beats; to examine carefully; (*coll*) to glance hastily at (a newspaper *etc*); (in television *etc*) to pass a beam of light over every part of. – *noun* **scansion** scanning of verse.

scandal *noun* something disgraceful or shocking, arousing general disapproval; talk or gossip about people's (supposed) misdeeds. – *verb* **scandalize** to shock, horrify. – *adjective* **scandalous** shameful, disgraceful; containing scandal. – *noun* **scandalmonger** a person who spreads gossip or scandal.

scant *adjective* not plentiful, hardly enough: *to pay scant attention*. – *adjective* **scanty** little or not enough in amount: *scanty clothing*.

scapegoat *noun* a person who bears the blame for the wrongdoing of others.

scapula *noun* the shoulderblade.

scar *noun* the mark left by a wound, a sore *etc*; any mark or blemish. – *verb* (*past tense* **scarred**) to mark with a scar.

scarce *adjective* not plentiful, not enough; rare, seldom found. – *adverb* **scarcely** only just, barely: *I could scarcely hear*; probably, or definitely, not: *You can scarcely expect me to work when I'm ill.* – *noun* (*plural* **scarcities**) **scarcity** want, shortage. – **make oneself scarce** to go, run away.

scare *verb* to drive away by frightening; to startle, frighten. – *noun* a sudden fright or alarm. – *noun* **scarecrow** a figure (dressed in old clothes) set up to scare birds away from crops.

scarf *noun* (*plural* **scarves** or **scarfs**) a piece or a strip of material worn round the neck, shoulders or head.

scarlatina *noun* scarlet fever, *esp* in a mild form.

scarlet *noun* a bright red colour. – Also *adjective*. – *noun* **scarlet fever** a type of infectious illness, causing a rash.

scathing *adjective* (of something said, written *etc*) cruel, bitter, hurtful.

scatter *verb* to throw loosely about, sprinkle; to spread widely, send in all directions; to go away or flee in all directions. – *noun* **scatterbrain** a thoughtless person. – *adjective* **scattered** thrown, sent or placed widely here and there. – *noun* **scattering** an act of spreading, or being spread, widely; a small number or amount thinly spread or scattered.

scavenger *noun* a person who cleans streets or picks up rubbish; an animal which feeds on dead flesh.

SCE *abbreviation* Scottish Certificate of Education.

scene *sēn*, *noun* the place where something, real or imaginary, happens; a view, landscape; a division of a play or opera; a particular area of activity: *the business scene*; a show of bad temper, a violent quarrel. – *noun* **scenery** the painted background on a theatre stage; the general appearance of a stretch of country. – *adjective* **scenic** of scenery; picturesque.

scent *sent*, *verb* to discover by the smell; to have a suspicion of, to sense: *scent* *danger;* to cause to smell pleasantly: *The roses scented the air.* – *noun* perfume; an odour, smell; the trail of smell by which an animal or person may be tracked.

sceptic *skep'tik, noun* a person who is always inclined to doubt what he is told. – *adjective* **sceptical** unwilling to believe, doubtful. – *noun* **scepticism** a doubting or questioning attitude.

sceptre *sep'ter, noun* the ornamental rod carried by a monarch on ceremonial occasions as a symbol of power.

schedule *shed'ūl, noun* the time set or fixed for doing something *etc*, a timetable: *The plane is 2 hours behind schedule;* a written statement of details; a form for filling in information. – *verb* to form into, put into a schedule or list; to plan, arrange.

scheme *schēm, noun* a plan or systematic arrangement; a dishonest or crafty plan. – *verb* to make (crafty) plans, to plot. – *adjective* **scheming** crafty, cunning.

schism *sizm* or *skizm, noun* a breaking away of some persons from the main group (*esp* in the Church).

schist *shist, noun* a type of rock that splits easily into layers.

schizophrenia *skit-sō-frē'niā, noun* a form of mental illness in which the patient's personality and behaviour undergo a complete change. – *noun, adjective* **schizophrenic.**

scholar *noun* a man of great learning; one who has been awarded a scholarship; a pupil, student. – *adjective* **scholarly** showing or having knowledge, high intelligence and love of accuracy. – *noun* **scholarliness.** – *noun* **scholarship** learning; a sum of money given to help a clever student to carry on further studies. – *adjective* **scholastic** of schools or scholars.

school *noun* a place for teaching *esp* children; a group of thinkers, artists *etc* who have the same ideas; a large number of fish, whales *etc*. – *verb* to send to, or educate in, a school; to train by practice. – *noun* **schoolfellow** or **schoolmate** a person taught at the same school as oneself. – *noun* **schooling** education (in a school); training. – **schoolmaster** (*masculine*), **schoolmistress** (*feminine*) a teacher at a school.

schooner *noun* a type of sailing ship with two masts; a large sherry glass; (*US, Austr*) a large beer glass.

sciatica *noun* severe pain in the upper part of the leg.

science *noun* knowledge obtained by observation and experiment; any branch of such knowledge *eg* chemistry, physics, biology *etc;* such sciences as a whole. – *adjective* **scientific.** – *noun* **scientist** a person who studies one or more branches of science. – *noun* **science fiction** stories dealing with life on earth in the future, space travel, life on other planets *etc.*

sci fi *abbreviation* science fiction.

scimitar *noun* a type of sword with a short curved blade.

scintillate *verb* to sparkle; to show brilliance in wit *etc.*

scion *sī'ŏn, noun* a young member of a family; a descendant; a cutting or twig for grafting on another plant.

scissors *noun plural* a type of cutting instrument with two blades.

scoff *verb* to express scorn; (with **at**) to make fun of, mock.

scold *verb* to find fault with, blame, rebuke, with angry words. – *noun* a bad-tempered person *esp* a woman. – *noun* **scolding.**

scone *noun* a kind of small plain cake.

scoop *noun* any of several kinds of instruments of a hollow shape, as a ladle, shovel *etc,* used for lifting up or digging out (loose material, water *etc*); a piece of news which one newspaper prints before others. – *verb* to lift up or dig out, as with a scoop.

scooter *noun* a kind of two-wheeled toy vehicle pushed along by the foot; a type of small motor-cycle.

scope *noun* opportunity or room (for something, to do something): *scope for improvement;* extent, range or area dealt with: *outside the scope of this dictionary.*

scorch *verb* to burn slightly, singe; to dry up with heat. – *adjective* **scorching** burning, singeing; very hot; harsh, severe: *scorching criticism.*

score *noun* a gash, notch or line; an account, a debt: *settle old scores;* the total number of points gained in a game, test *etc;* a written piece of music showing separately all the parts for voices and instruments; a set of twenty: *a score of soldiers;* (*plural*) a great many: *scores of people;* a reason, account: *Don't worry on* *that score.* – *verb* to mark with lines, notches *etc*, to scratch; to gain points; to keep a note of points gained, in a game *etc*. – *noun* **scorer**. – **score out** to cross out.

scorn *verb* to look down on, despise; to refuse (help *etc*) *esp* because of pride. – Also *noun*. – *adjective* **scornful** full of scorn.

scorpion *noun* a type of spider-like creature with a poisonous sting in its tail.

scotch *verb* to cut or wound slightly; to stamp out (a rumour *etc*).

Scotch *noun* (*coll*) whisky. – *noun* **Scotch tape**® (*US*) a kind of (transparent) adhesive tape. – *noun* **Scotch terrier** a breed of small rough-coated, short-legged dog.

scot-free *adjective* unhurt; unpunished.

scoundrel *noun* a rascal, a worthless person.

scour *verb* to clean (a pan *etc*) by hard rubbing, to scrub; to move swiftly over or along, *esp* in search of something or someone.

scourge *noun* a cause of suffering, *esp* widespread (as an infectious disease *etc*); a whip made of leather thongs. – *verb* to cause great suffering; to whip.

scout *noun* someone sent out to spy and bring in information. – *noun* **Scout** (formerly **Boy Scout**) a member of the Scout Association.

scowl *verb* to wrinkle the brows in displeasure or anger. – Also *noun*.

scrabble *verb* to scratch, scrape, or grope (about). – *noun* **Scrabble**® a kind of word-building game.

scraggy *adjective* long and thin; uneven, rugged.

scramble *verb* to struggle to seize something before others; to wriggle along on hands and knees; to mix or toss together: *scrambled eggs*; to jumble up (a message *etc*) so that it must be decoded before it can be understood. – *noun* an act of scrambling; a rush and struggle to get something; a motor-cycle race over rough country.

scrap *noun* a small piece, a fragment; a picture *etc* for pasting in a scrapbook; (*coll*) a fight; articles or parts (*eg* of a car) no longer required for the original purpose: *sold as scrap*: (*plural*) small pieces, odds and ends. – *verb* (*past tense* **scrapped**) to throw away, to abandon

as useless; (*coll*) to fight, quarrel. – *noun* **scrapbook** a blank book in which to stick pictures *etc*. – *noun* **scrap-heap** a heap of old metal *etc*, a rubbish heap. – *noun* **scrap metal** metal for melting and re-using. – *adjective* **scrappy** made up of odd scraps, not well put together.

scrape *verb* to rub and (*usu*) mark with something sharp; to drag or rub (something) against or across (a surface) with a harsh grating sound; (with **up** or **together**) to collect (money *etc*) with difficulty. – *noun* an act of scraping; a mark or sound made by scraping; (*coll*) a difficult situation. – **scrape through** only just to avoid failure.

scratch *verb* to draw a sharp point across the surface of; to mark by doing this; to tear or to dig with claws, nails *etc*; to rub with the nails to relieve or stop itching; to (cause to) withdraw from a competition. – *noun* (*plural* **scratches**) a mark or sound made by scratching; a slight wound. – *adjective* (in golf) too good to be allowed a handicap; (of a team) made up of players hastily got together. – **come up to scratch** to be satisfactory; **start from scratch** to start from nothing, right at the beginning.

scrawl *verb* to write or draw untidily or hastily. – *noun* untidy, hasty or bad writing; something scrawled.

scrawny *adjective* thin, skinny.

scream *verb* to utter a shrill, piercing cry as in pain, fear *etc*, to shriek. – Also *noun*.

scree *noun* loose stones covering a steep mountain side.

screech *verb* to utter a harsh, shrill and sudden cry. – Also *noun*.

screed *noun* a long (tiresome) speech or letter.

screen *noun* any of several kinds of movable pieces of furniture (*usu* a flat, (folding) covered framework) to shelter from view or protect from heat, cold *etc*; something that shelters from wind, danger, difficulties *etc*; the surface on which films *etc* are shown; the surface on which television pictures appear. – *verb* to shelter, hide; to make a film of; to show on a screen; to sift or sieve; to sort out (*eg* the good from the bad) by testing *etc*; to conduct (a series of) examinations on a person or group of people to test for disease. – **screen off** to hide behind, or separate by, a screen.

screw noun a kind of nail with a slotted head and a winding groove or ridge (called the **thread**) on its surface; a kind of propeller (a **screw-propeller**) with spiral blades, used in ships and aircraft; a turn or twist (of a screw etc). – verb to fasten or tighten with a screw; to fix (eg a stopper) in place with a twisting movement; to twist, turn round (one's head etc); to twist up, crumple, pucker. – noun **screwdriver** a kind of tool for turning screws.

scribble verb to write carelessly; to make untidy or meaningless marks with a pencil etc: The child loved to scribble. – noun careless writing; meaningless marks (eg written by a child).

scribe noun (hist) a clerk or secretary, or one who copied out manuscripts; (among the Jews) a teacher of law.

scrimp verb to be sparing or stingy (usu with money): He scrimps and saves for his holiday.

script noun the text of a play, talk etc; handwriting like print.

scripture noun sacred writings. – noun (often plural) **Scripture** the Bible.

scroll noun a piece of paper rolled up; an ornament shaped like this.

scrotum noun the bag of skin enclosing the testicles.

scrounge verb to cadge; to (try to) get by begging. – Also noun: He's on the scrounge. – noun **scrounger**.

scrub verb (past tense **scrubbed**) to rub hard in order to clean. – noun (country covered with) low bushes.

scruff noun the back of the neck. – adjective **scruffy** untidy.

scrum noun (in Rugby) a struggle for the ball by the forwards of the opposing sides bunched together.

scruple noun hesitation or doubt over what is right or wrong that keeps one from acting or doing something. – verb to hesitate because of a scruple. – adjective **scrupulous** careful over the smallest details.

scrutiny noun (plural **scrutinies**) careful examination, a close look. – verb **scrutinize** to examine very closely.

scuba noun breathing apparatus used by skin-divers.

scud verb (past tense **scudded**) to move or sweep along quickly: scudding waves.

scuffle noun a confused fight.

scull noun a short oar. – verb to move (a boat) with a pair of these or with one oar worked at the back of the boat.

scullery noun (plural **sculleries**) a room for rough kitchen work.

sculptor (masculine), **sculptress** (feminine) noun an artist who carves or models figures, designs etc in wood, stone, clay etc. – noun **sculpture** the art of the sculptor or sculptress; (a piece of) their work.

scum noun foam or skin that rises to the surface of liquids; the most worthless part of anything: the scum of the earth.

scupper noun (usu plural) a hole in the side of a ship to drain water from the deck. – verb to put an end to, ruin: scupper his chances.

scurf noun small flakes of dead skin (esp on the scalp).

scurrilous adjective insulting, abusive: a scurrilous attack on his rival's work.

scurry verb (past tense **scurried**) to hurry along, scamper. – Also noun.

scurvy noun a type of disease caused by a lack of fresh fruit and vegetables.

scuttle noun a wooden or metal fireside container for coal; an opening with a lid in a ship's deck or side. – verb to make a hole in (a ship) in order to sink it; to hurry along, scamper.

scythe sīTH, noun a large curved blade, on a long handle, for cutting grass etc by hand. – verb to cut with a scythe.

SDP abbreviation Social Democratic Party.

sea noun the mass of salt water covering most of the earth's surface; a great stretch of water of less size than an ocean; a great expanse or number: a sea of faces. – noun **sea anemone** a type of small plant-like animal found on rocks at the seashore. – noun **seaboard** land along the edge of the sea. – noun **sea dog** an old sailor; a pirate. – noun **seafarer** a traveller by sea, a sailor. – adjective **seafaring**. – noun **seafront** a promenade with its buildings facing the sea. – adjective **seagoing** (of a ship) sailing on the ocean. – noun **seagull** a type of web-footed sea bird. – noun **sea-horse** a type of small fish with a horse-like head and neck. – noun **sea level** the level of the surface of the sea. – noun **sea-lion** a large kind of seal the male of which has a mane. – noun

seaman (*plural* **seamen**) a sailor, *esp* a member of a ship's crew who is not an officer. – *noun* **seamanship** the art of steering and looking after ships at sea. – *noun* **sea-mew** the seagull. – *noun* **seaplane** an aeroplane which can take off from and land on the water. – *noun* **seascape** a picture of a scene at sea. – *noun* **seashore** the land next to the sea. – *adjective* **seasick** made ill by the rocking movement of a ship. – *noun* **seaside** the land beside the sea. – *noun* **sea-trout** a type of large trout living in the sea but spawning in rivers. – *noun* **sea urchin** a type of small sea creature with a spiny shell. – *adjective, adverb* **seaward** towards the sea. – *noun* **seaweed** any of many kinds of plants growing in the sea. – *adjective* **seaworthy** (of ships) in a good enough condition to go to sea. – **at sea** on the sea; completely puzzled.

seal *noun* a type of furry sea animal living partly on the land; a piece of wax *etc* having a design pressed into it, attached to a document to show that it is legal or official; a piece of wax used to keep (a parcel *etc*) closed; anything that joins tightly or closes up completely; a piece of sticky paper with a design or picture on it: *a Christmas seal*. – *v* to mark or fasten with a seal; to close up completely; to make (legally) binding and definite: *to seal a bargain*. – *n* **sealing wax** a hard kind of wax for sealing letters, documents *etc*.

seam *noun* the line formed by the sewing together of two pieces of cloth *etc*; a line or layer of metal, ore, coal *etc* in the earth. – *noun* **seamstress** a woman who sews *esp* for a living. – **the seamy side** the more unpleasant side (of life *etc*).

séance *noun* a meeting of people who believe that it is possible to receive messages from the spirits of dead people.

sear *verb* to scorch, burn, dry up; to hurt severely.

search *verb* to look over, examine (a place, a person) in order to find something; (with **for**) to look for, seek. – *noun* (*plural* **searches**) an act of searching; an attempt to find. – *adjective* **searching** examining closely and carefully: *a searching question*. – *noun* **searchlight** a strong beam of light used for picking out objects at night. – *noun* **search-warrant** permission given to the police

to search a house *etc* for stolen goods *etc*.

season *noun* one of the four divisions of the year (spring, summer, autumn, winter); the usual or proper time for anything; a time associated with a particular activity: *football season*. – *verb* to add (salt *etc*) to improve the flavour of (food); to dry (wood) till it is ready for use. – *adjective* **seasonable** happening at the proper time; (often of weather) suitable for the season. – *adjective* **seasonal** of the seasons or a season; (of work, sports *etc*) taking place in one particular season only: *Hotel work is often seasonal*. – *adjective* **seasoned** (of food) flavoured; (of wood) ready to be used; trained, experienced: *a seasoned traveller*. – *noun* **seasoning** something (as salt, pepper *etc*) added to food to give it more taste. – *noun* **season ticket** a ticket that can be used over and over again for a certain period of time.

seat *noun* a piece of furniture (as a chair, bench *etc*) for sitting on; the part of a chair *etc* on which one sits; the part of the body or a garment on which a person sits; a (country) mansion; a place in parliament, on a council *etc*; the place from which something is carried on *etc*: *London became the seat of government. His hostility was the seat of the trouble*. – *verb* to cause to sit down; to have seats for (a certain number): *The room seats forty people*. – *noun* **seat-belt** a belt fixed to a seat in a car, aircraft *etc* to prevent a passenger from being thrown out of the seat (also **safety belt**).

sec *noun* short for **second**. – *abbreviation* secretary.

secateurs *noun plural* a type of tool like scissors, for trimming bushes *etc*.

secede *verb* to break away from a group, society *etc*. – *noun* **secession**.

seclude *verb* to keep (*esp* oneself) apart or away (from people's notice or company). – *noun* **seclusion**.

second *adjective* next after, or following, the first in time, place *etc*; other, alternate: *every second week*; another of the same kind as. *They thought him a second Mozart*. – *noun* a person or thing that is second; one who acts as attendant to a person who boxes or fights a duel; the 60th part of a minute of time, or of a degree (in measuring angles); an article not quite perfectly made: *These* *tights are seconds.* – *verb* to support, back up: *He seconded his friend's appointment as chairman;* to transfer temporarily to a special job. – *adjective* **secondary** second in position or importance. – *adjective* **second-best** next to the best, not the best. – *adjective* **second-hand** not new; having been used by another: *second-hand clothes;* (of a shop *etc*) dealing in second-hand goods. – *adverb* **secondly** in the second place. – *adjective* **second-rate** not of the best quality, inferior. – *noun* **second nature** a firmly fixed habit: *Organizing people is second nature to her.* – *noun* **secondary school, education** a school, education, between primary school and university *etc*.

secret *adjective* hidden from, not known to, or told to, others; secretive. – *noun* a fact, purpose, method *etc* that is not told or is not known: *He intends to keep his secret.* – *noun* **secrecy** state of being secret, mystery. – *adjective* **secretive** inclined to hide or conceal one's feelings, activities *etc*. – *noun* **secret service** a government department dealing with spying *etc*.

secretary (*plural* **secretaries**) *noun* a person employed to write letters, keep records and carry out routine business arrangements; a person elected or employed to deal with the written business of a club *etc*. – *adjective* **secretarial** of a secretary or his or her work. – **Secretary of State** a government minister in charge of an administrative department: *Secretary of State for Industry;* (*US*) the person in charge of foreign affairs.

secrete *verb* to hide, conceal in a secret place; (of a part of the body, *eg* the liver *etc*) to store up and give out (a fluid). – *noun* **secretion** an act of secreting; fluid secreted.

sect *noun* a group of people who hold certain views *esp* in religious matters. – *adjective* **sectarian** of a sect; loyal, or devoted to, a sect; (of opinions, attitudes *etc*) narrow-minded.

section *noun* a part or division: *a section of the community;* a thin slice (of something) for examination under a microscope; the view of the inside of anything when it is cut right through or across: *a section of a plant.*

sector *noun* a three-sided part of a circle whose sides are two radii and a part of the circumference; a part or section: *the Communist sector of Germany.*

secular *adjective* of worldly, not spiritual or religious things; (of music *etc*) not sacred or religious.

secure *adjective* safe, free from danger or from fear; confident, without doubts or fears: *secure in the knowledge that she had no rivals;* firmly fixed or fastened: *The lock is secure.* – *verb* to make safe, firm or established: *secure her position;* to seize, get hold of: *secure the diamonds;* to fasten: *secure the lock.* – *noun* **security** safety; (*plural* **securities**) property or goods which a lender of money may keep until the loan is paid back.

secy *abbreviation* secretary.

sedan *noun* an enclosed chair for one person, carried on two poles by two bearers (also **sedan chair**); (*US*) a saloon car.

sedate *adjective* calm, serious, dignified. – *noun* **sedateness**. – *noun* **sedation** use of sedatives to calm a patient. – *noun, adjective* **sedative** (a medicine that is) calming, soothing.

sedentary *adjective* (of a job *etc*) requiring much sitting.

sedge *noun* a type of coarse grass growing in swamps and rivers.

sediment *noun* the grains or solid parts which settle at the bottom of a liquid.

sedition *noun* (the stirring up of) rebellion against the government. – *adjective* **seditious** encouraging rebellion, rebellious.

seduce *verb* to succeed in tempting (someone) away from right or moral behaviour, *esp* to persuade (someone) to have sexual intercourse; to attract. – *noun* **seducer**. – *noun* **seduction**. – *adjective* **seductive** attractive, tempting.

see *verb* (*past tense* **saw**, *past participle* **seen**) to have sight: *After years of blindness he found he could see;* to be aware of, notice by means of the eye: *He sees her coming;* to form a picture of in the mind; to understand: *I see what you mean;* to find out: *I'll see what is happening;* to make sure: *See that he finishes his homework;* to accompany: *I'll see you home;* to meet: *I'll see you at the usual time.* – *noun* the district over which a bishop or archbishop has authority. – *conjunction* **seeing that** since, because. – **see through** to take part in, or support, to the end; not to be deceived by (a person, trick *etc*); **see to** to attend to (the preparation of): *to see to a meal.*

seed noun the part of a tree, plant etc from which a new plant may be grown; a seed-like part of a plant (as a grain or a nut); the beginning from which anything grows: the seeds of rebellion; (in a tournament) a seeded player; (old) children, descendants. – verb (of a plant) to produce seed; to sow; to remove the seeds from (eg a fruit); to arrange (good players) in a tournament (of golf, tennis etc) so that they do not compete against each other till the later rounds. – noun **seedling** a young plant just sprung from a seed. – adjective **seedy** full of seeds; shabby; sickly, not very well. – **go to seed** or **run to seed** (of plants) to develop seeds; (of a person, area etc) to deteriorate, to become much worse in condition etc.

seek verb (past tense **sought**) to look or search for: He is seeking evidence of an old civilization; to try (to do something): seek to establish proof; to try to get (advice etc). – **sought after** popular, much in demand.

seem verb to appear to be: He seems kind; to appear: She seems to like it. – adjective **seeming** apparent but not actual or real: a seeming success. – adjective **seemly** suitable; decent.

seen see **see**.

seep verb to flow slowly through a small opening, leak: Water seeped from the cracked pipe.

seer noun one who sees; a prophet.

seesaw noun a plank balanced across a stand so that one end of it goes up when the other goes down, used as a plaything by children; an up-and-down movement like that of a seesaw. – verb to go up and down on a seesaw; to move with a seesaw-like movement.

seethe verb to boil; to be very angry. – adjective **seething**.

segment noun a part cut off; a part of a circle cut off by a straight line.

segregate verb to separate (a person or group) from others. – noun **segregation**.

seine noun a large type of fishing net.

seismic sīz'mik, adjective of earthquakes. – noun **seismograph** an instrument that records earthquake shocks and measures their force.

seize verb to take suddenly, esp by force; to overcome: He was seized with fury; (of

machinery etc, usu with **up**) to become stuck, to break down. – noun **seizure** the act of seizing; capture; a sudden attack (of illness, rage etc).

seldom adverb not often, rarely: You seldom see an owl during the day.

select verb to pick out from a number according to one's preference, to choose. – adjective picked out, chosen; very good; (of a club etc) allowing only certain people in. – noun **selection** the act of choosing; thing(s) etc chosen; number of things from which to choose. – adjective **selective** having or using the power of choice; selecting carefully; (of weedkiller) harmless to garden plants. – noun **selector** someone who or something that chooses.

self noun (plural **selves**) one's own person; one's personality, character. – adjective **self-assured** trusting in one's own power or ability, confident. – adjective **self-centred** concerned with one's own affairs, selfish. – adjective **self-confident** believing, trusting in one's own powers or abilities. – **self-conscious** too aware of oneself, one's faults, blemishes etc, and therefore embarrassed in the company of others. – adjective **self-contained** (of a house) complete in itself, not sharing any part with other houses. – noun **self-control** control over oneself, one's feelings etc. – noun **self-defence** (the act of) defending one's own person, property etc. – noun **self-denial** doing without something (esp in order to give to others). – adjective **self-effacing** keeping oneself from being noticed, modest. – noun **self-esteem** respect for oneself; conceit. – adjective **self-evident** clear enough to need no proof. – noun **self-expression** expressing one's own personality in one's activities, esp art, writing etc. – adjective **self-important** having a mistakenly high sense of one's importance. – adjective **self-indulgent** too ready to satisfy one's own inclinations and desires. – noun **self-interest** a selfish desire to consider only one's own interests or advantage. – adjective **selfish** caring only for one's own pleasure or advantage. – noun **selfishness**. – adjective **selfless** thinking of others before oneself, unselfish. – adjective **self-made** owing one's success etc to one's own efforts: a self-made man. – noun **self-portrait** an artist's portrait of himself. – adjective **self-possessed** calm in mind or manner, quietly confident. – **self-raising flour** flour already containing an ingredient to make it rise. – *adjective* **self-reliant** trusting in one's own abilities *etc*. – *noun* **self-respect** respect for oneself and concern for one's own character and reputation. – *adjective* **self-righteous** thinking (too) highly of one's own goodness and virtue. – *noun* **self-sacrifice** the act of giving up one's own life, possessions, adverbantages *etc* in order to do good to others. – *adjective* **selfsame** the very same. – *adjective* **self-satisfied** pleased, smug, satisfied with oneself. – *noun* **self-service** helping or serving oneself (as in a restaurant, petrol station *etc*). – Also *adjective*. – *adjective* **self-sufficient** needing no help or support from anyone else. – *adjective* **self-willed** determined to have one's own way, obstinate.

sell *verb* (*past tense* **sold**) to give or hand over for money; to have or keep for sale: *He sells newspapers*; to be sold for, cost: *This book sells for £5*. – *noun* **seller** a person who sells.

Sellotape® *noun* a kind of transparent adhesive tape, used *eg* for sticking pieces of paper together.

selvage *noun* the firm edge of a piece of cloth, that does not fray.

semaphore *noun* a form of signalling by means of two arms which form different positions for each letter.

semblance *noun* an outward, often false, appearance: *She gave a semblance of listening*.

semen *noun* the liquid that carries sperm.

semi- *prefix* half; (*coll*) partly. – *noun* **semibreve** (in music) a note equal to four crotchets in length. – *noun* **semicircle** half of a circle. – *noun* **semicolon** the punctuation mark (;). – *adjective* **semi-detached** (of a house) joined to another house on one side but not on the other. – *noun* **semi-final** the stage or match of a contest immediately before the final. – *adjective* **semi-precious** (of a stone) having some value, but not considered a gem.

seminar *noun* a group of students *etc* working on, or meeting to discuss, a particular subject.

seminary *noun* (*plural* **seminaries**) a school or college.

semolina *noun* the hard particles of wheat sifted from flour, used for puddings *etc*.

senate *noun* the upper house of parliament in some countries, as USA, Australia; the governing council of some universities; (*hist*) the law-making body in ancient Rome. – *noun* **senator** a member of a senate.

send *verb* (*past tense*, *pp* **sent**) to cause (a person) to go; to cause (a thing) to be carried (to a place). – *noun* **sender**. – *noun* **send-off** a start; a friendly farewell (or party) for someone departing on a journey *etc*. – **send for** to order (a person or thing) to be brought.

senile *adjective* of old age; showing the (mental) feebleness of old age. – *noun* **senility**.

senior *adjective* older in age or higher in rank. – Also *noun*. – *noun* **seniority** state of being senior.

senna *noun* the dried leaves of certain plants, used as a laxative.

sensation *noun* a feeling through any of the five senses; a feeling, a vague effect: *a floating sensation*; a great stir, a state of excitement. – *adjective* **sensational** (aimed at) causing great excitement, horror *etc*.

sense *noun* one of the five powers by which we feel or notice (hearing, taste, sight, smell, touch); a feeling: *a sense of loss*; an ability to understand or appreciate: *a sense of humour*; (*plural*) one's right mind: *to take leave of one's senses*; wisdom, ability to act in a reasonable or sensible way; that which can be understood or be meaningful: *Your sentence does not make sense*; meaning: *To what sense of this word are your referring?* – *verb* to feel, realize: *to sense someone's disapproval*. – *adjective* **senseless** stunned, unconscious; foolish. – *noun* **sensibility** (*plural* **sensibilities**) ability to feel, sensitivity. – *adjective* **sensible** wise; able to be felt or noticed; (with **of**) aware of. – *adjective* **sensitive** feeling, *esp* easily, strongly or painfully; strongly affected by light, small changes, movements *etc*. – *verb* **sensitize** to make sensitive (*esp* to light). – *adjective* **sensory** of the senses. – *adjective* **sensual** of the senses rather than the mind; inclined to indulge too much in bodily pleasures. – *adjective* **sensuous** affecting the senses in a pleasant way; easily affected through the senses.

sent *see* **send**.

sentence *noun* a number of words which together make a complete statement; a judgement or punishment announced by a judge or a court. – verb to condemn (a person) to a particular punishment.

sentiment noun a thought, opinion (expressed in words); (a show of) feeling or emotion, often excessive. – adjective **sentimental** having or showing too much feeling or emotion.

sentinel noun a soldier on guard.

sepal noun one of the green leaves beneath the petals of a flower.

separate verb to set or keep apart; to divide (something) into parts; to disconnect; to go different ways; to live apart by choice. – adjective placed, kept etc apart; divided; not connected; different. – noun **separation** a dividing or putting apart. – noun **separatism**. – noun **separatist** a person who withdraws or urges separation from an established church, state etc.

sepia noun a brown colour.

sept- prefix seven.

September noun the ninth month of the year.

septic adjective (of a wound etc) full of germs that are poisoning the blood. – noun **septic tank** a tank in which sewage is partially purified.

septuagenarian noun a person from seventy to seventy-nine years old.

sepulchre noun a tomb. – adjective **sepulchral** of sepulchres; dismal, gloomy; (of a voice) deep, hollow in tone.

sequel noun a result, consequence; a story that is a continuation of an earlier story.

sequence noun the order (of events) in time; a number of things following in order, a connected series.

sequestered adjective (of a place) lonely, quiet.

sequin noun a small round sparkling ornament sewn on a dress etc.

seraph noun (plural **seraphs** or **seraphim**) an angel of the highest rank. – adjective **seraphic** like an angel.

sere adjective (in poetry etc) dry, withered.

serenade noun music (suitable to be) played or sung in the open air at night, esp under a lady's window. – verb to sing or play a serenade (to).

serene adjective calm; not worried, happy, peaceful. – noun **serenity** calmness, peacefulness.

serf noun (hist) a slave bought and sold with the land on which he worked. – noun **serfdom** slavery.

serge noun a strong type of cloth.

sergeant noun an army rank above corporal; a rank in the police force above a constable. – noun **sergeant-major** an army rank above sergeant.

series noun (plural **series**) a number of things following each other in order; a set of things of the same kind: He wrote a series of books on sport. – noun **serial** a story which is published, broadcast or televised in instalments.

serious adjective grave, thoughtful: a serious expression on her face; not joking, in earnest: a serious remark; important, needing careful thought: a serious matter; causing worry, likely to have dangerous results: serious injury.

sermon noun a serious talk, esp one given in church.

serpent noun a snake. – adjective **serpentine** like a serpent; winding, full of twists.

serrated adjective (of the edge of a blade etc) having notches or teeth like a saw.

serried adjective crowded together: serried ranks.

serum noun a clear watery fluid in the blood that helps fight disease; any of several fluids injected into the body to help fight disease.

serve verb to work for and obey; to attend or wait upon at table etc; to give out food, goods etc; to be able to be used (as): The cave will serve as a shelter; to do what is required for, be suitable for: serve a purpose; to carry out duties (as a member of the armed forces etc); to undergo, be subjected to (a sentence in prison etc); in starting the play in tennis, to throw up the ball and hit it with the racket. – noun **servant** a person who is paid to work for another, esp in helping to run a house; one employed by the government or administration of a country: When he was elected, he proved to be a conscientious public servant. Government offices are staffed by civil servants. – noun **service** an act of serving; the duty required of a servant or other employee; a performance of (public) worship or other religious ceremony; use: It is time to bring the new machine into service; time spent in the army, navy, air force etc; (plural) the armed forces; (often *plural*) help: *He was thanked for his services to refugees*; a regular supply (of something, *eg* transport): *bus service*; (*plural*) public supply of water, gas, electricity to houses *etc*; a set of dishes: *dinner service*. – *verb* to keep (a car, machine *etc*) in good working order by regular repairs. – *adjective* **serviceable** useful; lasting a long time: *serviceable clothes*. – **active service** service in battle; **at one's service** ready to help or be of use; **serve someone right** to be deserved by someone.

serviette *noun* a table napkin.

servile *adjective* slave-like; showing lack of spirit: *a servile attitude to his employer*. – *noun* **servility**. – *noun* **servitude** slavery; the state of being under strict control.

session *noun* a meeting or a series of meetings of a court, council *etc*; the period of the year when classes are held in a school *etc*; a period of time spent on a particular activity: *We'll have a session on that particular problem this afternoon*.

set *verb* (*present participle* **setting**, *past tense, past participle* **set**) to place or put; to fix in the proper place (*eg* broken bones); to arrange (a table for a meal, jewels in a necklace *etc*); to fix (a date, a price *etc*); to fix hair (in waves or curls); to adjust (a clock *etc*, or a machine *etc* so that it is ready to work or perform some function); to give (a task *etc*): *set him three problems*; to put in a certain state or condition: *set free*; (with **off** or **out** or **forth**) to start (on a journey *etc*); (of a jelly *etc*) to become firm or solid; to compose music for: *He set the poem to music*; (of the sun) to go out of sight below the horizon. – *adjective* fixed or arranged beforehand; ready: *all set*; fixed, stiff: *a set expression on his face*. – *noun* a group of people; a number of things of a similar kind, or used together: *set of carving tools*; an apparatus: *a television set*; scenery made ready for a play *etc*; pose, position: *the set of his head*; a series of six or more games in tennis; a fixing of hair in waves or curls; a badger's burrow (also **sett**); a street paving-block (also **sett**). – *noun* **setback** a movement in the wrong direction, a failure. – *noun* **set-square** a triangular drawing instrument, with one right angle. – *noun* **setting** act of someone who or something that sets; an arrangement; a background: *against*

a setting of hills and lochs. – **set about** to begin (doing something); to attack; **set in** to begin: *Winter has set in*; **set on** or **upon** to (cause to) attack.

sett *see* **set**.

settee *noun* a kind of sofa.

setter *noun* a dog of certain breeds that can be trained to point out game in hunting.

settle *verb* to place in a position or at rest; to come to rest; to agree over (a matter): *settle the price*; (sometimes with **down**) to (come to) be calm or quiet; (sometimes with **down**) to make one's home in a place; to pay (a bill); to fix, decide (**on**); to bring (a quarrel *etc*) to an end; to sink to the bottom. – *noun* a long high-backed bench. – *noun* **settlement** the act of settling; a decision, arrangement, agreement; payment for a bill; money given to a woman on her marriage; a number of people who have come to live in a country. – *noun* **settler** one who, or that which, settles; someone who goes to live in a new country.

seven *noun* the number 7. – *adjective* 7 in number. – *adjective* **seventh** the last of seven (things *etc*). – *noun* one of seven equal parts.

seventeen *noun* the number 17. – *adjective* 17 in number. – *adjective* **seventeenth** the last of seventeen (things *etc*). – *noun* one of seventeen equal parts.

seventy *noun* the number 70. – *adjective* 70 in number. – *adjective* **seventieth** the last of seventy (things *etc*). – *noun* one of seventy equal parts.

sever *verb* to cut apart or away, to break off; to separate, part. – *noun* **severance**.

several *adjective* more than one or two, but not a great many; various; different: *The boys went their several ways*. – *pronoun* more than one or two people, things *etc*, but not a great many.

severe *adjective* serious: *a severe illness*; harsh; strict; very plain and simple, not fancy. – *noun* **severity**.

sew *verb* (*past tense* **sewed**, *past participle* **sewn**) to join together with a needle and thread; to make or mend in this way. – *noun* **sewer**.

sewer *noun* an underground drain for carrying off water and waste matter. – *noun* **sewage** water and waste matter.

sex *noun* either of the two classes (male or female) into which animals are divided according to the part they play in producing children or young; sexual intercourse. – *noun* **sexism** discrimination against, or the assigning of stereotyped rôles to, a person on the grounds of their sex. – *adjective, noun* **sexist**. – *adjective* **sexual** of sex; involving sex or sexual intercourse. – *noun* **sexual intercourse** physical union between a man and a woman involving the insertion of the penis into the vagina.

sex- *prefix* six.

sexagenarian *noun* a person from sixty to sixty-nine years old.

sextant *noun* an instrument used for calculating distances by means of measuring angles *eg* the distance between two stars.

sexton *noun* a man who has various responsibilities in a church, as bellringing, gravedigging *etc*.

SF *abbreviation* science fiction.

SFA *abbreviation* Scottish Football Association.

shabby *adjective* worn-looking; poorly dressed; (of behaviour *etc*) mean, unfair.

shack *noun* a roughly-built hut.

shackle *verb* to fasten with a chain; to hold back, prevent, hinder. – *noun plural* **shackles** chains fastening the legs or arms of prisoners.

shade *noun* slight darkness caused by cutting off some light; a place not in full sunlight; anything that screens or shelters from the heat or light; (*plural*) (*coll*) sunglasses; the deepness or a variation of a colour; the dark parts in a picture; a very small amount or difference: *a shade larger*; a ghost. – *verb* to shelter from the sun or light; to make parts of a picture darker; to change gradually (*eg* from one colour into another *etc*). – *noun* **shading** the act of making shade; the marking of the darker places in a picture. – *adjective* **shady** sheltered from light or heat; (*coll*) dishonest, underhand: *a shady character.*

shadow *noun* darkness, shade caused by some object coming in the way of a light; the dark shape of that object on the ground *etc*; a dark part, in *eg* a picture; a very small amount: *a shadow of doubt*. – *verb* to shade, darken; to follow a person about secretly and watch them closely. – *noun* **shadow**

cabinet leading members of the opposition in parliament.

shaft *noun* anything long and straight; the long rod on which the head of an axe, spear, arrow *etc* is fixed; an arrow; a revolving rod which turns a machine or engine; the pole of a cart *etc* to which the horses are tied; the deep, narrow passageway leading to a mine; a deep vertical hole, as that for a lift; a ray (of light).

shaggy *adjective* rough, hairy, or woolly.

shake *verb* (*past tense* **shook**, *past participle* **shaken**) to (cause to) move backwards and forwards, up and down, or from side to side with quick, jerky movements; to make or be made unsteady; to shock, disturb: *His parting words shook me*. – *noun* the act of shaking or trembling; a shock, a drink mixed by shaking or stirring quickly: *milk shake*. – *adjective* **shaky** unsteady; trembling.

shale *noun* a kind of rock from which oil can be obtained.

shall *verb* used to form future tenses of other verbs when the subject is **I** or **we**: *I shall tell you later*; used for emphasis, or to mean 'must', or to express a promise, when the subject is **you, he, she, it** or **they**: *You shall go if I say you must. You shall go if you want to*; *see* also **should**.

shallot *noun* a kind of onion.

shallow *adjective* not deep; (of a person's mind, a person *etc*) not capable of thinking or feeling deeply. – *noun* (often *pl*) a place where the water is not deep.

sham *noun* something which is not what it appears to be, a pretence, a deception. – *adjective* false, imitation, pretended: *a sham fight*. – *verb* (*past tense* **shammed**) to pretend: *He's shamming sleep. I think he's shamming.*

shamble *verb* to walk in a shuffling or awkward manner. – *noun plural* **shambles** (*coll*) a mess, confused disorder; a slaughterhouse.

shame *noun* an uncomfortable feeling caused by awareness or realization of guilt, fault or failure; disgrace, dishonour: *He brought shame on his family*; (*coll*) bad luck, a pity: *It's a shame that you can't go.* – *verb* to make to feel shame or ashamed; (with **into**) to cause (someone to do something) by making him ashamed: *They shamed him into paying his share.* – *adjective* **shamefaced** showing shame or embarrassment. – *adjective* **shameful** disgraceful. – *adjective*

shameless feeling, showing no shame. – **put to shame** to cause to feel ashamed.

shammy *see* **chamois**.

shampoo *verb* to wash (the hair and scalp). – *noun* an act of shampooing; a soapy preparation (*usu* a liquid) used for this; a similar substance for cleaning carpets or upholstery.

shamrock *noun* a type of plant like clover with leaves divided in three.

shank *noun* the part of the leg between the knee and the foot; a long straight part (of a tool *etc*).

shan't short for **shall not**.

shanty *noun* (*plural* **shanties**) a roughly-made hut *etc*; a sailors' song (also **chanty**).

shape *noun* the form or outline of anything; a mould (for a jelly *etc*); a jelly *etc*, turned out of a mould; condition: *in good shape*. – *verb* to make in or into a certain form or shape; to model, mould; to (cause to) develop (in a particular way): *Our plans are shaping well.* – *adjective* **shapeless** having no shape or regular form. – *adjective* **shapely** having an attractive shape.

share *noun* one of the parts of something that is divided among several people *etc*; one of the parts into which the money of a business firm is divided. – *verb* to divide out among a number of people; to allow others to use (one's books *etc*); to have, use, own in common with someone else or some others: *We share a liking for music.* – *noun* **shareholder** a person who owns shares in a business company.

shark *noun* a type of large, very fierce, flesh-eating fish; (*coll*) a wicked and greedy person, a swindler.

sharp *adjective* cutting, piercing; having a thin edge or fine point; hurting, stinging, biting: *The sharp wind stung her face. His sharp words brought tears to her eyes*; alert, quick-witted; severe, inclined to scold; (of a note in music) raised half a tone, or too high in pitch; (of a voice) shrill; (of an outline *etc*) clear. – *adverb* punctually: *Come at ten o'clock sharp.* – *noun* a sign (#) used in music to show that a note is to be raised half a tone. – *verb* **sharpen** to make or grow sharp. – *noun* **sharpener** an instrument for sharpening: *a pencil sharpener.* – *noun* **sharper** a cheat (*esp* at cards). – *noun*

sharp practice cheating. – *adjective* **sharp-sighted** having keen sight. – *adjective* **sharp-witted** alert, intelligent. – **look sharp** to hurry.

shatter *verb* to break in pieces; to upset, ruin (hopes, health *etc*).

shave *verb* to cut away hair with a razor; to scrape or cut away the surface of (wood *etc*); to touch lightly, or just avoid touching, in passing. – *noun* the act of shaving; a narrow escape: *a close shave.* – *adjective* **shaven** shaved. – *noun plural* **shavings** very thin slices *esp* of wood.

shawl *noun* a loose covering for the shoulders.

she *pronoun* some female person, animal, or thing (as a ship) thought of as female, already spoken about (used only as the subject of a verb): *When the girl saw us, she asked the time.*

sheaf *noun* (*plural* **sheaves**) a bundle (*eg* of corn, papers) tied together: – *plural* **sheaves**.

shear *verb* (*past tense* **sheared**, *past participle* **shorn**) to clip, cut (*esp* wool from a sheep); to cut through, cut off. – *noun plural* **shears** large scissors; a large type of cutting tool like scissors.

sheath *noun* a case for a sword or dagger; a long close-fitting covering; a condom. – *verb* **sheathe** to put into a sheath.

shed *noun* a building for storage or shelter: *The coalshed will hold 10 bagfuls. There is a bicycle shed at the back of the school*; an out-house. – *verb* to throw or cast off (leaves, a skin, clothing); to (let) pour out (tears, blood); to give out (light *etc*).

sheen *noun* brightness, gloss.

sheep *noun* a type of animal whose flesh is used as food and from whose wool clothing is made; a very meek person who lacks confidence. – *noun* **sheep-dip** a liquid for disinfecting sheep. – *noun* **sheepdog** a dog trained to look after sheep or of a breed used for this work. – *adjective* **sheepish** shy; embarrassed, shamefaced.– *noun* **sheepshank** a kind of knot, used for shortening a rope. – *noun* **sheepskin** the skin of a sheep; a kind of leather made from it.

sheer *adjective* very steep: *a sheer drop from the cliff*; pure, not mixed: *sheer delight*: *sheer nonsense*; (of cloth) very thin or fine. – *adverb* straight up and down, very steeply. – *verb* to (cause to) turn aside from a straight line, swerve.

sheet *noun* a large piece of linen, cotton, nylon *etc* for a bed; a large thin piece of anything as metal, glass, ice *etc*; a piece of paper; a sail; the rope fastened to the lower corner of a sail. – *noun* **sheet-anchor** a large anchor for use in emergencies. – *noun* **sheeting** any material from which sheets are made. – *noun* **sheet-lightning** lightning which appears in great sheets or flashes.

sheikh *noun* an Arab chief.

shekel *noun* (*hist*) a Jewish weight and coin; (*plural coll*) money.

shelf *noun* (*plural* **shelves**) a board fixed on a wall, for laying things on; a flat layer of rock, a ledge; a sandbank. – *verb* **shelve** to put up shelves in; to put aside (a problem *etc*) *usu* for later consideration; (of land) to slope gently.

shell *noun* a hard outer covering (of a shellfish, egg, nut *etc*); a husk or pod (*eg* of peas); a metal case filled with explosive fired from a gun; any framework, as of a building not yet completed, or burnt out: *Only the shell of the warehouse was left*. – *verb* to take the shell from (a nut, egg *etc*); to fire shells at. – *noun* **shellfish** a water creature covered with a shell (as oyster, limpet, mussel).

shelter *noun* a building or something else which acts as a protection from harm, rain, wind *etc*; the state of being protected from any of these. – *verb* to give protection to; to put in a place of shelter or protection; to go to, stay in, a place of shelter. – **take shelter** to go to a place of shelter.

shelve *see* **shelf**.

shepherd (*masculine*), **shepherdess** (*feminine*) *noun* a person who looks after sheep. – *verb* (**shepherd**) to watch over carefully, to guide. – *noun* **shepherd's pie** a dish of minced meat covered with mashed potatoes.

sherbet *noun* (powder for making) a fizzy drink.

sheriff *noun* the chief representative of the king *etc* in a county whose duties include keeping the peace; (in Scotland) the chief judge of county; (in the USA) the chief law-enforcement officer of a county.

sherry *noun* a strong kind of wine, often drunk before a meal.

shied *see* **shy**.

shield *noun* anything that protects from harm *etc*; (*hist*) a broad piece of metal *etc* carried as part of a soldier's armour as a defence against weapons; a shield-shaped trophy won in a competition *etc*; a shield-shaped plaque bearing a coat-of-arms. – *verb* to protect, defend, shelter.

shift *verb* to move (something), change the position of, transfer: *We shifted the furniture away from the leak in the roof. He tried to shift the blame on to his brother*; to change position or direction: *The wind shifted*; to get rid of. – *noun* a change: *shift of emphasis*; a change of position, transfer; a group of workers on duty at the same time: *Visitors to the factory can watch the day shift at work. We provide a bus to take the night shift home*; a specified period of work or duty; a kind of loose-fitting dress. – *adjective* **shiftless** having no set plan or purpose, lazy. – *adjective* **shifty** not to be trusted, looking dishonest. – **shift for oneself** to manage to get on by one's own efforts.

shilling *noun* before 1971, the name of the silver-coloured coin worth ½₀ of £1 (now the 5 pence piece).

shillyshally *verb* (*past tense* **shillyshallied**) to hesitate in making up one's mind, to waver.

shimmer *verb* to shine with a quivering or unsteady light. – Also *noun*.

shin *noun* the front part of the leg below the knee. – **shin up** to climb.

shindy *noun* (*plural* **shindies**) (*coll*) a noise, uproar.

shine *verb* (*past tense, past participle* **shone**) to (cause to) give out or reflect light; to be bright; to polish (shoes *etc*); to be very good at: *He shines at arithmetic*. – *noun* brightness; an act of polishing. – *adjective* **shining** very bright and clear; to be admired, distinguished: *a shining example*. – *adjective* **shiny** glossy, polished.

shingle *noun* coarse gravel (made up of rounded stones) on the shores of rivers or of the sea. – *noun plural* **shingles** a type of infectious disease causing a painful rash.

shinty *noun* in Scotland, a kind of ball game, something like hockey.

shiny *see* **shine**.

ship *noun* any large vessel for journeys across water. – *verb* (*past tense* **shipped**) to take on to a ship; to send by ship; to go by ship. – noun **ship chandler** a person who deals in ship's stores. – noun **shipmate** a fellow-sailor. – noun **shipment** an act of putting on board ship; a load of goods sent by ship. – noun **shipping**. – adjective **shipshape** in good order, neat, trim. – noun **shipwreck** the sinking or destruction of a ship (esp by accident); a wrecked ship; ruin. – adjective **shipwrecked** involved in a shipwreck. – noun **shipwright** a person who is employed to build or repair ships. – noun **shipyard** the yard in which ships are built or repaired.

shire noun a county.

shirk verb to avoid or evade (doing one's duty etc). – noun **shirker**.

shirt noun a kind of garment worn by men on the upper part of the body, usu having a collar, sleeves and buttons down the front; a similar garment for a woman.

shiver verb to tremble (as with cold or fear); to break into small pieces, shatter. – noun the act of shivering; a small broken piece: shivers of glass.

shoal noun a great number, esp of fishes, together in one place; a shallow place, a sandbank.

shock noun a sudden blow, coming with great force; a feeling of fright, horror, dismay etc; a state of weakness or illness that may follow such feelings; the effect on the body of an electric current passing through it; an earthquake; a bushy mass (of hair). – verb to give a shock to; to upset or horrify. – noun **shock-absorber** a device (in an aircraft, car etc) for lessening the impact or force of bumps. – adjective **shocking** causing horror or dismay; disgusting.

shod adjective wearing shoes. – verb see **shoe**.

shoddy adjective of poor material or quality: shoddy goods; mean: a shoddy trick.

shoe noun a stiff outer covering for the foot, not reaching above the ankle; a rim of iron nailed to the hoof of a horse. – verb (past tense, past participle **shod**) to put shoes on (a horse). – noun **shoehorn** a curved piece of horn, metal etc used for making one's shoe slip easily over one's heel. – noun **shoelace** a kind of cord or string used for fastening a shoe. – noun **shoemaker** a person who makes and mends shoes. – **on a shoestring** with very little money.

shone see **shine**.

shoo! interjection used to scare away birds, animals etc. – verb (**shoo**) to drive or scare away.

shook see **shake**.

shoot verb (past tense, past participle **shot**) to send a bullet from a gun, or an arrow from a bow; to hit or kill with an arrow, bullet etc; to send, let fly swiftly and with force; to kick for a goal; to score (a goal); (of plants) to grow new buds etc; to photograph or film; to move very swiftly or suddenly; to slide (a bolt). – noun a new sprout etc on a plant; an expedition to shoot game; land where game is shot. – noun **shooting-brake** (old) an estate car. – noun **shooting star** a meteor.

shop noun a place where goods are sold; a workshop or a place where any industry is carried on. – verb (past tense **shopped**) to visit shops and buy goods; (slang) to betray (to the police). – noun **shopkeeper** a person who owns and keeps a shop. – noun **shoplifter** a person who steals goods from a shop. – noun **shopper**. – noun **shop steward** in a factory etc, a worker elected by the other workers as their representative. – **talk shop** (coll) to talk about work when off duty.

shore noun the land bordering on a sea or lake. – verb to prop (up), support: We shored up the wall to hold the flood. We must borrow money to shore up this failing organization.

shorn see **shear**.

short adjective not long: a short piece of string; not tall: a short man; brief, not lasting long: a short talk; not enough, less than it should be; (of a person or his manner) rude, sharp, abrupt; (of pastry) crisp and crumbling easily. – adverb suddenly, abruptly: He stopped short; not as far as intended: The shot fell short. – noun a short film; a short-circuit; (plural) short trousers. – verb to short-circuit. – noun **shortage** a lack. – noun **shortbread** a kind of thick biscuit made of butter and flour etc. – noun **short-circuit** the missing out, usu accidentally, of a major part of an intended electric circuit, sometimes causing blowing of fuses. – verb (of an electrical appliance) to develop or undergo a short-circuit; to bypass (a difficulty etc). – noun **shortcoming** a fault, a defect. – noun **short cut** a short way of going somewhere or doing something. – verb **shorten** to make less in length. – *noun* **shorthand** a method of swift writing using strokes and dots to show sounds. – *adjective* **short-handed** having fewer workers than usual. – *noun* **short list** a list of candidates, *eg* for a job, who have been selected from the total number of those applying for it: *He's on the short list for the prize.* – *adjective* **shortlived** living or lasting only a short time. – *adverb* **shortly** soon; curtly, abruptly; briefly. – *adjective* **short-sighted** seeing clearly only things which are near; taking no account of what may happen in the future. – *adjective* **short-tempered** easily made angry. – *adjective* **short-term** intended to last only a short time. – **give short shrift to** to waste little time or consideration on; **in short** in a few words; **short of** not having enough; *short of money*; less than, not as much or as far as: *I have just £3 short of the price. We ran out of fuel 5 miles short of London; without going as far as: He did not know how to get the money, short of stealing it.*

shot *noun* something which is shot or fired; small lead bullets, used in cartridges; a single act of shooting; the sound of a gun being fired; the distance covered by a bullet, ball, arrow *etc*; a marksman; a throw, stroke, turn *etc* in a game or competition; an attempt (at doing something, at guessing *etc*); a photograph; a scene in a motion picture. – *adjective* (of silk *etc*) showing changing colours; streaked or mixed with (a colour *etc*). – *verb see* **shoot.** – *noun* **shotgun** a light type of gun which fires shot. – **a shot in the dark** a guess.

should *verb* the form of the verb **shall** used to express a condition: *I should go if I had time;* used to mean 'ought to': *You should know that already.*

shoulder *noun* the part of the body between the neck and the upper arm; the upper part of the foreleg of an animal; anything resembling a shoulder in shape: *the shoulder of the hill.* – *verb* to carry on the shoulder(s); to bear the full weight of (a burden *etc*); to push with the shoulder. – *noun* **shoulderblade** the broad flat bone of the shoulder.

shout *noun* a loud cry or call; a loud burst (of laughter *etc*). – Also *verb*.

shove *verb* to push with force, thrust, push aside. – Also *noun*.

shovel *noun* a kind of spade-like tool used for lifting or shifting coal, gravel *etc*. – *verb* to lift or move with a shovel.

show *verb* (*past tense* **showed**, *past participle* **shown**) to allow, or cause, to be seen: *Show her your new dress;* to be able to be seen: *Your underskirt is showing;* to exhibit, display (an art collection *etc*); to point out (the way *etc*); to direct, guide: *Show her to a seat;* to make clear, demonstrate: *That shows that I was right.* – *noun* the act of showing; display; an exhibition; a performance, an entertainment. – *noun* **show business** the branch of the theatre concerned with variety entertainments. – *noun* **showroom** a room where goods are laid out for people to see. – *adjective* **showy** bright, gaudy; (too) obvious, striking. – **show off** to show or display (something); to try to impress others with one's talents, possessions *etc*; **show up** to (cause to) stand out clearly; to expose, to make the faults of (someone, something) obvious.

shower *noun* a short fall of rain; a large quantity: *a shower of questions;* a showerbath; the apparatus which sprays water for this; the place where this apparatus is kept; (*US*) a party at which gifts are given *eg* to someone about to be married. – *verb* to pour (something) down on; to bathe under a shower. – *noun* **showerbath** a bath in which water is sprayed from above. – *adjective* **showerproof** (of material, a coat *etc*) able to withstand light rain. – *adjective* **showery** raining from time to time.

shown *see* **show.**

shrank *see* **shrink.**

shrapnel *noun* a shell containing bullets *etc* which scatter with explosion; splinters or fragments of the shell, metal, a bomb *etc*.

shred *noun* a long, narrow piece, cut or torn off; a scrap, a very small amount: *not a shred of evidence.* – *verb* (*past tense* **shredded**) to cut or tear into shreds.

shrew *noun* a small mouse-like type of animal with a long nose; a noisy, quarrelsome or scolding woman. – *adjective* **shrewish** quarrelsome, ill-tempered.

shrewd *adjective* clever, sometimes also cunning: *The teacher relied on shrewd commonsense. A shrewd businessman can foresee demand.*

shriek *verb* to utter (with) a shrill scream or laugh. – Also *noun*.

shrill *adjective* (of a sound or voice) high in tone, piercing. – *adverb* **shrilly.**

shrimp *noun* a small, long-tailed kind of eatable shellfish; (*coll*) a small person.

shrine *noun* a holy or sacred place.

shrink *verb* (*past tense* **shrank**, *past participle* **shrunk**) to (cause to) become smaller; to draw back in fear and disgust (from). – *noun* **shrinkage** the amount by which a thing grows smaller. – *adjective* **shrunken** shrunk.

shrivel *verb* (*past tense* **shrivelled**) to dry up, wrinkle, wither.

shroud *noun* the cloth round a dead body; anything which covers: *a shroud of mist*; (*plural*) the rope from the mast-head to a ship's sides. – *verb* to cover (up) as with a shroud.

shrub *noun* a small bush or plant. – *noun* **shrubbery** (*plural* **shrubberies**) a place where shrubs grow.

shrug *verb* (*past tense* **shrugged**) to show doubt, lack of interest *etc* by drawing up the shoulders. – Also. *noun* – **shrug off** to dismiss or to treat as being unimportant: *shrug off a problem*.

shrunk, shrunken *see* **shrink**.

shudder *verb* to tremble from fear, cold, disgust. – Also *noun*.

shuffle *verb* to mix, rearrange (*eg* playing-cards); to move by dragging or sliding the feet along the ground without lifting them; to move (the feet) in this way. – Also *noun*.

shun *verb* (*past tense* **shunned**) to avoid, keep clear of.

shunt *verb* to move (railway trains, engines *etc*) on to a side track.

shut *verb* (*present participle* **shutting**, *past tense* **shut**) to move (a door, window, lid *etc*) so that it covers an opening; to close, lock (a building *etc*): *We shut the shop at 12.30*; to become closed: *The door shut with a bang*; to confine, put (something or someone) in something to prevent from going free: *Shut the dog in his kennel.* – *noun* **shutter** a cover for a window or opening (as in a camera). – **shut down** to close (a factory *etc*); **shut up** to close completely; (*coll*) to (cause to) stop speaking or making other noise.

shuttle *noun* the part of a weaving loom which carries the cross thread from side to side. – *adjective* (of a bus or train service *etc*) going to and fro between two places. – *noun* **shuttlecock** a rounded cork stuck with feathers, used in the game of badminton. – *noun* **shuttle service** a transport service moving constantly between two points.

shy *adjective* (of a wild animal) easily frightened, timid; lacking confidence in the presence of others, *esp* strangers; not wanting to attract attention. – *verb* (*past tense* **shied**) to jump or turn suddenly aside in fear; to throw, toss. – *noun* a try, an attempt. – *adverb* **shyly.** – *noun* **shyness.** – **fight shy of** to avoid, keep away from.

SI *abbreviation* [*Fr*] Système International (d'Unités) – the metric unit system.

sibilant *adjective, noun* (of) a hissing sound.

sibling *noun* a brother or sister.

sibyl *noun* (*myth*) a woman able to tell the future, a prophetess.

sick *adjective* wanting to vomit; vomiting; not well, ill; (with **of**) tired of. – *noun* **sick bed** or **sick room** a bed or room, in which there is an ill person. – *verb* **sicken** to make or become sick. – *adjective* **sickening** causing sickness, disgust, weariness. – *noun* **sick leave** time off work for illness. *adjective* **sickly** unhealthy; causing sickness; feeble. – *noun* **sickness.**

sickle *noun* a hooked knife for cutting or reaping grain, hay *etc*.

side *noun* an edge, border or boundary line; a surface of something, *esp* one that is not the top, bottom, front or back; either surface of a piece of paper, cloth *etc*; the right or left part of the body (*esp* between the hip and armpit); a division or part: *the north side of the town*; an aspect, point of view: *all sides of the problem*; a slope (of a hill); a team or party which is opposing another. – *adjective* on or towards the side: *side door*; indirect, additional but less important: *side issue.* – *verb* (with **with**) to support (one person, group *etc* against another). – *noun* **sideboard** a piece of furniture in a dining room *etc* for holding dishes *etc*. – *noun* **sidecar** a small car for a passenger, attached to a motor-cycle. – *noun* **side effect** an additional (often bad) effect (*esp* of a medicine, drug *etc*). – *noun* **sideline** an extra bit of business, outside one's regular job or activity. – *adjective, adverb* **sidelong** from or to the side: *a sidelong glance.* – *noun* **sideshow** a less important show (that is part of a larger one). –

verb **sidestep** to avoid by stepping to one side. – *verb* **sidetrack** to turn (a person) away from what they were going to do or say. – *noun* **sidewalk** (*US*) a pavement, footpath. – *adverb* **sideways** with the side foremost; towards the side. – *noun* **siding** a short line of rails on which trucks *etc* are shunted off the main line. – **take sides** to choose to support (a party, person) against another.

sidle *verb* to go or move sideways; to move in a stealthy way.

siege *sēj*, *noun* an attempt to capture a town, fort *etc* by keeping it surrounded by an armed force; a constant attempt to gain control of. – **lay siege to** to besiege.

sierra *noun* a range of mountains with jagged peaks.

siesta *noun* a short sleep or rest, *esp* one taken in the afternoon.

sieve *siv*, *noun* a container with a mesh or very small holes used to separate liquids from solids, fine, small pieces from large, coarse pieces *etc*. – *verb* to put through a sieve.

sift *verb* to separate by passing through a sieve; to consider and examine closely: *sifting all the evidence*.

sigh *verb* to take a long, deep-sounding breath, showing tiredness, sadness, longing *etc*. – Also *noun*.

sight *noun* the act or power of seeing; a view, a glimpse: *He caught sight of her*; (often *plural*) something worth seeing: *the sights of London*; something or someone seen that is unusual, ridiculous, shocking *etc*: *She's quite a sight in that hat*; (on a gun) a guide to the eye in taking aim. – *verb* to get a view of, see suddenly; to look at through the sight of a gun. – *noun* **sight-reading** playing or singing from music that one has not seen previously. – *noun* **sightseeing** visiting the chief buildings, monuments *etc* of a place.

sign *noun* a mark with a special meaning, a symbol: *+ is the sign of addition*; a movement (such as a nod, wave of the hand) to show one's meaning; (a board with) an advertisement or notice giving information (*eg* the name of a shopkeeper); something which shows what is happening or what is going to happen: *signs of irritation: a sign of good weather*. – *verb* to write one's name (on a document, cheque *etc*); to make a sign

or gesture to; to show (one's meaning) by a sign or gesture. – *noun* **signboard** a board with a notice. – *noun* **signpost** a post with a sign, *esp* one showing the direction and distances of certain places. – **sign on** to enter one's name on a list for work, the army *etc*.

signal *noun* a sign (as a gesture, light, sound) giving a command, warning or other message; something used for this purpose: *railway signals*; the wave, sound received or sent out by a radio set *etc*. – *verb* (*past tense* **signalled**) to make signals (to); to send (information) by signal. – *adjective* remarkable: *a signal success*. – *noun* **signalman** a person who works railway signals, or who sends signals.

signature *noun* a signed name; an act of signing; the flats or sharps at the beginning of a piece of music which show its key, or the sign showing its time. – *noun* **signatory** (*plural* **signatories**) a person who has signed an agreement *etc*. – *noun* **signature tune** a tune used to identify a particular performer, radio or television series *etc* played at the beginning and/or end of the programme.

signet *noun* a small seal, *esp* one bearing one's initials *etc* and set into a ring (**signet ring**).

signify *verb* (*past tense* **signified**) to mean; to be a sign of; to show, make known by a gesture *etc*: *He signified his disapproval by a shake of the head*; to have meaning or importance. – *noun* **significance** meaning; importance. – *adjective* **significant** meaning much; important: *no significant change*.

silage *noun* green fodder preserved in a silo.

silence *noun* absence or lack of sound or speech; a time of quietness. – *verb* to cause to be silent. – *noun* **silencer** a device (on a car engine, gun *etc*) for making noise less. – *adjective* **silent** free from noise; not speaking.

silhouette *noun* an outline drawing (of a person) *esp* in profile, and *usu* filled in with black; a dark outline (of someone, something) seen against the light.

silica *noun* a white or colourless substance, of which flint, sandstone, quartz *etc* are mostly made up.

silk *noun* very fine, soft fibres, spun by silkworms; thread or cloth made from it. – *adjective* made of silk; like silk, soft, smooth. – *adjective* **silken** made of silk; like silk. – *noun* **silkworm** the caterpillar of certain moths which spins silk. – *adjective* **silky** like silk.

sill *noun* a ledge of wood, stone *etc* such as that below a window or a door.

silly *adjective* foolish, not sensible.

silo *noun* (*plural* **silos**) a tower-like building for storing grain *etc*; a pit or airtight chamber for holding silage; an underground chamber built to contain a guided missile.

silt *noun* sand or mud left behind by flowing water. – **silt up** to (cause to) become blocked by mud.

silver *noun* an element, a type of white metal, able to take on a high polish; money made of silver or of a metal alloy used instead of it; objects (*esp* cutlery) made of, or plated with, silver. – *adjective* made of, or looking like, silver. – *verb* to cover with silver; to become like silver. – *noun* **silverfish** a kind of wingless, silvery insect, sometimes found in houses. – *noun* **silver foil** or **silver paper** kinds of wrapping materials made of metal, having a silvery appearance. – *noun* **silversmith** one who makes or sells articles of silver. – *noun* **silver wedding** *etc* a 25th anniversary of a wedding *etc*. – *adjective* **silvery** like silver; (of sound) ringing and musical.

simian *adjective* ape-like.

similar *adjective* (almost) alike or like. – *noun* **similarity** (*plural* **similarities**). – *adverb* **similarly** in the same, or a similar, way; likewise, also.

simile *noun* a form of expression using 'like' or 'as', in which one thing is likened to another that is well-known for a particular quality (*eg* 'as black as night', 'to swim like a fish').

simmer *verb* to cook gently just below or just at boiling-point.

simper *verb* to smile in a silly manner; to say with a simper. – *noun* a silly smile.

simple *adjective* easy, not difficult, or not complicated; plain, not fancy: *a simple hairstyle*; ordinary: *simple, everyday objects*; of humble rank: *a simple peasant*; mere, nothing but: *the simple truth*; too trusting, easily cheated; foolish, half-witted. – *noun* **simpleton** a foolish person. – *noun* **simplicity** the state of being simple. – *noun* **simplification** an act of making simpler; a simple form. –

verb **simplify** (*past tense* **simplified**) to make simpler. – *adverb* **simply** in a simple manner; merely: *I do it simply for the pay*; absolutely: *simply beautiful*.

simulate *verb* to pretend, make a pretence of: *She simulated illness*; to have an appearance of, look like. – *adjective* **simulated** pretended; having the appearance of: *simulated leather*. – *noun* **simulation**.

simultaneous *adjective* happening, or done, at the same time. – *adverb* **simultaneously**.

sin *noun* a wicked act, *esp* one which breaks the laws of one's religion; wrongdoing; (*coll*) a shame, pity. – *verb* (*past tense* **sinned**) to commit a sin, do wrong. – *adjective* **sinful** wicked. – *noun* **sinner**. – **original sin** the supposed sinful nature of all human beings since the time of Adam's sin.

since *adverb* (often with **ever**) from that time onwards: *I have avoided him* (*ever*) *since*; at a later time: *We have since become friends*; ago: *long since*; from the time of: *since his arrival*. – *conjunction* after the time when: *I have been at home since I returned from Italy*; because: *Since you are going, I will go too*.

sincere *adjective* honest in word and deed, meaning what one says or does, true: *a sincere friend*; truly felt: *a sincere desire*. – *noun* **sincerity**.

sinecure *noun* a job in which one receives money but has little or no work to do.

sinew *noun* a tough cord or band that joins a muscle to a bone; (*plural*) equipment and resources necessary for (something): *sinews of war*. – *adjective* **sinewy** having (strong) sinews; strong, tough.

sing *verb* (*past tense* **sang**, *past participle* **sung**) to make musical sounds with one's voice; to utter (words, a song *etc*) by doing this. – *noun* **singer**. – *noun* **sing-song** a gathering of people singing informally together; an up-and-down tone of voice. – Also *adjective*.

singe *verb* to burn slightly on the surface, scorch. – Also *noun*.

single *adjective* one only; not double; not married; for one person: *a single bed*; between two people: *singularle combat*; for one direction of a journey: *a single ticket*. – *adjective* **single-handed** working *etc* by oneself. – *adjective* **single-minded** having one aim only. – *noun*

singleness the state of being single. – adverb **singly** one by one, separately. – **single out** to pick out, treat differently in some way.

singlet noun a vest, an undershirt, worn as underwear or as sportswear by runners etc.

singular adjective (in grammar, the opposite of. **plural**) showing one person, thing etc; exceptional: singular success; unusual, strange: a singular sight. – adverb **singularly** strangely, exceptionally: singularly ugly.

sinister adjective suggesting evil to; evil-looking.

sink verb (past tense **sank**, past participle **sunk**) to (cause to) go down below the surface of the water etc; to go down or become less: His hopes sank; (of a very ill person) to become weaker; to lower oneself (into): to sink into a chair; to make by digging (a well etc); to push (one's teeth etc) deep into (something); to invest (money etc) into a business. – noun a kind of basin in a kitchen, bathroom etc, with a water supply connected to it and a drain for carrying off dirty water etc. – noun **sinker** a weight fixed to a fishing line etc. – adjective **sunk** on a lower level than the surroundings; sunken; (coll) defeated, done for. – adjective **sunken** that has been sunk; (of cheeks etc) hollow.

sinuous adjective bending in and out, winding.

sinus noun (plural **sinuses**) a hollow or air cavity, esp an air cavity in the head connected with the nose. – noun **sinusitis** inflammation of (one of) the sinuses.

sip verb (past tense **sipped**) to drink in very small quantities. – Also noun.

siphon noun a bent tube for drawing off liquids from one container into another; a glass bottle, for soda water etc, containing such a tube. – verb to draw (off) through a siphon; (with **off**) to take (part of something) away gradually: He siphoned off some of the club's funds.

sir noun a polite form of address used to a man. – noun **Sir** the title of a knight or baronet.

sire noun a male parent (esp a horse); (hist) a title used in speaking to a king. – verb (of an animal) to be the male parent of.

siren noun a kind of instrument that gives out a loud hooting noise as a warning or signal; (myth) a sea nymph whose singing enchanted sailors and tempted them into danger; an attractive but dangerous woman.

sirloin noun the upper part of the loin of beef.

sisal noun a fibre from a kind of West Indian plant, used for making ropes.

sister noun a female born of the same parents as oneself; a senior nurse, often in charge of a hospital ward or department; a member of a religious group or community of women (eg a nun). – adjective closely related; alike eg in design: a sister ship. – noun **sisterhood** the state of being a sister; a group of women formed for purposes of religion, good works etc. – noun **sister-in-law** the sister of one's husband or of one's wife; the wife of one's brother or of one's brother-in-law. – adjective **sisterly** like a sister.

sit verb (present participle **sitting**, past tense, past participle **sat**) to rest on the buttocks, to be seated; (of birds) to perch; to rest on eggs in order to hatch them; to be an official member: Mr Smith sits in parliament. Each member sits on the committee for two years; (of a court, parliament etc) to meet officially; to pose (for) a photographer, painter etc; to take (an examination etc). – noun **sit-in** an occupation of a building etc by protestors. – noun **sitter** a person who poses for a portrait etc; a babysitter; a bird sitting on eggs. – noun **sitting** the state or time of sitting. – adjective seated; for sitting in or on; (of a member of parliament, tenant etc) actually in office or in possession. – noun **sitting-room** a room chiefly for sitting in. – **sit tight** to be unwilling to move; **sit up** to sit with one's back straight; to remain up instead of going to bed.

site noun a place where a building, town etc is, was or is to be put up or placed. – verb to select a place for (a building etc).

situated adjective placed. – noun **situation** the place where anything stands; a job, employment; a state of affairs, circumstances: in an awkward situation.

six noun the number 6. – adjective 6 in number. – adjective **sixth** the last of six (things etc). – noun one of six equal parts. – **at sixes and sevens** in confusion.

sixpence noun (old) a silver-coloured coin worth 1/40 of £1.

sixteen noun the number 16. – adjective 16 in number. – adjective **sixteenth** the last of sixteen (things etc). – noun one of sixteen equal parts.

sixty noun the number 60. – adjective 60 in number. – adjective **sixtieth** the last of sixty (things etc). – noun one of sixty equal parts.

size noun space taken up by anything; measurements, dimensions (of someone or something); largeness; one of a number of classes into which shoes and clothes are grouped according to size: He takes size 8 in shoes; a weak kind of glue. – adjective **sizeable** or **sizable** fairly large. – **size up** to form an opinion or estimation of a person, situation etc.

sizzle verb to make a hissing sound; to fry or scorch.

skate noun a steel blade attached to a boot for gliding on ice; see also **rollerskate**; a type of large flatfish. – verb to move on skates. – noun **skateboard** a narrow board on four rollerskate wheels. – noun **skateboarding** the sport of going on a skateboard.

skein noun a coil of thread or yarn, loosely tied in a knot.

skeleton noun the bony framework of an animal or person, without the flesh; any framework or outline. – adjective (of eg staff, crew etc) reduced to a very small or minimum number: Over Christmas only a skeleton staff was working. – adjective **skeletal** of, like a skeleton. – noun **skeleton key** a key from which the inner part has been cut away so that it can open many different locks.

sketch noun (plural **sketches**) a rough plan or painting or drawing; a short or rough account; a short play, dramatic scene etc. – verb to draw, describe a plan roughly; to give the chief points of; to draw in pencil or ink. – adjective **sketchy** roughly done; not thorough, incomplete: My knowledge of that period of history is rather sketchy.

skew adjective, adverb off the straight, slanting. – verb to set at a slant.

skewer noun a long pin of wood or metal for holding meat together while roasting etc. – verb to fasten, fix, with a skewer or with something sharp.

ski noun (plural **skis**) one of a pair of long narrow strips of wood etc that can be attached to boots for gliding over snow. – verb (present participle **skiing**, past tense **skied**) to travel on, use skis.

skid noun a slide sideways: The car went into a skid; a wedge etc put under a wheel to check it on a steep place; (plural) log(s), plank(s) etc on which things can be moved by sliding. – verb (of wheels) to slide along without turning; to slip sideways.

skiff noun a small light boat.

skill noun cleverness at doing a thing, either from practice or as a natural gift. – adjective **skilful** having or showing skill. – adjective **skilled** having skill, esp through training; (of a job) requiring skill.

skillet noun a small metal pan with a long handle for frying food.

skim verb (past tense **skimmed**) to remove floating matter (eg cream, scum etc) from the surface of (something); to move lightly and quickly over (a surface); to read quickly, missing parts. – noun **skim-milk** milk from which the cream has been skimmed.

skimp verb to give (someone) hardly enough; to do (a job) imperfectly; to spend too little money (on): She skimped on clothes. – adjective **skimpy** too small; (of clothes) too short or tight.

skin noun the natural outer covering of an animal or person; a thin outer layer, as on a fruit; a (thin) film or layer that forms on a liquid. – verb (past tense **skinned**) to strip the skin from. – adjective **skin-deep** as deep as the skin only, on the surface. – noun **skin-diver** originally a person who dived naked for pearls; a diver who wears simple equipment and is not connected to a boat. – noun **skinflint** a very mean person. – adjective **skinny** very thin. – **by the skin of one's teeth** very narrowly.

skip verb (past tense **skipped**) to go along with a rhythmic step and hop; to jump over a turning rope; to leap, esp lightly or joyfully; to leave out (parts of a book, a meal etc). – noun an act of skipping; the captain of a side at bowls etc; a large metal container for transporting refuse. – noun **skipping rope** a rope used in skipping.

skipper noun the captain of a ship, aeroplane or team.– Also verb.

skirmish noun (plural **skirmishes**) a fight between small parties of soldiers; a short sharp contest or disagreement. – Also *verb*.

skirt *noun* a garment, worn by women, that hangs from the waist; the lower part of a dress; (*plural*) the outer edge or border. – *verb* to pass along, or lie along, the edge of. – *noun* **skirting (board)** the narrow board next to the floor round the walls of a room.

skit *noun* a piece of writing, short play *etc* that makes fun of a person or event *etc*.

skittish *adjective* too frisky or lively.

skittle *noun* a bottle-shaped *usu* wooden object, a ninepin; (*plural*) a game in which skittles are knocked over by a ball.

skive *verb* (*coll*) to avoid doing a duty.

skulk *verb* to wait about, stay hidden (often for a bad purpose); to move in a stealthy way.

skull *noun* the bony case which encloses the brain; the head. – *noun* **skullcap** a cap which fits closely to the head. – **skull and crossbones** the sign on a pirate's flag.

skunk *noun* a kind of small American animal which defends itself by squirting out an evil-smelling liquid; a contemptible person.

sky *noun* (often in *plural* **skies**) the upper atmosphere, the heavens; the weather or climate. – *noun* **sky-diving** jumping with a parachute as a sport. – *noun* **skylark** the common lark which sings while hovering far overhead. – *noun* **skylarking** mischievous behaviour. – *noun* **skylight** a window in a roof or ceiling. – *noun* **skyline** the horizon. – *noun* **skyscraper** a high building of very many storeys.

slab *noun* a thick slice, or thick flat piece of anything: *A slab of stone covers the grave. He cut a slab of cake.*

slack *adjective* not firmly stretched; not firmly in position; not strict; lazy and careless; not busy: *the slack season in hotels.* – *noun* the loose part of a rope; small coal and coal-dust; (*plural*) trousers. – *verb* to do less work than one should, to be lazy; to slacken. – *verb* **slacken** to make or become looser; to make or become less active, less busy or less fast *etc*.

slag *noun* waste left from metal-smelting. – *verb* (*past tense* **slagged**) (*slang*) to criticize, make fun of cruelly.

slain *see* **slay**.

slake *verb* to quench, satisfy (thirst, longing *etc*); to put out (fire); to mix (lime) with water.

slalom *noun* a downhill, zigzag ski run among posts or trees; an obstacle race in canoes.

slam *verb* (*past tense* **slammed**) to shut (a door, lid *etc*) with a bang or loud noise; to put down with a loud noise. – *noun* the act of slamming; (also **grand slam**) a winning of every trick in cards or every contest in a competition *etc*.

slander *noun* untrue statement(s) made in speech, not in writing, with the purpose of doing harm to a person's reputation. – *verb* to speak slander against (someone). – *adjective* **slanderous**.

slang *noun* popular words and phrases (often in use only for a short time) that are used in informal, everyday speech or writing, but not in formal speech or writing; the special language of a particular group: *Cockney slang*. – *verb* to scold, abuse.

slant *verb* to slope; to place, lie, move diagonally or in a sloping position or way; to give or present (facts or information) in a special way, *esp* in a distorted way that suits one's own purpose. – *noun* a slope; a diagonal direction; a way of considering or thinking about something, point of view.

slap *noun* a blow with the palm of the hand or anything flat. – *verb* (*past tense* **slapped**) to give a slap to. – *adjective* **slapdash** hasty, careless. – *adjective* **slapstick** (of comedy) boisterous, funny in a very obvious way. – Also *n*.

slash *verb* to make long cuts in; to strike at violently. – *noun* (*plural* **slashes**) a long cut; a sweeping blow.

slat *noun* a thin strip of wood, metal or other material. – *adjective* **slatted** having slats.

slate *noun* an easily split rock of dull blue-grey, used for roofing or (formerly) commonly for writing upon. – *adjective* made of slate; slate-coloured. – *verb* to cover with slate; to say harsh things to or about: *to slate a play*.

slattern *noun* a woman of untidy or dirty appearance or habits.

slaughter *noun* the killing of animals, *esp* for food; cruel killing, *esp* of great numbers of people. – *verb* to kill for food; to kill brutally. – *noun* **slaughterhouse** a place where animals are killed in order to be sold for food.

slave *noun* (*hist*) a person forced to work for a master and owner; a person who serves another in a devoted way; a person who works very hard; a person who is addicted (to): *a slave to fashion*. – *verb* to work like a slave. – *noun* **slavery** the state of being a slave; the system of owning slaves. – *adjective* **slavish** slavelike; (thinking or acting) exactly according to rules or instructions.

slaver *noun* saliva running from the mouth. – *verb* to let the saliva run out of the mouth.

slay *verb* (*past tense* **slew** *past participle* **slain**) to kill.

SLD *abbreviation* Social and Liberal Democrats.

sledge *noun* a vehicle with runners, made for sliding upon snow (also **sled**). – *verb* to ride on a sledge. – *noun* **sledgehammer** a kind of large, heavy hammer.

sleek *adjective* smooth, glossy; well-fed and well-cared for; (of a woman *etc*) elegant, well-groomed.

sleep *verb* (*past tense* **slept**) to rest with one's eyes closed and in a state of natural unconsciousness. – *noun* **sleeper** one who sleeps; a beam of wood or metal *etc* supporting railway lines; a sleeping car or sleeping berth on a railway train. – *noun* **sleeping bag** a kind of large warm bag for sleeping in, used by campers *etc*. – *noun* **sleeping car** a railway coach with beds or berths. – *adjective* **sleepless** unable to sleep, without sleep. – *noun* **sleepwalker** someone who walks *etc* while asleep. – *adjective* **sleepy** drowsy, wanting to sleep; looking, seeming like this. – **go to sleep** to pass into the state of being asleep; (of the limbs) to become numb or to tingle; **put to sleep** to cause to go to sleep or to cause to become unconscious; to put (an animal) to death painlessly, *usu* by an injection of a drug; **sleep with** (*coll*) to have sexual intercourse with.

sleet *noun* rain mixed with snow or hail.

sleeve *noun* the part of a garment which covers the arm; a cover for a gramophone record; something (*esp* in machinery) that covers as a sleeve does. – *adjective* **sleeveless** without sleeves.

sleigh *noun* a sledge, sometimes a large horse-drawn one.

sleight: *noun* **sleight-of-hand** skill and quickness of hand movement in performing card tricks *etc*.

slender *adjective* thin or narrow; slim; small in amount: *by a slender margin*.

sleuth *noun* a person who tracks down criminals, a detective.

slew *verb see* slay; (*past tense* **slewed**) to (cause to) swing round.

slice *noun* a thin, broad piece (of something); a broad-bladed utensil for serving fish *etc*. – *verb* to cut into slices; to cut through; to cut (off from *etc*); in golf *etc*, to hit (a ball) in such a way that it curves away to the right.

slick *adjective* smart, clever, often in a sly way; sleek, smooth. – *noun* a thin layer of spilt oil.

slide *verb* (*past tense* **slid**) to (cause to) move smoothly over a surface; to slip; to pass quietly or secretly. – *noun* an act of sliding; a smooth, slippery slope or track; a chute; a groove or rail on which a thing slides; a fastening for the hair; a picture for showing on a screen; a piece of glass on which to place objects to be examined under a microscope. – *noun* **slide-rule** an instrument used for calculating, made up of one ruler sliding against another. – *noun* **sliding scale** a scale of wages, charges *etc* which can be changed as conditions change.

slight *adjective* of little amount or importance: *A slight breeze rose at dawn. We had a slight quarrel*; (of a person) small, slender. – *verb* to treat as unimportant, to insult by ignoring. – Also *noun*.

slim *adjective* slender, thin; small, slight: *a slim chance*. – *verb* (*past tense* **slimmed**) to make slender; to use means (such as eating less) to become slender.

slime *noun* thin, slippery mud, or other matter that is soft, sticky and half liquid. – *adjective* **slimy** covered with slime; like slime; oily, greasy.

sling *noun* a bandage hanging from the neck or shoulders to support an injured arm; a strap with a string attached to each end, for flinging a stone; a net of ropes, chains *etc* for hoisting, carrying and lowering heavy objects. – *verb* (*past tense* **slung**) to throw with a sling; to move or swing by means of a sling; (*coll*) to throw.

slink *verb* (*past tense* **slunk**) to sneak away, move stealthily.

slip *verb* (*past tense* **slipped**) to slide accidentally and lose one's footing or balance: *She slipped on the ice*; to fall out of place, or out of one's control: *The plate slipped from my grasp*; to (cause to) move quickly and easily; to (cause to) move quietly, quickly and secretly; to escape from: *to slip one's mind*. – *noun* act of slipping; an error, a slight mistake; a cutting from a plant; a strip or narrow piece of anything (*eg* paper); a slim, slight person: *a slip of a girl*; a smooth slope on which a ship is built (also **slipway**); a type of undergarment worn under a dress, a petticoat; a cover for a pillow; in cricket, a fielding position. – *noun* **slipknot** a knot made with a loop so that it can slip. – *noun* **slipped disc** displacement of one of the discs between the vertebrae causing severe back pain. – *noun* **slipper** a loose indoor shoe. – *adjective* **slippery** so smooth as to cause slipping; not trustworthy. – *noun* **slip road** a road by which vehicles join or leave a motorway. – *adjective* **slipshod** untidy, careless. – *noun* **slipstream** the stream of air driven back by an aircraft propeller *etc*. – *noun* **slipway** *see* **slip** (*noun*) above. – **slip up** to make a mistake (*noun* **slip-up**).

slit *verb* (*present participle* **slitting**, *past tense* **slit**) to make a long narrow cut in; to cut into strips. – *noun* a long narrow cut or opening.

slither *verb* to slide or slip about (*eg* on mud); to move with a gliding motion. – *adjective* **slithery** slippery.

sliver *noun* a thin strip or slice.

slobber *verb* to let saliva dribble from the mouth, slaver.

sloe *noun* the small black fruit of a type of shrub called **blackthorn.**

slog *verb* (*past tense* **slogged**) to work or plod on steadily, *esp* against difficulty. – Also *noun*.

slogan *noun* an easily remembered and frequently repeated phrase which is used in advertising *etc*.

sloop *noun* a type of one-masted sailing vessel.

slop *verb* (*past tense* **slopped**) to (cause to) flow over or spill; to splash. – *noun* spilt liquid; (*plural*) dirty water; (*plural*) thin, tasteless food. – *adjective* **sloppy** wet, muddy; careless, untidy; silly, sentimental.

slope *noun* a position or direction that is neither level nor upright, a slant; a surface with one end higher than the other (*eg* a hillside). – *verb* to (cause to) be in a slanting, sloping position.

slosh *verb* to splash; (*coll*) to hit.

slot *noun* a small, narrow opening (*esp* one to receive coins); a position. – *verb* (*past tense* **slotted**) to make a slot in; (sometimes with **into**) to find a position or place for. – *noun* **slot machine** a machine (often containing small articles for sale) worked by putting a coin in a slot.

sloth *noun* laziness; a kind of slow-moving animal that lives in trees in S. America. – *adjective* **slothful** lazy.

slouch *noun* a hunched-up body position.– *verb* to walk with shoulders rounded and head hanging.

slough[1] *slō*, *noun* a bog or marsh.

slough[2] *sluf*, *noun* the cast-off skin of a snake. – *verb* to cast off (*eg* a skin); (of skin *etc*) to come (off).

slovenly *adjective* untidy, careless, dirty.

slow *adjective* not fast; not hasty or hurrying; (of a clock *etc*) behind in time; not quick in learning, dull. – *verb* (often with **down**) to make or become slower. – *noun* **slowcoach** a person who moves, works *etc* slowly. – *adverb* **slowly.** – *adjective* **slow-motion** much slower than normal movement; (of a film) slower than actual motion. – Also *noun* and *adverb*. – *noun* **slow-worm** a kind of snake-like, legless lizard.

sludge *noun* soft, slimy mud.

slug *noun* a kind of snail-like animal with no shell; a small piece of metal used as a bullet; a heavy blow. – *noun* **sluggard** a person who has slow and lazy habits. – *adjective* **sluggish** moving slowly.

sluice *noun* a sliding gate for controlling a flow of water in an artificial channel (also **sluicegate**); the channel or the stream which flows through it. – *verb* to clean out with a strong flow of water.

slum *noun* an overcrowded part of a town where the houses are dirty and unhealthy; such a house.

slumber *verb* to sleep. – *noun* sleep.

slump *verb* to fall or sink suddenly and heavily; to lose value suddenly. – *noun* a sudden fall in values, prices *etc*.

slung *see* **sling.**

slunk *see* **slink.**

slur *verb* (*past tense* **slurred**) to pronounce indistinctly; to damage (a reputation *etc*), speak evil of. – *noun* a blot or stain (on one's reputation); a criticism, insult.

slush *noun* watery mud; melting snow; something very sentimental; sentimentality. – *adjective* **slushy** covered with, or like, slush; sentimental.

slut *noun* a dirty, untidy woman. – *adjective* **sluttish**.

sly *adjective* cunning; wily; deceitful. – *adverb* **slyly**. – *noun* **slyness**. – **on the sly** secretly, surreptitiously.

smack *verb* to strike smartly, slap; to have a trace or suggestion (of): *This smacks of treason*. – *noun* an act of smacking; the sound made by smacking; a boisterous kiss; a taste, flavour; a trace, suggestion; a small fishing vessel. – *adverb* with sudden violence: *He ran smack into the door*.

small *adjective* little, not big or much; not important: *a small matter*; not having a large or successful business: *a small businessman*; (of voice) soft. – *noun* the most slender or narrow part: *the small of the back*. – *adverb* into small pieces: *to cut up small*. – *noun plural* **small-arms** (weapons, *esp* pistols, rifles *etc*) that can be carried by a person. – *noun plural* **small hours** the hours just after midnight. – *adjective* **small-minded** having narrow opinions, ungenerous. – *noun* **smallpox** a serious infectious illness, causing a rash of large pimples (**pocks**). – *noun* **small talk** (polite) conversation about nothing very important.

smart *adjective* clever and quick in thought or action; well-dressed; brisk; sharp, stinging. – *noun* sharp, stinging pain. – *verb* (of the body, or part of it) to feel a sharp, stinging pain; to feel annoyed, resentful *etc* after being insulted *etc*.

smash *verb* to (cause to) break in pieces, shatter; to strike with force: *He smashed the ball with his racket*; to crash (into *etc*): *The car smashed into the wall*. – *noun* (*plural* **smashes**) an act of smashing; a crash or collision (of vehicles); the ruin of a business *etc*.

smattering *noun* a very slight knowledge (of a subject).

smear *verb* to spread (something sticky or oily); to spread, smudge (a surface) with (something sticky *etc*); to become smeared; to slander, insult (a person or reputation). – Also *noun*; *see* also **cervical** under **cervix**.

smell *noun* (*past tense* **smelled** or **smelt**) the sense, or power, of being aware of things through one's nose; an act of using this sense or the nose; that which is noticed by it. – *verb* to notice by using one's sense of smell: *I smell gas*; to use one's sense of smell on: *Smell this fish*; to give off a smell: *This room smells*. – *noun* **smelling-salts** strong-smelling chemicals in a bottle, used to revive fainting persons. – *adjective* **smelly** having a bad smell. – **smell out** to find out by prying or inquiring closely.

smelt *noun* a type of fish of the salmon kind. – *verb* to melt (ore) in order to separate the metal from other material; *see* also *verb* **smell**.

smile *verb* to show pleasure by drawing up the corners of the lips; (sometimes with **on**) to be favourable to: *Fortune smiled on him*. – *noun* an act of smiling.

smirch *verb* to stain, soil. – *noun* a stain.

smirk *verb* to smile in a self-satisfied or foolish manner. – Also *noun*.

smite *verb* (*past tense* **smote**, *past participle* **smitten**) to strike, hit hard. – **smitten with** affected by; strongly attracted by.

smith *noun* a worker in metals; a blacksmith. – *noun* **smithy** (*plural* **smithies**) the workshop of a smith.

smithereens *noun plural* fragments.

smitten *see* **smite**.

smock *noun* a loose shirt-like garment (sometimes worn over other clothes as a protection).

smog *noun* smoky fog.

smoke *noun* the cloud-like gases and particles of soot given off by anything burning; an act of smoking (a cigarette *etc*). – *verb* to give off smoke; to draw in and puff out the smoke of tobacco from a cigarette, pipe *etc*; to dry, cure, preserve (ham, fish *etc*) by applying smoke; to darken (*eg* glass) by applying smoke. – *adjective* **smokeless** having no smoke; burning without smoke; of an area where the emission of smoke is prohibited: *a smokeless zone*. – *noun* **smoker** a person who smokes; a railway compartment in which smoking is allowed. – *noun* **smokescreen** anything (*orig* smoke) meant to confuse or mislead: *His bookshop was a smokescreen for his drug trading*. – *adjective* **smoky** giving out smoke; full of smoke; like smoke.

smooth *adjective* not rough; having an even surface; without lumps: *a smooth* *sauce*; hairless; without breaks, stops or jolts: *smooth movement*: smooth journey; (too) agreeable in manner, often with the intention of deceiving. – *verb* to make smooth; to calm, soothe; to free from difficulty.

smote *see* **smite**.

smother *verb* to kill by keeping air from, *esp* by means of a thick covering over the nose and mouth; to die by this means; to cover up, conceal (feelings *etc*); to put down, suppress (a rebellion *etc*).

smoulder *verb* to burn slowly without bursting into flame; to exist in a hidden state; to show otherwise hidden emotion, *eg* anger, hate: *Her eyes smouldered with hate.*

smudge *noun* a smear. – *verb* to make dirty with spots or smears; to smear.

smug *adjective* well-satisfied, too obviously pleased with oneself.

smuggle *verb* to take (goods) into, or out of, a country without paying the taxes fixed by law; to send or take secretly. – *noun* **smuggler** a person who smuggles.

smut *noun* a spot of dirt or soot; vulgar or indecent talk *etc*. – *adjective* **smutty** dirty, grimy; (of talk *etc*) indecent, vulgar.

snack *noun* a light, hasty meal.

snag *noun* a difficulty, an obstacle: *A great many snags had to be overcome.* – *verb* (*past tense* **snagged**) to catch or tear on something sharp.

snail *noun* a kind of soft-bodied, small, crawling animal with a shell; a person who is very slow.

snake *noun* any of a group of legless reptiles with long bodies which move along the ground with a winding movement; anything snake-like in form or movement; a cunning, deceitful person.

snap *verb* (*past tense* **snapped**) to make a sudden bite; (with **up**) to eat up, or grab, eagerly; to break or shut suddenly with a sharp noise; to cause (the fingers) to make a sharp noise; to speak sharply; to take a photograph of. – *noun* an act of snapping; the noise made by snapping; a sudden spell (*eg* of cold weather); a simple type of card game; a photograph. – *noun* **snapdragon** a type of garden plant whose

flower, when pinched, opens and shuts like a mouth. – *adjective* **snappy** irritable, inclined to speak sharply. – *noun* **snapshot** a quickly taken photograph.

snare *noun* a noose or loop of string or wire *etc* that draws tight when pulled, for catching an animal; a trap; a hidden danger or temptation. – *verb* to catch in or with a snare.

snarl *verb* to growl, showing the teeth; to speak in a furious, spiteful tone; to (cause to) become tangled: *This piece of rope is snarled up.* – *noun* a growl or furious noise; a tangle or knot; a muddled or confused state or condition.

snatch *verb* to seize or grab suddenly; to take quickly when one has time: *to snatch an hour's sleep.* – *noun* (*plural* **snatches**) an attempt to seize; a small piece or quantity: *a snatch of music.*

sneak *verb* to creep or move in a stealthy, secretive way; to tell tales, tell on others. – *noun* a person who tells tales; a deceitful, underhand person. – *adjective* **sneaky**.

sneer *verb* to show contempt by a scornful expression, words *etc*. – Also *noun*.

sneeze *verb* to make a sudden, unintentional and violent blowing noise through the nose and mouth. – Also *noun*.

snicker *verb* to snigger; to neigh.

sniff *verb* to draw in air through the nose with a slight noise, sometimes because one has a cold *etc*, sometimes to show disapproval; to smell (a scent *etc*); (with **at**) to treat with scorn or suspicion. – Also *noun*.

snigger *verb* to laugh in a quiet, sly manner. – Also *noun*.

snip *verb* (*past tense* **snipped**) to cut off sharply, *esp* with a single cut of scissors *etc*. – *noun* a cut with scissors; a small piece snipped off; (*coll*) a bargain: *The dress was a snip at the price.* – *noun* **snippet** a little piece, *esp* of information or gossip.

snipe *noun* a type of bird with a long straight beak, found in marshy places. – *verb* (with **at**) to shoot at from a place of hiding; (with **at**) to attack with critical remarks. – *noun* **sniper** a person who shoots at a single person from cover.

snivel *verb* (*past tense* **snivelled**) to have a running nose (*eg* because of a cold); to whine or complain tearfully. – Also noun.

snob noun a person who admires people of high rank or social class, and looks down on those in a lower class etc than himself. – noun **snobbery**. – adjective **snobbish**. – noun **snobbishness**.

snooker noun a type of game like billiards, using twenty-two coloured balls.

snoop verb to spy or pry in a sneaking secretive way. – Also noun.

snooze verb to sleep lightly, doze. – Also noun.

snore verb to make a snorting noise in one's sleep as one breathes. – Also noun.

snorkel noun a tube or tubes with ends above the water, through which air is brought into a submarine; a similar device to enable an underwater swimmer to breathe.

snort verb to force air noisily through the nostrils as horses etc do; to make such a noise to express disapproval, anger, laughter etc. – Also noun.

snot noun mucus of the nose. – adjective **snotty** supercilious.

snout noun the sticking-out nose and mouth part of an animal, eg of a pig.

snow noun frozen water vapour which falls in light white flakes. – verb to fall down in, or like, flakes of snow. – noun **snowball** a ball made of snow pressed hard together. – verb to throw snowballs; to grow increasingly quickly: Unemployment has snowballed recently. – noun **snow blindness** dimness of sight caused by the brightness of light reflected from the snow. – noun **snowdrift** a bank of snow blown together by the wind. – noun **snowdrop** a kind of small white flower growing from a bulb in early spring. – noun **snowflake** a flake of snow. – noun **snowline** the height up a mountain above which there is always snow. – noun **snowman** a figure shaped like a human being, made of snow. – noun **snowplough** a large kind of vehicle for clearing snow from the roads etc. – noun **snow-shoe** a long broad frame with a mesh, one of a pair for walking on top of snow. – adjective **snowy** full of snow; covered with snow; white, pure. – **snowed under with** overwhelmed with (eg work).

SNP abbreviation Scottish National Party.

snub verb (past tense **snubbed**) to treat or speak to in an abrupt, scornful way,

insult. – noun an act of snubbing. – adjective (of the nose) short and turned up at the end.

snuff verb to put out or trim the wick of (a candle). – noun powdered tobacco for drawing up into the nose. – noun **snuffbox** a box for snuff.

snuffle verb to make a sniffing noise or talk through the nose (esp as the result of a cold). – Also noun.

snug adjective lying close and warm; cosy, comfortable; closely fitting; neat and trim. – verb **snuggle** to curl up comfortably; to draw close to for warmth, affection etc.

so adverb as shown: Holding his hand a few inches above the floor, he said 'It is so high.'; to such an extent, to a great extent: It was so heavy that we left it behind. I am so happy; in this or that way: Point your toe so; correct: Is that so?; (used in contradicting) indeed: It's not true. Yes, it is so. – conj therefore: You don't need it, so don't buy it. – noun **so-and-so** (coll) this or that person or thing; (coll) used instead of a stronger insulting word: She's a real so-and-so, betraying her husband like that!. – adjective **so-called** called (usu wrongly) by such a name: a so-called musician. – adjective **so-so** not particularly good. – **so as to** in order to: Leave early so as to be in time; **so far** up to this or that point; **so forth** more of the same sort of thing: pots, pans and so forth; **so much for** that is the end of: So much for that idea!; **so that** with the purpose that: Wash this dress so that you may wear it tomorrow; with the result that: The letter arrived torn so that he was unable to read it; **so what?** What difference does it make? Does it matter?

soak verb to (let) stand in a liquid until wet through; to drench (with); (with **up**) to suck up, absorb. – adjective **soaking** wet through. – Also adverb: soaking wet. – noun a wetting, drenching.

soap noun a mixture containing oils or fats and other substances, used in washing. – verb to use soap on. – noun **soap-box** a small box for holding soap; a makeshift platform for standing on when speaking to a crowd out of doors. – noun plural **soapsuds** soapy water worked into a froth. – adjective **soapy** like soap; covered with, or full of soap.

soar verb to fly high into the air; (of prices) to rise high and quickly.

sob verb (past tense **sobbed**) to weep noisily. – Also noun.

sober *adjective* not drunk; having a serious mind; of formal style; not brightly coloured. – *verb* (sometimes with **up**) to make or become sober. – *adverb* **soberly**. – *noun* **soberness** or **sobriety** the state of being sober.

Soc *abbreviation* Society.

soccer *noun* the game played under the rules of the Football Association, with eleven players a side.

sociable *adjective* fond of the company of others, friendly. – *noun* **sociability** or **sociableness**.

social *see* **society**.

society *noun* mankind considered as a whole; a community of people; a group of people joined together for a purpose, an association or club; the class of people who are wealthy, fashionable or of high rank; company, companionship: *I enjoy his society*. – *adjective* **social** of society; of the way of life or organization of people in a community; *social history*; living in communities: *Ants and wasps are social insects*; of companionship: *a social gathering*; of rank or level in society: *social class*. – *noun* **socialism** the belief that a country's wealth (its industries *etc*) should belong to the people as a whole, not to private owners; a system in which the state runs the country's wealth. – *noun* **socialist**. – *noun* **social security** the system (paid for by the community in general) of providing insurance against old age, illness, unemployment *etc*. – *noun* **social work** work which deals with the care of the people in a community, *esp* of the poor or underprivileged *etc*. – *noun* **social worker**. – *noun* **sociology** the science which studies human society.

sock *noun* a short stocking.

socket *noun* a hollow into which something is fitted: *an electric socket*.

sod *noun* a piece of earth with grass growing on it, a turf.

soda *noun* the name of several substances formed from sodium, *esp* one in the form of crystals (**sodium carbonate**) used for washing, or one in a powdery form (**sodium bicarbonate**) used in baking; soda-water. – *noun* **sodium** a metallic element from which many substances are formed, including common salt (**sodium chloride**). – *noun* **soda-water** water through which gas has been passed, making it fizzy.

sodden *adjective* soaked through and through.

sodium *see* **soda**.

sodomy *noun* anal intercourse.

sofa *noun* a kind of long, stuffed seat with back and arms.

soft *adjective* easily put out of shape when pressed; not hard or not firm; not loud; (of colours) not bright or glaring; not strict enough; lacking strength, courage, determination; lacking common sense, weak in the mind; (of drinks) not alcoholic; (of water) containing little calcium *etc*. – *adverb* gently, quietly. – *verb* **soften** to make or grow soft. – *adjective* **soft-hearted** (too) kind and generous. – *noun* **software** (*comput*) programs *etc* as opposed to the machines. – *noun* **softwood** the wood of a cone-bearing tree (as fir, larch).

SOGAT *abbreviation* Society of Graphical and Allied Trades.

soggy *adjective* soaked; soft and wet.

soil *noun* the upper layer of the earth in which plants grow; loose earth; dirt. – *verb* to make dirty.

sojourn *verb* to stay for a time. – Also *noun*.

solace *noun* something which makes pain or sorrow easier to bear, comfort. – *verb* to comfort.

solar *adjective* of the sun; influenced by the sun; powered by energy from the sun's rays. – *noun* **solar system** the sun with the planets (including earth) going round it.

sold *see* **sell**.

solder *noun* melted metal used for joining metal surfaces. – *verb* to join (with solder).

soldier *noun* a person in military service, *esp* one who is not an officer.

sole *noun* the underside of the foot, or of a boot or shoe; a small type of flat fish. – *adjective* only: *the sole survivor*; belonging to one person or group only: *a sole right*. – *verb* to put a sole on (a shoe). – *adverb* **solely** only, alone.

solemn *adjective* serious, earnest; (of an occasion *etc*) celebrated with special, *usu* religious, ceremonies. – *noun* **solemnity**. – *verb* **solemnize** to carry out (a wedding *etc*) with religious ceremonies.

sol-fa *noun* (in music) a system of syllables (do, ray, me *etc*) to be sung to the notes of a scale.

solicit verb to ask earnestly for (something): *solicit advice*; to ask (a person for something); to offer oneself as a prostitute. – noun **solicitor** a lawyer who advises people about legal matters. – adjective **solicitous** anxious; considerate, careful. – noun **solicitude** care or anxiety (about a matter or about a person).

solid adjective fixed in shape, not in the form of gas or liquid; of three dimensions, having length, breadth and height; not hollow; hard, firm or strongly made; made or formed completely of one substance: *solid silver*; reliable, sound: *a solid businessman*; (*coll*) without a break: *three solid hours' work*. – noun a substance that is solid; a figure that has three dimensions. – noun **solidarity** unity of arms, interests *etc*. – v **solidify** (*past tense* **solidified**) to make or become firm or solid. – noun **solidity** the state of being solid.

soliloquy noun (*plural* **soliloquies**) (a) speech to oneself, *esp* on the stage. – verb **soliloquize** to speak to oneself, *esp* on the stage.

solitary adjective lone, alone or lonely; single: *Not a solitary crumb remained.*

solitude noun the state of being alone; lack of company.

solo noun (*plural* **solos**) a musical piece for one singer or player. – adjective performed by one person alone: *a solo aeroplane flight.* – noun **soloist** a person who plays or sings a solo.

solstice noun the time of longest daylight (**summer solstice** about 21 June) or longest dark (**winter solstice** about 21 December).

soluble adjective able to be dissolved or made liquid; (of difficulties, problems *etc*) able to be solved. – noun **solubility**.

solution noun the act of dissolving; a liquid with something dissolved in it; the act of solving a problem *etc*; an answer to a problem, puzzle *etc*.

solve verb to clear up or explain (a mystery); to discover the answer or solution to. – noun **solvency** the state of being able to pay all debts. – adjective **solvent** able to pay all debts. – noun anything that dissolves another substance.

sombre adjective gloomy, dark, dismal.

sombrero noun (*plural* **sombreros**) a kind of broad-brimmed hat.

some adjective several: *some people in the garden*; a few: *some oranges, but not many*; a little: *some bread, but not much*; certain: *Some people are rich.* – pronoun a number or part out of a quantity: *It's very good – please try some!*; certain people: *Some will be jealous.* – pronoun **somebody** or **someone** an unknown or unnamed person: *somebody I'd never seen before*; a person of importance: *He really is somebody now.* – adverb **somehow** in some way or other. – pronoun **something** a thing not known or not stated; a thing of importance; a slight amount, degree: *He has something of his father's looks.* – adverb **sometime** at a time not known or stated definitely. – adverb **sometimes** at times, now and then. – adverb **somewhat** rather: *somewhat boring.* – adverb **somewhere** in some place.

somersault noun a forward or backward turning leap or roll in which the heels go over the head. – Also verb.

somnambulist noun a sleepwalker.

somnolence noun sleepiness. – adjective **somnolent** sleepy; causing sleepiness.

son noun a male child. – noun **son-in-law** one's daughter's husband.

sonata noun a piece of music with three or more movements, *usu* for one instrument.

song noun singing; something (intended to be) sung. – noun **songbird** a bird that sings. – noun **songster** (*masculine*), **songstress** (*feminine*) a singer. – **for a song** (bought, sold *etc*) very cheaply.

sonic adjective of sound waves. – noun **sonic boom** an explosive sound that can be heard when an aircraft travels faster than the speed of sound.

sonnet noun a type of poem in fourteen lines.

sonorous adjective giving a clear, loud sound.

soon adverb in a short time from now or from the time mentioned: *He will come soon*; early: *too soon to tell*; (with **as**) as readily, as willingly: *I would as soon stand as sit.* – adverb **sooner** more willingly, rather: *I would sooner stand than sit.* – **sooner or later** at some time in the future.

soot noun the black powder left by smoke. – adjective **sooty** like, or covered with, soot.

soothe verb to calm or comfort (a person, feelings *etc*); to help or ease (a pain *etc*). – adjective **soothing**.

sop *noun* bread dipped in soup *etc*; something (*eg* a bribe) given to keep a person quiet. – *verb* to soak (up). – *adjective* **sopping** wet through.

sophisticated *adjective* (of a person) full of experience, accustomed to an elegant, cultured way of life; (of ways of thought, or machinery *etc*) highly developed, complicated, elaborate.

soporific *adjective* causing sleep. – *noun* something which causes sleep.

soprano *noun* (*plural* **sopranos**) (a woman or boy with) a singing voice of high pitch.

sorcerer (*masculine*), **sorceress** (*feminine*) *noun* one who works magic spells; a wizard. – *noun* **sorcery** magic, witchcraft.

sordid *adjective* dirty, filthy; mean, selfish; contemptible.

sore *adjective* painful. – *noun* a painful, inflamed spot on the skin. – *adverb* **sorely** very greatly: *sorely in need.* – *noun* **soreness.**

sorrel *noun* a type of plant with sour-tasting leaves.

sorrow *noun* sadness (caused by a loss, disappointment *etc*). – *verb* to be sad. – *adjective* **sorrowful.**

sorry *adjective* feeling regret about something one has done: *I'm sorry I mentioned it*; feeling sympathy or pity (for): *sorry for you*; miserable: *in a sorry state.*

sort *noun* a kind of (person or thing): *the sort of sweets I like.* – *verb* to separate things, putting each in its place: *They sort letters at the post office.* – **a sort of** used of something which is like something else, but not exactly: *He wore a sort of crown*; **of a sort** or **of sorts** of a (*usu* poor) kind: *a party of sorts*; **out of sorts** not feeling very well.

sortie *noun* a sudden attack made by the defenders of a place on those who are trying to capture it.

SOS *noun* a code signal calling for help; any call for help.

sot *noun* a drunkard. – *adjective* **sottish** foolish; stupid with drink.

sotto voce *adverb* in a low voice, so as not to be overheard.

soufflé *noun* a kind of light cooked dish, made of whisked whites of eggs *etc*.

sough *verb* (of the wind) to make a sighing sound. – Also *noun*.

sought *see* **seek.**

soul *noun* the spirit, the part of a person which is not the body; a person: *a dear old soul*; a perfect example (of): *the soul of kindness.* – *adjective* **soulful** full of feeling. – *adjective* **soulless** (of a task) dull, very boring.

sound *noun* anything that can be heard, a noise; a distance from which something may be heard: *within the sound of Bow Bells*; a narrow passage of water, *esp* one connecting two seas. – *verb* to strike one as being: *That sounds awful*; (with **like**) to resemble in sound: *That sounds like Henry's voice*; to cause to make a noise: *He sounded his hooter*; to examine by listening carefully to: *to sound the patient's chest*; to measure (the depths of water); to try to find out a person's opinions: *I'll sound him out tomorrow.* – *adjective* healthy, strong; (of sleep) deep; thorough: *a sound beating*; reliable: *sound opinions.* – *adverb* deeply: *sound asleep.* – *noun* **sound-barrier** the point at which an aircraft's speed is near to the speed of sound. – *adjective* **sound-proof** built or made so that sound cannot pass in or out. – *noun* **sound-track** the strip on a film where the speech and music is recorded.

soup *noun* a liquid food made from meat, vegetables *etc*.

sour *adjective* having an acid or bitter taste, often as a stage in going bad: *sour milk*; bad-tempered. – *verb* to make sour.

source *noun* the place where something has its beginning or is found; a spring, *esp* one from which a river flows.

souse *verb* to soak (*eg* herrings) in salted water *etc*.

south *noun* one of the four chief directions, that to one's left as one faces the setting sun. – Also *adjective, adverb.* – *noun* **south-east** (or **south-west**) the point of the compass midway between south and east (or south and west). – Also *adjective.* – *adjective* **southerly** towards the south; (of wind) from the south. – *adjective* **southern** of, from or in the south. – *noun* **southerner** a person living in a southern region or country. – *noun* **South Pole** the southern end of the imaginary axis on which the earth turns. – *adverb* **southward** towards the south. – *noun* **sou'wester** a kind of waterproof hat.

souvenir *noun* something (bought or given) which reminds one of a person, place or occasion.

sovereign noun a king or queen; (old) a British gold coin worth £1. – adjective supreme, highest: our sovereign lord; having its own government: sovereign state. – noun **sovereignty** highest power.

sow[1] noun a female pig.

sow[2] verb (past tense **sowed**, past participle **sown** or **sowed**) to scatter (seeds so that they may grow); to cover (an area) with seeds. – noun **sower**.

soya bean noun a kind of bean, rich in protein, used as a substitute for meat etc (also **soy bean**). – noun **soya** or **soy sauce** a sauce made from soya beans used in Chinese etc cooking.

spa noun a place where people go to drink or bathe in the water from a natural spring.

space noun a gap or an empty place; the distance between objects; an uncovered part (as on a sheet of paper); length of time: in the space of a day; the empty region in which all stars, planets etc are situated. – verb to put things apart from each other, leaving room between them. – noun **spacecraft** a machine for travelling in space. – **spaceman** or **spacewoman** a traveller in space. – **spaceship** a manned spacecraft. – adjective **spacious** having plenty of room. – noun **spaciousness**.

spade noun a tool with a broad blade for digging in the earth; one of the four suits of playing-cards. – **call a spade a spade** to say plainly and clearly what one means.

spaghetti noun a type of pasta made into long sticks.

spake verb (old) spoke.

span noun the distance between the tips of a man's finger and thumb when the hand is spread out (about 23 centimetres, 9 inches); the full time anything lasts; an arch of a bridge. – verb (past tense **spanned**) to stretch across: The bridge spans the river.

spangle noun a thin sparkling piece of metal used as an ornament. – verb to sprinkle with spangles etc.

spaniel noun a breed of dog with large, hanging ears.

spank verb to strike with the flat of the hand. – noun a slap with the hand, esp on the buttocks. – noun **spanking**. – adjective fast: a spanking pace.

spanner noun a tool used to tighten or loosen nuts, screws etc.

spar noun a long piece of wood or metal used as a ship's mast or its crosspiece. – verb (past tense **sparred**) to fight with the fists; to indulge in an argument.

spare verb to do without: I can't spare you today; to afford, set aside: I can't spare the time to do it; to treat with mercy, hold oneself back from killing, injuring etc; to avoid causing (trouble etc) to (a person). – adjective extra, not yet in use: a spare tyre; thin, small: spare but strong. – noun another of the same kind (eg a tyre, part of a machine) kept for or available for emergencies. – adjective **sparing** careful, economical: Be sparing in your use of pencils. – **to spare** over and above what is needed.

spark noun a small red-hot part thrown off from something that is burning; a trace: a spark of humanity; a lively person. – verb to make sparks. – noun **sparking-plug** or **spark-plug** a device in a car engine that produces a spark to set on fire explosive gases.

sparkle noun a little spark; brightness or liveliness; bubbles, as in wine. – verb to shine in a glittering way; to be lively or witty; to bubble. – adjective **sparkling** glittering; witty; (of drinks) bubbling, fizzy.

sparrow noun a type of small dull-coloured bird. – noun **sparrowhawk** a type of short-winged hawk.

sparse adjective thinly scattered; not much, not enough.

spartan adjective (of conditions, life etc) hard, without luxury.

spasm noun a sudden jerk of the muscles which one cannot prevent; a strong, short burst (eg of anger, work). – adjective **spasmodic** occurring in spasms; coming etc now and again, not regularly. – adverb **spasmodically**.

spastic adjective, noun (one) suffering from brain damage which has resulted in extreme muscle spasm and paralysis.

spat see spit.

spate noun flood: The river is in spate; a sudden rush: a spate of new books.

spatial adjective of or relating to space.

spats noun plural short gaiters reaching just above the ankle.

spatter verb to splash (eg with mud).

spatula noun a kind of tool or utensil with a broad, blunt blade.

spawn *noun* a mass of eggs of fish, frogs etc. – *verb* (of fishes, frogs etc) to lay eggs; to cause, produce in large quantities.

spay *verb* to remove the ovaries of (a female animal).

speak *verb* (*past tense* **spoke**, *past participle* **spoken**) to say words, talk; to hold a conversation (with); to make a speech; to be able to talk (a certain language). – **speak one's mind** to give one's opinion boldly; **speak up** to speak more loudly or clearly; to give one's opinion boldly.

spear *noun* a long weapon, with an iron or steel point; a long, pointed shoot or leaf (*esp* of grass). – *verb* to pierce with a spear or something similar.

special *adjective* not ordinary, exceptional: *Her birthday was a special occasion. His neighbour was a special friend*; put on etc for a particular purpose: *a special train*; belonging to one person or thing and not to others: *His special skills are what are needed for this job. The plumber had a special tool for drilling holes in tiles.* – *noun* **specialist** a person who makes a very deep study of one branch of a subject or field: *Dr Brown is a heart specialist*. – *noun* **speciality** (*plural* **specialities**) something for which one is well-known: *Cream cakes are their speciality.* – *verb* **specialize** to work in, or study, a particular job, subject etc. – *noun* **specialization**. – *adjective* **specialized** (of knowledge) obtained by specializing. – *noun* **specialty** (*plural* **specialties**) a branch of work in which one specializes: *There are many specialties in medicine.*

species *noun* (*plural* **species**) a group of plants or animals which are alike in most ways; a kind (of anything). – *noun* **specie** *spē'shi*, gold and silver coins.

specific *adjective* giving all the details clearly; particular, exactly stated: *a specific purpose.* – *adverb* **specifically**. – *noun* **specification** the act of specifying or the thing specified; a full description of details (*eg* in a plan, contract). – *verb* **specify** (*past tense* **specified**) to set down or say clearly (what is wanted); to make particular mention of.

specimen *noun* something used as a sample of a group or kind of anything, *esp* for study or for putting in a collection.

specious *adjective* looking or seeming good but really not so good.

speck *noun* a small spot; a tiny piece (*eg* of dust). – *noun* **speckle** a spot on a different-coloured background. – *adjective* **speckled** dotted with speckles.

spectacle *noun* a sight, *esp* one which is striking or wonderful; (*plural*) glasses which a person wears to improve eyesight. – *adjective* **spectacular** making a great show or display; impressive.

spectator *noun* a person who watches (an event *eg* a football match).

spectre *noun* a ghost. – *adjective* **spectral** ghostly.

spectrum *noun* (*plural* **spectra** or **spectrums**) the band of colours as seen in a rainbow, sometimes formed when light passes through water or glass; the range or extent of anything.

speculate *verb* to guess; to wonder (about); to buy goods, shares etc in order to sell them again at a profit. – *noun* **speculation**. – *adjective* **speculative** speculating.

sped *see* **speed**.

speech *noun* the power of making sounds which have meaning for other people; a way of speaking: *His speech is always clear*; (*plural* **speeches**) a (formal) talk given to an audience. – *noun* **speech day** the day at the end of a school year when speeches are made and prizes given out. – *adjective* **speechless** so surprised *etc* that one cannot speak.

speed *noun* quickness of, or rate of, movement or action; (*slang*) amphetamine. – *verb* (*past tense* **sped**) to (cause to) move along quickly, to hurry; (*past tense* **speeded**) to drive very fast in a motor car etc (*esp* faster than is allowed by law). – *noun* **speeding** driving at (an illegally) high speed. – *noun* **speed limit** the greatest speed permitted on a particular road. – *noun* **speedometer** an instrument that shows how fast one is travelling. – **speedway** a motor-cycle racing track. – *adjective* **speedy** going quickly.

speedwell *noun* a type of small plant with blue flowers.

spell *noun* words which, when spoken, are supposed to have magic power; magic or other powerful influence; a (short) space of time; a turn (at work, rest, play). – *verb* (*past tense* **spelled** or **spelt**) to give or write correctly the letters which make up a word; to mean,

imply: *This defeat spells disaster for us all.*
– *adjective* **spellbound** charmed, held by a spell. – *noun* **spelling** the ability to spell words; the study of spelling words correctly. – **spell out** to say (something) very frankly or clearly.

spelt *see* **spell.**

spend *verb* (*past tense* **spent**) to use (money) for buying; to use (energy *etc*); to pass (time): *I spent a week there*; to use up energy, force: *The storm spent itself and the sun shone.* – *noun* **spendthrift** a person who spends money freely and carelessly. – *adjective* **spent** exhausted; having lost force or power: *a spent bullet.*

sperm *noun* (the fluid in a male carrying) the male sex-cell that fertilizes the female egg. – *noun* **sperm bank** a store of semen for use in artificial insemination. – *noun* **sperm-whale** a kind of whale from the head of which **spermaceti,** a waxy substance, is obtained.

spew *verb* to vomit.

sphagnum *noun* a kind of moss.

sphere *noun* a ball or similar perfectly round object; a position or level in society: *He moves in the highest spheres*; range (of influence or action). – *adjective* **spherical** having the shape of a sphere.

Sphinx *noun* (*myth*) a monster with the head of a woman and the body of a lioness; the large stone model of the Sphinx in Egypt. – *noun* **sphinx** a person whose real thoughts one cannot guess.

spice *noun* any substance used for flavouring *eg* pepper, nutmeg; anything that adds liveliness, interest. – *verb* to flavour with spice. – *adjective* **spicy** full of spices; lively and sometimes slightly indecent: *a spicy tale.* – *noun* **spiciness.**

spick-and-span *adjective* neat, clean and tidy.

spider *noun* a kind of small, insect-like creature with eight legs, that spins a web. – *adjective* **spidery** like a spider; (of handwriting) having fine, sprawling strokes.

spiel *spēl, noun* (*coll*) a (long or often repeated) story or speech.

spike *noun* a pointed piece of rod (of wood, metal *etc*); a type of large nail; an ear of corn; a head of flowers. – *verb* to pierce with a spike; to make useless; (*coll*) to add an alcoholic drink *esp* to a soft drink. – *adjective* **spiked** having spikes (*esp* of shoes for running). – *adjective* **spiky** having spikes or a sharp point.

spill *verb* (*past tense* **spilt** or **spilled**) to (allow liquid to) run out or overflow. – *noun* a fall; a thin strip of wood or twisted paper for lighting a candle, a pipe *etc*. – *noun* **spillage** an act of spilling or what is spilt. – **spill the beans** (*coll*) to give away a secret, *esp* unintentionally.

spin *verb* (*present participle* **spinning,** *past tense* **spun**) to draw out (cotton, wood, silk *etc*) and twist into threads; (to cause) to whirl round quickly; to travel quickly, *esp* on wheels; to produce a fine thread as a spider does. – *noun* a whirling motion; a ride (*esp* on wheels). – *noun* **spindrier** a machine for taking water out of clothes by whirling them round; – *noun* **spinner.** – *noun* **spinneret** in a spider *etc*, the organ for producing thread. – *noun* **spinning wheel** a machine for spinning thread, consisting of a wheel which drives spindles. – **spin a yarn** to tell a long story; **spin out** to make to last a long or longer time.

spinach *noun* a type of plant whose leaves are eaten as vegetables.

spinal *see* **spine.**

spindle *noun* the pin from which the thread is twisted in spinning wool or cotton; a pin on which anything turns round (*eg* that in the centre of the turntable of a record-player). – *adjective* **spindly** long and thin.

spindrift *noun* the spray blown from the tops of waves.

spine *noun* the line of linked bones running down the back in animals and humans, the backbone; a ridge, a stiff, pointed spike which is part of an animal's body (*eg* a porcupine); a thorn. – *noun* **spinal cord** a cord of nerve cells in the spine. – *adjective* **spineless** having no spine; weak.

spinet *noun* a kind of small harpsichord.

spinney *noun* (*plural* **spinneys**) a small clump of trees.

spinster *noun* a woman who is not married.

spiral *adjective* coiled round like a spring; winding round and round, getting further and further away from the centre. – *noun* anything with this shape; a movement of this kind; an increase *etc* which gets ever more rapid. – *verb* (*past tense* **spiralled**) to move in a spiral; to increase *etc* ever more rapidly.

spire *noun* a tall, sharp-pointed tower (*esp* on the roof of a church).

spirit *noun* the soul; a being without a body, a ghost: *an evil spirit*; liveliness, boldness: *He acted with spirit*; a feeling or attitude: *a spirit of kindness*; the intended meaning: *the spirit of the laws*; a distilled liquid, *esp* alcohol; (*plural*) strong alcoholic drinks in general (*eg* whisky); (*plural*) state of mind, mood: *in high spirits*. – *verb* (*esp* with **away**) to remove, as if by magic. – *adjective* **spirited** lively. – *adjective* **spiritual** having to do with the soul or with ghosts. – *noun* (also **Negro spiritual**) an emotional, religious song of a kind developed by the Negro slaves of America. – *noun* **spiritualism** the belief that living people can communicate with the souls of dead people. – *noun* **spiritualist** a person who holds this belief.

spit *noun* the liquid which forms in a person's mouth (also **spittle**). – *noun* a metal bar on which meat is roasted; a long piece of land running into the sea. – *verb* (*present participle* **spitting**, *past tense* **spat**) to throw liquid out from the mouth; to rain slightly; (*past tense* **spitted**) to pierce with something sharp. – *noun* **spitting image** an exact likeness. – *noun* **spittoon** a kind of dish into which people may spit.

spite *noun* the wish to hurt (*esp* feelings). – *verb* to annoy out of spite. – *adjective* **spiteful**. – **in spite of** taking no notice of: *He left in spite of his father's command*; although something has happened or is a fact: *The ground was dry in spite of all the rain that had fallen*.

spittle *see* spit.

splash *verb* to spatter with water, mud *etc*; to move or fall with a splash or splashes. – *noun* (*plural* **splashes**) the sound made by, or the scattering of liquid caused by, something hitting water *etc*; a mark made by splashing (*eg* on one's clothes); a bright patch: *a splash of colour*. – **make a splash** to attract a lot of attention.

splay *verb* to turn out at an angle. – *adjective* **splay-footed** with flat feet turned outward.

spleen *noun* a spongy, blood-filled organ inside the body, near the stomach; bad temper.

splendid *adjective* magnificent; brilliant; (*coll*) very good. – *noun* **splendour**.

splenetic *adjective* irritable.

splice *verb* to join (*esp* two ends of a rope by twining the threads together). – *noun* a joint so made.

splint *noun* a piece of wood *etc* tied to a broken limb to keep it in a fixed position. – *noun* **splinter** a sharp, thin, broken piece of wood, glass *etc*. – *verb* to split into splinters. – *noun* **splinter group** a group which breaks away from a larger one.

split *verb* (*present participle* **splitting**, *past tense* **split**) to cut or break lengthways; to crack or break; to divide into pieces or into groups *etc*. – *noun* a crack, break or division; (*plural*) (with **the**) the trick of going down on the floor with one leg stretched forward and the other back. – *adjective* **splitting** (of a headache) very bad. – **a split second** a fraction of a second; **split one's sides** to laugh very heartily.

splutter *verb* to make spitting noises; to speak hastily and unclearly. – Also *noun*.

spoil *verb* (*past tense* **spoilt** or **spoiled**) to make bad or useless, to damage or ruin; to give in to the wishes of (a child *etc*) and so possibly make his character, behaviour *etc* worse; (of food *etc*) to become bad or useless; (*past tense* **spoiled**) to rob, plunder. – *noun* (often *plural*) plunder. – *noun* **spoilsport** someone who spoils, or won't join in, other's fun. – **spoiling for** eager for (*esp* a fight).

spoke *noun* one of the ribs or bars from the centre to the rim of a wheel. – *verb see* **speak**.

spoken *see* **speak**.

spokesman (*masculine*), **spokeswoman** (*feminine*) *noun* a person who speaks on behalf of others.

spoliation *noun* plundering.

sponge *noun* a kind of sea animal; its soft, elastic skeleton which can soak up water and is used for washing *etc*; a manmade object like this used for washing *etc*; a kind of light cake or pudding. – *verb* to wipe with a sponge; to live off money *etc* given by others. – *noun* **sponger** one who lives at others' expense. – adjective **spongy** soft like a sponge. – **throw in the sponge** to give up a fight or struggle.

sponsor noun a person who takes responsibility for introducing something, a promoter; one who promises to pay a certain sum of money to a charity etc if another person completes a set task (eg a walk, swim etc); a business firm which pays for a radio or television programme etc and advertises its products during it. – verb to act as a sponsor to. – noun **sponsorship** the act of sponsoring.

spontaneous adjective done readily, not thought about beforehand; natural, not forced. – noun **spontaneity**.

spoof noun a trick played as a joke, a hoax. – Also verb, adjective.

spook noun a ghost. – adjective **spooky**.

spool noun a reel for thread, film etc.

spoon noun hollow-shaped piece of metal etc fixed to a handle and used for lifting food to the mouth. – verb to lift with a spoon. – verb **spoonfeed** to teach (someone) in a way that causes them not to think independently.

spoonerism noun a mistake in speaking in which the first sounds of words change position, as in every crook and nanny (every nook and cranny).

spoor noun the footmarks or trail left by an animal.

sporadic adjective happening here and there, or now and again. – adverb **sporadically**.

spore noun the seed of certain plants (eg ferns, fungi).

sporran noun kind of purse worn hanging in front of a kilt.

sport noun games such as football, cricket, fishing, hunting etc in general; any one game of this type; a good-natured, obliging person. – verb to have fun, play; to wear: He was sporting a pink tie. – adjective **sporting** of, or liking, sport; believing in fair play, good-natured. – noun **sporting chance** a reasonably good chance. – noun **sports car** a small, fast car with only two seats. – noun **sportsman** one who enjoys sports; one who shows a spirit of fairness in sports. – adjective **sportsmanlike**.

spot noun a small mark or stain (of mud, paint etc); a round mark as part of a pattern on material etc; a pimple; a

place: the spot where Nelson fell. – verb (past tense **spotted**) to mark with spots; to catch sight of. – adjective **spotless** very clean. – noun **spotlight** a light that is shone on an actor on the stage. – verb to show up clearly; to draw attention to. – adjective **spotted** or **spotty** covered with spots. – **in a spot** in trouble; **on the spot** in the place where a person or thing is most needed; right away, immediately; in an embarrassing or difficult position.

spouse noun a husband or wife.

spout noun the part of a kettle, teapot etc through which the liquid it contains is poured out; a strong jet of liquid. – verb to pour or spurt out: Water spouted from the hole in the tank.

sprain noun a painful twisting (eg of an ankle). – Also verb.

sprang see **spring**.

sprat noun a type of small fish similar to a herring.

sprawl verb to sit, lie or fall with the limbs spread out widely or carelessly; (of a town etc) to spread out in an untidy, irregular way.

spray noun a fine mist of liquid like that made by a waterfall; a device with many small holes (as on a watering-can or shower) or other instrument for producing spray; a liquid for spraying; a twig or shoot spreading out in branches or flowers. – verb to cover with a mist or fine jets of liquid.

spread verb (past tense **spread**) to put or go more widely or thinly over an area: He spread the butter on the slice of bread; to cover: He spread the bread with jam; to open out (eg one's arms, a map); to go, scatter, or distribute over a wide area, over a length of time, amongst many people etc. – noun the act of spreading; the extent or range (of something); a food which is spread on bread: sandwich spread; (coll) a (large) meal laid out on a table. – adjective **spread-eagled** with limbs spread out. – noun **spreadsheet (program)** (comput) a program with which data can be viewed on screen and manipulated to make calculations etc.

spree noun a careless, merry spell of some activity: a spending spree.

sprig noun a small twig or shoot.

sprightly adjective lively, brisk. – noun **sprightliness**.

spring *verb* (*past tense* **sprang**, *past participle* **sprung**) to jump, leap; to move swiftly (*usu* upwards); (with **back**) to return suddenly to an earlier shape or position when released (like the string of a bow *etc*); to set off (a trap *etc*); to give, reveal unexpectedly: *He sprang the news on me*; to come from: *His bravery springs from his love of adventure.* – *noun* a leap; a coil of wire, such as that used in a mattress; the ability to stretch and spring back; bounce, energy; a small stream flowing out from the ground; the season which follows winter when plants begin to grow again. – *noun* **springboard** a springy board from which swimmers may dive. – *noun* **springbok** a type of deer found in South Africa. – *noun* **spring-cleaning** a thorough cleaning of a house, *esp* in the spring. – *adjective* **springy** able to spring back into its former shape, position *etc*, elastic. – **spring a leak** to begin to leak; **spring up** to appear suddenly.

sprinkle *verb* to scatter or cover in small drops or pieces. – *noun* **sprinkler** something which sprinkles water. – *noun* **sprinkling** a few.

sprint *verb* to run at full speed. – *noun* a short running race. – *noun* **sprinter**.

sprite *noun* (*myth*) a fairy or elf.

sprocket *noun* one of a set of teeth on the rim of a wheel.

sprout *verb* to begin to grow; to put out new shoots. – *noun* a young bud; (*plural*) Brussels sprouts.

spruce *adjective* neat, smart. – *noun* a kind of fir-tree.

sprung *see* **spring**.

spry *adjective* lively, active.

spume *noun* froth, foam.

spun *see* **spin**.

spunk *noun* pluck.

spur *noun* a sharp point worn by a horse-rider on the heel and used to urge on the horse; a claw-like point at the back of a bird's (*esp* a cock's) leg; anything that urges a person on; a small line of mountains running off from a larger range. – *verb* (*past tense* **spurred**) to use spurs on (a horse); to urge on. – **on the spur of the moment** without thinking beforehand.

spurious *adjective* not genuine, false.

spurn *verb* to cast aside, reject with scorn: *He spurned my offer of help.*

spurt *verb* to pour out in a sudden stream. – *noun* a sudden stream pouring or squirting out; a sudden increase of effort.

sputnik *noun* a kind of small, manmade (*orig* Russian) earth satellite.

sputter *verb* to make a noise as of spitting and throw out moisture in drops.

sputum *noun* mucus and spittle from the nose, throat *etc*.

spy *noun* (*plural* **spies**) a person who secretly collects (and reports) information about another person, country, firm *etc*. – *verb* (*past tense* **spied**) to catch sight of; (with **on**) to watch secretly. – *noun* **spyglass** a small telescope.

sq *abbreviation* **square**.

squabble *verb* to quarrel noisily. – Also *noun*.

squad *noun* a group of soldiers, workmen *etc* doing a particular job; a group of people. – *noun* **squadron** a division of a regiment, section of a fleet or group of aeroplanes. – *noun* **squadron leader** in the air force, an officer below a wing commander.

squalid *adjective* very dirty, filthy; contemptible. – *noun* **squalor**.

squall *noun* a sudden violent storm, gust or shower; a squeal or scream. – *verb* to cry out loudly. – *adjective* **squally**.

squander *verb* to waste (one's money, goods, strength *etc*).

square *noun* a figure with four equal sides and four right angles shaped thus: □; an open space enclosed by buildings in a town *etc*; the answer when a number is multiplied by itself (*eg* the square of 3 is 9). – *adjective* shaped like a square; (in games) equal in scores; (of two or more people) not owing one another anything; straight, level. – *verb* to make like a square; to straighten (the shoulders); to multiply a number by itself; to (make to) fit or agree: *That doesn't square with what you said earlier*; (with **up**) to settle (a debt). – *adverb* in a straight or level position; directly; exactly: *hit square on the nose*. – *noun* **square deal** fair treatment. – *noun* **square foot** or **square metre** *etc* an area equal to that of a square each side of which is one foot or one metre *etc* long. – *noun* **square meal** a large, satisfying meal. – *noun* **square root** the number which, multiplied by itself, gives a certain other number (*eg* 3 is the square root of 9).

squash verb to crush flat or to a pulp; to put down, defeat (rebellion etc). – noun a crushing or crowding; a mass (usu of people) crowded together; a drink made from the juice of crushed fruit; a game with rackets and a rubber ball played in a walled court (also **squash rackets**).

squat verb (past tense **squatted**) to sit down on the heels; to settle without permission on land or in property which one does not pay rent for. – adjective short and thick. – noun **squatter** a person who squats in a building, on land etc.

squaw noun a North American Indian woman or wife.

squawk verb to give a harsh cry. – Also noun.

squeak verb to give a short, high-pitched sound. – Also noun. – adjective **squeaky**.

squeal verb to give a loud, shrill cry; (coll) to inform on. – Also noun.

squeamish adjective easily sickened or shocked; feeling sick.

squeeze verb to press together; to grasp tightly; to force out (liquid or juice from) by pressing; to force a way: He squeezed through the hole in the wall. – noun a squeezing or pressing; a few drops got by squeezing: a squeeze of lemon juice; a crowd of people crushed together.

squelch noun a sound made eg by walking through marshy ground. – Also verb.

squib noun a type of small firework.

squid noun a type of sea animal of the cuttlefish kind.

squiggle noun a curly or wavy mark. – Also verb. – adjective **squiggly**.

squint verb to screw up the eyes in looking at something; to have the eyes looking in different directions. – noun a fault in eyesight which causes squinting; (coll) a quick, close glance.

squire noun a country gentleman, esp one who owns a lot of the land in a certain district; (hist) a knight's servant.

squirm verb to wriggle, twist the body, esp in pain or embarrassment.

squirrel noun a type of small gnawing animal (usu either reddish-brown or grey) with a bushy tail.

squirt verb to shoot out, or wet with, a narrow jet of liquid. – Also noun.

Sr abbreviation senior.

SS abbreviation steamship.

St abbreviation saint; strait; street.

st abbreviation stone (weight).

stab verb (past tense **stabbed**) to wound or pierce with a pointed weapon; to poke (at). – noun the act of stabbing; a wound made by stabbing; a sharp feeling (of pain etc). – **have a stab at** to make an attempt at.

stable noun a building for keeping horses. – verb to put or keep (horses) in a stable. – adjective firm, steady. – noun **stability** steadiness. – verb **stabilize** to make steady.

staccato adjective (of speech, sounds) sharp and separate, like the sound of tapping; (in music) with each note sounded separately and clearly.

stack noun a large pile (of straw, hay, wood etc). – verb to pile in a stack.

stadium noun (plural **stadiums** or **stadia**) a large sports-ground or race-course with seats for spectators.

staff noun a stick or pole carried in the hand; the five lines and four spaces on which music is written or printed (also **stave**); workers employed in a business, school etc; a group of army officers who assist a commanding officer. – verb to supply (a school etc) with staff.

stag noun a male deer. – noun **stag party** a party for men only.

stage noun a platform esp for performing or acting on; (with **the**) the theatre, or the job of working as an actor: He chose the stage as a career; period, step in development (of something): the first stage of the plan; a landing place (eg for boats); a part of a journey; a stopping place on a journey. – verb to prepare and put on a performance of (a play etc); to arrange (an event, eg an exhibition). – noun **stage-coach** (hist) a coach running every day with passengers. – noun **stage-fright** an actor's fear when acting in public esp for the first time. – noun **stage whisper** a loud whisper. – noun **staging** scaffolding; putting on the stage. – **on the stage** in(to) the theatre-world.

stagger verb to walk unsteadily, totter; to astonish; to arrange (people's hours of work etc) so that they do not begin or end together. – adjective **staggered**. – adjective **staggering** astonishing.

stagnant *adjective* (of water) standing still, not flowing and therefore not pure. – *verb* **stagnate** (of water) to remain still and so become impure; to remain for a long time in the same (dull) circumstances and so become bored, inactive *etc*. – *noun* **stagnation**.

staid *adjective* set in one's ways, sedate.

stain *verb* to give a different colour to (wood *etc*); to mark or make dirty by accident. – *noun* a liquid which dyes or colours something; a mark which is not easily removed; something shameful in one's character or reputation. – *noun* **stained glass** glass with colour fixed into its surface. – *noun* **stainless steel** a mixture of steel and chromium which does not rust.

stair *noun* one or all of a number of steps one after the other; (*plural*) a series or flight of steps. – *noun* **staircase** a stretch of stairs with rails on one or both sides.

stake *noun* a strong stick pointed at one end; the money that one puts down as a bet; (*hist*) the post to which people were tied to be burned. – *verb* to mark the limits or boundaries (of a field *etc*) with stakes; to bet (money); to risk. – **at stake** to be won or lost; in great danger: *His life is at stake*; **have a stake in** to be concerned in (because one has something to gain or lose); **stake a claim** to establish one's ownership or right (to something).

stalactite *noun* an icicle-shaped spike of limestone hanging from the roof of a cave, formed by the dripping of water containing lime. – *noun* **stalagmite** a similar spike of limestone, like a stalactite, rising from the floor of a cave.

stale *adjective* (of food *etc*) no longer fresh; no longer interesting because heard, done *etc* too often before; not able to do one's best (because of overworking, boredom *etc*).

stalemate *noun* (in chess) a position in which a player cannot move without putting his king in danger; in a quarrel or argument, a position in which neither side can win.

stalk *noun* the stem of a plant or of a leaf or flower. – *verb* to walk stiffly or proudly; (in hunting) to go quietly up to animals (*eg* deer) in order to shoot at close range. – *noun* **stalker**.

stall *noun* (a division for one animal in) a stable, cowshed *etc*; a table *etc* on which things are laid out for sale; an open-fronted shop; a seat in a church (*esp* for choir or clergy); (*usu plural*) theatre seat(s) on the ground floor. – *verb* (of a car engine *etc*) to come to a halt without the driver intending it to do so; (of an aircraft) to lose flying speed and so fall out of control for a time; (*coll*) to avoid action or decision for the time being.

stallion *noun* a male horse, *esp* one kept for breeding purposes.

stalwart *adjective* brave, stout-hearted. – Also *noun*.

stamen *noun* one of the thread-like spikes in the middle of a flower which bear the pollen.

stamina *noun* strength, power to keep going.

stammer *verb* to have difficulty in saying the first letter of words in speaking; to stumble over words. – Also *noun*.

stamp *verb* to bring the foot down firmly (and noisily) on the ground; to stick a (postage) stamp on; to mark with a design, words *etc* using ink and a flat surface on which the design *etc* is moulded or cut; to fix or mark deeply: *stamped in his mind*. – *noun* the act of stamping; a design *etc* made by stamping; the object with which stamping is done; kind, sort: *a man of a different stamp; see* also **postage stamp**. – **stamp out** to put out (a fire) by stamping; to crush (*eg* a rebellion).

stampede *noun* a wild rush of frightened animals; a sudden, wild rush of people: *a stampede to the sale*. – Also *verb*.

stance *noun* one's manner of standing.

stanch or **staunch** *verb* to stop from flowing (*esp* blood from a wound).

stanchion *noun* an upright iron bar used as a support (*eg* in windows, ships).

stand *verb* (*past tense* **stood**) to be on one's feet (not lying or sitting down); to rise to one's feet; (of an object) to (cause to) be in a particular place: *The wardrobe stood by the door. He stood the case in the corner*; to bear: *I cannot stand this heat*; to treat (someone) to: *I will stand you tea*; to remain: *This law still stands*; to be a candidate (for): *He stood for parliament*; to be short (for): *PO stands for Post Office*. – *noun* something on which anything is placed; an object made to hold, or for hanging, things: *a hatstand*; lines of raised seats from which people may watch games *etc*; an effort made to support, defend, resist *etc*: *a stand against violence*; (*US*) a witness box in a law court. – *noun, adjective* **stand-alone** *(comput)* (of) a system, device *etc* that can operate unconnected to any other. – *noun* **standing** one's social position or reputation. – *adjective* on one's feet; placed on end; not moving; lasting, permanent: *a standing joke.* – *adjective* **stand-offish** unfriendly. – *noun* **standpoint** the position from which one looks at something (*eg* a question, problem), point of view. – *noun* **standstill** a complete stop. – **stand by** to be ready or available to be used or help in an emergency *etc* (*noun* **standby**); **stand down** to withdraw (from a contest) or resign (from a job); **stand fast** to refuse to give in; **stand in (for)** to take another's place, job *etc* for a time (*noun* **stand-in**); **stand out** to stick out, to be noticeable; **stand to reason** to be likely or reasonable; **stand up for** to defend strongly; **stand up to** to face or oppose bravely.

standard *noun* a level against which things may be judged; a level of excellence aimed at: *She has very high moral standards*; a large flag, badge *etc* on a pole. – *adjective* normal, usual: *£1 is the standard charge*; ordinary, without extras: *the standard model of this car.* – *verb* **standardize** to make all of one kind, size *etc*. – *noun* **standardization**. – *noun* **standard lamp** a kind of tall lamp which stands on the floor of a room *etc*. – **standard of living** a level of material comfort considered necessary by a particular group of society *etc*.

stank *see* **stink**.

stanza *noun* a group of lines making up a part of a poem, a verse.

staple *noun* a U-shaped iron nail; a piece of wire driven through sheets of paper and folded to fasten them together; the thing, material *etc* which forms the largest part (of a country's output, a person's diet *etc*); a fibre of wool, cotton *etc*. – *verb* to fasten with a staple. – *adjective* chief, main.

star *noun* any of the bodies in the sky appearing as points of light; the fixed bodies which are really distant suns, not the planets; an object, shape or figure with a number of pointed rays (often five); a leading actor or actress or other well-known performer. – *adjective* for or of a star (in a film *etc*). – *verb* (*past tense* **starred**) to act the chief part (in a play or film); (of a play *etc*) to have as its star. – *noun* **stardom** the state of being a leading performer. – *noun* **starfish** a type of small sea creature with five points or arms. – *adjective* **starry** full of stars; shining like stars. – **Stars and Stripes** the flag of the United States of America.

starboard *noun* the right side of a ship, as one looks towards the bow (or front). – Also *adjective*.

starch *noun* (*plural* **starches**) a white carbohydrate (found in flour, potatoes, bread, biscuits *etc*); a form of this used for stiffening clothes. – *adjective* **starchy** (of food) containing starch; stiff and unfriendly.

stare *verb* to look with a fixed gaze. – Also *noun*.

stark *adjective* barren, bare; harsh, severe; sheer: *stark idiocy.* – *adverb* completely: *stark naked.*

starling *noun* a type of common bird with dark, glossy feathers.

starry *see* **star**.

start *verb* to begin (an action): *He started to walk home*; to get (a machine *etc*) working: *He started the car*; to jump or jerk (*eg* in surprise). – *noun* the act of starting (*eg* on a task, journey); a sudden movement of the body; a sudden shock: *You gave me a start*; in a race *etc* the advantage of beginning before, or farther forward than, others, or the amount of this: *The youngest runner got a start of five metres.*

startle *verb* to give a shock or fright to. – *adjective* **startled**. – *adjective* **startling**.

starve *verb* to die for want of food; to suffer greatly from hunger; to deprive (of something needed or wanted badly): *I'm starved of company here.* – *noun* **starvation**.

state *noun* the condition (of something): *the bad state of the roads*; the people of a country under a government; (*US*) an area and its people with its own laws forming part of the whole country; a government and its officials; great show, pomp: *The king drove by in state.* – *adj* of the government; national and ceremonial: *state occasions*; (*US*) of a certain state of America: *The state capital of Texas is Austin.* – *verb* to tell, say or write (*esp* clearly and fully). – *adjective* **stately** noble-looking; dignified. – *noun* **stateliness**. – *noun* **statement** that which is said or written. – *noun* **stateroom** a large cabin in a ship. – *noun* **statesman** a person skilled in government. – *adjective* **statesmanlike**.

static *adjective* not moving. – *noun* atmospheric disturbances causing poor reception of radio or television programmes; electricity on the surface of objects which will not conduct it *eg* hair, nylons *etc* (also **static electricity**).

station *noun* a place with a ticket office, waiting rooms *etc* where trains, buses or coaches stop to pick up or set down passengers; a place which is the centre for work or duty of any kind: *The alarm rang in the fire station. The suspect was taken to the police station*; one's rank or position: *a humble station*. – *verb* to assign to a position or place; to take up a position: *He stationed himself at the corner of the road.* – *adjective* **stationary** standing still, not moving.

stationery *noun* writing paper, envelopes, pens *etc*. – *noun* **stationer** a person who sells these.

statistics *noun plural* figures and facts set out in order: *statistics of road accidents for last year*; the study of these: *Statistics is not an easy subject.* – *adjective* **statistical**. – *noun* **statistician** a person who produces or studies statistics.

statue *noun* a likeness of a person or animal carved in stone, metal *etc*. – *noun* **statuette** a small statue. – *adjective* **statuesque** like a statue in dignity *etc*.

stature *noun* height; importance, reputation.

status *noun* position, rank (of a person) in the eyes of others. – *noun* **status quo** the state of affairs now existing, or existing before a certain time or event. – *noun* **status symbol** a possession which is thought to show the high status of the owner (*eg* a powerful car).

statute *noun* a written law of a country. – *adjective* **statutory** according to law.

staunch *adjective* firm, loyal; trustworthy. – *verb see* **stanch**.

stave *noun* (in music) the staff; one of the strips of wood making the side of a cask or tub. – *verb* (*past tense* **staved** or **stove**) (with **in**) to crush in, make a hole in; (with **off**) to keep away, delay.

stay *verb* to continue to be: *He stayed calm despite his fear. Stay here while I go for help*; to live (for a time): *I stayed with my brother when I went to London*; (*old*) to stop. – *noun* time spent in a place; a strong rope running from the side of a ship to the mast-head; (*plural, old*) corsets. – **stay put** to remain in the same place.

St Bernard *see* **Saint Bernard**.

STD *abbreviation* subscriber trunk dialling.

stead *noun* place: *I shall go in your stead.* – **stand one in good stead** to turn out to be helpful to one: *His knowledge of German stood him in good stead.*

steadfast *adjective* steady, fixed; faithful and true.

steady *adjective* firm, not moving or changing; not easily upset or put off from doing something; even, regular, unchanging: *moving at a steady pace.* – *verb* (*past tense* **steadied**) to make or become steady. – *noun* **steadiness**.

steak *noun* a *usu* thick slice of meat *etc* for cooking.

steal *verb* (*past tense* **stole**, *past participle* **stolen**) to take (what does not belong to one) without permission; to move quietly; to take quickly or secretly: *He stole a look at her.*

stealth *noun* a secret way of doing, acting *etc*. – *adjective* **stealthy**. – *adverb* **stealthily**.

steam *noun* vapour from hot liquid, *esp* from boiling water; power produced by steam: *in the days of steam.* – *verb* to give off steam; to cook by steam; to open, loosen, by putting into steam: *to steam open an envelope*; to move, travel by steam. – *noun* **steamboat** a steamer. – *noun* **steam-engine** an engine (*esp* a railway engine) worked by steam. – *noun* **steamer** a ship driven by steam. – *noun* **steamroller** a steam-driven engine with large and very heavy wheels, used for flattening the surfaces of roads. – *noun* **steamship** a steamer. – *adjective* **steamy** full of, emitting steam; (*coll*) erotic. – **steam up** (of glass) to become covered with condensed steam in the form of small drops of water.

steed *noun* (*old*) a horse.

steel *noun* a very hard mixture of iron and carbon; a bar of steel on which knives may be sharpened. – *adjective* **steely** hard, cold, strong *etc* like steel. – **of steel** hard, like steel: *a grip of steel*; **steel oneself** to get up courage (to).

steep *adjective* (of a slope, hill *etc*) rising nearly straight up; (*coll*) (of a price) too great. – *verb* to soak (in a liquid); to fill with knowledge and experience (of a subject): *He is steeped in French literature.*

steeple *noun* a tower of a church *etc* rising to a point, a spire. – *noun* **steeplechase**

a race run across open country, over hedges *etc*; a race over a course on which obstacles (*eg* walls) have been made. – *noun* **steeplejack** a person who climbs steeples or other high buildings to make repairs.

steer *noun* a young ox raised for its beef. – *verb* to control the course of (a car, ship, discussion *etc*); to follow (a course). – *noun* **steerage** (*old*) the part of a ship set aside for the passengers who pay the lowest fares. *noun* **steering** the parts of a ship, motor-car *etc* which have to do with controlling its course. – *noun* **steering-wheel** the wheel in a car used by the driver to steer it. – **steer clear of** to keep away from.

stellar *adjective* of the stars.

stem *noun* the part of a plant from which the leaves and flowers grow; the thin support of a wine-glass. – *verb* (*past tense* **stemmed**) to stop (the flow *etc* of): *He tried to stem the bleeding without success*; to start, spring (from): *Hate stems from envy*.

stench *noun* a strong unpleasant smell.

stencil *noun* a sheet of metal, cardboard *etc* with a pattern cut out; the drawing or design made by rubbing ink or brushing paint *etc* over a cut-out pattern; a piece of waxed paper on which words are cut with a typewriter, and which is then used to make copies. – *verb* (*past tense* **stencilled**) to make a design or copy in one of these ways.

stenography *noun* (*US*) shorthand. – *noun* **stenographer** (*US*) a shorthand typist.

stentorian *adjective* (of the voice) very loud.

step *noun* one movement of the leg in walking, running *etc*; the distance covered by this; a particular movement of the feet, as in dancing; the sound made by the foot in walking *etc*; one of the parts of a stair or ladder on which one stands; a move in a plan, career *etc*: *The first step is to find out where we are*; a way of walking: *a proud step*; (*plural*) a flight of stairs; (*plural*) a step-ladder. – *verb* (*past tense* **stepped**) to take a step; to walk. – *noun* **step-ladder** a ladder with a support on which it rests. – *noun* **stepping-stone** a stone rising above water or mud, used to cross on; anything that helps one to advance. – **in step** (of two or more people walking) with the same foot going forward at the same time; acting *etc* in agreement

(with); **out of step** not in step (with); **step up** to increase (*eg* production); **take steps** to begin to do something for a certain purpose: *I shall take steps to have the guilty person punished*.

step- *prefix* showing a relationship between people which results from a second marriage, as in **stepfather, stepmother, stepson** or **stepdaughter**.

steppe *noun* a dry, grassy treeless plain in SE Europe and Asia.

stereo *adjective* short for **stereophonic**. – *noun* (*plural* **stereos**) stereophonic equipment, *esp* a record-player and/or tape recorder, with amplifier and loudspeakers.

stereo- *prefix* having to do with three dimensions.

stereophonic *adjective* (of sound, a recording *etc*) giving a life-like effect, with different instruments, voices *etc* coming from different directions.

stereotype *noun* a metal plate having on its surface moulded letters *etc* for printing; something fixed and unchanging; a person of a well-known type. – *adjective* **stereotyped** fixed, not changing: *He has stereotyped ideas*.

sterile *adjective* unable to have children, produce fruit, ideas *etc*; free from germs. – *noun* **sterility** the state of being sterile. – *verb* **sterilize** to make unable to have children, bear young *etc*; to kill germs by boiling or other means. – *noun* **sterilization**.

sterling *noun* a name for British money *esp* when used in international trading: *one pound sterling*. – *adjective* (of silver) of a certain standard of purity; worthy, good: *He has many sterling qualities*.

stern *adjective* angry or displeased in look, manner, or voice; severe, strict, harsh: *a stern prison sentence*. – *noun* the back part of a ship. – *noun* **sternness** the state or quality of being stern.

steroid *noun* any of a number of substances, including certain hormones; *see* also **anabolic steroids**.

stertorous *adjective* making a snoring noise.

stethoscope *noun* an instrument by means of which a doctor listens to a person's heartbeats, breathing *etc*.

stevedore *noun* one who loads and unloads ships.

stew *verb* to cook by boiling slowly. – *noun* a dish of stewed food, *esp* one containing meat and vegetables; *(coll)* a state of worry.

steward *noun* a passengers' attendant on a ship or aeroplane; a person who shows people to their seats at a meeting *etc*; an official at a race meeting *etc*; a person who manages an estate or farm for someone else. – *noun* **stewardess** a female steward, *esp* one who waits on passengers in an aeroplane (also **air hostess**).

stick *noun* a long thin piece of wood; a branch or twig from a tree; a piece of wood shaped for a special purpose: *hockey-stick: drumstick*; a long piece (*eg* of rhubarb). – *verb* (*past tense* **stuck**) to push or thrust (something): *Stick the knife in your belt*; to fix with glue *etc*: *I'll stick the pieces back together*; to be or become caught, fixed or held back: *The car is stuck in the ditch*; to hold fast to, keep to (*eg* a decision). – *noun* **sticking-plaster** a kind of tape with a sticky surface, used to protect slight cuts *etc*. – *noun* **stick-in-the-mud** a person who is against new ideas, change *etc*. – *adjective* **sticky** clinging closely (like glue, treacle *etc*); covered with something sticky; difficult: *a sticky problem*. – *noun* **stickiness**. – **stick up for** to speak in defence of.

stickleback *noun* a type of small river-fish with prickles on its back.

stickler *noun* a person who attaches great importance to a particular (often small) matter: *a stickler for punctuality*.

stiff *adjective* not easily bent or moved; (of a mixture, dough *etc*) thick, not easily stirred; cold and distant in one's manner; hard, difficult: *a stiff examination*; severe: *a stiff penalty*; strong: *a stiff drink*. – *verb* **stiffen** to make or become stiff. – *adjective* **stiff-necked** proud, obstinate.

stifle *verb* to suffocate; to put out (flames); to keep back (tears, a yawn *etc*). – *adjective* **stifling** very hot and stuffy.

stigma *noun* (*plural* **stigmata**) a mark of disgrace; (*plural* **stigmas**) in a flower, the top of the pistil. – *verb* **stigmatize** to mark, describe as something bad: *stigmatized for life*.

stile *noun* a step or set of steps for climbing over a wall or fence.

stiletto *noun* (*plural* **stilettos**) a dagger, or a type of instrument, with a narrow blade; (a shoe with) a stiletto heel. – *noun* **stiletto heel** a high, thin heel on a shoe.

still *adjective* not moving; calm, without wind; quiet; (of drinks) not fizzy. – *verb* to make calm or quiet. – *adverb* up to the present time or the time spoken of: *He was still there*; even so, nevertheless: *It's difficult but we must still try*; even: *still more people*. – *noun* an apparatus for distilling spirits (*eg* whisky). – *adjective* **stillborn** (of a child) dead at birth. – *noun* **still life** a picture of something that is not living (as a bowl of fruit *etc*). – *noun* **stillness** the state of being still. – *noun* **stillroom** a pantry or room where drinks, food *etc* are kept.

stilted *adjective* stiff, not natural.

stilts *noun plural* long poles with footrests on which a person may walk clear of the ground; tall poles (*eg* to support a house built above water).

stimulant *noun* something which makes a part of the body more active or which makes one feel livelier. – *verb* **stimulate** to make more active; to encourage; to excite. – *noun* **stimulus** (*plural* **stimuli**) something that brings on a reaction in a living thing; something that rouses (a person *etc*) to action or greater effort.

sting *noun* the part of some animals and plants (as the wasp, the nettle) which can prick the skin and cause pain or irritation; the act of piercing with a sting; the wound, swelling or pain caused by a sting. – *verb* (*past tense* **stung**) to pierce with a sting or cause pain like that of a sting; to be painful, to smart: *The smoke made his eyes sting*; to hurt the feelings of: *She was stung by his words*.

stingy *adjective* mean, not generous.

stink *noun* a bad smell. – *verb* (*past tense* **stank**, *past participle* **stunk**) to give out a bad smell.

stint *verb* to allow (someone) very little: *Although he says he's poor, he doesn't stint himself*. – *noun* limit: *praise without stint*; a fixed amount of work: *my daily stint*.

stipend *noun* pay (*esp* of a clergyman).

stipulate *verb* to state as a condition (of doing something). – *noun* **stipulation** something stipulated, a condition.

stir *verb* (*past tense* **stirred**) to set (liquid) in motion, *esp* with a spoon *etc* moved circularly; to move slightly: *He stirred in his sleep*; to arouse (a person, a feeling *etc*). – *noun* disturbance, fuss. – *adjective* **stirring** exciting. – **stir up** to rouse, cause (*eg* trouble).

stirrup *noun* a metal loop hung from a horse's saddle as a support for the rider's foot.

stitch *noun* (*plural* **stitches**) the loop made in a thread, wool *etc* by a needle in sewing or knitting; a sharp, sudden pain in one's side. – *verb* to put stitches in, to sew.

stoat *noun* a type of small fierce animal similar to a weasel, sometimes called an ermine when in its white winter fur.

stock *noun* family, race: *of ancient stock*; goods in a shop, warehouse *etc*; the capital of a business company divided into shares; the animals of a farm (also **livestock**); liquid (used for soup) obtained by boiling meat, bones *etc*; a type of scented garden flower; the handle of a whip, rifle *etc*; (*plural, hist*) a wooden frame, with holes for the ankles and wrists, in which criminals *etc* were fastened as a punishment; (*plural*) the wooden framework upon which a ship is supported when being built. – *verb* to keep a supply of (for sale); to supply (a farm with animals *etc*). – *adjective* usual, known by everyone; *a stock joke*; usually stocked (by a shop *etc*). – *noun* **stockbroker** a person who buys and sell shares in business companies on behalf of others. – *noun* **stock exchange** a place where stocks and shares are bought and sold; an association of people who do this. – *noun* **stock-in-trade** the necessary equipment *etc* for a particular trade *etc*; a person's usual ways of speaking, acting *etc*: *Sarcasm is part of his stock-in-trade.* – *noun* **stock market** the stock exchange; dealings in stocks and shares. – *noun* **stockpile** a store, a reserve supply. – *verb* to build up a store. – *adjective* **stock-still** perfectly still. – *noun* **stocktaking** a regular check of the goods in a shop or warehouse. – **take stock of** to form an opinion or estimation about (a situation *etc*).

stockade *noun* a fence of strong posts set up round an area or building for defence.

stocking *noun* a close fitting covering in a knitted fabric (wool, nylon *etc*) for the leg and foot.

stocky *adjective* short and stout. – *noun* **stockiness**.

stodgy *adjective* (of food) heavy, not easily digested; (of a person, book *etc*) dull. – *noun* **stodginess**.

stoic *noun* one who bears pain, hardship *etc* without showing any sign of feeling it. – *adjective* **stoical**. – *noun* **stoicism** the bearing of pain *etc* patiently.

stoke *verb* to put coal, wood, or other fuel on (a fire). – *noun* **stoker** a person who looks after a furnace.

stole *noun* a length of silk, linen or fur worn over the shoulders. – *verb* *see* **steal.**

stolen *see* **steal.**

stolid *adjective* (of a person *etc*) dull; not easily excited. – *noun* **stolidity**.

stomach *noun* the bag-like part of the body into which the food passes when swallowed; desire or courage (for something): *He had no stomach for the fight.* – *verb* to put up with, bear: *I can't stomach her rudeness.*

stone *noun* the material of which rocks are composed; a (small) loose piece of this; a piece of this shaped for a certain purpose: *tombstone*; a precious stone (*eg* a diamond); the hard shell around the seed of some fruits (*eg* peach, cherry); a measure of weight (14 lb, 6·35 kilogrammes); a piece of hard material that forms in the kidney, bladder *etc*, causing pain. – *verb* to throw stones at; to take the stones out of fruit. – *adjective* made of stone. – *adjective* **stone-cold** very cold. – *adjective* **stone-dead** or **stone-deaf** completely dead or deaf. – *noun* **stoneware** a kind of pottery made out of coarse clay. – *noun* **stonework** that which is built of stone *esp* the stone parts of a building. – *adjective* **stony** like stone; covered with stones; hard, cold in manner: *a stony stare*. – **a stone's throw** a very short distance; **leave no stone unturned** to do everything possible.

stood *see* **stand.**

stooge *noun* a person who is used by another to do a (*usu* humble or unpleasant) job.

stool *noun* a seat without a back.

stoop *verb* to bend the body forward and downward; to be low or wicked enough to do a certain thing: *I wouldn't stoop to stealing.* – *noun* the act of stooping; a forward bend of the body.

stop *verb* (*past tense* **stopped**) to bring to a halt: *stop the car*; to prevent from doing:

stop him from working; to put an end to: *stop this nonsense;* to come to an end: *The rain has stopped;* (with **up**) to block (a hole *etc*). – *noun* the state of being stopped; a place where something stops; a full stop; a knob on an organ which brings certain pipes into use. – *noun* **stopcock** a tap for controlling the flow of liquid through a pipe. – *noun* **stopgap** something which is used in an emergency until something better is found. – *noun* **stoppage** something which blocks up (*eg* a tube or a passage in the body); a halt (*eg* in work in a factory). – *noun* **stopper** something that stops up an opening (*esp* in the neck of a bottle, jar *etc*). – *noun* **stop press** a space in a newspaper for news put in at the last minute. – *noun* **stopwatch** a watch that can be stopped and started, used in timing races.

store *noun* a supply (*eg* of goods) from which things are taken when needed; a place where goods are kept; a shop; a collected amount or number. – *verb* to put aside for future use. – *noun* **storage** the act of storing; the state of being stored: *Our furniture is in storage.* – *noun* **storehouse** or **storeroom** a building or room where goods are stored. – **in store for** awaiting: *There is trouble in store for you;* **set (great) store by** to value highly.

storey *noun* (*plural* **storeys**) all that part of a building on the same floor.

stork *noun* a type of wading bird with a long bill, neck and legs.

storm *noun* a sudden burst of bad weather (*esp* with heavy rain, lightning, thunder, high wind); a violent outbreak (*eg* of anger). – *verb* to be in a fury; to rain, blow *etc* violently; to attack (a stronghold *etc*) violently. – *adjective* **stormy.**

story *noun* (*plural* **stories**) an account of an event or events, real or imaginary.

stout *adjective* fat; brave: *They put up a stout resistance;* strong: *a stout stick.* – *noun* a strong, dark-coloured kind of beer. – *adjective* **stout-hearted** having a brave heart. – *noun* **stoutness.**

stove *noun* an apparatus using coal, gas or electricity *etc*, used for heating, cooking *etc*. – *verb see* **stave.**

stow *verb* to pack or put away; to fill, pack. – *noun* **stowaway** a person who hides in a ship in order to travel without paying a fare.

straddle *verb* to stand or walk with legs apart; to sit with one leg on each side of (*eg* a chair or horse).

straggle *verb* to wander from the line of a march *etc*; to lag behind; to grow or spread beyond the intended limits: *His long beard straggled over his chest.* – *noun* **straggler** one who straggles. – *adjective* **straggly** spread out untidily.

straight *adjective* not bent or curved: *a straight line;* direct, frank, honest: *a straight answer;* in the proper position or order: *Your tie isn't straight;* (of a hanging picture *etc*) placed level with ceiling or floor; without anything added: *a straight vodka;* expressionless: *He kept a straight face.* – *adverb* by the shortest way, directly: *straight across the desert;* at once, without delay: *I came straight here after work;* fairly, frankly: *He's not playing straight with you.* – *noun* (with **the**) the straight part of a racecourse *etc*. – *verb* **straighten** to make straight. – *noun* **straight fight** a contest between two people only. – *adjective* **straightforward** without any difficulties; honest, frank. – *noun* **straightness** the state of being straight. – **straight away** immediately.

strain *verb* to hurt (a muscle or other part of the body) by overworking or misusing it; to work to or use to the fullest: *He strained his ears to hear the whisper;* to make a great effort: *He strained to reach the rope;* to stretch too far, to the point of breaking (a person's patience *etc*); to separate liquid from a mixture of liquids and solids by passing it through a sieve. – *noun* the act of straining; a hurt to a muscle *etc* caused by straining it; (the effect of) too much work, worry *etc*: *suffering from strain;* too great a demand: *a strain on my patience;* manner: *He grumbled on in the same strain for hours;* a streak: *a strain of selfishness;* a tune; a kind, breed: *a strain of fowls.* – *adjective* **strained** not natural, done with effort: *a strained conversation;* unfriendly: *strained relations.* – *noun* **strainer** a sieve.

strait *noun* a narrow strip of sea between two pieces of land; (*plural*) difficulties, hardships: *in sore straits.* – *adjective* **straitened** poor and needy. – *noun* **straitjacket** a jacket with long sleeves tied behind to prevent a violent or insane person from using their arms. – *adjective* **straitlaced** strict in attitude and behaviour.

strand *noun* a length of something soft and fine (*eg* hair, thread); (*old*) the shore of a sea or lake. – *adjective* **stranded** (of a ship) run aground on the shore; left helpless without money or friends.

strange *adjective* unusual, odd: *a strange look on his face*; not known, seen, heard *etc* before, unfamiliar: *The method was strange to me*; not accustomed (to); foreign: *a strange country.* – *adverb* **strangely.** – *noun* **strangeness.** – *noun* **stranger** a person who is unknown to one; a visitor. – **a stranger to** a person who is quite unfamiliar with: *He is no stranger to misfortune.*

strangle *verb* to kill by gripping or squeezing the throat tightly; to keep in, prevent oneself from giving (*eg* a scream, a sigh); to stop the growth of. – *noun* **stranglehold** a tight control over something which prevents it from escaping, growing *etc*.

strangulate *verb* to strangle, constrict. – *noun* **strangulation.**

strap *noun* a narrow strip of leather, cloth *etc* used to hold things in place or together *etc*. – *verb* (*past tense* **strapped**) to bind or fasten with a strap *etc*; to beat with a strap. – *adjective* **strapping** tall and strong: *a strapping young man.*

stratagem *noun* a cunning act, meant to deceive and outwit an enemy.

strategy *noun* (*plural* **strategies**) the art of guiding, forming or carrying out a plan. – *adjective* **strategic** of strategy; done according to a strategy: *a strategic retreat*; giving an advantage: *a strategic position.* – *noun* **strategist** a person who plans military operations.

stratify *see* **stratum.**

stratosphere *noun* the layer of the earth's atmosphere between 10 and 60 kilometres above the earth.

stratum *noun* (*plural* **strata**) a layer of rock or soil; a level of society. – *verb* **stratify** (*past tense* **stratified**) to form layers or levels. – *noun* **stratification.**

stratus *noun* low, spread-out clouds.

straw *noun* the stalk on which corn grows; a paper or plastic tube for sucking up a drink.

strawberry *noun* a type of small, juicy, red fruit or the low creeping plant which bears it.

stray *verb* to wander; to lose one's way, become separated (from companions *etc*). – *adjective* wandering, lost; happening *etc* here and there: *a stray example.* – *noun* a wandering animal which has been abandoned or lost.

streak *noun* a line or strip different in colour from that which surrounds it; a smear of dirt, polish *etc*; a flash (*eg* of lightning); a trace of some quality in one's character: *a streak of selfishness.* – *verb* to mark with streaks; (*coll*) to move very fast. – *adjective* **streaked.** – *noun* **streaker** (*coll*) a person who runs naked in public. – *adjective* **streaky** marked with streaks. – *noun* **streakiness.** – *noun* **streaky bacon** bacon with streaks of fat and lean.

stream *noun* a flow (of water, air, light *etc*); a small river, a brook; any steady flow of people or things: *a stream of traffic.* – *verb* to flow or pour out. – *noun* **streamer** a long strip *usu* of paper, used for decorating rooms *etc* (*esp* at Christmas); a narrow flag blowing in the wind. – *noun* **streamlet** a small stream. – *verb* **streamline** to shape (a vehicle *etc*) so that it may cut through the air or water as easily as possible; to make more efficient: *We've streamlined our methods of paying.*

street *noun* a road lined with houses *etc*. – **streets ahead of** much better *etc* than.

strength, strengthen *see* **strong.**

strenuous *adjective* making or needing great effort: *The builder's plans met strenuous resistance. Squash is a strenuous game.* – *noun* **strenuousness.**

stress *noun* (*plural* **stresses**) force, pressure, pull *etc* of one thing on another; physical or nervous pressure or strain; emphasis, importance; extra weight laid on a part of a word (as in *butter*); physical or nervous strain: *the stress of modern life.* – *verb* to put stress, pressure, emphasis or strain on.

stretch *verb* to draw out to greater length, or too far, or from one point to another: *Don't stretch that elastic too far. We will stretch a rope from post to post to hold back the crowds*; to be able to be drawn out to a greater length or width: *That material stretches*; to (cause to) exert (oneself): *The work stretched him to the full*; to hold (out); to make (something, *eg* words, the law) appear to mean more than it does. – *noun* (*plural* **stretches**) the act of stretching; the state of being stretched; a length in distance or time: *a stretch of bad road.* – *noun* **stretcher** a light folding bed with handles for carrying the sick or wounded. – **at a stretch** continuously: *They worked three hours at a stretch.*

strew *verb (past tense* **strewed**, *past participle* **strewn** or **strewed**) to scatter: *papers strewn over the floor*; to cover, sprinkle (with): *The floor was strewn with papers.*

stricken *adjective* wounded; deeply affected (*eg* by illness); struck.

strict *adjective* (of a person) insisting on exact obedience to rules; exact: *the strict meaning of a word*; allowing no exception: *strict orders*; severe. – *noun* **strictness**. – *noun* **stricture** criticism, blame.

stride *verb (past tense* **strode**, *past participle* **stridden**) to walk with long steps; to take a long step; to walk over, along *etc*. – *n* a long step; the distance covered by a step; a step forward.

strident *adjective* (of a sound) harsh, grating. – *noun* **stridency**.

strife *noun* quarrelling; fighting.

strike *verb (past tense, past participle* **struck**) to hit with force: *The bullet struck his helmet*; to give, deliver (a blow); to knock: *to strike one's head on the beam*; to attack: *The enemy struck at dawn*; to light (a match); to make (a musical note) sound; (of a clock) to sound (*eg* at ten o'clock with ten chimes); (often with **off** or **out**) to cross out, cancel; to hit or discover suddenly: *strike oil*; to take a course: *He struck out across the fields*; to stop working (in support of a claim for more pay *etc*); to give (someone) the impression of being: *Did he strike you as lazy?*; to affect, impress: *I am struck by her beauty*; to make (an agreement *etc*). – *adjective* **striking** noticeable: *a striking resemblance*; impressive. – **strike camp** to take down tents; **strike home** (of a blow) to hit the point aimed at; (of a remark) to have the intended effect; **strike up** to begin to play or sing (a tune); to begin (a friendship, conversation *etc*).

string *noun* a long narrow cord for binding, tying *etc* made of threads twisted together; a piece of wire, gut *etc* in a violin *etc*; (*plural*) the stringed instruments played by a bow in an orchestra; a line of objects threaded together: *a string of pearls*; a number of things coming one after another: *a string of curses*. – *verb (past tense, past participle* **strung**) to put on a string; to stretch out in a line. – *adjective* **stringed**

having strings. – *adjective* **stringy** like string; (of meat) having (unpleasant) fibres.

stringent *adjective* binding strongly, strictly enforced: *stringent rules*. – *noun* **stringency** strictness.

strip *verb (past tense* **stripped**) to pull (off) (in strips); to remove (*eg* leaves, fruit) from; to remove the clothes from; to deprive: *stripped of his disguise*; to make bare or empty: *strip the room*. – *noun* a long narrow piece (*eg* of paper). – *noun* **strip-cartoon** a line of drawings which tell a story (often an amusing one).

stripe *noun* a band of colour *etc* different from the background on which it lies; a blow with a whip or rod. – *verb* to make stripes on. – *adjective* **stripy**.

stripling *noun* a growing youth.

strive *verb (past tense* **strove**, *past participle* **striven**) to try hard; (*old*) to fight.

strode *see* **stride**.

stroke *noun* the act of striking; a blow (as with a sword, whip); something unexpected: *a stroke of good luck*; one movement (as of a pen, an oar); one chime of a clock; (in swimming) one complete movement of the arms and legs; a particular style of swimming: *breast stroke*; a way of striking the ball (*eg* in tennis, cricket); a single effort or action: *at a stroke*; an achievement; a sudden attack of illness causing paralysis or loss of feeling in the body. – *verb* to rub gently *esp* as a sign of affection.

stroll *verb* to walk slowly in a relaxed way. – Also *noun*.

strong *adjective* not easily worn away: *strong cloth*; not easily defeated *etc*; powerful in attack, not easily resisted: *a strong wind*; (of persons, animals) having great muscular strength, resistance to illness *etc*; (of a person or one's character) forceful, commanding respect or obedience; (of smells, colours *etc*) striking, very noticeable; (of a feeling) intense: *a strong dislike*; in number: *Their army was 2000 strong*. – *noun* **strength** the state of being strong; an available number or force (of soldiers, volunteers *etc*). – *verb* **strengthen** to make, or become strong or stronger. – *noun* **strongbox** a box for storing valuable objects or money. – *noun* **stronghold** a place built to withstand attack, a fortress. – *adverb* **strongly**. – *noun* **strongroom** a room for storing valuable objects or money. –

on the strength of encouraged by or counting on.

strop *noun* a strip of leather on which a razor is sharpened. – *verb* (*past tense* **stropped**) to sharpen a razor. – *adjective* **stroppy** (*coll*) quarrelsome, disobedient, rowdy.

strove *see* **strive**.

struck *see* **strike**.

structure *noun* a building; a framework; the way the parts of anything are arranged: *We made a diagram of the structure of a flower. Before you start to write consider the structure of the story.* – *adjective* **structural**.

struggle *verb* to try hard (to do something); to twist and fight to escape: *He struggled but they were too strong for him*; to fight (with or against someone); to move with difficulty: *He struggled through the mud.* – *noun* a great effort; a fight.

strum *verb* (*past tense* **strummed**) to play (on a guitar or piano) in a relaxed way. – Also *noun*.

strung *see* **string**.

strut *verb* (*past tense* **strutted**) to walk in a proud manner. – *noun* a proud way of walking; a bar *etc* which supports something.

strychnine *noun* a bitter, poisonous drug.

stub *noun* a small stump (as of a pencil, cigarette). – *verb* (*past tense* **stubbed**) to put out, (*eg* a cigarette) by pressure against something; to knock (one's toe) painfully against something.

stubble *noun* the short ends of the stalks of corn left after it is cut; a short growth of beard.

stubborn *adjective* unwilling to give way, obstinate; (of resistance, an attempt *etc*) strong, determined; difficult to manage or deal with. – *noun* **stubbornness**.

stubby *adjective* short, thick and strong: *stubby fingers*.

stucco *noun* (*plural* **stuccos**) a kind of plaster (used for covering walls, moulding ornaments *etc*); work done in stucco.

stuck *see* **stick**.

stud *noun* a nail with a large head; a knob on a surface (often for ornament); a button with two heads for fastening a collar; a collection of horses kept for breeding, or for racing or hunting. – *verb* to cover or fit with studs; to sprinkle, or be sprinkled over, thickly (with): *The meadow is studded with flowers.*

student *noun* a person who studies, *esp* at college, university *etc*.

studio *noun* (*plural* **studios**) the workshop of an artist or photographer; a building or place in which cinema films are made; a room from which television or radio programmes are broadcast.

study *verb* (*past tense* **studied**) to gain knowledge of (a subject) by reading, experiment *etc*; to look carefully at; to consider carefully (*eg* a problem). – *noun* (*plural* **studies**) the gaining of knowledge of a subject: *the study of history*; a room where one reads and writes; a piece of music which is meant to develop the skill of the player; a work of art done as an exercise, or to try out ideas for a later work. – *adjective* **studied** done on purpose, intentional: *a studied insult*; too careful, not natural: *a studied smile.* – *adjective* **studious** studying carefully and much; careful: *his studious avoidance of quarrels.* – *noun* **studiousness**.

stuff *noun* the material of which anything is made; cloth, fabric; substance or material of any kind (used *esp* if the name of it is not known): *What is that stuff all over the wall?* – *verb* to pack full; to fill the skin of (a dead animal) to preserve it, in such a way that it looks as it did when alive; (of a turkey *etc*) to fill with stuffing before cooking. – *noun* **stuffing** anything (*eg* feathers, scraps of material) used to stuff a cushion, chair *etc*; breadcrumbs, onions *etc* packed inside a fowl or other meat and cooked with it. – *adjective* **stuffy** (of a room *etc*) full of stale air, badly ventilated; (*coll*) dull, having old-fashioned ideas. – *noun* **stuffiness**.

stultify *verb* (*past tense* **stultified**) to dull the mind, make stupid.

stumble *verb* to trip in walking; to walk as if blind, unsteadily; to make mistakes or hesitate in speaking; (with **on**) to find by chance. – *noun* the act of stumbling. – *noun* **stumbling block** a difficulty in the way of a plan or of progress.

stump *noun* the part (of something, such as a tree, leg, tooth) left after the main part has been cut, worn *etc* away; (in cricket) one of the three wooden stakes which make up a wicket. – *verb* (in cricket) to put out (a batsman) by touching the stumps with the ball; to puzzle completely; to walk stiffly or heavily. – *adjective* **stumpy** short and thick.

stun *verb* (*past tense* **stunned**) to knock senseless (by a blow *etc*); to surprise or shock very greatly: *He was stunned by the news of her death.*

stung *see* **sting**.

stunk *see* **stink**.

stunt *noun* a daring trick; something done to attract attention: *a publicity stunt.* – *verb* to stop the growth of. – *adjective* **stunted** small and badly shaped.

stupefy *verb* (*past tense* **stupefied**) to make stupid, deaden the feelings of; to astonish. – *noun* **stupefaction.**

stupendous *adjective* wonderful, amazing (*eg* because of size and power).

stupid *adjective* foolish: *a stupid thing to do*; dull, slow at learning; stupefied (*eg* from lack of sleep). – *noun* **stupidity.** – *noun* **stupor** the state of being only partly conscious.

sturdy *adjective* strong, well built; healthy. – *noun* **sturdiness.**

sturgeon *noun* a type of large fish from which caviare is taken.

stutter *verb* to utter one's words in a halting, jerky way, to stammer. – *noun* a stammer.

sty(e) *noun* (*plural* **sties** or **styes**) an inflamed swelling on the eyelid; *see* also **pigsty.**

style *noun* manner of acting, writing, speaking, painting *etc*; fashion: *in the style of the late 19th century*; an air of elegance: *He has a certain style*; the middle part of the pistil of a flower. – *verb* to call, name: *He styled himself 'Lord John'.* – *adjective* **stylish** smart, elegant, fashionable. – **in style** with no expense or effort spared.

stylus *noun* (*plural* **styluses**) a needle for a record-player.

suave *adjective* (of a person or his manner) polite and pleasant (*esp* on the surface).

sub- *prefix* under, below; less than; less in rank or importance.

subaltern *noun* an officer in the army under the rank of captain.

subcommittee *noun* a committee with powers given to it by a larger one.

subconscious *adjective, noun* (of) the workings of the mind of which a person is not himself aware: *a subconscious desire for fame.*

subdivide *verb* to divide into smaller parts. – *noun* **subdivision** a part made by subdividing.

subdue *verb* to conquer (an enemy *etc*); to keep under control (*eg* a desire one has); to make less bright (as a colour, a light); to make quieter: *He seemed subdued after the fight.*

subject *adjective* under the power of another: *a subject nation*; (with **to**) liable to suffer from (*eg* colds, acne); (with **to**) depending on: *This plan is subject to your approval.* – *noun* one under the power of another: *the king's subjects*; a member of a nation: *a British subject*; something or someone spoken or written about, studied *etc*; in a sentence or clause, the word(s) standing for the person or thing which does the action shown by the verb (as in 'The *cat* sat on the mat'). – *verb* (often with **to**) to force to submit (to). – *noun* **subjection** the act of subjecting or the state of being subjected. – *adjective* **subjective** (of an attitude *etc*) arising only from one's own personal feelings, thoughts *etc*, not impartial.

sub judice [L] under (legal) consideration.

subjugate *verb* to bring under one's power; to make obedient.

sublieutenant *noun* an officer in the navy below the rank of lieutenant.

sublime *adjective* very noble, great or grand. – *noun* **sublimity.**

submarine *noun* a ship which can travel under water. – *adjective* under the surface of the sea.

submerge *verb* to cover with water; to sink. – *noun* **submergence.** – *noun* **submersion.**

submit *verb* (*past tense* **submitted**) to give in, yield; to place (a matter) before someone so that he can give his opinion. – *noun* **submission** an act of submitting; readiness to yield, meekness; something (as an idea, statement *etc*) offered for consideration. – *adjective* **submissive** meek, yielding easily.

subordinate *adjective* (often with **to**) lower in rank, power, importance *etc* (than). – noun a person who is subordinate. – verb (with **to**) to consider as of less importance than. – noun **subordination** state of being subordinate; act of subordinating.

suborn verb to persuade (a person) esp by bribery to do something illegal.

subpoena noun an order for a person to appear in court. – Also verb.

subscribe verb to make a contribution, esp of money towards (a charity etc); to promise to take and pay for a number of issues (of a magazine etc); (with **to**) to agree with (an idea, statement etc). – noun **subscription** an act of subscribing; money subscribed.

subsequent adjective following, coming after.

subservient adjective weak-willed, ready to do as one is told. – noun **subservience**.

subside verb to settle down, sink lower, in the earth; (of flood water, noise etc) to get less and less. – noun **subsidence** (of ground, a building etc) a falling or sinking down.

subsidy noun (plural **subsidies**) money paid by a government etc to help an industry etc. – adjective **subsidiary** acting as a help; of less importance; (of a company or firm) controlled by another company (also noun). – verb **subsidize** to give money as a help.

subsist verb to exist; (with **on**) to live on (a kind of food etc). – noun **subsistence** state of existing; means of living, of survival; (state of having) the bare necessities for survival.

subsoil noun the layer of the earth just below the surface soil.

substance noun a material or a material object that can be seen and felt: Glue is a sticky substance; general meaning (of a talk, essay etc); thickness, solidity; wealth, property: a man of substance. – adjective **substantial** solid, strong; large: a substantial building; able to be seen and felt; in the main, but not in detail: substantial agreement. – adverb **substantially** for the most part: substantially the same. – verb **substantiate** to give proof of, or evidence for. – noun **substantive** (in grammar) a noun.

substitute verb (with **for**) to put in place or instead of. – noun a person or thing acting or used instead of another. – noun **substitution**.

substratum noun (plural **substrata**) a layer lying underneath; a foundation.

subterfuge noun a cunning trick to get out of a difficulty etc.

subterranean adjective found under the ground.

subtitle noun a second additional title (of a book etc); on a film, a translation of foreign speech, appearing at the bottom of the screen.

subtle adjective difficult to describe or explain: a subtle difference; cunning: by a subtle means. – adverb **subtly**. – noun **subtlety** (plural **subtleties**) the state of being subtle; something subtle.

subtract verb to take away (a part from); to take away (one number from another). – noun **subtraction**.

suburb noun an area of houses etc on the outskirts of a town. – adjective **suburban** of suburbs. – noun **suburbia** suburbs.

subversive adjective likely to overthrow, destroy (government, discipline etc).

subway noun an underground way for pedestrians etc; an underground railway.

succeed verb (with **in**) to manage to do what one has been trying to do; to get on well; to take the place of, follow: He was succeeded as chairman by his son; (often with **to**) to follow in order (to the throne etc). – noun **success** (plural **successes**) the doing of what one has been trying to do; a person who succeeds; a thing that turns out well. – adjective **successful** having achieved what one aimed at; having achieved wealth, importance etc; turning out as one had planned. – noun **succession** the act of following after; the right of becoming the next holder (of a throne etc); a number of things coming one after the other: a succession of victories. – adjective **successive** following one after the other. – noun **successor** a person who comes after, follows in a post etc. – **in succession** one after another.

succinct adjective in a few words, brief, concise: a succinct reply.

succour verb to help in time of distress. – noun help.

succulent adjective juicy; (of a plant) having thick, juicy leaves or stems.

succumb verb to yield (to): He succumbed to temptation.

such *adjective* of a particular kind previously mentioned: *Such things are difficult to find*; similar: *doctors, nurses, and such people*; so great: *His excitement was such that he shouted out loud*; used for emphasis: *It's such a disappointment!* – *pronoun* thing(s), people *etc*, of a kind already mentioned: *Such as these are not to be trusted*. – *adjective, pronoun* **such-and-such** any given (person or thing): *such-and-such a book*. – **as such** by itself: *The music is unpleasant as such, but it suits my purpose*; **such as** of the same kind as: *birds such as ducks and swans*.

suck *verb* to draw into the mouth; to draw milk from with the mouth; to hold in the mouth and lick hard (*eg* a sweet); (often with **up, in**) to draw in, absorb. – *noun* a sucking action; the act of sucking. – *noun* **sucker** a side shoot rising from the root of a plant; an organ on an animal by which it sticks to objects; a pad (of rubber *etc*) which can stick to a surface; (*coll*) someone easily fooled. – *verb* **suckle** (of a woman or female animal) to give milk from the breast or teat. – *noun* **suckling** a baby or young animal which still sucks its mother's milk.

suction *noun* the act of sucking; the act or process of reducing the air pressure, and so producing a vacuum, on part of the surface of a substance (*eg* on a liquid so that it is drawn up into a tube *etc*) or between surfaces (*eg* a rubber pad and a wall so that they stick together).

sudden *adjective* happening all at once *etc* without being expected: *a sudden attack*. – *adverb* **suddenly**. – *noun* **suddenness**.

suds *noun plural* frothy, soapy water.

sue *verb* to start a law case against.

suede *noun* a kind of leather with a soft, dull surface. – Also *adjective*.

suet *noun* a kind of hard animal fat.

suffer *verb* to feel pain or punishment; to bear, endure; (*old*) to allow; to go through, undergo (a change *etc*). – *noun* **suffering**. – **on sufferance** allowed or tolerated but not really wanted: *He's here on sufferance*.

suffice *verb* to be enough, or good enough. – *adjective* **sufficient** enough.

suffix *noun* (*plural* **suffixes**) a small part added to the end of a word to make another word, as *-ness* to *good* to make *goodness*, *-ly* to *quick* to make *quickly etc*.

suffocate *verb* to kill by preventing the breathing of; to die from lack of air; to (cause to) feel unable to breathe freely. – *noun* **suffocation**.

suffrage *noun* a vote; the right to vote.

suffuse *verb* to spread over: *A blush suffused her face*. – *noun* **suffusion**.

sugar *noun* a sweet substance got mostly from sugar-cane and sugar-beet. – *verb* to mix or sprinkle with sugar. – *noun* **sugar-beet** a type of vegetable whose root yields sugar. – *noun* **sugar-cane** a type of tall grass from whose juice sugar is obtained. – *noun* **sugar daddy** an older man who lavishes gifts *etc* on a younger female, in exchange for companionship and, often, sex. – *adjective* **sugary** tasting of, or like, sugar; too sweet.

suggest *verb* to put forward, propose (an idea *etc*); to put into the mind, to hint. – *noun* **suggestion** an act of suggesting; an idea put forward; a slight trace: *a suggestion of anger in her voice*. – *adjective* **suggestible** easily influenced by suggestions. – *adjective* **suggestive** that suggests something particular, *esp* something improper: *He made suggestive remarks to her*; (with **of**) giving the idea of: *suggestive of mental illness*.

suicide *noun* the taking of one's own life; one who kills himself. – *adjective* **suicidal** of suicide; likely to cause one's death or ruin: *suicidal action*.

suit *noun* a set of clothes to be worn together; a case in a law court; a request for permission to court a lady; one of the four divisions (spades, hearts, diamond, clubs) of playing-cards. – *verb* to be convenient or suitable for, to please: *The climate suits me*; to look well on: *The dress suits you*; (with **to**) to make fitting or suitable for: *He suited his words to the occasion*. – *adjective* **suitable** fitting the purpose; just what is wanted, convenient. – *noun* **suitability**. – *noun* **suitcase** a travelling case for carrying clothes *etc*. – *noun* **suitor** a man who tries to gain the love of a woman. – **follow suit** to do just as someone else has done.

suite *noun* a number of things in a set, as rooms, furniture, pieces of music *etc*; the body of attendants who go with an important person.

sulk *verb* to keep silent because one is displeased. – *adjective* **sulky**. – **the sulks** a fit of sulking.

sullen *adjective* angry and silent, sulky. – *noun* **sullenness**.

sully verb (past tense **sullied**) to make less pure, to dirty.

sulphur noun an element, a yellow substance found in the ground which gives off a choking smell when burnt, used in matches, gunpowder etc. – noun **sulphuric acid** a powerful acid much used in industry.

sultan noun the king or ruler in some Eastern countries. – noun **sultana** a sultan's wife; a kind of raisin.

sultry adjective (of weather) very hot and close; passionate.

sum noun the amount or total made by two or more things added together; a quantity of money; a question or problem in arithmetic; the general meaning (of something said or written). – noun **sum total** the sum of several smaller sums; the main point, total effect. – **sum up** to give the main points of (a discussion, evidence in a trial etc (noun **summing-up**).

summary noun (plural **summaries**) a shortened form (of a story, statement etc) giving only the main points. – adjective short; quick; done without wasting time or words. – adverb **summarily**. – verb **summarize** to state briefly, make a summary of.

summer noun the warmest season of the year. – Also adjective.– noun **summerhouse** a small house for sitting in, in a garden.

summit noun the highest point (of a hill etc). – noun **summit conference** a conference between heads of governments.

summon verb to order (a person) to come to oneself, to a court of law etc; (with **up**) to gather up (one's courage, strength etc). – noun **summons** (plural **summonses**) an order to appear in court.

sump noun the part of a motor-engine which contains the oil; a small pit into which water drains and out of which it can be pumped.

sumptuous adjective costly, splendid.

sun noun the round body in the sky which gives light and heat to the earth and to the other planets revolving round it; sunshine. – verb (past tense **sunned**) (with **oneself**) to sit, lie in the sunshine, sunbathe. – verb **sunbathe** to lie or sit in the sun to acquire a suntan. – noun **sunbeam** a ray of light from the

sun. – noun **sunburn** a burning or redness to the sun. – adjective **sunburned** or **sunburnt** affected by sunburn. – noun **sundial** an instrument for telling the time from the shadow of a rod or plate on its surface cast by the sun. – noun **sunflower** a large type of yellow flower with petals like rays of the sun. – noun plural **sunglasses** spectacles with tinted lenses that shield the eyes from sunlight. – noun **sunlight** the light from the sun. – adjective **sunlit** lighted up by the sun. – adjective **sunny** full of sunshine; cheerful: a sunny nature. – noun **sunrise** the (time of the) rising of the sun in the morning. – noun **sunset** the (time of the) setting of the sun in the evening. – noun **sunshine** bright sunlight; cheerfulness. – noun **sunstroke** a serious type of illness caused by being out in very hot sunshine for too long. – noun **suntan** a browning of the skin caused by exposure to the sun, often acquired deliberately by sitting or lying in the sun.

sundae noun a type of sweet food made up of ice cream served with fruit, syrup etc.

Sunday noun the first day of the week, in the Christian religion set aside for worship.

sundry adjective several, various: sundry articles for sale. – noun plural **sundries** odds and ends.

sung see **sing**.

sunk, sunken see **sink**.

sup verb (past tense **supped**) to eat or drink in small mouthfuls: sup one's soup.

super adjective (coll) extremely good.

super- prefix above, beyond, very, too.

superannuate verb to cause (a person) to retire from a job because of old age, usu with a pension. – noun **superannuation** such a pension.

superb adjective magnificent, very fine, excellent: a superb view.

supercilious adjective looking down on others, haughty.

superficial adjective (of a wound etc) affecting the surface of the skin only, not deep; not thorough or detailed: a superficial interest; apparent at first glance, not actual: a superficial likeness; (of a person) not capable of deep thoughts or feelings. – noun **superficiality**.

superfluous *adjective* beyond what is enough or necessary. – *noun* **superfluity.**

superhuman *adjective* divine; greater than would be expected of an ordinary person: *superhuman effort.*

superimpose *verb* to lay or place (one thing on another thing).

superintend *verb* to be in charge or control, manage. – *noun* **superintendent** a person who is in charge of an institution, building *etc*; a police officer above a chief inspector.

superior *adjective* higher in place, rank or excellence; better or greater than others in some way: *The invaders have superior forces. We sell only superior goods Madam*; having an air of being better than others. – *noun* a person who is better than, or higher in rank than, others. – *noun* **superiority.**

superlative *adjective* better than, or going beyond, all others: *superlative skill*; (in grammar) an adjective or adverb of the highest degree of comparison, as *kindest, worst, most quickly.*

supermarket *noun* a kind of large self-service store selling food *etc.*

supernatural *adjective* not happening in the ordinary course of nature, miraculous.

supersede *verb* to take the place of: *He superseded his brother as headmaster*; to replace (something with something else).

supersonic *adjective* faster than the speed of sound: *supersonic flight.*

superstition *noun* belief in magic and in things which cannot be explained by reason; an example of such belief: *the superstition that one should not walk under ladders.* – *adjective* **superstitious** having superstitions.

supervise *verb* to be in charge of some work and see that it is properly done. – *noun* **supervision** the act of supervising; control, inspection. – *noun* **supervisor.**

supine *adjective* lying on the back; not showing any interest or energy.

supper *noun* a meal taken in the evening.

supplant *verb* to take the place of somebody (sometimes by cunning means) or of something: *The baby supplanted the dog in her affections.*

supple *adjective* bending or moving easily; (of an object) bending easily without breaking. – *noun* **suppleness.** – *adverb* **supply.**

supplement *noun* something added *esp* to supply a need or lack; a special part added to the ordinary part of a newspaper or magazine. – *verb* to make or be an addition to: *Her earnings supplemented his income.* – *adjective* **supplementary** added to supply a need; additional.

suppliant *adjective* asking earnestly and humbly. – *noun* one who asks in this way. – *noun* **supplication** a humble, earnest request.

supply *verb* (*past tense* **supplied**) to provide (what is wanted or needed); to provide (someone) with (something). – *noun* an act of supplying; (*plural* **supplies**) something supplied; a stock or store; (*plural*) a stock of necessary things, as food, equipment, money. – *adjective* (of a teacher *etc*) filling another's place or position for a time.

support *verb* to hold up, take part of the weight of; to help or encourage; to supply with a means of living: *to support a family*; to bear, put up with: *I can't support lies.* – *noun* an act of supporting; something that supports. – *noun* **supporter** a person who supports (*esp* football club *etc*).

suppose *verb* to take as true, assume (often for the sake of argument or discussion): *Let us suppose that we have £100 to spend*; to think, believe, think probable: *I suppose you know*; used in the form of a command to give a polite order: *Suppose you go now.* – *adjective* **supposed** believed (often mistakenly or with too little evidence) to be so: *his supposed kindness.* – *adverb* **supposedly** according to what is supposed. – **supposing (that)** if, in the event that: *Supposing it rains.* – *noun* **supposition** the act of supposing; something supposed. – **be supposed to** to be required or expected to (do).

suppress *verb* to crush, put down (a rebellion *etc*); to keep back (a yawn, a piece of news *etc*). – *noun* **suppression** the act of suppressing.

suppurate *verb* (of a wound *etc*) to be full of, or discharge, pus.

supra- *prefix* above.

supreme *adjective* highest, most powerful: *supreme ruler*; greatest: *supreme* *courage*. – *noun* **supremacy** the state of being supreme; highest power or authority.

surcharge *noun* an extra charge or tax.

sure *adjective* having no doubt: *I'm sure that I can be there*; certain (to do, happen *etc*): *He is sure to go*; reliable, dependable: *a sure method*. – Also *adverb*. – *adverb* **surely** certainly, without doubt; sometimes expressing a little doubt: *Surely you will not go?*; without hesitation, mistake, failure *etc*. – *adjective* **sure-footed** unlikely to slip or stumble. – *noun* **surety** (*plural* **sureties**) a person who promises that another person will do something (as appear in court *etc*); a pledge or guarantee. – **be sure** see to it that: *Be sure that he does it*; **make sure** to act so that, or to check that, something is sure; **sure of oneself** confident; **to be sure!** certainly!; undoubtedly: *To be sure, you are correct!*

surf *noun* the foam made by the breaking of waves. – *noun* **surfboard** a long, narrow board on which a person can ride over the surf. – *noun* **surfing** the sport of riding on a surfboard.

surface *noun* the outside or top part of anything (as of the earth, of a road *etc*). – *verb* to come up to the surface of (water *etc*); to put a (smooth) surface on. – *adjective* on the surface; travelling on the surface of land or water: *surface mail*.

surfeit *noun* too much of anything.

surge *verb* to move (forward) like waves; to rise suddenly or excessively. – *noun* the rising or swelling of a large wave; a movement like this; a sudden rise or increase (of pain *etc*).

surgeon *noun* a doctor who treats injuries and diseases by operations in which the body sometimes has to be cut (to remove a diseased part *etc*). – *noun* **surgery** (*plural* **surgeries**) the act, or art, of treating diseases, injuries, by operation; a doctor's or dentist's consulting room. – *adjective* **surgical.**

surly *adjective* gruff, rude, ill-mannered. – *noun* **surliness.**

surmise *verb* to suppose, to guess. – Also *noun*.

surmount *verb* to overcome (a difficulty *etc*); to be on the top of, to climb, or get, over. – *adjective* **surmountable.**

surname *noun* a person's last name or family name.

surpass *verb* to go beyond, to be more or better than: *His work surpassed my expectations.*

surplice *noun* a loose white gown worn by clergymen *etc*.

surplus *noun* the amount left over after what is needed has been used up. – Also *adjective*.

surprise *noun* the feeling or emotion caused by an unexpected or sudden happening; an unexpected happening *etc*. – *verb* to cause a person to feel surprise; to come upon (a person, an enemy *etc*) suddenly and without warning. – **take by surprise** to come upon (or capture) without warning.

surrender *verb* to give up, give in, yield: *He surrendered to the enemy*; to hand over: *He surrendered the note to the teacher*. – Also *noun*.

surreptitious *adjective* done in a secret, underhand way.

surrogate *noun* a substitute. – *noun* **surrogacy.**

surround *verb* to come, or be, all round (someone or something); to enclose, put round. – *noun* a border. – *noun plural* **surroundings** the country lying round (a place); the people and places with which one has to do in one's daily life.

surtax *noun* an extra tax *esp* on income.

surveillance *noun* a close watch or constant guard.

survey *verb* (*past tense* **surveyed**) to look over; to inspect, examine; to make careful measurements of (a piece of land *etc*). – *noun* (*plural* **surveys**) a general view; a detailed examination or inspection; a piece of writing *etc* giving results of this; a careful measuring of land *etc*; a map made with the measurements obtained. – *noun* **surveyor** a person who makes surveys of land, buildings *etc*.

survive *verb* to remain alive, to continue to exist (after an event *etc*); to live longer than: *He survived his wife*. – *noun* **survival** the state of surviving; anything (as a custom, relic *etc*) that remains from earlier times. – *noun* **survivor** a person who remains alive: *the only survivor of the crash.*

susceptible *adjective* (with **to**) liable to be affected by: *susceptible to colds*; (of a person or his feelings) easily affected or moved. – *noun* **susceptibility** (*plural* **susceptibilities**).

suspect verb to be inclined to think (a person etc) guilty. *I suspect her of the crime*; to distrust, have doubts about: *I suspected his air of frankness*; to guess: *I suspect that we're wrong.* – noun a person etc thought to be guilty of a crime etc. – adjective arousing doubt, suspected. – noun **suspicion** the act of suspecting; a feeling of doubt or mistrust; an opinion, a guess. – adjective **suspicious** suspecting, or inclined to suspect or distrust; arousing, causing suspicion.

suspend verb to hang; to keep from falling or sinking: *particles suspended in a liquid*; to stop for a time or postpone: *to suspend business*; to take away a job, privilege etc from, esp for a time: *They suspended the student from classes.* – noun **suspender** an elastic strap to keep up socks or stockings; (US, plural) braces. – noun **suspense** a state of being undecided; a state of uncertainty or worry. – noun **suspension** the act of suspending; the state of being suspended; the state of a solid which is mixed with a liquid or gas and does not sink or dissolve in it. – noun **suspension bridge** a bridge which is suspended from cables hanging from towers.

suspicion see **suspect.**

sustain verb to hold up, support; to bear (an attack etc) without giving way; to suffer (an injury etc); to give strength to: *This food will sustain you*; to keep up, keep going: *sustain a conversation.* – noun **sustenance** food, nourishment.

swab noun a mop for cleaning a ship's deck; a piece of cottonwool used for various medical purposes, as cleaning parts of the body. – verb (past tense **swabbed**) to clean with a swab.

swaddle verb to wrap up (a young baby) tightly. – noun plural **swaddling clothes** (old) strips of cloth used to wrap up a young baby.

swagger verb to walk proudly, swinging the arms and body; to boast. – Also noun.

swain noun (old) a young man.

swallow verb to make (food or drink) pass over the throat into the stomach; (with up) to cause to disappear; to receive (an insult etc) without objecting or rejecting; to keep back (tears, a laugh etc). – noun an act of swallowing; a type of bird with pointed wings and a forked tail.

swamp noun wet, marshy ground. – verb to cause (a boat) to fill with water; to overwhelm: *They were swamped with work.*

swan noun a large, stately type of water bird, usu white, with a long neck. – noun **swan song** the last work of a musician, writer etc.

swank verb (coll) to show off. – Also noun. – adjective **swanky.**

swap or **swop** verb (past tense **swapped** or **swopped**) to give one thing in exchange for another: *They swapped stamps.*

sward noun (in poetry etc) a patch of green turf.

swarm noun a large number of insects flying or moving together, eg bees; a dense moving crowd. – verb (of bees) to gather together in great numbers; to move in crowds; to be crowded with: *The ruins swarmed with tourists*; (with up) to climb up (a wall etc).

swarthy adjective dark-skinned.

swashbuckling adjective bold, swaggering: *a swashbuckling pirate.*

swat verb (past tense **swatted**) to crush (a fly etc). – noun an instrument for doing this.

swath or **swathe** noun a line of corn or grass cut by a scythe; a strip.

swathe verb to wrap round with clothes or bandages. – noun see **swath.**

sway verb to move, swing, in a rocking manner; to (cause to) bend in one direction or to one side; to influence: *He swayed the audience.* – noun the act of swaying; a swaying movement; rule, power: *to hold sway over.*

swear verb (past tense **swore**, past participle **sworn**) to promise or declare solemnly; to vow; to curse, using the name of God or other sacred things without respect; to make (someone) take an oath: *to swear a person to secrecy.* – noun **swear word** a word used in swearing or cursing. – adjective **sworn** holding steadily to one's attitude etc: *They had been sworn friends since childhood. The two rivals became sworn enemies.* – **swear by** to rely on, have complete faith in.

sweat noun the moisture from the skin, perspiration. – verb to give out sweat; (coll) to work hard. – noun **sweated labour** hard work for which very little pay is given. – noun **sweater** a jersey, a pullover. – adjective **sweaty** wet, or stained with, sweat.

swede *noun* a kind of large yellow turnip.

sweep *verb* (*past tense* **swept**) to clean (a floor *etc*) with a brush or broom; (often with **up**) to gather up or remove (dust *etc*) by sweeping; to carry (away, along, off) with a long brushing movement; to travel over quickly, to move with speed (and force): *This disease is sweeping the country*; to move quickly in a proud manner (*eg* from a ship); (with **of**) to clear (something) of: *to sweep the sea of enemy mines*; to curve widely or stretch far. – *noun* an act of sweeping; a sweeping movement; a curve or a stretch; a chimney sweeper; a sweepstake. – *adjective* **sweeping** that sweeps; (of a victory *etc*) great, overwhelming; (of a statement *etc*) too general, allowing no exceptions, rash. – *noun* **sweepstake** a system of gambling on a race *etc*, in which those who take part stake money which goes to the holder of the winning ticket *etc*.

sweet *adjective* having the taste of sugar, not salty, sour or bitter; pleasing to the taste; pleasant to hear or smell; kindly, agreeable, charming. – *noun* a small piece of sweet substance, as of chocolate, toffee, candy *etc*; something sweet served towards the end of a meal, a pudding. – *verb* **sweeten** to make or become sweet or sweeter. – *noun* **sweetener** a substance that sweetens *esp* one not containing sugar; (*coll*) a bribe. – *noun* **sweetheart** a boyfriend or girlfriend; a darling. – *noun* **sweetmeat** (*old*) a sweet, candy *etc*. – *noun* **sweetness**. – *noun* **sweet pea** a type of sweet-smelling climbing flower grown in gardens. – *noun* **sweet tooth** a liking for sweet-tasting things. – *noun* **sweet william** a sweet-smelling type of garden flower.

swell *verb* (*past participle* **swollen**) to grow or make larger, greater, louder *etc*; (of the sea) to rise into waves. – *noun* an act of swelling; an increase in size *etc*; large, heaving waves; a gradual rise in the height of the ground. – *adjective* (*coll*) fine, splendid. – *noun* a dandy. – *noun* **swelling** a swollen part of the body, a lump.

swelter *verb* to be too hot. – *adjective* **sweltering** very hot.

swept *see* **sweep**.

swerve *verb* to turn quickly to one side. – Also *noun*.

swift *adjective* moving quickly; rapid, quick. – *noun* a type of bird rather like the swallow. – *noun* **swiftness**.

swig *noun* (*coll*) a mouthful of liquid, a large drink. – *verb* (*past tense* **swigged**) (*coll*) to gulp down.

swill *verb* to wash out; (*coll*) to drink a great deal. – *noun* (partly) liquid food given to pigs; (*coll*) a big drink.

swim *verb* (*present participle* **swimming**, *past tense* **swam**, *past participle* **swum**) to move on or in water, using arms, legs, fins, tails *etc*; to cross by swimming: *to swim a river*; to float, not sink; to move with a gliding motion; to be dizzy; to be covered (with liquid): *meat swimming in grease*. – *noun* an act of swimming, or a motion like it. – *noun* **swimmer** one who swims. – *noun* **swimming bath** or **swimming pool** an area of water, *usu* a large kind of tank, designed for swimming, diving in *etc*. – *noun* **swimming costume** or **swimsuit** a brief close-fitting garment for swimming *etc* in. – *adverb* **swimmingly** smoothly, easily, successfully.

swindle *verb* to cheat (someone); to get (money *etc* from someone) by cheating. – *noun* a fraud, a deception. – *noun* **swindler**.

swine *noun* (*plural* **swine**) (*old*) a pig; (*coll*) a contemptible person. – *noun* **swineherd** (*old*) a person who looks after pigs.

swing *verb* (*past tense* **swung**) to move to and fro, to sway; to move backwards and forwards on a swinging seat; to (cause to) turn or whirl round; to walk quickly, moving the arms to and fro. – *noun* an act of swinging; a swinging movement; a seat for swinging, hung on ropes *etc* from a support. – *noun* **swing bridge** a kind of bridge that swings open to let ships pass. – **in full swing** going on busily.

swingeing *adjective* very great: *swingeing cuts in taxation*.

swipe *verb* to strike with a sweeping blow. – Also *noun*.

swirl *verb* to sweep along with a whirling motion. – Also *noun*.

swish *verb* to strike *etc* (something) with a whistling or rustling sound; to move making such a noise: *She swished out of the room in her long dress*. – Also *noun*.

switch *noun* (*plural* **switches**) a small lever or handle *eg* for turning an electric current on and off; an act of switching; a change: *a switch of support*; a thin stick. – *verb* to strike with a switch; to turn (off or on an electric current *etc*) by means of a switch; to (cause to) change or turn: *The men switched jobs. She hastily switched the conversation.* – *noun* **switch-back** a road or railway with steep ups and downs or sharp turns. – *noun* **switchboard** a board with equipment for making telephone connections.

swivel *noun* a type of joint between two parts of an object that enables one part to turn or pivot without the other. – *verb* (*past tense* **swivelled**) to turn on, or as if on, a swivel.

swollen *adjective* increased in size by swelling. – *verb see* **swell**.

swoon *verb* (*old*) to faint. – Also *noun*.

swoop *verb* to come down with a sweep (as a hawk does on its prey). – *noun* a sudden downward rush. – **at one fell swoop** all at one time, at a stroke.

swop *see* **swap**.

sword *noun* a type of weapon with a long blade for cutting or piercing. – *noun* **swordfish** a large type of fish with a long pointed upper jaw like a sword.

swore, sworn *see* **swear**.

sycamore *noun* a name given to several different types of trees, the maple, plane, and a kind of fig tree.

sycophant *noun* a person who flatters (someone) in order to gain some advantage for himself. – *adjective* **sycophantic**.

syllable *noun* a word or part of a word uttered by only one effort of the voice. (*Cheese* has one syllable, *but-ter* two, *mar-gar-ine* three). – *adjective* **syllabic**.

syllabus *noun* (*plural* **syllabuses** or **syllabi**) a programme or list *eg* of lectures, classes *etc*.

sylph *noun* (*myth*) a type of fairy supposed to inhabit the air; a slender, graceful woman.

symbol *noun* a thing that stands for or represents another, as the cross, which stands for Christianity; a sign used as a short way of stating something, as the signs + meaning plus, O meaning oxygen. – *adjective* **symbolic** or **symbolical** of, or using, symbols; standing as a symbol of. – *noun* **symbolism** the use of symbols to express ideas *esp* in art and literature. – *verb* **symbolize** to be a symbol of.

symmetry *noun* the state in which two parts, on either side of a dividing line, are equal in size, shape and position: *The extension spoiled the symmetry of the building.* – *adjective* **symmetrical** having symmetry, not lopsided in appearance.

sympathy *noun* (*plural* **sympathies**) a feeling of pity or sorrow for a person in trouble; the state of being in agreement with, or of being able to understand, the feelings, attitudes *etc* of others. – *adjective* **sympathetic** feeling, showing sympathy: (with **to** or **towards**) inclined to be in favour of: *sympathetic to the scheme.* – *verb* **sympathize** (sometimes with **with**) to express or feel sympathy.

symphony *noun* (*plural* **symphonies**) a long piece of music for an orchestra of many different instruments.

symposium *noun* a meeting or conference for the discussion of some subject; a collection of essays dealing with a single subject.

symptom *noun* something that indicates the existence of something, a sign (*esp* of a disease): *A rash is one symptom of measles.* – *adjective* **symptomatic**.

syn- *prefix* with, together.

synagogue *noun* a Jewish place of worship.

synchronize *verb* to happen at the same time; to (cause to) agree in time: *synchronize watches.*

syncopate *verb* to change the beat in music by putting the accent on beats not usually accented. – *noun* **syncopation**.

syndicate *noun* a number of persons who join together to manage some piece of business.

synod *noun* a meeting of clergymen.

synonym *noun* a word which has the same (or, nearly the same) meaning as another as 'ass' and 'donkey'; 'brave' and 'courageous', 'to hide' and 'to conceal'. – *adjective* **synonymous** (sometimes with **with**) having the same meaning.

synopsis *noun* (*plural* **synopses**) a short summary of the main points of a book, speech *etc*.

syntax *noun* (rules for) the correct putting together of words into sentences. – *adjective* **syntactic** or **syntactical**.

synthesis *noun* the act of making a whole by putting together its separate parts, *esp* the making of a substance by combining chemical elements. – *verb* **synthesize** to make (*eg* a drug) by synthesis. – *adjective* **synthetic** made artificially and looking like, but not the same as, the natural product: *These boots are made of synthetic rubber. Synthetic leather can be cheap*; not natural, pretended: *synthetic charm*.

syringe *noun* a tube with a rubber bulb or piston for sucking up, and squirting out, liquid; an instrument of this kind with a needle, used by doctors for injecting drugs *etc*. – *verb* to wash out, clean, with a syringe: *She's had her ears syringed*.

syrup *noun* water, or the juice of fruits, boiled with sugar and made thick and sticky; a purified form of treacle.

system *noun* an arrangement of many parts which work together: *The railway system requires more finance. The sun is at the centre of the solar system*; a way of organizing: *We have a democratic system of government*. A regular way of doing something, a plan, a method; the body, or parts of the body, thought of as working as a whole: *His system won't stand the treatment*. – *adjective* **systematic** following a system; methodical.

T

T: T-shirt *noun* same as **tee-shirt**.

tab *noun* a small tag or flap by which anything is gripped.

tabard *noun* a short sleeveless tunic-like garment.

tabby *noun* (*plural* **tabbies**) a striped cat, *esp* female. – *noun* **tabby-cat**.

tabernacle *noun* a place of worship.

table *noun* a piece of furniture with a flat top and standing on legs; food, supply of food on a table; a statement of facts or figures set out in columns: *This bus timetable is out of date. You must learn the multiplication tables*. – *verb* to make into a list or table; to put forward for discussion. – *noun* **tablecloth** a cloth for covering a table. – *noun* **tableland** a raised stretch of land with a level surface. – *noun* **table linen** tablecloths, napkins *etc*. – *noun* **tablespoon** a large size of spoon. – *noun* **table tennis** a type of game played on a table with small bats and a light ball.

tableau *noun* (*plural* **tableaux**) a striking group or scene.

table d'hôte *täb'l dōt* *noun* a meal of several courses at a fixed price.

tablet *noun* a small flat plate, slab or surface on which to write, cut inscriptions, paint, *etc*; a small flat cake or piece (of soap, chocolate *etc*); a pill.

tabloid *noun* a small-sized newspaper, *esp* one that gives news in shortened and often simplified form and often contains many pictures. – Also *adjective*.

taboo *noun*, *adjective* (something) forbidden for religious reasons or not approved by social custom: *Certain slang words are considered taboo*.

tabor *noun* a small kind of drum.

tabulate *verb* to set out (information *etc*) in columns or rows. – *adjective* **tabular**.

tachograph *noun* an instrument fitted to a commercial vehicle to show mileage, speed, number and location of stops *etc*.

tachometer *noun* an instrument for measuring the speed of rotation; an instrument fitted in a vehicle showing the speed of the engine.

tacit *tas'it*, *adjective* understood but not spoken aloud, silent: *tacit agreement*. – *adjective* **taciturn** not inclined to talk. – *noun* **taciturnity**.

tack *noun* a kind of short sharp nail with a broad head; a sideways movement of a sailing ship so that it may sail against the wind; a direction, a course; in sewing, a large stitch to be taken out later. – *verb* to fasten with tacks; to sew with tacks; (of sailing ships) to move from side to side across the face of the wind.

tackle *noun* the ropes, rigging, *etc* of a ship; equipment, tools, gear: *fishing tackle*; ropes and pulleys for raising heavy weights; an act of tackling. – *verb* to seize, come to grips with or try to deal with; (in football, hockey *etc*) to try to stop, or take the ball from, another player.

tacky *adjective* sticky; shabby, of poor quality.

tact *noun* care and skill in dealing with people so as to avoid hurting and offending. – *adjective* **tactful**. – *adjective* **tactless**.

tactics *noun* a way of acting in order to gain success or advantage; the art of arranging troops or warships successfully during a battle. – *adjective* **tactical** of tactics, of clever and successful planning. – *noun* **tactician** a person who plans and acts cleverly.

tadpole *noun* a young frog or toad in its first stage of life.

taffeta *noun* a kind of thin, glossy cloth made of silk *etc*.

tag *noun* a metal *etc* point at the end of a shoelace; a label: *a price tag*; any saying or quotation that is often repeated: *a Latin tag*; a kind of chasing game played by children (also **tig**). – *verb* to put a tag or tags on. – **tag on to** or **tag after** to follow (a person) closely and continually: *His little brother tags after him.*

tagliatelle *noun* pasta made in long ribbons.

tail *noun* the part of an animal, bird or fish which sticks out behind the rest of its body; anything like a tail in position or shape: *tail of an aeroplane*; (*plural*) the side of a coin that does not bear the head; (*plural*) a tail-coat. – *verb* (*coll*) to follow closely: *The detective tailed him for three days*; to remove the tails from (gooseberries *etc*). – *noun* **tailback** a line of traffic stretching back from anything obstructing traffic flow. – *noun* **tailboard** a moveable board at the back end of a cart, lorry *etc*. – *noun* **tail-coat** a type of coat with a divided tail, part of a man's evening dress. – *noun* **tail-end** the very end (of a procession *etc*). – *noun* **tail-gate** a door at the back of a car that opens upwards. – *noun* **tail-light** the light at the back of a motor-car, cycle, *etc*. – *noun* **tail-spin** (in aeroplanes) a steep, spinning, downward dive. – **tail off** to become less, fewer or worse: *The number of spectators tailed off*; **turn tail** to run away.

tailor *noun* a person who cuts out and makes suits, overcoats *etc*. – *verb* to make and fit (outer clothes); to make to fit the circumstances, adapt: *to tailor your expenditure to your earnings.*

taint *verb* to spoil by touching or bringing into contact with something bad or rotten; to corrupt. – *noun* a trace of decay or of evil.

take *verb* (*past tense* **took**, *past participle* **taken**) to lay hold of, grasp; to choose: *Take a card!*; to accept, agree to have (a seat, a biscuit, a rest, responsibility *etc*); to have room for: *The car takes eight passengers*; to eat, swallow (food, drink); to get or have regularly: *He takes sugar*; to capture (a fort *etc*); to subtract: *Take 3 from 6*; to lead, carry, drive: *to take pigs to market*; to use, make use of: *Take care!*; to require: *It takes courage*; to travel by (a train *etc*); to feel (pride, pleasure *etc*) (in); to photograph: *He took three shots of the village*; to understand (a statement *etc* in a certain way); (of an inoculation *etc*) to be effective; (of a plant) to root; to become popular, to please. – *noun* **take-away** a meal prepared and bought in a restaurant or shop but taken away and eaten somewhere else; a restaurant or shop providing such means. – Also *adjective*. – *adjective* **taking** pleasing, attractive. – *noun* an act of taking; (*plural*) money received from things sold. – **take account of** to consider, to remember; **take advantage of** to make use of (an opportunity); to treat or use (a person) unfairly; **take after** to be like in appearance or ways; **take care of** to look after; **take down** to write, note down; **take for** to believe (mistakenly) to be: *I took him for his brother*; **take heed** to pay careful attention; **take ill** to become ill; **take in** to include; to receive; to understand: *I didn't take in what you said*; to make something smaller: *take in a dress*; to cheat, deceive: *You took me in with your impersonation*; **take leave of** to say goodbye; to depart from; **take (someone's) life** to kill (someone); **taken with** attracted to; **take off** to remove (clothes *etc*); to imitate unkindly; (of an aircraft) to leave the ground (*noun* **take-off**); **take on** to undertake (work *etc*); to accept (as an opponent): *He will take you on at tennis*; **take over** to take control of (*eg* a business) (*noun* **takeover**); **take part (in)** to share, help (in); **take pity on** to show pity for; **take place** to happen; **take to** to turn to (flight *etc*) in an emergency: *He took to* *his heels and ran away;* to be attracted by; to begin to do or use regularly: *He took to rising early;* **take to heart** to be deeply affected or upset by; **take up** to lift, raise; to occupy (space, time *etc*); to begin to learn, show interest in: *He has taken up chess.*

talc *noun* a soft type of mineral, soapy to the touch. – *noun* **talcum powder** a fine kind of powder, used for rubbing on to the body, made from talc.

tale *noun* story; an untrue story, a lie.

talent *noun* a special ability or skill: *a talent for drawing;* (*hist*) a measure of weight or the value of this weight of gold or silver. – *adjective* **talented** skilled, gifted.

talisman *noun* an object supposed to have magic powers, a charm.

talk *verb* to speak; to gossip; to give information. – *noun* conversation; gossip; the subject of conversation; a discussion or lecture. – *adjective* **talkative** inclined to chatter. – *noun* **talking-to** a scolding. – **talk over** to discuss; to persuade; **talk round** to discuss (something) without coming to the main point; to persuade; **talk shop** *see* **shop.**

tall *adjective* high or higher than usual or normal: *A tall person can look over the wall. A tall building stands at the corner of the square;* hard to believe: *a tall story.* – *noun* **tallboy** a tall kind of chest of drawers. – *noun* **tallness.** – *noun* **tall order** (an instruction to do) something unreasonably difficult.

tallow *noun* the fat of animals, melted down to make soap, candles *etc*.

tally *noun* (*plural* **tallies**) an account; a ticket, label; (*old*) a stick with notches cut in it for keeping an account or score. – *verb* (*past tense* **tallied**) to agree (with): *His story tallies with yours.*

tally-ho! *interjection* a cry used by huntsmen.

talon *noun* the claw of a bird of prey.

tambourine *noun* a kind of small one-sided drum with tinkling metal discs set into the sides.

tame *adjective* (of animals) not wild, used to living with human beings; dull, not exciting. – *verb* to make tame; to subdue, make humble.

tamper *verb* (with **with**) to meddle with so as to damage, alter *etc*: *He tampered with the machine.*

tampon *noun* a piece of cotton-wool *etc* inserted in a wound *etc* to stop bleeding or absorb blood, *esp* a plug of cotton-wool inserted into the vagina during menstruation.

tan *verb* (*past tense* **tanned**) to make an animal's skin into leather by treating it with tannin; to make or become brown *esp* by exposure to the sun. – *noun* a yellowish-brown colour; suntan. – *noun* **tanner** a person whose work is tanning. – *noun* **tannery** (*plural* **tanneries**) a place where leather is made. – *noun* **tannin** any of several substances got from plants, used in tanning, dyeing *etc*; one of these substances present in tea.

tandem *noun* a long bicycle with two seats and two sets of pedals one behind the other. – *adjective* one behind the other. – **in tandem** together or in conjunction.

tang *noun* a strong taste, flavour or smell: *the tang of the sea.*

tangent *noun* a straight line which touches a circle or curve but does not cut into it. – **go off at a tangent** to go off suddenly in another direction or on a different line of thought.

tangerine *noun* a small type of orange.

tangible *adjective* able to be felt by touching; real, definite: *tangible profits.*

tangle *verb* to mix, twist together in knots; to make or become difficult or confusing. – Also *noun*.

tango *noun* (*plural* **tangos**) a type of dance, *orig* from S. America.

tank *noun* a large container for water, petrol, gas *etc*; a heavy steel-covered vehicle armed with guns and moving on caterpillar wheels. – *noun* **tanker** a ship or large lorry for carrying liquids *esp* oil; an aircraft carrying fuel.

tankard *noun* a large drinking mug of metal, glass *etc*.

tanner, tannery, tannin *see* **tan.**

tantalize *verb* to annoy, to torment, by offering something and keeping it out of reach. – *adjective* **tantalizing.**

tantamount: tantamount to coming to the same thing as, equivalent to: *tantamount to stealing.*

tantrum *noun* a fit of rage or bad temper.

tap *noun* a light touch or knock; any of several devices (*esp* one with a handle and a valve that can be opened and shut) for controlling the flow of liquid, gas *etc*. – *verb* (*past tense* **tapped**) to knock or strike lightly; to draw on, start using (a source, supply *etc*); to attach a listening device secretly to (telephone wires). – *noun* **tap-dance** a dance done with special shoes that make a tapping sound. – **on tap** ready, available, for use.

tape *noun* a narrow band or strip of strong cloth used for tying *etc*; a piece of string stretched above the finishing line on a racetrack; a narrow strip of paper, plastic, metal *etc* used for measuring, sound recording, filming *etc*. – *verb* to fasten with tape; to record (sound) on tape. – *noun* **tape-measure** a strong tape marked off in centimetres *etc* for measuring. – *noun* **tape-recorder** a kind of instrument for recording sound *etc* on magnetic tape. – *noun* **tapeworm** a type of long worm sometimes found in the intestines of humans and animals. – **have (someone or something) taped** to have a thorough understanding of the characteristics, worth *etc* (of a person or thing): *They've had him taped from the start.*

taper *noun* a long, thin kind of candle; a long waxed wick used for lighting lamps *etc*, a spill. – *verb* to make or become thinner at one end. – *adjective* **tapering**.

tapestry *noun* (*plural* **tapestries**) a cloth with designs or figures woven into it (hung on walls as a decoration or used to cover furniture).

tapioca *noun* a kind of food got from the root of the cassava plant and used for making puddings.

tapir *noun* a kind of wild animal something like a large pig.

tar *noun* any of several kinds of thick, black, sticky liquid, got from wood or coal, used in roadmaking *etc*; (*coll*) a sailor. – *verb* (*past tense* **tarred**) to smear with tar. – *adjective* **tarry** like, or covered with, tar. – **tarred with the same brush** having the same faults (as someone else).

tarantula *noun* a type of large, poisonous spider.

tardy *adjective* slow; late. – *noun* **tardiness**.

tare *noun* the weight of a box, truck *etc* when empty; (in the Bible) a weed found growing among corn.

target *noun* a mark to fire or aim at, in shooting, archery, darts *etc*; something

(*eg* a result) that is aimed at: *a target of £3000*; a person at whom unfriendly remarks *etc* are aimed: *He is always the target of her criticism.*

tariff *noun* a list of prices; a list of the taxes to be paid on goods brought into a country.

tarmacadam *noun* a mixture of small stones and tar used to make road surfaces *etc*. – *noun* **tarmac** the surface of a road or airport runway made of tarmacadam. – *noun* **Tarmac**® (*US*) tarmacadam.

tarnish *verb* (of metals) to (cause to) become dull or discoloured; to spoil (one's reputation *etc*).

tarpaulin *noun* (a sheet of) strong cloth made waterproof (with tar).

tarry *verb* to stay behind, linger; to be slow or late. – *adjective see* **tar.**

tart *noun* a small pie containing fruit, jam, vegetables *etc*. – *adjective* (of taste) sharp, sour.

tartan *noun* woollen (or other) cloth woven with a pattern of squares of different colours, originally used by clans of the Scottish Highlands; any one of these patterns: *the Cameron tartan*. – Also *adjective*.

tartar *noun* a substance that gathers on the teeth; a difficult, demanding and irritable person; a substance that forms inside wine casks. – **cream of tartar** a white powder obtained from the tartar from wine casks, used in baking.

task *noun* a set piece of work to be done. – *noun* **task force** a group of people gathered together with the purpose of performing a special or specific task. – *noun* **taskmaster** a person who sets and supervises tasks: *a hard taskmaster*. – **take to task** to scold, find fault with.

tassel *noun* a hanging bunch of threads, used as an ornament on a hat *etc*; anything like this, *esp* a hanging cluster of flowers such as a catkin.

taste *verb* to try by eating or drinking a little; to eat or drink a little of; to recognize (a flavour): *I can taste the lemon in this pudding*; to have a particular flavour: *to taste of garlic*; to experience: *to taste success*. – *noun* the act or sense of tasting; a flavour; a small quantity (of food or drink); a liking: *a taste for music*; the ability to judge what is suitable (in behaviour, dress *etc*) or what is fine, beautiful *etc*. – *adjective*

tasteful showing good taste and judgement. – *adjective* **tasteless** without flavour; not tasteful. – *adjective* **tasty** having a good flavour.

tatters *noun plural* torn, ragged pieces. – *adjective* **tattered** ragged.

tattle *noun* gossip. – Also *verb*.

tattoo *noun* a design marked on the skin by tattooing; a drumming or drumbeat; a military outdoor display at night with music *etc*. – *verb* to prick coloured designs into the skin. – *adjective* **tattooed** marked with tattoos.

taught *see* **teach.**

taunt *verb* to tease or jeer at unkindly. – Also *noun*.

taut *adjective* pulled tight; tense, in a state of strain. – *verb* **tauten** to make or become tight.

tautology *noun* a form of repetition in which the same thing is said in different ways, as in 'He *hit* and *struck* me'.

tavern *noun* a public house, an inn.

tawdry *adjective* cheap-looking and gaudy.

tawny *adjective* yellowish-brown.

tax *noun* (*plural* **taxes**) a charge made by the government on incomes, certain types of goods *etc*, to help pay for the running of the state; a strain, a burden: *a severe tax on his patience*. – *verb* to make (persons) pay a tax; to put a strain on: *She will tax her strength*; (with **with**) to accuse of: *I taxed him with laziness*. – *noun* **taxation** the act or system of taxing; taxes. – *noun* **taxpayer** a person who pays taxes.

taxi *noun* (*plural* **taxis**) a motor-car which may be hired, with a driver (also **taxi-cab**). – *verb* (*present participle* **taxiing**, *past tense* **taxied**) to travel in a taxi; (of aeroplanes) to run along the ground. – *noun* **taxi-rank** a place where taxis park to wait for hire.

taxidermy *noun* the art of preparing and stuffing the skins of animals to make them lifelike. – *noun* **taxidermist** a person who does this work.

TB *abbreviation* tuberculosis.

tea *noun* a type of plant grown in India, China *etc* or its dried and prepared leaves; a drink made by adding boiling water to these; any drink looking, or made, like tea: *His nurse gave him beef tea. I prefer herbal tea at night*; an

afternoon meal at which tea is drunk. – *noun* **teacake** a kind of light, flat bun. – *noun* **tea chest** a tall box of thin wood in which tea is packed for export, often used as a packing case for other goods. – *noun* **teacup** a cup of medium size from which to drink tea. – *noun* **teapot** a pot with a spout, for making and pouring tea. – *noun* **teaspoon** a small spoon. – *noun* **tea-towel** a cloth for drying crockery *etc*.

teach *verb* (*past tense* **taught**) to give (someone) skill or knowledge: *Miss Brown teaches my daughter*; to give knowledge of, or training in (a subject or an art): *He teaches French*; to be a teacher: *She decided to teach*. – *noun* **teacher** a person whose job is to give knowledge or skill. – *noun* **teaching** the work of a teacher; guidance, instruction; (often *plural*) beliefs, rules of conduct *etc* that are preached or taught.

teak *noun* a type of tree from the East Indies; its very hard wood; a type of African tree.

teal *noun* a small water bird of the duck kind.

team *noun* a group of people working together; a side in a game: *a football team*; two or more animals working together: *a team of oxen*. – *noun* **team spirit** willingness to work loyally as a team or as a member of a team. – **team (up) with** to join together with, join forces with.

tear[1] *n* a drop of liquid coming from the eye; (*plural*) grief. – *adjective* **tearful** inclined to weep; causing tears. – *noun* **tear gas** a type of gas which causes the eyes to stream with tears, used against rioters *etc*. – **in tears** weeping.

tear[2] *verb* (*past tense* **tore**, *past participle* **torn**) to pull with force (apart, away, down *etc*); to make a hole or split in (material *etc eg* by pulling it away from something it is attached to); to hurt deeply: *The story tears my heart*; (*coll*) to rush: *He tore off down the road*. – *noun* a hole, or split, made by tearing.

tease *verb* to annoy, irritate on purpose: *He's teasing the cat*; to pretend playfully to upset or annoy: *I'm only teasing*; to untangle (sheep's wool *etc*) with a comb; to sort out (a problem or puzzle). – *noun* a person who teases. – *noun* **teaser** a problem, a puzzle.

teasel *noun* a type of prickly plant.

teat *noun* the part of an animal through which milk passes to its young; a rubber object shaped like this attached to a baby's feeding bottle.

technical *adjective* of, belonging to, a particular art or skill, *esp* of a mechanical or industrial kind; *He learnt the technical term for each piece. We called in a technical expert*; according to strict laws or rules; *a technical defeat.* – *noun* **technicality** (*plural* **technicalities**) a technical detail or point; the state of being technical. – *adverb* **technically** in a technical way; in technique; according to strict legal or technical rules, strictly speaking. – *noun* **technician** a person who has trained skill in the practical side of an art. – *noun* **technique** the way in which a (skilled) process *etc* is carried out, a method. – *noun* **technology** (the study of) science applied to practical (*esp* industrial) purposes; technical means and skills of a particular civilization, period *etc*. – *adjective* **technological**. – *noun* **technologist**.

teddy or **teddybear** *noun* (*plural* **teddies** or **teddybears**) a stuffed toy bear.

tedious *adjective* long and tiresome. – *noun* **tedium** the quality of being tedious.

tee *noun* the square of level ground from which a golf-ball is driven; the peg or sand heap on which the ball is placed for driving. – *verb* (often with **up**) to place (a ball) on a tee.

teem *verb* (with **with**) to be full of; to rain heavily.

teens *noun plural* the years of one's age from thirteen to nineteen. – *adjective* **teenage** suitable for, or typical of, those in the teens. – *noun* **teenager** a person in the teens.

tee-shirt *noun* a short-sleeved light shirt pulled on over the head.

teeth *see* **tooth.**

teethe *verb* (of a baby) to grow the first teeth – *noun* **teething troubles** pain and irritation caused by teeth growing in; difficulties encountered at the beginning of any undertaking.

teetotal *adjective* never taking an alcoholic drink. – *noun* **teetotaller.**

tel. *abbreviation* telephone.

tele- *prefix* at a distance.

telecommunications *noun* the science of sending messages, information *etc* by telephone, radio, television *etc*.

telegram *noun* a message sent by telegraph (*see* **telemessage**).

telegraph *noun* an instrument or system for sending messages to a distance *esp* using electrical impulses. – *verb* to send (a message) by telegraph. – *adjective* **telegraphic** of a telegraph; short, brief, concise.

telemessage *noun* a message sent by telex or telephone (replacing telegram).

telepathy *noun* the communication of ideas *etc* from one person to another without the use of sight, hearing or the other bodily senses. – *adjective* **telepathic.**

telephone *noun* an instrument for speaking to a person at a distance, using an electric current which travels along a wire, or using radio waves. – *verb* to send (a message) by telephone. – *noun* **telephonist** a person whose job is operating a telephone switchboard.

telephoto *adjective* of a lens used for obtaining large images of distant objects.

teleprinter *noun* a telegraph system in which messages are sent out at one place, and received and printed at another, by machines resembling typewriters; one of these machines.

telescope *noun* a kind of tube fitted with lenses or magnifying glasses which makes distant objects seem larger and nearer. – *verb* to push or be pushed together so that one thing slides inside another; to fit, close or slide in such a way; to force together, compress.

teletex *noun* a means of transmitting data, similar to telex, but using high-speed electronic apparatus.

teletext *noun* news, financial information, weather forecasts *etc*, transmitted by television companies, that can be read on a specially adapted television.

television *noun* the sending of pictures from a distance, and the reproduction of them on a screen; (also **television set**) an apparatus for receiving these pictures. – *verb* **televise** to send a picture (of) by television: *They televised the football match.*

telex *noun* a service involving the sending of messages by means of teleprinters; a message sent in this way.

tell *verb* (*past tense* **told**) to say or express in words: *He is telling the truth*; to give the facts of (a story); to inform, give information: *He told me when the train left*; to order, command: *Tell her to go* *away!*; to make out, to distinguish: *Can you tell one twin from the other?*; to give away a secret; to be effective, produce results: *Good training will tell in the end.* – *noun* **teller** a person who tells; a bank clerk who receives and pays out money; a person who counts votes at an election. – *adjective* **telling** having a great or marked effect: *a telling remark.* – **all told** altogether, counting all; **tell off** (*coll*) to scold; **tell on** to have an effect on; to give information about (a person); **tell tales** to give away information not intended to be given about the misdeeds of others (*noun, adjective* **tell-tale**).

temerity *noun* rashness, boldness.

temp *abbreviation* temperature; temporary. – *noun* (*coll*) a temporarily employed secretarial worker. – *verb* (*coll*) to work as a temp.

temper *noun* one's state of mind: *He is of an even temper*; a passing mood: *in a good temper*; a tendency to get angry easily; (a mood of) anger; the amount of hardness in metal, glass *etc.* – *verb* to bring metal (or other material) to the right degree of hardness by heating and cooling; to make less severe. – **lose one's temper** to show anger.

temperament *noun* one's nature as it affects the way one feels, acts *etc*, disposition. – *adjective* **temperamental** of temperament; excitable, emotional.

temperate *adjective* moderate, well-controlled in temper, eating or drinking habits *etc*; (of climate) neither very hot nor very cold. – *noun* **temperance** the state of being temperate; the habit of not drinking much (or any) alcohol. – *noun* **temperature** amount, degree of heat or cold: *a body heat higher than normal: The little boy has a temperature.*

tempest *noun* a storm, with great wind. – *adjective* **tempestuous** very stormy, like a tempest; (of a person *etc*) passionate, violently emotional.

template *noun* a thin plate cut in a certain shape, for use as a pattern for drawing round.

temple *noun* a building in which people worship; a church; either of the flat parts of the head on each side of the forehead.

tempo *noun* (*plural* **tempos** or **tempi**) the speed at which music is played; the speed or rate of any activity: *the tempo of life.*

temporal *adjective* of, belonging to this world or this life only, not eternal or of the soul or spirit; belonging to time.

temporary *adjective* lasting, used *etc* only for a time, not permanent. – *verb* **temporize** to avoid taking a definite decision or action (in order to give oneself more time).

tempt *verb* to try to persuade or to entice, *esp* to evil; to attract; to cause to be inclined (to): *I am tempted to end the quarrel.* – *noun* **temptation** the act of tempting; the state or feeling of being tempted; that which tempts. – *adjective* **tempting** attractive.

ten *noun* the number 10. – *adjective* 10 in number. – *adjective* **tenth** the last of ten (things). – *noun* one of ten equal parts.

tenable *adjective* (of a position, a theory *etc*) able to be held or defended.

tenacious *adjective* keeping a firm hold or grip; obstinate, persistent, determined. – *noun* **tenacity.**

tenant *noun* a person who pays rent to another for the use of a house, building, land *etc*. – *noun* **tenancy** (*plural* **tenancies**) the holding of a house, farm *etc* by a tenant; the period of this holding. – *adjective* **tenanted** occupied, lived in.

tend *verb* to be likely or inclined (to do something): *These flowers tend to wilt*; (with **towards**) to move, lean, slope in a certain direction; to take care of, look after. – *noun* **tendency** (*plural* **tendencies**) a leaning or inclination (towards): *a tendency to alcoholism.*

tender *adjective* soft, not hard or tough; easily hurt or damaged; hurting when touched; very young: *of tender years*; loving, gentle. – *verb* to offer (a resignation *etc*) formally; to make a tender (for a job). – *noun* an offer, *esp* to take on work, supply goods *etc* for a fixed price; a small boat that carries stores for a large one; a truck for coal and water attached to a steam railway engine. – *adjective* **tender-hearted** inclined to be kind and sympathetic. – **legal tender** coins or notes which must be accepted when offered in payment.

tendon *noun* a tough cord joining a muscle to a bone or other part.

tendril *noun* a thin curling part of some kinds of climbing plants (as the pea) which attaches itself to a support; a curling strand of hair.

tenet *noun* a belief, opinion.

tennis *noun* a type of game for two or four players using rackets to hit a ball to each other over a net on the ground or floor. – *noun* **tennis court** a place made level and prepared for tennis.

tenon *noun* a projecting bit at the end of a piece of wood made to fit a **mortise**.

tenor *noun* (a man with) a singing voice of the highest normal pitch for an adult male; a musical part for such a voice; the general course: *the even tenor of country life*; the general meaning (of a speech *etc*).

tense *noun* the form of a verb that shows time of action, as in '*I was*' (**past tense**), '*I am*' (**present tense**), *I shall be* (**future tense**). – *adjective* tightly stretched; nervous, strained: *tense with excitement*. – *noun* **tension** the act of stretching; the state of being stretched; strain, anxiety.

tent *noun* a movable shelter made of canvas or other material, supported by poles, and secured by ropes and pegs to the ground.

tentacle *noun* a long thin flexible part of an animal used to feel, grasp *etc* (*eg* the arm of an octopus).

tentative *adjective* experimental, not fully worked out or developed: *a tentative offer*; uncertain, hesitating: *a tentative smile*.

tenterhooks: on tenterhooks uncertain and very anxious about what will happen.

tenth *see* **ten**.

tenuous *adjective* slender, weak: *a tenuous connection*.

tenure *noun* the holding of property, or of a post or employment; the terms or conditions, or the period, of this.

tepid *adjective* (only) slightly warm.

tercentenary *noun* the 300th anniversary of an event *etc*.

term *noun* a length of time: *a term of imprisonment*; a division of a school or university year: *the autumn term*; a word or expression: *medical terms*; (*plural*) the rules or conditions of an agreement or a bargain; (*plural*) fixed charges; (*plural*) footing, relationship, relations, between people: *He is on good terms with his neighbours.* – *verb* to name, to call. – **come to terms, make terms** to reach an agreement or understanding: **in terms of** from the point of view of; *in terms of numbers*.

termagant *noun* a bad-tempered, noisy woman.

terminal *adjective* of, or growing at, the end: *a terminal bud*; (of an illness) fatal, reaching its last stages. – *noun* an end; a point of connection in an electric circuit; a terminus; a building containing the arrival and departure areas at an airport; a place in a town centre connected by a bus service to a nearby airport.

terminate *verb* to bring, or come, to an end or limit: *He terminated the discussion.* – *noun* **termination** an act of ending; an end.

terminology *noun* the special words or expressions used in a particular art, science *etc*.

terminus *noun* (*plural* **termini** or **terminuses**) the end; one of the end places or points on a railway, bus route *etc*.

termite *noun* a pale-coloured wood-eating kind of insect, like an ant.

tern *noun* a type of sea bird like a small gull.

terrace *noun* a raised level bank of earth like a big step; any raised flat place; a connected row of houses. – *verb* to form into a terrace or terraces.

terracotta *noun* a brownish-red mixture of clay and sand used for small statues, pottery *etc*.

terra firma *noun* land as opposed to water.

terrain *noun* a stretch of country (*esp* considered with reference to its physical features or as a battle field): *The terrain is a bit rocky.*

terrestrial *adjective* of, or living on, the earth.

terrible *adjective* causing great fear: *a terrible sight*; causing great hardship or distress: *a terrible disaster*; (*coll*) very bad: *a terrible singer*.

terrier *noun* a name given to many breeds of small dog.

terrify *verb* (*past tense* **terrified**) to frighten greatly. – *adjective* **terrific** powerful, dreadful; huge, amazing; (*coll*) attractive, enjoyable *etc*: *a terrific party*.

territory *noun* (*plural* **territories**) a stretch of land, a region; the land under the control of a ruler or state; an area in which a salesman *etc* works; a field of activity or interest. – *adjective* **territorial**

of, belonging to a territory. – *noun plural* **territorial waters** seas close to, and considered to belong to, a country.

terror *noun* very great fear; anything which causes great fear. – *noun* **terrorism** the activity or methods of terrorists. – *noun* **terrorist** someone who tries to frighten people into doing what he wants. – Also *adjective*. – *verb* **terrorize** to frighten very greatly.

terse *adjective* (of a speech *etc*) using few words; (of a person) speaking in such a way, curt. – *noun* **terseness**.

tertiary *adjective* third in position or order. – *noun* **tertiary education** education at universities, polytechnics *etc*.

test *noun* a set of questions or exercises, a short examination; something done to find out whether a thing is good, reliable *etc*: *We carried out tests on the new car*; a means of finding the presence of: *test for radioactivity*; a happening that shows up a good or bad quality: *a test of one's courage*. – *verb* to try, to carry out tests on. – *noun* **test match** in cricket *etc*, one of a series of matches between two countries. – *noun* **test pilot** a pilot who tests new aircraft. – *noun* **test tube** a glass tube closed at one end used in chemical tests.

testament *noun* a written statement *esp* of what one desires to be done with one's personal property after death, a will. – *noun* **testator** (*masculine*), **testatrix** (*feminine*) the person who writes a will. – **Old Testament** and **New Testament** the two main divisions of the Bible.

testicle *noun* one of two glands in the male body in which sperm is produced.

testify *verb* (*past tense* **testified**) to give evidence *esp* in a law court; to make a (solemn) declaration of; (with **to**) to show, give evidence of: *His recent action testifies to his inadequacy*. – *noun* **testimonial** (written) statement telling what one knows about a person's character, abilities *etc*; a gift given to show respect or thanks for services given. – *noun* **testimony** (*plural* **testimonies**) the statement made by one who testifies; evidence.

testy *adjective* easily made angry, irritable.

tetanus *noun* a type of serious disease which causes the muscles of the jaw and other parts to become stiff, caused by an infected wound *etc*.

tête-à-tête *noun* a private talk between two people.

tether *noun* a rope or chain for tying an animal, allowing it to feed within a certain area only. – *verb* to tie with a tether; to limit the freedom of.

text *noun* the main part of a book, the written or printed words of the author, not the pictures, notes *etc*; a printed or written version of a speech, play *etc*; a passage from the Bible about which a sermon is preached; anything used as the subject of a speech, essay *etc*. – *noun* **textbook** a book used for instruction, giving the main facts about a subject. – *adjective* **textual** of, in, a text.

textile *adjective* of weaving; woven. – *noun* cloth or fabric formed by weaving.

texture *noun* the quality of cloth resulting from the way it has been woven: *loose texture*; the quality of a substance which is noticeable through touch or taste: *a rough texture*: *lumpy texture*.

TGWU *abbreviation* Transport and General Workers' Union.

than *conjunction, preposition* used in comparisons: *The recipe was easier than I thought. The meal was better than usual.*

thane *noun* (*hist*) a noble who held land from the king or a higher noble.

thank *verb* to express appreciation, gratitude to (someone) for a favour, service, gift *etc*. – *adjective* **thankful** grateful; relieved and glad. – *adjective* **thankless** (of a task *etc*) neither worthwhile nor appreciated. – *noun plural* **thanks** expression of gratitude. – *noun* **thanksgiving** the act of giving thanks; a church service giving thanks to God. – *noun* **Thanksgiving** (*US*) a day (the fourth Thursday of November) set apart for this. – **thanks to** with the help of: *We arrived on time, thanks to our friends*; owing to: *We were late, thanks to our car breaking down*; **thank you** or **thank you very much** or **thanks** polite expressions used to thank someone for something.

that *adjective, pronoun* (*plural* **those**) used to point out a thing, person *etc* (opposite of **this**): *that woman over there. Don't say that*. Also *relative pronoun*: *Those are the clothes that he wore. That is the person that we saw yesterday*. – *adverb* to such an extent or degree: *I didn't know you'd be that late*. – *conj* used in reporting speech: *I said that I knew*; or to connect clauses: *It's good to know that you are well*.

thatch *noun* straw, rushes *etc* used to make the roof of a house. – *verb* to cover with thatch.

thaw *verb* (of ice, snow *etc*) to melt; to cause to melt; (of frozen foods) to (cause to) cease to be frozen; to become friendly. – *noun* the (time of) melting of ice and snow by heat; the change in the weather that causes this.

the *adjective* used to refer to particular person(s), thing(s) *etc*: *I saw the boy in the park. I like the jacket I'm wearing*; or to refer to all or any of a general class or type: *The horse is of great use to man*.

theatre or (*US*) **theater** *noun* a place where public performances (of plays, *etc*) are seen; a room in a hospital for surgical operations; the profession of actors. – *adjective* **theatrical** of theatres or acting; behaving as if in a play, over-dramatic.

thee *pronoun* (*old*) you (*singular*) as the object of a sentence.

theft *noun* (an act of) stealing.

their *adjective* belonging to them: *their car*. – *pronoun* **theirs**: *The red car is theirs*.

them *pronoun* persons or things already spoken about (as object of a verb): *We've seen them*; those: *one of them over in the corner*. – *pronoun* **themselves** used reflexively: *They hurt themselves*; used for emphasis: *They'll have to do it by themselves*.

theme *noun* the subject of a discussion, essay *etc*; in music, a main melody which may often be repeated. – *noun* **theme song** or **theme tune** a tune that is repeated often in a play, film, television series *etc* and is connected with a certain character, subject *etc*.

then *adverb* at that time; after that: *And then where did you go?* – *conjunction* in that case, therefore: *If you're ill, then why are you not in bed?*

thence *adverb* (*old*) from that time or place.

theodolite *noun* a type of instrument for measuring angles, used in surveying land.

theology *noun* the science of the study of God, and of man's duty to Him. – *noun* **theologian** a person who makes a study of theology. – *adjective* **theological**.

theorem *noun* (in mathematics) something (to be) proved by reasoning, shown step by step.

theory *noun* (*plural* **theories**) an explanation which one thinks is correct but has not been proved or tested; the main ideas (*esp* as opposed to practice or performance) in an art, science *etc*. – *adjective* **theoretic** or **theoretical** of theory, not actual experience or practice. – *adverb* **theoretically**. – *verb* **theorize** to form theories.

therapy *noun* (*plural* **therapies**) treatment of disease, disorder *etc*. – *adjective* **therapeutic** of therapy; healing, curing. – *noun* **therapist** a person who gives therapeutic treatment: *a speech therapist*.

there *adverb* at, in or to that place: *What did you do there? There he is in the corner*. – *pron* used (with some form of the verb to be) as a subject of a sentence or clause when the real subject follows the verb: *There is no one at home*. – *adverb* **thereabouts** approximately in that place or of that number, time *etc*. – *adverb* **thereafter** after that. – *adverb* **thereby** by that means. – *adverb* **therefore** for this or that reason. – *adverb* **thereupon** because of this or that; immediately.

therm *noun* a unit of heat used in the measurement of gas. – *adjective* **thermal** of heat; of hot springs.

thermometer *noun* an instrument for measuring temperature of various kinds.

Thermos or **Thermos**⊛ **flask** *noun* a kind of vacuum flask.

thermostat *noun* a device for automatically controlling temperature (*eg* of a room).

thesaurus *noun* a book giving information (as a dictionary, encyclopaedia *etc*) *esp* one listing words and their synonyms.

these *see* **this**.

thesis *noun* (*plural* **theses**) a long piece of written work (often done for a university degree) discussing a particular subject in detail; a statement of a point of view.

they *pronoun* some persons, animals or things already spoken about (used only as the subject of a verb): *They followed the others*.

thick *adjective* not thin; having a large, or a certain, distance between opposite sides: *He cut a thick slice. The concrete was two metres thick*; (of a mixture *etc*) containing solid matter, semi-solid, stiff: *a thick soup*; dense, difficult to see through or to pass through: *We were caught in thick fog. Thick woods surrounded the village*; (of speech) not clear; (*coll*) stupid; (*coll*) very friendly. – *noun* the thickest, most crowded or active part: *in the thick of the fight*. – *verb* **thicken** to make or become thick or thicker: *to thicken a sauce*. – *noun* **thicket** a group of close-set trees and bushes. – *noun* **thickness** the quality of being thick; the distance between opposite sides; a layer. – *adjective* **thickset** closely set or planted; having a thick sturdy body. – *adjective* **thick-skinned** not sensitive or easily hurt.

thief *noun* (*plural* **thieves**) a person who steals. – *verb* **thieve** to steal. – *noun* **thieving** the act or activity of thieving. – *adjective* **thievish** inclined to thieve; of a thief.

thigh *noun* the thick, fleshy part of the leg between the knee and the hip.

thimble *noun* a kind of metal *etc* cap to protect the finger and push the needle in sewing.

thin *adjective* having little distance between opposite sides: *thin paper: thin slice*; slim, not fat; not dense or crowded: *a thin population*; poor in quality: *a thin wine*; (of a mixture *etc*) not thick or stiff, not containing solid matter: *a thin soup*. – *verb* (*past tense* **thinned**) to make or become thin or thinner. – *noun* **thinness**. – *adjective* **thin-skinned** sensitive, easily hurt.

thine *adjective* (*old*) belonging to you (used before words beginning with a vowel or a vowel sound): *thine enemies*. – *pronoun*: *My heart is thine*.

thing *noun* an object that is not living; (*coll*) a person: *a nice old thing*; (*plural*) belongings; any individual object, fact, quality, idea *etc* that one may think of or refer to: *Several things must be taken into consideration*.

think *verb* (*past tense* **thought**) to work things out, to reason; to form ideas in the mind; to believe, judge or consider: *I think that we should go. I think her stupid*; (with **of**) to intend: *He is thinking of leaving*. – **think better of** to change one's mind about; **think highly** or **much** or **well of** to have a good opinion of; **think nothing of** to have a poor opinion of; not to regard as difficult; **think out** to work out in the mind.

third *adjective* the last of three (things). – *noun* one of three equal parts. – *adjective* **third-rate** of very poor quality.

thirst *noun* the dry feeling in the mouth caused by lack of drink; an eager desire (for anything): *thirst for power*. – *verb* to feel thirsty; (with **for**) to desire eagerly. – *adjective* **thirsty** having thirst; (of earth) parched, dry; eager (for).

thirteen *noun* the number 13. – *adjective* thirteen in number. – *adjective* **thirteenth** the last of thirteen (things). – *noun* one of thirteen equal parts.

thirty *noun* the number 30. – *adjective* thirty in number. – *adjective* **thirtieth** the last of thirty (things). – *noun* one of thirty equal parts.

this *adjective, pronoun* (*plural* **these**) used to point out a thing, person *etc, esp* one nearby or close in time (opposite of **that**): *Look at this book in my hand. Take this instead*; to such an extent or degree: *this early*.

thistle *noun* a prickly type of plant with purple flowers. – *noun* **thistledown** the feathery bristles of the seeds of the thistle.

thither *adjective* to that place.

thong *noun* a piece or strap of leather to fasten anything; the lash of a whip.

thorax *noun* the chest in the human or animal body; the middle section of an insect's body.

thorn *noun* a sharp, woody prickly part sticking out from the stem of a plant; a bush or shrub with thorns, *esp* the hawthorn. – *adjective* **thorny** full of thorns; prickly; difficult, causing arguments: *a thorny problem*. – **thorn in the flesh** a cause of constant irritation.

thorough *adjective* complete, absolute: *a thorough muddle*; (of a person *etc*) very careful, attending to every detail. – *noun* **thoroughbred** an animal of pure breed. – *noun* **thoroughfare** a public street; a passage or way through or the right to use it: *no thoroughfare*. – *adjective* **thoroughgoing** thorough, complete. – *adverb* **thoroughly**.

those *see* **that.**

thou *pronoun* (*old*) you as the subject of a sentence.

though *conjunction* although: *Though he disliked it, he ate it all*. – *adverb* (*coll*) however: *I wish I'd never said it, though*.

thought *noun* (the act of) thinking; that which one thinks, an idea; an opinion; consideration: *after much thought*. – *verb see* **think.** – *adjective* **thoughtful** full of thought; thinking of others, considerate. – adjective **thoughtless** showing lack of thought; inconsiderate.

thousand noun the number 1000. – adjective a thousand in number. – adjective **thousandth** the last of a thousand (things). – noun one of a thousand equal parts.

thrall: in thrall enchanted or fascinated.

thrash verb to beat or flog soundly; to move or toss violently (about); (with **out**) to discuss (a problem etc) thoroughly; to thresh (grain). – noun **thrashing** a flogging, a beating.

thread noun a very thin line or cord of any substance (eg of cotton, wool, silk), esp one twisted and drawn out; the ridge which goes in a spiral round a screw; (in a story etc) a connected series of details in correct order. – verb to put a thread through a needle, a bead etc; to make (one's way) in a narrow space. – adjective **threadbare** (of clothes) worn thin. – noun **threadworm** a kind of tiny, thread-like worm which lives in the intestines of humans.

threat noun a warning that one intends to hurt or to punish; a warning of something bad that may come: a threat of war; something likely to cause harm: a threat to our plans. – verb **threaten** to make a threat: He threatened to kill himself; to suggest the approach of something unpleasant; to be a danger to.

three noun the number 3. – adjective 3 in number. – See also **third**.

thresh verb to beat out (grain) from straw (also **thrash**).

threshold noun a piece of wood or stone under the door of a building; a doorway; an entry or beginning: on the threshold of a new era.

threw see **throw**.

thrice adverb three times.

thrift noun careful management of money or goods, in order that one may save. – adjective **thrifty** careful about spending.

thrill noun an excited feeling; quivering, vibration. – verb to (cause to) feel excitement. – noun **thriller** an exciting story (usu about crime and detection). – adjective **thrilling** very exciting.

thrive verb to grow strong and healthy; to get on well, be successful.

thro' short for **through**.

throat noun the back part of the mouth where the openings to the stomach,

windpipe and nose are; the front part of the neck.

throb verb (past tense **throbbed**) (of pulse etc) to beat esp more strongly than normal; to beat or vibrate rhythmically and regularly.

throes noun plural great suffering or struggle. – **in the throes of** in the middle of (a struggle, doing a task etc).

thrombosis noun the forming of a clot in a blood vessel.

throne noun the seat of a king or bishop; the king etc or his power.

throng noun a crowd. – verb to move in a crowd; to crowd, fill (a place).

throttle noun (in engines) the part through which steam or petrol can be turned on or off. – verb to choke by gripping the throat.

through preposition into from one direction and out of in the other: through the tunnel; from end to end, side to side etc of: all through the performance; by way of: related through his grandmother; as a result of: through his mother's influence; (US) from . . . to (inclusive): Monday through Friday is five days. – adverb into and out, from beginning to end etc: He ran all the way through the tunnel. – adjective without break or change: a through train to London; (coll) finished: Are you through with the newspaper?; (of a telephone call) connected: I couldn't get through this morning. – adverb **through-and-through** completely, entirely: a gentleman through-and-through. – preposition **throughout** in all parts of: throughout the country; from start to finish of: throughout the journey. – Also adverb.

throw verb (past tense **threw**, past participle **thrown**) to send through the air with force; (of a horse etc) to cause (a person) to fall to the ground; to shape (pottery) on a wheel; to give (a party). – noun the act of throwing; the distance a thing is thrown: within a stone's throw of the house.

thru (US) short form of **through**.

thrush noun (plural **thrushes**) a type of singing bird with a speckled breast; a type of infectious disease of the mouth, throat or vagina.

thrust verb (past tense, past participle **thrust**) to push with force; to make a sudden push forward with a pointed weapon; (with **on, upon**) to force (something, oneself) upon. – *noun* a stab; a pushing force.

thud *noun* a dull, hollow sound like that made by a heavy body falling. – *verb* (*past tense* **thudded**) to move or fall with such a sound.

thug *noun* a violent, brutal person.

thumb *noun* the short, thick finger of the hand. – *verb* to turn over or dirty (the pages of a book) with the thumb or fingers. – *noun* **thumbscrew** (*hist*) an instrument of torture which worked by squashing the thumbs. – **under someone's thumb** under someone's control.

thump *noun* a heavy blow. – *verb* to beat heavily; to move or fall with a dull, heavy noise.

thunder *noun* the deep rumbling sound heard after a flash of lightning; any loud, rumbling noise. – *verb* to produce the sound of, or a sound like, thunder; to shout out angrily. – *noun* **thunderbolt** a flash of lightning followed by thunder; a very great and sudden surprise. – *noun* **thunderclap** a sudden roar of thunder. – *adjective* **thunderous** like thunder; very angry. – *adjective* **thunderstruck** overcome by surprise. – *adjective* **thundery** (of weather) sultry, bringing thunder.

Thursday *noun* the fifth day of the week.

thus *adverb* in this or that manner: *He always talks thus*; to this degree or extent: *thus far*; because of this, therefore: *Thus, we must go on.*

thwart *verb* to hinder (a person) from carrying out a plan, intention *etc*; to prevent (an attempt *etc*). – *noun* a cross seat for rowers in a boat.

thy *adjective* (*old*) belonging to you: *thy wife and children.*

thyme *noun* a kind of small sweet-smelling herb used for seasoning food.

thyroid gland *noun* a large gland in the neck which influences the rate at which energy is used by the body.

tiara *noun* a jewelled ornament for the head like a crown.

tibia *noun* the bone of the shin, the larger of the two bones between knee and ankle.

tic *noun* a twitching motion of certain muscles, *esp* of the face.

tick *noun* a light mark (√) used to mark as correct, to mark off in a list *etc*; a tiny blood-sucking animal; the cloth cover of a mattress, pillow *etc*; a small quick noise, made regularly by a clock, watch *etc*; (*coll*) a moment. – *verb* to mark with a tick; (of a clock *etc*) to produce regular ticks. – *noun* **ticker tape** paper tape used in a kind of automatic machine that prints the latest news of share prices *etc*. – *noun* **ticking** the noise made by a clock *etc*; the type of material from which mattress covers *etc* are made.

ticket *noun* a marked card or paper giving the owner a right to do something (*eg* travel by train *etc*, enter a theatre *etc*); a card or label stating the price *etc* of something.

tickle *verb* to excite the surface nerves of a part of the body by touching lightly and so cause to laugh; to please or amuse. – *adjective* **ticklish** tickly; not easy to deal with: *a ticklish problem*. – *adjective* **tickly** sensitive to tickling.

tiddly *adjective* slightly drunk; tiny.

tiddlywink *noun* a small plastic disc used in **tiddlywinks**, a game in which tiddlywinks are flipped into a cup.

tide *noun* the rise and fall of the sea which happens regularly twice each day; time, season: *Christmastide*. – *adjective* **tidal**. – *noun* **tidal wave** an enormous wave in the sea often caused by an earthquake *etc*. – **tide over** to help to get over a difficulty for a time.

tidings *noun plural* news.

tidy *adjective* in good order, neat; (*coll*) fairly big: *a tidy sum of money*. – *verb* (*past tense* **tidied**) to make neat. – *noun* **tidiness**.

tie *verb* (*past tense* **tied**) to fasten with a cord, string *etc*; to knot or put a bow in (string, shoelaces *etc*); to join, unite; to limit, restrict: *tied to a tight schedule*; to score the same number of points (in a game *etc*), to draw. – *noun* a band of fabric worn round the neck, tied with a knot or bow; something that connects: *ties of friendship*; something that restricts or limits; an equal score in a competition *etc*; a game or match to be played.

tier *tēr*, *noun* a row of seats *etc*, *usu* with others above or below it.

tiff *noun* a slight quarrel.

tig *see* **tag**.

tiger (*masculine*), **tigress** (*feminine*) *noun* a large, fierce, animal of the cat family with tawny coat striped with black. – *noun* **tiger lily** a kind of lily with large spotted flowers.

tight *adjective* packed closely; firmly stretched, not loose; fitting (too) closely; (of money *etc*) hard to obtain; (*coll*) drunk. – *verb* **tighten** to make or become tight or tighter. – *noun* **tight-rope** a tightly stretched rope on which acrobats perform. – *noun plural* **tights** a close-fitting garment covering the feet, legs and body as far as the waist. – **a tight corner** an awkward situation.

tile *noun* a piece of baked clay or other material used in covering floors, roofs *etc*. – *verb* to cover with tiles.

till *noun* in a shop, a container or drawer for money. – *verb* to prepare, cultivate (land); to plough. – *preposition, conjunction see* **until**. – *noun* **tillage** the act of tilling; tilled land.

tiller *noun* the handle of a boat's rudder.

tilt *verb* to fall into, or place in, a sloping position; (*hist*) to joust; (*hist*) (with **at**) to attack on horseback, using a lance. – *noun* a slant; a thrust, a jab. – **at full tilt** with full speed and force.

timber *noun* wood for building *etc*; trees suitable for this; a wooden beam in a house or ship.

timbre *tan*ᵍ*br*, *noun* the quality of a (musical) sound or voice.

time *noun* the hour of the day; the period at which something happens; (often *plural*) a particular period: *in modern times*; opportunity, interval of leisure: *no time to listen*; a suitable or right moment: *Now is the time to ask*; one of a number of occasions: *He won four times*; (*plural*) used to mean 'multiplied by': *two times four*; the rhythm or the rate of performance of a piece of music. – *adjective* of time; arranged to go off *etc*, at a particular time: *a time bomb*. – *verb* to measure the minutes, seconds *etc* taken by (work, someone racing *etc*); to choose the time for (well, badly *etc*): *to time one's entrance well*. – *adjective* **time-honoured** (of a custom *etc*) respected because it has lasted a long time. – *adjective* **timeless** not belonging *etc* to any particular time; never ending: *timeless beauty*. – *adjective* **timely** coming at the right moment: *a timely reminder*. – *noun* **timepiece** (*old*) a clock or watch. – *noun* **time-sharing** (*comput*) a system of using a computer so that it can deal with several programs at the same time; a scheme by which a person buys the right to use a holiday home for the same specified period of time each year for a specified number of years. – *noun* **timetable** a list showing times of classes, arrivals or departures of trains *etc*. – **at times** occasionally; **do time** (*slang*) to serve a prison sentence; **in time** early enough; **on time** or **up to time** punctual; **the time being** the present time.

timid *adjective* easily frightened; shy. – *noun* **timidity**.

timorous *adjective* very timid.

timpani or **tympani** *noun plural* kettle-drums. – *noun* **timpanist** or **tympanist** a person who plays these.

tin *noun* an element, a silvery-white kind of metal; a box or can made of **tinplate**, thin iron covered with tin or other metal. – *verb* (*past tense* **tinned**) to cover with tin; to pack (food *etc*) in tins. – *noun* **tinfoil** a very thin sheet of tin, aluminium *etc*, used for wrapping. – *adjective* **tinny** like tin; (of sound) thin, high-pitched.

tincture *noun* a slight tinge (of colour); a characteristic quality; a medicine mixed in alcohol.

tinder *noun* dry material easily set alight by a spark.

tine *noun* a spike of a fork or of a deer's antler.

tinge *verb* to tint, colour slightly; (with **with**) to add a slight amount of something to. – *noun* a slight amount (of colour, or other quality): *We put a tinge of blue in the white paint. I felt a tinge of sadness seeing him go.*

tingle *verb* to feel a sharp, thrilling or prickling sensation: *Thinking of her hero makes her tingle with excitement. My elbow tingled with pain.* – Also *noun*.

tinker *noun* a mender of kettles, pans *etc*. – *verb* to work clumsily or unskilfully; to meddle (with).

tinkle *verb* to (cause to) make a light, ringing sound, to clink or jingle. – Also *noun*.

tinsel *noun* a sparkling, glittering material used for decoration: *The children put strings of tinsel on the Christmas tree.*

tint *noun* a variety or shade of a colour. – *verb* to give slight colour to.

tiny *adjective* very small.

tip *noun* the top or point of anything *usu* of something thin or tapering; a piece of useful information, a hint; a small gift of money (to a waiter *etc*); a dump for rubbish; a tap or light stroke. – *verb* (*past tense* **tipped**) to (cause to) slant; (with **over**) to (cause to) overturn; (with **out** or **into**) to empty out, into; (also with **off**) to give a hint to; to give a small gift of money; to put a tip on; to strike lightly. – *noun* **tipster** a person who gives hints about racing.

tipple *verb* (*coll*) to take alcoholic drink in small quantities and often. – *noun* an alcoholic drink. – *noun* **tippler**.

tipsy *adjective* rather drunk.

tiptoe *verb* to walk on one's toes, often in order to go very quietly. – **on tiptoe(s)** (standing, walking *etc*) on one's toes.

tirade *noun* a long, bitter, scolding speech.

tire *verb* to make, or become, weary or without patience or interest to go on. – *noun* (*US*) a tyre. – *adjective* **tired** weary; (with **of**) bored with. – *adjective* **tireless** never becoming weary; never resting. – *adjective* **tiresome** making weary; long and dull; annoying: *a tiresome child*. – *adjective* **tiring** causing tiredness or weariness: *a tiring journey*.

tiro or **tyro** *noun* (*plural* **tiros** or **tyros**) a beginner.

tissue *noun* substance of which the organs of the body are made: *muscle tissue*; a mass, network (of lies, nonsense *etc*); a piece of soft absorbent paper, *esp* a paper handkerchief; finely woven cloth. – *noun* **tissue paper** a kind of thin, soft paper.

tit *noun* any of several types of small birds: *blue tit*: *great tit*; a teat; (*slang*) a woman's breast. – **tit for tat** blow for blow, repayment of injury with injury.

titanium *noun* an element, a light, strong type of metal used in aircraft.

titbit *noun* a tasty little piece of food *etc*.

tithe *noun* (*hist*) a tax paid to the church, a tenth part of one's income, produce *etc*.

titivate *verb* to make smarter, improve the appearance of: *She is always titivating (herself)*.

title *noun* the name of a book, poem *etc*; a word in front of a name to show rank, honour or office held (as *Sir, Lord, Major etc*) or used in addressing any person formally (as *Mr, Mrs etc*); right, claim (to money, an estate *etc*). – *adjective* **titled** having a title which shows noble rank. – *noun* **title deed** a document that proves a right to ownership (of a house *etc*). – *noun* **title page** the page of a book on which are the title, author's name *etc*. – *noun* **title rôle** the part in a play which is the same as the title *eg Hamlet*. – *adjective* **titular** having the title without the duties of an office *etc*.

titter *verb* to giggle. – Also *noun*.

tittle *noun* a very small part.

tittletattle *noun* gossip, idle chatter.

titular *see* **title**.

TNT *abbreviation* trinitrotoluene.

to *preposition* showing the place or direction aimed for: *Let's go to the cinema. We are moving to the west*; showing the indirect object in a phrase, sentence *etc*: *Give it to me*; used before a verb to indicate the infinitive: *To be great is to be misunderstood*; showing that one thing *etc* belongs with another in some way: *the key to the door*; compared with: *This is nothing to what happened before*; about, concerning: *What did he say to that?*; showing a ratio, proportion *etc*: *The odds are six to one against*; showing the purpose or result of an action: *Tear it to pieces*. – *adverb* (almost) closed: *Pull the door to*. – **to and fro** backwards and forwards.

toad *noun* a type of reptile like a large frog. – *noun* **toadstool** any of several kinds of mushroom-like fungi, often poisonous. – *verb* **toady** to give way to a person's wishes, or flatter him, to gain his favour. – *noun* a person who does this.

toast *verb* to make bread brown by means of the direct heat of fire, gas flame, or electricity; to take a drink and wish success or health to (a person); to warm (one's feet *etc*) at a fire. – *noun* bread toasted; the person to whom a toast is drunk; an act of drinking a toast; the call to drink a toast. – *noun* **toaster** an electric machine for toasting bread. – *noun* **toastmaster** the announcer of toasts at a public dinner. – *noun* **toastrack** a stand with partitions for slices of toast.

tobacco *noun* a type of plant whose dried leaves are used for smoking. – *noun* **tobacconist** a person who sells tobacco, cigarettes *etc*.

toboggan *noun* a kind of long, light sledge. – *verb* to go in a toboggan.

today *adverb, noun* (on) this day; (at) the present time.

toddle *verb* to walk unsteadily, with short steps. – *noun* **toddler** a young child just able to walk.

to-do *noun* a bustle, commotion.

toe *noun* one of the five finger-like end parts of the foot; the front part of an animal's foot; the front part of a shoe, golf club *etc*. – **on one's toes** alert, ready for action; **toe the line** to do as one is told.

toffee *noun* a kind of sweet made of sugar and butter.

tofu *noun* a paste of unfermented soya bean.

toga *noun* (*hist*) the loose outer garment worn by a citizen of ancient Rome.

together *adverb* with each other, in place or time: *The group must stay together. The two events may happen together*; in or into union or connection: *to nail planks together*; by joint action: *Together we won*.

togs *noun plural* (*coll*) clothes.

toil *verb* to work hard and long; to walk, move *etc* with effort. – *noun* hard work. – *noun* **toiler.**

toilet *noun* the act of washing oneself, doing one's hair *etc*; (a room containing) a receptacle for waste matter from the body, *usu* equipped with a water-supply for flushing this away. – *noun* **toilet water** a lightly perfumed, spirit-based liquid for the skin.

token *noun* a mark or sign; *a token of my friendship*; a piece of metal or plastic, or a card *etc*, with an official marking, for use in place of money: *He lost his bus token so he had to walk. Give her a book token for her birthday*. – *adjective* acting as a symbol of one's opinion, intentions *etc*: *a token strike*.

told *see* **tell.**

tolerable *adjective* able to be borne or endured; fairly good: *a tolerable pianist*. – *noun* **tolerance** putting up with and being fair to people whose ways and opinions are different from one's own; an ability to resist the effects of (hardship, a drug *etc*). – *adjective* **tolerant.** – *verb* **tolerate** to bear, endure; to put up with; to allow. – *noun* **toleration.**

toll *verb* to sound (a large bell) slowly, as for a funeral; (of a bell) to be sounded thus. – *noun* a tax charged for crossing a bridge *etc*; loss, damage. – **take toll** to cause damage or loss.

tomahawk *noun* (*hist*) a light kind of axe once used as a weapon and tool by the N. American Indians.

tomato *noun* (*plural* **tomatoes**) a type of fleshy, juicy fruit, *usu* red, used in salads, sauces *etc*.

tomb *noun* a grave; a vault or chamber in which a dead body is placed. – *noun* **tombstone** a stone placed over a grave in memory of the dead person.

tombola *noun* a kind of lottery.

tomboy *noun* a high-spirited active girl.

tomcat *noun* a male cat.

tome *noun* a large heavy (*usu* learned) book.

tomfoolery *noun* silly behaviour.

tomorrow *adverb, noun* (on) the day after today; (in) the future: *The children of tomorrow will learn from our mistakes*.

tomtit *noun* a kind of small bird.

tomtom *noun* a kind of Indian drum *usu* beaten with the hands.

ton *noun* a measure of weight equal to 2240 pounds, about 1016 kilogrammes; a unit (100 cubic feet) of space in a ship. – *noun* **tonnage** the space available in a ship, measured in tons. – **metric ton** (also **tonne**) 1000 kilogrammes.

tone *noun* sound; the quality of sound: *a harsh tone*; (in music) one of the larger intervals in a scale (as between C and D); the quality of the voice as it varies in pitch, loudness *etc*, expressing the mood of the speaker: *a gentle tone*; a shade of colour; bodily firmness or strength. – *verb* (sometimes with **in**) to blend, fit in well; (with **down**) to make or become softer, less harsh *etc*; (with **up**) to give strength to (muscles *etc*). – *noun* **tonic** something (*eg* a medicine) which gives one strength and energy; (in music) the keynote of a scale; tonic water. – *adjective* of tones or sounds; of a tonic. – *noun* **tonic water** aerated water with quinine.

tongs *noun plural* an instrument for lifting and grasping coals, sugar lumps *etc*.

tongue *noun* the fleshy organ inside the mouth, used in tasting, speaking, and swallowing; anything resembling this, as a flap in a shoe or a long, thin strip of land; the tongue of an animal served as food; a language: *his mother tongue.* – *adjective* **tongue-tied** not able to speak freely. – *noun* **tongue-twister** a phrase, sentence *etc* not easy to say quickly, *eg* She sells sea shells.

tonic *see* **tone.**

tonight *adverb, noun* (on) the night of the present day.

tonnage, tonne *see* **ton.**

tonsil *noun* one of a pair of soft, fleshy lumps at the back of the throat. – *noun* **tonsillitis** reddening and painfulness of the tonsils.

tonsure *noun* the shaving of the top of the head of priests and monks; the part of the head so shaved.

too *adverb* to a greater extent, in a greater quantity *etc* than is wanted or thought suitable: *He's too fat. It's too cold for swimming. There are too many people in the room*; (with a negative) very, particularly: *not feeling too well* (ie not feeling very well); also, as well: *I'm feeling quite cold, too.*

took *see* **take.**

tool *noun* an instrument for doing work, *esp* by hand.

toot *noun* the sound of a horn. – Also *verb.*

tooth *noun* (*plural* **teeth**) any of the hard, bony objects projecting from the gums, arranged in two rows in the mouth, used for biting and chewing; anything resembling a tooth; the points of a saw, cogwheel, comb *etc.* – *noun* **toothache** pain in a tooth. – *noun* **toothpaste** or **tooth-powder** a kind of paste or powder, used for cleaning the teeth. – *noun* **toothpick** a small sharp instrument for picking out anything (*eg* meat) from between the teeth. – *adjective* **toothsome** pleasant to the taste. – **tooth and nail** with all one's strength and fury.

top *noun* the highest part of anything; the upper surface; the highest place or rank; a lid; a circus tent; a kind of spinning toy. – *adjective* highest, chief. – *verb* (*past tense* **topped**) to cover on the top; to rise above; to do better than; to reach the top of; to take off the top of. – *noun* **topboot** a tall boot with a light-coloured band round the top. – *noun* **topcoat** an overcoat. – *noun* **top dog** (*coll*) a winner or leader. – *noun* **top hat** a man's tall silk hat. – *adjective* **top-heavy** having the upper part too heavy for the lower. – *adjective* **topmost**

highest, uppermost. – *adjective* **top-notch** of the highest quality. – *adjective* **top-secret** (of information *etc*) very secret. – *noun* **top ten, top twenty** *etc* list of the ten, twenty *etc* best-selling records, CDs *etc, usu* in a week.

topaz *noun* a type of precious stone, of various colours.

topi or **topee** *noun* a helmet-like hat used in hot countries as a protection against the sun.

topiary *noun* the art of trimming bushes, hedges *etc* into decorative shapes, *eg* animals.

topic *noun* a subject spoken or written about. – *adjective* **topical** of present interest, concerned with present events; of a topic.

topography *noun* (the description of) the features of the land in a certain region. – *adjective* **topographical.**

topple *verb* (cause to) be unsteady and fall.

topsyturvy *adjective, adverb* (turned) upside down.

torch *noun* (*plural* **torches**) a small hand-held light with a switch and electric battery; a flaming piece of wood or coarse rope once carried as a light, now sometimes in processions.

tore *see* **tear.**

toreador *noun* a bullfighter *esp* one mounted on horseback.

torment *verb* to treat cruelly and cause great suffering to; to worry greatly; to tease. – *noun* great pain, suffering, worry; a cause of these. – *noun* **tormentor.**

torn *see* **tear.**

tornado *noun* (*plural* **tornadoes**) a violent whirling wind that causes great damage.

torpedo *noun* (*plural* **torpedoes**) a large cigar-shaped type of missile fired by ships, planes *etc*. – *verb* (*past tense* **torpedoed**) to hit or sink (a ship) with a torpedo.

torpid *adjective* slow, dull, stupid. – *noun* **torpidity** or **torpor** dullness.

torrent *noun* a rushing stream; a heavy downpour of rain; a violent flow (of words *etc*): *a torrent of abuse.* – *adjective* **torrential** like a torrent.

torrid *adjective* parched by heat; very hot.

torso *noun* (*plural* **torsos**) the body, without head or limbs.

tortoise *noun* a four-footed, slow-moving kind of reptile, covered with a hard shell. – *noun* **tortoiseshell** the shell of a kind of sea turtle, used in making ornamental articles. – *adjective* made of this shell; of the colour of this shell, mottled brown, yellow and black: *a tortoiseshell cat*.

tortuous *adjective* winding, roundabout, not straightforward.

torture *verb* to treat a person cruelly or painfully, as a punishment or to force him to confess something; to cause to suffer. – *noun* the act, or activity, of torturing; great suffering.

Tory *noun* (*plural* **Tories**), *adjective* (a member) of the Conservative Party.

toss *verb* to throw up in the air; to throw up (a coin) to see which side is uppermost when it falls; to turn oneself restlessly from side to side; (of a ship) to be thrown about by rough water. – Also *noun*. – **toss up** to toss a coin.

tot *noun* a little child; a small amount of alcoholic drink, *usu* spirits. – **tot up** to add up.

total *adjective* whole: *total number*; complete: *The car was a total wreck.* – *noun* the entire amount; the sum of amounts added together. – *verb* (*past tense* **totalled**) to add up; to amount to. – *adjective* **totalitarian** of government by a single party that allows no rivals. – *noun* **totalizator** (for short, **tote**) a machine to work out the amount of money to be paid to those who bet on winning horses. – *adverb* **totally** completely.

tote *see* **total.**

totem *noun* among N. American Indians *etc*, an (image of an) animal or plant used as the badge or sign of a tribe. – *noun* **totem pole** a pole on which totems are carved and painted.

totter *verb* to shake as if about to fall; to stagger.

toucan *noun* a type of S. American bird with a very big beak.

touch *verb* to feel (with the hand); to come or be in contact (with): *A leaf touched his cheek*; to move, affect the feelings of: *The story touched those who heard it*; to mark slightly with colour: *The sky was touched with gold*; to reach the standard of. *I can't touch him at chess*; to have anything to do with: *I wouldn't touch a job like that*; to eat or drink: *He won't touch alcohol*; to concern (a person); (*coll*) to persuade (someone) to lend one money: *I touched him for £1*. – *noun* the act of touching; the physical sense of touch: *The blind man felt his way by touch*; a small quantity or degree: *a touch of salt*; (of an artist, pianist *etc*) skill or style; (in football) the ground beyond the edges of the pitch marked off by **touchlines**. – *adjective* **touch-and-go** very uncertain: *It's touch-and-go whether we'll get it done on time*. – *preposition* **touching** about, concerning. – *adjective* causing emotion, moving. – *noun* **touchstone** a test or standard of measurement of quality *etc*. – *adjective* **touchy** easily offended. – *noun* **touchiness.** – **in** (or **out of**) **touch with** in (or not in) communication or contact with; **touch down** (of an aircraft) to land (*noun* **touchdown**); **touch off** to cause to happen: *touch off a riot*; **touch on** to mention briefly; **touch up** to improve (a drawing or photograph *etc*) by making details clearer *etc*.

tough *adjective* strong, not easily broken; (of meat *etc*) hard to chew; (of persons) strong, able to stand hardship or strain; difficult to cope with or overcome: *tough opposition*. – *verb* **toughen** to (cause to) become tough.

toupee *noun* a small wig or piece of false hair worn to cover a bald spot.

tour *noun* a journey in which one visits various places; a pleasure trip. – *verb* to make a tour (of). – *noun* **tourism** the activities of tourists and of those who cater for their needs and pleasure. – *noun* **tourist** a person who travels for pleasure, and visits places of interest.

tournament *noun* a competition (in chess, tennis *etc*) involving many contests and players; (*hist*) a meeting at which knights fought together on horseback.

tourniquet *toor'ni-kā, noun* a bandage tied tightly round a limb to prevent great loss of blood from a wound.

tousled *adjective* (*esp* of hair) untidy, tangled.

tout *verb* to go about looking for support, votes, buyers *etc*. – *noun* one who does this; one who gives information useful to people who bet on horse races.

tow *verb* to pull (*eg* a ship, a barge, a motor-car) with a rope (attached to another ship, a horse or another vehicle). – *noun* the act of towing; the rope used for towing. – *noun* **towpath** a path alongside a canal used by horses which tow barges. – **in tow** under protection or guidance; **on tow** being towed.

towards or **toward** *preposition* (moving, keeping) in the direction of (a place, person *etc*): *He walked towards his house*; to (a person, thing *etc*): *his attitude towards his son*; as a help, contribution to: *He gave £1 towards the price of her present*; near, about (a time *etc*): *towards four o'clock*.

towel *noun* a cloth or piece of absorbent paper for drying or wiping (*eg* the skin after washing). – *verb* (*past tense* **towelled**) to rub with a towel. – *noun* **towelling** a kind of (cotton) cloth often used for making towels.

tower *noun* a high narrow building, or a high narrow part of another building (*eg* of a castle). – *verb* to rise high (over, above). – *adjective* **towering** rising high; violent: *a towering rage*.

town *noun* a place, larger than a village, in which there is a large collection of buildings, including houses, shops *etc*. – *noun* **town crier** (mainly *hist*) one whose job it is to make public announcements in a town. – *noun* **town hall** the building where the official business of a town is done. – *noun* **town planning** planning of the future development of a town.

toxin *noun* a naturally occurring poison (produced by animals, plants, bacteria *etc*). – *adjective* **toxic** poisonous; caused by poison.

toy *noun* an object made for a child to play with; an object for amusement only. – *noun* **toy-boy** (*coll*) a young male (*usu* paid) companion of an older woman. – **toy with** to play or trifle with.

trace *noun* a mark or sign left behind; a footprint; a small amount; a line drawn by an instrument recording a change (*eg* in temperature); (*plural*) the straps by which a horse pulls a cart *etc* along. – *verb* to follow the tracks of, or the course of; to copy (a drawing *etc*) on thin, transparent paper placed over it. – *adjective* **traceable** able to be traced (to). – *noun* **tracery** the decorated stonework holding the glass in some church windows. – *noun* **tracing** a traced copy.

track *noun* a mark left; (*plural*) footprints; a path or rough road; a racecourse (for

runners, cyclists *etc*); a railway line; an endless band on which wheels of a tank *etc* travel. – *verb* to follow by the marks, footprints *etc* left by (*eg* an animal). – *noun* **tracksuit** a warm suit worn while jogging *etc*, before and after an athletic performance *etc*. – **keep** or **lose track of** to keep or fail to keep aware of the whereabouts or progress of; **make tracks (for)** to set off (towards); **track down** to pursue or search for (someone or something) until caught or found.

tract *noun* a stretch of land; a short pamphlet, *esp* on a religious subject; a system made up of connected parts of the body: *the digestive tract*.

tractable *adjective* easily made to do what is wanted.

traction *noun* the act of pulling or dragging; the state of being pulled. – *noun* **traction engine** a road steam-engine.

tractor *noun* a motor vehicle for pulling loads, ploughs *etc*.

trade *noun* the buying and selling of goods; one's occupation, craft, job: *He is a carpenter by trade*. – *verb* to buy and sell; to have business dealings (with); to deal (in); to exchange, swap. – *noun* **trademark** a registered mark or name put on goods to show that they are made by a certain company (and forbidden to be used by others). – *noun* **trader** a person who buys and sells.– *noun* **tradesman** a shopkeeper; a workman in a skilled trade. – *noun* **trade union** a group of workers of the same trade who join together to bargain with employers for fair wages *etc*. – *noun* **trade unionist** a member of a trade union. – *noun* **tradewind** a wind which blows towards the equator (from the north-east and south-east). – **trade in** to give as part-payment for something else (*eg* an old car for a new one); **trade on** to take (*usu* unfair) advantage of: *He traded on the fact that the manager was his cousin*.

tradition *noun* the handing-down of customs, beliefs, stories *etc* from generation to generation; a custom, belief *etc* handed down in this way. – *adjective* **traditional**.

traffic *noun* the motor-cars, buses, cycles, boats *etc* which use roads, waterways *etc*; trade; dishonest dealings (as in drugs). – *verb* (*past tense* **trafficked**) to trade; to deal (in). – *noun plural* **traffic lights** lights of changing colours for controlling traffic at road junctions or street crossings.

tragedy noun (plural **tragedies**) a very sad event or one with very unfortunate results; a play about unhappy events and with a sad ending. – adjective **tragic** of tragedy; very sad.

trail verb to draw along, in or through: trailing his foot through the water; to hang down (from) or be dragged loosely behind; to hunt (animals) by following footprints etc; to walk wearily; (of a plant) to grow over (such as the ground, a wall). – noun a track (of an animal); a pathway through a wild region; something left stretching behind one: a trail of dust. – noun **trailer** a vehicle pulled behind a motor-car; in a cinema, a short film advertising a longer film to be shown at a later date.

train noun a railway engine with carriages or trucks; the part of a dress which trails behind the wearer; the attendants who follow an important person; a line (of thought, events etc); a line of animals carrying persons or baggage. – verb to prepare oneself by practice, exercise etc (as for a sporting event, a job or profession); to educate: a child trained in good habits; to exercise (animals or people) in preparation for a race etc; to tame and teach (an animal); (with **on** or **at**) to aim, point (a gun, telescope etc) at; to make (a tree or plant) grow (in a certain direction). – noun **trainbearer** one who carries the train of a person's dress, robe etc. – noun **trainee** a person who is being trained. – noun **trainer** a person who trains people or animals for a sport, or race, circus performance etc. – noun **training** preparation for a sport; experience or learning of the practical side of a job.

trait noun a point that stands out in a person's character: Patience is one of his good traits.

traitor noun a person who goes over to the enemy's side, or gives away secrets to the enemy; a person who betrays trust. – adjective **traitorous**.

trajectory noun (plural **trajectories**) the curved path of something (eg a bullet) moving through the air or through space.

tram noun a long car running on rails and driven usu by electric power for carrying passengers along streets (also **tramcar**). – noun **tramline** a rail of tramway; (plural) in tennis or badminton, the parallel lines marked at the sides of the court. – noun **tramway** a system of tracks on which trams run.

trammel noun (often plural) anything which hinders movement. – verb (past tense **trammelled**) to hinder.

tramp verb to walk with heavy footsteps; to walk along, over etc: He tramped the streets in search of a job. – noun a person with no fixed home and no job, who lives usu by begging; a journey made on foot; the sound of marching feet; a small cargo-boat with no fixed route.

trample verb to tread under foot, stamp on; (usu with **on**) to treat roughly or unfeelingly; to tread heavily.

trampoline noun a bed-like framework holding a sheet of elastic material for bouncing on, used by gymnasts etc.

trance noun a sleeplike or half-conscious state.

tranquil adjective quiet, peaceful. – noun **tranquillity**. – verb **tranquillize** to make calm. – noun **tranquillizer** a drug to calm the nerves or cause sleep.

trans- prefix across, through.

transact verb to do (a piece of business). – noun **transaction** a piece of business, a deal.

transatlantic adjective crossing the Atlantic Ocean: transatlantic yacht race; across or over the Atlantic: transatlantic friends.

transcend verb to be, or rise, above. He transcended the difficulty; to be, or do, better than.

transcribe verb to copy from one book etc into another or from one form of writing (eg shorthand) into another (eg ordinary writing); to adapt (a piece of music) for a particular instrument, group of instruments etc. – noun **transcription** the act of transcribing: a written copy.

transept noun the part of a church which lies across the main part.

transfer verb (past tense **transferred**) to remove to another place; to hand over to another person. – noun the act of transferring; a design or picture which can be transferred from one surface to another. – adjective **transferable** able to be transferred. – noun **transference**.

transfigure verb to change (greatly and for the better) the form or appearance of. – noun **transfiguration**.

transfix verb to make unable to move, act etc (eg because of surprise): transfixed by *the sight*; to pierce through (as with a sword).

transform *verb* to (cause to) change in shape or appearance *etc*. – *noun* **transformation**. – *noun* **transformer** an apparatus for changing electrical energy from one voltage to another.

transfuse *verb* to pass (liquid) from one thing to another; to transfer (blood of one person) to the body of another. – *noun* **transfusion** the act of transfusing *esp* the act of putting blood from one person into the veins of another for medical purposes.

transgress *verb* to break a rule, law *etc*. – *noun* **transgression** the act of breaking a rule, law *etc*; a sin. – *noun* **transgressor** a person who breaks a rule, law *etc*.

transient *adjective* not lasting, passing. – *noun* **transience**.

transistor *noun* a small device, made up of a crystal enclosed in plastic or metal, which controls the flow of an electrical current; a portable radio set using these.

transit *noun* the carrying or movement of goods, passengers *etc* from place to place; the passing of a planet between the sun and the earth. – *noun* **transition** a change from one form, place, appearance *etc* to another. – *adjective* **transitional**. – *adjective* **transitory** lasting only for a short time.

transitive *adjective* in grammar, of a verb, having an object (as the verb '*hit*' in 'He *hit* the ball').

translate *verb* to turn (something said or written) into another language: *to translate from French into English*. – *noun* **translation** the act of translating; something translated. – *noun* **translator** a person who translates.

translucent *adjective* allowing light to pass through, but not transparent. – *noun* **translucence**.

transmit *verb* (*past tense* **transmitted**) to pass on (*eg* a message, news, heat); (of a television or radio station) to send out signals which are received as programmes. – *noun* **transmission** the act of transmitting; a radio or television broadcast. – *noun* **transmitter** an instrument for transmitting (*esp* radio signals).

transom *noun* a beam across a window or the top of a door.

transparent *adjective* able to be seen through; easily seen to be true or false: *a transparent excuse*. – *noun* **transparency** (*plural* **transparencies**) the state of being transparent; a photograph that is printed on transparent material and viewed by means of light shining through it.

transpire *verb* (of secrets) to become known; to happen: *He told me what had transpired*; to pass out (moisture *etc*) through pores of the skin or through the surface of leaves.

transplant *verb* to lift and plant (a growing plant) in another place; to remove (skin) and graft it on another part of the same body; to remove (an organ, *eg* a kidney) and graft it in another person or animal. – *noun* the act of transplanting; a transplanted organ, plant *etc*. – *noun* **transplantation**.

transport *verb* to carry from one place to another; to overcome with strong feeling: *transported with delight*; (*hist*) to send (a prisoner) to a prison in a different country. – *noun* the act of transporting; any means of carrying persons or goods: *The company uses rail transport to send goods south. Air transport will get you there quickest*; strong feeling: *transports of joy*. – *noun* **transportation** the act of transporting; means of transport; (*hist*) punishment of prisoners by sending them to a prison in a different country.

transpose *verb* to cause (two things) to change places; to change (a piece of music) from one key to another. – *noun* **transposition**.

transverse *adjective* lying, placed *etc* across: *transverse beams in the roof*.

transvestite *noun* a person who likes to wear clothes for the opposite sex. – Also *adjective*.

trap *noun* a device for, or means of, catching animals *etc*; a plan or trick for taking a person by surprise; a bend in a pipe which is kept full of water, for preventing the escape of air or gas; a carriage with two wheels. – *verb* (*past tense* **trapped**) to catch in a trap, or in such a way that escape is not possible. – *noun* **trapdoor** a door in a floor or ceiling. – *noun* **trapper** a person who makes a living by catching animals, *usu* for their skins and fur.

trapeze *noun* a swing used in performing gymnastic exercises or feats (as in a circus).

trapezium *noun* a figure with four sides, two of which are parallel.

trappings *noun plural* clothes or ornaments suitable for a particular person or occasion; ornaments put on horses.

trash *noun* something of little worth, rubbish. – *noun* **trash-can** (*US*) a container for household rubbish, a dustbin. – *adjective* **trashy**.

trauma *noun* injury (*eg* a wound) to the body; a very violent or distressing experience which has a lasting effect on a person; a condition (of a person) caused in this way. – *adjective* **traumatic**.

travail *noun* (*old*) hard work. – Also *verb*.

travel *verb* (*past tense* **travelled**) to go on a journey; to move; to go along, across; to visit foreign countries. – *noun* the act of travelling. – *noun* **traveller** a person who travels; a travelling representative of a business firm who tries to obtain orders for his firm's products.

traverse *verb* to go across, pass through. – *noun* something that crosses or lies across; a going across a rock face *etc*; a zigzag track of a ship.

travesty *noun* (*past tense* **travesties**) a poor or ridiculous imitation (of something): *a travesty of justice*.

trawl *verb* to fish by dragging a trawl along the bottom of the sea. – *noun* a wide-mouthed, bag-shaped net. – *noun* **trawler** a boat used for trawling.

tray *noun* a flat piece of wood, metal *etc* with a low edge, on which dishes *etc* may be carried.

treachery *noun* (*plural* **treacheries**) the act of betraying those who have trusted one. – *adjective* **treacherous** betraying, or likely to betray; dangerous: *a treacherous path over the marsh.* – *adverb* **treacherously**.

treacle *noun* a thick, dark syrup produced from sugar when it is being refined.

tread *verb* (*past tense* **trod**, *past participle* **trodden**) to walk on or along; (with **on**) to put one's foot on; to crush, trample under foot. – *noun* a step; one's way of walking; the part of a tyre which touches the ground. – *noun* **treadle** the part of a machine which is worked by the foot. – *noun* **treadmill** (*hist*) a mill turned by the weight of persons who were made to walk on steps fixed round a big wheel; any tiring, routine work. – **tread on someone's toes** to offend or upset a person; **tread water** to keep oneself afloat in an upright position by moving the arms and legs.

treason *noun* disloyalty to one's own country or its government (*eg* by giving away its secrets to an enemy, trying to overthrow it) (also **high treason**). – *adjective* **treasonable** consisting of, or involving, treason.

treasure *noun* a store of money, gold, precious stones *etc*; anything of great value or highly prized. – *verb* to value greatly; to keep carefully because one values greatly: *She treasures the mirror her mother left her.* – *noun* **treasurer** a person who has charge of the money (*eg* of a club). – *noun* **treasure-trove** treasure or money found hidden, the owner of which is unknown. – *noun* **Treasury** or **treasury** (*plural* **treasuries**) the part of a government which has charge of the country's money.

treat *verb* to deal with, handle, use, act towards (in a certain manner): *I was treated very well in prison*; to try to cure a person (of a disease); to try to cure (a disease); to write or speak about; to buy (someone a meal, drink *etc*); to deal (with), try to arrange (a peace treaty *etc* with). – *noun* something special (*eg* an outing) that gives much pleasure: *They went to the pantomime as a treat.* – *noun* **treatment** the act of treating (*eg* a disease); remedies or medicine: *a new treatment for cancer*; the way in which any thing or person is dealt with: *rough treatment*.

treatise *noun* a long, detailed essay *etc* on some subject.

treaty *noun* (*plural* **treaties**) an agreement made between countries.

treble *adjective* threefold, three times the normal: *wood of treble thickness*; high in pitch: *treble note*. – *verb* to (cause to) become three times as great. – *noun* the highest part in singing; one (*esp* a child) who sings the treble part of a song.

tree *noun* the largest kind of plant with a thick, firm wooden stem and branches; anything like a tree in shape.

trek *noun* a long or wearisome journey; (*old*) a journey, *esp* by wagon. – *verb* (*past tense* **trekked**) to make a long hard journey; (*old*) to make a journey by wagon.

trellis *noun* (*plural* **trellises**) a network of strips, *usu* of wood, used for holding up growing plants *etc*.

tremble *verb* to shake (*eg* with cold, fear, weakness); to feel fear (for another person's safety *etc*). – *noun* the act of trembling; a fit of trembling.

tremendous *adjective* very great or strong; (*coll*) very good, excellent. – *adverb* **tremendously** (*coll*) very.

tremor *noun* a shaking or quivering.

tremulous *adjective* shaking; showing fear; *a tremulous voice.*

trench *noun* (*plural* **trenches**) a long narrow ditch dug in the ground (*eg* by soldiers as a protection against enemy fire). – *verb* to dig a trench in. – *noun* **trenchcoat** a kind of waterproof overcoat with a belt.

trenchant *adjective* going deep, hurting: *a trenchant remark*; (of a policy *etc*) effective, vigorous.

trencher *noun* (*old*) a wooden plate. – *noun* **trencherman** a person able to eat large meals: *a good trencherman.*

trend *noun* a general direction: *the trend of events.* – *adjective* **trendy** (*coll*) fashionable.

trepidation *noun* fear, nervousness.

trespass *verb* to go illegally (on another's land *etc*); (with **on**) to take or demand too much of: *She trespasses on my time*; to sin. – *noun* (*plural* **trespasses**) the act of trespassing. – *noun* **trespasser**.

tress *noun* (*plural* **tresses**) a (long) lock of hair; (*plural*) hair, *usu* long.

trestle *noun* a wooden support with legs, used for holding up a table, platform *etc*.

trews *noun plural* tartan trousers.

tri- *prefix* three.

trial *see* **try**.

triangle *noun* a figure with three sides and three angles: △; a triangular metal musical instrument, played by striking with a small rod. – *adjective* **triangular** having the shape of a triangle.

triathlon *noun* a sporting contest consisting of three events, *usu* swimming, running and cycling.

tribe *noun* a race or family who are all descended from the same ancestor; a group of families, *esp* of a primitive or wandering people ruled by a chief. – *adjective* **tribal**. – *noun* **tribesman** a man belonging to a tribe.

tribulation *noun* great hardship or sorrow.

tribunal *noun* a group of persons appointed to give judgement, *esp* on an appeal (*eg* against a high rent); a court of justice.

tribune *noun* (*hist*) a high official elected by the people in ancient Rome.

tributary *noun* (*plural* **tributaries**) a stream that flows into a river or other stream; a person who gives money as a tribute. – Also *adjective*.

tribute *noun* an expression, in word or deed, of praise, thanks *etc*: *a warm tribute to his courage*; money paid regularly by one nation or ruler to another in return for protection or peace.

trice: in a trice in a very short time.

trick *noun* a cunning or skilful action (to puzzle, deceive, amuse *etc*): *The magician amazed us with a conjuring trick. He only won by using dirty tricks*; in card games, the cards picked up by the winner when each player has played a card. – *adjective* meant to deceive: *trick photography*. – *verb* to cheat by some quick or cunning action. – *noun* **trickery** cheating. – *noun* **trickster** a person who deceives by tricks. – *adjective* **tricky** not easy to do.

trickle *verb* to flow in small amounts; to come, go *etc* slowly and in small numbers: *People began to trickle into the hall.* – Also *noun*.

tricolour or (*US*) **tricolor** *noun* the flag of France, which is made up of three upright stripes (red, white, blue).

tricycle *noun* a kind of cycle with three wheels.

trident *noun* a three-pronged spear.

tried *see* **try**.

triennial *adjective* lasting for three years; happening every third year.

tries *see* **try**.

trifle *noun* anything of little value; a small amount; a pudding of whipped cream, sponge-cake, wine *etc*. – *verb* (with **with**) to act towards without sufficient respect: *I am in no mood to be trifled with*; to amuse oneself in an idle way (with): *He trifled with her affections*; to behave in a light, thoughtless manner. – *adjective* **trifling** very small in value or quantity.

trigger *noun* a small lever on a gun which, when pulled with the finger, causes the bullet to be fired. – *verb* (*usu* with **off**) to start, be the cause of, an important event, chain of events *etc*.

trigonometry *noun* the branch of mathematics which has to do chiefly with the relationship between the sides and angles of triangles. – *adjective* **trigonometric(al)**.

trill *verb* to sing, play or utter in a quivering or bird-like way. – *noun* a trilled sound; in music, a rapid repeating of two notes several times.

trillion *noun* a million million millions; (*US*, now often in Britain) a million millions.

trilogy *noun* (*plural* **trilogies**) a group of three related plays, novels *etc* by the same author, meant to be seen or read as a whole.

trim *verb* (*past tense* **trimmed**) to clip the edges or ends of (*eg* a hedge, the hair); to arrange (sails, cargo) so that a boat is ready for sailing; to decorate (*eg* a hat). – *noun* the act of trimming; dress: *in hunting trim*. – *adjective* tidy, in good order, neat. – *noun* **trimming** a fancy part added (*eg* to a dress, cake, dish) as a decoration; a bit cut off while trimming (cloth, paper *etc*). – **in good trim** in good order; fit.

Trinity *noun* in Christian belief, (the union in one God of) Father, Son and Holy Ghost.

trinket *noun* a small ornament (*esp* one of little value).

trio *noun* (*plural* **trios**) (a piece of music for) three performers; three people or things.

trip *verb* (*plural* **tripped**) (often with **up**) to (cause to) stumble or fall; to move with short, light steps; (with **up**) to (cause to) make a mistake. – *noun* a voyage or journey for pleasure or business; a light short step. – *noun* **tripper** a person who goes on a short pleasure trip, *usu* a day trip.

tripartite *adjective* in, or having, three parts; (of an agreement *etc*) reached by, and binding, three countries.

tripe *noun* part of the stomach of the cow or sheep used as food; (*coll*) rubbish, nonsense.

triple *adjective* made up of three; three times as large (as something else, as usual *etc*). – *verb* to make or become three times as large. – *noun* **triplet** one of three children or animals born of the same mother at one time; three rhyming lines in a poem; (in music) a group of three notes played in the time of two.

triplicate: in triplicate in, or in the form of, three copies.

tripod *noun* a three-legged stand (*esp* for a camera).

trite *adjective* (of a remark, saying *etc*) used so often that it has little force or meaning.

triumph *noun* a great success or victory; a state of celebration, great joy, pride *etc* after a success: *ride in triumph through the streets*. – *verb* to win a victory; to rejoice openly because of a victory (*esp* over the person one has defeated). – *adjective* **triumphal** of triumph; used *etc* in celebrating a triumph. – *adjective* **triumphant** victorious; showing joy because of, or celebrating, triumph. – *adj* **triumphantly**

trivia *noun plural* unimportant matters or details. – *adjective* **trivial** of very little importance. – *noun* **triviality** (*plural* **trivialities**) something unimportant; trivialness. – *noun* **trivialness** the state of being trivial.

trod, trodden *see* **tread.**

troll *noun* (*myth*) a creature, giant or dwarf, who lives in a cave *etc*.

trolley *noun* (*plural* **trolleys**) a small cart (*eg* as used by porters at railway stations); in a supermarket, a large basket on wheels; in hospitals, a kind of bed on wheels, used for transporting patients; a table on wheels, *usu* with two or more surfaces one above the other, used for serving tea *etc*. – *noun* **trolleybus** a bus which gets its power from overhead wires.

trollop *noun* a careless, untidy woman; a sexually immoral woman.

trombone *noun* a type of brass wind instrument with a sliding tube which changes the notes.

troop *noun* a crowd or collection of people or animals; (*plural*) soldiers; a unit in cavalry *etc*. – *verb* to gather in numbers; to go in a group: *They all trooped out*. – *noun* **trooper** a horse-soldier. – *noun* **troopship** a ship for carrying soldiers. – **troop the colour(s)** to carry a regiment's flag past the lined-up soldiers of the regiment.

trophy *noun* (*plural* **trophies**) something taken from an enemy and kept in memory of the victory; a prize such as a silver cup won in a sports competition *etc*.

tropic *noun* either of two imaginary circles running round the earth at about 23 degrees north (*Tropic of Cancer*) or south (*Tropic of Capricorn*) of the equator; (*plural*) the hot regions near or between these circles. - *adjective (also* **tropical***)* of the tropics; growing in hot countries; very hot.

trot *verb (past tense* **trotted***)* (of a horse) to run with short, high steps; (of a person) to run slowly with short steps; to make (a horse) trot. - *noun* the pace of a horse or person when trotting. - *noun plural* **trotters** the feet of pigs or sheep, *esp* when used as food.

troubadour *noun (hist)* a wandering singer, *esp* in France.

trouble *verb* to cause worry, uneasiness, sorrow *etc* to; to cause inconvenience to; to make an effort, bother (to): *I didn't trouble to ring him.* - *noun* worry, uneasiness; difficulty; disturbance; something which causes worry, difficulty *etc*; a disease; care and effort put into doing something. - *noun* **troubleshooter** a person whose job is to solve difficulties (*eg* in a firm's business activities). - *adjective* **troublesome** causing difficulty or inconvenience.

trough *noun* a long, open container for holding animals' food, water *etc*; an area of low atmospheric pressure; a dip between two sea waves.

trounce *verb* to punish or beat severely; to defeat heavily.

troupe *troop, noun* a company (of actors, dancers *etc*).

trousers *noun plural* an outer garment for the lower part of the body which covers each leg separately. - *adjective* **trouser** of a pair of trousers: *trouser leg.*

trousseau *noun (plural* **trousseaux** or **trousseaus***)* a bride's outfit for her wedding.

trout *noun* a type of freshwater (or (**sea-trout**) sea) fish, used as food.

trowel *noun* a small spade used in gardening; a similar tool with a flat blade, used for spreading mortar *etc*.

troy weight *noun* a system of weights for weighing gold, gems *etc*.

truant *noun* someone who stays away from school *etc* without permission. - Also *adjective*. - *noun* **truancy**. - **play truant** to stay away from school, work *etc* without permission *etc*.

truce *noun* a rest from fighting or quarrelling agreed to by both sides.

truck *noun* a wagon for carrying goods (*esp* on a railway); a strong lorry for carrying heavy loads. - *noun* **trucker** (*esp US*) a lorry driver. - **have no truck with** to refuse to have dealings with (*eg* a person).

truculent *adjective* fierce and threatening, aggressive. - *noun* **truculence**.

trudge *verb* to walk with heavy steps, as if tired.

true *adjective* (of a story, book *etc*) telling of something which really happened; correct, not invented or wrong: *It's true that the earth is round*; accurate: *a true idea of its appearance*; faithful: *a true friend*; real, properly so called: *The spider is not a true insect*; rightful: *the true heir to the title*; in the correct or intended position. - *adjective* **truly**. - *noun* **truism** a statement which is so clearly true that it is not worth making; - *noun* **truth** the state of being true; a true statement; the facts. - *adjective* **truthful** (of a person) *usu* telling the truth, not lying; (of a statement *etc*) true. - *adverb* **truthfully**. - *noun* **truthfulness**.

truffle *noun* (often *plural*) a type of round fungus found underground and much valued as a flavouring for food.

trug *noun* a shallow basket used in gardening.

trump *noun* in some card games, (any card of) a suit having a higher value than cards of other suits. - *verb* to play a card which is a trump. - *noun* **trump card** a card which is a trump; something kept in reserve as a means of winning a contest, argument *etc*. - **trump up** to make up, invent (*eg* a story, evidence against a person); **turn up trumps** to play one's part nobly when things are difficult.

trumpery *noun (plural* **trumperies***)* something showy but worthless.

trumpet *noun* a brass musical instrument with a clear, high-pitched tone; the cry of an elephant. - *verb* to announce (*eg* news) so that all may hear; to blow a trumpet; (*esp* of an elephant) to make a noise like a trumpet.

truncated *adjective* cut off at the top or end; shortened: *a truncated version of the play.*

truncheon *noun* a short heavy staff or baton such as that used by policemen.

trundle *verb* to wheel or roll along: *He trundled his wheelbarrow down the path.*

trunk *noun* the main stem of a tree; the body (not counting the head, arms, or legs) of a person or animal; the long nose of an elephant; a large box or chest for clothes *etc*; (*US*) the luggage compartment of a motor-car; (*plural*) short pants worn by boys and men, *esp* for swimming. – *noun* **trunkcall** the former name for a **national call**. – *noun* **trunk road** a main road.

truss *noun* (*plural* **trusses**) a bundle (*eg* of hay, straw); a system of beams to support a bridge *etc*; a kind of supporting bandage. – *verb* to bind, tie tightly (up); (*usu* with **up**) to prepare (a bird ready for cooking) by tying up the legs and wings.

trust *noun* belief in the power, reality, truth or goodness (of a thing or person): *have trust in our leaders*; something (*eg* a task, a valuable) given one in the belief that one will do it, guard it faithfully; charge, keeping: *The child was put in my trust*; an arrangement by which something (*eg* money) is given to a person for use in a particular way; a number of business firms working closely together. – *verb* to have faith or confidence (in); to give (a person something) in the belief that he will use it well *etc*: *I can't trust your sister with my tennis racket*; to feel confident (that): *I trust that you can find your way here*. – *noun* **trustee** a person who keeps something in trust for another. – *adjective* **trustful**. – *adjective* **trusting** ready to trust, not suspicious. – *adjective* **trustworthy**. – *adjective* **trusty** able to be depended on. – **take on trust** to believe without checking or testing.

truth, truthful *see* **true**.

try *verb* (*plural* **tried**) to attempt, make an effort (to do something); to test by using: *try this new soap*; to test severely, strain: *You're trying my patience*; to attempt to use, open *etc*: *I tried the door but it was locked*; to judge (a prisoner) in a court of law. – *noun* (*plural* **tries**) an effort, attempt; one of the ways of scoring in Rugby football. – *noun* **trial** the act of testing or trying (*eg* something new, one's patience *etc*); a test; the judging (of a prisoner) in a court of law; suffering. – Also *adjective*. – *adjective* **trying** hard to bear; testing. – **on trial** being tried (*esp* in a court of law); for the purpose of trying out: *goods sent on trial*; being tested: *I'm on trial with this firm*; **trial and error** the trying of various methods or choices until the

right one is found; **try on** to put on (clothing) to see if it fits *etc*; **try out** to test by using.

tryst *noun* (*old*) an arrangement to meet someone at a certain place.

tsar or **tzar** or **czar** (*masculine*), **tsarina** or **tzarina** or **czarina** (*feminine*) *noun* the title of the former emperors and empresses of Russia.

tsetse *noun* a kind of African biting fly which causes dangerous diseases to men and animals (also **tsetse fly**).

TT *abbreviation* Tourist Trophy; tuberculin tested; teetotal.

tub *noun* a round wooden container used for washing *etc*; a bath; a round container (*esp* for ice cream).

tuba *noun* a large brass musical instrument giving a low note.

tubby *adjective* fat and round.

tube *noun* a hollow, cylinder-shaped object through which liquid may pass; an organ of this kind in humans, animals *etc*; a container from which something may be squeezed (*eg* toothpaste); an underground railway system; a cathode ray tube. – *noun* **tubing** a length or lengths of tube. – *adjective* **tubular** shaped like a tube.

tuber *noun* a swelling on the underground stem of a plant (*eg* a potato).

tuberculosis *noun* an infectious disease, *usu* affecting the lungs.

TUC *abbreviation* Trades Union Congress.

tuck *noun* a fold stitched in a piece of cloth; (*coll*) sweets, cakes *etc*. – *verb* to gather (cloth) together into a fold; to fold or push (into or under a place); (with **in** or **up**) to push bedclothes closely round (a person in bed). – *noun* **tuck shop** a shop (*esp* in a school) where sweets, cakes *etc* are sold. – **tuck in** (*coll*) to eat with enjoyment or greedily.

Tuesday *noun* the third day of the week.

tuft *noun* a bunch or clump of grass, hair *etc*.

tug *verb* (*past tense* **tugged**) to pull hard; to pull along. – *noun* a strong pull; a tugboat. – *noun* **tugboat** a small but powerful ship used for towing larger ones. – *noun* **tug-of-war** a contest in which two sides, holding the ends of a strong rope, pull against each other.

tuition *noun* teaching; private coaching or teaching.

tulip *noun* a type of flower with cup-shaped flowers grown from a bulb.

tulle *noun* a kind of cloth made of thin silk or rayon net.

tumble *verb* to (cause to) fall or come down suddenly and violently; to roll, toss (about); to do acrobatic tricks; to throw into disorder. – *noun* a fall; a confused state. – *adjective* **tumbledown** falling to pieces. – *noun* **tumbler** a large drinking glass; an acrobat. – **tumble to** to understand suddenly.

tumbrel or **tumbril** *noun* (*hist*) a two-wheeled cart of the kind used to take victims to the guillotine during the French Revolution.

tummy *noun* (*plural* **tummies**) (*coll*) stomach.

tumour *noun* an abnormal growth on or in the body.

tumult *noun* a great noise (made by a crowd); excitement, agitation: *the tumult within him*. – *adjective* **tumultuous**.

tumulus *noun* a man-made mound of earth, *esp* over a tomb.

tun *noun* a large cask, *esp* for wine.

tuna *noun* (*plural* **tuna** or **tunas**) a type of large sea fish, used as food (also **tunny** (*plural* **tunnies**)).

tundra *noun* a level treeless plain in Arctic regions.

tune *noun* notes put together in a certain order, a melody; the music of a song. – *verb* to put (a musical instrument) in tune; to adjust a radio set to a particular station; (sometimes with **up**) to improve the working of an engine. – *adjective* **tuneful** having a pleasant or easily heard tune; like a tune. – *adjective* **tunefully**. – *noun* **tuning fork** a steel fork which, when struck, gives a note of a certain pitch. – **change one's tune** to change one's opinions, attitudes *etc*; **in tune** (of a musical instrument) having each note adjusted to agree with the others or with the notes of other instruments *etc*; (of a person's voice) agreeing with the notes of other voices or instruments; (of a person) in agreement (with); **to the tune of** to the sum of.

tungsten *noun* an element, a grey metal.

tunic *noun* a soldier's or policeman's jacket; (*hist*) a loose garment reaching to the knees, worn in ancient Greece and Rome; any similar modern garment: *gym tunic*.

tunnel *noun* an underground passage (*eg* for a railway train), *esp* one cut through a hill or under a river *etc*. – *verb* (*past tense* **tunnelled**) to make a tunnel; (of an animal) to burrow.

tunny *see* **tuna**.

turban *noun* a long piece of cloth wound round the head, worn *esp* by Muslims; a kind of hat resembling this.

turbid *adjective* (of liquid *etc*) muddy, clouded.

turbine *noun* a kind of engine, *usu* with curved blades, turned by the action of water, steam, hot air *etc*.

turbo- *prefix* used of engines in which a turbine is used or of aeroplanes having such engines.

turbot *noun* a type of large flat sea fish, used as food.

turbulent *adjective* (of times, conditions *etc*) disturbed, in a restless state; (of persons) likely to cause a disturbance or riot. – *noun* **turbulence** the state of being turbulent; in the atmosphere, irregular movement of air currents, *esp* when affecting the flight of aircraft.

turd *noun* a lump of dung; (*slang*) a despicable person.

tureen *noun* a large dish for holding soup at table.

turf *noun* grass and the soil below it; (with **the**) (the world of) horseracing. – *verb* to cover with turf. – **turf out** (*coll*) to throw out.

turgid *adjective* swollen; (of language) sounding grand but meaning little, pompous.

turkey *noun* (*plural* **turkeys**) a type of large farmyard bird, used as food.

Turkish bath *noun* a type of hot air or steam bath in which a person is made to sweat heavily, is massaged and then slowly cooled.

turmeric *noun* (the yellow powder made from) the root of a ginger-like plant, used as a spice in curries *etc*.

turmoil *noun* state of wild, confused movement or disorder: *His mind was in a turmoil*.

turn *verb* to (make to) go round: *wheels turning*; to face or go in the opposite direction: *He turned and walked away*; to change direction: *The road turns sharply to the left*; to direct (*eg* attention); (with **on**) to move, swing *etc* (on something as a centre): *The door turns on its hinges*; (of milk) to go sour; to (cause to) become: *His hair turned white*; (of leaves) to change colour; to shape in a lathe; to pass (the age of): *She must have turned 40.* – *noun* the act of turning; a point where one may change direction *eg* where a road joins another: *Take the first turn on the left. His career took a new turn*; a bend (*eg* in a road); a chance or duty (to do something shared by several people): *your turn to wash the car*; an act (*eg* in a circus); a short stroll: *a turn along the beach*; a fit of dizziness, shock *etc*; requirement: *This will serve our turn.* – *noun* **turncoat** a person who betrays his party, his principles *etc*. – *noun* **turning** the act of turning; a point where a road *etc* joins another; the act of shaping in a lathe. – *noun* **turning-point** the point at which a turn or an important change takes place. – *noun* **turnover** rate of change or replacement (*eg* of workers in a firm *etc*); the total amount of sales made by a firm during a certain time. – *noun* **turnpike** (*hist*) a gate across a road which opened when the user paid a toll; (*US*) a road on which a toll is paid. – *noun* **turnstile** a gate which turns, allowing only one person to pass at a time. – *noun* **turntable** a revolving platform for turning a railway engine round; the revolving part of a record-player on which the record rests. – **by turns**, in turn, one after another in a regular order; **do someone a good** (or **bad**) **turn** to act helpfully (or unhelpfully) towards someone; **to a turn** exactly, perfectly: *lamb cooked to a turn*; **turn against** to become hostile to; **turn down** say no to, refuse (*eg* an offer, a request); to reduce, make less (heat, volume of sound *etc*); **turn in** to go to bed; to hand over to those in authority; **turn off** to stop the flow of (a tap); to switch off the power for (a television *etc*); **turn on** to set running (*eg* water from a tap); to switch on power for (a television *etc*); to depend (on): *Everything turns on the weather*; to become angry with (someone) unexpectedly; **turn one's head** to fill with pride or conceit; **turn out** to make to leave, drive out; to make, produce; to empty: *turn out the attic*; (of a crowd) to come out, gather for a special purpose (*noun* **turn-out**): *A large crowd turned out for the Queen's visit*; to switch off (a light); to prove (to be): *He*

turned out to be right; **turn to** to set to work; to go to for help *etc*; **turn up** to appear, arrive; to be found; to increase (*eg* heat, volume of sound *etc*).

turnip *noun* a type of plant with a large round root used as a vegetable.

turpentine *noun* an oil got from certain trees and used for mixing paints, cleaning paint brushes *etc*.

turpitude *noun* wickedness.

turquoise *noun* a type of greenish-blue precious stone.

turret *noun* a small tower on a castle or other building; a tower on which guns are mounted, *esp* on a warship. – *adjective* **turreted** having turrets.

turtle *noun* a kind of large tortoise which lives in water. – *noun* **turtledove** a type of dove noted for its sweet, soft song. – *noun* **turtleneck** (a garment with) a high, round neck. – *noun* **turtle soup** a soup made from the flesh of a type of turtle. – **turn turtle** (of a boat *etc*) to turn upside down, capsize.

tusk *noun* a large tooth (one of a pair) sticking out from the mouth of certain animals (*eg* the elephant, the walrus).

tussle *noun* a struggle. – Also *verb*.

tussock *noun* a tuft of grass.

tutelage *noun* the state of being protected (by a guardian). – *adjective* **tutelary** protecting.

tutor *noun* a teacher of students (*eg* in a college, a university *etc*); a teacher employed privately to teach one or a few pupils at a time. – *verb* to teach. – *adjective* **tutorial** of a tutor. – *noun* a meeting for study or discussion between tutor and student(s).

tutu *noun* a ballet dancer's short, stiff, spreading skirt.

tuxedo *noun* (*plural* **tuxedos** or **tuxedoes**) (*US*) a dinner-jacket.

TV *abbreviation* television.

TVP *abbreviation* texturized vegetable protein.

twaddle *noun* nonsense.

twain *noun* (*old*) two. – **in twain** (*old*) in two, apart.

twang *noun* a tone of voice in which the words seem to come through the nose; a sound like that of a tightly-stretched string being plucked. – *verb* to (cause to) make such a sound.

tweak verb to pull with a sudden jerk, twitch. – Also noun.

tweed noun a kind of woollen cloth with a rough surface; (plural) clothes, or a suit, made of this cloth. – Also adjective.

tweezers noun plural small pincers (for pulling out hairs, holding small things etc).

twelve noun the number 12. – adjective 12 in number. – adjective **twelfth** the last of twelve (things etc). – noun one of twelve equal parts.

twenty noun the number 20. – adjective 20 in number. – adjective **twentieth** the last of twenty (things etc). – noun one of twenty equal parts.

twice adverb two times.

twiddle verb to play with, twirl idly. – **twiddle one's thumbs** to turn the thumbs around one another; to have nothing to do.

twig noun a small branch of a tree.

twilight noun the faint light between sunset and night, or before sunrise; the state or time just before or esp after the greatest power (of something): the twilight of the dictator's power.

twill noun a kind of strong cloth with a ridged appearance.

twin noun one of two children or animals born of the same mother at the same birth; one of two things exactly the same. – adjective born at the same birth; very like another; made up of two parts or things which are alike. – noun **twin bed** one of two matching single beds. – adjective **twin-screw** (of an aeroplane) having two separate propellers. – noun **twinset** a matching cardigan and jumper.

twine noun a strong kind of string made of twisted threads. – verb to wind or twist together; to wind (about or around something).

twinge noun a sudden, sharp pain.

twinkle verb (of a star etc) to shine with light which seems to vary in brightness; (of eyes) to shine with amusement etc. – noun **twinkle** or **twinkling** the act or state of twinkling. – **in a twinkling** in an instant.

twirl verb to turn or spin round quickly and lightly; to turn (something) round and round with the fingers. – Also noun.

twist verb to wind (as two threads) together; to wind (round or about something); to make (eg a rope) into a coil; to bend out of shape: The great heat twisted the metal bars; to bend or wrench painfully (eg one's ankle); to make (eg facts) appear to have a meaning which is really false. – noun the act of twisting; a painful wrench; something twisted: a twist of tissue paper. – noun **twister** (coll) a dishonest and unreliable person.

twitch verb to pull with a sudden light jerk; to jerk slightly and suddenly: A muscle in his face twitched. – Also noun.

twitter noun high, rapidly repeated sounds, as made by small birds; slight nervous excitement. – verb (of a bird) to make a series of high quivering notes, chirp continuously; (of a person) to talk continuously (in a bird-like voice).

two noun the number 2. – adjective 2 in number. – adjective **two-faced** deceitful, insincere. – adjective **twofold** double. – See also **twice**.

tycoon noun a business man of great wealth and power.

tympani, tympanist see **timpani**.

type noun kind: a new type of farming; an example which has all the usual characteristics of its, his etc kind; a small block (usu of metal) on which is a raised letter or sign, used for printing; a set of these; printed lettering. – verb to print with a typewriter; to use a typewriter; to identify or classify as a particular type: to type blood. – verb **typecast** to give (an actor) the part of a character very like himself, or a part of a kind which he has successfully played before. – noun **typewriter** a machine with keys which, when struck, cause letters to be printed on a sheet of paper. – noun **typist** a person whose work is to use a typewriter and usu to do other secretarial or clerical tasks.

typhoid adjective, noun (of) an infectious disease caused by germs in infected food or drinking water.

typhoon noun a violent storm of wind and rain in Eastern seas.

typhus noun a dangerous fever carried by lice.

typical adjective having or showing the usual characteristics: That fellow is a typical Englishman. It's typical of her to put the blame on others. – adverb **typically**.

typify verb (past tense **typified**) to be a good example of: He typifies the Englishman abroad.

tyrant *noun* a ruler who governs cruelly and unjustly. – *adjective* **tyrannical** or **tyrannous** like a tyrant, cruel. – *verb* **tyrannize** to act as a tyrant; to rule (over) harshly. – *noun* **tyranny** (*pl* **tyrannies**) the rule of a tyrant.

tyre or (*US*) **tire** *noun* a thick rubber cover round a motor or cycle wheel.

tyro *see* **tiro.**

tzar *see* **tsar.**

U

ubiquitous *adjective* being everywhere at once; found everywhere. – *noun* **ubiquity.**

UDA *abbreviation* Ulster Defence Association.

UDI *abbreviation* Unilateral Declaration of Independence.

udder *noun* the bag-like part of a cow, goat *etc* with teats which supply milk for their young or for man.

UDR *abbreviation* Ulster Defence Regiment.

UEFA *abbreviation* Union of European Football Associations.

UFO *abbreviation* unidentified flying object.

ugly *adjective* unpleasant to look at or hear; threatening, dangerous: *an ugly situation.* – *noun* **ugliness.**

UHF *abbreviation* ultra high frequency.

UHT *abbreviation* ultra high temperature.

ukelele *noun* a type of small, stringed musical instrument played like a banjo.

ulcer *noun* an open sore on the inside or the outside of the body. – *adjective* **ulcerated** having an ulcer or ulcers.

ult *abbreviation* last month (*ultimo* [L]): *We refer to your letter of 12th ult.*

ulterior *adjective* beyond what is admitted or seen: *an ulterior motive.*

ultimate *adjective* last, final. – *adjective* **ultimately** finally, in the end.

ultimatum *noun* a final demand sent by one person, nation *etc* to another, with a threat to break off discussion, declare war *etc* if the demand is not met.

ultra- *prefix* very: *ultra-careful;* beyond: *ultramicroscopic.*

ultramarine *adjective, noun* (of) a deep blue colour.

ultrasonic *adjective* beyond the range of human hearing.

ultraviolet *adjective* (of light) having rays of slightly shorter wavelength than visible light, which cause objects they strike to glow with various colours and cause tanning of the skin.

umber *noun* a mineral substance used to produce a brown paint.

umbilical *adjective* of the navel. – *noun* **umbilical cord** a tube that connects an unborn baby mammal to its mother through the placenta; the lifeline of an astronaut outside the vehicle in space.

umbrage *noun* a feeling of offence or hurt: *He took umbrage at my words.*

umbrella *noun* an object made up of a folding covered framework on a stick which protects against rain.

umpire *noun* (in cricket, tennis *etc*) a person who sees that the game is played according to the rules and decides doubtful points; a judge who is asked to settle a dispute. – *verb* to act as an umpire.

UN *abbreviation* United Nations.

un- *prefix* not: *unequal;* (with verbs) used to show the reversal of an action: *unfasten.*

unable *adjective* lacking enough strength, power, skill *etc.*

unaccountable *adjective* not able to be explained. – *adjective* **unaccountably.**

unadulterated *adjective* pure, not mixed with anything else.

unanimous *adjective* all of the same opinion: *We were unanimous; agreed to* by all: *a unanimous decision.* – *noun* **unanimity.**

unapproachable *adjective* unfriendly and stiff in manner.

unassuming *adjective* modest.

unaware *adjective* not knowing, ignorant (of): *unaware of the danger.* – *adjective* **unawares** without warning; without meaning to, unintentionally.

unbalanced *adjective* mad; lacking balance: *an unbalanced view.*

unbeliever *noun* a person who does not follow a certain religion.

unbend *verb* to behave in a natural way without pride or stiffness. – *adjective* **unbending** severe.

unbounded *adjective* not limited, very great: *unbounded enthusiasm.*

unbridled *adjective* not kept under control: *unbridled fury.*

unburden: unburden oneself to tell one's secrets or problems freely (to another).

uncalled: uncalled for quite unnecessary: *His remarks were uncalled for.*

uncanny *adjective* strange, mysterious.

uncared: uncared for not looked after properly.

uncertain *adjective* not certain, doubtful; not definitely known; changeable: *uncertain weather.*

uncharted *adjective* not shown on a map or chart; little known.

uncle *noun* the brother of one's father or mother; the husband of one's father's or mother's sister.

unclean *adjective* dirty, impure.

uncoil *verb* to unwind.

uncommon *adjective* not common, strange. – *adjective* **uncommonly** very: *uncommonly well.*

uncompromising *adjective* not willing to give in or make concessions to others.

unconscionable *adjective* more than is reasonable: *unconscionable demands.*

unconscious *adjective* senseless, stunned (*eg* by an accident); not aware (of); not recognized by the person concerned: *an unconscious prejudice against women.* – *noun* the deepest level of the mind.

uncouth *adjective* clumsy, awkward; rude.

undaunted *adjective* fearless; not discouraged.

undeniable *adjective* not able to be denied, clearly true.

under *preposition* directly below or beneath: *under the stone;* less than: *bought for under £1;* for, within the authority or command of: *under General Montgomery;* going through, suffering: *under attack;* having, using: *under a false name;* in accordance with: *under our agreement.* – *adverb* in or to a lower position, condition *etc;* beneath the surface of the water. – **under age** younger than the legal age of independence or freedom; having less than the required age: *He's under age for this class;* immature; **under way** in motion, started.

under- *prefix* below, beneath; lower (in position or rank); too little.

undercarriage *noun* the wheels of an aeroplane and their supports.

underclothes *noun plural* clothes worn next to the skin under other clothes.

undercover *adjective* acting or done in secret: *an undercover agent* (*ie* a spy).

undercurrent *noun* a flow or movement under the surface; a half-hidden feeling, tendency *etc: an undercurrent of despair beneath his confident words.*

undercut *verb* to sell at a lower price than (someone else).

underdeveloped *adjective* not fully grown; (of a country) lacking modern agricultural and industrial systems, and with a low standard of living.

underdog *noun* the weaker side, or the loser in any conflict or fight.

underdone *adjective* (of food) not quite cooked.

underestimate *verb* to estimate at less than the real worth, value *etc.*

underfoot *adjective* under the feet.

undergo *verb* (*past tense* **underwent,** *past participle* **undergone**) to suffer or endure; to receive (*eg* as medical treatment).

undergraduate *noun* a university student who has not yet passed final examinations.

underground *adjective* below the surface of the ground; secret. – *noun* a railway which runs in a tunnel beneath the surface of the ground.

undergrowth *noun* shrubs or low plants growing amongst trees.

underhand *adjective* sly, deceitful. – Also *adjective*.

underlie *verb* to be the hidden cause or source of. – *adjective* **underlying**.

underline *verb* to draw a line under; to stress the importance of, emphasize.

underling *noun* a person of lower rank.

undermine *verb* to do damage to, weaken gradually (health, authority *etc*).

underneath *adjective, preposition* in a lower position (than), beneath: *Have you searched underneath (the table)? He wore a jacket underneath his overcoat.*

underpass *noun* a road passing under another one.

underpay *verb* to pay too little.

underprivileged *adjective* not having normal living standards or rights.

underrate *verb* to think too little of, underestimate: *He underrates his ability.*

undersigned *noun* (with **the**) the person or persons whose names are written at the end of a letter or statement.

underskirt *noun* a thin skirt worn under another skirt.

understand *verb* (*past tense* **understood**) to see the meaning of (something); to appreciate the reasons for: *I don't understand his behaviour*; to have a thorough knowledge of: *Do you understand children? I do not understand finance*; to have the impression that: *I understood that you had gone home*; to take for granted as part of an agreement. – *adjective* **understandable**. – *noun* **understanding** the act or power of seeing the full meaning (of something); an agreement; condition: *on the understanding that we both pay half the price*; appreciation of another's feelings, difficulties *etc*. – *adjective* able to understand another's feelings, sympathetic.

understatement *noun* a statement which does not give the whole truth, making less of certain details than is actually the case.

understudy *noun* an actor who learns the part of another actor so that he may take his place if necessary. – Also *verb*.

undertake *verb* to promise (to do something); to take upon oneself (a task, duty *etc*): *I undertook the task alone.* – *noun*

undertaker a person whose job is to organize funerals. – *noun* **undertaking** something which is being attempted or done; a promise; the business of an undertaker.

undertone *noun* a soft voice; a partly hidden meaning, feeling *etc*: *an undertone of discontent.*

undertow *noun* a current below the surface of the water which moves in a direction opposite to the surface movement.

undervalue *verb* to value (something) below the real worth.

underwear *noun* underclothes.

underworld *noun* the criminal world or level of society; (*myth*) the place where spirits go after death.

underwriter *noun* a person who insures ships. – *verb* **underwrite** to accept for insurance; to accept responsibility or liability for.

undo *verb* (*past tense* **undid**, *past participle* **undone**) to unfasten (a coat, parcel *etc*); to wipe out the effect of, reverse: *You will undo all the good he did*; (*hist*) to ruin (*esp* one's reputation): *Alas, I am undone.* – *noun* **undoing** ruin: *His boldness will be his undoing.*

undoubted *adjective* not to be doubted. – *adjective* **undoubtedly** without doubt, certainly.

undress *verb* to take the clothes off.

undue *adjective* too much, more than is necessary: *undue expense.* – *adverb* **unduly**: *unduly worried.*

undulate *verb* to move as waves do; to have a rolling, wavelike appearance: *The countryside undulated gently.* – *adjective* **undulating**. – *noun* **undulation**.

unearth *verb* to bring or dig out from the earth, or from a place of hiding. – *adjective* **unearthly** strange, as if not of this world; (*coll*) absurd, *esp* absurdly early: *at this unearthly hour.*

uneasy *adjective* anxious, worried. – *noun* **uneasiness**.

unemployed *adjective* without a job; not in use. – *noun plural* (with **the**) unemployed people as a group. – *noun* **unemployment** the state of being unemployed; the total number of unemployed people in a country.

unequal *adjective* not equal; unfair: *an unequal distribution of profits*; lacking enough strength, skill *etc* for (a task): *unequal to the job*. – *adjective* **unequalled** without an equal, unique.

unequivocal *adjective* clear, not ambiguous: *unequivocal orders*.

unerring *adjective* always right, never making a mistake: *unerring judgement*.

UNESCO *abbreviation* United Nations Educational, Scientific and Cultural Organization.

uneven *adjective* not smooth or level; not all of the same quality *etc*: *This work is very uneven*.

unexpected *adjective* not expected, sudden.

unfailing *adjective* never failing, never likely to fail: *unfailing accuracy*.

unfair *adjective* not just.

unfaithful *adjective* not true to one's marriage vows; failing to keep one's promises.

unfasten *verb* to loosen, undo (*eg* a buttoned coat).

unfeeling *adjective* harsh, hard-hearted.

unfit *adjective* not suitable; not good enough, or not in a suitable state (to, for): *This water is unfit for drinking. The patient is unfit to travel*; not as vigorous (physically or mentally) as one could be.

unflagging *adjective* not tiring or losing strength.

unflinching *adjective* brave, not put off by pain, opposition *etc*.

unfold *verb* to spread out; to give details of (as a story, plan); (of details of a plot *etc*) to become known.

unforgettable *adjective* of such a kind as never to be forgotten.

unfortunate *adjective* unlucky; regrettable: *an unfortunate manner in dealing with people*.

unfounded *adjective* not based on facts or reality, untrue.

unfurl *verb* to unfold (*eg* a flag).

ungainly *adjective* clumsy, awkward.

ungracious *adjective* rude, not polite.

ungrateful *adjective* not showing thanks for kindness.

unguarded *adjective* without protection; careless: *an unguarded remark*.

unguent *noun* ointment.

unhappy *adjective* miserable, sad; unfortunate. – *adjective* **unhappily**. – *noun* **unhappiness**.

unhealthy *adjective* not well, ill; harmful to health: *an unhealthy climate*; showing that one is not well: *an unhealthy complexion*.

unhinge *verb* to send (a person) mad.

unhorse *verb* to throw from a horse.

uni- *prefix* one, a single.

UNICEF *abbreviation* United Nations Children's Fund.

unicorn *noun* (*myth*) an animal like a horse, but with one straight horn on its forehead.

uniform *adjective* the same in all parts, at all times *etc*, never varying. – *noun* the form of clothes worn by soldiers, sailors, children at a certain school *etc*. – *noun* **uniformity** sameness.

unify *verb* (*past tense* **unified**) to make into one. – *noun* **unification**.

unilateral *adjective* one-sided; affecting or involving one person or group *etc* out of several. – *noun* **unilateralism**. – *noun* **unilateralist** a person who favours unilateral action *esp* in abandoning the production *etc* of nuclear weapons.

uninterrupted *adjective* not interrupted; continuing without a break or stoppage; (of a view) not blocked by anything.

union *noun* the act of joining together; the state of being joined together; marriage; countries or states joined together; a trade union. – *noun* **Union Jack** the flag of the United Kingdom.

unique *adjective* without a like or equal: *a unique sense of timing*.

unisex *adjective* in a style that can be worn, used *etc* by both males and females.

unison *noun* identity, exact sameness, of musical pitch; singing or playing (a musical passage) at the same pitch; agreement, accord. – **in unison** all together.

unit *noun* a single thing, person or group, *esp* when considered as part of a larger whole: *storage unit: army unit*; a fixed amount, length *etc* used as a standard by which other amounts *etc* are measured (*eg* metres, litres, centimetres *etc*); the smallest whole number *ie* the number one. – *adjective* **unitary** existing as a unit, not divided; using or based on units. – *noun* **unity** the state of being in complete agreement; the state of being one or a whole; the number one.

unite *verb* to join together; to become one; to act together. – *adjective* **united.**

universe *noun* all things, including the earth and all heavenly bodies; mankind. – *adjective* **universal** of the universe; of, affecting, including all, sometimes all mankind. – *adverb* **universally.**

university *noun* (*plural* **universities**) a place of learning where a wide range of subjects are taught to a high level, and which gives degrees to those of its students who pass its examinations.

unkempt *adjective* untidy.

unkind *adjective* not kind; harsh, cruel.

unleaded *adjective* of petrol, not containing lead compounds.

unleash *verb* to set free (a dog *etc*); to let loose (*eg* one's anger).

unless *conjunction* if . . . not: *Unless he's here soon, I'm going* (*ie* if he's not here soon). *Unless you come, I'm not going* (*ie* if you don't come as well).

unlike *adjective* different, not similar. – *preposition* different from; not characteristic of: *It was unlike her to run away.*

unlikely *adjective* not probable: *It's unlikely that it will rain today*; probably not true: *an unlikely tale.*

unload *verb* to take the load from; to remove the charge from a gun.

unlooked-for *adjective* not expected: *unlooked-for happiness.*

unloose *verb* to set free; to make loose.

unlucky *adjective* not lucky or fortunate; unsuccessful. – *adverb* **unluckily.**

unmanly *adjective* weak, cowardly.

unmask *verb* to take a mask or covering off; to show the true character of; to bring to light (a plot *etc*).

unmatched *adjective* without an equal.

unmentionable *adjective* not fit to be spoken of, scandalous, indecent: *unmentionable deeds.*

unmistakable *adjective* very clear; impossible to confuse with any other: *Jack's unmistakable shock of orange hair.*

unmitigated *adjective* complete, absolute: *an unmitigated disgrace.*

unmoved *adjective* not affected: *unmoved by her sobbing*; firm.

unnecessary *adjective* not necessary; avoidable.

UNO *abbreviation* United Nations Organization.

unobtrusive *adjective* not obvious or conspicuous; modest.

unpack *verb* to open (a piece of luggage) and remove the contents (*eg* clothes).

unpalatable *adjective* not pleasing to the taste; not pleasant to have to face up to: *the unpalatable facts.*

unparalleled *adjective* not having an equal: *an earthquake of unparalleled severity.*

unpick *verb* to take out (stitches) from (sewing *etc*).

unpremeditated *adjective* done without having been planned: *unpremeditated murder.*

unprepossessing *adjective* not attractive.

unpretentious *adjective* modest, not showy or affected.

unprincipled *adjective* without (moral) principles.

unravel *verb* (*past tense* **unravelled**) to unwind or take the knots out of; to solve (a problem or mystery).

unremitting *adjective* never stopping, unending: *unremitting rain.*

unrequited *adjective* (*esp* of love) not given in return.

unrest *noun* a state of trouble or discontent, *esp* among a group of people: *political unrest.*

unrivalled *adjective* without an equal.

unruly *adjective* badly behaved; not obeying laws or rules. – *noun* **unruliness.**

unsavoury *adjective* very unpleasant, causing a feeling of disgust.

unscathed *adjective* not harmed.

unscrew *verb* to loosen (something screwed in).

unseasonable *adjective* (of weather) not suitable to the time of year; not well-timed.

unseat *verb* to remove from a seat *esp* from a political seat: *He was unseated at the last* *election*; to throw from the saddle (of a horse).

unseen *adjective* not seen. – *noun* a passage from a foreign language to be translated without previous preparation.

unsettle *verb* to disturb, upset. – *adjective* **unsettled** disturbed; (of weather) changeable; (of a bill *etc*) unpaid.

unsightly *adjective* ugly.

unsolicited *adjective* not requested: *unsolicited advice*.

unsophisticated *adjective* simple; lacking experience of the world.

unsound *adjective* (of reasoning *etc*) not correct; (of one's mind) not sane; (of fruit *etc*) rotten.

unspeakable *adjective* incapable of being expressed in words, *esp* too bad to describe: *unspeakable rudeness*.

unstudied *adjective* natural, not forced: *unstudied charm*.

unsuspecting *adjective* not aware of coming danger.

unthinkable *adjective* very unlikely; too bad to be thought of.

until or **till** *prep* up to (the time of): *Wait until* (or *till*) *Saturday. I stayed until* (or *till*) *he died.* – *conjunction*: *Keep walking until* (or *till*) *you come to the church.*

untimely *adjective* happening before the proper time: *untimely arrival*; not suitable to the occasion: *untimely remark*.

unto *preposition* (*old*) equal in meaning to **to** in most senses; however, **unto** cannot indicate the infinitive.

untold *adjective* not told, too great to be counted or measured: *untold riches*.

untoward *adjective* unlucky, unfortunate; inconvenient.

untrue *adjective* not true, false; not faithful. – *noun* **untruth** a lie. – *adjective* **untruthful**.

unusual *adjective* not usual; rare, remarkable.

unvarnished *adjective* not varnished; plain, straightforward: *the unvarnished truth*.

unveil *verb* to remove a veil from; to remove a cover from (*esp* a statue, memorial *etc*); to bring to light (*eg* an evil plot).

unwaged *adjective* unemployed.

unwell *adjective* not in good health.

unwieldy *adjective* not easily moved or handled. – *noun* **unwieldiness**.

unwitting *adjective* unintended: *an unwitting insult*; unaware. – *adverb* **unwittingly**.

unwonted *adjective* unaccustomed, not usual: *unwonted cheerfulness*.

unworthy *adjective* not worthy; low, worthless, despicable; (with **of**) not deserving (*eg* of attention); less good than one would expect: *That drawing is unworthy of you*.

up *adverb* (*superlative* **uppermost**) towards or in a higher or more northerly position: *She came up the hill. They live up in the Highlands*; completely, so as to finish: *Drink up your tea*; to a larger size *etc*: *blow up a balloon*; as far as a given place: *He came up to me and shook hands*; towards a more important city *etc*, not necessarily from the south: *going up to London from Manchester*. – *preposition* towards or in the higher part of: *climbed up the ladder*; along: *walking up the street*. – *adjective* (*comparative* **upper**, *superlative* **uppermost** or **upmost**) ascending, going *etc* up: *Use the up escalator*; ahead (in score): *2 goals up*; better off, richer: *£2 up on the deal*; risen: *The sun is up*; (of a given length of time) ended: *Your time is up*; (*coll*) wrong: *What's up with her today?* – *adjective* **upfront** or **up-front** candid, open; foremost. – *noun* **upper** (often *plural*) the part(s) of a shoe *etc* above the sole. – *n* **uppercut** in boxing, a punch which swings up from below. – *adjective* **up-to-date** modern, in touch with recent ideas *etc*; belonging to the present time; containing all recent facts *etc*: *an up-to-date logbook*. – **the upper hand** control, dominance; **up and about** awake, out of bed (*esp* after an illness); **up front** at the front; (of money) paid in advance; candidly, openly; **ups and downs** times of good and bad luck, business *etc*; **up to** until: *up to the present*; capable of (doing): *Are you up to the job?*; a duty belonging to (someone): *It's up to you to do it*; doing, *esp* something cunning *etc*: *up to his tricks again*; **up to date** to the present time; containing recent facts *etc*; aware of recent developments: *He is not up to date in modern methods*.

upbeat *adjective* (*coll*) cheerful, optimistic.

upbraid *verb* to scold.

upbringing *noun* the rearing of or the training given to, or received by, a child.

up-country *adverb, adjective* inland.

update *verb* to bring up to date. – *noun* the act of updating; new information: *We have an update on yesterday's report*.

upgrade *verb* to raise to a more important position; to improve the quality of.

upheaval *noun* a violent shaking (*eg* an earthquake); a great disturbance or change.

uphill *adjective* going upwards; difficult: *an uphill struggle*. – *adverb* upwards.

uphold *verb* (*past tense* **upheld**) to support (*eg* a person, an action); to maintain, keep going (*eg* a tradition).

upholster *verb* to fit chairs, sofas *etc* with springs, stuffing, covers *etc*. – *noun* **upholsterer** a person who upholsters furniture. – *noun* **upholstery** covers, cushions *etc*.

upkeep *noun* the act of keeping (*eg* a house or car) in a good state of repair; the cost of this.

upland *noun* high ground; (*plural*) a hilly or mountainous region. – Also *adjective*.

upmost, upper, uppermost *see* **up**.

upon *preposition* on the top of: *upon the table*; at, after the time of: *upon completion of the task*.

upright *adjective* standing up, vertical; just and honest. – *noun* an upright post, piano *etc*.

uprising *noun* the act of rising against a government *etc*; a revolt.

uproar *noun* a noisy disturbance. – *adjective* **uproarious** very noisy *esp* because of laughter.

uproot *verb* to tear up by the roots; to cause (*eg* a family) to leave home and go to live in another place: *The Browns were uprooted again when Mr Brown changed his job*.

upset *verb* (*present participle* **upsetting,** *past tense* **upset**) to make unhappy, angry *etc*; to overturn; to be overturned; to disturb, put out of order (*eg* one's digestion); to ruin (plans *etc*). – *adjective* distressed, unhappy *etc*, ill. – *noun* an act of upsetting; state of being upset; distress; the cause of this.

upshot *noun* a result or end of a matter: *The upshot of all this was that they went home early*.

upside-down *adjective, adverb* with the top part underneath; in confusion.

upstage *adverb* away from the footlights on a theatre stage. – *adjective* (*coll*) haughty, proud. – *verb* to divert attention from (someone) to oneself.

upstairs *adverb* in or to the upper storey(s) of a house *etc*. – Also *noun, adjective*.

upstanding *adjective* honest, respectable; strong and healthy; standing up: *Be upstanding and drink the king's health*.

upstart *noun* a person who has recently risen quickly from a humble to a high position, *esp* one who claims to be more important than he is.

upstream *adverb* higher up a river or stream, towards the source.

uptake: quick on the uptake quick to understand.

uranium *noun* an element, a radioactive metal.

urban *adjective* of, consisting of or living in a town or city (opposite of **rural**).

urbane *adjective* polite in a smooth way. – *noun* **urbanity** state of being urbane; (*plural* **urbanities**) urbane actions.

urchin *noun* a small boy, *esp* a dirty, ragged one.

urge *verb* to drive (on); to try to persuade: *He urged me to go home*; to advise, adverbocate earnestly: *He urged caution*. – *noun* a strong desire or impulse. – *adjective* **urgent** requiring immediate attention or action; eagerly calling for immediate action. – *noun* **urgency**.

urine *noun* the waste liquid passed out of the body of animals and humans from the bladder. – *adjective* **urinary**. – *verb* **urinate** to pass urine from the bladder.

urn *noun* a vase for the ashes of the dead; a large metal vessel, with a tap, used for making and pouring out tea *etc*.

US(A) *abbreviation* United States (of America).

us *pronoun* the word used by a speaker or writer in mentioning himself or herself together with other people (as the object in a sentence): *They beat us. Show it to us*.

use *verb* to put to some purpose: *Use a knife to open it*; to bring into action: *Use your common sense*; (often with **up**) to spend, exhaust (*eg* one's patience, energy); to treat: *He used his wife cruelly*. – *noun* the act of using; value or suitability for a (or any) purpose: *no use* *to anybody*; state of being used: *It's in use at the moment*; custom. – *noun* **usage** act or manner of using; the established way of using (a word *etc*); custom, habit; treatment: *rough usage*. – *adjective* **used** employed, put to a purpose; not new: *used cars*. – *adjective* **useful** serving a purpose; helpful. – *adverb* **usefully**. – *noun* **usefulness**. – *adjective* **useless** having no use or effect. – *noun* **uselessness**. – *adjective* **user-friendly** easily understood, easy to use. – **no use** useless; **used to** accustomed to: *We're not used to poverty*; (with another verb) was or were in the habit of (doing something): *We used to go there every year*.

usher (*masculine*), **usherette** (*feminine*) *noun* a person who shows people to their seats in a theatre *etc*. – *verb* **usher** to lead (in, into, to).

USSR *abbreviation* Union of Soviet Socialist Republics.

usual *adjective* done, happening *etc* most often: *the usual way of doing things*; customary: *with his usual cheerfulness*; ordinary. – *adverb* **usually** on most occasions.

usurp *verb* to take possession of (*eg* a

throne) by force or without the right to do so. – *noun* **usurper**.

usury *noun* the lending of money in return for a (*usu* very) high rate of interest on the loan. – *noun* **usurer** a moneylender who demands a very high rate of interest.

utensil *noun* an instrument, vessel *etc* commonly used, *esp* in the home (*eg* a ladle, knife, pan).

uterus *noun* (*plural* **uteri**) the womb.

utility *noun* (*plural* **utilities**) usefulness; a useful public service (*eg* the supplying of water, gas *etc*).

utilize *verb* to make use of. – *noun* **utilization**.

utmost *adjective* greatest possible: *the utmost care*; furthest. – **do one's utmost** to make the greatest possible effort.

utter *verb* to give out, produce with the voice (words, a scream *etc*). – *adjective* complete, total: *utter darkness*. – *adverb* **utterly**.

uvula *noun* the small piece of flesh which hangs down from the palate right at the back of the mouth.

V

v *abbreviation* against (*versus* [L]); see (*vide* [L]); verb; verse; volume.

vacant *adjective* empty; not occupied; (of a look, expression *etc*) showing no interest or intelligence. – *noun* **vacancy** (*plural* **vacancies**) a post, job or place that has not been filled. – *verb* **vacate** to leave empty, to cease to occupy. – *noun* **vacation** the act of vacating; a holiday.

vaccine *noun* a substance made from the germs that cause a disease, given to people and animals to try to prevent them taking that disease. – *verb* **vaccinate** to protect against a disease by giving a vaccine to, *eg* by injecting it into the skin. – *noun* **vaccination**.

vacillate *verb* to move from one opinion to another, to waver.

vacuous *adjective* empty, stupid.

vacuum *noun* a space from which (almost) all air has been removed. – *noun* **vacuum cleaner** a machine which cleans carpets *etc* by sucking up the dust. – *noun* **vacuum flask** a container which has double walls with a vacuum between them, for keeping liquids *etc* hot or cold.

vagabond *noun* a person who has no settled home, a wanderer; a rascal, a rogue.

vagary *noun* (often *plural* **vagaries**) strange, unexpected behaviour: *the vagaries of human nature*.

vagina *noun* the passage connecting the female genital area to the womb.

vagrant *adjective* unsettled, wandering. – *noun* a wanderer or tramp, with no settled home. – *noun* **vagrancy** the state of being a tramp.

vague *adjective* not clear; not definite: *He has a vague idea. She has made a vague accusation. I can see a vague shape*; not practical or efficient, forgetful: *a vague old lady*.

vain *adjective* conceited; useless: *vain efforts*; empty, meaningless: *vain promises*. – *noun* **vanity** conceit; worthlessness; (*plural* **vanities**) something vain and worthless. – **in vain** without success.

vainglory *noun* boastfulness. – *adjective* **vainglorious** boastful.

valance *noun* a hanging frill round the edge of a bed.

vale *noun* a valley.

valediction *noun* a farewell. – *adjective* **valedictory** saying farewell.

valency *noun* (*plural* **valencies**) (in chemistry) the combining power of an atom or group. In water, H_2O, oxygen shows valency two.

valentine *noun* a greetings card sent on St Valentine's Day (14 February) or a sweetheart chosen then.

valet *noun* a manservant.

valetudinarian *adjective, noun* (of) a person who is over-anxious about health.

valiant *adjective* brave.

valid *adjective* sound, acceptable: *He has a valid reason for not going*; that can be lawfully used, legally in force: *a valid passport*. – *noun* **validity**.

Valium® *noun* a brand name for diazepam, a tranquillizing drug.

valley *noun* (*plural* **valleys**) low land between hills, often having a river flowing through it.

valour *noun* courage, bravery. – *adj* **valorous**.

value *noun* worth; price; purchasing power (of a coin *etc*); importance; usefulness; (in algebra) a number or quantity put as equal to an expression: *In this case the value of x is 8*. – *verb* to put a price on; to think highly of. – *adjective* **valuable** of great value. – *noun plural* **valuables** articles of worth. – *noun* **valuation** the act of valuing; an estimated price or value. – *noun* **value-added tax** a tax raised on the selling-price of an article at each stage of its manufacture or marketing, or charged on certain services. – *adjective* **valueless** worthless. – *noun* **valuer** or **valuator** a

person trained to estimate the value of property.

valve *noun* a device (*eg* that in a tyre) for allowing air, steam or liquid to flow in one direction only; a small flap with a similar effect, controlling the flow of blood in the body; a type of electronic component found in older television sets, radios *etc*.

vamp *noun* the upper part of a boot or shoe; a woman who sets out to attract men. – *verb* to patch; to play quickly made-up music on the piano; to try to attract men.

vampire *noun* a dead person supposed to rise at night and suck the blood of sleeping people. – *noun* **vampire bat** any of several types of bats, including a S. American type that sucks blood.

van *noun* a covered or closed-in vehicle or wagon for carrying goods by road or rail; short for **vanguard**.

vandal *noun* a person who pointlessly destroys or damages public buildings *etc*. – *noun* **vandalism** the activity of a vandal. – *verb* **vandalize** to damage by vandalism.

vane *noun* a weathercock; the blade of a windmill, propeller *etc*.

vanguard *noun* the part of an army going in front of the main body; the leading group in a movement *etc*.

vanilla *noun* a sweet-scented flavouring substance obtained from the pods of a type of orchid.

vanish *verb* to go out of sight; to fade away to nothing.

vanity *see* **vain**.

vanquish *verb* to defeat.

vantage point *noun* a position giving one an advantage or a clear view.

vapid *adjective* dull, uninteresting.

vapour *noun* the air-like or gas-like state of a substance that is usually liquid or solid: *water vapour*; mist or smoke in the air. – *verb* **vaporize** to (cause to) change into vapour. – *noun* **vaporizer** an apparatus for sending out liquid in a very fine spray.

variable, variance, variation *see* **vary**.

varicose *adjective* (of a vein *usu* of the leg) swollen, enlarged.

variegated *adjective* marked with different colours, varied in colour.

variety noun (plural **varieties**) the quality of being of many kinds, of being different; a mixed collection: a variety of books; a sort, kind: a variety of potato; mixed theatrical entertainment including dances, songs, comic acts etc. – adjective **various** of different kinds; several: After various attempts we gave up.

varlet noun (old) a rascal.

varnish noun a sticky liquid which gives a usu glossy surface to paper, wood etc. – verb to cover with varnish; to cover up (faults).

vary verb (past tense **varied**) to make, be, or become different; to make changes in (a routine etc); to differ, disagree. – adjective **variable** changeable; that may be varied. – noun something that varies eg in value. – noun **variance** a state of differing or disagreement. – noun **variant** a different form or version. – Also adjective. – noun **variation** a varying, a change; the extent of a difference or change: In the desert there are great variations of temperature; (in music etc) a repetition, in a slightly different form, of a main theme. – **at variance** in disagreement.

vase noun a jar of pottery, glass etc, used as an ornament or for holding cut flowers.

vasectomy noun (plural **vasectomies**) sterilization of a male by cutting (and removing part of) the sperm-carrying tubes.

Vaseline* noun a type of ointment made from petroleum.

vassal (hist) noun a person who held land from an overlord in return for certain services.

vast adjective of very great size or amount. – noun **vastness**.

VAT or **vat** noun short for **value-added tax**.

vat noun a large tub or tank, used esp in fermenting liquors and dyeing.

vaudeville noun an entertainment with dances and songs, usu comic.

vault noun an arched roof; an underground room, a cellar. – verb to leap, esp supporting one's weight on one's hands, or on a pole.

vaunt verb to boast.

VC abbreviation Victoria Cross.

VCR abbreviation video cassette recorder.

VD abbreviation venereal disease(s).

VDU abbreviation visual display unit.

veal noun the flesh of a calf, used as food.

veer verb to change direction; to change course; to change mood, opinions etc.

Vegan or **vegan** noun a vegetarian who uses no animal products.

vegetable noun a plant, esp one grown for food. – adjective of plants; made from or consisting of plants: The wool was coloured with vegetable dye. There is some vegetable matter in the water. – noun **vegetarian** a person who eats no meat but lives wholly on vegetable food, and (usu) milk, eggs etc. – verb **vegetate** to grow as a plant does; to lead a dull, aimless life: She sits at home and vegetates. – noun **vegetation** plants in general; the plants of a place or region.

vehement adjective emphatic and forceful in expressing one's opinions etc. – noun **vehemence**.

vehicle noun a means of transport esp one with wheels, used on land: motor vehicle; a means (as television, newspapers etc) of carrying information etc. – adjective **vehicular**.

veil noun a piece of cloth or netting worn to shade or hide the face; anything that hides or covers up. – verb to cover with a veil; to hide. – **take the veil** to become a nun.

vein noun one of the tubes which carry the blood back to the heart; a small rib of a leaf; a thin layer of mineral in a rock; a streak in wood, stone etc; a mood or personal characteristic: a vein of cheerfulness. – adjective **veined** marked with veins.

Velcro® noun a type of fastener for clothing etc made of two strips of specially treated fabric.

veldt noun (in S. Africa) open grass-country, with few or no trees.

vellum noun a fine parchment used for bookbinding etc, made from the skins of calves, kids or lambs; paper etc made in imitation of this.

velocity noun rate or speed of movement; swiftness.

velour(s) *vě-loor*, *noun* a type of material with a soft, velvet-like surface.

velvet *noun* a type of cloth made from silk *etc*, with a thick, soft surface; velveteen. – *adjective* made of velvet; like velvet. – *noun* **velveteen** a fabric looking like velvet, but made of cotton. – *adjective* **velvety** soft, like velvet.

venal *adjective* willing to be bribed; (of an act) unworthy, done for a bribe.

vend *verb* to sell. – *noun* **vending machine** a machine containing small articles for sale worked by putting coins in a slot. – *noun* **vendor** a person who sells (also **vender**).

vendetta *noun* a bitter, long-lasting quarrel or feud.

veneer *verb* to cover a piece of wood with another thin piece of finer quality; to (try to) give a good appearance to what is really bad. – *noun* a thin layer (of fine wood) forming a surface; a false outward show hiding some bad quality *etc*: *a veneer of good manners*.

venerable *adjective* worthy of respect because of age, exceptional goodness *etc*. – *verb* **venerate** to respect or honour greatly. – *noun* **veneration** the act of venerating; great respect.

venereal disease *noun* a type of disease which can be passed on through sexual intercourse.

Venetian blind *noun* a blind for windows, formed of thin movable strips of metal, plastic *etc* hung on tapes.

vengeance *noun* punishment given, harm done in return for wrong or injury, revenge. – *adjective* **vengeful** seeking revenge. – **with a vengeance** with unexpected force or enthusiasm.

venial *adjective* (of a sin *etc*) not very bad, pardonable.

venison *noun* the flesh of the deer, used as food.

venom *noun* poison; spite. – *adjective* **venomous** poisonous; spiteful.

vent *noun* a small opening; a hole to allow air, smoke *etc* to pass through; an outlet; a slit at the bottom of the back of a coat *etc*. – *verb* to pour out, express (one's rage or other strong feeling) in some way. – **give vent to** to vent.

ventilate *verb* to allow fresh air to pass through (a room *etc*); to talk about, discuss. – *noun* **ventilation**. – *noun*

ventilator a kind of grating or other device for bringing in fresh air.

ventricle *noun* a small cavity, *esp* in the brain or heart.

ventriloquist *noun* a person who can speak without any obvious movement of the lips, making the voice appear to come from a puppet *etc*. – *noun* **ventriloquism.**

venture *noun* a piece of business or other undertaking which involves some risk. – *verb* to risk; to dare; to do or say something at the risk of causing annoyance *etc*: *I ventured to remark that I didn't like her dress*. – *adjective* **venturesome.** – *adjective* **venturous.**

venue *noun* the scene of an event, *eg* a sports contest, a conference.

veracious *adjective* truthful. – *noun* **veracity** truthfulness.

veranda(h) *noun* a kind of terrace with a roof supported by pillars, extending along the side of a house.

verb *noun* the word that tells what a person or thing does or experiences: I *singular*. He *had* no idea. She *was hit*. – *adjective* **verbal** of verbs; of words; spoken, not written: *a verbal report*. – *adjective* **verbatim** in the exact words, word for word: *He told me what she said, verbatim*. – *adjective* **verbose** using more words than necessary. – *noun* **verbosity** the fault of being verbose, or of speaking too much.

verdant *adjective* green with grass or leaves. – *noun* **verdure** green vegetation.

verdict *noun* the decision given by a judge at the end of a trial; a person's opinion on a matter.

verdigris *noun* the greenish rust of copper, brass or bronze.

verge *noun* a border, *esp* the grassy border along the edge of a road; edge, brink: *on the verge of a mental breakdown*. – *verb* (with **on**) to be on the borderline of, close to: *It verges on the indecent*. – *noun* **verger** a church caretaker, or church official.

verify *verb* (*past tense* **verified**) to prove, show to be true, to confirm. – *adjective* **verifiable** able to be verified. – *noun* **verification.**

verily *adjective* (*old*) in truth.

verisimilitude *noun* likeness of life; appearance of truth.

verity *noun* truth. – *adjective* **veritable** true; real, genuine.

vermicelli *noun* a type of food like spaghetti but in much thinner pieces.

vermilion *adjective, noun* (of) a bright red colour.

vermin *noun* animals, insects *etc* that are considered pests, *eg* rats, mice, fleas, lice *etc*. – *adjective* **verminous** full of vermin.

vermouth *noun* a kind of drink containing white wine flavoured with wormwood.

vernacular *noun* the ordinary spoken language of a country or district. – Also *adjective*.

vernal *adjective* of the season of spring.

verruca *noun* a wart, used *esp* of one on the foot.

versatile *adjective* able to turn easily from one subject or task to another; (of a material, a tool or other object) useful in many different ways. – *noun* **versatility**.

verse *noun* a number of lines of poetry grouped according to a plan; poetry as opposed to prose; a short division of a chapter of the Bible; a line of poetry. – *noun* **version** an account from one point of view; a form: *another version of the same game*; a translation. – **versed in** knowing much about, skilled or experienced in.

versus *preposition* against (often shortened to **v**).

vertebra *noun* (*plural* **vertebrae**) one of the bones of the spine. – *noun* **vertebrate** an animal having a backbone.

vertex *noun* (*plural* **vertices**) the top or summit; the point of a cone, pyramid or angle. – *adjective* **vertical** standing upright; straight up and down.

vertigo *noun* giddiness, dizziness.

verve *noun* lively spirit, enthusiasm.

very *adverb* to a great extent or degree: *This painting is very beautiful. He ran very quickly*; exactly: *He has done the very same job for 30 years*. – *adjective* same, identical: *The very people who claimed to support him voted against him*; ideal, exactly what is wanted: *the very man for the job*; actual: *in the very act of stealing*; mere: *the very thought of blood*.

vespers *noun plural* a church service in the evening.

vessel *noun* a ship; a container, *usu* for a liquid; a tube conducting fluids in the body: *blood vessels*.

vest *noun* an undergarment for the top half of the body; (*esp US*) a waistcoat.

vestibule *noun* an entrance hall; a lobby.

vestige *noun* a trace, evidence (of something existing, being present *etc*): *no vestige of lie*. – *adjective* **vestigial** surviving only as a trace or indication that something once existed: *vestigial wings*.

vestment *noun* a ceremonial garment, *esp* part of the dress worn by clergymen during the service.

vestry *noun* (*plural* **vestries**) a room in a church in which vestments are kept.

vet *noun* short for **veterinary surgeon**. – *verb* (*past tense* **vetted**) to examine or check (and pass as correct).

vetch *noun* a type of plant of the pea family.

veteran *adjective* old, experienced. – *noun* a person who has given long service; an old soldier; (*US*) anyone who has served in the armed forces.

veterinary *adjective* having to do with the curing of diseases of animals. – *noun* **veterinary surgeon** or (*US*) **veterinarian** a doctor for animals.

veto *noun* (*plural* **vetoes**) the power or right to forbid; an act of forbidding. – *verb* (*present participle* **vetoing,** *past tense* **vetoed**) to forbid.

vex *verb* to annoy; to cause trouble to. – *noun* **vexation** the state of being vexed; something that vexes. – *adjective* **vexatious** causing trouble or annoyance.

VHF very high frequency.

via *preposition* by way of: *He travelled to Oxford via London. She came to films via small parts in the theatre*.

viable *adjective* capable of living or surviving; able to be managed, practicable. *Is this a viable proposition*?

viaduct *noun* a long bridge for carrying a railway or road over a valley, river *etc*.

viands *noun plural* (*old*) food.

vibrate *verb* to (cause to) shake, tremble or quiver; to (cause to) swing to and fro in a regular (and *usu* rapid) movement; (of sound) to resound, ring. – *adjective* **vibrant** full of energy; thrilling. – *noun* **vibration** the act of vibrating; the state of being vibrated; a rapid to-and-fro movement. – *adjective* **vibratory** of vibration.

vicar *noun* a clergyman in charge of a parish in the Church of England. – *noun* **vicarage** the house of a vicar.

vicarious *adjective* filling the place of another person; done or suffered on behalf of another person; not experienced personally but imagined through the experience of others: *vicarious pleasure*. – *adverb* **vicariously**.

vice *noun* a bad habit, a serious (moral) fault; wickedness, immorality; a kind of tool with two jaws for gripping objects firmly. – *adjective* **vicious** wicked; spiteful. – *noun* **vicious circle** a bad situation whose results cause it to get worse.

vice- *prefix* second in rank to, having authority to act in place of, as in **vice-admiral, vice-chairman, vice-president**.

viceroy *noun* a person who governs a large kingdom in the name of his king.

vice versa *adjective* the other way round: *I needed his help and vice versa (ie* he needed mine).

vicinity *noun* nearness; neighbourhood.

vicious *see* **vice**.

vicissitude *noun* a change from one state to another; (*plural*) changes of luck, ups and downs.

victim *noun* a person who is killed or harmed, intentionally or by accident: *She was the victim of a vicious attack. The firm was a victim of the financial situation*; an animal for sacrifice. – *verb* **victimize** to treat unjustly or with unnecessary harshness; to make a victim of.

victor *noun* a winner (of a contest *etc*). – *adjective* **victorious** successful in a battle or other contest. – *noun* **victory** (*plural* **victories**) success in any battle, struggle or contest.

victuals *vit'lz, noun plural* food.

video *adjective* having to do with the recording and broadcasting of TV pictures and sound; having to do with recording by video. – *noun* (*plural* **videos**) television; a videocassette recorder; a recording on videotape. – *verb* (*present participle* **videoing,** *past tense* **videoed**) to make a recording by video. – *noun* **videocassette** a cassette containing videotape. – *noun* **video-cassette recorder** a tape recorder

using videocassettes for recording and playing back TV programmes or films made on videotape. – *noun* **video game** an electronically-operated game played using a visual display unit. – *noun* **video nasty** a pornographic or horror film on videotape. – *noun* **video-tape** magnetic tape for carrying pictures and sound.

vie *verb* (*present participle* **vying,** *past tense* **vied**) (*usu* with **with**) to try to do better than.

view *noun* a sight; a range or field of sight: *a good view*; a scene; an opinion. – *verb* to look at; to watch (television); to consider. – *noun* **viewpoint** a place from which a scene is viewed; one's way of looking at a matter (also **point of view**). – **in view** in sight; in one's mind as an aim; **in view of** taking into consideration; **on view** on show; ready for inspecting; **with a view to** with the purpose or intention of.

vigil *noun* a time of watching or of keeping awake at night (sometimes before a religious festival). – *noun* **vigilance** watchfulness, alertness. – *adjective* **vigilant**. – *noun* **vigilante** a member of a group taking upon itself the task of keeping order in an unsettled or disorderly community.

vignette *noun* a little design or portrait; a short description or character sketch.

vigour *noun* a strength of body or mind, energy. – *adjective* **vigorous** strong, healthy; forceful: *a vigorous attack*.

Viking *noun* (*hist*) a Norse invader of W. Europe.

vile *adjective* wicked; very bad; disgusting. – *verb* **vilify** (*past tense* **vilified**) to say wicked things about.

villa *noun* a house, *usu* detached; a house in the country *etc* used for holidays.

village *noun* a collection of houses, not big enough to be called a town. – *noun* **villager** a person who lives in a village.

villain *noun* a wicked person, a scoundrel; a rascal. – *adjective* **villainous** wicked. – *noun* **villainy** (*plural* **villainies**) wickedness.

villein *noun* (*hist*) a serf.

vindicate *verb* to clear from blame; to justify.

vindictive *adjective* revengeful; spiteful.

vine *noun* a type of climbing plant that bears grapes; any climbing or trailing plant. – *noun* **vinery** a hot-house for growing vines. – *noun* **vineyard** a place planted with grape vines.

vinegar *noun* a sour-tasting kind of liquid made from wine, beer *etc*, used as seasoning, for pickling *etc*.

vintage *noun* the gathering of ripe grapes; the grapes gathered; wine of a particular year, *esp* when of very high quality; the time or period of origin or manufacture: – *adjective* of a vintage; (of wine) of a particular year and *usu* of very high quality; (of a play *etc*) of high quality and characteristic of the author *etc*: *vintage Shaw*. – *noun* **vintage car** one of a very early type, still able to run.

vintner *noun* a wineseller.

viola *noun* a kind of large violin; any member of the family of plants which include violets and pansies.

violate *verb* to break (a law, a treaty *etc*); to do harm to, *esp* to rape; to treat with disrespect; to disturb, interrupt. – *n* **violation**. – *noun* **violator**.

violent *adjective* acting or done with great force: *a violent storm*; caused by violence: *a violent death*; uncontrollable: *a violent temper*. – *noun* **violence** great roughness and force.

violet *noun* a kind of small bluish-purple flower.

violin *noun* a type of musical instrument with four strings, played with a bow. – *noun* **violinist** a person who plays the violin.

violoncello *see* **cello**.

VIP *abbreviation* very important person.

viper *noun see* **adder**; a vicious or treacherous person.

virago *noun* (*plural* **viragos**) a noisy, bad-tempered woman.

viral *see* **virus**.

virgin *noun* one, *esp* a woman, who has had no sexual intercourse. – *adjective* **virginal** of, like, a virgin. – **the Virgin Mary** the mother of Jesus.

virginal *noun* (often *plural*) an early type of musical instrument, with a keyboard. – *adjective see* **virgin**.

virile *adjective* manly; strong, vigorous. – *noun* **virility** manhood; manliness; strength, vigour.

virtue *noun* goodness of character and behaviour; a good quality *eg* honesty,

generosity *etc*; a good point: *One virtue of plastic crockery is that it doesn't break*. – *adjective* **virtual** in effect, though not in strict fact: *Because of the weakness of the king she was the virtual ruler*. – *adverb* **virtually**: *virtually in complete charge*. – *adjective* **virtuous** good, just, honest. – **by virtue of** because of.

virtuoso *noun* (*plural* **virtuosos**) a highly skilled performer on a musical instrument or in another art. – *noun* **virtuosity**.

virulent *adjective* full of poison; bitter, spiteful; (of a disease) dangerous. – *noun* **virulence**.

virus *noun* (*plural* **viruses**) any of several kinds of germs that are smaller than any bacteria, and cause certain diseases, as mumps, chicken pox *etc*. – *adjective* **viral**.

visa *noun* the mark put on one's passport by the authorities of a country, to show that one may travel in that country.

visage *noun* the face.

vis-à-vis *vēz-à-vē, preposition* in relation to, compared with: *his hopes vis-à-vis his abilities*.

viscera *vis'è-rà, noun plural* the inner parts of the body.

viscid *vis'id, adjective* viscous.

viscount *vī'kownt* (*masculine*), **viscountess** (*feminine*) *noun* a title of nobility next below an earl (*masculine*) or countess (*feminine*).

viscous (of a liquid) sticky, not flowing easily. – *noun* **viscosity**.

visible *adjective* to be seen. – *noun* **visibility** the clearness with which objects may be seen; the extent or range of vision as affected by fog, rain *etc*.

vision *noun* the act or power of seeing; something seen in the imagination; a strange, supernatural sight; the ability to foresee likely future events. – *adjective* **visionary** seen in imagination only, not real. – *noun* (*plural* **visionaries**) a person who forms plans which are difficult or impossible to carry out.

visit *verb* to go to see; to call on; to stay with as a guest. – *noun* a call at a person's house or at a place of interest *etc*; a short stay. – *noun* **visitation** a visit of an important official, or of a supernatural being; a great misfortune, seen as a punishment from God. – *noun* **visitor** someone who makes a visit.

visor noun a part of a helmet covering the face; a movable shade on a car's windscreen; the peak of a cap for shading the eyes.

vista noun a view, esp one seen through or along an avenue of trees, or other long, narrow opening.

visual adjective of, concerned with, or received through, sight: visual aids. – verb **visualize** to form a clear picture of in the mind. – **visual display unit** a device like a television set, on which data from a computer's memory can be displayed.

vital adjective of the greatest importance: vital information; necessary to life; of life; vigorous, energetic: a vital personality. – noun **vitality** life; liveliness, strength; ability to go on living. – verb **vitalize** to give life or vigour to. – noun plural **vitals** (old) parts of the body necessary for life.

vitamins noun plural any of a group of substances necessary for health, different ones occurring in different natural foods.

vitiate verb to spoil or damage.

vitreous adjective of, or like, glass. – verb **vitrify** (past tense **vitrified**) to make or become, glass-like.

vitriol noun sulphuric acid. – adjective **vitriolic** biting, scathing: vitriolic criticism.

vitro see **in vitro**.

vituperate verb to be rude to, abuse. – noun **vituperation**. – adjective **vituperative** abusive, very rude.

vivacious adjective lively, sprightly. – noun **vivacity** liveliness of behaviour.

viva vī vă, noun an oral examination.

vivarium noun a tank or other enclosure for keeping living creatures.

vivid adjective life-like; brilliant, striking.

vivisection noun the carrying out of experiments on living animals.

vixen noun a female fox; an ill-tempered woman.

viz adjective namely: Three games are played in this school, viz football, hockey and cricket.

vizier noun (mainly hist) a minister of state in some Eastern countries.

vocabulary noun (plural **vocabularies**) the stock or range of words used by a person or a group etc; the words of a language; a list of words in alphabetical order, with their meanings.

vocal adjective of the voice; expressing one's opinions etc loudly and fully. – noun **vocalist** a singer.

vocation noun an occupation or profession, esp one to which one feels called (by God) to dedicate oneself: Nursing is a vocation; a strong inclination or desire to follow a particular course of action or work.

vociferous adjective loud in speech, noisy.

vodka noun an alcoholic spirit made from grain or from potatoes.

vogue noun the fashion of the moment; popularity. – **in vogue** in fashion.

voice noun the sound produced from the mouth in speech or song; ability to sing; (the right to express) an opinion. – verb to express (an opinion) etc).

void adjective empty, vacant; not valid. – noun an empty space. – **void of** lacking completely.

vol. abbreviation volume.

volatile adjective (of a liquid) quickly turning into vapour; (of a person) changeable in mood or behaviour.

volcano noun (plural **volcanoes**) a mountain, usu cone-shaped, with an opening through which molten rock, ashes etc are, or have been, periodically thrown up from inside the earth. – adjective **volcanic** of volcanoes; caused or produced by heat within the earth.

vole noun any of several kinds of small rodents, including the water rat.

volition noun an act of will or of choosing: He did it of his own volition.

volley noun (plural **volleys**) a number of shots fired or missiles thrown at the same time; an outburst (of words); (in tennis) a return of a ball before it reaches the ground. – verb to shoot or throw in a volley; to return (a ball) before it reaches the ground.

volt noun the unit used in measuring the force of electricity. – noun **voltage** electrical force measured in volts.

voluble adjective (speaking) with a great flow of words. – noun **volubility**.

volume noun a book, often one of a series; the amount of space taken up by anything; amount: the volume of trade;

loudness or fullness (of sound). – *adjective* **voluminous** bulky, of great volume.

voluntary *adjective* done, or acting, by choice, not under compulsion; (working) without payment. – *noun* (*plural* **voluntaries**) a piece of organ music of the organist's choice played at a church service.

volunteer *noun* a person who offers to perform some task, service *etc* of their own accord. – *verb* to offer to do something of one's own accord; to give (information, an opinion *etc*) unasked.

voluptuous *adjective* full of, or too fond of, the pleasures of life.

vomit *verb* to throw up the contents of the stomach through the mouth. – *noun* the substance thrown up by vomiting.

voracious *adjective* very greedy, difficult to satisfy: *The boy has a voracious appetite. My daughter is a voracious reader.* – *noun* **voracity**.

vortex *noun* (*plural* **vortices** or **vortexes**) a whirlpool; a whirlwind.

votary *noun* (*plural* **votaries**) a person who has made a vow to do some good service; a devoted worshipper or admirer.

vote *verb* to give one's support to (a particular candidate, a proposal *etc*) by putting a mark on a paper, or by raising one's hand *etc*; to decide by voting. –

noun a formal expression of a wish or opinion by voting; the right to vote. – *noun* **voter** a person who votes.

vouch *verb* (with **for**) to say that one is sure of or can guarantee: *I can vouch for his courage.* – *noun* **voucher** a paper which says that money or goods will be given for it. – *verb* **vouchsafe** to give or grant (a reply, privilege *etc*).

vow *noun* a solemn promise or declaration *esp* one made to God. – *verb* to make a vow; to threaten (revenge *etc*).

vowel *noun* any of many simple sounds made by the voice that do not require the use of tongue, teeth or lips; the letters a, e, i, o, u (or various combinations of them), and sometimes y, which represent those sounds.

voyage *noun* a journey, *esp* one by sea. – *verb* to make a journey.

VSO *abbreviation* Voluntary Service Overseas.

vulgar *adjective* coarse, ill-mannered; indecent; of the common people. – *noun* **vulgarity**. – *noun* **vulgar fraction** a fraction not written as a decimal, *eg* a half written ½, not 0·5.

vulnerable *adjective* exposed to, in danger of, attack; liable to be hurt in body or feelings.

vulture *noun* a large type of bird that lives chiefly on the flesh of dead animals.

W

wad *noun* a mass or lump of loose material (as wool, cloth, paper) pressed together; a bunch of banknotes. – *noun* **wadding** soft material (*eg* cotton wool) used for packing, padding *etc*.

waddle *verb* to walk with short, unsteady steps, moving from side to side as a duck does. – Also *noun*.

wade *verb* to walk through water, mud *etc*; to get through (work, a book *etc*) with difficulty. – *noun* **wader** a type of long-legged bird that wades in search of food; (*plural*) high waterproof boots (as worn by anglers) for wading.

wadi *noun* in North Africa, the rocky bed of a river, dry except in the rainy season.

wafer *noun* a very thin, light type of biscuit, as that eaten with ice cream; a very thin slice of anything.

waffle *noun* (*esp US*) a kind of light, crisp cake made from batter, cooked in a **waffle-iron**; pointless, long-drawn-out talk. – *verb* to talk long and meaninglessly.

waft *verb* to carry or drift lightly through the air or over water.

wag verb (past tense **wagged**) to move from side to side or up and down. – noun an act of wagging; a person who is always joking. – adjective **waggish** always joking.

wage verb to carry on (a war etc). – noun (often plural) payment for work. – noun **wager** a bet. – verb to bet.

waggle verb to move from side to side in an unsteady manner. – Also noun.

wagon or **waggon** noun a strong four-wheeled vehicle for carrying loads; an open railway carriage for goods; (US) a trolley for carrying food.

wagtail noun a small black and white type of bird with a long tail which wags up and down.

waif noun an uncared-for or homeless child or other person or animal. – **waifs and strays** people, animals, without a home.

wail noun to cry or moan (for sorrow). – Also noun.

wain noun (old) a wagon.

wainscot noun the wooden lining or panelling sometimes found round (the lower part of) the walls of a room.

waist noun the narrow part of one's body, between ribs and hips. – noun **waist-coat** a short, sleeveless jacket (by men, worn under the outer jacket).

wait verb to put off or delay action (until a certain event occurs); (with **for**) to remain in expectation or readiness for (a person or thing), to await; to act as a waiter. – noun a delay; (plural) singers of Christmas carols. – noun **waiter** (masculine), **waitress** (feminine) a person whose job it is to serve people at table. – noun **waiting list** a list of people needing, and waiting for, something. – noun **waiting room** a room in which to wait (at a railway station, clinic etc). – **wait (up)on** to serve (someone) at table; to act as a servant to.

waive verb to give up (a claim or right). – noun **waiver** the act of waiving; a document indicating this.

wake verb (past tense **woke** or **waked**, past participle **woken** or **wakened**) (often with **up**) (to cause) to stop sleeping. – noun a night of watching beside a dead body; a feast or holiday; a streak of foamy water left in the track of a ship. – adjective **wakeful** not sleeping, unable to sleep. – verb **waken** to wake, arouse or be aroused. – adjective **waking** (of, belonging to the state of) being or becoming awake. – **in the wake of** immediately behind or after.

walk verb to cause to move along on foot; to travel along (the streets etc) on foot. – noun an act of walking; a manner of walking; a distance (to be) walked over; a place for walking: a covered walk. – noun **walkie-talkie** a wireless set for sending and receiving messages, carried on the body. – noun **walking stick** a stick used for support when walking. – noun **walk-over** an easy victory. – **walk of life** one's rank or occupation; **walk the plank** (hist) to be put to death by pirates by being made to walk off the end of a plank sticking out over a ship's side.

Walkman® noun (plural **Walkmans** or **Walkmen**) a brand of personal stereo.

wall noun something built of stone, brick etc used to separate, or to enclose; the side of a building. – verb (with **in, up, off** etc) to enclose or separate with a wall. – noun **wallflower** a kind of sweet-smelling spring flower; a person who is continually without a partner at a dance etc. – noun **wallpaper** paper used in house decorating for covering walls.

wallaby noun (plural **wallabies**) a small kind of kangaroo.

wallet noun a small flat case of a soft material (as leather etc) for holding bank notes, personal documents etc.

wallop verb (coll) to beat, to hit. – Also noun.

wallow verb to roll about with enjoyment (in water, mud etc).

walnut noun a type of tree whose wood is used for making furniture; its nut.

walrus noun (plural **walruses**) a large type of sea animal, like a seal, with two long tusks.

waltz noun (plural **waltzes**) a kind of dance with a whirling motion performed by couples; music (with three beats to each bar) for this. – verb to dance a waltz.

wan adjective pale and sickly looking.

wand noun a long slender rod as used by a conjuror, or, in stories etc, by fairies, magicians etc.

wander verb to go from place to place, to roam with no definite purpose; to go astray; to be disordered in one's mind because of illness *etc*. – *noun* **wanderer**. – *noun* **wanderlust** a keen desire for travel.

wane *verb* to become smaller (opposite of **wax**); to lose power, importance *etc*. – **on the wane** becoming less.

wangle *verb* to get, manage, achieve, through craftiness, skilful planning *etc*.

want *verb* to wish for; to need; to lack. – *noun* poverty; scarcity; need; lack. – *adjective* **wanted** looked for, *esp* by the police. – *adjective* **wanting** absent, missing; without; not good enough; feeble-minded; (with **in**) lacking.

wanton *adjective* (of a destructive act, of cruelty *etc*) thoughtless, pointless, without motive.

war *noun* an armed struggle, *esp* between nations. – *verb* (*present participle* **warring**) (with **against**) to fight in a war, make war against. – *noun* **war-cry** a phrase or word shouted aloud in battle, for encouragement. – *noun* **warfare** the carrying on of war, armed struggle. – *noun* **warhead** the part of a missile containing the explosive. – *adjective* **warlike** fond of war; threatening war. – *noun* **warrior** a fighting man, a great fighter. – *noun* **warship** a ship equipped for war, with guns *etc*. – **on the warpath** in a fighting or angry mood.

warble *verb* to sing like a bird, to trill. – *noun* **warbler** any of several types of singing birds.

ward *verb* (with **off**) to keep off, defend oneself against (a blow *etc*). – *noun* in a hospital *etc* a room containing a number of beds; one of the parts into which a town is divided for voting; a person who is in the care of a guardian. – *noun* **warden** a person who guards a game reserve *etc*; a person in charge of a hostel or college. – *noun* **warder** (*masculine*), **wardress** (*feminine*) a prison guard. – *noun* **wardrobe** a cupboard for clothes; a person's supply of clothes. – *noun* **wardroom** a room for officers on a warship.

ware *noun* manufactured material (often pottery); now *usu* used as part of a word: *earthenware; glassware: ironware; (pl)* goods for sale. – *noun* **warehouse** a building where goods are stored.

warm *adjective* fairly hot; (of clothes) keeping the wearer warm; (of a person or their behaviour *etc*) earnest, sincere, friendly, loving. – *verb* to make or become warm. – *adjective* **warm-blooded** having a blood temperature

higher than that of the surrounding atmosphere. – *adjective* **warm-hearted** kind, generous. – *noun* **warmth**.

warn *verb* to tell (a person) beforehand about possible danger, misfortune *etc*: *I warned him about the icy roads;* to give (cautionary) advice to: *I warned him not to be late*. – *noun* **warning** something (*eg* a person's words, a notice *etc*) that warns.

warp *verb* to (cause to) become twisted out of shape; to cause to think, reason *etc* wrongly: *His previous experiences had warped his judgement*. – *noun* the threads stretched lengthwise on a loom, to be crossed by the **weft**.

warrant *noun* something which gives a person the authority or right to do a certain thing; a certificate *etc* granting such authority: *a search warrant*. – *verb* to justify, be a good enough reason for: *Such a crime does not warrant such punishment*. – *adjective* **warranted** guaranteed. – **I warrant you** or **I'll warrant** you may be sure, I assure you.

warren *noun* a place full of rabbit burrows; a building or built-up area with many confusing passages.

wart *noun* a small hard growth on the skin. – *noun* **wart-hog** a kind of wild pig found in Africa.

wary *adjective* cautious, on one's guard. – *adverb* **warily**. – *noun* **wariness**.

was *see* **be**.

wash *verb* to clean with water, soap *etc*; to clean oneself with water *etc*; (of water) to flow over or against; to sweep (away, along *etc*) by force of water. – *noun* (*plural* **washes**) a washing; a streak of foamy water left behind by a moving boat; a liquid with which anything is washed; a thin coat of paint *etc*. – *noun* **washer** a person or thing that washes; a flat ring of metal, rubber *etc* for keeping nuts or joints tight. – *noun* **washerwoman** (*old*) a woman who is paid to wash clothes. – *noun* **washhand basin** a fixed bowl (with taps and a plug) in which to wash one's hands and face. – *noun* **washing** the act of cleaning by water; clothes (to be) washed. – *noun* **washing machine** a machine (*usu* driven by electricity) for washing clothes. – **wash one's hands of** to have nothing further to do with; **wash up** to wash dishes *etc*.

wasp *noun* a stinging, winged type of insect, with a slender, yellow and black striped body.

wassail (*old*) *verb* to hold a merry drinking meeting. – Also *noun*.

waste *adjective* thrown away, rejected as useless or worthless: *Pick up all the waste paper. We burn the waste materials*; (of ground or land) uncultivated, or barren and desolate. – *verb* to use or spend (money, time, energy, materials) extravagantly, or with too little result or profit; to (cause to) decay or wear away gradually. – *noun* extravagant use, squandering; rubbish, waste material; uncultivated land; an unbroken expanse, a stretch (of water, snow *etc*). – *noun* **wastage** amount wasted; loss through decay or (wasteful) use. – *adjective* **wasteful** involving or causing waste, extravagant. – *noun* **waster** or **wastrel** an idle, good-for-nothing person. – *noun* **wastepaper basket** a basket for (paper) rubbish. – *noun* **wastepipe** a pipe for carrying away dirty water or semi-liquid waste matter.

watch *verb* to look at, observe, closely; (often with **over**) to look after, to mind; (*old*) to keep awake. – *noun* (*plural* **watches**) the act of keeping guard; one who keeps, or those who keep, guard; a sailor's period of duty on deck (*usu* four hours); a kind of small clock for the pocket or wrist. – *adjective* **watchful** alert, cautious. – *noun* **watchman** a man who guards a building *etc*, *esp* at night. – *noun* **watchword** a motto or slogan.

water *noun* a clear liquid without taste or smell when pure, which falls as rain; any collection of it, as an ocean, sea, lake, river *etc*; saliva, urine or other bodily fluids. – *verb* to supply with water; to dilute or mix with water; (of the mouth) to fill with saliva; (of the eyes) to fill with tears. – *noun* **water biscuit** a crisp kind of biscuit, a cracker. – *noun* **water butt** a large barrel for rain water. – *noun* **water-closet** (*usu* **WC**) a toilet, a lavatory. – *noun* **water-colour** a paint used by mixing with water, not with oil; a painting done with this paint. – *noun* **watercress** a small type of plant found beside streams, used for salads *etc*. – *noun* **waterfall** a place where a river falls from a height, *usu* over a ledge of rock. – *noun* **waterhen** a dark-coloured type of bird which lives about ponds or rivers. – *noun* **waterlily** a type of plant growing in ponds *etc* with flat floating leaves and large flowers. – *adjective* **waterlogged** filled with water; saturated with, or soaked with, water. – *noun* **watermain** a large underground pipe carrying a public water supply. – *noun* **watermark** a faint design showing the maker's name, crest *etc* in a sheet of writing paper. – *noun* **watermelon** a type of large, very juicy, fruit. – *noun* **watermill** a mill driven by water. – *noun* **water polo** a type of game played by swimmers (seven on each side) with a floating ball. – *adjective* **waterproof** not allowing water to pass through. – *noun* an outer garment made of waterproof material. – *noun* **water rat** a kind of vole. – *noun* **watershed** a ridge or line separating the valleys of two rivers. – *adjective* **watertight** so closely fitted or made that water cannot leak through. – *noun* **waterway** a channel along which ships can sail. – *noun* **waterwheel** a wheel moved by water. – *noun plural* **waterworks** the place where the water of a town is made pure and stored. – *adjective* **watery** full of, or like, water; tasteless, dull.

watt *noun* a unit of electric power. – *noun* **wattage** electric power measured in watts.

wattle *noun* twigs and branches interwoven, used for fences *etc*; an Australian type of tree; a fleshy part hanging from the neck of a turkey.

wave *noun* a moving ridge on the surface of the water; anything resembling this, as a ridge or curve in the hair; a vibration travelling through the air or through space conveying light, sound *etc*; a gesture made with the hand; a rush of anything (as of despair, enthusiasm, crime *etc*). – *verb* to make a sign with the hand; to (cause to) move to and fro, or flutter; to (cause to) curl or curve. – *noun* **wavelength** the distance from one (high, low *etc*) point on a wave or vibration to the next similar point. – *adjective* **wavy** having waves.

waver *verb* to be unsteady or uncertain, to falter.

wax *noun* the sticky, fatty substance of which bees make their cells; any substance like it, as that in the ear; a quickly hardening substance used for sealing letters *etc*. – *adjective* made of wax. – *verb* to rub with wax; to grow, increase (opposite of **wane**). – *adjective* **waxen** made of, or like, wax; pale. – *noun plural* **waxworks** a place where wax models of well-known people are shown. – *adjective* **waxy** of, or like, wax.

way noun an opening, a passage: *the way out*; road, path; room to go forward or to pass: *to block the way*; direction: *He went that way*; route: *Do you know the way?*; distance: *a long way*; condition: *in a bad way*; means, method: *Find a way of doing this*; manner: *in a clumsy way*; one's own wishes or choice: *He always gets his own way*. – noun **wayfarer** a traveller, *usu* oh foot. – verb **waylay** to wait for and stop (a person). – **-ways** (used with another word) in the direction of: *lengthways*: *sideways*. — noun **wayside** the edge of a road or path. – Also *adjective*. – adjective **wayward** wilful, following one's own way. – **by the way** incidentally, in passing; **by way of** travelling through; as if, with the purpose of: *He did it by way of helping me*; **in the way** blocking one's progress; **make one's way** to go (to).

WC abbreviation water-closet.

we pronoun the word used by a speaker or writer in mentioning himself or herself together with other people (as the subject of a verb): *We chased them away from the fire.*

weak adjective not strong, feeble; lacking determination, easily persuaded; easily overcome: *weak opposition*. – verb **weaken** to make or become weak. – noun **weakling** a person or animal lacking strength. – adjective **weakly** lacking strength, sickly. – noun **weakness** lack of strength; a fault; a special fondness (for): *a weakness for chocolate*. – adjective **weak-kneed** lacking determination.

weal noun a raised mark on the skin caused by a blow from a whip *etc*. **wealth** noun riches; a large quantity: *a wealth of information*. – adjective **wealthy** rich.

wean verb to make (a child or other young animal) used to food other than (the mother's) milk; (with **from**) to cause (a person) gradually to give up (a bad habit *etc*).

weapon noun an instrument used for fighting, as a sword, gun *etc*; any means of attack.

wear verb (past tense **wore**, past participle **worn**) to be dressed in, to have on the body; to arrange (one's hair *etc*) in a particular way; to have (a beard, moustache) on the face; to damage, to make gradually less, by use, by rubbing *etc*; to be damaged, become less, in this way; to last: *to wear well*. – noun use by wearing: *for my own wear*; damage by

use; ability to last; clothes *etc*: *school wear*. – adjective **wearable** fit to be worn. – noun **wearer**. – adjective **wearing** tiring, exhausting. – adjective **worn** damaged by use; (also **worn-out**) tired. – **wear and tear** damage by ordinary use; **wear off** to pass away gradually; **wear on** to become later: *The afternoon wore on*; **wear out** to make or become unfit for further use; to exhaust (*adjective* **worn-out**).

weary adjective tired, having used up one's strength or patience; tiring, boring. – verb (past tense **wearied**) to make or become tired, bored or impatient. – adjective **wearisome** causing tiredness, boredom or impatience. – **weary of** tired of, bored with.

weasel noun a type of small wild animal with a long and slender body, that lives on mice, birds *etc*.

weather noun the state of the atmosphere (heat, coldness, cloudiness *etc*). – verb to (cause to) dry, wear away, become discoloured *etc*, through exposure to the air; to come safely through (a storm, difficulty *etc*). – adjective **weatherbeaten** showing signs of having been out in all weathers. – noun **weathercock** or **weathervane** a flat piece of metal (often in the shape of a cock) that swings round with, and shows the direction of, the wind.

weave verb (past tense **wove**, past participle **woven**) to pass threads over and under each other on a loom *etc* to form cloth; to plait cane *etc*; to put together (a story, plan *etc*); to move in and out between objects, or to move from side to side: *He wove his way through the traffic*. – noun **weaver** a person who weaves.

web noun the net made by a spider, a cobweb; the skin between the toes of ducks, swans, frogs *etc*; something woven. – adjective **webbed** (of feet) having the toes joined by a web. – noun **webbing** a type of strong, woven tape of nylon *etc*, used for belts *etc*. – adjective **web-footed** or **web-toed** having webbed feet or toes.

wed verb (past tense **wedded**) to marry. – noun **wedding** marriage; a marriage ceremony. – noun **wedlock** the state of being married.

we'd short for **we would** or **we should** or **we had.**

wedge noun a piece of wood, metal *etc* thick at one end but sloping to a thin edge at the other used in splitting wood, stone *etc*, forcing two surfaces apart, or for fixing firmly (doors *etc*); anything shaped like a wedge. – *verb* to fix, or to become fixed, with or as if with a wedge; to push or squeeze (in): *He wedged himself in amongst the crowd.*

Wednesday *noun* the fourth day of the week.

wee *adjective* (mainly *Scots*) small, tiny.

weed *noun* any useless, troublesome plant; a weak, worthless person; (*plural*) a widow's mourning clothes. – *verb* to clear (a garden *etc*) of weeds. – *adjective* **weedy** full of weeds; like a weed; (of a man) very thin and weak, unmanly.

week *noun* the space of seven days, *esp* from Sunday to Saturday; the working days of the week, not Saturday and Sunday. – *noun* **weekday** any day except Saturday and Sunday. – *noun* **weekend** the time from Saturday to Monday. – *adjective* **weekly** happening, or done, once a week. – *adverb* once a week. – *noun* (*plural* **weeklies**) a newspaper, magazine *etc* coming out once a week.

weep *verb* to shed tears; to ooze or drip: *a weeping wound*. – *adjective* **weeping** (of the willow tree *etc*) having drooping branches.

weevil *noun* any of several types of small beetles that destroy grain, flour *etc*.

weft *see* **warp.**

weigh *verb* to find out how heavy a thing is (by putting it on a scale *etc*); to have a certain heaviness: *It weighs 1 kilogramme*; to raise (a ship's anchor); (of burdens, cares *etc*) to press down, be heavy or troublesome; to consider (a matter, a point) carefully, to be of importance. – *noun* **weighbridge** a large scale for weighing vehicles. – *noun* **weight** the amount that anything weighs; a piece of metal weighing a certain amount (*eg* a 100 gramme weight *etc*); something heavy, a load or burden; importance. – *verb* to make heavy by adding or attaching a weight. – *adjective* **weightless**. – *noun* **weightlessness** absence of the pull of gravity. – *adjective* **weighty** heavy; important. – **weigh in** to test one's weight before a boxing match; **weigh out** to measure out a quantity by weighing it on a scale.

weir *noun* a dam across a stream.

weird *adjective* mysterious, supernatural; odd, strange.

welcome *verb* to receive with kindness or pleasure; to accept or undergo gladly: *I welcome the challenge.* – *noun* a welcoming, a kindly reception. – *adjective* received with gladness; causing gladness. – **welcome!** *interjection* used to express a greeting to a guest. – **welcome (to)** permitted (to do or take something): *You are welcome to help yourself;* **you're welcome!** polite expression used in reply to an expression of thanks.

weld *verb* to join (pieces of metal *etc*) by pressure, with or without heating; to join closely. – *noun* a joint made by welding. – *noun* **welder.**

welfare *noun* comfort, good health, freedom from want. – *noun* **welfare state** country with health service, insurance against unemployment, pensions for those who cannot work *etc*.

well *noun* a spring of water; a shaft (*usu* circular) made in the earth so as to obtain water, oil *etc*; any similar enclosed space, as that round which a staircase winds. – *verb* (often with **up**) to rise up and gush. – *adjective* in good health. – *adverb* (*comparative* **better,** *superlative* **best**) in a good and correct manner: *to speak well;* thoroughly: *He was well beaten;* successfully: *to do well;* conveniently: *That will fit in well with my plans.* – *interjection* expressing surprise, or used in explaining, narrating *etc*. – *adjective* **well-advised** wise. – *noun* **well-being** welfare; contentment. – *adjective* **well-bred** or **well-mannered** having good manners. – *adjective* **well-disposed** (with **to** or **towards**) inclined to favour. – *adjective* **well-informed** having or showing knowledge. – *adjective* **well-known** familiar; celebrated, famous. – *adjective* **well-meaning** having good intentions. – *adjective* **well-meant** rightly, kindly intended. – *adjective* **well-off** rich. – *adjective* **well-read** having read many good books. – *adjective* **well-to-do** rich. – *noun* **well-wisher** someone who wishes a person success. – **as well (as)** in addition (to); **it is well** or **as well** or **just as well** it is a good thing, fortunate.

we'll short for **we shall** or **will.**

wellingtons *noun plural* high rubber boots covering the lower part of the legs.

welsh rarebit *noun* a dish made of cheese melted on toast.

welt *noun* a firm edging or band (as on a garment, at the wrist, waist *etc*); a weal.

welter verb to roll about or wallow. –
noun a state of great disorder; a confused mass: a welter of information about
holiday travel.

wench noun (plural **wenches**) (old) a young
woman, a girl.

wend: wend one's way to make one's
way (slowly).

went see **go**.

wept see **weep**.

were see **be**.

we're short for **we are**.

werewolf noun (myth) a person supposed
to be able to change for a time into a
wolf.

west noun one of the four chief directions,
that in which the sun sets. – Also
adjective, adverb. – adjective **westerly**
lying or moving towards the west; (of
wind) from the west. – adjective **western** in, of, belonging to, to the west. –
noun a film or story about the life of the
early settlers in the western United
States (the **Wild West**). – noun **wester-
ner** a person belonging to the west. –
adjective **westernmost** most westerly;
adjective **westward** towards the west. –
Also adverb (often **westwards**).

wet adjective containing, soaked with,
covered with, water or other liquid;
rainy: a wet day. – noun water; rain. –
verb (past tense **wet** or **wetted**) to make
wet. – noun **wet suit** a suit for wearing
in water, that allows water to pass
through but retains body heat.

whack noun a loud slap or blow. – Also v.

whale noun a very large kind of mammal
(not fish) living in the sea. – verb to
catch whales. – noun **whalebone** a light
bendable substance obtained from the
upper jaw of certain whales. – noun
whale oil oil obtained from the blubber
of a whale. – noun **whaler** a person or
ship engaged in catching whales.

wharf noun (plural **wharfs** or **wharves**) a
landing stage for loading and unload-
ing ships. – noun **wharfinger** a person
who looks after a wharf.

what adjective, pronoun used to indicate
something about which a question is
being asked: What street is this? What are
you doing? – adjective any . . . that: Give
me what books you have. – conjunction
anything that: I'll take what you can give
me. – adjective, adv, pronoun used for
emphasis in exclamations: What clothes
she wears! What bad taste she has! You did
what! – pronoun , adjective **whatever**
anything (that): Show me whatever you
have; no matter what: whatever happens.
– adjective **whatsoever** at all: nothing
whatsoever to do with me. – **what about?**
used in asking whether the listener
would like (to do) something: What
about a glass of milk? – **what if?** what will
or would happen if . . .?: What if he
comes back? – **what with . . . and**
because of: What with having no exercise
and being overweight, he had a heart attack.

wheat noun a grain from which the flour
used for making bread etc is made. –
adjective **wheaten** made of wheat;
wholemeal. – noun **wheatear** a type of
small bird, visiting Britain in summer. –
noun **wheat germ** the vitamin-rich
embryo of wheat. – noun **wheat-meal**
meal made of wheat esp wholemeal. –
Also adjective.

wheedle verb to beg, to coax, using
flattery etc.

wheel noun a circular frame or disc
turning on an axle, used for transporting things etc; a steering-wheel (of
a car etc). – verb to move or push on
wheels; to turn like a wheel or in a wide
curve; to turn (round) suddenly: She
wheeled round in surprise. – noun
wheelbarrow a handcart with one
wheel in front, two handles and legs
behind. – noun **wheelchair** a chair on
wheels for an invalid. – noun
wheelhouse the shelter in which a
ship's steering-wheel is placed. – noun
wheelwright a person who makes
wheels and carriages.

wheeze verb to breathe with a whistling
or croaking sound and with difficulty:

whelk noun a type of small shellfish, used
as food.

whelp noun a young lion; a puppy. – verb
(of lions, dogs etc) to give birth to
young ones.

when adverb at what time?: When did you
arrive? – adverb, conjunction (at, during)
the time at which: I know when you left. I
fell when I was coming in. – relative pronoun
at which: at the time when I saw him. –
conjunction seeing that, since: Why walk
when you have a car? – adverb **whence**
(old) from what place?: Whence did you
appear? – conjunction (to the place) from
which: He's gone back (to the country)
whence he came. – adverb, conjunction
whenceforth (old) whence. – adverb,
conjunction **whenever** at any given time:

Come and see me whenever you're ready; at every time: *I go whenever I get the chance.*

where *adverb, conjunction* to or in what place (?): *Where are you going? I wonder where we are.* – *relative pronoun, conjunction* (in the place) in which, (to the place) to which: *Sit in the seat where you were put! Go where he tells you to go. It's still where it was.* – *adverb, conjunction* **whereabouts** near or in what place?: *Whereabouts is it? I don't know whereabouts it is.* – *noun* the place where a person or thing is: *I don't know his whereabouts.* – *conjunction* **whereas** when in fact: *He thought I was lying, whereas I was telling the truth*; but, on the other hand: *He's tall, whereas I'm short.* – *adverb, conjunction* **whereupon** at or after which time, event *etc.* – *adverb* **wherever** to what place?: *Wherever did you go?* – *conjunction* to any place: *wherever you may go.* – *noun* **wherewithal** the means of doing something; money.

wherry *noun* (*plural* **wherries**) a type of shallow, light boat.

whet *verb* (*past tense* **whetted**) to sharpen (a knife *etc*) by rubbing; to make (one's desire, appetite *etc*) keener. – *noun* **whetstone** a stone on which knives *etc* may be sharpened.

whether *conjunction* if: *I don't know whether it's possible (or not).*

which *adjective, pronoun* used (often in questions) to refer to a particular person or thing from a group: *Which (colour) do you like best?*; the one that: *Show me which (dress) you would like.* – *relative pron*: *This church, which will soon be pulled down, is very old: I bought the chair which you are sitting on.* – *adjective, pronoun* **whichever** any (one), no matter which: *I'll take whichever (book) you don't want. I saw trees whichever way I turned.* – **which is which** which is one and which is the other: *Mary and Susan are twins and I can't tell which is which.*

whiff *noun* a sudden puff (of scent, smoke, gas *etc*).

while or **whilst** *conjunction* during the time that: *while I'm at the office*; although: *While I sympathize, I can't really help.* – *noun* **while** a space of time. – *verb* (with **away**) to pass (time) without boredom: *He whiled away the time by reading.*

whim *noun* a sudden thought, fancy, or desire. – *adjective* **whimsical** full of whims, fanciful; humorous. – *noun* **whimsy** (*plural* **whimsies**) a whim.

whimper *verb* to cry with a low, whining voice. – Also *noun.*

whin *noun* gorse.

whine *verb* to utter a high-pitched, complaining cry; to complain unnecessarily. – Also *noun.*

whinge *verb* (*present participle* **whingeing**) to whine, complain peevishly. – *noun* a peevish complaint. – *adjective* **whingeing.** – *noun* **whinger.**

whinny *verb* (*present participle* **whinnying,** *past tense* **whinnied**) (of horses) to neigh. – Also *noun* (*plural* **whinnies**).

whip *noun* a lash, with a handle, for punishing or urging on (horses *etc*); in parliament, a member of a party whose duty it is to see that the party-members are there to give their vote when needed. – *verb* (*past tense* **whipped**) to hit, punish, drive, with a lash; to beat (eggs, cream *etc*) into a froth; to snatch (away, off, out, up *etc*): *to whip out a revolver*; to move fast, like a whip. – *noun* **whip-hand** the advantage in a fight, argument *etc.* – *noun* **whippersnapper** a small, unimportant, impertinent person. – *noun* **whipping** a beating with a whip.

whippet *noun* a breed of racing dog, like a small greyhound.

whir or **whirr** *noun* a sound of fast, continuous whirling. – *verb* (*past tense* **whirred**) to move, whirl, with a buzzing noise.

whirl *verb* to turn round quickly; to carry (off, away *etc*) quickly. – *noun* a fast round-and-round movement; great excitement, confusion: *Everyone was in a whirl over the wedding arrangements.* – *noun* **whirlpool** a place in a river, sea *etc* where the current moves in a circle. – *noun* **whirlwind** a very violent current of wind with a whirling motion.

whisk *verb* to move, carry, sweep, quickly and lightly; to beat or whip (a mixture). – *noun* a quick sweeping movement; a type of kitchen utensil for beating eggs or mixtures; a small bunch of twigs, bristles *etc* used to dust, brush *etc.*

whisker *noun* (*usu plural*) hair on the sides of a man's face; a long bristle on the upper lip of a cat *etc.*

whisky or (*Irish* and *US*) **whiskey** *noun* (*plural* **whiskies** or **whiskeys**) a kind of alcoholic spirit made from grain.

whisper *verb* to speak very softly, using the breath only, not the voice; to make a soft, rustling sound. – Also *noun.*

whist *noun* a type of card game for four players.

whistle *verb* to make a high-pitched sound by forcing breath through the lips or teeth; to make such a sound with an instrument; to move with such a sound, as a bullet or arrow does. – *noun* the sound made by whistling; any instrument for whistling.

whit *noun* a tiny bit: *not a whit better*.

white *adjective* of the colour of pure snow; pale or light-coloured: *white wine*; of a pale-coloured complexion. – *noun* something white; a person with a pale-coloured complexion of European race; the part of an egg surrounding the yolk. – *noun* **white ant** a termite. – *noun* **whitebait** the young of herring or sprats. – *noun* **white elephant** something useless and unwanted, *esp* something costly and troublesome to maintain. – *adjective* **white-hot** having reached a degree of heat at which metals *etc* glow with a white light (hotter than **red-hot**). – *noun* **white knight** (*stock exchange slang*) a company which comes to the aid of another facing an unwelcome takeover bid, by making a more favourable bid. – *verb* **whiten** to make or become white or whiter. – *noun* **whiteness.** – *noun* **white paper** a statement (printed on white paper) issued by the government for the information of parliament. – *noun* **whitewash** a mixture of whiting, or lime, and water, for whitening walls *etc*. – *verb* to put whitewash on; to (try to) cover up the faults of, give a good appearance to. – *noun* **whiting** a small type of fish related to the cod.

whither *adverb, conjunction* (*old*) to what place(?).

whitlow *noun* an infected swelling beside the finger or toenail.

Whitsun or **Whit** *adjective* of, or of the week beginning with, the seventh Sunday after Easter.

whittle *verb* to pare or cut (wood *etc*) with a knife; (with **away** or **down**) to make gradually less: *She whittled away his savings*.

whiz or **whizz** *verb* (*past tense* **whizzed**) to move with a hissing sound, as an arrow does; to move very fast. – *noun* **whiz** or **whizz kid** a person who achieves rapid success while relatively young.

WHO *abbreviation* World Health Organization.

who *pronoun* used (often in questions) to refer to a person or people unknown or unnamed (only as the subject of a verb): *Who is that woman in the green hat?*; (*coll*) used as the object in a sentence: *Who did you choose? Who did you give it to?* – *relative pronoun*: *I knew the woman who died. Do you know who those people are?* – *pronoun* **whoever** any person or people. – *pronoun* **whom** (often in questions) used to refer to a person or people unknown or unnamed (only as the object of a sentence): *Whom did you see? To whom shall I speak?* – *conjunction*: *Do you know to whom I gave it?* – *relative pronoun*: *the person whom I liked best.*

whole *adjective* complete; consisting of all, with nothing or no one missing; not broken; in good health. – *noun* the entire thing. – *noun* **wholefood** food produced without the aid of artificial fertilizers *etc*, and processed as little as possible. – *adjective* **wholehearted** enthusiastic, generous. – *noun* **wholemeal** flour made from the entire wheat grain. – Also *adjective*. – *noun* **wholesale** the sale of goods in large quantities to a shop *etc* from which they can be bought in small quantities by ordinary buyers. – *adjective* buying, selling, bought, sold, through wholesale; on a large scale: *wholesale killing*. – *adjective* **wholesome** giving health, healthy. – *adverb* **wholly** entirely, altogether. – **on the whole** when everything is taken into account.

who'll short for **who will** or **who shall.**

whom *see* **who.**

whoop *noun* a loud cry, rising in pitch. – Also *verb*. – *noun* **whooping-cough** an infectious type of disease in which violent bouts of coughing are followed by a whoop as the breath is drawn in.

whore *noun* a female prostitute.

whortleberry *noun* bilberry.

whose *adjective, pronoun* belonging to whom, which person(?): *Whose (jacket) is this?* – *relative pron*: *Show me the boy whose father is a policeman.* – *conj*: *Do you know whose pen this is?*

why *adverb, pronoun* for which (reason) (?): *Why are you not finished? Tell me (the reason) why you came here.* – **the whys and wherefores** (all) the reasons, details.

wick *noun* the twisted threads (of cotton *etc*) in a candle or lamp which draw up the oil or grease to the flame.

wicked *adjective* evil, sinful; mischievous, spiteful. – *noun* **wickedness.**

wicker *adjective* (of a chair *etc*) made of woven willow twigs *etc*.

wicket *noun* a small gate or door, *esp* in or beside a larger one; (in cricket) the set of three stumps, or one of these, at which the ball is bowled; the ground between the bowler and the batsman.

wide *adjective* broad, not narrow; stretching far; measuring a certain amount from side to side: *5 centimetres wide*. – *adverb* off the target: *The shots went wide*; (often with **apart**) far apart: *to hold one's arms wide*. – *adjective* **wide-awake** fully awake; alert. – *noun* **wide-boy** (*slang*) an astute or wily (often business) person. – *adjective* **wide-eyed** with eyes wide open (in surprise *etc*). – *adverb* **widely** over a wide area; among many: *widely believed*; far apart. – *verb* **widen** to make or become wide or wider. – *noun* **wideness.** – *adjective* **wide-open** opened to the full extent. – *adjective* **widespread** spread over a large area or among many: *a widespread belief*. – *noun* **width** measurement across, from side to side; large extent. – **wide of the mark** off the target, inaccurate.

widow *noun* a woman whose husband is dead. – *noun* **widower** a man whose wife is dead.

width *see* **wide.**

wield *verb* to swing or handle (a cricket bat, sword *etc*); to use (power, authority *etc*).

wife *noun* (*plural* **wives**) a married woman; the woman to whom a man is married.

wig *noun* an artificial covering of hair for the head.

wiggle *verb* to (cause to) move from side to side with jerky or twisting movements. – Also *noun*. – *adjective* **wiggly.**

wigwam *noun* a conical tent of skins, as formerly made by N. American Indians.

wild *adjective* (of animals) not tamed; (of plants) not cultivated in a garden *etc*; uncivilized, unruly, uncontrolled, violent; (of weather) stormy; frantic; mad: *wild with anxiety*; (of a remark, a guess *etc*) rash, inaccurate. – *noun* (*usu plural*) an uncultivated or uncivilized region. – *noun* **wild boar** a wild type of pig. – *noun* **wild cat** a wild type of European cat. – *adjective* **wildcat** (of a workers' strike) not supported or permitted by trade union officials. – *noun* **wildfire** lightning without thunder. – *noun* **wildfowl** wild birds, *esp* those shot as game. – *noun* **wild-goose chase** a troublesome and useless errand. – *noun* **wildlife** wild animals, birds *etc*, in their natural habitats. – **like wildfire** very quickly.

wilderness *noun* a wild, uncultivated, or desolate region.

wile *noun* a crafty trick. – *adjective* **wily.**

will *noun* the power to choose or decide; desire: *against my will*; determination: *the will to win*; feeling towards someone: *a sign of goodwill*; a written statement about what is to be done with one's property after one's death. – *verb* (*past tense* **willed**) to (try to) influence someone by exercising one's will: *He willed her to win*; to hand down (property *etc*) by will; (*past tense* **would**) also used to form future tenses of other verbs when the subject is **he, she, it, you** or **they**: *You will see me there*; (*coll*) often used for the same purpose when the subject is **I** or **we**: *I will tell you later*; used for emphasis, or to express a promise, when the subject is **I** or **we**: *I will do it if possible*. (*See* also **shall, would**). – *adjective* **wilful** fond of having one's own way; intentional: *wilful damage*. – *adjective* **willing** ready to do what is asked; eager. – **at will** as or when one chooses; **with a will** eagerly.

will-o'-the-wisp *noun* a pale light sometimes seen by night over marshy places.

willow *noun* a type of tree with long slender branches, or its wood (used in cricket bats). – *adjective* **willowy** slender, graceful: *a willowy figure*.

willynilly *adverb* whether one wishes or not.

wilt *verb* (of flowers) to droop; to lose strength: *He wilts in hot weather*.

wily *see* **wile.**

wimp *noun* (*coll*) an ineffectual person.

win *verb* (*past tense* **won**) to gain by contest (a victory *etc*), by luck (money in gambling *etc*), by effort (the love of someone *etc*); to come first in a contest, to be victorious; (often with **over**) to gain the support or friendship of: *He finally won over his mother-in-law*. – *noun* an act of winning; a victory. – *adjective* **winning** victorious, successful; charming, attractive: *a winning smile*. – *noun* *plural* **winnings** money *etc* that has been won.

wince *verb* to shrink or start back in pain *etc*, to flinch: *Her playing of the violin made him wince.*

winceyette *noun* a type of brushed cotton cloth.

winch *noun* (*plural* **winches**) a handle or crank for turning a wheel; a machine for lifting things up, worked by winding a rope round a revolving cylinder. – **winch up** to lift up with a winch.

wind¹ *noun* air in motion, a current of air; breath; air carrying a scent (of game *etc*); air or gas in the stomach or intestines; the wind instruments in an orchestra. – *verb* to put out of breath. – *noun* **windfall** a fruit blown from a tree; an unexpected gain or advantage, *eg* a sum of money. – *noun* **wind instrument** any of many kinds of musical instruments sounded by wind, *esp* by the breath. – *noun* **windjammer** a type of sailing ship. – *noun* **windmill** a type of mill whose machinery is driven by sails which are moved by the wind, used for pumping water, grinding grain *etc*. – *noun* **windpipe** the tube leading from the mouth to the lungs. – *noun* **windscreen** or (*US*) **windshield** a pane of glass in front of the driver of a motor-car *etc*. – *verb* **windsurf** to sail on a sailboard. – *noun* **windsurfer**. – *noun* **windsurfing**. – *adjective* **windswept** exposed to strong winds and showing the effects of it: *windswept hair*. – *noun, adj, adverb* **windward** (in) the direction from which the wind blows. – *adjective* **windy** (of weather) with a strong wind blowing; (of a place) exposed to strong winds. – **get the wind up** (*coll*) to become afraid; **get wind of** (*coll*) to hear about in an indirect way.

wind² *verb* (*past tense* **wound**) to turn, twist or coil; (sometimes with **up**) to screw up the spring of (a watch, clockwork toy *etc*); to wrap closely. – *noun* **winder** a knob, key *etc* for winding a clock *etc*. – *adjective* **winding** curving, twisting. – **wind one's way** to make one's way *esp* by turning and twisting; **wind up** to bring or come to an end: *He wound up the meeting;* **wound up** tense, agitated.

windlass *noun* a machine for lifting up or hauling a winch.

window *noun* an opening in the wall of a building *etc* (protected by glass) to let in light and air (or, in a shop, to display goods.

wine *noun* an alcoholic drink made from the fermented juice of grapes or other fruit; a rich dark red colour. – *noun* **winepress** a machine in which the juice is squeezed out of grapes.

wing *noun* one of the arm-like limbs of a bird, bat, or insect by means of which it flies; one of the two projections resembling these on the sides of an aeroplane; anything else resembling a wing, as a part of a house built out to the side; the side of a stage, where actors *etc* wait; (in football *etc*) a player at the edge of the field; a section, with specific opinions *etc*, of a political party. – *verb* to wound in the wing: *He's winged the grouse;* to soar. – *noun* **wing commander** a high-ranking officer in the air force. – *adjective* **winged** having wings; swift. – **on** or **upon the wing** flying, in motion; **under someone's wing** under the protection or care of someone.

wink *verb* to open and close an eye quickly; to give a hint by winking; (of lights *etc*) to flicker, twinkle. – *noun* an act of winking; a hint given by winking. – **forty winks** a short sleep.

winkle *noun* a type of shellfish, the periwinkle, used as food. – **winkle out** to force out gradually: *He winkled the information out of his son.*

winnow *verb* to separate the chaff from the grain by wind.

winsome *adjective* charming.

winter *noun* the cold season of the year. – *adjective* of, belonging to, or suitable for winter. – *verb* to pass the winter: *They wintered in the South of France;* to keep, feed (sheep *etc*) during the winter. – *noun plural* **winter quarters** a place to stay during the winter (*esp* for soldiers). – *noun plural* **winter sports** sports on snow or ice (skiing, tobogganing *etc*). – *adjective* **wintry** like winter, cold, stormy; cheerless, unfriendly: *a wintry smile.*

wipe *verb* to clean or dry by rubbing; (with **away, out, off** or **up**) to clear away. – *noun* the act of cleaning by rubbing. – *noun* **wiper** one of a pair of moving arm-like parts which wipe the windscreen of a car.

wire *noun* a thread-like length of metal; the metal thread used in communication by telephone *etc*; (*coll*) a telegram. – *adjective* made of wire. – *verb* to bind or fasten with wire; (*coll*) to send a telegram; to supply (a building *etc*) with wires for carrying an electric current. – *adjective* **wireless** (of communication by telephone, telegraph *etc*) by radio waves. – *noun* an apparatus for sending or receiving messages or broadcasts by radio waves, a radio set. – *noun* **wire-netting** mesh (used for hen-runs *etc*) made of wire. – *adjective* **wiry** made of, or like wire; (of a person) thin but strong.

wireless *see* **wire.**

wise *adjective* full of learning or knowledge; able to use knowledge well, judging rightly; sensible. – *noun* **wisdom** the quality of being wise. – *noun plural* **wisdom teeth** four large back teeth which do not appear in a person until after childhood. – **-wise** (used with another word) in the manner or way of: *crabwise*; of, with reference or regard to: *careerwise*.

wish *verb* to feel or express a desire or want: *I wish he'd go*; (*usu* with **for**) to long for, desire, want: *She wished for riches*; to hope for on behalf of (someone): *to wish someone luck*. – *noun* (*plural* **wishes**) desire, longing; a thing desired or wanted. *Her great wish was to go abroad*; an expression of desire: *She made a wish*; (*plural*) expression of hope for another's happiness, good fortune *etc*: *She sends you her good wishes*. – *noun* **wishbone** a forked bone in the breast of fowls. – *adjective* **wishful** wishing, eager. – *noun* **wishful thinking** basing one's belief on (false) hopes rather than known facts. – **wish someone well** to feel goodwill towards someone.

wishywashy *adjective* (of liquids) thin and weak; (of a person) feeble, not energetic or lively; lacking colour.

wisp *noun* a small tuft or strand: *a wisp of hair*. – *adjective* **wispy**.

wistful *adjective* thoughtful and rather sad, as if longing for something: *The child cast a wistful glance at the toys in the window*. – *adverb* **wistfully**.

wit *noun* (often *plural*) understanding, intelligence, common sense; the ability to express ideas cleverly, neatly, and funnily; a person who can do this. – **-witted** (used with another adjective) having wits (of a certain kind): *slow-witted*: *quick-witted*. – *noun* **witticism** a witty remark. – *adverb* **wittingly** knowingly. – *adjective* **witty** clever and amusing. – **at one's wits' end** unable to solve one's difficulties, desperate;

keep one's wits about one to keep alert; **to wit** namely, that is to say.

witch *noun* (*plural* **witches**) a woman supposed to have magic power obtained through evil spirits; an ugly old woman. – *noun* **witchcraft** magic performed by a witch. – *noun* **witch doctor** in African tribes, a person believed to have magical powers to cure illnesses *etc*. – *noun* **witch-hazel** a type of N. American shrub; a healing lotion made from its bark and leaves.

with *preposition* in the company of: *I was walking with my father*; by means of: *Cut it with a knife*; in the same direction as: *drifting with the current*; against: *fighting with his brother*; on the same side as; having: *a man with a limp*; in the keeping of: *Leave your bag with me*.

withdraw *verb* (*past tense* **withdrew,** *past participle* **withdrawn**) to go back or away; to take away, remove (troops, money from the bank *etc*); to take back (an insult *etc*). – *noun* **withdrawal** an act of withdrawing. – *adjective* **withdrawn** (of a place) lonely, isolated; (of a person) unwilling to communicate with others, unsociable.

wither *verb* to (cause to) fade, dry up or decay; to cause to feel very unimportant, embarrassed *etc*: *She withered him with a look*. – *adjective* **withering** drying up, dying; (of a remark, glance *etc*) scornful, sarcastic. – *noun plural* **withers** the ridge between the shoulder bones of a horse.

withhold *verb* (*past tense* **withheld**) to keep back, refuse to give.

within *preposition* inside (the limits of): *to keep within the law*. – *adverb* on the inside.

without *preposition* in the absence of: *They went without you*; not having: *without a penny*; outside (the limits of): *without the terms of the agreement*. – *adverb* (*old*) on the outside; out-of-doors.

withstand *verb* to oppose or resist successfully.

witness *noun* (*plural* **witnesses**) a person who sees or has direct knowledge of a thing; one who gives evidence, *esp* in a law court; (something that provides) proof or evidence. – *verb* to see, be present at; to sign one's name to show one's belief in the genuineness of (someone else's signature); to give or be evidence, to bear witness. – *noun* **witness box** the stand from which a

witness in a law court gives evidence. –
bear witness to give or be evidence of:
to bear witness to his honesty.

wizard *noun* a man who is supposed to
have the power of magic. – *noun*
wizardry magic.

wizened *adjective* dried up, shrivelled: *a
wizened old man.*

woad *noun* a blue dye; the plant from
which it is obtained.

wobble *verb* to rock unsteadily from side
to side. – Also *noun.* – *adjective* **wobbly.**

woe *noun* grief, misery; a cause of sorrow,
a trouble. – *adjective* **woebegone**
dismal, sad-looking. – *adjective* **woeful**
sorrowful; pitiful.

wolf *noun* (*plural* **wolves**) a type of wild
animal of the dog kind that hunts in
packs. – *verb* to eat greedily: *That child
wolfs (down) his food.* – *noun* **wolfhound**
a large breed of dog formerly used in
hunting wolves. – *adjective* **wolfish** of,
or like, a wolf. – **cry wolf** to give a false
alarm; **keep the wolf from the door** to
keep away hunger or want.

wolverine *noun* a type of wild animal of
the weasel family.

woman *noun* (*plural* **women**) an adult
human female; human females in
general; a domestic help. – *noun*
womanhood the state of being a
woman. – *adjective* **womanish** (of a
man) not manly. – *noun* **womankind** or
womenkind or **womenfolk** women
generally. – *adjective* **womanly** of, like,
suitable for, a woman.

womb *noun* the part of a female mammal's body in which the young develop
and stay till birth.

wombat *noun* a type of small, beaver-like,
Australian animal, with a pouch.

won *see* **win.**

wonder *noun* the state of mind produced
by something unexpected or extraordinary, surprise, awe; something
strange, amazing or miraculous. – *verb*
to be curious, or in doubt: *I wonder what
will happen. I wonder whether to go*; to feel
surprise or amazement (at, that). –
adjective **wonderful** or (*old*) **wondrous**
arousing wonder, strange, marvellous.
– *noun* **wonderland** a land of wonderful
things, a fairy-like place. – *noun* **won-
derment** (*old*) amazement.

wont *adjective* (*old*) accustomed (to do
something). – *noun* habit.

won't short for **will not.**

woo *verb* (*past tense* **wooed**) to try to win
the love of (someone), *esp* with the
intention of marrying; to try to gain (*eg*
success). – *noun* **wooer.**

wood *noun* (sometimes *plural*) a group of
growing trees; the hard part of a tree,
esp when cut or sawn for use in
building *etc*, or for fuel. – *noun*
woodbine the honeysuckle. – *noun*
woodchuck same as **marmot.** – *noun*
woodcock a type of game bird related
to the snipe. – *noun* **woodcut** a picture
engraved on wood or a print made
from it. – *noun* **woodcutter** a man who
fells trees, cuts up wood *etc.* – *adjective*
wooded covered with trees. – *adjective*
wooden made of, or like, wood; dull,
stiff, not lively. – *noun* **woodland** land
covered with trees. – *noun* **woodlouse**
(*plural* **woodlice**) a type of insect with a
jointed shell found under stones *etc.* –
noun **woodpecker** a bird that pecks
holes in the barks of trees with its beak,
in search of insects. – *noun* **woodwind**
wind instruments, made of wood (or
sometimes of metal, as silver) *eg* flute,
clarinet. – *noun* **woodwork** the making
of wooden articles, carpentry; the
wooden parts of a house, room *etc.* –
noun **woodworm** the larva of a certain
beetle that bores holes in wood and
destroys it. – *adjective* **woody** like
wood; wooded.

wool *noun* the soft hair of sheep and other
animals; yarn or cloth made of wool;
any light fluffy or fleecy material
resembling wool. – *noun* **woolgather-
ing** day-dreaming. – *noun, adjective*
woollen (a garment *etc*) made of wool.
– *adjective* **woolly** made of, or like,
wool; vague, hazy. – *noun* (*plural*
woollies) a knitted garment.

word *noun* a written or spoken sign
showing a thing or an idea; (*plural*)
speech, talk: *gentle words*; news: *word of
his death*; a promise: *to break one's word.* –
verb to choose words for: *He worded his
refusal carefully.* – *noun* **wording** choice,
or arrangement, of words. – *noun* **word
processor** an electronic machine (with
a screen) which can be used for storing,
organizing and printing out text. –
adjective **wordy** using too many words.
– **have words** (*coll*) to quarrel; **in a
word** in short, to sum up; **take someone at their word** to treat what
someone says as true; **take someone's
word for something** to trust that what
someone says is true; **word for word** in
the exact words.

work *noun* a physical or mental effort or exertion made to achieve or make something *etc*; a job, employment: *out of work*; a task: *I've got work to do*; anything made or done; something, as a book, a painting, a musical composition *etc*, produced by art; the manner of working, workmanship: *poor work*; (*plural*) a factory *etc*; (*plural*) the mechanism (of a watch *etc*); (*plural*) deeds: *good works*. – *verb* to be engaged in physical or mental work; to be employed; to (cause machinery *etc* to) run or operate smoothly and efficiently; (of a plan *etc*) to be successful; to get or put into a position or stated condition slowly and gradually: *The screw worked loose*; to organize, manage, control. – *adjective* **workable** able to be done, practical. – *adjective* **workaday** ordinary, unexciting. – *noun* **worker** a person who works *esp* in a manual job. – *noun* **working class** the social class including manual workers. – *noun* **working day** or **working hours** a day or the hours that one spends at work, on duty *etc*. – *noun* **working party** a group of people appointed to investigate a particular matter. – *noun* **workman** one who works with his hands. – *adjective* **workmanlike** done with skill. – *noun* **workmanship** the skill of a workman; the manner of making (something). – *noun* **workshop** a room or building where manufacturing, manual work *etc* is done. – **work out** to solve; to discover as a result of deep thought; (of a situation *etc*) to turn out all right in the end; **work up** to arouse, excite: *He worked himself up into a fury*.

world *noun* the earth and all things on it; mankind; any planet or star; the universe; a state of existence: *the next world*; a particular area of life or activity: *This book deals with the insect world. She always wished to enter the world of entertainment*; a great deal: *a world of good*. – *adjective* **worldly** belonging to, or concerned with, material things such as money, possessions *etc*, not the soul or spirit. – *adjective* **worldwide** stretching all over the world. – Also *adverb*.

worm *noun* an earthworm or any similar small creeping animal without a backbone; (*coll*) a low, contemptible person; anything spiral-shaped, *eg* the thread of a screw; (*plural*) the condition of having worms of some kind in the intestines (in humans *usu* threadworms). – *verb* to move like a worm, or gradually and stealthily (in or into); (*usu* with **out**) to obtain, draw out (information) bit by bit.

wormwood *noun* a type of plant with a bitter taste.

worn, worn-out *see* **wear.**

worry *verb* to shake or tear (something) with the teeth as a dog does; to annoy; to (cause to) be troubled and anxious. – *noun* (*plural* **worries**) uneasiness, anxiety, or a cause of this.

worse *adjective* bad or evil to a greater degree; more ill. – *adverb* badly to a greater degree, in a more severe or evil way: *It's raining worse than ever.* – *verb* **worsen** to (cause to) become worse. – **worse off** in a worse position, less wealthy *etc*.

worship *noun* a religious ceremony or service; deep reverence or adoration; a title of honour (used in addressing mayors of cities *etc*). – *verb* (*past tense* **worshipped**) to pay honour to (God, *esp* at a church service); to adore or admire deeply. – *adjective* **worshipful** full of reverence; worthy of honour.

worst *adjective* bad or evil to the greatest degree. – *adverb* badly to the greatest degree. – *verb* (*past tense* **worsted**) to beat, defeat. – **at worst** under the least favourable circumstances; **if the worst comes to the worst** if the worst possible circumstances occur.

worsted *noun* (a strong cloth made of) a type of fine woollen yarn. – *verb see* **worst.**

worth *noun* value; price; importance; excellence of character *etc*. – *adjective* equal in value to; deserving of: *worth considering*. – *adjective* **worthless** of no merit or value. – *adjective* **worthwhile** deserving time and effort. – *adjective* **worthy** (sometimes with **of**) deserving, suitable; of good character. – *noun* (*plural* **worthies**) a highly respected person *esp* a local person. – **worth one's while** worth the trouble spent.

would the form of the verb **will** used to express a condition: *He would go if he could*; used for emphasis: *I tell you I would do it if possible*; (*old*) expressing a wish: *I would (that) he were gone.*

would-be *adjective* trying to be or pretending to be: *a would-be actor: a would-be aristocrat.*

wound *noun* any cut or injury caused by force, as by a weapon, in an accident *etc*; a hurt to one's feelings. – *verb* to make a wound in; to hurt the feelings of. – *adjective* **wounded** having a wound, injured, hurt.

WPC *abbreviation* Woman Police Constable.

wrack *rak*, *noun* seaweed cast up on the shore.

wraith *rāth*, *noun* an apparition, *esp* of a living person; a ghost.

wrangle *rang'gl*, *verb* to quarrel noisily. – Also *noun*.

wrap *rap*, *verb* (*past tense* **wrapped**) to fold or roll (something round something); (often with **up**) to cover by folding or winding something round. – *noun* a covering such as a cloak or shawl. – *noun* **wrapper** a loose paper book cover, or other (paper) cover, as that round a sweet *etc*.

wrath *rōth*, *noun* violent anger. – *adjective* **wrathful** very angry.

wreak *rēk*, *verb* to carry out (*eg* vengeance); to cause (havoc *etc*); to give way to, act as prompted by (one's anger *etc*).

wreath *rēth*, *noun* a ring or garland of flowers or leaves; a curling wisp or drift of smoke, mist *etc*. – *verb* **wreathe** to twine about or encircle.

wreck *rek*, *noun* destruction, *esp* of a ship by the sea; the remains of anything destroyed *esp* a ship; a person whose health or nerves *etc* are in bad condition. – *verb* to destroy. – *noun* **wreckage** the remains of something wrecked.

wren *ren*, *noun* a very small type of bird.

wrench *rench*, *verb* to pull with a twisting motion, or violently; to sprain (one's ankle *etc*). – *noun* (*plural* **wrenches**) a violent twist; a type of tool for gripping and turning nuts, bolts *etc*; sadness caused by parting from someone or something.

wrest *rest*, *verb* to twist or take by force.

wrestle *res'l*, *verb* to struggle with someone, trying to bring him down; (with **with**) to think deeply about (and try to solve) (a problem *etc*). – *noun* **wrestler** a person who wrestles as a sport. – *noun* **wrestling** the sport in which two people struggle to throw each other to the ground.

wretch *rech*, *noun* (*plural* **wretches**) a miserable, pitiable person; a worthless or contemptible person. – *adjective*

wretched very miserable; worthless; very bad. – *noun* **wretchedness.**

wriggle *rig'l*, *verb* to twist to and fro; to move by doing this, as a worm does; to escape (out of a difficulty *etc*).

-wright *-rīt*, (used with another word) a maker: *shipwright*: *playwright*.

wring *ring*, *verb* (*past tense* **wrung**) to twist or squeeze (*esp* water out of wet clothes *etc*); to clasp and unclasp (one's hands) in grief, anxiety *etc*; to cause pain to: *The story wrung everybody's heart*; to force (something from a person *eg* a promise). – *noun* **wringer** a machine for forcing water from wet clothes.

wrinkle *rink'l*, *noun* a small crease or fold on the skin or other surface. – *verb* to make or become wrinkled. – *adjective* **wrinkly.**

wrist *rist*, *noun* the joint by which the hand is joined to the arm.

writ *rit*, *noun* a formal document which orders one to do something (as appear in a law court).

write *rīt*, *verb* (*past tense* **wrote,** *past participle* **written**) to form letters with a pen, pencil *etc*; to put into writing: *to write one's name*; to compose (a poem, a book *etc*); to send a letter (to). – *noun* **writer** a person who writes, *esp* an author. – *noun* **writing** putting (something) down in letters; (often *plural*) something composed and written. – **write down** to record in writing; **write off** to cancel, or to regard as lost for ever (*noun* **write-off**); **write to** (*comput*) to record on to (*eg* a disc); **write up** to make a written record of.

writhe *rīTH*, *verb* to twist or roll about in pain *etc*.

wrong *rong*, *adjective* not correct; not right or just; evil; not what is intended: *He took the wrong umbrella*; unsuitable: *the wrong weather for camping*; mistaken: *You are wrong if you think that*. – *noun* whatever is not right or just; an injury done to another. – *verb* to do wrong to, to harm. – *noun* **wrongdoer** a person who does wrong. – *noun* **wrongdoing.** – *adjective* **wrongful** not lawful or just. – *adverb* **wrongly.** – **go wrong** to fail to work properly; to fail to reach a successful conclusion; to make a mistake or mistakes; **in the wrong** guilty of injustice or error.

wrote *see* **write.**

wrought *röt*, *adjective* (*old*) made, manufactured. – *verb* old *past tense of* **work.** –

noun **wrought-iron** a form of iron, (able to be) hammered, rather than cast, into shape. – adjective **wrought-up** agitated, anxious.

wrung see **wring.**

wry rī, adjective twisted or turned to one side: a wry neck; slightly mocking or bitter: a wry remark. – adverb **wryly.**

WYSIWYG (comput) what you see (on the screen) is what you get (in the print-out).

X

X-rays noun plural rays that can pass through many substances impossible for light to pass through, and produce, on photographic film, a shadow picture (called an **X-ray**) of the object through which they have passed. – verb **X-ray** to photograph by X-rays.

xenophobia noun hatred of foreigners or strangers. – adjective **xenophobic.**

Xerox® noun a type of photographic process used for copying documents; a copy made in this way. – Also adjective. – verb to copy by Xerox.

Xmas noun short for Christmas.

xylophone noun a musical instrument made up of a series of wooden plates graded in size, which the player strikes with hammers.

Y

yacht noun a sailing or motor-driven vessel for racing, cruising etc. – noun **yachting** sailing a yacht. – noun **yachtsman.**

yak noun a long-haired type of ox, found in Tibet.

yam noun any of several types of potato-like tropical plants, used as food.

yank verb (coll) to tug or pull with a violent jerk. – Also noun.

yap verb (past tense **yapped**) to bark sharply.

yard noun a measure of length (0·9144 of a metre, or 3 feet); a long beam on a mast for spreading sails (of which each half is called a **yard-arm**); an enclosed space esp one near a building or one used for special work: The wagons are loaded in the railway yard. The ship-building yard is at the mouth of the river; (US) a garden. – noun **yardstick** a stick a yard long, for measuring; any standard of measurement.

yarn noun wool, cotton, etc spun into thread; one of the threads of a rope; a story, a tale, esp a long, improbable one. – verb to tell stories.

yarrow noun a strong-smelling type of plant with flat clusters of white flowers.

yashmak noun the veil worn by Muslim women, covering the face below the eyes.

yawl noun a ship's small rowing boat; a small fishing boat or type of sailing boat.

yawn verb unintentionally to take a deep breath usu with wide-open mouth, from boredom, sleepiness etc; (of a hole etc) to be wide open, to gape. – Also noun.

yd abbreviation **yard(s).**

ye pronoun (old) you.

yea interjection (old) yes.

year *noun* the time taken by the earth to go once round the sun, about 365 days; the period 1 January to 31 December, or a period of twelve months starting at any point; (*plural*) age: *wise for his years.* – *noun* **yearling** an animal a year old. – *adjective* **yearly** happening every year, once a year, or in one year. – Also *adverb.*

yearn *verb* to long (for, to do something *etc*); to feel pity or tenderness (for). – *noun* **yearning** an eager longing.

yeast *noun* a substance which causes fermentation, used in brewing beer, and to make the dough rise in bread-baking *etc.*

yell *verb* to utter a loud, shrill cry, to scream. – Also *noun.*

yellow *adjective, noun* (of) the colour of gold, the yolk of an egg, or butter. – *verb* to become yellow, *usu* with age. – *noun* **yellowhammer** a type of bird of the finch kind, yellow in colour.

yelp *noun* a sharp bark or cry. – Also *verb.*

yen *noun* the standard unit of Japanese currency; (*coll*) a strong desire, longing: *He has a yen to go back home.*

yeoman *yō'mán, noun* (*hist*) a farmer with his own land. – *noun* **yeomanry** (*hist*) farmers; (*hist*) a troop of cavalrymen serving voluntarily in the British army. – **Yeomen of the Guard** the company acting as bodyguard to the British king or queen on certain occasions.

yes *interjection* expressing agreement or consent. – *noun* an expression of agreement or consent; a vote in favour.

yesterday *adverb, noun* (on) the day before today; (in) the past.

yet *adverb* by now, by this time: *Have you heard yet?*; still, before the matter is finished: *He may win yet.* – *conjunction* but, nevertheless: *I am defeated, yet I shall not surrender.* – **yet another** and another one still; **yet more** a still greater number or quantity.

Yeti *see* **Abominable Snowman**.

yew *noun* a type of tree with dark green leaves and red berries or its wood.

YHA *abbreviation* Youth Hostels Association.

yield *verb* to give in, surrender, give up; to give way to pressure or persuasion; to produce (a crop, results *etc*). – *noun* amount produced. – *adjective* **yielding** giving way easily.

YMCA *abbreviation* Young Men's Christian Association.

yob or **yobbo** (*plural* **yobboes** or **yobbos**) *noun* a lout, a hooligan.

yodel *verb* (*past tense* **yodelled**) to sing changing frequently from an ordinary to a very high-pitched voice and back again.

yoga *noun* a Hindu system of philosophy and meditation, often involving special physical exercises.

yoghourt or **yoghurt** or **yogurt** *noun* a semi-liquid type of food made from fermented milk.

yoke *noun* a wooden frame joining oxen when pulling a plough, cart *etc*; a pair (of oxen, horses); something that joins together; a frame placed across the shoulders for carrying pails *etc*; slavery, domination; a part of a garment fitting over the neck and shoulders; a part of a skirt fitting closely over the hips. – *verb* to put a yoke on; to join together.

yokel *noun* a country man or boy, used insultingly.

yolk *noun* the yellow part of an egg.

yonder *adverb* in that place (at a distance but within sight). – Also *adjective.*

yore: of yore formerly, in times past.

you *pronoun* the person(s) spoken or written to, used as the *singular* or *plural* subject or object of a verb.

you'd short for **you would** or **you should** or **you had.**

you'll short for **you will** or **you shall.**

young *adjective* in early life; in the early part of growth. – *noun* the offspring of animals; (with **the**) young people. – *noun* **youngster** a young person.

your *adjective* belonging to you: *your father.* – *pronoun* **yours**: *This seat is yours.* – *pronoun* **yourself** (*plural* **yourselves**) used reflexively: *Don't worry yourself*; used for emphasis: *You yourself can't go, but your representative can.* – **Yours** or **Yours faithfully** or **Yours sincerely** or **Yours truly** expressions used before one's signature at the end of a letter.

you're short for **you are.**

youth *noun* the state of being young; the early part of life; a young man; young people in general. – *adjective* **youthful** young; fresh and vigorous. – *noun*

youth hostel a hostel where hikers *etc* may spend the night.

you've short for **you have**.

Yo-Yo® *noun* a type of toy consisting of a reel which spins up and down on a string.

yr *abbreviation* year.

Yule *noun* the season or feast of Christmas. – *noun* **Yuletide** Christmas time.

yuppie or **yuppy** *noun* (*plural* **yuppies**) a young well-paid ambitious urban professional.

YWCA *abbreviation* Young Women's Christian Association.

Z

zany *adjective* (*coll*) crazy, clown-like.

zeal *noun* enthusiasm; keenness, determination. – *noun* **zealot** *zel ot*, a person who is very keen, an enthusiast. – *adjective* **zealous** full of zeal.

zebra *noun* a type of striped African animal of the horse family. – *noun* **zebra crossing** a street crossing, painted in stripes, for pedestrians.

zenith *noun* the point of the heavens which is exactly overhead; the highest point (of achievement *etc*).

zephyr *noun* a soft, gentle breeze.

zero *noun* nothing or the sign for it (0); the point (marked 0) from which a scale (*eg* on a thermometer) begins. – *noun* **zero hour** the exact time fixed for some action, operation *etc*. – *noun* **zero option** a proposal to limit or abandon the deployment of (medium range) nuclear missiles if the opposing side does likewise. – *adjective* **zero-rated** of goods on which the purchaser pays no value-added tax and on which the seller can claim back any value-added tax already paid by him.

zest *noun* relish, keen enjoyment; orange or lemon peel. – *adjective* **zestful.**

zigzag *adjective* (of a line, road *etc*) having sharp bends or angles. – Also *adverb*. – *verb* (*past tense* **zigzagged**) to move in a zigzag manner or course.

Zimmer® *noun* a metal frame held in front of one, used as an aid to walking.

zinc *noun* an element, a bluish-white kind of metal.

zinnia *noun* a type of tropical American plant of the thistle family.

zip *noun* a zip fastener; a whizzing sound, like that of a flying bullet; (*coll*) energy, vigour. – *verb* (*past tense* **zipped**) to

fasten with a zip fastener; to whiz. – *noun* **zip fastener** a device for fastening (garments *etc*) in which two rows of metal or nylon teeth are caused to fit into each other when a sliding tab is pulled between them.

zither *noun* a type of flat, stringed musical instrument, played with the fingers.

zodiac *noun* an imaginary strip of the heavens, divided into twelve equal parts called the **signs of the zodiac**, each named after a particular group of stars.

zone *noun* any of the five great bands into which the earth's surface is divided according to temperature: *temperate zone*; an area, region, section of a country, town *etc*, *esp* one marked off for a particular purpose: *a no-parking zone: a smokeless zone*. – *verb* to divide into zones.

zombie *noun* a corpse reanimated by sorcery; a stupid or useless person; a very slow, lethargic person.

zonked *adjective* (*slang*) exhausted, drunk; under the influence of drugs.

zoo *noun* a zoological garden. – *adjective* **zoological** of animals; of a zoo. – *noun* **zoological garden** a place where wild animals are kept and shown. – *noun* **zoologist** a person who studies animal life. – *noun* **zoology** the science of animal life.

zoom *verb* to move with a loud, low buzzing noise; to make such a noise; (of an aircraft) to climb sharply at high speed for a short time; (of prices *etc*) to increase sharply; (of a special kind of camera lens (**zoom lens**)) to make a distant object appear gradually nearer without the camera being moved.

zucchini *zoo-kē'nē*, *noun* (*plural* **zucchini** or **zucchinis**) a courgette.

APPENDICES

Spelling rules

A few general rules of spelling are given here, but there are always exceptions to the rules. In cases of doubt, the dictionary will be helpful.

Derivatives of words ending in -y

(1) The plural of a noun in **-y, -ey** (also **-ay, -oy, -uy**):

A noun in **-y** following a consonant has its plural in **-ies.**

baby	babies	country	countries

A noun in **-y** following a vowel has its plural in **-eys** etc.

donkey	donkeys	valley	valleys
day	days	Monday	Mondays
alloy	alloys	guy	guys

(2) The parts of a verb when the verb ends in **-y, -ey** etc:

The formation is similar to that of noun plurals in (1) above.

cry	cries	cried
certify	certifies	certified
convey	conveys	conveyed
delay	delays	delayed
destroy	destroys	destroyed
buy	buys	

(3) Comparison of adjectives, or the formation of nouns or adverbs from them:

A rule similar to the above holds for words in **-y,** and in some cases for those in **-ey** etc.

shady	shadier	shadiest	shadiness	shadily
pretty	prettier	prettiest	prettiness	prettily
grey	greyer	greyest	greyness	greyly
coy	coyer	coyest	coyness	coyly

There are, however, exceptions and irregularities for which a dictionary should be consulted.

Derivatives of words ending in -c

When a suffix beginning with a vowel is added, and the consonant still has a hard k sound, **-c** becomes **-ck**:

picnic	picnicking	picnicked	picnicker
mimic	mimicking	mimicked	mimicker

-k- is not added in words such as *musician, electricity* etc, where the consonant has the soft sound of *sh* or *s*.

-ie- or -ei-?

'*i* before *e* except after *c*.'

(This rule applies only to words in which the sound is long $\bar{e}$.)

belief	believe	grief	pier	siege
ceiling	conceit	deceit	deceive	

Exceptions are *seize, weird* and personal names (for example *Neil, Sheila*).

The doubling of a final consonant before a following vowel

(1) In a word of one syllable with a short vowel, the final consonant is doubled:

man	*manning*	*manned*	*mannish*
red	*redder*	*reddest*	*redden*
sin	*sinning*	*sinned*	*sinner*
stop	*stopping*	*stopped*	*stopper*
drum	*drumming*	*drummed*	*drummer*

(2) In a word of more than one syllable with a short final vowel, the final consonant is doubled only if the accent is on the final syllable:

regret'	*regretting*	*regretted*	
begin'	*beginning*	*beginner*	
occur'	*occurring*	*occurred*	*occurrence*
en'ter	*entering*	*entered*	
prof'it	*profiting*	*profited*	
gall'op	*galloping*	*galloped*	

(3) In British English (but not in American) -**l** is doubled regardless of where the accent falls:

compel'	*compelling*	*compelled*	
trav'el	*travelling*	*travelled*	*traveller*

(4) Some derivatives of words ending in -**s**, *eg bias*, can be spelt in two ways: *biassed* or *biased*, *biassing* or *biasing*.

Certain words ending in -**p** are not treated according to the rule stated in (2) above:

handicap	*handicapped*	*handicapping*
kidnap	*kidnapped*	*kidnapping*

Derivatives of words with final -*e*

(1) Before a vowel (including **y**), -**e** is usually dropped:

come	*coming*	*hate*	*hating*	*rage*	*raging*
fame	*famous*	*pale*	*paling*	*use*	*usage*
ice	*icy*	*noise*	*noisy*	*stone*	*stony*

Some exceptions distinguish one word from another:
   holey (=full of holes), *holy*; *dyeing*, *dying*.

(2) Before a consonant, -**e** is usually kept:

   hateful   *useless*   *movement*   *strangeness*

but see *true*, *whole*, *judge* for exceptions.

(3) -**e**- is kept after soft -**c**- or -**g**- before -**a** and -**o**-:

   noticeable   *traceable*   *manageable*   *advantageous*

Irregular plurals

Where a noun has an irregular plural form it is usually shown in its entry in the dictionary.

Words confused and misused

The dictionary will help to distinguish and explain these words.

accept
except

access
excess

adverse
averse

advice
advise

affect
effect

allude
elude

allusion
delusion
illusion

amend
emend

amoral
immoral

aural
oral

bail
bale

berth
birth

born
borne

breath
breathe

cannon
canon

canvas
canvass

check
cheque

choir
quire

chord
cord

collaborate
corroborate

complement
compliment

comprise
consist

concert
consort

concise
precise

confidant
confident
confidante

contemptible
contemptuous

continual
continuous

co-respondent
correspondent

corps
corpse

council
counsel

councillor
counsellor

credible
creditable

currant
current

deduce
deduct

defective
deficient

deprecate
depreciate

desert
dessert

device
devise

draft
draught

dual
duel

elicit
illicit

eligible
legible

emigrant
immigrant

eminent
imminent

ensure
insure

exceedingly
excessively

exercise
exorcise

faint
feint

forceful
forcible

foreword
forward

gait
gate

gaol
goal

gild
guild

gilt
guilt

gorilla
guerrilla

hangar
hanger

hoard
horde

illegible
ineligible

imaginary
imaginative

imply
infer

impracticable
impractical

inapt
inept

ingenious
ingenuous

interment
internment

lair
layer

lath
lathe

lay
lie

licence
license

lightening
lightning

liqueur
liquor

439

loath	persecute	quiet	surplice
loathe	prosecute	quite	surplus
loose	personal	raise	swingeing
lose	personnel	raze	swinging
metal	pore	reverend	team
mettle	pour	reverent	teem
meter	practice	review	venal
metre	practise	revue	venial
naught	pray	sceptic	waive
nought	prey	septic	wave
negligent	premier	stationary	
negligible	première	stationery	
official	principal	storey	
officious	principle	story	
peal	prophecy	straight	
peel	prophesy	strait	

Common prefixes and suffixes

Prefix	Meaning	Example
a-	in, on	amid, ashore
a-, ab-, abs-	away from	avert, abdicate, absent
a-, ad-, al-, an-, at-	to, at	abase, admire, allure, annex, attract
ante-, anti-	before	anteroom, anticipate
ant(i)-	against	antipodes, antagonist
arch-	chief	archbishop
auto-	self	autobiography
circum-	round about	circumference
com-, con-	together, with	compile, connect
contra-, counter-	against	contradict, counterattack
de-	away from	debar, detract
dis-	apart, away	dissect, dispel
e-, ex-	from, out of	emerge, exceed, exodus
en-, em-	in, into	enlist, embark
fore-	before	foretell
hemi-	half	hemisphere
il-, im-, in-, ir-	not	illegal, improper, infirm, irregular
in-, il-, im-, *etc*	in, into	income, illuminate, imbibe
inter-	between	interval
intro-	into	introduce

Prefix	Meaning	Example
mis-	wrong	misbehave, misdeed
mono-	one	monoplane
multi-	many	multiply
non-	not	nonsense
ob-, op-	against, in the way of	obstruct, oppose
pen(e)-	almost	peninsula
per-	through	pervade
post-	after	postpone
pre-	before	predict
pro-	before, in front of	propose
re-	again	recast
semi-	half	semicircle
sub-	under	submarine
super-	over, beyond	superhuman
tele-	at a distance	telephone
trans-	beyond, across	transport, transgress
un-	not	unhappy, untruth

Suffix	Meaning	Example
-able,-ible,-uble	fit for, able (to be —)	eatable, edible, soluble
-age	used to make nouns	bondage, vicarage
-al, -ial	used to make nouns and adjectives	legal, editorial
-ana	belonging to, connected with	Victoriana
-ance, -ence	used to make nouns	repentance, conference
-ant, -ent	a doer	attendant
-dom	state, power	freedom, kingdom
-ee	one who is —	employee
-en	used to form verbs	harden, flatten
-ence, -ent	see -ance, -ant	
-er	a doer	baker, writer
-er	to a greater extent	higher, harder
-escent	growing, becoming	adolescent
-esque	in the style of	picturesque, Miltonesque
-ess	used to make feminine forms of words	countless, lioness
-est	to the greatest extent	highest, hardest
-ette	used to make feminine or diminutive (small) forms of words	usherette, cigarette
-fold	times	fourfold, twofold
-ful	full of	delightful
-hood	state of	manhood, childhood
-ible	see -able	
-ic	of, belonging to	gigantic, public
-ise, ize	used to make verbs	publicize

Suffix	Meaning	Example
-ish	rather like, slightly	childish, brownish
-ism	a belief or practice	Communism, terrorism
-ist	a doer	typist
-ite	a native of, follower of	Israelite, Hitlerite
-itis	inflammation of	tonsillitis
-less	free from, lacking	harmless, useless
-let	small	ringlet
-ly	used to make adverbs and adjectives	sweetly, quietly manly
-ment	used to make nouns	merriment
-ness	a state of being	kindness, redness
-ock	used to make diminutive (small) forms of words	hillock
-oid	like, in the form of	tabloid, humanoid
-or	a doer	sailor, tailor
-ous	used to make adjectives	dangerous
-ry	a place of work; also used to make many general nouns	bakery, laundry, slavery, poetry
-ship	a state of being	friendship
-some	full of	troublesome
-ster, -stress (fem)	member of a group, profession etc	gangster, seamstress
-ty	a state of being	cruelty
-uble	see -able	
-ward(s)	in a certain direction	eastward, homewards